Verify
Those Credentials

Do You Know Who You're Dealing with?

Verify Those Credentials

Do You Know Who You are Dealing With?

©1997 By Facts on Demand Press
4653 South Lakeshore Drive, Suite 3
Tempe, AZ 85282
(800) 929-3811

ISBN 1-889150-01-1

Edited by: Michael Sankey & Carl R. Ernst
Cover Design by Robin Fox & Associates

Cataloging-in-Publication Data

025.5   **Sankey, Michael L., 1949-**
SAN   Verify those credentials : do you know who you are dealing with? / [edited by: Michael L Sankey & Carl R. Ernst].- Tempe, Ariz. : Facts on Demand Press, © 1997.

       480 p. ; 7 x 10 in.

       Summary: Explains how to check and verify the representations people make to you in the day-to-day conduct of your business or personal life, including educational, professional licensing, certification and other representations.

       ISBN 1-889150-00-2

       1. Information retrieval - Handbooks, manuals, etc. 2. Personnel records 3. Public records 4. Records Management I. Ernst, Carl. R. II. Title

                                      025.5'2_dc20

Provided in cooperation with Unique Books, Inc.

Table of Contents

Before You Start v

Introduction

Do You Know Who You're Dealing With?... 1

"Just the Facts, Ma'am"

The Verification Process—Digging into Details... 4

Educational Records

Reading the Profiles 7
Performing the Verification.. 8
Other Searching Nuances to Keep in Mind.. 9

State Licensing Records

Using the State Licensing & Business Registration Section 11
The Quick Finder Section.. 11
The Agency Information Section 13
Search Fees.. 13
Searching Tip—Distinguish the Type of Agency 14
Other Forms of Licensing and Registration 14
Other Information Available 15

State Chapters

Alabama—Wyoming.. 17

Appendix I—Sample Release Form 461

Appendix II—Telephone Area Code Changes 1996-97 462

Appendix III—Privacy

Privacy—What is, What isn't and Why? 463
Federal Acts Impacting Privacy 467
Recent Interest in Information Regulation by the Feds... 470

Introduction

A sharp looking, articulate individual has just answered your help wanted ad. You look over his resume and application and it appears he is just what you need for the position. His educational background, prior employment record, and certification make him your number one candidate. So, all that remains is to tender an employment offer and bring him into your firm, right? NO!

Before you go much further, it would be first wise to **VERIFY THOSE CREDENTIALS** and assure yourself and your organization that the candidate is "as advertised."

Do You Know Who You're Dealing With?

Fact or Fiction

The story above can be re-written using a child care center, a business partner, a contractor, a company offering a service, or even a possible new lover. Regardless of the story line, you need to know the answers to these two questions—

Is he, she or it for real?

Is the information provided complete and honest?

Confirm Existence & Validity

Employers, human resource personnel, and professionals recognize the importance of verifying credentials and education. They know that too many times, a business will hire a new employee without verifying what is represented on the employment application and be embarrassed or suffer in some manner later. However, the verification of credentials is not limited to this group. Other users include; news reporters, financial institutions, private investigators, and consumers. A lawful investigation into an individual's past is recommended when considering promotion of, endorsement of, hiring, or strategic alignment with an individual or company.

Doing business with or having a relationship with a stranger can be unpredictable unless you *know who you are dealing with.*

Hired any liars?

A well-known, proven fact touted by professional pre-employment screening firms and corporate human resource departments is that **25% of applications contain misrepresentations!** Whoever receives information has a responsibility to check on the truth of the information presented.

The Tools to Verify Representations

This book—*Verify Those Credentials*—is designed to provide you with the tools necessary to **check on the representations people make to you in the day-to-day conduct of your business or personal life**. It is easy to say anything one wants on a resume or to distort the facts to one's benefit.

Using Smart Business Practices

We are trying neither to fuel paranoia nor to imply that everyone presents him or herself fraudulently. However, it is simply a smart business practice to check on those with whom you deal, particularly if money or property, real or intellectual, is at stake. Verifying facts in easily accessible public records will give you a "feel" for whether you need to dig deeper or whether you can accept the individual at face value and move on through the business or personal process, whether it is hiring, contracting, marrying, or whatever else is important to you and your life.

It's A Simple Process

Before you decide that this whole process is too much for you to handle, please be assured that we will make the process as clear and simple as possible between the covers of this book.

We'll provide tips and **clues** to help you plan and **execute a search** for the information you need. You will be able to verify, with ease, the educational, professional licensing, certification and other representations about people and businesses. We will provide you with up-to-date school and government agency names, addresses, phone and fax numbers along the requirements you must meet to obtain the information. You can even check yourself out!

"Just the Facts, Ma'am"

The first thing you need to understand is what "facts" are and why they might need verification. Consider these definitions—

Facts vs. Representations

Facts are information about an individual or organization that determines who he or she really is and what makes the individual unique and/or qualified to do or not do certain activities.

Representations are unsubstantiated facts about a person or organization as told by the person, organization or associates of theirs.

Some facts are difficult to misstate or claim fraudulently, such as physical facts like one's height. It's hard to say you are 6'9" tall if it is obvious you are about 5'2" tall. Other facts are rather simple to overstate or falsify, such as one's academic or work record; anyone can "claim" he or she has a Baccalaureate degree. These "facts" are in reality only representations; it is up to you to assure yourself that they are true, accurate and, in some situations, current.

Verifications

Verifications are confirmation of representations from an objective, unrelated third party.

You might ask why anyone would need to verify information presented to on most applications, when it is signed by the individual that the information provided is correct. Well, you don't call a mother to ask if her son is a good boy. For a representation to become fact, it must be verified!

The Bottom Line

Don't just accept representations. The proper and logical action is to get the facts—

Representation

⇩

Verification

⇩

Fact

The Verification Process—Digging into Details

What's Involved

Let's take a quick look at some of the facets involved in evaluating an individual.

Personal Data

Personal data includes such information as an individual's name, aliases, nicknames, height, weight, age, Social Security Number, address, employment history, and the like. Some of this is pretty easy to ascertain by merely looking at the person in front of you. However, items such as the Social Security Number may require additional verification to insure that the individual is really the holder of the social security account. Dates of birth, marriage and divorce may be checked through the state agency responsible for maintaining records of such events.

Judicial/ Legal Data

Judicial and legal data includes such information as civil litigation, criminal judgments, motor vehicle license issuance, liens, bankruptcies, and the like. As with personal data, the requirements for obtaining such information varies from jurisdiction to jurisdiction. However, this data is, with some exceptions, public information and is easily available to you. Facts On Demand's publication, *Find Public Records Fast,* is a valuable reference resource to over 8,000 public records locations in the US for this type of information.

Employment History

Verifying employment data may take time and effort, and you will have to decide if you want to "interview" prior employers by phone/fax or by writing a series of letters. Be prepared to get nothing more from previous employers than verification that the individual was indeed employed or, at best, dates of employment. In today's atmosphere of litigation, many employers are unwilling to offer anything more than the sketchiest of information. We will discuss this in a little more detail in the section on legal ramifications.

Credentials

Credentials include that set of representations, made by a person or organization, regarding these four specific areas—

- educational accomplishments

- professional certifications and status

- special knowledge base (programming languages, speaking foreign languages, etc.)

- indicators of professional competence (publications authored, awards, etc.)

The area in which people are most likely to misrepresent themselves is in **credentials** (the primary focus of this book).

Education Training

Education and training information includes such data as high school diplomas, college/university level education, trade schools, professional schools, extension courses, and similar activities.

Unfortunately, such accomplishments are often overstated or fraudulently reported, with individuals indicating successful completion of educational, trade, or professional schools when, indeed, that is not the case. Fortunately, **this data is very easy to verify**—attendance and completions can often be verified with only a phone call. If you require a transcript or written verification, this normally will take longer and usually require the signed approval of the individual concerned. (See Sample Release Form on page 461)

Be aware that many professional and trade schools enter and leave the market every year; when they leave, the records of graduates often leave with them.

Certification & Licensing

This category includes professional or occupational licensing, professional certification, and business registration. It encompasses both **individuals and businesses**. The information is generally maintained by the agency or licensing board granting the license/certification.

The amount and depth of information released will vary, but usually includes how long and/or at what level the individual or business is licensed/certified. Verification of this kind is crucial for such fields as health care, finance, real estate, and teaching. Fortunately, these are (usually) **very easy to verify** through the state agency granting the license/certificate.

Certifications granted by professional societies, associations or schools may not be as easy to verify. For example, it is sometimes difficult to verify that an individual is a linguist or that he or she is designated a CPM by NAPM (National Association of Purchasing Managers), or a CPIM by APICS (The American Production and Inventory Control Society). An excellent source of these professional organizations is the *Gale Encyclopedia of Business and Professional Associations* ($75, from BRB Publications at 800-929-3811).

A Word of Caution about Registrations

There is a clear **distinction between registration and licensing certification**. The latter requires having proved a level of professional competence, such as passing the CPA examination. Some "professions"—for example, a nurse assistant in some states—merely required registration of notice that such services are performed.

Registration of an **individual or organization** tells you **nothing** about **competence.**

Educational Records

The 3,880 degree granting educational institutions and 1,728 non-degree granting accredited trade school institutions profiled in *Verify Those Credentials* are organized into 51 state chapters.

Reading the Profiles

The first section of each state chapter contains the educational institutions, profiled in alphabetical order by name of institution. The address and phone number given is for the location maintaining the student records. Also, included are office hours, fax numbers, types (levels) of degrees granted, and, usually, an indication of how many years back records are maintained. Branch campuses are listed by city after the main campus. We have indicated when records are maintained at a different or central location.

Attendance and Degree Confirmation

The descriptive format of each profile falls into two categories: **attendance confirmation** and **degree confirmation**. Each category is then individually dissected as follows:

- **Permissible Access Modes**

  Phone, fax, mail or written requests only

- **General Search Requirements**

  Identifying information you must submit, such as years attended, signed release, Social Security Number, etc. Items which are optional, but helpful are also noted.

- **Fees and Payments**

  All costs involved

Don't Forget the SASE!

Some profiles also contain searching tips that you should be aware of regarding that particular school. We have included such items as whether the school requires a self-addressed stamped envelope (**SASE**) with your requests, or if credit cards are accepted for payment, and any comments or searching tips the school asked us to pass along.

Alumni
Associations

You will find many profiles include an alumni association address and phone number. However, some schools have no such organization since they are very technically oriented or narrow in their fields of study. (Note: An alumni association is a good place to a find a current address or a maiden name.)

Adverse Action
Record
Centers

Also, we have indicated 1,724 institutions that house an adverse incident record database. These are records of possible criminal actions, incidents or reprimands that give indication of trustworthiness or morals. The records may be at a center for student activities, the campus police or even the local jurisdictional police. Again, the larger institutions generally have some record center of this type, and the smaller institutions do not.

Performing the Verification

School Policies
Will Vary

Most schools are very willing to cooperate with an employer regarding the placement or hiring of a former student. However, how a record is released and the degree of authority needed to obtain the record are subject to **individual school policy**. Although most schools will confirm attendance over the phone, the policies of the admissions' or registrars' office can and do vary significantly from school to school. For example—

Some Statistics

69 %	require a Social Security Number to confirm attendance and/or degree
81 %	will confirm attendance and/or degree over the phone
15 %	require a signed release from the student to confirm a degree
95%	require a signed release from the student to release a transcript

Identifying
Information

Although it is obvious that you must give the name of the student or graduate in order to obtain information about him or her, you should not overlook the possibility that the person went by another name or name variation while in school. **Be prepared to search by the name at the time of attendance.** A clear example of this is a married woman, but there is also the possibility that someone who today goes by the moniker

C. Alexander Ernst, was just plain Carl A. Ernst when he was in school.

Always Try the Phone

Even when a college or university indicates that it does not take telephone calls for information about students and former students, **most of these institutions will accept a phone call to confirm or deny information that you already have in your possession.** Try this if you have the following kinds of questions—

- Did William White graduate with a B.S. in Biology in 1990? (yes or no response.)

- Did Marilou Beshara receive a degree from your school? (looking for a yes-no answer, not the details.)

Proper Identification

When you call with this kind of request, be sure to identify yourself up front as someone with an obvious proper need to know. For example—

- I'm a reporter doing a story on John Spensieri.

- I'm considering hiring a former student named Roberta Canier.

- Marc Dauphinais applied for a loan from our bank.

- I'm about to sign a large contract with Bill Brownlee.

Verifying by Mail

Always include in your letter of request a note that the Registrar should feel free to call you collect or at your free 800 number if she has any questions about your request.

Just as with a telephone call, include in your cover note a proper, valid reason for your request, and indicate the urgency of your request as well.

Even if not requested, we advise always to include a prepaid return envelope (SASE) for the results. This, again, is a matter of courtesy that is likely to get you a better than average level of service.

Requesting Copies of Transcripts

Although not covered in the profiles, be aware that the overwhelming majority of schools **require a signed release and a fee to obtain a transcript**. You will find a sample of a Release Form on page 461. When you are requesting a transcript (and have a signed release from the graduate), make certain that you have all the information the registrar will need to complete your request in a timely manner. This information might include the address and telephone number of the graduate in case the school wants to verify the request directly with the graduate. Also, if the college has an internal student identification number system, include that number as well if available. Since there will be a fee, we recommend sending a blank check with a limited dollar amount, (i.e., not more than $25.00).

Other Searching Nuances to Keep in Mind

Here are some **searching tips—**

- At larger universities, it will help if you know the student's degree or major. This is especially true if you are trying to obtain information by telephone.

- Older records are usually archived. Whether they are on microfiche or stored in a box in the basement, count on it taking longer for the school to complete your search.

- Branch campuses generally do not maintain official transcript files; however, many, when asked by a requester with a legitimate purpose, will confirm attendance or a degree.

- Some schools allow students to block or restrict access to their records. If this happens to you, a signed release is advised. On the other hand some schools, which are otherwise restrictive, will permit the student to leave a release in his/her file to facilitate a verification. It wouldn't hurt to ask if a school indicates they have such a policy.

- Many schools who accept fax requests, ask that a written request follow in the mail. Most schools consider any information faxed back to a requester to be unofficial or uncertified.

- If a subject or an employee claims to have a four-year (or higher) degree from an institution that offers only a two-year associate's degree, you have an immediate indication of that person's character or memory.

State Licensing Records

Using the State Licensing & Business Registration Section

The second part of each state chapter in *Verify Those Credentials* contains a broad list of **occupational licensing** and **business registration agencies**. You will find that these agencies maintain a wealth of information about each licensee or registrant in their files.

The Privacy Question

While some agencies consider this information private and confidential to one extent or another, most agencies freely release at least some basic data over the phone or by mail.

Our research indicates that many agencies appear to make their own judgments regarding what specifically is private and confidential in their files. For example, although most agencies will not release an SSN, 8% do. On the other side of the question, 45% of the agencies indicate that they will disclose adverse information about a registrant, and many of those will only disclose selected portions of the information.

In any event, the basic rule to follow when you contact a licensing agency is to **ask for the specific kinds of information available.**

What Information May Be Available

An agency may be willing to release part or all of the following—

Field of Certification

Status of License/Certificate

Date License/Certificate Issued

Date License/Certificate Expires

Current or Most Recent Employer

Social Security Number

Address of Subject

Complaints, Violations or Disciplinary Actions

The Quick Finder Section

The State Licensing & Business Registration portion of each state chapter is separated into two parts—**Quick Finder** and **Agency Information**. The two sections are tied together by a **Key Number**.

Using The Quick Finder

The place to start a verification search is in the **Quick Finder.** Here you will find, licenses, registrations or occupations are listed in alphabetical order, within these **12 general categories—**

The Agency Categories

Architecture, Engineering & Surveying

Business - Court & Legal Services

Business - General Services

Construction & Manufacturing

Education

Environmental & Agriculture

Finance - Real Estate, Insurance & Banking

Health & Beauty

Investigations & Security

Social Services

Sports & Entertainment

Transportation

License Name

Although we reflect the official name used in a state for most items, names of some of the major license types have been standardized to make them easier to locate. For example, some states use the word "Physician" rather than "Medical Doctor." We have chosen the latter usage.

Special Search Indicators

The majority of agencies will accept a telephone call to verify that a person or business is included in their records. In many cases, the agency will provide additional information as discussed on the previous page. In those cases where a telephone request will not be accepted, ⊠ will appear.

There are two indicators that summarize particularly important data which is included in the Agency Information for this license. The indicators are:

☎ Agency releases information freely over the telephone.

⊠ Agency will only release information with a written request.

Use the Key Number

The **Key Number** is the *identifying number* for the agency that maintains information about this license. By matching the Key Number found in the Quick Finder to the profile in the Agency Information, you will have the address and other details about how this agency operates.

An Example of the Quick Finder Section

Health and Beauty

Beautician #3 (1241).............................. ☎ 216-123-4536

Dentist #4 .... ☎ 216-321-3545

Medical Doctor #16 (945).................... ✉ 216-323-1234

In this example, the first two agencies indicate that a telephone call will get you the basics for free. For medical doctors, you must place your verification in writing.

The number in parenthesis indicates the number of current licenses within that agency or board.

The Agency Information Section

As stated above, the Key Number leads you to the Agency Information Section, where you will find the Agency or Board's address and phone number.

(3) Department of Health & Social Services, Division of Public Health, 123 Sesame Street, Mapletown, OH 44414, 216-123-4536

Search Fees

We observed several trends when we verified search fees of the various licensing agencies. They are as follows:

- There is no charge to verify if a particular person is licensed and this can usually be done over the phone.

- The fee for copies or faxes ranges from $0.25 to $2.00.

- A fee of $5 to $20 usually applies to written requests. This is due to the fact that the written certification releases more information than a verbal inquiry, i.e. disciplinary action or exam scores.

- A fee that is $25 or more is usually for a list of licensed professionals. For example, a hospital that needs a roster of registered nurses in a certain geographic area.

Searching Tip—Distinguish the Type of Agency

Within the agency category listings, it is important to note that there are five general types of agencies. When you are verifying credentials, you should be aware of what distinguishes each type, which in turn could alter the questions you ask.

Private
Certification

1. **Private Licensing and Certification**—requires a proven level of minimum competence before license is granted. These professional licenses separate the true "professions" from the third category below. In many of these professions, the certification body, such as the American Institute of Certified Public Accountants, is a private association whereas the licensing body, such as the New York State Education Department, is the licensing agency. Also, many professions may provide additional certifications in specialty areas.

State
Certification

2. **State Licensing and Certification**—requires certification through an **examination** and/or other **requirements supervised** directly **by the state** rather than by a private association.

By Individual

3. **Individual Registration**—required if an individual intends to offer specified products or services in the designated area, but does not require certification that the person has met minimum requirements. An everyday example would be registering a handgun in a state that does not require passing a gun safety course.

By Business

4. **Business Registration**—required if a business intends to do business or offer specified products or services in a designated area, such as registering a liquor license. Some business license agencies require testing or a background check. Others merely charge a fee after a cursory review of the application.

Special
Permits

5. **Permits**—give the grantee specific permission to do something, whether it is to sell hot-dogs on the corner or to put up a three story sign. Permits are usually granted at the local rather than state level of government.

Other Forms of Licensing and Registration

Although the state level is where much of the licensing and registration occurs, you should be aware of other places you may want to search.

Local Government Agencies	Local government agencies at both the **county** and **municipal levels** require a myriad of business registrations and permits in order to do business (construction, signage, etc.) within their borders. Even where you think a business or person, such as a remodeling contractor, should have local registrations you want to check out, it is still best to start at the state level using this book.
County Recorder's Office and City Hall	If you decide to check on local registrations and permits, call the offices at both the county—try the **county recorder**—and municipal level—**try city hall**—to find out what type of registrations may be required for the person or business you are checking out. (See the bibliography for sources of county level records.)
	Just as on the state level, you should expect that basic information will be just a phone call away and that you will not be charged for obtaining a status summary.
Professional Associations	As mentioned above, many professional licenses are based on completion of the requirements of professional associations. In addition, there are **many professional designations** from such associations that **are not recognized as official licenses by government**. Other designations are basic certifications in fields that are so specialized that they are not of interest to the states, but rather only to the professionals within an industry. For example, if your company needs to hire an investigator to check out a potential fraud against you, you might want to hire a CFE—Certified Fraud Examiner—who has meet the minimum requirements for that title from the Association of Certified Fraud Examiners.

Other Information Available

Mail Lists and Databases	Many agencies make their lists available in reprinted or computer form, and a few maintain online access to their files. If you are interested in the availability of licensing agency information in bulk (e.g., mailing lists, magnetic tapes, disks) or on–line, call the agency and ask about

formats that are available.

Online Searching and CD-ROMS

A number of private vendors also compile lists from these agencies and make them available online or on CD-ROM. We do not suggest these databases for credential searching because they may not be complete, may not be up to date, and may not contain all the information you can obtain directly from the licensing agency. However, these databases are extremely valuable as a general source of background information on an individual or company you wish to do business with. For a more complete discussion of general background checking and sources of such information, take a look at two other books in the Facts on Demand Press series—*Find Public Records Fast* and *Public Records Online.*

Alabama

Capitol: Montgomery (Montgomery County)	
State Population	4.3 Million
Number of Degree Granting Institutions:	72
Number of State Licensing & Business Registration Agencies:	121

Degree Granting Educational Institutions

Alabama Agricultural and Mechanical University, Registrar, PO Box 908, Normal, AL 35762, 205-851-5254 (Fax: 205-851-5253). Hours: 8AM-5PM. Enrollment: 4800. Degrees granted: Associate; Bachelors; Masters; Doctorate. Adverse incident record source- Public Safety, 205-851-5555.

Attendance and degree information available by phone, fax, mail. Search requires name plus SSN, approximate years of attendance. There is no fee.

Alabama Aviation and Technical College, Registrar, PO Box 1209, Ozark, AL 36361-1209, 334-774-5113 (Fax: 334-774-5113). Hours: 7:45AM-4:30PM. Enrollment: 300. Records go back to 1960. Alumni records are maintained here at the same phone number. Degrees granted: Associate. Adverse incident record source- Student Development, 334-774-5113.

Attendance and degree information available by fax, mail. Search requires name plus SSN. Also helpful: exact years of attendance. There is no fee.

Alabama Southern Community College, Registrar, PO Box 2000, Monroeville, AL 36461, 334-575-3156 X252. Hours: 7:30AM-4:30PM. Enrollment: 1800. Records go back to 1965. Degrees granted: Associate.

Attendance and degree information available by phone, mail. Search requires name plus SSN. There is no fee.

Alabama Southern Community College, (Thomasville), Registrar, Hwy 43 S, Thomasville, AL 36784, 334-575-3156 X252 (Fax: 334-575-5356). Records are not housed here. They are located at Alabama Southern Community College, Registrar, PO Box 2000, Monroeville, AL 36461.

Alabama State University, Registrar, 915 S Jackson St, Montgomery, AL 36101-0271, 334-229-4243 (Fax: 334-834-0336). Hours: 8AM-6PM M-Th, 8AM-5PM F. Enrollment: 5400. Records go back to 1874. Alumni records are maintained here also. Call 334-293-4280. Degrees granted: Associate; Bachelors; Masters. Adverse incident record source- Security, 334-293-4400.

Attendance and degree information available by phone, fax, mail. Search requires name plus SSN, date of birth, approximate years of attendance. Also helpful: exact years of attendance. There is no fee.

Athens State College, Records Office, 300 N Beaty St, Athens, AL 35611, 205-233-8165 (Fax: 205-233-8128). Hours: 8AM-4:30PM. Enrollment: 2600. Records go back to 1823. Alumni records are maintained here also. Call 205-233-8275. Degrees granted: Bachelors.

Attendance and degree information available by phone, fax, mail. Search requires name only. Also helpful: SSN, date of birth, exact years of attendance. There is no fee.

Auburn University, Registrar, 100 Mary Martin Hall, Auburn, AL 36849, 334-844-4770 (Fax: 334-844-6436). Hours: 7:45AM-4:45PM. Enrollment: 19780. Records go back to 1960. Alumni records are maintained here also. Call 334-844-2586. Degrees granted: Bachelors; Masters; Doctorate. Adverse incident record source- Campus Security, 205-844-4000.

Attendance and degree information available by phone, fax, mail. Search requires name plus SSN, approximate years of attendance. There is no fee.

Auburn University at Montgomery, Registrar, 7300 University Dr, Montgomery, AL 36117-3596, 334-244-3614 (Fax: 334-244-3795). Hours: 8AM-5PM. Enrollment: 5882. Records go back to 1976. Alumni records are maintained here also. Call 334-244-3356. Degrees granted: Bachelors; Masters. Adverse incident record source- Campus Police, 334-244-3424.

Attendance and degree information available by phone, mail. Search requires name plus SSN. There is no fee.

Bessemer State Technical College, Registrar, PO Box 308, Bessemer, AL 35021, 205-428-6391 (Fax: 205-424-5119). Hours: 8AM-4PM. Enrollment: 5121. Records go back to 1965. Degrees granted: Associate.

Attendance and degree information available by phone, mail. Search requires name plus SSN. There is no fee.

Bevill State Community College, Registrar, PO Box 800, Sumiton, AL 35148, 205-648-3271 (Fax: 205-648-2288). Hours: 8AM-4:30PM. Enrollment: 5000. Records go back to 1969. Alumni records are maintained here at the same phone number. Degrees granted: Associate.

Attendance information available by phone, fax, mail. Search requires name plus SSN. Also helpful: date of birth, exact years of attendance. There is no fee.

Degree information available by mail. Search requires name plus SSN. Also helpful: date of birth, exact years of attendance. There is no fee.

Bevill State Community College, (Brewer), Registrar, 2631 Temple Ave N, Fayette, AL 35555, 205-932-3221. Records are not housed here. They are located at Bevill State Community College, Registrar, PO Box 800, Sumiton, AL 35148.

Birmingham-Southern College, Registrar, 900 Arkadelphia Rd, PO Box 549018, Birmingham, AL 35254, 205-226-4698 (Fax: 205-226-3064). Hours: 8:15AM-4:45PM. Enrollment: 1565. Records go back to 1856. Alumni records are maintained here at the same phone number. Degrees granted: Bachelors; Masters. Special programs- Adult Study. Adverse incident record source- Student Affairs, 205-226-4722.

Attendance and degree information available by phone, fax, mail. Search requires name plus exact years of attendance. Also helpful: SSN. There is no fee.

Bishop State Community College, Registrar, 351 N Broad St, Mobile, AL 36603-5898, 334-690-6421 (Fax: 334-438-5403). Hours: 8AM-5PM. Enrollment: 4640. Records go back to 1960. Degrees granted: Associate.

Attendance and degree information available by phone, mail. Search requires name plus SSN, date of birth, approximate years of attendance. There is no fee.

Bishop State Community College, (Carver), Registrar, 414 Stanton St, Mobile, AL 36617, 334-473-8692 (Fax: 334-471-5961). Hours: 8AM-4:30PM. Degrees granted: Associate.

Attendance and degree information available by phone, mail. Search requires name plus SSN, exact years of attendance. There is no fee.

Bishop State Community College, (Southwest), Registrar, 925 Dauphin Island Pkwy, Mobile, AL 36605-3299, 334-479-7476 (Fax: 334-473-2049). Hours: 8AM-7PM M-Th; 8AM-4:30PM F. Records go back to 1955. Degrees granted: Associate.

Attendance and degree information available by phone, mail. Search requires name plus SSN, date of birth, approximate years of attendance. There is no fee.

Central Alabama Community College, Registrar, 908 Cherokee Rd, PO Box 699, Alexander City, AL 35010, 205-234-6346 (Fax: 205-234-0384). Hours: 7:30AM-4:30PM. Enrollment: 2500. Records go back to 1965. Degrees granted: Associate. Special programs- Tech Records prior 1989 merger, 205-378-5570 X6420. Adverse incident record source- Dean of Student Development, 205-234-6346 X6510.

Attendance and degree information available by phone, fax, mail. Search requires name only. Also helpful: SSN, date of birth, exact years of attendance. There is no fee.

Chattahoochee Valley State Community College, Director of Admissions, 2602 College Dr, Phenix City, AL 36869, 334-291-4928 (Fax: 334-291-4994). Hours: 8AM-5PM. Enrollment: 1367. Records go back to 1974. Alumni records are maintained here at the same phone number. Degrees granted: Associate. Adverse incident record source- 334-291-4946.

Attendance and degree information available by fax, mail. Search requires name plus SSN, exact years of attendance, signed release. Also helpful: date of birth. There is no fee.

Community College of the Air Force/RRR, Registrar, Simler Hall Ste 128, 130 W Maxwell Blvd, Maxwell Air Force Base, AL 36112-6613, 334-953-6436. Hours: 7AM-5PM. Enrollment: 42670. Records go back to 1976. Degrees granted: Associate. Adverse incident record source- Administrative Office, 205-953-6436.

Attendance and degree information available by phone, mail. Search requires name plus SSN, date of birth. There is no fee.

Concordia College, Registrar, 1804 Green St, PO Box 1329, Selma, AL 36701, 334-874-5700 (Fax: 334-874-5755). Hours: 8AM-4PM. Enrollment: 348. Degrees granted: Associate; Bachelors. Adverse incident record source- Dean's Office, 334-874-5730 .

Attendance information available by phone, fax, mail. Search requires name plus SSN, exact years of attendance. There is no fee.

Degree information available by phone, mail. Search requires name plus SSN, exact years of attendance. There is no fee.

Douglas MacArthur State Technical College, Registrar, 1708 N Main St, Opp, AL 36467, 334-493-3573 X233 (Fax: 334-493-7003). Hours: 7:30AM-4:30PM. Enrollment: 550. Records go back to 1965. Degrees granted: Associate.

Attendance and degree information available by phone, fax, mail. Search requires name plus SSN. Also helpful: date of birth, exact years of attendance. There is no fee.

Enterprise State Junior College, Registrar, 600 Plaza Dr, PO Box 1300, Enterprise, AL 36331, 334-347-2623 X233 (Fax: 334-347-1157). Hours: 7:45AM-4:30PM. Enrollment: 1900. Records go back to 1965. Degrees granted: Associate.

Attendance and degree information available by phone, fax, mail. Search requires name plus SSN, date of birth. Also helpful: exact years of attendance. There is no fee.

Faulkner University, Registrar, 5345 Atlanta Hwy, Montgomery, AL 36109-3398, 334-260-6241 (Fax: 334-260-6201). Hours: 8AM-5PM. Enrollment: 2090. Records go back to 1942. Alumni records are maintained here also. Call 334-260-6136. Degrees granted: Associate; Bachelors; JD. Adverse incident record source- Student Services, 334-260-6180.

Attendance and degree information available by phone, fax, mail. Search requires name plus approximate years of attendance. Also helpful: SSN, date of birth, exact years of attendance. There is no fee.

Gadsden State Community College, Registrar, PO Box 227, Gadsden, AL 35902-0227, 205-549-8261 (Fax: 205-549-8444). Hours: 7:30AM-4PM. Enrollment: 6200. Records go back to 1925. Alumni records are maintained here also. Call 205-549-8224. Degrees granted: Associate. Adverse incident record source- Registrar, 205-549-8261.

Attendance and degree information available by phone, fax, mail. Search requires name plus SSN, exact years of attendance. There is no fee.

George C. Wallace State Community College, Registrar, Route 6, Box 62, Dothan, AL 36303, 334-983-5321 X302 (Fax: 334-983-3600). Hours: 7:45AM-4:30PM. Records go back to 1949. Alumni records are maintained here at the same phone number. Degrees granted: Associate.

Attendance and degree information available by phone, fax, mail. Search requires name plus SSN. There is no fee.

George Corley Wallace State Community College, Registrar, PO Drawer 1049, 3000 Range Line Rd, Selma, AL 36702-1049, 334-875-2634 X36 (Fax: 334-874-7116). Hours: 7:30AM-4:30PM M-Th, 7:30AM-3PM F. Enrollment: 1590. Records go back to 1965. Alumni records are maintained here at the same phone number. Degrees granted: Associate.

Attendance and degree information available by phone, fax, mail. Search requires name plus SSN. There is no fee.

Harry M. Ayers State Technical College, Registrar, PO Box 1647, Anniston, AL 36202-1647, 205-835-5400 (Fax: 205-835-5474). Hours: 7:30AM-4:30PM. Enrollment: 372. Records go back to 1965. Degrees granted: Associate.

Attendance and degree information available by phone, fax, mail. Search requires name plus SSN, exact years of attendance. There is no fee.

Huntingdon College, Registrar, 1500 E Fairview Ave, Montgomery, AL 36106-2148, 334-833-4430 (Fax: 334-833-4502). Hours: 8AM-5PM Sep-May, 7:30AM-4PM Jun-Aug. Enrollment: 650. Records go back to 1900. Alumni records are maintained here also. Call 334-883-4504. Degrees granted: Associate; Bachelors.

Attendance and degree information available by phone, fax, mail. Search requires name only. Also helpful: SSN, date of birth, exact years of attendance. There is no fee.

International Bible College, Registrar, 3625 Helton Dr, PO Box IBC, Florence, AL 35630, 205-766-6610 (Fax: 205-760-0981). Hours: 8AM-4:30PM. Enrollment: 155. Records go back to 1971. Alumni Records Office: Alumni President, PO Box 716, Haleyville, AL 35565. Degrees granted: Associate; Bachelors.

Attendance and degree information available by phone, fax, mail. Search requires name plus SSN, date of birth, exact years of attendance. There is no fee.

J. F. Drake State Technical College, Registrar, 3421 Meridian St, Huntsville, AL 35811, 205-539-8161 X110 (Fax: 205-539-6439). Hours: 7:30AM-4PM. Enrollment: 575. Records go back to 1961. Alumni records are maintained here also. Call 205-539-8161. Degrees granted: Associate.

Attendance and degree information available by phone, fax, mail. Search requires name plus SSN, approximate years of attendance. There is no fee.

Jacksonville State University, Registrar, 700 N Pelham Rd, Jacksonville, AL 36265-9982, 205-782-5400 (Fax: 205-782-5121). Hours: 8AM-4:30PM. Enrollment: 6095. Alumni records are maintained here also. Call 205-782-5404. Degrees granted: Bachelors; Masters; Educational Specialists.

Attendance and degree information available by phone, fax, mail. Search requires name plus SSN, approximate years of attendance. There is no fee.

James H. Faulkner State Community College, Registrar, 1900 Hwy 31 S, Bay Minette, AL 36507, 334-937-9581 X311 (Fax: 334-580-2253). Hours: 8AM-5PM. Enrollment: 3418. Records go back to 1965. Degrees granted: Associate.

Attendance and degree information available by phone, fax, mail. Search requires name plus SSN, approximate years of attendance. There is no fee.

Jefferson Davis Community College, Registrar's Office, 220 Alco Dr, Brewton, AL 36426, 334-867-4832 X45 (Fax: 334-867-7399). Hours: 7:30AM-4:30PM. Enrollment: 1630. Records go back to 1965. Degrees granted: Associate. Adverse incident record source- Registrar, 205-867-4832.

Attendance and degree information available by phone, fax, mail. Search requires name plus SSN, exact years of attendance. Also helpful: approximate years of attendance. There is no fee.

Jefferson State Community College, Registrar, 2601 Carson Rd, Birmingham, AL 35215-3098, 205-853-1200 X6069. Hours: 8AM-4:30PM. Enrollment: 5000. Records go back to 1965. Degrees granted: Associate. Adverse incident record source- Security Office, 205-856-6093.

Attendance and degree information available by mail. Search requires name plus SSN, signed release. There is no fee.

John C. Calhoun State Community College, Registrar, PO Box 23216, Decatur, AL 35609-2216, 205-306-2601 (Fax: 205-306-2885). Hours: 8AM-8PM M-Th; 8AM-4PM F. Enrollment: 7800. Records go back to 1950. Alumni records are maintained here at the same phone number. Degrees granted: Associate. Adverse incident record source- Dean of Students: Security

Attendance and degree information available by phone, fax, mail. Search requires name plus SSN, date of birth. There is no fee.

John M. Patterson State Technical College, Registrar, 3920 Troy Hwy, Montgomery, AL 36116, 334-288-1080 (Fax: 334-284-9357). Hours: 8AM-6:30PM M-Th, 8AM-4PM F. Enrollment: 1100. Records go back to 1962. Alumni records are maintained here at the same phone number. Degrees granted: Associate.

Attendance and degree information available by phone, fax, mail. Search requires name plus SSN. Also helpful: exact years of attendance. There is no fee.

Judson College, Registrar, PO Box 120, Marion, AL 36756, 334-683-5129 (Fax: 334-683-5147). Hours: 8AM-5PM. Enrollment: 400. Records go back to 1838. Alumni records are maintained here also. Call 334-683-5169. Degrees granted: Bachelors. Certification: Teacher. Special programs- External Degree, 334-683-5123. Adverse incident record source- Student Services, 334-683-5108.

Attendance and degree information available by fax, mail. Search requires name plus approximate years of attendance, signed release. Also helpful: SSN, date of birth, exact years of attendance. There is no fee.

Lawson State Community College, Registrar, 3060 Wilson Rd SW, Birmingham, AL 35221, 205-929-6309 (Fax: 205-929-6316). Hours: 8AM-5PM. Enrollment: 1846. Degrees granted: Associate. Adverse incident record source- Security, 205-925-2515 X235.

Attendance and degree information available by phone, fax, mail. Search requires name plus SSN, approximate years of attendance. There is no fee.

Lurleen B. Wallace State Junior College, Registrar, PO Box 1418, Andalusia, AL 36420, 334-222-6591 X273 (Fax: 334-222-6567). Hours: 8AM-5PM. Enrollment: 995. Records go back to 1969. Degrees granted: Associate. Adverse incident record source- Dean of the College, 334-222-6591 X2213.

Attendance and degree information available by phone, fax, mail. Search requires name plus SSN, date of birth, approximate years of attendance. Also helpful: exact years of attendance. There is no fee.

Marion Military Institute, Registrar, 1101 Washington St, Marion, AL 36756, 334-683-2304 X334 (Fax: 334-683-2380). Hours: 8AM-4PM. Enrollment: 217. Records go back to 1920. Degrees granted: Associate. Adverse incident record source- Commandant Office, 334-683-2321 or 2322.

Attendance and degree information available by phone, fax, mail. Search requires name plus date of birth. Also helpful: exact years of attendance. Fee is $5.00.

Miles College, Registrar, PO Box 3800, Birmingham, AL 35208, 205-923-2771 X276 (Fax: 205-923-9292). Hours: 8AM-5PM. Enrollment: 1043. Records go back to 1905. Alumni records are maintained here also. Call 205-923-2771 X291. Degrees granted: Bachelors.

Attendance and degree information available by phone, fax, mail. Search requires name plus SSN. There is no fee.

Northeast Alabama State Community College, Registrar, PO Box 159, Hwy 35, Rainsville, AL 35986, 205-638-4418 X238 (Fax: 205-228-6861). Hours: 8AM-

4:30PM. Enrollment: 1061. Records go back to 1965. Alumni records are maintained here at the same phone number. Degrees granted: Associate. Adverse incident record source- Admissions, 205-638-4418 X222.

Attendance and degree information available by mail. Search requires name plus SSN, signed release. There is no fee.

Northwest Shoals Community College, Registrar, PO Box 2545, George Wallace Blvd, Muscle Shoals, AL 35662, 205-331-5200 (Fax: 205-331-5366). Hours: 7:30AM-4PM. Enrollment: 2530. Records go back to 1963. Degrees granted: Associate.

Attendance and degree information available by phone, fax, mail. Search requires name plus SSN. There is no fee.

Oakwood College, Registrar, Oakwood Rd NW, Huntsville, AL 35896, 205-726-7346 (Fax: 205-726-7199). Hours: 9AM-4PM M-Th, 9AM-Noon F. Enrollment: 1392. Records go back to 1896. Alumni records are maintained here also. Call 205-726-7039. Degrees granted: Associate; Bachelors. Adverse incident record source- Student Affairs, 205-726-7400 X7400.

Attendance and degree information available by phone, fax, mail. Search requires name plus SSN, approximate years of attendance. There is no fee.

Reid State Technical College, Registrar, I-65 at Hwy 83, Evergreen, AL 36401, 334-578-1313 X106 (Fax: 334-578-5345). Hours: 7AM-4PM. Enrollment: 518. Records go back to 1963. Alumni records are maintained here at the same phone number. Degrees granted: Associate. Adverse incident record source- Dean of Students, 334-578-1313.

Attendance and degree information available by phone, fax, mail. Search requires name plus SSN, approximate years of attendance. There is no fee.

Samford University, Registrar, 800 Lakeshore Dr, Birmingham, AL 35229, 205-870-2911 (Fax: 205-870-2908). Hours: 7:30AM-5PM. Enrollment: 4445. Records go back to 1887. Alumni records are maintained here at the same phone number. Degrees granted: Associate; Bachelors; Masters; Doctorate. Adverse incident record source- Campus Security, 205-870-2020.

Attendance and degree information available by phone, fax, mail. Search requires name plus SSN. There is no fee.

Selma University, Admissions & Records, Director, 1501 Lapsley St, Selma, AL 36701, 334-872-2533 (Fax: 334-872-7746). Hours: 8:30AM-4PM. Enrollment: 200. Records go back to 1892. Degrees granted: Associate; Bachelors.

Attendance and degree information available by phone, fax, mail. Search requires name plus SSN, approximate years of attendance. There is no fee.

Shelton State Community College, Registrar, 202 Skyland Blvd, Tuscaloosa, AL 35405, 205-391-2214 (Fax: 205-759-2495). Hours: 8AM-5PM. Enrollment: 6120. Records go back to 1950. Alumni records are maintained here also. Call 205-391-2221. Degrees granted: Associate.

Attendance and degree information available by phone, fax, mail. Search requires name plus SSN. There is no fee.

Snead State Community College, Registrar, PO Drawer D, 220 N Walnut St, Boaz, AL 35957, 205-593-5120 X207 (Fax: 205-593-7180). Hours: 7:30AM-4PM. Enrollment: 1700. Records go back to 1934. Alumni records are maintained here also. Call 205-593-5120. Degrees granted: Associate.

Attendance and degree information available by phone, fax, mail. Search requires name plus SSN. Also helpful: date of birth, exact years of attendance. There is no fee.

Southeastern Bible College, Registrar, 3001 Hwy 28 E, Birmingham, AL 35243, 205-970-9208 (Fax: 205-970-9207). Hours: 8AM-4:30PM. Enrollment: 134. Records go back to 1940. Alumni records are maintained here at the same number. Degrees granted: Associate; Bachelors; Masters. Adverse incident record source- Dean of Students, 205-969-0880.

Attendance and degree information available by phone, fax, mail. Search requires name plus approximate years of attendance. There is no fee.

Southern Christian University, Registrar, 1200 Taylor Rd, Montgomery, AL 36117-3553, 334-277-2277 (Fax: 334-271-0002). Hours: 9AM-5PM. Enrollment: 180. Alumni records are maintained here at the same phone number. Degrees granted: Bachelors; Masters; Doctorate. Adverse incident record source- Academic Dean, 334-277-2277.

Attendance and degree information available by phone, fax, mail. Search requires name plus SSN, approximate years of attendance. Fee is $10.00.

Southern Union State Community College, Registrar, PO Box 1000, Wadley, AL 36276, 334-395-2211 (Fax: 334-395-2215). Hours: 7:30AM-4:30PM. Records go back to 1922. Alumni records are maintained here also. Call 334-745-6437. Degrees granted: Associate. Adverse incident record source- Dean, 205-395-2211.

Attendance and degree information available by phone, fax, mail. Search requires name plus SSN, date of birth. Also helpful: exact years of attendance. There is no fee.

Sparks State Technical College, Registrar, PO Drawer 580, Eufala, AL 36072, 334-687-3543 (Fax: 334-681-0255). Hours: 8AM-5PM. Enrollment: 2500. Formerly Chauncey Sparks State Technical College Records go back to 1963. Alumni records are maintained here at the same phone number. Degrees granted: Associate. Adverse incident record source- Department of Security.

Attendance and degree information available by phone, fax. Search requires name plus SSN, exact years of attendance. There is no fee.

Spring Hill College, Registrar, 4000 Dauphin St, Mobile, AL 36608, 334-380-2240 (Fax: 334-460-2192). Hours: 8AM-5PM. Enrollment: 1090. Records go back to 1900. Alumni records are maintained here also. Call 334-380-2280. Degrees granted: Associate; Bachelors.

Attendance and degree information available by phone, fax, mail. Search requires name plus SSN, date of birth, approximate years of attendance. There is no fee.

Stillman College, Registrar, PO Drawer 1430, Tuscaloosa, AL 35403, 205-349-8816 (Fax: 205-366-8996). Hours: 8AM-5PM. Enrollment: 842. Records go back to 1955. Alumni records are maintained here also. Call 205-366-8885. Degrees granted: Bachelors. Adverse incident record source- VP, Student Affairs, 205-366-8833.

Attendance and degree information available by phone, fax, mail. Search requires name plus SSN, date of birth, exact years of attendance. There is no fee. Expedited service available for $5.00.

Talladega College, Registrar, 627 W Battle St, Talladega, AL 35160, 205-761-6219 (Fax: 205-362-2268). Hours: 8AM-5PM. Enrollment: 786. Records go back to 1867. Alumni records are maintained here also. Call 205-761-6203. Degrees granted: Bachelors. Adverse incident record source- Student Activities, 205-761-6233.

Attendance and degree information available by phone, fax, mail. Search requires name plus SSN, approximate years of attendance. There is no fee.

Trenholm State Technical College, Registrar, 1225 Air Base Blvd, Montgomery, AL 36108, 334-832-9000 (Fax: 334-832-9777). Hours: 8AM-5PM. Enrollment: 780. Rec-

ords go back to 1966. Alumni records are maintained here at the same phone number. Degrees granted: Associate.

Attendance information available by phone, mail. Search requires name plus SSN. Also helpful: date of birth, exact years of attendance. There is no fee.

Degree information available by mail. Search requires name plus SSN. Also helpful: date of birth, exact years of attendance. There is no fee.

Troy State University, University Records, University Ave, Troy, AL 36082, 334-670-3170 (Fax: 334-670-3538). Hours: 8AM-5PM. Enrollment: 9200. Records go back to 1887. Alumni records are maintained here at the same phone number. Degrees granted: Associate; Bachelors; Masters. Adverse incident record source- Student Services, 334-670-3000.

Attendance and degree information available by phone, fax, mail. Search requires name plus SSN, exact years of attendance. There is no fee.

Troy State University at Dothan, Registrar, PO Box 8368, 3601 US Hwy 231 N, Dothan, AL 36304-0368, 334-983-6556 X229 (Fax: 334-983-6322). Hours: 7:45AM-5:30PM M-Th; 8AM-Noon F. Enrollment: 2300. Records go back to 1981. Alumni records are maintained here at the same phone number. Degrees granted: Associate; Bachelors; Masters. Special programs- Tech Mgmt, 334-983-6556 X264: Edu Leadershp, 334-983-6556. Adverse incident record source- Financial Affairs, 334-983-6556 X212: Student Affairs, 334-983-6556 X204

Attendance and degree information available by phone, fax, mail. Search requires name plus SSN, approximate years of attendance. There is no fee.

Troy State University in Montgomery, Registrar's Office, 231 Montgomery, PO Drawer 4415, Montgomery, AL 36103-4415, 334-241-9511 (Fax: 334-241-9714). Hours: 8AM-5:30PM. Enrollment: 3400. Records go back to 1972. Alumni records are maintained here also. Call 334-241-9523. Degrees granted: Associate; Bachelors; Masters; ED.S.

Attendance and degree information available by phone, fax, mail. Search requires name only. Also helpful: SSN, date of birth, exact years of attendance. There is no fee.

Tuskegee University, Office of the Registrar, Tuskegee, AL 36088, 334-727-8507. Hours: 8AM-4:30PM. Enrollment: 3140. Records go back to 1881. Alumni records are maintained here also. Call 334-727-8342. Degrees granted: Associate; Bachelors; Masters; Doctorate.

Attendance and degree information available by phone, mail. Search requires name plus SSN, date of birth, exact years of attendance. There is no fee.

United States Sports Academy, Registrar, One Academy Dr, Daphne, AL 36526, 334-626-3303 (Fax: 334-626-1149). Hours: 8AM-5PM. Enrollment: 211. Records go back to 1974. Degrees granted: Bachelors; Masters.

Attendance and degree information available by phone, fax, mail. Search requires name plus SSN, approximate years of attendance. Also helpful: exact years of attendance. There is no fee.

University of Alabama, Records Office, PO Box 870134, Tuscaloosa, AL 35487-0134, 205-348-4886 (Fax: 205-348-8187). Hours: 8AM-4:45PM. Enrollment: 19000. Alumni Records Office: Alumni Hall, The University of Alabama, PO Box 1928, Tuscaloosa, AL 35486. Degrees granted: Bachelors; Masters; Doctorate. Adverse incident record source- Dept of Public Safety, 205-348-5454.

Attendance and degree information available by phone, fax, mail. Search requires name plus SSN, date of birth. Also helpful: exact years of attendance. There is no fee.

University of Alabama at Birmingham-Walker College, Registrar, 1411 Indiana Ave, Jasper, AL

35501, 205-387-0511 (Fax: 205-387-5175). Hours: 8AM-4:30PM. Enrollment: 1000. Records go back to 1938. Alumni records are maintained here at the same phone number. Degrees granted: Associate.

Attendance and degree information available by phone. Search requires name plus SSN. There is no fee.

University of Alabama in Huntsville, Office of Records, University Center #116, Huntsville, AL 35899, 205-895-6750 (Fax: 205-895-6073). Hours: 8:15AM-5PM. Enrollment: 7200. Records go back to 1968. Alumni records are maintained here at the same phone number. Degrees granted: Bachelors; Masters; Doctorate. Adverse incident record source- Student Affairs.

Attendance and degree information available by phone, fax, mail. Search requires name plus SSN. Also helpful: date of birth, exact years of attendance. There is no fee.

University of Mobile, Registrar, PO Box 13220, Mobile, AL 36663-0220, 334-675-5990 X235 (Fax: 334-675-9816). Hours: 8AM-4:30PM. Enrollment: 1865. Formerly Mobile College Records go back to 1963. Alumni records are maintained here also. Call 334-675-5990 X224. Degrees granted: Associate; Bachelors; Masters.

Attendance and degree information available by phone, fax, mail. Search requires name plus SSN, exact years of attendance. There is no fee.

University of Montevallo, Registrar, Station 6040, Montevallo, AL 35115-6001, 205-665-6040 (Fax: 205-665-6042). Hours: 8AM-5PM. Enrollment: 3000. Records go back to 1896. Alumni records are maintained here at the same phone number. Alumni Records Office: Station 6215, Montevallo, AL 35115-6001. Degrees granted: Bachelors; Masters. Adverse incident record source- Student Affairs, Station 6020.

Attendance and degree information available by phone, fax, mail. Search requires name only. Also helpful: SSN, date of birth, exact years of attendance. There is no fee.

University of North Alabama, Registrar, Box 5044, Florence, AL 35632-0001, 205-760-4316 (Fax: 205-760-4349). Hours: 8AM-4:30PM. Enrollment: 5200. Records go back to 1850. Alumni records are maintained here at the same phone number. Alumni Records Office: Box 5047, Florence, AL 35632-0001. Degrees granted: Bachelors; Masters. Adverse incident record source- Student Life, 205-760-4248.

Attendance and degree information available by phone, fax, mail. Search requires name plus date of birth. Also helpful: SSN, exact years of attendance. There is no fee.

University of South Alabama, Registrar, AD 165, Mobile, AL 36688-0002, 334-460-6251 (Fax: 334-460-7738). Hours: 8AM-5PM. Enrollment: 12000. Records go back to 1963. Alumni Records Office: Plantation Creole House, Mobile, AL 36688. Degrees granted: Bachelors; Masters; Doctorate. Adverse incident record source- Campus Security, 334-460-6312: Dean of Students, 334-460-6171

Attendance information available by fax, mail. Search requires name plus SSN, approximate years of attendance. Also helpful: date of birth. There is no fee.

Degree information available by phone, fax, mail. Search requires name plus approximate years of attendance. Also helpful: SSN, date of birth. There is no fee.

University of West Alabama (The), Registrar, 205 N Washington St, Livingston, AL 35470, 205-652-3400 (Fax: 205-652-4065). Hours: 8AM-5PM. Formerly Livingston University Records go back to 1913. Degrees granted: Associate; Bachelors; Masters.

Attendance and degree information available by phone, fax, mail. Search requires name plus SSN. Also helpful: date of birth, exact years of attendance. There is no fee.

Virginia College, (Branch Campus), Registrar, 1900 28th Ave, Birmingham, AL 35209, 205-802-1200 (Fax: 205-802-7045). Hours: 9AM-6PM M-Th, 9AM-4PM F. Enrollment: 400. Records go back to 1993. Degrees granted: Associate.

Attendance and degree information available by phone, mail. Search requires name plus SSN, exact years of attendance. There is no fee.

Virginia College-Huntsville, Registrar, 2800-A Bob Wallace Ave, Huntsville, AL 35805, 205-533-7387 (Fax: 205-533-7785). Hours: 8AM-5PM. Enrollment: 250. Records go back to 1993. Degrees granted: Associate. Adverse incident record source- Director of School.

Attendance and degree information available by mail. Search requires name plus SSN, date of birth, signed release. Also helpful: exact years of attendance. There is no fee.

Wallace State Community College, Registrar, PO Box 2000, Hanceville, AL 35077, 205-352-6403 (Fax: 205-352-6400). Hours: 7:30AM-4PM. Enrollment: 4350. Records go back to 1966. Degrees granted: Associate.

Attendance and degree information available by phone, fax, mail. Search requires name plus SSN, date of birth. Also helpful: exact years of attendance. There is no fee.

Trade and Vocational Schools

Alabama Reference Laboratories, Inc, PO Box 4600, Montgomery, AL 36103, 334-263-5745

Alabama State College of Barber Styling, 9480 Pkwy E, Birmingham, AL 35215-8308, 205-836-2404

Army Academy of Health Sciences (School of Aviation Medicine), Fort Rucker, AL 36362, 334-255-7393

Army Ordinance Missile and Munitions Center and School, Redstone Arsenal, Huntsville, AL 35897, 205-876-3349

Capps College, 3100 Cottage Hill Rd Bldg 4, Mobile, AL 36606, 334-473-1393

Career Development Institute, 2233 Fourth Ave N, Birmingham, AL 35203, 205-252-6396

Career Development Institute, 1060 Springhill Ave, Mobile, AL 36604, 334-433-5042

Career Development Institute, 505 and 507 Montgomery St, Montgomery, AL 36101, 334-262-3131

Career Development Institute, 516 14th St, Parkview Ctr, Tuscaloosa, AL 35401, 205-752-6025

Choctaw Training Institute, 218 W Church St, Butler, AL 36904, 205-459-4331

Extension Course Institute of the United States Air Force, 50 S Turner Blvd, Gunter Annex, Maxwell Afb, AL 36118, 334-416-4252

Gadsden Business College, 750 Forest Ave PO Box 1544, Gadsden, AL 35901, 205-546-2863

Gadsden Business College (Branch Campus), PO Box 1575, Anniston, AL 36202, 205-237-7517

Herzing Institute, 280 W Valley Ave, Homewood, AL 35209, 205-916-2800

Huntsville Business Institute School of Court Reporting, 3315 S Memorial Pkwy #5, Huntsville, AL 35801, 205-880-7530

J.R. Pittard Area Vocational School, 22401 Alabama Hwy 21, Alpine, AL 35014, 205-539-8161

John Pope Eden Area Vocational Education Center, Rte 2 Box 1855, Ashville, AL 35953, 205-594-7055

Mitchell Cosmetology College, 116 First St, Alabaster, AL 35007, 205-663-7126

New World College of Business, 1031 Noble St, Anniston, AL 36201, 205-236-7578

Prince Institute of Professional Studies, 7735 Atlanta Hwy, Montgomery, AL 36117, 334-271-1670

Rice College, 2116 Bessemer Rd, Birmingham, AL 35208, 205-781-8600

Southern Community College, 205 S Main St, Tuskegee, AL 36083, 334-727-5220

Tallapoosa-Alexander City Area Vocational Center, 100 E Junior College Dr, Alexander City, AL 35010, 205-329-8448

Winston County Technical Center, Holly Grove Rd, Double Springs, AL 35553, 205-489-2121

State Licensing & Business Registration Quick Finder Index

Architecture, Engineering & Surveying
Architect #8 (1850)..☎ 334-242-4179
Engineer #28 (10431)....................................☎ 334-242-5568
Geologist #42..205-349-2852
Landscape Architect #18 (192) ....☎ 334-262-7768
Surveyor #28 (789)..☎ 334-242-5568

Business - Court & Legal Services
Attorney #3 ....☎ 334-269-1515
Notary Public #48..334-242-7205
Shorthand Reporter #32..................................334-749-1020

Business - General Services
Auctioneer #9 (750)..☎ 205-739-0548
Pawn Shop #5 (638)..334-242-3452
Propane Gas Broker #46 (396) ....✉ 334-242-5649
Public Accountant-CPA #26 (7000)..............☎ 334-242-5700

Construction & Manufacturing
Educational Administrator #56......................☎ 334-242-9977
Electrical Contractor #14 (800) ....☎ 334-263-3407
Gas Fitter #50..205-349-2852
General Contractor #7 (5000)........................☎ 334-242-2839

Heating & Air Conditioning Contractor #43 (3500)☎ 334-242-5550
Journeyman Electrician #14 (250)................. ☎ 334-263-3407
Mobile Home Manufacturer #47 (549) 334-242-4036
Plumber #53.. ☎ 205-945-4857
School Counselor #56........................... ☎ 334-242-9977
Teacher #56 .... ☎ 334-242-9977

Education
Elementary Teacher #28 .... ☎ 217-782-2805

Environmental & Agriculture
Forester #27 (2) .... ☎ 334-240-9368
Livestock Market Operator #34 (50).............. ☎ 334-240-7208
Mine Personnel #39 (100) .... ☎ 205-254-1275
Pest Control #34 (455)............................. ☎ 334-240-7241
Pesticide Applicator #34 (196)................... ☎ 334-240-7239
Pesticide Dealer #34 (298) .... ☎ 334-240-7239
Professional Soil Classifier #1 .... ☎ 334-242-2620
Surface Mining #36 (623) .... ☎ 334-242-8055
Veterinarian #30 (1160) .... ☎ 205-353-3544
Veterinarian Technicians #30 (110)............... ☎ 205-353-3544
Veterinary Premise Permit #30...................... ☎ 205-353-3544

Financial - Real Estate, Insurance & Banking
Bank #5 (148) 334-242-3452
Broker Dealer Agents #55 (40000) .... ☒ 334-242-2984
Consumer Finance Company #5 (1398)............. 334-242-3452
Insurance Agent #45 (48000) .... ☎ 334-269-3550
Investment Advisor #55 (500)....................... ☒ 334-242-2984
Investment Advisor Representatives #55
  (5500) .... ☒ 334-242-2984
Real Estate Appraiser #49 .... ☎ 334-242-8747
Real Estate Broker #2............................ ☎ 334-242-5544
Real Estate Salesperson #2....................... ☎ 334-242-5544
Securities Broker/Dealer #55 (1260).............. ☒ 334-242-2984
Timeshare Seller #2 .... ☎ 334-242-5544

Health & Beauty
Abortion Centers #35 .... ☒ 334-240-3500
Ambulatory Surgery Centers #35 .... ☒ 334-240-3500
Apprentice Cosmetologist #11 (1523) .... ☒ 334-272-1110
Apprentice Esthetician #11 (22).................. ☒ 334-272-1110
Apprentice Manicurist #11 (905) .... ☒ 334-272-1110
Assisted Living Unit (Assisted Living Facilities) #35
  .... ☒ 334-240-3500
Beauty Shop #11 (10379)......................... ☒ 334-272-1110
Beauty Shop/Booth Rental #11 (2076) .... ☒ 334-272-1110
Birthing Centers #35.............................. ☒ 334-240-3500
Chiropractor #10 (775)............................ ☒ 334-947-5838
Cosmetic Studio #11 (86).......................... ☒ 334-272-1110
Cosmetologist & Cosmetology Instructor #11
  (12399)... ☒ 334-272-1110
Cosmetologist/Pending Exam #11 (3047)......☒ 334-272-1110
Dental Scholarship Award #13...................... 205-934-4384
Dentist/Dental Hygienist #12 .... ☎ 205-533-4638
Dietitian/Nutritionist #37............................ ☎ 334-242-4505
Embalmer #17 (212)................................ ☎ 334-242-4049
Emergency Medical Technician #57 (13000)
  .... ☎ 334-613-5383
Endstage Renal Disease and Treatment
  Centers #35 .... ☒ 334-240-3500
Esthetician #11 (44)................................ ☒ 334-272-1110
Esthetician Salon #11 (19)......................... ☒ 334-272-1110
Esthetician/Pending Exam #11 (12) .... ☒ 334-272-1110
Funeral Director #17 (1593)........................ ☎ 334-242-4049
Hearing Aid Dealer #40 (105)....................... ☎ 334-242-1925

Hospice #35 .... ☒ 334-240-3500
Hospital #35 .... ☒ 334-240-3500
Independent Clinical/Physiological Labs #35
  .... ☒ 334-240-3500
Instructor Esthetician #11 (1) .... ☒ 334-272-1110
Instructor Manicurist #11 (8)......................... ☒ 334-272-1110
Instructor-Cosmetology #11 (662) .... ☒ 334-272-1110
Managing Cosmetologist #11 (18522) ....☒ 334-272-1110
Managing Cosmetologist/Pending Exam #11
  (47) .... ☒ 334-272-1110
Managing Esthetician #11 (31)..................... ☒ 334-272-1110
Managing Manicurist #11 (751) .... ☒ 334-272-1110
Manicurist #11 (1601) .... ☒ 334-272-1110
Manicurist Salon #11 (292) .... ☒ 334-272-1110
Manicurist School #11 (1) .... ☒ 334-272-1110
Manicurist/Pending Exam #11 (542)............. ☒ 334-272-1110
Master Cosmetologist #11 (222) .... ☒ 334-272-1110
Maternity Homes #35 .... ☒ 334-240-3500
Medical Doctor #19 (7)............................. ☎ 334-242-4116
Natural Disaster Relief #38 205-280-2200
Nurse #20 334-242-4060
Nursing Home #35................................... ☒ 334-240-3500
Nursing Home Administrator #22 (1498) ...... ☎ 334-271-6214
Occupational Therapist #21 .... ☎ 334-265-9654
Optometrist #23 (525)............................. ☎ 205-538-9903
Osteopathic Physician #19 (6) .... ☎ 334-242-4116
Pharmacist #24 (56000)............................ ☎ 205-967-0130
Physical Therapist #25.............................. ☎ 334-242-4064
Physician's Assistant #19 .... ☎ 334-242-4116
Podiatrist #4 .... ☎ 205-995-8537
Rehabilitation Centers #35 .... ☒ 334-240-3500
Residential Treatment Centers #35................. ☒ 334-240-3500
Restricted Managing Cosmetologist #11 (12)
  .... ☒ 334-272-1110
Rural Primary Care Hospitals #35 .... ☒ 334-240-3500
School for Esthetician #11 (1) .... ☒ 334-272-1110
School of Cosmetology #11 (66).................... ☒ 334-272-1110
Shampoo Assistant #11 (2552)..................... ☒ 334-272-1110
Speech Pathologist/Audiologist #29 (602)..... ☎ 334-834-2415
Student Cosmetologist #11 (6914) .... ☒ 334-272-1110
Student Esthetician #11 (40)........................ ☒ 334-272-1110
Student Manicurist #11 (626)....................... ☒ 334-272-1110
Transitional Care Facilities #35..................... ☒ 334-240-3500

Investigations & Security
Firefighter #41 (2000).............................. 205-759-1508
Law Enforcement Personnel #51 (900) ....☒ 334-242-4047
Polygraph Examiner #54 (80)...................... ☎ 334-260-1182

Social Services
Counselor #15 (1200) .... ☎ 205-933-8100
Psychologist #16 (560) .... ☎ 334-242-4127

Sports & Entertainment
Athletic Trainer #44................................. 334-242-5655
Bear Creek Recreation (Swimming, fishing, camping) #6
  (42000) .... ☎ 205-332-4392
Boxing #31.. 334-242-1380
State Fairs #58.. 205-787-2641
Wrestling #31... 334-242-1380

Transportation
Airport/Landing Area #33 (146).................... ☎ 334-242-4480
Pilot #52 (12) .... ☒ 334-479-9247

State Licensing & Business Registration Agency Information

(1)　(1) Agricultural & Conservation Development Commission, PO BOX 304800, Montgomery, AL 36130-4800, 334-242-2620, Fax: 334-242-0551

(2)　Alabama Real Estate Commission, 1201 Carmichael Way, Montgomery, AL 36106, 334-242-5544

(3)　Alabama State Bar, 415 Dexter Ave (36104), PO Box 671, Montgomery, AL 36101, 334-269-1515

(4)　Alabama State Board of Podiatry, 13 Innisbrook Ln, Birmingham, AL 35242, 205-995-8537, Fax: 205-995-8537

(5)　Banking Department, 101 S Union St, Montgomery, AL 36130, 334-242-3452

(6)　Bear Creek Development Authority, PO Box 670, Russellville, AL 35653, 205-332-4392, Fax: 205-332-4372

(7)　Board for General Contractors, 400 S Union St, Suite 235, Montgomery, AL 36130, 334-242-2839, Fax: 334-240-3424

(8)　Board for Registration of Architects, 770 Washington Ave, Montgomery, AL 36130, 334-242-4179, Fax: 334-242-4531

(9)　Board of Auctioneers, 2015-C Cherokee Ave, SW, PO Box 1207, Cullman, AL 35056, 205-739-0548, Fax: 205-739-8776

(10)　Board of Chiropractic Examiners, 737 Logan Road, Clanton, AL 35045, 205-755-8000, Fax: 205-755-0081

(11)　Board of Cosmetology, 1000-A Interstate Dr, Montgomery, AL 36130, 334-272-1110, Fax: 334-270-9959

(12)　Board of Dental Examiners, 2327-B Pansy St, Huntsville, AL 35801, 205-533-4638, Fax: 205-533-4690

(13)　Board of Dental Scholarship Awards, 1600 University Blvd, Volker Hall P100, Box 802, Birmingham, AL 35294, 205-934-4384

(14)　Board of Electrical Contractors, 660 Adams Ave, Suite 254, Montgomery, AL 36104, 334-263-3407, Fax: 334-263-6115

(15)　Board of Examiners in Counseling, PO Box 550397, Birmingham, AL 35255, 205-933-8100, Fax: 205-933-6700

(16)　Board of Examiners in Psychology, 660 Adams Avenue Suite 360, Montgomery, AL 36104, 334-242-4127

(17)　Board of Funeral Service, PO Box 309522, 770 Washington Ave, Suite 226, Montgomery, AL 36130, 334-242-4049, Fax: 334-353-7988

(18)　Board of Landscape Architects, 908 S Hull St, Montgomery, AL 36104, 334-262-7768, Fax: 334-263-9370

(19)　Board of Medical Examiners, 848 Washington Ave, PO Box 36104-946, Montgomery, AL 36100-0946, 334-242-4116, Fax: 334-242-4155

(20)　Board of Nursing, 770 Washington Ave, Suite 250, Montgomery, AL 36130, 334-242-4060, Fax: 334-242-4360

(21)　Board of Nursing, PO Box 303900, Montgomery, AL 36130, 334-242-4278

(22)　Board of Nursing Home Administrators, 4156 Carmichael Road, Montgomery, AL 36106, 334-271-6214, Fax: 334-244-6509

(23)　Board of Optometry, PO Box 448, Attalla, AL 35954, 205-538-9903, Fax: 205-538-9904

(24)　Board of Pharmacy, 1 Perimeter Park, S, Suite 425, S, Birmingham, AL 35243, 205-967-0130, Fax: 205-967-1009

(25)　Board of Physical Therapy, 400 S Union St, Suite 315, Montgomery, AL 36130-5040, 334-242-4064, Fax: 334-240-3288

(26)　Board of Public Accounting, 770 Washington Ave, Suite 236, Montgomery, AL 36130, 334-242-5700, Fax: 334-242-2711

(27)　Board of Registration for Foresters, 513 Madison Ave, Montgomery, AL 36130, 334-240-9368, Fax: 334-240-9390

(28)　Board of Registration for Professional Engineers &, Land Surveyors, 100 N Union St #382, Montgomery, AL 36104, 334-242-5568

(29)　Board of Speech Pathology & Audiology, PO Box 20833, Montgomery, AL 36120-0833, 334-834-2415, Fax: 334-269-6379

(30)　Board of Veterinary Medicine, PO Box 1968, Decatur, AL 35602, 205-353-3544, Fax: 205-350-5629

(31)　Boxing & Wrestling Commission, Room 4131-Gordon Persons Bldg, 50 N Ripley St, Montgomery, AL 36130, 334-242-1380

(32)　CSR Chairperson, PO Box 70, Opelika, AL 36801, 334-749-1020

(33)　Department of Aeronautics, 770 Washington Ave, Suite 544, Montgomery, AL 36130, 334-242-4480, Fax: 334-240-3274

(34)　Department of Agriculture & Industries, 1445 Federal Dr, Montgomery, AL 36107, 334-240-7100, Fax: 334-223-7352

(35)　Department of Health, Division of Licensing, 434 Monroe St, Montgomery, AL 36130-3017, 334-240-3500, Fax: 334-240-3147

(36)　Department of Industrial Relations, 649 Monroe St, Montgomery, AL 36131, 334-242-8265, Fax: 334-242-8265

(37)　Dietetic/Nutrition Examiners Board, 400 S Union St, Suite 465, Montgomery, AL 36104, 334-242-4505, Fax: 334-834-6398

(38)　Emergency Management Agency, PO Drawer 2160, Clanton, AL 35045, 205-280-2200

(39)　Examiners of Mine Personnel, PO Box 10444, Birmingham, AL 35202, 205-254-1275, Fax: 205-254-1278

(40)　Executive Secretary, Hearing Aid Dealers, 400 S Union, Suite 125, Montgomery, AL 36130-3010, 334-242-1925, Fax: 334-834-6389

(41)　Fire College & Personnel Standards Commission, 2015 McFarland Blvd, E, Tuscaloosa, AL 35404-1399, 205-759-1508, Fax: 205-391-3747

(42)　Geological Survey, 420 Hackberry Ln, PO Box O, Tuscaloosa, AL 35486-9780, 205-349-2852, Fax: 205-349-2861

(43)　Heating & Air Conditioning Contractors Board, 100 N Union St, Montgomery, AL 36130, 334-242-5550, Fax: 334-353-7050

(44)　High School Athletic Association, 926 Pelham St, Montgomery, AL 36104, 334-242-5655

(45)　Insurance Department, 135 S Union St, Montgomery, AL 36130, 334-269-3550, Fax: 334-240-3282

(46)　Liquified Petroleum Gas Board, 818 S Perry St, PO Box 1742, Montgomery, AL 36104-5020, 334-242-5649, Fax: 334-240-3255

(47)　Manufactured Housing Commission, 350 S Decator St, Montgomery, AL 36104, 334-242-4036, Fax: 334-240-3178

(48)　Office of the Secretary of State, PO Box 5616, State Capitol, Bainbridge St, Montgomery, AL 36103-5616, 334-242-7205

(49)   Office of the Secretary of State, Real Estate Appraisers Licensing, 699 Interstate Park Drive, Suite 628, Montgomery, AL 36109, 334-242-8747, Fax: 334-242-8729

(50)   Oil & Gas Board, PO Box O, 420 Hackberry Ln, Tuscaloosa, AL 35486-9780, 205-349-2852, Fax: 205-349-2861

(51)   Peace Officers Standards & Training Commission, RSA Union Bldg, 100 Union St, Suite 600, Montgomery, AL 36130, 334-242-4047, Fax: 334-242-4633

(52)   Pilotage Commission, PO Box 273, Mobile, AL 36601, 334-432-2639, Fax: 334-432-2630

(53)   Plumbers & Gas Fitters Examining Board, 11 W Oxmoor, Suite 104, Birmingham, AL 35209, 205-945-4857, Fax: 205-945-9915

(54)   Polygraph Examiners Board, 2720-D W Gunter Park Dr, Montgomery, AL 36109, 334-260-1182, Fax: 334-260-8788

(55)   Securities Division, 770 Washington, Suite 570, Montgomery, AL 36130, 334-242-2984, Fax: 334-242-0240

(56)   State Department of Education, 50 N Ripley St, Montgomery, AL 36104, 334-242-9977, Fax: 334-242-0498

(57)   State Department of Health, Emergency Medical Services Division, 434 Monroe St, Montgomery, AL 36130-3017, 334-613-5383, Fax: 334-240-3061

(58)   State Fair Authority, PO Box 3800-B, Birmingham, AL 35208, 205-786-8100

Alaska

Capital: Juneau (Juneau Borough)	
State Population	.6 Million
Number of Degree Granting Institutions:	14
Number of State Licensing & Business Registration Agencies:	79

Degree Granting Educational Institutions

Alaska Bible College, Registrar, Box 289, Glennallen, AK 99588, 907-822-3201 (Fax: 907-822-5027). Hours: 8AM-Noon, 1-5PM. Enrollment: 54. Records go back to 1970. Degrees granted: Associate; Bachelors. Adverse incident record source- Alaska State Troopers, 907-822-3263.

Attendance and degree information available by phone, fax, mail. Search requires name only. There is no fee.

Alaska Pacific University, Registrar, 4101 University Dr, Anchorage, AK 99508, 907-564-8210 (Fax: 907-562-4276). Hours: 8AM-5PM. Enrollment: 1540. Records go back to 1961. Alumni records are maintained here also. Call 907-564-8256. Degrees granted: Associate; Bachelors; Masters.

Attendance and degree information available by phone, mail. Search requires name only. Also helpful: SSN, date of birth, exact years of attendance. Fee is $4.00. Expedited service available for $10.00.

Kenai Peninsula College, Registrar, 34820 College Dr, Soldotna, AK 99669, 907-262-0300 (Fax: 907-262-9280). Records are not housed here. They are located at University of Alaska Anchorage, Records Dept., 3211 Providence Dr, Anchorage, AK 99508-8038.

Kodiak College, Registrar, 117 Benny Benson Dr, Kodiak, AK 99615, 907-486-4161 X44 (Fax: 907-486-4166). Hours: 8AM-5PM. Records go back to 1970. Degrees granted: Associate.

Attendance and degree information available by phone, fax, mail. Search requires name plus SSN, date of birth, exact years of attendance. There is no fee.

Prince William Sound Community College, Registrar, PO Box 97, Valdez, AK 99686, 907-835-2697 (Fax: 907-835-2593). Hours: 8AM-5:30PM. Enrollment: 1500. Records go back to 1980. Alumni records are maintained here at the same phone number. Degrees granted: Associate. Special programs- Rural Alaska Teacher Education, 907-835-2678. Adverse incident record source- Police, 907-35-4560.

Attendance and degree information available by phone, fax, mail. Search requires name only. Also helpful: SSN, date of birth, exact years of attendance. There is no fee.

Sheldon Jackson College, Registrar, 801 Lincoln, Sitka, AK 99835, 907-747-5216 (Fax: 907-747-5212). Hours: 8AM-Noon, 1-5PM. Enrollment: 300. Records go back to 1898. Alumni records are maintained here also. Call 907-747-2589. Degrees granted: Associate; Bachelors.

Attendance and degree information available by phone, fax, mail. Search requires name only. Also helpful: SSN, exact years of attendance. There is no fee.

University of Alaska, (Kuskokwim), Registrar, Bethel, AK 99559, 907-543-4562 (Fax: 907-543-4527). Records are not housed here. They are located at University of Alaska Fairbanks, Office of the Registrar, PO Box 757495, Fairbanks, AK 99775-7495.

University of Alaska, (Northwest), Registrar, Pouch 400, Nome, AK 99762, 907-474-7521 (Fax: 907-474-5379). Records are not housed here. They are located at University of Alaska Fairbanks, Office of the Registrar, PO Box 757495, Fairbanks, AK 99775-7495.

University of Alaska Anchorage, Records Dept., 3211 Providence Dr, Anchorage, AK 99508-8038, 907-786-1480 (Fax: 907-786-4888). Hours: 8AM-4:30PM. Enrollment: 18100. Records go back to 1950's. Degrees granted: Associate; Bachelors; Masters; Doctorate.

Attendance and degree information available by phone, fax, mail. Search requires name plus SSN, date of birth, approximate years of attendance. Also helpful: exact years of attendance. There is no fee.

University of Alaska Fairbanks, Office of the Registrar, PO Box 757495, Fairbanks, AK 99775-7495, 907-474-6300 (Fax: 907-474-5379). Hours: 8AM-5PM. Enrollment: 7000. Records go back to 1922. Alumni records are maintained here also. Call 907-474-7081. Degrees granted: Associate; Bachelors; Masters; Doctorate. Special programs- Mineral & Petroleum Engineering, 907-474-7366: Wildlife Biology, 907-474-7671. Adverse incident record source- UAF Police, 907-474-5555.

Attendance and degree information available by phone, fax, mail. Search requires name only. Also helpful: SSN, date of birth, exact years of attendance. Fee is $1.00.

University of Alaska Fairbanks, (Chukchi),
Registrar, PO Box 297, Kotzebue, AK 99752, 907-474-7521 (Fax: 907-474-5379). Records are not housed here. They are located at University of Alaska Fairbanks, Office of the Registrar, PO Box 757495, Fairbanks, AK 99775-7495.

Unwwiversity of Alaska Southeast, Registrar,
11120 Glacier Hwy, Juneau, AK 99801, 907-465-6458 (Fax: 907-465-6365). Hours: 9AM-5PM. Enrollment: 5177. Records go back to 1970's. Alumni records are maintained here also. Call 907-465-6457. Degrees granted: Bachelors; Masters.

Attendance and degree information available by phone, fax, mail. Search requires name plus SSN, exact years of attendance. There is no fee.

University of Alaska Southeast, (Ketchikan),
Registrar, Ketchikan, AK 99901, 907-225-6177 (Fax: 907-225-3624). Hours: 8AM-5PM. Enrollment: 800. Records go back to 1980. Alumni records are maintained here at the same phone number. Degrees granted: Associate. Certification: Welding, Tourism, Accounting, Business Information.

Attendance and degree information available by fax, mail. Search requires name plus signed release. Also helpful: SSN, date of birth, exact years of attendance. There is no fee.

University of Alaska Southeast, (Sitka),
Registrar, 1332 Seward Ave, Sitka, AK 99835, 907-465-6268 (Fax: 907-465-6365). Records are not housed here. They are located at University of Alaska Southeast, Registrar, 11120 Glacier Hwy, Juneau, AK 99801.

Trade and Vocational Schools

Career Academy (The), 1415 E Tudor Rd, Anchorage, AK 99507-1033, 907-563-7575

State Licensing & Business Registration Quick Finder Index

Architecture, Engineering & Surveying
Architect #19 (549)............................... ☎ 907-465-2540
Engineer #14 (3536) .... ☎ 907-465-2540
Geologist #14 (442)............................. ☎ 907-465-2695
Surveyor #14 (669)............................... ☎ 907-465-2540

Business - Court & Legal Services
Attorney #11 .... ☎ 907-272-7469
Bondsman #13 (316) .... ☎ 907-465-2515
Lobbyist #9 (300) .... ☎ 907-465-4864
Notary Public #18............................... ☎ 907-465-3509

Business - General Services
CPA #19 (1683).................................... ☎ 907-465-2580
Employment Agency
    Operator #7 (6)............................... ☎ 907-269-4900

Construction & Manufacturing
Boiler Operator #5 .... ☎ 907-269-4925
Construction Contractor #19 .... ☎ 907-465-2546
Electrical Administrator #14 .... ☎ 907-465-2551
Electrical Worker #5........................... ☎ 907-269-4925
Explosives Handler #5 (100)............... ☎ 907-269-4925
Mechanical Administrator #14
    (550).. ☎ 907-465-2589
Painter #6.. 907-269-4952
Plumber #5... ☎ 907-269-4925
Residential Contractor #14 (912) ..... ☎ 907-465-2589

Education
Teacher #1 .... ☎ 907-465-2831

Environmental & Agriculture
Asbestos Removal Worker #5
    (300)... ☎ 907-269-4925
Pesticide Applicator #2 (1521)........... ☎ 907-745-3236

Underground Storage Tank Worker
    & Contractor #14 (364)................... ☎ 907-465-2547
Veterinarian #14 (401)........................ ☎ 907-465-5470
Veterinary Technician #14 (112).......... ☎ 907-465-5470
Waste Water Systems Operator #3 907-465-5140

Financial - Real Estate, Insurance & Banking
Agent in Securities #12 (30000)......... ☎ 907-465-5449
Broker-Dealer #12 (800)...................... ☎ 907-465-5449
Collection Agency/Operator #19
    (118)... ☎ 907-465-2695
Independent Adjuster #13 (297)......... ☎ 907-465-2515
Insurance Occupations #13
    (3697)... ☎ 907-465-2515
Insurance Producer #13 (3068).......... ☎ 907-465-2515
Investment Advisor #12 (7000)........... ☎ 907-465-2549
Investment Broker-Dealer
    & Related Occupation #12 .... ☎ 907-465-5449
Managing General Agent #13
    (89)... ☎ 907-465-2515
Real Estate Agent & Broker #14
    (2170) .... ☎ 907-465-2542
Real Estate Appraiser #14 (168)......... ☎ 907-465-2542
Reinsurance Intermediary Broker #13
    (3) .... ☎ 907-465-2515
Reinsurance Intermediary Manager #13
    (2) .... ☎ 907-465-2515
Surplus Lines Broker #13 (280) .... ☎ 907-465-2515

Health & Beauty
Acupuncturist #19 (28)........................ ☎ 907-465-2695
Audiologist/Hearing Aid Dealers #19
    (60) .... ☎ 907-465-2695
Barber #19 (300).................................. ☎ 907-465-2547

Chiropractor #19 (192) .... ☎ 907-465-2589
Defibillator Technician #16
(500) .... ☎ 907-465-3029
Dental Hygienist #14 (413) .... ☎ 907-465-2542
Dentist #14 (576) .... ☎ 907-465-2542
Emergency Medical Technician #16
(4000) .... ☎ 907-465-3027
Hairdresser & Cosmetologist #14
.... ⊠ 907-465-2541
Hearing Aid Dealer #14 .... ☎ 907-465-3811
Medical Doctor & Surgeon #14
(1883) .... ☎ 907-465-2541
Mortician-Embalmer #14 (52) .... ☎ 907-465-2695
Naturopathic Physician
(Naturopathic Doctor) #14 (20) .... ☎ 907-465-2695
Nurse (RN & LPN)-Nurse Anesthetist #14
(6835) .... ⊠ 907-465-2544
Nurse Practitioner (Advanced) #14
(398) .... ⊠ 907-465-2544
Nurses Aide #14 .... ☎ 907-269-8169
Nursing Home Administrator #14
.... ⊠ 907-465-2541
Occupational Therapist/Assistant #14
.... ☎ 907-465-2551
Optician #14 .... ☎ 907-465-2547
Optometrist #14 (150) .... ☎ 907-465-2580
Osteopathic Physician #14 .... ⊠ 907-465-2541
Paramedic #14 .... ⊠ 907-465-2541

Pharmacist #14 .... ☎ 907-465-2589
Physical Therapist/Assistant #14 .... ☎ 907-465-2551
Physician's Assistant #14 (231) .... ☎ 907-269-8163
Podiatrist #14 .... ⊠ 907-465-2541
Psychologist & Psychological Assistant #14
.... ☎ 907-465-2551

Investigations & Security
Security Guard #10 .... ☎ 907-258-8876

Social Services
Child Care Provider (Home & Center) #15 907-465-2145
Social Worker #14 .... ☎ 907-465-2551

Sports & Entertainment
Boxing & Wrestling Related Occupation #19
(17) .... ⊠ 907-465-2551
Commercial Fishing Operators #8 (100) .... ☎ 907-260-4882
Concert Promoter (Registration) #19
(18) .... ☎ 907-465-2695
Crewmember (Fishing Boat) #4 .... ☎ 907-465-2376
Examining Physician, Boxing #19 (3) .... ☎ 907-465-2534
Guide (Sport Fishing) #8 (400) .... ☎ 907-260-4882
Guide Outfitter (hunting) #14 (436) .... ☎ 907-465-2543

Transportation
Aircraft Related Occupation #17 (250) .... ☎ 907-271-5514
Marine Pilot #14 (76) .... ☎ 907-465-2548

State Licensing & Business Registration Agency Information

(1) Alaska Department of Education, Teacher Certification, Division of Teaching and Learning Support, 801 W 10th Street Suite 200, Juneau, AK 99801-1894, 907-465-2831, Fax: 907-465-2441

(2) Alaska Department of Environmental Conservation, Division of Environmental Health, 500 S Alaska St, Suite A, Palmer, AK 99645, 907-745-3236

(3) Alaska Department of Environmental Conservation, Facility Construction and Operation, 410 Willoughby Ave, Juneau, AK 99801-1795, 907-465-5140

(4) Alaska Department of Fish & Game, Fish & Game Licensing Section, PO Box 25525, Juneau, AK 99802-5525, 907-465-2376

(5) Alaska Department of Labor, Mechanical Inspection, PO Box 107020, Anchorage, AK 99510, 907-269-4925, Fax: 907-269-4932

(6) Alaska Department of Labor, Occupational Safety & Health, PO Box 107022, Anchorage, AK 99510, 907-269-4925, Fax: 907-269-4952

(7) Alaska Department of Labor, Wage & Hour Administration, PO Box 107021, Anchorage, AK 99510, 907-269-4900

(8) Alaska Department of Natural Resources, Division of Parks & Outdoor Recreation, 36130 Kenai Spur Highway, Soldotna, AK 99669, 907-260-4882, Fax: 907-260-5992

(9) Alaska Public Offices Commission, PO Box 110222, Juneau, AK 99811-0222, 907-465-4864, Fax: 907-465-4832

(10) Alaska State Troopers, Licensing & Permits, 117 W 4th Ave, Anchorage, AK 99501, 907-258-8892, Fax: 907-258-8893

(11) Board of Governors, Alaska Bar Association, PO Box 100279, Anchorage, AK 99510, 907-272-7469, Fax: 907-272-2932

(12) Department of Commerce & Economic Development, Division of Banking, Securities & Corporations, PO Box 110807, Juneau, AK 99811-0807, 907-465-2521, Fax: 907-465-2549

(13) Department of Commerce & Economic Development, Division of Insurance, PO Box 110805, Juneau, AK 99811-0805, 907-465-2515, Fax: 907-465-2816

(14) Department of Commerce & Economic Development, Division of Occupational Licensing, State Office Bldg, 9th Floor, PO Box 110806, Juneau, AK 99811-0806, 907-269-8163, Fax: 907-465-2974

(15) Department of Health & Social Services, Division of Family & Youth Services, PO Box 110630, Juneau, AK 99811-0630, 907-465-2145

(16) Department of Health & Social Services, Division of Public Health, PO Box 110616, Juneau, AK 99811-0616, 907-465-3027, Fax: 907-465-4101

(17) Federal Aviation Administration, Flight Standards Regional Office, 222 W 7th Ave, #14, Anchorage, AK 99513, 907-271-5514, Fax: 907-276-6207

(18) Office of Lieutenant Governor, State Capitol, PO Box 110015, Juneau, AK 99811, 907-465-3520

(19) State of Alaska, Division of Occupational Licensing, PO Box 110806, Juneau, AK 99811-0806, 907-465-2695, Fax: 907-465-2974

Arizona

Capitol: Phoenix (Maricopa County)	
State Population	4.2 Million
Number of Degree Granting Institutions:	52
Number of State Licensing & Business Registration Agencies:	258

Degree Granting Educational Institutions

Academy of Business College, Registrar, 2525 W Beryl Ave, Phoenix, AZ 85021, 602-942-4141 (Fax: 602-943-0960). Hours: 7:45AM-8PM M-Th, 7:45AM-5PM F. Enrollment: 200. Records go back to 1982. Degrees granted: Associate. Special programs- Business Tech: Paralegal Tech: PC Tech. Adverse incident record source- Education.

Attendance and degree information available by phone, fax, mail. Search requires name plus SSN, exact years of attendance. There is no fee.

American Graduate School of International Management, (Thunderbird Campus), Registrar, 15249 N 59 Ave, Glendale, AZ 85306, 602-978-7980 (Fax: 602-439-5432). Hours: 9AM-4:30PM. Enrollment: 1450. Records go back to 1947. Alumni records are maintained here also. Call 602-978-7135. Degrees granted: Masters.

Attendance and degree information available by phone, fax, mail. Search requires name only. Also helpful: exact years of attendance. There is no fee.

American Indian Bible College of the Assemblies of God, Registrar, 10020 N 15th Ave, Phoenix, AZ 85021, 602-944-3335 X32. Enrollment: 120. Formerly American Indian Bible College Alumni records are maintained here at the same phone number. Degrees granted: Associate; Bachelors.

Attendance and degree information available by phone, mail. Search requires name only. Also helpful: exact years of attendance. There is no fee.

American Institute, Registrar, 3343 N Central Ave, Phoenix, AZ 85012, 602-252-4986 (Fax: 602-252-7440). Hours: 8AM-6PM. Enrollment: 300. Records go back to 1980. Degrees granted: Associate.

Attendance and degree information available by phone, fax, mail. Search requires name plus SSN, date of birth. Also helpful: exact years of attendance. There is no fee.

Arizona College of the Bible, Registrar, 2045 W Northern Ave, Phoenix, AZ 85021, 602-995-2670 (Fax: 602-864-8183). Hours: 7:30AM-4:30PM. Enrollment: 150. Records go back to 1971. Alumni records are maintained here at the same phone number. Degrees granted: Associate; Bachelors.

Certification: 1yr Bible. Adverse incident record source- Dean of Students, 602-995-2670.

Attendance and degree information available by phone. Search requires name plus SSN, approximate years of attendance. Also helpful: date of birth, exact years of attendance. There is no fee.

Arizona Institute of Business and Technology, Registrar, 4136 N 75th Ave Ste 211, Phoenix, AZ 85033, 602-849-8208 (Fax: 602-849-0110). Hours: 8AM-10PM M-Th, 8AM-5PM F. Enrollment: 198. Records go back to 1980. Alumni records are maintained here at the same phone number. Alumni Records Office: Suite 104, Phoenix, AZ 85033. Degrees granted: Associate. Adverse incident record source- Student Services, 602-849-8208.

Attendance and degree information available by fax, mail. Search requires name plus signed release. Also helpful: SSN, date of birth, exact years of attendance. There is no fee.

Arizona Institute of Business and Technology, (Branch), Registrar, 925 S Gilbert Rd Ste 201, Mesa, AZ 85204, 602-545-8755 (Fax: 602-926-1371). Hours: 7:30AM-8PM M-Th, 8MA-4:30PM F. Enrollment: 300. Records go back to 1983. Degrees granted: Associate. Adverse incident record source- Student Services, 602-545-8755.

Attendance and degree information available by fax, mail. Search requires name plus SSN, signed release. There is no fee.

Arizona State University, Registrar, Tempe, AZ 85287-0312, 602-965-3124 (Fax: 602-965-2295). Hours: 8AM-5PM. Enrollment: 45000. Records go back to 1885. Alumni Records Office: Alumni Center, Arizona State University, Box 871004, Tempe, AZ 85287-1004. Degrees granted: Bachelors; Masters; Doctorate. Adverse incident record source- Registrar, 602-965-7276.

Attendance information available by phone, fax, mail. Search requires name plus SSN, date of birth, exact years of attendance. Also helpful: approximate years of attendance. There is no fee.

Degree information available by phone, fax, mail. Search requires name plus SSN, date of birth, exact years of attendance. There is no fee.

Arizona State University West, Registrar, 4701 W Thunderbird Rd, PO Box 37100, Phoenix, AZ 85069-7100, 602-543-8123 (Fax: 602-543-8312). Hours: 8AM-6PM M-Th, 8AM-

4PM F. Enrollment: 4800. Records go back to 1980. Alumni Records Office: Alumni Center, Arizona State University, Box 871004, Tempe, AZ 85287-1004. Degrees granted: Bachelors; Masters. Adverse incident record source- Registrar, 602-543-8123.

Attendance and degree information available by phone, mail. Search requires name plus SSN, exact years of attendance. There is no fee.

Arizona Western College, Registrar, PO Box 929, Yuma, AZ 85366, 520-726-1050 (Fax: 520-344-7730). Hours: 7AM-5PM M-Th. Enrollment: 8000. Records go back to 1962. Degrees granted: Associate. Adverse incident record source-Student Services, 520-726-1000.

Attendance information available by written request only. Search requires name plus SSN. Also helpful: date of birth, exact years of attendance. Fee is $2.00.

Degree information available by written request only. Search requires name only. Also helpful: exact years of attendance. There is no fee.

Central Arizona College, Registrar, 8470 N Overfield Rd, Coolidge, AZ 85228, 520-426-4444 (Fax: 520-426-4234). Hours: 8AM-4:30PM. Enrollment: 5000. Records go back to 1969. Degrees granted: Associate.

Attendance and degree information available by phone, fax, mail. Search requires name only. Also helpful: SSN, date of birth, approximate years of attendance. There is no fee.

Chandler-Gilbert Community College, Registrar, 2626 E Pecos Rd, Chandler, AZ 85225-2479, 602-732-7308 (Fax: 602-732-7099). Hours: 8:30AM-7PM. Enrollment: 3500. Records go back to 1987. Degrees granted: Associate. Special programs- Aviation, 602-732-7054. Adverse incident record source- Jose Garcia, 602-732-7280.

Attendance and degree information available by phone, fax, mail. Search requires name only. Also helpful: SSN, date of birth. There is no fee.

Chaparral College, Registrar, 4585 E Speedway Blvd Ste 204, Tucson, AZ 85712, 520-327-6866 (Fax: 520-325-0108). Hours: 7:30AM-10:05PM. Enrollment: 450. Formerly Chaparral Career College Records go back to 1973. Degrees granted: Associate. Adverse incident record source- Student Services, 520-327-6866.

Attendance and degree information available by phone, fax, mail. Search requires name plus SSN, approximate years of attendance. Also helpful: date of birth, exact years of attendance. There is no fee.

Cochise College, Registrar, 4190 Hwy 80, Douglas, AZ 85607-9724, 520-364-0241 (Fax: 520-364-0236). Hours: 8AM-4:30PM. Enrollment: 4500. Records go back to 1965. Degrees granted: Associate. Special programs- Aviation, 520-364-0314.

Attendance and degree information available by phone, fax, mail. Search requires name plus SSN, exact years of attendance. There is no fee.

DeVry Institute of Technology, Phoenix, Registrar, 2149 W Dunlap Ave, Phoenix, AZ 85021, 602-870-9222 (Fax: 602-870-1209). Hours: 8AM-5PM. Enrollment: 2600. Records go back to 1967. Alumni Records Office: Alumni Association, One Oakbrook Tower Ste 100, Oak Brook, IL 60181-4624. Degrees granted: Associate; Bachelors.

Attendance and degree information available by phone, fax, mail. Search requires name plus SSN, date of birth, approximate years of attendance. Also helpful: exact years of attendance. There is no fee.

Denver Business College, (Branch), Registrar, 1457 W Southern Ave #8, Mesa, AZ 85202, 602-834-1000 (Fax: 602-491-2970). Hours: 8AM-7PM. Records go back to 1987. Degrees granted: Associate.

Attendance information available by fax, mail. Search requires name plus SSN, approximate years of attendance, signed release. There is no fee.

Degree information available by phone, fax, mail. Search requires name plus SSN, approximate years of attendance. There is no fee.

Eastern Arizona College, Records Office, Thatcher, AZ 85552-0769, 520-428-8250 (Fax: 520-428-8462). Hours: 9AM-4PM. Enrollment: 5000. Records go back to 1895. Alumni records are maintained here also. Call 520-428-8295. Degrees granted: Associate.

Attendance and degree information available by phone, fax, mail. Search requires name plus SSN, date of birth. Also helpful: exact years of attendance. There is no fee.

Embry-Riddle Aeronautical University, (Branch), Registrar, 3200 N Willow Creek Rd, Prescott, AZ 86301, 520-776-3808 (Fax: 520-776-3806). Hours: 8AM-5PM. Enrollment: 1400. Records go back to 1978. Alumni records are maintained here also. Call 904-226-6161. Degrees granted: Associate; Bachelors; Masters. Adverse incident record source-Police Dept, 520-778-1444.

Attendance information available by phone, fax, mail. Search requires name only. Also helpful: SSN. There is no fee.

Degree information available by phone, fax, mail. Search requires name only. Also helpful: SSN, approximate years of attendance. There is no fee.

Frank Lloyd Wright School of Architecture, Registrar, Taliesin West, Scottsdale, AZ 85261, 602-860-2700 (Fax: 602-391-4009). Hours: 9AM-4:30PM. Enrollment: 35. Records go back to 1945. Alumni records are maintained here at the same phone number. Degrees granted: Bachelors; Masters.

Attendance and degree information available by phone, fax, mail. Search requires name plus exact years of attendance. Also helpful: approximate years of attendance. There is no fee.

Gateway Community College, Registrar, 108 N 40th St, Phoenix, AZ 85034, 602-392-5189 (Fax: 602-392-5209). Hours: 8AM-7PM M-Th; 8AM-5PM F. Enrollment: 7000. Records go back to 1968. Degrees granted: Associate. Adverse incident record source- Security, 602-392-5025.

Attendance and degree information available by phone, fax, mail. Search requires name only. Also helpful: SSN, date of birth, approximate years of attendance. There is no fee.

Glendale Community College, Registrar, 600 W Olive Ave, Glendale, AZ 85302, 602-435-3319. Hours: 8AM-7:30PM M-Th, 9AM-4PM F. Enrollment: 18000. Records go back to 1965. Alumni records are maintained here also. Call 602-435-3014. Degrees granted: Associate.

Attendance and degree information available by phone, mail. Search requires name plus SSN, date of birth, exact years of attendance. There is no fee.

Grand Canyon University, Registrar, 3300 W Camelback Rd, PO Box 11097, Phoenix, AZ 85061, 602-589-2850 (Fax: 602-589-2594). Hours: 8AM-5PM M-Th; 9AM-4PM F. Enrollment: 1878. Records go back to 1949. Alumni records are maintained here also. Call 602-249-3300. Degrees granted: Bachelors; Masters. Special programs- College of Continuing Education. Adverse incident record source- Academic Records, 602-589-2460.

Attendance and degree information available by phone, fax, mail. Search requires name plus SSN, date of birth, exact years of attendance. There is no fee.

ITT Technical Institute, Registrar, 4837 E McDowell Rd, Phoenix, AZ 85008-4292, 602-252-2331 (Fax: 602-267-8727). Hours: 7AM-7PM M-Th; 8AM-5PM F. Enrollment: 400. Records go back to 1968. Alumni Records Office: Alumni Association, 5975 Castle Creek Pkwy N Dr, Indianapolis, IN

46250. Degrees granted: Associate. Adverse incident record source- Safety, 602-252-2331.

Attendance and degree information available by phone, fax, mail. Search requires name plus SSN, exact years of attendance. There is no fee.

ITT Technical Institute, Registrar, 1840 E Benson Hwy, Tucson, AZ 85714-1770, 520-294-2944. Hours: 8AM-10PM. Records go back to 1980. Degrees granted: Associate.

Attendance and degree information available by phone, mail. Search requires name plus SSN. There is no fee.

Interstate Career College, Registrar, 6367 E Tanque Verde Rd Ste 100, Tucson, AZ 85715, 520-327-6851 (Fax: 520-298-0722). Hours: 8AM-5PM. Enrollment: 125. Formerly Lamson Business College Records go back to 1960. Degrees granted: Associate. Adverse incident record source- Registrar's Office, 602-327-6851   .

Attendance and degree information available by phone, mail. Search requires name plus SSN, date of birth, exact years of attendance. There is no fee.

Keller Graduate School of Management, (East Valley Center), Registrar, 1201 S Alma School Rd Ste 5450, Mesa, AZ 85210, 602-827-1511 (Fax: 602-827-2552). Records are not housed here. They are located at Keller Graduate School of Management, (Phoenix/Northwest Center), Registrar, 2149 W Dunlap Ave, Phoenix, AZ 85021.

Keller Graduate School of Management, (Phoenix/Northwest Center), Registrar, 2149 W Dunlap Ave, Phoenix, AZ 85021, 602-870-0117 (Fax: 602-870-0022). Hours: 8:30AM-8PM M-Th, 8:30AM-5PM, Sat by appointment. Enrollment: 500. Records go back to 1973. Alumni records are maintained here also. Call 602-870-0117. Degrees granted: Masters. Special programs- Project Management: Human Resources: Business Administration. Adverse incident record source- Registrar, 602-870-0117.

Attendance and degree information available by phone, mail. Search requires name plus SSN, exact years of attendance. There is no fee.

Mesa Community College, Registrar, 1833 W Southern Ave, Mesa, AZ 85202, 602-461-7478 (Fax: 602-471-7805). Hours: 8AM-8PM M-Th. Enrollment: 22300. Records go back to 1965. Alumni records are maintained here also. Call 602-461-7501. Degrees granted: Associate. Adverse incident record source- Public Safety, 602-461-7000.

Attendance and degree information available by fax, mail. Search requires name plus SSN, signed release. Also helpful: date of birth. There is no fee.

Mohave Community College, Registrar, 1971 Jagerson Ave, Kingman, AZ 86401, 520-757-0847 (Fax: 520-757-0808). Hours: 8AM-5PM. Enrollment: 5800. Records go back to 1971. Degrees granted: Associate.

Attendance and degree information available by phone, fax, mail. Search requires name plus SSN. Also helpful: date of birth, exact years of attendance. There is no fee.

National Education Center-Arizona Automotive Institute, Director of Graduate Placement, 6829 N 46th Ave, Glendale, AZ 85301, 602-934-7273. Formerly Arizona Automotive Institute

Attendance and degree information available by phone, mail. Search requires name plus SSN, exact years of attendance. There is no fee.

Navajo Community College, Records/Admissions Officer, Tsaile, AZ 86556, 520-724-6630 (Fax: 520-724-3349). Hours: 8AM-5PM. Enrollment: 2017. Records go back to 1991. Degrees granted: Associate. Adverse incident record source- Security Office, 520-724-6628.

Attendance and degree information available by written request only. Search requires name plus SSN, exact years of attendance, signed release. There is no fee.

Northern Arizona University, Registrar, Box 4103, Flagstaff, AZ 86011-4092, 520-523-9011. Hours: 8AM-5PM Fall/Spring; 7:30AM-4:30PM Summer. Enrollment: 13931. Records go back to 1900. Degrees granted: Bachelors; Masters; Doctorate. Adverse incident record source- Campus Safety & Security, 602-523-3611.

Attendance information available by phone, mail. Search requires name plus SSN, approximate years of attendance. Also helpful: date of birth, exact years of attendance. There is no fee.

Degree information available by phone, mail. Search requires name plus SSN, approximate years of attendance. Also helpful: date of birth, exact years of attendance. There is no fee.

Northland Pioneer College, Registrar, 103 First Ave at Hopi Dr, PO Box 610, Holbrook, AZ 86025, 520-524-1993 (Fax: 520-524-1997). Hours: 8AM-5PM. Enrollment: 1800. Records go back to 1974. Degrees granted: Associate. Certification: CAS. Special programs- Nursing: Legal Assistant, 520-537-2976. Adverse incident record source- Student Services, 520-524-1993.

Attendance and degree information available by phone, fax, mail. Search requires name plus SSN. Also helpful: approximate years of attendance. There is no fee.

Paradise Valley Community College, Registrar, 18401 N 32nd St, Phoenix, AZ 85032, 602-493-2610 (Fax: 602-493-2983). Hours: 8AM-7PM M-Th; 8AM-5PM F. Enrollment: 5235. Records go back to 1987. Degrees granted: Associate. Adverse incident record source- Security Office, 602-493-2650.

Attendance information available by phone, fax. Search requires name plus approximate years of attendance. Also helpful: SSN, exact years of attendance. There is no fee.

Degree information available by phone, fax. Search requires name plus approximate years of attendance. Also helpful: SSN, exact years of attendance. There is no fee.

Paralegal Institute, Inc., Registrar, 3602 W Thomas Rd Ste 9, PO Drawer 11408, Phoenix, AZ 85061-1408, 602-272-1855 (Fax: 602-269-0793). Hours: 8AM-5PM. Records go back to 1975. Degrees granted: Associate. Special programs- Home Study Program.

Attendance and degree information available by phone, fax, mail. Search requires name plus SSN. There is no fee.

Parks College, (Branch Campus), Registrar, 6992 E Broadway, Tucson, AZ 85710, 520-886-7979 (Fax: 520-886-2395). Hours: 8AM-5PM M-Th; 8AM-3PM F. Records go back to 1987. Degrees granted: Associate.

Attendance and degree information available by fax, mail. Search requires name plus SSN, approximate years of attendance, signed release. There is no fee.

Phoenix College, Registrar, 1202 W Thomas Rd, Phoenix, AZ 85013, 602-285-7500 (Fax: 602-285-7813). Hours: 7:30AM-7:30PM M-Th; 7:30AM-4:30PM F. Enrollment: 12000. Records go back to 1920. Alumni records are maintained here at the same phone number. Degrees granted: Associate. Certification: Fire Science

Attendance and degree information available by phone, fax, mail. Search requires name plus SSN, date of birth. Also helpful: exact years of attendance. There is no fee.

Pima County Community College District, Registrar, 4907 E Broadway Blvd, Tucson, AZ 85709-1120, 520-884-6060 (Fax: 520-748-4790). Hours: 8:15AM-4:45PM. Enrollment: 27950. Records go back to 1969. Alumni Records Office: Alumni Association, Pima County Community College, 4905 E Broadway Blvd, Tucson, AZ 85709. Degrees granted: Associate; Basic, Advanced & Technical. Special programs-

Associate, 520-748-4903: Advanced & Technical, 520-478-4961. Adverse incident record source- Department of Public Safety, 520-748-2692.

Attendance and degree information available by phone, fax, mail. Search requires name plus SSN. Also helpful: date of birth, approximate years of attendance. There is no fee.

Pima Medical Institute, Registrar, 3350 E Grant Rd, Tucson, AZ 85716, 520-326-1600 (Fax: 520-795-3643). Hours: 7:15AM-8:30PM M-Th, 8AM-5PM F. Records go back to 1972. Alumni records are maintained here also. Call 520-326-1600. Degrees granted: Associate. Adverse incident record source- Student Services.

Attendance and degree information available by phone, fax, mail. Search requires name plus SSN, date of birth, exact years of attendance. There is no fee.

Pima Medical Institute, (Branch), Registrar, 957 S Dobson Rd, Mesa, AZ 85202, 602-345-777. Hours: 8AM-5PM. Records go back to 1970. Degrees granted: Associate.

School will not confirm attendance information.

Degree information available by phone, mail. Search requires name only. There is no fee.

Prescott College, Registrar, 220 Grove Ave, Prescott, AZ 86301, 520-776-5164 (Fax: 520-776-5175). Hours: 8AM-5PM. Enrollment: 870. Records go back to 1966. Alumni records are maintained here also. Call 520-776-5223. Degrees granted: Bachelors; Masters.

Attendance and degree information available by phone, fax, mail. Search requires name only. Also helpful: SSN, date of birth, approximate years of attendance. There is no fee.

Rio Salado Community College, Registrar, 2323 W 14th St, Tempe, AZ 85281, 602-517-8150 (Fax: 602-517-8199). Hours: 8:15AM-5:45PM M-Th; 8:15AM-4:45PM F. Enrollment: 20000. Records go back to 1978. Alumni records are maintained here also. Call 602-517-8000. Degrees granted: Associate. Special programs- Chemical Dependency: Mentally Ill. Adverse incident record source- Administration, 602-517-8149.

Attendance information available by phone, fax, mail. Search requires name only. Also helpful: SSN. There is no fee.

Degree information available by phone, mail. Search requires name only. Also helpful: SSN. Fee is $5.00.

Scottsdale Community College, Registrar, 9000 E Chaparral Rd, Scottsdale, AZ 85250, 602-423-6000 (Fax: 602-423-6200). Hours: 8AM-7PM M-Th, 8AM-4PM F. Enrollment: 10000. Records go back to 1976. Degrees granted: Associate.

Attendance and degree information available by phone, fax, mail. Search requires name plus SSN. Also helpful: date of birth, exact years of attendance. There is no fee.

South Mountain Community College, Admissions & Records, 7050 S 24th St, Phoenix, AZ 85040, 602-243-8000 (Fax: 602-243-8199). Enrollment: 2500. Records go back to 1980. Alumni records are maintained here at the same phone number. Degrees granted: Associate. Adverse incident record source- Dr. Harrid, 602-243-8064.

Attendance and degree information available by phone, mail. Search requires name plus SSN. Also helpful: date of birth, exact years of attendance. There is no fee.

Southwestern College, Registrar, 2625 E Cactus Rd, Phoenix, AZ 85032, 602-992-6101 (Fax: 602-404-2159). Hours: 8:30AM-4:30PM. Enrollment: 200. Records go back to 1960. Degrees granted: Associate; Bachelors.

Attendance and degree information available by phone, fax, mail. Search requires name only. Also helpful: SSN, date of birth, exact years of attendance. There is no fee.

Southwestern Conservative Baptist Bible College, Registrar, 2625 E Cactus Rd, Phoenix, AZ 85032, 602-992-6101 (Fax: 602-404-2159). Enrollment: 200. Records go back to 1936. Degrees granted: Associate; Bachelors. Adverse incident record source- Student Services.

Attendance and degree information available by phone. Search requires name plus SSN, exact years of attendance. There is no fee.

University of Arizona, Registrar, Tucson, AZ 85721, 520-621-3393 (Fax: 520-621-8944). Hours: 8AM-5PM. Enrollment: 34000. Records go back to 1885. Alumni records are maintained here also. Call 520-621-2211. Degrees granted: Bachelors; Masters; Doctorate. Adverse incident record source- Registrar's Office, 602-621-3393 .

Attendance and degree information available by phone, mail. Search requires name plus SSN, date of birth, exact years of attendance. There is no fee.

University of Phoenix, Registrar, 4615 E Elwood St 3rd Flr, Phoenix, AZ 85072-2069, 602-966-9577 (Fax: 602-894-1758). Hours: 8AM-6PM. Enrollment: 31000. Records go back to 1979. Alumni records are maintained here at the same phone number. Degrees granted: Associate; Bachelors; Masters.

Attendance information available by phone, fax, mail. Search requires name plus SSN. Also helpful: date of birth, exact years of attendance. There is no fee. Expedited service available for $7.50.

Degree information available by phone, fax, mail. Search requires name plus SSN. Also helpful: date of birth, exact years of attendance. There is no fee. Expedite service available for $7.50.

University of Phoenix, (Center for Distance Education), Registrar, PO Box 52069, Phoenix, AZ 85072, 602-921-8014 (Fax: 602-894-1758). Hours: 8AM-6PM. Enrollment: 36000. Records go back to 1980. Alumni records are maintained here at the same phone number. Degrees granted: Bachelors; Masters; Nursing. Adverse incident record source- Safety & Security, 602-966-7400.

Attendance and degree information available by fax, mail. Search requires name plus SSN, approximate years of attendance. There is no fee.

University of Phoenix, (Phoenix Main), Registrar, 4605 E Elmwood St, PO Box 52076, Phoenix, AZ 85072-2076, 602-804-7600. Enrollment: 12030. Records go back to 1976. Transcript records are housed at University of Phoenix, Registrar, PO Box 52069, Phoenix, AZ 85072. Degrees granted: Bachelors; Masters.

Attendance and degree information available by phone, mail. Search requires name plus SSN, approximate years of attendance. There is no fee.

University of Phoenix, (Tucson Main), Registrar, 5099 E. Grant Rd, Tucson, AZ 85712, 520-881-6512 (Fax: 520-759-6177). Transcript records are housed at University of Phoenix, Registrar, PO Box 52069, Phoenix, AZ 85072.

Attendance and degree information available by written request only. Search requires name plus SSN, approximate years of attendance.

Yavapai College, Registrar, 1100 E Sheldon St, Prescott, AZ 86301, 520-776-2150 (Fax: 520-776-2151). Hours: 8:30AM-4:30PM. Enrollment: 7000. Records go back to 1994. Degrees granted: Associate. Adverse incident record source- Judicial Coordinator, 520-776-2207.

Attendance and degree information available by phone, fax, mail. Search requires name plus SSN, date of birth, approximate years of attendance. Also helpful: exact years of attendance. There is no fee.

Trade and Vocational Schools

AIBT (Branch Campus), 925 S Gilbert Rd #201, Mesa, AZ 85204, 602-545-8755

AIBT (Branch Campus), 4023 E Grant Rd Ste A, Tucson, AZ 85712, 520-881-1541

Al Collins Graphic Design School, 1140 S Priest Dr, Tempe, AZ 85281, 602-966-3000

American Institute of Technology, 440 S 54th Ave, Phoenix, AZ 85043, 602-233-2222

Apollo College (Phoenix), 8503 N 27th Ave, Phoenix, AZ 85051, 602-864-1571

Apollo College (Tri-City), 630 W Southern Ave, Mesa, AZ 85210, 602-831-6585

Apollo College (Tucson), 3870 N Oracle Rd, Tucson, AZ 85705, 520-888-5885

Apollo College (Westside), 2701 West Bethany Home Rd, Phoenix, AZ 85017, 602-433-1333

Arizona College of Allied Health, 7900 E Greenway Rd Ste 210, Scottsdale, AZ 85260, 602-951-0629

Arizona Paralegal Training Program, First American Title Bldg, 111 West Monroe Ave Ste 800, Phoenix, AZ 85003, 602-252-2171

Art Center (The), 2525 N Country Club Rd, Tucson, AZ 85716, 520-325-0123

AzTech College, 941 S Dobson Rd Ste 120, Mesa, AZ 85202, 602-897-9898

Bryman School (The), 4343 N 16th St, Phoenix, AZ 85016, 602-274-4300

Clinton Technical Institute, 2844 W Deer Valley Rd, Phoenix, AZ 85027, 602-869-9644

Conservatory of Recording Arts & Sciences, 2300 E Broadway Rd, Tempe, AZ 85282, 602-265-5566

Desert Institute of the Healing Arts, 639 N Sixth Ave, Tucson, AZ 85705, 520-882-0899

Distance Learning International, 500 N Kimball Ave, Southdale, AZ 79029, 817-488-6797

High-Tech Institute, 1515 E Indian School Rd, Phoenix, AZ 85014, 602-279-9700

Long Medical Institute, 4126 N Black Canyon Hwy, Phoenix, AZ 85017, 602-279-9333

Metropolitan College of Court Reporting, 4640 E Elwood St #12, Phoenix, AZ 85040, 602-955-5900

Mundus Institute, 4745 N Seventh St #100, Phoenix, AZ 85014, 602-248-8548

National Education Center - Arizona Automotive Institute, 6829 N 46th Ave, Glendale, AZ 85301, 800-528-0717

North American Technical College, 1131 W Broadway, Tempe, AZ 85282, 602-829-1903

Northern Arizona College of Health Careers, 2575 E Seventh Ave, Flagstaff, AZ 86004, 520-526-0763

Refrigeration School (The), 4210 E Washington St, Phoenix, AZ 85034, 602-275-7133

Rice Aviation, a Division of A&J Enterprises (Branch Campus), 3201 E Broadway, Phoenix, AZ 85040, 602-243-6611

Roberto-Venn School of Luthiery, 4011 S 16th St, Phoenix, AZ 85040, 602-243-1179

Scottsdale Culinary Institute, 8100 E Camelback Rd, Scottsdale, AZ 85251, 602-990-3773

Southwest Academy of Technology, 1660 S Alma School Rd #227, Mesa, AZ 85210, 602-820-3003

Tucson College, 7302-10 E 22nd St, Tucson, AZ 85710, 520-296-3261

Universal Technical Institute, 3121 W Weldon Ave, Phoenix, AZ 85017, 602-264-4164

University of Advancing Computer Technology, 4100 E Broadway Rd Ste 150, Phoenix, AZ 85040, 602-437-0405

Western Truck School (Branch Campus), 3201 E Broadway Rd, Phoenix, AZ 85040, 602-437-5303

State Licensing & Business Registration Quick Finder Index

Architecture, Engineering & Surveying
Architect #28 .... ☎ 602-255-4053
Engineer #28 .... ☎ 602-255-4053
Geologist #28 .... ☎ 602-255-4053
Landscape Architect #28 .... ☎ 602-255-4053
Surveyor #28 .... ☎ 602-255-4053

Business - Court & Legal Services
Attorney #29 (17573) .... ☎ 602-252-4804
Bondsman #50 (100) .... ☎ 602-912-8470
Court Reporter #64 520-325-1055
Lobbyist #71 .... ☎ 602-542-4086
Notary Public #71 (90000) .... ☎ 602-542-4086

Business - General Services
Bottled Water Processor #65 (25) .... ☎ 602-506-6970
Food Establishment #65 (8694) .... ☎ 602-506-6970
Public & Semi-Public Bathing Place #65 (7134)
.... ☎ 602-506-6970
Public Accountant-CPA #6 (7641) .... ☎ 602-255-3648
Public Accountant-PA #6 (17) .... ☎ 602-255-3648
Public Accounting Firm-CPA & PA #6 (76)
.... ☎ 602-255-3648
Public Weighmaster #58 (200) .... ☎ 602-451-2979
Publishing #55 602-542-4565
Restaurant & Bar #55 602-542-4565
Retail Sales Outlet #55 602-542-4565
Telemarketing Firm #71 (3) .... ☎ 602-542-4086
Tobacco Products Distributor #55 602-542-4565
Weights & Measures - Registered Service Agency #58
.... ☎ 602-255-5211
Weights & Measures - Registered Serviceman #58
.... ☎ 602-255-5211

Construction & Manufacturing
Bedding/Furniture Manufacturer #65 .... ☎ 602-506-6970
Contractor #70 (31700) .... ☎ 602-542-1525
Mobile Home Dealer/Broker #36 (417) .... ☎ 602-255-4072
Mobile Home Installer #36 (185) .... ☎ 602-255-4072
Mobile Home Manufacturer #36 (149) .... ☎ 602-255-4072
Pipeline #55 602-542-4565
Renovator or Sterilizer or Spray Process
    Applicator #65 .... ☎ 602-506-6970

Education
Community College Teacher #30 (4260) .... ☎ 602-255-5582
Elementary & Special Education Teacher #38.... 602-542-4368
Guidance Counselor #38 602-542-4368
Postsecondary Vocational Programs - Private #5
.... ✉ 602-542-5709
School Bus Driver (Certification) #1 (6000)
.... ☎ 602-223-2646
School Librarian #38 602-542-4368
School Psychologist & Psychometrist #38 602-542-4368
School Superintendent #38 602-542-4368
School Supervisor #38 602-542-4368
Vocational Rehabilitation #61 602-542-3739

Environmental & Agriculture
Agricultural Aircraft Pilot #35 (117) .... ☎ 602-542-0904
Agricultural Grower Permit #35 .... ☎ 602-542-4499
Agricultural Pest Control Advisor #35 (314)
.... ☎ 602-542-0904
Agricultural Seller Permit #35 .... ☎ 602-542-4499
Agriculture Broker, Distributor, Jobber #34 602-542-6309

Agriculture Wholesale Distributor &
    Producer-Distributor #34 602-542-6309
Air Pollution Sources #39 .... ✉ 602-207-2338
Aquaculture #34 602-542-6309
Aquifer Protection Permit #41 602-207-4524
Assayer #28 .... ☎ 602-255-4053
Beef Cattle Feedlot #34 602-542-6309
Cheese & Ice Cream Plant #34 602-542-6309
Citrus Fruit Broker, Dealer, Packer, Shipper #32
.... ☎ 602-542-4373
Cloud Seeder or Weather Modifier #57 .... ☎ 602-417-2400
Dairy Farms & Facility #34 602-542-6309
Dry Well Registration #41 602-207-4524
Egg & Egg Product Salesperson/Firm #34 602-542-6309
Environmental Laboratory #44 (210) .... ☎ 602-255-3454
Equine Trader #34 602-542-6309
Feedlot #34 602-542-6309
Feeds Distribution - Commercial #33 602-253-1920
Fertilizer Distribution - Commercial #33 602-253-1920
Food Brand #34 602-542-6309
Food Inspector #45 .... ☎ 602-230-5912
Food Packer or Grower/Shipper - Contract #32
    (28) .... ☎ 602-542-4373
Forester #63 602-542-4627
Fruit & Vegetable Broker, Dealer #32 .... ☎ 602-542-4373
Fur Dealer #59 602-942-3000
Garbage Fed to Swine #34 602-542-6309
Hay Broker/Dealer #32 (63) .... ☎ 602-542-4373
Hazardous Waste Facility #40 602-207-4524
Land Disposition Division #62 602-542-1704
Livestock or Poultry Slaughterer #34 602-542-6309
Meat & Poultry Processor #34 602-542-6309
Mining #55 602-542-4565
Mining Elevator & Diesel #67 (170) .... ✉ 602-542-5971
Mining Operator-Start-up #67 (170) .... ✉ 602-542-5971
Natural Resources Division #63 602-542-4625
Oil & Gas Production #55 602-542-4565
Pesticide Applicator #35 (1009) .... ☎ 602-542-0904
Pesticide Applicator, Supervisor or Advisor #72
.... ☎ 602-255-3664
Pesticide Distribution #33 602-253-1920
Pesticide Salesperson #32 .... ☎ 602-542-4373
Plant Operator #41 602-207-4524
Pollutant Discharge Permit #41 602-207-4524
Prospector (Mineral Exploration Permit) #63 (1)
.... ☎ 602-542-4628
Radioactive Material Possession #66 602-255-4845
Seed Dealer #32 (858) .... ☎ 602-542-4373
Seed Labeler #32 (181) .... ☎ 602-542-4373
Sewage, Sludge and Septic Pumping
    Vehicle #40 602-207-4524
Solid Waste Management Facility #40 602-207-4524
Timbering #55 602-542-4565
Urban Lands Division #63 602-542-3671
Vehicle Emission-Fleet Inspection Station #42
    (350) .... ☎ 602-207-7000
Vehicle Emissions-Fleet Inspector #42 (1000)
.... ☎ 602-207-7000
Veterinary Medicine & Surgery #73 (1375)
.... ☎ 602-542-3095
Veterinary Premise (Hospital) #73 (520) .... ☎ 602-542-3095
Veterinary Technician #73 (220) .... ☎ 602-542-3095
Waste Water Collection, Treatment,
    Construction #41 602-207-4692

Waste Water Facility Operator #41 602-207-4524
Waste Water Reuse #41 602-207-4524
Water Distribution System Operator #41 602-207-4524
Water Quality Certification #41 602-207-4524
Water Rights Assignment #57 .... ☎ 602-417-2400
Water Transporter (out of state) #57 .... ☎ 602-417-2400
Well Driller (Drilling Firm) #57 (649) .... ☎ 602-417-2470
Well Registration & Construction #57 (6000)
.... ☎ 602-417-2400
Wholesale Feed #55 602-542-4565

Financial - Real Estate, Insurance & Banking

Campground Membership Broker &
  Salesman #54 (90) .... ☎ 602-468-1414
Collection Agency #4 (254) .... ☎ 602-255-4421
Commercial Leasing #55 602-542-4565
Consumer Lender #4 (32) .... ☎ 602-255-4421
Debt Management #4 (7) .... ☎ 602-255-4421
Escrow Agent #4 (57) .... ☎ 602-255-4421
Insurance Broker #50 (2944) .... ☎ 602-912-8470
Insurance Sales Agent/Solicitor #50 (128) ..... ☎ 602-912-8470
Money Transmitter #4 (22) .... ☎ 602-255-4421
Mortgage Banker #4 (215) .... ☎ 602-255-4421
Mortgage Broker #4 (497) .... ☎ 602-255-4421
Motor Vehicle Dealer & Sales Finance #4
  (643) .... ☎ 602-255-4421
Property Tax Agent #7 (1650) .... ☎ 602-542-1539
Real & Personal Property Appraisal #55 602-542-4565
Real Estate Appraiser #7 (400) .... ☎ 602-542-1539
Real Estate Broker & Salesman #54 (31680)
.... ☎ 602-468-1414
Real Estate School #54 (43) .... ☎ 602-468-1414
Real Estate School Instructor & Course #54
  (1000) .... ☎ 602-468-1414
Rental of Personal Property #55 602-542-4565
Securities Dealer #31 602-542-4242
Securities Salesperson #31 602-542-4242
Self Insurance #60 (133) .... ✉ 602-542-1836
Trust Company #4 (11) .... ☎ 602-255-4421

Health & Beauty

Acupuncture #10 (26) .... ☎ 602-255-1444
Adult Care Home Manager #68 602-542-3095
Advanced Life Support Base Hospital #43 .... ☎ 602-255-1272
Aesthetician, Cosmetologist & Nail
  Technician #11 (28000) .... ☎ 602-542-3769
Aesthetics, Cosmetology & Nail
  Technology Instructor #11 .... ☎ 602-542-3769
Ambulance Service #43 .... ☎ 602-255-1272
Ambulatory Surgical Center #43 .... ☎ 602-255-1177
Audiologist #49 .... ☎ 602-255-1177
Barber #8 (3358) .... ☎ 602-542-4498
Barber Establishment #8 (1041) .... ☎ 602-542-4498
Barber Instructor #8 (43) .... ☎ 602-542-4498
Barber School #8 (9) .... ☎ 602-542-4498
Behavioral Health Center #43 .... ☎ 602-255-1272
Birthing Center #43 .... ☎ 602-255-1272
Cannabis & Controlled Substance Dealer #55 602-542-4565
Cemetery Broker & Salesman #54 (207) .... ☎ 602-468-1414
Chiropractor #10 (2383) .... ☎ 602-255-1444
Clinical Laboratory #44 (482) .... ☎ 602-255-3454
Cosmetology or Nail Technology Salon or
  School #11 .... ☎ 602-542-3769
Dental Assistant #12 .... ☎ 602-255-3696
Dental Hygienist #12 (1918) .... ☎ 602-255-3696
Dentist #12 (2971) .... ☎ 602-255-3696
Denturist #12 (14) .... ☎ 602-255-3696
Drug Manufacturer #23 (13) .... ✉ 602-255-5125
Drug Wholesaler #23 (177) .... ✉ 602-255-5125
Embalmer #14 .... ☎ 602-542-3095

Emergency Medical Technician &
  Paramedic #43 (19000) .... ☎ 602-255-1170
Emergency Medical Technician
  Instructor #47 .... ✉ 602-255-1272
Funeral Director #14 .... ☎ 602-542-3095
Health Screening Service #44 .... ☎ 602-255-3454
Hearing Aid Dispenser #49 (375) .... ☎ 602-255-1177
Home Health Agency #43 .... ☎ 602-255-1272
Homeopathic Physician #15 (65) .... ☎ 602-542-3095
Hospice #43 .... ☎ 602-255-1272
Hospital #43 .... ☎ 602-255-1272
Infirmary #43 .... ☎ 602-255-1272
Intern & Resident #16 (1100) .... ☎ 602-255-3751
Lay Midwife #48 (37) .... ☎ 602-255-1177
Mammography Screening #43 .... ☎ 602-255-1272
Medicaid Service #46 .... ☎ 602-255-1127
Medical Doctor #16 (945) .... ☎ 602-255-3751
Naturopathic Physician #18 (210) .... ☎ 602-542-3095
Nurse #19 .... ☎ 602-255-5092
Nurse Practitioner #19 (1537) .... ☎ 602-255-5092
Nurses Aide #19 (40000) .... ☎ 602-255-5092
Nursing Care Institution Administrator #68
.... 602-255-3095
Occupational Therapist/Assistant #20 (4) ...... ☎ 602-542-6784
Optical Establishments #13 (300) .... ☎ 602-542-3095
Optician #13 (800) .... ☎ 602-542-3095
Optometrist #21 .... ☎ 602-542-3095
Osteopathic Physician #22 (1570) .... ☎ 602-255-1747
Outpatient Surgical Center & Outpatient
  Treatment Clinic #43 .... ☎ 602-255-1272
Pharmacist #23 (5215) .... ✉ 602-255-5125
Pharmacy Intern #23 (500) .... ✉ 602-255-5125
Physical Therapist #24 (2400) .... ☎ 602-542-3095
Physician's Assistant #17 .... ☎ 602-255-3751
Physiotherapy #10 (166) .... ☎ 602-255-1444
Podiatrist #25 (291) .... ☎ 602-542-3095
Radiation Machine Possession #66 (3687) 602-255-4845
Radiation Therapy Technologist #66 (151) 602-255-4845
Radiologic Technologist #66 (2920) 602-255-4845
Radiology - Practical Technologist #66
  (550) 602-255-4845
Rehabilitation & Psychiatric Unit #43 .... ☎ 602-255-1272
Rehabilitation Agency #43 .... ☎ 602-255-1272
Renal Disease Facility #43 .... ☎ 602-255-1272
Respiratory Therapist #27 (4100) .... ☎ 602-542-5995
Sanitarian #45 .... ☎ 602-230-5912
Speech-Language Pathologist #49 .... ☎ 602-255-1177
X-Ray Supplier - Portable #43 .... ☎ 602-255-1272

Investigations & Security

Polygraph Examiner & Polygraph Examiner
  Intern #52 .... ☎ 602-223-2361
Private Investigator #52 .... ☎ 602-223-2361
Security Guard #52 .... ☎ 602-223-2361

Social Services

Behavioral Health Emergency Service #46 .... ☎ 602-255-1127
Behavioral Health Residential #46 .... ☎ 602-255-1127
Behavioral Health Service Agency #46 .... ☎ 602-255-1127
Child Adoption Agency #37 (16) .... ☎ 602-542-2287
Child Foster Home #37 (255) .... ☎ 602-542-2287
Child Placing Agency #37 (17) .... ☎ 602-542-2287
Child Residential & Shelter Care #37
  (221) .... ☎ 602-542-2287
DUI Education Agency #46 .... ☎ 602-255-1127
DUI Screening Agency #46 .... ☎ 602-255-1127
DUI Treatment Agency #46 .... ☎ 602-255-1127
Day Care Establishment #43 .... ☎ 602-255-1272
Detoxification Services #46 .... ☎ 602-255-1127
Family Day Care Home #37 .... ☎ 602-542-2287
Foster Care Home #43 .... ☎ 602-255-1272

Headstart #43 .... ☎ 602-255-1272
Marriage & Family Therapist #9 (338) .... ☎ 602-542-1895
Mental Health Screening, Evaluation &
   Treatment #46 .... ☎ 602-255-1127
Mentally Retarded Intermediate Care
   Facility #43 .... ☎ 602-255-1272
Preschool #43 .... ☎ 602-255-1272
Professional Counselor #9 (1411) .... ☎ 602-542-1884
Psychologist #26 (1399) .... ☎ 602-542-3095
Social Worker #9 (2168) .... ☎ 602-542-1895
Substance Abuse Counselor #9 (972) .... ☎ 602-542-1895
Substance Abuse Treatment Service #46 .... ☎ 602-255-1127

Sports & Entertainment

Amusement Printing & Advertising #55 602-542-4565
Amusements #55 602-542-4565
Big and Small Game Resident Guide #59 602-942-3000
Bingo Operation #55 602-542-4565
Boxer #2 .... ☎ 602-542-1417
Boxing #2 (430) .... ☎ 602-542-1417
Concession on State Park Lands #69 .... ☎ 602-542-2155
Field Trial License #59 602-942-3000
Horse or Greyhound Racing #53 (6576) .... ☎ 602-277-1704
Hunting & Fishing License Dealer #59 602-942-3000
Liquor Producer #51 (530) .... ☎ 602-542-5141

Liquor Retail Co-Operative, Agent &
   Manager (Liquor Retail) #51 (8149) .... ☎ 602-542-5141
Liquor Wholesaler #51 (66) .... ☎ 602-542-5141
Lottery Retailer #3 602-921-4400
Minnow Dealer #59 602-942-3000
Taxidermy #59 602-942-3000
Trailer Coach Park #65 (561) .... ☎ 602-506-6970
Watercraft Registration Agent #59 602-942-3000
Zoo #59 602-942-3000

Transportation

Aircraft Dealer #56 (38) .... ☎ 602-255-7691
Aircraft Dealer for Wreckers or Salvage #56
   .... ☎ 602-255-7691
Aircraft Manufacturer, Distributor, Retail or
   Importer #56 .... ☎ 602-255-7691
Aircraft Owner #56 (5260) .... ☎ 602-255-7691
Aircraft Pilot Trainer School or Instructor #56
   .... ☎ 602-255-7691
Aircraft Transporter #56 .... ☎ 602-255-7691
Aircraft Use Fuel Dealer, Manufacturer #56
   .... ☎ 602-255-7691
Hotel, Motel & Tourist Court #65 (335) .... ☎ 602-506-6970
Mobile Home Salesperson #36 (1551) .... ☎ 602-255-4072
Private Car, Rail & Aircraft #55 602-542-4565
Transporting & Towing #55 602-542-4565

State Licensing & Business Registration Agency Information

(1) Arizona Department of Public Safety, Student Transportaion, 2102 W Encanto Blvd, PO Box 6638, Phoenix, AZ 85005, 602-223-2646, Fax: 602-223-2923

(2) Arizona State Boxing Commission, 1400 W Washington, Phoenix, AZ 85007, 602-542-1417, Fax: 602-542-1458

(3) Arizona State Lottery, 4740 E University Dr, Phoenix, AZ 85034, 602-921-4400

(4) Banking Department, 2910 N 44th St, Suite 310, Phoenix, AZ 85018, 602-255-4421, Fax: 602-381-1225

(5) Board for Private Postsecondary Education, 1400 W Washington Room 260, Phoenix, AZ 85007, 602-542-5709

(6) Board of Accountancy, 3877 N Seventh Street 106, Phoenix, AZ 85014, 602-255-3648

(7) Board of Appraisal, 1400 W Washington, Suite 360, Phoenix, AZ 85007, 602-542-1539

(8) Board of Barbers, 1400 W Washington, Room 220, Phoenix, AZ 85007, 602-542-4498

(9) Board of Behavioral Health Examiners, 1400 W Washington, Room 350, Phoenix, AZ 85007, 602-542-1882, Fax: 602-542-1830

(10) Board of Chiropractic Examiners, 5060 N 19th Ave., Room 416, Phoenix, AZ 85015, 602-255-1444, Fax: 602-255-4289

(11) Board of Cosmetology, Information Services, 1510 W. Adams, Phoenix, AZ 85007, 602-542-4769, Fax: 602-542-6533

(12) Board of Dental Examiners, 5060 N 19th Ave, Suite 406, Phoenix, AZ 85015, 602-255-3696, Fax: 602-255-3589

(13) Board of Dispensing Opticians, 1400 W Washington, Room 230, Phoenix, AZ 85007, 602-542-3095, Fax: 602-542-3093

(14) Board of Funeral Directors & Embalmers, 1400 W Washington, Room 230, Phoenix, AZ 85007, 602-542-3095, Fax: 602-542-3093

(15) Board of Homeopathic Medical Examiners, 1400 W Washington, Room 230, Phoenix, AZ 85007, 602-542-3095, Fax: 602-542-3093

(16) Board of Medical Examiners, 1651 E Morton, Suite 210, Phoenix, AZ 85020, 602-255-3751, Fax: 602-255-8148

(17) Board of Medical Examiners, 1651 E Morton, Suite 210, Phoenix, AZ 85020, 602-255-3751, Fax: 602-255-1848

(18) Board of Naturopathic Physicians Examiners, 1400 W Washington, Room 230, Phoenix, AZ 85007, 602-542-3095, Fax: 602-542-3093

(19) Board of Nursing, 1651 E Morton, #150, Phoenix, AZ 85020, 602-255-5092

(20) Board of Occupational Therapy Examiners, 1400 W Washington #340, Phoenix, AZ 85007, 602-542-6784, Fax: 602-542-5469

(21) Board of Optometry, 1400 W Washington, Room 230, Phoenix, AZ 85007, 602-542-3095

(22) Board of Osteopathic Medicine & Surgery Examiners, 141 E Palm Lane #205, Phoenix, AZ 85004, 602-255-1747 X21

(23) Board of Pharmacy, 5060 N 19th Ave, Room 101, Phoenix, AZ 85015, 602-255-5125, Fax: 602-255-5940

(24) Board of Physical Therapy Examiners, 1400 W Washington, Room 230, Phoenix, AZ 85007, 602-542-3095, Fax: 602-542-3093

(25) Board of Podiatry Examiners, 1400 W Washington, Room 230, Phoenix, AZ 85007, 602-542-3095

(26) Board of Psychologist Examiners, 1400 W Washington, Rm 235, Phoenix, AZ 85007, 602-542-3095, Fax: 602-542-3093

(27) Board of Respiratory Care Examiners, 1400 W Washington, Suite 200, Phoenix, AZ 85007, 602-542-5995, Fax: 602-542-5900

(28) Board of Technical Registration, 1951 W Camelback, Suite 250, Phoenix, AZ 85015, 602-255-4053, Fax: 602-255-4051

(29) Committee on Examinations of Character & Fitness, 111 W Monroe, Suite 1800, Phoenix, AZ 85003-1742, 602-252-4804, Fax: 602-271-4930

(30) Community College Board of Directors, 3225 N Central, Suite 1220,Century Plaza, Phoenix, AZ 85012, 602-255-5582, Fax: 602-279-3464

(31) Corporation Commission, Securities Division, 1300 W Washington, 3rd Floor, Phoenix, AZ 85007, 602-542-4242

(32) Department of Agriculture, 1688 W Adams St, Phoenix, AZ 85007, 602-542-0958, Fax: 602-542-1004

(33) Department of Agriculture, Agricultural Laboratory, 2422 W Holly Ave, Phoenix, AZ 85009, 602-253-1920

(34) Department of Agriculture, Animal Services, Dairy & Dairy Products Control, 1688 W Adams, Room 332, Phoenix, AZ 85007, 602-542-6309

(35) Department of Agriculture, Environmental Services Div, 1688 W Adams St, Phoenix, AZ 85007, 602-542-3578, Fax: 602-542-0466

(36) Department of Building and Fire Safety, 99 East Virginia Suite 100, Phoenix, AZ 85004, 602-255-4072, Fax: 602-255-4962

(37) Department of Economic Security, Social Services Division, 1789 W Jefferson, Site Code 940A, Phoenix, AZ 85007, 602-542-2287, Fax: 602-542-3330

(38) Department of Education, Teacher Certification Unit, 1535 W Jefferson, Phoenix, AZ 85007, 602-542-4368

(39) Department of Environmental Quality, Office of Air Quality, 3033 N Central Ave, Phoenix, AZ 85012, 602-207-2338, Fax: 602-207-2336

(40) Department of Environmental Quality, Office of Waste Programs, 3033 N Central Ave, Phoenix, AZ 85012.ll Department of Environmental Quality, Office of Water Quality, 3033 N Central Ave, Phoenix, AZ 85012, 602-207-4524

(41) Department of Environmental Quality, Vehicle Emissions Section, 600 N 40th St, Phoenix, AZ 85008, 602-207-7000, Fax: 602-207-7020

(42) Department of Health Services, 1647 E Morten, Suite 230, Phoenix, AZ 85020, 602-255-1272

(43) Department of Health Services, Div of State Laboratory Services/Licensure/Cert, 3443 N Central Avenue Suite 810, Phoenix, AZ 85012, 602-255-3454, Fax: 602-255-3462

(44) Department of Health Services, Food Protection & Institutional Sanitation Section, 3815 N Black Canyon Hwy, Phoenix, AZ 85015, 602-230-5912, Fax: 602-230-5817

(45) Department of Health Services, Office of Behavioral Health Licensure, 1647 E Morten, Suite 240, Phoenix, AZ 85020, 602-255-1127, Fax: 602-255-1225

(46) Department of Health Services, Office of EMS, 1647 E Morten, Suite 120, Phoenix, AZ 85020, 602-255-1170

(47) Department of Health Services, Office of Health Care Licenses, 1647 E Morten Avenue Suite 110, Phoenix, AZ 85020, 602-542-1875, Fax: 602-255-1109

(48) Department of Health Services, Office of Health Care Licensure, 1647 E Morten Avenue, Phoenix, AZ 85020, 602-255-1177, Fax: 602-255-1109

(49) Department of Insurance, Licensing Section, 2910 N 44th St, Suite 210, Phoenix, AZ 85018-7256, 602-912-8470, Fax: 602-912-8421

(50) Department of Liquor License & Control, 800 W Washington, 5th Floor, Phoenix, AZ 85007, 602-542-5141, Fax: 602-542-5707

(51) Department of Public Safety, PO Box 6328, Phoenix, AZ 85005-6328, 602-223-2361

(52) Department of Racing, Licensing Division, 3877 N 7th Street Suite 201, Phoenix, AZ 85014, 602-277-1704, Fax: 602-277-1165

(53) Department of Real Estate, 2910 N 44th St, Phoenix, AZ 85018, 602-468-1414, Fax: 602-468-0562

(54) Department of Revenue, License & Registration, PO Box 29002, Phoenix, AZ 85038-9002, 602-542-4565

(55) Department of Transportation, Aeronautics Division, PO Box 13588, Mail Drop 426M, Phoenix, AZ 85002-3588, 602-255-7691, Fax: 602-407-3007

(56) Department of Water Resources, 500 N 3rd St, Phoenix, AZ 85004-3903, 602-417-2470, Fax: 602-417-2421

(57) Department of Weights & Measures, 9535 E Doubletree Ranch Rd, Scottsdale, AZ 85258-5539, 602-255-5211, Fax: 602-255-1950

(58) Game & Fish Department, 2222 W Greenway Rd, Phoenix, AZ 85023, 602-942-3000

(59) Industrial Commission of Arizona, Division of Administration, 800 W Washington, 3rd Floor, Phoenix, AZ 85007, 602-542-4653, Fax: 602-542-3070

(60) Industrial Commission of Arizona, Special Fund Division, 800 W Washington, 2nd Floor, Phoenix, AZ 85007, 602-542-3739

(61) Land Department, 1616 W Adams, Phoenix, AZ 85007, 602-542-1704

(62) Land Department, 1616 W Adams, Phoenix, AZ 85007, 602-542-4628, Fax: 602-542-4668

(63) Management Plus, 1604 N Country Club Rd, Tucson, AZ 85716, 520-325-1055

(64) Maricopa Environmental Services, 2406 S 24th St, Park Center Complex, E-204, Phoenix, AZ 85034, 602-506-6970, Fax: 602-506-6925

(65) Medical Radiologic Technology Board of Examiners, 4814 S 40th St, Phoenix, AZ 85040, 602-255-4845

(66) Mine Inspector, 1700 W Washington, Suite 403, Phoenix, AZ 85007-2805, 602-542-5971, Fax: 602-542-5335

(67) Nursing Care Board, 1400 W Washington, Suite 230, Phoenix, AZ 85007, 602-255-3095

(68) Parks Board, 1300 W Washington, Phoenix, AZ 85007, 602-542-2155, Fax: 602-542-4180

(69) Registrar of Contractors, 800 W Washington, 6th Floor, Phoenix, AZ 85007, 602-542-1525, Fax: 602-542-1599

(70) Secretary of State, 1700 W Washington, Phoenix, AZ 85007, 602-542-4086, Fax: 602-542-6172

(71) Structural Pest Control Commission, 9545 E Doubletree Ranch Rd, Scottsdale, AZ 85258, 602-255-3664, Fax: 602-255-1281

(72) Veterinary Medical Examining Board, 1400 W Washington, Suite 230, Phoenix, AZ 85007, 602-542-3095, Fax: 602-542-3093

Arkansas

Capitol: Little Rock (Pulaski County)	
State Population	2.9 Million
Number of Degree Granting Institutions:	35
Number of State Licensing & Business Registration Agencies:	168

Degree Granting Educational Institutions

Arkansas Baptist College, Registrar, 1600 Bishop St, Little Rock, AR 72202, 501-374-7856 (Fax: 501-372-0321). Hours: 8:30AM-4:30PM. Enrollment: 315. Records go back to 1884. Alumni records are maintained here at the same phone number. Degrees granted: Bachelors.

Attendance and degree information available by mail. Search requires name plus SSN, date of birth, approximate years of attendance, signed release. There is no fee.

Arkansas State University, Registrar, PO Box 1570, State University, AR 72467, 501-972-2031. Hours: 8AM-5PM. Records go back to 1909. Degrees granted: Associate; Bachelors; Masters; Doctorate; Specialist.

Attendance and degree information available by phone, fax, mail. Search requires name plus SSN. Also helpful: date of birth, exact years of attendance. There is no fee.

Arkansas State University, (Beebe Branch), Registrar, Drawer H, Beebe, AR 72012, 501-882-8260 (Fax: 501-882-8370). Hours: 8AM-5PM. Enrollment: 2000. Records go back to 1927. Alumni records are maintained here also. Call 501-882-6452. Degrees granted: Associate. Adverse incident record source- Student Services, 501-882-8245.

Attendance and degree information available by fax, mail. Search requires name plus SSN, date of birth, approximate years of attendance. There is no fee.

Arkansas Tech University, Registrar, Russellville, AR 72801, 501-968-0272 (Fax: 501-968-0683). Hours: 8AM-5PM. Enrollment: 4. Records go back to 1909. Alumni records are maintained here also. Call 501-968-0242. Degrees granted: Associate; Bachelors; Masters. Certification: Medical Transcription. Adverse incident record source- 501-968-0222.

Attendance and degree information available by phone, fax, mail. Search requires name only. Also helpful: SSN, date of birth, exact years of attendance. There is no fee.

Black River Technical College, Registrar, Hwy 304 E, PO Box 468, Pocahontas, AR 72455, 501-892-4565 (Fax: 501-892-3546). Hours: 8AM-4:30PM. Enrollment: 3031. Records go back to 1991. Degrees granted: Associate.

Attendance and degree information available by mail. Search requires name plus SSN, date of birth, exact years of attendance, signed release. Fee is $2.00.

Central Baptist College, Registrar, 1501 College Ave, Conway, AR 72032, 501-329-6872 (Fax: 501-329-2941). Hours: 8AM-4:30PM. Enrollment: 300. Records go back to 1966. Alumni records are maintained here at the same phone number. Degrees granted: Associate; Bachelors. Adverse incident record source- Dean of Students.

Attendance and degree information available by phone, fax, mail. Search requires name only. Also helpful: SSN. There is no fee.

Crowley's Ridge College, Registrar, 100 College Dr, Paragould, AR 72450, 501-236-6901 (Fax: 501-236-7748). Enrollment: 200. Records go back to 1964. Alumni records are maintained here at the same phone number. Degrees granted: Associate. Special programs- Liberal Arts. Adverse incident record source- Student Services.

Attendance and degree information available by phone, mail. Search requires name plus SSN, exact years of attendance. There is no fee.

East Arkansas Community College, Registrar, 1700 Newcastle Rd, Forrest City, AR 72335-9598, 501-633-4480 (Fax: 501-633-7222). Hours: 8AM-8PM M-Th; 8AM-5PM F. Enrollment: 1200. Records go back to 1974. Degrees granted: Associate. Adverse incident record source- Carolyn Bowlin, 501-633-4480.

Attendance and degree information available by fax, mail. Search requires name only. Also helpful: SSN, date of birth, exact years of attendance. There is no fee.

Garland County Community College, Registrar, 101 College Dr, Hot Springs, AR 71913-9174, 501-767-9371 (Fax: 501-767-6896). Hours: 8AM-4:30PM. Enrollment: 2000. Records go back to 1973. Degrees granted: Associate. Special programs- Nursing Program, 501-767-9371. Adverse incident record source- Student Services, 501-767-9371.

Attendance and degree information available by phone, fax, mail. Search requires name plus SSN. Also helpful: date of birth, exact years of attendance. There is no fee.

Harding University, Registrar, Box 776, 900 E Center Ave, Searcy, AR 72149-0001, 501-279-4403 (Fax: 501-279-4388). Hours: 8AM-5PM. Enrollment: 4000. Records go back to 1924. Alumni records are maintained here at the same phone number. Alumni Records Office: Box 768, Searcy, AR 72149-0001. Degrees granted: Associate; Bachelors; Masters. Adverse incident record source- Student Services.

Attendance and degree information available by phone, fax, mail. Search requires name only. Also helpful: SSN, date of birth, exact years of attendance. There is no fee.

Henderson State University, Registrar, 1100 Henderson St, Arkadelphia, AR 71999-0001, 501-230-5135 (Fax: 501-230-5144). Hours: 8AM-5PM. Enrollment: 3614. Records go back to 1890. Alumni records are maintained here also. Call 501-230-5401. Degrees granted: Associate; Bachelors. Special programs- Masters Aviation Program. Adverse incident record source- Security Office, 501-230-5098.

Attendance and degree information available by phone, fax, mail. Search requires name plus SSN, date of birth, exact years of attendance. There is no fee.

Hendrix College, Registrar, 1600 Washington Ave, Conway, AR 72032-3080, 501-329-6811 (Fax: 501-450-1200). Hours: 8AM-5PM. Enrollment: 1000. Records go back to 1886. Alumni records are maintained here also. Call 501-450-1223. Degrees granted: Bachelors. Adverse incident record source- Student Development.

Attendance and degree information available by phone, fax, mail. Search requires name only. Also helpful: SSN, date of birth, exact years of attendance. Fee is $2.00.

John Brown University, Registrar, Siloam Springs, AR 72761, 501-524-7103 (Fax: 501-524-9548). Hours: 7:30AM-5PM. Enrollment: 1300. Records go back to 1919. Alumni records are maintained here also. Call 501-524-7330. Degrees granted: Associate; Bachelors. Special programs- Adult Ed (Advance Program),501-524-7259. Adverse incident record source- Student Life, 501-524-7252.

Attendance and degree information available by phone, fax, mail. Search requires name plus approximate years of attendance. Also helpful: SSN, date of birth, exact years of attendance. There is no fee.

Lyon College, Office of the Registrar, PO Box 2317, 2300 Highland Rd, Batesville, AR 72503, 501-698-4204 (Fax: 501-698-4622). Hours: 8AM-5PM. Enrollment: 630. Formerly Arkansas College Alumni records are maintained here also. Call 501-698-4238. Degrees granted: Bachelors. Special programs- National Testing Information, 501-698-4311. Adverse incident record source- Dean of Students, 501-698-4314.

Attendance and degree information available by phone, fax, mail. Search requires name only. Also helpful: SSN, date of birth, exact years of attendance. There is no fee.

Mississippi County Community College, Registrar, PO Drawer 1109, Blytheville, AR 72316, 501-762-1020 (Fax: 501-763-3704). Hours: 8AM-4:30PM. Enrollment: 1800. Records go back to 1975. Degrees granted: Associate.

Attendance and degree information available by fax, mail. Search requires name plus SSN. Also helpful: approximate years of attendance. There is no fee.

North Arkansas Community/Technical College, Registrar, Pioneer Ridge, Harrison, AR 72601, 501-743-3000 (Fax: 501-743-3577). Hours: 8AM-5PM. Enrollment:

1700. Records go back to 1974. Alumni records are maintained here at the same phone number. Degrees granted: Associate.

Attendance and degree information available by phone, fax, mail. Search requires name plus SSN. Also helpful: date of birth, exact years of attendance. There is no fee.

Northwest Arkansas Community College, Registrar, One College Dr, Bentonville, AR 72712, 501-636-9222 (Fax: 501-619-4116). Hours: 8AM-5:30PM. Enrollment: 3000. Records go back to 1990. Alumni records are maintained here also. Call 501-619-4184. Degrees granted: Associate. Special programs- Nursing, 501-619-4257. Adverse incident record source- Student Services.

Attendance and degree information available by fax, mail. Search requires name only. Also helpful: SSN. There is no fee.

Ouachita Baptist University, Registrar, OBU Box 3757, Arkadelphia, AR 71998-0001, 501-245-5578 (Fax: 501-245-5500). Hours: 8AM-5PM. Enrollment: 1477. Records go back to 1940's. Alumni records are maintained here at the same phone number. Alumni Records Office: Box 3762, Arkadelphia, AR 71998-0001. Degrees granted: Bachelors. Adverse incident record source- Dean of Students.

Attendance and degree information available by phone, fax, mail. Search requires name only. Also helpful: SSN, date of birth, exact years of attendance. There is no fee.

Philander Smith College, Registrar, 812 W 13th St, Little Rock, AR 72202, 501-370-5220 (Fax: 501-370-5278). Hours: 8:30AM-5PM. Enrollment: 956. Records go back to 1989. Alumni records are maintained here at the same phone number. Degrees granted: Bachelors. Special programs- Degree Completion Program, 501-370-5283. Adverse incident record source- Dean of Students, 501-370-5335.

Attendance information available by phone, fax, mail. Search requires name plus SSN, approximate years of attendance. Also helpful: exact years of attendance. There is no fee.

Degree information available by phone, fax, mail. Search requires name plus SSN. Also helpful: date of birth, exact years of attendance. There is no fee.

Pulaski Technical College, Registrar, 3000 W Scenic Drive, North Little Rock, AR 72118-3399, 501-771-1000 (Fax: 501-771-2844). Hours: 8AM-5PM. Enrollment: 1170. Records go back to 1900. Degrees granted: Associate.

Attendance and degree information available by fax, mail. Search requires name plus SSN, exact years of attendance, signed release. Also helpful: date of birth. Fee is $2.00.

Rich Mountain Community College, Registrar, 1100 Bush St, Mena, AR 71953, 501-394-5012 (Fax: 501-394-2828). Hours: 8AM-4:30PM. Enrollment: 765. Records go back to 1976. Alumni records are maintained here also. Call 501-394-5012 X56. Degrees granted: Associate. Adverse incident record source- Registrar's Office   .

Attendance and degree information available by fax, mail. Search requires name plus SSN, signed release. Also helpful: date of birth, exact years of attendance. There is no fee.

Shorter College, Registrar, 604 Locust St, North Little Rock, AR 72114, 501-374-6305 (Fax: 501-374-9333). Hours: 8:30AM-5pm. Enrollment: 305. Records go back to 1995. Alumni records are maintained here at the same phone number. Degrees granted: Associate.

Attendance information available by phone, fax, mail. Search requires name plus SSN, date of birth. Also helpful: exact years of attendance. There is no fee.

Degree information available by mail. Search requires name plus SSN, date of birth. Also helpful: exact years of attendance. There is no fee.

South Arkansas Community College, Registrar, PO Box 7010, El Dorado, AR 71731-7010, 501-862-8131 (Fax:

501-864-7122). Hours: 8AM-5PM. Enrollment: 1200. Records go back to 1975. Alumni records are maintained here also. Call 501-862-8131. Degrees granted: Associate. Adverse incident record source- Student Affairs, 501-862-8131.

Attendance and degree information available by phone, fax, mail. Search requires name plus SSN. There is no fee.

Southern Arkansas University, Registrar, SAU Box 1404, Magnolia, AR 71753, 501-235-4031 (Fax: 501-235-4931). Hours: 8AM-5PM. Enrollment: 2745. Records go back to 1920. Alumni Records Office: SAU Box 1416, Magnolia, AR 71753, 501-235-4079. Degrees granted: Associate; Bachelors; Masters. Adverse incident record source- Student Affairs, 501-235-4012.

Attendance and degree information available by phone, mail. Search requires name plus SSN. Also helpful: date of birth, exact years of attendance. There is no fee.

Southern Arkansas University Tech, Registrar, SAU Tech Station, Camden, AR 71701, 501-574-4500 (Fax: 501-574-4520). Hours: 8AM-5:30PM. Enrollment: 900. Records go back to 1979. Alumni records are maintained here at the same phone number. Degrees granted: Associate. Adverse incident record source- Student Affairs, 501-574-4500.

Attendance information available by phone, fax, mail. Search requires name plus SSN, approximate years of attendance. There is no fee.

Degree information available by mail. Search requires name plus SSN, approximate years of attendance. There is no fee.

University of Arkansas, Registrar, Silas Hunt Hall, Fayetteville, AR 72701, 501-575-5346 (Fax: 501-575-7515). Hours: 8AM-5PM. Enrollment: 14900. Formerly University of Arkansas, Fayetteville Records go back to 1870. Alumni records are maintained here at the same phone number. Degrees granted: Bachelors; Masters; Doctorate. Special programs- 200 Majors.

Attendance and degree information available by phone, fax, mail. Search requires name only. Also helpful: SSN, date of birth, exact years of attendance. There is no fee.

University of Arkansas, (Phillips Community College), Registrar, Helena, AR 72342, 501-338-6474 (Fax: 501-338-7542). Hours: 8AM-4:30PM. Formerly Phillips County Community College Records go back to 1905. Degrees granted: Associate. Special programs- Nursing Program: Medical Lab Tech. Adverse incident record source- 501-338-6474 X242.

Attendance information available by phone, fax, mail. Search requires name plus SSN. Also helpful: date of birth, exact years of attendance. There is no fee.

Degree information available by phone, fax. Search requires name plus SSN. Also helpful: date of birth, exact years of attendance. There is no fee.

University of Arkansas at Little Rock, Registrar, 2801 S University Ave, Little Rock, AR 72204, 501-569-3111 (Fax: 501-569-8956). Hours: 8AM-5PM. Enrollment: 9900. Records go back to 1950. Alumni records are maintained here at the same phone number. Degrees granted: Associate; Bachelors; Masters.

Attendance and degree information available by phone, fax, mail. Search requires name plus SSN. Also helpful: approximate years of attendance. There is no fee.

University of Arkansas at Monticello, Registrar, Monticello, AR 71656, 501-460-1035 (Fax: 501-460-1935). Hours: 8AM-4:30PM. Enrollment: 2300. Records go back to 1950. Alumni records are maintained here also. Call 501-460-1027. Degrees granted: Bachelors.

Attendance and degree information available by phone, fax, mail. Search requires name plus SSN, approximate years of attendance. There is no fee.

University of Arkansas at Pine Bluff, Registrar, 1200 N University Dr, Pine Bluff, AR 71601, 501-543-8486 (Fax: 501-543-8014). Hours: 8AM-5PM. Enrollment: 3000. Records go back to 1923. Alumni records are maintained here also. Call 501-543-8499. Degrees granted: Associate; Bachelors; Masters. Special programs- Fish Biology. Adverse incident record source- Dean of Students, 501-543-8360.

Attendance and degree information available by phone, fax, mail. Search requires name plus SSN, approximate years of attendance. There is no fee.

University of Arkansas for Medical Sciences, Registrar, 4301 W Markham St, Little Rock, AR 72205, 501-686-5000. Hours: 8AM-4:30PM. Alumni records are maintained here also. Call 501-686-5000. Degrees granted: Associate; Bachelors; Masters; Doctorate; PhD, MD, Pharm.

Attendance information available by phone, fax, mail. Search requires name plus SSN, approximate years of attendance. There is no fee.

Degree information available by phone, fax, mail. Search requires name plus SSN. There is no fee.

University of Central Arkansas, Registrar, 201 Donaghey Ave, Conway, AR 72035-0001, 501-450-5200 (Fax: 501-450-5734). Hours: 8AM-4:45PM. Enrollment: 9000. Records go back to 1908. Alumni records are maintained here also. Call 501-450-3114. Degrees granted: Associate; Bachelors; Masters; Ed. S. Adverse incident record source- Dean of Students, 501-450-3416.

Attendance and degree information available by phone, fax, mail. Search requires name only. Also helpful: SSN, date of birth, exact years of attendance. There is no fee.

University of the Ozarks, Registrar, 415 N College Ave, Clarksville, AR 72830, 501-979-1215 (Fax: 501-979-1355). Hours: 8AM-Noon,1-4:30PM. Enrollment: 563. Records go back to 1915. Alumni records are maintained here also. Call 501-979-1237. Degrees granted: Associate; Bachelors; Masters. Adverse incident record source- Student Affairs, 501-979-1211.

Attendance and degree information available by phone, fax, mail. Search requires name only. Also helpful: SSN, exact years of attendance. There is no fee.

Westark Community College, Registrar, PO Box 3649, Fort Smith, AR 72913, 501-788-7230 (Fax: 501-788-7016). Hours: 8AM-7PM M-Th, 8AM-4:30PM F. Enrollment: 4130. Records go back to 1929. Alumni records are maintained here also. Call 501-788-7021. Degrees granted: Associate. Adverse incident record source- Student Life, 501-788-7013: Security, 501-788-7140

Attendance and degree information available by phone, fax, mail. Search requires name plus SSN, date of birth, approximate years of attendance. There is no fee.

Williams Baptist College, Registrar, Box 3663, Walnut Ridge, AR 72476, 501-886-6741 X104 (Fax: 501-886-3924). Hours: 8AM-4:30PM Winter, 9AM-4PM Summer. Enrollment: 600. Records go back to 1941. Alumni records are maintained here also. Call 501-886-6741. Degrees granted: Bachelors. Adverse incident record source- Student Affairs, 501-886-6741.

Attendance and degree information available by phone, fax, mail. Search requires name plus SSN, approximate years of attendance. There is no fee.

Trade and Vocational Schools

Arkansas College of Barbering and Hair Design, 200 Washington Ave, North Little Rock, AR 72114, 501-376-9696

Arkansas Valley Technical Institute, 1311 S I St, Fort Smith, AR 72901, 501-441-5256

CARTI School of Radiation Therapy Technology, PO Box 5210, Little Rock, AR 72215, 501-664-8573

Cotton Boll Technical Institute, Box 36, Burdette, AR 72321, 501-763-1486

Eastern College of Health Vocations, 6423 Forbing Rd, Little Rock, AR 72209, 501-568-0211

Fayetteville College, 3348 N College St, Fayetteville, AR 72703, 501-442-2364

New Tyler Barber College Inc., 1221 E Seventh St, North Little Rock, AR 72114, 501-375-0377

Red River Technical College, PO Box 140, Hope, AR 71801, 501-777-5722

Remington College, 7601 Scott Hamilton Dr, Little Rock, AR 72209, 501-565-7000

Remington College (Branch Campus), 3348 N College St, Fayetteville, AR 72703, 501-442-2364

State Licensing & Business Registration Quick Finder Index

Architecture, Engineering & Surveying
Architect #7 .... ✉ 501-375-1310
Engineer #22 (5244) .... ✉ 501-324-9085
Engineer-in-Training #22 (1416) .... ✉ 501-324-9085
Geologist #24 (1788) .... ☎ 501-663-9714
Landscape Architect #7 .... ✉ 501-682-3171
Surveyor #22 (720) .... ✉ 501-324-9085
Surveyor-in-Training #22 (59) .... ✉ 501-324-9085

Business - Court & Legal Services
Attorney #47 (6800) .... ☎ 501-682-6849
Bondsman #3 .... ✉ 501-686-9050
Court Reporter #9 (243) .... ☎ 501-682-6844
Lobbyist #42 (346) .... ☎ 501-682-1010
Notary Public #42 .... ✉ 501-682-3409

Business - General Services
Appliance Server #34 501-371-1008
Auctioneer #6 (865) .... ✉ 501-375-3858
Certified Public Accountant #21 .... ☎ 501-682-1520
Employment Agency Manager #31 (70) .... ☎ 501-682-4505
Employment Agent & Counselor #31
(204) .... ☎ 501-682-4505
Public Accountant #21 (455) .... ☎ 501-682-1520

Construction & Manufacturing
Boiler Inspector (State) #31 .... ☎ 501-682-4513
Boiler Installer #31 (531) .... ☎ 501-682-4513
Boiler Operator #31 (5785) .... ☎ 501-682-4513
Boiler Repairer #31 .... ☎ 501-682-4547
Combination Welder #39 501-771-1000
Contractor #27 (7000) .... ✉ 501 372 4661
Electrical Contractor #31 (547) .... ☎ 501-682-4549
Elevator/Lifting Device Inspector #31 (12) ... ☎ 501-682-4531
Gas Fitter #29 (427) .... ☎ 501-661-2000
Gas Fitter Trainee #29 (12) .... ☎ 501-661-2262
Hospital Maintenance Plumber #29 (10) .... ☎ 501-661-2262
Industrial Maintenance Electrician #31 (206)
.... ☎ 501-682-4849
Journeyman Electrician #31 (3188) .... ☎ 501-682-4549
Journeyman Plumber #29 (1205) .... ☎ 501-661-2262
Limited Plumber #29 .... ☎ 501-661-2262
Master Electrician #31 (4186) .... ☎ 501-682-4549
Master Plumber #29 .... ☎ 501-661-2262

Plumber Apprentice #29 .... ☎ 501-661-2262
Plumbing & Gas Inspector #29 .... ☎ 501-661-2262
Pump Installer #49 (300) .... ☎ 501-682-1025
Safety Supervisor #34 (837) .... ☎ 501-324-9228
Special Gas Fitter #29 .... ☎ 501-661-2262
Water Well Contractor #49 (234) .... ☎ 501-682-1025

Education
Administrator #36 .... ☎ 501-682-4344
Business Education #36 .... ☎ 501-682-4344
Career Orientation #36 .... ☎ 501-682-4344
Coordinated Career Education #36 .... ☎ 501-682-4344
Elementary School Teacher #36 .... ☎ 501-682-4344
Elementary Secondary Principal #36 .... ☎ 501-682-4344
General Cooperative Education #36 .... ☎ 501-682-4344
Health Occupations Education #36 .... ☎ 501-682-4344
Home Economics Education #36 .... ☎ 501-682-4344
Marketing/Distributive Education #36 .... ☎ 501-682-4344
School Counselor #36 .... ☎ 501-682-4344
School Library Media Administrator #36 .... ☎ 501-682-4344
School Superintendent #36 .... ☎ 501-682-4344
Secondary School Teacher #36 .... ☎ 501-682-4344
Trade/Industrial Education #36 .... ☎ 501-682-4344

Environmental & Agriculture
Agricultural Consultant #37 .... ✉ 501-225-1598
Agricultural Seed Dealer #37 .... ✉ 501-225-1598
Agriculture Education #36 .... ☎ 501-682-4344
Asbestos Removal Worker #32 (845) .... ☎ 501-682-0718
Commercial Applicator #37 .... ✉ 501-225-1598
Custom Applicator #37 .... ✉ 501-225-1598
Equine Dentist #40 .... ☎ 501-682-1467
Fertilizer Facility #37 .... ✉ 501-225-1598
Forester #23 (325) .... ☎ 501-225-8619
Grain Warehouseman #37 .... ✉ 501-225-1598
Lime Vender #37 .... ✉ 501-225-1598
Nurseryman #37 .... ✉ 501-225-1598
Pest Exterminator #37 .... ✉ 501-225-1598
Plant Breeder #37 .... ✉ 501-225-1598
Private Pesticide Applicator #37 .... ✉ 501-225-1598
Seed Treatment - Commercial Applicator #37
.... ✉ 501-225-1598
Solid Waste Facility Operator #32 (630) .... ☎ 501-682-0585
Tree Injector (Forester Worker) #37 .... ✉ 501-225-1598

Veterinarian #48 (989) .... ☎ 501-224-2836
Veterinarian-Poultry Specialty #48 (10) .... ☎ 501-224-2836
Veterinary Technician #48 (27)..................... ☎ 501-224-2836
Waste Water Treatment Plant Operator #32
(2700) .... ☎ 501-682-2700
Water Supply Operator #29...................... ☎ 501-661-2262
Water Well Driller #49 (315) .... ☎ 501-682-1025

Financial - Real Estate, Insurance & Banking

Claims Adjuster #3 .... ✉ 501-371-2750
Collection Agency Collector #11 .... ☎ 501-376-9814
Collection Agency Manager #11..................... ☎ 501-376-9814
Insurance Inspector (Boiler) #31 .... ☎ 501-682-4547
Insurance Sales Agent #3 (28000).................✉ 501-371-2750
Investment Advisor #43 (2510)...................... ☎ 501-324-9260
Real Estate Appraiser #41 .... ☎ 501-682-2732
Real Estate Broker #41 (4100) .... ☎ 501-682-2732
Real Estate Sales Agent #41 (5500)............... ☎ 501-682-2732
Securities Agent #43 (37008)........................ ☎ 501-324-9260
Securities Broker/Dealer #43 (1039).............. ☎ 501-324-9260

Health & Beauty

Acupuncturist #35 .... ☎ 501-296-1802
Aesthetician #12 .... ☎ 501-682-2168
Anesthetist #18 (282) .... ☎ 501-686-2700
Audiologist #45 501-320-4319
Barber #8 (2100)... ☎ 501-682-4035
Barber Instructor #8 (28) .... ☎ 501-682-4035
Barber Technician #8 (8) .... ☎ 501-682-4035
Chiropractor #10.......................................✉ 501-682-9015
Cosmetologist #12 .... ☎ 501-682-2168
Cosmetology Instructor #12 .... ☎ 501-682-2168
Dental Assistant #13 (1300)......................... ☎ 501-682-2085
Dental Hygienist #13 (865) .... ☎ 501-682-2085
Dentist #13 (1250)....................................... ☎ 501-682-2085
Dentist's Anesthesia Permit #13 (78) .... ☎ 501-682-2085
Dietitian #33 501-374-8212
Dispensing Optician #14 501-268-4351
Dispensing Optician Apprentice #14 501-268-4351
Electrologist #12.. ☎ 501-682-2168
Electrology Instructor #12 .... ☎ 501-682-2168
Embalmer #15 (700) .... ☎ 501-682-0574
Embalmer Apprentice #15 (40) .... ☎ 501-682-0574
Emergency Medical Technician #29 (6000)
.... ☎ 501-661-2262
Emergency Medical Technician-Paramedic #29 (200)
.... ☎ 501-661-2262
Funeral Director #15 (1500)........................... ☎ 501-682-0574
Funeral Director Apprentice #15 (100) .... ☎ 501-682-0574
Hearing Aid Dispenser #17 (119) .... ☎ 501-663-5869
Licensed Certified Social Worker #44 (900)
.... ✉ 501-372-5071
Manicurist #12... ☎ 501-682-2168
Medical Doctor/Surgeon #35 (7514)............... ☎ 501-296-1802
Nurse #18 (27153)....................................... ☎ 501-686-2700
Nurse Midwife #18 (13) .... ☎ 501-686-2700

Nurse Practitioner #18 (1103) .... ☎ 501-686-2700
Nursing Home Administrator #30 .... ☎ 501-682-1001
Occupational Therapist #35 (1541)................ ☎ 501-296-1802
Optometrist #19 (340).................................. ☎ 501-268-4351
Osteopathic Physician #35............................ ☎ 501-296-1802
PTA #4 .... ☎ 501-228-7100
Pharmacist #20 (3097).................................. ☎ 501-682-0190
Pharmacist Intern #20 (398) .... ☎ 501-682-0190
Pharmacy #20 (723)..................................... ☎ 501-682-0190
Physical Therapist #4 (1200) .... ☎ 501-228-7100
Physical Therapist Assistant #4 (400) .... ☎ 501-228-7100
Podiatrist #38 (80) .... ☎ 501-664-3668
Practical Nurse #18 (23) .... ☎ 501-686-2700
Professional Counselor #2 .... ☎ 501-235-4314
Psychiatric Technician-Nurse #18 (695) .... ☎ 501-686-2700
Respiratory Care Practitioner #35 (945).......... ☎ 501-296-1802
Sanitarian-Registered #25 (220) .... ✉ 501-535-2142
Speech Pathologist #45................................. 501-320-4319
Therapy Technician (Masseur/Masseuse) #26
.... 501-534-4734
Wholesaler-Controlled/Legend #20 (430)...... ☎ 501-682-0190
Wholesaler-DME-MED Gas #20 (160).......... ☎ 501-682-0190

Investigations & Security

Armored Car Guard #46 (300)...................... ☎ 501-221-8245
Burglar Alarm Installer #46 (3000) .... ☎ 501-221-8245
Burglar Alarm Servicer (Oper) #46................ ☎ 501-221-8245
Polygraph Examiner #46 (50)........................ ☎ 501-221-8245
Private Investigator #46 (400) .... ☎ 501-221-8245
Security Guard #46 (7000) .... ☎ 501-221-8245

Social Services

Child Care Provider #30 (3000) .... ☎ 501-682-1001
Counselor/Associate Counselor #2................ ☎ 501-235-4314
Master Social Worker #44 (250) .... ✉ 501-372-5071
Psychological Examiner #16 (412).................. ✉ 501-682-6167
Psychologist #16 (406) .... ✉ 501-682-6167
Social Worker-Licensed #44 (900)................. ✉ 501-372-5071

Sports & Entertainment

Athletic Manager #5 (15).............................. ✉ 501-666-5544
Athletic Promoter/Matchmaker #5 (25).......... ✉ 501-666-5544
Athletic Trainer #4 (150) .... ☎ 501-228-7100
Boxer #5 (30) .... ✉ 501-666-5544
Boxing/Wrestling Referee #5 (10) .... ✉ 501-666-5544
Event Sponsor #5 .... ✉ 501-666-5544
Greyhound Racing #40 (1197) .... ☎ 501-682-1467
Horse Racing #40 (5692).............................. ☎ 501-682-1467
Liquor Distributor #1 (7) .... ☎ 501-682-1105
Ring Announcer #5 (10) .... ✉ 501-666-5544
Timekeeper #5 (10)...................................... ✉ 501-666-5544
Wrestler #5 (60) .... ✉ 501-666-5544

Transportation

Chauffeur #28 (89051) .... ☎ 501-371-1741

State Licensing & Business Registration Agency Information

(1) Alcoholic Beverage Control Division, 100 Main St, Suite 503, Little Rock, AR 72201, 501-682-1105

(2) Arkansas Board of Examiners in Counseling, Box 1396, Magnolia, AR 71753-5000, 501-235-4314, Fax: 501-234-1842

(3) Arkansas Insurance Department, Licensing Division, 1200 West 3rd, Little Rock, AR 72201, 501-371-2750, Fax: 501-371-2618

(4) Arkansas State Board of Physical Therapy, 9 Shackelford Plaza Suite 1, Little Rock, AR 72211, 501-228-7100, Fax: 501-228-5535

(5) Athletic Commission, 809 North Palm Street, Little Rock, AR 72205-1946, 501-666-5544, Fax: 501-666-5546

(6) Auctioneers Licensing Board, 101 E Capital Suite 112 B, Little Rock, AR 72201, 501-945-7874, Fax: 501-682-1158

(7) Board of Architecture, 101 E Capitol, Suite 208, Little Rock, AR 72201, 501-682-3171, Fax: 501-682-3172

(8) Board of Barber Examiners, 103 E 7th St, Room 212, Little Rock, AR 72201-4512, 501-682-4035

(9) Board of Certified Court Reporter Examiners, 625 Marshall St, Justice Bldg, Little Rock, AR 72201, 501-682-6844

(10) Board of Chiropractic Examiners, 101 East Capital Suite 209, Little Rock, AR 72201, 501-682-9015, Fax: 501-682-9016

(11) Board of Collection Agencies, 523 S Louisiana St, Suite 460, Little Rock, AR 72201, 501-376-9814, Fax: 501-375-7013

(12) Board of Cosmetology, 101 E Capitol, Suite 108, Little Rock, AR 72201, 501-682-2168, Fax: 501-682-5640

(13) Board of Dental Examiners, 101 E Captiol Ave, Suite 111, Little Rock, AR 72201, 501-682-2085, Fax: 501-682-3543

(14) Board of Dispensing Opticians, PO Box 512, Searcy, AR 72145, 501-268-4351

(15) Board of Embalmers & Funeral Directors, 101 E Capitol Ave, Suite 113, Little Rock, AR 72201, 501-682-0574, Fax: 501-682-0575

(16) Board of Examiners in Psychology, 101 E Capitol Ave, Suite 415, Little Rock, AR 72201, 501-682-6167, Fax: 501-682-6165

(17) Board of Hearing Aid Dispensers, 305 N Monroe, Little Rock, AR 72205, 501-663-5869, Fax: 501-663-6359

(18) Board of Nursing, 1123 S University, Suite 800, Little Rock, AR 72204, 501-686-2700, Fax: 501-686-2714

(19) Board of Optometry, PO Box 512, Searcy, AR 72143, 501-268-4351

(20) Board of Pharmacy, 101 E Capitol, Suite 218, Little Rock, AR 72201, 501-682-0190, Fax: 501-682-0195

(21) Board of Public Accountancy, 101 East Capitol, Suite 430, Little Rock, AR 72201, 501-682-1520, Fax: 501-682-5538

(22) Board of Registration for Engineers/Land Surveyors, PO Box 3750, Little Rock, AR 72203, 501-324-9085

(23) Board of Registration for Foresters, PO Box 7424, Little Rock, AR 72207, 501-225-8619

(24) Board of Registration for Professional Geologists, 3815 W Roosevelt Rd, Little Rock, AR 72204, 501-663-9714, Fax: 501-663-7360

(25) Board of Sanitarians, 4815 W Markham, Little Rock, AR 72205, 501-661-2171, Fax: 501-536-3006

(26) Board of Therapy Technology, 256 State Capitol, Little Rock, AR 72201, 501-624-0673, Fax: 501-624-4955

(27) Contractors Licensing Board, 621 E Capitol, Little Rock, AR 72202, 501-372-4661, Fax: 501-372-2247

(28) Department of Finance & Administration, Division of Revenues, Ledbetter Bldg, 7th & Wolfe Sts #215, Little Rock, AR 72203, 501-324-9057, Fax: 501-682-7075

(29) Department of Health, 4815 W Markham, Slot 38, Little Rock, AR 72205-3867, 501-661-2262, Fax: 501-280-4901

(30) Department of Human Services, Division of Social Services, PO Box 1437, Little Rock, AR 72203-1437, 501-682-1001, Fax: 501-682-2317

(31) Department of Labor, 10421 W Markham, Little Rock, AR 72205, 501-682-4547, Fax: 501-682-4562

(32) Department of Pollution Control & Ecology, PO Box 8913, Little Rock, AR 72219-8913, 501-682-0744

(33) Dietetics Licensing Board, PO Box 1016, Little Rock, AR 72115, 501-374-8212

(34) Liquefied Petroleum Gas Board, 1421 W 6th St, Little Rock, AR 72201, 501-324-9228

(35) Medical Board, 2100 Riverside, Suite 200, Little Rock, AR 72202, 501-296-1802, Fax: 501-296-1805

(36) Office of Teacher Education & Licensure, Arkansas Department of Education, State Education Bldg, Room 106B, Capitol Mall #4, Little Rock, AR 72201, 501-682-4344, Fax: 501-682-4898

(37) Plant Board, PO Box 1069, Little Rock, AR 72203, 501-225-1598, Fax: 501-225-3590

(38) Podiatry Examining Board, 2001 Georgia Ave, Little Rock, AR 72207, 501-664-3668, Fax: 501-666-3338

(39) Pulaski Vo-Tech School, 3000 W Scenic Dr, North Little Rock, AR 72118, 501-771-1000

(40) Racing Commission, PO Box 3076, Little Rock, AR 72203, 501-682-1467, Fax: 501-682-5273

(41) Real Estate Commission, 612 Summit St, Little Rock, AR 72201, 501-682-2732, Fax: 501-682-2729

(42) Secretary of State, 256 State Capitol, Little Rock, AR 72201, 501-682-3409, Fax: 501-682-3437

(43) Securities Department, 201 W Markham, 3rd Floor, Heritage West Bldg, Little Rock, AR 72201, 501-324-9260, Fax: 501-324-9268

(44) Social Work Licensing Board, PO Box 250381, 503 Executive Bldg, Little Rock, AR 72225, 501-372-5071

(45) Speech Pathology & Audiology, 800 Marhsall St, Arkansas Children's Hospital, Little Rock, AR 72202, 501-320-4319, Fax: 501-320-6881

(46) State Police, PO Box 5901, Little Rock, AR 72215, 501-221-8245

(47) Supreme Court, 625 Marshall, Justice Building, Little Rock, AR 72201, 501-682-6849, Fax: 501-682-6877

(48) Veterinary Medical Examining Board, PO Box 5497, Little Rock, AR 72215, 501-224-2836

(49) Waterwell Construction Commission, #1 Capitol Mall, Suite 2-D, Little Rock, AR 72201, 501-682-1025

California

Capitol: Sacramento (Sacramento County)	
State Population	31.5 Million
Number of Degree Granting Institutions:	339
Number of State Licensing & Business Registration Agencies:	185

Degree Granting Educational Institutions

Academy of Art College, Registrar, 79 New Montgomery, San Francisco, CA 94105, 415-274-2251. Hours: 9AM-5PM. Enrollment: 4500. Records go back to 1930. Degrees granted: Bachelors.

Attendance and degree information available by phone, mail. Search requires name plus SSN. Also helpful: exact years of attendance. There is no fee.

Academy of Chinese Culture and Health Sciences, Registrar, 1601 Clay St, Oakland, CA 94612, 510-763-7787 (Fax: 510-834-8646). Hours: 9AM-5PM. Enrollment: 140. Records go back to 1984. Degrees granted: Masters. Special programs- Chinese Medicine. Adverse incident record source- Administration, 510-763-7787.

Attendance and degree information available by written request only. Search requires name plus signed release. Also helpful: SSN, date of birth, exact years of attendance. There is no fee.

Allan Hancock College, Registrar, 800 S College Dr, Santa Maria, CA 93454-6399, 805-922-6966 X3248 (Fax: 805-922-3477). Hours: 8AM-6PM M-Th; 8AM-4PM F. Enrollment: 10000. Records go back to 1954. Degrees granted: Associate. Adverse incident record source- 805-922-6966 X3651.

Attendance and degree information available by phone, fax, mail. Search requires name plus SSN. Also helpful: date of birth, exact years of attendance. There is no fee.

American Academy of Dramatic Arts West, Registrar, 2550 Paloma St, Pasadena, CA 91107, 818-798-0777 (Fax: 818-798-5047). Hours: 8:30AM-5PM. Enrollment: 300. Degrees granted: Associate.

Attendance and degree information available by phone. Search requires name plus SSN, exact years of attendance. There is no fee.

American Baptist Seminary of the West, Registrar, 2606 Dwight Way, Berkeley, CA 94704-3029, 510-841-1905. Hours: 8AM-4:30PM. Degrees granted: Masters.

Attendance and degree information available by phone, mail. Search requires name plus SSN. There is no fee.

American College in Los Angeles, (Branch), Registrar, 1651 Westwood Blvd, Los Angeles, CA 90024, 310-470-2000 (Fax: 310-477-8640). Hours: 9AM-5PM. Formerly American College for the Applied Arts Records go back to 1984. Alumni records are maintained here at the same phone number. Degrees granted: Associate; Bachelors. Special programs- Business Administration: Visual Communications: Fashion Design: Fashion Marketing: Interior Design. Adverse incident record source- Safety Department, 310-470-2000.

Attendance and degree information available by phone, mail. Search requires name only. Also helpful: SSN, date of birth, exact years of attendance. There is no fee.

American College of Traditional Chinese Medicine, Registrar, 455 Arkansas St, San Francisco, CA 94107, 415-282-7600 (Fax: 415-287-0856). Hours: 9AM-5PM. Enrollment: 56. Records go back to 1980. Degrees granted: Masters. Certification: TCM.

Attendance information available by written request only. Search requires name only. Also helpful: SSN, date of birth, exact years of attendance. There is no fee.

Degree information available by phone, fax, mail. Search requires name only. Also helpful: SSN, date of birth, exact years of attendance. There is no fee.

American Conservatory Theater, Registrar, 30 Grant Ave, San Francisco, CA 94108, 415-834-3350. Enrollment: 120. Records go back to 1972. Alumni records are maintained here at the same phone number. Degrees granted: Masters.

Attendance information available by phone, fax, mail. Search requires name plus SSN. Also helpful: exact years of attendance. There is no fee.

Degree information available by phone, fax, mail. Search requires name only. Also helpful: exact years of attendance. There is no fee.

American Film Institute Center for Advanced Film/TV Studies, Registrar, 2021 N Western Ave, Los Angeles, CA 90027, 213-856-7714 (Fax: 213-467-4578). Hours: 9AM-5:30PM. Enrollment: 210. Records go back to 1914. Alumni records are maintained here also. Call 213-886-7680. Degrees granted: Masters. Adverse incident record source- 213-856-7714.

Attendance and degree information available by written request only. Search requires name plus SSN, date of birth, exact years of attendance, signed release. Fee is $5.00.

American River College, Registrar, 4700 College Oak Dr, Sacramento, CA 95841, 916-484-8261 (Fax: 916-484-8864). Hours: 7:30AM-8PM M-Th, 7:30AM-5PM F. Enrollment: 20000. Records go back to 1955. Alumni records are maintained here also. Call 916-568-3100 X8990. Degrees granted: Associate. Adverse incident record source- 916-484-8591.

Attendance and degree information available by mail. Search requires name plus SSN, date of birth, exact years of attendance, signed release. There is no fee.

Antelope Valley College, Registrar, 3041 W Ave K, Lancaster, CA 93536, 805-943-3241 X620. Hours: 8AM-4:30PM. Records go back to 1929. Alumni records are maintained here at the same phone number. Degrees granted: Associate.

Attendance and degree information available by mail. Search requires name plus SSN, date of birth, exact years of attendance, signed release. There is no fee.

Antioch University, (Southern California (Los Angeles)), Registrar, 13274 Fiji Way, Marina Del Rey, CA 90292, 310-578-1080 (Fax: 310-822-4824). Hours: 9AM-7PM M,W; 9AM-5PM T,Th; 9AM-1PM F. Records go back to 1972. Records prior to 7/85 housed at Administrative Headquarters; Yellow Springs, OH. Alumni records are maintained here also. Call 310-578-1080 X115. Degrees granted: Bachelors; Masters. Special programs- Liberal Arts. Adverse incident record source- Student Affairs.

Attendance information available by mail. Search requires name plus signed release. Also helpful: SSN, date of birth, exact years of attendance. There is no fee.

Degree information available by mail. Search requires name plus signed release. Also helpful: SSN, date of birth, exact years of attendance. There is no fee.

Antioch University, (Southern California (Santa Barbara)), Registrar, 801 Garden St, Santa Barbara, CA 93101, 805-962-8179 (Fax: 805-962-4786). Hours: 8AM-5PM M-Th; 9AM-2PM F. Enrollment: 250. Records go back to 1985. Pre-1985 records are housed at Antioch University, 795 Livermore St, Yellow Springs, OH 45387, 513-767-6401. Alumni records are maintained here at the same phone number. Degrees granted: Bachelors; Masters. Special programs- Liberal Arts. Adverse incident record source- Student Services.

Attendance and degree information available by phone, fax, mail. Search requires name only. Also helpful: SSN. There is no fee.

Armstrong University, Registrar, 2222 Harold Way, Berkeley, CA 94704, 510-848-2500 (Fax: 510-848-9438). Hours: 8:30AM-5:30PM M-Th; 8:30AM-4PM F. Enrollment: 180. Records go back to 1977. Degrees granted: Associate; Bachelors; Masters.

Attendance information available by phone, fax, mail. Search requires name plus approximate years of attendance. Also helpful: SSN, date of birth, exact years of attendance. There is no fee.

Degree information available by fax, mail. Search requires name plus approximate years of attendance. Also helpful: SSN, date of birth, exact years of attendance. There is no fee.

Art Center College of Design, Registrar, 1700 Lida St, PO Box 7197, Pasadena, CA 91109, 818-396-2316 (Fax: 818-568-0258). Hours: 8:30AM-4:30PM M-Th; 8:30AM-4PM F. Enrollment: 1200. Records go back to 1930. Alumni records are maintained here also. Call 818-396-2305. Degrees granted: Bachelors; Masters.

Attendance and degree information available by phone, fax, mail. Search requires name plus SSN, date of birth. Also helpful: exact years of attendance. There is no fee.

Art Institute of Southern California, Registrar, 2222 Laguna Canyon Rd, Laguna Beach, CA 92651, 714-497-3309. Hours: 8AM-5PM. Enrollment: 129. Records go back to 1979. Alumni records are maintained here at the same phone number. Degrees granted: Bachelors.

Attendance and degree information available by mail. Search requires name plus SSN, signed release. Also helpful: date of birth. There is no fee.

Azusa Pacific University, Registrar, 901 E Alosta, Azusa, CA 91702-7000, 818-969-3434 X3391. Hours: 8AM-5PM. Records go back to 1880. Alumni records are maintained here also. Call 818-812-3026. Degrees granted: Bachelors; Masters.

Attendance and degree information available by phone, mail. Search requires name plus SSN, date of birth. There is no fee.

Bakersfield College, Registrar, 1801 Panorama Dr, Bakersfield, CA 93305, 805-395-4011. Hours: 8:30AM-4:45PM M-Th, 8:30AM-Noon F. Records go back to 1913. Alumni records are maintained here at the same phone number. Degrees granted: Associate. Adverse incident record source- Security, 805-395-4554: Dean of Students, 805-395-4204

Attendance and degree information available by mail. Search requires name plus SSN, exact years of attendance, signed release. There is no fee.

Barstow College, Registrar, 2700 Barstow Rd, Barstow, CA 92311, 619-252-2411 (Fax: 619-252-1875). Hours: 8AM-5PM. Enrollment: 1709. Records go back to 1964. Degrees granted: Associate. Adverse incident record source- HRDO Office, 619-252-2411.

Attendance and degree information available by mail. Search requires name plus SSN, approximate years of attendance, signed release. Also helpful: date of birth, exact years of attendance. There is no fee.

Bethany College of the Assemblies of God, Registrar, 800 Bethany Dr, Scotts Valley, CA 95066, 408-438-3800 X1444 (Fax: 408-438-1621). Hours: 8AM-5PM. Enrollment: 550. Records go back to 1919. Alumni records are maintained here also. Call 408-438-3800 X1470. Degrees granted: Associate; Bachelors. Adverse incident record source- Campus Life, 408-438-3800 X1417.

Attendance information available by phone, fax, mail. Search requires name plus SSN, date of birth. Also helpful: exact years of attendance. There is no fee.

Degree information available by phone, mail. Search requires name plus SSN, date of birth. Also helpful: exact years of attendance. There is no fee.

Bethel Seminary College, (West), Registrar, 6116 Arosa St, San Diego, CA 92115, 619-582-8188 (Fax: 619-265-1714). Hours: 8AM-5PM. Enrollment: 150. Records go back to 1977. Alumni Records Office: Alumni Association, 390 Bethel Dr, St Paul, MN 55112. Degrees granted: Masters; Doctorate.

Attendance and degree information available by phone, mail. Search requires name plus SSN, exact years of attendance. There is no fee.

Biola University, Registrar, 13800 Biola Ave, La Mirada, CA 90639, 310-903-4720 (Fax: 310-903-4748). Hours: 8AM-4:30PM. Enrollment: 2982. Records go back to 1913. Alumni records are maintained here also. Call 310-903-4728. Degrees granted: Bachelors; Masters; Doctorate. Adverse incident record source- Registrar's Office, 310-903-4720 .

Attendance and degree information available by phone, fax, mail. Search requires name plus SSN, date of birth, exact years of attendance. There is no fee.

Brooks College, Registrar, 4825 E Pacific Coast Hwy, Long Beach, CA 90804, 310-597-6611 (Fax: 310-597-7412). Hours: 8AM-5PM. Enrollment: 153. Records go back to 1970. Degrees granted: Associate. Adverse incident record source- Registrar's Office, 310-597-6611

Attendance and degree information available by fax, mail. Search requires name plus SSN, exact years of attendance. There is no fee.

Brooks Institute of Photography, Registrar, 801 Alston Rd, Santa Barbara, CA 93108, 805-966-3888 X229 (Fax: 805-564-1475). Hours: 8AM-5PM. Records go back to 1947. Alumni records are maintained here at the same phone number. Degrees granted: Bachelors.

Attendance and degree information available by phone, fax, mail. Search requires name plus SSN, date of birth, exact years of attendance. There is no fee.

Bryman College, Registrar, 3505 N Hart Ave, Rosemead, CA 91770, 818-573-5470 X171 (Fax: 818-280-4011). Hours: 9AM-5PM. Enrollment: 400. Formerly National Education Center (Bryman) Records go back to 1970. Degrees granted.

Attendance and degree information available by fax, mail. Search requires name plus SSN, date of birth, approximate years of attendance, signed release. Also helpful: exact years of attendance. There is no fee.

Butte College, Registrar, 3536 Butte Campus Dr, Oroville, CA 95965, 916-895-2511. Hours: 8:30AM-4PM. Records go back to 1974. Degrees granted: Associate.

Attendance and degree information available by mail. Search requires name plus SSN, date of birth, exact years of attendance, signed release. There is no fee.

Cabrillo College, Registrar, 6500 Soquel Dr, Aptos, CA 95003, 408-479-6213 (Fax: 408-479-5782). Hours: 8AM-9PM M-Th, 8AM-5PM F. Enrollment: 13520. Records go back to 1959. Alumni records are maintained here also. Call 408-479-6100. Degrees granted: Associate. Adverse incident record source- Registrar, 408-479-6212.

Attendance information available by phone, fax, mail. Search requires name plus SSN, date of birth, exact years of attendance. Also helpful: approximate years of attendance. There is no fee.

Degree information available by phone, fax, mail. Search requires name plus SSN, date of birth, exact years of attendance. There is no fee.

California Baptist College, Registrar, 8432 Magnolia Ave, Riverside, CA 92504, 909-689-5771 X222 (Fax: 909-351-1808). Hours: 8AM-5PM. Enrollment: 1200. Alumni records are maintained here also. Call 909-343-4226. Degrees granted: Bachelors; Masters. Certification: Athletic Training; Church Business; Church Growth; Church Music; Computer (Bus. Applications, Programming); Public Adm. Adverse incident record source- Student Life, 909-689-5771 X217.

Attendance and degree information available by phone, fax, mail. Search requires name only. Also helpful: SSN, date of birth, exact years of attendance. There is no fee.

California College for Health Sciences, Registrar, 222 W 24th St, National City, CA 91950-9998, 619-477-4800 (Fax: 619-477-4360). Hours: 8AM-5PM. Records go back to 1978. Degrees granted: Associate; Bachelors; Masters.

Attendance and degree information available by phone, fax, mail. Search requires name plus SSN. There is no fee.

California College of Arts and Crafts, Registrar, 5212 Broadway, Oakland, CA 94618, 510-597-3651. Hours: 8AM-4:30PM. Records go back to 1907. Alumni records are maintained here also. Call 510-597-3634.

Attendance and degree information available by phone, mail. Search requires name only. Also helpful: date of birth, exact years of attendance. There is no fee.

California College of Podiatric Medicine, Registrar, 1210 Scott St, San Francisco, CA 94115, 415-292-0414 (Fax: 415-292-0439). Hours: 9AM-5:30PM. Enrollment: 414. Records go back to 1916. Alumni records are maintained here also. Call 415-292-0484. Degrees granted: Doctorate.

Attendance information available by phone, fax, mail. Search requires name plus exact years of attendance. Also helpful: SSN, date of birth. There is no fee.

Degree information available by fax, mail. Search requires name plus exact years of attendance. Also helpful: SSN, date of birth. There is no fee.

California Institute of Integral Studies, Registrar, 9 Peter Yorke Way, San Francisco, CA 94109, 415-753-6100 X488. Hours: 10AM-12:30PM, 2-5PM. Degrees granted: Bachelors; Masters; Doctorate. Certification: ODT,EXA.

Attendance and degree information available by phone, fax, mail. Search requires name only. Also helpful: SSN, date of birth, exact years of attendance. There is no fee.

California Institute of Technology, Registrar, 1201 E California Blvd, Pasadena, CA 91125, 818-395-6354 (Fax: 818-577-4215). Hours: 8AM-Noon, 1:00-5PM. Enrollment: 2000. Records go back to 1940. Alumni Records Office: 345 S Hill Ave, Pasadena, CA 91125. Degrees granted: Bachelors; Masters; Doctorate. Adverse incident record source- Undergraduate Dean's Office, 818-395-6351 : Graduate Dean's Office, 818-395-6346

Attendance and degree information available by phone, fax, mail. Search requires name only. Also helpful: SSN, date of birth, approximate years of attendance. There is no fee.

California Institute of the Arts, Registrar, 24700 McBean Pkwy, Valencia, CA 91355, 805-253-7843 (Fax: 805-254-8352). Hours: 8:30AM-4PM. Enrollment: 1030. Records go back to 1930. Alumni records are maintained here also. Call 805-255-1050 X2749. Degrees granted: Bachelors; Masters.

Attendance and degree information available by phone, fax, mail. Search requires name plus approximate years of attendance. Also helpful: SSN, date of birth, exact years of attendance. There is no fee.

California Lutheran University, Registrar, 60 W Olsen Rd, Thousand Oaks, CA 91360, 805-493-3105. Hours: 8AM-4:30PM. Enrollment: 3000. Records go back to 1959. Alumni records are maintained here also. Call 805-493-3170. Degrees granted: Bachelors; Masters.

Attendance and degree information available by phone, mail. Search requires name plus SSN, date of birth, exact years of attendance. There is no fee.

California Maritime Academy, Registrar, 200 Maritime Academy Dr, PO Box 1392, Vallejo, CA 94590-0644, 707-648-4262 (Fax: 707-649-4773). Hours: 9AM-4:30PM. Enrollment: 400. Records go back to 1920. Alumni records are maintained here also. Call 707-648-5386. Degrees granted: Bachelors.

Attendance and degree information available by phone, fax, mail. Search requires name only. Also helpful: exact years of attendance. There is no fee.

California Polytechnic State University, San Luis Obispo, Academic Records, San Luis Obispo, CA 93407, 805-756-2531 (Fax: 805-756-7237). Hours: 8AM-5PM. Enrollment: 14110. Records go back to 1901. Degrees granted: Bachelors; Masters. Adverse incident record source- Public Safety, 805-756-2281.

Attendance and degree information available by phone, mail. Search requires name only. Also helpful: SSN, date of birth, exact years of attendance. There is no fee.

California School of Professional Psychology, (Alameda),

Registrar, 1005 Atlantic Ave, Alameda, CA 94501, 510-523-2300 (Fax: 510-521-0728). Hours: 9AM-5PM. Enrollment: 800. Records go back to 1970. Degrees granted: Masters; Doctorate.

Attendance and degree information available by fax, mail. Search requires name plus SSN, signed release. Also helpful: date of birth, exact years of attendance. There is no fee.

California School of Professional Psychology, Fresno,

Registrar, 5130 E Clinton Wy, Fresno, CA 93727, 209-456-2777 (Fax: 209-253-2777). Hours: 9AM-4:30PM. Enrollment: 400. Records go back to 1973. Alumni Records Office: 1000 S Fremont, Alhambra, CA 91803-1360. Degrees granted: Masters; Doctorate.

Attendance and degree information available by fax, mail. Search requires name plus signed release. There is no fee.

California School of Professional Psychology, Los Angeles,

Registrar, 1000 S Fremont Ave, Alhambra, CA 91803-1360, 818-284-2777. Hours: 8:30AM-4PM. Records go back to 1969. Alumni records are maintained here at the same phone number. Degrees granted: Doctorate.

Attendance and degree information available by mail. Search requires name plus SSN, date of birth, exact years of attendance, signed release. There is no fee.

California School of Professional Psychology, San Diego,

Registrar, 6160 Cornerstone Ct E, San Diego, CA 92121-3725, 619-452-1664 (Fax: 619-552-1974). Hours: 8:30AM-5:00PM. Enrollment: 630. Records go back to 1971. Alumni records are maintained here at the same phone number. Degrees granted: Masters; Doctorate. Certification: Doctoral Respecialization.

Attendance and degree information available by fax, mail. Search requires name plus signed release. Also helpful: SSN, date of birth, exact years of attendance. There is no fee.

California State Polytechnic University, Pomona,

Registrar, 3801 W Temple Ave, Pomona, CA 91768, 909-869-7659. Hours: 9AM-4PM. Degrees granted: Bachelors; Masters.

Attendance and degree information available by phone, mail. Search requires name plus SSN, date of birth, exact years of attendance. There is no fee.

California State University, Bakersfield,

Registrar, 9001 Stockdale Hwy, Bakersfield, CA 93311-1099, 805-664-2147 (Fax: 805-664-3389). Hours: 8AM-5PM. Enrollment: 5300. Records go back to 1970. Alumni records are maintained here also. Call 805-664-3211. Degrees granted: Bachelors; Masters. Adverse incident record source- Dean of Students, 805-664-2161.

Attendance and degree information available by fax, mail. Search requires name plus SSN, date of birth. Also helpful: exact years of attendance. There is no fee.

California State University, Chico,

Admissions & Records, 180 - Meriam Library, Chico, CA 95929-0220, 916-898-5143 (Fax: 916 898 4359). Hours: 8AM-5PM. Enrollment: 12625. Records go back to 1927. Alumni records are maintained here also. Call 916-898-6472. Degrees granted: Bachelors; Masters.

Attendance and degree information available by phone, mail. Search requires name plus SSN, exact years of attendance. Also helpful: date of birth. There is no fee.

California State University, Dominguez Hills,

Registrar, 1000 E Victoria St, Carson, CA 90747, 310-243-3300 (Fax: 310-516-4513). Hours: 10AM-7PM M,Th; 10AM-7:30PM T,W. Enrollment: 12500. Records go back to 1960. Alumni Records Office: Alumni Relations, 1000 E Victoria St, ERCG-521, Carson, CA 90747, 310-243-4237. Degrees granted: Bachelors; Masters.

Attendance and degree information available by phone, fax, mail. Search requires name plus SSN, date of birth. Also helpful: exact years of attendance. Fee is $4.00.

California State University, Fresno,

Registrar, 5150 N Maple Ave, Fresno, CA 93740-0057, 209-278-2191 (Fax: 209-278-4812). Hours: 8AM-5PM. Enrollment: 17500. Records go back to 1911. Alumni Records Office: Alumni Association, 5150 N Maple Ave Rm 148, Fresno, CA 93740-0045, 209-278-2586. Degrees granted: Bachelors; Masters; Doctorate. Adverse incident record source- Dean of Students, 209-278-2541.

Attendance and degree information available by fax, mail. Search requires name plus SSN, date of birth, signed release. Also helpful: exact years of attendance. Fee is $5.00. Expedited service available for $10.00.

California State University, Fullerton,

Registrar, PO Box 34080, Fullerton, CA 92634, 714-773-2011. Degrees granted: Bachelors; Masters.

Attendance and degree information available by phone, fax, mail. Search requires name plus SSN, date of birth. Also helpful: exact years of attendance. There is no fee.

California State University, Hayward,

Registrar, 25800 Carlos Bee Blvd, Hayward, CA 94542, 510-885-3075 (Fax: 510-885-3816). Hours: 8AM-5PM M-Th. Enrollment: 10650. Records go back to 1960. Degrees granted: Bachelors; Masters.

Attendance and degree information available by phone, fax, mail. Search requires name plus SSN, date of birth, exact years of attendance. There is no fee.

California State University, Long Beach,

Records Transcripts, 1250 Bellflower Blvd, Long Beach, CA 90840, 310-985-5487. Degrees granted: Bachelors; Masters.

Attendance information available by phone, fax, mail. Search requires name plus SSN, approximate years of attendance. Also helpful: date of birth, exact years of attendance. There is no fee.

Degree information available by phone, fax, mail. Search requires name plus approximate years of attendance. Also helpful: SSN, date of birth, exact years of attendance. There is no fee.

California State University, Los Angeles,

Registrar, 5151 State University Dr, Los Angeles, CA 90032, 213-343-3940 (Fax: 213-343-3840). Hours: 8AM-4:30PM. Records go back to 1965. Degrees granted: Bachelors; Masters; Doctorate.

Attendance and degree information available by phone, mail. Search requires name plus SSN, date of birth, exact years of attendance. There is no fee.

California State University, Northridge,

Registrar, 18111 Nordhoff St, Northridge, CA 91330, 818-677-3776 (Fax: 818-677-3766). Hours: 8AM-5PM M; 10AM-7PM T&W; 8AM-5PM Th; 8AM-4PM F. Enrollment: 26000. Records go back to 1957. Alumni Records Office: Alumni Association, 9528 Etiwanda, Northridge, CA 91330. Degrees granted: Bachelors; Masters. Adverse incident record source- Campus Police, 818 677-2111.

Attendance information available by fax, mail. Search requires name plus SSN. Also helpful: date of birth, exact years of attendance. There is no fee.

Degree information available by phone, fax, mail. Search requires name plus SSN. Also helpful: date of birth, exact years of attendance. There is no fee.

California State University, Sacramento,

Admissions & Records, 6000 J St, Sacramento, CA 95819-6048, 916-278-7111 (Fax: 916-278-5603). Hours: 9AM-4PM. Enrollment: 23000. Records go back to 1949. Alumni Records Office: 7750 College Town Dr #203, Sacramento, CA 95826. Degrees granted: Bachelors; Masters.

Attendance information available by phone, fax, mail. Search requires name plus SSN, exact years of attendance. There is no fee.

Degree information available by phone, fax, mail. Search requires name plus SSN, exact years of attendance. Also helpful: approximate years of attendance. There is no fee.

California State University, San Bernardino,
Registrar, 5500 State University Pkwy, San Bernardino, CA 92407-2397, 909-880-5200 (Fax: 909-880-7021). Hours: 8AM-6PM M-Th; 8AM-5PM F. Records go back to 1970's. Degrees granted: Bachelors; Masters.

Attendance and degree information available by phone, fax, mail. Search requires name plus SSN, date of birth. Fee is $4.00.

California State University, San Marcos,
Registrar, San Marcos, CA 92096, 619-750-4800 (Fax: 619-750-3285). Hours: 9AM-5PM. Enrollment: 1995. Records go back to 1990. Alumni records are maintained here also. Call 619-750-4970. Degrees granted: Bachelors; Masters; Teaching Credential. Adverse incident record source- Public Safety, 619-750-4562.

Attendance and degree information available by phone, fax, mail. Search requires name only. Also helpful: SSN, date of birth. There is no fee.

California State University, Stanislaus,
Registrar, 801 W Monte Vista Ave, Turlock, CA 95382, 209-667-3264 (Fax: 209-667-3788). Hours: 8AM-5PM. Enrollment: 6100. Records go back to 1960. Alumni records are maintained here also. Call 209-667-3131. Degrees granted: Bachelors; Masters. Adverse incident record source- Campus Police, 209-667-3114.

Attendance and degree information available by phone, fax, mail. Search requires name only. Also helpful: SSN. Fee is $5.00. Expedited service available for $10.00.

California Western School of Law,
Registrar's Office, 225 Cedar St, San Diego, CA 92101, 619-525-1414 (Fax: 619-525-7092). Hours: 8AM-5PM. Records go back to 1962. Alumni records are maintained here also. Call 619-239-0391 X7644.

Attendance and degree information available by phone, fax, mail. Search requires name plus SSN. Also helpful: exact years of attendance. There is no fee.

Canada College,
Dottie Shiloh, 4200 Farm Hill Blvd, Redwood City, CA 94061, 415-306-3124 (Fax: 415-306-3475). Hours: 8AM-8:15PM M-Th; 8AM-4:30PM F. Enrollment: 5710. Records go back to 1968. Degrees granted: Associate.

Attendance information available by phone, fax, mail. Search requires name plus SSN, approximate years of attendance. Also helpful: exact years of attendance. There is no fee.

Degree information available by phone, mail. Search requires name plus SSN. Also helpful: exact years of attendance. There is no fee.

Center for Early Education,
Registrar, 563 N Alfred St, Los Angeles, CA 90048, 213-651-0707 (Fax: 213-651-0860). Enrollment: 475. Records go back to 1939. Degrees granted: Associate; Masters. Special programs- Nursery Education. Adverse incident record source- Security.

Attendance and degree information available by phone, mail. Search requires name plus SSN, date of birth. There is no fee.

Cerritos College,
Registrar, 11110 Alondra Blvd, Norwalk, CA 90650, 310-860-2451 (Fax: 310-467-5005). Hours: 8AM-9PM M-Th, 8AM-4:30PM F. Records go back to 1955. Alumni records are maintained here also. Call 310-860-2451. Degrees granted: Associate.

Attendance and degree information available by phone, mail. Search requires name plus SSN, date of birth, exact years of attendance. There is no fee.

Cerro Coso Community College,
Registrar, 3000 College Heights Blvd, Ridgecrest, CA 93555-7777, 619-384-6357 (Fax: 619-375-4776). Hours: 8AM-7PM M-Th; 8AM-4PM F. Enrollment: 6000. Records go back to 1973. Alumni records are maintained here also. Call 619-375-5001 X230. Degrees granted: Associate. Adverse incident record source- Administrative Services.

Attendance and degree information available by phone, fax, mail. Search requires name plus SSN. Also helpful: date of birth, approximate years of attendance. There is no fee.

Chabot College,
Registrar, 25555 Hesperian Blvd, Hayward, CA 94545, 510-786-6703 (Fax: 510-732-0212). Hours: 8AM-7:30PM M-Th, 8AM-1PM F. Enrollment: 12500. Records go back to 1960. Alumni records are maintained here also. Call 510-786-6600. Degrees granted: Associate.

Attendance and degree information available by phone, mail. Search requires name plus SSN, exact years of attendance. There is no fee.

Chaffey College,
5885 Haven Ave, Rancho Cucamonga, CA 91737, 909-941-2100. Enrollment: 13500. Records go back to 1950. Degrees granted: Associate. Adverse incident record source- Mike Edwards, 909-941-2382.

Attendance and degree information available by mail. Search requires name plus SSN, date of birth, signed release. Also helpful: exact years of attendance. There is no fee. Expedited service available for $10.00.

Chapman University,
Registrar, 333 N Glassell St, Orange, CA 92866, 714-997-6701 (Fax: 714-997-6986). Hours: 8AM-4:30PM. Enrollment: 5600. Records go back to 1958. Alumni records are maintained here also. Call 714-997-6783. Degrees granted: Associate; Bachelors; Masters; Teaching Credential. Adverse incident record source- Campus Safety, 714-997-6763.

Attendance and degree information available by phone, mail. Search requires name plus SSN. Also helpful: date of birth, exact years of attendance. There is no fee.

Charles R. Drew University of Medicine and Science,
Registrar, 1730 E 118th St, Los Angeles, CA 90059, 213-563-4800 (Fax: 213-563-4957). Hours: 8AM-5PM. Enrollment: 625. Records go back to 1966. Alumni records are maintained here at the same phone number. Degrees granted: Doctorate.

Attendance information available by phone, fax, mail. Search requires name plus SSN. There is no fee.

Degree information available by fax, mail. Search requires name plus SSN. There is no fee.

Christian Heritage College,
Registrar, 2100 Greenfield Dr, El Cajon, CA 92019, 619-590-1784 (Fax: 619-440-0209). Hours: 8:30AM-3PM. Enrollment: 500. Records go back to 1977. Alumni records are maintained here also. Call 619-590-1750. Degrees granted: Bachelors.

Attendance and degree information available by phone, fax, mail. Search requires name plus SSN. Also helpful: date of birth, exact years of attendance. There is no fee.

Church Divinity School of the Pacific,
Registrar, 2451 Ridge Rd, Berkeley, CA 94709-1211, 510-204-0715 (Fax: 510-644-0712). Hours: 8AM-4PM. Enrollment: 110. Records go back to 1920's. Alumni records are maintained here also. Call 510-204-0709. Degrees granted: Masters. Adverse incident record source- Security Officer.

Attendance information available by phone, fax, mail. Search requires name only. There is no fee.

Degree information available by fax, mail. Search requires name only. There is no fee.

Citrus College, Registrar, 1000 W Foothill Blvd, Glendora, CA 91741-1899, 818-914-8511 (Fax: 818-335-3159). Hours: 8AM-9PM M-Th, 8AM-4:30PM F. Records go back to 1915. Alumni records are maintained here also. Call 818-963-0323. Degrees granted: Associate. Adverse incident record source- Dean of Students, 818-914-8534.

Attendance and degree information available by phone, fax, mail. Search requires name plus SSN. There is no fee.

City College of San Francisco, Registrar, 50 Phelan Ave, San Francisco, CA 94112, 415-239-3838 (Fax: 415-239-3936). Hours: 8AM-3PM M-Th; 8AM-Noon F. Enrollment: 75000. Records go back to 1935. Degrees granted: Associate.

Attendance and degree information available by fax, mail. Search requires name plus SSN, signed release. Also helpful: date of birth, approximate years of attendance. Fee is $5.00.

Claremont Graduate School, Registrar's Office, 170 E 10th St, Claremont, CA 91711, 909-621-8285 (Fax: 909-607-7285). Hours: 8:30AM-5PM. Enrollment: 200. Records go back to 1925. Alumni records are maintained here also. Call 909-621-8204. Degrees granted: Masters; Doctorate.

Attendance information available by phone, fax, mail. Search requires name plus SSN. Also helpful: date of birth, exact years of attendance. There is no fee.

Degree information available by phone, fax, mail. Search requires name only. Also helpful: SSN, date of birth, exact years of attendance. There is no fee.

Claremont McKenna College, (Bauer Center), Registrar, 500 E 9th St, Claremont, CA 91711-6400, 909-621-8101. Hours: 8AM-5PM. Records go back to 1946. Alumni Records Office: Alumni Association, 850 Columbia Ave, Claremont, CA 91711-6400. Degrees granted: Bachelors. Adverse incident record source- Registrar's Office, 909-621-8101 .

Attendance and degree information available by phone, mail. Search requires name plus SSN, exact years of attendance. There is no fee.

Cleveland Chiropractic College, Registrar, 590 N Vermont Ave, Los Angeles, CA 90004, 213-660-6166 X58 (Fax: 213-660-3190). Hours: 7AM-3:30PM. Enrollment: 460. Records go back to 1908. Alumni records are maintained here at the same phone number. Adverse incident record source- Same as above.

Attendance information available by fax, mail. Search requires name plus SSN, date of birth, signed release. Also helpful: exact years of attendance. There is no fee.

Degree information available by fax, mail. Search requires name plus SSN, signed release. Also helpful: date of birth, exact years of attendance. There is no fee.

Coastline Community College, Registrar, 11460 Warner Ave, Fountain Valley, CA 92708, 714-241-6168 (Fax: 714-241-6288). Hours: 8AM-6:30PM M-Th, 8AM-2PM F. Records go back to 1976. Degrees granted: Associate.

Attendance and degree information available by phone, fax, mail. Search requires name plus SSN, exact years of attendance. There is no fee.

Cogswell Polytechnical College, Registrar, 1175 Bordeaux Dr, Sunnyvale, CA 94089-1299, 408-541-0100 X110 (Fax: 408-747-0764). Hours: 9AM-5:45PM. Enrollment: 340. Formerly Cogswell College Records go back to 1956. Alumni records are maintained here at the same phone number. Degrees granted: Associate; Bachelors.

Attendance information available by mail. Search requires name plus SSN, date of birth, exact years of attendance, signed release. There is no fee.

Degree information available by fax, mail. Search requires name plus SSN, date of birth, exact years of attendance, signed release. There is no fee.

Coleman College, Registrar, 7380 Parkway Dr, La Mesa, CA 91942-1532, 619-475-3990 (Fax: 619-463-0162). Hours: 9AM-8PM M-Th. Enrollment: 900. Records go back to 1963. Alumni records are maintained here at the same phone number. Degrees granted: Associate; Bachelors; Masters.

Attendance and degree information available by phone, fax, mail. Search requires name plus date of birth. Also helpful: SSN, exact years of attendance. There is no fee.

College of Alameda, Registrar, 555 Atlantic Ave, Alameda, CA 94501, 510-748-2228 (Fax: 510-769-6019). Hours: 9AM-7 M,T; 9AM-3PM W-F. Enrollment: 5595. Records go back to 1974. Alumni records are maintained here also. Call 510-522-7221. Degrees granted: Associate.

Attendance and degree information available by fax, mail. Search requires name plus SSN, date of birth, exact years of attendance, signed release. There is no fee.

College of Marin, Admissions, 1800 Ignacio Blvd, Novato, CA 94949, 415-883-2211. Hours: 9AM-3PM M-Th; 9AM-Noon F. Enrollment: 8500. Records go back to 1926. Alumni records are maintained here at the same phone number. Degrees granted: Associate.

Attendance and degree information available by written request only. Search requires name only. There is no fee.

College of Notre Dame, Registrar's Office, 1500 Ralston Ave, Belmont, CA 94002, 415-508-3521 (Fax: 415-508-3736). Hours: 8:30AM-7PM M-Th; 8:30AM-4PM F. Enrollment: 1725. Records go back to 1851. Alumni records are maintained here also. Call 415-508-3515. Degrees granted: Associate; Bachelors; Masters. Adverse incident record source- Head of Security, 415-508-5502.

Attendance and degree information available by phone, fax, mail. Search requires name only. Also helpful: SSN, date of birth, exact years of attendance. There is no fee.

College of Oceaneering, Registrar, Los Angeles Harbor, 272 S Fries Ave, Wilmington, CA 90744, 310-834-2501 (Fax: 310-834-7132). Hours: 7:30AM-4:30PM. Enrollment: 400. Records go back to 1976. Alumni records are maintained here at the same phone number. Degrees granted: Associate.

Attendance information available by fax, mail. Search requires name plus SSN, exact years of attendance, signed release. Also helpful: date of birth. There is no fee.

Degree information available by fax, mail. Search requires name plus SSN, exact years of attendance. Also helpful: date of birth. There is no fee.

College of Osteopathic Medicine of the Pacific, Student Affairs Office, 309 E Second St, College Plaza, Pomona, CA 91766-1889, 909-469-5340 (Fax: 909-623-9623). Hours: 8:30AM-5PM. Enrollment: 850. Records go back to 1978. Alumni records are maintained here also. Call 909-469-5275. Degrees granted: Masters; Doctorate. Certification: P.A. Special programs- Rotations, 909-469-5260: Academic Affairs, 909-469-5267: Allied Health, 909-469-5378. Adverse incident record source- Deans' Office, 909-469-5267

Attendance and degree information available by fax, mail. Search requires name plus signed release. Also helpful: SSN, exact years of attendance. There is no fee.

College of San Mateo, Registrar, 1700 W Hillsdale Blvd, San Mateo, CA 94402, 415-574-6165. Hours: 8AM-4:30PM. Records go back to 1922. Alumni records are maintained here also. Call 415-574-6141. Degrees granted: Associate.

Attendance and degree information available by phone, mail. Search requires name plus SSN, date of birth. There is no fee.

College of the Canyons, Admissions & Records Officed, 26455 N Rockwell Canyon Rd, Santa Clarita, CA 91355, 805-259-7900 (Fax: 805-259-8302). Hours: 9AM-7PM M-Th. Enrollment: 7272. Records go back to 1969. Degrees granted: Associate.

Attendance and degree information available by phone, fax, mail. Search requires name plus SSN, date of birth, approximate years of attendance. There is no fee.

College of the Desert, Registrar, 43-500 Monterey Ave, Palm Desert, CA 92260, 619-773-2518 (Fax: 619-776-0136). Hours: 8:30AM-7PM M-Th; 8:30AM-3PM F. Enrollment: 10000. Records go back to 1963. Alumni records are maintained here also. Call 619-773-2567. Degrees granted: Associate. Adverse incident record source- Administrative Support Services.

Attendance information available by written request only. Search requires name plus SSN, date of birth, signed release. Also helpful: exact years of attendance. There is no fee.

Degree information available by phone, fax, mail. Search requires name plus SSN, date of birth. Also helpful: exact years of attendance. There is no fee.

College of the Redwoods, Dir, Admissions & Records, Attn: Transcripts, 7358 Tompkins Hill Rd, Eureka, CA 95501, 707-445-6717 (Fax: 707-445-6990). Hours: 8AM-7PM M-Th; 8AM-5PM F. Enrollment: 7000. Records go back to 1965. Alumni records are maintained here also. Call 707-445-6992. Degrees granted: Associate. Adverse incident record source- 707-445-6933.

Attendance and degree information available by written request only. Search requires name plus SSN, signed release. Also helpful: date of birth, exact years of attendance. There is no fee.

College of the Sequoias, Student Records Ofc, 915 S Mooney Blvd, Visalia, CA 93277, 209-730-3775 (Fax: 209-730-3894). Hours: 8:30AM-4PM. Enrollment: 9000. Records go back to 1922. Alumni records are maintained here also. Call 209-730-3861. Degrees granted: Associate.

Attendance and degree information available by phone, fax, mail. Search requires name plus SSN, date of birth. Also helpful: exact years of attendance. There is no fee.

College of the Siskiyous, Registrar, 800 College Ave, Weed, CA 96094, 916-938-5215 (Fax: 916-938-5367). Hours: 9AM-3PM. Enrollment: 2774. Records go back to 1937. Degrees granted: Associate.

Attendance and degree information available by fax, mail. Search requires name plus date of birth, signed release. Also helpful: SSN, exact years of attendance. There is no fee.

Columbia College, Admissions and Records, 11600 Columbia College Dr, Sonora, CA 95370-8582, 209-533-5231 (Fax: 209-533-5104). Hours: 8AM-6:30PM M-Th; 8AM-4:30PM F. Records go back to 1968. Degrees granted: Associate. Certification: Vocational. Adverse incident record source- Student Services.

Attendance and degree information available by phone, fax, mail. Search requires name only. Also helpful: SSN, date of birth, exact years of attendance. There is no fee.

Columbia College Hollywood, Registrar, 925 N La Brea Ave, Los Angeles, CA 90038-2392, 213-851-0550 (Fax: 213-851-6401). Hours: 8AM-4:30PM. Enrollment: 210. Records go back to 1952. Degrees granted: Associate.

Attendance and degree information available by phone, fax, mail. Search requires name plus SSN, exact years of attendance. There is no fee.

Compton Community College, Registrar, 1111 E Artesia Blvd, Compton, CA 90221, 310-637-2660 X2043 (Fax: 310-639-8260). Hours: 8AM-7PM M-W; 8AM-4:30PM Th-F. Records go back to 1929. Degrees granted: Associate. Adverse incident record source- Campus Police, 310-637-2660 X2790.

Attendance and degree information available by phone, fax, mail. Search requires name plus date of birth. Also helpful: SSN, approximate years of attendance. There is no fee.

Concordia University, Registrar, 1530 Concordia W, Irvine, CA 92715-3299, 714-854-8002 (Fax: 714-854-6854). Hours: 8AM-4:30PM. Enrollment: 1500. Formerly Christ College Records go back to 1978. Alumni records are maintained here at the same phone number. Degrees granted: Bachelors; Masters. Certification: Lutheran Teaching; Director of Christian.

Attendance information available by phone, fax, mail. Search requires name plus SSN. Also helpful: date of birth, exact years of attendance. There is no fee.

Degree information available by phone, fax, mail. Search requires name plus SSN. Also helpful: exact years of attendance. There is no fee.

Contra Costa College, Registrar, 2600 Mission Bell Dr, San Pablo, CA 94806, 510-235-7800 X382 (Fax: 510-236-6768). Hours: 8AM-4:30PM M-F; 5:30-8:30PM M-Th. Enrollment: 8500. Records go back to 1950. Alumni records are maintained here at the same phone number. Degrees granted: Associate.

Attendance and degree information available by phone, mail. Search requires name plus SSN, exact years of attendance. Also helpful: approximate years of attendance. There is no fee.

Cosumnes River College, Admissions & Records, 8401 Center Pkwy, Sacramento, CA 95823, 916-688-7410 (Fax: 916-688-7467). Hours: 8AM-8PM M-Th; 8AM-5PM F. Enrollment: 11303. Records go back to 1970. Degrees granted: Associate.

Attendance and degree information available by mail. Search requires name plus SSN, date of birth, signed release. There is no fee.

Crafton Hills College, Registrar, 11711 Sand Canyon Rd, Yucaipa, CA 92399, 909-389-3372 (Fax: 909-389-9141). Hours: 10AM-8AM M-Th; 10AM-4:30PM F. Enrollment: 5200. Records go back to 1972. Degrees granted: Associate.

Attendance and degree information available by phone, fax, mail. Search requires name only. Also helpful: SSN, date of birth, exact years of attendance. There is no fee.

Cuesta College, Records Office Rm 3110, Hwy 1, San Luis Obispo, CA 93403, 805-546-3139 (Fax: 805-546-3904). Hours: 9AM-4PM M-Th; 9AM-3PM F. Enrollment: 8000. Records go back to 1965. Alumni records are maintained here also. Call 805-546-3915. Degrees granted: Associate. Adverse incident record source- Dean of Students, 805-546-3130.

Attendance information available by phone, fax, mail. Search requires name only. Also helpful: SSN, exact years of attendance. There is no fee.

Degree information available by phone, fax, mail. Search requires name only. Also helpful: SSN, exact years of attendance. There is no fee.

Cuyamaca College, Registrar, 900 Rancho San Diego Parkway, El Cajon, CA 92019, 619-670-1980 (Fax: 619-670-7204). Hours: 8AM-7PM M-Th; 8AM-2PM F; 9AM-1PM S. Enrollment: 5000. Records go back to 1978. Alumni records are maintained here also. Call 619-670-1980. Degrees granted: Associate.

Attendance and degree information available by mail. Search requires name plus SSN, date of birth, signed release. Also helpful: exact years of attendance. Fee is $3.00. Expedited service available for $5.00.

Cypress College, Registrar, 9200 Valley View St, Cypress, CA 90630, 714-826-2220 (Fax: 714-826-4224). Hours: 8AM-7PM M-Th; 8AM-1PM F. Enrollment: 14600. Records go back to 1966. Degrees granted: Associate.

Attendance and degree information available by phone, mail. Search requires name plus date of birth. Also helpful: SSN, exact years of attendance. Fee is $3.00. Expedited service available for $10.00.

D-Q University, Registrar, PO Box 409, Davis, CA 95617-0409, 916-758-0470 (Fax: 916-758-4891). Hours: 8AM-4:30PM. Enrollment: 535. Records go back to 1971. Alumni records are maintained here at the same phone number. Degrees granted: Associate.

Attendance and degree information available by mail. Search requires name plus SSN, date of birth, exact years of attendance. There is no fee.

De Anza College, Registrar, 21250 Stevens Creek Blvd, Cupertino, CA 95014, 408-864-5300 (Fax: 408-864-8329). Hours: 8AM-7:30PM M-Th; 8AM-3PM F. Records go back to 1967. Degrees granted: Associate.

Attendance and degree information available by mail. Search requires name plus SSN, signed release. Also helpful: date of birth, exact years of attendance. Fee is $3.00. Expedited service available for $7.50.

DeVry Institute of Technology, Registrar's Office, 901 Corporate Center Dr, Pomona, CA 91768, 909-622-9800. Hours: 8:30AM-4:30PM M,T,W,F; 8:30AM-8PM Th. Enrollment: 3000. Records go back to 1983. Alumni records are maintained here at the same phone number. Degrees granted: Associate; Bachelors.

Attendance and degree information available by phone, mail. Search requires name plus SSN. There is no fee.

Design Institute of San Diego, Registrar, 8555 Commerce Ave, San Diego, CA 92121, 619-566-1200 (Fax: 619-566-2711). Hours: 8:30AM-4:30PM. Enrollment: 210. Records go back to 1977. Alumni records are maintained here also. Call 619-566-1200. Degrees granted: Bachelors.

Attendance and degree information available by phone, fax, mail. Search requires name plus SSN. There is no fee.

Diablo Valley College, Registrar, 321 Golf Club Rd, Pleasant Hill, CA 94523, 510-685-1230 X327 (Fax: 510-685-1551). Hours: 8AM-8PM M-Th; 8AM-4:30PM F. Records go back to 1949. Degrees granted: Associate.

Attendance and degree information available by phone, fax, mail. Search requires name plus date of birth. Also helpful: SSN, exact years of attendance. There is no fee.

Dominican College of San Rafael, Registrar, 50 Acacia St, San Rafael, CA 94901, 415-457-4440 X260. Hours: 9AM-5PM. Records go back to 1890. Alumni records are maintained here also. Call 415-457-4440. Degrees granted: Bachelors; Masters.

Attendance and degree information available by phone, mail. Search requires name plus SSN, exact years of attendance. There is no fee.

Dominican School of Philosophy and Theology, Registrar, 2401 Ridge Rd, Berkeley, CA 94709, 510-849-2030. Degrees granted: Bachelors; Masters. Certification: Theology.

Attendance and degree information available by mail. Search requires name plus approximate years of attendance, signed release. Also helpful: date of birth, exact years of attendance. Fee is $3.00.

Don Bosco Technical Institute, Registrar, 1151 San Gabriel Blvd, Rosemead, CA 91770-4299, 818-307-6522 (Fax: 818-280-9316). Hours: 8AM-3:30PM. Enrollment: 200. Records go back to 1968. Alumni records are maintained here also. Call 818-307-6528. Degrees granted: Associate.

Attendance and degree information available by phone, fax, mail. Search requires name only. Also helpful: SSN, date of birth, exact years of attendance. There is no fee.

East Los Angeles College, Registrar, 1301 Brooklyn Ave, Monterey Park, CA 91754, 213-265-8650. Hours: 8AM-5PM. Records go back to 1956. Alumni records are maintained here also. Call 213-265-8650. Degrees granted: Associate.

Attendance and degree information available by mail. Search requires name plus SSN, date of birth, exact years of attendance. Fee is $1.00.

El Camino College, Registrar, 16007 Crenshaw Blvd, Torrance, CA 90506, 310-660-3418 (Fax: 310-660-3818). Hours: 8AM-7:30PM. Records go back to 1945. Alumni records are maintained here also. Call 310-660-3500. Degrees granted: Associate. Adverse incident record source- Campus Security, 310-532-3670.

Attendance and degree information available by fax, mail. Search requires name plus SSN, date of birth, exact years of attendance. There is no fee.

Emperor's College of Traditional Oriental Medicine, Registrar, 1807-B Wilshire Blvd, Santa Monica, CA 90403, 310-453-8300 (Fax: 310-829-3838). Hours: 8AM-5PM. Enrollment: 300. Records go back to 1982. Alumni records are maintained here at the same phone number. Degrees granted: Masters. Adverse incident record source- CEO Fairness Committee.

Attendance and degree information available by mail. Search requires name plus SSN, date of birth, signed release. Also helpful: exact years of attendance. Fee is $5.00.

Emperor's College of Traditional Oriental Medicine, (Branch), Registrar, 3625 W 6th St Ste 220, Los Angeles, CA 90020, 310-453-8300. Records are not housed here. They are located at Emperor's College of Traditional Oriental Medicine, Registrar, 1807-B Wilshire Blvd, Santa Monica, CA 90403.

Empire College, Registrar, 3033 Cleveland Ave Ste 102, Santa Rosa, CA 95403, 707-546-4000 (Fax: 707-546-4058). Hours: 8AM-5PM. Degrees granted: Associate; JD.

Attendance and degree information available by mail. Search requires name plus SSN, date of birth, exact years of attendance, signed release. There is no fee.

Evergreen Valley College, Registrar, 3095 Yerba Buena Rd, San Jose, CA 95135, 408-270-6441 (Fax: 408-223-9351). Hours: 8AM-5PM. Enrollment: 10000. Records go back to 1975. Degrees granted: Associate.

Attendance information available by written request only. Search requires name plus SSN. Also helpful: date of birth, exact years of attendance. There is no fee.

Degree information available by phone, fax, mail. Search requires name plus SSN. Also helpful: date of birth, exact years of attendance. There is no fee.

Fashion Institute of Design and Merchandising, Registrar, 919 S Grand Ave, Los Angeles, CA 90015, 213-624-1200 (Fax: 213-624-4777). Hours: 8AM-5PM. Enrollment: 2225. Records go back to 1970. Alumni records are maintained here at the same phone number. Degrees granted: Associate. Adverse incident record source- Student Advisory, 213-624-1200.

Attendance and degree information available by phone, fax, mail. Search requires name plus SSN. There is no fee.

Fashion Institute of Design and Merchandising, (Branch), Registrar, 3420 S Bristol St, Suite 400, Costa Mesa, CA 92626, 714-546-0930 (Fax: 714-540-8118). Records are not housed here. They are located at Fashion Institute of Design and Merchandising, Registrar, 919 S Grand Ave, Los Angeles, CA 90015.

Fashion Institute of Design and Merchandising, (Branch), Registrar, 1010 Second Ave Ste 200, San Diego, CA 92101, 619-235-4515 (Fax: 619-232-4322). Records are not housed here. They are located at Fashion Institute of Design and Merchandising, Registrar, 919 S Grand Ave, Los Angeles, CA 90015.

Fashion Institute of Design and Merchandising, (Branch), Registrar, 55 Stockton St, San Francisco, CA 94108, 415-433-6691 (Fax: 415-296-7299). Enrollment: 400. Records go back to 1980. Alumni records are maintained here at the same phone number. Degrees granted: Associate.

Attendance and degree information available by phone, fax, mail. Search requires name plus SSN, exact years of attendance. There is no fee.

Feather River College, Registrar, PO Box 11110, Quincy, CA 95971, 916-283-0202 X285 (Fax: 916-283-3757). Hours: 8AM-5PM. Enrollment: 1434. Records go back to 1988. Alumni records are maintained here at the same phone number. Degrees granted: Associate.

Attendance and degree information available by written request only. Search requires name plus SSN, date of birth, approximate years of attendance, signed release. Also helpful: exact years of attendance. There is no fee.

Fielding Institute, Registrar, 2112 Santa Barbara St, Santa Barbara, CA 93105, 805-687-1099 (Ext 3108) (Fax: 805-687-9793). Hours: 9AM-5PM. Enrollment: 965. Records go back to 1975. Alumni records are maintained here at the same phone number. Degrees granted: Masters; Doctorate. Certification: Neurobehavioral Certificate Program. Special programs- CE Program - Group Psychotherapy, 805-687-1099. Adverse incident record source- Registrar's Office, 805-687-1099 X3108

Attendance and degree information available by phone, fax, mail. Search requires name only. Also helpful: SSN. There is no fee.

Foothill College, Registrar, 12345 El Monte Rd, Los Altos Hills, CA 94022, 415-949-7325 (Fax: 415-949-7048). Hours: 9AM-7:30PM M-Th, 9AM-4PM F. Enrollment: 15000. Records go back to 1958. Degrees granted: Associate. Adverse incident record source- Dean of Students, 415-949-7241.

Attendance and degree information available by phone, fax, mail. Search requires name plus SSN, approximate years of attendance. There is no fee.

Franciscan School of Theology, Registrar, 1712 Euclid Ave, Berkeley, CA 94709, 510-848-5232 (Fax: 510-549-9466). Hours: 8:30AM-12:30PM, 1:30-4:30pm. Enrollment: 100. Records go back to 1968. Alumni records are maintained here at the same phone number. Degrees granted: Masters.

Attendance information available by written request only. Search requires name plus signed release. Also helpful: exact years of attendance. There is no fee.

Degree information available by written request only. Search requires name plus signed release. Also helpful: date of birth, exact years of attendance. There is no fee.

Fresno City College, Registrar, 1101 E University Ave, Fresno, CA 93741, 209-442-4600 (Fax: 209-485-7304). Hours: 8AM-6:45PM M-Th; 8AM-5PM F; 7AM-3:30PM Summer. Enrollment: 18240. Records go back to 1948. Alumni Records Office: 1525 E Weldon Ave, Fresno, CA 93704. Degrees granted: Associate.

Attendance and degree information available by fax, mail. Search requires name plus SSN, signed release. Also helpful: date of birth, exact years of attendance. There is no fee.

Fresno Pacific College, Registrar, 1717 S Chestnut Ave, Fresno, CA 93702, 209-453-2037 (Fax: 209-453-2007). Hours: 8AM-5PM. Enrollment: 1040. Records go back to 1965. Alumni records are maintained here also. Call 209-453-2058. Degrees granted: Associate; Bachelors; Masters; Teaching Credential. Special programs- Graduate Office, 209-453-2016: Center/Degree Completion, 209-453-2280. Adverse incident record source- Personnel Office, 209-453-2245: Safety & Security, 209-453-2298

Attendance and degree information available by phone. Search requires name plus SSN. Also helpful: date of birth, exact years of attendance. There is no fee.

Fuller Theological Seminary, Registrar, 135 N Oakland Ave, Pasadena, CA 91182, 818-584-5408. Hours: 8AM-5PM. Records go back to 1947. Alumni records are maintained here also. Call 818-584-5498. Degrees granted: Associate; Bachelors; Masters; Doctorate.

Attendance and degree information available by phone, mail. Search requires name plus SSN, date of birth, approximate years of attendance. There is no fee.

Fullerton College, Admissions and Records, 321 E Chapman Ave, Fullerton, CA 92634-2095, 714-992-7568 (Fax: 714-870-7751). Hours: 8AM-7PM M-Th; 8AM-3PM F. Enrollment: 18700. Records go back to 1913. Degrees granted: Associate. Adverse incident record source- Student Affairs, 714-992-7248.

Attendance and degree information available by phone, mail. Search requires name plus date of birth. Also helpful: SSN, exact years of attendance. Fee is $3.00. Expedited service available for $13.00.

Gavilan College, Admissions Office, 5055 Santa Teresa Blvd, Gilroy, CA 95020, 408-848-4735 (Fax: 408-848-4801). Hours: 8AM-5PM. Enrollment: 4555. Records go back to 1919. Degrees granted: Associate.

Attendance and degree information available by phone, fax, mail. Search requires name plus SSN. Also helpful: date of birth, exact years of attendance. There is no fee. Expedited service available for $5.00.

Glendale Community College, Office of Admissions & Records, 1500 N Verdugo Rd, Glendale, CA 91208, 818-240-1000 (Fax: 818-549-9436). Hours: 8AM-8PM M-Th, 9AM-Noon F. Enrollment: 14149. Records go back to 1927. Alumni records are maintained here also. Call 818-240-1000 X5126. Degrees granted: Associate.

Attendance and degree information available by fax, mail. Search requires name plus SSN, date of birth, approximate years of attendance, signed release. Fee is $5.00. Expedited service available for $5.00.

Golden Gate Baptist Theological Seminary, Registrar Box 97, 201 Seminary Dr, Mill Valley, CA 94941-3197, 415-388-8080 X209 (Fax: 415-383-0723). Hours: 8:30AM-4:30PM. Enrollment: 1500. Records go back to 1944. Alumni records are maintained here at the same phone number. Degrees granted: Masters; Doctorate. Special programs- Ethnic Leadership Development, 415-388-8080 X280: Continuing Education, 415-388-8080 X203. Adverse incident record source- Student Affairs, 415-388-8080 X292.

Attendance and degree information available by phone, fax, mail. Search requires name only. Also helpful: SSN, date of birth, exact years of attendance. There is no fee.

Golden Gate University, Records Office, 536 Mission St, San Francisco, CA 94105-2968, 415-442-7211 (Fax: 415-442-7807). Hours: 9AM-6:30PM M-Th; 9AM-5:30PM F. Enrollment: 4172. Records go back to 1900. Alumni Records Office: 562 Mission St, San Francisco, CA 94105-2968. Degrees granted: Associate; Bachelors; Masters; Doctorate. Special programs- LLB, J.D., 415-442-6600. Adverse incident record source- Dean of Student Services, 415-442-7285.

Attendance and degree information available by phone, mail. Search requires name plus SSN, approximate years of attendance. Also helpful: date of birth, exact years of attendance. There is no fee.

Golden West College, Registrar, 15744 Golden West St, PO Box 2710, Huntington Beach, CA 92647-0710, 714-895-8128 (Fax: 714-895-8960). Hours: 8AM-7PM M-Th; 8AM-3PM F. Enrollment: 13094. Records go back to 1966. Alumni records are maintained here also. Call 714-895-8315. Degrees granted: Associate. Special programs- Office of Instruction, 714-895-8134. Adverse incident record source- Safety/Security, 714-895-8924.

Attendance and degree information available by phone, fax, mail. Search requires name plus SSN, date of birth. Also helpful: exact years of attendance. There is no fee.

Graduate Theological Union, Registrar, 2400 Ridge Rd, Berkeley, CA 94709, 510-649-2462 (Fax: 510-649-1730). Hours: 9AM-5PM. Enrollment: 420. Records go back to 1962. Degrees granted: Masters; Doctorate.

Attendance and degree information available by phone, fax, mail. Search requires name plus exact years of attendance. Also helpful: SSN, date of birth. There is no fee.

Grossmont College, Registrar, 8800 Grossmont College Dr, El Cajon, CA 92020, 619-465-1700 (Fax: 619-461-3396). Hours: 8AM-7PM M-Th; 8AM-3PM F. Enrollment: 15000. Records go back to 1935. Alumni records are maintained here also. Call 619-465-1700 X169. Degrees granted: Associate.

Attendance and degree information available by mail. Search requires name plus signed release. Also helpful: SSN, date of birth, exact years of attendance. Fee is $3.00. Expedited service available for $5.00.

Hartnell College, Registrar, 156 Homestead Ave, Salinas, CA 93901, 408-755-6711 (Fax: 408-759-6014). Hours: 8AM-7PM M-Th; 8AM-5PM F. Enrollment: 7550. Records go back to 1920. Degrees granted: Associate.

Attendance information available by written request only. Search requires name plus SSN, date of birth, exact years of attendance, signed release. There is no fee.

Degree information available by phone, fax, mail. Search requires name plus SSN, date of birth, exact years of attendance. There is no fee.

Harvey Mudd College, Registrar, 301 E 12th St, Claremont, CA 91711, 909-621-8090 (Fax: 909-621-8494). Hours: 8AM-Noon, 1-5PM. Enrollment: 670. Transcripts available since founding; other records for past 10 years. Alumni records are maintained here also. Call 909-621-8560. Degrees granted: Bachelors; Masters.

Attendance and degree information available by phone, fax, mail. Search requires name only. Also helpful: exact years of attendance. There is no fee.

Heald Business College-Concord, Registrar, 2150 John Glenn Dr Ste 100, Concord, CA 94520, 510-827-1300 (Fax: 510-827-1486). Hours: 7:30AM-6PM. Enrollment: 500. Records go back to 1970. Degrees granted: Associate.

Attendance and degree information available by phone, fax, mail. Search requires name plus SSN, approximate years of attendance. Also helpful: date of birth, exact years of attendance. There is no fee.

Heald Business College-Fresno, Registrar, 255 W Bullard Ave, Fresno, CA 93704, 209-438-4222 (Fax: 209-438-6368). Hours: 8AM-7PM. Degrees granted: Associate.

Attendance and degree information available by phone, fax, mail. Search requires name plus SSN, approximate years of attendance. There is no fee.

Heald Business College-Hayward, Registrar, 777 Southland Dr, Suite 210, Hayward, CA 94545, 510-784-7000 (Fax: 510-784-7050). Hours: 8AM-5PM. Records go back to 1863. Degrees granted: Associate.

Attendance and degree information available by phone, fax, mail. Search requires name plus SSN. There is no fee.

Heald Business College-Oakland, Registrar, 1000 Broadway, Ste 290, Oakland, CA 94607, 510-444-0201 (Fax: 510-839-2084). Hours: 8AM-6PM. Records go back to 1975. Degrees granted: Associate.

Attendance and degree information available by phone, fax, mail. Search requires name plus SSN, approximate years of attendance. There is no fee.

Heald Business College-Sacramento, Registrar, 2910 Prospect Park Dr, Rancho Cordova, CA 95670, 916-638-1616 (Fax: 916-638-1580). Hours: 7:30AM-8PM. Enrollment: 32. Records go back to 1950. Degrees granted: Associate. Adverse incident record source- Corporate Office, 415-864-5060.

Attendance and degree information available by phone, fax, mail. Search requires name plus SSN, approximate years of attendance. There is no fee.

Heald Business College-Salinas, Registrar, 1333 Schilling Pl, PO Box 3167, Salinas, CA 93901, 408-443-1700 (Fax: 408-443-1050). Hours: 8AM-5PM. Enrollment: 500. Records go back to 1992. Alumni records are maintained here at the same phone number. Degrees granted: Associate. Adverse incident record source- Director, 408-443-1700.

Attendance information available by phone, fax, mail. Search requires name only. Also helpful: SSN, date of birth, exact years of attendance. There is no fee.

Degree information available by phone, fax, mail. Search requires name plus approximate years of attendance. Also helpful: SSN, date of birth, exact years of attendance. There is no fee.

Heald Business College-San Francisco, Registrar, 1453 Mission St, San Francisco, CA 94103, 415-673-5500 (Fax: 415-626-1404). Hours: 8AM-5PM. Enrollment: 303. Records go back to 1965. Degrees granted: Associate. Special programs- Hospitality & Tourism. Adverse incident record source- Dean's Office

Attendance and degree information available by phone, fax, mail. Search requires name plus SSN, date of birth. Also helpful: exact years of attendance. Fee is $2.00.

Heald Business College-San Jose, Registrar, 2665 N First St Ste 110, San Jose, CA 95134, 408-955-9555 (Fax: 408-955-9580). Hours: 8AM-5PM. Records go back to 1970. Degrees granted: Associate.

Attendance and degree information available by phone. Search requires name plus SSN, approximate years of attendance. There is no fee.

Heald Business College-Santa Rosa, Registrar, 2425 Mendocino Ave, Santa Rosa, CA 95403, 707-525-1300 (Fax: 707-527-0251). Hours: 9AM-4:30PM. Degrees granted: Associate.

Attendance and degree information available by phone, fax, mail. Search requires name plus SSN. Also helpful: exact years of attendance. There is no fee.

Heald Business College-Stockton, Registrar, 1605 E March Ln, Stockton, CA 95210, 209-477-1114 (Fax: 209-477-2739). Hours: 7:30AM-7PM. Records go back to 1863. Degrees granted: Associate.

Attendance and degree information available by fax, mail. Search requires name plus SSN, signed release. There is no fee.

Heald Business College-Walnut Creek, Dean of Instruction, 2150 John Glenn Dr, Ste 100, Concord, CA 94520, 510-827-1300 (Fax: 510-827-1486). Enrollment: 335. Records go back to 1863. Degrees granted: Associate. Special programs- Arts: Science. Adverse incident record source- Department of Security.

Attendance and degree information available by phone, mail. Search requires name plus SSN, exact years of attendance. There is no fee.

Heald Institute of Technology, Office of the Dean of Instruction, 684 El Paso de Saratoga, San Jose, CA 95130, 408-295-8000 (Fax: 408-934-7777). Enrollment: 600. Records go back to 1863. Degrees granted: Associate. Adverse incident record source- Department of Student Affairs.

Attendance and degree information available by mail. Search requires name plus SSN, exact years of attendance, signed release. There is no fee.

Heald Institute of Technology-Hayward, Registrar, 24301 Southland Dr Ste 500, Hayward, CA 94545, 510-783-2100 (Fax: 510-783-3287). Hours: 8AM-4:30PM. Records go back to 1920. Degrees granted: Associate.

Attendance and degree information available by phone, fax, mail. Search requires name plus SSN. There is no fee.

Heald Institute of Technology-Martinez, Registrar, 2860 Howe Rd, Martinez, CA 94553, 510-228-9000 (Fax: 510-228-6991). Hours: 8AM-5PM. Enrollment: 475. Records go back to 1985. Degrees granted: Associate.

Attendance and degree information available by phone, fax, mail. Search requires name plus SSN, exact years of attendance. There is no fee.

Heald Institute of Technology-Sacramento, Registrar, 2910 Prospect Park Dr, Rancho Cordova, CA 95670, 916-638-1616 (Fax: 916-638-1580). Hours: 8AM-5PM. Enrollment: 32. Records go back to 1868. Degrees granted: Associate.

Attendance and degree information available by fax, mail. Search requires name plus SSN, date of birth, exact years of attendance. There is no fee.

Heald Institute of Technology-San Francisco, Registrar, 1453 Mission St, San Francisco, CA 94103, 415-673-5500 (Fax: 415-626-1404). Hours: 8AM-5PM. Records go back to 1863. Degrees granted: Associate.

Attendance and degree information available by phone, fax, mail. Search requires name plus SSN, date of birth, exact years of attendance. There is no fee.

Heald Institute of Technology-San Jose, Registrar, 2665 N 1st St, San Jose, CA 95134, 408-955-9555 (Fax: 408-955-9580). Hours: 8AM-5PM. Records go back to 1863. Degrees granted: Associate.

Attendance and degree information available by fax, mail. Search requires name plus SSN, signed release. There is no fee.

Hebrew Union College-Jewish Institute of Religion, Registrar, 3077 University Ave, Los Angeles, CA 90007, 213-749-3424 (Fax: 213-747-6128). Hours: 8AM-5PM. Enrollment: 68. Records go back to 1972. Alumni records are maintained here also. Call 213-749-3424. Degrees granted: Bachelors; Masters; Doctorate. Special programs- U of S CA Judaic Studies Dept, 212-749-3424. Adverse incident record source- Registrar's Office, 213-749-3424 .

Attendance and degree information available by phone, fax, mail. Search requires name only. Also helpful: SSN, exact years of attendance. There is no fee.

Holy Names College, Registrar, 3500 Mountain Blvd, Oakland, CA 94619-9989, 510-436-1133 (Fax: 510-436-1137). Hours: 9:30AM-3:30PM. Enrollment: 970. Records go back to 1868. Alumni records are maintained here also. Call 510-436-1240. Degrees granted: Bachelors; Masters.

Attendance information available by phone, fax, mail. Search requires name plus SSN, approximate years of attendance. Also helpful: date of birth, exact years of attendance. There is no fee.

Degree information available by phone, fax, mail. Search requires name plus approximate years of attendance. Also helpful: SSN, date of birth, exact years of attendance. There is no fee.

Humboldt State University, Registrar, Arcata, CA 95521, 707-826-4402 (Fax: 707-826-6194). Hours: 9AM-4PM. Enrollment: 6600. Records go back to 1922. Alumni records are maintained here also. Call 707-826-5101. Degrees granted: Bachelors; Masters. Adverse incident record source- Registrar, 707-826-4402.

Attendance and degree information available by phone, fax, mail. Search requires name plus SSN. Also helpful: date of birth. There is no fee.

Humphrey's College, Registrar, 6650 Inglewood St, Stockton, CA 95207, 209-478-0800. Hours: 7:30AM-8:30PM M-Th, 8AM-5PM F. Records go back to 1896. Alumni records are maintained here at the same phone number. Degrees granted: Bachelors.

Attendance and degree information available by mail. Search requires name plus SSN, date of birth, exact years of attendance, signed release. There is no fee.

ITT Technical Institute, Registrar, 7100 Knott Ave Plaza, Buena Park, CA 90620-1374, 714-535-3700 (Fax: 714-535-1802). Hours: 8AM-5PM. Enrollment: 560. Records go back to 1983. Alumni Records Office: ITT Technical Institute, 9511 Angola Ct, Indianapolis, IN 46268. Degrees granted: Associate.

Attendance and degree information available by phone, fax, mail. Search requires name plus SSN. There is no fee.

ITT Technical Institute, Registrar, 2035 E 223rd St, Carson, CA 90810-1698, 310-835-5595 (Fax: 310-835-8986). Hours: 8AM-5PM M-W,F; 11AM-8PM Th. Enrollment: 500. Records go back to 1989. Alumni Records Office: ITT Technical Institute, 9511 Angola Ct, Indianapolis, IN 46268. Degrees granted: Associate.

Attendance and degree information available by phone, fax, mail. Search requires name plus SSN, exact years of attendance. There is no fee.

ITT Technical Institute, Registrar, 9700 Goethe Rd, Sacramento, CA 95827-5281, 916-366-3900 (Fax: 916-366-9225). Hours: 8AM-5PM. Records go back to 1984. Degrees granted: Associate; Bachelors.

Attendance and degree information available by phone, fax, mail. Search requires name only. There is no fee.

ITT Technical Institute, Registrar, 630 E Brier Dr Ste 150, San Bernardino, CA 92408-2800, 909-889-3800 (Fax: 909-888-6970). Hours: 8AM-5PM. Records go back to 1907. Alumni Records Office: ITT Technical Institute, 9511 Angola Ct, Indianapolis, IN 46268. Degrees granted: Associate; Bachelors.

Attendance information available by mail. Search requires name plus exact years of attendance, signed release. Also helpful: SSN, date of birth. There is no fee.

Degree information available by phone, mail. Search requires name plus exact years of attendance. Also helpful: SSN, date of birth. There is no fee.

ITT Technical Institute, Registrar, 9680 Granite Ridge Dr, San Diego, CA 92123-2662, 619-571-8500 (Fax: 619-571-1277). Hours: 7AM-6PM. Records go back to 1980. Alumni Records Office: ITT Technical Institute, 9511 Angola Ct, Indianapolis, IN 46268. Degrees granted: Associate; Bachelors.

Attendance and degree information available by phone, fax, mail. Search requires name plus SSN, exact years of attendance. There is no fee.

ITT Technical Institute, Registrar, 6723 Van Nuys Blvd, Van Nuys, CA 91405-4620, 818-989-1177 (Fax: 818-989-2093). Hours: 8AM-5PM. Records go back to 1985. Alumni Records Office: ITT Technical Institute, 9511 Angola Ct, Indianapolis, IN 46268. Degrees granted: Associate.

Attendance and degree information available by phone, fax, mail. Search requires name only. Also helpful: SSN. There is no fee.

ITT Technical Institute, Registrar, 1530 W Cameron Ave, West Covina, CA 91790-2767, 818-960-8681 (Fax: 818-337-5271). Hours: 8AM-5PM. Records go back to 1982. Alumni Records Office: ITT Technical Institute, 9511 Angola Ct, Indianapolis, IN 46268. Degrees granted: Associate; Bachelors.

Attendance and degree information available by phone, fax, mail. Search requires name plus SSN, exact years of attendance. There is no fee.

Imperial Valley College, Registrar, PO Box 158, Imperial, CA 92251, 619-352-8320 (Fax: 619-355-2663). Enrollment: 5000. Alumni records are maintained here at the same phone number. Degrees granted: Associate.

Attendance and degree information available by phone, mail. Search requires name plus SSN. Also helpful: date of birth, exact years of attendance. There is no fee.

Institute of Transpersonal Psychology, Registrar, 744 San Antonio Rd, Palo Alto, CA 94303, 415-493-4430 (Fax: 415-493-6835). Enrollment: 325. Records go back to 1975. Alumni records are maintained here at the same phone number. Degrees granted: Masters; Doctorate. Adverse incident record source- Admissions, 415-493-4430.

Attendance and degree information available by phone, fax, mail. Search requires name only. Also helpful: SSN, date of birth, exact years of attendance. There is no fee.

Interior Designers Institute, Registrar, 1061 Camelback Rd, Newport Beach, CA 92660, 714-675-4451. Hours: 8AM-5PM. Enrollment: 248. Records go back to 1961. Degrees granted: Associate; Bachelors.

Attendance and degree information available by mail. Search requires name plus exact years of attendance, signed release. There is no fee.

Irvine Valley College, Admissions & Records, Transcript Unit, 5500 Irvine Center Dr, Irvine, CA 92620, 714-559-3461 (Fax: 714-559-3443). Hours: 9AM-7PM M-Th; 9AM-3PM F. Enrollment: 10284. Records go back to 1969. Alumni records are maintained here also. Call 714-559-3216. Degrees granted: Associate.

Attendance information available by fax, mail. Search requires name plus SSN, date of birth, signed release. Also helpful: approximate years of attendance. Fee is $3.00. Expedited service available for $8.00.

Degree information available by fax, mail. Search requires name plus SSN, date of birth, signed release. Fee is $3.00. Expedite service available for $8.00.

Jesuit School of Theology at Berkeley, Registrar, 1735 LeRoy Ave, Berkeley, CA 94709-1193, 510-841-8804 (Fax: 510-649-1730). Hours: 8:30AM-5PM. Enrollment: 190. Records go back to 1969. Degrees granted: Masters; Doctorate.

Attendance and degree information available by phone, fax, mail. Search requires name plus exact years of attendance. Also helpful: SSN, date of birth. There is no fee.

John F. Kennedy University, Registrar, 12 Altarinda Rd, Orinda, CA 94563, 510-254-0200 (Fax: 510-254-6949). Hours: 10AM-6PM. Records go back to 1964. Degrees granted: Bachelors; Masters.

Attendance and degree information available by phone, fax, mail. Search requires name only. Also helpful: SSN, exact years of attendance. There is no fee.

Kelsey-Jenney College, Registrar, 201 "A" St, San Diego, CA 92101, 619-549-5070 (Fax: 619-549-2027). Hours: 7:30AM-9:40PM. Enrollment: 950. Records go back to 1960. Degrees granted: Associate.

Attendance and degree information available by fax, mail. Search requires name plus SSN, approximate years of attendance, signed release. Also helpful: date of birth, exact years of attendance. There is no fee.

Kings River Community College, Registrar, 995 N Reed Ave, Reedley, CA 93654, 209-638-3641. Hours: 8AM-4PM. Records go back to 1926. Degrees granted: Associate. Adverse incident record source- Dean of Students: Campus Police

Attendance and degree information available by phone, mail. Search requires name plus SSN. Also helpful: date of birth, exact years of attendance. There is no fee.

L.I.F.E Bible College, Registrar, 1100 Covina Blvd, San Dimas, CA 91773, 909-599-5433 X304 (Fax: 909-599-6690). Hours: 8AM-5PM. Records go back to 1930. Degrees granted: Associate; Bachelors.

Attendance and degree information available by phone, fax, mail. Search requires name plus SSN, date of birth, approximate years of attendance. There is no fee.

La Sierra University, Registrar, 4700 Pierce St, Riverside, CA 92515, 909-785-2006 (Fax: 909-785-2447). Hours: 8:30AM-4:30PM M-Th; 8:30AM-Noon F. Enrollment: 1500. Records go back to 1922. Alumni records are maintained here at the same phone number. Degrees granted: Associate; Bachelors; Masters; Doctorate. Adverse incident record source- Student Life.

Attendance and degree information available by fax, mail. Search requires name plus signed release. Also helpful: SSN, date of birth, exact years of attendance. There is no fee.

Lake Tahoe Community College, Registrar, One College Dr, South Lake Tahoe, CA 96150, 916-541-4660 X211 (Fax: 916-541-7852). Hours: 8AM-5PM. Enrollment: 2700. Records go back to 1976. Alumni records are maintained here also. Call 916-541-4660. Degrees granted: Associate. Special programs- Intensive Spanish Summer Institute, 916-541-4660 X252.

Attendance and degree information available by phone, fax, mail. Search requires name plus SSN, date of birth. Also helpful: exact years of attendance. There is no fee.

Laney College, Registrar, 900 Fallon St, Oakland, CA 94607, 510-464-3122. Hours: 9AM-7PM M-T, 9AM-3PM W-F. Records go back to 1940. Degrees granted: Associate.

Attendance and degree information available by mail. Search requires name plus SSN, date of birth, exact years of attendance, signed release. There is no fee.

Las Positas College, Admissions & Records, 3033 Collier Canyon Rd, Livermore, CA 94550, 510-373-5800 (Fax: 510-606-6437). Hours: 9AM-7:30PM M-Th, 9AM-5PM F. Records go back to 1960. Degrees granted: Associate.

Attendance and degree information available by fax, mail. Search requires name plus SSN, signed release. There is no fee.

Lassen College, Registrar, PO Box 3000, Susanville, CA 96130, 916-257-6181 (Fax: 916-257-8964). Hours: 8AM-4:30PM. Records go back to 1927. Degrees granted: Associate.

Attendance and degree information available by phone, fax, mail. Search requires name plus SSN, exact years of attendance. Also helpful: date of birth. There is no fee.

Life Chiropractic College-West, Registrar, 2005 Via Barrett, San Lorenzo, CA 94580, 510-276-9013 (Fax: 510-276-4893). Hours: 8AM-5PM. Records go back to 1979. Alumni records are maintained here at the same phone number. Degrees granted: Doctorate. Adverse incident record source- Dean of Students, 510-276-9013 X251.

Attendance and degree information available by fax, mail. Search requires name plus signed release. There is no fee.

Lincoln University, Registrar, 281 Masonic Ave, San Francisco, CA 94118, 415-221-1212 (Fax: 415-387-9730). Hours: 9AM-5PM. Records go back to 1926. Degrees granted: Bachelors; Masters.

Attendance and degree information available by phone, fax, mail. Search requires name plus date of birth, approximate years of attendance. Also helpful: exact years of attendance. There is no fee.

Loma Linda University, Office of University Records, Loma Linda, CA 92350, 909-824-4508 (Fax: 909-824-4879). Hours: 8:30AM-4PM M,T; 9AM-4PM W; 9AM-6PM Th; 8:30AM-2PM F. Enrollment: 3000. Records go back to 1905. Alumni records are maintained here at the same phone number. Degrees granted: Associate; Bachelors; Masters; Doctorate.

Attendance and degree information available by fax, mail. Search requires name plus SSN, signed release. Also helpful: date of birth, exact years of attendance. There is no fee.

Long Beach City College, Registrar, 4901 E Carson St, Long Beach, CA 90808, 310-420-4139 (Fax: 310-420-4118). Hours: 8AM-7PM M-Th, 8AM-4:30PM F. Records go back to 1927. Alumni records are maintained here also. Call 310-420-4203. Degrees granted: Associate. Adverse incident record source- Dean of Students, 310-420-4155.

Attendance and degree information available by phone, mail. Search requires name plus SSN, date of birth, approximate years of attendance. Fee is $3.00.

Los Angeles City College, Registrar, 855 N Vermont Ave, Los Angeles, CA 90029, 213-953-4448 (Fax: 213-953-4536). Hours: 9AM-7PM. Records go back to 1990. Alumni records are maintained here also. Call 213-953-4415. Degrees granted: Associate. Adverse incident record source- Campus Police, 213-953-4311.

Attendance and degree information available by phone, fax, mail. Search requires name plus SSN, approximate years of attendance. There is no fee.

Los Angeles College of Chiropractic, Registrar, 16200 E Amber Valley Dr, Whittier, CA 90604, 310-902-3380 (Fax: 310-947-5724). Hours: 8AM-5PM. Records go back to 1911. Alumni records are maintained here also. Call 310-947-8755. Degrees granted: Bachelors; Doctorate. Adverse incident record source- Academic Dean, 310-947-8755 X313.

Attendance and degree information available by mail. Search requires name plus SSN, date of birth, approximate years of attendance, signed release. Fee is $10.00. Expedited service available for $15.00.

Los Angeles Harbor College, Registrar, 1111 Figueroa Pl, Wilmington, CA 90744, 310-522-8216 (Fax: 310-834-1882). Hours: 9AM-7PM M-Th; 9AM-3PM F. Enrollment: 8000. Records go back to 1949. Degrees granted: Associate.

Attendance and degree information available by mail. Search requires name plus SSN, date of birth, exact years of attendance, signed release. Fee is $1.00. Expedited service available for $5.00.

Los Angeles Mission College, Registrar, 13356 Eldridge Ave, Sylmar, CA 91342-3245, 818-364-7663 (Fax: 818-364-7755). Hours: 9AM-7PM. Records go back to 1975. Degrees granted: Associate.

Attendance and degree information available by fax, mail. Search requires name plus SSN, date of birth, approximate years of attendance, signed release. There is no fee.

Los Angeles Pierce College, Registrar, 6201 Winnetka Ave, Woodland Hills, CA 91371, 818-347-5553 (Fax: 818-710-9844). Hours: 8:30AM-8:30PM M-Th, 8:30AM-4PM F. Records go back to 1940. Alumni records are maintained here at the same phone number. Degrees granted: Associate. Adverse incident record source- Academic, 818-347-6448.

Attendance and degree information available by phone, fax, mail. Search requires name plus SSN, approximate years of attendance. There is no fee.

Los Angeles Southwest College, Admission Office, 1600 W Imperial Hwy, Los Angeles, CA 90047, 213-241-5320 (Fax: 213-241-5325). Hours: 8:30AM-8PM M-Th. Enrollment: 5000. Records go back to 1967. Degrees granted: Associate. Adverse incident record source- Campus Police, 213-241-5311.

Attendance information available by fax, mail. Search requires name plus SSN, date of birth, signed release. Also helpful: exact years of attendance. Fee is $1.00. Expedited service available for $5.00.

Degree information available by mail. Search requires name plus date of birth, signed release. Also helpful: SSN, exact years of attendance. Fee is $1.00. Expedite service available for $5.00.

Los Angeles Trade-Technical College, Registrar, 400 W Washington Blvd, Los Angeles, CA 90015, 213-744-9420 (Fax: 213-744-9425). Hours: 8:30AM-8PM M-Th; 8:30AM-4PM F. Enrollment: 13000. Records go back to 1928. Alumni records are maintained here also. Call 213-744-9003. Degrees granted: Associate.

Attendance information available by fax, mail. Search requires name plus SSN, approximate years of attendance, signed release. Also helpful: date of birth, exact years of attendance. First two transcripts/verifications free. Additional ones are $1.00 each.

Degree information available by fax, mail. Search requires name plus SSN, signed release. Also helpful: date of birth, exact years of attendance. First two transcripts/verifications free. Additional ones are $1.00 each.

Los Angeles Valley College, Registrar, 5800 Fulton Ave, Van Nuys, CA 91401, 818-781-1200 X255 (Fax: 818-781-4672). Hours: 8:30AM-8:30PM M-Th, 8:30AM-4PM F. Records go back to 1940. Degrees granted: Associate.

Attendance information available by mail. Search requires name plus SSN, date of birth, approximate years of attendance, signed release. Fee is $1.00.

Degree information available by fax, mail. Search requires name plus SSN, date of birth, approximate years of attendance, signed release. Fee is $1.00.

Los Medanos College, Registrar, 2700 E Leland Rd, Pittsburg, CA 94565, 510-439-2181 (Fax: 510-427-1599). Hours: 9AM-8PM M-Th; 9AM-3PM F. Enrollment: 7800. Records go back to 1974. Degrees granted: Associate.

Attendance and degree information available by phone, fax, mail. Search requires name only. Also helpful: SSN, date of birth. There is no fee.

Louise Salinger Academy of Fashion, Registrar, 101 Jessie St, San Francisco, CA 94105-3593, 415-974-6666 (Fax: 415-982-0113). Hours: 9AM-5PM. Enrollment: 100. Records go back to 1939. Degrees granted: Associate; Bachelors. Special programs- Fashion Design and Merchandising.

Attendance and degree information available by phone, fax, mail. Search requires name only. Also helpful: SSN, date of birth, exact years of attendance. There is no fee.

Loyola Marymount University, Registrar, Loyola Blvd at W 80th St, Los Angeles, CA 90045, 310-338-2740 (Fax: 310-338-4466). Hours: 8AM-5PM. Degrees granted: Bachelors; Masters.

Attendance and degree information available by phone, fax, mail. Search requires name only. Also helpful: SSN, date of birth, exact years of attendance. There is no fee.

Marin Community College, Admissions and Records Office, 1800 Ignacia Blvd, Navato, CA 94949, 415-883-2211. Enrollment: 8300. Records go back to 1926. Alumni records are maintained here at the same phone number. Degrees granted: Associate.

Attendance and degree information available by written request only. Search requires name only. There is no fee.

Marymount College, Registrar, 30800 Palos Verdes Dr E, Rancho Palos Verdes, CA 90274-6299, 310-377-5501 X214 (Fax: 310-377-6223). Hours: 8AM-5PM. Records go back to 1972. Degrees granted: Associate. Adverse incident record source- Ofc of Student Development, 310-377-5501 X254.

Attendance and degree information available by phone, fax, mail. Search requires name plus approximate years of attendance. Also helpful: SSN, date of birth, exact years of attendance. There is no fee.

Master's College (The), Registrar's Office #42, 21726 Placerita Canyon Rd, Santa Clarita, CA 91321-1200, 805-259-3540 X317 (Fax: 805-288-1037). Hours: 8:30AM-5PM. Enrollment: 850. Records go back to 1927. Alumni records are maintained here at the same phone number. Degrees granted: Bachelors; Masters. Adverse incident record source- Campus Security, 805-259-3540 X344.

Attendance and degree information available by phone, fax, mail. Search requires name only. Also helpful: SSN, date of birth, exact years of attendance. There is no fee.

Masters College (The), Registrar, PO Box 221450, Newhall, CA 91322, 805-259-3540 X317 (Fax: 805-288-1037). Enrollment: 800. Formerly Los Angeles Baptist College Records go back to 1927. Alumni records are maintained here at the same phone number. Degrees granted: Bachelors; Masters. Adverse incident record source- Security.

Attendance and degree information available by phone, mail. Search requires name plus SSN, exact years of attendance. There is no fee.

Mendocino College, Registrar, PO Box 3000, Ukiah, CA 95482, 707-468-3103 (Fax: 707-468-3120). Hours: 8AM-5PM. Enrollment: 4100. Records go back to 1973. Degrees granted: Associate. Adverse incident record source- Student Services, 707-468-3105.

Attendance and degree information available by phone, fax, mail. Search requires name plus SSN, date of birth. Also helpful: exact years of attendance. There is no fee.

Menlo College, Office of the Registrar, 1000 El Camino Real, Atherton, CA 94027-4185, 415-688-3764 (Fax: 415-324-2347). Hours: 9AM-5PM. Enrollment: 440. Records go back to 1930. Alumni Records Office: c/o External Relations, 1000 El Camino Real, Atherton, CA 94027-4185. Degrees granted: Associate; Bachelors. Adverse incident record source- Office of Student Life, 415-688-3751: Security & Facilities, 415-688-3714

Attendance and degree information available by phone, mail. Search requires name plus SSN, exact years of attendance. There is no fee.

Mennonite Brethren Biblical Seminary, Registrar, 4824 E Butler Ave, Fresno, CA 93727-5097, 209-452-1723 (Fax: 209-251-7212). Hours: 8AM-5PM. Enrollment: 175. Records go back to 1955. Alumni records are maintained here at the same phone number. Degrees granted: Masters.

Attendance and degree information available by phone, fax, mail. Search requires name plus SSN. Also helpful: date of birth, exact years of attendance. There is no fee.

Merced College, Registrar, 3600 M St, Merced, CA 95340, 209-384-6188 (Fax: 209-384-6339). Hours: 8AM-5PM. Records go back to 1965. Degrees granted: Associate. Adverse incident record source- Dean's Office, 209-384-6191   .

Attendance and degree information available by phone, fax, mail. Search requires name plus SSN. There is no fee.

Mills College, Registrar, Oakland, CA 94613, 510-430-2083 (Fax: 510-430-3314). Hours: 9AM-4PM. Enrollment: 1165. Records go back to 1871. Alumni records are maintained here also. Call 510-430-2110. Degrees granted: Bachelors; Masters. Certification: Post Bac.

Attendance information available by phone, fax, mail. Search requires name plus exact years of attendance. Also helpful: SSN, date of birth, approximate years of attendance. There is no fee.

Degree information available by phone, fax, mail. Search requires name plus exact years of attendance. Also helpful: date of birth, approximate years of attendance. There is no fee.

Mira Costa College, Registrar, One Barnard Dr, Oceanside, CA 92056, 619-757-2121 (Fax: 619-721-8760). Hours: 8AM-7PM M-Th; 8AM-4:30PM F. Enrollment: 8432. Records go back to 1937. Alumni records are maintained here also. Call 619-757-2121 X259. Degrees granted: Associate. Adverse incident record source- Dick Robertson, 619-757-2121 X295.

Attendance and degree information available by mail. Search requires name plus SSN, date of birth, exact years of attendance, signed release. There is no fee.

Mission College, Registrar, 3000 Mission College Blvd, Santa Clara, CA 95054, 408-748-2700 (Fax: 408-980-8980). Hours: 9:30AM-6:30PM M-Th, 9:30AM-1PM F. Enrollment: 9390. Degrees granted: Associate.

Attendance and degree information available by phone, fax, mail. Search requires name plus SSN, date of birth, approximate years of attendance. There is no fee.

Modesto Junior College, Registrar, 435 College Ave, Modesto, CA 95350, 209-575-6470 (Fax: 209-575-6666). Hours: 8AM-5PM. Enrollment: 13500. Records go back to 1921. Alumni records are maintained here also. Call 209-575-6308. Degrees granted: Associate. Adverse incident record source- Dr. Wilma McLeod, 209-575-6060.

Attendance information available by phone, fax, mail. Search requires name plus SSN. Also helpful: date of birth, exact years of attendance. There is no fee.

Degree information available by mail. Search requires name plus SSN. Also helpful: date of birth, exact years of attendance. There is no fee.

Monterey Institute of International Studies, Registrar, 425 Van Buren, Monterey, CA 93940, 408-647-4121 (Fax: 408-647-4199). Hours: 8:30AM-5PM. Enrollment: 720. Records go back to 1959. Alumni records are maintained here also. Call 408-647-4130. Degrees granted: Bachelors; Masters.

Attendance and degree information available by phone, fax, mail. Search requires name only. Also helpful: SSN, date of birth, exact years of attendance. There is no fee.

Monterey Peninsula College, Admissions & Records, 980 Fremont St, Monterey, CA 93940, 408-646-4002 (Fax: 408-655-2627). Hours: 8AM-6:30PM M-Th; 8AM-2:30PM F. Enrollment: 8750. Records go back to 1947. Degrees granted: Associate. Adverse incident record source- Campus Security, 408-646-4099.

Attendance and degree information available by phone, fax, mail. Search requires name only. Also helpful: SSN, date of birth, exact years of attendance. Fee is $2.00. Expedited service available for $2.00.

Moorpark College, Registrar, 7075 Campus Rd, Moorpark, CA 93021, 805-378-1429 (Fax: 805-378-1583). Hours: 7:30AM-7PM M-Th; 7:30AM-5PM F. Enrollment: 10220. Records go back to 1967. Degrees granted: Associate.

Attendance and degree information available by fax, mail. Search requires name plus SSN, date of birth, signed release. Also helpful: exact years of attendance. Fee is $3.00. Expedited service available for $5.00.

Mount San Jacinto College, Registrar, 1499 N State St, San Jacinto, CA 92583, 909-487-6752 (Fax: 909-654-6738). Hours: 8AM-8PM M-Th, 8AM-4:30PM F. Enrollment: 6000. Records go back to 1963. Degrees granted: Associate.

Attendance information available by mail. Search requires name plus SSN, exact years of attendance, signed release. Also helpful: date of birth. There is no fee.

Degree information available by mail. Search requires name plus SSN, exact years of attendance, signed release. There is no fee.

Mount St. Mary's College, Registrar, 12001 Chalon Rd, Los Angeles, CA 90049, 310-471-9560 (Fax: 310-471-

9566). Hours: 8:30AM-4:30PM. Records go back to 1925. Degrees granted: Associate; Bachelors; Masters.

Attendance and degree information available by phone, fax, mail. Search requires name plus exact years of attendance. Also helpful: SSN, date of birth. Fee is $5.00.

Mount St. Mary's College, (Doheny), Registrar, 10 Chester Pl, Los Angeles, CA 90007, 213-746-0450. Hours: 8:30AM-4PM. Enrollment: 2000. Records go back to 1949. Alumni Records Office: 12001 Chalon, Los Angeles, CA 90049. Degrees granted: Associate; Bachelors; Masters.

Attendance and degree information available by mail. Search requires name plus SSN, date of birth, signed release. Also helpful: exact years of attendance. There is no fee.

Mt. San Antonio College, Director, Admissions & Records, 1100 N Grand Ave, Walnut, CA 91789, 909-594-5611 X4419 (Fax: 909-468-3932). Hours: 8AM-8PM M-Th, 8AM-4:30PM F. Enrollment: 22330. Records go back to 1947. Alumni records are maintained here at the same phone number. Degrees granted: Associate.

Attendance information available by fax, mail. Search requires name plus SSN, date of birth, signed release. Also helpful: exact years of attendance. Fee is $2.00.

Degree information available by phone, fax, mail. Search requires name plus SSN, date of birth. Also helpful: exact years of attendance. There is no fee.

Napa Valley College, Admissions & Records, 2277 Napa-Vallejo Hwy, Napa, CA 94558, 707-253-3000 (Fax: 707-253-3064). Hours: 7:30AM-8PM M-Th; 7:30AM-5PM F. Enrollment: 8000. Records go back to 1942. Alumni records are maintained here at the same phone number. Degrees granted: Associate; Associate of Arts, Associate of Science.

Attendance and degree information available by mail. Search requires name plus SSN, date of birth, exact years of attendance. There is no fee.

National Education Center, (Skadron), Registrar, 825 E Hospitality Lane, San Bernardino, CA 92408, 909-885-3896 (Fax: 909-885-2396). Hours: 7:30AM-5PM. Records go back to 1970. Degrees granted: Associate.

Attendance and degree information available by phone, fax, mail. Search requires name plus SSN, approximate years of attendance. There is no fee.

National University, Registrar, 11255 N Torrey Pines Rd, La Jolla, CA 92034, 619-642-8260 (Fax: 619-642-8717). Hours: 8AM-5:30PM. Enrollment: 9000. Records go back to 1971. Alumni records are maintained here at the same phone number. Degrees granted: Associate; Bachelors; Masters.

Attendance and degree information available by phone, fax, mail. Search requires name plus SSN. Also helpful: date of birth, exact years of attendance. There is no fee.

Naval Postgraduate School, Registration & Scheduling, Code 61, 589 Dyer Rd, Monterey, CA 93943-5133, 408-656-2591 (Fax: 408-656-2891). Hours: 8AM-4:30PM. Enrollment: 1600. Records go back to 1948. Alumni records are maintained here also. Call 408-656-4011. Degrees granted: Masters; Doctorate. Certification: Aviation Safety.

Attendance and degree information available by phone, fax, mail. Search requires name plus SSN. Also helpful: exact years of attendance. There is no fee.

Nazarene Bible College, (Emmanuel Bible College), Registrar, 1605 E Elizabeth St, Pasadena, CA 91104, 818-791-2575 (Fax: 818-398-2424). Hours: 8AM-5PM. Records go back to 1983.

Attendance and degree information available by fax, mail. Search requires name plus SSN, date of birth, exact years of attendance, signed release. There is no fee.

Nazarene Bible College, (Instituto Teologico Nazareno), Registrar, 1539 E Howard St, Pasadena, CA 91104, 619-221-2200 (Fax: 619-221-2579). Hours: 8AM-4:30PM. Enrollment: 25. Records go back to 1902. Alumni records are maintained here also. Call 619-221-2586. Degrees granted: Bachelors; Masters. Adverse incident record source- Student Development, 619-221-2255.

Attendance information available by phone, fax, mail. Search requires name plus SSN, date of birth. There is no fee.

Degree information available by phone, fax, mail. Search requires name only. There is no fee.

New College of California, Registrar, 50 Fell St, San Francisco, CA 94102, 415-6226-1694. Hours: 8AM-4:30PM. Records go back to 1972. Alumni records are maintained here at the same phone number. Degrees granted: Bachelors; Masters.

Attendance and degree information available by phone, mail. Search requires name plus SSN. There is no fee.

Occidental College, Registrar, 1600 Campus Rd, Los Angeles, CA 90041-3314, 213-259-2686 (Fax: 213-341-4886). Hours: 8AM-5PM. Records go back to 1887. Alumni records are maintained here at the same phone number. Degrees granted: Bachelors; Masters.

Attendance and degree information available by phone, fax, mail. Search requires name plus SSN, date of birth, exact years of attendance. There is no fee.

Ohlone College, Admissions & Records, 43600 Mission Blvd, Fremont, CA 94539, 510-659-6100 (Fax: 510-659-6057). Hours: 9AM-8PM M-Th; 9AM-4PM F. Enrollment: 8000. Records go back to 1970. Degrees granted: Associate.

Attendance and degree information available by fax, mail. Search requires name plus SSN, signed release. Also helpful: date of birth, exact years of attendance. Fee is $4.00.

Orange Coast College, Student Records, 2701 Fairview Rd, PO Box 5005, Costa Mesa, CA 92628, 714-432-5771 (Fax: 714-432-5736). Hours: 8:00AM-7PM M-Th; 8AM-3PM F. Enrollment: 24500. Alumni records are maintained here also. Call 714-432-5645. Degrees granted: Associate.

Attendance and degree information available by phone, mail. Search requires name only. Also helpful: SSN, date of birth, exact years of attendance. Fee is $3.00. Expedited service available for $5.00.

Otis College of Art and Design, Office of Registration & Records, 2401 Wilshire Blvd, Los Angeles, CA 90057, 213-251-0510. Hours: 8:30AM-5PM. Records go back to 1950. Alumni records are maintained here also. Call 213-251-0522. Degrees granted: Bachelors; Masters. Adverse incident record source- Dean of Students, 213-251-0540.

Attendance information available by mail. Search requires name plus signed release. Also helpful: SSN, date of birth, approximate years of attendance. There is no fee.

Degree information available by phone, mail. Search requires name only. Also helpful: SSN, date of birth, approximate years of attendance. There is no fee.

Oxnard College, Registrar, 4000 S Rose Ave, Oxnard, CA 93033-6699, 805-986-5810 (Fax: 805-986-5806). Hours: 8AM-5PM. Records go back to 1975. Alumni records are maintained here also. Call 805-986-5808. Degrees granted: Associate.

Attendance and degree information available by phone, fax, mail. Search requires name plus SSN. There is no fee.

Pacific Christian College, Registrar, 2500 E Nutwood Ave, Fullerton, CA 92831, 714-879-3901 X256 (Fax: 714-526-0231). Hours: 8AM-5PM. Enrollment: 1000. Records go back to 1928. Alumni records are maintained here at the same phone number. Degrees granted: Associate; Bachelors; Masters. Special programs- Traditional Undergrad, 714-879-3901: Escel-Degree Completion, 714-879-3901 X600: Spanish Certificate,

714-879-3901 X269: Supplemental Transfer Program,714-879-3901: Graduate Program, 714-879-3901 X604.

Attendance information available by phone, fax, mail. Search requires name plus date of birth. Also helpful: SSN, exact years of attendance. There is no fee.

Degree information available by phone, fax, mail. Search requires name only. Also helpful: SSN, date of birth, exact years of attendance. There is no fee.

Pacific College of Oriental Medicine, Registrar,
7445 Mission Valley Rd Ste 105, San Diego, CA 92108-4407, 619-574-6909 (Fax: 619-574-6641). Hours: 9AM-5PM. Enrollment: 87. Records go back to 1986. Degrees granted: Masters.

Attendance and degree information available by mail. Search requires name plus SSN, signed release. There is no fee.

Pacific Graduate School of Psychology, Registrar, 935 E Meadow Dr, Palo Alto, CA 94306, 415-494-7477
(Fax: 415-493-6147). Hours: 9:30AM-5:30PM. Records go back to 1975. Alumni records are maintained here also. Call 415-843-3403. Degrees granted: Doctorate.

Attendance and degree information available by phone, fax, mail. Search requires name plus SSN, approximate years of attendance. There is no fee.

Pacific Lutheran Theological Seminary, Registrar, 2700 Marin Ave, Berkeley, CA 94708-5264, 510-524-5264. Hours: 8AM-4:30PM. Records go back to 1950. Alumni
records are maintained here at the same phone number. Degrees granted: Masters. Adverse incident record source- Business Office, 510-524-5264.

Attendance and degree information available by mail. Search requires name plus date of birth, signed release. There is no fee.

Pacific Oaks College, Registrar, 5 Westmoreland Pl,
Pasadena, CA 91103, 818-397-1342 (Fax: 818-577-6144). Hours: 8:30AM-4:30PM. Records go back to 1959. Alumni records are maintained here also. Call 818-397-1314. Degrees granted: Bachelors; Masters. Certification: Post-Grad. Special programs- Extension Division, 818-397-1375.

Attendance information available by phone, fax, mail. Search requires name only. Also helpful: SSN, date of birth, exact years of attendance. There is no fee.

Degree information available by phone, fax, mail. Search requires name plus approximate years of attendance. Also helpful: SSN, date of birth, exact years of attendance. There is no fee.

Pacific School of Religion, Registrar, 1798 Scenic
Ave, Berkeley, CA 94709, 510-849-8200 (Fax: 510-845-8948). Hours: 8:30AM-5PM. Enrollment: 200. Alumni records are maintained here at the same phone number. Degrees granted: Masters; Doctorate.

Attendance and degree information available by phone, fax, mail. Search requires name only. There is no fee.

Pacific Union College, Records Office, Angwin, CA
94508-9707, 707-965-6673 (Fax: 707-965-6432). Hours: 8:30AM-4:30PM M-Th; 8:30AM-Noon F. Enrollment: 1600. Records go back to 1887. Alumni records are maintained here also. Call 707-965-6306. Degrees granted: Associate; Bachelors; Masters. Adverse incident record source- Student Services, 707-965-7362.

Attendance and degree information available by phone, fax, mail. Search requires name only. Also helpful: SSN, date of birth, exact years of attendance. There is no fee.

Palmer College of Chiropractic-West, Registrar, 90 E Tasman Dr, San Jose, CA 95134, 408-944-6099 (Fax:
408-944-6017). Hours: 8AM-4:30PM. Enrollment: 650. Records go back to 1981. Alumni records are maintained here also. Call 408-944-6043. Degrees granted: Doctorate.

Attendance and degree information available by mail. Search requires name plus SSN, exact years of attendance, signed release. There is no fee.

Palo Verde College, Registrar, 811 W Chanslorway,
Blythe, CA 92225, 619-922-6168 (Fax: 619-922-0230). Hours: 8AM-5PM. Enrollment: 2300. Records go back to 1955. Degrees granted: Associate. Special programs- LVN Program, 619-921-5346. Adverse incident record source- Student Services.

Attendance and degree information available by mail. Search requires name plus SSN, date of birth, signed release. Also helpful: exact years of attendance. There is no fee.

Palomar College, Registrar, 1140 W Mission Rd, San
Marcos, CA 92069, 619-744-1150 X2169 (Fax: 619-744-2932). Hours: 7:30AM-7PM M-Th; 7:30AM-2PM F. Enrollment: 24437. Degrees granted: Associate. Adverse incident record source- James Bowen, 619-744-1150 X2594.

Attendance and degree information available by phone, fax, mail. Search requires name plus SSN. Also helpful: date of birth, approximate years of attendance. Fee is $3.00. Expedited service available for $5.00.

Pasadena City College, Records Office, 1570 E Colorado Blvd, Pasadena, CA 91106, 818-585-7475. Hours: 8AM-
7:30PM. Records go back to 1945. Alumni records are maintained here at the same phone number. Degrees granted: Associate. Special programs- Financial Aid, 818-585-7401. Adverse incident record source- Safety Office, 818-585-7484.

Attendance and degree information available by mail. Search requires name plus SSN, date of birth, approximate years of attendance, signed release. Also helpful: exact years of attendance. Fee is $3.00. Expedited service available for $6.00.

Patten College, Registrar, 2433 Coolidge Ave, Oakland,
CA 94601, 510-533-8300 X220. Hours: 9AM-5PM. Records go back to 1989. Alumni records are maintained here also. Call 510-533-8300 X255. Degrees granted: Bachelors.

Attendance and degree information available by mail. Search requires name plus SSN, date of birth, approximate years of attendance, signed release. There is no fee.

Pepperdine University, Registrar, 24255 Pacific Coast
Hwy, Malibu, CA 90263, 310-456-4542 (Fax: 310-456-4358). Hours: 8AM-5PM. Records go back to 1937. Alumni records are maintained here also. Call 310-456-4248. Degrees granted: Bachelors; Masters; Doctorate.

Attendance and degree information available by phone, fax, mail. Search requires name plus SSN, date of birth, approximate years of attendance. There is no fee.

Phillips College Inland Empire Campus, Registrar, 4300 Central Ave, Riverside, CA 92506, 909-787-9300
(Fax: 909-787-9452). Hours: 9AM-5PM. Records go back to 1975. Degrees granted: Associate.

Attendance and degree information available by fax, mail. Search requires name plus SSN, signed release. Also helpful: approximate years of attendance. There is no fee.

Phillips Graduate Institute, Registrar, 5445 Balboa
Blvd, Encino, CA 91316-1509, 818-509-5959 X252 (Fax: 818-386-5699). Hours: 8AM-5PM. Enrollment: 300. Formerly California Family Study Center Records go back to 1983. Alumni records are maintained here also. Call 818-386-5600. Degrees granted: Masters. Adverse incident record source- Graduate Advisor, 818-509-5959.

Attendance and degree information available by phone, mail. Search requires name plus SSN, date of birth. There is no fee.

Phillips Junior College, Registrar, 15350 Sherman
Way, Ste 350, Van Nuys, CA 91406, 818-895-2220 X115 (Fax: 818-376-8414). Hours: 8AM-6:30PM M-Th, 8AM-5PM F. Records go back to 1989. Degrees granted: Associate.

Attendance and degree information available by phone, fax, mail. Search requires name plus SSN. There is no fee.

Phillips Junior College, (Branch), Registrar, One
Civic Plaza Ste 110, Carson, CA 90745-2264, 310-518-2600

(Fax: 310-518-3652). Hours: 9AM-5PM. Records go back to 1988. Degrees granted: Associate. Special programs- Paralegal: Electronics: Computer Info Systems. Adverse incident record source- Academic, 310-518-2600.

Attendance and degree information available by phone, fax, mail. Search requires name plus SSN, date of birth, exact years of attendance. There is no fee.

Phillips Junior College Condie Campus,
Registrar, One W Campbell Ave, Campbell, CA 95008, 408-866-6666 (Fax: 408-866-5542). Hours: 9AM-12:30PM M-Th. Records go back to 1979. Degrees granted: Associate.

Attendance information available by written request only. Search requires name plus SSN, approximate years of attendance, signed release. Also helpful: exact years of attendance. There is no fee.

Degree information available by phone, fax, mail. Search requires name plus SSN. Also helpful: approximate years of attendance. There is no fee.

Pitzer College, Registrar, 1050 N Mills Ave, Claremont,
CA 91711-6110, 909-621-8000 X3036. Hours: 8AM-5PM. Records go back to 1963. Alumni records are maintained here also. Call 909-621-8000 X8130. Degrees granted: Bachelors.

Attendance and degree information available by phone, fax, mail. Search requires name plus exact years of attendance. Also helpful: SSN, date of birth. There is no fee.

Point Loma Nazarene College, Registrar, 3900
Lomaland Dr, San Diego, CA 92106, 619-849-2286 (Fax: 619-849-2579). Hours: 8AM-4:30PM. Enrollment: 2459. Records go back to 1902. Alumni records are maintained here also. Call 619-849-2586. Degrees granted: Bachelors; Masters; EDS.

Attendance and degree information available by mail. Search requires name plus date of birth, approximate years of attendance, signed release. Also helpful: SSN, exact years of attendance. There is no fee.

Pomona College, Registrar, 550 N College Ave, Clare-
mont, CA 91711, 909-621-8147 (Fax: 909-621-8671). Hours: 8AM-5PM. Enrollment: 1500. Records go back to 1887. Alumni records are maintained here also. Call 909-621-8110. Degrees granted: Bachelors. Special programs- Liberal Arts. Adverse incident record source- Student Affairs, 909-621-8131.

Attendance and degree information available by phone, fax, mail. Search requires name plus date of birth, approximate years of attendance. There is no fee.

Porterville College, Registrar, 100 E College Ave,
Porterville, CA 93257, 209-791-2220 (Fax: 209-791-2349). Hours: 8AM-7PM M-Th; 8AM-4:30PM F. Enrollment: 3400. Records go back to 1927. Alumni records are maintained here also. Call 209-791-2270. Degrees granted: Associate.

Attendance information available by phone, fax, mail. Search requires name only. Also helpful: SSN, date of birth, exact years of attendance. There is no fee.

Degree information available by fax, mail. Search requires name only. Also helpful: SSN, date of birth, exact years of attendance. There is no fee.

Queen of the Holy Rosary College, Registrar, PO
Box 3908, Mission San Jose, CA 94539, 510-657-2468. Hours: 8AM-4PM. Enrollment: 224. Records go back to 1930. Degrees granted: Associate.

Attendance and degree information available by mail. Search requires name plus SSN, date of birth, exact years of attendance. Fee is $3.00.

Rancho Santiago Community College, Regis-
trar, 1530 W 17th St, Santa Ana, CA 92706, 714-564-6000 (Fax: 714-564-6379). Hours: 8AM-9PM. Alumni records are maintained here at the same phone number. Degrees granted: Associate.

Attendance information available by mail. Search requires name plus SSN, signed release. Also helpful: date of birth, exact years of attendance. Fee is $2.00.

Degree information available by phone, fax, mail. Search requires name plus SSN. Also helpful: date of birth, exact years of attendance. Fee is $2.00.

Rand Graduate School of Policy Studies,
Registrar, 1700 Main St, PO Box 2138, Santa Monica, CA 90407-2138, 310-393-0411 X1690 (Fax: 310-451-6978). Hours: 8AM-5PM. Enrollment: 58. Records go back to 1948. Alumni records are maintained here at the same phone number. Degrees granted: Doctorate.

Attendance and degree information available by phone, fax, mail. Search requires name plus exact years of attendance. There is no fee.

Rio Hondo College, Registrar, 3600 Workman Mill Rd,
Whittier, CA 90601-1699, 310-692-0921 X3153 (Fax: 310-692-8318). Hours: 8AM-8PM M-Th, 8AM-4PM F. Records go back to 1963. Alumni records are maintained here also. Call 310-692-0921 X3445. Degrees granted: Associate.

Attendance and degree information available by phone, fax, mail. Search requires name plus SSN, date of birth. There is no fee.

Riverside Community College, Registrar, 4800
Magnolia Ave, Riverside, CA 92506-1299, 909-222-8603 (Fax: 909-222-8028). Hours: 7:30AM-7PM,M-Th;7:30AM-4:00PM,F. Degrees granted: Associate. Adverse incident record source- Safety & Security.

Attendance information available by fax, mail. Search requires name plus SSN, date of birth, exact years of attendance, signed release. There is no fee.

Degree information available by phone, fax, mail. Search requires name plus SSN, date of birth, exact years of attendance. There is no fee.

Sacramento City College, Registrar, 3835 Freeport
Blvd, Sacramento, CA 95822, 916-558-2351 (Fax: 916-558-2190). Hours: 7:30AM-8PM M-Th; 7:30AM-4:30PM F. Records go back to 1916. Degrees granted: Associate.

Attendance information available by phone, mail. Search requires name plus SSN, date of birth. Also helpful: approximate years of attendance. There is no fee.

Degree information available by mail. Search requires name plus SSN, date of birth. Also helpful: approximate years of attendance. There is no fee.

Saddleback College, Office of Admissions & Records,
28000 Marguerite Pkwy, Mission Viejo, CA 92692, 714-582-4555. Hours: 8AM-5PM. Records go back to 1968. Degrees granted: Associate. Adverse incident record source- VP Student Service, 714-582-4566.

Attendance information available by phone, fax, mail. Search requires name plus date of birth. Also helpful: SSN, exact years of attendance. There is no fee.

Degree information available by mail. Search requires name plus date of birth. Also helpful: SSN, exact years of attendance. Fee is $3.00. Expedite service available for $5.00.

Saint Mary's College of California, Office of the
Registrar, PO Box 4748, Moraga, CA 94575-4748, 510-631-4214 (Fax: 510-376-8339). Hours: 8:30AM-4:30PM. Enrollment: 4875. Records go back to 1875. Alumni Records Office: Alumni Association, Saint Mary's College of California, PO Box 3400, Moraga, CA 94575-3400. Degrees granted: Associate; Bachelors; Masters.

Attendance and degree information available by phone, fax, mail. Search requires name only. Also helpful: SSN, date of birth, exact years of attendance. There is no fee.

Salvation Army School for Officers' Train-
ing, Registrar, 30840 Hawthorne Blvd, Rancho Palos Verdes,

CA 90275, 310-544-6467 (Fax: 310-265-6506). Hours: 8:15AM-4:15PM. Enrollment: 83. Records go back to 1900's. Degrees granted: Associate.

Attendance and degree information available by phone, fax, mail. Search requires name plus exact years of attendance. There is no fee.

Samra University of Oriental Medicine, Registrar, 600 St Paul Ave, Los Angeles, CA 90017, 213-482-8448 (Fax: 213-842-9020). Hours: 10:30AM-6:30PM. Enrollment: 350. Records go back to 1982. Degrees granted: Masters.

Attendance and degree information available by fax, mail. Search requires name plus SSN, date of birth, signed release. Also helpful: exact years of attendance. Fee is $5.00.

Samuel Merritt College, Registrar, 370 Hawthorne Ave, Oakland, CA 94609, 510-869-6131 (Fax: 510-869-6525). Hours: 8AM-5PM. Enrollment: 600. Records go back to 1909. Alumni records are maintained here also. Call 510-869-6614. Degrees granted: Bachelors; Masters.

Attendance and degree information available by phone, fax, mail. Search requires name plus exact years of attendance. Also helpful: SSN, date of birth. There is no fee.

San Bernardino Valley College, Registrar, 701 S Mt Vernon Ave, San Bernardino, CA 92410, 909-888-6511 (Fax: 909-889-4988). Hours: 8AM-7PM. Records go back to 1926. Degrees granted: Associate.

Attendance information available by written request only. Search requires name plus SSN, approximate years of attendance, signed release. Also helpful: date of birth, exact years of attendance. There is no fee.

Degree information available by phone, fax, mail. Search requires name plus SSN, approximate years of attendance. Also helpful: date of birth, exact years of attendance. There is no fee.

San Diego City College, Registrar, 1313 Twelfth Ave, San Diego, CA 92101, 619-584-6925 (Fax: 619-230-2135). Hours: 8AM-7:30PM. Records go back to 1950. Degrees granted: Associate.

Attendance and degree information available by fax, mail. Search requires name plus SSN, date of birth, approximate years of attendance, signed release. There is no fee.

San Diego Mesa College, Registrar, 7250 Mesa College Dr, San Diego, CA 92111, 619-627-2805 (Fax: 619-627-2808). Hours: 8AM-6PM M-Th, 8AM-3:30PM F. Enrollment: 24101. Records go back to 1964. Degrees granted: Associate.

Attendance information available by phone, fax, mail. Search requires name plus SSN, date of birth. There is no fee.

Degree information available by phone, fax, mail. Search requires name only. There is no fee.

San Diego Miramar College, Registrar, 10440 Black Mountain Rd, San Diego, CA 92126, 619-584-6931 (Fax: 619-584-6946). Hours: 8AM-5PM M-Th; 8AM-3PM F. Enrollment: 9773. Records go back to 1946. Degrees granted: Associate. Special programs- Continuing Education, 619-527-5280: Law Enforcement Academy, 619-536-7320. Adverse incident record source- Campus Police, 619-230-2910.

Attendance and degree information available by fax, mail. Search requires name plus SSN, date of birth, signed release. Also helpful: exact years of attendance. There is no fee.

San Diego State University, Registrar, 5500 Campanile Dr, San Diego, CA 92182-7455, 619-594-6871 (Fax: 619-594-4902). Hours: 8AM-4:30PM. Enrollment: 29000. Records go back to 1890. Alumni records are maintained here also. Call 619-594-ALUM. Degrees granted: Bachelors; Masters; Doctorate. Special programs- College of Extended Studies, 619-594-5821. Adverse incident record source- Judicial Procedures, 619-594-6455: Public Safety, 619-594-1991

Attendance and degree information available by phone, fax, mail. Search requires name only. Also helpful: SSN, date of birth, exact years of attendance. There is no fee.

San Francisco Art Institute, Registrar, 800 Chestnut St, San Francisco, CA 94133, 415-749-4535 (Fax: 415-749-4590). Hours: 9AM-5PM. Records go back to 1930's. Alumni records are maintained here also. Call 415-749-5842. Degrees granted: Bachelors; Masters.

Attendance and degree information available by phone, fax, mail. Search requires name plus SSN, approximate years of attendance. There is no fee.

San Francisco College of Mortuary Science, Registrar, 1598 Dolores St, San Francisco, CA 94110, 415-824-1313 (Fax: 415-824-1390). Hours: 8AM-4:30PM. Enrollment: 80. Records go back to 1965. Alumni records are maintained here at the same phone number. Degrees granted: Associate. Adverse incident record source- Registrar's Office   .

Attendance and degree information available by phone, fax, mail. Search requires name plus SSN, date of birth. There is no fee.

San Francisco Conservatory of Music, Registrar, 1201 Ortega St, San Francisco, CA 94122, 415-759-3422 (Fax: 415-759-3499). Hours: 9AM-5PM. Enrollment: 255. Records go back to 1956. Alumni records are maintained here also. Call 415-759-3445. Degrees granted: Bachelors; Masters.

Attendance and degree information available by phone, fax, mail. Search requires name plus date of birth. Also helpful: SSN, approximate years of attendance. There is no fee.

San Francisco State University, Registrar, 1600 Holloway Ave, San Francisco, CA 94132, 415-338-2077. Hours: 8:30AM-5PM. Records go back to 1960. Alumni records are maintained here also. Call 415-338-2217. Degrees granted: Bachelors; Masters.

Attendance and degree information available by phone, mail. Search requires name plus SSN, approximate years of attendance. There is no fee.

San Francisco Theological Seminary, Registrar, 2 Kensington Rd, San Anselmo, CA 94960, 415-258-6553 (Fax: 415-454-2493). Hours: 9AM-5PM. Enrollment: 700. Records go back to 1900. Alumni records are maintained here at the same phone number. Degrees granted: Bachelors; Masters; Doctorate. Certification: Spir. Direction. Adverse incident record source- Facilities, 415-258-6606.

Attendance and degree information available by phone, fax, mail. Search requires name only. Also helpful: exact years of attendance. There is no fee.

San Joaquin College of Law, Registrar, 3385 E Shields Ave, Fresno, CA 93726, 209-225-4953 (Fax: 209-225-4322). Hours: 9AM-5PM. Enrollment: 235. Records go back to 1974. Alumni records are maintained here at the same phone number. Degrees granted: Masters; Doctorate; Juris.

Attendance information available by phone, fax, mail. Search requires name plus SSN. Also helpful: date of birth, exact years of attendance. There is no fee.

Degree information available by fax, mail. Search requires name plus SSN. Also helpful: date of birth, exact years of attendance. There is no fee.

San Joaquin Delta College, Registrar, 5151 Pacific Ave, Stockton, CA 95207, 209-474-5635 (Fax: 209-474-5600). Hours: 8AM-8:30PM M-Th; 8AM-5PM F. Enrollment: 16000. Records go back to 1963. Degrees granted: Associate.

Attendance and degree information available by phone, fax, mail. Search requires name plus SSN, date of birth. Also helpful: exact years of attendance. There is no fee.

San Jose Christian College, Registrar, PO Box 1090, 790 S 12th St, San Jose, CA 95112, 408-293-9058 (Fax:

408-293-7352). Hours: 8AM-4:30PM. Enrollment: 325. Records go back to 1939. Degrees granted: Associate; Bachelors. Certification: Bible Counseling.

Attendance and degree information available by phone, fax, mail. Search requires name plus exact years of attendance. There is no fee.

San Jose City College, Registrar, 2100 Moorpark Ave, San Jose, CA 95128, 408-298-2181 (Fax: 408-298-1935). Hours: 8AM-7PM M-Th; 9AM-5PM F. Enrollment: 11000. Records go back to 1955. Alumni records are maintained here at the same phone number. Degrees granted: Associate.

Attendance and degree information available by phone, fax, mail. Search requires name plus SSN, date of birth. Also helpful: exact years of attendance. Fee is $2.00.

San Jose State University, Registrar, One Washington Square, San Jose, CA 95192, 408-283-7500 (Fax: 408-924-2050). Hours: 9AM-4PM. Records go back to 1917. Alumni records are maintained here also. Call 408-924-6515. Degrees granted: Bachelors.

Attendance and degree information available by phone, fax, mail. Search requires name plus SSN, date of birth. There is no fee.

San Mateo Count Community College, District Office, Admissions Office, 1700 W Hillsdale Blvd, San Mateo, CA 94402, 415-574-6165 (Fax: 415-574-6506). Enrollment: 12000. Records go back to 1922. Alumni records are maintained here at the same phone number. Degrees granted: Associate. Adverse incident record source- Security.

Attendance and degree information available by phone. Search requires name plus SSN, date of birth, exact years of attendance. There is no fee.

Santa Barbara City College, Registrar, 721 Cliff Dr, Santa Barbara, CA 93109, 805-965-0581 (Fax: 805-963-7222). Hours: 8AM-7:30PM M-Th; 8AM-4:15PM F. Enrollment: 11500. Records go back to 1958. Alumni records are maintained here at the same phone number. Degrees granted: Associate. Adverse incident record source- Campus Security, 805-965-0581 X2264: Dean of Students, 805-965-0581 X2278

Attendance information available by fax, mail. Search requires name plus SSN, signed release. Also helpful: date of birth, exact years of attendance. There is no fee.

Degree information available by phone, fax, mail. Search requires name plus SSN, approximate years of attendance. Also helpful: exact years of attendance. There is no fee.

Santa Clara University, Registrar, Santa Clara, CA 95053, 408-554-4331 (Fax: 408-554-6926). Hours: 8AM-5PM. Enrollment: 7451. Records go back to 1800's. Alumni records are maintained here also. Call 408-554-6800. Degrees granted: Bachelors; Masters; Doctorate.

Attendance and degree information available by phone, fax, mail. Search requires name plus SSN, date of birth. Also helpful: exact years of attendance. There is no fee.

Santa Monica College, Admissions & Records, 1900 Pico Blvd, Santa Monica, CA 90405, 310-452-9382 (Fax: 310-399-1730). Hours: 8AM-5PM M-Th. Enrollment: 19890. Degrees granted: Associate.

Attendance and degree information available by mail. Search requires name plus date of birth, signed release. Also helpful: SSN, exact years of attendance. Fee is $3.00.

Santa Rosa Junior College, Admissions & Records, Transcripts, 1501 Mendocino Ave, Santa Rosa, CA 95401, 707-527-4513 (Fax: 707-527-4798). Hours: 8AM-5PM. Records go back to 1917. Alumni records are maintained here also. Call 707-527-4733. Degrees granted: Associate.

Attendance and degree information available by fax, mail. Search requires name plus SSN, signed release. Also helpful: date of birth, exact years of attendance. There is no fee.

Saybrook Institute Graduate School & Research Center, Registrar, 450 Pacific Ave 3rd Flr, San Francisco, CA 94133, 415-433-9200 (Fax: 415-433-9271). Hours: 8:30AM-4:30pm. Enrollment: 292. Records go back to 1971. Alumni records are maintained here at the same phone number. Degrees granted: Masters; Doctorate.

Attendance information available by fax, mail. Search requires name plus signed release. Also helpful: exact years of attendance. There is no fee.

Degree information available by phone, fax, mail. Search requires name only. Also helpful: exact years of attendance. There is no fee.

School of Theology at Claremont, Registrar, 1325 N College Ave, Claremont, CA 91711-3199, 909-626-3521 (Fax: 909-626-7062). Hours: 9AM-Noon, 1-5PM. Records go back to 1965. Degrees granted: Masters; Doctorate.

Attendance information available by phone, fax, mail. Search requires name only. Also helpful: SSN, date of birth, exact years of attendance. There is no fee.

Degree information available by phone, fax, mail. Search requires name only. Also helpful: SSN. There is no fee.

Scripps College, Registrar, 1030 N Columbia Ave, Claremont, CA 91711, 909-621-8273 (Fax: 909-621-8323). Hours: 9AM-Noon, 1-4PM. Enrollment: 675. Records go back to 1926. Alumni records are maintained here at the same phone number. Degrees granted: Bachelors. Certification: Post-Bac Pre-Med.

Attendance and degree information available by phone, mail. Search requires name only. Also helpful: SSN, date of birth, exact years of attendance. There is no fee.

Scripps Research Institute (The), Registrar, 10550 N Torrey Pines Rd, La Jolla, CA 92037, 619-554-8469 (Fax: 619-554-6602). Hours: 8:30AM-5PM. Enrollment: 100. Records go back to 1989. Degrees granted: Doctorate; PhD.

Attendance and degree information available by phone, fax, mail. Search requires name plus SSN, date of birth, approximate years of attendance. There is no fee.

Shasta College, Registrar, PO Box 496006, Redding, CA 96049, 916-225-4841 (Fax: 916-225-4995). Hours: 8AM-8PM M-Th, 8AM-5PM F Summer: 8AM-8PM M-Th, 8AM-4:30PM F. Enrollment: 11595. Records go back to 1950's. Alumni records are maintained here at the same phone number. Degrees granted: Associate. Adverse incident record source- Campus Security, 916-225-4631.

Attendance and degree information available by fax, mail. Search requires name plus SSN, date of birth, approximate years of attendance, signed release. There is no fee.

Sierra College, Assistant Dean, 5000 Rocklin Rd, Rocklin, CA 95677, 916-781-0430 (Fax: 916-781-0403). Hours: 7:30AM-7:30PM M-Th; 7:30AM-3PM F. Enrollment: 17000. Records go back to 1937. Alumni records are maintained here also. Call 916-773-5659. Degrees granted: Associate. Adverse incident record source- Campus Police, 916-781-0570.

Attendance and degree information available by fax, mail. Search requires name plus approximate years of attendance, signed release. Also helpful: SSN, date of birth, exact years of attendance. There is no fee.

Simpson College, Registrar, 2211 College View Dr, Redding, CA 96003, 916-224-5600 X2111 (Fax: 916-224-5608). Hours: 8AM-6PM. Enrollment: 950. Records go back to 1921. Alumni records are maintained here also. Call 916-224-5600 X2503. Degrees granted: Associate; Bachelors; Masters. Adverse incident record source- Student Development.

Attendance and degree information available by phone, fax, mail. Search requires name plus SSN, date of birth, approximate years of attendance. There is no fee.

Skyline College, Admissions & Records Office, 3300 College Dr, San Bruno, CA 94066, 415-738-4252. Hours: 8AM-

10PM M-Th, 8AM-4:30PM F, 8AM-Noon Sat. Records go back to 1969. Degrees granted: Associate. Adverse incident record source- Campus Security, 415-738-4199 (day), 415-738-4256 (eve.).

Attendance information available by mail. Search requires name plus SSN, approximate years of attendance, signed release. Fee is $1.00.

Degree information available by phone, mail. Search requires name plus SSN, approximate years of attendance. Fee is $1.00.

Solano Community College, Admissions & Records, 4000 Suisun Valley Rd, Suisun, CA 94585, 707-864-7171 (Fax: 707-864-7175). Hours: 8AM-8:30PM M-Th; 8AM-3PM F. Enrollment: 10000. Records go back to 1945. Degrees granted: Associate. Adverse incident record source- Campus Police, 707-864-7000.

Attendance and degree information available by fax, mail. Search requires name plus SSN, signed release. Also helpful: date of birth, exact years of attendance. There is no fee.

Sonoma State University, Registrar, 1801 E Cotati Ave, Rohnert Park, CA 94928, 707-664-2778 (Fax: 707-664-2060). Hours: 8AM-4:30PM. Records go back to 1960. Alumni records are maintained here also. Call 707-664-2426. Degrees granted: Bachelors.

Attendance and degree information available by phone, fax, mail. Search requires name plus SSN, date of birth, exact years of attendance. There is no fee.

South Baylo University, Registrar, 1126 N Brookhurst St, Anaheim, CA 92801, 714-533-1495 (Fax: 714-533-1640). Hours: 10AM-6PM. Enrollment: 235. Records go back to 1982. Degrees granted: Masters.

Attendance and degree information available by phone, fax, mail. Search requires name plus SSN. There is no fee.

South Baylo University, (Branch), Registrar, 1543 W Olympic Blvd, Los Angeles, CA 90015, 213-738-1974. Records are not housed here. They are located at South Baylo University, Registrar, 1126 N Brookhurst St, Anaheim, CA 92801.

Southern California College, Registrar, 55 Fair Dr, Costa Mesa, CA 92626, 714-556-3610 (Fax: 714-966-5471). Hours: 8AM-4:30PM. Enrollment: 1200. Records go back to 1920. Alumni records are maintained here at the same phone number. Degrees granted: Bachelors; Masters. Adverse incident record source- Student Life, 714-668-6194 X224.

Attendance and degree information available by phone, fax, mail. Search requires name plus SSN. Also helpful: date of birth, exact years of attendance. There is no fee.

Southern California College of Optometry, Registrar, 2575 Yorba Linda Blvd, Fullerton, CA 92631-1699, 714-449-7445 (Fax: 714-992-7878). Hours: 8AM-5PM. Records go back to 1906. Alumni records are maintained here also. Call 714-449-7461. Degrees granted: Doctorate.

Attendance information available by phone, fax, mail. Search requires name only. Also helpful: SSN, date of birth, exact years of attendance. There is no fee.

Degree information available by phone, fax, mail. Search requires name only. Also helpful: SSN, exact years of attendance. There is no fee.

Southern California Institute of Architecture, Registrar, 5454 Beethoven St, Los Angeles, CA 90066, 310-574-1123 (Fax: 310-574-3801). Enrollment: 440. Records go back to 1792. Alumni records are maintained here at the same phone number. Degrees granted: Bachelors; Masters.

Attendance and degree information available by phone, fax, mail. Search requires name plus SSN, exact years of attendance. Also helpful: date of birth. Fee is $5.00.

Southwestern College, Admissions Center, 900 Otay Lakes Rd, Chula Vista, CA 91910, 619-482-6550 (Fax: 619-482-6413). Hours: 7:30AM-8PM M-Th; 7:30AM-5PM F. Records go back to 1800. Degrees granted: Associate. Adverse incident record source- Student Activities, 619-421-6700 X5432.

Attendance information available by fax, mail. Search requires name plus SSN, date of birth, signed release. Also helpful: exact years of attendance. There is no fee.

Degree information available by fax, mail. Search requires name plus SSN, date of birth. There is no fee.

Southwestern University School of Law, Registrar, 675 S Westmoreland Ave, Los Angeles, CA 90005, 213-738-6734 (Fax: 213-383-1688). Enrollment: 1200. Records go back to 1913. Alumni records are maintained here also. Call 213-738-6814.

Attendance and degree information available by mail. Search requires name plus SSN. There is no fee.

St. John's Seminary, Registrar, 5012 Seminary Rd, Camarillo, CA 93012-2598, 805-482-2755 (Fax: 805-484-4074). Hours: 8AM-4:30PM. Enrollment: 110. Records go back to 1939. Alumni records are maintained here at the same phone number. Degrees granted: Masters.

Attendance and degree information available by phone, fax, mail. Search requires name plus SSN, date of birth. Also helpful: exact years of attendance. There is no fee.

St. John's Seminary College, Registrar, 5118 E Seminary Rd, Camarillo, CA 93012-2599, 805-482-2755 X202 (Fax: 805-987-5097). Hours: 8AM-4PM. Enrollment: 71. Records go back to 1940. Alumni Records Office: 1531 W Ninth St, Los Angeles, CA 90015. Degrees granted: Bachelors.

Attendance and degree information available by mail. Search requires name plus SSN, date of birth, signed release. Also helpful: approximate years of attendance. There is no fee.

St. Patrick's Seminary, Registrar, 320 Middlefield Rd, Menlo Park, CA 94025, 415-325-5621 (Fax: 415-322-0997). Hours: 9AM-Noon, 1-4PM. Enrollment: 50. Records go back to 1896. Alumni records are maintained here at the same phone number. Degrees granted: Masters.

Attendance and degree information available by phone, fax, mail. Search requires name plus SSN, date of birth. Also helpful: exact years of attendance. There is no fee.

Stanford University, Transcripts & Registration, Old Union Bldg, Stanford, CA 94305, 415-723-2086 (Fax: 415-725-7248). Hours: 9AM-Noon, 1-5PM. Records go back to 1891. Alumni records are maintained here also. Call 415-723-2021. Degrees granted: Bachelors; Masters; Doctorate. Adverse incident record source- Campus Police, 415-723-9633.

Attendance and degree information available by phone, fax, mail. Search requires name only. There is no fee.

Starr King School for the Ministry, Registrar, 2441 LeConte Ave, Berkeley, CA 94709, 510-845-6232 (Fax: 510-845-6273). Hours: 9AM-5PM. Records go back to 1900's. Alumni records are maintained here at the same phone number. Degrees granted: Masters.

Attendance and degree information available by phone, fax, mail. Search requires name only. There is no fee.

State Center Community College, Registrar, 1101 E University Ave, Fresno, CA 93741, 209-442-4600 (Fax: 209-485-3367). Enrollment: 19000. Records go back to 1910. Degrees granted: Associate. Special programs- Liberal Arts: Business. Adverse incident record source- Security.

Attendance and degree information available by phone, mail. Search requires name plus SSN, exact years of attendance. There is no fee.

Taft College, Registrar, 29 Emmons Park Dr, Taft, CA 93268, 805-763-4282 (Fax: 805-763-1038). Hours: 8AM-5PM. Records go back to 1922. Degrees granted: Associate.

Attendance and degree information available by phone, fax. Search requires name plus SSN, date of birth, exact years of attendance. There is no fee.

Thomas Aquinas College, Registrar, 10000 N Ojai Rd, Santa Paula, CA 93060, 805-525-4417 X308 (Fax: 805-525-0620). Hours: 8AM-5PM. Enrollment: 220. Records go back to 1971. Alumni records are maintained here also. Call 805-525-4417. Degrees granted: Bachelors.

Attendance and degree information available by phone, fax, mail. Search requires name plus SSN. There is no fee.

Thomas Jefferson School of Law, Registrar, 2121 San Diego Ave, San Diego, CA 92110, 619-297-9700. Hours: 8AM-6PM. Enrollment: 495. Formerly Western State University College of Law of San Diego Records go back to 1969. Alumni records are maintained here at the same phone number. Degrees granted: Bachelors; Juris Doctor.

Attendance and degree information available by mail. Search requires name plus signed release. Also helpful: SSN, date of birth, exact years of attendance. There is no fee.

United States International University, Registrar, 10455 Pomerado Rd, San Diego, CA 92131, 619-635-4580 (Fax: 619-693-8562). Hours: 8AM-5:30PM. Enrollment: 1300. Records go back to 1950. Alumni records are maintained here at the same phone number. Degrees granted: Associate; Bachelors; Masters; Doctorate. Certification: Education.

Attendance information available by phone, fax, mail. Search requires name plus approximate years of attendance. Also helpful: exact years of attendance. There is no fee.

Degree information available by phone, fax, mail. Search requires name only. Also helpful: exact years of attendance. There is no fee.

University of California, Berkeley, Registrar, 128 Sproul Hall, Berkeley, CA 94720-5404, 510-642-4814 (Fax: 510-643-8050). Hours: 9AM-Noon, 1-4PM. Enrollment: 33000. Records go back to 1902. Alumni records are maintained here also. Call 510-642-7026. Degrees granted: Bachelors; Masters; Doctorate. Certification: Teaching Cred. Adverse incident record source- Student Conduct, 510-643-9069.

Attendance and degree information available by phone, fax, mail. Search requires name plus approximate years of attendance. Also helpful: SSN, date of birth, exact years of attendance. There is no fee.

University of California, Davis, Office of the Registrar, 124 Mrak Hall, Davis, CA 95616, 916-752-2980 (Fax: 916-752-6906). Hours: 8AM-5PM. Records go back to 1960. Degrees granted: Bachelors; Masters; Doctorate.

Attendance and degree information available by phone, fax, mail. Search requires name plus SSN, date of birth, exact years of attendance. There is no fee.

University of California, Hastings College of the Law, Registrar, 200 McAllister St, San Francisco, CA 94102, 415-565-4613 (Fax: 415-565-4863). Hours: 9AM-3:30PM. Enrollment: 1250. Records go back to 1975. Alumni records are maintained here also. Call 415-565-4667. Degrees granted: Doctorate.

Attendance and degree information available by phone, fax, mail. Search requires name only. Also helpful: SSN, exact years of attendance. There is no fee.

University of California, Irvine, Registrar, Irvine, CA 92717-4975, 714-824-6124 (Fax: 714-824-7896). Hours: 8AM-5PM. Records go back to 1965. Degrees granted: Associate; Bachelors; Masters; Doctorate.

Attendance and degree information available by phone, mail. Search requires name plus SSN, date of birth. Fee is $3.00.

University of California, Los Angeles, Office of the Registrar, Transcripts, 405 Hilgard Ave, Rm 1105 Murphy House, Los Angeles, CA 90095-1429, 310-825-3801. Hours: 9AM-5PM. Records go back to 1898. Degrees granted: Bachelors; Masters; Doctorate.

Attendance and degree information available by phone, mail. Search requires name plus SSN, date of birth. Also helpful: exact years of attendance. There is no fee.

University of California, Riverside, Registrar, Riverside, CA 92521, 909-787-7284 (Fax: 909-787-7368). Hours: 8AM-5PM. Enrollment: 9300. Alumni Records Office: Alumni Association, 3127 Hinderacker Hall, Riverside, CA 92521. Degrees granted: Bachelors; Masters; Doctorate. Certification: EDUC. Special programs- Extension Office, 909-787-7105.

Attendance and degree information available by phone, fax, mail. Search requires name plus SSN. Also helpful: date of birth, exact years of attendance. There is no fee.

University of California, San Diego, Office of the Registrar, 9500 Gilman Dr, La Jolla, CA 92093, 619-534-3150 (Fax: 619-534-5723). Hours: 8AM-4:30PM. Enrollment: 18000. Records go back to 1960. Alumni records are maintained here at the same phone number. Degrees granted: Bachelors; Masters; Doctorate; MD. Adverse incident record source- Campus Police, 619-534-4357.

Attendance and degree information available by phone, mail. Search requires name plus SSN. Also helpful: date of birth, exact years of attendance. Fee is $4.00.

University of California, San Francisco, Registrar, 513 Parnassus Ave, San Francisco, CA 94143, 415-476-4527. Hours: 8AM-5PM. Records go back to 1920. Alumni records are maintained here also. Call 415-476-1471.

Attendance and degree information available by phone, mail. Search requires name plus SSN, approximate years of attendance. There is no fee.

University of California, Santa Barbara, Registrar, Santa Barbara, CA 93106, 805-893-3135 (Fax: 805-893-2985). Hours: 8AM-5PM. Enrollment: 17834. Records go back to 1900's. Alumni Records Office: 6550 Hollister Ave, Golita, CA 93117. Degrees granted: Bachelors; Masters; PhD.

Attendance and degree information available by phone, fax, mail. Search requires name plus SSN. Also helpful: date of birth, approximate years of attendance. There is no fee.

University of California, Santa Cruz, Registrar, 190 Hahn Student Services, Santa Cruz, CA 95064, 408-459-4412. Hours: 8AM-5PM. Enrollment: 10000. Records go back to 1966. Phone number for transcripts is 408-459-2902. Alumni Records Office: Carriage House, Santa Cruz, CA 95064, 408-459-2530. Degrees granted: Bachelors; Masters; Doctorate. Certification: Post-Bac. Special programs- University Extension,740 Front St, Santa Cruz, CA 95060.

Attendance information available by mail. Search requires name plus signed release. Also helpful: SSN, date of birth, exact years of attendance. There is no fee.

Degree information available by phone, mail. Search requires name plus approximate years of attendance. Also helpful: SSN, date of birth, exact years of attendance. Fee is $5.00.

University of Judaism, Registrar, 15600 Mulholland Dr, Los Angeles, CA 90077, 310-476-9777 (Fax: 310-471-1278). Hours: 9AM-5PM. Enrollment: 200. Records go back to 1947. Alumni records are maintained here at the same phone number. Degrees granted: Bachelors; Masters.

Attendance and degree information available by phone, fax, mail. Search requires name only. Also helpful: SSN, exact years of attendance. There is no fee.

University of La Verne, Registrar, 1950 Third St, La Verne, CA 91750, 909-593-3511 X4000 (Fax: 909-392-2703). Hours: 8AM-5PM M,W,F; 8AM-7PM T,Th. Enrollment: 6000. Records go back to 1891. Alumni records are maintained here also. Call 909-593-3511 X4680. Degrees granted: Associate; Bachelors; Masters; Doctorate.

Attendance and degree information available by phone, fax, mail. Search requires name only. Also helpful: SSN, date of birth, exact years of attendance. There is no fee.

University of Phoenix, (Fountain Valley Main), Registrar, 10540 Talbert Ave, Fountain Valley, CA 92708, 714-968-2299. Transcript records are housed at University of Phoenix, Registrar, PO Box 52069, Phoenix, AZ 85072.

Attendance and degree information available by written request only. Search requires name plus SSN, approximate years of attendance.

University of Phoenix, (Online), Registrar, 100 Spear St #110, San Francisco, CA 94105, 415-541-0141 (Fax: 415-541-0761). Enrollment: 1700. Records go back to 1976. Transcript records are housed at University of Phoenix, Registrar, PO Box 52069, Phoenix, AZ 85072. Alumni Records Office: Alumni Association, 4615 E Elwood ST, Phoenix, AZ 85072, 800-795-2586. Degrees granted: Bachelors; Masters.

Attendance and degree information available by phone, fax, mail. Search requires name plus SSN, approximate years of attendance. There is no fee.

University of Phoenix, (San Diego), Registrar, 3870 Murphy Canyon Rd Ste 200, San Diego, CA 92123, 619-576-7469 (Fax: 619-576-0032). Records go back to 1976. Transcript records are housed at University of Phoenix, Registrar, PO Box 52069, Phoenix, AZ 85072. Degrees granted: Bachelors. Special programs- Business Management: Nursing.

Attendance and degree information available by mail. Search requires name plus SSN, approximate years of attendance. There is no fee.

University of Phoenix, (San Jose Main), Registrar, 3590 N 1st St, San Jose, CA 95134-1805, 408-435-8500 (Fax: 408-435-8250). Transcript records are housed at University of Phoenix, Registrar, PO Box 52069, Phoenix, AZ 85072. Degrees granted: Bachelors; Masters.

Attendance and degree information available by written request only. Search requires name plus SSN, approximate years of attendance.

University of Redlands, Registrar, 1200 E Colton Ave, Redlands, CA 92373-0999, 909-793-2121 (Fax: 909-793-2029). Hours: 8AM-5PM. Enrollment: 3723. Records go back to 1903. Alumni records are maintained here at the same phone number. Degrees granted: Bachelors; Masters. Special programs- Masters Communicative Disorders: Masters Music.

Attendance and degree information available by phone, fax, mail. Search requires name plus SSN, date of birth, exact years of attendance. There is no fee.

University of San Diego, Registrar, 5998 Alcala Park, San Diego, CA 92110-2492, 619-260-4557 (Fax: 619-260-4649). Hours: 8:30AM-5PM. Records go back to 1949. Alumni records are maintained here also. Call 619-260-4819. Degrees granted: Bachelors; Masters.

Attendance and degree information available by phone, fax, mail. Search requires name plus SSN, exact years of attendance. There is no fee.

University of San Francisco, Registrar, 2130 Fulton St, San Francisco, CA 94117-1080, 415-666-6316 (Fax: 415-666-6321). Hours: 8:30AM-5PM M-F, 10:30AM-3:30PM Sat. Records go back to 1986. Alumni records are maintained here also. Call 415-666-6431. Degrees granted: Bachelors; Masters; Doctorate.

Attendance and degree information available by phone, fax, mail. Search requires name plus SSN. There is no fee.

University of Southern California, Registrar, Los Angeles, CA 90089-0912, 213-740-7445 (Fax: 213-740-8710).

Hours: 8:30AM-5PM. Enrollment: 28000. Records go back to 1880. Alumni records are maintained here also. Call 213-740-1234. Degrees granted: Bachelors; Masters; Doctorate. Adverse incident record source- Student Affairs, 213-740-2311.

Attendance and degree information available by phone, mail. Search requires name plus SSN. Also helpful: date of birth, exact years of attendance. Fee is $5.00. Expedited service available for $15.00.

University of West Los Angeles, Registrar, 1155 W Arbor Vitae St, Inglewood, CA 90301-2902, 310-215-3339 (Fax: 310-641-4736). Hours: 8:30AM-6:30PM. Enrollment: 595. Alumni records are maintained here also. Call 310-215-3339. Degrees granted: Bachelors; Doctorate; Para-Legal. Adverse incident record source- Academic Office, 310-215-3339.

Attendance and degree information available by mail. Search requires name plus approximate years of attendance. There is no fee.

University of West Los Angeles-Law School, Registrar, 1155 W Arbor Vitae St, Inglewood, CA 91301-2902, 310-342-5200 (Fax: 310-342-5295). Enrollment: 750. Records go back to 1966. Alumni records are maintained here at the same phone number. Degrees granted: Bachelors; Doctorate.

Attendance and degree information available by mail. Search requires name plus signed release. Also helpful: SSN, date of birth, exact years of attendance. Fee is $5.00. Expedited service available for $5.00.

University of the Pacific, Registrar, 3601 Pacific Ave, Stockton, CA 95211, 209-946-2135 (Fax: 209-946-2596). Hours: 8AM-5PM. Enrollment: 5850. Records go back to 1900. Alumni records are maintained here also. Call 209-946-2391. Degrees granted: Bachelors; Masters; Doctorate.

Attendance and degree information available by phone, fax, mail. Search requires name only. Also helpful: SSN, date of birth, exact years of attendance. There is no fee.

Ventura College, Registrar, 4667 Telegraph Rd, Ventura, CA 93003, 805-654-6457 (Fax: 805-654-6466). Hours: 8AM-7:30PM M-Th, 9AM-5PM F. Enrollment: 10500. Records go back to 1945. Alumni records are maintained here also. Call 805-648-8927. Degrees granted: Associate. Adverse incident record source- Dean of Student Services, 805-654-6455.

Attendance and degree information available by phone, fax, mail. Search requires name plus SSN, date of birth, approximate years of attendance. There is no fee.

Victor Valley College, Admissions & Records Dept, 18422 Bear Valley Rd, Victorville, CA 92392, 619-245-4271 (Fax: 619-245-9745). Hours: 8:30AM-5PM. Enrollment: 8329. Records go back to 1961. Alumni records are maintained here at the same phone number. Degrees granted: Associate. Certification: Occupation. Adverse incident record source- Vice President, 619-245-4271 X271.

Attendance information available by phone, fax, mail. Search requires name plus SSN, date of birth. Also helpful: exact years of attendance. Fee is $2.00. Expedited service available for $2.00.

Degree information available by fax, mail. Search requires name plus SSN, date of birth. Also helpful: exact years of attendance. Fee is $2.00. Expedite service available for $2.00.

Vista College, Registrar, 2020 Milvia St, Berkeley, CA 94704, 510-841-8860 X245 (Fax: 510-841-7333). Hours: 9AM-3PM. Enrollment: 3500. Records go back to 1960. Alumni records are maintained here also. Call 510-841-8431 X267. Degrees granted: Associate.

Attendance and degree information available by fax, mail. Search requires name plus SSN, signed release. Also helpful: date of birth, exact years of attendance. There is no fee.

West Coast University, Records Department, 440 S Shatto Pl, Los Angeles, CA 90020-1765, 213-427-4400 (Fax: 213-380-4362). Hours: 9AM-5PM. Enrollment: 750. Records go back to 1950. Some records go back to 1950. Alumni records are maintained here at the same phone number. Degrees granted: Associate; Bachelors; Masters. Certification: CEU. Adverse incident record source- Records Dept, 213-427-4400.

Attendance information available by written request only. Search requires name plus SSN, signed release. Also helpful: date of birth, exact years of attendance. There is no fee.

Degree information available by phone, fax, mail. Search requires name plus SSN, approximate years of attendance. Also helpful: date of birth, exact years of attendance. There is no fee.

West Coast University Orange County Center, Registrar, 440 Shatto Pl, Los Angeles, CA 90020, 213-953-2700 (Fax: 213-380-4362). Enrollment: 600. Records go back to 1909. Alumni records are maintained here at the same phone number. Degrees granted: Associate; Bachelors. Special programs- Computer Engineering: Business. Adverse incident record source- Security.

Attendance and degree information available by phone, mail. Search requires name plus SSN, date of birth, exact years of attendance. There is no fee.

West Hills Community College, Registrar, 300 Cherry Lane, Coalinga, CA 93210, 209-935-0801 (Fax: 209-935-5655). Hours: 8AM-5PM. Enrollment: 3000. Records go back to 1932. Alumni records are maintained here also. Call 209-935-0801 X3224. Degrees granted: Associate. Adverse incident record source- Local police, 209-935-1525.

Attendance and degree information available by phone, fax, mail. Search requires name only. Also helpful: SSN, date of birth, exact years of attendance. There is no fee.

West Los Angeles College, Attn: Admissions, 4800 Freshman Dr, Culver City, CA 90230, 310-287-4329 (Fax: 310-841-0396). Hours: 9AM-8PM M-Th; 9AM-3:30PM F. Degrees granted: Associate.

Attendance and degree information available by fax, mail. Search requires name plus SSN, exact years of attendance, signed release. Also helpful: date of birth. Fee is $1.00.

West Valley College, Registrar, 14000 Fruitvale Ave, Saratoga, CA 95070, 408-867-2200 (Fax: 408-867-5033). Hours: 10AM-7PM M-Th; 10PM-4PM F. Enrollment: 11000. Records go back to 1964. Degrees granted: Associate.

Attendance and degree information available by written request only. Search requires name plus SSN, date of birth, approximate years of attendance, signed release. Also helpful: exact years of attendance. There is no fee.

Western State University College of Law of Orange County, Registrar, 1111 N State College Blvd, Fullerton, CA 92631, 714-738-1000 (Fax: 714-525-2786). Hours: 9AM-6PM. Enrollment: 1300. Records go back to 1966. Alumni records are maintained here at the same phone number. Degrees granted: Doctorate; Juris Doctor.

Attendance and degree information available by fax, mail. Search requires name plus exact years of attendance, signed release. Also helpful: SSN, date of birth. There is no fee.

Westminster Theological Seminary in California, Registrar, 1725 Bear Valley Pkwy, Escondido, CA 92027, 619-480-8474 (Fax: 619-480-0252). Hours: 8AM-4:30PM. Enrollment: 126. Records go back to 1991. Alumni records are maintained here at the same phone number. Degrees granted: Masters; Doctorate.

Attendance and degree information available by phone, fax, mail. Search requires name only. Also helpful: SSN, date of birth, exact years of attendance. There is no fee.

Westmont College, Registrar, 955 La Paz Rd, Santa Barbara, CA 93108-1089, 805-565-6060 (Fax: 805-565-6234).

Hours: 8AM-4:30PM. Enrollment: 1250. Records go back to 1940. Alumni records are maintained here also. Call 805-565-6056. Degrees granted: Bachelors. Adverse incident record source- Dean of Students, 805-565-6028.

Attendance information available by phone, fax, mail. Search requires name plus SSN. Also helpful: date of birth, exact years of attendance. There is no fee.

Degree information available by phone, fax, mail. Search requires name only. Also helpful: SSN, date of birth, exact years of attendance. There is no fee.

Whittier College, Office of the Registrar, 13406 E Philadelphia St, Whittier, CA 90601, 310-907-4241 (Fax: 310-698-4067). Hours: 8AM-5PM. Records go back to 1902. Alumni records are maintained here at the same phone number. Degrees granted: Bachelors; Masters. Adverse incident record source- Student Services, 310-907-4233.

Attendance and degree information available by phone, fax, mail. Search requires name plus SSN, date of birth, approximate years of attendance. Also helpful: exact years of attendance. There is no fee.

Woodbury University, Registrar's Office, PO Box 7846, Burbank, CA 91510-7846, 818-767-0888 X270 (Fax: 818-768-8628). Hours: 8AM-8PM M-Th; 8AM-5PM F. Enrollment: 1072. Records go back to 1930. Alumni records are maintained here at the same phone number. Degrees granted: Bachelors; Masters.

Attendance and degree information available by phone, fax, mail. Search requires name plus SSN, date of birth, approximate years of attendance. Also helpful: exact years of attendance. There is no fee.

Wright Institute, Registrar, 2728 Durant Ave, Berkeley, CA 94704, 510-841-9230. Enrollment: 242. Records go back to 1969. Alumni records are maintained here at the same phone number. Degrees granted: Doctorate.

Attendance and degree information available by phone, mail. Search requires name only. There is no fee.

Yeshiva Ohr Elchonon Chabad/West Coast Seminary, Registrar, 7215 Waring Ave, Los Angeles, CA 90046, 213-937-3763. Enrollment: 60. Records go back to 1977. Alumni records are maintained here at the same phone number. Degrees granted: Bachelors. Adverse incident record source- Student Services.

Attendance and degree information available by mail. Search requires name plus SSN, exact years of attendance, signed release. There is no fee.

Yeshiva Ohr Elchonon-Chabad/West Coast Talmudic Seminary, Registrar, 7215 Waring Ave, Los Angeles, CA 90046, 213-937-3763 (Fax: 213-937-9456). Hours: 8:30AM-4PM. Enrollment: 35. Records go back to 1956. Alumni records are maintained here at the same phone number. Degrees granted: Bachelors.

Attendance and degree information available by phone, fax, mail. Search requires name plus SSN, date of birth, approximate years of attendance. Also helpful: exact years of attendance. There is no fee.

Yo San University of Traditional Chinese Medicine, Registrar, 1314 Second St, Santa Monica, CA 90401, 310-917-2202 (Fax: 310-917-2267). Hours: 9AM-7PM. Enrollment: 26. Alumni records are maintained here also. Call 310-917-2202. Degrees granted: Masters.

Attendance and degree information available by phone, fax, mail. Search requires name plus SSN, date of birth, approximate years of attendance. There is no fee.

Yuba College, Records Office, 2088 N Beale Rd, Marysville, CA 95901, 916-741-6871. Hours: 8AM-6PM M-Th; 8AM-5PM F. Enrollment: 9247. Records go back to 1926. Degrees granted: Associate. Adverse incident record source- Campus Police, 916-741-6771.

Attendance information available by mail. Search requires name plus signed release. Also helpful: SSN, date of birth, exact years of attendance. There is no fee.

Degree information available by phone, mail. Search requires name only. Also helpful: SSN, date of birth, exact years of attendance. There is no fee.

Trade and Vocational Schools

Academy Pacific Business and Travel College, 1777 N Vine St, Hollywood, CA 90028, 213-462-3211

Advertising Arts College (The), 10025 Mesa Rim Rd, San Diego, CA 92121, 619-546-0602

American Academy of Nutrition, 3408 Sausalito, Corona Del Mar, CA 92625, 714-760-5081

American Career College, 4021 Rosewood Ave, Los Angeles, CA 90004, 213-383-2862

American College of Hotel and Restaurant Manager, 11336 Camarillo St, North Hollywood, CA 91602, 818-505-9800

American Nanny College, 4650 Aroow Hwy Ste A10, Montclair, CA 91763, 909-624-7711

Ameritech Colleges, 5445 Lankershim Blvd, North Hollywood, CA 91601, 818-761-3656

Ameritech Colleges of Bakersfield, 3845 30th St E Ste B-1, Palmdale, CA 93550, 805-274-1570

Andon College at Modesto, 1314 H St, Modesto, CA 95354, 209-571-8777

Andon College at Stockton, 1201 N El Dorado St, Stockton, CA 95202, 209-462-8777

Associated Technical College, 1177 N Magnolia Ave, Anaheim, CA 92801, 714-229-8785

Associated Technical College, 1670 Wilshire Blvd, Los Angeles, CA 90017, 213-484-2444

Associated Technical College, 395 N E St, San Bernardino, CA 92401, 909-885-1888

Associated Technical College, 1475 Sixth Ave, San Diego, CA 92101, 619-234-2181

Bryan College (San Francisco), 731 Market St, San Francisco, CA 94103, 415-957-0663

Bryan College of Court Reporting, 2511 Beverly Blvd, Los Angeles, CA 90057, 213-484-8850

Cabot College, 41 E 12th St, National City, CA 91950, 619-474-8017

California Academy of Merchandising, Art & Design, 2035 Hurley Way #3000, Sacramento, CA 95825, 916-649-8168

California Career Schools, 392 W Cerritos Ave, Anaheim, CA 92805, 714-635-6585

California Culinary Academy, 625 Polk St, San Francisco, CA 94102, 415-771-3536

California Institute of Locksmithing, 14721 Oxnard St, Van Nuys, CA 91411, 818-994-7426

California Nannie College, 910 Howe Ave, Sacramento, CA 95825, 916-921-2400

California Paramedical & Technical College, 3745 Long Beach Blvd, Long Beach, CA 90807, 310-426-9359

California Paramedical & Technical College, 4550 LaSierra Ave, Riverside, CA 92505, 909-687-9006

California School of Court Reporting, 3510 Adams St, Riverside, CA 92504, 909-359-0293

Career Management Institute, 1855 W Katella Ave #150, Orange, CA 92667, 714-771-5077

Career West Academy, 2505B Zanella Wy, Chico, CA 95928, 916-893-1481

Central California School of Continuing Education, 3195 McMillan St Ste F, San Luis Obispo, CA 93401, 805-543-9123

Champion Institute of Cosmetology, 72261 Hwy 111, Palm Desert, CA 92260, 619-322-2227

Champion Institute of Cosmetology, 559 S Palm Canyon Dr, Palm Springs, CA 92260, 619-322-2227

College for Recording Arts, 665 Harrison St, San Francisco, CA 94107, 415-781-6306

CollegeAmerica - San Francisco, 814 Mission St Ste 300, San Francisco, CA 94103, 415-882-4545

Combat Systems Technical Schools Command, Mare Island, Vallejo, CA 94592, 707-554-8550

Computer Learning Center, 222 S Harbor Blvd, Anaheim, CA 92805, 714-956-8060

Computer Learning Center, 3130 Wilshire Blvd, Los Angeles, CA 90010, 213-386-6311

Computer Learning Center, 661 Howard St, San Francisco, CA 94105, 415-498-0800

Computer Learning Center, 111 N Market St, San Jose, CA 95113, 408-983-5950

ConCorde Career Institute, 1717 S Brookhurst St, Anaheim, CA 92804, 714-635-3450

ConCorde Career Institute, 4150 Lankershim Blvd, North Hollywood, CA 91602, 818-766-8151

ConCorde Career Institute, 570 W 4th St #107, San Bernardino, CA 92410, 909-884-8891

ConCorde Career Institute, 123 Camino de la Reina, San Diego, CA 92108, 619-688-0800

ConCorde Career Institute, 1290 N First St, San Jose, CA 95112, 408-441-6411

Consolidated Welding Schools, 4343 E Imperial Hwy, Lynwood, CA 90262, 310-638-0418

Court Reporting Institute (Branch Campus), 1333 Camino del Rio S, San Diego, CA 92108, 619-294-5700

Dell'Arte School of Physical Theatre, PO Box 816, Blue Lake, CA 95525, 707-668-5663

Dickinson-Warren Business College, 2702 Clayton Rd Ste 201, Concord, CA 94519, 510-609-1770

EDUTEK Professional Colleges, 780 Bay Blvd #101, Chula Vista, CA 91910, 619-425-3200

EDUTEK Professional Colleges (Branch Campus), 5952 El Cajon Blvd, San Diego, CA 92120, 619-582-1319

East Los Angeles Occupational Center, 2100 Marengo St, Los Angeles, CA 90033, 213-223-1283

Educorp Career College, 230 E Third St, Long Beach, CA 90802, 310-437-0501

Eldorado College, 2204 El Camino Real, Oceanside, CA 92054, 619-433-3660

Eldorado College, 1901 Pacific Ave, West Covina, CA 91790, 818-960-5173

Eldorado College (Branch Campus), 385 N Escondido Blvd, Escondido, CA 92025, 619-743-2100

Eldorado College (Branch Campus), 2255 Camino Del Rio, San Diego, CA 92108, 619-294-9256

Elegance International, 4929 Wilshire Blvd, Los Angeles, CA 90010, 213-937-4838

Elite Progressive School of Cosmetology, 5522 Garfield Ave, Sacramento, CA 95841, 916-338-1885

Fashion Careers of California, 1923 Morena Blvd, San Diego, CA 92110, 619-275-4700

Fresno Institute of Technology, 1545 N Fulton St, Fresno, CA 93720, 209-442-3574

Galen College of Medical and Dental Assistants, 1325 N Wishon Ave, Fresno, CA 93728, 209-527-5084

Galen College of Medical and Dental Assistants (Branch Campus), 1604 Ford Ave #10, Modesto, CA 95350, 209-264-9726

Galen College of Medical and Dental Assistants (Branch Campus), 3746 W Mineral King Ave Ste C, Visalia, CA 93291, 209-264-9726

Gemological Institute of America, PO Box 2110, 1660 Steward St, Santa Monica, CA 90404-4088, 310-829-2991

Glendale Career College, 1021 Grandview Ave, Glendale, CA 91201, 818-243-1131

Golf Academy of San Diego, 2022 University Dr #311, Vista, CA 96083, 619-756-2486

Hacienda La Puente Adult Education, 15540 E Fairgrove Ave, La Puente, CA 91744, 818-855-3138

Health Staff Training Institute, 1505 E 17th St No 122, Santa Ana, CA 92701, 714-543-9828

Helicopter Adventures, 81 John Glenn Dr, Concorde, CA 94520, 510-686-2917

Hemphill Schools, 510 S Alvarado St, Los Angeles, CA 90057, 213-413-6323

High-Tech Institute (Branch Campus), 1111 Howe Ave #250, Sacramento, CA 95825, 800-322-4128

Hospitality Management Training Institute, 814 Mission St Ste 500, San Francisco, CA 94103, 415-896-0370

Huntington College of Dental Technology, 7466 Edinger Ave, Huntington Beach, CA 92647, 714-841-9500

Hypnosis Motivation Institute, 18607 Ventura Blvd #310, Tarzana, CA 91356, 800-6000-HMI

Institute for Business & Technology (National Career Education), 6060 Sunrise Vista Dr #3000, Citrus Heights, CA 95610, 916-969-4900

Institute of Computer Technology, 3200 Wilshire Blvd #400, Los Angeles, CA 90010, 213-381-3333

International Air Academy (Branch Campus), 2980 Inland Empire Blvd, Ontario, CA 91764, 909-989-5222

International Dealers School, 6329 E Washington Blvd, Commerce, CA 90040, 213-890-0030

Irvine College of Business, 16591 Noyes Ave, Irvine, CA 92714, 714-863-1145

John Tracy Clinic, 806 W Adams Blvd, Los Angeles, CA 90007, 800-522-4582

Learning Tree University, 20916 Knapp St, Chatsworth, CA 91311, 818-882-5685

Lederwolff Culinary Academy, 3300 Stockton Blvd, Sacramento, CA 95820, 916-456-7002

Leicester School, 1106 W Olympic Blvd, Los Angeles, CA 90015, 213-746-7666

Los Angeles ORT Technical Institute, 635 S Harvard Blvd, Los Angeles, CA 90005, 213-387-4244

Los Angeles ORT Technical Institute (Valley Branch), 15130 Ventura Blvd #250, Sherman Oaks, CA 91403, 818-788-7222

MTI Business College of Stockton Inc., 6006 N El Dorado St, Stockton, CA 95207, 209-957-3030

MTI College, 2011 W Chapman Ave #100, Orange, CA 92668, 714-385-1132

MTI College (Branch Campus), 760 Via Lata #300, Colton, CA 92324, 909-424-0123

Management College of San Francisco, 1255 Post St #450, San Francisco, CA 94109, 405-776-7244

Maric College of Medical Careers, 3666 Kearny Villa Rd, San Diego, CA 92123, 619-583-8232

Maric College of Medical Careers, 1300 Rancheros Dr, San Marcos, CA 92069, 619-747-1555

Maric College of Medical Careers (Branch Campus), 1593-C E Vista Way, Vista, CA 92084, 619-758-8640

Marin Ballet School, 100 Elm St, San Rafael, CA 94901, 415-453-6705

Masters Institute, 50 Airport Pkwy #8, San Jose, CA 95110, 408-441-1800

Microcomputer Education Center, 2212 M Winery No 122, Fresno, CA 93703, 209-456-0623

Modern Technology School of X-Ray, 1232 E Katella Ave, Anaheim, CA 92805, 714-978-7702

Modern Technology School of X-Ray, 6180 Laurel Canyon Blvd, North Hollywood, CA 91606, 818-763-2563

Moler Barber College, 3500 Broadway St, Oakland, CA 94611, 510-652-4177

Moler Barber College, 727 J St, Sacramento, CA 95814, 916-441-0072

Moler Barber College, 50 Mason St, San Francisco, CA 94102, 415-362-5885

Moler Barber College (Branch Campus), 2645 El Camino Ave, Sacramento, CA 95821, 916-482-0871

Moler Barber College (Branch Campus), 410 E Weber Ave, Stockton, CA 95202, 209-465-3218

Monterey Park College, 583 Monterey Pass Rd, Monterey Park, CA 91754, 818-576-2444

Musicians Institute, 1655 N McCadden Pl, Hollywood, CA 90028, 213-462-1384

NA Professional Bartenders, 7132 Garden Grove Blvd, Westminster, CA 92683, 714-895-9818

National Career Education, 6060 Sunrise Vista Dr Ste 3000, Citrus Heights, CA 95610-7053, 916-969-4900

National Education Center - Bryman Campus, 1120 N Brookhurst St, Anaheim, CA 92801, 714-954-6500

National Education Center - Bryman Campus, 5350 Atlantic Ave, Long Beach, CA 90805, 310-422-6007

National Education Center - Bryman Campus, 1017 Wilshire Blvd, Los Angeles, CA 90017, 213-481-1640

National Education Center - Bryman Campus, 3505 N Hart Ave, Rosemead, CA 91770, 818-573-5470

National Education Center - Bryman Campus, 731 Market St, San Francisco, CA 94103, 415-777-2500

National Education Center - Bryman Campus, 2015 Naglee Ave, San Jose, CA 95128, 408-275-8800

National Education Center - Bryman Campus, 4212 W Artesia Blvd, Torrance, CA 90504, 310-542-6951

National Education Center - Bryman Campus, 20835 Sherman Way, Winnetka, CA 91306, 818-887-7911

National Education Center Sawyer Campus, 8475 Jackson Rd, Sacramento, CA 95826, 916-383-1909

National Hispanic University (The), 14271 Story Rd, San Jose, CA 95112, 408-254-6900

Naval Construction Training Center, 343, Port Hueneme, CA 93043, 805-982-4153

Naval Expeditionary Warfare Training Group (Pacific), 3423 Guadalcanal Rd Bldg 401, San Diego, CA 92155-5099, 619-437-3726

Naval Fleet Anti-Submarine Warfare Training Center (Pacific), 32444 Echo Ln Ste 100, San Diego, CA 92147-5199, 619-524-1664

Naval Health Sciences Education and Training Command (Field Medical Service School), Camp Pendleton, CA 92055, 619-725-2672

Naval Health Sciences Education and Training Command (School of Dental Assisting), Naval Station, San Diego, CA 92136, 619-556-8262

Naval Health Sciences Education and Training Command (School of Health Science), San Diego, CA 92134, 619-532-7700

Naval Service School Command, 32224 Naval Training Ctr, San Diego, CA 92133, 619-524-4857

Naval Technical Training Center Detachment, Treasure Island, 1070 M Ave, San Francisco, CA 94130, 415-395-3073

Naval Transportation Management School, Oakland Army Base Bldg 790, Oakland, CA 94626, 510-466-2155

Newbridge College, 700 El Camino Real, Tustin, CA 92680, 714-573-8787

Newschool of Architecture, 1249 F St, San Diego, CA 92101, 619-235-4100

North Park College, 3956 30th St, San Diego, CA 92104, 619-297-3333

North Park College (Branch Campus), 4718 Clairemont Mesa Blvd, San Diego, CA 92117, 619-483-3088

North Valley Occupational Center, 11450 Sharp Ave, Mission Hills, CA 91345, 818-365-9645

Northwest College of Medical & Dental Assistants, 530 E Union Ave, Pasadena, CA 91101, 818-796-5815

Northwest College of Medical & Dental Assistants, 134 W Holt Ave, Pomona, CA 91768, 909-623-1552

Northwest College of Medical & Dental Assistants, 2121 W Garvey Ave, West Covina, CA 91790, 818-961-3495

Northwest College of Medical & Dental Assistants (Branch Campus), 124 S Glendale Ave, Glendale, CA 91205, 818-242-0205

Nova Institute of Health Technolgy, 3000 S Robertson Blvd, Los Angeles, CA 90034, 310-840-5777

Nova Institute of Health Technolgy, 520 N Euclid Ave, Ontario, CA 91762, 909-984-5027

Nova Institute of Health Technolgy, 11416 Whittier Blvd, Whittier, CA 90601, 310-695-0771

Orange County Business College, 2035 E Ball Rd, Anaheim, CA 92806, 714-772-6941

Pacific Gateway College, 3018 Carmel St, Los Angeles, CA 90065, 818-247-9544

Pacific Travel School, 2515 N Main St, Santa Ana, CA 92701, 714-543-9495

Platt College, 10900 E 183rd St #290, Cerritos, CA 90701, 310-809-5100

Platt College, 7470 N Figueroa St, Los Angeles, CA 90041, 213-258-8050

Platt College, 3901 MacAuther Blvd, Newport Beach, CA 92600, 714-833-2300

Platt College, 9521 Business Center Dr, Rancho Cucamonga, CA 91730, 909-989-1187

Platt College, 6250 El Cajon Blvd, San Diego, CA 92115, 619-265-0107

Platt College, 301 Mission St #450, San Francisco, CA 94105, 415-495-4000

Practical Schools, 900 E Ball Rd, Anaheim, CA 92805, 714-535-6000

Premier Career College, 12901 Ramona Blvd Ste D, Irwindale, CA 91706, 818-814-2080

Professional Skills Institute (Santa Barbara Campus), 4213 State St #302, Santa Barbara, CA 93110, 805-683-1902

Rice Aviation, a Division of A&J Enterprises (Branch Campus), 8911 Aviation Blvd, Inglewood, CA 90301, 310-337-4444

Riverland Community College, 17911 Bushard St, Fountain Valley, CA 92708, 714-378-4510

Rosston School of Hair Design, 673 W Fifth St, San Bernardino, CA 92410, 909-884-2719

SUTECH School of Vocational-Technical Training, 3427 E Olympic Blvd, Los Angeles, CA 90023, 213-262-3210

SUTECH School of Vocational-Technical Training (Branch Campus), 1885 S Santa Cruz St, Anaheim, CA 92805, 714-939-7860

San Francisco Ballet School, 455 Franklin St, San Francisco, CA 94102, 415-861-5600

San Francisco Barber College, 64 Sixth St, San Francisco, CA 94103, 415-621-6802

San Joaquin Valley College, 201 New Stine Rd, Bakersfield, CA 93309, 805-834-0126

San Joaquin Valley College, 3333 N Bond St, Fresno, CA 93726, 209-229-7800

San Joaquin Valley College, 8400 W Mineral King Ave, Visalia, CA 93291, 209-651-2500

San Joaquin Valley College of Aeronautics, 4985 E Andersen Ave, Fresno, CA 93726, 209-229-7800

Santa Barbara Business College, 211 S Real Rd, Bakersfield, CA 93301, 805-322-3006

Santa Barbara Business College, 4333 Hansen Ave, Fremont, CA 94536, 510-793-4342

Santa Barbara Business College, 5266 Hollster Ave, Santa Barbara, CA 93111, 805-967-9677

Santa Barbara Business College, 303 E Plaza Dr, Santa Maria, CA 93454, 805-922-8256

Sawyer College, 441 W Trimble Rd, San Jose, CA 95131, 408-954-8200

Sawyer College at Ventura, 2101 E Gonzales Rd, Oxnard, CA 93030, 805-485-6000

School of Communications Electronics, 184 Second St, San Francisco, CA 94105, 415-896-0858

Sequoia Institute, 420 Whitney Pl, Fremont, CA 94539, 510-490-6900

Sierra Academy of Aeronautics Technicians Institute, Oakland International Airport, PO Box 2429, Oakland, CA 94614, 510-568-6100

Sierra Valley Business College, 4747 N First St Bldg D, Fresno, CA 93726, 209-222-0947

Silicon Valley College, 41350 Christy St, Fremont, CA 94538, 510-623-9966

Simi Valley Adult School, 3192 Los Angeles Ave, Simi Valley, CA 93065, 805-527-4840

South Coast College of Court Reporting, 1380 S Sanderson Ave, Anaheim, CA 92806, 714-635-6464

Southern California College of Business and Law, 595 W Lambert Rd, Brea, CA 92621, 714-529-1055

Southern California College of Court Reporting, 1100 S Claudina Pl, Anaheim, CA 92805, 714-758-1500

Southern California Institute of Technology, 1900 W Cresent Ave, Anaheim, CA 92801, 714-520-5552

Systems Programming Development Institute, 4900 Triggs St, City of Commerce, CA 90022, 213-261-8181

Travel University International, 3655 Ruffin Rd N #225, San Diego, CA 92123, 619-292-9755

Travel and Trade Career Institute, 3635 Atlantic Ave, Long Beach, CA 90807, 310-426-8841

Travel and Trade Career Institute (Branch Campus), 12541 Brookhurst St #100, Garden Grove, CA 92640, 714-636-2611

Truck Driving Academy, 5168 N Blythe Ave #102, Fresno, CA 93722, 209-276-5708

Truck Driving Academy, 5711 Florin-Perkins Rd, Sacramento, CA 95828, 916-381-2285

Truck Marketing Institute, PO Box 5000, Carpinteria, CA 93014, 805-684-4558

Valley Commercial College, 1207 I St, Modesto, CA 95354, 209-578-0616

Watterson College, 150 S Los Robles Ave #100, Pasadena, CA 91101, 818-449-3990

Watterson College, 1422 S Azusa Ave, West Covina, CA 91791, 818-919-8701

Watterson College Pacific, 815 N Oxnard Blvd, Oxnard, CA 93030, 805-656-5566

Watterson College Pacific (Branch Campus), 2030 University Dr, Vista, CA 92083, 619-724-1500

Westech College, 500 W Mission Blvd, Pomona, CA 91766, 714-622-6486

Western Career College, 8909 Folsom Blvd, Sacramento, CA 95826, 916-361-1660

Western Career College, 170 Bayfair Mall, San Leandro, CA 94578, 510-278-2888

Western Pacific Truck School, 4565 N Golden State Blvd, Fresno, CA 93722, 209-276-1220

Western Truck School, 4521 W Capitol Ave, West Sacramento, CA 95691, 916-372-6500

Western Truck School (Branch Campus), 5800 State Rd, Bakersfield, CA 93308, 805-399-0701

Western Truck School (Branch Campus), 8775 Aero Dr, San Diego, CA 92123, 619-514-8902

Western Truck School (Branch Campus), 1053 N Broadway, Stockton, CA 95205, 209-465-1191

Westlake Institute of Technology, 31826A Village Center Rd, Westlake Village, CA 91361, 818-991-9992

State Licensing & Business Registration Quick Finder Index

Architecture, Engineering & Surveying

Architect #6 (26527)	☎ 916-445-3393
Engineer #10 (84938)	☎ 916-263-2275
Engineering Geologist #20 (1450)	☎ 916-263-2113
Geologist #20 (4100)	☎ 916-263-2113
Geophysicist #20 (350)	☎ 916-263-2113
Hydrogeologist #20 (300)	☎ 916-263-2113
Landscape Architect #14 (3396)	☎ 916-445-4954
Surveyor #10 (3776)	☎ 916-263-2275
Surveyor-in-Training #10 (5644)	☎ 916-263-2275

Business - Court & Legal Services

Attorney #25	✉ 415-561-8303
Automobile Manufacturer Arbitration Program (Third Party Dispute Resolution) #3 (3)	☎ 916-323-3406
Court Reporter #31	☎ 916-263-3660
Notary Public #39	☎ 916-327-4202
Shorthand Reporter #32	☎ 916-445-5101

Business - General Services

Dry Cleaning Plant #23	☎ 916-574-2040
Fund-Raising to Establish Training Schools #44	☎ 916-445-9041
Locksmith #24	☎ 800-952-5210
Public Accountant #5	☎ 916-263-3680
Public Accountant-CPA #5	☎ 916-263-3680
Tax Interviewer #46	916-324-4977
Tax Preparer #46	916-324-4977

Construction & Manufacturing

Bedding Manufacturer, Renovator, Retailer & Wholesaler #23	☎ 916-574-2040
Boiler, Hot Water & Steam Fitting #30	☎ 916-255-3985
Building Moving/Demolition #30 (1665)	☎ 916-255-3985
Cabinet & Mill Work #30 (4744)	☎ 916-255-3985
Concrete #30 (7936)	☎ 916-255-3985
Custom Upholsterer #23	☎ 916-574-2040
Drywall #30 (4644)	☎ 916-255-3985
Earthwork & Paving #30 (3591)	☎ 916-255-3985
Electrical (General) & Electrical Sign #30	☎ 916-255-3985
Electrical Repair Establishment #22	☎ 916-324-4384
Elevator Installation #30	☎ 916-255-3985
Fencing #30 (1466)	☎ 916-255-3985
Flooring & Floor Covering #30 (7923)	☎ 916-255-3985
Furniture & Bedding Retailer #23	☎ 916-574-2040
Furniture Manufacturer, Retailer & Wholesaler #23	☎ 916-574-2040
General Building Contractor-Class B #30	☎ 916-255-3985
General Engineering Contractor-Class A #30	☎ 916-255-3985
General Manufactured Housing #30 (932)	☎ 916-255-3985
Glazier #30	☎ 916-255-3985
Insulation & Acoustical #30 (2083)	☎ 916-255-3985
Insulation Manufacturer #23	☎ 916-574-2040
Landscaping #30 (11140)	☎ 916-255-3985
Lathing #30 (518)	☎ 916-255-3985
Limited Specialty (60 Sublicenses) #30 (14801)	☎ 916-255-3985
Masonry #30 (4371)	☎ 916-255-3985
Ornamental Metal #30 (898)	☎ 916-255-3985
Painting & Decorating #30 (17996)	☎ 916-255-3985
Pipeline #30 (859)	☎ 916-255-3985
Plastering #30 (2827)	☎ 916-255-3985
Plumber #30	☎ 916-255-3985
Refrigeration #30 (2659)	☎ 916-255-3985
Roofing #30 (7408)	☎ 916-255-3985
Sheet Metal #30 (2579)	☎ 916-255-3985
Solar #30 (175)	☎ 916-255-3985
Specialty Contractor-Class C #30	☎ 916-255-3985
Steel, Reinforcing & Structural #30	☎ 916-255-3985
Supply Dealer #23	☎ 916-574-2040
Tile (Ceramic & Mosaic) #30 (5245)	☎ 916-255-3985
Warm-air Heating, Ventilating & Air Conditioning #30	☎ 916-255-3985

Education

Apprenticeship Training Establishment #13	☎ 916-445-7921
School Administrator #28 (2000)	☎ 916-445-7254
School Library Media Specialist #28 (100)	☎ 916-445-7254
Teacher #28 (15000)	☎ 916-445-7254

Environmental & Agriculture

Agricultural Engineer #10 (354)	☎ 916-263-2275
Animal Health Technician #2	☎ 916-263-2613
Fumigation #45	☎ 916-263-2540
General Pest Control #45	☎ 916-263-2540
Pest Control Field Representative #45	☎ 916-263-2540
Pest Control Operator #45	☎ 916-263-2540
Pesticide Appplicator #45	☎ 916-263-2540
Pesticide Dealer #45	☎ 916-263-2540
Smog Check Technician #21 (15000)	☎ 916-322-4010
Termite Control #45	☎ 916-263-2540
Veterinarian #11	☎ 916-263-2610
Veterinarian Hospital #11	☎ 916-263-2610
Well Drilling (Water) #30 (1061)	☎ 916-255-3985

Financial - Real Estate, Insurance & Banking

Collection Agency/Manager, Collector & Bookkeeper #24	☎ 800-952-5210
Insurance Adjuster #35	☎ 916-322-3555
Insurance Agent #35	☎ 916-322-3555
Insurance Broker #35	☎ 916-322-3555
Investment Advisor #33	☎ 916-327-0308
Real Estate Appraiser #36	☎ 415-904-5900
Real Estate Broker #36 (110839)	☎ 916-227-0931
Real Estate Sales Agent #36 (212200)	☎ 916-227-0931
Repossessor Employee & Company Manager #24	☎ 800-952-5210
Securities Broker/Dealer #33	☎ 916-327-0308

Health & Beauty

Acupuncturist #1 (5500)	☎ 916-263-2680
Audiologist #43	☎ 916-263-2685

Barber & Apprentice #7 (22228).................... ☎ 916-445-7061
Barber College & Instructor #7 (196) .... ☎ 916-445-7061
Barber Shop #7 .... ☎ 916-445-7061
Cemetery, Cemetery Sales Agent &
   Cemetery Broker #27 916-263-2660
Cosmetician & Cosmetologist #7 (255421) ... ☎ 916-445-7061
Cosmetology Establishment, Instructor &
   School #7 (3687)...................................... ☎ 916-445-7061
Cremated Remains Disposer #27 916-263-2660
Crematory #27 916-263-2660
Dental Assistant #29 (46215) .... ☎ 916-263-2595
Dental Assistant-Extended Functions #29
   (432) .... ☎ 916-263-2595
Dental Hygienist #29 (17000) .... ☎ 916-263-2595
Dentist #9 (29000)....................................... ☎ 916-263-2300
EFE (Retired/Military/Disabled) #17 (300) ... ☎ 916-263-2382
EL (Residency) #17 (100) .... ☎ 916-263-2382
Electrologist #7 (9) .... ☎ 916-445-7061
Electrology Establishment, Instructor &
   School #7.. ☎ 916-445-7061
Electroneuromyographer #40 .... ☎ 916-263-2550
Embalmer #13... ☎ 916-445-7921
Embalmer Apprentice #13.............................. ☎ 916-445-7921
FNP (Fictitious Name Permit) #17 (400) .... ☎ 916-263-2382
Funeral Arrangement Trust #13 .... ☎ 916-445-7921
Funeral Director #13...................................... ☎ 916-445-7921
Hearing Aid Dispenser #37 (1865) .... ☎ 916-263-2288
Hypodermic Needle & Syringe Distributor #16
   .... ☎ 916-327-6308
Kinesiological Electromyographer #40.......... ☎ 916-263-2550
Licensed Midwife #38 (3) .... ☎ 916-263-2393
Medical Doctor & Surgeon #38 (103130)...... ☎ 916-263-2635
Medical Provider Consultant #24................... ☎ 800-952-5210
Nonprofit Surgical Clinic #16 .... ☎ 916-327-6308
Nuclear Medicine Technologist #34 .... ☎ 916-445-6695
Nurse #19 (254822)...................................... ☎ 800-838-6828
Nurse Anesthetist #19 (1378)........................ ☎ 800-838-6828
Nurse Midwife #19 (850) .... ☎ 800-838-6828
Nurse Practitioner #19 (7625) .... ☎ 800-838-6828
Nursing Home Administrator #12 .... ☎ 916-263-2685
Optometric Corporation #15.......................... ☎ 916-323-8720
Optometrist #15 .... ☎ 916-323-8720
Optometry Branch Office #15 .... ☎ 916-323-8720
Out-of-State Distributor #16 .... ☎ 916-327-6308
Pharmaceutical Wholesaler & Exemptee #16
   .... ☎ 916-327-6308
Pharmacist #16.. ☎ 916-327-6308
Pharmacist Intern #16.................................... ☎ 916-327-6308
Pharmacy #16 .... ☎ 916-327-6308
Pharmacy Continuing Education Provider #16
   .... ☎ 916-327-6308
Physical Therapist/Assistant #40.................... ☎ 916-263-2550
Physician's Assistant #41............................... ☎ 916-263-2670
Podiatrist #17 (1750) .... ☎ 916-263-2382
Psychiatric Mental Health Nurse #19 (424)... ☎ 800-838-6828
Radiation Therapy Technologist #34 .... ☎ 916-445-6695
Radiologic Technologist #34.......................... ☎ 916-445-6695
Registered Dispensing Optician #38
   (6033) .... ☎ 916-263-2634
Research Psychoanalyst #38 (70)................... ☎ 916-263-2634
Respiratory Care Practitioner #42 (19000) .... ☎ 916-263-2626

Sanitation System #30 (1887)......................... ☎ 916-255-3985
Sanitizer #23 .... ☎ 916-574-2040
Speech Pathologist #43 .... ☎ 916-263-2685
Supervising Physician #41.............................. ☎ 916-263-2670
Vocational Nurse #47 .... ☎ 916-445-0793

Investigations & Security
Burglar Alarm Agent & Company Operator &
   Manager #24... ☎ 800-952-5210
Fire Protection #30 (2607)............................. ☎ 916-255-3985
Fire Protection Engineer #10 (944) .... ☎ 916-263-2275
Private Investigator #24................................. ☎ 800-952-5210
Private Patrol Operator #24 .... ☎ 800-952-5210
Protection Dog Operator & Employee #24 .... ☎ 800-952-5210
Security Guard/Armored Car Guard #24........ ☎ 800-952-5210
Training School #44....................................... ☎ 916-445-9041

Social Services
Clinical Social Worker Corporation &
   Worker #8 (13480).................................... ☎ 916-445-4933
Educational Psychologist #8 (1567)............... ☎ 916-445-4933
Instructor #44 .... ☎ 916-445-9041
Marriage, Family & Child Counselor #8
   (22957) .... ☎ 916-445-4933
Marriage, Family & Child Counselor
   Registered Intern #8 (8353) .... ☎ 916-445-4933
Psychiatric Technician #47............................ 916-263-2499
Psychological Assistant #18 .... ☎ 916-263-2699
Psychologist #18 .... ☎ 916-263-2699
Registered Associate Clinical Social
   Worker #8 (3835).................................... ☎ 916-445-4933

Sports & Entertainment
Amateur Kickboxer #4 (146).......................... ☎ 916-263-2195
Announcer #4 (9)... ☎ 916-263-2195
Box Office Employee #4 .... ☎ 916-263-2195
Boxer #4 (300).. ☎ 916-263-2195
Doorperson #4... ☎ 916-263-2195
Firearms/Baton Training Facility &
   Instructor #24 .... ☎ 800-952-5210
Full Contact Karate (Kickboxer) #4 (52) .... ☎ 916-263-2195
Gym #4 (3) .... ☎ 916-263-2195
Horse Racing #26.. ☎ 916-920-7178
Judge, Manager, Promoter & Matchmaker #4
   (106) .... ☎ 916-263-2195
Matchmaker #4 (4).. ☎ 916-263-2195
Referee #4 (7) .... ☎ 916-263-2195
Seconds #4 (542) .... ☎ 916-263-2195
Sparring Permit #4 .... ☎ 916-263-2195
Swimming Pool #30 (1811).......................... ☎ 916-255-3985
Ticket Seller #4 .... ☎ 916-263-2195
Timekeeper #4... ☎ 916-263-2195
Trainer/Second #4... ☎ 916-263-2195

Transportation
Automotive Repair Dealer #21 (36000) .... ☎ 916-322-4010
Lamp, Brake & Smog Inspection Certification
   Station #21 (3000)................................... ☎ 916-322-4010
Parking & Highway Improvement #30
   (640) .... ☎ 916-255-3985

State Licensing & Business Registration Agency Information

(1) Acupuncture Committee, 1424 Howe Ave, Suite 37, Sacramento, CA 95825-3233, 916-263-2680, Fax: 916-263-2654

(2) Animal Health Technician Examining Committee, 1420 Howe Ave, Suite 6, Sacramento, CA 95825, 916-263-2613, Fax: 916-263-2621

(3) Arbitration Review Program, 400 R Street, Sacramento, CA 95814, 916-323-3406, Fax: 916-323-3968

(4) Athletic Commission, 1424 Howe Ave, Suite 33, Sacramento, CA 95825, 916-263-2195, Fax: 916-263-2197

(5) Board of Accountancy, 2000 Evergreen, #250, Sacramento, CA 95815-3832, 916-263-3680

(6) Board of Architectural Examiners, 400 R St, Suite 4000, Sacramento, CA 95814-6200, 916-445-3393, Fax: 916-445-8524

(7) Board of Barber Examiners & Cosmetology, 400 R St, Suite 4080, Sacramento, CA 95814-6200, 916-445-7061, Fax: 916-445-8893

(8) Board of Behavioral Science Examiners, 400 R St, Suite 3150, Sacramento, CA 95814-6200, 916-445-4933

(9) Board of Dental Examiners, 1432 Howe Ave, Suite 85-B, Sacramento, CA 95825-3241, 916-263-2300, Fax: 916-263-2140

(10) Board of Engineers & Land Surveyors, 2535 Capitol Oaks Dr, Suite 300, Sacramento, CA 95833, 916-263-2275, Fax: 916-263-2246

(11) Board of Examiners in Veterinary Medicine, 1420 Howe Ave, Suite 6, Sacramento, CA 95825-3228, 916-263-2610, Fax: 916-263-2621

(12) Board of Examiners of Nursing Home Administrators, 1420 Howe Ave, Suite 2, Sacramento, CA 95825-3227, 916-263-2685

(13) Board of Funeral Directors & Embalmers, 400 R St, Suite 3080, Sacramento, CA 95814-6200, 916-332-7720, Fax: 916-455-1694

(14) Board of Landscape Architects, 400 R St, Suite 4020, Sacramento, CA 95814-6200, 916-445-4954, Fax: 916-324-2333

(15) Board of Optometry, 400 R St, Suite 1070, Sacramento, CA 95814-6200, 916-323-8720

(16) Board of Pharmacy, 400 R St, Suite 4070, Sacramento, CA 95814-6200, 916-445-5014, Fax: 916-327-6308

(17) Board of Podiatric Medicine, 1420 Howe Ave, Suite 8, Sacramento, CA 95825-3229, 916-263-2647

(18) Board of Psychology, 1426 Howe Ave, Suite 54, Sacramento, CA 95825-3236, 916-263-2699

(19) Board of Registered Nursing, 400 R St, Suite 4030, Sacramento, CA 95814-6200, 916-322-3350

(20) Board/Registration for Geologists & Geophysicists, 2535 Capitol Oaks Drive, Suite 300A, Sacramento, CA 95814, 916-263-2113, Fax: 916-263-2099

(21) Bureau of Automotive Repair, PO Box 989001 Pkwy, West Sacramento, CA 95798-9001, 916-322-4010, Fax: 916-322-4374

(22) Bureau of Electronic & Appliance Repair, Department of Consumer Affairs, 400 R St, #3080, Sacramento, CA 95814, 916-445-4751

(23) Bureau of Home Furnishings & Thermal Insulation, 400 R St, Sacramento, CA 95814, 916-445-1591, Fax: 916-323-6639

(24) Bureau of Security & Investigative Services, 400 R St, Suite 3080, Sacramento, CA 95814, 800-952-5210, Fax: 916-445-1964

(25) California Committee of Bar Examiners, State Bar of California, 555 Franklin St, Box 7908, San Francisco, CA 94102, 415-561-8303

(26) California Horse Racing Board, 1010 Hurley Way, Suite 190, Sacramento, CA 95825, 916-263-6000

(27) Cemetery Board, 400 R St., Suite 3080, Sacramento, CA 95825, 916-327-5729, Fax: 916-445-4694

(28) Commission on Teacher Credentialing, PO Box 944270, Sacramento, CA 94244, 916-445-7254, Fax: 916-445-7255

(29) Committee on Dental Auxiliaries, 1428 Howe Ave, Suite 58, Sacramento, CA 95825-3235, 916-263-2595, Fax: 916-263-2709

(30) Contractors State License Board, PO Box 26000, (9835 Goethe Rd 95827), Sacramento, CA 95826, 916-255-3900, Fax: 916-361-7497

(31) Court Reporters Board of California, 2535 Capitol Oaks Drive Suite 230, Sacramento, CA 95833, 916-263-3660, Fax: 916-263-3664

(32) Department of Consumer Affairs, CSR Board, 2535 Capital Oaks Dr, Suite 230, Sacramento, CA 95833, 916-263-3660

(33) Department of Corporations, 3700 Wilshire Blvd, Suite 600, Los Angeles, CA 90010, 213-736-2741, Fax: 213-736-3543

(34) Department of Health Services, Radiological Health Branch, PO Box 942732, (601 N 7th St, MS #178 95814), Sacramento, CA 94234-7320, 916-445-6695, Fax: 916-324-3610

(35) Department of Insurance/License Bureau, PO Box 1139, (320 Capital Mall 95814), Sacramento, CA 95812-1139, 415-557-1126

(36) Department of Real Estate, 185 Berry St, Room 3400, San Francisco, CA 94107, 916-227-0931, Fax: 916-227-0925

(37) Hearing Aid Dispensers Examining Committee, 1420 Howe Ave, Suite 12, Sacramento, CA 95825-3230, 916-263-2288, Fax: 916-263-2290

(38) Medical Board of California, 1430 Howe Ave Suite 54, Sacramento, CA 95825-3236, 916-263-2433

(39) Office of the Secretary of State, PO Box 942877, (1500 11th St, 2nd Flr 95814), Sacramento, CA 94277-0001, 916-263-3520

(40) Physical Therapy Examining Committee, 1434 Howe Ave, Suite 92, Sacramento, CA 95825-3291, 916-263-2550, Fax: 916-263-2560

(41) Physican Assistant Examining Committee, 1424 Howe Ave, Suite 35, Sacramento, CA 95825-3237, 916-263-2670

(42) Respiratory Care Examining Committee, 1426 Howe Ave, Suite 48, Sacramento, CA 95825-3234, 916-263-2626

(43) Speech Pathology & Audiology Examining Committee, 1434 Howe Ave, Suite 86, Sacramento, CA 95825-3240, 916-263-2666, Fax: 916-263-2668

(44) State Department of Rehabilitation, 830 K St Mall, Room 222, Sacramento, CA 95814, 916-332-2929, Fax: 916-327-9487

(45) Structural Pest Control Board, 1422 Howe Ave, Suite 3, Sacramento, CA 95825-3280, 916-263-2540, Fax: 916-263-2469

(46) Tax Preparer Program, 400 R St, Suite 3140, Sacramento, CA 95814-6200, 916-324-4977

(47) Vocational Nurse/Psychiatric Technician Examiners, Medical Licensing, 2535 Capitol Oaks Dr, Suite 200, Sacramento, CA 95833, 916-263-7800

Colorado

Capitol: Montgomery (Montgomery County)	
State Population	3.7 Million
Number of Degree Granting Institutions:	63
Number of State Licensing & Business Registration Agencies:	91

Degree Granting Educational Institutions

Adams State College, Registrar, Alamosa, CO 81102, 719-589-7321 (Fax: 719-589-7522). Hours: 8AM-4:45PM. Enrollment: 2140. Records go back to 1925. Alumni records are maintained here also. Call 719-587-7121. Degrees granted: Associate; Bachelors; Masters. Adverse incident record source-Public Safety, 719-589-7901: Dean of Students, 719-589-7221

Attendance and degree information available by phone, fax, mail. Search requires name plus SSN, date of birth, exact years of attendance. There is no fee.

Aims Community College, Registrar, PO Box 69, Greeley, CO 80632, 970-330-8008 X440 (Fax: 970-339-6669). Hours: 8AM-5PM Summers closed Friday. Enrollment: 7000. Records go back to 1967. Degrees granted: Associate. Adverse incident record source- Dean of Student Services, 303-330-8008 X225.

Attendance and degree information available by phone, fax, mail. Search requires name only. Also helpful: SSN, date of birth, exact years of attendance. There is no fee.

Arapahoe Community College, Registrar, 2500 W College Dr, PO Box 9002, Littleton, CO 80160-9002, 303-797-5621 (Fax: 303-797-5970). Hours: 8AM-5PM. Enrollment: 7500. Records go back to 1966. Degrees granted: Associate. Adverse incident record source- Public Safety, 303-797-5800.

Attendance and degree information available by phone, fax, mail. Search requires name plus SSN, date of birth, approximate years of attendance. There is no fee.

Bel-Rea Institute of Animal Technology, Registrar, 1681 S Dayton St, Denver, CO 80321-3048, 303-751-8700. Hours: 8AM-5PM. Enrollment: 350. Records go back to 1970. Degrees granted: Associate.

School will not confirm attendance information.

Degree information available by phone, fax, mail. Search requires name plus approximate years of attendance. Also helpful: SSN, date of birth. There is no fee.

Beth-El College of Nursing, Registrar, 2790 N Academy Blvd Ste 200, Colorado Springs, CO 80917-5338,

719-475-5170 (Fax: 719-475-5198). Hours: 8AM-4:30PM. Enrollment: 450. Records go back to 1907. Alumni records are maintained here at the same phone number. Degrees granted: Bachelors; Masters. Certification: NNP, Forensics, Post Masters Certificate, Nurse Practitioner.

Attendance and degree information available by phone, fax, mail. Search requires name plus SSN, exact years of attendance. Also helpful: date of birth. There is no fee.

Blair Junior College, Registrar, 828 Wooten Rd, Colorado Springs, CO 80915, 719-574-1082 (Fax: 719-574-4493). Hours: 7:30AM-7PM. Enrollment: 270. Records go back to 1900. Degrees granted: Associate. Adverse incident record source- Same as above.

Attendance information available by phone, fax, mail. Search requires name plus SSN, approximate years of attendance. Also helpful: date of birth, exact years of attendance. There is no fee.

Degree information available by phone, mail. Search requires name plus SSN, approximate years of attendance. Also helpful: date of birth, exact years of attendance. There is no fee.

Colorado Christian University, Registrar, 180 S Garrison St, Lakewood, CO 80226, 303-238-5386 X140 (Fax: 303-274-7560). Hours: 8AM-5PM. Enrollment: 1698. Records go back to 1915. Alumni records are maintained here at the same phone number. Degrees granted: Associate; Bachelors; Masters. Certification: Education, LPC, Comp, OM.

Attendance and degree information available by phone, fax, mail. Search requires name plus SSN, approximate years of attendance. There is no fee.

Colorado College, Registrar, 14 E Cache la Pourde St, Colorado Springs, CO 80903, 719-389-6610 (Fax: 719-389-6931). Hours: 8:30AM-5PM. Enrollment: 1963. Records go back to 1895. Alumni records are maintained here also. Call 719-389-6000. Degrees granted: Bachelors; Masters.

Attendance information available by phone, fax, mail. Search requires name only. Also helpful: date of birth, exact years of attendance. There is no fee.

Degree information available by phone, fax, mail. Search requires name only. There is no fee.

Colorado Institute of Art, Registrar, 200 E Ninth Ave, Denver, CO 80203-9947, 303-837-0825 (Fax: 303-860-8520). Hours: 7:30AM-5PM. Enrollment: 1500. Records go back to 1960's. Alumni records are maintained here at the same phone number. Degrees granted: Associate. Special programs-Culinary Arts, 303-837-0825.
Attendance information available by fax, mail. Search requires name plus SSN, signed release. Also helpful: exact years of attendance. There is no fee.
Degree information available by phone, fax, mail. Search requires name plus SSN. Also helpful: exact years of attendance. There is no fee.

Colorado Mountain College, Registrar, Box 10001, 215 Ninth St, Glenwood Springs, CO 81602, 800-621-8559 (Fax: 970-928-8633). Hours: 8AM-5PM. Enrollment: 2000. Records go back to 1967. Second phone number is 970-945-8691. Alumni records are maintained here at the same phone number. Degrees granted: Associate.
Attendance and degree information available by fax, mail. Search requires name plus approximate years of attendance. There is no fee.

Colorado Mountain College, (Alpine), Registrar, 1370 Bob Adams Dr, Steamboat Springs, CO 80477, 970-870-4444 (Fax: 970-870-0845). Records are not housed here. They are located at Colorado Mountain College, Registrar, Box 10001, 215 Ninth St, Glenwood Springs, CO 81602.

Colorado Mountain College, (Roaring Fork), Registrar, 3000 County Rd 114, Glenwood Springs, CO 81601, 970-945-7841. Records are not housed here. They are located at Colorado Mountain College, Registrar, Box 10001, 215 Ninth St, Glenwood Springs, CO 81602.

Colorado Mountain College, (Timberline), Registrar, 901 S Hwy 24, Leadville, CO 80461, 719-486-2015 (Fax: 719-486-3212). Records are not housed here. They are located at Colorado Mountain College, Registrar, Box 10001, 215 Ninth St, Glenwood Springs, CO 81602.

Colorado Northwestern Community College, Registrar, 500 Kennedy Dr, Rangely, CO 81648, 970-675-3218 (Fax: 970-675-3343). Hours: 8AM-5PM. Enrollment: 1800. Records go back to 1960. Alumni records are maintained here also. Call 970-675-3346. Degrees granted: Associate. Special programs- Dental Hygiene: Aviaation. Adverse incident record source- Student Services, 970-675-3222.
Attendance and degree information available by phone, fax, mail. Search requires name plus SSN. Also helpful: exact years of attendance. There is no fee.

Colorado School of Mines, Registrar, 1500 Illinois St, Golden, CO 80401, 303-273-3200 (Fax: 303-273-3278). Hours: 8AM-5PM. Enrollment: 3000. Records go back to 1876. Alumni records are maintained here also. Call 303-273-3295. Degrees granted: Bachelors; Masters; PhD, Professional. Special programs- Office of Special Programs & Continuing Ed. Adverse incident record source- Dean of Students, 303-273-3350.
Attendance and degree information available by phone, fax, mail. Search requires name plus SSN. Also helpful: date of birth, exact years of attendance. There is no fee.

Colorado State University, Records & Registration, Rm 200 Admin Annex, Fort Collins, CO 80523, 970-491-7148 (Fax: 970-491-2283). Hours: 7:45AM-4:45PM Winter; 7:30AM-4:30PM Summer. Enrollment: 21000. Records go back to 1875. Alumni Records Office: 645 S Shields St, Fort Collins, CO 80521. Degrees granted: Bachelors; Masters; Doctorate. Adverse incident record source- Judicial Affairs, 970-491-5312.
Attendance and degree information available by phone, fax, mail. Search requires name only. Also helpful: SSN, date of birth. There is no fee.

Colorado Technical University, Records, 4435 N Chestnut St, Colorado Springs, CO 80907, 719-598-0200 (Fax: 719-598-3740). Hours: 8AM-6PM. Enrollment: 1600. Formerly Colorado Technical College Records go back to 1926. Degrees granted: Associate; Bachelors; Masters; Doctorate.
Attendance information available by phone, fax, mail. Search requires name plus SSN. Also helpful: exact years of attendance. There is no fee.
Degree information available by fax, mail. Search requires name plus SSN. Also helpful: exact years of attendance. There is no fee.

Community College of Aurora, Registrar, 16000 E Centretech Pkwy, Aurora, CO 80011, 303-361-7411 (Fax: 303-361-7432). Hours: 9AM-6PM M-Th, 8AM-5PM F. Enrollment: 4600. Records go back to 1983. Degrees granted: Associate. Adverse incident record source- Dean of Students, 303-360-4752.
Attendance and degree information available by phone, fax, mail. Search requires name plus SSN, approximate years of attendance. There is no fee.

Community College of Denver, Registrar, PO Box 173363, Denver, CO 80217-3363, 303-556-2430 (Fax: 303-446-2461). Hours: N/A. Records go back to 1969. Degrees granted: Associate. Adverse incident record source- Auraria Public Safety, 303-556-3271.
Attendance and degree information available by phone, fax, mail. Search requires name plus SSN. Also helpful: date of birth, exact years of attendance. There is no fee.

Denver Business College, Registrar, 7350 N Broadway, Denver, CO 80221, 303-426-1000. Enrollment: 440. Records go back to 1958. Degrees granted: Associate.
Attendance and degree information available by fax, mail. Search requires name plus signed release. Also helpful: SSN, date of birth, exact years of attendance. There is no fee.

Denver Conservative Baptist Seminary, Registrar, PO Box 10000, Denver, CO 80250-0100, 303-761-2482 X221 (Fax: 303-761-8060). Hours: 8AM-4:30PM. Enrollment: 625. Records go back to 1950. Alumni records are maintained here at the same phone number. Degrees granted: Masters; Doctorate.
Attendance and degree information available by phone, fax, mail. Search requires name only. Also helpful: SSN, date of birth, exact years of attendance. There is no fee.

Denver Institute of Technology, Registrar, 7350 N Broadway, Denver, CO 80221-3653, 303-426-1111 X362 (Fax: 303-426-1818). Hours: 7:30AM-7PM M-Th, 8AM-Noon F, Sat. Degrees granted: Associate; Bachelors.
Attendance and degree information available by phone, fax, mail. Search requires name plus SSN, exact years of attendance. There is no fee.

Denver Institute of Technology, (Health Careers Division), Registrar, 7350 N Broadway Annex HCD, Denver, CO 80221-3653, 303-650-5050 (Fax: 303-426-1832). Records are not housed here. They are located at Denver Institute of Technology, Registrar, 7350 N Broadway, Denver, CO 80221-3653.

Denver Technical College, Registrar, 925 S Niagara St, Denver, CO 80224-1658, 303-329-3340 (Fax: 303-321-3412). Hours: 7AM-5PM. Enrollment: 850. Records go back to 1986. Degrees granted: Associate; Bachelors; Masters.
Attendance and degree information available by phone, fax, mail. Search requires name only. Also helpful: SSN, exact years of attendance. There is no fee.

Denver Technical College at Colorado Springs, Registrar, 225 S Union Blvd, Colorado Springs, CO

80910-3138, 719-632-3000 X123 (Fax: 719-632-1909). Hours: 8AM-6PM M-Th, 8AM-Noon. Records go back to 1985. Alumni records are maintained here at the same phone number. Degrees granted: Associate; Bachelors. Adverse incident record source-Student Services, 719-632-3000 X112.

Attendance and degree information available by phone, fax, mail. Search requires name plus SSN. Also helpful: approximate years of attendance. There is no fee.

Fort Lewis College, Records Office, 108MSC, 1000 Rim Dr, Durango, CO 81301-3999, 970-247-7350. Hours: 9AM-Noon, 1-4PM. Records go back to 1925. Alumni records are maintained here also. Call 970-247-7427. Degrees granted: Associate; Bachelors. Adverse incident record source- Dean of Student Affairs, 970-247-7331.

Attendance and degree information available by phone, mail. Search requires name plus SSN, date of birth. Also helpful: exact years of attendance. There is no fee.

Front Range Community College, Registrar, 3645 W 112th Ave, Westminster, CO 80030, 303-466-8811 X53413 (Fax: 303-439-2614). Hours: 9AM-5PM M,Th; 9AM-7PM T,W; 9AM-4PM F. Enrollment: 13000. Records go back to 1970. Degrees granted: Associate. Adverse incident record source- Security, 303-466-8811 X5403 info 5 yrs back: Current info, 303-466-8811 X5313

Attendance and degree information available by mail. Search requires name plus SSN, signed release. There is no fee.

ITT Technical Institute, Registrar, 2121 S Blackhawk St, Aurora, CO 80014-1416, 303-695-1913 (Fax: 303-751-5603). Hours: 8AM-5PM. Enrollment: 250. Records go back to 1989. Alumni Records Office: Alumni Association, 5975 Castle Creek Pkwy N, Indianapolis, IN 46250-0466. Degrees granted: Associate; Bachelors.

Attendance information available by phone, fax, mail. Search requires name only. Also helpful: exact years of attendance. There is no fee.

Degree information available by phone, fax, mail. Search requires name only. Also helpful: exact years of attendance. There is no fee.

Iliff School of Theology, Registrar, 2201 S University Blvd, Denver, CO 80210, 303-744-1287 X227 (Fax: 303-777-3387). Hours: 8AM-4:30PM. Enrollment: 350. Records go back to 1892. Alumni records are maintained here also. Call 303-744-127 X285. Degrees granted: Masters.

Attendance and degree information available by phone, fax, mail. Search requires name plus SSN. Also helpful: date of birth, exact years of attendance. There is no fee.

Johnson & Wales University, (Branch Campus), Registrar, 616 W Lionshead Cir, Vail, CO 81657, 970-476-2993 (Fax: 970-476-2994). Hours: 8AM-5PM. Enrollment: 40. Records go back to 1993. Alumni Records Office: 8 Abbott Park Pl, Providence, RI 02903. Degrees granted: Associate. Special programs- Culinary Arts (1 year program). Adverse incident record source- Directors Office.

Attendance and degree information available by phone, mail. Search requires name plus SSN, exact years of attendance. There is no fee.

Lamar Community College, Registrar, 2401 S Main St, Lamar, CO 81052, 719-336-2248 X125 (Fax: 719-336-2448). Hours: 8AM-5PM. Enrollment: 1000. Records go back to 1937. Alumni Records Office: Alumni Association, 2401 S Main St, Lamar, CO 81052. Degrees granted: Associate. Adverse incident record source- Student Affairs, 719-336-2248 X241.

Attendance and degree information available by phone, fax, mail. Search requires name plus exact years of attendance. Also helpful: SSN, date of birth. There is no fee.

Mesa State College, Registrar, PO Box 2647, Grand Junction, CO 81502, 970-248-1641 (Fax: 970-248-1131). Hours: 8AM-5PM. Enrollment: 4382. Records go back to 1928. Degrees granted: Associate; Bachelors. Adverse incident record source-Disciplinary Officer: Mesa State College

Attendance and degree information available by phone, fax, mail. Search requires name plus SSN, date of birth, approximate years of attendance. There is no fee.

Metropolitan State College of Denver, Registrar, PO Box 173362, Denver, CO 80217-3362, 303-556-3991 (Fax: 303-556-3999). Hours: 8AM-5:30PM Summer; 7:30AM-6:30PM M-Th, 8AM-5PM F Fall. Enrollment: 17550. Records go back to 1963. Alumni records are maintained here also. Call 303-556-8320. Degrees granted: Associate; Bachelors; Masters; Doctorate. Special programs- Recreation and Leisure Services.

Attendance information available by fax, mail. Search requires name plus SSN, approximate years of attendance, signed release. There is no fee.

Degree information available by phone, fax, mail. Search requires name plus SSN, approximate years of attendance. There is no fee.

Morgan Community College, Registrar, 17800 Rd 20, Fort Morgan, CO 80701, 970-867-3081 (Fax: 970-867-6608). Hours: 8AM-5PM. Enrollment: 1000. Records go back to 1971. Degrees granted: Associate.

Attendance and degree information available by phone, fax, mail. Search requires name plus SSN. Also helpful: date of birth, exact years of attendance. There is no fee.

Naropa Institute, Registrar, 2130 Arapahoe Ave, Boulder, CO 80302, 303-546-3500 (Fax: 303-546-3536). Hours: 9AM-3PM M-Th. Records go back to 1974. Degrees granted: Bachelors; Masters. Adverse incident record source- Student Services, 303-546-3562.

Attendance and degree information available by phone, fax, mail. Search requires name plus SSN. There is no fee.

National Technological University, Registrar, 700 Centre Ave, Fort Collins, CO 80526, 970-495-6403 (Fax: 970-498-0601). Hours: 8AM-5PM. Enrollment: 1943. Records go back to 1984. Alumni records are maintained here at the same phone number. Degrees granted: Masters.

Attendance and degree information available by fax, mail. Search requires name plus SSN, signed release. There is no fee.

National Theatre Conservatory, Registrar, 1050 13th St, Denver, CO 80204, 303-446-4855 (Fax: 303-821-2117). Hours: 9AM-5PM. Enrollment: 24. Records go back to 1985. Alumni records are maintained here also. Call 303-446-4855. Degrees granted: Masters. Adverse incident record source- Registrar, 303-446-4855.

Attendance and degree information available by fax, mail. Search requires name plus SSN, exact years of attendance. There is no fee.

Nazarene Bible College, Registrar, PO Box 15749, 1111 Chapman Dr, Colorado Springs, CO 80916, 719-596-5110 (Fax: 719-550-9437). Hours: 8AM-4:30PM. Enrollment: 420. Records go back to 1968. Alumni records are maintained here at the same phone number. Degrees granted: Associate; Bachelors.

Attendance and degree information available by phone, fax, mail. Search requires name plus SSN. Also helpful: date of birth, exact years of attendance. There is no fee.

Northeastern Junior College, NJC Records Office, 100 College Dr, Sterling, CO 80751, 970-522-6600 X658 (Fax: 970-522-4664). Hours: 8AM-4:30PM. Enrollment: 3500. Records go back to 1989. Alumni records are maintained here also. Call 970-522-6600 X2690. Degrees granted: Associate. Adverse incident record source- Student Services.

Attendance and degree information available by written request only. Search requires name plus SSN, date of birth, signed release. Also helpful: approximate years of attendance. There is no fee.

Otero Junior College, Registrar, 1802 Colorado Ave, La Junta, CO 81050, 719-384-6833 (Fax: 719-384-6800). Hours: 7:30AM-9PM M-Th, 7:30AM-5PM F. Enrollment: 1000. Records go back to 1942. Degrees granted: Associate.

Attendance and degree information available by phone, fax, mail. Search requires name plus SSN, approximate years of attendance. There is no fee.

Parks Junior College, Registrar, 9065 Grant St, Denver, CO 80229, 303-457-2757 (Fax: 303-457-4030). Hours: 10:30AM-7:30PM. Records go back to 1970. Degrees granted: Associate.

Attendance information available by phone, fax, mail. Search requires name plus SSN, exact years of attendance. Also helpful: date of birth. There is no fee.

Degree information available by mail. Search requires name plus SSN, exact years of attendance. Also helpful: date of birth. There is no fee.

Parks Junior College, (Branch), Registrar, 6 Abilene St, Aurora, CO 80011, 303-367-2757 (Fax: 303-461-9706). Hours: 7AM-6PM. Records go back to 1895. Degrees granted: Associate.

Attendance and degree information available by fax, mail. Search requires name plus SSN, approximate years of attendance. There is no fee.

Pikes Peak Community College, Records Office, Box 8, 5675 S Academy Blvd, Colorado Springs, CO 80906-5498, 719-540-7116 (Fax: 719-540-7614). Hours: 8AM-8PM M,T; 8AM-5PM W-F. Enrollment: 6900. Records go back to 1969. Alumni records are maintained here also. Call 719-540-7554. Degrees granted: Associate. Adverse incident record source- Public Safety, 719-540-7162.

Attendance and degree information available by phone, mail. Search requires name plus SSN. Also helpful: date of birth, exact years of attendance. There is no fee.

Pima Medical Institute, (Branch), Registrar, 1701 W 72nd Ave #130, Denver, CO 80221, 303-426-1800 (Fax: 303-430-4048). Hours: 7:30AM-6:30PM M-Th; 8AM-5PM F. Enrollment: 290. Records go back to 1989. Degrees granted: Associate. Adverse incident record source- Student Services.

Attendance information available by phone, fax, mail. Search requires name plus SSN, date of birth. There is no fee.

Degree information available by phone, fax, mail. Search requires name plus SSN. There is no fee.

Pueblo College of Business and Technology, Registrar, 330 Lake Ave, Pueblo, CO 81004, 719-545-3100 (Fax: 719-545-4530). Hours: 7:30AM-4:30PM. Enrollment: 180. Records go back to 1983. Degrees granted: Associate.

Attendance and degree information available by phone, mail. Search requires name plus SSN. Also helpful: date of birth, exact years of attendance. There is no fee.

Pueblo Community College, Registrar, 900 W Orman Ave, Pueblo, CO 81004, 719-549-3016 (Fax: 719-543-7566). Hours: 8AM-6PM M-Th; 8AM-5PM F. Enrollment: 4000. Records go back to 1979. Alumni records are maintained here also. Call 719-549-3213. Degrees granted: Associate. Special programs- 6/1974 & Previous, U of CO, 719-549-2261. Adverse incident record source- PCC Security, 719-549-3291.

Attendance and degree information available by phone, fax, mail. Search requires name plus SSN. Also helpful: date of birth, exact years of attendance. There is no fee.

Red Rocks Community College, Registrar, 13300 W Sixth Ave, Lakewood, CO 80401-5398, 303-988-6160 (Fax: 303-988-6191). Hours: 8AM-7PM M-Th, 9AM-5PM F. Enrollment: 6832. Records go back to 1969. Degrees granted: Associate. Adverse incident record source- Security, 303-988-6160.

Attendance and degree information available by phone, fax, mail. Search requires name plus SSN, exact years of attendance. There is no fee.

Regis University, Registrar, 3333 Regis Blvd, Denver, CO 80221-1099, 303-458-4114 (Fax: 303-964-5536). Hours: 8:30AM-5PM. Enrollment: 9505. Records go back to 1877. Alumni records are maintained here at the same phone number. Degrees granted: Associate; Bachelors; Masters. Certification: Teacher. Adverse incident record source- Student Life Office: Probation/suspension posted to transcript

Attendance and degree information available by phone, fax, mail. Search requires name plus SSN, date of birth. Also helpful: exact years of attendance. There is no fee.

Rocky Mountain College of Art and Design, Registrar, 6875 E Evans Ave, Denver, CO 80224-2359, 303-753-6046 (Fax: 303-759-4970). Hours: 8AM-4:30PM. Enrollment: 400. Records go back to 1963. Alumni records are maintained here also. Call 800-888-2787. Degrees granted: Bachelors.

Attendance and degree information available by phone, fax, mail. Search requires name plus SSN, exact years of attendance. There is no fee.

Technical Trades Institute, Registrar, 2315 E Pikes Peak, Colorado Springs, CO 80909, 719-632-7626 (Fax: 719-632-7451). Enrollment: 260. Records go back to 1965. Degrees granted: Associate. Adverse incident record source- Student Services.

Attendance and degree information available by phone, mail. Search requires name plus SSN, exact years of attendance. There is no fee.

Trinidad State Junior College, Registrar, 600 Prospect St, Trinidad, CO 81082, 719-846-5621 (Fax: 719-846-5667). Hours: 8AM-5PM. Enrollment: 1500. Records go back to 1940. Alumni records are maintained here also. Call 719-846-5649. Degrees granted: Associate. Special programs- Gunsmithing: Recreation Vehicle Service Technician: Aqua Farm, 719-846-5621. Adverse incident record source- Student Services, 719-846-5621.

Attendance and degree information available by phone, fax, mail. Search requires name plus SSN. Also helpful: date of birth, exact years of attendance. Fee is $3.00.

United States Air Force Academy, (Department of the Air Force), HQ USAFA/DFRR, 2354 Fairchild Dr Ste 6D106, USAF Academy, CO 80840-6210, 719-472-3970 (Fax: 719-472-2943). Hours: 7AM-4:30PM. Enrollment: 4000. Records go back to 1959. Alumni Records Office: Alumni Association, 3116 Academy Dr Ste 100, USAF Academy, CO 80840-4425. Degrees granted: Bachelors.

Attendance and degree information available by phone, fax, mail. Search requires name only. Also helpful: SSN, exact years of attendance. There is no fee.

University of Colorado Health Sciences Center, Admissions & Records, 4200 E 9th Ave, Box A054, Denver, CO 80262, 303-399-1211 (Fax: 303-270-3358). Hours: 8AM-4:30PM. Enrollment: 720. Alumni Records Office: Alumni Development, Box A065, Denver, CO 80262, 303-270-5271. Degrees granted: Bachelors; Masters; Doctorate.

Attendance and degree information available by phone, fax, mail. Search requires name only. Also helpful: SSN, date of birth, exact years of attendance. There is no fee.

University of Colorado at Boulder, Office of the Registrar, Campus Box 68, Boulder, CO 80309, 303-492-6907 (Fax: 303-492-4884). Enrollment: 25000. Records go back to 1896. Alumni Records Office: Campus Box 459, Boulder, CO 80309, 303-492-8484. Degrees granted: Bachelors; Masters; Doctorate. Certification: Teacher. Adverse incident record source- Student Conduct, 303-492-5550.

Attendance and degree information available by phone, fax, mail. Search requires name only. Also helpful: SSN, date of birth, exact years of attendance. There is no fee.

University of Colorado at Colorado Springs, Registrar, PO Box 7150, Colorado Springs, CO 80933-7150, 719-262-3361 (Fax: 719-262-3116). Hours: 8AM-7PM M, 8AM-5PM T-F. Enrollment: 6000. Records go back to 1970. Alumni records are maintained here also. Call 719-262-3465. Degrees granted: Bachelors; Masters; Doctorate.

Attendance information available by fax, mail. Search requires name plus SSN, date of birth, signed release. Also helpful: approximate years of attendance. There is no fee.

Degree information available by phone, fax, mail. Search requires name plus SSN, date of birth. There is no fee.

University of Colorado at Denver, Transcript Office, Campus Box 167, PO Box 173364, Denver, CO 80217-3364, 303-556-3415 (Fax: 303-556-4829). Hours: 8AM-5PM. Enrollment: 11000. Records go back to 1960. Alumni records are maintained here also. Call 303-556-2549. Degrees granted: Bachelors; Masters; Doctorate.

Attendance and degree information available by phone, fax, mail. Search requires name only. Also helpful: SSN, date of birth, exact years of attendance. There is no fee.

University of Denver, Registrar, 2199 S University Blvd, Denver, CO 80208, 303-871-2284 (Fax: 303-871-4300). Hours: 8AM-4:30PM. Enrollment: 8492. Records go back to 1882. Alumni records are maintained here also. Call 303-871-2103. Degrees granted: Bachelors; Masters; Doctorate. Adverse incident record source- COMMUNICATIONS, 303-871-2711.

Attendance and degree information available by phone, fax, mail. Search requires name plus SSN, exact years of attendance. Also helpful: date of birth. There is no fee.

University of Denver, College of Law, Registrar, 7039 E 18th St, Denver, CO 80220, 303-871-6132 (Fax: 303-871-6378). Enrollment: 10000. Records go back to 1864. Alumni records are maintained here at the same phone number. Degrees granted: Doctorate. Adverse incident record source- Security.

Attendance and degree information available by phone, mail. Search requires name plus SSN, date of birth, exact years of attendance. There is no fee.

University of Northern Colorado, Registrar's Office, Carter Hall 3002, Greeley, CO 80639, 970-351-2231 (Fax: 970-351-1870). Hours: 8AM-5PM. Enrollment: 10450. Records go back to 1890. Alumni Records Office: Alumni Association, University of Northern Colorado, Faculty Apartments, Greeley, CO 80639. Degrees granted: Bachelors; Masters; Doctorate. Certification: Teacher. Adverse incident record source-Police, 970-351-2245.

Attendance information available by phone, fax, mail. Search requires name only. Also helpful: SSN, date of birth, exact years of attendance. There is no fee.

Degree information available by phone, fax, mail. Search requires name only. Also helpful: SSN, date of birth, exact years of attendance. There is no fee.

University of Phoenix, (Denver Main), Registrar, 7800 E Dorado Pl, Englewood, CO 80111, 303-755-9090 (Fax: 303-694-6084). Enrollment: 3000. Records go back to 1976. Transcript records are housed at University of Phoenix, Registrar, PO Box 52069, Phoenix, AZ 85072. Alumni Records Office: Alumni Association, PO Box 52069, Phoenix, AZ 85072. Degrees granted: Bachelors; Masters.

Attendance and degree information available by written request only. Search requires name plus SSN, approximate years of attendance. Also helpful: date of birth, exact years of attendance. There is no fee.

University of Southern Colorado, Registrar, 2200 Bonforte Blvd, Pueblo, CO 81001, 719-549-2261 (Fax: 719-549-2419). Hours: 8AM-5PM. Enrollment: 4800. Records go back to 1933. Alumni records are maintained here also. Call 719-549-2114. Degrees granted: Bachelors; Masters.

School will not confirm attendance information.

Degree information available by phone, fax, mail. Search requires name plus SSN, date of birth, exact years of attendance. There is no fee.

Western State College of Colorado, Registrar, Gunnison, CO 81231, 970-943-2047 (Fax: 970-943-2212). Hours: 8AM-5PM. Enrollment: 2445. Records go back to 1911. Alumni records are maintained here also. Call 970-943-2090. Degrees granted: Bachelors.

Attendance information available by phone, fax, mail. Search requires name plus SSN. Also helpful: exact years of attendance. There is no fee.

Degree information available by phone, fax, mail. Search requires name plus SSN. Also helpful: date of birth, exact years of attendance. There is no fee.

Yeshiva Toras Chaim Talmudic Seminary, Registrar, 1400 Quitman St, PO Box 4067, Denver, CO 80204, 303-629-8200 (Fax: 303-623-5949). Hours: 8AM-5PM. Enrollment: 18. Records go back to 1967. Degrees granted: Masters; 1st Professional Degree.

Attendance and degree information available by phone, fax, mail. Search requires name plus SSN, approximate years of attendance. There is no fee.

Trade and Vocational Schools

Academy of Floral Design, 837 Acoma St, Denver, CO 80204], 303-623-8855

Army Academy of Health Sciences (Medical Equipment and Optician School), Aurora, CO 80045, 303-361-8898

Boulder School of Massage Therapy, 3285 30th St, Boulder, CO 80301, 303-443-5131

Boulder Valley Area Vocational-Technical Center, 6600 E Arapahoe Ave, Boulder, CO 80303, 303-447-5247

CollegeAmerica - Denver, 720 S Colorado Blvd #260, Denver, CO 80222, 303-691-9756

Colorado Aero Tech, 10851 W 120th Ave, Broomfield, CO 80021, 800-888-3995

Colorado Association of Paramedical Education, Inc., 9191 Grant St, Thornton, CO 80229, 303-451-7800

Colorado School of Trades, 1575 Hoyt St, Lakewood, CO 80215, 303-233-4697

Colorado School of Travel, 608 Garrison St #J, Lakewood, CO 80215, 303-233-8654

ConCorde Career Institute, 770 Grant St, Denver, CO 80203, 303-861-1151

Denver Academy of Court Reporting, 7290 Samuel Dr 2nd Flr #200, Denver, CO 80221, 303-427-5292

Denver Automotive and Diesel College, 405 S Platte Rive Dr, Denver, CO 80223, 303-722-5724

Denver Paralegal Institute, 1401 19th St, Denver, CO 80202, 800-848-0550

Denver Paralegal Institute (Branch Campus), 105 E Vermijo Ave #415, Colorado Springs, CO 80903, 719-444-0190

Durango Air Service, 1300 County Rd 309, Durango, CO 81301, 970-247-5535

Emily Griffith Opportunity School, 1250 Welton St, Denver, CO 80204, 303-572-8218

Heritage College of Health Careers, 12 Lakeside Ln, Denver, CO 80212, 303-477-7240

Institute of Business Medical Careers, 1609 Carridge Dr #102, Fort Collins, CO 80525, 970-223-2669

Institute of Business and Medical Careers, 1609 Oakridge Dr Ste 102, Fort Collins, CO 80525, 303-223-2669

PPI Health Careers School, 2345 N Academy Blvd, Colorado Springs, CO 80909, 719-596-7400

Platt College, 3100 S Parker Rd, Aurora, CO 80014, 303-369-5151

Presbyterian-St. Luke Center for Health Science Foundation, 1719 E 19th Ave, Denver, CO 80218, 303-839-6740

T.H. Pickens Technical Center, 500 Buckley Rd, Aurora, CO 80011, 303-344-4910

Technical Trades Institute, 2315 E Pikes Peak Ave, Colorado Springs, CO 80909, 719-632-7626

Technical Trades Institute, 772 Horizon Dr, Grand Junction, CO 81501, 970-245-8101

State Licensing & Business Registration Quick Finder Index

Architecture, Engineering & Surveying
Architect #15 .... ✉ 303-894-7801
Engineer #19 (15500) .... ☎ 303-894-7788
Engineer-in-Training (Engineer Intern) #19
.... ☎ 303-894-7788
Land Surveyor Intern #19 .... ☎ 303-894-7788
Land Surveyor-Professional #19 (1800) .... ☎ 303-894-7788

Business - Court & Legal Services
Attorney #3 .... ✉ 303-893-8096
Bonding Agent #10 (300) .... ☎ 303-894-7499
Notary Public #37 (100000) .... ☎ 303-894-2680
Shorthand Reporter #36 303-837-3695

Business - General Services
Public Accountant-CPA & PA #13 303-894-7800
Solicitor #2 (600) .... ☎ 303-866-5706

Construction & Manufacturing
Electrical Apprentice #41 303-894-2300
Electrical Contractor #41 303-894-2300
Electrical Inspector #41 303-894-2300

Electrician-Journeyman #41 303-894-2300
Electrician-Master #41 303-894-2300
Manufactured Housing Dealer #22 .... ☎ 303-894-7802
Manufactured Housing Salesperson #22 .... ☎ 303-894-7802
Plumber #35 .... ☎ 303-894-2319
Plumber-Apprentice #35 .... ☎ 303-894-2319
Plumber-Residential #35 .... ☎ 303-894-2319
Residential Wireman #41 303-894-2300

Education
School Administrator #40 (953) .... ☎ 303-866-6628
School Special Service Associate #40
(1199) .... ☎ 303-866-6628
Substitute Teacher #40 .... ☎ 303-866-6968
Teacher #40 (12382) .... ☎ 303-866-6628
Vocational Education Teacher #40 (15) .... ☎ 303-866-6628

Environmental & Agriculture
Asbestos Certification #5 (1600) .... ☎ 303-692-3158
Butcher #1 .... ✉ 303-239-4140
Milk & Cream Sampler #6 (130) .... ☎ 303-692-3642
Milk & Cream Tester #6 (60) .... ☎ 303-692-3642

Nursery #1 .... ⊠ 303-239-4140
Pesticide Applicator #1 .... ⊠ 303-239-4140
Veterinarian #31 .... ☎ 303-894-7755
Veterinary Student #31 .... ☎ 303-894-7755

Financial - Real Estate, Insurance & Banking

Claims Adjuster #10 .... ☎ 303-894-7499
Collection Agency #2 (370) .... ☎ 303-866-5706
Credit Union (State Chartered) #9 .... ☎ 303-894-2336
Debt Management Company #8 (7) .... ☎ 303-894-7575
Industrial Bank #8 (5) .... ☎ 303-894-7575
Insurance Agent #10 .... ☎ 303-894-7499
Insurance Broker #10 (40000) .... ☎ 303-894-7499
Money Order Company #8 (17) .... ☎ 303-894-7575
Real Estate Broker #12 .... ☎ 303-894-2166
Real Estate Salesperson #12 .... ☎ 303-894-2166
Savings & Loan Association - State Chartered #9
.... ☎ 303-894-2336
Securities Broker #34 .... ☎ 303-894-2320
Securities Dealer #34 .... ☎ 303-894-2320
Securities Sales Promoter #34 .... ☎ 303-894-2320
Small Business Development Credit Corporation
(Life Care Institutions) #9 .... ☎ 303-894-2336
State Chartered Commercial Bank #8
(126) .... ☎ 303-894-7575
Trust Company #8 (9) .... ☎ 303-894-7575

Health & Beauty

Acupuncturist #14 .... ☎ 303-894-2464
Artificial Inseminator #31 .... ☎ 303-894-7755
Barber #16 .... ☎ 303-894-7772
Child Health Associate #21 .... ☎ 303-894-7690
Chiropractor #17 .... ☎ 303-894-7762
Cosmetician #16 .... ☎ 303-894-7772
Cosmetologist #16 .... ☎ 303-894-7772
Dental Hygienist #18 303-894-7758
Dentist #18 303-894-7758

Hearing Aid Dealer/Dispenser #2 .... ☎ 303-866-3617
Kennel #5 .... ☎ 303-692-2000
Manicurist #16 .... ☎ 303-894-7772
Medical Doctor #21 (14707) .... ☎ 303-894-7690
Nurse #4 (45000) .... ☎ 303-894-2430
Nurses Aide #4 (18000) .... ☎ 303-894-2816
Nursing Home Administrator #23 (506) ...... ⊠ 303-894-7760
Optometrist #33 (950) .... ☎ 303-894-7750
Pharmacist #26 .... ☎ 303-894-7750
Pharmacy #26 .... ☎ 303-894-7750
Pharmacy Intern #26 .... ☎ 303-894-7750
Physical Therapist #32 (5520) .... ☎ 303-894-2440
Physician's Assistant #21 (649) .... ☎ 303-894-7690
Physiotherapist #32 (5520) .... ☎ 303-894-2440
Podiatrist #27 .... ☎ 303-894-7690
Practical Nurse #4 .... ☎ 303-894-2430

Social Services

Clinical Social Worker #30 .... ☎ 303-894-7766
Family Therapist #20 .... ⊠ 303-894-7766
Marriage Therapist #20 .... ⊠ 303-894-7766
Professional Counselor #28 (1500) .... ☎ 303-894-7766
Psychiatric Technician #4 (1600) .... ☎ 303-894-2430
Psychologist #29 .... ☎ 303-894-7766

Sports & Entertainment

Greyhound Racing (10 types) #11 .... ☎ 303-205-2990
Horse Racing (17 types) #11 .... ☎ 303-205-2990
Liquor Control #39 (12000) .... ☎ 303-205-2300
Outfitter #24 .... ☎ 303-894-7778
Pet Animal/Bird Dealer #5 .... ☎ 303-692-2000
River Outfitter #38 .... ☎ 303-866-3311

Transportation

Commercial Driving School #7 303-866-3091
Tramway #25 (292) .... ☎ 303-894-7785

State Licensing & Business Registration Agency Information

(1) Agriculture Department, 700 Kipling St, Suite 4000, Lakewood, CO 80215-5894, 303-239-4140, Fax: 303-239-4125

(2) Attorney General's Office, 1525 Sherman St, 5th Floor, Denver, CO 80203, 303-866-5706, Fax: 303-866-5691

(3) Board of Law Examiners, 600 17th St, Suite 520 S, Denver, CO 80202, 303-893-8096

(4) Board of Nursing, 1560 Broadway, Suite 670, Denver, CO 80202, 303-894-2430, Fax: 303-894-2821

(5) Department of Health, 4300 Cherry Creek Dr S, Denver, CO 80222-1530, 303-692-3150, Fax: 303-782-0278

(6) Department of Health, Consumer Protection Division, 4300 Cherry Creek Dr South, Denver, CO 80222-1530, 303-692-3642, Fax: 303-253-6809

(7) Department of Revenue, 1375 Sherman St, Denver, CO 80261, 303-866-3091

(8) Division of Banking, 1560 Broadway, Suite 1175, Denver, CO 80202, 303-894-7575, Fax: 303-894-7570

(9) Division of Financial Services, 1560 Broadway, Suite 1520, Denver, CO 80202, 303-894-2336, Fax: 303-894-7885

(10) Division of Insurance, 1560 Broadway, Suite 850, Denver, CO 80202, 303-894-7499, Fax: 303-894-7455

(11) Division of Racing Events, 1881 Pierce St., Suite 108, Lakewood, CO 80214, 303-205-2990, Fax: 303-205-2950

(12) Division of Real Estate, 1900 Grant St, Suite 600, Denver, CO 80203, 303-894-2166

(13) Division of Registrations, 1560 Broadway, Suite 1370, Denver, CO 80202, 303-894-7800

(14) Division of Registrations, 1560 Broadway, Suite 680, Denver, CO 80202, 303-866-5000

(15) Division of Registrations, 1560 Broadway, Suite 1370, Denver, CO 80202, 303-894-7801

(16) Division of Registrations, 1560 Broadway, Suite 1340, Denver, CO 80202, 303-894-7772

(17) Division of Registrations, 1560 Broadway, Suite 1340, Denver, CO 80202, 303-894-7762

(18) Division of Registrations, 1560 Broadway, Suite 1310, Denver, CO 80202, 303-894-7758, Fax: 303-894-7764

(19) Division of Registrations, 1560 Broadway, Suite 1370, Denver, CO 80202, 303-894-7788, Fax: 303-894-7790

(20) Division of Registrations, 1560 Broadway, Suite 1340, Denver, CO 80202, 303-894-7766

(21) Division of Registrations, 1560 Broadway, Suite 1300, Denver, CO 80202, 303-894-7690, Fax: 303-894-7692

(22) Division of Registrations, 525 Canyon Blvd, Suite A, Denver, CO 80302, 303-442-4402, Fax: 303-442-4430

(23) Division of Registrations, 1560 Broadway, Suite 1310, Denver, CO 80202, 303-894-7760, Fax: 303-894-7764

(24) Division of Registrations, 1560 Broadway, Suite 1340, Denver, CO 80202, 303-894-7778

(25) Division of Registrations, 1560 Broadway, Suite 1370, Denver, CO 80202, 303-894-7785, Fax: 303-894-7790

(26) Division of Registrations, 1560 Broadway, Suite 1310, Denver, CO 80202-5146, 303-894-7750, Fax: 303-894-7764

(27) Division of Registrations, 1560 Broadway, Suite 680, Denver, CO 80202, 303-894-2464, Fax: 303-894-2821

(28) Division of Registrations, 1560 Broadway, Suite 1340, Denver, CO 80202, 303-894-7766

(29) Division of Registrations, 1560 Broadway, Suite 1340, Denver, CO 80202, 303-894-7766

(30) Division of Registrations, 1560 Broadway, Suite 1340, Denver, CO 80202, 303-894-7766

(31) Division of Registrations, 1560 Broadway, Suite 1340, Denver, CO 80202-5146, 303-894-7755, Fax: 303-894-7764

(32) Division of Registrations, Physical Therapy Registration, 1560 Broadway, Suite 670, Denver, CO 80202, 303-894-2440, Fax: 303-894-2821

(33) Division of Registrations, State Board of Optometry Examiners, 1560 Broadway, Suite 1310, Denver, CO 80202, 303-894-7750, Fax: 303-894-7764

(34) Division of Securities, 1580 Lincoln, Suite 420, Denver, CO 80202, 303-894-2320

(35) Examing Board of Plumbers, 1580 Logan St, Suite 550, Denver, CO 80203-1941, 303-894-2319, Fax: 303-894-2310

(36) Human Resources Office, Colorado Judicial Department, 1301 Pennsylvania St, Ste 300, Denver, CO 80203, 303-837-3695

(37) Office of Secretary of State, 1560 Broadway, Suite 200, Denver, CO 80202, 303-894-2680, Fax: 303-894-7732

(38) Outfitters Registration, 13787 S Highway 85, Littleton, CO 80125, 303-791-1954, Fax: 303-470-0782

(39) Revenue Department, Alcohol Control Division, 1375 Sherman St, Suite 600, Denver, CO 80261, 303-205-2300, Fax: 303-205-2341

(40) State Department of Education, 201 E Colifax, Denver, CO 80203, 303-866-6628, Fax: 303-866-6968

(41) State Electrical Board, Electrical Apprentice & Related Licensing, 1580 Logan St., Suite 550, Denver, CO 80203-1939, 303-894-2300, Fax: 303-894-2310

Connecticut

Capitol: Hartford (Hartford County)	
State Population	3.3 Million
Number of Degree Granting Institutions:	47
Number of State Licensing & Business Registration Agencies:	103

Degree Granting Educational Institutions

Albertus Magnus College, Registrar, New Haven, CT 06511-1189, 203-773-8514 (Fax: 203-773-3117). Hours: 9AM-5PM. Enrollment: 1000. Records go back to 1925. Alumni records are maintained here also. Call 203-773-8502. Degrees granted: Associate; Bachelors; Masters. Adverse incident record source- Student Services, 203-773-8541.

Attendance information available by phone, fax, mail. Search requires name plus SSN, approximate years of attendance. There is no fee.

Degree information available by phone, mail. Search requires name plus SSN, approximate years of attendance. There is no fee.

Asnuntuck Community-Technical College, Registrar, 170 Elm St, Enfield, CT 06082, 203-253-3000 (Fax: 203-253-3016). Hours: 8:30AM-4:30PM. Enrollment: 835. Records go back to 1973. Degrees granted: Associate.

Attendance information available by phone, fax, mail. Search requires name plus SSN. There is no fee.

Degree information available by phone, fax, mail. Search requires name plus SSN, date of birth. There is no fee.

Bais Binyomin Academy, Registrar, 132 Prospect St, Stamford, CT 06901, 203-325-4351 (Fax: 203-325-4352). Enrollment: 100. Records go back to 1976. Alumni records are maintained here at the same phone number. Degrees granted. Special programs- Rabbinical College.

Attendance and degree information available by phone, mail. Search requires name plus SSN, exact years of attendance. There is no fee.

Briarwood College, Registrar, 2279 Mt Vernon Rd, Southington, CT 06489, 860-628-4751 (Fax: 860-628-6444). Enrollment: 540. Records go back to 1968. Alumni records are maintained here also. Call 860-628-4751. Degrees granted: Associate.

Attendance and degree information available by phone, fax, mail. Search requires name only. There is no fee.

Capital Community-Technical College, Registrar, 61 Woodland St, Hartford, CT 06105, 860-520-7898 (Fax: 860-520-7906). Hours: 8:30AM-5PM. Enrollment: 3000. Records go back to 1947. Degrees granted: Associate. Adverse incident record source- Security Office, 203-520-7813.

Attendance and degree information available by phone, fax, mail. Search requires name only. Also helpful: SSN, exact years of attendance. There is no fee.

Central Connecticut State University, Registrar's Office, 1615 Stanley St, New Britain, CT 06050, 860-832-2244 (Fax: 860-832-2522). Hours: 8AM-8:30PM. Enrollment: 11500. Records go back to 1974. Degrees granted: Bachelors; Masters.

Attendance and degree information available by phone, mail. Search requires name plus SSN, approximate years of attendance. Also helpful: date of birth. There is no fee.

Charter Oak State College, Registrar, 66 Cedar St #301, Newington, CT 06111-2646, 860-666-4595 (Fax: 860-666-4852). Hours: 8:30AM-5PM. Enrollment: 1300. Records go back to 1974. Alumni records are maintained here at the same phone number. Degrees granted: Associate; Bachelors.

Attendance and degree information available by phone, fax, mail. Search requires name plus SSN. Also helpful: date of birth. There is no fee.

Connecticut College, Registrar, New London, CT 06320, 860-439-2068 (Fax: 860-439-5421). Hours: 8:30AM-5PM. Enrollment: 1780. Records go back to 1920. Alumni records are maintained here also. Call 860-439-2300. Degrees granted: Bachelors.

Attendance and degree information available by phone, fax, mail. Search requires name plus exact years of attendance. There is no fee.

Eastern Connecticut State University, Registrar's Office, 83 Windham St, Willimantic, CT 06226-2295, 860-465-5224 (Fax: 860-465-4382). Hours: 8:15AM-4:45PM. Enrollment: 4700. Records go back to 1889. Alumni records are maintained here also. Call 860-465-5238. Degrees granted: Associate; Bachelors; Masters.

Attendance and degree information available by phone, fax, mail. Search requires name plus SSN. Also helpful: date of birth, exact years of attendance. There is no fee.

Fairfield University, Registrar, Fairfield, CT 06430, 203-254-4000 (Fax: 203-254-4109). Enrollment: 5000. Alumni records are maintained here also. Call 203-254-4280. Degrees granted: Associate; Bachelors; Masters; Masters in Nursing, Business, Education. Special programs- Florence Italy Campus,

203-254-4220. Adverse incident record source- Dean's of Students, 203-254-4000 .

Attendance and degree information available by phone, fax, mail. Search requires name plus SSN. Also helpful: date of birth, exact years of attendance. There is no fee.

Gateway Community-Technical College,

Registrar, 60 Sargent Dr, New Haven, CT 06511, 203-789-7041 (Fax: 203-777-8415). Hours: 8:30AM-4:30PM. Enrollment: 4843. Records go back to 1992. Student records are at 88 Basset, New Haven, CT, 06473, 203-234-3373. Alumni records are maintained here at the same phone number. Degrees granted: Associate. Special programs- Auto Tech: Alternative Fuel Certification: Dietetic Tech: Graphic Communications Tec: Postal Service Management: Pharmacy. Adverse incident record source- Dean of Students, 203-789-7016.

Attendance information available by fax, mail. Search requires name plus SSN, approximate years of attendance, signed release. Also helpful: date of birth, exact years of attendance. There is no fee.

Degree information available by phone, fax, mail. Search requires name plus SSN, approximate years of attendance. Also helpful: date of birth, exact years of attendance. There is no fee.

Gateway Community-Technical College,

(North Haven), Registrar, 88 Bassett Rd, North Haven, CT 06473, 203-234-3325 (Fax: 203-234-3372). Hours: 8:30AM-4:30PM. Enrollment: 5000. Records go back to 1978. Alumni records are maintained here also. Call 203-234-3342. Degrees granted: Associate.

Attendance information available by phone, fax, mail. Search requires name plus SSN. There is no fee.

Degree information available by phone, fax, mail. Search requires name only. There is no fee.

Hartford College for Women, Registrar, 1265 Asy-

lum Ave, Hartford, CT 06105, 860-768-5600 (Fax: 860-768-5693). Enrollment: 250. Records go back to 1932. Alumni records are maintained here at the same phone number. Degrees granted: Associate; Bachelors. Adverse incident record source- Dept. of Student Services.

Attendance and degree information available by phone, mail. Search requires name plus SSN. Also helpful: exact years of attendance. There is no fee.

Hartford Graduate Center, Registrar, 275 Windsor

St, Hartford, CT 06120, 860-548-2425 (Fax: 860-548-7823). Records are not housed here. They are located at Rensselaer Polytechnic Institute, Registrar, 110 Eighth St, Troy, NY 12180-3590.

Hartford Seminary, Registrar, 77 Sherman St, Hartford,

CT 06105, 860-509-9500 (Fax: 860-509-9509). Hours: 9AM-5PM. Enrollment: 400. Records go back to 1945. Alumni records are maintained here at the same phone number. Degrees granted: Masters; Doctorate.

Attendance and degree information available by phone, fax, mail. Search requires name plus approximate years of attendance. Also helpful: SSN, date of birth, exact years of attendance. There is no fee.

Holy Apostles College and Seminary, Regis-

trar, Cromwell, CT 06416, 860-632-3000 (Fax: 860-632-0176). Hours: 9AM-5PM. Enrollment: 33. Records go back to 1953. Degrees granted: Bachelors; Masters; M. Div.

Attendance and degree information available by phone, fax, mail. Search requires name plus approximate years of attendance. Also helpful: SSN, date of birth. Fee is $5.00.

Housatonic Community-Technical College,

Registrar, 510 Barnum Ave, Bridgeport, CT 06608, 203-579-6400 (Fax: 203-579-6408). Hours: 8AM-4:30PM. Enrollment: 2750. Records go back to 1966. Alumni records are maintained

here at the same phone number. Degrees granted: Associate. Adverse incident record source- Student Affairs, 203-579-6454.

Attendance and degree information available by phone, fax, mail. Search requires name only. Also helpful: SSN, date of birth, exact years of attendance. There is no fee.

Katharine Gibbs School, Registrar, 142 East Ave,

Norwalk, CT 06851, 203-838-4173 (Fax: 203-899-0788). Hours: 7:30AM-5PM. Degrees granted: Associate.

Attendance and degree information available by phone, fax, mail. Search requires name plus approximate years of attendance. Also helpful: SSN, exact years of attendance. There is no fee.

Manchester Community-Technical College,

Registrar, PO Box 1046, Manchester, CT 06045-1046, 860-647-6147 (Fax: 860-647-6328). Hours: 8AM-4:30PM. Enrollment: 6000. Records go back to 1963. Alumni records are maintained here also. Call 860-647-6137. Degrees granted: Associate.

Attendance and degree information available by phone, fax, mail. Search requires name plus SSN. Also helpful: date of birth. There is no fee.

Middlesex Community-Technical College,

Registrar, 100 Training Hill Rd, Middletown, CT 06457, 860-343-5720 (Fax: 860-344-7488). Hours: 8:30AM-4:30PM. Enrollment: 2800. Records go back to 1966. Alumni records are maintained here also. Call 860-343-5744. Degrees granted: Associate. Special programs- Environmental Science-BioTechnology, 860-343-4880: Broadcast Communications, 860-343-5896: Ophthalmic Design & Dispensing, 860-343-5845. Adverse incident record source- Dean of Students, 860-343-5708.

Attendance and degree information available by phone, fax, mail. Search requires name only. Also helpful: SSN, exact years of attendance. There is no fee.

Mitchell College, Registrar, New London, CT 06320,

860-443-2811 (Fax: 860-437-0632). Hours: 8:30AM-4:30PM. Enrollment: 600. Records go back to 1939. Alumni records are maintained here at the same phone number. Degrees granted: Associate. Special programs- Intensive English, 860-701-5037. Adverse incident record source- Security, 860-701-5179.

Attendance and degree information available by fax, mail. Search requires name only. Also helpful: SSN, date of birth, exact years of attendance. There is no fee.

Naugatuck Valley Community-Technical

College, Registrar, 750 Chase Pkwy, Waterbury, CT 06708, 203-575-8040 (Fax: 203-596-8766). Hours: 8:30AM-4:30PM. Enrollment: 5000. Records go back to 1967. Alumni records are maintained here also. Call 203-596-8757. Degrees granted: Associate. Special programs- Nursing: Physical Therapy: Automotive Tech: Respiratory Care: Manfuacturing Engineer: Computer Drafting Design. Adverse incident record source- Dean of Students, 203-575-8081.

Attendance and degree information available by phone, fax, mail. Search requires name plus approximate years of attendance. Also helpful: SSN, date of birth. There is no fee.

Northwestern Connecticut Community-

Technical College, Registrar, Park Place E, Winsted, CT 06098, 860-738-6314 (Fax: 860-379-4465). Hours: 8:30AM-4:30PM. Enrollment: 900. Records go back to 1965. Alumni records are maintained here also. Call 860-738-6349. Degrees granted: Associate.

Attendance information available by fax, mail. Search requires name plus SSN, exact years of attendance, signed release. There is no fee.

Degree information available by phone, fax, mail. Search requires name plus SSN, exact years of attendance. There is no fee.

Norwalk Community-Technical College, Registrar, 188 Richards Ave, Norwalk, CT 06854, 203-857-7035 (Fax: 203-857-7012). Hours: 9AM-6:30PM M-Th; 9AM-4PM F. Enrollment: 5300. Records go back to 1961. Alumni records are maintained here also. Call 203-857-7270. Degrees granted: Associate. Special programs- Nursing: EMT: Architural Engineering. Adverse incident record source- Dean of Students, 203-857-7018.

Attendance information available by phone, fax, mail. Search requires name plus SSN. Also helpful: date of birth, exact years of attendance. There is no fee.

Degree information available by fax, mail. Search requires name plus SSN. Also helpful: date of birth, exact years of attendance. There is no fee.

Paier College of Art, Registrar, 20 Gorham Ave, Hamden, CT 06154, 203-287-3032 (Fax: 203-287-3021). Hours: 9AM-4PM. Records go back to 1950. Alumni records are maintained here also. Call 203-287-3036. Degrees granted: Associate; Bachelors. Adverse incident record source- President, 203-287-3054.

Attendance and degree information available by phone, fax, mail. Search requires name plus SSN. There is no fee.

Quinebaug Valley Community-Technical College, Records Office, 742 Upper Maple St, Danielson, CT 06239, 860-774-1130 (Fax: 860-774-7768). Hours: 8:30AM-4:30PM. Enrollment: 1170. Records go back to 1972. Degrees granted: Associate.

Attendance information available by phone, fax, mail. Search requires name plus SSN. Also helpful: date of birth, exact years of attendance. There is no fee.

School will not confirm degree information.

Quinnipiac College, Registrar, 275 Mount Carmel Ave, Hamden, CT 06518-0569, 203-281-8695 (Fax: 203-248-4703). Hours: 8AM-6PM M-Th, 8AM-4PM F. Enrollment: 5000. Records go back to 1929. Alumni records are maintained here also. Call 203-281-8667. Degrees granted: Bachelors; Masters.

Attendance and degree information available by phone, fax, mail. Search requires name plus SSN, date of birth, exact years of attendance. There is no fee.

Sacred Heart University, Registrar, 5151 Park Ave, Fairfield, CT 06432, 203-371-7890 (Fax: 203-365-7509). Hours: 8AM-8PM M-Th, 8AM-4PM F. Enrollment: 5600. Records go back to 1963. Alumni records are maintained here also. Call 203-371-7861. Degrees granted: Associate; Bachelors; Masters. Adverse incident record source- Dean of Students, 203-371-7916.

Attendance and degree information available by phone, fax, mail. Search requires name only. Also helpful: SSN, date of birth, exact years of attendance. There is no fee.

Saint Basil's College, Registrar, 195 Glenbrook Rd, Stamford, CT 06902, 203-324-4578 (Fax: 203-357-7681). Enrollment: 55. Records go back to 1939. Degrees granted: Bachelors.

Attendance and degree information available by phone, mail. Search requires name plus SSN, exact years of attendance. There is no fee.

Southern Connecticut State University, Registrar, New Haven, CT 06505-0901, 203-392-5300 (Fax: 203-392-5320). Hours: 8:30AM-4:30PM. Enrollment: 10000. Alumni Records Office: 501 Crescent St, New Haven, CT 06515. Degrees granted: Associate; Bachelors; Masters.

Attendance information available by fax, mail. Search requires name plus SSN, date of birth, approximate years of attendance, signed release. Also helpful: exact years of attendance. There is no fee.

Degree information available by fax, mail. Search requires name plus SSN, date of birth, signed release. Also helpful: exact years of attendance. There is no fee.

St. Joseph College, Registrar, 1678 Asylum Ave, West Hartford, CT 06117, 860-232-4571 (Fax: 860-233-5695). Hours: 8:30AM-4:30PM. Enrollment: 1077. Records go back to 1933. Alumni records are maintained here at the same phone number. Degrees granted: Bachelors; Masters. Certification: Six year.

Attendance and degree information available by phone, fax, mail. Search requires name only. Also helpful: approximate years of attendance. There is no fee.

Teikyo Post University, Registrar, 800 Country Club Rd, Waterbury, CT 06708, 203-596-4619 (Fax: 203-596-4699). Hours: 8AM-8PM M-Th; 8AM-5PM F. Enrollment: 1661. Records go back to 1950's. Alumni records are maintained here also. Call 860-546-4605. Degrees granted: Associate; Bachelors. Adverse incident record source- Dean of Students, 203-596-4510.

Attendance and degree information available by phone, fax, mail. Search requires name only. Also helpful: SSN, exact years of attendance. There is no fee.

Three Rivers Community-Technical College, Registrar, PO Box 629, Mahan Dr, Norwich, CT 06360, 860-886-1931 (Fax: 860-823-2983). Hours: 8:30AM-4:30PM. Enrollment: 2000. Degrees granted: Associate. Adverse incident record source- Dean's Office, 860-823-2828 .

Attendance and degree information available by fax, mail. Search requires name plus SSN, exact years of attendance, signed release. Also helpful: date of birth. There is no fee.

Three Rivers Community-Technical College, (Thames), Registrar, 574 New London Tpke, Norwich, CT 06360, 860-885-2301 (Fax: 860-886-4960). Hours: 8AM-4PM. Enrollment: 4100. Records go back to 1966. Alumni Records Office: Mahan Drive, Norwich, CT 06360. Degrees granted: Associate.

Attendance information available by fax, mail. Search requires name plus SSN, signed release. Also helpful: date of birth, exact years of attendance. There is no fee.

Degree information available by phone, fax, mail. Search requires name plus SSN. Also helpful: date of birth, exact years of attendance. There is no fee.

Trinity College, Registrar, 300 Summit St, Hartford, CT 06106, 860-297-2118 (Fax: 860-297-5179). Hours: 10AM-Noon, 1-3PM. Enrollment: 1939. Records go back to 1910. Alumni records are maintained here also. Call 860-297-2400. Degrees granted: Bachelors; Masters. Adverse incident record source- Dean of Students, 203-297-2156.

Attendance and degree information available by phone, fax, mail. Search requires name only. Also helpful: SSN, date of birth, exact years of attendance. There is no fee.

Tunxis Community-Technical College, Registrar, 271 Scott Swamp Rd, Farmington, CT 06032, 860-679-9511 (Fax: 860-676-8906). Hours: 8:30AM-7:30PM. Enrollment: 3700. Records go back to 1971. Alumni records are maintained here at the same phone number. Degrees granted: Associate. Special programs- Dental Hygiene, 860-679-9521: Drug & Alcohol Rehab Counselor: Physical Therapist Assistant. Adverse incident record source- Student Affairs, 860-679-9520.

Attendance information available by fax, mail. Search requires name plus SSN, date of birth, signed release. Also helpful: exact years of attendance. There is no fee.

Degree information available by mail. Search requires name plus SSN, date of birth, signed release. There is no fee.

United States Coast Guard Academy, Registrar, 15 Mohegan Ave, New London, CT 06320-4195, 860-444-8214 (Fax: 860-444-8216). Hours: 7:30AM-4:30PM. Enrollment: 930. Records go back to 1930. Alumni records are maintained here also. Call 861-444-8238. Degrees granted: Bachelors.

Attendance and degree information available by phone, fax, mail. Search requires name plus SSN, exact years of attendance. There is no fee.

University of Bridgeport, Registrar, 380 University Ave, Bridgeport, CT 06601, 203-576-4636 (Fax: 203-576-4941). Hours: 8:30AM-4:30PM. Records go back to 1927. Alumni records are maintained here also. Call 203-576-4508. Degrees granted: Associate; Bachelors; Masters; Doctorate. Certification: Six year certificate.

Attendance and degree information available by phone, fax, mail. Search requires name plus approximate years of attendance. Also helpful: SSN, date of birth, exact years of attendance. There is no fee.

University of Connecticut, Office of the Registrar, Certifications Office, U-77E, 233 Glenbrook Rd, Wilbur Cross Bldg RM 153, Storrs, CT 06269, 860-486-3328 (Fax: 860-486-4199). Hours: 8:30AM-4:30PM. Enrollment: 23500. Records go back to 1900. Alumni Records Office: Alumni Association, U-53, 2384 Alumni Dr, Storrs, CT 06269-3053. Degrees granted: Bachelors; Masters; Doctorate. Special programs- School of Law, 203-241-5638: School of Social Work, 203-241-4737: School of Medicine, 203-679-3872: School of Dentistry, 203-679-2175. Adverse incident record source- Alumni Office, 203-486-2240.

Attendance information available by phone, fax, mail. Search requires name plus approximate years of attendance. Also helpful: SSN, date of birth, exact years of attendance. There is no fee.

Degree information available by phone, fax, mail. Search requires name only. Also helpful: SSN, date of birth, exact years of attendance. There is no fee.

University of Connecticut School of Medicine, Registrar, UCONN School of Medicine, Farmington, CT 06030-1905, 860-679-2153 (Fax: 860-679-1282). Hours: 8AM-5PM. Enrollment: 350. Records go back to 1968. Alumni records are maintained here also. Call 860-679-2819. Degrees granted: Doctorate.

Attendance and degree information available by phone, fax, mail. Search requires name only. Also helpful: SSN, date of birth. There is no fee.

University of Hartford, Registrar, 200 Bloomfield Ave, West Hartford, CT 06117, 860-768-5589 (Fax: 860-768-4593). Hours: 8:30AM-7:30PM M-Th, 8:30AM-4:30PM F. Enrollment: 5630. Records go back to 1950. While the majority of the records date back to the 1950's, there may be records as old as the 1800's. Alumni Records Office: Alumni Relations, 312 Bloomfield Ave, West Hartford, CT 06117. Degrees granted: Associate; Bachelors; Masters; Doctorate; Engineering. Adverse incident record source- Student Affairs, 203-768-4165.

Attendance and degree information available by phone, fax, mail. Search requires name plus SSN, exact years of attendance. Also helpful: date of birth. There is no fee.

University of New Haven, Registrar, 300 Orange Ave, West Haven, CT 06516, 203-932-7301 (Fax: 203-932-7429). Hours: 8:30AM-4:30PM. Enrollment: 3487. Records go back to 1920. Alumni records are maintained here also. Call 203-932-7268. Degrees granted: Associate; Bachelors; Masters; Doctorate. Adverse incident record source- Student Affairs, 203-932-7199.

Attendance and degree information available by phone, fax, mail. Search requires name only. Also helpful: SSN, date of birth, approximate years of attendance. There is no fee.

Weselyan University, Registrar, Middletown, CT 06459, 860-685-2748 (Fax: 860-685-2601). Hours: 9AM-4PM. Enrollment: 3000. Records go back to 1800's. Alumni records are maintained here also. Call 860-685-2200. Degrees granted: Bachelors; Masters; Ph.D. Special programs- Studies Abroad. Adverse incident record source- Dean's Office, 203-685-2600 .

Attendance and degree information available by phone, fax, mail. Search requires name plus SSN. Also helpful: approximate years of attendance. There is no fee.

Western Connecticut State University, Registrar, Danbury, CT 06810, 203-837-9200 (Fax: 203-837-9049). Hours: 8AM-4:30PM. Enrollment: 5600. Records go back to 1904. Alumni records are maintained here also. Call 203-837-8278. Degrees granted: Associate; Bachelors; Masters.

Attendance and degree information available by phone, fax, mail. Search requires name only. Also helpful: SSN, date of birth, approximate years of attendance. There is no fee.

Wilcox College of Nursing, Registrar, 28 Crescent St, Middletown, CT 06547, 860-344-6719 (Fax: 860-344-6999). Hours: 8AM-4:30PM. Enrollment: 100. Records go back to 1911. This school will be closing in December 1997. Alumni records are maintained here also. Call 860-344-6401. Degrees granted: Associate.

Attendance and degree information available by phone, fax, mail. Search requires name only. Also helpful: SSN, exact years of attendance. There is no fee.

Yale Divinity School, Registrar, 409 Prospect St, New Haven, CT 06511, 203-432-5312 (Fax: 203-432-5356). Hours: 9AM-5PM. Enrollment: 330. Records go back to 1800's. Alumni records are maintained here also. Call 203-432-5033. Degrees granted: Masters.

Attendance and degree information available by phone, fax, mail. Search requires name only. Also helpful: date of birth, exact years of attendance. There is no fee.

Yale University, Registrar, New Haven, CT 06520, 203-432-4771 (Fax: 203-432-2324). Hours: 8:30AM-4:30PM. Enrollment: 10986. Records go back to 1700's. Alumni records are maintained here also. Call 203-432-2586. Degrees granted: Associate; Bachelors; Masters; Doctorate.

Attendance and degree information available by fax, mail. Search requires name plus SSN, approximate years of attendance. There is no fee.

Trade and Vocational Schools

Albert I. Prince Regional Vocational-Technical School, 500 Bookfield St, Hartford, CT 06106, 860-246-8594

Allstate Tractor Trailer Training School, 2064 Main St, Bridgeport, CT 06004, 203-336-9567

Baran Institute of Technology, 611 Day Hill Rd, Windsor, CT 06095, 860-688-3353

Basic Enlisted Submarine School, Box 700 Bldg 84, Code 01A, Groton, CT 06340-5700, 860-449-4369

Branford Hall Career Institute, 9 Business Park Dr, Branford, CT 06405, 203-488-2525

Butler Business School, 2710 North Ave, Bridgeport, CT 06604, 203-333-3601

Connecticut Business Institute, 605 Broad St, Stratford, CT 06497, 203-377-1775

Connecticut Business Institute (Branch Campus), 809 Main St, East Hartford, CT 06108, 860-291-2880

Connecticut Business Institute (Branch Campus), 447 Washington Ave, New Haven, CT 06473, 203-239-7660

Connecticut Center for Massage Therapy, 75 Kitts La, Newington, CT 06111, 203-667-1886

Connecticut Center for Massage Therapy (Branch Campus), 25 Sylvan Rd S, Westport, CT 06880, 203-221-7325

Connecticut Culinary, 230 Farmington Ave US 1, Farmington, CT 06032, 860-677-7869

Connecticut Institute of Art, 581 W Putnam Ave, Greenwich, CT 06830, 860-869-4430

Connecticut Institute of Hair Design, 1681 Meriden Rd, Wolcott, CT 06716, 203-879-4247

Connecticut School of Electronics, 586 Ella T. Grasso Blvd, New Haven, CT 06519, 203-624-2121

Data Institute, 745 Burnside Ave, East Hartford, CT 06108, 860-528-4111

Data Institute (Branch Campus), 101 Pierpont Rd, Waterbury, CT 06705, 203-756-5500

Eli Whitney Regional Vocational-Technical School, 71 Jones Rd, Hamden, CT 06514, 203-397-4031

Fox Institute of Business, 765 Asylum Ave, Hartford, CT 06105, 860-522-2888

Hartford Camerata Conservatory, 834 Asylum Ave, Hartford, CT 06105, 860-246-2588

Huntington Institute, 193 Broadway, Norwich, CT 06360, 860-886-0507

Industrial Management and Training, Inc., 233 Mill St, Waterbury, CT 06706, 203-753-7910

Lyme Academy of Fine Arts, 84 Lyme St, Old Lyme, CT 06371, 860-434-5232

Morse School of Business, 275 Asylum St, Hartford, CT 06103, 860-522-2261

NRI Schools, 4401 Connecticut Ave NW, Washington, CT 20008, 202-244-1600

Naval Health Sciences Education and Training Command (Undersea Medical Institute), Groton, CT 06349, 860-449-2874

New England Technical Institute of Connecticut, 200 John Downey Dr, New Britain, CT 06051, 860-225-8641

New England Tractor Trailer Training School of Connecticut, 32 Field Rd, Somers, CT 06071, 860-749-0711

Porter and Chester Institute, PO Box 364, Stratford, CT 06497, 203-375-4463

Porter and Chester Institute (Branch Campus), 138 Weymouth St, Enfield, CT 06082, 800-870-6789

Porter and Chester Institute (Branch Campus), 320 Sylvan Lake Rd, Watertown, CT 06779, 860-274-9294

Porter and Chester Institute (Branch Campus), 125 Silas Deane Hwy, Wethersfield, CT 06109, 860-529-2519

Ridley-Lowell Business and Technical Institute, 470 Bank St, New London, CT 06320, 860-443-7441

Roffler Academy for Hairstylists, 454 Park St, Hartford, CT 06106, 860-522-2359

Roffler Academy for Hairstylists (Branch Campus), 709 Queen St, Southington, CT 06489, 860-620-9260

Sawyer School (Branch Campus), 1125 Dixwell Ave, Hamden, CT 06514, 203-239-6200

School of the Hartford Ballet, Hartford Courant Arts Ctr, 224 Farmington Ave, Hartford, CT 06105, 860-525-9396

Stone Academy, 1315 Dixwell Ave, Hamden, CT 06514, 203-288-7474

Technical Careers Institute, 11 Kimberly Ave, West Haven, CT 06516, 203-932-2282

Technical Careers Institute (Branch Campus), 605 Day Hill Rd, Windsor, CT 06095, 860-688-8351

Westlawn School of Marine Technology, 733 Summer St, Stamford, CT 06901, 203-359-0500

Windham Regional Vocational-Technical School, 210 Birch St, Willimantic, CT 06226, 860-456-3879

State Licensing & Business Registration Quick Finder Index

Architecture, Engineering & Surveying
Architect #3 .... ☎ 860-566-2093
Engineer #4 .... ☎ 860-566-3290
Surveyor #4 .... ☎ 860-566-3290

Business - Court & Legal Services
Attorney #1 (1500) .... ☎ 860-568-3762
Lobbyist #18 (2500) .... ☎ 860-566-4472
Notary Public #16 .... ☎ 860-566-5273

Business - General Services
Public Accountant-CPA #16 .... ☎ 860-566-5273
Weigher #8 .... ☎ 860-566-4778
Weights & Measures Dealer/Repairer #8 .... ☎ 860-566-4778

Construction & Manufacturing
Antenna Service Dealer #5 .... ☎ 860-566-3275
Antenna Technician #5 .... ☎ 860-566-3275
Electrical Journeyman/Apprentice #4 .... ☎ 860-566-3290
Electronics Service Dealer #5 .... ☎ 860-566-3275
Electronics Service Technician #5 .... ☎ 860-566-3275
Elevator Contractor/Journeyman #4 .... ☎ 860-566-3290
Heating & Cooling Contractor #4 .... ☎ 860-566-3290
Plumber Journeyman #4 .... ☎ 860-566-3290
Solar Contractor/Journeyman #4 .... ☎ 860-566-3290

Education
School Administrator/Supervisor #9 .... ☎ 860-566-4561
School Library Media Associate #9 .... ☎ 860-566-4561
School Superintendent #9 .... ☎ 860-566-4561
Teacher #9 .... ☎ 860-566-4561

Environmental & Agriculture
Arborist #7 .... ☎ 860-566-3290
Pesticide Dealer/Applicator #14 .... ☎ 860-424-3001
Solid Waste Facility Operator #10 .... ☎ 860-566-5599
Veterinarian #11 .... ☎ 860-528-0400
Well Drilling Contractor/Journeyman #4 .... ☎ 860-566-3290

Financial - Real Estate, Insurance & Banking
Agent of Issuer #6 .... ☎ 860-240-8299
Auto Adjuster #2 .... ☎ 860-297-3845
Auto Appraiser #2 .... ☎ 860-297-3845
Branch Office-Bank #6 .... ☎ 860-240-8299
Broker-Dealer Agent #6 .... ☎ 860-240-8299
Business Opportunity Offerings for Sale #6
.... ☎ 860-240-8299
Check Cashing Service #6 .... ☎ 860-240-8299
Consumer Collection Agency #6 (368) .... ☎ 860-240-8299
Debt Adjuster #6 (4) .... ☎ 860-240-8299
Insurance Agent/Broker #2 .... ☎ 860-297-3845
Insurance Company #2 .... ☎ 860-297-3845
Insurance Consultant #2 .... ☎ 860-297-3845
Investment Adviser #6 (1140) .... ☎ 860-240-8299
Investment Adviser Agent #6 (10278) .... ☎ 860-240-8299
Money Forwarder #6 .... ☎ 860-240-8299
Money Orders & Travelers Checks Service #6
.... ☎ 860-240-8299
Mortgage Lender/Broker #6 (1228) .... ☎ 860-240-8299
Nondepository Banking offices #6 .... ☎ 860-240-8299
Real Estate Appraiser #17 .... ☎ 860-566-5130
Real Estate Broker #17 .... ☎ 860-566-5130
Real Estate Salesperson #17 .... ☎ 860-566-5130
Sales Finance Company #6 (222) .... ☎ 860-240-8299
Savings & Loan Association Bank #6 .... ☎ 860-240-8299
Savings Bank #6 .... ☎ 860-240-8299
Securities Agent #6 .... ☎ 860-566-4560
Securities Broker/Dealer #6 (2026) .... ☎ 860-240-8299
Small Loan Company #6 .... ☎ 860-566-4560
State Chartered Bank & Trust Company #6 ... ☎ 860-566-4560
Surplus Lines Broker #2 .... ☎ 860-297-3845

Health & Beauty
Advanced Practice R.N. #11 .... ☎ 860-528-0400
Audiologist #11 .... ☎ 860-528-0400
Barber #11 .... ☎ 860-528-0400
Chiropractor #11 .... ☎ 860-528-0400
Cosmetician #11 .... ☎ 860-528-0400
Dentist/Dental Hygienist #11 .... ☎ 860-528-0400
Electrologist #11 .... ☎ 860-528-0400
Embalmer #11 .... ☎ 860-528-0400
Emergency Medical Techician #11 .... ☎ 860-528-0400
Funeral Director #11 .... ☎ 860-528-0400
Hairdresser #11 .... ☎ 860-528-0400
Hearing Aid Dealer #11 .... ☎ 860-528-0400
Homeopathic Physician #11 .... ☎ 860-528-0400
Hypertrichologist #11 (291) .... ☎ 860-509-7569
Massage Therapist #11 .... ☎ 860-528-0400
Medical Doctor #11 .... ☎ 860-528-0400
Naturopathic Physician #11 .... ☎ 860-528-0400
Nurse #11 .... ☎ 860-528-0400
Nurse Midwife #11 .... ☎ 860-528-0400
Nurses Aide #11 .... ☎ 860-528-0400
Nursing Home Administrator #11 .... ☎ 860-528-0400
Occupational Therapist #11 .... ☎ 860-528-0400
Occupational Therapist/Assistant #11 .... ☎ 860-528-0400
Optician #11 .... ☎ 860-528-0400
Optometrist #11 (2429) .... ☎ 860-509-7562
Osteopathic Physician #11 .... ☎ 860-528-0400
Pharmacist #4 .... ☎ 860-566-3290
Physical Therapist #11 .... ☎ 860-528-0400
Physician's Assistant #11 .... ☎ 860-528-0400
Podiatrist #11 .... ☎ 860-528-0400
Practical Nurse #11 .... ☎ 860-528-0400
Radiographer #11 .... ☎ 860-528-0400
Respiratory Care Practitioner #11 .... ☎ 860-528-0400
Speech Pathologist #11 .... ☎ 860-528-0400

Investigations & Security
Fire Protection-Sprinkler System Contractor
/Journeyman #4 .... ☎ 860-566-3290
Private Investigator #13 .... ☎ 860-685-8046

Social Services
Marriage & Family Therapist #11 .... ☎ 860-528-0400
Psychologist #11 .... ☎ 860-528-0400
Social Worker #11 (3951) .... ☎ 860-509-7567

Sports & Entertainment
Boxing & Wrestling #7 .... ☎ 860-566-3290
Casino #12 .... ☎ 860-594-0565
Greyhound Racing #12 .... ☎ 860-566-2756
Horse Racing #12 .... ☎ 860-566-2756
Jai Alai #12 .... ☎ 860-667-5073
Liquor License #15 (7000) .... ☎ 860-566-5926
Lottery #12 .... ☎ 860-667-5073
Off Track Betting #12 .... ☎ 860-667-5073

State Licensing & Business Registration Agency Information

(1)   Bar Examining Committee, 287 Main Street, East Hartford, CT 06118-1885, 860-721-0025

(2)   Connecticut Department of Insurance, Licensing Section, PO Box 816, Hartford, CT 06142-0816, 860-297-3845, Fax: 860-297-3872

(3)   Consumer Protection Department, Board of Architects, 165 Capitol Ave, Hartford, CT 06106, 860-566-3290, Fax: 860-566-7630

(4)   Consumer Protection Department, Board of Trades Division, 165 Capitol Ave, Hartford, CT 06106, 860-566-3290, Fax: 860-566-7630

(5)   Consumer Protection Dept/Occupational Licensing, Board of Television & Radio Service Examiners, 165 Capitol Ave, Hartford, CT 06106, 860-566-3275, Fax: 860-566-7630

(6)   Department of Banking, 260 Constitution Plaza, Hartford, CT 06103-1800, 860-240-8299, Fax: 860-240-8178

(7)   Department of Consumer Protection, Occupational Licensing Division, 165 Capitol Ave, Room 110, Hartford, CT 06106, 860-566-3290, Fax: 860-566-7630

(8)   Department of Consumer Protection, Weights & Measures Division, 165 Capitol Ave, State Office Bldg, Hartford, CT 06106, 860-566-4778, Fax: 860-566-7630

(9)   Department of Education, Teacher Certification Chief, 165 Capitol Ave, PO Box 2219, Hartford, CT 06145-2219, 860-566-4561, Fax: 860-566-8929

(10)   Department of Environmental Protection, 79 Elms St, Hartford, CT 06106, 860-424-3000, Fax: 860-424-4072

(11)   Department of Public Health & Addiction Services, 410 Capital Ave, Hartford, CT 06134, 860-509-8000

(12)   Division of Special Revenue, 555 Russell Rd, PO Box 11424, Newington, CT 06111-0424, 860-594-0501, Fax: 860-594-0509

(13)   Division of State Police, 111 Country Club Rd, Middletown, CT 06457-9294, 860-685-8046, Fax: 860-685-8355

(14)   Environmental Protection Department, 79 Elm St, Hartford, CT 06106, 860-424-3001, Fax: 860-424-4051

(15)   Liquor Control Department, 165 Capitol Ave, Room 556, Hartford, CT 06106, 860-566-5926, Fax: 860-566-6060

(16)   Office of the Secretary of the State, PO Box 150470, Hartford, CT 06115-0470, 860-566-5273, Fax: 860-566-5757

(17)   Real Estate Division, Consumer Protection Department, 165 Capitol Ave, Room 110, Hartford, CT 06106, 860-566-5130, Fax: 860-566-7630

(18)   State Ethics Commission, 20 Trinity St, Hartford, CT 06106, 860-566-4472, Fax: 860-566-3806

Delaware

Capitol: Dover (Kent County)	
State Population	.7 Million
Number of Degree Granting Institutions:	10
Number of State Licensing & Business Registration Agencies:	62

Degree Granting Educational Institutions

Delaware State University, Records Department, 1200 N Dupont Hwy, Dover, DE 19901-2277, 302-739-4917 (Fax: 302-739-2856). Hours: 8:30AM-4:30PM. Enrollment: 3175. Records go back to 1891. Alumni Records Office: Alumni Association, Thomasson Bldg, 1200 N DuPont Hwy, Dover, DE 19901. Degrees granted: Bachelors; Masters. Adverse incident record source- Student Affairs, 302-739-4943.

Attendance and degree information available by fax, mail. Search requires name plus SSN, signed release. Also helpful: date of birth, exact years of attendance. There is no fee.

Delaware Technical & Community College, (Stanton/Willington), Registrar, 400 Stanton Christiana Rd, Newark, DE 19713, 302-454-3959 (Fax: 302-454-3184). Hours: 8:30AM-8PM M-Th; 8:30AM-4:30PM F. Enrollment: 6422. Records go back to 1968. Alumni Records Office: Alumni Association, 333 Shipley St, Wilmington, DE 19801. Degrees granted: Associate. Adverse incident record source- Student Services.

Attendance and degree information available by phone, fax, mail. Search requires name plus SSN. Also helpful: date of birth. There is no fee.

Delaware Technical & Community College, (Terry), Registrar, 1832 N Dupont Pkwy, Dover, DE 19901, 302-741-2718 (Fax: 302-741-2778). Hours: 8:30AM-7:30PM M-Th, 8:30AM-4PM F. Enrollment: 1700. Records go back to 1975. Alumni records are maintained here also. Call 302-741-2782. Degrees granted: Associate.

Attendance and degree information available by phone, fax, mail. Search requires name plus SSN. Also helpful: approximate years of attendance. There is no fee.

Delaware Technical Community College Southern, Registrar, 333 Shipley St, Wilmington, DE

19801, 302-571-5317 (Fax: 302-577-6432). Enrollment: 3000. Records go back to 1973. Alumni records are maintained here at the same phone number. Degrees granted: Associate. Adverse incident record source- Security.

Attendance and degree information available by phone, mail. Search requires name plus SSN, exact years of attendance. There is no fee.

Delaware Technical & Community College, (Southern), Registrar, PO Box 610, Georgetown, DE 19947, 302-856-5400 (Fax: 302-856-5392). Records are not housed here. They are located at Delaware Technical & Community College, (Terry), Registrar, 1832 N Dupont Pkwy, Dover, DE 19901.

Goldey-Beacom College, Registrar, 4701 Limestone Rd, Wilmington, DE 19808, 302-998-8814 (Fax: 302-998-8631). Hours: 8AM-5PM. Enrollment: 1700. Records go back to 1886. Alumni records are maintained here also. Call 302-998-8814. Degrees granted: Associate; Bachelors; Masters. Adverse incident record source- Student Affairs, 302-998-8814 X332.

Attendance and degree information available by fax, mail. Search requires name plus SSN, date of birth, exact years of attendance, signed release. There is no fee.

University of Delaware, Office of the Registrar, Student Services Bldg, Newark, DE 19716-6220, 302-831-2131 (Fax: 302-831-3005). Hours: 8AM-5PM. Enrollment: 21585. Alumni records are maintained here also. Call 302-831-8741. Degrees granted: Associate; Bachelors; Masters; PhD. Adverse incident record source- Dean of Students, 302-831-2116.

Attendance and degree information available by phone, fax, mail. Search requires name only. Also helpful: SSN, date of birth, exact years of attendance. There is no fee.

Wesley College, Registrar, 120 N State St, Dover, DE 19901, 302-736-2434 (Fax: 302-736-2301). Hours: 8:30AM-4:30PM. Enrollment: 1399. Records go back to 1946. Alumni records are maintained here also. Call 302-736-2355. Degrees granted: Associate; Bachelors; Masters.

Attendance information available by phone, fax, mail. Search requires name plus approximate years of attendance. Also helpful: SSN, exact years of attendance. Fee is $4.00.

Degree information available by phone, fax, mail. Search requires name only. Also helpful: SSN, exact years of attendance. Fee is $4.00.

Widener University, (School of Law), Registrar, 4601 Concord Pike, PO Box 7474, Wilmington, DE 19803-0474, 302-477-2170 (Fax: 302-477-2258). Hours: 9AM-5PM. Enrollment: 2000. Records go back to 1971. Alumni records are maintained here at the same phone number. Degrees granted: Masters; Juris Doctor. Special programs- Legal Education Institute (Paralegal) prior 1989, 610-499-4000.

Attendance and degree information available by phone, fax, mail. Search requires name plus SSN. Also helpful: date of birth, exact years of attendance. There is no fee.

Wilmington College, Registrar, 320 Dupont Hwy, New Castle, DE 19720, 302-328-9401 X110 (Fax: 302-328-7918). Hours: 8:30AM-6PM M-Th, 8:30AM-4:30PM. Enrollment: 5000. Records go back to 1968. Alumni records are maintained here also. Call 302-328-9401 X101. Degrees granted: Associate; Bachelors; Masters; Doctorate.

Attendance and degree information available by phone, fax, mail. Search requires name plus SSN, approximate years of attendance. There is no fee.

Trade and Vocational Schools

Career Institute (The) (Branch Campus), 711 Market St Mall, Wilmington, DE 19801, 302-575-1400

Dawn Training Institute, 120 Old Churchmans Rd, New Castle, DE 19720, 302-328-9695

Star Technical Institute, 631 W Newport Pike, Wilmington, DE 19804, 302-999-7827

State Licensing & Business Registration Quick Finder Index

Architecture, Engineering & Surveying
Architect #2 .... ☎ 302-739-4522
Engineer #2 .... ☎ 302-739-4522
Geologist #2 .... ☎ 302-739-4522
Land Surveyor #2 .... ☎ 302-739-4522
Landscape Architect #2 .... ☎ 302-739-4522

Business - Court & Legal Services
Attorney #3 .... ☎ 302-651-3113
Lobbyist #11 .... ✉ 302-739-6479
Notary Public #11 .... ✉ 302-739-6479

Business - General Services
Employment Agency #2 .... ☎ 302-739-4522
Public Accountant-CPA #2 .... ☎ 302-739-4522

Construction & Manufacturing
Electrician #2 .... ☎ 302-739-4522
General Contractor #7 .... ☎ 302-577-3363
Heating & Air Conditioning Mechanic #2 ..... ☎ 302-739-4522

Education
Administrative Supervisor/Assistant #5 .... ☎ 302-739-4661
School Counselor #5 .... ☎ 302-739-4661
School Librarian Media Specialist #6 .... ☎ 302-739-4601
School Principal #5 .... ☎ 302-739-4661
School Superintendent #5 .... ☎ 302-739-4661
Teacher #6 .... ☎ 302-739-4601
Teacher #5 .... ☎ 302-739-4661

Environmental & Agriculture
Pesticide Applicator #12 (2550) .... ☎ 302-739-4811

Veterinarian #2 .... ☎ 302-739-4522

Financial - Real Estate, Insurance & Banking
Insurance Adjuster #10 .... ✉ 302-739-4251
Insurance Advisor #10 .... ✉ 302-739-4251
Insurance Agent/Consultant #10 .... ✉ 302-739-4251
Insurance Broker #10 .... ✉ 302-739-4251
Real Estate Appraiser #2 .... ☎ 302-739-4522
Real Estate Broker/Agent #2 .... ☎ 302-739-4522
Securities Agent #10 .... ✉ 302-739-4251
Securities Broker/Dealer #10 .... ✉ 302-739-4251

Health & Beauty
Ambulance Attendant #9 .... ✉ 302-739-4773
Barber #2 .... ☎ 302-739-4522
Chiropractor #2 .... ☎ 302-739-4522
Cosmetologist #2 .... ☎ 302-739-4522
Dentist #2 .... ☎ 302-739-4522
Emergency Medical Technician #9 (400) .... ✉ 302-739-4710
Emergency Medical Technician-Paramedic #9
.... ✉ 302-739-6637
Funeral Director #2 .... ☎ 302-739-4522
Hearing Aid Dealer/Fitter #2 .... ☎ 302-739-4522
Massage #2 .... ☎ 302-739-4522
Medical Doctor/Surgeon #2 .... ☎ 302-739-4522
Nurse #2 .... ☎ 302-739-4522
Nursing Home Administrator #2 .... ☎ 302-739-4522
Occupational Therapist/Assistant #2 .... ☎ 302-739-4522
Optometrist #2 .... ☎ 302-739-4522
Osteopathic Physician #2 .... ☎ 302-739-4522

Pharmacist #2 .... ☎ 302-739-4522
Physical Therapist/Assistant #2 .... ☎ 302-739-4522
Podiatrist #2 .... ☎ 302-739-4522
Speech Pathologist/Audiologist #2 .... ☎ 302-739-4522

Investigations & Security
Private Detective #4 .... ☎ 302-739-5991
Private Investigator Agency #4 (75) .... ☎ 302-739-5991

Social Services
Professional Counselor #2 .... ☎ 302-739-4522
Psychologist #2 .... ☎ 302-739-4522
Social Worker #2 .... ☎ 302-739-4522

Sports & Entertainment
Adult Entertainment #2 .... ☎ 302-739-4522
Alcoholic Beverage Establishment #1 .... ☎ 302-577-3760
Athletic Trainer #2 .... ☎ 302-739-4522
Deadly Weapons Dealer #2 .... ☎ 302-739-4522
Gaming Control #2 .... ☎ 302-739-4522
Harness Racing #8 302-739-4811

Transportation
River Pilot #2 .... ☎ 302-739-4522

State Licensing & Business Registration Agency Information

(1) Alcoholic Beverage Control Division, 820 N French St, Carvel State Office Bldg, Wilmington, DE 19801, 302-577-3760, Fax: 302-577-3204

(2) Board of Accountancy, Cannon Bldg, PO Box 1401, Dover, DE 19903, 302-739-4522, Fax: 302-739-2711

(3) Board of Bar Examiners, 200 W 9th St, Suite B, Wilmington, DE 19801, 302-658-9200, Fax: 302-658-4605

(4) Delaware State Police, Detectitve Licensing, PO Box 430, Dover, DE 19903, 302-739-5991, Fax: 302-739-5888

(5) Department of Public Instruction, PO Box 1402, Dover, DE 19903, 302-739-4661, Fax: 302-739-3092

(6) Division of Professional Regulations, Margaret M. O'Neill Bldg, PO Box 1401, Dover, DE 19903, 302-739-4522

(7) Division of Revenue, 820 N French St, Carvel State Office Bldg, Wilmington, DE 19801, 302-577-3300, Fax: 302-577-3689

(8) Harness Racing Commission, 2320 S DuPont Hwy, Dover, DE 19901, 302-739-4811, Fax: 302-697-6287

(9) Health & Social Services Department, Division of Public Health, PO Box 637, Dover, DE 19903, 302-739-4701, Fax: 302-739-6617

(10) Insurance Department, 841 Silver Lake Blvd, Dover, DE 19904, 302-739-4251, Fax: 302-739-5280

(11) Office of Secretary of State, Notary Division, PO Box 898, Dover, DE 19903, 302-739-6479, Fax: 302-739-3812

(12) Pesticide Section, Department of Agriculture, 2320 S DuPont Hwy, Dover, DE 19901, 302-739-4811, Fax: 302-697-6287

District of Columbia

General Statistics	
State Population	**.5 Million**
Number of Degree Granting Institutions:	**20**
Number of State Licensing & Business Registration Agencies:	**65**

Degree Granting Educational Institutions

American University, Registrar, 4400 Massachusetts Ave NW, Washington, DC 20016, 202-885-2200 (Fax: 202-885-1046). Hours: 9AM-6PM M-Th, 9AM-5PM F. Records go back to 1973. Alumni Records Office: Penley Campus, 140 Constitution Hall, Washington, DC 20016. Degrees granted: Bachelors; Masters; Doctorate. Adverse incident record source- Dean, 202-885-3310.

Attendance and degree information available by phone, fax, mail. Search requires name plus SSN, approximate years of attendance. There is no fee.

Catholic University of America, Registrar, 620 Michigan Ave NE, Washington, DC 20064, 202-319-5311 (Fax: 202-319-5831). Hours: 9AM-5PM. Enrollment: 6000. Records go back to 1876. Alumni records are maintained here also. Call 202-319-5608. Degrees granted: Bachelors; Masters; Doctorate; Licentuate. Adverse incident record source- V.P's Office .

Attendance and degree information available by phone, fax, mail. Search requires name plus date of birth. Also helpful: SSN, exact years of attendance. There is no fee.

Corcoran School of Art, Registrar, 500 17th St NW, Washington, DC 20006-4899, 202-638-0561 (Fax: 202-347-4826). Hours: 9AM-5PM. Enrollment: 1400. Records go back to 1965. Alumni records are maintained here at the same phone number. Degrees granted: Bachelors.

Attendance and degree information available by phone, fax, mail. Search requires name plus approximate years of attendance. Also helpful: SSN, date of birth, exact years of attendance. There is no fee.

De Sales School of Theology, Registrar, 721 Lawrence St NE, Washington, DC 20017, 202-269-9412 (Fax: 202-526-2720). Hours: 9AM-4PM. Enrollment: 33. Records go back to 1985. Degrees granted: Masters. Adverse incident record source- Dean of Students, 202-269-9412.

Attendance and degree information available by phone, fax, mail. Search requires name plus SSN. There is no fee.

District of Columbia School of Law, Registrar, 719 13th St NW, Washington, DC 20005, 202-274-7340 (Fax: 202-727-9608). Hours: 9AM-5:30PM. Enrollment: 243. Records go back to 1991. Alumni records are maintained here at the same phone number. Degrees granted: Doctorate.

Attendance and degree information available by phone, fax, mail. Search requires name plus exact years of attendance. Also helpful: SSN, date of birth. There is no fee.

Dominican House of Studies, Registrar, 487 Michigan Ave NE, Washington, DC 20017, 202-529-5300 (Fax: 202-636-4460). Hours: 9AM-4PM. Enrollment: 35. Records go back to 1945. Degrees granted: Masters; M. Div; S.T.L.

Attendance and degree information available by written request only. Search requires name only. Also helpful: exact years of attendance. Fee is $3.00.

Gallaudet University, Registrar, 800 Florida Ave NE, Washington, DC 20002, 202-651-5393 (Fax: 202-651-5182). Hours: 8:30AM-4:30PM. Enrollment: 2130. Alumni records are maintained here also. Call 202-651-5060. Degrees granted: Associate; Bachelors; Masters; Doctorate. Adverse incident record source- Student Life, 202-651-5255.

Attendance and degree information available by phone, fax, mail. Search requires name plus SSN, date of birth. There is no fee.

George Washington University, Registrar, 2121 I St NW Ste 101, Washington, DC 20052, 202-994-4900 (Fax: 202-994-4448). Hours: 8AM-5PM. Enrollment: 19000. Records go back to 1820. Alumni records are maintained here also. Call 202-994-6435. Degrees granted: Associate; Bachelors; Masters; Doctorate. Adverse incident record source- Dean of Students, 202-994-6710.

Attendance and degree information available by fax, mail. Search requires name only. Also helpful: SSN, date of birth, exact years of attendance. There is no fee.

Georgetown University, Registrar, 37th and O Sts NW, Washington, DC 20057, 202-687-4020 (Fax: 202-687-3608). Hours: 9AM-5PM. Enrollment: 12618. Records go back to 1977. Alumni records are maintained here also. Call 202-687-1789. Degrees granted: Associate; Bachelors; Masters; Doctorate.

Attendance and degree information available by phone, fax, mail. Search requires name plus SSN, approximate years of attendance. Also helpful: date of birth, exact years of attendance. There is no fee.

Howard University, Registrar, 2400 Sixth St NW, Washington, DC 20059, 202-806-2712 (Fax: 202-806-4466). Hours: 8AM-5PM. Enrollment: 10952. Records go back to 1867.

Alumni records are maintained here also. Call 202-806-8010. Degrees granted: Bachelors; Masters; Doctorate. Adverse incident record source- Security Office, 202-806-1073: Student Affaris, 202-806-2120

Attendance information available by phone, fax, mail. Search requires name plus SSN. Also helpful: date of birth, exact years of attendance. There is no fee.

Degree information available by phone, fax, mail. Search requires name plus SSN. Also helpful: date of birth, exact years of attendance. There is no fee.

Johns Hopkins University, (School of Advanced International Studies), Registrar, 1740 Massachusetts Ave NW, Washington, DC 20036, 202-663-5708 (Fax: 202-663-5615). Hours: 9AM-4:45PM. Enrollment: 450. Records go back to 1943. Alumni records are maintained here at the same phone number. Degrees granted: Masters; Doctorate.

Attendance and degree information available by phone, fax, mail. Search requires name plus SSN, approximate years of attendance. There is no fee.

Joint Military Intelligence College, Registrar, Defense Intelligence Analysis Ctr, Washington, DC 20340-5485, 202-646-1333. Enrollment: 35. Degrees granted: Masters.

Attendance information available by phone, fax, mail. Search requires name plus SSN. Also helpful: date of birth, approximate years of attendance. There is no fee.

Degree information available by phone, fax, mail. Search requires name plus SSN. Also helpful: date of birth. There is no fee.

Mount Vernon College, Registrar, 2100 Foxhall Rd NW, Washington, DC 20007, 202-625-4527 (Fax: 202-625-6735). Hours: 9AM-5PM. Enrollment: 600. Alumni records are maintained here also. Call 202-625-4685. Degrees granted: Associate; Bachelors; Masters.

Attendance and degree information available by phone, fax, mail. Search requires name plus SSN, approximate years of attendance. Also helpful: date of birth, exact years of attendance. There is no fee.

Oblate College, Registrar, 391 Michigan Ave NE, Washington, DC 20017-1587, 202-529-6544. Hours: 9AM-3PM. Enrollment: 25. Records go back to 1950. Degrees granted: Bachelors; Masters. Adverse incident record source- Dean, 202-529-6544.

Attendance and degree information available by phone, mail. Search requires name only. Also helpful: SSN, date of birth, exact years of attendance. There is no fee.

Southeastern University, Registrar, 501 Eye St SW, Washington, DC 20024, 202-488-8162 X264 (Fax: 202-488-8093). Hours: 10AM-7PM. Enrollment: 458. Records go back to

1990. Alumni records are maintained here also. Call 202-488-8162 X251. Degrees granted: Bachelors; Masters.

Attendance and degree information available by phone, fax, mail. Search requires name plus SSN, date of birth, approximate years of attendance. There is no fee.

Trinity College, Registrar, 125 Michigan Ave NE, Washington, DC 20017, 202-884-9200 (Fax: 202-884-9229). Hours: 9AM-5PM. Enrollment: 1400. Records go back to 1902. Alumni records are maintained here at the same phone number. Degrees granted: Bachelors; Masters. Adverse incident record source- Mr. William Merritt, 202-884-9110.

Attendance and degree information available by fax, mail. Search requires name plus SSN, signed release. Also helpful: date of birth, exact years of attendance. There is no fee.

University of the District of Columbia, Registrar, 4200 Connecticut Ave NW, Washington, DC 20008, 202-274-6072 (Fax: 202-274-6073). Hours: 8AM-5PM M,W,F; 8AM-6PM T,Th. Enrollment: 9660. Records go back to 1851. Alumni Records Office: Alumni Affairs, 4250 Connecticut Ave, Washington, DC 20008, 202-274-5117. Degrees granted: Masters; Undergrad. Adverse incident record source- Student Affairs, 202-274-5088.

Attendance and degree information available by mail. Search requires name plus SSN, exact years of attendance, signed release. Also helpful: date of birth. There is no fee.

University of the District of Columbia, (Georgia/Harvard Street), 11th and Harvard Sts NW, Washington, DC 20009, 202-274-5000. Records are not housed here. They are located at University of the District of Columbia, Registrar, 4200 Connecticut Ave NW, Washington, DC 20008.

Washington Theological Union, Registrar, 6896 Laurel St,NW, Washington, DC 20012, 202-541-5216 (Fax: 202-726-1716). Hours: 8AM-5PM. Enrollment: 250. Records go back to 1970. Alumni records are maintained here at the same phone number. Degrees granted: Masters. Adverse incident record source- Academic Dean.

Attendance and degree information available by phone, fax, mail. Search requires name plus exact years of attendance. Also helpful: SSN, date of birth. There is no fee.

Wesley Theological Seminary, Registrar, 4500 Massachusetts Ave NW, Washington, DC 20016, 202-885-8650 (Fax: 202-885-8605). Hours: 9AM-4PM. Enrollment: 609. Records go back to 1984. Degrees granted: Masters; Doctorate.

Attendance and degree information available by phone, fax, mail. Search requires name only. There is no fee.

Trade and Vocational Schools

Hannah Harrison Career Schools, 4470 MacArthur Blvd NW, Washington, DC 20007, 202-333-3500

Levine School of Music, 1690 36th St NW, Washington, DC 20007, 202-337-2227

Margaret Murray Washington Vocational School, 27 O St NW, Washington, DC 20001, 202-673-7224

Marine Corps Institute, 8th and Eye Sts SE, Washington, DC 20390, 202-433-2728

McGraw-Hill Continuing Education Center, 4401 Connecticut Ave NW, Washington, DC 20008, 202-244-1600

McGraw-Hill Continuing Education Center (NRI Schools), 4401 Connecticut Ave NW, Washington, DC 20008, 202-244-1600

National Conservatory of Dramatic Arts, 1556 Wisconsin Ave NW, Washington, DC 20007, 202-333-2202

Washington Conservatory of Music, Inc., PO Box 5758, Washington, DC 20816, 301-320-2770

State Licensing & Business Registration Quick Finder Index

Architecture, Engineering & Surveying
Architect #5 .... ☎ 202-727-7480
Engineer #5 .... ☎ 202-727-7480

Business - Court & Legal Services
Attorney #3 .... ☎ 202-727-7900
Lobbyist #7 .... ☎ 202-939-8717
Notary Public #13 .... ⊠ 202-727-3117

Business - General Services
Auctioneer #5 .... ☎ 202-727-7480
Interior Designer #5 .... ☎ 202-727-7480
Motor Vehicle Dealer/Salesperson #5 .... ☎ 202-727-7480
Public Accountant #6 .... ☎ 202-727-7170
Solicitor #5 .... ☎ 202-727-7480

Construction & Manufacturing
Contractor #5 .... ☎ 202-727-7480
Electrician #5 .... ☎ 202-727-7480
Gas Fitter #5 .... ☎ 202-727-7480
Master Mechanic #5 .... ☎ 202-727-7480
Plumber #5 .... ☎ 202-727-7170
Refrigeration/Air Conditioning #5 .... ☎ 202-727-7480

Environmental & Agriculture
Pesticide Applicator #4 .... ☎ 202-727-7070
Pesticide Dealer #4 .... ☎ 202-727-7100
Pesticide Employee/Operator #4 .... ☎ 202-645-6617
Solid Waste Collector #5 .... ☎ 202-727-7480
Veterinarian #6 .... ☎ 202-727-7170

Financial - Real Estate, Insurance & Banking
Auto Repossessor #5 .... ☎ 202-727-7480
Bank #8 .... ☎ 202-727-1563
Credit Union #8 .... ☎ 202-727-1563
Insurance Broker/Agent #10 .... ☎ 202-727-7425
Property Manager #5 .... ☎ 202-727-7480
Real Estate Appraiser #5 .... ☎ 202-727-7480
Real Estate Broker/Salesperson #5 .... ☎ 202-727-7480
Savings & Loan Company #8 .... ☎ 202-727-1563
Securities Agent #14 .... ⊠ 202-626-5105
Securities Broker/Dealer #14 .... ⊠ 202-626-5105

Health & Beauty
Acupuncturist #2 .... ⊠ 202-727-5365
Barber #6 .... ☎ 202-727-7170
Chiropractor #6 .... ☎ 202-727-7170
Cosmetologist #6 .... ☎ 202-727-7170
Dental Hygienist #5 .... ☎ 202-727-7480
Dentist #6 .... ☎ 202-727-7170
Dietitian/Nutritionist #6 .... ☎ 202-727-7170
Emergency Medical Technician #9 .... ☎ 202-939-8739
Funeral Director #5 .... ☎ 202-727-7480
Hearing Aid Dispenser #5 .... ☎ 202-727-7480
Medical Doctor #2 .... ⊠ 202-727-7170
Nurse #6 .... ☎ 202-727-7170
Nurse Midwife #5 .... ☎ 202-727-7480
Nursing Home Administrator #6 .... ☎ 202-727-7170
Occupational Therapist #5 .... ☎ 202-727-7480
Optometrist #5 .... ☎ 202-727-7480
Osteopathic Physician #2 .... ⊠ 202-727-5365
Pharmacist #6 .... ☎ 202-727-7170
Physical Therapist #5 .... ☎ 202-727-7480
Physician's Assistant #6 .... ☎ 202-727-7170
Podiatrist #5 .... ☎ 202-727-7480

Investigations & Security
Private Investigator #12 .... ⊠ 202-939-8722
Security Alarm Dealer/Agent #5 .... ☎ 202-727-7480
Security Guard #5 .... ☎ 202-727-7480

Social Services
Professional Counselor #5 .... ☎ 202-727-7480
Psychologist #6 .... ☎ 202-727-7170
Social Worker #6 .... ☎ 202-727-7170

Sports & Entertainment
Alcohol Distributor #1 .... ☎ 202-727-7375
Alcohol Manufacturer #1 .... ☎ 202-727-7375
Alcohol Vendor #1 .... ☎ 202-727-7375
Boxing/Wrestling Commission #6 .... ☎ 202-727-7170
Lottery Retailer #11 .... ☎ 202-433-8000
Tour Guide #5 .... ☎ 202-727-7480

Transportation
Parking Lot Attendant #5 .... ☎ 202-727-7480

State Licensing & Business Registration Agency Information

(1) Alcohol & Beverage Control Board, 614 H St NW, Room 807, Washington, DC 20001, 202-727-7375, Fax: 202-727-8030

(2) Board of Medicine, 614 H St NW, Rm 108, Washington, DC 20001, 202-727-5365, Fax: 202-727-4087

(3) Court of Appeals, 500 Indiana Ave NW, Rm 4200, Washington, DC 20001, 202-879-2710

(4) Department of Consumer & Regulatory Affairs, Environmental Control Division-Pesticides, 2100 Martin Luther King Jr Ave SE, Ste 203, Washington, DC 20020, 202-645-6080

(5) Department of Consumer & Regulatory Affairs, License & Certification Division, PO Box 37200, 614 H St NW, 9th Flr, Washington, DC 20001, 202-727-7480

(6) Department of Consumer & Regulatory Affairs, Occupational & Professional Licensing Admin, PO Box 37200, 614 H St NW, Washington, DC 20001, 202-727-7170, Fax: 202-727-7961

(7) Director of Campaign Finance, Office of Campaign Finance, 2000 - 14th St NW, Ste 420, Washington, DC 20009, 202-939-8717, Fax: 202-939-7160

(8) Economic Development, Banking & Financial Institutions Office, 717 - 14th St NW, Ste 1100, Washington, DC 20005, 202-727-1563, Fax: 202-727-1588

(9) Emergency Medical Services Office, 2000 14th St NW, 4th Flr, Washington, DC 20009, 202-939-8739, Fax: 202-673-2132

(10) Insurance Administration, 1 Judiciary Square, 441 - 4th St NW, Rm 870N, Washington, DC 20001, 202-727-7425, Fax: 202-727-7940

(11) Lottery & Charitable Games Control Board, 2101 Martin Luther King Jr Ave SE, Washingtin, DC 20020, 202-645-8000

(12) Metropolitian Police Department, Licensing Division, 2000 - 14th St NW, 3rd Flr, Washington, DC 20001, 202-939-8722, Fax: 202-673-7418

(13) Office of the Secretary, Notary Commissions & Authentications Section, 717 14th St NW, Suite 230, Washington, DC 20005, 202-727-3117, Fax: 202-727-8457

(14) Public Service Commission, Division of Securities, 450 - 5th St NW, Ste 821, Washington, DC 20001, 202-626-5105

Florida

Capitol: Tallahassee (Leon County)	
State Population	14.1 Million
Number of Degree Granting Institutions:	116
Number of State Licensing & Business Registration Agencies:	149

Degree Granting Educational Institutions

American Trade Institute, Registrar, 1395 SW 167th St, Ste 200, Miami, FL 33169, 305-628-1000 (Fax: 305-628-1461). Enrollment: 250. Formerly Flagler Career Institute Records go back to 1976. Degrees granted: Associate. Adverse incident record source- Director of Student Affairs.

Attendance and degree information available by phone, mail. Search requires name plus SSN, exact years of attendance. There is no fee.

Art Institute of Fort Lauderdale, Registrar, 1799 SE 17th St, Fort Lauderdale, FL 33316-3000, 954-463-3000 X451 (Fax: 954-523-7676). Hours: 8AM-5PM. Enrollment: 2000. Records go back to 1971. Degrees granted: Associate; Bachelors.

Attendance information available by fax, mail. Search requires name plus SSN, signed release. Also helpful: exact years of attendance. There is no fee.

Degree information available by phone, fax, mail. Search requires name plus SSN. Also helpful: exact years of attendance. There is no fee.

Barry University, Registrar, 11300 NE Second Ave, Miami Shores, FL 33161-6695, 305-899-3948 (Fax: 305-899-3946). Hours: 8:30AM-5PM. Enrollment: 7048. Records go back to 1940. Alumni records are maintained here also. Call 305-899-3175. Degrees granted: Bachelors; Masters; Doctorate. Adverse incident record source- VP Student Services, 305-899-3085.

Attendance and degree information available by phone, fax, mail. Search requires name plus SSN, date of birth. Also helpful: exact years of attendance. There is no fee.

Bethune-Cookman College, Registrar, 640 Dr Mary McLeod Bethune Blvd, Daytona Beach, FL 32114-3099, 904-255-1401 (Fax: 904-257-5338). Hours: 8:30AM-5PM. Enrollment: 2400. Records go back to 1904. Alumni records are maintained here also. Call 904-255-1401. Degrees granted: Bachelors.

Attendance information available by fax, mail. Search requires name plus SSN, signed release. There is no fee.

Degree information available by phone, fax, mail. Search requires name plus SSN. There is no fee.

Brevard Community College, Enrollment Services, 1519 Clearlake Rd, Cocoa, FL 32922, 407-632-1111 X3700 (Fax: 407-634-3752). Hours: 8AM-4:30PM Summer; 8AM-5PM Fall. Enrollment: 12500. Records go back to 1962. Degrees granted: Associate.

Attendance and degree information available by phone, mail. Search requires name plus SSN, date of birth, approximate years of attendance. There is no fee.

Broward Community College, Registrar, 225 E Las Olas Blvd, Fort Lauderdale, FL 33301, 954-761-7465 (Fax: 954-761-7466). Hours: 8AM-4PM. Enrollment: 77122. Records go back to 1951. Alumni records are maintained here also. Call 954-761-7414. Degrees granted: Associate.

Attendance and degree information available by phone, fax, mail. Search requires name plus SSN. Also helpful: approximate years of attendance. There is no fee.

Caribbean Center for Advanced Studies, (Miami Institute of Psychology), Registrar, 8180 NW 36th St 2nd Fl, Miami, FL 33166-6653, 305-593-1223 (Fax: 305-592-7930). Hours: 9AM-6PM. Enrollment: 550. Records go back to 1980. Degrees granted: Bachelors; Masters; Doctorate. Adverse incident record source- Chancellor's Office .

Attendance and degree information available by fax, mail. Search requires name plus SSN, exact years of attendance, signed release. There is no fee.

Central Florida Community College, Registrar, PO Box 1388, Ocala, FL 34478, 904-237-2111 (Fax: 904-237-3747). Hours: 8AM-7PM M-Th, 8AM-4:30PM F. Enrollment: 6000. Records go back to 1957. Alumni records are maintained here at the same phone number. Degrees granted: Associate.

Attendance and degree information available by fax, mail. Search requires name plus SSN. Also helpful: date of birth, exact years of attendance. There is no fee.

Chipola Junior College, Registrar, 3094 Indian Circle, Marianna, FL 32446-2053, 904-526-2761 (Fax: 904-718-2344). Hours: 7:30AM-4:30PM. Enrollment: 2500. Records go back to 1947. Alumni records are maintained here at the same phone number. Degrees granted: Associate. Adverse incident record source- Marianna Police Dept, 904-526-3125.

Attendance and degree information available by phone, mail. Search requires name only. Also helpful: SSN, date of birth, exact years of attendance. There is no fee.

City College, **(Branch)**, Registrar, 2400 SW 13th St, Gainesville, FL 32608, 352-335-4000 (Fax: 352-335-4303). Hours: 8AM-8PM. Enrollment: 330. Formerly Career College (Branch) Records go back to 1989. Degrees granted: Associate. Special programs- Specialized Phlebotony Lab. Adverse incident record source- Local Police.

Attendance information available by phone, fax, mail. Search requires name plus SSN, date of birth. Also helpful: exact years of attendance. There is no fee.

Degree information available by mail. Search requires name plus SSN, date of birth. Also helpful: exact years of attendance. There is no fee.

Clearwater Christian College, Registrar, 3400 Gulf-to-Bay Blvd, Clearwater, FL 34619, 813-726-1153 (Fax: 813-726-8597). Hours: 8AM-4:30PM. Enrollment: 530. Records go back to 1966. Alumni records are maintained here at the same phone number. Degrees granted: Associate; Bachelors.

Attendance information available by phone, fax, mail. Search requires name plus SSN. There is no fee.

Degree information available by fax, mail. Search requires name plus SSN. There is no fee.

Cooper Career Institute, Registrar, 2247 Palm Beach Lakes Blvd, West Palm Beach, FL 33409, 516-640-6999 (Fax: 516-686-8778). Hours: 8:30AM-5:30PM. Enrollment: 200. Formerly Cooper Academy of Court Reporting Records go back to 1900's. Alumni records are maintained here at the same phone number. Degrees granted: Associate. Special programs- Court Reporting: Medical Stenoscription.

Attendance and degree information available by phone, fax, mail. Search requires name plus SSN. Also helpful: exact years of attendance. There is no fee.

Daytona Beach Community College, Records Office, PO Box 2811, Daytona Beach, FL 32120-2811, 904-255-8131 (Fax: 904-254-4489). Hours: 8AM-7PM M-Th; 8AM-4:30PM F. Enrollment: 12400. Records go back to 1958. Alumni records are maintained here also. Call 904-255-8131 X4436. Degrees granted: Associate. Adverse incident record source- VP Student Development, 904-255-8131 X3797.

Attendance information available by fax, mail. Search requires name plus SSN, signed release. Also helpful: date of birth, exact years of attendance. There is no fee.

Degree information available by phone, fax, mail. Search requires name plus SSN. Also helpful: date of birth, exact years of attendance. There is no fee.

Eckerd College, Registrar, 4200 54th Ave S, St Petersburg, FL 33711, 813-864-8217 (Fax: 813-864-8060). Hours: 8:30AM-5PM. Enrollment: 1380. Records go back to 1960. Alumni records are maintained here also. Call 813-864-8219. Degrees granted: Bachelors.

Attendance and degree information available by phone, fax, mail. Search requires name only. There is no fee.

Edison Community College, Registrar, 8099 College Pkwy SW, PO Box 60210, Fort Myers, FL 33906-6210, 941-489-9317 (Fax: 941-489-9217). Hours: 8:30AM-7PM M-Th; 8:30AM-4PM F. Enrollment: 10000. Records go back to 1950's. Alumni records are maintained here at the same phone number. Degrees granted: Associate. Adverse incident record source- Registrar.

Attendance information available by mail. Search requires name plus SSN, signed release. Also helpful: date of birth, exact years of attendance. There is no fee.

Degree information available by phone, fax, mail. Search requires name plus SSN. Also helpful: date of birth, exact years of attendance. There is no fee.

Education America, Registrar, 2410 E Busch Blvd, Tampa, FL 33612, 813-935-5700 (Fax: 813-935-7415). Enrollment: 1250. National Education Center-Tampa Technical Institute Records go back to 1948. Degrees granted: Bachelors.

Attendance and degree information available by fax, mail. Search requires name plus SSN, signed release. Also helpful: exact years of attendance. There is no fee.

Edward Waters College, Registrar, 1658 Kings Rd, Jacksonville, FL 32209, 904-366-2717 (Fax: 904-366-2760). Hours: 8AM-5PM. Records go back to 1866. Degrees granted: Bachelors. Adverse incident record source- Student Affairs, 904-366-2514.

Attendance and degree information available by phone, fax, mail. Search requires name plus SSN. There is no fee.

Embry-Riddle Aeronautical University, Registrar, 600 S Clyde Morris Blvd, Daytona Beach, FL 32114-3900, 904-226-6030 (Fax: 904-226-7070). Hours: 8AM-4PM. Records go back to 1945. Alumni records are maintained here also. Call 904-226-6160. Degrees granted: Associate; Bachelors; Masters. Special programs- Aviation Maintenance Technology, 904-226-6779: Extended Campus, active records, 904-226-6910: Extended Campus, inactive records, 904-226-6920. Adverse incident record source- Office of Student Affairs, Daytona, 904-226-6326: Office of Student Affairs, Prescott, 602-776-3774

Attendance and degree information available by phone, fax, mail. Search requires name plus SSN. Also helpful: date of birth, exact years of attendance. There is no fee.

Flagler Career Institute, Registrar, 3225 University Blvd S, Jacksonville, FL 32216-2736, 904-721-1622 (Fax: 904-723-3117). Degrees granted: Associate.

Attendance information available by written request only. Search requires name plus SSN, date of birth, approximate years of attendance, signed release. Also helpful: exact years of attendance. There is no fee.

Degree information available by written request only. Search requires name plus SSN, date of birth, approximate years of attendance, signed release. Also helpful: exact years of attendance. There is no fee.

Flagler College, Registrar, PO Box 1027, 74 King St, St Augustine, FL 32085-1027, 904-829-6481 (Fax: 904-826-0094). Hours: 8AM-Noon, 1-5PM. Enrollment: 1400. Records go back to 1968. Alumni records are maintained here at the same phone number. Degrees granted: Bachelors.

Attendance and degree information available by phone, fax, mail. Search requires name only. Also helpful: SSN. There is no fee.

Florida Agricultural and Mechanical University, Registrar's Office, Foote Hilyer Admin Ctr #112, Tallahassee, FL 32307-3200, 904-599-3115 (Fax: 904-561-2428). Hours: 8AM-5PM. Enrollment: 10500. Records go back to 1887. Alumni records are maintained here also. Call 904-599-3861. Degrees granted: Associate; Bachelors; Masters; Doctorate. Adverse incident record source- Police, 904-599-3256: Ofc of Judicial Officer, 904-599-3541

Attendance and degree information available by phone, fax, mail. Search requires name plus SSN. Also helpful: date of birth, exact years of attendance. There is no fee.

Florida Atlantic University, Registrar, 777 Glades Rd, PO Box 3091, Boca Raton, FL 33431-0991, 561-367-2711 (Fax: 561-367-2756). Hours: 8AM-6PM M-Th, 8AM-5PM F. Enrollment: 18000. Records go back to 1965. Alumni records are maintained here also. Call 561-367-3010. Degrees granted:

Associate; Bachelors; Masters; Doctorate. Adverse incident record source- Dean of Students, 561-367-3546.

Attendance and degree information available by phone, fax, mail. Search requires name plus SSN, approximate years of attendance. There is no fee.

Florida Baptist Theological College, Registrar, PO Box 1306, Graceville, FL 32440, 904-263-3261 (Fax: 904-263-7506). Hours: 8AM-4:30PM. Enrollment: 491. Records go back to 1947. Alumni records are maintained here also. Call 904-263-3261 X85. Degrees granted: Associate; Bachelors. Adverse incident record source- Admininstrative VP, 904-263-3261 X31.

Attendance and degree information available by phone, fax, mail. Search requires name plus date of birth, exact years of attendance. Also helpful: SSN, approximate years of attendance. There is no fee.

Florida Christian College, Registrar, 1011 Bill Beck Blvd, Kissimmee, FL 34744, 407-847-8966 (Fax: 407-847-3925). Hours: 8:30AM-4:30PM. Enrollment: 150. Records go back to 1976. Alumni records are maintained here also. Call 407-847-8966 X313. Degrees granted: Associate; Bachelors.

Attendance information available by phone, fax, mail. Search requires name only. Also helpful: SSN, date of birth, exact years of attendance. There is no fee.

Degree information available by fax. Search requires name only. Also helpful: SSN, date of birth, exact years of attendance. There is no fee.

Florida College, Registrar, 119 Glen Arven Ave, Temple Terrace, FL 33617, 813-988-5131 (Fax: 813-899-6772). Hours: 8AM-5PM. Enrollment: 400. Records go back to 1945. Alumni records are maintained here at the same phone number. Degrees granted: Associate; Bachelors. Special programs- Biblical Studies. Adverse incident record source- Student Services, 813-899-6745.

Attendance and degree information available by phone, fax, mail. Search requires name only. Also helpful: SSN, date of birth, exact years of attendance. There is no fee.

Florida Community College at Jacksonville, Registrar, 501 W State St, Jacksonville, FL 32202, 904-632-3100 (Fax: 904-632-3109). Enrollment: 19000. Records go back to 1966. Degrees granted: Associate. Special programs- Nursing Program: Vocational & Adult Studies. Adverse incident record source- Security, 904-632-3396.

Attendance and degree information available by phone, fax, mail. Search requires name plus SSN, exact years of attendance.

Florida Computer & Business School, Registrar, 8300 Flagler St Ste 200, Miami, FL 33144, 305-553-6065 (Fax: 305-225-0128). Hours: 7:30AM-4:30PM. Enrollment: 140. Records go back 5 years in-house; the rest are off-site. Degrees granted: Associate; Diploma, Specialized Associate Degree. Adverse incident record source- Director of Schools.

Attendance and degree information available by fax, mail. Search requires name plus SSN, exact years of attendance, signed release. Also helpful: date of birth. There is no fee.

Florida Institute of Technology, Registrar, 150 W University Blvd, Melbourne, FL 32901-6988, 407-768-8000 X8115 (Fax: 407-727-2419). Hours: 8AM-5PM. Enrollment: 4500. Records go back to 1990. Alumni records are maintained here also. Call 407-768-8000 X7190. Degrees granted: Associate; Bachelors; Masters; Doctorate.

Attendance and degree information available by phone, fax, mail. Search requires name plus SSN, approximate years of attendance. There is no fee.

Florida International University, Registrar, University Park, Miami, FL 33199, 305-348-2383 (Fax: 305-348-2941). Hours: 8AM-7PM M-Th; 8AM-5PM F. Enrollment: 28000. Records go back to 1973. Alumni records are maintained here at the same phone number. Degrees granted: Bachelors; Masters; Doctorate. Special programs- School of Hospitality Management, 305-948-4500: School of Journalism & Mass Communications, 305-940-5625: School of Nursing, 305-940-5915: School of Policy Management, 305-940-5890: School of Social Work, 305-940-5880: Continuing Education (non-credit), 305-940-5669: College of Business Administration, 305-348-2751. Adverse incident record source- Judicial Affairs, 305-348-3939: Public Safety, 305-348-2623

Attendance and degree information available by phone, fax, mail. Search requires name plus SSN. Also helpful: date of birth. There is no fee.

Florida Keys Community College, Registrar, 5901 W College Rd, Key West, FL 33040, 305-296-9081 (Fax: 305-292-5155). Hours: 8:30AM-4PM. Enrollment: 3800. Records go back to 1965. Degrees granted: Associate.

Attendance and degree information available by phone, fax, mail. Search requires name plus SSN. Also helpful: date of birth. There is no fee.

Florida Memorial College, Registrar, 15800 NW 42nd Ave, Miami, FL 33054, 305-626-3752 (Fax: 305-626-3669). Hours: 8AM-5PM. Enrollment: 1600. Records go back to 1879. Alumni records are maintained here also. Call 305-626-3657. Degrees granted: Bachelors. Adverse incident record source- Student Development, 305-626-1410.

Attendance information available by phone, fax, mail. Search requires name plus SSN, date of birth, approximate years of attendance. There is no fee.

Degree information available by fax, mail. Search requires name plus SSN, date of birth, approximate years of attendance. There is no fee.

Florida Metropolitan University, (Tampa College, Pinellas Campus), Registrar, 2471 N McMullen Booth Rd, Clearwater, FL 34619-1354, 813-725-2688 (Fax: 813-796-3722). Hours: 8AM-8PM. Enrollment: 700. Formerly Tampa College Records go back to 1989. Alumni records are maintained here at the same phone number. Degrees granted: Associate; Bachelors; Masters.

Attendance information available by mail. Search requires name plus SSN, date of birth, signed release. Also helpful: exact years of attendance. There is no fee.

Degree information available by phone, fax, mail. Search requires name plus SSN, date of birth. Also helpful: exact years of attendance. There is no fee.

Florida Southern College, Registrar, 111 Lake Hollingsworth Dr, Lakeland, FL 33801, 941-680-4127 (Fax: 941-680-4565). Hours: 8AM-5PM. Enrollment: 1600. Records go back to 1915. Alumni records are maintained here also. Call 941-680-4110. Degrees granted: Bachelors; Masters. Special programs- Orlando Program, 407-855-1302: Charlotte-DeSoto Program, 813-494-7373. Adverse incident record source- Dean, 813-680-4206.

Attendance and degree information available by phone, fax, mail. Search requires name plus SSN, approximate years of attendance. Also helpful: date of birth, exact years of attendance. There is no fee.

Florida State University, Registrar, Tallahassee, FL 32306-1011, 904-644-1050 (Fax: 904-644-1597). Hours: 8AM-5PM. Enrollment: 29000. Records go back to 1857 as the Seminary West of Suwannee; to 1909 as the FL State College for Women; to 1947 as the FL State University. Alumni Records Office: Alumni Office, Florida State University, 114 Longmire Bldg, Tallahassee, FL 32306-1052. Degrees granted: Associate; Bachelors; Masters; Doctorate.

Attendance and degree information available by phone, fax, mail. Search requires name only. Also helpful: SSN, date of birth, exact years of attendance. There is no fee.

Florida Technical College, Registrar, 8711 Lone Star Rd, Jacksonville, FL 32211, 904-724-2229 (Fax: 904-720-0920). Hours: 8AM-6PM. Records go back to 1984. Degrees granted: Associate. Adverse incident record source- Site Admin., 904-724-2229.

Attendance and degree information available by fax, mail. Search requires name plus SSN, exact years of attendance, signed release. There is no fee.

Fort Lauderdale College, Registrar, 1040 Bayview Dr, Fort Lauderdale, FL 33304, 954-568-1600 (Fax: 954-568-2008). Hours: 8AM-8PM M-Th; 9AM-1PM F. Enrollment: 450. Records go back to 1940. Degrees granted: Associate; Bachelors. Adverse incident record source- Academic Dean.

Attendance information available by fax, mail. Search requires name plus SSN, signed release. Also helpful: date of birth, exact years of attendance. There is no fee.

Degree information available by phone, fax, mail. Search requires name plus SSN. Also helpful: date of birth, exact years of attendance. There is no fee.

Gulf Coast Community College, Admissions & Records, 5230 W US Hwy 98, Panama City, FL 32401-1041, 904-872-3892 (Fax: 904-913-3308). Hours: 7:30AM-7:30PM M-Th; 7:30AM-4PM F. Enrollment: 8000. Records go back to 1960. Degrees granted: Associate; PSAV Certification.

Attendance and degree information available by phone, fax, mail. Search requires name plus SSN, date of birth. Also helpful: exact years of attendance. There is no fee.

Hillsborough Community College, HCC Admissions Office, PO Box 5096, Tampa, FL 33631-3127, 813-253-7004 (Fax: 813-253-7578). Hours: 8AM-4:30PM. Enrollment: 9870. Records go back to 1970. Alumni Records Office: Alumni Association, PO Box 31127, Tampa, FL 33631. Degrees granted: Associate. Adverse incident record source- Campuses: Student Services at 253-7280; Ybor City, 253-7680: Brandon, 253-7880; Plant City, 757-2102

Attendance and degree information available by phone, fax, mail. Search requires name plus SSN. Also helpful: date of birth, exact years of attendance. There is no fee.

Hobe Sound Bible College, Registrar, PO Box 1065, 11298 SE Gomez Ave, Hobe Sound, FL 33455, 561-546-5534 (Fax: 561-545-1422). Hours: 8AM-5PM. Enrollment: 144. Records go back to 1960. Degrees granted: Associate; Bachelors.

Attendance information available by phone, fax, mail. Search requires name plus approximate years of attendance. Also helpful: exact years of attendance. There is no fee.

Degree information available by phone, fax, mail. Search requires name only. Also helpful: date of birth, exact years of attendance. There is no fee.

ITT Technical Institute, Registrar, 2600 Lake Lucien Dr, Maitland, FL 32751-9754, 407-660-2900 (Fax: 407-660-2566). Enrollment: 450. Records go back to 1990. Alumni records are maintained here at the same phone number. Degrees granted: Associate; Bachelors. Adverse incident record source- Registrar's Office   .

Attendance and degree information available by fax, mail. Search requires name only. Also helpful: exact years of attendance. There is no fee.

ITT Technical Institute, Registrar, 4809 Memorial Hwy, Tampa, FL 33634-7350, 813-885-2244 (Fax: 813-888-6078). Hours: 8AM-5PM. Enrollment: 600. Records go back to 1984. Alumni records are maintained here at the same phone number. Degrees granted: Associate; Bachelors. Special programs- Electronics Engineering. Adverse incident record source- Registrar's Office   .

Attendance and degree information available by phone, fax, mail. Search requires name plus SSN. There is no fee.

ITT Technical Institute, (Branch of Fort Wayne, IN), Registrar, 3401 S University Dr, Fort Lauderdale, FL 33328, 954-476-9300 (Fax: 954-476-6889). Hours: 8AM-5PM. Enrollment: 450. Records go back to 1991. Alumni records are maintained here at the same phone number. Degrees granted: Associate. Special programs- Electrical Engineering. Adverse incident record source- Student Affairs.

Attendance information available by phone, fax, mail. Search requires name only. Also helpful: SSN, date of birth, exact years of attendance. There is no fee.

Degree information available by fax, mail. Search requires name only. Also helpful: SSN, date of birth, exact years of attendance. There is no fee.

ITT Technical Institute, (Branch of Tampa, FL), Registrar, 6600 Youngerman Cir #10, Jacksonville, FL 32244, 904-573-9100 (Fax: 904-573-0512). Hours: 8AM-5PM. Enrollment: 450. Records go back to 1991. Alumni Records Office: Alumni Association, 5975 Castle Creek Pkwy N, Indianapolis, IN 46250. Degrees granted: Associate; Bachelor's in Electronics. Adverse incident record source- Director of Education, 904-573-9100.

Attendance and degree information available by phone, mail. Search requires name only. Also helpful: SSN. There is no fee.

Indian River Community College, Registrar, 3209 Virginia Ave, Fort Pierce, FL 34981-5599, 561-462-4766 (Fax: 561-462-4699). Hours: 8AM-5PM. Enrollment: 4370. Records go back to 1960. Alumni records are maintained here also. Call 561-462-4786. Degrees granted: Associate. Special programs- Education Services Dept, 561-462-4740. Adverse incident record source- Dean of Students, 561-462-4706.

Attendance and degree information available by mail. Search requires name plus SSN, signed release. Also helpful: date of birth, exact years of attendance. There is no fee.

International Academy of Merchandising and Design, Registrar, 211 S Hoover St, Tampa, FL 33609-9785, 813-881-0007 X235 (Fax: 813-881-0008). Hours: 8AM-4:30PM. Records go back to 1985. Degrees granted: Associate.

Attendance and degree information available by phone, fax, mail. Search requires name plus SSN, exact years of attendance. There is no fee.

International College, Registrar, 2654 E Tamiami Trail, Naples, FL 33962-5790, 941-774-4700 (Fax: 941-774-4593). Hours: 9AM-6:30PM. Enrollment: 500. Records go back to 1990. Alumni records are maintained here at the same phone number. Degrees granted: Associate; Bachelors.

Attendance and degree information available by phone, fax, mail. Search requires name plus SSN. Also helpful: date of birth, exact years of attendance. There is no fee.

International College, (Branch), Registrar, 8695 College Pkwy Ste 217, Fort Myers, FL 33919, 941-482-0019 (Fax: 941-482-1714). Records are not housed here. They are located at International College, Registrar, 2654 E Tamiami Trail, Naples, FL 33962-5790.

International Fine Arts College, Registrar, 1737 N Bayshore Dr, Miami, FL 33132, 305-373-4684 (Fax: 305-374-7946). Hours: 7AM-6PM. Enrollment: 700. Records go back to 1971. Alumni records are maintained here at the same phone number. Degrees granted: Associate. Special programs- Film Animation: Visual Arts. Adverse incident record source- Registrar's Office   .

Attendance and degree information available by phone, fax, mail. Search requires name only. Also helpful: SSN, date of birth, exact years of attendance. There is no fee.

Jacksonville University, Registrar, 2800 University Blvd N, Jacksonville, FL 32211, 904-745-7090 (Fax: 904-745-7086). Hours: 8:30AM-5PM. Enrollment: 2416. Records go back to 1934. Alumni records are maintained here also. Call 904-745-7201. Degrees granted: Bachelors; Masters. Special programs- Marine Science, 904-745-7301. Adverse incident record source- Dean of Students, 904-745-7070: Security, 904-744-3950 X2213

Attendance information available by phone, mail. Search requires name plus SSN, approximate years of attendance. Also helpful: date of birth, exact years of attendance. There is no fee.

Degree information available by phone, mail. Search requires name plus SSN. Also helpful: date of birth, exact years of attendance. There is no fee.

Johnson & Wales University, (Branch Campus), Registrar, 1701 NE 127th St, North Miami, FL 33181, 305-892-7038 (Fax: 305-892-7019). Hours: 8:30AM-4:30PM. Enrollment: 850. Records go back to 1991. Degrees granted: Associate; Bachelors. Adverse incident record source- Chris Magnan, 305-892-7006.

Attendance and degree information available by phone, fax, mail. Search requires name plus SSN. There is no fee.

Jones College, Registrar, 5353 Alrington Expy, Jacksonville, FL 32211-5588, 904-743-1122 (Fax: 904-743-4446). Hours: 8AM-5PM. Alumni records are maintained here at the same phone number. Degrees granted: Associate; Bachelors.

Attendance and degree information available by fax, mail. Search requires name plus SSN, signed release. Also helpful: date of birth, exact years of attendance. There is no fee.

Jones College, (Branch), Registrar, 5975 Sunset Dr Ste 100, South Miami, FL 33143, 904-743-1122 (Fax: 904-669-9504). Records are not housed here. They are located at Jones College, Registrar, 5353 Alrington Expy, Jacksonville, FL 32211-5588.

Keiser College, Registrar, 1500 NW 49th St, Fort Lauderdale, FL 33309-3779, 954-776-4456. Hours: 8AM-5PM M-Th, 8AM-Noon F. Enrollment: 950. Records go back to 1979. Alumni records are maintained here at the same phone number. Degrees granted: Associate. Adverse incident record source- Registrar, 954-776-4456.

Attendance and degree information available by mail. Search requires name plus SSN, exact years of attendance, signed release. There is no fee.

Keiser College, (Branch), Registrar, 1800 W International Speedway Blvd #3, Daytona Beach, FL 32114, 904-255-1707 (Fax: 904-239-0995). Hours: 7:30AM-8PM M-Th; 7:30AM-4PM F. Formerly Phillips Junior College Records go back to 1989. Degrees granted: Associate. Adverse incident record source- Director's Office

Attendance and degree information available by fax, mail. Search requires name plus SSN, date of birth, signed release. Also helpful: exact years of attendance. There is no fee.

Keiser College, (Branch), Registrar, 701 S Babcock St, Melbourne, FL 32901-1461, 407-255-2255. Hours: 7:30AM-8PM. Records go back to 1977. Degrees granted: Associate.

Attendance and degree information available by mail. Search requires name plus SSN, exact years of attendance, signed release. There is no fee.

Keiser College, (Branch), Registrar, 1605 E Plaza Dr, Tallahassee, FL 32308, 904-942-9494 (Fax: 904-942-9497). Hours: 8AM-10:30PM M-F; 8AM-3:30PM S. Enrollment: 350. Records go back to 1992. Alumni records are maintained here at the same phone number. Degrees granted: Associate. Special programs- Computer Graphics & Design. Adverse incident record source- Registrar, 904-942-9494: Local Police

Attendance information available by phone, fax, mail. Search requires name plus SSN. Also helpful: exact years of attendance. There is no fee.

Degree information available by phone, fax, mail. Search requires name plus SSN. Also helpful: date of birth, exact years of attendance. There is no fee.

Lake City Community College, Registrar, Rte 19 Box 1030, Lake City, FL 32025, 904-752-1822 (Fax: 904-755-1521). Hours: 8AM-4:30PM. Enrollment: 2139. Records go back to 1964. Degrees granted: Associate.

Attendance information available by phone, mail. Search requires name plus SSN, exact years of attendance. Also helpful: date of birth. There is no fee.

Degree information available by mail. Search requires name plus SSN, exact years of attendance. Also helpful: date of birth. There is no fee.

Lake-Sumter Community College, Registrar, 9501 US Hwy 441, Leesburg, FL 34788-8751, 352-365-3572 (Fax: 352-365-3501). Hours: 8AM-9PM M-Th, 8AM-4:30PM F. Records go back to 1962. Alumni records are maintained here also. Call 352-787-3747. Degrees granted: Associate.

Attendance and degree information available by phone, mail. Search requires name plus SSN, date of birth, exact years of attendance. There is no fee.

Lynn University, Registrar, 3601 N Military Tr, Boca Raton, FL 33431, 407-994-0770 X177 (Fax: 407-241-3552). Hours: 9AM-6PM M-Th; 9AM-5PM F. Enrollment: 1500. Records go back to 1966. Alumni records are maintained here also. Call 407-994-0770 X238. Degrees granted: Associate; Bachelors; Masters.

Attendance and degree information available by phone, fax, mail. Search requires name only. Also helpful: SSN, date of birth, exact years of attendance. There is no fee.

Manatee Community College, Registrar, 5840 26th St W, Bradenton, FL 34207, 941-755-1511 X4231 (Fax: 941-755-1511 X4331). Hours: 8AM-4:30PM. Enrollment: 8000. Records go back to 1958. Alumni records are maintained here also. Call 941-755-1511 X4389. Degrees granted: Associate.

Attendance and degree information available by fax. Search requires name plus SSN, signed release. Also helpful: date of birth, approximate years of attendance. There is no fee.

Miami-Dade Community College, Registrar, 300 NE Second Ave, Miami, FL 33132, 305-237-3336. Hours: 8AM-4:30PM. Records go back to 1959. Alumni records are maintained here also. Call 305-237-4000. Degrees granted: Associate. Adverse incident record source- Campus Security, 305-237-4000.

Attendance and degree information available by phone, mail. Search requires name plus SSN. There is no fee.

Miami-Dade Community College-Kendall Campus, Registrar, 11011 S W 104 St, Miami, FL 33176, 305-237-2222 (Fax: 305-237-2964). Enrollment: 19000. Formerly Miami-Dade Community College-South Campus Records go back to 1960. Alumni records are maintained here at the same phone number. Degrees granted: Associate.

Attendance information available by fax, mail. Search requires name plus SSN, date of birth. Also helpful: exact years of attendance. Fee is $3.00. Expedited service available for $3.00.

Degree information available by phone, fax, mail. Search requires name plus SSN, date of birth. Also helpful: exact years of attendance. Fee is $3.00. Expedite service available for $3.00.

North Florida Community College, Registrar, 100 Turner Davis Dr, Madison, FL 32340, 904-973-2288 X151 (Fax: 904-973-2288). Hours: 8AM-4:30PM. Enrollment: 1073. Formerly North Florida Junior College Records go back to 1958. Alumni records are maintained here at the same phone number. Degrees granted: Associate.

Attendance and degree information available by phone, fax, mail. Search requires name plus SSN. Also helpful: date of birth, exact years of attendance. There is no fee.

Northwood University, (Branch), Registrar, 2600 N Military Trail, West Palm Beach, FL 33409, 407-478-5500 (Fax: 407-640-3328). Hours: 9AM-5PM. Enrollment: 1200. Records go back to 1986. Alumni records are maintained here at the same phone number. Degrees granted: Associate; Bachelors.

Attendance information available by phone, mail. Search requires name plus SSN. Also helpful: approximate years of attendance. There is no fee.

Degree information available by phone, mail. Search requires name plus SSN, approximate years of attendance. There is no fee.

Nova Southeastern University, Registrar, 3301 College Ave, Fort Lauderdale, FL 33314, 954-475-7300 (Fax: 954-452-7265). Hours: 8:30AM-7PM M-Th, 8:30AM-6PM F. Enrollment: 18000. Formerly Nova University Records go back to 1967. Alumni records are maintained here at the same phone number. Degrees granted: Bachelors; Masters; Doctorate. Adverse incident record source- Registrar, 305-475-7300.

Attendance and degree information available by phone, fax, mail. Search requires name plus SSN. Also helpful: approximate years of attendance. There is no fee.

Nova Southeastern University, Registrar, 3301 College Ave, Fort Lauderdale, FL 33314, 954-475-7400 (Fax: 954-452-7265). Hours: 8:30AM-7PM M-Th; 8:30AM-6PM F, 9AM-Noon S. Enrollment: 13950. Formerly Southeastern University of the Health Sciences Records go back to 1979. Alumni records are maintained here also. Call 954-475-7418. Degrees granted: Bachelors; Masters; Doctorate; Physician Asst., Occupational Therapy Cert. Adverse incident record source- VP Student Affairs, 954-475-7017.

Attendance and degree information available by phone, fax, mail. Search requires name plus SSN. Also helpful: exact years of attendance. There is no fee.

Okaloosa-Walton Community College, Registrar, 100 College Blvd, Niceville, FL 32578, 904-678-5111 (Fax: 904-729-5323). Enrollment: 16000. Records go back to 1968. Degrees granted: Associate.

Attendance and degree information available by mail. Search requires name plus SSN, signed release. Also helpful: date of birth, exact years of attendance. There is no fee.

Orlando College, Registrar, 5421 Diplomat Cir, Orlando, FL 32810, 407-628-5870 (Fax: 407-628-1344). Hours: 10AM-7PM M-W; 8:30AM-7PM Th; 8:30AM-5PM F. Records go back to 1956. Degrees granted: Associate; Bachelors; Masters. Adverse incident record source- Dean's Office .

Attendance and degree information available by phone, fax, mail. Search requires name plus SSN. Also helpful: approximate years of attendance. There is no fee.

Orlando College, (Branch), Registrar, 2411 Sand Lake Rd, Orlando, FL 32809, 407-851-2525 (Fax: 407-851-1477). Hours: 9AM-7:30PM M-Th; 9AM-5PM F. Enrollment: 800. Records go back to 1991. Degrees granted: Associate; Bachelors; Masters. Special programs- Medical Assistant. Adverse incident record source- Dean's Office, 407-851-2525 .

Attendance information available by phone, mail. Search requires name only. Also helpful: SSN. There is no fee.

Degree information available by phone, mail. Search requires name only. Also helpful: SSN, date of birth, approximate years of attendance. There is no fee.

Palm Beach Atlantic College, Registrar, 901 S Flagler Dr, PO Box 24708, West Palm Beach, FL 33416-4708, 561-803-2075 (Fax: 561-803-2081). Hours: 8AM-7PM M-Th, 8MA-5PM F, 9AM-1PM Sat. Enrollment: 2000. Records go

back to 1968. Alumni records are maintained here also. Call 561-803-2016. Degrees granted: Bachelors; Masters.

Attendance and degree information available by mail. Search requires name plus SSN, signed release. Also helpful: date of birth, exact years of attendance. There is no fee.

Palm Beach Community College, Registrar, 4200 Congress Ave, Lake Worth, FL 33461-4796, 407-439-8000 (Fax: 407-439-8255). Hours: 8AM-7PM M-Th; 8AM-4PM F. Enrollment: 18000. Records go back to 1933. Alumni records are maintained here also. Call 407-439-8072. Degrees granted: Associate. Special programs- Nursing: Criminal Justice Degree. Adverse incident record source- Registrar, 407-439-8000.

Attendance information available by phone, fax, mail. Search requires name only. Also helpful: SSN, exact years of attendance. There is no fee.

Degree information available by fax, mail. Search requires name only. Also helpful: SSN, exact years of attendance. There is no fee.

Pasco-Hernando Community College, Registrar, 36727 Blanton Rd, Dade City, FL 33525-7599, 813-847-2727 (Fax: 813-844-7244). Hours: 8AM-4:30PM. Enrollment: 7200. Records go back to 1972. Degrees granted: Associate.

Attendance and degree information available by phone, fax, mail. Search requires name plus SSN. There is no fee.

Pensacola Junior College, Registrar, 1000 College Blvd, Pensacola, FL 32504-8998, 904-484-1600 (Fax: 904-484-1689). Hours: 7:30AM-4PM. Enrollment: 17341. Records go back to 1948. Alumni records are maintained here at the same phone number. Degrees granted: Associate. Adverse incident record source- Adverse Info: Student Life: Incident Reports: Public Safety

Attendance and degree information available by phone, fax, mail. Search requires name plus SSN, date of birth, approximate years of attendance. Also helpful: exact years of attendance. There is no fee.

Polk Community College, Registrar, 999 Ave H NE, Winter Haven, FL 33881-4299, 941-297-1000 (Fax: 941-297-1060). Hours: 8AM-5PM. Enrollment: 6000. Records go back to 1966. Alumni records are maintained here at the same phone number. Degrees granted: Associate. Certification: EMT & Paramedic.

Attendance information available by fax, mail. Search requires name plus approximate years of attendance, signed release. Also helpful: SSN, date of birth, exact years of attendance. There is no fee.

Degree information available by phone, fax, mail. Search requires name plus approximate years of attendance. Also helpful: SSN, date of birth, exact years of attendance. There is no fee.

Prospect Hall School of Business, Registrar, 2620 Hollywood Blvd, Hollywood, FL 33020, 954-923-8100. Hours: 8AM-8PM. Enrollment: 200. Records go back to 1973. Degrees granted: Associate. Special programs- All computer-oriented courses. Adverse incident record source- Registrar's Office .

Attendance and degree information available by written request only. Search requires name plus SSN, date of birth, exact years of attendance, signed release. There is no fee.

Ringling School of Art and Design, Registrar, 2700 N Tamiami Tr, Sarasota, FL 34234, 941-351-5100 (Fax: 941-359-7517). Hours: 8:30AM-4:30PM. Enrollment: 825. Records go back to 1931. Alumni records are maintained here at the same phone number. Degrees granted: Bachelors. Certification: BFA. Adverse incident record source- Security RSAD.

Attendance information available by fax, mail. Search requires name plus SSN. Also helpful: date of birth, exact years of attendance. There is no fee.

Degree information available by fax, mail. Search requires name plus SSN, date of birth, approximate years of attendance. Also helpful: exact years of attendance. There is no fee.

Rollins College, Registrar, 1000 Holt Ave, Winter Park, FL 32789-4499, 407-646-2144 (Fax: 407-646-1576). Hours: 8:30AM-5PM. Enrollment: 3500. Records go back to 1895. Alumni records are maintained here also. Call 407-646-2266. Degrees granted: Associate; Bachelors; Masters. Adverse incident record source- Safety, 407-646-2401.

Attendance and degree information available by phone, fax, mail. Search requires name plus SSN, date of birth, approximate years of attendance. Also helpful: exact years of attendance. There is no fee.

Santa Fe Community College, Registrar, 3000 NW 83rd St, Gainesville, FL 32606, 352-395-5443 (Fax: 352-395-5922). Hours: 8AM-4:30PM. Enrollment: 12500. Records go back to 1966. Degrees granted: Associate; Bachelors. Adverse incident record source- Registrar: Local Police

Attendance and degree information available by phone, fax, mail. Search requires name plus SSN. Also helpful: date of birth, exact years of attendance. There is no fee.

Seminole Community College, Registrar, 100 Weldon Blvd, Sanford, FL 32773-6199, 407-328-2025 (Fax: 407-328-2029). Hours: 8:30AM-7:30PM M-Th; 8:30AM-4PM F. Enrollment: 7500. Records go back to 1966. Alumni records are maintained here at the same phone number. Degrees granted: Associate.

Attendance information available by phone, fax, mail. Search requires name plus SSN, date of birth. Also helpful: exact years of attendance. There is no fee.

Degree information available by fax, mail. Search requires name plus SSN, date of birth. Also helpful: exact years of attendance. There is no fee.

South College, Registrar, 1760 N Congress Ave, West Palm Beach, FL 33409, 407-697-9200 (Fax: 407-697-9944). Hours: 8AM-7PM M-Th; 8AM-5PM F; 9AM-Noon S. Enrollment: 375. Records go back to 1986. Degrees granted: Associate. Special programs- Physical Therapy Assistants Program. Adverse incident record source- Academic Affairs,407-697-9200.

Attendance and degree information available by mail. Search requires name plus SSN, date of birth. Also helpful: exact years of attendance. There is no fee.

South Florida Community College, Registrar, 600 W College Dr, Avon Park, FL 33825, 941-453-6661 (Fax: 941-453-2365). Enrollment: 13000. Degrees granted: Associate. Adverse incident record source- Student Services, 813-453-6661 X104.

Attendance and degree information available by fax, mail. Search requires name plus signed release. Also helpful: SSN, approximate years of attendance. There is no fee.

Southeastern Academy, Inc., Registrar, 233 Academy Dr, PO Box 421768, Kissimmee, FL 32742, 407-847-4444 (Fax: 407-847-8793). Hours: 8:30AM-5PM. Enrollment: 400. Records go back to 1975. Adverse incident record source- Dean of Students, 407-847-4444 X391.

Attendance and degree information available by phone, fax, mail. Search requires name plus SSN, exact years of attendance. There is no fee.

Southeastern College of the Assemblies of God, Registrar, 1000 Longfellow Blvd, Lakeland, FL 33801, 941-667-5200 (Fax: 941-667-5200). Hours: 8AM-4:30PM. Enrollment: 1200. Records go back to 1935. Alumni records are maintained here at the same phone number. Degrees granted: Bachelors.

Attendance and degree information available by phone, fax, mail. Search requires name only. Also helpful: SSN, date of birth, exact years of attendance. There is no fee.

Southern College, Registrar, 5600 Lake Underhill Rd, Orlando, FL 32807, 407-273-1000 (Fax: 407-273-0492). Hours: 8AM-5PM. Enrollment: 450. Records go back to 1968. Degrees granted: Associate.

Attendance information available by fax, mail. Search requires name plus SSN, signed release. Also helpful: date of birth, exact years of attendance. There is no fee.

Degree information available by phone, fax, mail. Search requires name plus SSN. Also helpful: date of birth, exact years of attendance. There is no fee.

Southwest Florida College of Business, Registrar, 1685 Medical Lane Ste 200, Fort Myers, FL 33907, 941-939-4766 (Fax: 941-936-4040). Hours: 8AM-7PM. Enrollment: 250. Records go back to 1983. Degrees granted: Associate.

Attendance and degree information available by phone, fax, mail. Search requires name only. Also helpful: SSN, date of birth. There is no fee.

Spurgeon Baptist Bible Collge, Registrar, 4440 Spurgeon Dr, Mulberry, FL 33860, 941-425-3429 (Fax: 941-425-3861). Enrollment: 40. Records go back to 1970. Alumni records are maintained here at the same phone number. Degrees granted: Associate; Bachelors. Adverse incident record source- Main Office, 941-425-3421.

Attendance and degree information available by phone, fax, mail. Search requires name only. There is no fee.

St. John Vianney College Seminary, Registrar, 2900 SW 87th Ave, Miami, FL 33165, 305-223-4561 (Fax: 305-223-0650). Hours: 8:30AM-4:30PM. Enrollment: 40. Records go back to 1959. Alumni records are maintained here at the same phone number. Degrees granted: Bachelors. Adverse incident record source- Rector's Office, 305-223-4561 .

Attendance information available by phone, fax, mail. Search requires name plus SSN. There is no fee.

Degree information available by mail. Search requires name plus SSN. Also helpful: approximate years of attendance. There is no fee.

St. Johns River Community College, Registrar, 5001 St Johns Ave, Palatka, FL 32177-3897, 904-328-1571 X133 (Fax: 904-312-4292). Hours: 8AM-5PM. Records go back to 1958. Degrees granted: Associate.

Attendance and degree information available by mail. Search requires name plus SSN, date of birth, signed release. Also helpful: exact years of attendance. There is no fee.

St. Leo College, Registrar, PO Box 6665, MC 2278, Saint Leo, FL 33574, 352-588-8234 (Fax: 352-588-8390). Hours: 8AM-5PM. Enrollment: 6500. Records go back to 1920. Alumni Records Office: Alumni/Parent Relations, PO Box 6665 MC 2244, Saint Leo, FL 33574. Degrees granted: Bachelors; Masters. Special programs- Restaurant/Hotel Management. Adverse incident record source- Student Affairs, 352-588-8992.

Attendance and degree information available by phone, fax, mail. Search requires name plus SSN, date of birth. Also helpful: exact years of attendance. There is no fee.

St. Petersburg Junior College, Registrar, PO Box 13489, St Petersburg, FL 33733-3489, 813-341-3600 (Fax: 813-341-3150). Hours: 8AM-4PM. Enrollment: 19000. Records go back to 1928. Alumni records are maintained here also. Call 813-341-3600. Degrees granted: Associate. Adverse incident record source- Dean of Students, 813-341-3600.

Attendance and degree information available by phone, fax, mail. Search requires name plus SSN. Also helpful: date of birth, exact years of attendance. There is no fee.

St. Thomas University, Registrar, 16400 NW 32nd Ave, Miami, FL 33054, 305-628-6537 (Fax: 305-628-6551). Hours: 9AM-5PM M,Th,F; 9AM-6:30PM T,W. Enrollment: 2200. Records go back to 1961. Alumni records are maintained here also. Call 305-628-6641. Degrees granted: Bachelors; Masters. Special programs- Sports Administration Programs. Adverse incident record source- Student Affairs, 305-628-6687.

Attendance information available by phone, fax, mail. Search requires name plus SSN, exact years of attendance. There is no fee.

Degree information available by phone, mail. Search requires name plus SSN, exact years of attendance. There is no fee.

St. Vincent de Paul Regional Seminary, Registrar, 10701 S Military Tr, Boynton Beach, FL 33436-4899, 561-732-4424 (Fax: 561-737-2205). Hours: 9AM-4PM. Enrollment: 70. Records go back to 1963. Degrees granted: Masters. Adverse incident record source- Rector's Office, 561-732-4424

Attendance and degree information available by phone, fax, mail. Search requires name only. Also helpful: SSN, exact years of attendance. There is no fee.

Stetson University, Registrar, 421 N Woodland Blvd, Deland, FL 32720, 904-822-7140 (Fax: 904-822-7146). Hours: 8AM-4:30PM. Enrollment: 2000. Alumni records are maintained here also. Call 904-822-7480. Degrees granted: Bachelors; Masters; EDS. Adverse incident record source- Campus Life, 904-822-7201.

Attendance and degree information available by phone, mail. Search requires name only. Also helpful: SSN, date of birth, exact years of attendance. There is no fee.

Tallahassee Community College, Registrar, 444 Appleyard Dr, Tallahassee, FL 32304-2895, 904-921-2269 (Fax: 904-921-0563). Hours: 8AM-7PM M-Th; 8AM-5PM F. Enrollment: 10000. Records go back to 1966. Degrees granted: Associate.

Attendance and degree information available by phone, fax, mail. Search requires name only. Also helpful: SSN. There is no fee.

Talmudic College of Florida, Registrar, 1910 Alton Rd, Miami Beach, FL 33139-1507, 305-534-7050 (Fax: 305-534-8444). Hours: 9AM-5:30PM. Enrollment: 40. Records go back to 1974. Alumni records are maintained here at the same phone number. Degrees granted: Bachelors; Masters; Doctorate; 1st Talmudic Degree. Adverse incident record source- Registrar.

Attendance and degree information available by phone, fax, mail. Search requires name plus SSN, date of birth. Also helpful: exact years of attendance. There is no fee.

Tampa College, Registrar, 3319 W Hillsborough Ave, Tampa, FL 33614, 813-879-6000 (Fax: 813-871-2483). Enrollment: 850. Records go back to 1950. Degrees granted: Associate; Bachelors; Masters. Adverse incident record source- Registrar's Office, 813-879-6000

Attendance and degree information available by fax, mail. Search requires name plus SSN, date of birth, signed release. Also helpful: exact years of attendance. There is no fee.

Tampa College, (Branch), Registrar, 1200 US Hwy 98 S, Lakeland, FL 33801, 941-686-1444 (Fax: 941-682-1077). Hours: 7:30AM-5PM. Enrollment: 400. Records go back to 1970. Degrees granted: Associate; Bachelors; Masters. Adverse incident record source- Lakeland Police, 813-499-6936.

Attendance information available by fax, mail. Search requires name plus SSN, signed release. Also helpful: date of birth, exact years of attendance. There is no fee.

Degree information available by phone, fax, mail. Search requires name plus SSN. Also helpful: date of birth, exact years of attendance. There is no fee.

Tampa College, (Branch), Registrar, Sabal Business Ctr, 3924 Coconut Palm Dr, Tampa, FL 33619, 813-621-0041 (Fax: 813-623-5769). Hours: 8:30AM-8PM. Enrollment: 600. Records go back to 1990. Degrees granted: Associate; Bachelors; Masters.

Attendance and degree information available by phone, fax, mail. Search requires name plus SSN, exact years of attendance. There is no fee.

Trinity International University, Registrar, 500 NE First Ave, PO Box 019674, Miami, FL 33101-9674, 305-577-4600 X131 (Fax: 305-577-4612). Hours: 8AM-3PM. Enrollment: 400. Records go back to 1939. Alumni records are maintained here at the same phone number. Degrees granted: Bachelors.

Attendance and degree information available by phone, fax, mail. Search requires name only. Also helpful: SSN, date of birth, exact years of attendance. There is no fee.

United Electronics Institute of Florida, Registrar, 3924 Coconut Palm Dr, Tampa, FL 33619, 813-626-2999 (Fax: 813-623-5769). Enrollment: 250. Records go back to 1890. Degrees granted: Associate.

Attendance and degree information available by phone, mail. Search requires name plus SSN, exact years of attendance. There is no fee.

University of Central Florida, Registrar, 4000 Central Florida Blvd, PO Box 160114, Orlando, FL 32816-0114, 407-823-3100 (Fax: 407-823-5652). Hours: 8AM-6PM M-Th; 8AM-5PM F. Enrollment: 27000. Records go back to 1965. Alumni records are maintained here also. Call 407-823-2556. Degrees granted: Bachelors; Masters; Doctorate. Adverse incident record source- Student Affairs, 407-823-2821.

Attendance and degree information available by phone, fax, mail. Search requires name plus SSN. Also helpful: exact years of attendance. There is no fee.

University of Florida, Office of the Registrar, PO Box 114000, Gainesville, FL 32611-4000, 352-392-1374 (Fax: 352-392-3987). Hours: 8AM-4:30PM. Enrollment: 39951. Records go back to 1800's. Alumni Records Office: 2012 W University Ave, Gainesville, FL 32611. Degrees granted: Associate; Bachelors; Masters; Doctorate; Specialist; Engineer,Professional Degrees. Adverse incident record source- University Police: Office for Judicial Affairs

Attendance and degree information available by phone, mail. Search requires name plus SSN, date of birth, exact years of attendance. Also helpful: approximate years of attendance. There is no fee.

University of Miami, Office of the Registrar, PO Box 248026, Coral Gables, FL 33124-4627, 305-284-5455 (Fax: 305-284-3144). Hours: 8:30AM-5PM. Enrollment: 12496. Records go back to 1926. Degrees granted: Bachelors; Masters; Doctorate. Certification: Continuing Studies. Special programs- Continuing Studies, 305-284-4000. Adverse incident record source- Public Safety, 305-284-6666.

Attendance information available by fax, mail. Search requires name plus SSN, approximate years of attendance. Also helpful: date of birth, exact years of attendance. There is no fee.

Degree information available by fax, mail. Search requires name plus SSN, date of birth, approximate years of attendance. Also helpful: exact years of attendance. There is no fee.

University of North Florida, Registrar, 4567 St Johns Bluff Rd S, Jacksonville, FL 32224-2645, 904-646-2620 (Fax: 904-646-2703). Hours: 8AM-5PM. Enrollment: 10700. Records go back to 1972. Alumni records are maintained here also. Call 904-646-2513. Degrees granted: Bachelors; Masters; Doctorate. Adverse incident record source- Student Affairs, 904-646-2600: Police, 904-646-2804

Attendance and degree information available by fax, mail. Search requires name plus SSN, signed release. There is no fee.

University of Sarasota, Registrar, 5250 17th St, Sarasota, FL 34235, 941-379-0404 (Fax: 941-379-9464). Hours: 10AM-4PM. Enrollment: 1000. Records go back to 1969. Alumni records are maintained here also. Call 941-379-0404. Degrees granted: Bachelors; Masters; Doctorate. Adverse incident record source- Dean of Students, 941-379-0404.

Attendance and degree information available by phone, fax, mail. Search requires name plus SSN, exact years of attendance. Also helpful: date of birth. There is no fee.

University of South Florida, Registrar's Office, SVC 1034, 4202 E Fowler Ave, Tampa, FL 33620-6100, 813-974-2000 (Fax: 813-974-5271). Hours: 8AM-5PM. Enrollment: 36000. Records go back to 1956. Alumni records are maintained here also. Call 813-974-9127. Degrees granted: Associate; Bachelors; Masters; Doctorate. Special programs- Marine Science: Medical. Adverse incident record source- Student Affairs, same address, ADM 151 USF.

Attendance and degree information available by phone, fax, mail. Search requires name plus SSN. Also helpful: date of birth, exact years of attendance. There is no fee.

University of Tampa, Registrar, 401 W Kennedy Blvd, Tampa, FL 33606-1490, 813-253-6251 (Fax: 813-258-7238). Hours: 8:30AM-5PM. Enrollment: 2500. Records go back to 1933. Alumni records are maintained here at the same phone number. Degrees granted: Associate; Bachelors; Masters.

Attendance and degree information available by phone, fax, mail. Search requires name only. Also helpful: SSN, date of birth, exact years of attendance. There is no fee.

University of West Florida, Registrar, 11000 University Pkwy, Pensacola, FL 32514-5750, 904-474-2244 (Fax: 904-474-3360). Hours: 8AM-5PM. Enrollment: 8000. Records go back to 1967. Alumni records are maintained here also. Call 904-474-2758. Degrees granted: Associate; Bachelors; Masters; Doctorate; Specialist. Special programs- Marine Biology: Accounting. Adverse incident record source- Public Safety, 904-474-2415: Student Affairs, 904-474-2384

Attendance and degree information available by phone, fax, mail. Search requires name plus SSN. There is no fee.

Valencia Community College, (West), Registrar, PO Box 3028, 1800 S Kirkman Rd, Orlando, FL 32811, 407-299-5000 X1506. Hours: 7:30AM-9PM M-Th, 7:30AM-5PM F. Enrollment: 14301. Records go back to 1971. Alumni Records Office: Alumni Association, 190 N Orange Ave, Orlando, FL 32801. Degrees granted: Associate. Adverse incident record source- Provost, 407-299-5000 X1372.

Attendance information available by mail. Search requires name plus SSN, signed release. Also helpful: date of birth, exact years of attendance. There is no fee.

Degree information available by mail. Search requires name plus SSN, signed release. Also helpful: exact years of attendance. There is no fee.

Ward Stone College, Registrar, 9020 SW 137th Ave, Miami, FL 33186, 305-386-9900 (Fax: 305-388-1740). Hours: 8AM-6PM. Enrollment: 500. Records go back to 1981. Degrees granted: Associate; SAD. Adverse incident record source- Registrar's Office   .

Attendance information available by phone, fax, mail. Search requires name plus SSN. Also helpful: exact years of attendance. There is no fee.

Degree information available by fax, mail. Search requires name plus SSN. Also helpful: date of birth, exact years of attendance. There is no fee.

Warner Southern College, Registrar, 5301 US Hwy 27 S, Lake Wales, FL 33853-8725, 941-638-7204 (Fax: 941-638-1472). Enrollment: 581. Records go back to 1969. Alumni records are maintained here at the same phone number. Degrees granted: Associate; Bachelors. Adverse incident record source- Student Life.

Attendance and degree information available by phone, fax, mail. Search requires name plus SSN. Also helpful: exact years of attendance. There is no fee.

Webber College, Registrar, PO Box 96, Babson Park, FL 33827, 941-638-2929 (Fax: 941-638-2823). Hours: 8AM-5PM. Enrollment: 460. Records go back to 1927. Alumni records are maintained here also. Call 941-638-2941. Degrees granted: Bachelors. Adverse incident record source- Registrars Office, 813-638-2929.

Attendance information available by phone, fax, mail. Search requires name plus SSN. Also helpful: date of birth, exact years of attendance. There is no fee.

Degree information available by phone, fax, mail. Search requires name plus SSN. Also helpful: exact years of attendance. There is no fee.

Webster College, (Branch Campus), Registrar, N Bridge Plaza, 2192 N US Rte 1, Fort Pierce, FL 34946, 407-464-7474. Hours: 8AM-5PM. Records go back to 1981. Degrees granted: Associate.

Attendance and degree information available by phone, mail. Search requires name plus SSN, exact years of attendance. There is no fee.

Webster College, (Branch Campus), Registrar, 2002 NW 13th St, Gainesville, FL 32601, 352-867-5565. Hours: 8AM-5PM. Records go back to 1984. Degrees granted: Associate.

Attendance and degree information available by phone, mail. Search requires name plus SSN, date of birth, exact years of attendance. There is no fee.

Webster College, (Branch Campus), Registrar, 5623 US Hwy 19 Ste 300, New Port Richey, FL 34652, 813-849-4993. Hours: 8AM-5PM. Records go back to 1984. Degrees granted: Associate.

Attendance and degree information available by phone, mail. Search requires name plus SSN, exact years of attendance. There is no fee.

Webster College, (Branch Campus), Registrar, 1530 SW Third Ave, Ocala, FL 34474, 352-629-1941 (Fax: 352-629-0926). Hours: 8AM-9:30PM. Enrollment: 210. Records go back to 1984. Degrees granted: Associate. Adverse incident record source- Academic Dean, 352-629-1941.

Attendance and degree information available by phone, fax, mail. Search requires name plus SSN, exact years of attendance. There is no fee.

Trade and Vocational Schools

ATI Career Training Center, 3501 NW 9th Ave, Oakland Park, FL 33309, 954-563-5899

ATI Career Training Center (Branch Campus), One NE 19th St, Miami, FL 33132, 305-573-1600

ATI Career Training Center (Electronic Campus), 2880 NW 62nd St, Fort Lauderdale, FL 33309, 954-973-4760

ATI-Health Education Center, 1395 NW 167th St #200, Miami, FL 33169, 305-628-1000

Academy of Creative Hair Design, 2911 Jacksonville Rd, Ocala, FL 34470, 904-351-5900

Academy of Healing Arts, Message & Facial Skin Care, 3141 S Military Tr, Lake Worth, FL 33463, 407-965-5550

American Flyers College, 5400 NW 21st Terr, Fort Lauderdale, FL 33309, 954-772-7500

Atlantic Vocational-Technical Center, 4700 Coconut Creek Pkwy, Coconut Creek, FL 33063, 954-977-2000

Atlantic Vocational-Technical Center (Branch Campus), 1400 NE 6th St, Pompano Beach, FL 33060, 954-786-7600

Automotive Transmission School, 453 E Okeechobee Rd, Hialeah, FL 33010, 305-888-4898

Avanti Hair Tech, 905 E Memorial Blvd, Lakeland, FL 33801, 941-686-2224

Avanti Hair Tech, 8803 N Florida Ave, Ste B, Tampa, FL 33604, 813-933-6603

Avanti Hair Tech, 8851 N 56th St, Temple Terrace, FL 33617, 813-985-8785

Avanti Hair Tech (Branch Campus), 5433 Lake Howell Rd, Winter Park, FL 32792, 305-657-0700

Aviation Career Institute, 2945 Medulla Rd, Lakeland, FL 33811, 813-648-2004

Beacon Career Institute, 2900 NW 183rd St, Miami, FL 33056, 305-620-4637

Beauty Schools of America, 1305 W 49th St, Hialeah, FL 33012, 954-362-9003

Beauty Schools of America (Branch Campus), 1176 SW 67th Ave, Miami, FL 33144, 305-267-6604

Business & Technology Institute, 8991 SW 107 Ave Ste 323, Miami, FL 33176, 305-273-4499

Business Training Institute, 1270 Wickham Rd Ste 26, Melbourne, FL 32935, 407-255-9232

Career Training Institute, 101 W Main St, Leesburg, FL 34748, 904-326-5134

Career Training Institute, 2120 W Colonial Dr, Orlando, FL 32804, 407-843-3984

Charlotte Vocational-Technical Center, 18300 Toledo Blade Blvd, Port Charlotte, FL 33948, 941-629-6819

Clinton Technical Institute (Motorcycle/Marine Mechanics Institute), 9751 Delegates Dr, Orlando, FL 32837, 407-240-2422

ConCorde Career Institute, 7960 Arlington Expy, Jacksonville, FL 32211, 904-725-0525

ConCorde Career Institute, 4000 N State Rd 7, Lauderdale Lakes, FL 33319, 954-731-8880

ConCorde Career Institute, 4202 W Spruce St, Tampa, FL 33607, 813-874-0094

ConCorde Career Institute (Branch Campus), 285 NW 199th St, Miami, FL 33169, 305-652-0055

David G. Erwing Technical Center, 2010 E Hillsborough Ave, Tampa, FL 33610, 813-231-1800

Defense Equal Opportunity Management Institute, EOMI Library Bldg 560, Patrick Air Force Base, FL 32925, 407-494-6976

Euro Hair Design Institute, 1964 W Tennessee St #14, Tallahassee, FL 32304, 904-576-2174

Euro-Skill Therapeutic Training Center, 500 NE Spanish River Blvd #25-26, Boca Raton, FL 33431, 407-395-3089

FAA Center for Management Development, 4500 Palm Coast Pkwy SE, Palm Coast, FL 32137, 904-446-7136

Federal Correctional Institution, 501 Capital Cir NE, Tallahassee, FL 32301, 904-878-2173

FlightSafety International, PO Box 2708, Vero Beach, FL 32961, 407-567-5178

Florida Institute of Massage Therapy & Esthetics, 5453 N University Dr, Lauderhill, FL 33351, 954-742-8399

Florida Institute of Massage Therapy & Esthetics (Miami Campus), 7925 NW 12th St, Ste 201, Miami, FL 33126, 305-597-9599

Florida Institute of Traditional Chinese Medicine, 5335 66th St N, St Petersburg, FL 33709, 813-546-6565

Florida Institute of Ultrasound, Inc., 8800 University Pkwy, Pensacola, FL 32514, 904-478-7300

Florida School of Business, 2990 NW 81st Terrace, Miami, FL 33147, 305-696-6312

Florida School of Business, 4817 N Florida Ave, Tampa, FL 33603, 813-239-3334

Florida Technical College, 1819 N Semoran Blvd, Orlando, FL 32807, 407-678-5600

Florida Technical College, 4750 E Adamo Dr, Tampa, FL 33605, 813-247-1700

Full Sail Center for the Recording Arts, 3300 University Blvd, Ste 160, Winter Park, FL 32792, 407-679-6333

Garces Commercial College, 1301 SW First St, Miami, FL 33135, 305-643-1044

Garces Commercial College (Branch Campus), 5385 NW 36th St, Miami Springs, FL 33166, 305-871-6535

George Stone Vocational-Technical Center, 2400 Longleaf Dr, Pensacola, FL 32526, 904-944-1424

George T. Baker Aviation School, 3275 NW 42nd Ave, Miami, FL 33142, 305-871-3143

Golf Academy of San Diego (Golf Academy of the South), 307 Daneswood Way, Castlebury, FL 32707, 407-669-1990

Hair Design School (The), 5110 University Blvd Bldg C, Jacksonville, FL 32216, 904-731-7500

Health Institute of Louisville (The) (Branch Campus), 9549 Koger Blvd, Gadsden Blvd #100, St. Petersburg, FL 33716, 813-577-1497

Henry W. Brewster Technical Center, 2222 N Tampa St, Tampa, FL 33602, 813-276-5448

Hi-Tech School of Miami, 10350 W Flagler St, Miami, FL 33174, 305-221-3423

Hialeah Technical Center, 1780 E 4th Ave, Hialeah, FL 33012, 305-884-4387

Humanities Center Institute of Allied Health/School of Message, 4045 Park Blvd, Pinellas Park, FL 34665, 813-541-5200

Institute of Career Education, 1750 45th St, West Palm Beach, FL 33407, 407-881-0220

James L. Walker Vocational-Technical Center, 3702 Estey Ave, Naples, FL 33942, 941-643-0919

Lake County Area Vocational-Technical Center, 2001 Kurt St, Eustis, FL 32726, 904-747-6486

Lee County Vocational High Tech Center, 3800 Michigan Ave, Fort Myers, FL 33916, 941-334-4544

Lindsey Hopkins Technical Education Center, 750 NW 20th St, Miami, FL 33127, 305-324-6070

Lively Area Vocational Technical Center (Florida State Hospital Campus), HRS, Dist 2, Chattahoochee, FL 32324, 904-663-7202

Lively Area Vocational Technical Center (Lively Aviation Center), 390 Capital Cir SW, Tallahassee, FL 32310, 904-488-4161

Lively Area Vocational Technical Center (Lively Criminal Justice Training Academy), Rte 1 Box 3250, Havana, FL 32333, 904-487-2258

Lively Area Vocational-Technical Center, 500 N Appleyard Dr, Tallahassee, FL 32304, 904-487-7401

Manatee Area Vocational-Technical Center, 5603 34th St W, Bradenton, FL 34210, 941-751-7904

Marion County School of Radiologic Technology, 438 SW Third St, Ocala, FL 32674, 904-629-7545

Martin College, 1901 NW Seventh St, Miami, FL 33125, 305-541-8140

Master Schools, 824 SW 24th St, Fort Lauderdale, FL 33315, 954-467-8140

Medical Arts Training Center, Inc., 441 S State Rd 7, Margate, FL 33068, 954-968-3500

Medical Career Center, 4700 Bayou Blvd, Pensacola, FL 32503, 904-494-9784

Miami Institute of Technology, 1001 SW First St, Miami, FL 33130, 305-324-6781

Miami Job Corps Center, 3050 NW 183rd St, Miami, FL 33056, 305-325-1276

Miami Lakes Technical Education Center, 5780 NW 158th St, Miami, FL 33014, 305-557-1100

Miami Technical Institute, 14701 NW 7th Ave, North Miami, FL 33168, 305-688-8811

Miami Technical Institute (Branch Campus), 7061 W Flagler St, Miami, FL 33144, 305-263-9832

Motorcycle/Marine Mechanics Institute, 9751 Delegates Dr, Orlando, FL 32837-9835, 407-240-2422

National Aviation Academy, 5770 Roosevelt Blvd #105, Clearwater, FL 34620, 813-531-2080

National Career Institute, 3910 US Hwy 301 N #200, Tampa, FL 33619, 813-620-1446

National Education Center - Tampa Technical Institute, 2410 E Busch Blvd, Tampa, FL 33612, 813-935-5700

National School of Technology, 16150 NE 17th Ave, N Miami Beach, FL 33162, 305-949-9500

National School of Technology (Branch Campus), 4410 W 16th Ave, Hialeah, FL 33012, 305-558-9500

National Training, Inc., PO Box 1899, Orange Park, FL 32067, 904-272-4000

Naval Diving and Salvage Training Center, Panama City, FL 32407, 904-235-5207

Naval Health Sciences Education and Training Command (Aerospace Medical Institute), Pensacola, FL 32508, 904-452-4554

Naval Service School Command, 2200 Leahy Ave, Naval Training Center, Orlando, FL 32813, 407-646-4315

Naval Technical Training Center, Corry St, 640 Roberts Ave #112, Pensacola, FL 32511, 904-452-6558

New England Institute of Technology at Palm Beach, 1126 53rd Ct, West Palm Beach, FL 33407, 407-842-8324

New England Institute of Technology at Palm Beach (Branch Campus), 2400 Metro Center Blvd, West Palm Beach, FL 33407, 407-842-8324

North Technical Education Center, 7071 Garden Rd, Riviera Beach, FL 33404, 407-881-4639

Ohio State College of Barber Styling (Branch Campus), 2463 E Semoran Blvd, Apoplea, FL 32703, 407-884-1816

Ohio State College of Barber Styling (Career Training Institute), 2120 W Colonial Dr, Orlando, FL 32804-6948, 407-843-3984

Okaloosa Applied Technical Center, 1976 Lewis Turner Blvd, Fort Walton Beach, FL 32547, 904-833-3500

Omni Technical School, 2242 W Broward Blvd, Fortlauderdale, FL 33312, 954-584-4730

Omni Technical School, 1710 NW Seventh St, Miami, FL 33125, 305-541-6200

Orange Technical Education Center (Edgewood Ranch Campus), Edgewood Ranch, 2499 Edgewood Ranch Rd, Orlando, FL 32811, 407-295-2464

Orange Technical Education Center (Mid Florida Tech), 2900 W Oak Ridge Rd, Orlando, FL 32809-3799, 407-855-5880

Orange Technical Education Center (Technology Information Center Campus), Technology Information Center, 6628 Old Winter Garden Rd, Orlando, FL 32811, 407-292-8696

Orange Technical Education Center (Westside Tech), 955 E Story Rd, Winter Garden, FL 34787, 407-656-2851

Orange Technical Education Center (Winter Park Tech), 901 Webster Ave, Winter Park, FL 32789, 407-647-6366

Orlando Technical Education Center-Orlando Tech, 301 W Amelia St, Orlando, FL 32801, 407-425-2756

PHD Hair Academy, 27380 US Hwy 19 N, Clearwater, FL 34621, 813-791-7438

Palm Beach Beauty & Barber School, 4645 Gun Club Rd, West Palm Beach, FL 33415, 407-683-1238

Paralegal Careers, 1211 N Westshore Blvd #100, Tampa, FL 33607, 813-289-6025

Pinellas Technical Education Center, 6100 154th Ave N, Clearwater, FL 34620, 813-538-7167

Pinellas Technical Education Center (Branch Campus), 14400 49th St N, Clearwater, FL 34620, 813-531-3531

Pinellas Technical Education Center (Branch Campus), 2375 Whitney Rd, Clearwater, FL 34620, 813-530-0617

Pinellas Technical Education Center-St. Petersburg Campus, 910 34th St, St. Petersburg, FL 33711, 813-893-2500

Politechnical Institute, 1321 SW 107th Ave #202-B, Miami, FL 33174, 305-226-8099

Pompano Academy of Aeronautics, 1006 NE 10th St, Pompano Beach, FL 33060, 800-545-7262

Poynter Institute for Media Studies (The), 801 Third St S, St Petersburg, FL 33701, 813-821-9494

QUALTEC Institute for Competitive Advantage, 11760 US Hwy 1, North Palm Beach, FL 33408, 407-775-8300

RTI Technical Institute, 1412 W Fairfield Dr, Pensacola, FL 32501, 904-433-6547

Radford M. Locklin Vocational-Technical Center, 5330 Berryhill Rd, Milton, FL 32570, 904-983-5700

Recreational Vehicle Service Academy, 1127 Ellenton Gillette Rd, Ellenton, FL 34222, 941-722-7244

Rice College (Branch Campus), 5430 Norwood Ave, Jacksonville, FL 32208, 904-765-7300

Ridge Vocational-Technical Center, 7700 State Rd 544, Winter Haven, FL 33881, 914-422-6402

Robert Morgan Vocational-Technical Center, 18180 SW 122nd Ave, Miami, FL 33177, 305-253-9920

Ross Medical Education Center (Ross Technical Institute), 1490 S Military Tr #11, West Palm Beach, FL 33415, 407-433-1288

SER-IBM Business Institute, 42 NW 27th Ave #421, Miami, FL 33125, 305-649-7500

Sarasota County Technical Institute, 4748 Beneva Rd, Sarasota, FL 34235, 941-924-1365

Segal Institute of Court Reporting, 18850 US Hwy 19 N #565, Clearwater, FL 34624, 813-535-0608

Sheridan Vocational-Technical Center, 5400 Sheridan St, Hollywood, FL 33021, 954-985-3220

South Technical Education Center, 1300 SW 30th Ave, Boynton Beach, FL 33426, 407-369-7000

Southeastern Academy, Inc., PO Box 421768, Kissimmee, FL 32742, 407-847-4444

Southeastern Academy, Inc. (Peoples College of Independent Studies), PO Box 421768, Kissimmee, FL 32742, 407-847-4444

Southern Technical Center, 19151 S Dixie Hwy, Miami, FL 33157, 305-254-0995

St. Augustine Technical Center, 2980 Collins Ave, St. Augustine, FL 32095, 904-824-4401

St. Augustine Technical Center (Branch Campus), 113 Putnam County Blvd, East Palatka, FL 32131, 914-329-2550

Stenotype Institute of Jacksonville, 500 Ninth Ave N, Jacksonville Beach, FL 32250, 904-246-7466

Suncoast Center for Natural Health/Suncoast School, 4910 Cypress St, Tampa, FL 33607, 813-287-1099

Sunstate Academy of Hair Design, 2418 Colonial Blvd, Fort Myers, FL 33907, 941-278-1311

Sunstate Academy of Hair Design, 1825 Tamiami Tr #E6, Port Charlotte, FL 33948, 941-255-1366

Sunstate Academy of Hair Design, 4424 Bee Ridge Rd, Sarasota, FL 34233, 941-377-4880

Suwanee-Hamilton Area Vocational-Technical & Adult Education Ctr, 415 Pinewood Dr SW, Live Oak, FL 32060, 904-364-2750

Taylor Technical Institute, 3233 Hwy 19 S, Perry, FL 32347, 904-838-2545

Technical Career Institute, 720 NW 27th Ave, Miami, FL 33125, 305-842-2200

Tom P. Haney Vocational-Technical Center, 3016 Hwy 77, Panama City, FL 32405, 904-747-5565

Traviss Vocational-Technical Center, 3225 Winter Lake Rd, Eaton Park, FL 33813, 941-449-2700

U.S. Schools, 100 N Plaza, Miami, FL 33147, 305-836-7424

Ultrasound Diagnostic School (Branch Campus), 10199 Southside Blvd #106, Jacksonville, FL 32256, 904-363-6221

Ultrasound Diagnostic School (Branch Campus), 2760 E Atlantic Blvd, Pompano Beach, FL 33062, 954-942-6551

Ultrasound Diagnostic School (Branch Campus), 9950 Princess Palm Ave, Registry 2 Ste 120, Tampa, FL 33619, 813-621-0072

Washington-Holmes Area Vocational-Technical Center, 757 Hoyt St, Chipley, FL 32428, 904-638-1180

Webster Institute of Technology, 3910 US Hwy 301 N, Ste 200, Tampa, FL 33619-1259, 813-620-1446

West Technical Education Center, 2625 State Rd #715, Belle Glade, FL 33430, 407-996-4930

Westside Vocational-Technical Center, 955 E Story Rd, Winter Garden, FL 34787, 407-656-2851

Westside Vocational-Technical Center (Branch Campus), 2499 Edgewood Ranch Rd, Orlando, FL 32811, 407-295-2464

William T. McFatter Vocational-Technical Center, 6500 Nova Dr, Davie, FL 33317, 954-370-8324

William T. McFatter Vocational-Technical Center (Broward Fire Academy Branch Campus), 2600 SW 71 Terrace, Davie, FL 33314, 954-747-8217

Winter Park Adult Vocational Center, 901 Webster Ave, Winter Park, FL 32789, 407-647-6366

Withlacoochee Technical Institute, 1201 W Main St, Inverness, FL 34450, 904-726-2430

State Licensing & Business Registration Quick Finder Index

Architecture, Engineering & Surveying
Architect #14 (12000)...................................... ☎ 904-488-6685
Architect Firm #14... ☎ 904-488-6685
Engineer #15.. ✉ 904-488-9912
Geologist #15... ✉ 904-488-1105
Landscape Architect #15 .... ✉ 904-488-6685
Landscape Architecture, Business and
   Individual #14 .... ☎ 904-488-6685
Surveyor #15.. ✉ 904-488-9912

Business - Court & Legal Services
Attorney #25 (2400) .... ✉ 904-487-1292
Bondsman #13 .... ☎ 904-922-3156
Lobbyist/Principal #30 (7577)........................ ☎ 904-922-4990
Notary Public #20.. ☎ 904-488-7521
Registered Professional Reporter #31 904-488-8628
Shorthand Reporter #31....................................... 904-488-8628

Business - General Services
Auction Business #14....................................... ☎ 904-488-5189
Auctioneer #14 (2200)..................................... ☎ 904-488-5189
Food Services Establishment #6 (34890)....... ☎ 904-922-5335
Interior Decorator/Designer #15 .... ✉ 904-488-6685
Interior Design Individual #14 .... ☎ 904-488-6685
Lodging Establishment #6............................... ☎ 904-922-5335
Pawnbroker #22... ☎ 904-922-2967
Public Accountant-CPA #24 .... ☎ 904-336-2165
Resale Shop #18 .... ☎ 904-487-7000
Used/Second-Hand Dealer #18 .... ☎ 904-487-7000
Yacht & Ship Broker/Salesman #6 (1600)..... ☎ 904-488-1636

Construction & Manufacturing
Air Conditioning Contractor #16 .... ✉ 904-359-6310
Building Contractor #16.................................. ✉ 904-359-6310
Electrical Contractor #16................................ ☎ 904-488-3109
Elevator Certificates of Operation #6............. ☎ 904-922-5335
General Contractor #16 .... ✉ 904-359-6310
Mechanical Contractor #16 .... ✉ 904-359-6310
Mobile Home Manufacturer #12 (65) .... ✉ 904-488-4958
Plumbing Contractor #16 .... ✉ 904-359-6310

Education
Guidance Counselor #2 .... ☎ 904-488-2317
School Administrator/Supervisor #2 .... ☎ 904-488-2317
School Educational Media Specialist #2 .... ☎ 904-488-8198
School Principal #2... ☎ 904-488-2317
Teacher #2... ☎ 904-488-8198

Environmental & Agriculture
Animal Registration (Livestock Marks and
   Brands) #3 (5800) .... ☎ 904-922-0187
Asbestos Remover/Contractor #16................. ✉ 904-359-6310
Asbestos Surveyor Consultant #16................. ✉ 904-488-9912
Commercial Fresh Water Fishing #27............ ☎ 904-488-4066
Livestock Hauler #3.. ☎ 904-922-0187
Milk Hauler/Tester #3..................................... ☎ 904-487-1460
Pest Control Operator #4 .... ✉ 904-798-4609
Pesticide Applicator (Commercial, Private,
   Public) #3 (12000)..................................... ☎ 904-488-6838
Pesticide Dealer #3 (700)................................... 904-488-6838
Solid Waste Facility Operator #8 .... ☎ 904-922-6104
Underground Utility Contractor #16 .... ✉ 904-359-6310
Veterinarian #15 (6000).................................. ☎ 904-487-1820
Veterinary Establishment #15......................... ☎ 904-487-1820

Financial - Real Estate, Insurance & Banking
Adjuster/Agent/Title Agent #13 .... ☎ 904-922-3137
Automobile Repossession #19......................... ☎ 904-488-5381
Bank and Trust Company #5 (240) .... ☎ 904-487-1410
Broker Dealer Associated Person #5 .... ☎ 904-488-9805
Broker Dealer/Branch Office #5..................... ☎ 904-488-9805
Community Association Manager/
   Condominium Manager #17 .... ☎ 904-488-0725
Credit Union #5 .... ☎ 904-487-0570
Financial Institution #5 .... ☎ 904-488-0382
Interior Design Business #14.......................... ☎ 904-488-6685
International Bank Offices #5.......................... ☎ 904-487-1410
Investment Advisor (Credit Unions) #5
   (115) .... ☎ 904-487-1410
Investment-Securities Dealer #5.................... ✉ 904-488-9805
Money Transmitters #5 .... ☎ 904-921-2365
Mortgage Broker #17...................................... 407-423-6071
Real Estate Appraiser #26............................... ☎ 407-423-6053
Real Estate Broker #26 .... ☎ 904-423-6053
Securities Registration #5 .... ☎ 904-488-9805
Timeshare Agent #17....................................... 407-423-6071

Health & Beauty

Acupuncturist #14 (736)................................. ☎ 904-488-6039
Ambulance Service/Paramedic/Emergency
   Medical Technician #23 (36000)............... ☎ 904-487-1911
Audiologist #14 (615)................................... ☎ 904-487-3041
Audiologist Assistant #14 .... ☎ 904-488-8595
Audiologist Provisional #14.......................... ☎ 904-487-3041
Barber #14 (13720)...................................... ☎ 904-488-6888
Beautician/Cosmetology #14 (147720).......... ☎ 904-488-5702
Cemetery Lot Salesperson #17...................... 407-423-6071
Chiropractor #14 (6600)............................... ☎ 904-487-2395
Clinical Laboratory #1................................. ☎ 904-487-2527
Clinical Laboratory Director #15 .... ☎ 904-488-2224
Clinical Laboratory Supervisor #15 .... ☎ 904-488-2224
Clinical Laboratory Technician #15
   (3129)... ☎ 904-657-1425
Clinical Laboratory Technologist #15........... ☎ 904-488-2224
Clinical Laboratory Trainer #15.................... ☎ 904-488-2224
Consultant Pharmacist #15 .... ☎ 904-488-7546
Crematory/Funeral Dir.-Embalmer/Direct Dis-
   poser/Establishment
   /Funeral Home #15 (3000)....................... ☎ 904-488-8690
Dentist/Dental Hygienist/Dental Laboratory #15
   (10869) .... ☎ 904-488-6015
Dietitian/Nutrition Counselors #1 (2600) ...... ☎ 904-487-3372
Health Care Board #1 .... ☎ 904-487-2527
Health Facility #1.. ☎ 904-487-2527
Hearing Aid Specialist #15........................... ☎ 904-487-1813
Home Health Care Agency #11...................... ☎ 904-488-8922
Hospital #1... ☎ 904-487-2527
Laboratory Technician #9............................. 904-487-2299
Massage #15 904-488-6021
Medical Doctor/Surgeon #15 .... ☎ 904-488-0595
Medical Technologist #15 .... ☎ 904-488-0595
Midwife #15 .... ☎ 904-488-0595
Nuclear Medicine Technologist #9 .... ☎ 904-487-1111
Nuclear Pharmacist #15............................... ☎ 904-488-7546
Nurse #15 .... ☎ 904-359-6331
Nursing Home Administrator #28 .... ☎ 904-488-1295
Occupational Therapist/Assistant #1
   (5300)... ☎ 904-487-3372
Optician #15 .... ☎ 904-487-2397
Optometrist #15 .... ☎ 904-488-7484
Osteopathic Physician #1 (3549)................... ☎ 904-414-7209
Pharmacist/Pharmacy #15 (17900)............... ✉ 904-488-7546
Pharmacy #15 .... ☎ 904-488-7546
Physical Therapist/Assistant #1 (11000)........ ☎ 904-487-3372
Podiatrist #15... ☎ 904-487-1814
Radiology Technician/X-Ray Technologist #9
   .... ☎ 904-487-3451
Respiratory Technician/Therapist/Grandfather
   RT #1 (10000)... ☎ 904-487-3372
Speech-Language Pathologist #15 (3139) ..... ☎ 904-487-3041

Speech/Language Provisional Pathologist #15
   .... ☎ 904-487-3041
Speech/language Pathologist Assistant #15 ... ☎ 904-487-3041

Investigations & Security

Alarm System Contractor #15 .... ☎ 904-455-6685
Concealed Weapon License #19..................... ☎ 904-488-5381
Fire Equipment Dealer/Installer #13 .... ☎ 904-922-3172
Firearms (Armed Guards) #19 .... ☎ 904-488-5381
Guns (concealed weapon) #29....................... ☎ 904-488-0039
Private Invesigator/Agency #19 .... ☎ 904-488-5381
Private Investigator #29 .... ☎ 904-487-0482
Security Guard (Offices and Agencies) #19
   .... ☎ 904-488-5381

Social Services

Adoption Service #9 .... ☎ 904-488-8000
Adult & Foster Care #9................................ ☎ 904-487-1111
Counselor #15 .... ✉ 904-922-6728
Day Care Center/Child Care Center
   /Nursery School #10................................ ☎ 904-488-4900
Foster Family Home #9 .... ☎ 904-487-1111
Marriage Counselor/Mental Health
   Counselor #15 .... ☎ 904-487-2520
Orphanage #9... ☎ 904-487-1111
Psychologist/School #15 (2743).................... ☎ 904-922-6728
Social Worker #15 .... ☎ 904-487-2520

Sports & Entertainment

Alcoholic Beverages/Tobacco #6................... ☎ 904-488-7891
Athletic Agent #15...................................... ✉ 904-488-7487
Athletic Commission/Boxing/Kickboxing #6
   .... ☎ 904-488-8500
Charter (Savings and Loan Association) #5
   (4) .... ☎ 904-487-1410
Firearms #29 .... ☎ 904-487-0482
Liquor Store #6 .... ☎ 904-488-8288
Pari-Mutuel Wagering #7 .... ☎ 904-488-9161
Pet Shop #27 .... ☎ 904-488-6253
Racing-Dog/Horse #6.................................. ☎ 904-488-9130
Recreational Vehicle Dealer #12 .... ✉ 904-488-4958
Sweepstakes Operator (Registration) #19 ...... ☎ 904-488-5381
Zoo #27 .... ☎ 904-488-6253

Transportation

Airport #21 .... ☎ 904-488-8444
Automobile Dealer-New Cars #12 .... ✉ 904-488-4958
Automobile Sales/Dealer (Automobile
   Dealer-Used Cars) #12 (8000) .... ✉ 904-488-4958
Mobile Home Dealer/Broker #12 (1375) .... ✉ 904-488-4958
Motel/Restaurant #7.................................... ☎ 904-488-1133
Pilot #15 .... ✉ 904-488-0698

State Licensing & Business Registration Agency Information

(1) Agency for Health Care Administration, 2727 Mahan Dr, Tallahassee, FL 32308, 904-487-2513, Fax: 904-487-6240

(2) Bureau of Teacher Certification, Florida Education Center, 325 W Gaines, Suite 701, Tallahassee, FL 32399, 904-488-1899, Fax: 904-488-3352

(3) Department of Agriculture & Consumer Services, 407 S Calhoun, Mayo Bldg, Room 312, Tallahassee, FL 32399, 904-922-0187, Fax: 904-487-3641

(4) Department of Agriculture & Consumer Services, 644 Cessory Blvd, Suite 200, Jacksonville, FL 32211-7194, 904-727-6591, Fax: 904-727-6563

(5) Department of Banking & Finance, Fletcher Bldg Suite 636, 101 E Gaines St, Tallahassee, FL 32399-0350, 904-488-9805, Fax: 904-681-2428

(6) Department of Business & Professional Regulation, 1940 N Monroe St, Tallahassee, FL 32399, 904-922-5335, Fax: 904-488-1514

(7) Department of Business Regulations, The Johns Bldg, 725 S Bronough St, Tallahassee, FL 32399, 904-488-9161, Fax: 904-488-0550

(8) Department of Environmental Regulation, Division of Waste Management, 2600 Blair Stone Rd, Tallahassee, FL 32399-2400, 904-922-6104

(9) Department of Health & Rehabilitative Services, 1317 Winewood Blvd, Tallahassee, FL 32399-0700, 904-487-1111, Fax: 904-487-0688

(10) Department of Health & Rehabilitative Services, 3401 W Tharp, Tallahassee, FL 32303, 904-487-1111, Fax: 904-487-7956

(11) Department of Health & Rehabilitative Services, 2727 Mahan Dr, Tallahassee, FL 32308, 904-487-3513, Fax: 904-487-6240

(12) Department of Highway Safety & Motor Vehicles, Bureau of Motor Homes & Recreational Vehicles, Neil Kirkman Bldg, Room A129, 2900 Apalachee Pky, Tallahassee, FL 32399-0640, 904-488-4958, Fax: 904-922-9840

(13) Department of Insurance & Treasurer, 200 E Gaines St, Larson Bldg, Tallahassee, FL 32399-0319, 904-922-3137

(14) Department of Professional Regulation, 1940 N Monroe St, Tallahassee, FL 32399, 904-488-8595

(15) Department of Professional Regulation, 1940 N Monroe St, Tallahassee, FL 32399, 904-487-2252, Fax: 904-921-7865

(16) Department of Professional Regulation, Construction Industry Licensing Board, 1940 N Monroe St, Tallahassee, FL 32399-0781, 904-488-9912, Fax: 904-922-2918

(17) Department of Professional Regulation, Division of Real Estate, 1940 N Monroe St, Northwood Center, Tallahassee, FL 32399-1033, 407-423-6071, Fax: 904-488-7473

(18) Department of Revenue, Resale Shop & Related Licensing, 5050 W Tennessee St, Bldg K, Tallahassee, FL 32399-0100, 904-487-7000, Fax: 904-922-5938

(19) Department of State, 2520 N Monroe St, Tallahassee, FL 32303, 904-487-0482, Fax: 904-487-7950

(20) Department of State, Bureau of Notaries Public, The Capitol Bldg, Rm 1801, Tallahassee, FL 32399-0250, 904-488-7521, Fax: 904-488-1768

(21) Department of Transportation, 605 Suwannee St, Tallahassee, FL 32399-0450, 904-488-8444, Fax: 904-922-4942

(22) Division of Consumer Affairs, Pawnbroker Licensing, 207 S. Calhoun St., Tallahassee, FL 32399-0100, 904-922-2967, Fax: 904-487-4177

(23) Emergency Medical Services, 2002D Old St Augustine Rd, Tallahassee, FL 32301-4881, 904-487-1911, Fax: 904-488-2512

(24) Florida Board of Accountancy, 2610 NW 43rd St, Suite 1A, Gainesfille, FL 32606, 352-955-2165, Fax: 352-955-2164

(25) Florida Board of Bar Examiners, 1891 Elder Ct., Tallahassee, FL 32399-1750, 904-487-1292

(26) Florida Real Estate Commission, 400 W Robinson St, Room N-309, Hudson North Tower, Orlando, FL 32801, 407-296-4441

(27) Game & Fresh Water Fish Commission, 620 S Meridian St, Tallahassee, FL 32399-1600, 904-488-3641, Fax: 904-414-2628

(28) Health Care Administration, Fort Knox Executive Center, 2727 Mahan Dr, Tallahassee, FL 32308-5401, 904-487-4221, Fax: 904-487-6240

(29) Licensing Board, 325 John Knox Rd, Tallahassee, FL 32303, 904-487-0482, Fax: 904-487-7950

(30) Lobbyist Registration, 111 W Madison St, Room G-68, Claude Pepper Bldg, Tallahassee, FL 32399-1400, 904-922-4990

(31) Supreme Court of Florida, 500 N Duvall, Tallahassee, FL 32399-1900, 904-488-8628

Georgia

Capitol: Atlanta (DeKalb County)	
State Population	7.2 Million
Number of Degree Granting Institutions:	81
Number of State Licensing & Business Registration Agencies:	93

Degree Granting Educational Institutions

Abraham Baldwin Agricultural College, Registrar's Office, ABAC 3, 2802 Moore Hwy, Tifton, GA 31794-2601, 912-386-3236 (Fax: 912-386-7006). Hours: 8AM-5PM. Enrollment: 2300. Records go back to 1930's. Alumni records are maintained here also. Call 912-386-3265. Degrees granted: Associate. Adverse incident record source- Public Safety, 912-386-3274.

Attendance and degree information available by phone, fax, mail. Search requires name only. Also helpful: SSN, date of birth, exact years of attendance. There is no fee.

Agnes Scott College, Registrar, 141 E College Ave, Decatur, GA 30030, 404-638-6137 (Fax: 404-638-6177). Hours: 8:30AM-4:30PM. Enrollment: 36959. Records go back to 1889. Alumni records are maintained here also. Call 404-638-6323. Degrees granted: Bachelors; Masters.

Attendance and degree information available by phone, fax, mail. Search requires name only. Also helpful: approximate years of attendance. There is no fee.

Albany State College, Registrar, 504 College Dr, Albany, GA 31705-2794, 912-430-4638 (Fax: 912-430-2953). Hours: 8AM-5PM. Enrollment: 3200. Records go back to 1903. Alumni records are maintained here also. Call 912-430-4658. Degrees granted: Bachelors; Masters. Adverse incident record source- Registrar, 912-430-4638.

Attendance information available by mail. Search requires name plus SSN, exact years of attendance, signed release. Also helpful: date of birth. There is no fee.

Degree information available by phone, fax, mail. Search requires name plus SSN, exact years of attendance. Also helpful: date of birth. There is no fee.

American College, Registrar, 3330 Peachtree Rd NE, Atlanta, GA 30326, 404-231-9000 (Fax: 404-231-1062). Hours: 8AM-4:30PM. Enrollment: 2000. Records go back to 1971. Alumni records are maintained here at the same phone number. Degrees granted: Associate; Bachelors.

Attendance and degree information available by phone, fax, mail. Search requires name only. Also helpful: SSN, date of birth, exact years of attendance. There is no fee.

American Schools of Professional Psychology, (Georgia School of Professional Psychology), Registrar, 990 Hammond Dr NE, Atlanta, GA 30328, 770-671-1200 (Fax: 770-671-0476). Hours: 8:30AM-5:30PM. Enrollment: 450. Records go back to 1990. Degrees granted: Masters; Doctorate. Special programs- Clinical Psychology. Adverse incident record source- Registrar, 770-671-1200.

Attendance and degree information available by phone, fax, mail. Search requires name plus SSN. There is no fee.

Andrew College, Registrar, 413 College St, Cuthbert, GA 31740-1395, 912-732-2171 (Fax: 912-732-2176). Hours: 8:30AM-Noon, 1-4:30PM. Enrollment: 350. Records go back to 1883. Alumni records are maintained here at the same phone number. Degrees granted: Associate.

Attendance information available by phone, fax. Search requires name plus SSN, exact years of attendance. Also helpful: date of birth. There is no fee.

Degree information available by phone, fax. Search requires name plus SSN, date of birth, exact years of attendance. There is no fee.

Armstrong Atlantic State University, Registrar, 11935 Abercorn Ext, Savannah, GA 31419-1997, 912-927-5278 (Fax: 912-921-5462). Hours: 8:15AM-7PM M-Th; 8:15AM-5PM. Enrollment: 4160. Records go back to 1935. Degrees granted: Associate; Bachelors. Adverse incident record source- Public Safety, 912-927-2367.

Attendance information available by phone, fax, mail. Search requires name plus SSN, exact years of attendance. There is no fee.

Degree information available by phone, mail. Search requires name plus SSN, exact years of attendance. There is no fee.

Art Institute of Atlanta, Registrar, 3376 Peachtree Rd NE, Atlanta, GA 30326, 404-266-1341 (Fax: 404-266-1383).

Hours: 7:30AM-7PM. Enrollment: 1420. Records go back to 1975. Art Institute records available since 1975; formerly Massey Junior College 1949-1975. Degrees granted: Associate; Bachelors. Adverse incident record source- Registrar: Student Services Director

Attendance and degree information available by phone, fax, mail. Search requires name plus SSN. Also helpful: date of birth, exact years of attendance. There is no fee.

Athens Area Technical Institute, Registrar, 800 Hwy 29 N, Athens, GA 30601-1500, 706-355-5012 (Fax: 706-369-5753). Hours: 8AM-5PM M-Th, 8AM-4PM F. Enrollment: 7000. Records go back to 1967. Degrees granted: Associate.

Attendance and degree information available by phone, fax, mail. Search requires name plus SSN, exact years of attendance. There is no fee.

Atlanta Christian College, Registrar, 2605 Ben Hill Rd, East Point, GA 30344, 404-669-2093 (Fax: 404-669-2024). Hours: 8:30AM-4:30PM. Enrollment: 270. Records go back to 1937. Alumni records are maintained here also. Call 404-669-2091. Degrees granted: Associate; Bachelors.

Attendance and degree information available by phone, fax, mail. Search requires name only. Also helpful: SSN, date of birth, exact years of attendance. There is no fee.

Atlanta College of Art, Registrar, 1280 Peachtree St NE, Atlanta, GA 30309, 404-733-5001 (Fax: 404-733-5201). Hours: 8AM-5PM M-Th, 8:45AM-3:30PM F. Enrollment: 420. Records go back to 1950. Alumni records are maintained here also. Call 404-733-5001. Degrees granted: Bachelors.

Attendance and degree information available by phone, mail. Search requires name plus SSN, exact years of attendance. There is no fee.

Atlanta Metropolitan College, Registrar, 1630 Stewart Ave SW, Atlanta, GA 30310, 404-756-4001 (Fax: 404-756-5686). Hours: 8:30AM-5PM. Enrollment: 1800. Records go back to 1974. Degrees granted: Associate.

Attendance and degree information available by phone, fax, mail. Search requires name plus SSN. Also helpful: approximate years of attendance. There is no fee.

Augusta State University, Registrar, 2500 Walton Way, Augusta, GA 30904-2200, 706-737-1408 (Fax: 706-737-1777). Enrollment: 5700. Formerly Augusta College Records go back to 1957. Alumni records are maintained here also. Call 706-737-1759. Degrees granted: Associate; Bachelors; Masters; Education Specialist.

Attendance and degree information available by phone, fax, mail. Search requires name only. Also helpful: SSN, date of birth, exact years of attendance. There is no fee.

Augusta Technical Institute, Registrar, 3116 Deans Bridge Rd, Augusta, GA 30906, 706-771-4035 (Fax: 706-771-4016). Hours: 8AM-4:30PM. Enrollment: 2325. Records go back to 1961. Alumni records are maintained here at the same phone number. Degrees granted: Associate.

Attendance and degree information available by phone, mail. Search requires name only. Also helpful: SSN, exact years of attendance. There is no fee.

Bainbridge College, Registrar, Hwy 84 E, Bainbridge, GA 31717, 912-248-2504 (Fax: 912-248-2525). Hours: 8AM-6PM M,T; 8AM-5PM W,Th,F. Enrollment: 1180. Records go back to 1973. Alumni records are maintained here also. Call 912-248-2506. Degrees granted: Associate. Certification: Technical Studies. Adverse incident record source- Vice President of Student Affairs, 912-248-2506.

Attendance and degree information available by fax, mail. Search requires name plus SSN, signed release. Fee is $3 days.

Bauder College, Registrar, Phipps Plaza, 3500 Peachtree Rd NE, Atlanta, GA 30326-9975, 404-237-7573 (Fax: 404-237-1642). Hours: 8AM-4PM. Enrollment: 410. Records go back to 1970. Degrees granted: Associate.

Attendance and degree information available by phone, fax, mail. Search requires name plus SSN, exact years of attendance. There is no fee.

Berry College, Registrar, Box 49400, Mt Berry, GA 30149-0400, 706-236-2282 (Fax: 706-290-2179). Hours: 8AM-5PM. Enrollment: 1756. Records go back to 1902. Alumni records are maintained here also. Call 706-236-2256. Degrees granted: Bachelors; Masters; Ed.S. Adverse incident record source- Campus Safety, 706-236-2572.

Attendance and degree information available by phone, fax, mail. Search requires name plus SSN. There is no fee.

Brenau University, Registrar, One Centennial Cir, Gainesville, GA 30501, 770-534-6203. Hours: 8:30AM-5PM. Enrollment: 2300. Records go back to 1800's. Alumni records are maintained here also. Call 770-534-6164. Degrees granted: Bachelors; Masters; Education Specialist. Adverse incident record source- Student Development, 770-534-6130.

Attendance and degree information available by mail. Search requires name plus SSN. Also helpful: exact years of attendance. There is no fee.

Brewton Parker College, Registrar, Hwy 280, Mount Vernon, GA 30445, 912-583-2241 (Fax: 912-583-4498). Hours: 8AM-5PM. Enrollment: 1660. Records go back to 1904. Alumni records are maintained here at the same phone number. Degrees granted: Associate; Bachelors. Adverse incident record source- Business Office, 912-583-3290.

Attendance information available by phone, fax, mail. Search requires name plus SSN, date of birth. Also helpful: exact years of attendance. There is no fee.

Degree information available by phone, fax, mail. Search requires name plus SSN. Also helpful: date of birth, exact years of attendance. There is no fee.

Chattahochee Technical Institute, Registrar, 980 S Cobb Dr, Marietta, GA 30060, 770-528-4545 (Fax: 770-528-4578). Hours: 7:30AM-7:30PM M-Th; 7:30AM-4PM F. Enrollment: 2000. Records go back to 1966. Degrees granted: Associate. Adverse incident record source- Registrar, 770-528-4545.

Attendance and degree information available by phone, fax, mail. Search requires name plus SSN. Also helpful: date of birth, exact years of attendance. There is no fee.

Clark Atlanta University, Registrar, James P Brawley Dr at Fair St SW, Atlanta, GA 30314, 404-880-8759 (Fax: 404-880-6083). Hours: 9AM-5PM. Enrollment: 5300. Records go back to 1988. Alumni records are maintained here also. Call 404-880-8022. Degrees granted: Bachelors; Masters; Doctorate; Specialist. Adverse incident record source- Student Affairs, 404-880-8063.

Attendance and degree information available by phone, mail. Search requires name plus SSN, date of birth, exact years of attendance. There is no fee.

Clayton State College, Registrar, PO Box 285, Morrow, GA 30260, 770-960-5110 (Fax: 770-961-3752). Hours: 8AM-9PM M-Th; 8AM-4PM F; 8AM-Noon S. Enrollment: 5000. Records go back to 1969. Alumni records are maintained here also. Call 770-961-3580. Degrees granted: Associate; Bachelors.

Attendance and degree information available by fax, mail. Search requires name plus SSN. Also helpful: date of birth, exact years of attendance. There is no fee.

Coastal Georgia Community College, Registrar, 3700 Altama Ave, Brunswick, GA 31520-3644, 912-264-7235 (Fax: 912-262-3072). Hours: 8AM-5PM. Enrollment: 1920.

Formerly Brunswick College Records go back to 1969. Alumni records are maintained here also. Call 912-262-3303. Degrees granted: Associate.

Attendance and degree information available by phone, fax, mail. Search requires name plus SSN, exact years of attendance. There is no fee.

Columbia Theological Seminary, Registrar, PO
Box 520, 701 Columbia Dr, Decatur, GA 30031, 404-378-8821 (Fax: 404-377-9696). Hours: 8:30AM-4:30PM. Enrollment: 650. Records go back to 1930. Alumni records are maintained here at the same phone number. Degrees granted: Masters; Doctorate; M.Div; TH.M; MATS; D.Min; TH.D. Adverse incident record source- Business Office.

Attendance information available by fax, mail. Search requires name plus approximate years of attendance, signed release. Also helpful: exact years of attendance. There is no fee.

Degree information available by phone, fax, mail. Search requires name plus approximate years of attendance. Also helpful: exact years of attendance. There is no fee.

Columbus State University, Registrar, 4225 University Ave, Columbus, GA 31907-5645, 706-568-2237 (Fax: 706-568-2462). Hours: 8AM-6PM M-Th; 8AM-5PM F. Enrollment: 5500. Formerly Columbus College Records go back to 1957. Alumni records are maintained here also. Call 706-568-2280. Degrees granted: Associate; Bachelors; Masters. Certification: Comp Sci, Criminal Justice. E.D.S. Special programs- COMPASS, 706-568-2410. Adverse incident record source- VP for Student Affairs, 706-568-2033.

Attendance and degree information available by phone, fax, mail. Search requires name plus SSN, date of birth. Also helpful: approximate years of attendance. There is no fee.

Covenant College, Registrar, Scenic Hwy, Lookout
Mountain, GA 30750, 706-820-1560 X1134 (Fax: 706-820-2165). Hours: 8AM-4:30PM. Enrollment: 850. Records go back to 1955. Alumni records are maintained here also. Call 706-820-1560. Degrees granted: Associate; Bachelors; Masters. Adverse incident record source- Student Development, 706-820-1560.

Attendance and degree information available by phone, fax, mail. Search requires name plus SSN. There is no fee.

Dalton College, Registrar's Office, 213 N College Dr,
Dalton, GA 30720, 706-272-4436 (Fax: 706-272-2530). Hours: 8AM-5PM. Enrollment: 3200. Records go back to 1969. Alumni records are maintained here at the same phone number. Degrees granted: Associate.

Attendance information available by phone, fax, mail. Search requires name plus SSN, date of birth. Also helpful: exact years of attendance. There is no fee.

Degree information available by written request only. Search requires name plus SSN, date of birth. Also helpful: exact years of attendance. There is no fee.

Darton College, Registrar, 2400 Gillionville Rd, Albany,
GA 31707-3098, 912-430-6740 (Fax: 912-430-2926). Hours: 8AM-5PM. Enrollment: 2650. Records go back to 1966. Alumni records are maintained here also. Call 912-430-6000. Degrees granted: Associate. Adverse incident record source- Student Affairs, 912-430-6728.

Attendance and degree information available by phone, fax, mail. Search requires name plus SSN, date of birth. There is no fee.

DeKalb College, Admissions & Records, 555 N Indian
Creek Dr, Clarkston, GA 30021, 404-299-4566. Hours: 8AM-5PM M-Th; 8AM-4:30PM F. Enrollment: 16000. Records go back to 1964. Degrees granted: Associate.

Attendance and degree information available by phone, fax, mail. Search requires name plus SSN. Also helpful: date of birth, exact years of attendance. There is no fee.

DeVry Institute of Technology, Atlanta, Registrar, 250 N Arcadia Ave, Decatur, GA 30030, 404-292-7900 (Fax: 404-292-8117). Hours: 8:30PM 5PM M,W,F; 8:30PM-6PM T,Th. Enrollment: 3000. Records go back to 1971. Transcripts available for all years; other information for last five years only. Alumni Records Office: Alumni Association, DeVry National Offices, One Tower Lane, Oakbrook Terrace, IL 60181-4624. Degrees granted: Associate; Bachelors.

Attendance and degree information available by phone, fax, mail. Search requires name plus SSN. Also helpful: exact years of attendance. There is no fee.

East Georgia College, Registrar, 131 College Circle,
Swainsboro, GA 30401, 912-237-7831 (Fax: 912-237-5161). Hours: 8AM-5PM. Enrollment: 950. Records go back to 1973. Alumni records are maintained here at the same phone number. Degrees granted: Associate. Adverse incident record source- Student Affairs, 912-237-7831.

Attendance and degree information available by phone, fax, mail. Search requires name plus SSN. There is no fee.

Emmanuel College, Registrar, 212 Spring St, PO Box
129, Franklin Springs, GA 30639, 706-245-7226 (Fax: 706-245-4424). Hours: 8-11:30AM, 12:30-4PM. Enrollment: 600. Records go back to 1919. Alumni records are maintained here at the same phone number. Degrees granted: Associate; Bachelors.

Attendance and degree information available by phone, fax, mail. Search requires name only. Also helpful: SSN, date of birth, exact years of attendance. There is no fee.

Emory University, Office of the Registrar, 100 Boisfeuillet Jones Center, Atlanta, GA 30322-1970, 404-727-6042. Hours: 8AM-4:30PM. Enrollment: 11308. Records go back to 1836. Alumni records are maintained here also. Call 404-727-6400. Degrees granted: Associate; Bachelors; Masters; Doctorate. Adverse incident record source- Registrar, 404-727-6042.

Attendance and degree information available by phone, mail. Search requires name only. Also helpful: SSN, date of birth, exact years of attendance. There is no fee.

Floyd College, Registrar, PO Box 1864, Rome, GA
30162-1864, 706-802-5000 (Fax: 706-295-6341). Hours: 8:30AM-5PM. Enrollment: 3000. Records go back to 1970. Alumni records are maintained here at the same phone number. Degrees granted: Associate. Adverse incident record source- Student Services, 706-295-6363.

Attendance and degree information available by phone, fax, mail. Search requires name plus SSN. There is no fee.

Fort Valley State University, Registrar, 1005 State
College Dr, Fort Valley, GA 31030-3298, 912-825-6282. Hours: 8AM-5PM. Enrollment: 3100. Records go back to 1895. Alumni records are maintained here also. Call 912-825-6315. Degrees granted: Associate; Bachelors; Masters; Ed.S.

Attendance and degree information available by phone, mail. Search requires name plus SSN. Also helpful: date of birth, exact years of attendance. There is no fee.

Gainesville College, Registrar, PO Box 1358, Gainesville, GA 30503-1358, 770-535-6244 (Fax: 770-535-6359). Hours: 8AM-5PM. Enrollment: 2800. Records go back to 1964. Alumni records are maintained here also. Call 770-718-3648. Degrees granted: Associate. Adverse incident record source- Vice President of Student Development, 770-718-3360.

Attendance and degree information available by phone, fax, mail. Search requires name plus SSN, approximate years of attendance. There is no fee.

Georgia College, Registrar, CPO Box 23, Milledgeville,
GA 31061, 912-454-2772 (Fax: 912-453-1914). Hours: 8AM-6PM M-Th, 8AM-5PM F. Enrollment: 5710. Records go back to 1889. Alumni Records Office: CPO 98, Milledgeville, GA 31061, 912-453-5400. Degrees granted: Bachelors; Masters.

Adverse incident record source- Dept of Public Safety, 912-453-4400.

Attendance and degree information available by phone, fax, mail. Search requires name plus SSN, approximate years of attendance. There is no fee.

Georgia Institute of Technology, Registrar, 225 North Ave NW, Atlanta, GA 30332-0315, 404-894-4151 (Fax: 404-894-0167). Hours: 8AM-4:30PM. Enrollment: 14000. Records go back to 1888. Alumni records are maintained here also. Call 404-894-2391. Degrees granted: Bachelors; Masters; Doctorate.

Attendance and degree information available by phone, fax, mail. Search requires name only. Also helpful: SSN, date of birth, exact years of attendance. There is no fee.

Georgia Military College, Registrar, 201 E Greene St, Milledgeville, GA 31061, 912-454-2684 (Fax: 912-454-2688). Hours: 8AM-5PM. Enrollment: 650. Records go back to 1940. Alumni records are maintained here also. Call 912-454-2695. Degrees granted: Associate. Special programs- Pre-Nursing Degree: Criminal Justice: Behafvioral Science: Business Administration: Education. Adverse incident record source- Commandant, 912-454-2710.

Attendance and degree information available by fax, mail. Search requires name plus SSN, signed release. There is no fee.

Georgia Southern University, Registrar, PO Box 8092, Statesboro, GA 30460-8092, 912-681-0070 (Fax: 912-681-0081). Hours: 8AM-5PM. Enrollment: 14000. Records go back to 1924. Alumni records are maintained here also. Call 912-681-5691. Degrees granted: Bachelors; Masters; Doctorate; Education Specialist. Adverse incident record source- Judicial Affairs, 912-681-5409.

Attendance and degree information available by phone, fax, mail. Search requires name plus SSN, approximate years of attendance. Also helpful: date of birth, exact years of attendance. There is no fee.

Georgia Southwestern State University, Registrar, 800 Wheatley St, Americus, GA 31709-4693, 912-928-1331 (Fax: 912-931-2059). Hours: 8AM-5PM. Enrollment: 2500. Records go back to 1926. Alumni records are maintained here also. Call 912-928-1373. Degrees granted: Associate; Bachelors; Masters. Adverse incident record source- Student Affairs, 912-928-1387.

Attendance and degree information available by fax, mail. Search requires name plus SSN, signed release. Also helpful: date of birth, exact years of attendance. There is no fee.

Georgia State University, Student Service, PO Box 4017, Atlanta, GA 30302, 404-651-2383 (Fax: 404-651-1419). Hours: 8:30AM-5:15PM. Enrollment: 19200. Records go back to 1920. Degrees granted: Bachelors; Masters; Doctorate. Adverse incident record source- Dean of Students, 404-651-2200: Campus Police, 404-651-2100

Attendance and degree information available by phone, fax, mail. Search requires name only. Also helpful: SSN, exact years of attendance. There is no fee.

Gordon College, Registrar, 419 College Dr, Barnesville, GA 30204, 770-358-5022 (Fax: 770-358-3031). Hours: 8AM-8PM M; 8AM-5PM T-F. Enrollment: 2200. Records go back to 1955. Degrees granted: Associate. Certification: Assoc of Applied Science Cooperative Degree Pgm. Adverse incident record source- Student Affairs, 770-358-5056.

Attendance and degree information available by phone, fax, mail. Search requires name plus SSN. Also helpful: date of birth, exact years of attendance. There is no fee.

Gupton-Jones College of Funeral Service, Registrar, 5141 Snapfinger Woods Dr, Decatur, GA 30035-4022, 770-593-2257 (Fax: 770-593-1891). Hours: 7:30AM-4PM. Enrollment: 350. Records go back to 1970. Alumni records are maintained here at the same phone number. Degrees granted: Associate.

Attendance and degree information available by phone, mail. Search requires name only. Also helpful: SSN, approximate years of attendance. There is no fee.

Gwinnett Technical Institute, Registrar, 1250 Atkinson Rd, PO Box 1505, Lawrenceville, GA 30246-1505, 770-962-7580 X121 (Fax: 770-962-7985). Hours: 8AM-6:30PM M-Th; 8AM-5PM F. Enrollment: 3448. Records go back to 1986. Alumni records are maintained here also. Call 770-962-7580 X205. Degrees granted: Associate.

Attendance and degree information available by phone, fax, mail. Search requires name plus SSN. Also helpful: date of birth. There is no fee.

Herzing College of Business & Technology, Registrar, 3355 Lenox Rd Ste 100, Atlanta, GA 30326, 404-816-4533 (Fax: 404-816-5576). Hours: 8AM-6PM M-Th; 8AM-3PM F. Enrollment: 300. Records go back to 1980. Degrees granted: Associate. Special programs- Before 1979: Atlanta Art Institute, 404-266-2662. Adverse incident record source- Registrar's Office, 404-816-4533

Attendance and degree information available by phone, fax, mail. Search requires name plus SSN, exact years of attendance. Also helpful: date of birth. There is no fee.

Institute of Paper Science and Technology, Registrar, 500 10th St NW, Atlanta, GA 30318, 404-894-7764 (Fax: 404-894-4778). Hours: 8AM-5PM. Enrollment: 80. Records go back to 1929. Alumni records are maintained here also. Call 404-894-7764. Degrees granted: Masters; PhD.

Attendance and degree information available by phone, fax, mail. Search requires name plus SSN. There is no fee.

Interdenominational Theological Center, Registrar, 700 Martin Luther King Jr Dr, Atlanta, GA 30314, 404-527-7708 (Fax: 404-527-0901). Hours: 9AM-5PM. Enrollment: 400. Records go back to 1958. Alumni records are maintained here also. Call 404-527-7784. Degrees granted: Masters; Doctorate.

Attendance and degree information available by phone, fax, mail. Search requires name plus SSN, approximate years of attendance. Also helpful: date of birth, exact years of attendance. There is no fee.

Kennesaw State University, Registrar, 1000 Chastain Rd, Kennesaw, GA 30144, 770-423-6200 (Fax: 770-423-6541). Hours: 8AM-7PM M-Th; 8AM-5PM F. Enrollment: 12000. Records go back to 1964. Alumni records are maintained here also. Call 770-423-6333. Degrees granted: Associate; Bachelors; Masters. Adverse incident record source- 770-423-6666.

Attendance and degree information available by phone, fax, mail. Search requires name plus SSN. Also helpful: date of birth, exact years of attendance. There is no fee.

LaGrange College, Registrar, 601 Broad St, Lagrange, GA 30240-2999, 706-812-7237 (Fax: 706-884-7358). Hours: 8:15AM-5PM. Enrollment: 1000. Records go back to 1896. Alumni records are maintained here also. Call 706-812-7244. Degrees granted: Associate; Bachelors; Masters.

Attendance and degree information available by phone, fax, mail. Search requires name only. Also helpful: SSN, date of birth, exact years of attendance. There is no fee.

Life College, Registrar, 1269 Barclay Cir, Marietta, GA 30060, 770-426-2780 (Fax: 770-429-1512). Hours: 8AM-5PM. Enrollment: 4000. Records go back to 1977. Alumni records are maintained here also. Call 770-426-2925. Degrees granted: Bachelors; Masters; Doctorate. Adverse incident record source- Registrar: Dean of Students

Attendance and degree information available by mail. Search requires name plus signed release. Also helpful: SSN, exact years of attendance. There is no fee.

Macon College, Registrar, 100 College Station Dr, Macon, GA 31297, 912-471-2855 (Fax: 912-471-5343). Hours: 8AM-6PM M-Th; 8AM-4:30PM F. Enrollment: 3600. Records go back to 1968. Alumni records are maintained here also. Call 912-471-2732. Degrees granted: Associate. Adverse incident record source- Student Affairs, 912-471-2732.

Attendance and degree information available by phone, fax, mail. Search requires name plus SSN. Also helpful: date of birth, exact years of attendance. There is no fee.

Medical College of Georgia, Registrar, 1120 15th St, Augusta, GA 30912, 706-721-2201 (Fax: 706-721-0186). Hours: 8AM-5PM. Enrollment: 2500. Records go back to 1828. Alumni records are maintained here at the same phone number. Degrees granted: Associate; Bachelors; Masters; Doctorate. Adverse incident record source- Public Safety, 706-721-2911.

Attendance information available by phone, fax, mail. Search requires name plus SSN. Also helpful: exact years of attendance. There is no fee.

Degree information available by phone, fax, mail. Search requires name plus SSN. Also helpful: date of birth, exact years of attendance. There is no fee.

Mercer University, Registrar, 1400 Coleman Ave, Macon, GA 31207, 912-752-2683 (Fax: 912-752-2455). Hours: 8:30AM-5PM. Enrollment: 2600. Records go back to 1833. Alumni records are maintained here also. Call 912-752-2715. Degrees granted: Masters. Adverse incident record source- Student Life, 912-752-2685.

Attendance information available by fax, mail. Search requires name plus SSN, approximate years of attendance. There is no fee.

Degree information available by fax, mail. Search requires name plus SSN, approximate years of attendance. There is no fee.

Mercer University Southern School of Pharmacy, Registrar, 3001 Mercer University Dr, Atlanta, GA 30341, 770-986-3000 (Fax: 770-986-3135). Enrollment: 520. Records go back to 1930. Alumni Records Office: University Advancement, Koger Ctr, Oxford Bldg Ste 217, Atlanta, GA 30341. Degrees granted: Bachelors; Masters; Doctorate. Special programs- Pharmacy Administration, 770-986-3254: Pharmacy Practice, 770-986-3209: Pharmacy Sciences, 770-986-3237. Adverse incident record source- Dean's Office, 770-986-3304 .

Attendance and degree information available by phone, fax, mail. Search requires name only. Also helpful: SSN, date of birth, exact years of attendance. There is no fee.

Middle Georgia College, Registrar, 1100 Second St SE, Cochran, GA 31014, 912-934-3036 (Fax: 912-934-3049). Hours: 8AM-5PM. Enrollment: 1200. Records go back to 1884. Alumni records are maintained here also. Call 912-934-3301. Degrees granted: Associate. Adverse incident record source- Student Affairs, 912-934-3027.

Attendance and degree information available by phone, fax, mail. Search requires name plus SSN, approximate years of attendance. There is no fee.

Morehouse College, Registrar, 830 Westview Dr SW, Atlanta, GA 30314, 404-215-2641 (Fax: 404-215-2600). Hours: 9AM-5PM. Enrollment: 2800. Records go back to 1870. Alumni records are maintained here also. Call 404-215-2707. Degrees granted: Bachelors.

Attendance and degree information available by phone, fax, mail. Search requires name only. Also helpful: SSN, exact years of attendance. There is no fee.

Morehouse School of Medicine, Office of Admissions, 720 Westview Dr SW, Atlanta, GA 30310-1495, 404-752-1652 (Fax: 404-752-1512). Hours: 9AM-5PM. Enrollment: 157. Records go back to 1978. Alumni records are maintained here also. Call 404-752-1733. Degrees granted: Doctorate.

Attendance and degree information available by phone, fax, mail. Search requires name plus SSN, date of birth, exact years of attendance. Fee is $2.00.

Morris Brown College, Registrar, 643 Martin Luther King, Jr. Dr NW, Atlanta, GA 30314, 404-220-0145 (Fax: 404-659-4315). Hours: 9AM-5PM. Enrollment: 2000. Records go back to 1885. Alumni records are maintained here also. Call 404-220-0124. Degrees granted: Bachelors. Adverse incident record source- Student Affairs, 404-220-0300.

Attendance and degree information available by phone, fax, mail. Search requires name plus SSN, exact years of attendance. Also helpful: date of birth. There is no fee.

North Georgia College, Registrar, College Ave, Dahlonega, GA 30597, 706-864-1881. Hours: 7:30AM-4:30PM. Enrollment: 2898. Records go back to 1873. Degrees granted: Associate; Bachelors; Masters.

Attendance information available by phone, fax, mail. Search requires name plus SSN. Also helpful: exact years of attendance. There is no fee.

Degree information available by phone, fax, mail. Search requires name plus SSN. Also helpful: exact years of attendance. There is no fee.

Oglethorpe University, Registrar, 4484 Peachtree Rd NE, Atlanta, GA 30319-2797, 404-364-8315 (Fax: 404-364-8500). Hours: 8:30AM-5PM. Enrollment: 1100. Records go back to 1916. Alumni records are maintained here also. Call 404-364-8326. Degrees granted: Bachelors; Masters. Certification: Teacher Cert. Adverse incident record source- Dean Community Life, 404-364-8335.

Attendance and degree information available by phone, fax, mail. Search requires name plus SSN. Also helpful: approximate years of attendance. There is no fee.

Paine College, Registrar, 1235 15th St, Augusta, GA 30901-3182, 706-821-8311 (Fax: 706-821-8293). Hours: 9AM-5PM. Enrollment: 723. Records go back to 1920. Alumni records are maintained here also. Call 706-821-8247. Degrees granted: Bachelors. Adverse incident record source- Dean of Students, 706-821-8302.

Attendance and degree information available by phone, fax, mail. Search requires name plus SSN, exact years of attendance. There is no fee.

Piedmont College, Registrar, PO Box 10, Demorest, GA 30535, 706-778-3000 (Fax: 706-776-2811). Hours: 8AM-5PM. Enrollment: 900. Records go back to 1897. Alumni records are maintained here at the same phone number. Degrees granted: Bachelors; Masters.

Attendance and degree information available by phone, fax, mail. Search requires name plus SSN. Also helpful: exact years of attendance. There is no fee.

Reinhardt College, Registrar, 7300 Reinhardt College Parkway, Waleska, GA 30183, 770-720-5534 (Fax: 770-720-5602). Hours: 8:30AM-5PM. Enrollment: 1000. Records go back to 1960's. Alumni records are maintained here also. Call 770-720-5545. Degrees granted: Associate; Bachelors. Adverse incident record source- Registrar, 770-720-5534.

Attendance and degree information available by phone, fax, mail. Search requires name plus SSN, date of birth. Also helpful: exact years of attendance. There is no fee.

Savannah College of Art and Design, Registrar, 26 W Harris St, Savannah, GA 31401, 912-238-2400 (Fax: 912-238-2436). Hours: 9AM-6PM. Enrollment: 2800. Records go back to 1979. Records on computer from 1979. Alumni records are maintained here also. Call 912-238-2400. Degrees granted: Bachelors; M.F.A., M.A.

Attendance and degree information available by mail. Search requires name plus SSN, approximate years of attendance, signed release. Also helpful: date of birth, exact years of attendance. There is no fee.

Savannah State University, Registrar, PO Box 20479, Savannah, GA 31404, 912-356-2212 (Fax: 912-356-2296). Hours: 8AM-5PM. Enrollment: 2725. Records go back to 1931. Alumni records are maintained here also. Call 912-356-2427. Degrees granted: Bachelors; Masters. Special programs-Marine Biology. Adverse incident record source- 912-356-2194.

Attendance and degree information available by phone, fax, mail. Search requires name plus SSN, date of birth. Also helpful: exact years of attendance. There is no fee.

Savannah Technical Institute, Registrar, 5717 White Bluff Rd, Savannah, GA 31405-5594, 912-351-6362 (Fax: 912-352-4362). Hours: 8AM-6PM M-Th, 8AM-4PM F. Enrollment: 1350. Records go back to 1960. Alumni records are maintained here also. Call 912-351-4450. Degrees granted: Associate. Adverse incident record source- Registrar, 912-351-6362.

Attendance information available by phone, fax, mail. Search requires name plus SSN, date of birth, approximate years of attendance. Also helpful: exact years of attendance. There is no fee.

Degree information available by fax, mail. Search requires name plus SSN, date of birth, approximate years of attendance. Also helpful: exact years of attendance. There is no fee.

Shorter College, Registrar, 315 Shorter Ave, Rome, GA 30165-4298, 770-291-2121 (Fax: 770-236-1515). Hours: 8AM-5PM. Enrollment: 1390. Records go back to 1911. Alumni records are maintained here also. Call 706-233-7242. Degrees granted: Bachelors; Masters. Special programs- School of Prof. Programs, Marietta, GA, 770-989-5671: Davis Center for Ministry Ed, Rome, GA, 770-233-7293. Adverse incident record source- Student Development, 770-233-7231.

Attendance and degree information available by phone, fax, mail. Search requires name only. Also helpful: SSN, date of birth, exact years of attendance. There is no fee.

South College, Registrar's Office, 709 Mall Blvd, Savannah, GA 31406, 912-651-8100 (Fax: 912-356-1409). Hours: 8:30AM-5PM. Enrollment: 730. Records go back to 1977. Degrees granted: Associate; BBA. Adverse incident record source-Dean of Students.

Attendance and degree information available by phone, fax, mail. Search requires name plus SSN, exact years of attendance. Also helpful: date of birth. There is no fee.

South Georgia College, Registrar, 100 W College Park Dr, Douglas, GA 31533-5098, 912-383-4200 (Fax: 912-383-4392). Hours: 8AM-5PM. Enrollment: 1100. Records go back to 1906. Alumni records are maintained here at the same phone number. Degrees granted: Associate. Adverse incident record source- Robert Bidwell, 912-383-4281.

Attendance and degree information available by phone, fax, mail. Search requires name only. Also helpful: SSN, date of birth, approximate years of attendance. There is no fee.

Southern Polytechnic State University, Registrar, 100 S Marietta Pkwy, Marietta, GA 30060-2896, 770-528-7267 (Fax: 770-528-7292). Hours: 9AM-7PM M-Th; 9AM-5PM F. Enrollment: 4000. Formerly Southern College of Technology Records go back to 1948. Alumni records are maintained here at the same phone number. Degrees granted: Associate; Bachelors; Masters. Special programs- Technical & Professional Communi-cations: Architecture, 770-528-5483. Adverse incident record source- Student Affairs, 770-528-7225.

Attendance and degree information available by phone, fax, mail. Search requires name only. Also helpful: SSN, approximate years of attendance. There is no fee.

Spelman College, Registrar, 350 Spelman Lane,SW, Atlanta, GA 30314-4399, 404-223-2127 (Fax: 404-223-1449). Hours: 9AM-5PM. Enrollment: 1900. Records go back to 1881. Alumni records are maintained here also. Call 404-223-1427. Degrees granted: Bachelors. Adverse incident record source-Student Affairs, 404-223-1469.

Attendance and degree information available by phone, fax, mail. Search requires name plus SSN, exact years of attendance. There is no fee.

Thomas College, Student Services, 1501 Millpond Rd, Thomasville, GA 31792, 912-226-1621 (Fax: 912-226-1653). Hours: 8AM-5PM. Enrollment: 800. Records go back to 1950. Alumni records are maintained here at the same phone number. Degrees granted: Associate; Bachelors.

Attendance and degree information available by phone, fax, mail. Search requires name plus SSN, approximate years of attendance. Also helpful: date of birth. There is no fee.

Toccoa Falls College, Registrar's Office, PO Box 800896, Toccoa Falls, GA 30598, 706-886-6831 X5330 (Fax: 706-886-6412). Hours: 8:30AM-5PM. Enrollment: 1000. Records go back to 1912. Alumni Records Office: PO Box 800809, Toccoa Falls, GA 30598, 706-886-6831 X5222 (Fax: 706-886-0262). Degrees granted: Associate; Bachelors; Masters. Adverse incident record source- Student Affairs.

Attendance and degree information available by phone, fax, mail. Search requires name only. Also helpful: SSN, date of birth, exact years of attendance. There is no fee.

Truett-McConnell College, Registrar, 100 Alumni Dr, Cleveland, GA 30528, 706-865-2134 (Fax: 706-865-5135). Hours: 8AM-4:30PM. Enrollment: 1530. Records go back to 1947. Alumni records are maintained here at the same phone number. Degrees granted: Associate.

Attendance and degree information available by phone, fax, mail. Search requires name only. Also helpful: SSN, date of birth, exact years of attendance. There is no fee.

University of Georgia, Registrar's Office, 105 Academic Bldg, Athens, GA 30602-6113, 706-542-4040 (Fax: 706-542-6578). Hours: 8AM-5PM. Enrollment: 29500. Records go back to 1785. Limited records available back to 1785. Alumni records are maintained here at the same phone number. Degrees granted: Associate; Bachelors; Masters; Doctorate; Specialist. Adverse incident record source- Student Judiciary, 706-542-1131.

Attendance and degree information available by phone, fax, mail. Search requires name plus SSN. Also helpful: date of birth, exact years of attendance. There is no fee.

Valdosta State University, Registrar, 1500 N Patterson St, Valdosta, GA 31698, 912-333-5727 (Fax: 912-333-5475). Hours: 8AM-5:30PM M-Th, 8AM-3PM F. Enrollment: 9600. Records go back to 1919. Alumni records are maintained here also. Call 912-333-5797. Degrees granted: Associate; Bachelors; Masters. Adverse incident record source- Student Affairs, 912-333-5941: University Police, 912-333-7816

Attendance and degree information available by phone, fax, mail. Search requires name plus SSN. Also helpful: date of birth, exact years of attendance. There is no fee. Expedited service available for $5.00.

Waycross College, Registrar, 2001 South Georgia Parkway, Waycross, GA 31503, 912-285-6133 (Fax: 912-287-4909). Hours: 8AM-9PM. Enrollment: 900. Records go back to 1976. Alumni records are maintained here also. Call 912-285-

6130. Degrees granted: Associate. Special programs- P.S.O. Program (Public School Option): "Hope" Program - State Grant providing Freshman Tuition. Adverse incident record source- Student Affairs, 912-285-6012.

Attendance and degree information available by phone, fax, mail. Search requires name plus SSN. Also helpful: approximate years of attendance. There is no fee.

Wesleyan College, Registrar, 4760 Forsyth Rd, Macon, GA 31297-4299, 912-477-1110 (Fax: 912-757-4030). Hours: 8:30AM-5PM. Enrollment: 450. Records go back to 1836. Alumni records are maintained here at the same phone number. Degrees granted: Bachelors. Adverse incident record source- Student Life, 912-477-1110.

Attendance and degree information available by phone, fax, mail. Search requires name plus SSN, approximate years of attendance. There is no fee.

West Georgia College, Registrar, Carrollton, GA 30118-0001, 770-836-6438 (Fax: 770-836-6638). Hours: 8AM-5PM. Enrollment: 7947. Records go back to 1933. Alumni records are maintained here also. Call 770-836-6582. Degrees granted: Associate; Bachelors; Masters.

Attendance and degree information available by phone, fax, mail. Search requires name plus SSN. Also helpful: date of birth, exact years of attendance. There is no fee.

Young Harris College, Registrar, PO Box 96, Young Harris, GA 30582, 706-379-3111 X5699 (Fax: 706-379-4306). Hours: 8:30AM-4:30PM. Enrollment: 524. Records go back to 1911. Alumni Records Office: Alumni Association, PO Box 145, Young Harris, GA 30582. Degrees granted: Associate. Adverse incident record source- Dean of Students.

Attendance and degree information available by phone, fax, mail. Search requires name plus SSN. Also helpful: date of birth, exact years of attendance. There is no fee.

Trade and Vocational Schools

Albany Technical Institute, 1021 Lowe Rd, Albany, GA 31708, 912-430-3500

Alliance Tractor Trailer Training Center, PO Box 1008, McDonough, GA 30253, 770-957-6401

Altamaha Technical Institute, 1777 W Cherry St, Jessup, GA 31545, 912-427-5800

Altamaha Technical Institute (Branch Campus), Cromatie St, Hazlehurst, GA 31539, 912-375-6740

Army Signal Center and School, Fort Gordon, GA 30905, 706-791-6208

Artistic Beauty College, 1820 Hwy 20 #200, Conyers, GA 30208, 770-922-7653

Asher School of Business, 100 Pinnacle Wy #110, Norcross, GA 30071, 770-368-0800

Atlanta Area Technical School, 1560 Stewart Ave SW, Atlanta, GA 30310, 404-756-3703

Atlanta Area Technical School (Branch Campus), 4191 Northside Dr NW, Atlanta, GA 30342, 404-842-3117

Atlanta Institute of Music, 6145-D Northbelt Pkwy, Norcross, GA 30071, 770-242-7717

Atlanta Job Corps Center, 239 W Lake Ave NW, Atlanta, GA 30314, 404-794-9512

Atlanta School of Massage, 2300 Peachford Rd #3200, Atlanta, GA 30338, 770-454-7167

Ben Hill-Irwin Technical Institute, 667 Perry House Rd, Fitzgerald, GA 31750, 912-468-7487

Ben Hill-Irwin Technical Institute (Douglas Campus), 210 W Jackson St, Douglas, GA 31533, 912-384-7520

Brown College of Court Reporting & Medical Transcription, 1100 Spring St NW #200, Atlanta, GA 30376, 770-867-1227

Business Travel Institute, 5555 Oakbrook Pkwy, Ste 645, Norcross, GA 30093, 770-662-3090

Carroll Technical Institute, 997 S Hwy 16, Carrollton, GA 30116, 770-836-6800

Cobb Beauty College, 3096 Cherokee St, Kennesaw, GA 30144, 770-424-6915

Coosa Valley Technical Institute, 785 Cedar Ave, Rome, GA 30161, 770-295-6927

Creative Circus (The), 1935 Cliff Valley Way, No 210, Atlanta, GA 30329, 404-633-1990

Dalfort Aircraft Tech (Branch Campus), 990 Toffie Terrace, Atlanta, GA 30320, 770-428-9056

Dalton Vocational School of Health Occupations, 1221 Elkwood Dr, Dalton, GA 30720, 770-278-8922

DeKalb Beauty College, 6254 Memorial Dr #M, Stone Mountain, GA 30083, 770-879-6673

Derma Clinic Academy, 5600 Roswell Rd #110, Atlanta, GA 30066, 404-250-9600

Draughons College, 1430 W Peachtree St #101, Atlanta, GA 30309, 404-892-0814

Executive Travel Institute, 5775 Peachtree Dunwoody Rd #300E, Atlanta, GA 30342, 404-303-2929

Flint River Technical Institute, 1533 Hwy 19 S, Thomaston, GA 30286, 706-647-9616

Georgia Institute of Cosmetology, 3341 Lexington Rd, Athens, GA 30605, 706-549-6400

Georgia Medical Institute, 40 Marietta St Flrs 5 & 13, Atlanta, GA 30303, 404-525-3272

Georgia Medical Institute (Branch Campus), 1895 Phoenix Blvd #310, Atlanta, GA 30349, 770-994-1900

Georgia Medical Institute (Branch Campus), 1395 S Marietta Pkwy, Bldg 500 Ste 202, Marietta, GA 30067, 770-428-6303

Griffin Technical Institute, 501 Varsity Rd, Griffin, GA 30223, 770-228-7366

Gwinnett College, 4230 Hwy 29 Ste 11, Liburn, GA 30247, 770-381-7200

Heart of Georgia Technical Institute, 560 Pinehill Rd, Dublin, GA 31021, 912-275-6590

Heart of Georgia Technical Institute (Branch Campus), 109 Airport Rd, Eastman, GA 31023, 912-374-6980

Interactive College of Technology, 200 Cleveland Rd #6, Athens, GA 30622, 706-548-9800

Interactive College of Technology, 5600 Roswell Rd NE, Atlanta, GA 30342, 404-250-9000

Interactive College of Technology (Branch Campus), 4814 Old National Hwy, College Park, GA 30337, 404-765-9777

Interactive College of Technology (Branch Campus), 2759 Delk Rd #101, Marietta, GA 30067, 770-951-2367

Interactive College of Technology (Branch Campus), 2171 Northlake Pkwy #100, Tucker, GA 30084, 770-939-6008

International School of Skin & Nailcare, 5600 Roswell Rd NE, Atlanta, GA 30342, 404-843-1005

Kerr Business College, PO Box 976, Lagrange, GA 30241, 706-884-1751

Kerr Business College (Branch Campus), PO Box 1986, Augusta, GA 30903, 770-738-5046

LaGrange Cosmetology School, 1008 Colquitt St, Lagrange, GA 30240, 706-884-5750

Lanier Technical Institute, 2990 Landrum Education Dr, Oakwood, GA 30566, 770-531-6304

Mable Bailey Fashion College, 3121 Cross Country Hill, Columbus, GA 31906, 706-563-0606

Macon Beauty School, 630-J North Ave, Macon, GA 31211, 912-746-3243

Macon Technical Institute, 3300 Macon Tech Dr, Macon, GA 31206, 912-757-3501

Macon Technical Institute (Branch Campus), 940 Forsyth St, Macon, GA 31206, 912-744-4812

Medix School (The) (Branch Campus), 2480 Windy Hill Rd, Marietta, GA 30067, 770-980-0002

Metropolitan College of Business, 4319 Covington Hwy #300, Decatur, GA 30032, 404-288-6241

Metropolitan School of Hair Design, 5244 Memorial Dr #E 1002, Stone Mountain, GA 30083, 404-294-5697

Middle Georgia Technical Institute, 1311 Corder Rd, Warner Robins, GA 31088, 912-929-6800

Middle Georgia Technical Institute (Branch Campus), Robbins Air Force Museum, Robins Air Force Base, GA 31098, 912-929-6849

Moultrie Area Technical Institute, 361 Industrial Dr, Moultrie, GA 31768, 912-891-7000

Moultrie Area Technical Institute (Branch Campus), 314 E 14th St, Tifton, GA 31794, 912-891-7000

National Business Institute (The), 243 W Ponce de Leon Ave, Decatur, GA 30030, 404-352-0800

National Center for Paralegal Training (The), 3414 Peachtree Rd NE, Ste 528, Atlanta, GA 30326, 404-266-1060

Navy Supply Corps School, 1425 Prince Ave, Athens, GA 30606, 706-354-7200

North Fulton Beauty College, 10930 Crabapple Rd #4A & 4B, Roswell, GA 30075, 770-552-9570

North Georgia Technical Institute, Hwy 197 N, Clarksville, GA 30523, 706-754-7700

North Metro Technical Institute, 5198 Ross Rd, Acworth, GA 30080, 770-975-4052

Occupational Education Center-Central, 3075 Alton Rd, Chamblee, GA 30341, 770-457-3393

Occupational Education Center-North, 1995 Womack Rd, Dunwoody, GA 30338, 770-394-0321

Occupational Education Center-South, 3303 Pantherville Rd, Decatur, GA 30034, 404-241-9400

Ogeechee Technical Institute, One Joe Kennedy Blvd, Statesboro, GA 30458, 912-681-5500

Okefenokee Technical Institute, 1701 Carswell Ave, Waycross, GA 31503, 912-283-2002

Pickens Technical Institute, 100 Pickens Tech Dr, Jasper, GA 30143, 706-692-3411

Portfolio Center, 125 Bennett St NW, Atlanta, GA 30309, 404-351-5055

Pro-Way Hair School, 8649 Tara Blvd, Jonesboro, GA 30263, 404-477-2651

Professional Career Development Institute, 3597 Parkway Ln #100, Norcross, GA 30092, 770-729-8400

Quality Plus Office Skills and Motivational Training Center, 1655 Peachtree St #450, Atlanta, GA 30309, 404-892-6669

Roffler Moler Hairstyling College, PO Box 518, Forest Park, GA 30050, 404-366-2838

Roffler Moler Hairstyling College (Branch Campus), 1311 Roswell Rd, Marietta, GA 30062, 770-565-3285

SamVerly College, 210 Edgewood Ave NE, Atlanta, GA 30303, 404-522-4370

South Georgia Technical Institute, 728 Sotherfield Rd, Americus, GA 31709, 912-931-2150

Southeastern School fo Aeronautics, Herbert Smart Airport, Macon, GA 31201, 912-745-0964

Southeastern Technical Institute, 3001 E First St, Vidalia, GA 30474, 912-537-0386

Swainsboro Technical Institute, 201 Kite Rd, Swainsboro, GA 30401, 346-237-6465

Thomas Technical Institute, Hwy 19 at Rte 19, Thomasville, GA 31799, 912-225-4096

Trident Training Facility, 1040 USS Georgia Ave, Kings Bay, GA 31547, 912-673-3472

Turner Job Corps Center, 2000 Schilling Ave, Albany, GA 31705, 912-431-1821

Valdosta Technical Institute, 4089 Val-Tech Rd, Valdosta, GA 31603, 912-333-2100

Walker Technical Institute, 265 Bicentennial Trl, Rock Spring, GA 30739, 404-706-3530

West Georgia Technical Institute, 303 Fort Dr, Lagrange, GA 30240, 706-883-8324

State Licensing & Business Registration Quick Finder Index

Architecture, Engineering & Surveying
Architect #14 .... ☎ 404-656-2281
Engineer #10 .... ☎ 404-656-3926
Geologist #43 (100) .... ☎ 404-656-2281
Landscape Architect #26 (100) .... ☎ 404-656-2281
Surveyor #10 .... ☎ 404-656-3926

Business - Court & Legal Services
Attorney #47 .... ☎ 404-656-3490
Notary Public #45 (140000) .... ☎ 404-656-2899
Registered Professional Reporter #1 .... ☎ 404-656-6422
Shorthand Court Reporter/Stenomask #1
(1100) .... ☎ 404-656-6422

Business - General Services
Auctioneer #12 .... ☎ 404-656-2282
Public Accountant #13 (1000) .... ☎ 404-656-2281
Public Accountant-CPA #13 (1000) .... ☎ 404-656-2281
Salvage Pool Operator #11 .... ☎ 404-656-2282
Salvage Yard Dealer #11 .... ☎ 404-656-2282

Construction & Manufacturing
Conditioned Air Contractor #8 .... ☎ 404-656-3939
Electrical Contractor #8 .... ☎ 404-656-3939
General Contractor #8 .... ☎ 404-656-3939
Low Voltage Contractor #8 .... ☎ 404-656-3939
Plumber Journeyman #8 .... ☎ 404-656-3939
Plumbing Contractor #8 .... ☎ 404-656-3939
Rebuilder #11 .... ☎ 404-656-2282
Utility Contractor #8 .... ☎ 404-656-3939

Education
School Administrator/Supervisor #6 (13300)
.... 404-657-9000
School Librarian #39 .... ☎ 404-656-2281
Teacher #6 (229200) 404-657-9000

Environmental & Agriculture
Forester #35 (100) .... ☎ 404-656-2281
Landfill Inspector/Operator #4 .... ☎ 404-362-2696
Pesticide Applicator #3 .... ☎ 404-656-4958
Pesticide Contractor/Employee #3 .... ☎ 404-656-4958
Veterinarian #38 .... ☎ 404-656-3912
Veterinary Technician #38 .... ☎ 404-656-3912
Waste Water Collection System
Operator #42 .... ☎ 404-656-3933
Waste Water Laboratory Analyst #42 .... ☎ 404-656-3933
Waste Water Treatment System Operator #42
.... ☎ 404-656-3933
Water Distribution System Operator #42 .... ☎ 404-656-3933
Water Supply System Operator #42 .... ☎ 404-656-3933

Financial - Real Estate, Insurance & Banking
Insurance Adjuster #7 404-656-2100
Insurance Agent #7 404-656-2100
Insurance Counselor #7 404-656-2100
Public Adjuster #7 404-656-2100
Real Estate Appraiser #46 (4000) 404-656-3916
Real Estate Broker #46 (12500) 404-656-3916
Real Estate Sales Agent #46 (35000) 404-656-3916
Securities Dealer #44 (1845) .... ☎ 404-656-2895
Securities Salesperson #44 (76113) .... ☎ 404-656-2895

Health & Beauty
Acupuncturist #40 .... ✉ 404-656-3913
Barber #16 .... ☎ 404-656-3909
Cardiac Technician #40 .... ✉ 404-656-3913
Chiropractor #17 .... ☎ 404-656-3912
Cosmetologist #18 (41000) .... ✉ 404-656-3907
Dental Hygienist #19 (300) .... ☎ 404-656-3925
Dentist #19 (150) .... ☎ 404-656-3925
Dietitian #22 (1125) .... ☎ 404-656-3921
Embalmer #24 .... ☎ 404-656-3933
Esthetician #18 .... ✉ 404-656-3907
Funeral Apprentice #24 .... ☎ 404-656-3933
Funeral Director #24 .... ☎ 404-656-3933
Funeral Establishment #24 .... ☎ 404-656-3933
Hearing Aid Dealer/Dispenser #25 .... ☎ 404-656-3912
Medical Doctor #40 .... ✉ 404-656-3913
Nail Care #18 .... ✉ 404-656-3907
Nuclear Pharmacist #30 .... ☎ 404-656-3912
Nurse #27 .... ☎ 404-656-3943
Nursing Home Administrator #28 .... ☎ 404-656-3933
Occupational Therapist #29 (1335) .... ☎ 404-656-3921
Occupational Therapy Assistant #29 .... ☎ 404-656-3921
Optician #20 .... ☎ 404-656-3912
Optometrist #21 .... ☎ 404-656-3912
Osteopathic Physician #40 .... ✉ 404-656-3913
Paramedic #40 .... ✉ 404-656-3913
Pharmacist #30 .... ☎ 404-656-3912
Physical Therapist #31 (2920) .... ☎ 404-656-3921
Physical Therapist Assistant #31 .... ☎ 404-656-3921
Physician's Assistant #40 .... ✉ 404-656-3913
Podiatrist #32 .... ☎ 404-656-3912
Practical Nurse #2 (27800) .... ☎ 404-656-3921
Speech Pathologist/Audiologist #37 .... ☎ 404-656-3933
Therapeutic Recreation Specialist #48 404-656-3921

Investigations & Security
Polygraph Examiner #33 404-656-2282
Private Detective #34 404-656-3921
Security Guard #34 404-656-3929

Social Services
Counselor #9 (1619) .... ☎ 404-656-3933
Family Therapist #9 (554) .... ☎ 404-656-3933
Marriage Counselor #9 (1748) .... ☎ 404-656-3933
Psychologist #23 .... ☎ 404-656-3933
Social Worker #9 (1074) .... ☎ 404-656-3933

Sports & Entertainment

Athletic Agent #41... ☎ 404-656-3933
Athletic Trainer #15....................................... ☎ 404-656-3933
Liquor Control #5 404-656-0606
Recreation Administrator #48 404-656-3921
Recreation Leader/Supervisor #48 404-656-3921
Recreation Specialist #48 404-656-3921

Transportation

Used Car Dealer #36...................................... ☎ 404-656-2282

State Licensing & Business Registration Agency Information

(1) Board of Court Reporting, Clerk of the Board, 244 Washington St SW, Suite 550, Atlanta, GA 30334, 404-656-6422, Fax: 404-651-6449

(2) Board of Examiners of Licensed Practical Nurses, 166 Pryor St, SW, Atlanta, GA 30303, 404-656-3921

(3) Department of Agriculture, Pesticide Division, Capitol Sq, Room 550, Atlanta, GA 30334, 404-656-4958, Fax: 404-657-8378

(4) Department of Natural Resources, Environmental Protection Division, 4244 International Pkwy, Suite 104, Atlanta, GA 30354, 404-362-2537, Fax: 404-362-2693

(5) Department of Revenue, Centralized Tax Payer Registration, 270 Washington St, Room 310, Atlanta, GA 30374-0390, 404-656-4060, Fax: 404-651-6705

(6) Education Department, Teacher Certification, 1452 Twin Towers E, Atlanta, GA 30334, 404-657-9000

(7) Insurance Commissioner's Office, Licensing Division, Two Martin Luther King, Jr Dr, West Tower, 7th Fl, Atlanta, GA 30334, 404-656-2100

(8) Licensing Boards, 166 Pryor St, SW, Atlanta, GA 30303, 404-656-3939

(9) Licensing Boards, 166 Pryor St, SW, Atlanta, GA 30303, 404-656-3933, Fax: 404-656-3989

(10) Licensing Boards, 166 Pryor St, SW, Atlanta, GA 30303, 404-656-3926, Fax: 404-657-4220

(11) Licensing Boards, 166 Pryor St, SW, Atlanta, GA 30303, 404-656-2282

(12) Licensing Boards, Auctioneers Commission, 166 Pryor St, SW, Atlanta, GA 30303, 404-656-2282, Fax: 404-657-4220/651-9532

(13) Licensing Boards, Board of Accountancy, 166 Pryor St, SW, Atlanta, GA 30303, 404-656-2281, Fax: 404-651-9532

(14) Licensing Boards, Board of Architects, 166 Pryor St, SW, Atlanta, GA 30303, 404-656-2281

(15) Licensing Boards, Board of Athletic Trainers, 166 Pryor St, SW, Atlanta, GA 30303, 404-656-3933

(16) Licensing Boards, Board of Barbers & Cosmetology, 166 Pryor St, SW, Atlanta, GA 30303, 404-656-3909, Fax: 404-651-9532

(17) Licensing Boards, Board of Chiropractic Examiners, 166 Pryor St, SW, Atlanta, GA 30303, 404-656-3912, Fax: 404-657-4220

(18) Licensing Boards, Board of Cosmetology, 166 Pryor St, SW, Atlanta, GA 30303, 404-656-3909, Fax: 404-651-9532

(19) Licensing Boards, Board of Dentistry, 166 Pryor St, SW, Atlanta, GA 30303, 404-656-3925

(20) Licensing Boards, Board of Dispensing Opticians, 166 Pryor St, SW, Atlanta, GA 30303, 404-656-3912

(21) Licensing Boards, Board of Examiners in Optometry, 166 Pryor St, SW, Atlanta, GA 30303, 404-656-3912

(22) Licensing Boards, Board of Examiners of Licensed Dietitians, 166 Pryor St, SW, Atlanta, GA 30303, 404-656-3921

(23) Licensing Boards, Board of Examiners of Psychologists, 166 Pryor St, SW, Atlanta, GA 30303, 404-656-3933, Fax: 404-656-3989

(24) Licensing Boards, Board of Funeral Service, 166 Pryor St, SW, Atlanta, GA 30303, 404-656-3933, Fax: 404-656-3989

(25) Licensing Boards, Board of Hearing Aid Dealers & Dispensers, 166 Pryor St, SW, Atlanta, GA 30303, 404-656-3912, Fax: 404-657-4220

(26) Licensing Boards, Board of Landscape Architects, 166 Pryor St, SW, Atlanta, GA 30303, 404-656-2281, Fax: 404-651-9532

(27) Licensing Boards, Board of Nursing, Corner of Mitchell & Pryor, 166 Pryor St SW, Atlanta, GA 30303, 404-656-3943, Fax: 404-657-7489

(28) Licensing Boards, Board of Nursing Home Administrators, 166 Pryor St, SW, Atlanta, GA 30303, 404-656-3933, Fax: 404-656-3989

(29) Licensing Boards, Board of Occupational Therapy, 166 Pryor St, SW, Atlanta, GA 30303, 404-656-3921

(30) Licensing Boards, Board of Pharmacy, 166 Pryor St, SW, Atlanta, GA 30303, 404-656-3912

(31) Licensing Boards, Board of Physical Therapy, 166 Pryor St, SW, Atlanta, GA 30303, 404-656-3921

(32) Licensing Boards, Board of Podiatry Examiners, 166 Pryor St, SW, Atlanta, GA 30303, 404-656-3912, Fax: 404-656-4220

(33) Licensing Boards, Board of Polygraph Examiners, 166 Pryor St, SW, Atlanta, GA 30303, 404-656-2282

(34) Licensing Boards, Board of Private Detectives & Security Agencies, 166 Pryor St, SW, Atlanta, GA 30303, 404-656-3929

(35) Licensing Boards, Board of Registration for Foresters, 166 Pryor St, SW, Atlanta, GA 30303, 404-656-2281, Fax: 404-651-9532

(36) Licensing Boards, Board of Registration of Used Car Dealers, 166 Pryor St, SW, Atlanta, GA 30303, 404-656-2282, Fax: 404-657-4220/651-9532

(37) Licensing Boards, Board of Speech Pathology & Audiology, 166 Pryor St, SW, Atlanta, GA 30303, 404-656-3933

(38) Licensing Boards, Board of Veterinary Medicine, 166 Pryor St, SW, Atlanta, GA 30303, 404-656-3912, Fax: 404-657-4220

(39) Licensing Boards, Board of the Certification of Librarians, 166 Pryor St, SW, Atlanta, GA 30303, 404-656-2281

(40) Licensing Boards, Composite State Board of Medical Examiners, 166 Pryor St, SW, Atlanta, GA 30303, 404-656-3913, Fax: 404-656-9723

(41) Licensing Boards, Georgia Athletic Agent Commission, 166 Pryor St, SW, Atlanta, GA 30303, 404-656-3933, Fax: 404-656-3989

(42) Licensing Boards, Laboratory Analyst, 166 Pryor St, SW, Atlanta, GA 30303, 404-656-3933, Fax: 404-656-3989

(43) Licensing Boards, Registration for Professional Geologists, 166 Pryor St, SW, Atlanta, GA 30303, 404-656-2281, Fax: 404-651-9532

(44) Office of Secretary of State, Business Services & Regulation, 2 Martin Luther King, Jr Dr, West Tower, Suite 315, Atlanta, GA 30334-1530, 404-656-2895

(45) Office of Secretary of State, Notary Public Division, 2 Martin Luther King Dr, W Tower, Suite 820, Atlanta, GA 30334, 404-656-2899, Fax: 404-651-9530

(46) Real Estate Commission/Appraisor Board, 148 International Blvd NE, Suite 500, Atlanta, GA 30303, 404-656-3916

(47) State Bar of Georgia, 800 The Hurt Bldg, 50 Hurt Plaza, Atlanta, GA 30303, 404-656-3490, Fax: 404-527-8700/8717

(48) State Board of Recreational Examiners, Allied Health Fields, Professional Examining Board, 166 Pryor St SW, Atlanta, GA 30303, 404-656-3921

Hawaii

Capitol: Honolulu (Honolulu County)	
State Population	1.2 Million
Number of Degree Granting Institutions:	19
Number of State Licensing & Business Registration Agencies:	79

Degree Granting Educational Institutions

Brigham Young University, (Hawaii), Registrar, Snow Administration Bldg, 55-220 Kulanui St, Laie, HI 96762, 808-293-3736 (Fax: 808-293-3745). Hours: 8AM-5PM. Enrollment: 2000. Records go back to 1955. Alumni records are maintained here also. Call 808-293-3648. Degrees granted: Associate; Bachelors; Professional Diploma.

Attendance information available by phone, fax, mail. Search requires name plus SSN. Also helpful: date of birth, exact years of attendance. There is no fee.

Degree information available by phone, fax, mail. Search requires name only. Also helpful: SSN, exact years of attendance. There is no fee.

Chaminade University of Honolulu, Registrar, 3140 Waialae Ave, Honolulu, HI 96816-1578, 808-735-4773 (Fax: 808-735-4777). Hours: 8AM-4PM. Enrollment: 1280. Records go back to 1956. Alumni Records Office: CUH-Alumni Association, 2636 Pamao Rd, Honolulu, HI 96822. Degrees granted: Associate; Bachelors; Masters.

Attendance and degree information available by phone, fax, mail. Search requires name plus SSN. Also helpful: exact years of attendance. There is no fee.

Denver Business College, (Branch), Registrar, 419 South St #174, Honolulu, HI 96813, 808-942-1000 (Fax: 808-533-3064). Hours: 8AM-5PM. Records go back to 1910. Alumni records are maintained here at the same phone number. Degrees granted: Associate.

Attendance information available by phone, fax, mail. Search requires name plus SSN, approximate years of attendance. Also helpful: date of birth, exact years of attendance. Fee is $5.00.

Degree information available by fax, mail. Search requires name plus SSN, approximate years of attendance. Also helpful: date of birth, exact years of attendance. Fee is $5.00.

Hawaii Community College, Registrar, 200 W Kauili, Hilo, HI 96720-4091, 808-933-3662 (Fax: 808-933-3692). Hours: 8AM-4:30PM. Enrollment: 2700. Records go back to 1992. Degrees granted: Associate.

Attendance and degree information available by phone, fax, mail. Search requires name plus SSN, date of birth. Also helpful: exact years of attendance. There is no fee.

Hawaii Loa College, Registrar, 45-045 Kamehameha Hwy, Kaneohe, HI 96744, 808-233-3100 (Fax: 808-544-1168).

Enrollment: 8000. Records go back to 1965. Alumni records are maintained here at the same phone number. Degrees granted: Associate; Bachelors; Masters. Special programs- Liberal Arts. Adverse incident record source- Department of Student Services.

Attendance and degree information available by phone, mail. Search requires name plus SSN, exact years of attendance. There is no fee.

Hawaii Pacific University, Registrar's Office, 1164 Bishop St #200, Honolulu, HI 96813, 808-544-0239 (Fax: 808-544-1136). Hours: 8AM-5PM. Enrollment: 8036. Records go back to 1965. Alumni Records Office: 1154 Fort St Mall #216, Honolulu, HI 96813. Degrees granted: Associate; Bachelors; Masters. Certification: T.E.S.L.Q.M. Special programs- Travel Industry Management, 808-544-0229. Adverse incident record source- Barbara Bonson, 808-544-9358.

Attendance information available by phone, fax, mail. Search requires name plus approximate years of attendance. Also helpful: SSN. There is no fee.

Degree information available by phone, fax, mail. Search requires name only. Also helpful: SSN. There is no fee.

Honolulu Community College, Registrar, 874 Dillingham Blvd, Honolulu, HI 96817, 808-845-9120 (Fax: 808-845-9173). Hours: 7:45AM-4:30PM. Enrollment: 4740. Records go back to 1966. Alumni records are maintained here also. Call 808-956-7547. Degrees granted: Associate. Adverse incident record source- Dean of Student Services, 808-845-9236.

Attendance information available by phone, mail. Search requires name only. Also helpful: SSN, date of birth, exact years of attendance. There is no fee.

Degree information available by phone, mail. Search requires name only. Also helpful: SSN. There is no fee.

Kansai Gaidai Hawaii College, Registrar, 5257 Kalanianaole Hwy, Honolulu, HI 96821, 808-377-5402 (Fax: 808-373-4754). Hours: 8AM-5PM. Enrollment: 200. Records go back to 1980. Alumni records are maintained here at the same phone number. Degrees granted: Associate.

Attendance and degree information available by phone, mail. Search requires name plus exact years of attendance. There is no fee.

Kapiolani Community College, Registrar, 4303 Diamond Head Rd, Honolulu, HI 96816, 808-734-9532. Hours: 8AM-4:30PM. Enrollment: 6500. Records go back to 1960.

Degrees granted: Associate. Special programs- Liberal Arts: Health Education: Legal Education: Business Education: Food Service & Hotel Operations.

Attendance and degree information available by phone, mail. Search requires name plus SSN. Also helpful: date of birth, exact years of attendance. There is no fee.

Kauai Community College, Registrar, 3-1901 Kaumualii Hwy, Lihue, HI 96766, 808-245-8226 (Fax: 808-246-6377). Hours: 8AM-4:30PM. Enrollment: 1452. Records go back to 1952. Alumni records are maintained here also. Call 808-245-8271. Degrees granted: Associate.

Attendance and degree information available by phone, mail. Search requires name plus SSN. Also helpful: date of birth, exact years of attendance. There is no fee.

Leeward Community College, Registrar, 96-045 Ala Ike, Pearl City, HI 96782, 808-455-0219 (Fax: 808-455-0471). Hours: 7:45AM-4:30PM. Enrollment: 6400. Records go back to 1968. Degrees granted: Associate.

Attendance and degree information available by phone, fax, mail. Search requires name plus SSN, exact years of attendance. Also helpful: date of birth. There is no fee.

Maui Community College, Registrar, 310 Kaahumanu Ave, Kahului, HI 96732, 808-242-1267 (Fax: 808-244-0268). Hours: 9AM-4:30PM. Enrollment: 1915. Records go back to 1931. Degrees granted: Associate.

Attendance and degree information available by fax, mail. Search requires name plus SSN. There is no fee.

Tai Hsuan Foundation College of Acupuncture and Herbal Medicine, Registrar, 2600 S King St #206, Honolulu, HI 96826, 808-947-4788 (Fax: 808-947-1152). Hours: 9AM-5PM. Enrollment: 35. Records go back to 1970. Degrees granted: Masters; Doctorate. Special programs- Acupuncture and Oriental Medicine.

Attendance and degree information available by phone, fax. Search requires name only. Also helpful: SSN, date of birth, exact years of attendance. There is no fee.

University of Hawaii at Hilo, Records Office, 200 W Kawili St, Hilo, HI 96720-4091, 808-933-3385 (Fax: 808-933-3691). Hours: 8AM-4:30PM. Enrollment: 2736. Records go back to 1941. Alumni records are maintained here also. Call 808-933-3567. Degrees granted: Bachelors.

Attendance and degree information available by phone, mail. Search requires name plus SSN. Also helpful: date of birth, exact years of attendance. There is no fee.

University of Hawaii at Manoa, Registrar, 2600 Campus Rd Rm 101, Honolulu, HI 96822, 808-956-8010. Hours: 8AM-4:30PM. Enrollment: 19500. Records go back to 1907. Alumni records are maintained here also. Call 808-956-7547. Degrees granted: Bachelors; Masters; Doctorate.

Attendance and degree information available by phone, mail. Search requires name plus SSN, date of birth, exact years of attendance. There is no fee.

University of Hawaii at West Oahu, Student Services Office, 96-043 Ala Ike, Pearl City, HI 96782, 808-453-6179 (Fax: 808-456-5009). Hours: 8AM-6PM. Enrollment: 700. Records go back to 1976. Alumni records are maintained here at the same phone number. Degrees granted: Bachelors.

Attendance and degree information available by mail. Search requires name plus SSN. Also helpful: exact years of attendance. There is no fee.

University of Hawaii, Maui Community College, Registrar, 310 Kaahumanu Ave, Kahului, HI 96732, 808-242-1267 (Fax: 808-242-9618). Enrollment: 2700. Formerly Maui Community College Records go back to 1931. Alumni records are maintained here also. Call 808-242-4522. Degrees granted: Associate. Special programs- Science: Liberal Arts. Adverse incident record source- Security.

Attendance and degree information available by phone, mail. Search requires name plus SSN, date of birth, exact years of attendance. There is no fee.

University of Phoenix, (Hawaii Main), Registrar, 1601 Kapiolani Blvd #1250, Honolulu, HI 96814-4725, 808-949-0573 (Fax: 808-949-1064). Enrollment: 600. Records go back to 1993. Transcript records are housed at University of Phoenix, Registrar, PO Box 52069, Phoenix, AZ 85072. Alumni records are maintained here at the same phone number. Degrees granted: Bachelors; Masters. Special programs- Nursing: Business: Organization in Management.

Attendance and degree information available by written request only. Search requires name plus SSN, approximate years of attendance. There is no fee.

Windward Community College, Registrar, 45-720 Keaahala Rd, Kaneohe, HI 96744, 808-235-7432. Hours: 8:30AM-4:30PM. Records go back to 1972. Degrees granted: Associate.

Attendance and degree information available by phone, mail. Search requires name plus SSN, exact years of attendance. There is no fee.

Trade and Vocational Schools

Electronic Institute, 1270 Queen Emma St #107, Honolulu, HI 96813, 808-521-5290

Hawaii Business College, 33 N King St. Fourth, Honolulu, HI 96813, 808-524-4014

Hawaii Institute of Hair Design, 71 S Hotel St, Honolulu, HI 96813, 808-533-6596

Med-Assist School of Hawaii, 1149 Bethel St #605, Honolulu, HI 96813, 808-524-3363

New York Technical Institute of Hawaii, 1375 Dillingham Blvd, Honolulu, HI 96817, 808-841-5827

Travel Institute of the Pacific, 1314 S King St #1164, Honolulu, HI 96814, 808-591-2708

Travel University International (Branch Campus), 1441 Kapiolani Blvd #1414, Honolulu, HI 96814, 808-946-3535

State Licensing & Business Registration Quick Finder Index

Architecture, Engineering & Surveying
Architect #23 (2161)..................................☎ 808-586-2702
Engineer #23 (5012)..................................☎ 808-586-2702
Landscape Architect #23 ....☎ 808-586-2702
Surveyor #23 (244)...................................☎ 808-586-2702

Business - Court & Legal Services
Attorney #40 ....☎ 808-537-1868
Lobbyist #43 (250)...................................☎ 808-587-0460
Notary Public #3 (10000).........................☎ 808-586-1216
Shorthand Reporter #1 (200).....................☎ 808-539-4226

Business - General Services
Public Accountant-CPA #25 (3300) ....☎ 808-586-2694
Public Broadcasting #26...........................808-586-2620

Construction & Manufacturing
Contractor #30 ....☎ 808-586-2700
Electrician #11 (2991) ....☎ 808-586-3000
Elevator Mechanic #32.............................☎ 808-586-2699
General Contractor #35 ....☎ 808-586-2711
Plumber #11 (1122)..................................☎ 808-586-3000

Education
Educational Administrator #37...................☎ 808-586-3264
School Bus Driver #41 ....☎ 808-532-2503
Teacher #37 ....☎ 808-586-3392

Environmental & Agriculture
Commercial Pesticide Applicator #2.............☎ 808-973-9401
Fumigation Operator #34 ....☎ 808-586-2694
Pest Control Field Representative #34 ....☎ 808-586-2694
Pest Control Operator #34 ....☎ 808-586-2694
Pesticide Dealer #2 (60) ....☎ 808-973-9401
Pesticide Product #2 ....☎ 808-973-9418
Private Applicator (Pesticides) #2.................☎ 808-973-9401
Veterinarian #28 (370) ....☎ 808-586-2701

Financial - Real Estate, Insurance & Banking
Condominium Hotel Operator #36.................☎ 808-548-4100
Condominium Managing Agent #36.............☎ 808-548-4100
Credit Union #31 ....☎ 808-586-2730
Insurance Agent #33.................................☎ 808-586-2790
Investment Advisor/Representative #4 ....☎ 808-586-2730
Real Estate Agent #36 ....☎ 808-586-2643
Securities Salesperson #4 ....☎ 808-586-2730

Health & Beauty
Acupuncturist #5 (339)..............................☎ 808-586-2704
Barber #6 (771)...✉ 808-586-2699
Barber Shop #6 ....✉ 808-586-2699
Chiropractor #7 (454) ....☎ 808-586-3000
Clinical Laboratory Cryotechnologist #42.....☎ 808-453-6777

Clinical Laboratory Technician #42 ....☎ 808-453-6654
Clinical Laboratory Technologist
   /Specialist #42 ....☎ 808-453-6654
Cosmetologist #8 ....☎ 808-586-2699
Dental Hygienist #9 ....☎ 808-586-2702
Dentist #9 (1567) ....☎ 808-586-2702
Dispensing Optician #10............................☎ 808-586-3000
Embalmer #42 ....☎ 808-586-4540
Hearing Aid Dealer/Fitter #15 (47) ....☎ 808-586-2693
Massage Establishment #16........................✉ 808-586-2696
Massage Therapist #16 (2381).....................✉ 808-586-2696
Medical Doctor #17 808-586-2708
Naturopathic Physician #12........................☎ 808-586-2698
Nurse #18 ....☎ 808-586-2695
Nursing Home Administrator #14 ....☎ 808-586-2695
Optician #10 (152)....................................☎ 808-586-3000
Optometrist #13 (440)................................☎ 808-586-2694
Osteopathic Physician #19..........................☎ 808-586-2708
Out-of-state Pharmacy #20 ....☎ 808-586-3000
Pharmacist #20 (1253)...............................☎ 808-586-3000
Pharmacy #20...☎ 808-586-3000
Physical Therapist #21 (759) ....☎ 808-586-3000
Physician, Boxing #29 ....☎ 808-586-2701
Speech Pathologist/Audiologist #27.............☎ 808-586-3000
Wholesale Prescription, Drug Distributor #20
   ....☎ 808-586-3000

Investigations & Security
Detective Agency #22................................☎ 808-586-2701
Guard Agency #22.....................................☎ 808-586-2701
Private Detective #22 (102)..........................☎ 808-586-2701
Security Guard #22 (67) ....☎ 808-586-2701

Social Services
Psychologist #24 (432) ....✉ 808-586-2704

Sports & Entertainment
Boxer #29 (40)..☎ 808-586-2701
Boxing Judge #29 ....☎ 808-586-2701
Boxing Manager #29 ....☎ 808-586-2701
Boxing Matchmakers #29............................☎ 808-586-2701
Boxing Promoter #29.................................☎ 808-586-2701
Boxing Referee #29 ....☎ 808-586-2701
Boxing Second #29 ....☎ 808-586-2701
Boxing Timekeeper #29..............................☎ 808-586-2701

Transportation
Aircraft Related #39...................................☎ 808-837-8300
Bus Driver #41 ....☎ 808-532-2503
Commercial Marine License #38...................☎ 808-587-0100
Taxi Driver #41 ....☎ 808-532-2503

State Licensing & Business Registration Agency Information

(1) Board of Certified Shorthand Reporters, PO Box 619, Honolulu, HI 96809, 808-539-4226, Fax: 808-539-4322

(2) Department of Agriculture, PO Box 22159, Honolulu, HI 96823-2159, 808-973-9401, Fax: 808-973-9410

(3) Department of Attorney General, 425 Queen St, Honolulu, HI 96813, 808-586-1500

(4) Department of Commerce & Consumer Affairs, PO Box 40, 1010 Richards St, Honolulu, HI 96810, 808-586-2820, Fax: 808-586-2733

(5) Department of Commerce & Consumer Affairs, Board of Acupuncture, 1010 Richards St (96813), PO Box 3469, Honolulu, HI 96801, 808-586-2704

(6) Department of Commerce & Consumer Affairs, Board of Barbers, 1010 Richards St (96813), PO Box 3469, Honolulu, HI 96801, 808-586-2699

(7) Department of Commerce & Consumer Affairs, Board of Chiropractic Examiners, 1010 Richards St (96813), PO Box 3469, Honolulu, HI 96801, 808-586-3000

(8) Department of Commerce & Consumer Affairs, Board of Cosmetology, 1010 Richards St (96813), PO Box 3469, Honolulu, HI 96801, 808-586-3000

(9) Department of Commerce & Consumer Affairs, Board of Dental Examiners, 1010 Richards St (96813), PO Box 3469, Honolulu, HI 96801, 808-586-2702

(10) Department of Commerce & Consumer Affairs, Board of Dispensing Opticians, 1010 Richards St (96813), PO Box 3469, Honolulu, HI 96801, 808-586-3000

(11) Department of Commerce & Consumer Affairs, Board of Electricians & Plumbers, 1010 Richards St (96813), PO Box 3469, Honolulu, HI 96801, 808-586-2696

(12) Department of Commerce & Consumer Affairs, Board of Examiners in Naturopathy, 1010 Richards St (96813), PO Box 3469, Honolulu, HI 96801, 808-586-3000

(13) Department of Commerce & Consumer Affairs, Board of Examiners in Optometry, 1010 Richards St (96813), PO Box 3469, Honolulu, HI 96801, 808-586-2694

(14) Department of Commerce & Consumer Affairs, Board of Examiners of Nursing Home Administrators, 1010 Richards St (96813), PO Box 3469, Honolulu, HI 96801, 808-586-2695

(15) Department of Commerce & Consumer Affairs, Board of Hearing Aid Dealers & Fitters, 1010 Richards St (96813), PO Box 3469, Honolulu, HI 96801, 808-586-2693

(16) Department of Commerce & Consumer Affairs, Board of Massage, 1010 Richards St (96813), PO Box 3469, Honolulu, HI 96801, 808-586-2696

(17) Department of Commerce & Consumer Affairs, Board of Medical Examiners, 1010 Richards St (96813), PO Box 3469, Honolulu, HI 96801, 808-586-2708

(18) Department of Commerce & Consumer Affairs, Board of Nursing, 1010 Richards St (96813), PO Box 3469, Honolulu, HI 96801, 808-586-3000

(19) Department of Commerce & Consumer Affairs, Board of Osteopathic Examiners, 1010 Richards St (96813), PO Box 3469, Honolulu, HI 96801, 808-586-3000

(20) Department of Commerce & Consumer Affairs, Board of Pharmacy, 1010 Richards St (96813), PO Box 3469, Honolulu, HI 96801, 808-586-3000

(21) Department of Commerce & Consumer Affairs, Board of Physical Therapy, 1010 Richards St (96813), PO Box 3469, Honolulu, HI 96801, 808-586-3000

(22) Department of Commerce & Consumer Affairs, Board of Private Detectives & Guards, 1010 Richards St (96813), PO Box 3469, Honolulu, HI 96801, 808-586-2701, Fax: 808-586-2589

(23) Department of Commerce & Consumer Affairs, Board of Prof. Engineers, Architects & Surveyors, 1010 Richards St (96813), PO Box 3469, Honolulu, HI 96801, 808-586-2702

(24) Department of Commerce & Consumer Affairs, Board of Psychology, 1010 Richards St (96813), PO Box 3469, Honolulu, HI 96801, 808-586-2702

(25) Department of Commerce & Consumer Affairs, Board of Public Accountancy, 1010 Richards St (96813), PO Box 3469, Honolulu, HI 96801, 808-586-2694

(26) Department of Commerce & Consumer Affairs, Board of Public Broadcasting, 1010 Richards St (96813), PO Box 3469, Honolulu, HI 96801, 808-586-2620

(27) Department of Commerce & Consumer Affairs, Board of Speech Pathology & Audiology, 1010 Richards St (96813), PO Box 3469, Honolulu, HI 96801, 808-586-3000

(28) Department of Commerce & Consumer Affairs, Board of Veterinary Examiners, 1010 Richards St (96813), PO Box 3469, Honolulu, HI 96801, 808-586-2701

(29) Department of Commerce & Consumer Affairs, Boxing Commission, 1010 Richards St (96813), PO Box 3469, Honolulu, HI 96801, 808-586-2701, Fax: 808-586-2689

(30) Department of Commerce & Consumer Affairs, Contractors License Board, 1010 Richards St (96813), PO Box 3469, Honolulu, HI 96801, 808-586-3000

(31) Department of Commerce & Consumer Affairs, Credit Union Review Board, PO Box 40, (1010 Richards St, 96813), Honolulu, HI 96810, 808-586-2820, Fax: 808-586-2733

(32) Department of Commerce & Consumer Affairs, Elevator Mechanics Licensing Board, 1010 Richards St (96813), PO Box 3469, Honolulu, HI 96801, 808-586-2699

(33) Department of Commerce & Consumer Affairs, Insurance Division, Licensing Branch, PO Box 3469, (1010 Richards St, 96813), Honolulu, HI 96811, 808-586-2790, Fax: 808-586-2876

(34) Department of Commerce & Consumer Affairs, Pest Control Board, PO Box 3469, Honolulu, HI 96801, 808-586-3000

(35) Department of Commerce & Consumer Affairs, Professional & Vocational Licensing Division, 1010 Richards St (96813), PO Box 3469, Honolulu, HI 96801, 808-586-3000

(36) Department of Commerce & Consumer Affairs, Real Estate Commission, 250 S King St, Rm 702, Honolulu, HI 96813, 808-586-2643

(37) Department of Education, Board of Education, PO Box 2360, Honolulu, HI 96804, 808-586-3000, Fax: 808-586-3433

(38) Department of Land & Natural Resources, Division of Aquatic Resources, 1151 Punch Bowl St, Rm 330, Honolulu, HI 96813, 808-587-0100

(39) Department of Transportation, Airports Division, Certification, Gate 29, Honolulu International Airport, Honolulu, HI 96819, 808-586-3000

(40) Hawaii Bar Association, 1136 Union Mall, Penthouse 1, Honolulu, HI 96813, 808-586-3000, Fax: 808-521-7936

(41) Motor Vehicle Licensing Division, CDO, Sec 30360, 1370 Maunahia St, Honolulu, HI 96820-0360, 808-536-2694

(42) State Department of Health, Laboratory Licensing, 2725 Ramano St, Pearl City, HI 96782, 808-453-6654

(43) State Ethics Commission, Bishop Sq, Pacific Tower 970, 1001 Bishop St, Honolulu, HI 96813, 808-587-0460, Fax: 808-587-0470

Idaho

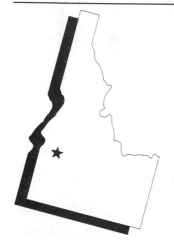

Capitol: Boise (Ada County)	
State Population	1.2 Million
Number of Degree Granting Institutions:	12
Number of State Licensing & Business Registration Agencies:	200

Degree Granting Educational Institutions

Albertson College, Registrar, 2112 Cleveland Blvd, Caldwell, ID 83605, 208-459-5201 (Fax: 208-459-5826). Hours: 9AM-4PM. Enrollment: 650. Records go back to 1891. Alumni records are maintained here also. Call 208-459-5300. Degrees granted: Bachelors. Adverse incident record source- Student Affairs, 208-459-5508.

Attendance and degree information available by phone, fax, mail. Search requires name plus date of birth. Also helpful: SSN. There is no fee.

Boise Bible College, Registrar, 8695 Marigold St, Boise, ID 83714, 208-376-7731 (Fax: 208-376-7743). Hours: 8:30AM-4:30PM. Enrollment: 140. Alumni records are maintained here at the same phone number. Degrees granted: Associate; Bachelors. Certification: 1yr bible.

School will not confirm attendance or degree information.

Boise State University, Registrars Office, 1910 University Dr, Boise, ID 83725, 208-385-3486 (Fax: 208-385-3169). Hours: 8AM-5PM. Enrollment: 15000. Records go back to 1930. Alumni records are maintained here also. Call 208-385-1959. Degrees granted: Associate; Bachelors; Masters; Doctorate.

Attendance and degree information available by phone, fax, mail. Search requires name only. Also helpful: SSN, date of birth, approximate years of attendance. There is no fee.

College of Southern Idaho, Registrar, 315 Falls Ave, PO Box 1238, Twin Falls, ID 83303-1238, 208-733-9554 (Fax: 208-736-3014). Hours: 8AM-7PM M-Th; 8AM-4:30PM F. Enrollment: 4092. Records go back to 1965. Degrees granted: Associate.

Attendance and degree information available by fax, mail. Search requires name plus SSN, signed release. Also helpful: date of birth, exact years of attendance. There is no fee.

Eastern Idaho Technical College, Registrar, 1600 S 2500 E, Idaho Falls, ID 83404, 208-524-3000 (Fax: 208-524-3007). Hours: 8AM-5PM. Enrollment: 412. Records go back to 1971. Degrees granted: Associate.

Attendance and degree information available by phone, fax, mail. Search requires name plus SSN, approximate years of attendance. Also helpful: date of birth, exact years of attendance. There is no fee.

ITT Technical Institute, Registrar, 12302 W Explorer Dr, Boise, ID 83713-1529, 208-344-8376 (Fax: 208-345-0056). Hours: 8AM-5PM. Enrollment: 325. Records go back to 1968. Alumni Records Office: Alumni Association, ITT Technical Institute, 9511 Angola Ct, Indianapolis, IN 46268. Degrees granted: Associate.

Attendance and degree information available by phone, fax, mail. Search requires name plus SSN, exact years of attendance. There is no fee.

Idaho State University, Registration & Records, PO Box 8196, Pocatello, ID 83209, 208-236-2661 (Fax: 208-236-4231). Hours: 8AM-5PM. Enrollment: 11877. Records go back to 1901. Alumni records are maintained here at the same phone number. Alumni Records Office: PO Box 8033, Pocatello, ID 83209. Degrees granted: Associate; Bachelors; Masters; Doctorate. Adverse incident record source- Public Safety & Security, 208-236-2515.

Attendance and degree information available by phone, fax, mail. Search requires name only. Also helpful: SSN, date of birth, exact years of attendance. There is no fee.

Lewis-Clark State College, Registrar, 500 8th Ave, Lewiston, ID 83501, 208-799-2223 (Fax: 208-799-2429). Hours: 8AM-5PM. Enrollment: 3500. Records go back to 1893. Alumni records are maintained here also. Call 208-799-2216. Degrees granted: Associate; Bachelors. Adverse incident record source- Student Services, 208-799-2218.

Attendance information available by phone, fax, mail. Search requires name plus SSN. Also helpful: date of birth. There is no fee.

Degree information available by phone, fax, mail. Search requires name plus SSN. Also helpful: date of birth. There is no fee.

North Idaho College, Registrar, Coeur D' Alene, ID 83814, 208-769-3320 (Fax: 208-769-3431). Hours: 7:30AM-

5PM M-Th; 7:30AM-2:30PM F. Enrollment: 3500. Records go back to 1933. Alumni records are maintained here at the same phone number. Degrees granted: Associate. Adverse incident record source- Dean of Students, 208-769-3370.

Attendance information available by fax, mail. Search requires name plus SSN, approximate years of attendance. Also helpful: date of birth, exact years of attendance. There is no fee.

Degree information available by phone, fax, mail. Search requires name plus SSN, approximate years of attendance. Also helpful: date of birth, exact years of attendance. There is no fee.

Northwest Nazarene College, Office of the Registrar, Dewey at Holly Sts, Nampa, ID 83686, 208-467-8541 (Fax: 208-467-1098). Hours: 8AM-5PM. Enrollment: 1200. Records go back to 1913. Alumni records are maintained here at the same phone number. Degrees granted: Associate; Bachelors; Masters.

Attendance and degree information available by phone, fax, mail. Search requires name only. Also helpful: SSN, date of birth, approximate years of attendance. There is no fee.

Ricks College, Transcripts, Rexburg, ID 83460-4125, 208-356-1011 (Fax: 208-356-1035). Hours: 8AM-5PM. Enrollment: 7500. Records go back to 1888. Alumni records are maintained here also. Call 208-356-2234. Degrees granted: Associate. Special programs- Nursing, 208-356-1325: Interior Design, 208-356-1340: Drafting, 208-356-1862: Elementary Ed, 208-356-1348. Adverse incident record source- Dean of Students, 208-356-1120.

Attendance and degree information available by phone, fax, mail. Search requires name only. Also helpful: SSN, date of birth, exact years of attendance. There is no fee.

University of Idaho, Registrar, Moscow, ID 83844, 208-885-6731 (Fax: 208-885-9061). Hours: 8AM-5PM. Enrollment: 12000. Records go back to 1889. Alumni records are maintained here also. Call 208-885-6154. Degrees granted: Bachelors; Masters; Doctorate.

Attendance and degree information available by phone, fax, mail. Search requires name plus SSN. There is no fee.

Trade and Vocational Schools

American Institute of Health Technology, Inc.,
6600 Emerald St, Boise, ID 83704, 208-377-8080

State Licensing & Business Registration Quick Finder Index

Architecture, Engineering & Surveying
Architect #19 (1152)..................................... ☎ 208-334-3233
Engineer #17.. ☎ 208-334-3860
Geologist #18 (700)..................................... ☎ 208-334-2268
Landscape Architect #19 .... ☎ 208-334-3233
Surveyor #17.. ☎ 208-334-3860

Business - Court & Legal Services
Attorney #30 .... ☎ 208-342-8958
Lobbyist #29 (308) .... ☎ 208-334-2852
Notary Public #29 (18000)........................... ☎ 208-334-2810
Shorthand Reporter #4 (400)........................ ☎ 208-334-2517

Business - General Services
Bakery #11.. ☎ 208-327-7450
Bed & Breakfast #11 .... ☎ 208-327-7450
Bottling Plant #11 .... ☎ 208-327-7450
Commission Merchant #20........................... ☎ 208-334-3240
Grocery Store #11... ☎ 208-327-7450
Public Accountant-CPA #12 .... ☎ 208-334-2490
Weighmaster #20.. ☎ 208-334-3240

Construction & Manufacturing
Boiler Inspector #10 .... ☎ 208-334-6000
Boiler Safety Code #10 .... ☎ 208-334-6000
Building Inspector #10 .... ☎ 208-334-6000
Contractor #32 .... ☎ 208-334-2966
Electrical Inspector, Contractor, Apprentice &
    Journeyman #10 .... ☎ 208-334-3950
Elevator #10... ☎ 208-334-6000
Manufactured Commercial Building #36....... ☎ 208-334-2327
Manufactured Homes & Housing #36........... ☎ 208-334-2327
Manufactured Housing Dealer, Broker,
    Manufacturer #36..................................... ☎ 208-334-2327
Manufactured Recreational Vehicle #36........ ☎ 208-334-2327

Mixer-Loader #20.. ☎ 208-334-3240
Plumbing Inspector, Contractor, Apprentice &
    Journeyman #36 .... ☎ 208-334-3442
Utility #27 208-334-0300
Welder #35..✉ 208-377-2100

Education
Director of Special Education #5................... ☎ 208-334-3475
Exceptional Child School Program Advisor #5
    .... ☎ 208-334-3475
School Counselor #5..................................... ☎ 208-334-3475
School Nurse #5.. ☎ 208-334-3475
School Principal #5....................................... ☎ 208-334-3475
School Superintendent #5............................. ☎ 208-334-3475
Standard Communications Disorders School
    Specialist #5 .... ☎ 208-334-3475
Teacher #5.. ☎ 208-334-3475

Environmental & Agriculture
Aquaculture (Commercial) #20 .... ☎ 208-334-3240
Asbestos Worker Certificaiton #10 .... ☎ 208-334-6000
Beekeeper #20.. ☎ 208-334-3240
Bulk Water Plant #11.................................... ☎ 208-327-7450
Chemigator #20.. ☎ 208-334-3240
Commercial Applicator #20.......................... ☎ 208-334-3240
Commercial Feed Manufacturer #20............. ☎ 208-334-3240
Commercial Fertilizer Manufacturer #20 .... ☎ 208-334-3240
Commercial Fish Hatchery #22 .... ☎ 208-334-3736
Commercial Fishing #22................................ ☎ 208-334-3736
Dairy Product Processor, Bulk Milk Hauler,
    Dairy Farm #20 .... ☎ 208-334-3240
Dam Construction #26................................... ☎ 208-327-7900
Discharge of Wastewater through Injection
    Wells #26... ☎ 208-327-7900
Egg Distributor/Grader #20 .... ☎ 208-334-3240

Farm Produce Dealer/Broker #20.................☎ 208-334-3240
Florist/Nurseryman #20...............................☎ 208-334-3240
Food Processing/Manufacturing Plant #11 ....☎ 208-327-7450
Food Warehouse, Cold Storage #11.............☎ 208-327-7450
Fur Buyer #22...☎ 208-334-3736
Handling of Critical Materials #11................☎ 208-327-7450
Livestock Auction Market #20......................☎ 208-334-3240
Livestock Brand #25....................................✉ 208-884-7130
Logging #10..☎ 208-334-6000
Milk Storage & Handling of Milk &
   Dairy Products #20 ....☎ 208-334-3240
Mine Safety Training #36.............................☎ 208-334-2327
Organic Certification #20 ....☎ 208-334-3240
Pest Control Consultant #20........................☎ 208-334-3240
Pesticide Applicator/Operator/Dealer
   /Manufacturer #20..................................☎ 208-334-3240
Private Applicator #20.................................☎ 208-334-3240
Public Commodity Warehouse #20................☎ 208-334-3240
Seed Company #20......................................☎ 208-334-3240
Septic Tank Pumping #11 ....☎ 208-375-5230
Small Water Supplies #11 ....☎ 208-375-5230
Soil & Plant Amendment Manufacturer #20
   ....☎ 208-334-3240
Stream Channel Alteration Subsurface #26 ...☎ 208-327-7900
Subdivision Approval (Sanitary) #11............☎ 208-375-5230
Subsurface Sewage Installation #11..............☎ 208-375-5230
Trapper #22..☎ 208-334-3736
Underground Storage Tank Technician #24
   ....☎ 208-334-4370
Veterinarian #1 (1040) ....☎ 208-332-8588
Veterinary Drug Outlet & Technician #16 (55)
   ....☎ 208-334-2356
Water Laboratory #2...................................☎ 208-334-2235
Water Rights/Well Driller #26 ....☎ 208-327-7900

Financial - Real Estate, Insurance & Banking

Bank #21..☎ 208-334-3313
Collection Agency/Collector #21..................☎ 208-334-3313
Collector/Solicitor #6 ....☎ 208-334-2945
Consumer Loans & Credit Sales #21 ....☎ 208-334-3313
Credit Union #21 ....☎ 208-334-3313
Domestic & Mutual Insurer #23....................☎ 208-334-4320
Finance Company #21 ....☎ 208-334-3313
Foreign & Alien Insurer #23 ....☎ 208-334-4320
Insurance Agent Corporation or Partnership #23
   ....☎ 208-334-4320
Insurance Agent Licensure Examination #23
   (11000)..☎ 208-334-4320
Insurance Broker License #23 (600) ....☎ 208-334-4320
Investment Advisor #21 ....☎ 208-334-3313
Mortgage Broker/Banker #21.......................☎ 208-332-8000
Mortgage Company #21...............................☎ 208-334-3313
Non-resident Insurance Agent #23................☎ 208-334-4320
Real Estate Appraiser #19 ....☎ 208-334-3233
Real Estate Broker #28 (2200) ....☎ 208-334-3285
Real Estate Salesperson #28 (4600) ....☎ 208-334-3285
Savings & Loan Association #21 ....☎ 208-334-3313
Securities Broker/Dealers Seller & Issuer #21
   ....☎ 208-334-3313
Time Share Registration #28 ....☎ 208-334-3285
Trust Company #21 ....☎ 208-334-3313

Health & Beauty

Artificial Inseminator #20 ....☎ 208-334-3240
Barber School Instructor #19 (3)..................☎ 208-334-3233
Barber, Barbershop, Barber School #19
   (881)..☎ 208-334-3233
Cemeterian #19...☎ 208-334-3233
Chiropractor #19 (419)................................☎ 208-334-3233
Clinical Laboratory Registration #2..............☎ 208-334-2235

Controlled Substance #16 (877) ....☎ 208-334-2356
Cosmetologist, Salon, School #19 (10697) ....☎ 208-334-3233
Cosmetology Instructor #19 (572)................☎ 208-334-3233
Crematory #3 (16).......................................☎ 208-334-3233
Dental Hygienist #13 (731) ....☎ 208-334-2369
Dentist #13 (910) ....☎ 208-334-2369
Denturist #19 (31).......................................☎ 208-334-3233
Dietitian #31...☎ 208-334-2822
Drug Manufacturer #16 ....☎ 208-334-2356
Drug Outlet (i.e. Nursing Home) #16 (75) .....☎ 208-334-2356
Drug Repackaging #16 ....☎ 208-334-2356
Drug Store/Pharmacy #16 (224) ....☎ 208-334-2356
Drug Wholesaler #16 (410) ....☎ 208-334-2356
Electrolysis #19 (79)....................................☎ 208-334-3233
Emergency Medical Service #9 ....☎ 208-334-5994
Environmental Health Specialist #19 ....☎ 208-334-3233
Esthetician #19..☎ 208-334-3233
Funeral Establishment #3.............................☎ 208-334-3233
Hearing Aid Dealer/Fitter #19 ....☎ 208-334-3233
Hospital #8 (51) ....☎ 208-334-6626
Intermediate Care Facility for the Mentally
   Retarded #8 (49)......................................☎ 208-334-6626
Mail Service Pharmacy #16 (116) ....☎ 208-334-2356
Mammography #2..☎ 208-334-2235
Medical Doctor #31 (2793)..........................☎ 208-334-2822
Medical Resident #31 ....☎ 208-334-2822
Mortician #19...☎ 208-334-3233
Mortician License #3 ....☎ 208-334-3233
Mortician Resident Trainee License #3.........☎ 208-334-3233
Non-Pharmacy Drug Sales (i.e. Grocery
   Store) #16 (1348) ....☎ 208-334-2356
Nurse #14 (11000)......................................☎ 208-334-3110
Nurse Anesthetist #14 (300) ....☎ 208-334-3110
Nurse Practitioner #14 (200) ....☎ 208-334-3110
Nursing Assistant #14 (12000) ....☎ 208-334-3110
Nursing Home Administrator #19 (142).........☎ 208-334-3233
Occupational Therapist/Assistant #31 (303)
   ....☎ 208-334-2822
Optometrist #19 (306)..................................☎ 208-334-3233
Oral Surgeon #13 ....☎ 208-334-2369
Orthodontist #13 (111) ....☎ 208-334-2369
Osteopathic Physician #31 (124)...................☎ 208-334-2822
Paramedic (EMT) #31..................................☎ 208-334-2822
Pharmacist, Intern, Preceptor #16 (1608).......☎ 208-334-2356
Physical Therapist/Assistant #31 (750) ....☎ 208-334-2822
Physician's Assistant #31 (99) ....☎ 208-334-2822
Podiatrist #19 ....☎ 208-334-3233
Practical Nurse #14 (5500) ....☎ 208-334-3110
Radiation Equipment #3 ....☎ 208-334-5945
Rehabilitation Facility #8 ....☎ 208-334-6626
Residential Care Administrator #19 ....☎ 208-334-3233
Residential Care Facility #8 (185)..................☎ 208-334-6626
Respiratory Therapist #31 (452) ....☎ 208-334-2822
Restaurant Sanitation Standards #11 ....☎ 208-375-5230
Skilled Nursing Care Facility #8 (84).............☎ 208-334-6626
X-ray Equipment #2....................................☎ 208-334-2235

Investigations & Security

Commodity Dealer #20................................☎ 208-334-3240
Fire Sprinkler System Contractor #24 ....☎ 208-334-4370
Peace Officer #25..✉ 208-884-7130

Social Services

Child Care Institution/Agency #7.................✉ 208-334-5700
Child Care Licensure #7 ....✉ 208-334-5700
Counselor #19 ....☎ 208-334-3233
Day Care Center Inspector #11....................☎ 208-327-7450
Day Care Center/Home #7...........................✉ 208-334-5700
Foster Home #7..✉ 208-334-5700
Labor Relations #10....................................☎ 208-334-6000
Professional Counselor #19 (588) ....☎ 208-334-3233

Psychologist #19 .... ☎ 208-334-3233
Residential School #7 .... ⊠ 208-334-5700
Social Worker #19 .... ☎ 208-334-3233
Substance Abuse Treatment Center #7 .... ⊠ 208-334-5700

Sports & Entertainment
Athletic Trainer #31 (80) .... ☎ 208-334-2822
Boxer #33 .... ☎ 208-334-3888
Brewery License #25 (15) .... ☎ 208-334-2521
Fish & Game Retailing #22 .... ☎ 208-334-3736
Game Farm #22 .... ☎ 208-334-3736
Guide #15 (2000) .... ☎ 208-327-7380
Horse Racing #34 .... ☎ 860-884-7130
Idaho State Racing #25 .... ⊠ 208-884-7080
Jockey #34 .... ☎ 860-884-7130
Outfitter #15 (400) .... ☎ 208-327-7380
Retail Beer & Wine License #25 .... ⊠ 208-884-7130

Retail Liquor License #25 .... ⊠ 208-884-7130
Shooting Preserve #22 .... ☎ 208-334-3736
Swimming Pool Installation #11 .... ☎ 208-375-5230
Tavern #11 .... ☎ 208-375-5230
Taxidermist #22 .... ☎ 208-334-3736
Trainer #34 .... ☎ 860-884-7130
Wholesale Beer & Wine License #25 .... ☎ 208-884-7130
Winery #25 .... ☎ 208-334-2521
Wrestler #33 .... ☎ 208-334-3888

Transportation
Interstate Common Carrier #27 208-334-0300
Intrastate Common & Contract Carrier #27 208-334-0300
Intrastate Private Carrier #27 208-334-0300

State Licensing & Business Registration Agency Information

(1) Board of Veterinary Medicine, PO Box 7249, Boise, ID 83707, 208-332-8588, Fax: 208-334-4062

(2) Bureau of Laboratories, 2220 Old Penitentiary Rd, Boise, ID 83712, 208-334-2235

(3) Bureau of Occupational Licenses, Mortitian Board of Examiners, 1109 Main Street, Suite 220, Boise, ID 83702, 208-334-3233, Fax: 208-334-3945

(4) Certified Shorthand Reporters Board, 650 W State St, Room B-83, Boise, ID 83720, 208-334-2517

(5) Department of Education, PO Box 83720, Boise, ID 83720-0027, 208-334-3475, Fax: 208-334-4664

(6) Department of Finance, PO Box 83720, Boise, ID 83720-0031, 208-334-2945, Fax: 208-332-8099

(7) Department of Health & Welfare, 450 W State St, Boise, ID 83720, 208-334-5700

(8) Department of Health & Welfare, 450 W State St, Boise, ID 83720, 208-334-6626, Fax: 208-332-7204

(9) Department of Health & Welfare, 450 W State St, Boise, ID 83720, 208-334-5994, Fax: 208-334-4015

(10) Division of Building Safety, PO Box 83720, Boise, ID 83720, 208-334-3950, Fax: 208-334-2683

(11) Environmental Health Department, Bakery & Related Licensing, 707 N. Armstrong Place, Boise, ID 83704, 208-375-5230, Fax: 208-327-7113

(12) Idaho Board of Accountancy, PO Box 83720, Boise, ID 83702-0002, 208-334-2490, Fax: 208-334-2615

(13) Idaho Board of Dentistry, 708 1/2 W Franklin St, Statehouse Mail, Boise, ID 83720, 208-334-2369, Fax: 208-334-3247

(14) Idaho Board of Nursing, 280 N 8th St, Suite 210, Boise, ID 83720, 208-334-3110, Fax: 208-334-3262

(15) Idaho Board of Outfitters & Guides, 1365 N Orchard, Room 172, Boise, ID 83706, 208-327-7380, Fax: 208-327-7382

(16) Idaho Board of Pharmacy, 280 N 8th St, Suite 204, Boise, ID 83702, 208-334-2356, Fax: 208-334-3536

(17) Idaho Board of Professional Engineers & Surveyors, 600 S Orchard, Suite A, Boise, ID 83705, 208-334-3860

(18) Idaho Board of Professional Geologists, 550 W State St, Room, Boise, ID 83720-3033, 208-334-2268

(19) Idaho Bureau of Occupational Licenses, 1109 Main St, Suite 220, Owyhee Plaza, Boise, ID 83702, 208-334-3233, Fax: 208-334-3945

(20) Idaho Department of Agriculture, 2270 Old Penitentiary Rd, Boise, ID 83712, 208-332-8500

(21) Idaho Department of Finance, 700 W State St, Boise, ID 83720, 208-332-8000, Fax: 208-332-8048

(22) Idaho Department of Fish & Game, PO Box 25, Boise, ID 83707, 208-334-3700, Fax: 208-334-2114

(23) Idaho Department of Insurance, 500 S 10th St, Boise, ID 83720, 208-334-4320, Fax: 208-334-4398

(24) Idaho Department of Insurance, 500 S 10th St, Boise, ID 83720, 208-334-4370, Fax: 208-334-4398

(25) Idaho Department of Law Enforcement, 700 Stratford St, Meridian, ID 83680, 208-884-7080, Fax: 208-884-7098

(26) Idaho Department of Water Resources, 1301 N Orchard St, Boise, ID 83706-2237, 208-327-7900, Fax: 208-327-7866

(27) Idaho Public Utilities Commission, PO Box 83720, (472 W Washington St 83702), Boise, ID 83720-0074, 208-334-0300, Fax: 208-334-3762

(28) Idaho Real Estate Commission, PO Box 83720, Boise, ID 83720-4500, 208-334-3285, Fax: 208-334-2050

(29) Idaho Secretary of State, Statehouse, Room 203, Boise, ID 83720, 208-334-2300, Fax: 208-334-2282

(30) Idaho State Bar Association, 525 W Jefferson, Boise, ID 83702, 208-334-4500

(31) Idaho State Board of Medicine, PO Box 83720, 280 N 8th St, Suite 202, Boise, ID 83720-0058, 208-334-2822, Fax: 208-334-2801

(32) Public Works Contractors Board, PO Box 83720, Boise, ID 83720-0073, 208-334-2966, Fax: 208-334-2785

(33) State Athletic Department, 10 S Lath, Suite 208, Boise, ID 83705, 208-334-3888, Fax: 208-345-1145

(34) State Horse Racing Commission, 700 S Stratford Dr, Meridian, ID 83642, 208-884-7080, Fax: 208-884-7098

(35) Welder Licensing, 370 Benjamin Ln, Boise, ID 83707, 208-377-2100

(36) Worker Certification & Licensing, Division of Building Safety, 217 N 6th St, Boise, ID 83702, 208-334-3896

Illinois

Capitol: Springfield (Sangamon County)	
State Population	11.8 Million
Number of Degree Granting Institutions:	176
Number of State Licensing & Business Registration Agencies:	161

Degree Granting Educational Institutions

Adler School of Professional Psychology, Registrar, 65 E Wacker Pl Ste 2100, Chicago, IL 60601-7203, 312-201-5900 (Fax: 312-201-5917). Hours: 9AM-5PM. Enrollment: 413. Records go back to 1970. Alumni records are maintained here also. Call 312-201-5900. Degrees granted: Masters; Doctorate. Adverse incident record source- Dean, 312-201-5900.

Attendance and degree information available by mail. Search requires name plus SSN, exact years of attendance, signed release. There is no fee.

American Academy of Art, Registrar, 332 S Michigan Ave #300, Chicago, IL 60604-4301, 312-461-0600. Hours: 8AM-3:30PM. Records go back to 1923. Degrees granted: Associate; Bachelors.

Attendance and degree information available by phone, fax, mail. Search requires name plus SSN, date of birth. Also helpful: exact years of attendance. Fee is $3.00.

American Conservatory of Music, Registrar, 16 N Wabash Ave Ste 1850, Chicago, IL 60602-4792, 312-263-4161 (Fax: 312-263-5832). Hours: 9AM-6PM. Records go back to 1886. Alumni records are maintained here at the same phone number. Degrees granted: Associate; Bachelors; Masters; Doctorate.

Attendance and degree information available by phone, mail. Search requires name plus exact years of attendance. There is no fee.

American Islamic College, Registrar, 640 W Irving Park Rd, Chicago, IL 60613, .

Attendance and degree information available by phone, mail. Search requires name plus SSN. Also helpful: date of birth, exact years of attendance. There is no fee.

American Schools of Professional Psychology, Registrar, 20 S Clark St 3rd Fl, Chicago, IL 60603, 312-201-0200 X610 (Fax: 312-201-1907). Hours: 8:30AM-5PM. Enrollment: 1250. Records go back to 1976. Alumni records are maintained here also. Call 312-201-0200 X610. Degrees granted: Masters; Doctorate. Adverse incident record source- Registrar, 312-201-0200 X610.

Attendance and degree information available by phone, fax, mail. Search requires name plus SSN. There is no fee.

Augustana College, Registrar, 639 38th St, Rock Island, IL 61201-2296, 309-794-7277 (Fax: 309-794-7422). Hours: 8AM-4:30PM. Enrollment: 2150. Records go back to 1900. Alumni records are maintained here also. Call 309-794-7336. Degrees granted: Bachelors.

Attendance and degree information available by phone, fax, mail. Search requires name plus date of birth. Also helpful: SSN, exact years of attendance. There is no fee.

Aurora University, Registrar, 347 S Gladstone Ave, Aurora, IL 60506, 708-844-5464 (Fax: 708-844-5463). Hours: 8AM-7PM M-Th; 8AM-6PM F; 9AM-1PM S. Enrollment: 2200. Records go back to 1893. Alumni records are maintained here also. Call 708-844-5486. Degrees granted: Bachelors; Masters. Adverse incident record source- Student Life, 708-844-5446.

Attendance and degree information available by phone, fax, mail. Search requires name only. Also helpful: SSN, date of birth, exact years of attendance. There is no fee.

Barat College, Registrar, 700 E Westleigh Rd, Lake Forest, IL 60045, 847-234-3000 (Fax: 847-234-1084). Hours: 8:30AM-4:30PM. Enrollment: 720. Records go back to 1922. Alumni records are maintained here at the same phone number. Degrees granted: Bachelors. Adverse incident record source- Dean of Students, 847-234-3000.

Attendance and degree information available by fax, mail. Search requires name plus SSN. There is no fee.

Belleville Area College, Registrar, 2500 Carlyle Ave, Belleville, IL 62221, 618-235-2700 X223 (Fax: 618-235-1578). Hours: 8AM-8PM M-Th, 8AM-4PM F. Enrollment: 14000. Records go back to 1946. Alumni records are maintained here at the same phone number. Degrees granted: Associate. Adverse incident record source- Special Services, 618-235-2700.

Attendance and degree information available by phone, fax, mail. Search requires name only. Also helpful: SSN, date of birth, exact years of attendance. There is no fee.

Black Hawk College, Registrar, 6600 34th Ave, Moline, IL 61265, 309-796-1311 (Fax: 309-792-5976). Hours: 7:30AM-6PM M-T, 7:30AM-5PM W-F. Enrollment: 7000. Records go back to 1966. Alumni records are maintained here also. Call 309-796-1311. Degrees granted: Associate. Adverse incident record source- Registrar, 309-796-1311.

Attendance information available by fax, mail. Search requires name plus SSN. There is no fee.

Degree information available by mail. Search requires name plus SSN. There is no fee.

Black Hawk College East Campus, Records and Admissions Office, Box 489, Kewanee, IL 61443, 309-852-5671 X220 (Fax: 309-856-6005). Enrollment: 750. Records go back to 1967. Alumni records are maintained here at the same phone number. Degrees granted: Associate. Adverse incident record source- Security.

Attendance and degree information available by phone. Search requires name plus SSN. Also helpful: exact years of attendance. There is no fee.

Blackburn College, Registrar, 700 College Ave, Carlinville, IL 62626, 217-854-3231 X4210 (Fax: 217-854-3713). Hours: 8AM-5PM. Enrollment: 575. Alumni records are maintained here at the same phone number. Degrees granted: Bachelors.

Attendance and degree information available by phone, fax, mail. Search requires name plus exact years of attendance. Also helpful: date of birth. There is no fee.

Blessing-Rieman College of Nursing, Registrar, Broadway at 11th St, PO Box 7005, Quincy, IL 62301-7005, 217-223-5520 X6992 (Fax: 217-223-1781). Hours: 8:30AM-5PM. Enrollment: 180. Records go back to 1908. Alumni records are maintained here also. Call 217-223-5520 X6961. Degrees granted: Bachelors.

Attendance and degree information available by phone, fax, mail. Search requires name only. Also helpful: SSN, date of birth, exact years of attendance. There is no fee.

Bradley University, Registrar, 1501 W Bradley Ave, Peoria, IL 61625, 309-677-3101 (Fax: 309-677-2715). Hours: 8AM-5PM. Records go back to 1897. Degrees granted: Bachelors; Masters. Adverse incident record source- Student Judicial System, 309-677-2428.

Attendance and degree information available by phone, fax, mail. Search requires name plus SSN, date of birth. Also helpful: exact years of attendance. There is no fee.

Brisk Rabbinical College, Registrar, 2965 W Peterson, Chicago, IL 60659, 312-274-1177 (Fax: 312-274-6559). Enrollment: 40. Records go back to 1984. Degrees granted: Bachelors. Special programs- Hebrew Religious Studies. Adverse incident record source- Student Records.

Attendance and degree information available by phone, mail. Search requires name plus SSN, exact years of attendance. There is no fee.

Carl Sandburg College, Registrar, 2232 S Lake Storey Rd, Galesburg, IL 61401, 309-344-2518 (Fax: 309-344-3291). Hours: 8AM-5PM. Records go back to 1967. Degrees granted: Associate.

Attendance and degree information available by phone, fax, mail. Search requires name plus SSN. There is no fee.

Catholic Theological Union, Registrar, 5401 S Cornell Ave, Chicago, IL 60615-5698, 312-753-5320 (Fax: 312-324-4360). Hours: 8:30AM-4PM. Enrollment: 360. Records go back to 1969. Alumni records are maintained here also. Call 312-753-5318. Degrees granted: Masters; Doctorate.

Attendance and degree information available by mail. Search requires name plus SSN, signed release. Also helpful: exact years of attendance. There is no fee.

Chicago College of Commerce, Registrar, 11 E Adams St, Chicago, IL 60603, 312-236-3312 (Fax: 312-236-0015). Hours: 9AM-5PM. Enrollment: 2000. Records go back to 1956. Degrees granted: Associate. Certification: Machine Shorthand, Legal Trans., Medical Trans, Court Reporting.

Attendance and degree information available by phone. Search requires name only. Also helpful: SSN, date of birth, exact years of attendance. There is no fee.

Chicago School of Professional Psychology, Registrar, 806 S Plymouth Ct, Chicago, IL 60605, 312-786-9443 (Fax: 312-332-3273). Hours: 9AM-5PM. Enrollment: 265. Records go back to 1979. Degrees granted: Doctorate.

Attendance and degree information available by phone, fax, mail. Search requires name plus SSN. There is no fee.

Chicago State University, Registrar, 9501 S King Dr, Chicago, IL 60628, 312-995-2461 (Fax: 312-995-3618). Hours: 8:30AM-5PM M,T,W,F; 8:30AM-7PM Th. Enrollment: 9000. Records go back to 1905. Alumni records are maintained here also. Call 312-995-2050. Degrees granted: Bachelors; Masters. Adverse incident record source- 312-995-2111.

Attendance information available by fax, mail. Search requires name plus SSN, signed release. Also helpful: date of birth, exact years of attendance. There is no fee.

Degree information available by phone, fax, mail. Search requires name plus SSN. Also helpful: date of birth, exact years of attendance. There is no fee.

Chicago Theological Seminary, Registrar, 5757 S University Ave, Chicago, IL 60637, 312-752-5757 X227 (Fax: 312-752-5925). Hours: 8:30AM-4:30PM. Enrollment: 210. Records go back to 1971. Alumni records are maintained here also. Call 312-752-5757 X264. Degrees granted: Masters; Doctorate.

Attendance and degree information available by phone, fax, mail. Search requires name plus exact years of attendance. Also helpful: date of birth. There is no fee.

City Colleges of Chicago-Wright College-North, Records Office, 4300 North Narragensett, Chicago, IL 60634, 312-777-7900 (Fax: 312-481-8053). Enrollment: 7000. Records go back to 1936. Alumni records are maintained here at the same phone number. Degrees granted: Associate. Special programs- 2 Year Arts & Science Programs. Adverse incident record source- Security.

Attendance and degree information available by fax, mail. Search requires name plus SSN, date of birth, exact years of attendance, signed release. There is no fee.

College of DuPage, Registrar, 22nd St and Lambert Rd, Glen Ellyn, IL 60137, 708-858-2800. Hours: 8:30AM-5PM. Records go back to 1967. Alumni records are maintained here also. Call 708-858-2800. Degrees granted: Associate.

Attendance and degree information available by mail. Search requires name plus SSN, exact years of attendance, signed release. There is no fee.

College of Lake County, Registrar, 19351 W Washington St, Grayslake, IL 60030, 708-223-6601 (Fax: 708-223-1017). Hours: 8AM-8PM M-Th; 8AM-4PM F. Enrollment: 14994. Records go back to 1969. Alumni records are maintained here at the same phone number. Degrees granted: Associate.

Attendance and degree information available by phone, fax, mail. Search requires name plus SSN, date of birth. There is no fee.

College of St. Francis, Registrar, 500 N Wilcox St, Joliet, IL 60435, 815-740-3391 (Fax: 815-740-4285). Hours: 8AM-4:30PM. Enrollment: 4300. Records go back to 1936. Alumni records are maintained here at the same phone number. Degrees granted: Bachelors; Masters. Adverse incident record source- Student Life, 815-740-3399.

Attendance and degree information available by phone, fax, mail. Search requires name only. Also helpful: SSN, approximate years of attendance. There is no fee.

Columbia College, Registrar, 600 S Michigan Ave, Chicago, IL 60605, 312-663-1600 (Fax: 312-663-5543). Hours: 9AM-5PM. Enrollment: 8000. Records go back to 1894. Alumni Records Office: 624 S Michigan, Chicago, IL 60605. Degrees granted: Bachelors; Masters.

Attendance and degree information available by phone, fax, mail. Search requires name only. Also helpful: SSN, date of birth, exact years of attendance. There is no fee.

Commonwealth Business College, (Branch), Registrar, 1527 47th Ave, Moline, IL 61265, 309-762-2100 (Fax: 309-762-2374). Hours: 8AM-9:30PM. Enrollment: 120. Records go back to 1986. Degrees granted: Associate. Adverse incident record source- Student Services.

Attendance information available by fax, mail. Search requires name plus SSN, signed release. Also helpful: date of birth, exact years of attendance. There is no fee.

School will not confirm degree information.

Concordia University, Registrar, 7400 Augusta St, River Forest, IL 60305, 708-383-7100 (Fax: 708-209-3176). Hours: 8AM-4:30PM. Enrollment: 2400. Records go back to 1913. Degrees granted: Bachelors; Masters. Certification: CAS.

Attendance and degree information available by phone, fax, mail. Search requires name plus SSN, date of birth. Also helpful: approximate years of attendance. There is no fee.

Danville Area Community College, Registrar, 2000 E Main St, Danville, IL 61832, 217-443-8797 (Fax: 217-443-8560). Hours: 8AM-5PM Winter; 7:30AM-4PM Summer. Enrollment: 3000. Degrees granted: Associate.

Attendance and degree information available by phone, fax, mail. Search requires name plus SSN. Also helpful: date of birth, exact years of attendance. There is no fee.

DePaul University, Registrar, 1 E Jackson Blvd, Chicago, IL 60604, 312-362-8610 (Fax: 312-362-5143). Hours: 8AM-6PM. Enrollment: 17133. Records go back to 1898. Alumni Records Office: 25 East Jackson Blvd, Chicago, IL 60604. Degrees granted: Bachelors; Masters; Doctorate. Adverse incident record source- Dean of Students, 312-325-7294.

Attendance and degree information available by phone, fax, mail. Search requires name plus SSN. Also helpful: date of birth, exact years of attendance. There is no fee.

DeVry Institute of Technology, Chicago, Registrar, 3300 N Campbell Ave, Chicago, IL 60618, 312-929-8500 X2060 (Fax: 312-348-1780). Hours: 7:30AM-4:30PM M,T,F; 7:30AM-7:30PM W,Th. Records go back to 1948. Alumni Records Office: Alumni Association, DeVry Institute, One Tower Ln, Oakbrook Terrace, IL 60181. Degrees granted: Associate; Bachelors.

Attendance and degree information available by phone, fax, mail. Search requires name plus SSN, exact years of attendance. There is no fee.

DeVry Institute of Technology, DuPage, Registrar, 1221 N Swift Rd, Addison, IL 60101-6106, 708-953-1300 (Fax: 708-953-1236). Hours: 8:30AM-10PM M-Th, 8:30AM-5PM F. Enrollment: 3000. Records go back to 1980. Alumni Records Office: Alumni Association, DeVry Institute, One Tower Ln, Oakbrook Terrace, IL 60181. Degrees granted: Associate; Bachelors. Adverse incident record source- Dean.

Attendance and degree information available by phone, fax, mail. Search requires name plus SSN, exact years of attendance. There is no fee.

Dr. William M. Scholl College of Podiatric Medicine, Registrar, 1001 N Dearborn St, Chicago, IL 60610, 312-280-2943 (Fax: 312-280-2495). Hours: 8:30AM-5PM. Enrollment: 400. Records go back to 1916. Alumni records are maintained here also. Call 312-280-2880. Degrees granted: Bachelors; Doctorate. Adverse incident record source- Department Chair or Dean.

Attendance and degree information available by phone, fax, mail. Search requires name plus SSN, exact years of attendance. There is no fee.

East-West University, Registrar, 816 S Michigan Ave, Chicago, IL 60605, 312-934-0111 X16 (Fax: 312-939-0083). Hours: 8:30AM-5PM. Records go back to 1980. Degrees granted: Associate.

Attendance information available by phone, fax. Search requires name plus SSN. There is no fee.

Degree information available by phone, fax. Search requires name plus SSN. Also helpful: date of birth, approximate years of attendance. There is no fee.

Eastern Illinois University, Registrar, 600 Lincoln Ave, Charleston, IL 61920, 217-581-3511 (Fax: 217-581-3412). Hours: 8AM-4PM. Enrollment: 10500. Records go back to 1895. Alumni records are maintained here also. Call 217-581-6616. Degrees granted: Bachelors; Masters. Adverse incident record source- Registrar, 217-581-3511.

Attendance and degree information available by phone, fax, mail. Search requires name plus SSN, date of birth, exact years of attendance. There is no fee.

Elgin Community College, Registrar, 1700 Spartan Dr, Elgin, IL 60123, 847-888-7386 (Fax: 847-697-9209). Hours: 8AM-7PM. Enrollment: 9000. Records go back to 1949. Alumni records are maintained here also. Call 847-697-1000 X7423. Degrees granted: Associate.

Attendance and degree information available by fax, mail. Search requires name plus SSN, signed release. Also helpful: date of birth, exact years of attendance. There is no fee.

Elmhurst College, Registration & Records, 190 Prospect St, Elmhurst, IL 60126-3296, 708-617-3052 (Fax: 708-617-3245). Hours: 8AM-9PM M-Th; 8AM-4PM F. Enrollment: 2000. Records go back to 1871. Degrees granted: Bachelors.

Attendance and degree information available by phone, fax, mail. Search requires name only. Also helpful: SSN, exact years of attendance. There is no fee.

Eureka College, Registrar, 300 E College Ave, Eureka, IL 61530, 309-467-3721 (Fax: 309-467-6437). Hours: 8AM-5PM. Enrollment: 500. Records go back to 1855. Alumni records are maintained here also. Call 309-467-6317. Degrees granted: Bachelors. Adverse incident record source- Registrar, 309-467-6305.

Attendance and degree information available by phone, fax, mail. Search requires name plus SSN, exact years of attendance. There is no fee.

Frontier Community College, Registrar, #2 Frontier Dr, Fairfield, IL 62837, 618-842-3111 (Fax: 618-842-4425). Enrollment: 3500. Records go back to 1973. Degrees granted: Associate; 2-year Associate in Applied Science, 1-year Certificates. Adverse incident record source- Dean's Office, 618-842-3111 .

Attendance and degree information available by written request only. Search requires name plus signed release. Also helpful: SSN, date of birth. There is no fee.

Garrett-Evangelical Theological Seminary, Registrar, 2121 Sheridan Rd, Evanston, IL 60201, 847-866-3905 (Fax: 847-866-3957). Hours: 8:30AM-4:30PM. Enrollment: 520. Records go back to 1892. Alumni records are maintained here at the same phone number. Degrees granted: Masters; Doctorate. Adverse incident record source- Student Life.

Attendance and degree information available by phone, fax, mail. Search requires name plus approximate years of attendance. Also helpful: exact years of attendance. There is no fee.

Gem City College, Registrar, PO Box 179, 700 State St, Quincy, IL 62306, 217-222-0391 (Fax: 217-222-1559). Hours: 8AM-4:40PM. Records go back to 1871.

Attendance and degree information available by written request only. Search requires name plus SSN, date of birth, signed release. Also helpful: exact years of attendance. There is no fee.

Governors State University, Registrar, University Park, IL 60466, 708-534-5000 X4120 (Fax: 708-534-8397). Hours: 8AM-8PM M-Th, 8AM-5PM F. Enrollment: 4260. Records go back to 1971. Alumni records are maintained here also. Call 708-534-5000. Degrees granted: Bachelors; Masters. Adverse incident record source- Student Affairs, 708-534-5000.

Attendance and degree information available by phone, mail. Search requires name plus SSN, exact years of attendance. There is no fee.

Greenville College, Registrar, 315 E College Ave, Greenville, IL 62246, 618-664-1840 X216 (Fax: 618-664-1323). Hours: 8AM-4:30PM. Enrollment: 824. Records go back to 1892. Alumni records are maintained here at the same phone number. Degrees granted: Bachelors. Adverse incident record source- Registrar, 618-664-1840 X4222.

Attendance and degree information available by phone, fax, mail. Search requires name plus SSN, exact years of attendance. Also helpful: date of birth. There is no fee.

Harold Washington College, Registrar, 30 E Lake St, Chicago, IL 60601, 312-553-6060 (Fax: 312-553-6077). Hours: 9AM-6PM. Records go back to 1962. Degrees granted: Associate.

Attendance and degree information available by phone, fax, mail. Search requires name only. Also helpful: SSN, date of birth, exact years of attendance. There is no fee.

Harrington Institute of Interior Design, Registrar, 410 S Michigan Ave, Chicago, IL 60605-1496, 312-939-4975 (Fax: 312-939-8005). Hours: 8:30AM-5:00PM. Enrollment: 350. Records go back to 1961. Degrees granted: Associate; Bachelors.

Attendance and degree information available by fax, mail. Search requires name only. Also helpful: exact years of attendance. There is no fee.

Harry S. Truman College, Registrar, 1145 W Wilson Ave, Chicago, IL 60640, 312-907-4755 (Fax: 312-907-4464). Hours: 8:30AM-7PM M-Th, 8:30AM-3PM. Records go back to 1958. Alumni records are maintained here also. Call 312-907-4755. Degrees granted: Associate.

Attendance and degree information available by phone, mail. Search requires name plus SSN, exact years of attendance. There is no fee.

Hebrew Theological College, Registrar, 7135 N Carpenter Rd, Skokie, IL 60077, 847-982-2500 (Fax: 847-674-6381). Enrollment: 250. Records go back to 1922. Alumni records are maintained here at the same phone number. Degrees granted: Bachelors. Adverse incident record source- Office of the Chancellor.

Attendance and degree information available by fax, mail. Search requires name plus SSN, signed release. Also helpful: approximate years of attendance. There is no fee.

Herman M. Finch University of Health Sciences, (The Chicago Medical School), Registrar, 3333 Green Bay Rd, North Chicago, IL 60046, 708-578-3228 (Fax: 708-578-3284). Hours: 8:30AM-4:30PM. Enrollment: 1300. Formerly The University of Health Sciences Records go back to 1932. Alumni Records Office: AMOCCO Bldg, North Chicago, IL 60046. Degrees granted: Bachelors; Masters; Doctorate. Special programs- Medical. Adverse incident record source- Dean of Medical School.

Attendance and degree information available by phone, fax, mail. Search requires name only. Also helpful: SSN, date of birth, exact years of attendance. There is no fee.

Highland Community College, Registrar, 2998 Pearl City Rd, Freeport, IL 61032, 815-235-6121 (Fax: 815-235-6130). Hours: 8AM-5PM. Enrollment: 2682. Records go back to 1962. Alumni records are maintained here also. Call 815-235-6121 X205. Degrees granted: Associate. Adverse incident record source- Vice President's Office, 815-235-6121 X216

Attendance and degree information available by phone, fax, mail. Search requires name plus SSN, exact years of attendance. There is no fee.

ITT Technical Institute, (Branch of Indianapolis, IN), Director of Education, 375 W Higgins Rd, Hoffman Estates, IL 60195, 847-519-9300 X20 (Fax: 847-519-0153). Hours: 8AM-5PM. Enrollment: 500. Records go back to 1986. Alumni records are maintained here at the same phone number. Degrees granted: Associate; Bachelors. Special programs- Electrical Engineering. Adverse incident record source- Student Services.

Attendance and degree information available by fax, mail. Search requires name plus signed release. Also helpful: exact years of attendance. There is no fee.

Illinois Benedictine University, Registrar, 5700 College Rd, Lisle, IL 60532, 708-960-1500 (Fax: 708-960-1126). Hours: 8AM-6:30PM M-Th; 8AM-4PM F. Enrollment: 2602. Records go back to 1901. Alumni records are maintained here at the same phone number. Degrees granted: Bachelors; Masters. Certification: IFM.

Attendance and degree information available by phone, fax, mail. Search requires name only. Also helpful: SSN, date of birth, exact years of attendance. There is no fee.

Illinois Central College, Registrar L-211, One College Dr, East Peoria, IL 61635, 309-694-5235 (Fax: 309-694-5450). Hours: 8AM-4:30PM. Enrollment: 12000. Records go back to 1967. Alumni records are maintained here also. Call 309-694-5530. Degrees granted: Associate. Adverse incident record source- Student Services, 309-694-5784.

Attendance and degree information available by phone, mail. Search requires name plus SSN. Also helpful: date of birth, exact years of attendance. There is no fee.

Illinois College, Registrar, 1101 W College Ave, Jacksonville, IL 62650, 217-245-3013 (Fax: 217-245-3034). Hours: 8:30AM-4:30PM. Enrollment: 950. Records go back to 1829. Alumni records are maintained here also. Call 217-245-3047. Degrees granted: Bachelors.

Attendance and degree information available by phone, fax, mail. Search requires name only. Also helpful: SSN, date of birth, exact years of attendance. There is no fee.

Illinois College of Optometry, Registrar, 3241 S Michigan Ave, Chicago, IL 60616, 312-225-1700 (Fax: 312-225-3405). Hours: 8:30AM-5PM. Enrollment: 544. Records go back to 1920. Alumni records are maintained here also. Call 312-225-1700 X612. Degrees granted: Bachelors; Doctorate. Adverse incident record source- Student Services, 312-225-1700.

Attendance and degree information available by phone, fax, mail. Search requires name only. Also helpful: SSN, date of birth, exact years of attendance. There is no fee.

Illinois Institute of Art (The), (Branch), Registrar, 1051 Perimeter Dr, Schaumburg, IL 60173-5070, 708-619-3450 (Fax: 708-619-3064). Hours: 8:30AM-4:30PM. Enrollment: 250. Records go back to 1984. Records go back 12 years for branch campus. Degrees granted: Associate; Bachelors.

Attendance information available by mail. Search requires name plus SSN, signed release. Also helpful: date of birth, exact years of attendance. There is no fee.

Degree information available by phone, fax, mail. Search requires name plus SSN, approximate years of attendance. Also helpful: date of birth, exact years of attendance. There is no fee.

Illinois Institute of Technology, Registrar, 3300 S Federal St, Chicago, IL 60616, 312-567-3310 (Fax: 312-567-3313). Hours: 8:30AM-5PM. Enrollment: 7158. Records go back to 1890. Alumni Records Office: Alumni Association, 10 W 33rd St Rm 203, Chicago, IL 60606. Degrees granted: Bachelors; Masters; Doctorate. Adverse incident record source-Registrar.

Attendance and degree information available by phone, fax, mail. Search requires name plus SSN, exact years of attendance. Also helpful: date of birth. There is no fee.

Illinois Institute of Technology-Rice Campus, Registrar,MCE, 201 E Loop Rd, Wheaton, IL 60187, 630-682-6000 (Fax: 630-682-6010). Formerly Midwest College of Engineering Records go back to 1967. Alumni records are maintained here at the same phone number. Degrees granted: Bachelors; Masters.

Attendance and degree information available by phone, fax, mail. Search requires name only. Also helpful: SSN. There is no fee.

Illinois State University, Registrar, Normal, IL 61761-1000, 309-438-2188/438-2181 (Fax: 309-438-7324). Hours: 8AM-4:30PM. Enrollment: 19605. Records go back to 1857. Alumni Records Office: Campus Box 3100, Normal, IL 61761-1000, 309-438-2586. Degrees granted: Bachelors; Masters; Doctorate. Special programs- Criminal Justice: Teacher Education. Adverse incident record source- Registrar, 309-438-2586.

Attendance and degree information available by phone, mail. Search requires name plus SSN, date of birth, exact years of attendance. There is no fee.

Illinois Valley Community College, Registrar, 815 N Orlando Smith Ave, Oglesby, IL 61348-9691, 815-224-2720. Degrees granted: Associate. Adverse incident record source- Student Development, 815-224-2720 X435.

Attendance and degree information available by phone, fax, mail. Search requires name only. Also helpful: SSN, date of birth, exact years of attendance. There is no fee.

Illinois Wesleyan University, Registrar, PO Box 2900, Bloomington, IL 61702, 309-556-3161 (Fax: 309-556-3411). Hours: 8AM-5PM. Enrollment: 1800. Records go back to 1850. Alumni records are maintained here also. Call 309-556-3091. Degrees granted: Bachelors. Adverse incident record source- Dean of Students, 309-556-3111.

Attendance and degree information available by phone, fax, mail. Search requires name plus exact years of attendance. Also helpful: SSN. There is no fee.

International Academy of Merchandising and Design, Registrar, One N State St #400, Chicago, IL 60602, 312-541-3910 (Fax: 312-541--3929). Hours: 8AM-5PM. Enrollment: 650. Records go back to 1979. Degrees granted: Associate; Bachelors.

Attendance and degree information available by phone, fax, mail. Search requires name only. Also helpful: SSN, approximate years of attendance. There is no fee.

John A. Logan College, Registrar, Carterville, IL 62918, 618-985-2828. Hours: 8AM-8PM M-Th; 8AM-4:30PM F. Enrollment: 4895. Records go back to 1967. Degrees granted: Associate.

Attendance and degree information available by phone, fax, mail. Search requires name plus SSN. Also helpful: date of birth, exact years of attendance. There is no fee.

John Marshall Law School, Registrar, 315 S Plymouth Ct, Chicago, IL 60604, 312-427-2737 X466 (Fax: 312-427-2922). Hours: 9AM-5:30PM. Enrollment: 1300. Records go back to 1898. Alumni records are maintained here also. Call 312-427-2737 X411. Degrees granted: Masters; JD.

Attendance and degree information available by phone, mail. Search requires name plus SSN, exact years of attendance. There is no fee.

John Wood Community College, Registrar, 150 S 48th St, Quincy, IL 62301, 217-224-6500 (Fax: 217-224-4208). Hours: 8AM-5PM. Enrollment: 2000. Records go back to 1976. Degrees granted: Associate; Vocational. Adverse incident record source- Dean of Students, 217-224-6500 X4301.

Attendance information available by fax, mail. Search requires name plus SSN. Also helpful: date of birth, exact years of attendance. There is no fee.

Degree information available by phone, fax, mail. Search requires name plus SSN. Also helpful: date of birth, exact years of attendance. There is no fee.

Joliet Junior College, JJC-Transcript Request, 1215 Houbolt Ave, Joliet, IL 60436-9352, 815-729-9020 X2242. Hours: 7:30AM-4PM. Enrollment: 10500. Records go back to 1910. Alumni records are maintained here also. Call 815-729-6620. Degrees granted: Associate. Special programs- Nursing Dept holds limited records for 5 years. Adverse incident record source- Current, Campus Police, 815-729-9020 X2234: Older records, Student Services, 815-729-9020 X2308

Attendance and degree information available by phone, mail. Search requires name plus SSN, approximate years of attendance. Also helpful: date of birth. There is no fee.

Judson College, Registrar, 1151 N State St, Elgin, IL 60123, 847-695-2500 X2210 (Fax: 847-695-4410). Hours: 8AM-4PM. Enrollment: 1000. Records go back to 1963. Alumni records are maintained here also. Call 708-695-2500. Degrees granted: Bachelors. Adverse incident record source- Dean of Students, 847-695-2500.

Attendance and degree information available by phone, fax, mail. Search requires name plus SSN, date of birth, exact years of attendance. There is no fee.

Kankakee Community College, Registrar, PO Box 888, Kankakee, IL 60901, 815-933-0246 (Fax: 815-933-0217). Hours: 8AM-5PM. Enrollment: 4000. Records go back to 1968. Alumni records are maintained here also. Call 815-933-0345. Degrees granted: Associate. Adverse incident record source- Student Services, 814-933-0345.

Attendance and degree information available by phone, fax, mail. Search requires name plus SSN. There is no fee.

Kaskaskia College, Registrar, 27210 College Rd, Centralia, IL 62801, 618-532-1981 X241 (Fax: 618-532-1990). Hours: 7:30AM-3:30PM. Records go back to 1965. Alumni records are maintained here also. Call 618-532-1981. Degrees granted: Associate.

Attendance and degree information available by phone, fax, mail. Search requires name plus SSN. Also helpful: date of birth, approximate years of attendance. There is no fee.

Keller Graduate School of Management, Registrar, 10 S Riverside Plaza, Chicago, IL 60606, 312-454-0880 (Fax: 312-454-6103). Hours: 9AM-4:30PM M-Th, 9AM-5PM F. Enrollment: 3800. Records go back to 1973. Alumni records are maintained here at the same phone number. Degrees granted: Masters. Adverse incident record source- Registrar, 708-574-1960.

Attendance and degree information available by phone, mail. Search requires name plus SSN, exact years of attendance. There is no fee.

Keller Graduate School of Management,
(North Suburban Center), Registrar, Tri State Intl Office Ctr, Bldg 25 Ste 13, Lincolnshire, IL 60069-4460, 708-940-7768. Records are not housed here. They are located at Keller Graduate School of Management, Registrar, 10 S Riverside Plaza, Chicago, IL 60606.

Keller Graduate School of Management,
(Northwest Suburban Center), Registrar, 1051 Perimeter Dr, Schaumburg, IL 60173-5009, 708-574-1960. Hours: 9AM-6PM M-Th, 9AM-5PM F. Enrollment: 3800. Records go back to 1971. Degrees granted: Masters.
Attendance and degree information available by phone, mail. Search requires name plus SSN, exact years of attendance. There is no fee.

Keller Graduate School of Management,
(South Suburban Center), Registrar, 15255 S 94th Ave, Orland Park, IL 60462-3823, 708-460-9580 (Fax: 708-460-0827). Records are not housed here. They are located at Keller Graduate School of Management, Registrar, 10 S Riverside Plaza, Chicago, IL 60606.

Keller Graduate School of Management,
(West Suburban Center), Registrar, 1101 31st St, Downers Grove, IL 60515-5515, 708-969-6624. Records are not housed here. They are located at Keller Graduate School of Management, Registrar, 10 S Riverside Plaza, Chicago, IL 60606.

Kendall College, Registrar, 2408 Orrington Ave, Evanston, IL 60201, 847-866-1325 (Fax: 847-866-6842). Hours: 8AM-4:30PM. Enrollment: 500. Records go back to 1960. Alumni records are maintained here at the same phone number. Degrees granted: Associate; Bachelors. Special programs- Continuing Education. Adverse incident record source- Student Services.
Attendance and degree information available by phone, mail. Search requires name plus SSN, exact years of attendance. Also helpful: date of birth. There is no fee.

Kennedy-King College, Registrar, 6800 S Wentworth Ave, Chicago, IL 60621, 312-602-5081 (Fax: 312-602-5247). Hours: 8:30AM-7PM M-Th, 8:30AM-5PM F. Enrollment: 2502. Records go back to 1900. Alumni records are maintained here at the same phone number. Degrees granted: Associate. Adverse incident record source- Security Office, 312-602-5149.
Attendance and degree information available by fax, mail. Search requires name plus SSN, date of birth, exact years of attendance, signed release. There is no fee.

Kishwaukee College, Admissions, Registration & Records, 21193 Malta Rd, Malta, IL 60150-9699, 815-825-2086 X218 (Fax: 815-825-2306). Hours: 7:30AM-7PM M-Th; 7:30AM-5PM F. Enrollment: 3800. Records go back to 1969. Alumni records are maintained here also. Call 815-825-2086 X266. Degrees granted: Associate; GED. Adverse incident record source- Student Services, 815-825-2086 X249.
Attendance and degree information available by phone, fax, mail. Search requires name only. Also helpful: SSN, date of birth, exact years of attendance. There is no fee.

Knowledge Systems Institute, Registrar, 3420 Main St, Skokie, IL 60076, 847-679-3135 (Fax: 847-679-3166). Hours: 10:30AM-6:30PM. Enrollment: 58. Records go back to 1989. Alumni records are maintained here at the same phone number. Degrees granted: Masters. Special programs- Computer Science. Adverse incident record source- Registrar, 708-679-3135.
Attendance and degree information available by fax, mail. Search requires name plus SSN, exact years of attendance, signed release. There is no fee.

Knox College, Registrar, Galesburg, IL 61401, 308-341-7205 (Fax: 308-341-7708). Hours: 8AM-4:30PM. Enrollment: 1100. Records go back to 1837. Alumni records are maintained here also. Call 309-341-7337. Degrees granted: Bachelors. Special programs- Studies Abroad. Adverse incident record source- Student Affairs, 309-341-7222.
Attendance and degree information available by phone, mail. Search requires name plus exact years of attendance. There is no fee.

Lake Forest College, Registrar, 555 N Sheridan Rd, Lake Forest, IL 60045, 708-735-5025 (Fax: 708-735-6292). Hours: 8:30AM-5PM. Enrollment: 1000. Records go back to 1860. Alumni records are maintained here also. Call 708-735-6016. Degrees granted: Bachelors; Masters. Adverse incident record source- Dean of Students, 708-735-5200.
Attendance and degree information available by phone, fax, mail. Search requires name plus exact years of attendance. There is no fee.

Lake Forest Graduate School of Management, Registrar, 280 N Sheridan Rd, Lake Forest, IL 60045, 847-234-5005 (Fax: 847-295-3656). Hours: 8:30AM-4:30PM. Enrollment: 750. Records go back to 1960. Alumni records are maintained here at the same phone number. Degrees granted: Masters.
Attendance and degree information available by phone, fax, mail. Search requires name plus SSN, date of birth. Also helpful: exact years of attendance. There is no fee.

Lake Land College, Registrar, 5001 Lake Land Blvd, Mattoon, IL 61938, 217-234-5378 (Fax: 217-234-5390). Hours: 7:30AM-6:30PM M-Th, 7:30AM-5PM F. Enrollment: 5100. Records go back to 1970. Alumni records are maintained here also. Call 217-234-5253. Degrees granted: Associate. Special programs- AG Technology, John Deere, 217-234-5308: Associate Degree Nursing, 217-234-5204: Civil Engineering, 217-234-5342: Dental Hygiene, 217-234-5203: Physical Therapist Assistant, 217-342-0955.
Attendance and degree information available by phone, mail. Search requires name plus SSN, date of birth, exact years of attendance. There is no fee.

Lewis University, Registrar, Route 53, Romeoville, IL 60446, 815-838-0500 X5217 (Fax: 815-838-9456). Hours: 8:30AM-5PM. Enrollment: 4144. Records go back to 1932. Alumni records are maintained here also. Call 815-838-0500 X244. Degrees granted: Associate; Bachelors; Masters. Special programs- Associate Degrees in all Phases of Aviation & FFA Approved: FLight Certification by the State of Illinois. Adverse incident record source- 815-838-0500.
Attendance and degree information available by phone, fax, mail. Search requires name plus SSN. Also helpful: date of birth, exact years of attendance. There is no fee.

Lewis and Clark Community College, Registrar, 5800 Godfrey Rd, Godfrey, IL 62035, 618-466-3411 X5112 (Fax: 618-467-2210). Hours: 8AM-4PM M,Th,F; 8AM-7PM T,W. Enrollment: 6000. Records go back to 1970. Degrees granted: Associate.
Attendance and degree information available by phone, fax, mail. Search requires name plus SSN. Also helpful: date of birth. There is no fee.

Lexington College, Registrar, 10840 S Western Ave, Chicago, IL 60643, 312-779-3800 (Fax: 312-779-7450). Hours: 8:45AM-4PM. Enrollment: 50. Formerly Lexington Institute of Hospitality Careers Records go back to 1977. Alumni records are maintained here at the same phone number. Degrees granted: Associate.

Attendance and degree information available by mail. Search requires name plus SSN, exact years of attendance, signed release. There is no fee.

Lincoln Christian College and Seminary,
Registrar, 100 Campus View Dr, Lincoln, IL 62656, 217-732-3168 X2244 (Fax: 217-732-5914). Hours: 7:30AM-4:30PM. Enrollment: 800. Records go back to 1946. Alumni records are maintained here at the same phone number. Degrees granted: Associate; Bachelors; Masters.

Attendance and degree information available by phone, fax, mail. Search requires name only. Also helpful: exact years of attendance. There is no fee.

Lincoln College,
Registrar, 300 Keokuk St, Lincoln, IL 62656, 217-732-3155 (Fax: 217-732-2992). Hours: 8AM-5PM. Enrollment: 850. Records go back to 1800's. Alumni records are maintained here also. Call 217-735-4902. Degrees granted: Associate. Adverse incident record source- Dean of Students, 217-732-3155 X300.

Attendance and degree information available by fax, mail. Search requires name plus SSN, signed release. Also helpful: date of birth, exact years of attendance. There is no fee.

Lincoln Land Community College,
Admissions and Records, Shepherd Rd, Springfield, IL 62794-9256, 217-786-2200 (Fax: 217-786-2492). Hours: 8AM-5PM. Enrollment: 11000. Records go back to 1969. Alumni records are maintained here at the same phone number. Degrees granted: Associate. Adverse incident record source- Enrollment Services, 217-786-2212.

Attendance and degree information available by phone. Search requires name only. Also helpful: SSN, date of birth, exact years of attendance. There is no fee.

Lincoln Trail College,
Registrar, 11220 State Hwy 1, Robinson, IL 62454-5707, 618-544-8657 X1137 (Fax: 618-544-9384). Hours: 8AM-5PM. Enrollment: 650. Records go back to 1971. Degrees granted: Associate. Special programs- Telecommunications: Nursing. Adverse incident record source- Dean of Students, 618-544-8657.

Attendance and degree information available by phone, fax, mail. Search requires name plus SSN. Also helpful: date of birth, approximate years of attendance. There is no fee.

Loyola University of Chicago,
Registrar, 820 N Michigan Ave, Chicago, IL 60611, 312-915-7221 (Fax: 312-915-6448). Hours: 8:30AM-5PM. Enrollment: 13806. Records go back to 1870. Alumni Records Office: 6525 N Sheridan Rd, Chicago, IL 60626. Degrees granted: Bachelors; Masters; Doctorate. Special programs- Stritch School of Medicine, 708-216-3222. Adverse incident record source- Dean of Students, 312-915-6000.

Attendance and degree information available by phone, fax, mail. Search requires name plus SSN, approximate years of attendance. Also helpful: date of birth, exact years of attendance. There is no fee.

Lutheran School of Theology,
Registrar, 1100 E 55 St, Chicago, IL 60615, 312-256-0700 (Fax: 312-256-0782). Enrollment: 384. Alumni records are maintained here also. Call 312-256-0785. Degrees granted: Masters; Doctorate.

Attendance and degree information available by phone, fax, mail. Search requires name plus exact years of attendance. Also helpful: SSN, date of birth. There is no fee.

Lutheran School of Theology at Chicago,
Registrar, 1100 E 55th St, Chicago, IL 60615-5199, 312-256-0700 (Fax: 312-256-0782). Hours: 8:30AM-4:30PM. Enrollment: 384. Records go back to 1940. Alumni records are maintained here also. Call 312-256-0785. Degrees granted: Masters; Doctorate. Certification: Theology.

Attendance information available by phone, mail. Search requires name plus SSN. Also helpful: date of birth, exact years of attendance. There is no fee.

Degree information available by phone, fax, mail. Search requires name plus SSN. Also helpful: date of birth, exact years of attendance. There is no fee.

MacCormac Junior College,
Registrar, 506 S Wabash Ave, Chicago, IL 60605-1667, 312-922-1884. Hours: 8AM-5PM. Enrollment: 415. Records go back to 1979. Degrees granted: Associate.

Attendance and degree information available by phone, fax, mail. Search requires name only. Also helpful: SSN. There is no fee.

MacMurray College,
Records and Registration, 477 E College Ave, Jacksonville, IL 62650, 217-479-7012 (Fax: 217-245-0405). Hours: 8AM-4:30PM. Enrollment: 700. Alumni records are maintained here also. Call 217-479-7024. Degrees granted: Associate; Bachelors.

Attendance information available by phone, fax, mail. Search requires name only. Also helpful: exact years of attendance. There is no fee.

Degree information available by phone, mail. Search requires name only. Also helpful: exact years of attendance. There is no fee.

Malcolm X College,
Registrar, 1900 W Van Buren St, Chicago, IL 60612, 312-850-7098 (Fax: 312-850-7092). Hours: 8:30AM-6PM. Enrollment: 5000. Records go back to 1966. Alumni records are maintained here at the same phone number. Degrees granted: Associate. Adverse incident record source- Security, 312-850-7000.

Attendance and degree information available by phone, fax, mail. Search requires name plus SSN. Also helpful: date of birth, exact years of attendance. There is no fee.

McCormick Theological Seminary,
Registrar, 5555 S Woodlawn Ave, Chicago, IL 60637, 312-947-6285 (Fax: 312-947-0376). Hours: 8:30AM-4:30PM. Enrollment: 450. Records go back to 1918. Alumni records are maintained here also. Call 312-947-9821. Degrees granted: Masters; Doctorate.

Attendance and degree information available by phone, fax, mail. Search requires name only. Also helpful: exact years of attendance. There is no fee.

McHenry County College,
Registrar, 8900 US Hwy 14, Crystal Lake, IL 60012-2794, 815-455-3700 (Fax: 815-455-3766). Hours: 8AM-7:30PM M-Th; 8AM-4PM F. Records go back to 1967. Degrees granted: Associate.

Attendance and degree information available by phone, fax, mail. Search requires name only. Also helpful: SSN, date of birth. There is no fee.

McKendree College,
Registrar, 701 College Rd, Lebanon, IL 62254, 618-537-6818 (Fax: 618-537-6259). Hours: 8AM-5PM. Enrollment: 1632. Records go back to 1928. Alumni records are maintained here also. Call 618-537-4481. Degrees granted: Associate; Bachelors.

Attendance and degree information available by phone, fax, mail. Search requires name only. Also helpful: SSN, exact years of attendance. There is no fee.

Meadville/Lombard Theological School,
Registrar, 5701 S Woodlawn Ave, Chicago, IL 60637, 312-753-3282 (Fax: 312-753-1323). Hours: 9AM-5PM. Enrollment: 83. Records go back to 1935. Alumni records are maintained here also. Call 312-753-3195. Degrees granted: Masters; Doctorate. Adverse incident record source- Dean of Students, 312-753-3195.

Attendance and degree information available by mail. Search requires name plus SSN, date of birth, exact years of attendance, signed release. There is no fee.

Mennonite College of Nursing, Registrar, 804 N East St, Bloomington, IL 61701, 309-829-0715 (Fax: 309-829-0765). Hours: 8AM-4:30PM. Enrollment: 210. Records go back to 1919. Alumni records are maintained here at the same phone number. Degrees granted: Bachelors. Adverse incident record source- 309-829-0715.

Attendance and degree information available by phone, fax, mail. Search requires name only. Also helpful: SSN, date of birth, exact years of attendance. There is no fee.

Midstate College, Registrar, 244 SW Jefferson St, Peoria, IL 61602, 309-673-6365 (Fax: 309-673-5814). Hours: 8AM-4:30PM. Enrollment: 350. Records go back to 1950's. Degrees granted: Associate.

Attendance and degree information available by phone, fax, mail. Search requires name plus SSN. Also helpful: date of birth, approximate years of attendance. There is no fee.

Midwestern University, Registrar, 555 31st St, Downers Grove, IL 60515, 708-515-6074 (Fax: 708-515-7140). Hours: 8AM-5PM. Enrollment: 14000. Formerly Chicago College of Osteopathic Medicine Records go back to 1921. Alumni records are maintained here at the same phone number. Degrees granted: Bachelors; Masters; Doctorate. Special programs-Medical: Pharmacy: Allied Health. Adverse incident record source- Student Affairs, 708-515-6470.

Attendance and degree information available by phone, fax, mail. Search requires name only. Also helpful: SSN, date of birth, exact years of attendance. There is no fee.

Millikin University, Registrar, 1184 W Main St, Decatur, IL 62522, 217-424-6217 (Fax: 217-424-3993). Hours: 8AM-5PM. Enrollment: 1850. Records go back to 1903. Alumni records are maintained here also. Call 217-424-6384. Degrees granted: Bachelors. Adverse incident record source- Student Development, 217-424-6240.

Attendance and degree information available by phone, fax, mail. Search requires name plus SSN, date of birth, exact years of attendance. There is no fee.

Monmouth College, Registrar, 700 E Broadway, Monmouth, IL 61462, 309-457-2326 (Fax: 309-457-2141). Hours: 8AM-Noon, 1-4:30PM. Enrollment: 950. Records go back to 1920's. Alumni records are maintained here also. Call 309-457-2336. Degrees granted: Bachelors. Adverse incident record source- Dean of Students.

Attendance and degree information available by phone, fax, mail. Search requires name only. Also helpful: SSN, date of birth, exact years of attendance. There is no fee.

Montay College, Registrar, 3750 W Peterson Ave, Chicago, IL 60659, 312-539-1919 (Fax: 312-539-1913). Hours: 8AM-4PM. Records go back to 1966. Degrees granted: Associate.

Attendance and degree information available by fax, mail. Search requires name plus approximate years of attendance, signed release. Also helpful: SSN, date of birth, exact years of attendance. There is no fee.

Moody Bible Institute, Registrar, 820 N La Salle Blvd, Chicago, IL 60610, 312-329-4261 (Fax: 312-329-8987). Hours: 8AM-4:30PM. Enrollment: 5697. Records go back to 1885. Alumni records are maintained here also. Call 312-329-4412. Degrees granted: Masters. Adverse incident record source- Student Development.

Attendance and degree information available by phone, fax, mail. Search requires name plus SSN, exact years of attendance. There is no fee.

Moraine Valley Community College, Registrar, 10900 S 88th Ave, Palos Hills, IL 60465, 708-974-5346 (Fax: 708-974-0974). Hours: 8:30AM-7:30PM M,T; 8:30AM-5PM W-F. Records go back to 1969. Degrees granted: Associate. Adverse incident record source- Public Safety, 708-974-5500.

Attendance and degree information available by phone, mail. Search requires name plus SSN, date of birth. Also helpful: exact years of attendance. There is no fee.

Morrison Institute of Technology, Registrar, 701 Portland Ave, Morrison, IL 61270-0410, 815-772-7218 (Fax: 815-772-7584). Hours: 8AM-4:30PM. Enrollment: 175. Records go back to 1975. Alumni records are maintained here at the same phone number. Degrees granted: Associate. Adverse incident record source- Student Affairs, 815-772-7218.

Attendance and degree information available by phone, mail. Search requires name plus SSN. There is no fee.

Morton College, Registrar, 3801 S Central Ave, Cicero, IL 60650, 708-656-8000 (Fax: 708-656-9592). Hours: 9AM-8PM M-Th, 9AM-4PM F. Enrollment: 4200. Records go back to 1925. Degrees granted: Associate.

Attendance information available by fax, mail. Search requires name plus SSN, date of birth, signed release. Also helpful: exact years of attendance. There is no fee.

Degree information available by phone, fax, mail. Search requires name plus SSN, date of birth. Also helpful: exact years of attendance. There is no fee.

NAES College, Registrar, 2838 W Peterson Ave, Chicago, IL 60659, 312-761-5000 (Fax: 312-761-3808). Hours: 9AM-5PM. Enrollment: 118. Records go back to 1977. Alumni records are maintained here also. Call 312-761-5000. Degrees granted: Bachelors. Adverse incident record source- President, 312-761-5000.

Attendance and degree information available by phone, fax, mail. Search requires name plus SSN. There is no fee.

National College of Chiropractic, Registrar, 200 E Roosevelt Rd, Lombard, IL 60148, 708-889-6548 (Fax: 708-889-6554). Hours: 8:30AM-6:30PM. Enrollment: 900. Records go back to 1945. Alumni records are maintained here also. Call 708-629-9664. Degrees granted: Bachelors; Doctorate. Adverse incident record source- Registrar, 708-889-6548.

Attendance and degree information available by mail. Search requires name plus SSN. Fee is $15.00.

National-Louis University, Transcript Department, 1000 Capitol Dr, Wheeling, IL 60090, 847-465-0575. Hours: 8:30AM-4:30PM. Enrollment: 2727. Records go back to 1886. Degrees granted: Bachelors; Masters; Doctorate.

Attendance and degree information available by phone, mail. Search requires name plus SSN. Also helpful: exact years of attendance. There is no fee.

North Central College, Registrar, 30 N Brainerd St, PO Box 3063, Naperville, IL 60566-7063, 630-637-5253 (Fax: 630-637-5121). Hours: 8AM-4PM. Enrollment: 2500. Alumni records are maintained here at the same phone number. Degrees granted: Bachelors; Masters. Adverse incident record source-Dispute Resolution Program.

Attendance and degree information available by phone, mail. Search requires name plus exact years of attendance. Also helpful: SSN, date of birth. There is no fee.

North Park College and Theological Seminary, Registrar, 3225 W Foster Ave, Chicago, IL 60625-4895, 773-244-5560 (Fax: 773-244-4954). Hours: 8AM-4:30PM M,Th,F; 8AM-7PM T,W. Enrollment: 1790. Records go back to 1886. Alumni records are maintained here also. Call 708-244-5754. Degrees granted: Bachelors; Masters. Certification: Teacher.

Attendance and degree information available by phone, fax, mail. Search requires name plus SSN, approximate years of attendance. Also helpful: exact years of attendance. There is no fee.

Northeastern Illinois University, Admissions and
Records, 5500 N St Louis Ave, Chicago, IL 60625, 312-583-4050 X3650 (Fax: 312-794-6246). Hours: 8:30AM-4:30PM. Enrollment: 10000. Records go back to 1962. Alumni Records Office: 5350 St Louis Ave, Chicago, IL 60625. Degrees granted: Bachelors; Masters. Adverse incident record source- Dean of Students, 312-583-4050 X 3167.

Attendance and degree information available by phone, fax, mail. Search requires name only. Also helpful: SSN, exact years of attendance. There is no fee.

Northern Baptist Theological Seminary, Registrar, 660 E Butterfield Rd, Lombard, IL 60148, 630-620-2105 (Fax: 630-620-2194). Hours: 8:30AM-4:30PM. Enrollment: 450. Alumni records are maintained here at the same phone number. Degrees granted: Masters; Doctorate. Adverse incident record source- Registrar, 630-620-2105.

Attendance and degree information available by written request only. Search requires name plus signed release. Also helpful: SSN, date of birth, exact years of attendance. There is no fee.

Northern Illinois University, Office of Registration & Records, Altgeld Hall Rm 212, De Kalb, IL 60115, 815-743-0689 (Fax: 815-743-0149). Hours: 8AM-4:30PM. Enrollment: 2200. Records go back to 1899. Alumni records are maintained here also. Call 815-753-1452. Degrees granted: Bachelors; Masters; Doctorate.

Attendance and degree information available by phone, fax, mail. Search requires name plus SSN. Also helpful: date of birth, exact years of attendance. Fee is $3.50.

Northwestern Business College, Registrar, 4829 N Lipps Ave, Chicago, IL 60630, 312-777-4220 (Fax: 312-777-2861). Hours: 8AM-4PM. Enrollment: 990. Alumni records are maintained here at the same phone number. Degrees granted: Associate.

Attendance and degree information available by fax, mail. Search requires name plus SSN, date of birth, approximate years of attendance, signed release. There is no fee.

Northwestern Business College, (Southwestern), Registrar, 8020 W 87th St, Hickory Hills, IL 60457, 708-430-0990 (Fax: 708-430-0995). Hours: 8AM-8PM. Degrees granted: Associate.

Attendance and degree information available by phone, mail. Search requires name plus SSN, date of birth. Also helpful: exact years of attendance. There is no fee.

Northwestern University, Registrar, 633 Clark St, Evanston, IL 60208, 708-491-5234 (Fax: 708-491-8458). Hours: 8:30AM-5PM. Enrollment: 17000. Records go back to 1882. Alumni Records Office: Alumni Agency, 1800 Sheridan Rd, Evanston, IL 60208. Degrees granted: Bachelors; Masters; Doctorate. Adverse incident record source- Student Affairs, 708-491-8430.

Attendance and degree information available by phone, fax, mail. Search requires name only. Also helpful: SSN, date of birth, exact years of attendance. There is no fee.

Oakton Community College, Registrar, 1600 E Golf Rd, Des Plaines, IL 60016, 847-635-1991 (Fax: 847-635-1706). Hours: 8:30AM-8PM M-Th, 8:30AM-5PM F, 9AM-Noon Sat Fall;8:30AM-8PM M-Th Summer. Records go back to 1970. Degrees granted: Associate. Adverse incident record source- Public Safety, 708-635-1880.

Attendance and degree information available by phone, fax, mail. Search requires name plus SSN. There is no fee.

Olive-Harvey College, Registrar, 10001 S Woodlawn Ave, Chicago, IL 60628, 312-291-6346 (Fax: 312-291-6304). Hours: 8AM-7PM M-Th, 9AM-5PM F. Enrollment: 3306. Records go back to 1961. Alumni records are maintained here at the

same phone number. Degrees granted: Associate. Adverse incident record source- Security, 312-291-6348.

Attendance information available by phone, fax, mail. Search requires name plus SSN, approximate years of attendance. Also helpful: date of birth, exact years of attendance. There is no fee.

Degree information available by fax, mail. Search requires name plus SSN, approximate years of attendance. Also helpful: date of birth, exact years of attendance. There is no fee.

Olivet Nazarene University, Registrar, Kankakee, IL 60901, 815-939-5201 (Fax: 815-935-4992). Hours: 8AM-5PM. Enrollment: 2000. Records go back to 1907. Alumni records are maintained here also. Call 815-939-5258. Degrees granted: Associate; Bachelors; Masters. Adverse incident record source- Dean of Students, 815-939-5333.

Attendance and degree information available by phone, fax, mail. Search requires name only. Also helpful: SSN, date of birth, exact years of attendance. There is no fee.

Olney Central College, Registrar, 305 N West St, Olney, IL 62450, 618-395-4351 X2230 (Fax: 618-392-3293). Hours: 8AM-5PM Fall, 7:30AM-4PM Summer. Enrollment: 1500. Records go back to 1963. Alumni records are maintained here also. Call 618-395-4351 X2226. Degrees granted: Associate; Vocational.

Attendance and degree information available by phone, fax, mail. Search requires name plus SSN, approximate years of attendance. There is no fee.

Parkland College, Registrar, 2400 W Bradley Ave, Champaign, IL 61821, 217-353-2625 (Fax: 217-353-2640). Hours: 7:30AM-8PM M-Th; 7:30AM-5PM F; 9AM-Noon S. Enrollment: 9500. Records go back to 1966. Alumni records are maintained here at the same phone number. Degrees granted: Associate.

Attendance and degree information available by phone, fax, mail. Search requires name plus SSN, approximate years of attendance. Also helpful: date of birth. There is no fee.

Prairie State College, Registrar, 202 S Halsted St, Chicago Heights, IL 60411, 708-709-3514 (Fax: 708-755-2587). Hours: 8AM-4:30PM. Enrollment: 5000. Records go back to 1958. Alumni records are maintained here also. Call 708-709-3734. Degrees granted: Associate. Adverse incident record source- Information Office.

Attendance and degree information available by phone, fax, mail. Search requires name plus SSN. Also helpful: date of birth, exact years of attendance. There is no fee.

Principia College, Registrar, Elsah, IL 62028, 618-374-5100 (Fax: 618-374-5122). Hours: 8AM-5PM. Enrollment: 560. Records go back to 1934. Alumni Records Office: 13202 Clayton Rd, St Louis, MO 63131-1099. Degrees granted: Bachelors. Adverse incident record source- Student Life, 618-374-2131.

Attendance and degree information available by phone, fax, mail. Search requires name only. Also helpful: exact years of attendance. There is no fee.

Quincy University, Registrar, 1800 College Ave, Quincy, IL 62301, 217-228-5280. Hours: 8AM-5PM. Enrollment: 1000. Formerly Quincy College Records go back to 1860. Alumni records are maintained here at the same phone number. Degrees granted: Bachelors; Masters.

Attendance and degree information available by phone, mail. Search requires name only. Also helpful: SSN, date of birth, exact years of attendance. There is no fee.

Ray College of Design, Registrar, 350 N Orleans St #136, Chicago, IL 60654-3532, 312-280-3500 (Fax: 312-280-3528). Hours: 9AM-4PM. Records go back to 1960's. Alumni records are maintained here at the same phone number. Degrees granted: Associate; Bachelors; Diploma.

Attendance information available by written request only. Search requires name plus SSN, approximate years of attendance, signed release. Also helpful: exact years of attendance. There is no fee.

Degree information available by mail. Search requires name plus SSN. Also helpful: exact years of attendance. There is no fee.

Rend Lake College, Registrar, Rural Rte 1, Ina, IL 62846, 618-437-5321 (Fax: 618-437-5677). Hours: 8AM-4:30PM M-Th; 8AM-4PMF. Enrollment: 8500. Records go back to 1956. Alumni records are maintained here at the same phone number. Degrees granted: Associate.

Attendance information available by phone, fax, mail. Search requires name plus SSN. Also helpful: date of birth, exact years of attendance. There is no fee.

Degree information available by phone, fax, mail. Search requires name only. There is no fee.

Richard J. Daley College, Registrar, 7500 S PUlaski Rd, Chicago, IL 60652, 312-838-7600 (Fax: 312-838-7605). Hours: 8AM-7PM. Records go back to 1960. Degrees granted: Associate.

Attendance and degree information available by phone, fax, mail. Search requires name plus SSN, exact years of attendance. There is no fee.

Richland Community College, Registrar, One College Park, Decatur, IL 62521, 217-875-7200 (Fax: 217-875-6965). Hours: 8AM-8PM M-Th; 8AM-5PM F. Enrollment: 4000. Records go back to 1972. Degrees granted: Associate.

Attendance and degree information available by phone, fax, mail. Search requires name plus SSN, date of birth. Also helpful: exact years of attendance. There is no fee.

Robert Morris College, Registrar, 180 N LaSalle St, Chicago, IL 60601, 312-836-4888 (Fax: 312-836-4853). Hours: 8:30AM-5PM. Enrollment: 3500. Records go back to 1950. Alumni records are maintained here also. Call 312-836-5469. Degrees granted: Associate; Bachelors.

Attendance and degree information available by phone, fax, mail. Search requires name plus SSN, exact years of attendance. There is no fee.

Rock Valley College, Registrar, 3301 N Mulford Rd, Rockford, IL 61114, 815-654-4306 (Fax: 815-654-5568). Hours: 8AM-5PM. Enrollment: 8910. Records go back to 1965. Alumni records are maintained here also. Call 815-654-4277. Degrees granted: Associate. Adverse incident record source- Dean of Students, 815-654-4270.

Attendance and degree information available by phone, fax, mail. Search requires name plus SSN. Also helpful: date of birth, exact years of attendance. There is no fee.

Rockford Business College, Registrar, 730 N Church St, Rockford, IL 61103, 815-965-8616 (Fax: 815-965-0360). Hours: 8AM-9PM. Records go back to 1950's. Alumni records are maintained here at the same phone number. Degrees granted: Associate. Adverse incident record source- Financial Aide, 815-965-8616.

Attendance information available by phone, fax, mail. Search requires name plus SSN, approximate years of attendance. Also helpful: exact years of attendance. There is no fee.

Degree information available by phone, fax, mail. Search requires name plus approximate years of attendance. Also helpful: SSN, exact years of attendance. There is no fee.

Rockford College, Registrar, 5050 E State St, Rockford, IL 61108, 815-226-4070 (Fax: 815-226-4119). Hours: 8AM-5PM. Enrollment: 1500. Records go back to 1925. Alumni records are maintained here also. Call 815-226-4080. Degrees granted: Bachelors; Masters.

Attendance and degree information available by phone, fax, mail. Search requires name plus SSN. Also helpful: date of birth, exact years of attendance. There is no fee.

Roosevelt University, Registrar, 430 S Michigan Ave, Chicago, IL 60605, 312-341-3526 (Fax: 312-341-3660). Hours: 9AM-6PM M,T; 9AM-5PM W,Th; 9AM-3PM F. Enrollment: 6000. Records go back to 1945. Alumni records are maintained here also. Call 312-341-3624. Degrees granted: Bachelors; Masters; Doctorate. Special programs- Lawyers Assistance: Continuing Ed. Adverse incident record source- Student Affairs, 312-341-3540.

Attendance and degree information available by phone, fax, mail. Search requires name plus SSN. Also helpful: date of birth, exact years of attendance. There is no fee.

Rosary College, Registrar, 7900 W Division St, River Forest, IL 60305, 708-366-2490. Enrollment: 850. Records go back to 1920. Alumni records are maintained here at the same phone number. Degrees granted: Bachelors; Masters.

Attendance and degree information available by phone, mail. Search requires name only. Also helpful: SSN, date of birth, exact years of attendance. There is no fee.

Rush University, Registrar, 1653 W Congress Pkwy, Chicago, IL 60612, 312-942-5681 (Fax: 312-942-6219). Hours: 8AM-5PM. Alumni records are maintained here also. Call 312-942-7165. Degrees granted: Doctorate; PhD.

Attendance information available by phone, fax, mail. Search requires name plus SSN, approximate years of attendance. There is no fee.

Degree information available by mail. Search requires name plus SSN, approximate years of attendance. There is no fee.

Sauk Valley Community College, Registrar, 173 Illinois Rte 2, Dixon, IL 61021, 815-288-5511 (Fax: 815-288-3190). Hours: 8AM-4:30PM. Enrollment: 3000. Records go back to 1965. Alumni records are maintained here at the same phone number. Degrees granted: Associate.

Attendance information available by phone, fax, mail. Search requires name plus SSN, approximate years of attendance. Also helpful: date of birth, exact years of attendance. There is no fee.

Degree information available by phone, fax, mail. Search requires name plus SSN. There is no fee.

School of the Art Institute of Chicago, Registrar, 37 S Wabash Ave, Chicago, IL 60603, 312-899-5117 (Fax: 312-263-0141). Hours: 8:30AM-4:30PM. Enrollment: 3000. Records go back to 1890. Alumni records are maintained here also. Call 312-899-5217. Degrees granted: Bachelors; Masters; Post Graduate. Adverse incident record source- Student Affairs, 312-899-5105.

Attendance and degree information available by phone, fax, mail. Search requires name plus SSN, approximate years of attendance. Also helpful: date of birth, exact years of attendance. There is no fee.

Seabury-Western Theological Seminary, Registrar, 2122 Sheridan Rd, Evanston, IL 60201, 708-328-9300 (Fax: 708-328-9624). Hours: 8:30AM-5PM; 9AM-4PM Jun-Aug. Enrollment: 115. Records go back to 1931. Alumni records are maintained here at the same phone number. Degrees granted: Masters; Doctorate.

Attendance and degree information available by phone, fax, mail. Search requires name plus date of birth, approximate years of attendance. Also helpful: SSN, exact years of attendance. There is no fee.

Shawnee Community College, Registrar, Rural Rte 1 Box 53, Ullin, IL 62992-9725, 618-634-2242 (Fax: 618-634-9028). Hours: 8AM-4PM. Enrollment: 2233. Records go back to 1969. Degrees granted: Associate.

Attendance and degree information available by phone, fax, mail. Search requires name plus SSN, date of birth. Also helpful: approximate years of attendance. There is no fee.

Sherwood Conservatory of Music, Registrar, Box A500, Chicago, IL 60605, 312-427-6267 (Fax: 312-427-6677). Enrollment: 1000. Records go back to 1920. Degrees granted: Music. Adverse incident record source- Student Services.

Attendance and degree information available by mail. Search requires name plus SSN, exact years of attendance, signed release. There is no fee.

Shimer College, Registrar, PO Box A500, 438 N Sheridan Rd, Waukegan, IL 60079, 708-249-7183 (Fax: 708-249-7171). Hours: 9AM-5PM. Enrollment: 125. Records go back to 1853. Alumni records are maintained here also. Call 708-249-7191. Degrees granted: Bachelors. Special programs- Academic, 708-623-8400.

Attendance and degree information available by phone, fax, mail. Search requires name only. There is no fee.

South Suburban College of Cook County, Registrar, 15800 S State St, South Holland, IL 60473, 708-596-2000 (Fax: 708-210-5746). Hours: 8AM-4:30PM. Enrollment: 8677. Records go back to 1986. Alumni records are maintained here also. Call 708-596-2000 X456. Degrees granted: Associate. Adverse incident record source- Campus Police, 708-596-2000 X235.

Attendance information available by phone, mail. Search requires name plus SSN, date of birth. Also helpful: approximate years of attendance. There is no fee.

Degree information available by phone, mail. Search requires name plus SSN. Also helpful: date of birth, approximate years of attendance. There is no fee.

Southeastern Illinois College, Registrar, 3575 College Rd, Harrisburg, IL 62946, 618-252-6376 (Fax: 618-252-6376). Hours: 8AM-4:30PM. Enrollment: 3382. Records go back to 1960. Degrees granted: Associate. Special programs- Incarcerated Students: Vienna Corr Cen, 618-658-2211.

Attendance and degree information available by phone, fax, mail. Search requires name only. Also helpful: SSN, date of birth, exact years of attendance. There is no fee.

Southern Illinois University at Carbondale, Admissions & Records, Carbondale, IL 62901, 618-453-4381 (Fax: 618-453-3250). Hours: 8AM-4:30PM. Enrollment: 23000. Records go back to 1869. Alumni Records Office: Alumni Association, Stone Center 6809, Carbondale, IL 62901. Degrees granted: Associate; Bachelors; Masters; Doctorate. Special programs- Law, 618-536-7711: Medicine, 217-782-3625. Adverse incident record source- Campus Police, 618-453-2381.

Attendance and degree information available by phone, fax, mail. Search requires name plus SSN, date of birth. Also helpful: exact years of attendance. There is no fee.

Southern Illinois University at Edwardsville, Admissions & Records, Campus Box 1047, Edwardsville, IL 62026, 618-692-2080 (Fax: 618-692-2081). Hours: 8AM-8PM M-Th, 8AM-4:30PM F, 8AM-2PM Sat. Enrollment: 11047. Records go back to 1957. Alumni records are maintained here at the same phone number. Degrees granted: Bachelors; Masters.

Attendance information available by phone, fax, mail. Search requires name plus SSN. Also helpful: date of birth, exact years of attendance. There is no fee.

Degree information available by phone, fax, mail. Search requires name plus SSN. There is no fee.

Spertus Institute of Jewish Studies, Registrar, 618 S Michigan Ave, Chicago, IL 60605, 312-922-9012 (Fax: 312-922-6406). Hours: 9AM-5PM. Enrollment: 140. Formerly Spertus College of Judaica Records go back to 1924. Degrees granted: Masters; Doctorate. Adverse incident record source- Student Services.

Attendance and degree information available by phone, fax, mail. Search requires name only. Also helpful: exact years of attendance. There is no fee.

Spoon River College, Records Dept, 23235 N Co 22, Canton, IL 61520, 309-647-4645 (Fax: 309-647-6498). Hours: 8AM-5PM. Enrollment: 2000. Records go back to 1959. Alumni records are maintained here at the same phone number. Degrees granted: Associate.

Attendance and degree information available by phone, fax, mail. Search requires name plus SSN. Also helpful: date of birth, exact years of attendance. There is no fee.

Springfield College in Illinois, Registrar, 1500 N Fifth St, Springfield, IL 62702, 217-525-1420 X213. Hours: 8AM-4:30PM Fall; 7:30AM-4PM M-Th Summer. Records go back to 1929. Alumni records are maintained here also. Call 217-525-1420 X228. Degrees granted: Associate.

Attendance and degree information available by mail. Search requires name plus SSN, exact years of attendance, signed release. There is no fee.

St. Augustine College, Registrar, 1333 W Argyle St, Chicago, IL 60640, 312-878-8756 (Fax: 312-878-9032). Hours: 9AM-8PM. Enrollment: 1450. Records go back to 1981. Degrees granted: Associate. Adverse incident record source- Student Affairs, 312-878-8756.

Attendance and degree information available by phone, fax, mail. Search requires name plus SSN. There is no fee.

St. Francis Medical Center College of Nursing, Registrar, 511 NE Greenleaf St, Peoria, IL 61603, 309-655-2596 (Fax: 309-655-3648). Hours: 7AM-3:30PM. Enrollment: 150. Records go back to 1956. School of Nursing records from 1956; College of Nursing records from 1986. Alumni records are maintained here also. Call 309-655-4125. Degrees granted: Bachelors.

School will not confirm attendance or degree information.

St. Joseph College of Nursing, Registrar, 290 N Springfield Ave, Joliet, IL 60435, 815-741-7143 (Fax: 815-741-7131). Hours: 8AM-4PM. Enrollment: 200. Records go back to 1922. Alumni records are maintained here at the same phone number. Degrees granted: Bachelors.

Attendance and degree information available by phone, fax, mail. Search requires name plus SSN, approximate years of attendance. Also helpful: date of birth. There is no fee.

St. Louis University, (Parks College), Registrar, Falling Springs Rd, Cahokia, IL 62206, 618-337-7575 (Fax: 618-336-7908). Hours: 8AM-4:30PM. Enrollment: 600. Records go back to 1927. Alumni Records Office: 221 N Grand Dubourg Hall 318, St Louis, MO 63103. Degrees granted: Bachelors. Adverse incident record source- Risk Management, 314-977-3952.

Attendance and degree information available by phone, fax, mail. Search requires name plus SSN, approximate years of attendance. Also helpful: date of birth, exact years of attendance. There is no fee.

St. Xavier University, Office of the Registrar, 3700 W 103rd St, Chicago, IL 60655, 312-298-3501 (Fax: 312-298-3508). Hours: 8:30AM-7PM. Enrollment: 4170. Records go back to 1925. Alumni records are maintained here also. Call 312-298-3318. Degrees granted: Bachelors; Masters. Special programs- Field Based Masters in Education, 312-298-3155. Adverse incident record source- Dean of Students.

Attendance and degree information available by phone, mail. Search requires name plus SSN, exact years of attendance. Also helpful: date of birth. There is no fee.

State Community College of East St. Louis, Registrar, 601 James R Thompson Blvd, East St Louis, IL 62201, 618-583-2609 (Fax: 618-583-2661). Hours: 8:30AM-5PM. Records go back to 1969. Alumni records are maintained here also. Call 618-583-2575. Degrees granted: Associate. Adverse incident record source- Campus Police, 618-583-2525.

Attendance and degree information available by fax, mail. Search requires name plus SSN, signed release. There is no fee.

Taylor Business Institute, Registrar, 36 S State St Ste 800, Chicago, IL 60603, 312-236-6400 X33 (Fax: 312-853-0390). Hours: 8:30AM-6PM. Records go back to 1975. Degrees granted: Associate.

Attendance information available by phone, fax, mail. Search requires name only. There is no fee.

Degree information available by fax, mail. Search requires name only. There is no fee.

Telshe Yeshiva-Chicago, Registrar, 3535 W Foster Ave, Chicago, IL 60625, 312-463-7738 (Fax: 312-463-2849). Hours: 8AM-5PM. Records go back to 1960. Degrees granted: Masters.

Attendance and degree information available by mail. Search requires name plus SSN. There is no fee.

Trinity Christian College, Registrar, 6601 W College Dr, Palos Heights, IL 60463, 708-597-3000 (Fax: 708-239-3986). Hours: 8AM-4:30PM. Enrollment: 600. Records go back to 1960. Alumni records are maintained here at the same phone number. Degrees granted: Bachelors.

Attendance and degree information available by phone, fax, mail. Search requires name plus approximate years of attendance. Also helpful: exact years of attendance. There is no fee.

Trinity Evangelical Divinity School, Registrar, 2065 Half Day Dr, Deerfield, IL 60015, 847-317-8050 (Fax: 847-317-8097). Hours: 8AM-5PM. Enrollment: 2049. Records go back to 1897. Alumni records are maintained here at the same phone number. Degrees granted: Bachelors; Masters; Doctorate.

Attendance and degree information available by mail. Search requires name plus date of birth, exact years of attendance. There is no fee.

Trinity International University, (College of Liberal Arts), Records Office, 2065 Half Day Rd, Deerfield, IL 60015, 708-317-7050 (Fax: 708-317-7081). Hours: 9AM-4PM. Enrollment: 800. Records go back to 1890. Alumni records are maintained here also. Call 708-317-8145. Degrees granted: Bachelors. Special programs- Continuing Education & Extension, 708-317-6550.

Attendance and degree information available by phone, fax, mail. Search requires name only. Also helpful: SSN, date of birth, exact years of attendance. There is no fee.

Triton College, Registrar, 2000 Fifth Ave, River Grove, IL 60171, 708-456-0300 X3748 (Fax: 708-583-3108). Hours: 8:30AM-7:30PM M-Th, 8:30AM-4PM F. Enrollment: 18000. Records go back to 1969. Degrees granted: Associate. Adverse incident record source- Police Dept, 708-456-0300 X2203.

Attendance and degree information available by phone, fax, mail. Search requires name plus SSN. Also helpful: date of birth, exact years of attendance. There is no fee.

University of Chicago, Registrar, 5801 S Ellis Ave, Chicago, IL 60637, 312-702-7880 (Fax: 312-702-3562). Hours: 9AM-4PM. Enrollment: 11226. Records go back to 1892. Alumni records are maintained here also. Call 312-702-2150. Degrees granted: Bachelors; Masters; Doctorate.

Attendance information available by phone, fax, mail. Search requires name plus SSN, date of birth. Also helpful: exact years of attendance. There is no fee.

Degree information available by phone, fax, mail. Search requires name plus SSN, date of birth, approximate years of attendance. There is no fee.

University of Illinois at Chicago, Registrar, PO Box 5220, Chicago, IL 60680, 312-996-4350. Hours: 8:30AM-4:45PM. Records go back to 1936. Alumni records are maintained here at the same phone number. Degrees granted: Bachelors; Masters; Doctorate; MD,DDS,PharmD. Adverse incident record source- University Police, 312-996-2830.

Attendance and degree information available by phone, mail. Search requires name plus SSN. Also helpful: date of birth, exact years of attendance. Fee is $4.00.

University of Illinois at Springfield, Registrar, Springfield, IL 62794-9243, 217-786-6709 (Fax: 217-786-6620). Hours: 8:30AM-5PM. Enrollment: 4700. Formerly Sangamon State University Records go back to 1970. Degrees granted: Bachelors; Masters.

Attendance and degree information available by phone, fax, mail. Search requires name only. Also helpful: SSN, date of birth, approximate years of attendance. There is no fee.

University of Illinois at Urbana-Champaign, Transcript Department, Rm 10 Henry Admin. Bldg, 506 S Wright St, Urbana, IL 61801, 217-333-0210 (Fax: 217-333-3100). Hours: 8:30AM-5PM. Enrollment: 36000. Records go back to 1897. Alumni Records Office: 227 Illini Union, 1401 W Green St, Urbana, IL 61801. Degrees granted: Bachelors; Masters; Doctorate.

Attendance and degree information available by phone, fax, mail. Search requires name only. Also helpful: SSN, date of birth, exact years of attendance. Fee is $4.00.

University of St. Mary of the Lake Mundelein Seminary, Registrar, 1000 E Maple Ave, Mundelein, IL 60060, 847-566-6401 (Fax: 847-566-0330). Hours: 8AM-4:30PM. Enrollment: 180. Records go back to 1929. Alumni records are maintained here at the same phone number. Degrees granted: Masters.

Attendance and degree information available by mail. Search requires name plus SSN, date of birth, signed release. There is no fee.

VanderCook College of Music, Registrar, 3140 S Federal St, Chicago, IL 60616, 312-225-6288 (Fax: 312-225-5211). Hours: 9AM-5PM. Enrollment: 810. Records go back to 1928. Alumni records are maintained here at the same phone number. Degrees granted: Bachelors; Masters.

Attendance and degree information available by phone, fax, mail. Search requires name plus SSN, approximate years of attendance. There is no fee.

Wabash Valley College, Admissions and Records, 2200 College Dr, Mount Carmel, IL 62863, 618-262-8641 (Fax: 618-262-8641). Hours: 8AM-5PM. Enrollment: 1200. Records go back to 1967. Degrees granted: Associate.

Attendance and degree information available by phone, fax, mail. Search requires name plus SSN, date of birth. Also helpful: exact years of attendance. There is no fee.

Waubonsee Community College, Registrar, Illinois Rte 47 at Harter Rd, Sugar Grove, IL 60554, 630-466-4811 X2373 (Fax: 630-466-4964). Hours: 8AM-8PM M-Th; 8AM-4PM F. Enrollment: 7500. Records go back to 1967. Alumni records are maintained here also. Call 708-892-3334 X149. Degrees granted: Associate.

Attendance and degree information available by phone, fax, mail. Search requires name plus SSN, date of birth. Also helpful: exact years of attendance. There is no fee.

West Suburban College of Nursing, Registrar, Erie at Austin Blvd, Oak Park, IL 60302, 708-383-3901 (Fax:

708-383-8783). Hours: 8:30AM-5:30PM. Enrollment: 240. Records go back to 1915. Alumni records are maintained here at the same phone number. Degrees granted: Bachelors. Special programs- Nursing. Adverse incident record source- Dean of Students, 708-383-3901.

Attendance and degree information available by phone, mail. Search requires name plus SSN, date of birth, exact years of attendance. There is no fee.

Western Illinois University, Registrar, 1 University Circle, Macomb, IL 61455, 309-298-1891 (Fax: 309-298-2787). Hours: 8AM-4:30PM. Enrollment: 12700. Records go back to 1899. Alumni records are maintained here also. Call 309-298-1914. Degrees granted: Bachelors; Masters; Education Specialist.

Attendance and degree information available by phone, fax, mail. Search requires name plus SSN, date of birth. There is no fee.

Wheaton College, Registrar, 501 E College Ave, Wheaton, IL 60187, 630-752-5045 (Fax: 630-752-5245). Hours: 9AM-4:30PM. Enrollment: 2600. Records go back to 1860. Alumni records are maintained here also. Call 630-752-5047. Degrees granted: Bachelors; Masters; Doctorate.

Attendance and degree information available by phone, fax, mail. Search requires name only. Also helpful: SSN, date of birth, exact years of attendance. There is no fee.

Wilbur Wright College, Registrar, 4300 N Narragansett Ave, Chicago, IL 60634, 312-481-8060 (Fax: 312-481-8053). Hours: 9AM-8PM M-Th; 9AM-4PM F. Enrollment: 7500. Records go back to 1936. Alumni records are maintained here at the same phone number. Degrees granted: Associate. Adverse incident record source- Security, 312-481-8911.

Attendance and degree information available by phone, fax, mail. Search requires name plus SSN. Also helpful: date of birth, exact years of attendance. There is no fee.

William Rainey Harper College, Registrar, 1200 W Algonquin Rd, Palatine, IL 60067-7398, 847-925-6501 (Fax: 847-925-6032). Hours: 8AM-8PM M-Th, 8AM-4:30PM F, 9AM-Noon Sat. Enrollment: 16212. Records go back to 1969. Degrees granted: Associate.

Attendance and degree information available by phone, fax, mail. Search requires name plus SSN. There is no fee.

Trade and Vocational Schools

American Career Training, 237 S State St, Chicago, IL 60604, 312-461-0700

American College of Technology, 1300 W Washington St, Bloomington, IL 61701, 309-828-5151

American Health Information Management Association, 919 N Michigan Ave #1400, Chicago, IL 60611, 312-787-2672

Belleville Barber College, 329 N Illinois St, Belleville, IL 62220, 618-234-4424

Cain's Barber College, 365 E 51st St, Chicago, IL 60615, 312-536-4623

Capital Area Vocational Center, 12201 Toronto Rd, Springfield, IL 62707, 217-529-5431

Cave Technical Institute, 2842 S State St, Lockport, IL 60441, 815-727-1576

Computer Learning Center, 200 S Michigan Ave 2nd Flr, Chicago, IL 60604, 312-427-2700

Computer Learning Center (Lombard Campus), 1919 S Highland Ave, Ste 325-A, Lombard, IL 60148, 708-889-0252

Connecticut School of Broadcasting, 200 W 22nd St #202, Lombard, IL 60148, 708-916-1700

Cooking and Hospitality Institute of Chicago, 361 W Chestnut St, Chicago, IL 60610, 312-944-2725

Coyne American Institute, 1235 W Fullerton Ave, Chicago, IL 60614, 312-935-2520

Echols International Tourism Institute, 28 E Jackson #1800, Chicago, IL 60604, 800-342-2733

Environmental Technical Institue, 1101 W Thorndale Ave, Itasca, IL 60143, 708-285-9100

Environmental Technical Institue (Branch Campus), 13010 S Division St, Blue Island, IL 60406, 708-385-0707

Fox Secretarial College, 4201 W 93rd St, Oak Lawn, IL 60453, 708-636-7700

Hadley School for the Blind (The), 700 Elm St, Winnetka, IL 60093, 708-446-8111

Heartland School of Business, 211 W State St #204, Jacksonville, IL 62650, 217-243-9001

ITT Technical Institute (Branch Campus), 600 Holiday Plaza Dr, Matteson, IL 60443, 708-747-2571

Illinois School of Health Careers, 1607 W Howard St #305, Chicago, IL 60626, 312-973-0299

Lincoln Technical Institute, 7320 W Agatite Ave, Norridge, IL 60656, 312-625-1535

Lincoln Technical Institute, 8920 S Cicero Ave, Oak Lawn, IL 60453, 708-423-9000

M G Institute, 40 E Delaware Pl, Chicago, IL 60611, 312-943-4190

Medical Careers Institute, 116 S Michigan Ave 2nd Flr, Chicago, IL 60603, 312-782-9804

Midwest Institute of Technology, 3712 W Montrose, Chicago, IL 60618, 312-478-0119

Moler Hairstyling College, 5840 W Madison St, Chicago, IL 60644, 312-287-2552

Music Center of the North Shore, 300 Green Bay Rd, Winnetka, IL 60093, 708-446-3822

Napoleon Hill Foundation, 1440 Paddock Dr, Northbrook, IL 60062, 847-998-0408

Naval Health Sciences Education and Training Command (Hospital Corps School), Great Lakes, IL 60088, 708-688-5680

Pathfinder Training Institute, 19 E 21st St, Chicago, IL 60616, 312-842-7272

Quincy Technical Schools, 501 N Third St, Quincy, IL 62301, 800-438-5621

Rockford School of Practical Nursing, 978 Haskell Ave, Rockford, IL 61103, 815-966-3716

SER Business and Technical Institute (Chicago Campus), 5150 W Roosevelt, Chicago, IL 60650, 312-379-1152

Sanford-Brown Business College, 3237 W Chain of Rocks Rd, Granite City, IL 62040, 618-931-0300

Spanish Coalition for Jobs, 2011 W Pershing Rd, Chicago, IL 60609, 312-247-0707

Sparks College, 131 S Morgan St, Shelbyville, IL 62565, 217-774-5112

Tyler School of Secretarial Sciences, 8030 S Kedzie Ave, Chicago, IL 60652, 312-436-5050

Universal Technical Institute (Branch Campus), 601 Regency Dr, Glendale Heights, IL 60139, 708-529-2662

Worsham College of Mortuary Science, 495 Northgate Pkwy, Wheeling, IL 60090, 708-808-8444

State Licensing & Business Registration Quick Finder Index

Architecture, Engineering & Surveying
Architect #12 .... ✉ 217-785-0800
Engineer #12 .... ✉ 217-785-0800
Engineer, Structural #12 .... ✉ 217-785-0800
Landscape Architect #12 .... ✉ 217-785-0800
Surveyor #12 .... ✉ 217-785-0800

Business - Court & Legal Services
Attorney #1 .... ☎ 217-522-6838
Lobbyist #32 217-782-7017
Notary Public #32 217-782-0641
Shorthand Reporter #12 .... ✉ 217-785-0800

Business - General Services
Employment Agency #23 .... ☎ 312-793-2810
Interior Designer #12 .... ✉ 217-785-0800
Public Accountant #12 .... ✉ 217-785-0800
Restaurant & Retail Food Store #15 217-785-2439

Construction & Manufacturing
Boiler Inspector #36 .... ☎ 217-782-2696
Demolition (Non-Explosive) #18 217-785-1743
Explosives #8 (300) .... ☎ 217-782-9976
Explosives Detonater/Storekeeper #8 (900)... ☎ 217-782-9976
Plumber #15 (6100) 217-524-0791
Plumber Apprentice #14 .... ☎ 217-524-0791
Registered Serviceman, Weighing & Measuring
  Devices #22 (1325) .... ☎ 217-782-3817
Roofer #12 .... ✉ 217-785-0800
Salvage Firm #14 .... ☎ 217-785-2439
Scrap Processor #30 .... ✉ 217-782-7817
Sewage System Contractor #15 .... ☎ 217-782-5830

Education
Chief School Business Official #35 .... ✉ 217-782-2805
Early Childhood Teacher #35 .... ✉ 217-782-2805
High School Teacher #35 .... ✉ 217-782-2805
School Administrator #35 .... ✉ 217-782-2805
School Guidance Counselor #35 .... ✉ 217-782-2805
School Media Specialist/Librarian #35 .... ✉ 217-782-2805
School Principal #35 .... ✉ 217-782-2805
School Superintendent #35 .... ✉ 217-782-2805
School Supervisor #35 .... ✉ 217-782-2805
Special Teacher #35 .... ✉ 217-782-2805
Substitute Teacher #35 .... ✉ 217-782-2805

Teacher #35 .... ✉ 217-782-2805
Transitional Bilingual Teacher #35 .... ✉ 217-782-2805

Environmental & Agriculture
Animal Breeder #7 .... ☎ 217-785-3423
Aquaculturist #7 .... ☎ 217-785-3423
Asbestos Contractor #14 .... ☎ 217-785-2080
Blaster #8 .... ☎ 217-782-4970
Coal Mine Worker #9 .... ☎ 217-782-6791
Commercial Fisherman #7 .... ☎ 217-785-3423
Cross-Connection Control Device Inspector #24
  .... ☎ 217-782-1020
Distribution System Operator #24 .... ☎ 217-782-1869
Fish Dealer #7 .... ☎ 217-785-3423
Food Processing Plants & Warehouses #14 ... ☎ 217-785-2439
Fur Buyer, Tanner or Dyer #5 .... ☎ 217-782-2138
Landfill Chief Operator #24 .... ☎ 217-785-8604
Mine Engineer #9 .... ☎ 217-782-6791
Mine Foreman #9 .... ☎ 217-782-6791
Mine Rescue Supervisor/Assistant #9 .... ☎ 217-782-6791
Mine Supervisor #9 .... ☎ 217-782-6791
Pest Control Technician/Business/Non-commercial #15
  (3500) 217-782-4674
Pesticide Applicator #15 .... ☎ 217-782-5830
Radon Measurement Specialist #11 (386) ...... ✉ 217-786-7127
Timber Buyer #4 .... ☎ 217-782-2361
Underground Shot Firer #9 .... ☎ 217-782-6791
Underground Storage Tank Worker #37 217-782-4542
Veterinarian #12 .... ✉ 217-785-0800
Waste Water Treatment Plant Operator #24
  .... ☎ 217-782-1020
Water Supply Operator #24 .... ☎ 217-782-1020
Water Well & Pump Installation Contractor #15
  (257) .... ☎ 217-782-5830
Water Well Contractor/IDPH #15 (450) 217-782-5830

Financial - Real Estate, Insurance & Banking
Collection Agency #12 .... ✉ 217-785-0800
Insurance Adjuster/Agent #6 .... ☎ 217-782-6366
Investment Adviser #33 .... ☎ 217-785-4929
Land Sales #12 .... ✉ 217-785-0800
Mortgage Banking #28 .... ☎ 217-782-6181
Real Estate Appraiser #12 .... ✉ 217-785-0800
Real Estate Broker/Salesperson #12 .... ✉ 217-785-0800

Savings & Loan Association #29 .... ☎ 217-782-6181
Securities Dealer/Salesperson #34 .... ☎ 217-782-2256
Stock Broker #34 (107500) .... ☎ 217-782-2256
Time Share #12 .... ✉ 217-785-0800

Health & Beauty

Ambulance Provider #14 .... ☎ 217-785-2080
Ambulance/Ambulance Provider (Ambulance) #14
  (2224) .... ☎ 217-785-2080
Barber #12 .... ✉ 217-785-0800
Chiropractor #12 .... ✉ 217-785-0800
Controlled Substance #12 .... ✉ 217-785-0800
Cosmetologist #12 .... ✉ 217-785-0800
County Coroner #19 .... ✉ 217-782-4540
Cytotechnologist #2 (11393) .... ☎ 312-738-1336
Dentist/Dental Hygienist #12 .... ✉ 217-785-0800
Dietitian/Nutrition Counselor #12 .... ✉ 217-785-0800
Emergency Medical Technician #14
  (28700) .... ☎ 217-785-2080
Environmental Health Practitioner #12 .... ✉ 217-785-0800
Esthetician #12 .... ✉ 217-785-0800
Food Service Sanitation Manager #14 (115000)
  .... ☎ 217-785-2439
Funeral Director/Embalmer #12 .... ✉ 217-785-0800
Hearing Aid Dispenser #14 .... ☎ 217-782-4733
Histologic Technician #2 (16384) .... ☎ 312-738-1336
Home Health Aide #14 .... ☎ 217-785-5133
Home Health Care Agency #14 .... ☎ 217-782-0514
Hospital #14 .... ☎ 217-782-0514
Hospital Administrator #14 .... ☎ 217-785-5133
Industrial Radiographer #10 .... ✉ 217-785-9913
Laboratory Analysis Technician #14 .... ☎ 217-785-8820
Medical Corporation #12 .... ✉ 217-785-0800
Medical Doctor/Physician's Assistant #12 ..... ✉ 217-785-0800
Medical Laboratory Technician #2 (53781)
  .... ☎ 312-738-1336
Nail Technician #12 .... ✉ 217-785-0800
Naprapath #12 .... ✉ 217-785-0800
Nuclear Medicine Technologist #10 (1435)
  .... ✉ 217-785-9913
Nurse #12 .... ✉ 217-785-0800
Nurses Aide #14 (221000) .... ☎ 217-782-3070
Nursing Assistant #14 .... ☎ 217-785-5133
Nursing Home Administrator #15 .... ☎ 217-782-0514
Occupational Aide #13 217-782-0545
Occupational Therapist #12 .... ✉ 217-785-0800
Optometrist #12 .... ✉ 217-785-0800
Osteopathic Physician #12 .... ✉ 217-785-0800
Pharmacist/Pharmacy #12 .... ✉ 217-785-0800
Physical Aide #13 217-782-0545
Physical Therapist #12 .... ✉ 217-785-0800
Podiatrist #12 .... ✉ 217-785-0800
Radiation Therapist #11 (929) .... ✉ 217-785-9913
Radiographer #11 (13574) .... ✉ 217-785-9913
Rehabilitation Aide #13 217-782-0545
School Nurse #35 .... ✉ 217-782-2805
Speech-Language Pathologist/Audiologist #12
  .... ✉ 217-785-0800

Tanning Facility #15 (2500) 217-785-2439
Vision Screening Technician #16 .... ☎ 217-782-4733
Wholesale Drug Distributor #12 .... ✉ 217-785-0800

Investigations & Security

Accident Reconstruction Specialist #19 .... ✉ 217-782-4540
Breath Analyzer Operator #14 .... ☎ 217-782-1571
County Correction Officer #19 .... ✉ 217-782-4540
County Sheriff Law Enforcement Officer #19
  .... ✉ 217-782-4540
Electronic Criminal Surveillance Officer #19
  .... ✉ 217-782-4540
Fire Equipment Distributor #37 217-782-4542
Fire Equipment Employee #37 217-782-4542
Firefighter #37 217-782-4542
Lie Detector Operator #12 .... ✉ 217-785-0800
Private Alarm Contractor #12 .... ✉ 217-785-0800
Private Detective #12 .... ✉ 217-785-0800
Private Security Contractor #12 .... ✉ 217-785-0800

Social Services

Alcoholism Counselor #21 (5500) .... ☎ 217-698-8110
Child Care Facility #3 .... ☎ 217-785-2688
Day Care #3 .... ☎ 217-785-2688
Marriage & Family Therapist #12 .... ✉ 217-785-0800
Professional Counselor/Clinical Professional
  Counselor #12 .... ✉ 217-785-0800
Psychologist #12 .... ✉ 217-785-0800
School Psychologist #35 .... ✉ 217-782-2805
Social Worker #12 .... ✉ 217-785-0800

Sports & Entertainment

Athletic Trainer #12 .... ✉ 217-785-0800
Bingo #17 (1900) .... ☎ 217-785-5864
Blacksmith (Farrier) #26 (75) .... ☎ 312-814-2600
Boxing/Wrestling #12 .... ✉ 217-785-0800
Firearms Regulation (Firearm Owner's Regulation) #27
  (250000) .... ✉ 217-782-7980
Gambling Employee #20 .... ☎ 217-524-0226
Horseshoeing #26 .... ☎ 312-814-2600
Hunting Area Operator #5 .... ☎ 217-782-2138
Liquor License (Retail, Distributor, Manufacturer) #25
  (28000) .... ✉ 312-814-3930
Riverboat Employee #20 .... ☎ 217-524-0226
Taxidermist #7 .... ☎ 217-785-3423
Track #26 .... ☎ 312-814-2600

Transportation

Automotive Parts Recycler #30 .... ✉ 217-782-7817
Boat Operator #5 .... ☎ 217-782-2138
Driving Instructor #31 .... ☎ 708-437-3953
New Vehicle Dealer #30 .... ✉ 217-782-7817
Used Vehicle Dealer #30 .... ✉ 217-782-7817
Vehicle Auctioneer #30 .... ✉ 217-782-7817
Vehicle Rebuilder #30 .... ✉ 217-782-7817
Vehicle Repair #30 .... ✉ 217-782-7817

State Licensing & Business Registration Agency Information

(1) Attorney Registration & Disciplinary Commission of, the Supreme Court of Illinois, Hilton Offices, Suite 201, 700 E Adams St, Springfield, IL 62701, 217-522-6838, Fax: 217-522-2417

(2) Board of Registry, PO Box 12277, Chicago, IL 60612-0277, 312-738-1336, Fax: 312-738-5808

(3) Department of Children & Family Services, 406 E Monroe St, Sta 60, Springfield, IL 62701, 217-785-2688, Fax: 217-524-3327

(4) Department of Commerce, Division of Forest Services, PO Box 19225, 600 N Grande Ave W, Springfield, IL 62794-9225, 217-782-2361, Fax: 217-785-5517

(5) Department of Conservation, 524 S 2nd St, Springfield, IL 62701, 217-782-2138, Fax: 217-782-5016

(6) Department of Insurance, 320 W Washington, Springfield, IL 62767, 217-782-6366

(7) Department of Natural Resources, 524 S 2nd St, Springfield, IL 62701, 217-785-3423, Fax: 217-782-5016

(8) Department of Natural Resources, Office of Mines & Minerals, 524 S 2nd, Springfield, IL 62701-1787, 217-782-9976, Fax: 217-524-4819

(9) Department of Natural Resources, Office of mine & Minerals, 525 S 2nd, (300 W Jefferson St, Suite 300, 62791), Springfield, IL 62701-1787, 217-782-6791, Fax: 217-524-4819

(10) Department of Nuclear Safety, 1035 Outer Park Dr, Springfield, IL 62704, 217-785-9900, Fax: 217-782-1938

(11) Department of Nuclear Safety, 1035 Outer Park Dr, Springfield, IL 62704, 217-785-9900, Fax: 217-782-1938

(12) Department of Professional Regulation, Professions/Occupations/Entities, 320 W Washington St, 3rd Floor, Springfield, IL 62786, 217-785-0800, Fax: 217-782-7645

(13) Department of Public Aid, Bureau of Long-Term Quality Care, 201 S Grand Ave, E, Springfield, IL 62763-0001, 217-782-0545, Fax: 217-524-7114

(14) Department of Public Health, 535 W Jefferson, Springfield, IL 62761, 217-785-2080, Fax: 217-785-5247

(15) Department of Public Health, 525 W Jefferson, Springfield, IL 62761, 217-785-2439, Fax: 217-524-0802

(16) Department of Public Health, Division of Health Assessment & Screening, 535 W Jefferson St, Springfield, IL 62761, 217-782-4733, Fax: 217-785-5247

(17) Department of Revenue, Bingo Division, PO Box 19480, Level 3 SW, 101 W Jefferson, Springfield, IL 62794, 217-785-5864

(18) Environmental Protection Agency, 2300 Churchill Rd, Springfield, IL 62754, 217-782-7327

(19) Ilinois Law Enforcement & Standards Training Board, 600 S Second St, Suite 300, Springfield, IL 62704, 217-782-4540, Fax: 217-524-5350

(20) Illinios Gaming Board, PO Box 19474, Willard Ice Bldg, Springfield, IL 62794-9474, 312-814-4700, Fax: 312-814-4602

(21) Illinois Alcoholism Counselor, Certification Board, 1305 Wabash Ave, Suite L, Springfield, IL 62704, 217-698-8110, Fax: 217-698-8234

(22) Illinois Department of Agriculture, PO Box 19281, Springfield, IL 62794-9281, 217-782-3817, Fax: 217-524-7801

(23) Illinois Department of Labor, 160 N. LaSalle 13th Floor, Chicago, IL 60611, 312-793-2810, Fax: 312-793-5257

(24) Illinois Environmental Protection Agency, 2200 Churchill Rd, PO Box 19276, Springfield, IL 62794-9276, 217-782-1869, Fax: 217-782-2465

(25) Illinois Liquor Control Commission, Freedom of Information Compliance Officer, 100 W. Randolph #5-300, Chicago, IL 60601, 312-814-3930, Fax: 312-814-2241

(26) Illinois Racing Board, 100 W Randolph, Suite 11-100, Chicago, IL 60601, 312-814-2600, Fax: 312-814-5062

(27) Illinois State Police, 100 Iles Park Place, Springfield, IL 62708, 217-782-7980

(28) Savings & Loan Commission, 500 E Monroe Ave, Suite 800, Springfield, IL 62701, 217-782-3000, Fax: 217-524-5941

(29) Savings & Loan Commission, 500 E Monroe Ave, Suite 800, Springfield, IL 62701, 217-782-3000, Fax: 217-524-5941

(30) Secretary of State, Howlett Bldg, Room 008, Springfield, IL 62756, 217-782-7817, Fax: 217-524-0120

(31) Secretary of State, Commercial Driver Training, 650 Roppolo Dr, Elk Grove, IL 60007, 847-437-3953, Fax: 847-437-3911

(32) Secretary of State, Index Department, 111 E Monroe St, Springfield, IL 62756, 217-782-7017, Fax: 217-524-0930

(33) Secretary of State, Securities Department, Lincoln Tower, Suite 200, 520 S 2nd St, Springfield, IL 62701, 217-782-2256, Fax: 217-524-2172

(34) Secretary of State, Securities Department, Lincoln Towers, 520 S. Second St. Ste. 200, Springfield, IL 62701, 217-782-2256, Fax: 217-524-2172

(35) State Board of Education, 100 N 1st St, Springfield, IL 62777, 217-782-2805, Fax: 217-524-1289

(36) State Fire Marshall, 1035 Stevenson Dr, Springfield, IL 62703, 217-782-2696

(37) State Fire Marshall, 1035 Stevenson Dr, Springfield, IL 62703, 217-782-4542

Indiana

Capitol: Indianapolis (Marion County)	
State Population	5.8 Million
Number of Degree Granting Institutions:	94
Number of State Licensing & Business Registration Agencies:	89

Degree Granting Educational Institutions

Ancilla College, Registrar, PO Box 1, Donaldson, IN 46513, 219-936-8898 (Fax: 219-935-1773). Hours: 8AM-4:30PM. Enrollment: 709. Records go back to 1937. Alumni records are maintained here at the same phone number. Degrees granted: Associate. Adverse incident record source- Student Affairs.

Attendance information available by phone, fax, mail. Search requires name plus SSN. There is no fee.

Degree information available by mail. Search requires name plus SSN. There is no fee.

Anderson University, Registrar, 1100 E Fifth St, Anderson, IN 46012-3462, 317-641-4160 (Fax: 317-641-3851). Hours: 8AM-5PM. Enrollment: 2200. Records go back to 1917. Alumni records are maintained here at the same phone number. Degrees granted: Associate; Bachelors; Masters; Doctorate. Adverse incident record source- Dean of Students, 317-641-4192.

Attendance and degree information available by phone, fax, mail. Search requires name plus SSN. Also helpful: date of birth, exact years of attendance. There is no fee.

Associated Mennonite Biblical Seminary, Registrar, 3003 Benham Ave, Elkhart, IN 46517-1999, 219-295-3726 X200 (Fax: 219-295-0092). Hours: 8AM-4PM. Enrollment: 160. Records go back to 1958. Degrees granted: Bachelors; Masters. Adverse incident record source- Student Affairs.

Attendance and degree information available by phone, mail. Search requires name only. Also helpful: SSN. There is no fee.

Ball State University, Registrar, 2000 University Ave, Muncie, IN 47306, 317-285-1722 (Fax: 317-285-8765). Hours: 8AM-5PM. Enrollment: 19500. Records go back to 1919. Alumni records are maintained here also. Call 317-285-1413. Degrees granted: Associate; Bachelors; Masters; Doctorate.

Attendance information available by phone, mail. Search requires name plus SSN. There is no fee.

Degree information available by mail. Search requires name plus SSN. There is no fee.

Bethany Theological Seminary, Coordinator of Academic Services, 615 National Road W, Richmond, IN 47374-4019, 317-983-1816 (Fax: 317-983-1840). Hours: 8AM-5PM. Enrollment: 80. Records go back to 1905. Alumni records are maintained here also. Call 317-983-1806. Degrees granted: Masters. Certification: Theological Studies. Special programs-Bethany Academy for Ministry Training, 317-983-1820.

Attendance and degree information available by phone, fax, mail. Search requires name only. Also helpful: SSN, date of birth, exact years of attendance. There is no fee.

Bethel College, Registrar, 1001 W McKinley Ave, Mishawaka, IN 46545, 219-257-3302 (Fax: 219-257-3277). Hours: 8AM-5PM. Enrollment: 1352. Records go back to 1947. Alumni records are maintained here also. Call 219-257-3310. Degrees granted: Associate; Bachelors; Masters.

Attendance information available by phone, fax. Search requires name only. Also helpful: SSN, date of birth, exact years of attendance. There is no fee.

Degree information available by phone, fax, mail. Search requires name only. Also helpful: SSN, date of birth, exact years of attendance. There is no fee.

Butler University, Registrar, 4600 Sunset Ave, Indianapolis, IN 46208, 317-940-9203. Hours: 8:30AM-5PM. Enrollment: 4457. Records go back to 1900. Alumni records are maintained here also. Call 317-940-9900. Degrees granted: Bachelors; Masters. Adverse incident record source- Registrar, 317-940-9203.

Attendance and degree information available by phone, mail. Search requires name plus SSN, exact years of attendance. There is no fee.

Calumet College of St. Joseph, Registrar's Office, 2400 New York Ave, Whiting, IN 46394, 219-473-4211 (Fax: 219-473-4259). Hours: 9AM-5PM. Enrollment: 1100. Records go back to 1951. Alumni records are maintained here also. Call 219-473-4326. Degrees granted: Associate; Bachelors. Adverse incident record source- Student Services.

Attendance and degree information available by phone, fax, mail. Search requires name plus SSN, date of birth, exact years of attendance. There is no fee.

Christian Theological Seminary, Registrar, 1000 W 42nd St, Indianapolis, IN 46208-3301, 317-931-2382 (Fax: 317-923-1961). Hours: 8AM-4:30PM. Enrollment: 376. Records go back to 1958. Alumni records are maintained here also. Call 317-931-2310. Degrees granted: Masters; Doctorate. Special programs- Advanced Studies, 317-931-2440.

Attendance and degree information available by phone, fax, mail. Search requires name plus SSN, date of birth. Also helpful: exact years of attendance. There is no fee.

Columbus IVY Tech, Records, 4475 Central Ave, Columbus, IN 47203, 812-372-9925 X30 (Fax: 812-372-9925 X121). Enrollment: 1500. Records go back to 1967. Alumni records are maintained here at the same phone number. Degrees granted: Associate; Technical. Adverse incident record source- Student Services.

Attendance and degree information available by phone, mail. Search requires name plus SSN, date of birth, exact years of attendance. There is no fee.

Commonwealth Business College, Registrar, 4200 W 81st Ave, Merrillville, IN 46410, 219-769-3321 (Fax: 219-738-1076). Hours: 8AM-5PM. Enrollment: 200. Records go back to 1991. Degrees granted: Associate.

Attendance and degree information available by written request only. Search requires name plus SSN, signed release. Also helpful: exact years of attendance. Fee is $2.00.

Commonwealth Business College, (LaPorte), Registrar, 8895 N State Rte 39, La Porte, IN 46350, 219-362-3338 (Fax: 219-324-0112). Hours: 7:30AM-9:30PM M-Th; 8AM-5PM F. Enrollment: 130. Records go back to 1890. Alumni records are maintained here at the same phone number. Degrees granted: Associate. Adverse incident record source- Merrillville Campus, 219-769-3321.

Attendance information available by phone, mail. Search requires name plus SSN, exact years of attendance. Also helpful: date of birth. There is no fee.

Degree information available by phone, mail. Search requires name plus SSN. Also helpful: date of birth, exact years of attendance. There is no fee.

Concordia Theological Seminary, Registrar, 6600 N Clinton St, Fort Wayne, IN 46825-4996, 219-481-2153 (Fax: 219-481-2121). Hours: 8AM-4:30PM. Enrollment: 311. Records go back to 1900. Alumni records are maintained here also. Call 219-481-2150. Degrees granted: Masters; Doctorate; First Professional, M.Div.

Attendance and degree information available by phone, fax, mail. Search requires name only. Also helpful: SSN, date of birth, exact years of attendance. There is no fee.

Davenport College of Business, (Branch), Registrar, 7121 Grape Rd, Granger, IN 46530, 219-277-8447 (Fax: 219-272-2967). Hours: 8AM-5PM. Enrollment: 400. Records go back to 1985. Alumni records are maintained here at the same phone number. Degrees granted: Associate. Adverse incident record source- Director of Security, 219-277-8447.

Attendance and degree information available by phone, fax, mail. Search requires name only. Also helpful: SSN, exact years of attendance. There is no fee.

Davenport College of Business, (Branch), Registrar, 8200 Georgia St, Merrillville, IN 46410, 219-769-5556 (Fax: 219-756-8911). Hours: 9AM-5PM M-Th, 8AM-4PM F. Enrollment: 550. Records go back to 1987. Degrees granted: Associate. Adverse incident record source- 219-769-5556 X237.

Attendance and degree information available by phone, mail. Search requires name plus SSN. There is no fee.

DePauw University, Registrar, Greencastle, IN 46135, 317-658-4000 (Fax: 317-658-4139). Hours: 8AM-4:30PM. Enrollment: 2100. Records go back to 1837. Alumni records are maintained here also. Call 317-658-4208. Degrees granted: Bachelors. Adverse incident record source- Dean of Students, 317-658-4270.

Attendance and degree information available by phone, fax, mail. Search requires name plus SSN, date of birth, exact years of attendance. There is no fee.

Earlham College, Registrar, National Rd W, Drawer 34, Richmond, IN 47374, 317-983-1515 (Fax: 317-983-1234). Hours: 8AM-5PM. Enrollment: 1017. Records go back to 1847. Alumni Records Office: Drawer 193, Richmond, IN 47374, 317-983-1313. Degrees granted: Bachelors; Masters.

Attendance information available by phone, fax, mail. Search requires name only. Also helpful: SSN, date of birth, exact years of attendance. There is no fee.

Degree information available by phone, mail. Search requires name only. Also helpful: SSN, date of birth, exact years of attendance. There is no fee.

Franklin College of Indiana, Registrar, 501 E Monroe St, Franklin, IN 46131, 317-738-8018 (Fax: 317-634-0471). Hours: 8AM-5PM. Enrollment: 600. Records go back to 1844. Alumni records are maintained here also. Call 317-738-1834. Degrees granted: Bachelors. Adverse incident record source- Student Services.

Attendance and degree information available by phone, mail. Search requires name plus SSN, date of birth. There is no fee.

Goshen College, Registrar, 1700 S Main St, Goshen, IN 46526, 219-535-7517 (Fax: 219-535-7660). Hours: 8AM-5PM. Enrollment: 1000. Records go back to 1894. Alumni records are maintained here also. Call 219-535-7566. Degrees granted: Bachelors. Adverse incident record source- Student Development Office, 219-535-7539.

Attendance and degree information available by phone, fax, mail. Search requires name plus date of birth. Also helpful: SSN, exact years of attendance. There is no fee.

Grace College, Registrar, 200 Seminary Dr, Winona Lake, IN 46590, 219-372-5110 (Fax: 219-372-5114). Hours: 8AM-4:30PM. Enrollment: 641. Records go back to 1948. Alumni records are maintained here also. Call 219-372-5289. Degrees granted: Associate; Bachelors; Masters. Adverse incident record source- Jim Swanson, 219-372-5700.

Attendance and degree information available by phone, fax. Search requires name only. Also helpful: SSN, date of birth. There is no fee.

Grace Theological Seminary, Registrar, 200 Seminary Dr, Winona Lake, IN 46590, 219-372-5111 (Fax: 219-372-5114). Hours: 8AM-4:30PM. Enrollment: 79. Records go back to 1937. Alumni records are maintained here also. Call 219-372-5289. Degrees granted: Masters; Doctorate. Adverse incident record source- Dave Plaster, 219-372-5104.

Attendance and degree information available by phone, fax. Search requires name only. Also helpful: SSN, date of birth. There is no fee.

Hanover College, Registrar, PO Box 108, Hanover, IN 47243-0108, 812-866-7051 (Fax: 812-866-2164). Hours: 8AM-5PM. Enrollment: 1093. Records go back to 1827. Alumni records are maintained here at the same phone number. Degrees granted: Bachelors. Adverse incident record source- Student Affairs, 812-866-7075.

Attendance and degree information available by phone, fax, mail. Search requires name only. Also helpful: SSN, exact years of attendance. There is no fee.

Holy Cross College, Registrar, Box 308, Notre Dame, IN 46556, 219-233-6813 (Fax: 219-233-7427). Hours: 8AM-

5PM. Enrollment: 450. Records go back to 1966. Alumni records are maintained here at the same phone number. Degrees granted: Associate.

Attendance and degree information available by phone, fax, mail. Search requires name only. Also helpful: SSN, exact years of attendance. There is no fee.

Huntington College, Registrar, 2303 College Ave, Huntington, IN 46750, 219-356-6000 (Fax: 219-356-9448). Hours: 8AM-5PM. Enrollment: 700. Records go back to 1897. Alumni records are maintained here at the same phone number. Degrees granted: Associate; Bachelors; Masters.

Attendance and degree information available by phone, fax, mail. Search requires name only. Also helpful: SSN, date of birth, exact years of attendance. There is no fee. Expedited service available for $3.00.

ITT Technical Institute, Registrar, 5115 Oak Grove Rd, Evansville, IN 47715-2340, 812-479-1441 (Fax: 812-479-1460). Hours: 8AM-5PM. Enrollment: 314. Evansville information only at this location. Degrees granted: Associate.

Attendance information available by mail. Search requires name plus SSN, signed release. Also helpful: date of birth. There is no fee.

Degree information available by phone, mail. Search requires name plus SSN. Also helpful: date of birth. There is no fee.

ITT Technical Institute, Registrar, 4919 Coldwater Rd, Fort Wayne, IN 46825-5532, 219-484-4107 X209 (Fax: 219-484-0860). Hours: 8AM-5PM. Enrollment: 700. Records go back to 1968. Degrees granted: Associate. Adverse incident record source- Supvr of Education, 219-484-4107 X212.

Attendance and degree information available by phone, mail. Search requires name plus SSN. There is no fee.

ITT Technical Institute, Registrar, 9511 Angola Ct, Indianapolis, IN 46268-1119, 317-875-8640 X249 (Fax: 317-875-8641). Hours: 8AM-5PM. Enrollment: 900. Records go back to 1968. Alumni records are maintained here at the same phone number. Degrees granted: Associate. Adverse incident record source- Student Services.

Attendance and degree information available by phone, mail. Search requires name plus exact years of attendance. There is no fee.

Indian Vocational State Technical College, Registrar, One W 26th St, Box 1763, Indianapolis, IN 46206, 317-921-4745 (Fax: 317-921-4753). Enrollment: 6000. Formerly Indian Vocational Technical College Records go back to 1969. Alumni records are maintained here at the same phone number. Degrees granted: Associate. Adverse incident record source- Security Department.

Attendance and degree information available by phone, mail. Search requires name plus SSN, exact years of attendance. There is no fee.

Indiana Business College, Registrar, 802 N Meridian St, Indianapolis, IN 46204, 317-264-5656 (Fax: 317-634-0471). Hours: 7:30AM-7:30PM. Enrollment: 600. Records go back to 1902. Degrees granted: Associate. Adverse incident record source- Student Affairs.

Attendance and degree information available by phone, fax, mail. Search requires name plus SSN. Also helpful: exact years of attendance. There is no fee.

Indiana Business College, (Branch), Registrar, Applegate Business Park, 140 E 53rd St, Anderson, IN 46103, 317-644-7514 (Fax: 317-644-5724). Hours: 7:30AM-5PM. Enrollment: 150. Records go back to 1902. Degrees granted: Associate.

Attendance information available by mail. Search requires name plus SSN, date of birth, signed release. Also helpful: approximate years of attendance. There is no fee.

Degree information available by phone, fax, mail. Search requires name plus SSN, date of birth. Also helpful: approximate years of attendance. There is no fee.

Indiana Business College, (Branch), Registrar, 3550 Two Mile House Rd, PO Box 1906, Columbus, IN 47201, 812-342-1000 (Fax: 812-342-1058). Hours: 7:30AM-9PM M-Th; 7:30AM-4:30PM F. Enrollment: 150. Records go back to 1985. Degrees granted: Associate. Adverse incident record source- Student Services.

Attendance and degree information available by phone, fax, mail. Search requires name plus SSN, exact years of attendance. There is no fee.

Indiana Business College, (Branch), Registrar, 4601 Theater Dr, Evansville, IN 47715, 812-476-6000 (Fax: 812-471-8576). Hours: 8AM-5PM. Enrollment: 170. Records go back to 1993. Degrees granted: Associate; Medical Assisting, Medical Records.

Attendance and degree information available by phone, fax, mail. Search requires name plus SSN, date of birth, exact years of attendance. There is no fee.

Indiana Business College, (Branch), Registrar, 5460 Victory Dr Ste 100, Indianapolis, IN 46203, 317-783-5100 (Fax: 317-783-4898). Hours: 8AM-6PM. Enrollment: 200. Records go back to 1993. Degrees granted: Associate; Medical Assisting, Medical Records, Medical Transcription.

Attendance and degree information available by fax, mail. Search requires name plus SSN, signed release. There is no fee.

Indiana Business College, (Branch), Registrar, 2 Executive Dr, Lafayette, IN 47905, 317-447-9550 (Fax: 317-447-0868). Hours: 8AM-5PM. Enrollment: 105. Records go back to 1907. Degrees granted: Associate.

Attendance and degree information available by phone, fax, mail. Search requires name plus SSN, date of birth, exact years of attendance. There is no fee.

Indiana Business College, (Branch), Registrar, 830 N Miller Ave, Marion, IN 46952, 317-662-7497 (Fax: 317-651-9421). Hours: 8AM-5PM. Enrollment: 188. Records go back to 1902. Degrees granted: Associate.

Attendance and degree information available by fax, mail. Search requires name plus SSN, signed release. There is no fee.

Indiana Business College, (Branch), Registrar, 1809 N Walnut St, Muncie, IN 47303, 317-288-8681 (Fax: 317-288-8797). Hours: 8AM-5PM. Enrollment: 250. Records go back to 1902. Degrees granted: Associate. Adverse incident record source- Student Affairs, 317-288-8681.

Attendance and degree information available by mail. Search requires name plus SSN, exact years of attendance, signed release. There is no fee.

Indiana Business College, (Branch), Registrar, 3175 S Third St, Terre Haute, IN 47802, 812-232-4458 (Fax: 812-234-2361). Hours: 7:30AM-5PM. Enrollment: 298. Records go back to 1981. Degrees granted: Associate. Adverse incident record source- Main Campus, 317-264-5656.

Attendance and degree information available by phone, fax, mail. Search requires name plus SSN. There is no fee.

Indiana Business College, (Branch), Registrar, 1431 Willow St, Vincennes, IN 47591, 812-882-2550 (Fax: 812-882-2270). Hours: 8AM-4PM. Enrollment: 85. Records go back to 1922. Degrees granted: Associate. Adverse incident record source- Director's Office

Attendance and degree information available by phone, fax, mail. Search requires name plus SSN, approximate years of attendance. Also helpful: exact years of attendance. There is no fee.

Indiana Institute of Technology, Registrar, 1600 E Washington Blvd, Fort Wayne, IN 46803, 219-422-5561 (Fax: 219-422-7696). Hours: 8:30AM-5PM. Enrollment: 1200. Records go back to 1930. Degrees granted: Associate; Bachelors. Adverse incident record source- Student Services.

Attendance and degree information available by phone, fax, mail. Search requires name plus SSN. Also helpful: date of birth, exact years of attendance. There is no fee.

Indiana State University, Registrar, 200 N 7th St, Terre Haute, IN 47809, 812-237-2020 (Fax: 812-237-8039). Hours: 8AM-4:30PM. Records go back to 1865. Alumni records are maintained here also. Call 812-237-2020 X3707. Degrees granted: Bachelors; Masters. Adverse incident record source- Registrar, 812-237-2020.

Attendance and degree information available by phone, fax, mail. Search requires name plus SSN, exact years of attendance. There is no fee.

Indiana University East, Student Records, 116 Whitewater Hall, Richmond, IN 47374, 317-973-8270 (Fax: 317-973-8388). Hours: 8AM-7PM M-Th; 8AM-5PM F. Enrollment: 2400. Alumni records are maintained here at the same phone number. Degrees granted: Associate; Bachelors.

Attendance and degree information available by phone, fax, mail. Search requires name only. Also helpful: SSN. There is no fee.

Indiana University Northwest, Registrar, 3400 Broadway, Gary, IN 46408-1197, 219-980-6815 (Fax: 219-981-4200). Hours: 8AM-6PM M,Th; 8AM-5PM T,W,F. Enrollment: 5300. Records go back to 1966. Alumni records are maintained here also. Call 219-980-6768. Degrees granted: Associate; Bachelors; Masters; PBC.

Attendance and degree information available by phone, fax, mail. Search requires name only. Also helpful: SSN, exact years of attendance. There is no fee.

Indiana University Southeast, LB100, Registrar, 4201 Grant Line Rd, New Albany, IN 47150, 812-941-2240 (Fax: 812-941-2493). Hours: 8AM-5PM. Enrollment: 5400. Records go back to 1941. Alumni records are maintained here at the same phone number. Degrees granted: Associate; Bachelors; Masters; Doctorate.

Attendance and degree information available by phone, mail. Search requires name plus SSN. Also helpful: date of birth, exact years of attendance. There is no fee.

Indiana University at Bloomington, Registrar, Franklin Hall Room 100, Bloomington, IN 47405, 812-855-0121. Hours: 9AM-4PM. Enrollment: 35500. Records go back to 1820. Alumni Records Office: Alumni Association, Indiana University, Fountain Square Ste 219, Bloomington, IN 47404. Degrees granted: Bachelors; Masters; Doctorate.

Attendance and degree information available by phone, fax, mail. Search requires name plus SSN, exact years of attendance. Also helpful: approximate years of attendance. There is no fee.

Indiana University at Kokomo, Registrar, PO Box 9003, Kokomo, IN 46904-9003, 317-455-9514 (Fax: 317-455-9475). Hours: 8AM-5PM. Enrollment: 3065. Records go back to 1965. Alumni records are maintained here also. Call 317-455-9411. Degrees granted: Bachelors; Masters. Adverse incident record source- Student Services, 317-455-9514 X363.

Attendance and degree information available by phone, mail. Search requires name plus SSN. There is no fee.

Indiana University at South Bend, Registrar, 1700 Mishawaka Ave, PO Box 7111, South Bend, IN 46634, 219-237-4451 (Fax: 219-237-4834). Hours: 8AM-5PM. Enrollment: 8000. Records go back to 1965. Alumni records are maintained here also. Call 219-237-4381. Degrees granted: Bache-

lors; Masters. Adverse incident record source- Student Affairs, 219-237-4499.

Attendance and degree information available by phone, fax, mail. Search requires name plus SSN. Also helpful: exact years of attendance. There is no fee.

Indiana University-Purdue University at Fort Wayne, Registrar, 2101 Coliseum Blvd E, Fort Wayne, IN 46805, 219-481-6815 (Fax: 219-481-6880). Hours: 8AM-5PM. Enrollment: 10000. Records go back to 1960. Alumni records are maintained here at the same phone number. Degrees granted: Associate; Bachelors; Masters.

Attendance and degree information available by phone, fax, mail. Search requires name plus SSN. Also helpful: date of birth, exact years of attendance. There is no fee.

Indiana University-Purdue University at Indianapolis, Registrar, 425 University Blvd, Indianapolis, IN 46202, 317-274-1501 (Fax: 317-278-2240). Hours: 8AM-7PM M-Th, 8AM-5PM. Enrollment: 27000. Records go back to 1965. Alumni records are maintained here also. Call 317-274-8828. Degrees granted: Associate; Bachelors; Masters; Doctorate. Adverse incident record source- Student Affairs.

Attendance and degree information available by phone, fax, mail. Search requires name plus SSN. There is no fee.

Indiana Wesleyan University, Registrar, 4201 S Washington St, Marion, IN 46953, 317-677-2131 (Fax: 317-677-2809). Hours: 8AM-5PM. Enrollment: 5000. Records go back to 1920. Alumni records are maintained here also. Call 317-677-2110. Degrees granted: Bachelors; Masters. Adverse incident record source- Registrar, 317-677-2131.

Attendance and degree information available by phone, fax, mail. Search requires name plus exact years of attendance. There is no fee.

International Business College, Registrar, 3811 Illinois Rd, Fort Wayne, IN 46804, 219-432-8702 (Fax: 219-436-1896). Hours: 8:30AM-9PM M-Th; 8:30AM-5PM F. Enrollment: 500. Records go back to 1918. Degrees granted: Associate. Adverse incident record source- Department of Security.

Attendance information available by phone, fax, mail. Search requires name plus SSN, exact years of attendance. There is no fee.

Degree information available by phone, fax, mail. Search requires name plus SSN, date of birth, exact years of attendance. There is no fee.

International Business College, Registrar, 7205 Shadeland Station, Indianapolis, IN 46256, 317-841-6400 (Fax: 317-841-6419). Hours: 8AM-4:30PM. Enrollment: 180. Records go back to 1986. Degrees granted: Associate. Adverse incident record source- 317-841-6400.

Attendance information available by written request only. Search requires name plus date of birth, signed release. Also helpful: SSN, approximate years of attendance. There is no fee.

Degree information available by phone, fax, mail. Search requires name plus date of birth. Also helpful: SSN, approximate years of attendance. There is no fee.

Ivy Tech State College, Registrar, One W 26th St, PO Box 1763, Indianapolis, IN 46206-1763, 317-921-4745 (Fax: 317-921-4753). Hours: 8AM-6PM M-Th, 9AM-5PM F. Enrollment: 6000. Records go back to 1968. Alumni records are maintained here also. Call 317-921-4882. Degrees granted: Associate. Adverse incident record source- Department of Security.

Attendance and degree information available by phone, fax, mail. Search requires name plus SSN, date of birth, exact years of attendance. There is no fee.

Ivy Tech State College, Registrar, 8204 Hwy 311 W, Sellersburg, IN 47172, 812-246-3301 X4139 (Fax: 812-246-9905). Hours: 9AM-6PM M-Th; 8AM-5PM F. Enrollment:

1800. Alumni records are maintained here also. Call 812-246-3301 X4129. Degrees granted: Associate. Certification: Technical Certificate. Adverse incident record source- Student Services, 812-246-4127.

Attendance information available by written request only. Search requires name plus SSN, signed release. Also helpful: date of birth, exact years of attendance. There is no fee.

Degree information available by phone, fax, mail. Search requires name plus SSN. Also helpful: date of birth, exact years of attendance. There is no fee.

Ivy Tech State College-Columbus/Bloomington Tech. Inst.,
Registrar, 4475 Central Ave, Columbus, IN 47203, 812-372-9925 X130 (Fax: 812-372-9925 X121). Hours: 8AM-7:30PM M-Th, 8AM-5PM F. Enrollment: 1000. Records go back to 1968. Degrees granted: Associate. Adverse incident record source- Department of Security.

Attendance and degree information available by phone, fax, mail. Search requires name plus SSN. There is no fee.

Ivy Tech State College-Eastcentral Technical Institute,
Registrar, 4301 S Cowan Rd, PO Box 3100, Muncie, IN 47307, 317-289-2291 (Fax: 317-289-2291 X502). Hours: 8AM-5PM. Enrollment: 2200. Records go back to 1969. Alumni records are maintained here at the same phone number. Degrees granted: Associate. Certification: Technical. Adverse incident record source- Department of Security.

Attendance information available by fax, mail. Search requires name plus SSN, signed release. Also helpful: date of birth, exact years of attendance. There is no fee.

Degree information available by phone, fax, mail. Search requires name plus SSN. Also helpful: date of birth, exact years of attendance. There is no fee.

Ivy Tech State College-Kokomo Technical Institute,
Registrar, 1815 E Morgan St, Kokomo, IN 46901, 317-459-0561 (Fax: 317-454-5111). Hours: 7:30AM-5:30PM. Enrollment: 2100. Alumni records are maintained here at the same phone number. Degrees granted: Associate. Certification: Technical. Adverse incident record source- Security Office, 317-459-0561.

Attendance and degree information available by written request only. Search requires name plus SSN. Also helpful: exact years of attendance. There is no fee.

Ivy Tech State College-Lafayette,
Registrar, 3101 S Creasy Ln, PO Box 6299, Lafayette, IN 47903, 317-477-9119 (Fax: 317-477-9214). Hours: 8AM-5PM. Enrollment: 2400. Records go back to 1971. Alumni records are maintained here also. Call 317-477-9193. Degrees granted: Associate. Adverse incident record source- Jim Jovanovic, 317-477-9117.

Attendance and degree information available by phone, fax, mail. Search requires name plus approximate years of attendance. Also helpful: SSN, date of birth. There is no fee.

Ivy Tech State College-Northcentral,
Registrar, 1534 W Sample St, South Bend, IN 46619, 219-289-7001 X326 (Fax: 219-236-7165). Hours: 8AM-6PM M-F; 8AM-Noon S. Enrollment: 2815. Records go back to 1968. Alumni records are maintained here at the same phone number. Degrees granted: Associate. Special programs- Technical Certificates, 219-289-7001 X326; Career Development Certificates, 219-289-7001 X326. Adverse incident record source- Director of Students, 219-289-7001 X354.

Attendance information available by phone, fax, mail. Search requires name plus SSN. Also helpful: approximate years of attendance. There is no fee.

Degree information available by fax, mail. Search requires name plus SSN. Also helpful: approximate years of attendance. There is no fee.

Ivy Tech State College-Northeast Technical Inst.,
Registrar, 3800 N Anthony Blvd, Fort Wayne, IN 46805, 219-480-4255 (Fax: 219-480-4177). Hours: 8AM-5PM. Enrollment: 3500. Records go back to 1970. Alumni records are maintained here also. Call 219-480-4211. Degrees granted: Associate. Adverse incident record source- Student Services, 219-480-4212.

Attendance and degree information available by phone, fax, mail. Search requires name plus SSN. Also helpful: date of birth, approximate years of attendance. There is no fee.

Ivy Tech State College-Northwest Technical Inst.,
(Branch), Registrar, 1440 E 35th Ave, Gary, IN 46409, 219-981-1111 X272 (Fax: 219-981-4415). Hours: 8AM-5PM. Enrollment: 950. Records go back to 1969. Alumni records are maintained here at the same phone number. Degrees granted: Associate. Adverse incident record source- Department of Security.

Attendance and degree information available by phone, mail. Search requires name plus SSN, date of birth. There is no fee.

Ivy Tech State College-Southeast Tech. Inst.,
Registrar, 590 Ivy Tech Dr, Madison, IN 47250, 812-265-2580 X4130 (Fax: 812-265-4028). Hours: 8AM-5PM. Enrollment: 1200. Records go back to 1971. Alumni records are maintained here at the same phone number. Degrees granted: Associate. Certification: Technical. Adverse incident record source- Same as above.

Attendance and degree information available by phone, fax, mail. Search requires name only. Also helpful: SSN, date of birth, exact years of attendance. There is no fee.

Ivy Tech State College-Southwest Tech. Inst.,
Registrar, 3501 First Ave, Evansville, IN 47710, 812-429-1433 (Fax: 812-429-9834). Hours: 8AM-6PM. Enrollment: 3500. Records go back to 1965. Alumni records are maintained here at the same phone number. Degrees granted: Associate. Certification: TC. Adverse incident record source- Director of Facilities, 812-429-1488.

Attendance and degree information available by phone, fax, mail. Search requires name plus SSN. Also helpful: date of birth, exact years of attendance. There is no fee.

Ivy Tech State College-Wabash Valley Tech. Inst.,
Registrar, 7999 US Hwy 41, Terre Haute, IN 47802, 812-299-1121 (Fax: 812-299-5723). Hours: 8AM-8PM M-Th; 8AM-4:45PM F. Enrollment: 2000. Records go back to 1969. Degrees granted: Associate. Adverse incident record source- Records/Registration.

Attendance information available by mail. Search requires name plus SSN, signed release. Also helpful: date of birth, exact years of attendance. There is no fee.

Degree information available by fax, mail. Search requires name plus SSN, signed release. Also helpful: date of birth, exact years of attendance. There is no fee.

Ivy Tech State College-Whitewater Tech. Inst.,
Registrar, 2325 Chester Blvd, Richmond, IN 47374, 317-966-2656 (Fax: 317-962-8741). Hours: 8AM-5PM. Enrollment: 1100. Records go back to 1968. Degrees granted: Associate. Certification: Technical. Adverse incident record source- Student Services.

Attendance and degree information available by fax, mail. Search requires name plus SSN, date of birth, approximate years of attendance, signed release. Also helpful: exact years of attendance. There is no fee.

Lutheran College of Health Professions,
Registrar, 3024 Fairfield Ave, Fort Wayne, IN 46807, 219-458-2453 (Fax: 219-458-3077). Hours: 8AM-4:30PM. Enrollment: 650. Records go back to 1904. Alumni records are maintained

here at the same phone number. Degrees granted: Associate; Bachelors.

Attendance and degree information available by written request only. Search requires name plus SSN, approximate years of attendance, signed release. Also helpful: date of birth, exact years of attendance. There is no fee.

Manchester College, Registrar, 604 College Ave, North Manchester, IN 46962, 219-982-5234 (Fax: 219-982-5043). Hours: 8AM-Noon,1-5PM. Enrollment: 1020. Records go back to 1800's. Alumni Records Office: Alumni Association, Manchester College, Box 175, North Manchester, IN 46962. Degrees granted: Associate; Bachelors; MACCTY. Adverse incident record source- Student Development, 219-982-5052.

Attendance and degree information available by phone, fax, mail. Search requires name only. Also helpful: date of birth, exact years of attendance. There is no fee.

Marian College, Registrar, 3200 Cold Spring Rd, Indianapolis, IN 46222, 317-929-0213 (Fax: 317-929-0263). Hours: 8AM-4:30PM. Enrollment: 1300. Records go back to 1851. Alumni records are maintained here also. Call 317-929-0227. Degrees granted: Bachelors. Adverse incident record source- Dean of Students, 317-929-0123.

Attendance and degree information available by mail. Search requires name plus SSN, date of birth. There is no fee.

Martin University, Registrar, 2171 Avondale Pl, PO Box 18567, Indianapolis, IN 46218, 317-543-3249 (Fax: 317-543-3257). Hours: 8AM-4:30PM. Enrollment: 950. Records go back to 1977. Alumni records are maintained here also. Call 317-543-4822. Degrees granted: Bachelors; Masters. Adverse incident record source- Student Services.

Attendance and degree information available by phone, mail. Search requires name plus SSN, date of birth. There is no fee.

Michiana College, Registrar, 1030 E Jefferson Blvd, South Bend, IN 46617, 219-237-0774 (Fax: 219-237-3585). Enrollment: 390. Records go back to 1882. Degrees granted: Associate.

Attendance and degree information available by mail. Search requires name plus SSN, exact years of attendance, signed release. Also helpful: date of birth. Fee is $5.00.

Michiana College, (Branch), Registrar, 4807 Illinois Rd, Fort Wayne, IN 46804, 219-436-2738 (Fax: 219-436-2958). Hours: 8AM-5:30PM. Enrollment: 60. Records go back to 1993. Degrees granted: Associate. Special programs- Medical Assistant. Adverse incident record source- Department of Security.

Attendance and degree information available by phone, mail. Search requires name plus SSN. There is no fee.

Mid-America College of Funeral Service, Registrar, 3111 Hamburg Pike, Jeffersonville, IN 47130, 812-288-8878 (Fax: 812-288-5942). Hours: 7:30AM-4PM. Enrollment: 120. Records go back to 1920. Degrees granted: Associate. Adverse incident record source- President of School.

Attendance and degree information available by phone, fax, mail. Search requires name plus SSN, approximate years of attendance. Also helpful: date of birth, exact years of attendance. There is no fee.

Oakland City University, Registrar, 143 N Lucretia St, Oakland City, IN 47660, 812-749-1238 (Fax: 812-749-1233). Hours: 8AM-Noon, 1-4:30PM. Enrollment: 1069. Formerly Oakland City College Records go back to 1885. Alumni records are maintained here also. Call 812-749-1223. Degrees granted: Associate; Bachelors; Masters. Adverse incident record source- Student Services, 812-745-4781.

Attendance and degree information available by phone, fax, mail. Search requires name only. Also helpful: SSN, date of birth, approximate years of attendance. There is no fee.

Purdue University, Office of the Registrar, 1095 Hovde Hall Rm55, West Lafayette, IN 47907-1095, 317-494-6153 (Fax: 317-494-0570). Hours: 8:30AM-5PM. Enrollment: 36172. Records go back to 1875. Phone number for transcripts is 317-494-6151. Alumni records are maintained here also. Call 317-494-5189. Degrees granted: Associate; Bachelors; Masters; Doctorate.

Attendance and degree information available by phone, fax, mail. Search requires name only. Also helpful: SSN, date of birth, exact years of attendance. There is no fee.

Purdue University Calumet, Registrar, Hammond, IN 46323, 219-989-2993. Records are not housed here. They are located at Purdue University, Office of the Registrar, 1095 Hovde Hall Rm55, West Lafayette, IN 47907-1095.

Purdue University North Central, Registrar, 1401 S US Hwy 421, Westville, IN 46391, 219-785-5200 (Fax: 219-785-5538). Enrollment: 3400. Records go back to 1981. Alumni records are maintained here at the same phone number. Degrees granted: Associate; Bachelors; Masters.

Attendance and degree information available by phone, fax, mail. Search requires name only. Also helpful: approximate years of attendance. There is no fee.

Rose-Hulman Institute of Technology, Registrar, 5500 Wabash Ave, Terre Haute, IN 47803, 812-877-1511 X298 (Fax: 812-877-8141). Hours: 8AM-5PM. Enrollment: 1400. Records go back to 1874. Alumni records are maintained here also. Call 812-877-8359. Degrees granted: Bachelors; Masters.

Attendance and degree information available by phone, fax, mail. Search requires name only. Also helpful: date of birth, approximate years of attendance. There is no fee.

Saint Joseph's College, Registrar's Office, PO Box 929, Rensselaer, IN 47978, 219-866-6161 (Fax: 219-866-6100). Hours: 8AM-Noon, 1-4:30PM. Enrollment: 950. Records go back to 1891. Alumni Records Office: Alumni Association, PO Box 870, Rensselaer, IN 47978. Degrees granted: Associate; Bachelors; Masters. Certification: Music. Adverse incident record source- Student Affairs, 219-866-6000.

Attendance and degree information available by phone, fax, mail. Search requires name only. Also helpful: SSN, date of birth, exact years of attendance. There is no fee.

Saint Mary's College, Registrar, Notre Dame, IN 46556, 219-284-4560 (Fax: 219-284-4716). Hours: 8AM-Noon, 1-4:30PM. Enrollment: 1550. Records go back to 1900. Alumni Records Office: Alumnae Relations, LeMans Hall, Notre Dame, IN 46556. Degrees granted: Bachelors. Adverse incident record source- Public Relations, 219-284-4595.

Attendance and degree information available by phone, fax, mail. Search requires name only. Also helpful: SSN, date of birth, exact years of attendance. There is no fee.

Sawyer College, Inc., Registrar, 6040 Hohman Ave, Hammond, IN 46320, 219-931-0436 (Fax: 219-933-1239). Hours: 8AM-5PM. Enrollment: 250. Records go back to 1990. Alumni records are maintained here at the same phone number. Degrees granted: Associate. Adverse incident record source- Department of Security.

Attendance and degree information available by fax, mail. Search requires name plus SSN, exact years of attendance, signed release. There is no fee.

Sawyer College, Inc., (Branch), Registrar, 3803 E Lincoln Hwy, Merrillville, IN 46410, 219-736-0436 (Fax: 219-942-3762). Hours: 8AM-5PM. Enrollment: 230. Records go back to 1985. Degrees granted: Associate. Adverse incident record source- Department of Security.

Attendance and degree information available by mail. Search requires name plus SSN, exact years of attendance, signed release. There is no fee.

St. Francis College, Registrar, 2701 Spring St, Fort Wayne, IN 46808, 219-434-3252 (Fax: 219-434-3183). Hours: 8:30AM-Noon,12:30-5PM. Enrollment: 1000. Records go back to 1890. Alumni records are maintained here at the same phone number. Degrees granted: Associate; Bachelors; Masters.

Attendance and degree information available by phone, fax, mail. Search requires name plus SSN. Also helpful: exact years of attendance. There is no fee.

St. Mary-Of-The-Woods College, Registrar, St. Mary-of-the-Woods, IN 47876, 812-535-5269 (Fax: 812-535-4613). Hours: 8:30AM-Noon, 1-4:30PM. Enrollment: 1250. Records go back to 1898. Alumni records are maintained here also. Call 812-535-5211. Degrees granted: Associate; Bachelors; Masters. Certification: Gerontology. Special programs- Music: Therapy: Education. Adverse incident record source- Le Fer Hall, 812-535-5216.

Attendance and degree information available by phone, fax, mail. Search requires name only. Also helpful: exact years of attendance. There is no fee.

St. Meinrad College, Registrar, St Meinrad, IN 47577, 812-357-6525 (Fax: 812-357-6964). Hours: 8AM-4:30PM. Enrollment: 100. Records go back to 1880. Degrees granted: Bachelors. Adverse incident record source- Physical Facilities.

Attendance and degree information available by phone, fax, mail. Search requires name only. Also helpful: SSN, date of birth, exact years of attendance. There is no fee.

St. Meinrad School of Theology, Registrar, St Meinrad, IN 47577, 812-357-6525 (Fax: 812-357-6964). Hours: 8AM-4:30PM. Enrollment: 145. Records go back to 1880. Degrees granted: Masters. Adverse incident record source- Physical Facilities, 812-357-6593.

Attendance and degree information available by phone, fax, mail. Search requires name only. Also helpful: SSN, date of birth, exact years of attendance. There is no fee.

Taylor University, Registrar's Office, 500 W Reade Ave, Upland, IN 46989, 317-998-5330/998-5193 (Fax: 317-998-4910). Hours: 8AM-5PM. Enrollment: 1850. Records go back to 1846. Alumni records are maintained here also. Call 317-998-5115. Degrees granted: Associate; Bachelors. Adverse incident record source- Student Development, 317-998-5379.

Attendance and degree information available by phone, fax, mail. Search requires name plus SSN, approximate years of attendance. Also helpful: date of birth, exact years of attendance. There is no fee. Expedited service available for $10.00.

Taylor University, (Fort Wayne), Registrar, 1025 W Rudisill Blvd, Fort Wayne, IN 46807, 219-456-2111 (Fax: 219-456-2119). Hours: 8AM-5pM. Records go back to 1890. Alumni records are maintained here also. Call 219-456-2211 X3331. Degrees granted: Associate; Bachelors. Adverse incident record source- Student Affairs, 219-456-2211 X3314.

Attendance and degree information available by phone, fax, mail. Search requires name plus SSN, exact years of attendance. There is no fee.

Tri-State University, Registrar, Angola, IN 46703, 219-665-4240 (Fax: 219-665-4292). Hours: 8AM-5PM. Enrollment: 1200. Records go back to 1900. Alumni records are maintained here also. Call 219-665-4122. Degrees granted: Associate; Bachelors.

Attendance and degree information available by phone, fax, mail. Search requires name only. Also helpful: SSN, date of birth, exact years of attendance. There is no fee.

University of Evansville, Registrar, 1800 Lincoln Ave, Evansville, IN 47722, 812-479-2267 (Fax: 812-474-2583). Hours: 8AM-5PM. Enrollment: 3162. Records go back to 1854. Alumni records are maintained here also. Call 812-479-2000. Degrees granted: Bachelors; Masters. Adverse incident record source- Registrar, 812-479-2267.

Attendance and degree information available by phone, fax, mail. Search requires name plus SSN. There is no fee.

University of Indianapolis, Registrar's Office, 1400 E Hanna Ave, Indianapolis, IN 46227, 317-788-3219 (Fax: 317-788-3300). Hours: 7:30AM09PM M-Th; 7:30AM-4:30PM F. Enrollment: 4000. Records go back to 1908. Alumni records are maintained here also. Call 317-788-3295. Degrees granted: Associate; Bachelors; Masters; PsyD. Adverse incident record source- Safety & Police, 317-788-3386.

Attendance and degree information available by phone, fax, mail. Search requires name only. Also helpful: SSN, date of birth, exact years of attendance. There is no fee.

University of Notre Dame, Registrar, 215 Main Bldg, Notre Dame, IN 46556, 219-631-7045 (Fax: 219-631-5872). Hours: 8AM-5PM. Enrollment: 10300. Records go back to 1842. Alumni Records Office: 201 Main Bldg, Notre Dame, IN 46556, 219-631-6000. Degrees granted: Bachelors; Masters; Doctorate; J.D.(Law).

Attendance and degree information available by phone, fax, mail. Search requires name plus SSN, exact years of attendance. There is no fee.

University of Southern Indiana, Registrar, 8600 University Blvd, Evansville, IN 47712, 812-464-1763 (Fax: 812-464-1960). Hours: 8AM-4:30PM. Enrollment: 7500. Records go back to 1962. Alumni records are maintained here at the same phone number. Degrees granted: Associate; Bachelors. Adverse incident record source- Student Services.

Attendance and degree information available by phone, fax, mail. Search requires name plus SSN. There is no fee.

Valparaiso University, Registrar, Valparaiso, IN 46383, 219-464-5212 (Fax: 219-464-5381). Hours: 8AM-5PM. Enrollment: 3500. Records go back to 1859. Alumni records are maintained here also. Call 219-464-5110. Degrees granted: Associate; Bachelors; Masters. Adverse incident record source- Registrar, 219-464-5212.

Attendance and degree information available by phone, fax, mail. Search requires name plus SSN, date of birth, exact years of attendance. There is no fee.

Vincennes University, Registrar, 1002 N First St, Vincennes, IN 47591, 812-888-4220 (Fax: 812-888-5868). Hours: 8AM-4:30PM. Enrollment: 8000. Records go back to 1806. Alumni records are maintained here also. Call 812-888-4354. Degrees granted: Associate. Adverse incident record source- Public Relations, 812-888-4358.

Attendance information available by phone, fax, mail. Search requires name only. Also helpful: SSN, date of birth, exact years of attendance. There is no fee.

Degree information available by phone, fax, mail. Search requires name only. Also helpful: SSN, date of birth. There is no fee.

Wabash College, Registrar, 301 W Wabash Ave, Crawfordsville, IN 47933, 317-364-4245 (Fax: 317-364-4432). Hours: 8AM-4:30PM. Enrollment: 800. Records go back to 1900. Degrees granted: Bachelors. Adverse incident record source- Dean of Students.

Attendance and degree information available by phone, fax, mail. Search requires name only. Also helpful: date of birth. There is no fee.

Trade and Vocational Schools

Academy of Hair Design, 2150 Lafayette Rd, Indianapolis, IN 46222, 317-637-7227

College of Court Reporting, 111 W 10th St #111, Hobart, IN 46342, 219-942-1459

Defense Information School, Bldg 400, Fort Benjamin Harrison, IN 46216, 317-542-4046

Horizon Career College, 8315 Virginia St Ste A, Merrillville, IN 46307, 219-756-6811

Indiana Barber/Stylist College, 121 S Ridgeview Dr, Indianapolis, IN 46219, 317-356-8222

PJ's College of Cosmetology (Branch Campus), 113 N Washington St, Crawfordsville, IN 47933, 800-627-2566

PJ's College of Cosmetology (Branch Campus), 1400 W Main St, Greenfield, IN 46140, 800-627-2566

PJ's College of Cosmetology (Branch Campus), 5539 S Madison Ave, Indianapolis, IN 46227, 800-627-2566

PJ's College of Cosmetology (Branch Campus), 2006 N Walnut St, Muncie, IN 47303, 800-627-2566

PJ's College of Cosmetology (Branch Campus), 2026 Stafford Rd, Plainfield, IN 46168, 800-627-2566

Professional Careers Institute, 2611 Waterfront Pkwy, Indianapolis, IN 46214, 317-299-6001

State Licensing & Business Registration Quick Finder Index

Architecture, Engineering & Surveying
Architect #17 .... ☎ 317-232-2980
Engineer #17 .... ☎ 317-232-2980
Surveyor #17 .... ☎ 317-232-2980

Business - Court & Legal Services
Attorney #14 317-639-5465
Lobbyist #16 .... ☎ 317-232-6542
Notary Public #16 .... ☎ 317-232-6542
Shorthand Reporter #10 219-873-7008

Business - General Services
Auctioneer #17 .... ☎ 317-232-2980
Public Accountant #17 .... ☎ 317-232-2980
TV-Radio Service #17 .... ☎ 317-232-2980

Construction & Manufacturing
Boiler & Pressure Vessel Inspector #7 (500)
.... ☎ 317-232-1921
Elevator Safety Contractor #7 317-232-6609
Manufactured Home Builder #7 317-232-1408
Plumber #17 .... ☎ 317-232-2980
Warehouse #11 .... ☎ 317-232-1358
Warehouseman #11 .... ☎ 317-232-1356

Education
School Administrator #13 .... ☎ 317-232-9010
School Counselor #13 .... ☎ 317-232-9010
School Principal #13 .... ☎ 317-232-9010
Teacher #13 .... ☎ 317-232-9010

Environmental & Agriculture
Asbestos Contractor #4 (400) .... ☎ 317-232-8232
Asbestos Disposal Manager/Worker #4 .... ☎ 317-232-8603
Asbestos Inspector/Supervisor #4 (10000) .... ☎ 317-232-8232
Asbestos Project Designer #4 .... ☎ 317-232-8603
Asbestos Training Course Provider #4 .... ☎ 317-232-8232
Environmental Health #9 (309) .... ✉ 317-233-2960
Grain Inspector #11 (1000) .... ☎ 317-232-1358

Livestock Dealer #2 (370) .... ☎ 317-232-1339
Pesticide Applicator #3 (5400) .... ☎ 317-494-1594
Pesticide Technician/Consultant #3 (1700) .... ☎ 317-494-1594
Underground Storage Tank #7 .... ☎ 317-232-2228
Veterinarian #9 (2145) .... ✉ 317-233-2960
Waste Water Treatment Plant Operator #4 (5300)
.... ☎ 317-232-8666

Financial - Real Estate, Insurance & Banking
Bank & Trust #5 .... ☎ 317-232-5846
Building & Loan/Credit Union #5 .... ☎ 317-232-5851
Check Casher #5 .... ☎ 317-232-3955
Consumer Credit #5 .... ☎ 317-232-5849
Insurance Adjuster #6 317-232-2585
Insurance Agent/Consultant #6 .... ☎ 317-232-2413
Investment Advisor #18 (950) .... ☎ 317-232-6681
Lender #5 .... ☎ 317-232-3955
Money Transmitter #5 .... ☎ 317-232-3955
Pawnbroker #5 .... ☎ 317-232-3955
Real Estate Agent #17 .... ☎ 317-232-2980
Real Estate Appraiser #17 .... ☎ 317-232-2980
Securities Broker/Dealer #18 (1590) .... ☎ 317-232-6690
Securities Sales Agent #18 (59000) .... ☎ 317-232-6690

Health & Beauty
Audiologist #9 .... ✉ 317-233-2960
Barber #17 .... ☎ 317-232-2980
Beauty Colorist #17 .... ☎ 317-232-2980
Chiropractor #9 (807) .... ✉ 317-233-2960
Clinical Social Worker #9 .... ✉ 317-233-2960
Cosmetologist #17 .... ☎ 317-232-2980
Dental Hygienist #9 (2913) .... ✉ 317-233-2960
Dentist #9 (3386) .... ✉ 317-233-2960
Dietitian #9 .... ✉ 317-233-2960
Emergency Medical Technician #17 .... ☎ 317-232-2980
Funeral/Cemetery Director #17 .... ☎ 317-232-2980
Health Services Administrator #9 .... ✉ 317-233-2960

Hearing Aid Dealer #9 (164)..........................✉ 317-233-2960
Licensed Practical Nurse #9 ....✉ 317-233-2960
Medical Doctor #9 (18213)...........................✉ 317-233-2960
Nurse #9..✉ 317-233-2960
Nurse Midwife #9 (24) ....✉ 317-233-2960
Nursing Home Administrator #9 (1464) ....✉ 317-233-2960
Occupational Therapist #9 (1695)..................✉ 317-233-2960
Optometrist #9 ....☎ 317-233-4413
Osteopathic Physician #9 (1040)...................✉ 317-233-2960
Pharmacist/Pharmacist Intern #9 (7490) ....✉ 317-233-2960
Physical Therapist #9.................................✉ 317-233-2960
Physical Therapist Assistant #9....................✉ 317-233-2960
Physician's Assistant #9 (119)......................✉ 317-233-2960
Podiatrist #9 (368) ....✉ 317-233-2960
Radiologic Technologist #19........................☎ 317-233-7147
Registered Nurse #9..................................✉ 317-233-2960
Respiratory Care Practitioner #9 (3600) ....✉ 317-233-2960
Sanitarian #9 ....✉ 317-233-2960
Speech Pathologist #9 (1404)........................✉ 317-233-2960

Investigations & Security
Polygraph Examiner #20 ....☎ 317-232-8263
Private Detective #17....................................☎ 317-232-2980

Social Services
Certified Clinical Social Worker #8 ....☎ 317-233-4397
Marriage & Family Therapist #9 (1248) ....✉ 317-233-2960
Psychologist #9 (1463) ....✉ 317-233-2960
Social Worker #8 (3474)...............................☎ 317-233-4937

Sports & Entertainment
Alcoholic Beverage Distributor #1.................☎ 317-232-2455
Athletic Trainer #9......................................✉ 317-233-2960
Boxer #17 (300)...☎ 317-232-3897
Horse Racing #12 (3295)...............................☎ 317-233-3110
Lottery Retailer #15 ....☎ 317-264-4800

State Licensing & Business Registration Agency Information

(1)   Alcoholic Beverage Commission, 402 W Washington St, IGS-S, Room E114, Indianapolis, IN 46204, 317-232-2455

(2)   Board of Animal Health, Licensing/Enforcement Division, 805 Beachway Dr, Ste 50, Indianapolis, IN 46224, 317-232-1339

(3)   Department of Biochemistry, Office of State Chemist & Seed Commissioner, Purdue University, West Lafayette, IN 47907, 317-494-1594

(4)   Department of Environmental Management, PO Box 7060, Indianapolis, IN 46202-7060, 317-232-8603, Fax: 317-232-8406

(5)   Department of Financial Institutions, 402 W Washington St, IGC-S, Room W066, Indianapolis, IN 46204-2759, 317-232-3955, Fax: 317-232-7655

(6)   Department of Insurance, 311 W Washington St, Ste 300, Indianapolis, IN 46204-2787, 317-232-2413, Fax: 317-232-5251

(7)   Fire & Building Services, 402 W Washington St, IGC-S, Room W246, Indianapolis, IN 46204, 317-232-6609, Fax: 317-232-0146

(8)   Health Professions Bureau, 402 W Washington St, Ste 041, Indianapolis, IN 46204-2739, 317-232-2960, Fax: 317-233-4236

(9)   Health Professions Bureau, 402 W Washington St, Rm W041, Indianapolis, IN 46204, 317-233-4413, Fax: 317-243-4236

(10)   ISRA President, PO Box 1103, Michigan City, IN 46340, 219-873-7008

(11)   Indiana Commodity Warehouse Licensing Agency, 150 W Market St, Room 416, Indianapolis, IN 46204, 317-232-1356, Fax: 317-232-1362

(12)   Indiana Horse Racing Licensing, 150 W Market St, Indianapolis, IN 46204, 317-233-3110

(13)   Indiana Professional Standards Board, 251 East Ohio Suite 201, Indianapolis, IN 46204-2133, 317-232-9010, Fax: 317-232-9023

(14)   Indiana Supreme Court, 217 State House, Indianapolis, IN 46204, 317-639-5465

(15)   Lottery Commission of Indiana, 201 S Capitol Ave, Ste 1100, Indianapolis, IN 46225, 317-264-4800, Fax: 317-264-4908

(16)   Office of Secretary of State, Statehouse, Suite 201, Indianapolis, IN 46204, 317-232-6542, Fax: 317-233-3283

(17)   Professional Licensing Agency, Boards & Commissions, 302 N Washington St, Rm E034, Indianapolis, IN 46204, 317-232-3897, Fax: 232-233-5559

(18)   Secretary of State, Securities Division, 302 W Washington St, RME-111, Indianapolis, IN 46204, 317-232-6681, Fax: 317-233-3675

(19)   State Board of Health, Division of End. & Radiologic Health, 2 N Meridian St, Indianapolis, IN 46204-3003, 317-233-7150

(20)   State Police, Government Center N, 100 N Senate Ave, Rm 302, Indianapolis, IN 46204, 317-232-8263

Iowa

Capitol: Des Moines (Polk County)	
State Population	2.8 Million
Number of Degree Granting Institutions:	65
Number of State Licensing & Business Registration Agencies:	101

Degree Granting Educational Institutions

American Institute of Business, Registrar, 2500 Fleur Dr, Des Moines, IA 50321, 515-244-4221 (Fax: 515-244-6773). Hours: 7AM-4:30PM. Enrollment: 764. Records go back to 1930's. Alumni records are maintained here at the same phone number. Degrees granted: Associate. Adverse incident record source- Dean of Students, 515-244-4221.

Attendance and degree information available by phone, mail. Search requires name plus approximate years of attendance. Also helpful: SSN, date of birth. There is no fee.

American Institute of Commerce, Registrar, 1801 E Kimberly Rd, Davenport, IA 52807, 319-355-3500 (Fax: 319-355-1320). Hours: 8AM-5PM. Enrollment: 370. Records go back to 1946. Degrees granted: Associate. Adverse incident record source- Student Services, 319-355-3500.

Attendance and degree information available by phone, fax, mail. Search requires name only. Also helpful: SSN, date of birth, approximate years of attendance. There is no fee.

American Institute of Commerce, (Branch), Registrar, 2302 W First St, Cedar Falls, IA 50613, 319-277-0220 (Fax: 319-268-0978). Hours: 8AM-5PM. Enrollment: 200. Records go back to 1987. Degrees granted: Associate. Special programs- Legal Assistant: Paralegal.

Attendance information available by written request only. Search requires name plus SSN, exact years of attendance. Also helpful: date of birth. Fee is $4.00.

Degree information available by written request only. Search requires name plus exact years of attendance. Also helpful: SSN, date of birth. Fee is $4.00.

Briar Cliff College, Registrar, 3033 Rebecca St, Sioux City, IA 51104, 712-279-5448 (Fax: 712-279-5410). Hours: 8AM-4:30PM. Enrollment: 1150. Alumni records are maintained here also. Call 712-279-5396. Degrees granted: Associate; Bachelors. Adverse incident record source- Student Development, 712-279-5406: Security, 712-279-5464

Attendance and degree information available by phone, fax, mail. Search requires name plus SSN. Also helpful: date of birth, exact years of attendance. There is no fee.

Buena Vista University, Registrar, 610 W Fourth St, Storm Lake, IA 50588, 712-749-2234. Hours: 8AM-5PM. Enrollment: 1150. Formerly Buena Vista College Records go back to 1891. Alumni records are maintained here at the same phone number. Degrees granted: Bachelors; Masters. Adverse incident record source- Dean of Students, 712-749-2123.

Attendance and degree information available by phone, mail. Search requires name only. Also helpful: SSN, date of birth, exact years of attendance. There is no fee.

Central College, Registrar, 812 University, Pella, IA 50219, 515-628-5267 (Fax: 515-628-5316). Hours: 8AM-5PM. Enrollment: 1400. Alumni records are maintained here also. Call 515-628-5281. Degrees granted: Bachelors.

Attendance and degree information available by phone, fax, mail. Search requires name only. Also helpful: SSN, date of birth, exact years of attendance. There is no fee.

Central University of Iowa, Registrar, 812 University, Pella, IA 50219, 515-628-5267 (Fax: 515-628-5316). Enrollment: 1538. Records go back to 1925. Alumni records are maintained here at the same phone number. Degrees granted: Bachelors. Special programs- Arts. Adverse incident record source- Student Services.

Attendance and degree information available by phone, mail. Search requires name plus SSN, exact years of attendance. There is no fee.

Clarke College, Registrar, 1550 Clarke Dr, Dubuque, IA 52001, 319-588-6314 (Fax: 319-588-6789). Hours: 8AM-4:30PM. Enrollment: 1020. Records go back to 1904. Alumni records are maintained here at the same phone number. Degrees granted: Associate; Bachelors; Masters.

Attendance information available by phone, fax, mail. Search requires name only. Also helpful: SSN, date of birth. There is no fee.

Degree information available by phone, fax, mail. Search requires name only. Also helpful: SSN. There is no fee.

Clinton Community College, Registrar, 1000 Lincoln Blvd, Clinton, IA 52732, 319-242-6841 (Fax: 319-242-7868). Hours: 7:30AM-5PM. Enrollment: 1100. Records go back to 1948. Alumni records are maintained here at the same phone number. Degrees granted: Associate.

School will not confirm attendance information.

Degree information available by phone, fax, mail. Search requires name plus SSN. Also helpful: date of birth, approximate years of attendance. There is no fee.

Coe College, Registrar, Cedar Rapids, IA 52402, 319-399-8526 (Fax: 319-399-8748). Hours: 8AM-4:30PM. Enrollment:

1343. Records go back to 1885. Alumni records are maintained here also. Call 319-399-8608. Degrees granted: Bachelors; Masters.

Attendance and degree information available by phone, fax, mail. Search requires name plus approximate years of attendance. Also helpful: SSN, date of birth, exact years of attendance. There is no fee.

Cornell College, Registrar, 600 First St W, Mount Vernon, IA 52314, 319-895-4372 (Fax: 319-895-4492). Hours: 8AM-4:30PM. Enrollment: 1150. Records go back to 1853. Alumni records are maintained here also. Call 319-895-4204. Degrees granted: Bachelors.

Attendance and degree information available by phone, fax, mail. Search requires name plus exact years of attendance. Also helpful: SSN, date of birth. There is no fee.

Des Moines Area Community College, Student Records Bldg 1, 2006 S Ankeny Blvd, Ankeny, IA 50021, 515-964-6224 (Fax: 515-964-6391). Hours: 8AM-5PM Fall, Spring; 7:30AM-4PM Summer. Enrollment: 11000. Records go back to 1920. Alumni records are maintained here also. Call 515-964-6376. Degrees granted: Associate. Adverse incident record source- Physical Plant, 515-964-6253.

Attendance information available by phone, fax, mail. Search requires name plus SSN. Also helpful: exact years of attendance. There is no fee.

Degree information available by phone, fax, mail. Search requires name plus SSN. Also helpful: exact years of attendance. There is no fee.

Divine Word College, Registrar, S Center Ave, Epworth, IA 52045, 319-876-3353 X205. Hours: 9AM-5PM. Records go back to 1964. Alumni records are maintained here also. Call 319-876-3353. Degrees granted: Bachelors. Adverse incident record source- Registrar, 319-876-3353.

Attendance and degree information available by phone, mail. Search requires name plus SSN. There is no fee.

Dordt College, Registrar, Sioux Center, IA 51250, 712-722-6030 (Fax: 712-722-4496). Hours: 8AM-Noon, 1-5PM. Enrollment: 1200. Records go back to 1955. Alumni records are maintained here also. Call 712-722-6022. Degrees granted: Associate; Bachelors; Masters. Adverse incident record source- Student Services.

Attendance and degree information available by phone, fax, mail. Search requires name plus SSN. Also helpful: date of birth, exact years of attendance. There is no fee.

Drake University, Registrar, 25th St and University Ave, Des Moines, IA 50311, 515-271-3901 (Fax: 515-271-3977). Hours: 8AM-4:30PM. Enrollment: 6000. Records go back to 1881. Alumni Records Office: Alumni Development, Drake University, 2507 University, Des Moines, IA 50310. Degrees granted: Bachelors; Masters; Doctorate.

Attendance and degree information available by phone, fax, mail. Search requires name plus SSN, date of birth, approximate years of attendance. Also helpful: exact years of attendance. There is no fee.

Eastern Iowa Community College District, Transcript Department, 500 Belmont Rd, Bettendorf, IA 52722, 319-359-7531 X316. Enrollment: 4000. Degrees granted: Associate.

School will not confirm attendance information.

Degree information available by phone, fax, mail. Search requires name plus SSN, exact years of attendance. Also helpful: date of birth, approximate years of attendance. There is no fee.

Ellsworth Community College, Registrar, 1100 College Ave, Iowa Falls, IA 50126, 800-322-9235 X436 (Fax: 515-648-3128). Hours: 8AM-5PM. Enrollment: 800. Records go

back to 1940's. Alumni records are maintained here also. Call 800-322-9235 X247. Degrees granted: Associate.

Attendance and degree information available by phone, fax, mail. Search requires name plus SSN. Also helpful: date of birth, exact years of attendance. There is no fee.

Emmaus Bible College, Registrar, 2570 Asbury Rd, Dubuque, IA 52001, 319-588-8000 (Fax: 319-588-1216). Hours: 8AM-5PM. Enrollment: 230. Records go back to 1945. Alumni records are maintained here also. Call 319-588-8000. Degrees granted: Associate; Bachelors. Adverse incident record source- 319-588-8000 X308.

Attendance and degree information available by phone, fax, mail. Search requires name plus SSN, approximate years of attendance. Also helpful: date of birth, exact years of attendance. There is no fee.

Faith Baptist Bible College and Theological Seminary, Registrar, 1900 NW Fourth St, Ankeny, IA 50021, 515-964-0601 X208 (Fax: 515-964-1638). Hours: 8AM-4:30PM. Enrollment: 203. Records go back to 1921. Alumni records are maintained here at the same phone number. Degrees granted: Associate; Bachelors; Masters.

Attendance and degree information available by phone, fax, mail. Search requires name only. Also helpful: SSN, date of birth, exact years of attendance. There is no fee.

Graceland College, Registrar, Lamoni, IA 50140, 515-784-5220 (Fax: 515-784-5474). Hours: 8AM-5PM. Enrollment: 3892. Alumni records are maintained here at the same phone number. Degrees granted: Bachelors; Masters.

Attendance and degree information available by phone, fax, mail. Search requires name plus SSN, approximate years of attendance. Also helpful: date of birth, exact years of attendance. There is no fee.

Grand View College, Registrar, 1200 Grandview Ave, Des Moines, IA 50316, 515-263-2818 (Fax: 515-263-6095). Hours: 8:15AM-4PM. Enrollment: 1480. Records go back to 1895. Alumni records are maintained here also. Call 515-263-2957. Degrees granted: Associate; Bachelors. Adverse incident record source- Dean of Students, 515-263-2885.

Attendance and degree information available by phone, fax, mail. Search requires name only. Also helpful: SSN, date of birth, exact years of attendance. There is no fee.

Grinnell College, Registrar, PO Box 805, Grinnell, IA 50112, 515-269-3450 (Fax: 515-269-4415). Hours: 8AM-5PM. Enrollment: 1270. Records go back to 1846. Alumni records are maintained here also. Call 515-269-4801. Degrees granted: Bachelors.

Attendance and degree information available by phone, mail. Search requires name plus SSN. Also helpful: exact years of attendance. There is no fee.

Hamilton Technical College, Registrar, 1011 E 53rd St, Davenport, IA 52807-2616, 319-386-3570 (Fax: 319-386-6756). Hours: 8AM-6PM M-Th; 8AM-Noon F. Enrollment: 350. Records go back to 1969. Degrees granted: Associate; Bachelors.

Attendance and degree information available by phone, fax, mail. Search requires name only. Also helpful: SSN, date of birth, exact years of attendance. There is no fee.

Hawkeye Community College, Registrar, 1501 E Orange Rd, Waterloo, IA 50704, 319-296-2320 (Fax: 319-296-2874). Enrollment: 3530. Records go back to 1966. Degrees granted: Associate. Adverse incident record source- Registrar's Office, 319-296-2320   .

Attendance and degree information available by phone, fax, mail. Search requires name plus approximate years of attendance. Also helpful: SSN, date of birth, exact years of attendance. There is no fee.

Indian Hills Community College, Registrar, 525 Grandview Ave, Ottumwa, IA 52501, 515-683-5151 (Fax: 515-683-5184). Hours: 8:30AM-4:30PM. Enrollment: 3336. Records go back to 1966. Alumni records are maintained here at the same phone number. Degrees granted: Associate.

Attendance and degree information available by phone, fax, mail. Search requires name plus SSN, exact years of attendance. There is no fee.

Indian Hills Community College, (Centerville), Registrar, Centerville, IA 52544, 515-856-2143 (Fax: 515-856-5527). Hours: 8AM-4PM. Records go back to 1930. Degrees granted: Associate.

Attendance and degree information available by phone, fax, mail. Search requires name plus SSN, approximate years of attendance. There is no fee.

Iowa Central Community College, Registrar, 330 Ave M, Fort Dodge, IA 50501, 515-576-7201 X2409 (Fax: 515-576-7206). Hours: 8AM-5PM M-Th, 8AM-4:30PM F. Enrollment: 2227. Records go back to 1966. Degrees granted: Associate.

Attendance information available by phone, fax, mail. Search requires name plus SSN. Also helpful: exact years of attendance. There is no fee.

Degree information available by phone, fax, mail. Search requires name plus SSN. There is no fee.

Iowa Lakes Community College, (Emmetsburg Campus), Registrar, 3200 College Dr, Emmetsburg, IA 50536, 712-852-3554 X265 (Fax: 712-852-2152). Hours: 8AM-5PM. Enrollment: 2050. Records go back to 1928. Alumni Records Office: 350 S 18th St, Estherville, IA 51334. Degrees granted: Associate.

Attendance and degree information available by phone, fax, mail. Search requires name only. Also helpful: SSN, date of birth, approximate years of attendance. There is no fee.

Iowa Lakes Community College, (Estherville), Registrar, 19 S 7th St, Estherville, IA 51334, 712-362-2604 X122 (Fax: 712-362-7649). Hours: 8AM-5PM. Enrollment: 2050. Records go back to 1928. Alumni records are maintained here also. Call 712-362-7923. Degrees granted: Associate.

Attendance and degree information available by phone, fax, mail. Search requires name only. Also helpful: SSN, date of birth, approximate years of attendance. There is no fee.

Iowa State University, Office of the Registrar, 214 Alumni Hall, Ames, IA 50011, 515-294-1840 (Fax: 515-294-1088). Hours: 8AM-5PM. Enrollment: 24000. Records go back to 1858. Alumni Records Office: Alumni Suite, Memorial Union, Ames, IA 50011, 515-294-6525 (Fax: 515-294-9402). Degrees granted: Bachelors; Masters; Doctorate; Doctor Veterinary Medicine, Specialist.

Attendance and degree information available by phone, fax, mail. Search requires name only. Also helpful: SSN, exact years of attendance. There is no fee. Expedited service available for $2.00.

Iowa Wesleyan College, Registrar, 601 N Main St, Mount Pleasant, IA 52641, 319-385-6225 (Fax: 319-385-6296). Hours: 8AM-Noon, 1-5PM. Enrollment: 820. Records go back to 1842. Alumni records are maintained here also. Call 319-385-6215. Degrees granted: Bachelors. Adverse incident record source- 319-385-6256.

Attendance and degree information available by phone, fax, mail. Search requires name only. Also helpful: SSN, date of birth, exact years of attendance. There is no fee.

Iowa Western Community College, Registrar, 2700 College Rd, Council Bluffs, IA 51502, 712-325-3200. Enrollment: 3600. Records go back to 1967. Alumni records are maintained here at the same phone number. Degrees granted: Associate.

Attendance and degree information available by phone, fax, mail. Search requires name plus SSN. Also helpful: date of birth, exact years of attendance. There is no fee.

Kirkwood Community College, Office of the Registrar, 6301 Kirkwood Blvd SW, PO Box 2068, Cedar Rapids, IA 52406-2068, 319-398-5603 (Fax: 319-398-4928). Hours: 8AM-6PM M-Th; 8AM-5PM F. Enrollment: 10000. Records go back to 1966. Alumni records are maintained here at the same phone number. Degrees granted: Associate. Special programs-Community Relation (non-credit), 319-398-5412: Truck Driving, 319-398-5690: Skills Center, 319-398-5455: GED/HS Completion, 319-366-0142.

Attendance and degree information available by phone, fax, mail. Search requires name plus SSN, date of birth. Also helpful: exact years of attendance. There is no fee.

Loras College, Registrar, 1450 Alta Vista, Dubuque, IA 52004, 319-588-7106 (Fax: 319-588-7964). Hours: 8AM-4:30PM. Enrollment: 1809. Records go back to 1839. Alumni records are maintained here also. Call 319-588-7170. Degrees granted: Bachelors; Masters.

Attendance and degree information available by phone, fax, mail. Search requires name plus SSN, exact years of attendance. There is no fee.

Luther College, Registrar's Office, 700 College Dr, Decorah, IA 52101-1045, 319-387-1167 (Fax: 319-387-2158). Hours: 8AM-5PM. Enrollment: 2350. Alumni records are maintained here also. Call 319-387-1861. Degrees granted: Bachelors.

Attendance and degree information available by phone, fax, mail. Search requires name plus SSN. Also helpful: date of birth, exact years of attendance. There is no fee. Expedite fee: $9.00 to $11.00.

Maharishi University of Management, Registrar, Fairfield, IA 52557, 515-472-1144 (Fax: 515-472-1133). Hours: 10AM-4PM. Enrollment: 500. Formerly Maharishi International University Records go back to 1971. Alumni records are maintained here also. Call 515-472-1190. Degrees granted: Associate; Bachelors; Masters; Doctorate.

Attendance and degree information available by phone, fax, mail. Search requires name only. Also helpful: SSN, date of birth, exact years of attendance. There is no fee.

Marshalltown Community College, Registrar's Office, 3700 S Center, Marshalltown, IA 50158, 515-752-7106 (Fax: 515-752-8149). Hours: 8AM-4:30PM. Enrollment: 1200. Records go back to 1950's. Alumni records are maintained here at the same phone number. Degrees granted: Associate.

Attendance and degree information available by phone, fax, mail. Search requires name plus SSN. Also helpful: date of birth, exact years of attendance. There is no fee.

Marycrest International University, Registrar, 1607 W 12th St, Davenport, IA 52804, 319-326-9216 (Fax: 319-327-9606). Hours: 8AM-5PM. Enrollment: 1000. Formerly Teikyo Marycrest University Records go back to 1939. Alumni records are maintained here also. Call 319-326-9492. Degrees granted: Associate; Bachelors; Masters.

Attendance and degree information available by phone, fax, mail. Search requires name only. Also helpful: SSN, date of birth, approximate years of attendance. There is no fee.

Morningside College, Registrar, 1501 Morningside Ave, Sioux City, IA 51106, 712-274-5110 (Fax: 712-274-5101). Hours: 8AM-5PM. Enrollment: 1214. Records go back to 1894. Alumni records are maintained here also. Call 712-274-5107. Degrees granted: Bachelors; Masters.

Attendance and degree information available by phone, fax, mail. Search requires name plus SSN. There is no fee.

Mount Mercy College, Registrar, 1330 Elmhurst Dr NE, Cedar Rapids, IA 52402, 319-363-8213 (Fax: 319-363-5270). Hours: 8:30AM-5PM. Enrollment: 1227. Records go back to 1928. Alumni records are maintained here also. Call 319-363-8213. Degrees granted: Bachelors.

Attendance and degree information available by phone, fax, mail. Search requires name plus SSN, date of birth, approximate years of attendance. There is no fee.

Mount St. Clare College, Registrar, 400 N Bluff Blvd, Clinton, IA 52732, 319-242-4023 (Fax: 319-242-2003). Hours: 7:30AM-4:30PM. Enrollment: 525. Alumni records are maintained here at the same phone number. Degrees granted: Associate; Bachelors. Adverse incident record source- Student Life, 319-242-4023.

Attendance and degree information available by phone, fax, mail. Search requires name only. Also helpful: SSN, date of birth, exact years of attendance. There is no fee.

Muscatine Community College, Registrar, 152 Colorado St, Muscatine, IA 52761, 319-263-8250 (Fax: 319-263-1010). Hours: 8AM-5PM. Enrollment: 1200. Records go back to 1929. Alumni records are maintained here at the same phone number. Degrees granted: Associate.

Attendance and degree information available by fax, mail. Search requires name plus SSN, signed release. Also helpful: date of birth, approximate years of attendance. There is no fee.

North Iowa Area Community College, Registrar, 500 College Dr, Mason City, IA 50401, 515-422-4205 (Fax: 515-422-1711). Hours: 7:45AM-4:15PM. Enrollment: 2700. Records go back to 1918. Alumni records are maintained here also. Call 515-422-4397. Degrees granted: Associate. Adverse incident record source- Student Services, 515-422-4003.

Attendance and degree information available by phone, fax, mail. Search requires name plus SSN, exact years of attendance. Also helpful: date of birth. There is no fee.

Northeast Iowa Community College, Registrar, Box 400 Hwy 150, Calmar, IA 52132, 319-562-3263 X233 (Fax: 319-562-3719). Hours: 7:30AM-4PM. Enrollment: 4000. Records go back to 1967. Alumni records are maintained here also. Call 319-562-3263 X300. Degrees granted: Associate.

Attendance and degree information available by phone, fax, mail. Search requires name plus SSN. There is no fee.

Northwest Iowa Community College, Registrar, 603 W Park St, Sheldon, IA 51201, 712-324-5061 X141 (Fax: 712-324-4136). Hours: 8AM-4:30PM. Enrollment: 988. Records go back to 1967. Alumni records are maintained here also. Call 712-324-5061 X220. Degrees granted: Associate. Adverse incident record source- Director, 712-324-5061 X141.

Attendance information available by phone, fax, mail. Search requires name only. Also helpful: SSN, exact years of attendance. There is no fee.

Degree information available by fax, mail. Search requires name only. Also helpful: SSN, exact years of attendance. There is no fee.

Northwestern College, Registrar, 101 7th St SW, Orange City, IA 51041-1996, 712-737-7145 (Fax: 712-737-7117). Hours: 8AM-5PM. Enrollment: 1200. Records go back to 1888. Alumni records are maintained here also. Call 712-737-7106. Degrees granted: Associate; Bachelors; Masters. Adverse incident record source- Student Affairs, 712-737-7200.

Attendance and degree information available by phone, fax, mail. Search requires name only. Also helpful: SSN, date of birth, exact years of attendance. There is no fee.

Palmer College of Chiropractic, Registrar, 1000 Brady St, Davenport, IA 52803, 319-326-9862 (Fax: 319-327-0181). Hours: 8AM-4:30PM. Enrollment: 1800. Records go back to 1900. Alumni records are maintained here at the same

phone number. Degrees granted: Associate; Bachelors; Masters; Doctorate; C.T. Adverse incident record source- Student Affairs, 319-326-9643.

Attendance information available by phone, mail. Search requires name only. Also helpful: SSN, date of birth, approximate years of attendance. There is no fee.

Degree information available by phone, mail. Search requires name only. Also helpful: SSN, approximate years of attendance. There is no fee.

Scott Community College, Registrar, 500 Belmont Rd, Bettendorf, IA 52722, 319-359-7531 (Fax: 319-359-0519). Hours: 8AM-5:30PM M-Th; 7:30AM-4:30PM F. Enrollment: 4000. Degrees granted: Associate. Adverse incident record source- Dean of Students, 319-359-7531 X225.

Attendance information available by fax, mail. Search requires name plus SSN. There is no fee.

Degree information available by phone, fax, mail. Search requires name plus SSN. Also helpful: date of birth, approximate years of attendance. There is no fee.

Simpson College, Registrar, 701 N C St, Indianola, IA 50125, 515-961-1642 (Fax: 515-961-1498). Hours: 8AM-4:30PM. Enrollment: 1150. Records go back to 1880's. Records are on computer from 1983. Alumni records are maintained here also. Call 515-961-1547. Degrees granted: Bachelors. Adverse incident record source- Security, 515-961-7111.

Attendance and degree information available by phone, fax, mail. Search requires name only. Also helpful: SSN, date of birth, exact years of attendance. There is no fee.

Southeastern Community College, Registrar, Drawer F, West Burlington, IA 52655, 319-752-2731 X133 (Fax: 319-752-4957). Hours: 8AM-4:30PM. Enrollment: 2400. Records go back to 1920. Alumni records are maintained here at the same phone number. Degrees granted: Associate.

Attendance information available by phone, fax, mail. Search requires name only. Also helpful: SSN, date of birth. There is no fee.

Degree information available by phone, fax, mail. Search requires name only. There is no fee.

Southwestern Community College, Registrar, 1501 Townline St, Creston, IA 50801, 515-782-7081 (Fax: 515-782-3312). Hours: 8AM-4:30PM. Enrollment: 1100. Records go back to 1932. Degrees granted: Associate.

Attendance and degree information available by phone, fax, mail. Search requires name only. Also helpful: SSN, date of birth, exact years of attendance. There is no fee.

Spencer College, Registrar, PO Box 465, 217 W Fifth St, Spencer, IA 51301, 800-383-7290. Degrees granted: Associate.

Attendance and degree information available by mail. Search requires name plus SSN. There is no fee.

St. Ambrose University, Registrar, 518 W Locust St, Davenport, IA 52803-2898, 319-333-6202 (Fax: 319-333-6243). Hours: 9AM-4PM. Enrollment: 2640. Records go back to 1908. Alumni records are maintained here also. Call 319-386-2225. Degrees granted: Bachelors; Masters. Special programs- AC-CEL, 319-386-2225. Adverse incident record source- Dean of Students, 319-333-6258.

Attendance and degree information available by phone, fax, mail. Search requires name plus date of birth. Also helpful: SSN, exact years of attendance. There is no fee.

University of Dubuque, Registrar, 2000 University Ave, Dubuque, IA 52001, 319-589-3126 (Fax: 319-556-8633). Hours: 8AM-5PM. Degrees granted: Associate; Bachelors; Masters; Doctorate.

Attendance and degree information available by phone, fax, mail. Search requires name plus SSN, approximate years of attendance. Also helpful: date of birth. There is no fee.

University of Iowa, Registrar, 1 Jessup Hall, Iowa City, IA 52242-1316, 319-335-0229 (Fax: 319-335-1999). Hours: 8:30AM-4:30PM. Enrollment: 26932. Records go back to 1965. Phone for transcripts is 319-335-0230. Records are on computer or film since 1965. Alumni records are maintained here at the same phone number. Degrees granted: Bachelors; Masters; Doctorate. Adverse incident record source- Campus Security, 319-335-5022.

Attendance and degree information available by phone, fax, mail. Search requires name plus SSN. Also helpful: approximate years of attendance. There is no fee.

University of Northern Iowa, Registrar, Cedar Falls, IA 50614, 319-273-2241 (Fax: 319-273-6792). Hours: 8AM-5PM. Enrollment: 12800. Records go back to 1876. Alumni records are maintained here also. Call 319-273-2355. Degrees granted: Bachelors; Masters; Doctorate. Adverse incident record source- Student Services, 319-273-2332.

Attendance and degree information available by phone, fax, mail. Search requires name plus SSN. Also helpful: approximate years of attendance. There is no fee.

University of Osteopathic Medicine and Health Sciences, Registrar, 3200 Grand Ave, Des Moines, IA 50313, 515-271-1460 (Fax: 515-271-1578). Hours: 8AM-4:30PM. Enrollment: 1200. Records go back to 1900. Alumni records are maintained here also. Call 515-271-1573. Degrees granted: Bachelors; Masters; D.D., DPM.

Attendance and degree information available by phone, fax, mail. Search requires name only. Also helpful: SSN. There is no fee.

Upper Iowa University, Registrar, Box 1857, College and Washington Sts, Fayette, IA 52142, 319-425-5268 (Fax: 319-425-5287). Hours: 8AM-5PM. Enrollment: 3804. Alumni records are maintained here at the same phone number. Degrees granted: Associate; Bachelors; Masters.

Attendance information available by phone, fax, mail. Search requires name plus SSN. Also helpful: date of birth, exact years of attendance. There is no fee.

Degree information available by phone, fax, mail. Search requires name plus SSN, date of birth. Also helpful: exact years of attendance. There is no fee.

Vennard College, Registrar, Eighth Ave E, PO Box 29, University Park, IA 52595, 515-673-8391 X205 (Fax: 515-673-8365). Hours: 8AM-5PM. Enrollment: 107. Records go back to 1910. Alumni records are maintained here also. Call 515-673-8391 X209. Degrees granted: Associate; Bachelors. Adverse incident record source- Student Development, 515-673-8391 X250.

Attendance and degree information available by phone, fax, mail. Search requires name plus SSN, approximate years of attendance. There is no fee.

Waldorf College, Registrar, Forest City, IA 50436, 515-582-8139 (Fax: 515-582-8194). Hours: 8AM-5PM. Enrollment: 585. Alumni records are maintained here at the same phone number. Degrees granted: Associate; Bachelors.

Attendance and degree information available by phone, fax, mail. Search requires name plus SSN, exact years of attendance. Also helpful: date of birth. There is no fee.

Wartburg College, Registrar, 222 9th St NW, Waverly, IA 50677, 319-352-8272 (Fax: 319-352-8514). Hours: 8AM-4:30PM. Enrollment: 1450. Records go back to 1852. Alumni records are maintained here also. Call 319-352-8491. Degrees granted: Bachelors.

Attendance and degree information available by phone, fax, mail. Search requires name only. Also helpful: SSN, date of birth. There is no fee.

Wartburg Theological Seminary, Registrar, 333 Wartburg Pl, Dubuque, IA 52003-7797, 319-589-0211 (Fax: 319-589-0333). Hours: 8AM-4:30PM. Enrollment: 180. Alumni records are maintained here also. Call 319-589-0220. Degrees granted: Masters.

Attendance and degree information available by phone, fax, mail. Search requires name only. Also helpful: date of birth, exact years of attendance. There is no fee.

Western Iowa Tech Community College, Registrar, 4647 Stone Ave, PO Box 265, Sioux City, IA 51102, 712-274-6400 (Fax: 712-274-6412). Hours: 8AM-5PM. Enrollment: 2664. Records go back to 1968. Alumni records are maintained here at the same phone number. Degrees granted: Associate; GED. Special programs- GED's, 712-255-7632. Adverse incident record source- Student Development, 712-274-6400.

Attendance and degree information available by phone, fax, mail. Search requires name plus SSN, exact years of attendance. There is no fee.

Westmar University, Registrar, 1002 Third Ave SE, Le Mars, IA 51031, 712-546-2006 (Fax: 712-546-2020). Hours: 8AM-5PM. Enrollment: 500. Formerly Teikyo Westmar University Alumni records are maintained here also. Call 712-546-2030. Degrees granted: Bachelors. Adverse incident record source- Student Affairs, 712-546-2090.

Attendance and degree information available by phone, fax, mail. Search requires name only. Also helpful: SSN, date of birth, exact years of attendance. There is no fee.

William Penn College, Registrar, 201 Trueblood Ave, Oskaloosa, IA 52577, 515-673-1082 (Fax: 515-673-1396). Hours: 8AM-Noon, 1-5PM. Records go back to 1873. Degrees granted: Bachelors.

Attendance and degree information available by phone, fax, mail. Search requires name only. Also helpful: SSN, date of birth, exact years of attendance. There is no fee.

Trade and Vocational Schools

American College of Hairstyling (Cedar Rapids), 1531 First Ave SE, Cedar Rapids, IA 52402, 319-362-1488

American College of Hairstyling (Des Moines Branch), 603 E 6th St, Des Moines, IA 50309-5478, 515-244-0971

Capri College, 315 2nd Ave SE, Cedar Rapids, IA , 319-364-1541

Capri College, PO Box 873, Dubuque, IA 52004, 319-588-4545

Capri College (Davenport Branch), 1815 E Kimberly Rd, Davenport, IA 52807, 319-359-1306

College of Hair Design, 810 LaPorte Rd, Waterloo, IA 50702, 319-232-9995

Iowa School of Barbering and Hairstyling, 603 E Sixth St, Des Moines, IA 50309, 515-244-0971

State Licensing & Business Registration Quick Finder Index

Architecture, Engineering & Surveying
Architect #7 .... ☎ 515-281-4126
Engineer #6 .... ☎ 515-281-5602
Landscape Architect #8 515-281-7362
Surveyor #6 .... ☎ 515-281-5602

Business - Court & Legal Services
Attorney #27 (100) .... ☎ 515-281-5911
Lobbyist #28 .... ☎ 515-281-5204
Notary Public #28 (39000) .... ☎ 515-281-5209
Shorthand Reporter #27 .... ☎ 515-281-5911
Voting Booth #30 .... ☎ 515-281-5865
Voting Equipment #30 .... ☎ 515-281-5865

Business - General Services
Public Accountant #6 .... ☎ 515-281-7363
Public Accountant-CPA #6 .... ☎ 515-281-7363

Construction & Manufacturing
Boiler Inspector #24 .... ☎ 515-281-3606
Contractor #24 .... ☎ 515-281-3606

Education
Instructor - Community College or
   Vocational/Technical School #10 .... ☎ 515-281-5849
School Counselor #10 .... ☎ 515-281-5849
School Principal #10 .... ☎ 515-281-5849
Superintendent of Schools #10 .... ☎ 515-281-5849
Teacher #10 .... ☎ 515-281-5849

Environmental & Agriculture
Asbestos Abatement Contractor/Worker #24
   (1500) .... ☎ 515-281-3606
Asbestos Inspector #24 (121) .... ☎ 515-281-3606
Asbestos Project Designer/Management
   Planner #24 (200) .... ☎ 515-281-3606
Landfill Operator #19 .... ☎ 515-281-5972
Pesticide Dealer/Applicator #1 (1800) .... ☎ 515-281-5601
Pesticide- Private Applicator #1 .... ☎ 515-281-4339
Pesticide-Commercial Applicator #1 .... ☎ 515-281-5601
Pesticide-Commercial Certified Applicator #1
   .... ☎ 515-281-5601
Radon Measurement Specialist #26 (18) .... ✉ 515-281-6549
Radon Mitigation Specialist #26 (12) .... ✉ 515-281-6549
Solid Waste Incinerator Operator #19 .... ☎ 515-281-5972
Veterinarian #20 .... ☎ 515-281-5304
Waste Water Lagoon/Treatment Operator #19
   (1660) .... ☎ 515-281-5972
Water Distribution Operator #19 (244) .... ☎ 515-281-5972
Water Treatment Operator #19 .... ☎ 515-281-5972
Well Driller #19 (423) .... ☎ 515-281-5972

Financial - Real Estate, Insurance & Banking
Bank #2 (427) .... ☎ 515-281-4014
Credit Union #4 .... ☎ 515-281-6514
Debt Management Company #2 (21) .... ☎ 515-281-4014
Finance Company #2 (290) .... ☎ 515-281-4014
Insurance Agent #5 .... ☎ 515-281-4037
Insurance Exams & Licensing #5 .... ☎ 515-281-4450
Mortgage Banker #2 (222) 515-281-8432
Mortgage Broker #2 (39) 515-281-8432
Mortgage Loan Service #2 .... ☎ 515-281-4014
Real Estate Appraiser #29 (1000) 515-281-7393
Real Estate Broker/Salesman #9 515-281-3183

Securities Bureau (Securities Agent/Registered
   Rep./Broker) #5 (42344) .... ☎ 515-281-4441
Trust Company #2 (2) 515-281-8432

Health & Beauty
Advanced Emergency Medical Technician &
   Paramedic #12 .... ☎ 515-281-5171
Advanced Registered Nurse Practitioner #13
   .... ☎ 515-281-6488
Audiologist #21 .... ☎ 515-281-4408
Barber #20 (6216) .... ☎ 515-281-4408
Chiropractor #20 (3346) .... ☎ 515-281-4416
Community & Institutional Pharmacy #25
   (1100) .... ☎ 515-281-5944
Controlled Substances Registrant #25 (10000)
   .... ☎ 515-281-5944
Cosmetologist #20 (48099) .... ☎ 515-281-5936
Dental Hygienist #11 .... ☎ 515-281-5157
Dentist #11 .... ☎ 515-281-5157
Dietitian #21 (1204) .... ☎ 515-281-4422
Drug Distributor/Drug Wholesaler #25
   (500) .... ☎ 515-281-5944
Drug Manufacturer #25 .... ☎ 515-281-5944
Drug Wholesaler #13 .... ☎ 515-281-5944
Emergency Medical Technician (Basic) #20
   (6800) .... ☎ 515-281-3239
Emergency Medical Technician-
   Intermediate #20 .... ☎ 515-281-3239
Emergency Medical Technician-Paramedic #20
   .... ☎ 515-281-3239
First Response Paramedic #20 .... ☎ 515-281-4958
Funeral Director #20 (2079) .... ✉ 515-281-4287
Hearing Aid Dealer #20 (715) .... ☎ 515-281-4287
Massage Therapist #15 (830) .... ☎ 515-281-4422
Medical Doctor #12 .... ☎ 515-281-5171
Nuclear Medicine Technologist #26 .... ✉ 515-281-4942
Nurse #13 .... ☎ 515-281-6488
Nursing Home Administrator #20 (1913) ...... ✉ 515-281-4401
Occupational Therapy #20 .... ☎ 515-281-4401
Optometrist #20 (1056) .... ✉ 515-281-4287
Osteopathic Physician #12 .... ☎ 515-281-5171
Pharmacist #14 (4000) .... ☎ 515-281-5944
Pharmacy #13 .... ☎ 515-281-5944
Physical & Occupational Therapist #20
   (2744) .... ✉ 515-281-4401
Physician's Assistant #20 .... ☎ 515-242-5937
Podiatrist #20 (491) .... ☎ 515-242-4287
Practical Nurse #13 .... ☎ 515-281-6488
Radiation Therapist #26 .... ✉ 515-281-4942
Radiographer (Medical) #26 (3000) .... ✉ 515-281-4942
Respiratory Therapist #21 (840) .... ☎ 515-281-4408
Speech Pathologist/Audiologist #21 (1073)
   .... ☎ 515-281-4408

Investigations & Security
Polygraph Examiner #22 (207) .... ☎ 515-281-8422
Private Investigator #22 (207) .... ☎ 515-281-7610
Private Security Guard #22 (94) .... ☎ 515-281-7610

Social Services
Adoption Investigator #16 (40) .... ☎ 515-281-6802
Day Care #17 .... ☎ 515-242-5994
Group Foster Care #17 .... ☎ 515-281-6802
Marital & Family Therapist #20 (135) .... ☎ 515-281-4422

Mental Health Counselor #20 (217)............... ☎ 515-281-4422
Psychologist #21 (793).................................. ☎ 515-281-4401
Social Worker #21 (1158) .... ☎ 515-281-4422

Sports & Entertainment
Alcoholic Beverage Licensing Retail/Wholesale #3
(8715)... ⊠ 515-281-7430

Alcoholic Beverage Manufacturer #3
(9104) ....⊠ 515-281-7430
Excursion Boat Gambling #18.......................... 515-281-7352
Lottery Retailer #23 .... ☎ 515-281-3204
Pari-Mutuel Wagering Facility #18 515-281-7352

State Licensing & Business Registration Agency Information

(1) Department of Agriculture, Laboratory Division, Wallace State Office Bldg, Des Moines, IA 50319, 515-281-5001, Fax: 515-281-6800

(2) Department of Commerce, 200 E Grand Ave, Des Moines, IA 50309, 515-281-4014, Fax: 515-281-4862

(3) Department of Commerce, Alcoholic Beverage Division, 1918 SE Hulsizer Ave, Ankeny, IA 50021, 515-281-7430, Fax: 515-281-7375

(4) Department of Commerce, Credit Union Division, 200 E Grand Ave, Suite 370, Des Moines, IA 50309, 515-281-6514, Fax: 515-281-7595

(5) Department of Commerce, Insurance Division, Lucas State Office Bldg, Des Moines, IA 50319, 515-281-4037

(6) Department of Commerce, Professional Licensing & Regulation Division, 1918 SE Hulsizer Ave, Ankeny, IA 50021, 515-281-5910, Fax: 515-281-7411

(7) Department of Commerce, Professional Licensing & Regulation Division, 1918 SE Hulsizer, Ankeny, IA 50021, 515-281-5910, Fax: 515-281-7411

(8) Department of Commerce, Professional Licensing & Regulation Division, 1918 SE Hulsizer, Ankeny, IA 50021, 515-281-5910, Fax: 515-281-7411

(9) Department of Commerce, Professional Licensing & Regulation Division, 1918 SE Hulsizer, Ankeny, IA 50021, 515-281-5910, Fax: 515-281-7411

(10) Department of Education, Board of Educational Examiners, Grimes State Office Bldg, Des Moines, IA 50319, 515-281-5849

(11) Department of Health, Board of Dental Examiners, 1209 E Court Ave, Executive Hills West, Des Moines, IA 50319, 515-281-5157, Fax: 515-281-7969

(12) Department of Health, Board of Medical Examiners, 1209 E Court Ave, Executive Hills West, Des Moines, IA 50319, 515-281-5171, Fax: 515-242-5908

(13) Department of Health, Board of Nursing, 1223 E Court Ave, Des Moines, IA 50319, 515-281-6488

(14) Department of Health, Board of Pharmacy, 1209 E Court Ave, Des Moines, IA 50319, 515-281-5944, Fax: 515-281-4609

(15) Department of Health, Massage Therapist Licensing, 1209 E Court Ave, Des Moines, IA 50319, 515-242-5937, Fax: 515-281-3121

(16) Department of Human Services, Adoption Investigator Certification, Hoover State Office Building, Des Moines, IA 50319-0014, 515-281-6802, Fax: 515-281-4597

(17) Department of Human Services, Children, Adult & Family Services, Hoover State Office Bldg, 5th Flr, Des Moines, IA 50319-0114, 515-281-5521, Fax: 515-281-4597

(18) Department of Inspections & Appeals, Iowa Racing & Gaming Commission, Lucas State Office Bldg, 2nd Floor, Des Moines, IA 50319, 515-281-7352, Fax: 515-242-6560

(19) Department of Natural Resources, Wallace State Office Bldg, Des Moines, IA 50319, 515-281-5972, Fax: 515-281-6794

(20) Department of Public Health, Division of Professional Licensure, Lucas State Office Bldg, Des Moines, IA 50319, 515-281-5304

(21) Department of Public Health, Division of Professional Licensure, Lucas State Office Bldg, Des Moines, IA 50319, 515-281-5596, Fax: 515-281-3121

(22) Department of Public Safety, Old Credit Union Bldg, Des Moines, IA 50319, 515-281-5261, Fax: 515-281-4569

(23) Department of Revenue & Finance, Iowa Lottery Board, 2015 Grand Ave, Des Moines, IA 50312, 515-281-7900, Fax: 515-281-7882

(24) Division of Labor, Iowa Workforce Development, 1000 E Grand, Des Moines, IA 50319, 515-281-3606, Fax: 515-281-7995

(25) Iowa Board of Pharmacy Examiners, 1209 E Court Ave, Des Moines, IA 50319-0187, 515-281-5944, Fax: 515-281-4609

(26) Iowa Department of Public health, Bureau of Radiological Health, Lucas State Office Bldg, Des Moines, IA 50319-0075, 515-281-3478, Fax: 515-242-6284

(27) Legal Boards, Supreme Court Clerk's Office, Statehouse, Des Moines, IA 50319, 515-281-5911, Fax: 515-242-6164

(28) Office of Secretary of State, Hoover Office Bldg, 2nd Floor, Des Moines, IA 50319, 515-281-5204, Fax: 515-242-5953

(29) Real Estate Commission, 1918 SE Hulsizer, Ankeny, IA 50021, 515-281-7393

(30) Voting Machines & Electronic Voting Systems, c/o Secretary of State, Statehouse, Des Moines, IA 50319, 515-281-5865, Fax: 515-242-5953

Kansas

Capitol: Topeka (Shawnee County)	
State Population	2.6 Million
Number of Degree Granting Institutions:	52
Number of State Licensing & Business Registration Agencies:	69

Degree Granting Educational Institutions

Allen County Community College, Registrar, 1801 N Cottonwood, Iola, KS 66749, 316-365-5116 (Fax: 316-365-3284). Hours: 8AM-5PM. Enrollment: 1700. Records go back to 1923. Alumni records are maintained here at the same phone number. Degrees granted: Associate.

Attendance and degree information available by phone, fax, mail. Search requires name plus SSN, date of birth. Also helpful: exact years of attendance. There is no fee.

Baker University, Registrar, 606 W 8th St, PO Box 65, Baldwin City, KS 66006-0065, 913-594-6451 X530 (Fax: 913-594-2522). Hours: 9AM-5PM. Enrollment: 1800. Records go back to 1859. Alumni records are maintained here also. Call 913-594-6451 X526. Degrees granted: Bachelors; Masters. Special programs- School/Professional & Graduate Studies, 913-491-4432. Adverse incident record source- Student Services, 913-594-6451 X484.

Attendance and degree information available by phone, fax, mail. Search requires name plus SSN, approximate years of attendance. Also helpful: exact years of attendance. There is no fee.

Barclay College, Registrar, 607 N Kingman, PO Box 288, Haviland, KS 67059, 316-862-5252 (Fax: 316-862-5403). Hours: 8AM-5PM. Enrollment: 100. Records go back to 1917. Alumni records are maintained here also. Call 316-862-5252. Degrees granted: Associate; Bachelors. Certification: Bible. Adverse incident record source- Business Office, 316-862-5252.

Attendance and degree information available by phone, fax, mail. Search requires name plus exact years of attendance. Also helpful: date of birth. There is no fee.

Barton County Community College, Registrar, Rural Rte # Box 136Z, Great Bend, KS 67530, 316-792-2701 (Fax: 316-792-3056). Hours: 7:30AM-4:30PM. Enrollment: 4567. Records go back to 1971. Degrees granted: Associate.

Attendance and degree information available by phone, fax, mail. Search requires name plus SSN. There is no fee.

Benedictine College, Registrar, 1020 N Second St, Atchison, KS 66002, 913-367-5340 X2550 (Fax: 913-367-3673). Hours: 8AM-Noon, 1-5PM. Enrollment: 800. Records go back to 1858. Records are hard copy before 1980. Alumni rec-

ords are maintained here also. Call 913-367-5340 X2417. Degrees granted: Associate; Bachelors; Masters. Special programs-Executive MBA. Adverse incident record source- Student Affairs, 913-367-5340 X2500.

Attendance and degree information available by phone, fax, mail. Search requires name only. Also helpful: SSN, date of birth, exact years of attendance. There is no fee.

Bethany College, Registrar, 421 N First St, Lindsborg, KS 67456, 913-227-3311 (Fax: 913-227-2004). Hours: 8AM-5PM. Enrollment: 725. Records go back to 1888. Alumni records are maintained here at the same phone number. Degrees granted: Bachelors.

Attendance information available by phone, fax, mail. Search requires name plus SSN. Also helpful: date of birth, exact years of attendance. There is no fee.

Degree information available by phone, fax, mail. Search requires name plus SSN. There is no fee.

Bethel College, Registrar, 300 E 27th St, North Newton, KS 67117, 316-283-2500 (Fax: 316-284-5286). Hours: 8AM-Noon, 1-5PM. Enrollment: 620. Records go back to 1893. Alumni records are maintained here at the same phone number. Degrees granted: Bachelors.

Attendance and degree information available by phone, fax, mail. Search requires name plus exact years of attendance. Also helpful: SSN, date of birth, approximate years of attendance. There is no fee.

Brown Mackie College, Registrar, 126 S Santa Fe Ave, Salina, KS 67401, 913-825-5422 (Fax: 913-823-7448). Hours: 8AM-5PM. Enrollment: 350. Records go back to 1950. Degrees granted: Associate.

Attendance information available by phone, fax, mail. Search requires name plus SSN. Also helpful: date of birth, exact years of attendance. Fee is $2.00.

Degree information available by phone, fax, mail. Search requires name plus SSN, approximate years of attendance. Also helpful: exact years of attendance. There is no fee.

Butler County Community College, Registrar, 901 S Haverhill Rd, El Dorado, KS 67042, 316-322-3124 (Fax: 316-322-3316). Hours: 8AM-5PM. Enrollment: 8000. Records go back to 1926. Alumni records are maintained here also. Call

316-322-3198. Degrees granted: Associate. Adverse incident record source- Dean of Students, 316-322-3297.

Attendance and degree information available by phone, fax, mail. Search requires name plus SSN, approximate years of attendance. Also helpful: exact years of attendance. There is no fee.

Central Baptist Theological Seminary, Registrar, 741 N 31st St, Kansas City, KS 66102-3964, 913-371-5313 (Fax: 913-371-8110). Hours: 8AM-4:30PM. Enrollment: 100. Records go back to 1901. Alumni Records Office: 741 N 31st St, Kansas City, MO 66102. Degrees granted: Masters. Adverse incident record source- Business Office, 913-371-5313.

Attendance and degree information available by phone. Search requires name plus SSN. There is no fee.

Central College, Registrar, 1200 S Main St, McPherson, KS 67460, 316-241-0723 (Fax: 316-241-6032). Hours: 8AM-5PM. Enrollment: 300. Records go back to 1914. Alumni records are maintained here at the same phone number. Degrees granted: Associate; Bachelors. Adverse incident record source- Student Services, 316-241-0723.

Attendance information available by phone, fax, mail. Search requires name plus SSN, date of birth, exact years of attendance. Fee is $2.00.

Degree information available by phone, fax, mail. Search requires name plus SSN, exact years of attendance. Also helpful: date of birth. There is no fee.

Cloud County Community College, Office of Student Records, 2221 Campus Dr, PO Box 1002, Concordia, KS 66901-1002, 913-243-1435 (Fax: 913-243-1043). Hours: 8AM-5PM. Enrollment: 3500. Records go back to 1965. Alumni records are maintained here also. Call 913-243-1435. Degrees granted: Associate. Adverse incident record source- 913-243-1435 X268.

Attendance and degree information available by phone, fax, mail. Search requires name plus SSN, approximate years of attendance. There is no fee.

Coffeyville Community College, Registrar, 400 W 11th, Coffeyville, KS 67337, 316-251-7700 X2083 (Fax: 316-252-7040). Hours: 8AM-5PM. Enrollment: 2195. Records go back to 1971. Alumni records are maintained here also. Call 316-251-7700 X2069. Degrees granted: Associate.

Attendance and degree information available by phone, mail. Search requires name plus SSN. Also helpful: date of birth, exact years of attendance. There is no fee.

Colby Community College, Registrar, 1255 S Range, Colby, KS 67701, 913-462-4675 (Fax: 913-462-4600). Hours: 8AM-5PM. Enrollment: 2400. Records go back to 1965. Alumni records are maintained here also. Call 913-462-3984. Degrees granted: Associate.

Attendance and degree information available by mail. Search requires name plus signed release. Also helpful: SSN, date of birth, exact years of attendance. Fee is $3.00.

Cowley County Community College, Registrar, 125 S Second St, PO Box 1147, Arkansas City, KS 67005, 316-442-0430 (Fax: 316-441-5350). Hours: 8AM-4:30PM. Enrollment: 2930. Records go back to 1922. Alumni records are maintained here at the same phone number. Degrees granted: Associate.

Attendance and degree information available by phone, fax, mail. Search requires name plus SSN, approximate years of attendance. Also helpful: exact years of attendance. There is no fee.

Dodge City Community College, Registrar, 2501 N 14th Ave, Dodge City, KS 67801, 316-225-1321 (Fax: 316-227-9277). Hours: 8AM-5PM. Enrollment: 2277. Records go back to 1934. Alumni records are maintained here at the same

phone number. Degrees granted: Associate. Certification: Vocational. Adverse incident record source- Student Service, 800-742-9519.

Attendance and degree information available by phone, fax, mail. Search requires name plus SSN. There is no fee.

Donnelly College, Registrar, 608 N 18th St, Kansas City, KS 66102, 913-621-6070 X33 (Fax: 913-621-0354). Hours: 8:30AM-4:30PM. Enrollment: 850. Records go back to 1949. Alumni records are maintained here at the same phone number. Degrees granted: Associate.

Attendance and degree information available by phone, mail. Search requires name plus SSN, date of birth. There is no fee.

Emporia State University, Registrar, 1200 Commercial St, Emporia, KS 66801, 316-341-5154 (Fax: 316-341-5073). Hours: 8AM-5PM; 7:30AM-4PM Summer. Enrollment: 6000. Records go back to 1900. Alumni Records Office: PO Box 4047, Emporia, KS 66801, 316-341-5440. Degrees granted: Bachelors; Masters; Doctorate. Adverse incident record source- 316-341-5337.

Attendance and degree information available by phone, fax, mail. Search requires name only. Also helpful: SSN, date of birth, exact years of attendance. There is no fee.

Fort Hays State University, Registrar, 600 Park St, Hays, KS 67601, 913-628-4222 (Fax: 913-628-4046). Hours: 8AM-4:30PM. Enrollment: 5600. Records go back to 1902. Alumni records are maintained here also. Call 913-628-4430. Degrees granted: Associate; Bachelors; Masters.

Attendance and degree information available by phone, fax, mail. Search requires name plus SSN. Also helpful: date of birth, exact years of attendance. There is no fee.

Fort Scott Community College, Registrar, 2108 S Horton St, Fort Scott, KS 66701, 316-223-2700 (Fax: 316-223-6530). Hours: 7:30AM-5PM. Enrollment: 1695. Records go back to 1919. Degrees granted: Associate. Adverse incident record source- Dean of Students, 316-223-2700.

Attendance and degree information available by phone, fax, mail. Search requires name plus SSN, approximate years of attendance. Also helpful: date of birth, exact years of attendance. There is no fee.

Friends University, Registrar, 2100 University Ave, Wichita, KS 67213, 316-261-5860 (Fax: 316-269-3538). Hours: 8AM-6PM M-Th; 8AM-5PM F. Enrollment: 2330. Records go back to 1900. Alumni records are maintained here also. Call 316-261-5802. Degrees granted: Associate; Bachelors; Masters.

Attendance and degree information available by phone, fax, mail. Search requires name plus SSN. There is no fee.

Garden City Community College, Registrar, 801 Campus Dr, Garden City, KS 67846, 316-276-7611 (Fax: 316-276-9573). Hours: 8AM-4:30PM. Enrollment: 2400. Records go back to 1919. Degrees granted: Associate. Adverse incident record source- Campus Police, 316-275-0005.

Attendance and degree information available by phone, fax, mail. Search requires name only. Also helpful: SSN, date of birth, exact years of attendance. There is no fee.

Haskell Indian Junior College, Registrar, 155 Indian Ave #1305, Lawrence, KS 66046-4800, 913-749-8454 (Fax: 913-749-8429). Hours: 9AM-4:30PM. Enrollment: 793. Degrees granted: Associate.

Attendance and degree information available by phone, fax, mail. Search requires name plus SSN. There is no fee.

Hesston College, Registrar, PO Box 3000, Hesston, KS 67062, 316-327-8231 (Fax: 316-327-8300). Hours: 8AM-5PM. Enrollment: 450. Records go back to 1909. Alumni records are maintained here also. Call 316-327-8110. Degrees granted: Associate.

Attendance and degree information available by phone, fax, mail. Search requires name plus SSN, approximate years of attendance. Also helpful: exact years of attendance. There is no fee.

Highland Community College, Registrar, PO Box 68, Highland, KS 66035, 913-442-6025 (Fax: 913-442-6100). Hours: 8:30AM-4:30PM. Enrollment: 2294. Degrees granted: Associate.

Attendance and degree information available by phone, fax, mail. Search requires name plus SSN, approximate years of attendance. There is no fee.

Hutchinson Community College, Registrar, 1300 N Plum St, Hutchinson, KS 67501, 316-665-3520 (Fax: 316-665-3301). Hours: 8AM-5PM. Enrollment: 5000. Records go back to 1928. Alumni records are maintained here also. Call 316-665-3516. Degrees granted: Associate.

Attendance and degree information available by phone, fax, mail. Search requires name plus SSN, approximate years of attendance. Also helpful: date of birth, exact years of attendance. There is no fee.

Independence Community College, Registrar, College Ave and Brookside Dr, Independence, KS 67301, 316-331-4100 (Fax: 316-331-0946). Hours: 8AM-5PM. Enrollment: 2000. Records go back to 1925. Alumni records are maintained here at the same phone number. Degrees granted: Associate. Adverse incident record source- Student Services, 316-331-4100.

Attendance and degree information available by mail. Search requires name plus SSN, date of birth, approximate years of attendance, signed release. There is no fee.

Johnson County Community College, Records Office, 12345 College Blvd, Overland Park, KS 66210-1299, 913-469-8500. Hours: 8AM-5PM. Enrollment: 16000. Records go back to 1971. Alumni records are maintained here at the same phone number. Degrees granted: Associate. Adverse incident record source- Security, 913-469-8500.

Attendance information available by phone, mail. Search requires name plus SSN, approximate years of attendance. Also helpful: date of birth, exact years of attendance. There is no fee.

Degree information available by phone, mail. Search requires name plus SSN. Also helpful: date of birth, exact years of attendance. There is no fee.

Kansas City College and Bible School, Registrar, 7401 Metcalf, Overland Park, KS 66204, 913-722-0272 X136 (Fax: 913-722-2135). Enrollment: 50. Records go back to 1938. Alumni records are maintained here at the same phone number. Degrees granted: Associate; Bachelors. Special programs- Ministerial: Missions: Teacher Education: General Business: Secretarial Science: Music Ministry: General Studies, 913-722-0272.

Attendance and degree information available by phone, fax, mail. Search requires name only. Also helpful: SSN, date of birth, exact years of attendance. There is no fee.

Kansas City Kansas Community College, Registrar, 7250 State Ave, Kansas City, KS 66112, 913-334-1100 (Fax: 913-596-9609). Hours: 7:30AM-4:30PM. Enrollment: 6000. Records go back to 1923. Alumni records are maintained here also. Call 913-334-1100 X623. Degrees granted: Associate.

Attendance and degree information available by phone, fax, mail. Search requires name plus SSN. Also helpful: date of birth, exact years of attendance. There is no fee.

Kansas Newman College, Registrar, 3100 McCormick Ave, Wichita, KS 67213, 316-942-4291 X121 (Fax: 316-942-4483). Hours: 8AM-6PM M-Th; 8AM-5PM F; 7:30-10:30AM S. Enrollment: 2000. Records go back to 1933.

Alumni records are maintained here at the same phone number. Degrees granted: Associate; Bachelors; Masters. Adverse incident record source- Human Resource Dept, 316-942-4291 X311.

Attendance and degree information available by phone, fax, mail. Search requires name plus SSN, approximate years of attendance. There is no fee.

Kansas State University, Registrar's Office, 118 Anderson Hall, Manhattan, KS 66506-0114, 913-532-6254 (Fax: 913-532-6393). Hours: 8AM-Noon, 1-5PM. Enrollment: 20000. Records go back to 1863. Alumni Records Office: 2323 Anderson Ave, Manhattan, KS 66502. Degrees granted: Associate; Bachelors; Masters; Doctorate.

Attendance and degree information available by phone, fax, mail. Search requires name only. Also helpful: SSN, date of birth, exact years of attendance. There is no fee. Expedited service available for $3.00.

Kansas State University, (Salina College of Technology), Registrar, 2409 Scanlan Ave, Salina, KS 67401-8196, 913-826-2607 (Fax: 913-826-2936). Hours: 8AM-5PM. Records go back to 1965. Alumni records are maintained here also. Call 913-826-2632. Degrees granted: Associate; Bachelors.

Attendance and degree information available by phone, fax, mail. Search requires name plus SSN. There is no fee.

Kansas Wesleyan University, Registrar, 100 E Clafin, Salina, KS 67401, 913-827-5541 X1260 (Fax: 913-827-0927). Hours: 8:15AM-Noon, 1-5PM. Enrollment: 720. Records go back to 1890's. Alumni records are maintained here at the same phone number. Degrees granted: Associate; Bachelors; Masters. Certification: Education. Adverse incident record source- Registrar's Office, 913-827-5541 .

Attendance and degree information available by phone, fax, mail. Search requires name plus SSN. Also helpful: date of birth, exact years of attendance. There is no fee.

Labette Community College, Registrar, 200 S 14th St, Parsons, KS 67357, 316-421-6700 X68 (Fax: 316-421-0180). Hours: 8AM-8PM M-Th, 8AM-4:30PM F. Enrollment: 2023. Records go back to 1923. Alumni records are maintained here also. Call 316-421-0180 X40. Degrees granted: Associate. Adverse incident record source- Dean of Instructors, 316-421-6700 X24.

Attendance and degree information available by phone, fax, mail. Search requires name plus SSN, approximate years of attendance. There is no fee.

Manhattan Christian College, Registrar, 1415 Anderson Ave, Manhattan, KS 66502, 913-539-3571 (Fax: 913-539-0832). Hours: 8AM-5PM. Enrollment: 300. Records go back to 1927. Alumni records are maintained here at the same phone number. Degrees granted: Associate; Bachelors.

Attendance and degree information available by phone, fax, mail. Search requires name plus SSN, exact years of attendance. There is no fee.

McPherson College, Registrar, 1600 E Euclid, PO Box 1402, McPherson, KS 67460, 316-241-0731 (Fax: 316-241-8443). Hours: 8AM-5PM. Enrollment: 500. Records go back to 1934. Alumni records are maintained here at the same phone number. Degrees granted: Bachelors. Certification: Education. Adverse incident record source- Student Affairs, 316-241-1104.

Attendance and degree information available by phone, fax, mail. Search requires name only. Also helpful: SSN, exact years of attendance. There is no fee.

MidAmerica Nazarene College, Registrar, 2030 E College Wy, Olathe, KS 66062-1899, 913-782-3750 (Fax: 913-791-3290). Hours: 8AM-5PM. Enrollment: 1445. Records go back to 1968. Alumni records are maintained here at the same phone number. Degrees granted: Associate; Bachelors; Masters;

MEd, MBA. Adverse incident record source- Campus Police, 913-782-3750.

Attendance and degree information available by phone, fax, mail. Search requires name plus SSN. Also helpful: date of birth, exact years of attendance. There is no fee.

Neosho County Community College, Registrar, 1000 S Allen, Chanute, KS 66720, 316-431-2820 (Fax: 316-431-0082). Hours: 8AM-5PM. Enrollment: 1500. Records go back to 1981. Degrees granted: Associate.

Attendance and degree information available by phone, fax, mail. Search requires name plus SSN, exact years of attendance. There is no fee.

Ottawa University, Registrar, 1001 S Cedar #5, Ottawa, KS 66067-3399, 913-242-5200 X5582 (Fax: 913-242-7429). Hours: 8AM-Noon, 1-5PM. Enrollment: 575. Alumni Records Office: 1001 S Cedar #16, Ottawa, KS 66067-3399, 800-755-5200. Degrees granted: Bachelors; Masters.

Attendance and degree information available by phone, fax, mail. Search requires name plus SSN. Also helpful: date of birth, exact years of attendance. There is no fee.

Pittsburg State University, Registrar, 1701 S Broadway, Pittsburg, KS 66762, 316-235-4206 (Fax: 316-235-4015). Hours: 8AM-4:30PM. Enrollment: 6500. Records go back to 1903. Alumni records are maintained here also. Call 316-235-4759. Degrees granted: Associate; Bachelors; Masters. Adverse incident record source- Student Affairs, 316-235-4233.

Attendance and degree information available by phone, fax, mail. Search requires name plus SSN, date of birth, approximate years of attendance. Also helpful: exact years of attendance. There is no fee.

Pratt Community College, Registrar, 348 NE SR61, Pratt, KS 67124, 316-672-5641 (Fax: 316-672-5288). Hours: 8AM-5PM. Enrollment: 1291. Alumni records are maintained here at the same phone number. Degrees granted: Associate.

Attendance and degree information available by phone, fax, mail. Search requires name plus SSN, approximate years of attendance. There is no fee.

Seward County Community College, Registrar, 1801 N Kansas St, Box 1137, Liberal, KS 67901, 316-629-2616 (Fax: 316-629-2725). Hours: 7:45AM-4:45PM. Enrollment: 1631. Alumni records are maintained here also. Call 316-629-2664. Degrees granted: Associate.

Attendance and degree information available by phone, fax, mail. Search requires name plus SSN, approximate years of attendance. There is no fee.

Southwestern College, Registrar, 100 College St, Winfield, KS 67156, 316-221-8268 (Fax: 316-221-8224). Hours: 8AM-Noon, 1-5PM. Enrollment: 750. Records go back to 1886. Degrees granted: Bachelors; Masters.

Attendance and degree information available by phone, fax, mail. Search requires name only. Also helpful: SSN, date of birth, exact years of attendance. There is no fee.

St. Mary College, Registrar, 4100 S 4th St Trafficway, Leavenworth, KS 66048-5082, 913-682-5151 (Fax: 913-758-6140). Hours: 8AM-4:30PM. Enrollment: 700. Records go back to 1928. Alumni records are maintained here at the same phone number. Degrees granted: Associate; Bachelors; Masters. Adverse incident record source- Student Services, 913-758-6120.

Attendance and degree information available by phone, fax, mail. Search requires name plus SSN, date of birth. Also helpful: exact years of attendance. There is no fee.

Sterling College, Registrar, Sterling, KS 67579, 316-278-4280 (Fax: 316-278-3690). Hours: 8AM-5PM. Enrollment: 840. Records go back to 1887. Alumni records are maintained here also. Call 316-278-4329. Degrees granted: Bachelors. Adverse incident record source- Student Affairs, 316-278-4222.

Attendance and degree information available by phone, fax, mail. Search requires name plus SSN, approximate years of attendance. Also helpful: exact years of attendance. There is no fee.

Tabor College, Registrar, 400 S Jefferson St, Hillsboro, KS 67063, 316-947-3121 (Fax: 316-947-2607). Hours: 8AM-5PM. Enrollment: 500. Records go back to 1920. Alumni records are maintained here at the same phone number. Degrees granted: Associate; Bachelors. Adverse incident record source- Student Development, 316-947-3121 X259.

Attendance and degree information available by phone, fax, mail. Search requires name only. Also helpful: SSN, date of birth, exact years of attendance. There is no fee.

United States Army Command and General Staff College, Registrar, Reynolds Ave, Fort Leavenworth, KS 66027-1352, 913-684-2312 (Fax: 913-684-4648). Hours: 7PM-4:30PM. Records go back to 1881. Degrees granted: Masters.

Attendance and degree information available by phone, fax, mail. Search requires name plus SSN, approximate years of attendance. There is no fee.

University of Kansas, Registrar, Lawrence, KS 66045, 913-864-3911 (Fax: 913-864-3256). Hours: 8AM-5PM. Enrollment: 26000. Records go back to 1866. Alumni records are maintained here also. Call 913-864-4760. Degrees granted: Bachelors; Masters; PhD. Adverse incident record source- Student Life, 913-864-4060.

Attendance and degree information available by phone, fax, mail. Search requires name plus SSN, approximate years of attendance. There is no fee.

University of Kansas Medical Center, Registrar, 3901 St & Rainbow Blvd, Kansas City, KS 66160-7190, 913-588-4698 (Fax: 913-588-4697). Hours: 8AM-4:30PM. Records go back to 1902. Alumni records are maintained here also. Call 913-588-1255. Degrees granted: Bachelors; Masters; Doctorate.

Attendance and degree information available by phone, fax, mail. Search requires name plus SSN, date of birth. There is no fee.

Washburn University of Topeka, Registrar, 17th and College Sts, Topeka, KS 66621, 913-231-1010 X1074. Hours: 8AM-5PM. Enrollment: 6300. Records go back to 1865. Alumni records are maintained here also. Call 913-231-1010 X1641. Degrees granted: Associate; Bachelors; Masters; J.D.

Attendance and degree information available by phone, mail. Search requires name plus SSN. Also helpful: date of birth, exact years of attendance. There is no fee.

Wichita State University, Registrar, 1845 Fairmount, Wichita, KS 67260-0058, 316-978-3092 (Fax: 316-978-3795). Hours: 8AM-5PM. Enrollment: 14568. Records go back to 1892. Alumni records are maintained here also. Call 316-978-3290. Degrees granted: Associate; Bachelors; Masters; Doctorate. Adverse incident record source- Campus Police, 316-978-3450.

Attendance and degree information available by phone, fax, mail. Search requires name plus SSN, date of birth, approximate years of attendance. Also helpful: exact years of attendance. Fee is $5.00.

Trade and Vocational Schools

Advanced Hair Tech, 4323 State Ave, Kansas City, KS 66101, 913-321-0214

Amtech Institute, 4011 E 31st St S, Wichita, KS 67210, 316-682-6548

Bryan Institute, 1004 S Oliver St, Wichita, KS 67214, 316-685-2284

Bryan Travel College, 1527 Fairlawn Rd, Topeka, KS 66604, 913-272-7511

Capitol City Barber College, 812 N Kansas Ave, Topeka, KS 66608-1211, 913-234-5401

Center for Training in Business and Industry, 2211 Silicon Ave, Lawrence, KS 66046, 913-841-9640

Climate Control Institute, 3030 N Hillside St, Wichita, KS 67219, 316-686-7355

Flint Hills Technical School, 3301 W 18th Ave, Emporia, KS 66801, 316-342-6404

Kansas School of Hairstyling, 1207 E Douglas Ave, Wichita, KS 67211, 316-264-4891

North Central Kansas Area Vocational-Technical School, PO Box 507, Beloit, KS 67420, 913-738-2276

North Central Kansas Area Vocational-Technical School (Hays Campus), 2205 Wheatland, Hays, KS 67601, 913-625-2437

Remington College, 2443 S Meridian, Wichita, KS 67213-1993, 316-681-6700

Topeka Technical College, 1620 NW Gage Blvd, Topeka, KS 66618, 913-232-5858

Wichita Area Vocational-Technical School, 324 N Emporia St, Wichita, KS 67202, 316-833-4664

Wichita Business College, 501 E Pawnee St#515, Wichita, KS 67211, 316-263-1261

Wichita Technical Institute, 942 S West St, Wichita, KS 67213, 316-943-2241

Wright Business School, 9500 Marshall Dr, Lenexa, KS 66215, 913-492-2888

State Licensing & Business Registration Quick Finder Index

Architecture, Engineering & Surveying
Architect #14 (2398)...................................☎ 913-296-3053
Engineer #14 (8281)....................................☎ 913-296-3053
Landscape Architect #14 (401) ....☎ 913-296-3053
Surveyor #14 (850).....................................☎ 913-296-3053

Business - Court & Legal Services
Attorney #18 (11000) ....☎ 913-296-8409
Lobbyist #27 (1200) ....☎ 913-296-0080
Notary Public #27 (1100) ....☎ 913-296-2744
Shorthand Reporter #17...............................☎ 913-296-8410

Business - General Services
Broadcaster #28 ....☎ 913-532-5851
Public Accountant-CPA #4 (7900) ....☎ 913-296-2162
Vendor License #20.....................................☎ 913-296-3946

Construction & Manufacturing
General Contractor #21 913-296-3160

Education
School Administrator #7................................☎ 913-296-2288
School Counselor #7....................................☎ 913-296-2288
School Library Media Specialist #7 ....☎ 913-296-2288
School Nurse #7..☎ 913-296-2288
Teacher #7 ....☎ 913-296-2288

Environmental & Agriculture
Livestock Brand #2 (1000)...........................☎ 913-296-2326
Pesticide Applicator #24...............................☎ 913-296-0673
Pesticide Dealer #24 ....☎ 913-296-2263
Veterinarian #15 ....☎ 316-355-6358

Financial - Real Estate, Insurance & Banking
Abstractor #1 (500).....................................☎ 316-544-2311
Insurance Agent #22 (5000) 913-296-2283
Investment Advisor #30 (458) ....☎ 913-296-3307
Real Estate Agent #29.................................913-296-0706
Real Estate Appraiser #29............................913-296-0706
Real Estate Broker #29................................913-296-0706
Securities Agent #30 (35577) ....☎ 913-296-3307
Securities Broker/Dealer #30 (1306).............☎ 913-296-3307

Health & Beauty
Ambulance Attendant #8 (9306) ....✉ 913-296-7299
Assistant Funeral Director #11 ....✉ 913-296-3980
Audiologist #16...☎ 913-296-1284
Barber #5 (1800)...✉ 913-296-2211
Certified Medication Aide #16 ....☎ 913-296-1284
Certified Nurse Aide #16..............................☎ 913-296-1284
Chiropractor #10...☎ 913-296-7413
Cosmetologist #6 (25000)............................✉ 913-296-3155
Dental Hygienist #19 ....☎ 913-273-0780
Dentist/Dental Hygienist #19 (2116).............☎ 913-273-0780
Dietitian #16 (856)......................................☎ 913-296-0061
Embalmer #11 (700) ....✉ 913-296-3980
Emergency Medical Techician #8 (5830).......✉ 913-296-7299
Funeral Branch Establishment #11 ....✉ 913-296-3980
Funeral Director #11 (80) ....✉ 913-296-3980
Funeral Establishment #11............................✉ 913-296-3980
Hearing Aid Dispenser #9 ....✉ 316-263-0774
Home Health Aide #16 (4539) ....☎ 913-296-1284
Medical Doctor #10 ....☎ 913-296-7413
Nurse #12 913-296-4929
Nursing Home Administrator #16 (2625) ......☎ 913-296-0061
Occupational Therapist/Assistant #10............☎ 913-296-7413

Optometrist #26 .... ☎ 913-296-0824
Osteopathic Physician #10 .... ☎ 913-296-7413
Pharmacist #13 (3100) .... ✉ 913-296-8420
Physical Therapist/Assistant #10 .... ☎ 913-296-7413
Physician's Assistant #10 .... ☎ 913-296-7413
Podiatrist #10 .... ☎ 913-296-7413
Respiratory Care Practitioner #10 .... ☎ 913-296-7413
Respiratory Therapist #10 .... ☎ 913-296-7413
Speech/Language Pathologist #16 .... ☎ 913-296-1284

Investigations & Security

Private Investigator #23 (500) .... ☎ 913-296-8200

Social Services

Adult Care Home Administrator #16 .... ☎ 913-296-1284
Marriage & Family Therapist #3 .... ✉ 913-296-3240
Professional Counselor #3 .... ✉ 913-296-3240
Psychologist #3 .... ✉ 913-296-3240
Social Worker #3 .... ✉ 913-296-3240

Sports & Entertainment

Racing Concessionaire #25 .... ☎ 913-296-5800
Racing Occupation License #25 .... ☎ 913-296-5800
Track Occupation Licenses #25 (6000) .... ☎ 913-296-5800

State Licensing & Business Registration Agency Information

(1) Abstracters Board of Examiners, 521 S Main, Box 549, Hugoton, KS 67951-0549, 316-544-2311, Fax: 316-544-8029

(2) Animal Health Department, 712 Kansas Ave, Suite 4B, Topeka, KS 66603-3808, 913-296-2326, Fax: 913-296-1765

(3) Behavorial Sciences Regulatory Board, 712 S Kansas, Topeka, KS 66603, 913-296-3240

(4) Board of Accountancy, 900 SW Jackson, Suite 556, Topeka, KS 66612-1239, 913-296-2162

(5) Board of Barbering, 700 SW Jackson, Suite 1002, Topeka, KS 66603, 913-296-2211

(6) Board of Cosmetology, 2708 NW Topeka Blvd, Topeka, KS 66617-1139, 913-296-3155, Fax: 913-296-3002

(7) Board of Education, 120 SW 10th Ave, Topeka, KS 66612-1182, 913-296-2288, Fax: 913-296-7933

(8) Board of Emergency Medical Services, 109 SW 6th, Topeka, KS 66603-3826, 913-296-7299, Fax: 913-296-6212

(9) Board of Examiners for Hearing Aid Dispensers, 600 N St Francis (67214-3810), PO Box 252, Wichita, KS 67201-0252, 316-263-0774, Fax: 316-264-2681

(10) Board of Healing Arts, 235 S Topeka Blvd, Topeka, KS 66603-3059, 913-296-7413, Fax: 913-296-0852

(11) Board of Mortuary Arts, 700 SW Jackson, Suite 904, Topeka, KS 66603-3758, 913-296-3980, Fax: 913-296-0891

(12) Board of Nursing, 900 SW Jackson, Room 551S, Topeka, KS 66612-1230, 913-296-2967, Fax: 913-296-3929

(13) Board of Pharmacy, 900 SW Jackson, Room 513, Topeka, KS 66612-1231, 913-296-4056, Fax: 913-296-8420

(14) Board of Technical Professions, 900 SW Jackson, Room 507, Topeka, KS 66612-1257, 913-296-3053

(15) Board of Veterinary Examiners, PO Box 242, Wamego, KS 66547-0242, 913-456-8781

(16) Bureau of Adult & Child Care, Department of Health & Environment, Mills Bldg, #400B, 109 SW 9th St, Topeka, KS 66612-2218, 913-296-1284, Fax: 913-296-7025

(17) Clerk of Appellate Court, Kansas Judicial Center, 301 W 10th St, Topeka, KS 66612, 913-296-8410, Fax: 913-296-1028

(18) Clerk of the Supreme Court, 301 W 10th, Topeka, KS 66612, 913-296-8409, Fax: 913-296-1028

(19) Dental Board, 3601 SW 29th St, Suite 134, Topeka, KS 66614-2062, 913-273-0780, Fax: 913-273-7545

(20) Department of Revenue, Alcohol Beverage Control, 4 Townsite Plaza, Suite 210, 200 SE 6th St, Topeka, KS 66603-3512, 913-296-3946

(21) Department of Revenue, Division of Taxation, Robert B Docking State Office Bldg, Topeka, KS 66625-0001, 913-296-3160

(22) Insurance Department, 420 SW 9th, Topeka, KS 66612-1678, 913-296-7858, Fax: 913-296-2283

(23) Kansas Bureau of Investigations, Attorney General's Office, 1620 Tyler, Topeka, KS 66612, 913-296-8200

(24) Kansas Department of Agriculture, Div of Plant Health, 901 S Kansas Ave, Topeka, KS 66612, 913-296-2263, Fax: 913-296-0673

(25) Kansas Racing Commission, 3400 Van Buren, Topeka, KS 66611, 913-296-5800, Fax: 913-296-0900

(26) Kansas State Board of Examiners in Optometry, 1001 SW Mulvane St, Topeka, KS 66604-1419, 913-296-0824, Fax: 913-296-0824

(27) Office of Secretary of State, State Capitol, 2nd Floor, Topeka, KS 66612, 913-296-2744, Fax: 913-296-4570

(28) Public Broadcasting Council, 20 McCain Auditorium, Kansas State University, Manhattan, KS 66506-4701, 913-532-5709

(29) Real Estate Commission, Real Estate Appraisal Board, 900 SW Jackson, Room 501, Topeka, KS 66612-1220, 913-296-0706

(30) Securities Commissioner of Kansas, 618 S Kansas, 2nd Floor, Topeka, KS 66603-3804, 913-296-3307, Fax: 913-296-6872

Kentucky

Capitol: Louisville (Jefferson County)	
State Population	3.9 Million
Number of Degree Granting Institutions:	68
Number of State Licensing & Business Registration Agencies:	134

Degree Granting Educational Institutions

Alice Lloyd College, Registrar, Purpose Rd, Pippa Passes, KY 41844, 606-368-2101 X4502 (Fax: 606-368-2125). Hours: 8AM-4:30PM. Enrollment: 500. Records go back to 1923. Alumni records are maintained here also. Call 606-368-2101. Degrees granted: Bachelors. Adverse incident record source- Student Affairs, 606-368-2101 X7101.

Attendance and degree information available by phone, fax, mail. Search requires name only. Also helpful: SSN, date of birth, exact years of attendance. There is no fee.

Asbury College, Registrar, One Macklem Dr, Wilmore, KY 40390-1198, 606-858-3511 X2325 (Fax: 606-858-3511 X3921). Hours: 8AM-5PM. Records go back to 1890. Alumni records are maintained here also. Call 606-858-3511 X2167. Degrees granted: Bachelors. Adverse incident record source- Student Affairs, 606-858-3511 X2322.

Attendance and degree information available by phone, fax, mail. Search requires name plus SSN, date of birth, exact years of attendance. There is no fee.

Asbury Theological Seminary, Registrar, 204 N Lexington Ave, Wilmore, KY 40390-1199, 606-858-3581 (Fax: 606-858-2248). Hours: 8AM-4:30PM. Enrollment: 1000. Records go back to 1923. Alumni records are maintained here also. Call 606-858-2305. Degrees granted: Masters; Doctorate. Adverse incident record source- Dean of Students, 606-858-2313.

Attendance and degree information available by phone, mail. Search requires name plus approximate years of attendance. Also helpful: SSN, date of birth, exact years of attendance. There is no fee.

Ashland Community College, Registrar, 1400 College Dr, Ashland, KY 41101-3683, 606-329-2999 (Fax: 606-325-9403). Hours: 8AM-5PM. Enrollment: 2700. Records go back to 1940. Alumni records are maintained here at the same phone number. Degrees granted: Associate. Adverse incident record source- Student Affairs, 606-329-2999 X280.

Attendance information available by phone, fax, mail. Search requires name plus SSN. There is no fee.

Degree information available by fax, mail. Search requires name plus SSN. There is no fee.

Bellarmine College, Registrar, 2001 Newburg Rd, Louisville, KY 40205, 502-452-8133 (Fax: 502-456-3331). Hours: 8AM-5PM. Records go back to 1938. Alumni records are maintained here also. Call 502-452-8333. Degrees granted: Associate; Bachelors; Masters.

Attendance and degree information available by phone, fax, mail. Search requires name plus SSN, approximate years of attendance. Also helpful: date of birth, exact years of attendance. There is no fee.

Berea College, Registrar, Berea, KY 40404, 606-986-9341 X5185 (Fax: 606-986-4506). Hours: 8AM-Noon, 1-5PM. Records go back to 1855. Degrees granted: Bachelors.

Attendance and degree information available by phone, fax, mail. Search requires name only. Also helpful: SSN, exact years of attendance. There is no fee.

Brescia College, Registrar, 717 Frederica St, Owensboro, KY 42301-3023, 505-685-3131. Enrollment: 700. Alumni records are maintained here at the same phone number. Degrees granted: Associate; Bachelors; Masters.

Attendance and degree information available by mail. Search requires name plus SSN, signed release. Also helpful: date of birth, exact years of attendance. There is no fee. Expedited service available for $5.00.

Campbellsville University, Director of Student Records, 200 W College St, Campbellsville, KY 42718-2799, 502-789-5233 (Fax: 502-789-5050). Hours: 8AM-5PM. Enrollment: 1366. Formerly Campbellsville College Alumni records are maintained here also. Call 502-789-5211. Degrees granted: Associate; Bachelors; Masters. Adverse incident record source- Student Development, 502-789-5005.

Attendance and degree information available by phone, fax, mail. Search requires name plus SSN. Also helpful: date of birth, approximate years of attendance. There is no fee.

CareerCom Junior College of Business, Registrar, 1102 S Virginia St, Hopkinsville, KY 42240, 502-886-1302 (Fax: 502-886-3544). Hours: 8AM-10PM M-Th; 8AM-4PM F. Enrollment: 129. Records go back to 1984. Degrees granted: Associate. Adverse incident record source- Registrar, 506-886-1302.

Attendance and degree information available by phone, fax, mail. Search requires name plus SSN, date of birth. Also helpful: exact years of attendance. There is no fee.

Centre College, Registrar's Office, 600 W Walnut St, Danville, KY 40422, 606-238-5360 (Fax: 606-236-9610).

Hours: 8:30AM-4:30PM. Enrollment: 975. Records go back to 1900. Degrees granted: Bachelors. Adverse incident record source- Dean of Students, 606-238-5471.

Attendance and degree information available by phone, fax, mail. Search requires name plus approximate years of attendance. Also helpful: SSN, date of birth, exact years of attendance. There is no fee.

Clear Creek Baptist Bible College, Registrar's Office, 300 Clear Creek Rd, Pineville, KY 40977, 606-377-3196 (Fax: 606-337-2372). Hours: 8AM-4:30PM. Enrollment: 135. Records go back to 1926. Alumni records are maintained here at the same phone number. Degrees granted: Associate; Bachelors. Adverse incident record source- Office of Student Life, 606-337-3196.

Attendance information available by fax, mail. Search requires name plus SSN, date of birth, signed release. Also helpful: approximate years of attendance. There is no fee.

Degree information available by fax, mail. Search requires name plus signed release. Also helpful: SSN, date of birth, approximate years of attendance. There is no fee.

Cumberland College, Registrar, 6174 College Station Dr, Williamsburg, KY 40769, 606-539-4316 (Fax: 606-539-4490). Hours: 8:30AM-5PM. Enrollment: 1500. Records go back to 1889. Transcripts permanent. Other records five years from last enrollment. Alumni records are maintained here also. Call 606-539-4277. Degrees granted: Bachelors; Masters.

Attendance and degree information available by phone, fax, mail. Search requires name plus SSN, date of birth. Also helpful: exact years of attendance. There is no fee. Expedited service available for $10.00.

Draughons Junior College, (Branch Campus), Registrar, 2424 Airway Dr and Lovers Lane, Bowling Green, KY 42103, 502-843-6750 (Fax: 502-843-6976). Hours: 8AM-5:30PM. Enrollment: 200. Records go back to 1989. Degrees granted: Associate. Special programs- Business. Adverse incident record source- Student Affairs.

Attendance and degree information available by phone, mail. Search requires name plus SSN, exact years of attendance. There is no fee.

Eastern Kentucky University, Records Office, Coates Box 28-A, Richmond, KY 40457-3101, 606-622-1102 (Fax: 606-622-6207). Hours: 8:30AM-4PM. Enrollment: 16500. Records go back to 1906. Alumni records are maintained here also. Call 606-622-1260. Degrees granted: Associate; Bachelors; Masters.

Attendance and degree information available by fax, mail. Search requires name only. Also helpful: SSN, date of birth. There is no fee.

Elizabethtown Community College, Registrar, 600 College Street Rd, Elizabethtown, KY 42701, 502-769-1632 (Fax: 502-769-0736). Hours: 8AM-5PM M-Th, 8AM-3PM F. Enrollment: 3766. Records go back to 1965. Alumni records are maintained here at the same phone number. Degrees granted: Associate.

Attendance and degree information available by phone, mail. Search requires name plus SSN. Also helpful: date of birth, exact years of attendance. There is no fee.

Franklin College Truck Driving School, Transcript Department, 218 N Fifth St, Paducah, KY 42001, 502-443-8478. Formerly CareerCom Junior College & Draughons College of Business Degrees granted.

Attendance and degree information available by phone, fax, mail. Search requires name plus SSN, approximate years of attendance. There is no fee.

Fugazzi College, Registrar, 406 Lafayette Ave, Lexington, KY 40502, 606-266-0401 (Fax: 606-266-2118). Hours:

9AM-5PM. Enrollment: 150. Records go back to 1993. Degrees granted: Associate.

Attendance and degree information available by fax, mail. Search requires name plus SSN, signed release. There is no fee.

Georgetown College, Registrar, 400 E College St, Georgetown, KY 40324, 502-863-8024. Hours: 8AM-5PM. Enrollment: 1400. Records go back to 1900. Alumni records are maintained here also. Call 502-863-8041. Degrees granted: Bachelors; Masters.

Attendance and degree information available by phone, mail. Search requires name plus SSN. There is no fee.

Hazard Community College, Registrar, One Community College Dr, Hazard, KY 41701, 606-436-5721 (Fax: 606-439-2988). Hours: 8AM-4:30PM. Enrollment: 1800. Records go back to 1989. Alumni Records Office: Alumni Association, 400 Rd St, Lexington, KY 40505. Degrees granted: Associate.

Attendance and degree information available by phone, fax, mail. Search requires name plus SSN. There is no fee.

Henderson Community College, Registrar, 2660 S Green St, Henderson, KY 42420, 502-827-1867 (Fax: 502-827-8635). Hours: 8AM-7PM M-Th; 8AM-5PM F. Enrollment: 1200. Records go back to 1960. Alumni records are maintained here also. Call 502-827-1867 X236. Degrees granted: Associate.

Attendance and degree information available by phone, mail. Search requires name plus SSN. Also helpful: date of birth. There is no fee.

Hopkinsville Community College, Registrar, PO Box 2100, Hopkinsville, KY 42241-2100, 502-886-3921 (Fax: 502-886-0237). Hours: 8AM-4:30PM. Enrollment: 3000. Records go back to 1966. Alumni records are maintained here at the same phone number. Degrees granted: Associate. Adverse incident record source- Student Affairs, 502-886-3921.

Attendance and degree information available by phone, mail. Search requires name plus SSN. Also helpful: approximate years of attendance. There is no fee.

ITT Technical Institute, (Branch of Evansville, IN), Registrar, 10509 Timberwood Cir, Louisville, KY 40223, 502-527-7424 (Fax: 502-327-7624). Hours: 8AM-10PM. Enrollment: 280. Records go back to 1993. Started in June 1993. Alumni Records Office: PO Box 50466, Indianapolis, IN 46250-0466. Degrees granted: Associate. Special programs- Electronics Engineering Technology: Computer Aided Drafting.

Attendance and degree information available by phone, fax, mail. Search requires name plus approximate years of attendance. Also helpful: SSN, date of birth, exact years of attendance. There is no fee.

Institute of Electronic Technology, Registrar, PO Box 8252, 509 s 30th St, Paducah, KY 42002-8252, 502-444-9676 (Fax: 502-441-7202). Hours: 8:30AM-5PM. Enrollment: 159. Records go back to 1976. Degrees granted: Associate.

Attendance and degree information available by phone, fax, mail. Search requires name plus SSN, approximate years of attendance. Also helpful; exact years of attendance. There is no fee.

Institute of Electronic Technology, (Lexington Electronics Institute), Registrar, 3340 Holwyn Rd, Lexington, KY 40503-9938, 606-223-9608 (Fax: 606-223-3310). Hours: 8AM-5PM. Enrollment: 200. Records go back to 1989. Degrees granted: Associate. Special programs- Financial Aid, 606-223-9608. Adverse incident record source- Registrar's Office

Attendance and degree information available by phone, fax, mail. Search requires name plus SSN, approximate years of attendance. There is no fee.

Jefferson Community College, Registrar, 109 E Broadway, Louisville, KY 40202, 502-584-0181 X2128. Hours: 8AM-5PM M-Th, 8AM-4:30PM. Enrollment: 6962. Records go back to 1968. Degrees granted: Associate.

Attendance and degree information available by phone, mail. Search requires name plus SSN. There is no fee.

Kentucky Christian College, Registrar, 100 Academic Pkwy, Grayson, KY 41143-2205, 606-474-3212 (Fax: 606-474-3154). Hours: 8:30AM-4:30PM. Enrollment: 515. Records go back to 1919. Alumni records are maintained here also. Call 606-474-3277. Degrees granted: Associate; Bachelors.

Attendance and degree information available by phone, fax, mail. Search requires name only. Also helpful: SSN, date of birth, exact years of attendance. There is no fee.

Kentucky College of Business, Registrar, 628 E Main St, Lexington, KY 40508, 606-253-0621 (Fax: 606-233-3054). Hours: 8AM-4:30PM. Enrollment: 700. Records go back to 1941. Alumni records are maintained here at the same phone number. Degrees granted: Associate. Adverse incident record source- Administration, 606-253-0621.

Attendance and degree information available by phone, fax, mail. Search requires name plus SSN, date of birth, exact years of attendance. There is no fee.

Kentucky College of Business, (Branch), Registrar, 115 E Lexington Ave, Danville, KY 40422, 606-236-6991 (Fax: 606-236-1063). Records are not housed here. They are located at National Business College, Registrar, PO Box 6400, Roanoke, VA 24017.

Kentucky College of Business, (Branch), Registrar, 7627 Ewing Blvd, Florence, KY 41042, 606-525-6510 (Fax: 606-525-2815). Records are not housed here. They are located at National Business College, Registrar, PO Box 6400, Roanoke, VA 24017.

Kentucky College of Business, (Branch), Registrar, 3950 Dixie Hwy, Louisville, KY 40216, 502-447-7634. Records are not housed here. They are located at National Business College, Registrar, PO Box 6400, Roanoke, VA 24017.

Kentucky College of Business, (Branch), Registrar, 198 S Mayo Trail, Pikeville, KY 41501, 606-432-5477 (Fax: 606-437-4952). Records are not housed here. They are located at National Business College, Registrar, PO Box 6400, Roanoke, VA 24017.

Kentucky College of Business, (Branch), Registrar, 139 Killarney Lane, Richmond, KY 40475, 606-623-8956. Records go back to 1989. Degrees granted: Associate.

Attendance information available by phone, mail. Search requires name plus SSN. Also helpful: exact years of attendance. There is no fee.

Degree information available by phone, fax, mail. Search requires name plus SSN, approximate years of attendance. Also helpful: date of birth, exact years of attendance. There is no fee.

Kentucky State University, Registrar, E Main St, Frankfort, KY 40601, 502-227-6340 (Fax: 502-227-6239). Hours: 8AM-4:30PM. Enrollment: 2700. Records go back to 1880. Alumni records are maintained here at the same phone number. Degrees granted: Associate; Bachelors; Masters. Adverse incident record source- Registrar, 502-227-6340.

Attendance information available by phone, fax, mail. Search requires name plus SSN, approximate years of attendance. Also helpful: date of birth, exact years of attendance. There is no fee.

Degree information available by phone, fax. Search requires name plus SSN, approximate years of attendance. Also helpful: date of birth, exact years of attendance. There is no fee.

Kentucky Wesleyan College, Registrar, 3000 Frederica St, PO Box 1039, Owensboro, KY 42302-1039, 502-926-3111 (Fax: 502-926-3196). Hours: 8AM-5PM. Enrollment: 650. Records go back to 1900. Alumni records are maintained here at the same phone number. Degrees granted: Associate; Bachelors. Adverse incident record source- Student Life, 502-926-3111.

Attendance and degree information available by phone, fax, mail. Search requires name only. Also helpful: SSN, date of birth, exact years of attendance. There is no fee.

Lees College, Registrar, 601 Jefferson Ave, Jackson, KY 41339, 606-666-7521 (Fax: 606-666-8910). Hours: 8AM-5PM. Records go back to 1900's. Degrees granted: Associate.

Attendance and degree information available by mail. Search requires name plus SSN, signed release. Also helpful: date of birth, exact years of attendance. There is no fee.

Lexington Community College, Registrar, Oswald Bldg, Cooper Dr, Lexington, KY 40506-0235, 606-257-4460 (Fax: 606-257-2634). Hours: 8AM-7:30PM M-Th, 8AM-4:30PM F. Enrollment: 5225. Records go back to 1965. Alumni records are maintained here at the same phone number. Degrees granted: Associate.

Attendance and degree information available by phone, fax, mail. Search requires name plus SSN. Also helpful: date of birth, exact years of attendance. There is no fee.

Lexington Theological Seminary, Registrar, 631 S Limestone St, Lexington, KY 40508, 606-252-0361 (Fax: 606-281-6042). Hours: 8AM-4:45PM. Enrollment: 190. Records go back to 1865. Alumni records are maintained here also. Call 606-252-0361. Degrees granted: Masters; Doctorate.

Attendance and degree information available by fax, mail. Search requires name plus SSN, signed release. There is no fee.

Lindsey Wilson College, Registrar, 210 Lindsey Wilson St, Columbia, KY 42728, 502-384-2126 X8024 (Fax: 502-384-8200). Hours: 7:30AM-4:30PM. Enrollment: 1317. Records go back to 1923. Alumni records are maintained here also. Call 502-384-8400. Degrees granted: Associate; Bachelors; Masters. Adverse incident record source- Dean of Students, 502-384-2126 X8036.

Attendance and degree information available by phone, fax, mail. Search requires name plus SSN. Also helpful: date of birth, exact years of attendance. There is no fee.

Louisville Presbyterian Theological Seminary, Registrar, 1044 Alta Vista Rd, Louisville, KY 40205, 502-895-3411 (Fax: 502-895-1096). Hours: 8:30AM-5PM. Enrollment: 250. Records go back to 1920. Alumni records are maintained here at the same phone number. Degrees granted: Masters; Doctorate.

Attendance and degree information available by phone, fax, mail. Search requires name plus approximate years of attendance. Also helpful: SSN, date of birth, exact years of attendance. There is no fee.

Louisville Technical Institute, Registrar, 3901 Atkinson Dr, Louisville, KY 40218, 502-456-6509 (Fax: 502-456-2341). Enrollment: 500. Records go back to 1970. Degrees granted: Associate. Special programs- Marine Mechanics Tecnician: Architectural Computer Ad Design Drafting: Mechanical Engineer: Electrical Engineer: Computer Graphics: Interior Design. Adverse incident record source- Corporate Office, 502-451-0815.

Attendance and degree information available by mail. Search requires name plus SSN, approximate years of attendance. There is no fee.

Madisonville Community College, Registrar, 2000 College Dr, Madisonville, KY 42431, 502-821-2250 (Fax: 502-821-1555). Hours: 8AM-4:30PM. Enrollment: 2500.

Alumni records are maintained here at the same phone number. Degrees granted: Associate.

Attendance and degree information available by phone, fax, mail. Search requires name plus SSN. Also helpful: date of birth, exact years of attendance. There is no fee.

Maysville Community College, Registrar, 1755 US 68, Maysville, KY 41056, 606-759-7141 X225 (Fax: 606-759-7176). Hours: 8AM-4:30PM. Enrollment: 1300. Records go back to 1968. Alumni records are maintained here at the same phone number. Degrees granted: Associate.

Attendance and degree information available by phone, fax, mail. Search requires name plus SSN. Also helpful: approximate years of attendance. There is no fee.

Midway College, Starks Hall/101, Registrar, 512 E Stephens St, Midway, KY 40347-1120, 606-846-5340 (Fax: 606-846-5774). Hours: 8AM-5PM. Enrollment: 975. Records go back to 1848. Degrees granted: Associate; Bachelors.

Attendance and degree information available by fax, mail. Search requires name only. Also helpful: SSN, date of birth, exact years of attendance. There is no fee.

Morehead State University, Registrar, University Blvd, Morehead, KY 40351, 606-783-2221 (Fax: 606-783-5038). Hours: 8AM-4:30PM. Enrollment: 8300. Records go back to 1922. Alumni records are maintained here also. Call 606-783-2221. Degrees granted: Associate; Bachelors; Masters. Adverse incident record source- Public Safety.

Attendance and degree information available by mail. Search requires name plus date of birth, exact years of attendance. Also helpful: SSN. There is no fee.

Murray State University, Registrar, PO Box 9, Murray, KY 42071-0009, 502-762-3753 (Fax: 502-762-3050). Hours: 8:30AM-4:30PM. Enrollment: 7135. Records go back to 1923. Alumni records are maintained here also. Call 502-762-3011. Degrees granted: Associate; Bachelors; Masters. Adverse incident record source- Security, 502-762-2222.

Attendance and degree information available by phone, fax, mail. Search requires name plus SSN. Also helpful: approximate years of attendance. There is no fee.

Northern Kentucky University, Office of Registrar, Service Center LAC 301, Highland Heights, KY 41099-7011, 606-572-5556 (Fax: 606-572-6094). Hours: 8:15AM-6:15PM M-Th; 8:15AM-4:30PM F. Enrollment: 11000. Records go back to 1970. Alumni records are maintained here also. Call 606-572-5486. Degrees granted: Associate; Bachelors; Masters. Adverse incident record source- Dean of Students, 606-572-5500.

Attendance and degree information available by phone, mail. Search requires name plus SSN. Also helpful: exact years of attendance. There is no fee.

Owensboro Community College, Registrar, 4800 New Hartford Rd, Owensboro, KY 42303, 502-686-4400 (Fax: 502-686-4648). Hours: 8AM-4:30PM. Enrollment: 2300. Records go back to 1986. Alumni records are maintained here at the same phone number. Degrees granted: Associate.

Attendance and degree information available by fax, mail. Search requires name plus SSN, signed release. Also helpful: exact years of attendance. There is no fee.

Owensboro Junior College of Business, Registrar, 1515 E 18th St, Owensboro, KY 42303, 502-926-4040 X25. Hours: 7:30AM-4:30PM. Records go back to 1963. Degrees granted: Associate.

Attendance and degree information available by phone, mail. Search requires name plus SSN, exact years of attendance. There is no fee.

Paducah Community College, Registrar, PO Box 7380, Paducah, KY 42002-7380, 502-554-9200 (Fax: 502-554-

6217). Hours: 8AM-5PM. Enrollment: 1983. Records go back to 1968. Alumni records are maintained here at the same phone number. Degrees granted: Associate. Adverse incident record source- Registrar, 502-554-6213.

Attendance and degree information available by written request only. Search requires name plus SSN, exact years of attendance, signed release. There is no fee.

Pikeville College, Registrar, 214 Sycamore St, Pikeville, KY 41501, 606-432-9369 (Fax: 606-432-9328). Hours: 8:30AM-5PM. Enrollment: 846. Records go back to 1936. Alumni records are maintained here also. Call 606-432-9326. Degrees granted: Associate; Bachelors.

Attendance and degree information available by phone, fax, mail. Search requires name plus SSN, date of birth. Also helpful: exact years of attendance. There is no fee.

Prestonsburg Community College, Registrar, One Bert T. Combs Dr, Prestonsburg, KY 41653, 606-886-3863 X224 (Fax: 606-886-6943). Hours: 8AM-4:30PM. Enrollment: 2388. Records go back to 1964. Degrees granted: Associate.

Attendance and degree information available by phone, fax, mail. Search requires name plus SSN. Also helpful: date of birth. There is no fee.

RETS Electronic Institute, Registrar, 4146 Outer Loop, Louisville, KY 40219, 502-968-7191 X271 (Fax: 502-968-1727). Enrollment: 300. Records go back to 1971. Alumni records are maintained here at the same phone number. Degrees granted: Associate. Adverse incident record source- Department of Student Services.

Attendance and degree information available by phone, mail. Search requires name plus SSN, exact years of attendance. There is no fee.

Somerset Community College, Registrar, 808 Monticello Rd, Somerset, KY 42501, 606-679-8501 (Fax: 606-676-9065). Hours: 8AM-5PM. Enrollment: 2145. Records go back to 1965. Degrees granted: Associate. Special programs-Business Technology: Registered Nurse: Clinical Lab Technician.

Attendance and degree information available by phone, fax, mail. Search requires name plus SSN, approximate years of attendance. Also helpful: date of birth, exact years of attendance. There is no fee.

Southeast Community College, Registrar, 700 College Rd, Cumberland, KY 40823, 606-589-2145. Hours: 8:30AM-4:30PM. Formerly Southeastern Nebraska Technical Community College Records go back to 1935. Degrees granted: Associate.

Attendance and degree information available by phone, mail. Search requires name plus SSN. Also helpful: exact years of attendance. There is no fee.

Southern Baptist Theological Seminary, Registrar, 2825 Lexington Rd, Louisville, KY 40280, 502-897-4209 (Fax: 502-899-1781). Hours: 8AM-4:30PM. Enrollment: 1770. Records go back to 1859. Degrees granted: Associate; Masters; Doctorate.

Attendance and degree information available by phone, mail. Search requires name plus SSN. Also helpful: date of birth, exact years of attendance. There is no fee.

Southern Ohio College, (Northern Kentucky), Registrar, 309 Buttermilk Pike, Fort Mitchell, KY 41017, 606-341-5627 (Fax: 606-341-6483). Hours: 9AM-6PM. Degrees granted: Associate.

Attendance information available by fax, mail. Search requires name plus SSN. Also helpful: date of birth, exact years of attendance. There is no fee.

Degree information available by fax, mail. Search requires name plus SSN. Also helpful: date of birth, exact years of attendance. There is no fee.

Southwestern College of Business, Registrar,
2929 S Dixie Hwy, Crestview Hills, KY 41017, 606-341-6633. Hours: 9AM-7PM M-Th; 9AM-1PM F. Enrollment: 140. Degrees granted: Associate.

Attendance and degree information available by phone, mail. Search requires name plus SSN, approximate years of attendance. Also helpful: date of birth, exact years of attendance. Fee is $2.00.

Spalding University, Registrar's Office, 851 S Fourth
St, Louisville, KY 40203-2188, 502-585-7110 (Fax: 502-585-7158). Hours: 8AM-5PM. Enrollment: 1350. Records go back to 1920. Alumni records are maintained here at the same phone number. Degrees granted: Associate; Bachelors; Masters; Doctorate.

Attendance and degree information available by phone, fax, mail. Search requires name only. Also helpful: SSN, date of birth, exact years of attendance. There is no fee.

St. Catharine College, Registrar, 2735 Bardstown Rd,
St Catharine, KY 40061, 606-336-5082 (Fax: 606-336-5031). Hours: 8AM-5PM. Enrollment: 386. Alumni records are maintained here at the same phone number. Degrees granted: Associate.

Attendance and degree information available by phone, fax, mail. Search requires name plus SSN, approximate years of attendance. Also helpful: date of birth. There is no fee.

Sue Bennett College, Registrar, 151 College St, Lon-
don, KY 40741, 606-864-2238. Hours: 8AM-4:30PM. Records go back to 1900. Alumni records are maintained here also. Call 606-864-2238 X1125. Degrees granted: Associate; Bachelors.

Attendance and degree information available by fax, mail. Search requires name plus signed release. Also helpful: SSN, date of birth. There is no fee.

Sullivan College, Registrar, 3101 Bardstown Rd, Louis-
ville, KY 40205, 502-456-6504 (Fax: 502-454-4880). Hours: 7:30AM-8PM M-Th; 7:30AM-4:30PM F; 8AM-2PM S. Enrollment: 2000. Records go back to 1960's. Alumni records are maintained here at the same phone number. Degrees granted: Associate; Bachelors. Adverse incident record source- Registrar's Office   .

Attendance and degree information available by phone, fax, mail. Search requires name plus SSN, approximate years of attendance. Also helpful: exact years of attendance. There is no fee.

Sullivan College, (Branch), Registrar, 2659 Regency Rd,
Lexington, KY 40503, 606-276-4357. Records are not housed here. They are located at Sullivan College, Registrar, 3101 Bardstown Rd, Louisville, KY 40205.

Thomas More College, Registrar, 333 Thomas More
Pkwy, Crestview Hills, KY 41017, 606-344-3380 (Fax: 606-344-3345). Hours: 8:30AM-5PM. Enrollment: 1500. Records go back to 1921. Formerly Villa Madonna College (founded 1921). Alumni records are maintained here also. Call 606-344-3346. Degrees granted: Associate; Bachelors; Masters. Special programs- TAP Program (accelerated), 606-341-4554. Adverse incident record source- Student Life, 606-344-3317.

Attendance and degree information available by mail. Search requires name plus SSN, date of birth, approximate years of attendance, signed release. Also helpful: exact years of attendance. There is no fee.

Transylvania University, Registrar, 300 N Broadway,
Lexington, KY 40508, 606-233-8116. Hours: 8AM-5PM. Records go back to 1900. Alumni records are maintained here also. Call 606-233-8275. Degrees granted: Bachelors.

Attendance information available by mail. Search requires name plus SSN. There is no fee.

Degree information available by phone, mail. Search requires name plus SSN. There is no fee.

Union College, Registrar, 310 College St, Barbourville,
KY 40906, 606-546-1208 (Fax: 606-546-1217). Hours: 8AM-4:30PM. Enrollment: 1000. Records go back to 1870. Alumni records are maintained here also. Call 606-546-1218. Degrees granted: Associate; Bachelors; Masters. Adverse incident record source- Dean of Students, 606-546-1230.

Attendance and degree information available by phone, fax, mail. Search requires name plus SSN, approximate years of attendance. Also helpful: date of birth. There is no fee.

University of Kentucky, Registrar's Office, 10 Funk-
houser Bldg, Lexington, KY 40506-0054, 606-257-3671 (Fax: 606-257-7160). Hours: 8AM-4:30PM. Enrollment: 26000. Records go back to 1900. Alumni Records Office: Alumni Association, 125 King, Lexington, KY 40506-0119. Degrees granted: Bachelors; Masters; Doctorate; Juris Doctor, MD, DD. Special programs- Dental School, 606-323-6071: Medical School, 606-323-5261. Adverse incident record source- Dean of Students, 606-257-3754.

Attendance and degree information available by phone, fax, mail. Search requires name plus SSN. Also helpful: date of birth, exact years of attendance. There is no fee.

University of Louisville, Registrar, 2301 S Third St,
Louisville, KY 40292, 502-852-6522 (Fax: 502-852-4776). Hours: 9AM-5PM. Enrollment: 22000. Records go back to 1900. Alumni records are maintained here also. Call 502-852-6186. Degrees granted: Bachelors; Masters. Adverse incident record source- Student Life, 502-852-5787.

Attendance and degree information available by phone, fax, mail. Search requires name plus SSN, date of birth, approximate years of attendance. There is no fee.

Western Kentucky University, Office of the Regis-
trar, Potter Hall, #1 Big Red Wy, Bowling Green, KY 42101-3576, 502-745-3351 (Fax: 502-745-4830). Hours: 8AM-4:30PM. Enrollment: 15000. Alumni records are maintained here also. Call 502-745-4395. Degrees granted: Associate; Bachelors; Masters. Adverse incident record source- Dean of Student Life, 502-745-2791.

Attendance and degree information available by phone, fax, mail. Search requires name plus SSN. Also helpful: date of birth, exact years of attendance. There is no fee.

Trade and Vocational Schools

Ballard County Area Vocational Center, Rte 1, US Hwy 60, Box 214, Barlow, KY 42024, 502-665-5112

Barrett & Company School of Hair Design, 973 Kimberly Sq, Nicholasville, KY 40356, 606-885-9135

Carl D. Perkins Job Corps Center, 363 Meadows Branch Rd, Prestonsburg, KY 41653, 606-886-1037

Computer Education Services, 981 S Third St #106, Louisville, KY 40203, 502-583-2860

Computer School (The), 820 Lane Allen Rd, Lexington, KY 40504, 606-276-1929

Earle C. Clements Job Corps Center, 2302 Hwy 60 E, Morganfield, KY 42437, 502-389-2419

Health Institute of Louisville (The), 612 S Fourth St #400, Louisville, KY 40202, 502-583-6525

Interactive College of Technology (Branch Campus), 11 S Main St, Day Ridge, KY 41097, 606-824-3573

Interactive College of Technology (Branch Campus), 6612 Dixie Hwy #2, Florence, KY 41042, 606-282-8989

Kentucky College of Barbering and Hairstyling, 1230 S Third St, Louisville, KY 40203, 502-634-0521

Kentucky Tech-Ashland State Vocational-Technical School, 4818 Roberts Dr, Ashland, KY 41102, 606-928-6427

Kentucky Tech-Barren County Area Technology Center, 491 Trojan Tr, Glasgow, KY 42141, 502-651-2196

Kentucky Tech-Belfry Area Technology Center, PO Box 280, Belfry, KY 41514, 606-353-4951

Kentucky Tech-Bell County Area Technology Center, Box 199-A, Rte 7, Pineville, KY 40977, 606-337-3094

Kentucky Tech-Boone County Center, 3320 Cougar Path, Hebron, KY 41048, 606-689-7855

Kentucky Tech-Bowling Green State Vocational-Technical School, 1845 Loop Dr, Bowling Green, KY 42101, 502-746-7461

Kentucky Tech-Breathitt County Area Vocational Education Center, PO Box 786, Jackson, KY 41339, 606-666-5153

Kentucky Tech-Breckenridge County Area Vocational Education Ctr, PO Box 68, Harned, KY 40144, 502-756-2138

Kentucky Tech-Bullitt County Area Vocational Education Ctr, 395 High School Dr, Shepherdsville, KY 40165, 502-543-7018

Kentucky Tech-CE McCormick Center, 50 Orchard Ln, Alexandria, KY 41001, 606-635-4101

Kentucky Tech-Caldwell County Area Vocational Education Ctr, PO Box 350, Princeton, KY 42445, 502-365-5563

Kentucky Tech-Carroll County Area Center, 1704 Highland Ave, Carrollton, KY 41008, 502-732-4479

Kentucky Tech-Casey County Area Vocational Education Center, Rte 4, Box 49, Liberty, KY 42539, 606-787-6241

Kentucky Tech-Central Campus, 104 Vo-Tech Rd, Lexington, KY 40510, 606-255-8501

Kentucky Tech-Christian County Area Center, 705 North Elm St, Hopkinsville, KY 42240, 502-886-3734

Kentucky Tech-Clark County Center, 650 Boone Ave, Winchester, KY 40391, 606-744-1250

Kentucky Tech-Clay County Area Vocational Education Center, Rte 2, Box 256, Manchester, KY 40962, 606-598-2194

Kentucky Tech-Clinton County Area Vocational Education Center, Rte 5 Box 5033, Albany, KY 42602, 606-387-6448

Kentucky Tech-Corbin Area Vocational Education Center, 1909 S Snyder Ave, Corbin, KY 40701, 606-528-5338

Kentucky Tech-Cumberland Valley Health Occupations Center, PO Box 187, Pineville, KY 40977, 606-337-3106

Kentucky Tech-Danville School of Health Occupations, 340 S Third St, Danville, KY 40423, 606-236-2053

Kentucky Tech-Daviess County Vocational-Technical School, 1901 Southeastern Pkwy, Owensboro, KY 42303, 502-687-7620

Kentucky Tech-Elizabethtown State Vocational-Technical School, 505 University Dr, Elizabethtown, KY 42701, 502-766-5137

Kentucky Tech-Fulton County Area Vocational Education Center, 2720 Moscow Ave, Hickman, KY 42050, 502-236-2517

Kentucky Tech-Garrard County Center, 306 W Maple Ave, Lancaster, KY 40444, 606-792-2144

Kentucky Tech-Garth Area Vocational Education Center, HC79, Box 205, Martin, KY 41649, 606-285-3088

Kentucky Tech-Glasgow Health Occupations School, 1215 N Race St, Glasgow, KY 42141, 502-651-5673

Kentucky Tech-Green County Area Vocational Education Center, PO Box 167, Greensburg, KY 42743, 502-932-4263

Kentucky Tech-Greenup County Area Vocational Education Center, PO Box 4009, South Shore, KY 41144, 606-437-9344

Kentucky Tech-Harlan State Vocational-Technical School, 21 Ballpark Rd, Harlan, KY 40831, 606-573-1506

Kentucky Tech-Harrison County Center, 551 Webster Ave, Cynthiana, KY 41031, 606-234-5286

Kentucky Tech-Harrodsburg Center, PO Box 628, Harrodsburg, KY 40330, 606-734-9329

Kentucky Tech-Hazard State Vocational-Technical School, 101 Vo-Tech Dr, Hazard, KY 41701, 606-435-6101

Kentucky Tech-Henderson County Area Center, 2440 Zion Rd, Henderson, KY 42420, 502-827-3810

Kentucky Tech-JD Patton Center, 3234 Turkeyfoot Rd, Fort Mitchell, KY 41017, 606-341-2266

Kentucky Tech-Jefferson State Vocational-Technical Center, 727 W Chestnut St, Louisville, KY 40203, 502-595-4136

Kentucky Tech-Kentucky Advanced Technology Center, 1127 Morgantown Rd, Bowling Green, KY 42101, 502-746-7807

Kentucky Tech-Knott County Area Vocational Education Center, HCR 60, Box 1100, Hindman, KY 41822, 606-785-5350

Kentucky Tech-Knox County Area Vocational Education Center, 210 Wall St, Barbourville, KY 40906, 606-546-5320

Kentucky Tech-Laurel County State Vocational-Technical School, 235 S Laurel, London, KY 40741, 606-864-7311

Kentucky Tech-Lee County Area Vocational Education Center, PO Box B, Beattyville, KY 41311, 606-464-5018

Kentucky Tech-Leslie County Area Vocational Education Center, PO Box 902, Hyden, KY 41749, 606-672-2859

Kentucky Tech-Letcher County Area Vocational Education Center, 610 Circle Dr, Whitesburg, KY 41858, 606-633-5053

Kentucky Tech-Madison County Center, PO Box 809, Richmond, KY 40475, 606-624-4520

Kentucky Tech-Madisonville Health Occupations School, 750 N Luffoon, Madisonville, KY 42431, 502-824-7552

Kentucky Tech-Madisonville State Vocational-Technical School, 150 School Ave, Madisonville, KY 42431, 502-824-7544

Kentucky Tech-Marion County Area Vocational Education Center, 721 E Main, Lebanon, KY 40033, 502-692-3155

Kentucky Tech-Martin County Area Vocational Education Center, HC 68 Box 2177, Inez, KY 41224, 606-298-3879

Kentucky Tech-Mason County Area Vocational Education Center, 646 Kent Station Rd, Maysville, KY 41056, 606-759-7101

Kentucky Tech-Mayfield Area Vocational Education Center, 710 Doughtit Rd, Mayfield, KY 42066, 502-247-4710

Kentucky Tech-Mayo State Vocational-Technical School, 513 Third St, Paintsville, KY 41240, 606-789-5321

Kentucky Tech-Meade County Area Vocational Education Center, 110 Greer St, Brandenburg, KY 40108, 502-422-3955

Kentucky Tech-Millard Area Vocational Education Center, 7925 Millard Hwy, Pikeville, KY 41501, 606-437-6059

Kentucky Tech-Monroe County Area Vocational Education Center, 309 Eberton St, Tompkinsville, KY 42167, 502-487-8261

Kentucky Tech-Montgomery County Area Vocational Education Center, 682 Woodford Dr, Mount Sterling, KY 40353, 606-498-1103

Kentucky Tech-Morgan County Area Vocational Education Center, PO Box 249, West Liberty, KY 41472, 606-743-4321

Kentucky Tech-Muhlenberg County Area Vocational Education Center, 201 Airport Rd, Greenville, KY 42345, 502-338-1271

Kentucky Tech-Murray Area Vocational Education Center, 1800 Sycamore St, Murray, KY 42071, 502-753-1870

Kentucky Tech-Nelson County Area Vocational Education Center, 1060 Bloomfield Rd, Bardstown, KY 40004, 502-348-9096

Kentucky Tech-Northern Campbell County Campus, 90 Campbell Dr, Highland Heights, KY 41076, 606-441-2010

Kentucky Tech-Northern Kentucky Campus, 1025 Amsterdam Rd, Covington, KY 41011, 606-292-2930

Kentucky Tech-Northern Kentucky Health Occupations Center, 790 Thomas More Pkwy, Edgewood, KY 41017, 606-341-5200

Kentucky Tech-Ohio County Area Vocational Education Center, 1406 Main St, Hartford, KY 42347, 502-274-9612

Kentucky Tech-Oldham County Area Vocational Education Center, PO Box 127, Buckner, KY 40010, 502-222-0131

Kentucky Tech-Owensboro Vocational-Technical School, 1501 Frederica St, Owensboro, KY 42301, 502-825-6546

Kentucky Tech-Paducah Area Vocational Education Center, 2400 Adams St, Paducah, KY 42001, 502-443-6592

Kentucky Tech-Phelps Area Vocational Education Center, 11500 Phelps, Phelps, KY 41553, 606-456-8136

Kentucky Tech-Rockcastle County Area Vocational Education Center, PO Box 275, Mount Vernon, KY 40456, 606-256-4346

Kentucky Tech-Rowan State Vocational-Technical School, 609 Viking Dr, Morehead, KY 40351, 606-783-1538

Kentucky Tech-Russell Area Vocational Education Center, 705 Red Devil Ln, Russell, KY 41169, 606-836-1256

Kentucky Tech-Russell County Area Vocational Education Center, PO Box 599, Russell Springs, KY 42642, 502-866-6175

Kentucky Tech-Russellville Area Vocational Education Center, 1103 W 9th St, Russellville, KY 42276, 502-726-8432

Kentucky Tech-Shelby County Area Vocational Education Center, 230 Rocket Ln, Shelbyville, KY 40065, 502-633-6554

Kentucky Tech-Somerset State Vocational Education Center, 230 Airport Rd, Somerset, KY 42501, 606-677-4049

Kentucky Tech-Wayne County Area Vocational Education Center, 150 Cardinal Wy, Monticello, KY 42633, 606-348-8424

Kentucky Tech-Webster County Area Vocational Education Center, 325 State Rd, Dixon, KY 42409, 502-639-5035

Kentucky Tech-West Kentucky State Vocational-Technical School, 5200 Blandville Rd, Paducah, KY 42002, 502-554-9754

Madisonville Health Technology Center, PO Box 608, Madisonville, KY 42431, 502-825-6546

New Image Careers, 109 E Sixth St, Corbin, KY 40701, 606-528-1490

Nu-Tek Academy of Beauty, Maysville Rd, Mount Sterling, KY 40391, 606-498-4460

PJ's College of Cosmetology, 1901 Russellville Rd, Bowling Green, KY 42101, 502-842-8149

PJ's College of Cosmetology, 124 W Washington St, Glasgow, KY 42141, 502-651-6553

Roy's of Louisville Beauty Academy, 151 Chenoweth Ln, Louisville, KY 40207, 502-897-9401

Roy's of Louisville Beauty Academy (Branch Campus), 5200 Dixie Hwy, Louisville, KY 40216, 502-448-1016

School of Business and Banking, 5045 Preston Hwy, Louisville, KY 40213, 502-969-2004

Spencerian College, PO Box 16418, Louisville, KY 40216, 502-447-1000

Tri-State Beauty Academy, 219 W Main St, Morehead, KY 40351, 606-784-6725

State Licensing & Business Registration Quick Finder Index

Architecture, Engineering & Surveying
Architect #7 (2400).. ☎ 606-246-2069
Engineer #39 (10500)..................................... ☎ 502-573-2680
Engineer and Land Surveyor Firm #39 .... ☎ 502-573-2680
Geologist #15... ✉ 502-564-3296
Landscape Architect #39 (250) .... ☎ 502-573-3263
Surveyor #39 (2000)...................................... ☎ 502-573-2680

Business - Court & Legal Services
Attorney #2 (12090) .... ☎ 502-564-3795
Lobbyist #27 (1100) .... ☎ 502-573-2863
Notary Public #30.. ☎ 502-564-3490

Business - General Services
Auctioneer #4 .... ☎ 502-595-4453
Public Accountant-CPA #3 (5000) .... ☎ 502-595-3037

Construction & Manufacturing
Blacksmith #31 .... ☎ 606-246-2040
Boiler Contractor #26 502-564-8044
Boiler Installer/Inspector #26 502-564-8044
Building Inspector #26 502-564-8044
Electrical Contractor #26................................ 502-564-8044
Electrical Inspector #26 502-564-8044
Elevator Inspector #26................................... 502-564-8044
Manufacturer #12 .... ✉ 502-573-1580
Plans & Specifications Inspector #26.............. 502-564-8044
Plumber #26... 502-564-8044
Wholesaler #12.. ✉ 502-573-1580

Education
Proprietary Education School #15.................. ✉ 502-564-3296
School Guidance Counselor #25 .... ☎ 502-564-4606
School Media Librarian #25 .... ☎ 502-564-4606
School Principal #25....................................... ☎ 502-564-4606
Teacher #25... ☎ 502-564-4606

Environmental & Agriculture
Compost Operator #24.................................... ☎ 502-565-6716
Drinking Water Treatment/Distribution
　System Operator #29 (3030) .... ✉ 502-564-3410
Fur Buyer #20 .... ☎ 502-564-4224
Fur Processor #20 .... ☎ 502-564-4224
Landfarm Operator #24 .... ☎ 502-564-6716
Landfill Manager #24 .... ☎ 502-564-6716
Landfill Operator #24 (250)........................... ☎ 502-564-6716
Milk Sampler-Weigher #44 (450) .... ☎ 606-257-2785
Milk Tester #44 (60) .... ☎ 606-257-2785
Miner #22.. ☎ 606-254-0367
Mining Blaster #22 .... ☎ 606-254-0367
Mining Fire Boss #22 .... ☎ 606-254-0367
Mining Foreman #22 .... ☎ 606-254-0367
Mining Inspector #22..................................... ☎ 606-254-0367
Mining Safety Instructor #22.......................... ☎ 606-254-0367
Pesticide Applicator #16 (4939) .... ☎ 502-564-7274
Pesticide Dealer #16 (495)............................. ☎ 502-564-7274
Pesticide Exterminator #16 (388) .... ☎ 502-564-7274
Veterinarian #15.. ✉ 502-564-3296
Veterinarian/Veterinarian Assistant #31 .... ☎ 606-246-2040
Veterinary Dental Technician #31.................. ☎ 606-246-2949
Wastewater System Operator #29.................. ✉ 502-564-3410

Financial - Real Estate, Insurance & Banking
Bank #19... 502-573-3390
Broker/Dealer/Agent #19............................... 502-573-3390
Check Casher #19 502-573-3390

Check Seller #19.......................................✉ 502-573-3390
Insurance Adjuster #21...502-564-3630
Insurance Agent #21...502-564-3630
Insurance Consultant #21 502-564-3630
Insurance Solicitor #21 (450)........................☎ 502-564-6078
Investment Advisor/Representative #19 ....✉ 502-573-3390
Loan Company #19 502-573-3390
Mortgage Broker #19 502-573-3390
Mortgage Loan Company #19......................✉ 502-573-3390
Property Valuation Administrator #34 502-564-8338
Real Estate Appraiser #32 (1200) ....☎ 606-246-2017
Real Estate Broker #33 (11000) ....☎ 502-425-4273
Real Estate Sales Associate #33 ....☎ 502-424-4273
Savings & Loan #19 ....✉ 502-573-3390
Securities Agent #18...502-573-3370
Securities Broker/Dealer #18 502-573-3370

Health & Beauty
Barber #5 (3174)...✉ 502-595-4754
Chiropractor #35 (1031).................................☎ 502-651-2522
Coroner #17 (300) ....☎ 606-622-6165
Cosmetologist #37 ....✉ 502-564-4262
Dental Hygienist #6 (1423) ....☎ 502-423-0573
Dental Laboratory #6.......................................☎ 502-423-0573
Dental Laboratory Technician #6 (1314).......☎ 502-423-0573
Dentist #6 (2717)..☎ 502-423-0573
Dietitian/Nutritionist #15................................✉ 502-564-3296
Embalmer #36 (4) ....☎ 502-241-3918
Emergency Medical Technician #14 (14500)
....☎ 502-564-8950
Funeral Director #36 (505)..............................☎ 502-241-3918
Health Care Facility #13..................................☎ 502-564-2800
Hearing Instrument Specialist #15 ....✉ 502-564-3296
Medical Doctor/Surgeon (Medical Doctor
  /Osteopathic Doctor) #41 (11734)..............☎ 502-429-8046
Nurse #9 (58718)...☎ 502-329-7000
Nurse Anesthetist #9 (1293)............................☎ 502-329-7000
Nurse Clinical Specialist #9 ....☎ 502-329-7000
Nurse Midwife #9...☎ 502-329-7000
Nurses Aide Instructor #40..............................☎ 502-564-2800
Nursing Home Administrator #15.................✉ 502-564-3296
Occupational Therapist #15............................✉ 502-564-3296
Ophthalmic Dispenser/Optician
  /Apprentices #10 (800) ....☎ 502-564-3296
Optometrist #11 (573) ....☎ 502-863-5816
Osteopathic Physician #8 (329)........................502-429-8046
Paramedic #41 ....☎ 502-564-8950
Pharmacist #12 (4500).....................................✉ 502-573-1580
Pharmacy #12 ....✉ 502-573-1580
Physical Therapist #38 (1800)........................☎ 502-595-4687

Physical Therapist Assistant #38 ....☎ 502-595-4687
Physician's Assistant #41 (250) ....☎ 502-429-8046
Podiatrist #43 (90) ....☎ 502-897-2047
Radiation Operator #13 (5549)........................☎ 502-564-3700
Respiratory Care Practitioner #15 ....✉ 502-564-3296
Respiratory Therapist #15.................................✉ 502-564-3296
Sanitarian #13 ....☎ 502-564-7900
Speech-Language Pathologist/Audiologist #15
....✉ 502-564-3296

Investigations & Security
Fire Alarm System Inspector #26 502-564-8044
Fire Protection Sprinkler Installer #26 502-564-8044
Law Enforcement Training Instructor #17 (200)
....☎ 606-622-6165
Police Officer #17 (7000) ....☎ 606-622-6165
Polygraph Examiner #28 (36)..........................☎ 502-564-7110
Polygraph Examiner-Trainee #28 ....☎ 502-564-7110
Suppression System Inspector #26 502-564-8044

Social Services
Psychologist #15 ....✉ 502-564-3296
Rehabilitation Counselor #23 ....☎ 502-564-4440
Social Worker #15 ....✉ 502-564-3296

Sports & Entertainment
Athletic Commission/Boxer/Wrestler/Trainer
  /Manager #15...✉ 502-564-3296
Commercial Fishing License #20 ....☎ 502-564-4224
Farm Manager/Trainer/Owner #31 ....☎ 606-254-7021
Guide, Hunting & Fishing #20 (152) ....☎ 502-564-4224
Horse Owner #31 ....☎ 606-254-7021
Horse Trainer #31 ....☎ 606-254-7021
Jockey #31 ....☎ 606-254-7021
Jockey Agent #31...☎ 606-254-7021
Liquor License #1 (4700) ....☎ 502-573-4850
Malt Beverage Distributor #1 ....☎ 502-573-4850
Pari-Mutuel Clerk #31 ....☎ 606-254-7021
Pay Lake Operator #20 ....☎ 502-564-4224
Racing Official #31..☎ 606-254-7021
Racing Vendor/Vendor Employee #31...........☎ 606-246-2040
Racing-Authorized Agent #31 ....☎ 606-246-2040
Stable Employee #31 ....☎ 606-254-7021
Taxidermist #20 ....☎ 502-564-4224
Track Occupational Employee (Popcorn
  Seller, etc.) #31...☎ 606-254-7021

Transportation
Driver Training Instructor #42........................☎ 502-564-8292

State Licensing & Business Registration Agency Information

(1) Alcoholic Beverage Control Department, 1003 Twilight Trail, Suite A-2, Frankfort, KY 40601, 502-564-4850, Fax: 502-564-1442

(2) Bar Association, 514 W Main St, Frankfort, KY 40601, 502-564-3795, Fax: 502-564-3225

(3) Board of Accountancy, 332 W Broadway, Suite 310, Louisville, KY 40202, 502-595-3037, Fax: 502-595-4281

(4) Board of Auctioneers, 9112 Leesgate Rd, Louisville, KY 40222, 502-595-4453, Fax: 502-595-4854

(5) Board of Barbering, 9114 Leesgate Rd, Louisville, KY 40222, 502-595-4754, Fax: 502-429-5223

(6) Board of Dentistry, 10101 Linn Station Rd, Louisville, KY 40223, 502-423-0573, Fax: 502-423-1239

(7) Board of Examiners & Registration of Architects, 841 Corporate Drive, Suite 200B, Lexington, KY 40503, 606-246-2069, Fax: 606-246-2431

(8) Board of Medical Licensure, 310 Whittington, Suite 1B, Louisville, KY 40222, 502-429-8046

(9) Board of Nursing, 312 Whittington Pky, Suite 300, Louisville, KY 40222, 502-329-7000, Fax: 502-329-7011

(10) Board of Ophthalmic Dispensers, PO Box 456, Frankfort, KY 40602, 502-564-3296 X227, Fax: 502-564-4818

(11) Board of Optometric Examiners, 1000 W Main St, Georgetown, KY 40324, 502-863-5816, Fax: 502-863-0176

(12) Board of Pharmacy, 1228 US 127 South, Frankfort, KY 40601, 502-573-1580, Fax: 502-573-1582

(13) Cabinet for Health Services, Division of Licensing & Regulations, CHR Bldg 4th Flr East, Frankfort, KY 40621-0001, 502-564-7900

(14) Cabinet for Human Resources, Emergency Medical Services Branch, 275 Main St, 1 R East Wing, Frankfort, KY 40621, 502-564-8950, Fax: 502-564-6533

(15) Department of Administration, Division of Occupations & Professions, PO Box 456, Frankfort, KY 40602, 502-564-3296, Fax: 502-564-4818

(16) Department of Agriculture, Division of Pesticide, 100 Fair Oak Ln, Frankfort, KY 40601, 502-564-7274, Fax: 502-564-3773

(17) Department of Criminal Justice Training, 3137 Kit Carson DR, Funderburk Bldg, Richmond, KY 40475, 606-622-6165, Fax: 606-622-2740

(18) Department of Financial Institutions, 911 Leawood Dr, Frankfort, KY 40601.ll Department of Financial Institutions, Division of Law & Regulatory Compliance, 477 Versailles Rd, Frankfort, KY 40601, 502-573-3390, Fax: 502-573-8787

(19) Department of Fish & Wildlife, 1 Game Farm Rd, Frankfort, KY 40602, 502-564-4224, Fax: 502-564-6508

(20) Department of Insurance, Licensing Division, 215 W Main St, Frankfort, KY 40601, 502-564-3630, Fax: 502-564-6090

(21) Department of Mines & Minerals, PO Box 14080, Lexington, KY 40512, 606-246-2026, Fax: 606-246-2038

(22) Department of Vocational Rehabilitation, 209 St Clair St, Frankfort, KY 40601, 502-564-4440, Fax: 502-564-6745

(23) Division of Waste Management, 18 Reilly Rd, Frankfort, KY 40601, 502-564-6716, Fax: 502-564-4049

(24) Education Department, Teacher Education/Certification Office, Capitol Plaza Tower, 500 Mero St, 18th Floor, Frankfort, KY 40601, 502-573-4606

(25) Housing, Buildings & Construction Department, 1047 US 127 S, Suite 1, Frankfort, KY 40601, 502-564-8044

(26) Kentucky Legislative Ethics Commission, 22 Mill Creek Park, Frankfort, KY 40601, 502-573-2863, Fax: 502-573-2929

(27) Kentucky State Police, Polygraph Unit, 1250 Louisville Rd, Frankfort, KY 40601, 502-564-7110, Fax: 502-564-5956

(28) Natural Resources & Environmental Protection, Division of Water, 14 Reilly Rd., Frankfort, KY 40601, 502-564-3410, Fax: 502-564-4245

(29) Office of Secretary of State, Notary Commissions, Capitol Bldg, PO Box 821, Frankfort, KY 40602-0821, 502-564-3490 X413, Fax: 502-564-4075

(30) Racing Commission, 4063 Iron Works Pike, Lexington, KY 40511, 606-254-2040, Fax: 606-246-2039

(31) Real Estate Appraisers Board, 3572 Iron Works Pike, Suite 308, Lexington, KY 40511-8410, 606-255-0144, Fax: 606-246-2020

(32) Real Estate Commission, 10200 Linn Station Rd, Suite 201, Louisville, KY 40223, 502-425-4273, Fax: 502-595-3040

(33) Revenue Cabinet, Department of Property Taxation, 592 E Main St, Frankfort, KY 40620, 502-564-5620

(34) State Board of Chiropractic Examiners, 211 S Green St, PO Box 183, Glasgow, KY 42142-0183, 502-651-2522, Fax: 502-651-8784

(35) State Board of Embalmers & Funeral Directors, PO Box 324, Crestwood, KY 40014, 502-241-3918, Fax: 502-241-4297

(36) State Board of Hairdressers & Cosmetologists, 314 W Second St, Frankfort, KY 40601, 502-564-4262

(37) State Board of Physical Therapy, 9110 Leesgate Rd, Suite 6, Louisville, KY 40222-5159, 502-595-4687, Fax: 502-595-4687

(38) State Board of Registration, Professional Engineers & Land Surveyors, 160 Democrat Dr, Frankfort, KY 40601, 502-573-2680, Fax: 502-573-6687

(39) State Department of Education, Teacher Certification, 275 E Main St, 4th Floor East, Frankfort, KY 40621, 502-564-2800

(40) State Medical Board, 310 Whittington Pky, Suite 1B, Louisville, KY 40222, 502-429-8046

(41) State Police Driver Testing Section, 919 Versailles Rd, Frankfort, KY 40601, 502-564-8292, Fax: 502-564-8314

(42) Stiver's Agency, 2414 Tavener Dr, Louisville, KY 40242-4000, 502-897-2047, Fax: 502-425-1333

(43) University of Kentucky Regulatory Services, College of Agriculture, Regulatory Services Bldg, Room 103, Lexington, KY 40546-0275, 606-257-2785, Fax: 606-323-9931

Louisiana

Capitol: Baton Rouge (East Baton Rouge Parish)	
State Population	4.3 Million
Number of Degree Granting Institutions:	34
Number of State Licensing & Business Registration Agencies:	103

Degree Granting Educational Institutions

Bossier Parish Community College, Registrar, 2719 Airline Dr at I-220, Bossier City, LA 71111, 318-746-9851 (Fax: 318-742-8664). Hours: 8AM-4PM M-Th, 8AM-4PM F. Enrollment: 4700. Records go back to 1967. Alumni records are maintained here at the same phone number. Degrees granted: Associate. Adverse incident record source- Student Affairs, 318-746-9851 X64.

Attendance and degree information available by phone, fax, mail. Search requires name only. Also helpful: SSN, approximate years of attendance. There is no fee.

Centenary College of Louisiana, Registrar, PO Box 41188, Shreveport, LA 71134-1188, 318-869-5146 (Fax: 318-869-5026). Hours: 8AM-4:30PM. Enrollment: 1000. Records go back to 1920's. Degrees granted: Bachelors; Masters.

Attendance and degree information available by phone, mail. Search requires name plus SSN. Also helpful: date of birth, exact years of attendance. There is no fee.

Delgado Community College, Registrar, 501 City Park Ave, New Orleans, LA 70119, 504-483-4153 (Fax: 504-483-4090). Hours: 8:30AM-4:30PM. Enrollment: 10952. Records go back to 1924. Alumni records are maintained here also. Call 504-483-4400. Degrees granted: Associate.

Attendance and degree information available by phone, fax, mail. Search requires name plus SSN, date of birth, exact years of attendance. There is no fee.

Delta School of Business and Technology, Registrar, 517 Broad St, Lake Charles, LA 70601, 318-439-5765 (Fax: 318-436-5151). Hours: 8AM-5PM. Degrees granted: Associate.

Attendance and degree information available by phone, fax, mail. Search requires name plus SSN, approximate years of attendance. Also helpful: date of birth, exact years of attendance. There is no fee.

Dillard University, Registrar, 2601 Gentilly Blvd, New Orleans, LA 70122, 504-286-4688. Hours: 8AM-5PM. Enrollment: 1562. Records go back to 1898. Alumni records are main-

tained here also. Call 504-286-4666. Degrees granted: Bachelors. Adverse incident record source- Security, 504-286-4793.

Attendance and degree information available by phone, mail. Search requires name plus SSN, approximate years of attendance. There is no fee.

Grambling State University, Registrar's Office, PO Box 589, Grambling, LA 71245, 318-274-2385 (Fax: 318-274-3292). Hours: 8MA-5PM. Enrollment: 7400. Records go back to 1930's. Alumni records are maintained here also. Call 318-274-2385. Degrees granted: Associate; Bachelors; Masters; Doctorate. Adverse incident record source- Office of the Provost, 318-274-2291.

Attendance and degree information available by phone, mail. Search requires name plus SSN. Also helpful: date of birth, exact years of attendance. There is no fee.

Grantham College of Engineering, Registrar, 34641 Grantham College Rd, PO Box 5700, Slidell, LA 70469, 504-649-4191 (Fax: 504-649-4183). Hours: 9AM-5:30PM. Enrollment: 1200. Records go back to 1951. Degrees granted: Bachelors.

Attendance and degree information available by phone, fax, mail. Search requires name only. There is no fee.

Louisiana College, Registrar, 1140 College Dr, Pineville, LA 71359, 318-487-7222 (Fax: 318-487-7191). Hours: 8AM-4:30PM. Enrollment: 1024. Records go back to 1990. Alumni records are maintained here also. Call 318-487-7301. Degrees granted: Associate; Bachelors; Masters.

Attendance and degree information available by fax, mail. Search requires name plus SSN, date of birth, approximate years of attendance, signed release. Also helpful: exact years of attendance. There is no fee.

Louisiana State University Medical Center, Registrar, 433 Bolivar St, New Orleans, LA 70112, 504-568-4829 (Fax: 504-568-5545). Hours: 8AM-4:30PM. Enrollment: 3074. Records go back to 1979. Alumni records are maintained here also. Call 504-568-4894. Degrees granted: Associate; Bachelors; Masters; Doctorate; PhD. Adverse incident record source- Student Affairs.

Attendance and degree information available by phone, mail. Search requires name plus SSN, date of birth, approximate years of attendance. There is no fee.

Louisiana State University and Agricultural & Mechanical College, Office of Records & Registration, 112 Thomas Boyd Hall, Baton Rouge, LA 70803, 504-388-1686 (Fax: 504-388-5991). Hours: 8:30AM-5PM. Enrollment: 22950. Records go back to 1960's. Alumni records are maintained here at the same phone number. Degrees granted: Bachelors.

Attendance and degree information available by phone, fax, mail. Search requires name plus SSN, exact years of attendance. There is no fee.

Louisiana State University at Alexandria, Registrar, 8100 Hwy 71 S, Alexandria, LA 71302, 318-473-6541 (Fax: 318-473-6418). Hours: 8AM-4:30PM. Enrollment: 1961. Records go back to 1960. Degrees granted: Associate.

Attendance information available by phone, fax, mail. Search requires name only. Also helpful: SSN, exact years of attendance. There is no fee.

Degree information available by phone, fax, mail. Search requires name only. Also helpful: SSN, date of birth, exact years of attendance. There is no fee.

Louisiana State University at Eunice, Registrar, PO Box 1129, Eunice, LA 70535, 318-457-7311 (Fax: 318-546-6620). Hours: 8AM-4:30PM. Enrollment: 2800. Records go back to 1967. Alumni records are maintained here at the same phone number. Degrees granted: Associate.

Attendance and degree information available by fax, mail. Search requires name plus SSN. Also helpful: date of birth, exact years of attendance. There is no fee.

Louisiana State University at Shreveport, Registrar, One University Pl, Shreveport, LA 71115, 318-797-5061 (Fax: 318-797-5286). Hours: 8AM-4:30PM. Enrollment: 4500. Records go back to 1957. Alumni records are maintained here also. Call 318-797-5202. Degrees granted: Bachelors; Masters; Specialist. Adverse incident record source- Student Affairs, 318-797-5116.

Attendance and degree information available by phone, mail. Search requires name plus SSN, date of birth, approximate years of attendance. There is no fee.

Louisiana Tech University, Registrar, PO Box 3155 Tech Station, Ruston, LA 71272, 318-257-2176 (Fax: 318-257-4041). Hours: 8AM-5PM. Enrollment: 10000. Records go back to 1894. Alumni records are maintained here at the same phone number. Degrees granted: Associate; Bachelors; Masters; Doctorate. Adverse incident record source- 318-257-4018.

Attendance and degree information available by phone, fax, mail. Search requires name only. Also helpful: SSN, date of birth, exact years of attendance. There is no fee.

Loyola University, Registrar, 6363 St. Charles Ave, New Orleans, LA 70118, 504-865-3237 (Fax: 504-865-2110). Hours: 8:30AM-4:45PM. Enrollment: 4485. Records go back to 1920. Alumni records are maintained here at the same phone number. Degrees granted: Bachelors; Masters; Law School. Adverse incident record source- Public Safety, 504-865-3434.

Attendance and degree information available by phone, mail. Search requires name plus SSN. There is no fee.

McNeese State University, Registrar, 4100 Ryan St, Lake Charles, LA 70609, 318-475-5356 (Fax: 318-475-5189). Hours: 7:45AM-4:30PM. Enrollment: 7380. Records go back to 1939. Degrees granted: Associate; Bachelors; Masters.

Attendance and degree information available by phone, fax, mail. Search requires name plus SSN, date of birth, approximate years of attendance. There is no fee.

New Orleans Baptist Theological Seminary, Registrar, 3939 Gentilly Blvd, New Orleans, LA 70126, 504-282-4455 X3337 (Fax: 504-286-3591). Hours: 8AM-5PM. Enrollment: 2300. Records go back to 1919. Alumni records are maintained here at the same phone number. Degrees granted: Associate; Bachelors; Masters.

Attendance and degree information available by phone, fax, mail. Search requires name plus SSN. There is no fee.

Nicholls State University, Office of Records, PO Box 2059, Thibodaux, LA 70310, 504-448-4153 (Fax: 504-448-4929). Hours: 8AM-4:30PM. Enrollment: 7300. Records go back to 1948. Alumni Records Office: PO Box 2158, Thibodaux, LA 70310. Degrees granted: Associate; Bachelors; Masters. Special programs- Center for Women in Government. Adverse incident record source- Student Life, 504-448-4525.

Attendance information available by mail. Search requires name plus SSN, date of birth, signed release. Also helpful: approximate years of attendance. There is no fee.

Degree information available by phone, mail. Search requires name plus SSN, date of birth. Also helpful: approximate years of attendance. There is no fee.

Northeast Louisiana University, Registrar, 700 University Ave, Monroe, LA 71209, 318-342-5262 (Fax: 318-342-5274). Hours: 8AM-4:30PM. Enrollment: 10975. Records go back to 1932. Alumni records are maintained here also. Call 318-342-5420. Degrees granted: Associate; Bachelors; Masters; Doctorate. Adverse incident record source- Student Life, 318-342-5230.

Attendance and degree information available by phone, fax, mail. Search requires name plus SSN, date of birth. Also helpful: exact years of attendance. There is no fee.

Northwestern State University, Registrar, College Ave, Natchitoches, LA 71497, 318-357-6171 (Fax: 318-357-5823). Hours: 8AM-4:30PM. Enrollment: 9040. Records go back to 1885. Alumni records are maintained here at the same phone number. Degrees granted: Associate; Bachelors; Masters; Doctorate. Certification: Teacher. Special programs- Louisiana Scholar's College, 318-357-4577. Adverse incident record source- News Bureau, 318-357-4577.

Attendance and degree information available by phone, fax, mail. Search requires name only. Also helpful: SSN, date of birth, exact years of attendance. There is no fee.

Notre Dame Seminary Graduate School of Theology, Registrar, 2901 S Carrollton Ave, New Orleans, LA 70118-4391, 504-866-7426. Hours: 8AM-4PM. Enrollment: 125. Records go back to 1950. Alumni records are maintained here at the same phone number. Degrees granted: Masters.

Attendance information available by mail. Search requires name plus signed release. Also helpful: SSN. There is no fee.

Degree information available by written request only. Search requires name plus signed release. Also helpful: SSN. There is no fee.

Nunez Community College, Registrar, 3700 LaFontaine St, Chalmette, LA 70043, 504-278-7440 X222 (Fax: 504-278-7353). Hours: 8AM-7PM M-W 8AM-4:30PM Th,F. Enrollment: 852. Formerly Elaine P. Nunez Community College Records go back to 1966. Degrees granted: Associate. Special programs- Environmental Technology, 504-278-7440. Adverse incident record source- VP of Student Affairs, 504-278-7440 X216.

Attendance and degree information available by phone, fax, mail. Search requires name only. Also helpful: SSN, date of birth, exact years of attendance. There is no fee.

Nunez Community College, (Branch), Registrar, PO Drawer 944, Port Sulphur, LA 70083, 504-564-2701. Records

are not housed here. They are located at Nunez Community College, Registrar, 3700 LaFontaine St, Chalmette, LA 70043.

Our Lady of Holy Cross College, Registrar, 4123
Woodland Dr, New Orleans, LA 70131, 504-394-7744. Hours: 8:30AM-5PM. Enrollment: 1350. Records go back to 1916. Alumni records are maintained here at the same phone number. Degrees granted: Associate; Bachelors; Masters.

Attendance information available by phone, fax, mail. Search requires name plus SSN. Also helpful: exact years of attendance. There is no fee.

Degree information available by written request only. Search requires name plus SSN. Also helpful: date of birth, exact years of attendance. There is no fee.

Remington College, Registrar, 303 Rue Louis XIV,
Lafayette, LA 70508, 318-981-4010 (Fax: 318-983-7130). Hours: 7:30AM-9PM. Records go back to 1991. Formerly known as Southern Technical College. Degrees granted: Associate.

Attendance and degree information available by phone, fax, mail. Search requires name plus SSN, approximate years of attendance. Also helpful: exact years of attendance. There is no fee.

Southeastern Louisiana University, Registrar,
PO Box 784 University Station, Hammond, LA 70402, 504-549-2062 (Fax: 504-549-5632). Hours: 7:45AM-4:30PM. Enrollment: 14377. Records go back to 1925. Alumni records are maintained here also. Call 504-549-2150. Degrees granted: Masters. Adverse incident record source- Dean of Students, 504-549-2212.

Attendance and degree information available by phone, fax, mail. Search requires name plus SSN, approximate years of attendance. There is no fee.

Southern University & Agricultural & Mech. College at Baton Rouge, Registrar, Southern Branch
PO Box 9454, Baton Rouge, LA 70813, 504-771-5050 (Fax: 504-771-5064). Hours: 8AM-5PM. Enrollment: 10359. Records go back to 1920's. Alumni records are maintained here also. Call 504-771-4200. Degrees granted: Associate; Bachelors; Masters; Doctorate.

Attendance information available by phone, fax, mail. Search requires name plus SSN, exact years of attendance. Also helpful: date of birth, approximate years of attendance. There is no fee.

Degree information available by phone, fax, mail. Search requires name plus SSN, exact years of attendance. Also helpful: date of birth. There is no fee.

Southern University at New Orleans, Registrar,
6400 Press Dr, New Orleans, LA 70126, 504-286-5175 (Fax: 504-286-5131). Hours: 8AM-5PM. Enrollment: 3810. Records go back to 1967. Alumni records are maintained here also. Call 504-286-5341. Degrees granted: Masters.

Attendance and degree information available by phone, fax, mail. Search requires name plus SSN. There is no fee.

Southern University/Shreveport Bossier,
Registrar, 3050 Martin Luther King, Jr. Dr, Shreveport, LA

71107, 318-674-3343 (Fax: 318-674-3331). Hours: 8AM-5PM. Enrollment: 1500. Records go back to 1967. Degrees granted: Associate. Adverse incident record source- Student Affairs.

Attendance and degree information available by phone, mail. Search requires name plus SSN. There is no fee.

St. Joseph Seminary College, Registrar, St Bene-
dict, LA 70457, 504-892-1800 (Fax: 504-892-3723). Hours: 8AM-5PM. Enrollment: 65. Records go back to 1891. Alumni records are maintained here at the same phone number. Degrees granted: Bachelors. Adverse incident record source- President.

Attendance and degree information available by phone, fax, mail. Search requires name plus SSN. Also helpful: date of birth. There is no fee.

Tulane University, Office of the Registrar, 110 Gibson
Hall, New Orleans, LA 70118, 504-865-5231 (Fax: 504-865-6760). Hours: 8:30AM-5PM. Enrollment: 11000. Alumni Records Office: Alumni Association, 6319 Willow St, New Orleans, LA 70118. Degrees granted: Associate; Bachelors; Masters; Doctorate. Special programs- School of Medicine, 504-588-5497: School of Public Health & Tropical Medicine, 504-588-5387.

Attendance and degree information available by phone, fax, mail. Search requires name plus approximate years of attendance. Also helpful: SSN, date of birth, exact years of attendance. There is no fee.

University of New Orleans, Registrar, Lakefront,
New Orleans, LA 70148, 504-286-6216 (Fax: 504-286-6217). Hours: 8AM-4:30PM. Enrollment: 16000. Records go back to 1959. Alumni records are maintained here also. Call 504-286-6368. Degrees granted: Bachelors; Masters; Doctorate. Adverse incident record source- Campus Police.

Attendance and degree information available by fax, mail. Search requires name plus SSN, date of birth. Also helpful: exact years of attendance. There is no fee.

University of Southwestern Louisiana, Regis-
trar, 200 E University Ave, Lafayette, LA 70504, 318-482-1000 (Fax: 318-482-6286). Hours: 8AM-4:30PM. Enrollment: 16902. Records go back to 1901. Alumni records are maintained here also. Call 318-482-1000. Degrees granted: Bachelors; Masters; Doctorate. Adverse incident record source- Dean of Students, 318-482-6272.

Attendance and degree information available by phone, mail. Search requires name plus SSN, exact years of attendance. There is no fee.

Xavier University of Louisiana, Registrar, 7325
Palmetto St, New Orleans, LA 70125, 504-483-7583 (Fax: 504-486-4852). Hours: 8AM-5PM. Enrollment: 3500. Records go back to 1925. Alumni records are maintained here also. Call 504-483-7614. Degrees granted: Bachelors; Masters; Pharm D.

Attendance and degree information available by phone, fax, mail. Search requires name only. Also helpful: SSN, date of birth, exact years of attendance. There is no fee. Expedited service available for $5.00.

Trade and Vocational Schools

Abbeville Beauty Academy, 1828 Veterans Memorial Dr, Abbeville, LA 70510, 318-893-1228

Acadian Technical Institute, 1933 W Hutchinson Ave, Crowley, LA 70526, 318-788-7520

Alexandria Regional Technical Institute, 4311 S MacArthur Dr, Alexandria, LA 71307, 318-487-5443

American School of Business, 702 Professional Dr N, Shreveport, LA 71105, 318-798-3333

Ascension College, 320 E Ascension St, Gonzales, LA 70737, 504-647-6609

Ascension Technical Institute, 9697 Airline Hwy, Sorrento, LA 70778, 504-675-5397

Avoyelles Technical Institute, Hwy 107, Cottonport, LA 71327, 318-876-2701

Ayers Institute, 2924 Knight St #318, Shreveport, LA 71105, 318-868-3000

Bastrop Technical Institute, Kammell St, Bastrop, LA 71221, 318-283-0836

Baton Rouge Regional Technical Institute (J.M. Frazier Vo-Tech School), 555 Julia St, Baton Rouge, LA 70802, 504-359-9201

Camelot Career College, 2618 Wooddale Blvd #A, Baton Rouge, LA 70805, 504-928-3005

Cameron College, 2740 Canal St, New Orleans, LA 70119, 504-821-5881

Career Training Specialists, 1611 Louisville Ave, Monroe, LA 71201, 318-323-2889

Charles B. Coreil Technical Institute, Industrial Park Ward I, Ville Platte, LA 70586, 318-363-2197

Claiborne Technical Institute, 3001 Minden Rd, Homer, LA 71040, 318-927-2034

Cloyd's Beauty School No. 2, 1311 Winnsboro Rd, Monroe, LA 71202, 318-323-2138

Cloyd's Beauty School No. 3, 2514 Ferrand St, Monroe, LA 71201, 318-388-3710

Coastal College (Branch Campus), 4301 Yokum Rd, Hammond, LA 70403, 504-345-3200

Commercial College of Baton Rouge, 5677 Florida Blvd, Baton Rouge, LA 70806, 504-927-3470

Commercial College of Shreveport, 2640 Youree Dr, Shreveport, LA 71104, 318-865-6571

Concordia Technical Institute, E.E. Wallace Blvd, Ferriday, LA 71334, 318-757-6501

Culinary Arts Institute of Louisiana, 427 Lafayette St, Baton Rouge, LA 70802, 504-343-6233

Cumberland School of Technology (Branch Campus), 4173 Government St, Baton Rouge, LA 70806, 504-338-9085

Delta Career College, 1702 Hudson Ln, Monroe, LA 71201, 318-322-8870

Delta-Ouachita Regional Technical Institute, 609 Vocational Pkwy, West Monroe, LA 71292, 318-396-7431

Denham Springs Beauty College, 923 Florida Ave SE, Denham Springs, LA 70726, 504-665-6188

Diesel Driving Academy, 8136 Airline Hwy, Baton Rouge, LA 70815, 504-929-9990

Diesel Driving Academy, 4709 Greenwood Rd, Shreveport, LA 71133, 318-636-6300

Domestic Health Care Institute, 4826 Jamestown Ave, Baton Rouge, LA 70808, 504-925-5312

Eastern College of Health Vocations, 3540 I-10 Service Rd S, Metairie, LA 70001, 504-834-8644

Evangeline Technical Institute, 600 S M.L.K., Jr. Dr, Martinville, LA 70582, 318-394-6108

Florida Parishes Technical Institute, 100 College Dr, Greensburg, LA 70441, 504-222-4251

Franklin College of Court Reporting, 1200 S Clearview Pkwy, New Orleans, LA 70123, 504-734-1000

Gulf Area Technical Institute, 1115 Clover St, Abbeville, LA 70510, 318-893-4984

Hammond Area Technical Institute, 111 Pride Blvd, Hammond, LA 70404, 504-543-4120

Huey P. Long Technical Institute, 303 S Jones St, Winnfield, LA 71483, 318-628-4342

Huey P. Long Technical Institute (Rod Brady Branch Campus), 117 E Bradford St, Jena, LA 71342, 318-992-2910

JM Frazier Vocational-Technical School, 555 Julia St, Baton Rouge, LA , 504-359-9204

Jefferson Davis Technical Institute, 1230 N Main St, Jennings, LA 70546, 318-824-4811

Jefferson Technical Institute, 5200 Blair Dr, Metairie, LA 70001, 504-736-7076

Jumonville Memorial Technical Institute, Hwy 3131, Hospital Rd, New Roads, LA 70760, 504-638-8613

Jumonville Memorial Technical Institute (Branch Campus), Louisiana State Penentiary, Angola, LA 70712, 504-688-8613

Jumonville Memorial Technical Institute (Branch Campus), Hunt Corr. Ctr, PO Box 40, St. Gabriel, LA 70776, 504-642-3306

Lafayette Regional Technical Institute, 1101 Bertrand Dr, Lafayette, LA 70506, 318-265-5962

Lamar Salter Technical Institute, 15014 Lake Charles, Leesville, LA 71446, 318-537-3135

Louisiana Art Institute, 7380 Exchange Pl, Baton Rouge, LA 70806, 504-928-7770

Louisiana Hair Design College, 7909 Airline Hwy, Metairie, LA 70003, 504-737-2376

Louisiana Institute of Technology, 6666 Coliseum Blvd, Alexandria, LA 71303, 318-442-1864

Louisiana Institute of Technology (Branch Campus), 115 Henderson Rd, Lafayette, LA 70508, 318-233-0776

Louisiana Technical College, 3250 N Acadian Thruway, Baton Rouge, LA 70805, 504-359-9201

Louisiana Technical College (Folkes Technical Institute), Dixon Correctional Institute, Jackson, LA 70748, 504-634-2636

Louisiana Technical College (LaFourche Campus), 1425 Tiger Dr, Thibodaux, LA 70302-1831, 504-447-0924

Louisiana Technical College (Shelby M. Jackson Campus), 2100 N EE Wallace Blvd, Ferriday, LA 71334-1995, 318-757-6501

Louisiana Training Center, 942-A Arizona St, Sulphur, LA 70663, 318-625-9469

Mansfield Technical Institute, 943 Oxford Rd, Mansfield, LA 71052, 318-872-2243

Medical Career Academy, 3333 Drusilla Ln, Baton Rouge, LA 70809, 504-929-7041

Natchitoches Technical Institute, 6587 Hwy 3111 S Bypass, Natchitoches, LA 71458, 318-357-3162

National Education Center - Bryman Campus (Branch Campus), 2322 Canal St, New Orleans, LA 70119, 504-822-4500

New Orleands Regional Technical Institute, 980 Navarre Ave, New Orleans, LA 70124, 504-483-4666

Nick Randazzo Vocational Training Institute, 125 Lafayette St, Gretna, LA 70053, 504-366-5409

North Central Technical Institute, 605 N Boundary, Farmerville, LA 71241, 318-368-3179

Northeast Louisiana Technical Institute, 1710 Warren St, Winnsboro, LA 71295, 318-435-2163

Northwest Louisiana Technical Institute, 814 Constable St, Minden, LA 71058, 318-371-3035

Oakdale Technical Institute, Old Pelican Hwy, Oakdale, LA 71463, 318-335-3944

Ochsner School of Allied Health Sciences, 880 Commerce Rd W, New Orleans, LA 70123, 504-842-3700

Refrigeration School of New Orleans, 1201 Mazant St, New Orleans, LA 70117, 504-949-2712

River Parishes Technical Institute, 251 Regala Park Rd, Reserve, LA 70084, 504-536-4418

Ruston Technical Institute, 1010 James St, Ruston, LA 71270, 318-251-4145

Sabine Valley Technical Institute, Hwy 171 S, Many, LA 71449, 318-256-4101

Shreveport-Bossier Regional Technical Institute, 2010 N Market St, Shreveport, LA 71137, 318-676-7811

Sidney N. Collier Technical Institute, 3727 Louisa St, New Orleans, LA 70126, 504-942-8333

Slidell Technical Institute, 1000 Canulette Rd, Slidell, LA 70458, 504-646-6430

South Louisiana Beauty College, 300 Howard Ave, Houma, LA 70363, 504-873-8978

South Louisiana Regional Technical Institute, 201 St. Charles St, Houma, LA 70361, 504-857-3655

South Louisiana Regional Technical Institute (Branch Campus), Station 1 Box 10251, Houma, LA 70361, 504-857-3698

Sowela Regional Technical Institute, 3820 Legion St, Lake Charles, LA 70616, 318-491-2698

Sowela Regional Technical Institute (Branch Campus), PO Box 1056, Dequincy, LA 70633, 318-491-2688

Sullivan Technical Institute, 1710 Sullivan Dr, Bogalusa, LA 70427, 504-732-6640

Sullivan Technical Institute (Branch Campus), Rte 2 Box 500, Angie, LA 70426, 504-732-6640

T.H. Harris Technical Institute, 337 E South St, Opelousas, LA 70570, 318-948-0239

Tallulah Technical Institute, Old Hwy 65 S, Tallulah, LA 71284, 318-574-4820

Tallulah Technical Institute (Branch Campus), Hwy 803-1, Lake Providence, LA 71254, 318-559-0864

Teche Area Technical Institute, Acadiana Airport, New Iberia, LA 70562, 318-373-0011

Thibodaux Area Technical Institute, 1425 Tiger Dr, Thibodaux, LA 70302, 504-447-0924

West Jefferson Technical Institute, 475 Manhattan Blvd, Harvey, LA 70058, 504-361-6464

Westside Technical Institute, 59125 Bayou Rd, Plaquemine, LA 70765, 504-687-6392

Young Memorial Technical Institute, 900 Youngs Rd, Morgan City, LA 70380, 504-380-2436

State Licensing & Business Registration Quick Finder Index

Architecture, Engineering & Surveying

Architect #50 (2530)...................................☎ 504-925-4802
Engineer #39 (14746) ....✉ 504-295-8522
Landscape Architect #38 (326) ....☎ 504-925-7772
Surveyor #58..☎ 504-295-8522

Business - Court & Legal Services

Attorney #49 (17500)...................................☎ 504-566-1600
Lobbyist #54 ....☎ 504-342-4981

Notary Public #54 (50000) .... ☎ 504-342-4981
Shorthand Reporter #36 .... ☎ 504-523-4306

Business - General Services
Auctioneer #43 (500) .... ☎ 504-925-3921
Interior Designer #11 .... ☎ 504-925-3921
Public Accountant-CPA #2 (5100) .... ☎ 504-566-1252
Retail and Wholesale Florist #38 .... ☎ 504-925-7772

Construction & Manufacturing
Boiler Inspector #55 .... ☎ 504-925-4911
Contractor #40 .... ☎ 504-765-2301
Explosives Dealer #37 (400) .... ☎ 504-925-6178
Explosives Handler #37 .... ☎ 504-925-6178
General Contractor #29 504-736-7125
Landscape Contractor #38 (1088) .... ☎ 504-925-7772
Manufactured Housing Dealer/Salesman #55
.... ☎ 504-925-4911
Plumber (Plumber, Master) #51 (1500) .... ☎ 504-826-2382
Plumber-Journeyman #51 .... ☎ 504-826-2382

Education
Parish or City School Superintendent #41 ..... ☎ 504-342-3490
School Counselor #41 .... ☎ 504-342-3490
School Librarian #41 .... ☎ 504-342-3490
School Principal #41 .... ☎ 504-342-3490
Teacher/Aides #8 .... ☎ 504-342-3490

Environmental & Agriculture
Agricultural Consultant #30 (95) .... ⊠ 504-925-3787
Arborist/Utility Arborist #38 (438) .... ☎ 504-925-7772
Horticulturist #38 (714) .... ☎ 504-925-7772
Livestock Branding #42 (10000) .... ☎ 504-925-3980
Pesticide Applicator #30 .... ⊠ 504-925-3787
Pesticide Dealer #56 (270) .... ☎ 504-925-3796
Pesticide Operator #56 (650) .... ☎ 504-925-3796
Veterinarian #44 (1270) .... ⊠ 504-342-2176

Financial - Real Estate, Insurance & Banking
Appraiser #27 504-925-4771
Bank #31 .... ☎ 504-925-4661
Consumer Credit #31 (1568) .... ☎ 504-925-4668
Insurance Agent #32 (14565) .... ☎ 504-342-0860
Insurance Agent-LHA #32 .... ☎ 504-342-0806
Insurance Broker #32 (1405) .... ☎ 504-342-0860
Investment Advisor #28 .... ⊠ 504-568-5515
Real Estate #59 (20000) .... ⊠ 504-925-4771
Real Estate Appraiser #60 504-925-4771
Real Estate Broker #60 504-925-4771
Real Estate Salesperson #60 504-925-4771
Savings & Loan & Credit Union #31 .... ☎ 504-925-4676
Securities Dealer #28 .... ⊠ 504-568-5515
Securities Salesperson #28 .... ⊠ 504-568-5515
Solicitor #32 (1772) .... ☎ 504-342-0860
Timeshare Interest Salesperson #60 504-925-4771

Health & Beauty
Acupuncturist #17 .... ⊠ 504-524-6763
Barber #1 .... ☎ 504-342-3099
Barber Instructor #1 .... ☎ 504-342-3099

Barber School #1 .... ☎ 504-342-3099
Barber Shop #1 .... ☎ 504-342-3099
Cemetery #45 (1500) .... ⊠ 504-838-5267
Chiropractor #4 .... ☎ 504-765-2322
Cosmetologist #5 (25062) .... ⊠ 504-756-3404
Dentist/Dental Hygienist #6 .... ⊠ 504-568-8574
Dietitian/Nutritionist #10 (800) .... ☎ 504-763-5490
Electrologist #7 504-336-1409
Embalmer #9 (930) .... ☎ 504-838-5109
Funeral Director #9 (434) .... ☎ 504-838-5109
Funeral Establishment #9 .... ☎ 504-838-5109
Funeral Home Internship #9 .... ☎ 504-838-5109
Funeral Home Work Permit #9 .... ☎ 504-838-5109
Hearing Aid Dealer #16 504-342-0818
Medical Doctor #17 .... ⊠ 504-524-6763
Medical Gas Piping Installer #51 .... ☎ 504-826-2382
Nuclear Medicine Technologist #13 (350) ..... ☎ 504-838-5231
Nurse #18 .... ⊠ 504-568-5464
Nursing Home Administrator #35 .... ☎ 504-925-4132
Optometrist #19 504-295-8540
Osteopathic Physician #17 .... ⊠ 504-524-6763
Pharmacist #20 (5400) .... ☎ 504-925-6496
Pharmacy #20 .... ☎ 504-925-6494
Physical Therapist #21 (1900) .... ⊠ 318-262-1043
Physician's Assistant #17 .... ⊠ 504-524-6763
Podiatrist #17 .... ⊠ 504-524-6763
Practical Nurse #22 .... ⊠ 504-568-6480
Radiation Therapy Technologist #13 .... ☎ 504-838-5231
Radiographer #13 .... ☎ 504-838-5231
Respiratory Therapist #17 .... ⊠ 504-524-6763
Respiratory Therapy Technician #17 .... ⊠ 504-524-6763
Sanitarian #14 .... ☎ 504-568-5181
Speech Pathologist/Audiologist #15 (2700)
.... ☎ 504-763-5480

Investigations & Security
Fire Protection Sprinkler Contractor #55 .... ☎ 504-925-4911
Polygraphist #57 (90) .... ⊠ 504-568-5397
Private Security #23 (8500) .... ☎ 504-295-8486

Social Services
Adoption Agency #34 (40) .... ☎ 504-922-0015
Adoption Homefinding #33 504-568-7448
Counselor #46 (1350) .... ☎ 504-765-2515
Foster Care Program #33 504-568-7448
Psychologist #12 (465) .... ☎ 504-293-2238
Social Worker #3 (3000) .... ☎ 504-763-5470
Substance Abuse Counselor #26 318-988-4378

Sports & Entertainment
Alcoholic Beverage Vendor #24 (700) .... ⊠ 318-673-6129
Boxing & Wrestling Personnel #25 .... ☎ 504-632-4422
Lottery #47 (3000) 504-297-2000
Lottery Claims Center #48 504-568-6860
Racing #52 (15000) .... ☎ 504-483-4000

Transportation
Motor Vehicle Inspector #53 (1800) .... ⊠ 504-925-6984
Used Vehicle Salesperson #61 (5560) .... ☎ 504-925-3870

State Licensing & Business Registration Agency Information

(1) Board of Barber Examiners, 1000 Scenic Hwy, Baton Rouge, LA 70809, 504-342-3099, Fax: 504-342-3100

(2) Board of Certified Public Accountants, 601 Poydres St, Suite 1770, New Orleans, LA 70130, 504-566-1244, Fax: 504-566-1252

(3) Board of Certified Social Work Examiners, 11930 Perkins Rd. Suite B, Baton Rouge, LA 70810, 504-763-5470, Fax: 504-763-5400

(4) Board of Chiropractic Examiners, 8621 Summa Ave, Baton Rouge, LA 70809, 504-765-2322

(5) Board of Cosmetology, 11622 Sunbelt Court, Baton Rouge, LA 70809, 504-756-3404, Fax: 504-756-3410/3109

(6) Board of Dentistry, 1515 Poydras St, Suite 1850, New Orleans, LA 70112, 504-568-8574, Fax: 504-568-8598

(7) Board of Electrolysis Examiners, PO Box 1468, Baton Rouge, LA 70821, 504-295-8566

(8) Board of Elementary & Secondary Education, 626 N 4th St, Baton Rouge, LA 70804-9064, 504-342-3490

(9) Board of Embalmers & Funeral Directors, 3500 N. Causeway Blvd, Suite 1232, New Orleans, LA 70002, 504-838-5109, Fax: 504-838-5112

(10) Board of Examiners of Dietitians & Nutritionists, Oak Grove Estates, Prairieville, LA 70769, 504-763-5490, Fax: 504-763-5400

(11) Board of Examiners of Interior Designers, 8017 Jefferson Hwy, Baton Rouge, LA 70812, 504-925-3921

(12) Board of Examiners of Psychologists, 11924 Justice A, Suite A, Baton Rouge, LA 70816, 504-293-2238, Fax: 504-293-2297

(13) Board of Examiners of Radiologic Technologists, 3108 Cleary Ave, Metairie, LA 70004, 504-838-5231, Fax: 504-838-5232

(14) Board of Examiners of Sanitarians, 1525 Fairfield Ave., Room 569, Shreveport, LA 71101-4388, 318-676-7489, Fax: 318-676-7560

(15) Board of Examiners of Speech Pathology & Audiology, Oak Grove Estates, Prairieville, LA 70769, 504-763-5480, Fax: 504-763-5400

(16) Board of Hearing Aid Dealers, PO Box 6016, Monroe, LA 71211-6016, 318-362-3014, Fax: 318-362-3019

(17) Board of Medical Examiners, PO Box 20350, 630 Camp St (70130), New Orleans, LA 70190, 504-599-1536, Fax: 504-568-8893

(18) Board of Nursing, 3510 N Causeway, Metairie, LA 70002, 504-838-5332, Fax: 504-838-5349

(19) Board of Optometry Examiners, PO Box 555, Oakdale, LA 71463, 318-335-2989, Fax: 318-335-3276

(20) Board of Pharmacy, 5615 Corporate Blvd, Baton Rouge, LA 70812, 504-925-6496, Fax: 504-925-6499

(21) Board of Physical Therapy, 2014 W Pinhook Rd, Suite 701, Lafayette, LA 70508, 318-262-1043, Fax: 318-262-1054

(22) Board of Practical Nurse Examiners, 3421 N Causeway Blvd, #203, Metairie, LA 70002, 504-838-5791, Fax: 504-838-5279

(23) Board of Private Security Examiners, PO Box 86510, Baton Rouge, LA 70879-6510, 504-295-8486, Fax: 504-295-8498

(24) Board of Wholesale Drug Distributors, PO Box 31107, (410 Kay Ln 71120), Shreveport, LA 71130, 318-673-6129, Fax: 318-673-6112

(25) Boxing & Wrestling Commission, 16150 W. Main, New Orleans, LA 70345, 504-632-4422, Fax: 504-632-5560

(26) Certification for Substance Abuse Counselors, 141 Ridgeway, Lafayette, LA 70502, 318-988-4378

(27) Certified Appraisers Subcommittee, 9071 Interline Ave, Baton Rouge, LA 70809, 504-925-4771

(28) Commissioner of Securities, 1100 Poydras St, #2250, New Orleans, LA 70163, 504-568-5515

(29) Contractors Licensing Board, 1221 Elmwood Park Blvd, New Orleans, LA 70141, 504-736-7125

(30) Department of Agriculture & Forestry, Pesticide Division, 5825 Florida Blvd, Baton Rouge, LA 70806, 504-925-3787, Fax: 504-925-3760

(31) Department of Economic Development, Office of Financial Institutions, 8660 United Plaza Blvd 2nd Floor, Baton Rouge, LA 70809, 504-925-4660, Fax: 504-925-4548

(32) Department of Insurance, Agent's License Division, 950 N 5th, Baton Rouge, LA 70814, 504-342-0860, Fax: 504-342-7401

(33) Department of Social Services, 2026 St Charles Ave, New Orleans, LA 70141, 504-568-7448

(34) Department of Social Services, Bureau of Licensing, PO Box 3078, Baton Rouge, LA 70821, 504-922-0015, Fax: 504-922-0014

(35) Examiners for Nursing Facility Administrators, 5615 Corporte Blvd, #8D, Baton Rouge, LA 70808, 504-922-0009, Fax: 504-922-4583

(36) Examiners of Certified Shorthand Reporters, 325 Loyola Ave, Suite 306, New Orleans, LA 70141, 504-523-4306, Fax: 504-523-2623

(37) Explosives Control Unit, PO Box 66614, (7901 Independence Blvd 70806), Baton Rouge, LA 70896, 504-925-6178, Fax: 504-925-4048

(38) Horticulture Commission, PO Box 3118, Baton Rouge, LA 70821, 504-925-7772, Fax: 504-925-3760

(39) LA State Bd. Of Reg. of Prof. Engineers & Surveyor, 10500 Coursey Blvd, Suite 107, Baton Rouge, LA 70816, 504-295-8522, Fax: 504-295-8525

(40) Licensing Board for Contractors, 7434 Perkins Rd, Baton Rouge, LA 70808, 504-765-2301, Fax: 504-765-2431

(41) Licensing Bureau of Higher Education Certification, Department of Education, PO Box 94064, 626 N 4th St, Baton Rouge, LA 70804-9064, 504-342-3490, Fax: 504-342-3499

(42) Livestock Brand Commission, PO Box 4048, 5825 Florida Blvd, Baton Rouge, LA 70806, 504-925-3980, Fax: 504-925-4103

(43) Louisiana Auctioneers Licensing Board, 8017 Jefferson Hwy, Baton Rouge, LA 70809, 504-925-3921, Fax: 504-925-1892

(44) Louisiana Board of Veterinary Medicine, 200 Lafayette St, Suite 604, Baton Rouge, LA 70814, 504-342-2176, Fax: 504-342-2142

(45) Louisiana Cemetery Board, 2901 Ridgelake Dr, Suite 101, Metairie, LA 70002-4946, 504-838-5267, Fax: 504-838-5289

(46) Louisiana Licensed Professional Counselors, Board of Examiners, 8631 Summa Ave., Suite A, Baton Rouge, LA 70809, 504-765-2515, Fax: 504-765-2514

(47) Louisiana Lottery Corporation, State Headquarters, 11200 Industriplex, Suite 190, Baton Rouge, LA 70809, 504-297-2000, Fax: 504-297-2005

(48) Louisiana Lottery Corporation, Region 1 Claims Center, 300 Poydras St, Suite 110, New Orleans, LA 70141, 504-568-6860

(49) Louisiana State Bar Association, 601 St Charles Ave, New Orleans, LA 70130, 504-566-1600, Fax: 504-566-0930

(50) Louisiana State Board of Architectural Examiners, 8017 Jefferson Hwy, Baton Rouge, LA 70809, 504-925-4802

(51) Louisiana State Plumbing Board, 2714 Canal St, Suite 512, New Orleans, LA 70119, 504-826-2382, Fax: 504-826-2175

(52) Louisiana State Racing Commission, 320 N Carrollton Ave., Suite 2B, New Orleans, LA 70119-5100, 504-483-4000, Fax: 504-483-4898

(53) Office of Motor Vehicles, State Police Safety & Enforcement, PO Box 64886, Baton Rouge, LA 70896, 504-925-6984, Fax: 504-925-3966

(54) Office of Secretary of State, PO Box 94125, Baton Rouge, LA 70804-9125, 504-342-4981, Fax: 504-342-3066

(55) Office of the State Fire Marshall, 5150 Florida Blvd, Baton Rouge, LA 70806, 504-925-4911, Fax: 504-925-4241

(56) Pest Control Commission, 5825 Florida Blvd, Baton Rouge, LA 70809, 504-925-3796, Fax: 504-925-3780

(57) Polygraph Board, 2025 Canal St, Suite 121, New Orleans, LA 70112, 504-568-5397

(58) Professional Engineers & Land Surveyors, 1055 St Charles Ave, New Orleans, LA 70143, 504-295-8522, Fax: 504-295-8525

(59) Real Estate Commission, 9071 Interline Ave, Baton Rouge, LA 70809, 504-925-4771, Fax: 504-925-4431

(60) Real Estate Commission, 9071 Interline Ave, Baton Rouge, LA 70809, 504-925-4771

(61) Used Motor Vehicle & Parts Commission, 3132 Valley Creek Dr, Baton Rouge, LA 70814, 504-925-3870, Fax: 504-925-3869

Maine

Capitol: Augusta (Kennebec County)	
State Population	1.3 Million
Number of Degree Granting Institutions:	32
Number of State Licensing & Business Registration Agencies:	85

Degree Granting Educational Institutions

Andover College, Registrar, 901 Washington Ave, Portland, ME 04103, 207-774-6126 (Fax: 207-774-1715). Hours: 9AM-5PM. Enrollment: 600. Records go back to 1927. Degrees granted: Associate.

Attendance and degree information available by phone, fax, mail. Search requires name plus SSN. Also helpful: date of birth, exact years of attendance. There is no fee.

Bangor Theological Seminary, Registrar, 300 Union St, Bangor, ME 04401, 207-942-6781 X36 (Fax: 207-990-1267). Hours: 8AM-4:30PM. Enrollment: 263. Records go back to 1814. Alumni records are maintained here at the same phone number. Degrees granted: Masters; Doctorate.

Attendance and degree information available by fax, mail. Search requires name plus date of birth, exact years of attendance. There is no fee.

Bates College, Registrar, 2 Andrews Rd, Lewiston, ME 04240, 207-786-6096 (Fax: 207-786-6123). Hours: 8AM-4:30PM. Enrollment: 1600. Records go back to 1900. Alumni records are maintained here also. Call 207-786-6127. Degrees granted: Bachelors. Adverse incident record source- Dean of Students, 207-786-6222.

Attendance and degree information available by phone, fax, mail. Search requires name plus date of birth, exact years of attendance. There is no fee.

Beal College, Registrar, 629 Main St, Bangor, ME 04401, 207-947-4591 (Fax: 207-947-0208). Records go back to 1960's. Degrees granted: Associate. Adverse incident record source-Registrar, 207-947-4591.

Attendance and degree information available by fax, mail. Search requires name plus SSN, date of birth, signed release. Also helpful: exact years of attendance. There is no fee.

Bowdoin College, Office of Student Records, Brunswick, ME 04011, 207-725-3226 (Fax: 207-725-3338). Hours: 8:30AM-5PM. Enrollment: 1450. Records go back to 1954. Earlier records in archives. Alumni records are maintained here also. Call 207-725-3266. Degrees granted: Bachelors.

Attendance and degree information available by phone, fax, mail. Search requires name only. Also helpful: exact years of attendance. There is no fee.

Casco Bay College, Registrar, 477 Congress St, Portland, ME 04101-3483, 207-772-0196 (Fax: 207-772-0636).

Hours: 8AM-5PM. Enrollment: 300. Records go back to 1960's. Degrees granted: Associate. Adverse incident record source-Registrar, 207-772-0196.

Attendance and degree information available by phone, fax, mail. Search requires name plus SSN. There is no fee.

Central Maine Medical Center School of Nursing, Registrar, Lewiston, ME 04240, 207-795-2858 (Fax: 207-795-2849). Hours: 8:30AM-5PM. Enrollment: 85. Records go back to 1891. Alumni records are maintained here also. Call 207-795-2884. Degrees granted: Associate.

Attendance and degree information available by phone, fax, mail. Search requires name only. Also helpful: date of birth, exact years of attendance. There is no fee.

Central Maine Technical College, Registrar, 1250 Turner St, Auburn, ME 04210, 207-784-2385 (Fax: 207-777-7353). Hours: 8AM-4:30PM. Enrollment: 1200. Records go back to 1965. Alumni records are maintained here at the same phone number. Degrees granted: Associate.

School will not confirm attendance information.

Degree information available by phone. Search requires name plus SSN. Also helpful: date of birth, exact years of attendance. There is no fee.

Colby College, Office of the Registrar, 4620 Mayflower Hill, Waterville, ME 04901-8846, 207-872-3197 (Fax: 207-872-3076). Hours: 8:30AM-4:30PM. Enrollment: 1700. Records go back to 1911. Degrees granted: Bachelors.

Attendance and degree information available by phone, fax, mail. Search requires name plus SSN, date of birth, exact years of attendance. There is no fee.

College of the Atlantic, Registrar, 105 Eden St, Bar Harbor, ME 04609, 207-288-5015 (Fax: 207-288-4126). Hours: 9AM-5PM. Enrollment: 230. Records go back to 1972. Alumni records are maintained here at the same phone number. Degrees granted: Bachelors; Masters. Adverse incident record source-Administrative Dean, 207-288-5015.

Attendance and degree information available by phone, fax, mail. Search requires name plus exact years of attendance. Also helpful: SSN. There is no fee.

Eastern Maine Technical College, Registrar, 354 Hogan Rd, Bangor, ME 04401, 207-941-4625 (Fax: 207-941-4666). Hours: 9AM-4PM. Enrollment: 2000. Records go back to

1971. Alumni records are maintained here at the same phone number. Degrees granted: Associate.

Attendance and degree information available by phone, fax, mail. Search requires name plus SSN, date of birth. Also helpful: exact years of attendance. There is no fee.

Husson College, Registrar, One College Circle, Bangor, ME 04401, 207-941-7000. Hours: 7:30AM-4:30PM. Enrollment: 2100. Records go back to 1920's. Alumni records are maintained here also. Call 207-941-7073. Degrees granted: Associate; Bachelors; Masters.

Attendance and degree information available by phone, mail. Search requires name plus SSN. Also helpful: date of birth, exact years of attendance. There is no fee.

Kennebec Valley Technical College, Registrar's Office, 92 Western Ave, Fairfield, ME 04937-1367, 207-453-5000 (Fax: 207-453-5010). Hours: 9AM-Noon, 1-4PM. Enrollment: 1200. Records go back to 1979. Records to 1957 for ME State School of Practical Nursing. Alumni records are maintained here at the same phone number. Degrees granted: Associate.

Attendance information available by phone, fax, mail. Search requires name plus SSN, approximate years of attendance. Also helpful: date of birth, exact years of attendance. There is no fee.

Degree information available by phone, fax, mail. Search requires name plus SSN, approximate years of attendance. Also helpful: date of birth. There is no fee.

Maine College of Art, Registrar, 97 Spring St, Portland, ME 04101, 207-775-3052 (Fax: 207-772-5069). Hours: 9AM-5PM. Enrollment: 300. Records go back to 1882. Alumni records are maintained here also. Call 207-775-5095. Degrees granted: Bachelors. Special programs- Only Independent College of Art & Design in New England. Adverse incident record source- Director of Student Life, 207-773-1546: Registrar, 207-775-3052

Attendance and degree information available by mail. Search requires name plus SSN, date of birth, exact years of attendance. There is no fee.

Maine Maritime Academy, Registrar, Castine, ME 04420, 207-326-2441. Hours: 7:30AM-4PM. Enrollment: 650. Records go back to 1941. Alumni records are maintained here also. Call 207-326-2337. Degrees granted: Associate; Bachelors; Masters.

Attendance and degree information available by phone, mail. Search requires name plus SSN, exact years of attendance. There is no fee.

Mid-State College, Registrar, 88 Hardscrabble Rd, Auburn, ME 04210, 207-783-1478 (Fax: 207-783-1477). Hours: 8AM-4PM. Enrollment: 350. Records go back to 1986. Alumni records are maintained here at the same phone number. Degrees granted: Associate. Adverse incident record source- Registrar, 207-784-1478.

Attendance and degree information available by written request only. Search requires name plus SSN, date of birth, signed release. There is no fee.

Mid-State College, (Branch), Registrar, 218 Water St, Augusta, ME 04430, 207-623-3962. Hours: 8AM-8PM M-Th, 8AM-4PM. Enrollment: 350. Records go back to 1950. Alumni records are maintained here at the same phone number. Degrees granted: Associate. Adverse incident record source- Registrar, 207-623-3962.

Attendance and degree information available by mail. Search requires name plus SSN, signed release. There is no fee.

Northern Maine Technical College, Registrar, 33 Edgemont Dr, Presque Isle, ME 04769, 207-768-2791 (Fax: 207-768-2831). Hours: 8AM-5PM. Enrollment: 600. Records go back to 1963. Graduate and Withdrawal files - 5 years. Alumni

records are maintained here also. Call 207-768-2808. Degrees granted: Associate. Adverse incident record source- Registrar, 207-768-2791.

Attendance and degree information available by phone, fax, mail. Search requires name plus SSN, date of birth. Also helpful: exact years of attendance. There is no fee.

Southern Maine Technical College, Registrar, Fort Road, South Portland, ME 04106, 207-767-9538 (Fax: 207-767-9671). Hours: 8AM-5PM. Enrollment: 2500. Records go back to 1948. Alumni records are maintained here also. Call 207-767-9507. Degrees granted: Associate.

Attendance information available by phone, fax, mail. Search requires name plus SSN. Also helpful: date of birth, exact years of attendance. There is no fee.

Degree information available by phone, fax, mail. Search requires name plus SSN. Also helpful: exact years of attendance. There is no fee.

St. Joseph's College, Registrar, Standish, ME 04084-5263, 207-892-6766 (Fax: 207-893-7861). Hours: 8:30AM-4:30PM. Enrollment: 2500. Records go back to 1912. Alumni records are maintained here at the same phone number. Degrees granted: Associate; Bachelors; Masters. Adverse incident record source- Dean of Students: Academic Dean

Attendance and degree information available by phone, fax, mail. Search requires name only. Also helpful: SSN, date of birth. There is no fee. Expedited service available for $10.00.

Thomas College, Registrar, 180 W River Rd, Waterville, ME 04901, 207-873-0771 (Fax: 207-877-0114). Hours: 8AM-4:30PM. Enrollment: 900. Records go back to 1920's. Alumni records are maintained here at the same phone number. Degrees granted: Associate; Bachelors; Masters.

Attendance and degree information available by phone, fax, mail. Search requires name plus SSN. Also helpful: date of birth, exact years of attendance. There is no fee.

Unity College, Registrar's Office, HC78 Box 1, Unity, ME 04988, 207-948-3131 X244 (Fax: 207-948-6277). Hours: 8:30AM-5PM. Enrollment: 500. Records go back to 1966. Alumni records are maintained here at the same phone number. Degrees granted: Associate; Bachelors.

Attendance and degree information available by phone, fax, mail. Search requires name only. Also helpful: SSN, date of birth, exact years of attendance. There is no fee.

University of Maine, Registrar, Orono, ME 04469, 207-581-1290 (Fax: 207-581-1314). Hours: 8AM-4:30PM. Enrollment: 10000. Records go back to 1865. Alumni records are maintained here also. Call 207-581-1138. Degrees granted: Bachelors; Masters; Doctorate. Adverse incident record source- Judicial Affairs, 207-581-1409.

Attendance and degree information available by phone, fax, mail. Search requires name plus SSN. Also helpful: date of birth, exact years of attendance. There is no fee.

University of Maine at Augusta, Admission & Records, 46 University Dr, Augusta, ME 04330, 207-621-3185 (Fax: 207-621-3116). Enrollment: 6166. Records go back to 1968. Alumni records are maintained here at the same phone number. Degrees granted: Associate; Bachelors.

Attendance and degree information available by phone, fax, mail. Search requires name plus SSN. Also helpful: exact years of attendance. There is no fee.

University of Maine at Farmington, Registrar, 86 Main St, Farmington, ME 04938, 207-778-7000 (Fax: 207-778-7247). Hours: 8AM-4:30PM. Enrollment: 2000. Records go back to 1864. Alumni records are maintained here also. Call 207-778-7090. Degrees granted: Bachelors. Adverse incident record source- Registrar, 207-778-7000.

Attendance and degree information available by phone, fax, mail. Search requires name plus SSN. Also helpful: exact years of attendance. There is no fee.

University of Maine at Fort Kent, Registrar, Pleasant St, Fort Kent, ME 04743, 207-834-7521 (Fax: 207-834-7503). Hours: 8AM-4:30PM. Enrollment: 600. Records go back to 1878. Alumni records are maintained here also. Call 207-834-7557. Degrees granted: Associate; Bachelors. Adverse incident record source- Physical Plant, 207-834-7671.

Attendance and degree information available by fax, mail. Search requires name plus SSN. Also helpful: date of birth. There is no fee.

University of Maine at Machias, Registrar, Machias, ME 04654, 207-255-3313 (Fax: 207-255-4864). Hours: 8AM-5PM. Enrollment: 950. Records go back to 1912. Alumni records are maintained here at the same phone number. Degrees granted: Associate; Bachelors. Adverse incident record source- Student Affairs, 207-255-3313 X202.

Attendance information available by phone, mail. Search requires name only. Also helpful: SSN, date of birth, exact years of attendance. There is no fee.

Degree information available by phone, mail. Search requires name only. Also helpful: SSN, exact years of attendance. There is no fee.

University of Maine at Presque Isle, Registrar, 181 Main St, Presque Isle, ME 04769, 207-768-9540 (Fax: 207-768-9458). Hours: 8AM-5PM. Enrollment: 1350. Records go back to 1903. Alumni records are maintained here also. Call 207-768-9525. Degrees granted: Bachelors.

Attendance and degree information available by phone, mail. Search requires name plus SSN. There is no fee.

University of New England, Registrar, 11 Hills Beach Rd, Biddeford, ME 04005-9599, 207-283-0171 X2473 (Fax: 207-282-6379). Hours: 9AM-4PM. Enrollment: 180. Records go back to 1940's. Alumni records are maintained here also. Call 207-283-0171 X2161. Degrees granted: Associate; Bachelors; Masters; Doctorate. Adverse incident record source- Student affairs, 207-283-0171 X2329.

Attendance information available by phone, fax, mail. Search requires name plus SSN, date of birth. Also helpful: exact years of attendance. There is no fee.

Degree information available by phone, fax, mail. Search requires name plus SSN. Also helpful: date of birth, exact years of attendance. There is no fee.

University of Southern Maine, Registrar, 96 Falmouth St, Portland, ME 04103, 207-780-5230 (Fax: 207-780-5517). Hours: 8AM-4:30PM. Enrollment: 9500. Records go back to 1896. Alumni records are maintained here also. Call 207-780-4110. Degrees granted: Associate; Bachelors; Masters; L.L.D.

Attendance and degree information available by phone, mail. Search requires name only. Also helpful: SSN, date of birth, exact years of attendance. There is no fee.

Washington County Technical College, Registrar, RR1 Box 22C, Calais, ME 04619, 207-454-1000 (Fax: 207-454-1026). Hours: 8AM-4:30PM. Enrollment: 300. Records go back to 1969. Alumni records are maintained here also. Call 207-454-1000. Degrees granted: Associate. Adverse incident record source- Dean of Students, 207-454-1047.

Attendance and degree information available by phone, fax, mail. Search requires name plus SSN. Also helpful: exact years of attendance. There is no fee.

Westbrook College, Registrar, Stevens Ave, Portland, ME 04103, 207-797-7261 (Fax: 207-797-7725). Hours: 8:30AM-5PM. Enrollment: 300. Records go back to 1940. Alumni records are maintained here at the same phone number. Degrees granted: Associate; Bachelors. Certification: CNA (in past).

Attendance and degree information available by fax, mail. Search requires name plus signed release. Also helpful: SSN, date of birth, approximate years of attendance. There is no fee.

Trade and Vocational Schools

Air-Tech, Inc., RR 1 Box 170, Limerick, ME 04048, 207-793-8020

Landing School of Boat Building and Design (The), PO Box 1490, Kennebunkport, ME 04046, 207-985-7976

New England School of Broadcasting, One College Cir, Bangor, ME 04401, 207-947-6083

State Licensing & Business Registration Quick Finder Index

Architecture, Engineering & Surveying
Architect #13 .... ☎ 207-624-8500
Engineer #17 .... ☎ 207-287-3236
Geologist & Soil Scientist #13 .... ☎ 207-624-8500
Landscape Architect #13 .... ☎ 207-624-8500
Surveyor #13 .... ☎ 207-624-8500

Business - Court & Legal Services
Attorney #22 .... ✉ 207-623-2464
Lobbyist #1 (285) .... ☎ 207-287-6221
Notary Public #24 .... ☎ 207-287-4173

Business - General Services
Auctioneer #13 .... ☎ 207-624-8500
Charitable Solicitation #13 .... ☎ 207-624-8500
Itinerant Vendor #13 .... ☎ 207-624-8500
Public Accountant #13 .... ☎ 207-582-8723

Construction & Manufacturing
Bedding, Upholstering, Furniture & Stuffed
   Toy Manufacturer #12 207-624-6411
Boiler, Elevator, Tramway Contractor #21 207-624-6420
Electrician #13 .... ☎ 207-624-8500
Manufactured Housing #13 .... ☎ 207-582-8723
Plumber #13 .... ☎ 207-624-8500

Education
School Guidance Counselor #4 .... ☎ 207-287-5944
School Library Media Specialist #4 .... ☎ 207-287-5944
School Principal #4 .... ☎ 207-287-5944
School Superintendent #4 .... ☎ 207-287-5944
Teacher #4 .... ☎ 207-287-5944

Environmental & Agriculture
Air Quality Control #5 .... ☎ 207-287-2437
Arborist #13 .... ☎ 207-624-8500
Forester #13 .... ☎ 207-624-8500
Hazardous Material/Solid Waste Operator #6
.... ☎ 207-287-2651
Oil & Solid Fuel #13 .... ☎ 207-624-8500
Pesticide Applicator #3 (4000) .... ☎ 207-287-2731
Pesticide Dealer #3 (75) 207-287-2731
Veterinarian #13 .... ☎ 207-624-8500

Financial - Real Estate, Insurance & Banking
Bank Personnel #14 .... ☎ 207-582-8713
Certified General Real Estate Appraiser #13
.... ☎ 207-624-8603
Certified Residential Real Estate Appraiser #13
.... ☎ 207-624-8603
Licensed Real Estate Appraiser #13 .... ☎ 207-624-8603
Real Estate Appraiser (Trainee) #13 (39) .... ☎ 207-624-8603
Securities Personnel #15 .... ☎ 207-624-8475
Self Insurance #15 .... ☎ 207-582-8707

Health & Beauty
Acupuncturist #13 .... ☎ 207-624-8500
Barber & Cosmetologist #13 .... ☎ 207-624-8500
Chiropractor #13 .... ☎ 207-624-8500

Dental Hygienist #16 .... ☎ 207-287-3333
Dental Radiographer #16 .... ☎ 207-287-3333
Dentist #16 (917) .... ☎ 207-287-3333
Dietitian #13 .... ☎ 207-624-8500
Emergency Medical Technician #10 207-624-5443
Funeral Service #13 .... ☎ 207-624-8500
Hearing Aid Dealer & Fitter #13 .... ☎ 207-624-8500
Hospital #9 (42) .... ☎ 207-624-5443
Massage Therapist #13 .... ☎ 207-624-8500
Medical Doctor #23 .... ☎ 207-287-3601
Nurse #8 .... ☎ 207-624-8500
Nursing Home #9 (136) .... ☎ 207-624-5443
Nursing Home Administrator #13 .... ☎ 207-624-8500
Occupational Therapist #13 .... ☎ 207-624-8500
Optometrist #18 (182) .... ☎ 207-287-2535
Osteopathic Physician #26 (505) .... ☎ 207-287-2480
Osteopathic Physician's Assistant #26 .... ☎ 207-287-2480
Osteopathic Resident/Intern #26 .... ☎ 207-287-2480
Ostepathic Physician Extender #26 .... ☎ 207-287-2480
Pharmacist #13 .... ☎ 207-624-8500
Physical Therapist #13 .... ☎ 207-624-8500
Podiatrist #23 .... ☎ 207-287-3601
Radiologic Technician #13 .... ☎ 207-624-8500
Respiratory Care Therapist #13 .... ☎ 207-624-8500
Speech Pathologist/Audiologist #13 .... ☎ 207-624-8500
Substance Abuse #13 .... ☎ 207-624-8500

Investigations & Security
Non-Resident Concealed Firearm Permit #25
.... ☎ 207-624-8775
Polygraph Examiner #19 207-624-7068
Private Investigator #25 .... ☎ 207-624-8775

Social Services
Counselor #13 (1305) .... ☎ 207-624-8603
Marriage & Family Therapist #13 .... ☎ 207-624-8500
Pastoral Counselor #13 .... ☎ 207-624-8500
Psychologist #13 .... ☎ 207-624-8500
Residential Child Care Provider #7 .... ☎ 207-287-5060
Social Worker #13 .... ☎ 207-624-8500

Sports & Entertainment
Alcoholic Beverage Distributor #20 (3975) ... ☎ 207-624-8745
Athletic Trainer #13 .... ☎ 207-624-8500
Firearm Permit (Resident-Concealed) #25
   (6000) .... ☎ 207-624-8775
Lottery Combined Instant and On-line
   Vendor #20 .... ☎ 207-287-6824
Lottery Instant Ticket Vendor #20 .... ☎ 207-287-6824
Lottery Retailer #2 .... ☎ 207-287-6824
Lottery Vending #20 .... ☎ 207-287-6824
Registration-ATV, Watercraft, Snowmobile #11
.... ☎ 207-287-2043

Transportation
Commercial Driver Education #13 .... ☎ 207-624-8500
Pilot #13 .... ☎ 207-624-8500

State Licensing & Business Registration Agency Information

(1) Commission on Governmental Ethics & Elections, Registrar, State House Station #135, Augusta, ME 04333, 207-287-6221, Fax: 207-287-6775

(2) Department of Administrative & Financial Services, Bureau of Alcoholic Beverages & Lottery Operations, 8 State House Station, Augusta, ME 04333, 207-287-6824, Fax: 207-287-6769

(3) Department of Agriculture, Food & Rural Resources, Board of Pesticides Control, AMHI Complex-Deering Bldg, Augusta, ME 04332, 207-287-2731, Fax: 207-287-6558

(4) Department of Education, Certification & Placement, 23 State House Station, Augusta, ME 04333-0023, 207-287-5800

(5) Department of Environmental Protection, Bureau of Air Quality Control, #17 State House Station, Augusta, ME 04333-0017, 207-287-2437, Fax: 207-287-7691

(6) Department of Environmental Protection, Bureau/Hazardous Materials & Solid Waste Control, State House Station #17, Augusta, ME 04333, 207-287-2651, Fax: 207-287-7826

(7) Department of Human Services, 221 State St, Station #11, Augusta, ME 04333, 207-287-5060

(8) Department of Human Services, Board of Nursing, 35 Anthony Ave, State House Station #158, Augusta, ME 04333, 207-624-8500, Fax: 207-287-1149

(9) Department of Human Services, Division of Licensure, 35 Anthony Ave, Station #11, Augusta, ME 04333, 207-624-5443, Fax: 207-624-5378

(10) Department of Human Services, Medical Services Bureau Licensing & Certification, State House Station 11, Augusta, ME 04333, 207-624-5443

(11) Department of Inland Fisheries & Wildlife, Licensing & Registration Division, 284 State St, Station #41, Augusta, ME 04333, 207-287-8000, Fax: 207-287-8094

(12) Department of Labor, #45 State House Station, Augusta, ME 04333, 207-624-6411, Fax: 207-624-6449

(13) Department of Professional & Financial Regulation, State House Station #35, Augusta, ME 04333, 207-624-8500, Fax: 207-624-8637

(14) Department of Professional & Financial Regulation, Bureau of Banking, State House Station #36, Augusta, ME 04333, 207-624-8570, Fax: 207-624-8590

(15) Department of Professional & Financial Regulation, Bureau of _____, State House Station #34, Augusta, ME 04333, 207-624-8475, Fax: 207-624-8637

(16) Department of Professional & Financial Regulations, Board of Dental Examiners, State House Station #143, Augusta, ME 04333, 207-287-3333, Fax: 207-287-3333

(17) Department of Professional & Financial Regulations, Bureau of Engineering, State House Station #92, Augusta, ME 04333, 207-287-3236, Fax: 207-287-2805

(18) Department of Professional & Financial Regulations, Bureau of Optometry, State House Station #113, Augusta, ME 04333, 207-287-2535, Fax: 207-287-8441

(19) Department of Public Safety, 36 Hospital St, Station #42, Augusta, ME 04333, 207-624-7068

(20) Department of Public Safety, Licensing & Inspection-Licquor, 164 State House Station, Augusta, ME 04333, 207-624-8745, Fax: 207-624-8767

(21) Labor Standards Bureau, 20 Union Street, PO Box 309, Augusta, ME 04333, 207-624-6420, Fax: 207-624-8637

(22) Main Board of Bar Examiners, PO Box 30, Augusta, ME 04332-0030, 207-623-2464, Fax: 207-623-4175

(23) Medical Doctor & Physician Assistant Licensing, Board of Licensure & Medicine, State House Station #137, Augusta, ME 04333, 207-287-3601, Fax: 207-287-6590

(24) Office of Secretary of State, Bureau of Corporations, Elections & Commissions, State House Station #101, Augusta, ME 04333, 207-287-4173, Fax: 207-287-5874

(25) State Police Licensing Division, State House Station #164, Augusta, ME 04333, 207-624-8775, Fax: 207-624-8767

(26) State of Maine, Board of Osteopathic Licensure, State House Station #142, Augusta, ME 04333, 207-287-2480, Fax: 207-287-2480

Maryland

Capitol: Annapolis (Anne Arundel County)	
State Population	5.0 Million
Number of Degree Granting Institutions:	65
Number of State Licensing & Business Registration Agencies:	89

Degree Granting Educational Institutions

Allegany Community College, Registrar, 12401 Willowbrook Rd SE, Cumberland, MD 21502, 301-724-7700 X212 (Fax: 301-724-6892). Hours: 9AM-5PM. Enrollment: 2800. Records go back to 1961. Alumni records are maintained here at the same phone number. Degrees granted: Associate.

Attendance and degree information available by phone, mail. Search requires name plus SSN. There is no fee.

Anne Arundel Community College, Registrar, 101 College Pkwy, Arnold, MD 21012, 410-541-2243/541-2241 (Fax: 410-541-2489). Hours: 8:30AM-8PM M-Th, 8:30-4:30PM F, 9AM-1PM Sat. Enrollment: 11800. Records go back to 1961. Alumni records are maintained here also. Call 410-541-2515. Degrees granted: Associate.

Attendance and degree information available by phone, mail. Search requires name plus SSN, exact years of attendance. There is no fee.

Antioch University, **(George Meany Center for Labor Studies)**, Registrar, 10000 New Hampshire Ave, Silver Spring, MD 20903, 301-431-5410 (Fax: 301-434-0371). Hours: 9AM-4:30PM. Records go back to 1974. Alumni records are maintained here at the same phone number. Degrees granted: Bachelors. Adverse incident record source- Student Affairs.

Attendance and degree information available by phone, fax, mail. Search requires name plus SSN, approximate years of attendance. There is no fee.

Baltimore City Community College, Registrar, 2901 Liberth Heights Ave, Baltimore, MD 21215, 410-462-7777 (Fax: 410-462-7677). Hours: 8AM-5PM. Enrollment: 6500. Records go back to 1947. Alumni Records Office: 600 E Lombard St, Baltimore, MD 21201. Degrees granted: Associate. Adverse incident record source- Student Affairs, 410-462-7676.

Attendance and degree information available by phone, fax, mail. Search requires name plus SSN. Also helpful: date of birth, exact years of attendance. There is no fee.

Baltimore City Community College, **(Harbor)**, Registrar, 600 E Lombard St, Baltimore, MD 21202, 410-986-5599 (Fax: 410-986-5577). Hours: 8AM-5PM. Degrees granted: Associate.

Attendance and degree information available by phone, mail. Search requires name plus SSN, exact years of attendance. There is no fee.

Baltimore Hebrew University, Registrar, 5800 Park Heights Ave, Baltimore, MD 21209, 410-578-6918 (Fax: 410-578-6940). Hours: 9AM-5PM. Enrollment: 340. Records go back to 1920's. Alumni records are maintained here also. Call 410-578-6915. Degrees granted: Associate; Bachelors; Masters; Doctorate.

Attendance and degree information available by written request only. Search requires name plus SSN, signed release. Also helpful: date of birth, exact years of attendance. There is no fee.

Baltimore International Culinary College, Registrar, 17 S Commerce St, Baltimore, MD 21202, 410-752-4710 (Fax: 410-545-5000). Hours: 8AM-4:30PM. Enrollment: 800. Records go back to 1972. Alumni records are maintained here also. Call 410-752-1446. Degrees granted: Associate. Special programs- Hotel Management. Adverse incident record source- Registrar, 410-752-4710.

Attendance and degree information available by phone, fax, mail. Search requires name plus SSN. There is no fee.

Bowie State University, Admissions Records & Reg., 14000 Jericho Park Rd, Bowie, MD 20715, 301-464-6570 (Fax: 301-464-7521). Hours: 10AM-7PM M,W; 8AM-6PM T,Th; 10AM-6PM F. Enrollment: 5200. Records go back to 1930's. Alumni records are maintained here also. Call 301-464-6584. Degrees granted: Bachelors; Masters. Adverse incident record source- Campus Safety, 301-464-7165.

Attendance information available by mail. Search requires name plus SSN, approximate years of attendance, signed release. Also helpful: date of birth, exact years of attendance. There is no fee.

Degree information available by phone, mail. Search requires name plus SSN, approximate years of attendance. Also helpful: date of birth, exact years of attendance. There is no fee.

Capitol College, Registrar, 11301 Springfield Rd, Laurel, MD 20708, 301-369-2800 (Fax: 301-953-3876). Hours: 9AM-5PM M, 9AM-7PM T,W,Th, 9AM-3PM F. Enrollment: 800. Records go back to 1964. Alumni records are maintained here at the same phone number. Degrees granted: Associate; Bachelors; Masters.

Attendance and degree information available by phone, fax, mail. Search requires name only. Also helpful: SSN, date of birth, exact years of attendance. There is no fee.

Catonsville Community College, Registrar, 800 S Rolling Rd, Baltimore, MD 21228, 410-455-4380 (Fax: 410-455-4504). Hours: 8AM-8PM M-Th; 8AM-4PM F. Enrollment: 10000. Records go back to 1961. Alumni records are maintained here also. Call 410-455-4400. Degrees granted: Associate. Adverse incident record source- Student Life, 410-455-4322: Campus Security, 410-455-4455

Attendance information available by phone, fax, mail. Search requires name plus SSN, approximate years of attendance. Also helpful: date of birth, exact years of attendance. There is no fee.

Degree information available by mail. Search requires name plus SSN, approximate years of attendance. Also helpful: date of birth, exact years of attendance. There is no fee.

Cecil Community College, Registrar, 1000 North East Rd, North East, MD 21901, 410-287-1004 (Fax: 410-287-1001). Hours: 8:30AM-4:30PM. Enrollment: 1348. Records go back to 1969. Alumni records are maintained here also. Call 410-287-1000. Degrees granted: Associate.

Attendance and degree information available by phone, fax, mail. Search requires name plus SSN. Also helpful: date of birth. There is no fee.

Charles County Community College, Registrar, Mitchell Rd, PO Box 910, La Plata, MD 20646, 301-870-3008 X7006 (Fax: 301-934-5255). Hours: 8:30AM-4:30PM. Records go back to 1974. Degrees granted: Associate.

Attendance information available by phone, mail. Search requires name plus SSN, date of birth, exact years of attendance. There is no fee.

Degree information available by phone, mail. Search requires name plus SSN, exact years of attendance. Also helpful: date of birth. There is no fee.

Chesapeake College, Registrar, PO Box 8, Wye Mills, MD 21679, 410-822-5400 (Fax: 410-827-9466). Hours: 8AM-4PM. Enrollment: 2000. Records go back to 1965. Alumni records are maintained here also. Call 410-827-5808. Degrees granted: Associate.

Attendance and degree information available by phone, mail. Search requires name plus SSN, date of birth, exact years of attendance. There is no fee.

College of Notre Dame of Maryland, Registrar, 4701 N Charles St, Baltimore, MD 21210, 410-435-0100 (Fax: 410-532-5937). Hours: 8AM-5PM. Enrollment: 3200. Records go back to 1895. Alumni records are maintained here also. Call 410-435-0100. Degrees granted: Bachelors; Masters.

Attendance and degree information available by phone, mail. Search requires name plus SSN. Also helpful: exact years of attendance. There is no fee.

Columbia Union College, Registrar, 7600 Flower Ave, Takoma Park, MD 20912, 301-891-4119 (Fax: 301-891-4022). Hours: 9AM Noon, 1-4PM M,T,Th; 9-11AM,1-4PM W; 9AM-Noon F. Enrollment: 1000. Records go back to 1904. Alumni records are maintained here also. Call 301-891-4132. Degrees granted: Associate; Masters.

Attendance and degree information available by phone, fax, mail. Search requires name plus SSN, approximate years of attendance. Also helpful: date of birth, exact years of attendance. There is no fee. Expedited service available for $10.00.

Coppin State College, Registrar, 500 W North Ave, Baltimore, MD 21216, 410-383-5550 (Fax: 410-523-7238). Hours: 8AM-5PM. Enrollment: 3380. Records go back to 1960's. Alumni records are maintained here also. Call 410-383-5960. Degrees granted: Bachelors; Masters.

Attendance and degree information available by phone, fax, mail. Search requires name plus SSN, exact years of attendance. Also helpful: date of birth. There is no fee.

Dundalk Community College, Registrar, 7200 Sollers Point Rd, Dundalk, MD 21222, 410-282-6700 (Fax: 410-285-9903). Enrollment: 3200. Records go back to 1971. Alumni records are maintained here also. Call 410-285-9935. Degrees granted: Associate. Adverse incident record source- Dean of Students, 410-285-9855.

Attendance and degree information available by phone, fax, mail. Search requires name plus SSN, exact years of attendance. There is no fee.

Essex Community College, Registrar, 7201 Rossville Blvd, Baltimore, MD 21237, 410-780-6363 (Fax: 410-686-9503). Hours: 8:30AM-8:30PM M-Th; 8:30AM-3:30PM F. Enrollment: 9653. Records go back to 1957. Alumni records are maintained here also. Call 410-780-6316. Degrees granted: Associate.

Attendance information available by phone, fax, mail. Search requires name plus SSN. Also helpful: date of birth, exact years of attendance. There is no fee.

Degree information available by mail. Search requires name plus SSN. Also helpful: date of birth, exact years of attendance. There is no fee.

Frederick Community College, Admissions/Registration Ofc, 7932 Opposumtown Pike, Frederick, MD 21702, 301-846-2430 (Fax: 301-846-2498). Hours: 8:30AM-8PM M-Th; 8:30AM-4:30PM F. Enrollment: 4000. Records go back to 1957. Degrees granted: Associate. Adverse incident record source- Dean of Student Development, 301-846-2470.

Attendance and degree information available by phone, fax, mail. Search requires name plus SSN. There is no fee.

Frostburg State University, Registrar, Frostburg, MD 21532, 301-687-4346 (Fax: 301-687-4597). Hours: 8AM-4:30PM. Enrollment: 5050. Records go back to 1902. Alumni records are maintained here at the same phone number. Degrees granted: Bachelors; Masters. Adverse incident record source- Student & Educational Services, 301-687-4311.

Attendance and degree information available by phone, fax, mail. Search requires name plus SSN, exact years of attendance. Also helpful: date of birth. There is no fee.

Garrett Community College, Registrar, PO Box 151, Mosser Rd, McHenry, MD 21541, 301-387-3040 (Fax: 301-387-3055). Hours: 8:30AM-4:30PM. Enrollment: 725. Records go back to 1971. Alumni records are maintained here also. Call 301-387-3056. Degrees granted: Associate. Special programs- Arts & Sciences: Liberal Arts: Teacher Ed: Business: Secretarical Science: Agricultural Technology: Adventure Sports. Adverse incident record source- Student Services, 301-387-3011.

Attendance and degree information available by phone, fax, mail. Search requires name plus SSN. Also helpful: exact years of attendance. There is no fee.

Goucher College, Registrar, 1021 Dulaney Valley Rd, Baltimore, MD 21204, 410-337-6090 (Fax: 410-337-6123). Hours: 8:45AM-5PM. Enrollment: 1130. Records go back to 1885. Alumni records are maintained here also. Call 410-337-6180. Degrees granted: Bachelors; Masters. Special programs- Master Historic Preservatory, 440-337-6200: Master Education & Arts in Teaching, 410-337-6047: Post Bac Pre-Med, 410-337-6207.

Attendance and degree information available by phone, fax, mail. Search requires name only. Also helpful: SSN, date of birth, exact years of attendance. There is no fee.

Hagerstown Business College, Registrar, 18618 Crestwood Dr, Hagerstown, MD 21742, 301-739-2670 (Fax: 301-791-7661). Hours: 8AM-5PM. Enrollment: 500. Records go back to 1958. Alumni records are maintained here at the same

phone number. Degrees granted: Associate. Adverse incident record source- Registrar.

Attendance and degree information available by fax, mail. Search requires name only. Also helpful: SSN, date of birth, exact years of attendance. There is no fee.

Hagerstown Junior College, Registrar, 11400 Robinwood Dr, Hagerstown, MD 21742, 301-790-2800 X239 (Fax: 301-791-9165). Hours: 8AM-4PM. Enrollment: 3000. Records go back to 1946. Planning purge back 5-10 years. Alumni records are maintained here also. Call 301-790-2800 X346. Degrees granted: Associate.

Attendance and degree information available by phone, fax, mail. Search requires name plus SSN. Also helpful: date of birth, exact years of attendance. There is no fee.

Harford Community College, Registrar, 401 Thomas Run Rd, Bel Air, MD 21015, 410-836-4222 (Fax: 410-836-4169). Hours: 8AM-7:30PM M-Th; 8AM-4:30PM F; 9AM-1PM S. Enrollment: 5304. Records go back to 1957. Alumni records are maintained here also. Call 410-836-4428. Degrees granted: Associate. Adverse incident record source- Campus Security, 410-836-4272.

Attendance information available by phone, fax, mail. Search requires name plus SSN, approximate years of attendance. Also helpful: date of birth, exact years of attendance. There is no fee.

Degree information available by phone, fax, mail. Search requires name plus SSN, date of birth, approximate years of attendance. Also helpful: exact years of attendance. There is no fee.

Home Study International, Registrar, 12501 Old Columbia Pike, PO Box 4437, Silver Spring, MD 20914, 301-680-6570 (Fax: 301-680-5157). Hours: 8:30AM-4:30PM M-Th, 8:30-11:30AM F. Records go back to 1954. Degrees granted: Associate.

Attendance and degree information available by phone, fax, mail. Search requires name only. Also helpful: SSN, date of birth, exact years of attendance. There is no fee.

Hood College, Registrar, 401 Rosemont Ave, Frederick, MD 21701, 301-696-3616 (Fax: 301-696-3597). Hours: 8AM-5PM. Enrollment: 2000. Records go back to 1893. Alumni records are maintained here also. Call 301-696-3900. Degrees granted: Bachelors; Masters. Adverse incident record source- Student Affairs, 301-696--3573.

Attendance and degree information available by phone, fax, mail. Search requires name plus SSN. Also helpful: exact years of attendance. There is no fee.

Howard Community College, Registrar, 10901 Little Patuxent Pkwy, Columbia, MD 21044, 410-992-4800 (Fax: 410-715-2426). Hours: 8:30AM-5PM. Enrollment: 5000. Records go back to 1970. Alumni records are maintained here at the same phone number. Degrees granted: Associate. Adverse incident record source- Security, 410-992-4882.

Attendance and degree information available by phone, fax, mail. Search requires name plus SSN, exact years of attendance. There is no fee.

Johns Hopkins University, Registrar, 75 Garland Hall, 3400 N Charles St, Baltimore, MD 21218-2688, 410-516-8600 (Fax: 410-516-6477). Hours: 8:30AM-5PM. Enrollment: 12000. Records go back to 1879. Alumni Records Office: Alumni Relations, Johns Hopkins University, 3211 N Charles St, Baltimore, MD 21218. Degrees granted: Associate; Bachelors; Masters; Doctorate. Adverse incident record source- Dean of Students, 410-516-8208.

Attendance and degree information available by phone, fax, mail. Search requires name plus SSN. Also helpful: date of birth, exact years of attendance. There is no fee.

Johns Hopkins University, (Columbia Center), Registrar, 6740 Alexander Bell Dr, Columbia, MD 21046, 410-

516-7088 (Fax: 410-516-6477). Hours: 8:30AM-4:30PM. Enrollment: 16120. Records go back to 1880. Alumni Records Office: Alumni Association, Johns Hopkins University (Columbia Centre), 3400 N Charles St, Baltimore, MD 21218. Degrees granted: Associate; Bachelors; Masters; Doctorate. Special programs- Medicine, 410-955-3080: Hygiene, 410-955-3552: Nursing, 410-955-9840. Adverse incident record source- Registrar, 410-516-7088.

Attendance and degree information available by phone, fax, mail. Search requires name plus SSN, exact years of attendance. There is no fee.

Johns Hopkins University, (Peabody Institute of the Johns Hopkins University), Registrar, One E Mount Vernon Pl, Baltimore, MD 21202, 410-659-8266 (Fax: 410-659-8129). Hours: 8:30AM-5PM. Enrollment: 625. Records go back to 1932. Alumni records are maintained here also. Call 410-659-8176. Degrees granted: Bachelors; Masters; Doctorate; Artist Diploma, Graduate Performance Diploma. Adverse incident record source- Campus Policy, 410-396-2525.

Attendance and degree information available by phone, fax, mail. Search requires name plus exact years of attendance. Also helpful: date of birth. There is no fee.

Lincoln Christian College East Coast, Registrar, PO Box 629, Bel Air, MD 21014, 410-836-2000. Enrollment: 40. Formerly Eastern Christian College Records go back to 1946. Degrees granted: Associate; Bachelors.

Attendance and degree information available by mail. Search requires name plus SSN, exact years of attendance. There is no fee.

Loyola College in Maryland, Registrar, Records Office MH 121, 4501 N Charles St, Baltimore, MD 21210-2699, 410-617-2504 (Fax: 410-617-5031). Hours: 7AM-7:45PM M-Th; 7AM-3PM F. Enrollment: 6000. Records go back to 1900. Alumni records are maintained here also. Call 410-617-2475. Degrees granted: Bachelors; Masters; Doctorate. Certification: 30 credit beyond the Masters.

Attendance information available by phone, fax, mail. Search requires name plus SSN, exact years of attendance. Also helpful: date of birth. There is no fee.

Degree information available by phone, fax, mail. Search requires name plus SSN, exact years of attendance. Also helpful: date of birth, approximate years of attendance. There is no fee.

Maryland College of Art and Design, Registrar, 10500 Georgia Ave, Silver Spring, MD 20902, 301-649-4454 (Fax: 301-649-2940). Hours: 8AM-5PM. Enrollment: 80. Records go back to 1986. Degrees granted: Associate.

Attendance and degree information available by fax, mail. Search requires name plus SSN, exact years of attendance, signed release. There is no fee.

Maryland Institute College of Art, Registrar, 1300 W Mt Royal Ave, Baltimore, MD 21217, 410-225-2236. Hours: 8:30AM-4PM. Enrollment: 1050. Records go back to 1925. Alumni records are maintained here also. Call 410-225-2339. Degrees granted: Bachelors; Masters.

Attendance and degree information available by phone, mail. Search requires name plus SSN, approximate years of attendance. Also helpful: date of birth, exact years of attendance. There is no fee.

Montgomery College-Germantown Campus, Registrar, 20200 Observation Dr, Germantown, MD 20876, 301-353-7821 (Fax: 301-353-7815). Hours: 8:30AM-6:30PM M-Th; 8:30AM-5PM F. Enrollment: 3730. Records go back to 1947. Alumni records are maintained here at the same phone number. Degrees granted: Associate.

Attendance and degree information available by mail. Search requires name plus SSN, date of birth, signed release. Also helpful: exact years of attendance. Fee is $5.00.

Montgomery College-Rockville Campus,
Registrar, 51 Mannakee St, Rockville, MD 20850, 301-279-5046 (Fax: 301-279-5037). Records are not housed here. They are located at Montgomery College-Germantown Campus, Registrar, 20200 Observation Dr, Germantown, MD 20876.

Montgomery College-Takoma Park Campus,
Registrar, Takoma Ave and Fenton St, Takoma Park, MD 20912, 301-650-1500 (Fax: 301-650-1497). Hours: 8:30AM-6:30PM M-Th; 8:30AM-4:30PM F. Enrollment: 4050. Records go back to 1945. Alumni records are maintained here at the same phone number. Degrees granted: Associate. Adverse incident record source- Dean of Student Services, 301-650-1469.

Attendance and degree information available by mail. Search requires name plus SSN. Also helpful: date of birth, exact years of attendance. There is no fee.

Morgan State University,
Registrar, Hillen Rd and Cold Spring Lane, Baltimore, MD 21239, 410-319-3301 (Fax: 410-319-3259). Hours: 8AM-5PM. Enrollment: 5800. Records go back to 1916. Alumni Records Office: Alumni Association, McKeldin Center Rm 206, Baltimore, MD 21239. Degrees granted: Bachelors; Masters; Doctorate. Adverse incident record source- MSU Police, 410-319-3103.

Attendance and degree information available by phone, fax, mail. Search requires name plus SSN. Also helpful: date of birth, exact years of attendance. There is no fee.

Mount St. Mary's College and Seminary,
Registrar, Emmitsburg, MD 21727, 301-447-5215 (Fax: 301-447-5755). Hours: 9AM-Noon, 1-5PM. Enrollment: 1500. Records go back to 1808. Alumni records are maintained here also. Call 301-447-5362. Degrees granted: Bachelors; Masters. Adverse incident record source- Registrar, 301-447-5215.

Attendance and degree information available by phone, fax, mail. Search requires name plus SSN. Also helpful: date of birth, exact years of attendance. There is no fee.

Ner Israel Rabbinical College,
Registrar, 400 Mount Wilson Lane, Baltimore, MD 21208, 410-484-7200 X234 (Fax: 410-484-3060). Hours: 1-6PM. Enrollment: 400. Records go back to 1933. Alumni records are maintained here at the same phone number. Degrees granted: Bachelors; Masters; Doctorate.

Attendance and degree information available by phone, fax, mail. Search requires name only. There is no fee.

Prince George's Community College,
Registrar, 301 Largo Rd, Largo, MD 20774, 301-322-0801 (Fax: 301-322-0119). Hours: 8:30AM-7:30PM. Enrollment: 12000. Records go back to 1958. Alumni records are maintained here also. Call 301-322-0854. Degrees granted: Associate. Adverse incident record source- Student Services, 301-322-0854.

Attendance and degree information available by phone, fax, mail. Search requires name plus SSN. Also helpful: exact years of attendance. There is no fee.

Prince George's Community College,
(Branch), Registrar, Andrews AFB Degree Center, Bldg 1413 Arkansas Rd, Andrews Air Force Base, MD 20762, 301-322-0778. Records are not housed here. They are located at Prince George's Community College, Registrar, 301 Largo Rd, Largo, MD 20774.

Salisbury State University,
Registrar, Salisbury, MD 21801, 410-543-6150 (Fax: 410-548-5979). Hours: 8AM-5PM. Enrollment: 6048. Records go back to 1926. Alumni records are maintained here also. Call 410-543-6042. Degrees granted: Bachelors; Masters. Adverse incident record source- Dean of Students, 410-543-6080.

Attendance information available by phone, fax, mail. Search requires name plus SSN. There is no fee.

Degree information available by phone, fax, mail. Search requires name plus SSN, date of birth, approximate years of attendance. There is no fee.

Sojourner-Douglass College,
Registrar, 500 N Caroline St, Baltimore, MD 21205, 410-276-0306. Hours: 8AM-4:30PM. Enrollment: 258. Records go back to 1980. Alumni records are maintained here also. Call 410-276-0306. Degrees granted: Bachelors.

Attendance and degree information available by mail. Search requires name plus SSN, exact years of attendance. There is no fee.

St. John's College,
Registrar, 60 College Ave, PO Box 2800, Annapolis, MD 21404, 410-626-2513 (Fax: 410-626-0789). Hours: 8:30AM-Noon; 1PM-4:30PM. Enrollment: 530. Records go back to 1700's. Alumni records are maintained here also. Call 410-626-2531. Degrees granted: Bachelors; Masters. Adverse incident record source- Registrar, 410-626-2513.

Attendance and degree information available by fax, mail. Search requires name plus signed release. Also helpful: SSN, exact years of attendance. There is no fee.

St. Mary's College of Maryland,
Registrar, St. Mary's City, MD 20686, 301-862-0336 (Fax: 301-862-0449). Hours: 8AM-5PM. Enrollment: 1500. Records go back to 1924. Alumni records are maintained here also. Call 301-862-0280. Degrees granted: Bachelors. Adverse incident record source- Dean of Students, 301-862-0208.

Attendance and degree information available by phone, fax, mail. Search requires name plus SSN, exact years of attendance. There is no fee.

St. Mary's Seminary and University,
Registrar, 5400 Roland Ave, Baltimore, MD 21210, 410-323-3200 (Fax: 410-323-3554). Hours: 8:30AM-4:30PM. Enrollment: 241. Alumni records are maintained here also. Call 410-323-3200 X74. Degrees granted: Bachelors; Masters.

Attendance and degree information available by phone, fax, mail. Search requires name plus SSN, date of birth, exact years of attendance. There is no fee.

Towson State University,
Records Office, 8000 York Rd, Towson, MD 21204, 410-830-3240 (Fax: 410-830-3443). Hours: 8:30AM-4:30PM. Enrollment: 13700. Records go back to 1920. Alumni Records Office: Alumni Association, Arburn Dr, Arburn House, Towson, MD 21204. Degrees granted: Bachelors; Masters. Adverse incident record source- Student Services.

Attendance information available by phone, fax, mail. Search requires name plus SSN. There is no fee.

Degree information available by phone, fax, mail. Search requires name plus SSN. Also helpful: approximate years of attendance. There is no fee.

Traditional Acupuncture Institute,
Registrar, American City Bldg Ste 100, 10227 Wincopin Cir, Columbia, MD 21044, 410-997-4888 (Fax: 410-964-3544). Hours: 9AM-5PM. Enrollment: 160. Records go back to 1981. Degrees granted: Masters. Adverse incident record source- Registrar, 410-997-4888.

Attendance and degree information available by mail. Search requires name plus SSN, date of birth, exact years of attendance, signed release. There is no fee.

Uniformed Services University of the Health Sciences,
Registrar, 4301 Jones Bridge Rd, Bethesda, MD 20814, 301-295-3197 (Fax: 301-295-3545). Hours: 7:30AM-4PM. Enrollment: 165. Records go back to 1976. Alumni records are maintained here also. Call 301-295-3578. Degrees granted: Masters; Doctorate; Graduate Nursing. Special pro-

grams- Graduate School of Nursing, 301-295-1989. Adverse incident record source- Student Affairs, 301-295-3185.

Attendance and degree information available by phone, fax, mail. Search requires name plus SSN. Also helpful: date of birth, exact years of attendance. There is no fee.

United States Naval Academy, Registrar, 589 McNair Rd, Annapolis, MD 21402, 410-293-6389 (Fax: 410-293-2327). Hours: 8AM-4:30PM. Enrollment: 165. Records go back to 1845. Alumni records are maintained here also. Call 410-293-1000. Degrees granted: Bachelors.

Attendance and degree information available by phone, fax, mail. Search requires name plus SSN, date of birth, exact years of attendance. There is no fee.

Univeristy of Maryland at Baltimore, Registrar, 621 W Lombard St, Rm 326, Baltimore, MD 21201, 410-706-7480 (Fax: 410-706-4053). Enrollment: 5750. Records go back to 1807. Alumni records are maintained here at the same phone number. Degrees granted: Bachelors; Masters; Doctorate. Special programs- Nursing: Medical. Adverse incident record source- Student Services.

Attendance and degree information available by phone, mail. Search requires name plus SSN, exact years of attendance. There is no fee.

University of Baltimore, Registrar, 1420 N Charles St, Baltimore, MD 21201, 410-837-4825 (Fax: 410-837-4820). Hours: 8:30AM-7PM M-Th, 8:30AM-4:30PM F. Enrollment: 5000. Records go back to 1925. Alumni records are maintained here also. Call 410-837-6131. Degrees granted: Bachelors; Masters. Special programs- Law. Adverse incident record source- Enrollment Mgmt Student Services, 410-837-4755.

Attendance and degree information available by phone, fax, mail. Search requires name plus SSN, date of birth, exact years of attendance. There is no fee.

University of Maryland, (College Park), Registrar, Mitchell Bldg Room 1101, College Park, MD 20742, 301-314-7934 (Fax: 301-314-9568). Hours: 9AM-5PM. Enrollment: 32440. Records go back to 1947. Alumni records are maintained here at the same phone number. Degrees granted: Doctorate.

Attendance and degree information available by phone, fax, mail. Search requires name plus SSN. There is no fee.

Universlty of Maryland Baltimore County, Registrar, 5401 Wilkens Ave, Baltimore, MD 21228, 410-455-3727 (Fax: 410-455-1094). Hours: 8:30AM-4:30PM. Enrollment: 10000. Records go back to 1966. Alumni records are maintained here also. Call 410-455-2904. Degrees granted: Bachelors; Masters; Doctorate.

Attendance and degree information available by phone, fax, mail. Search requires name plus SSN. There is no fee.

University of Maryland College Park, Registrar, College Park, MD 20742, 301-314-8240 (Fax: 301-314-9568). Hours: 8:30AM-4:30PM. Records go back to 1900. Degrees granted: Bachelors; Masters; Doctorate. Special programs- Adult Ed Center, U of M, College Park, MD 20742. Adverse incident record source- Campus Police, 301-405-3555.

Attendance and degree information available by phone, fax, mail. Search requires name plus SSN, date of birth, exact years of attendance. There is no fee.

University of Maryland Eastern Shore, Registrar, Princess Anne, MD 21853, 410-651-2200 X6410 (Fax: 410-651-7922). Hours: 8:30AM-4:30PM. Enrollment: 2925. Records go back to 1886. Alumni records are maintained here also. Call 410-651-2200. Degrees granted: Bachelors; Masters; Doctorate.

Attendance and degree information available by phone, mail. Search requires name plus SSN, date of birth, exact years of attendance. There is no fee.

University of Maryland at Baltimore, Registrar, 621 W Lombard St Room 326, Baltimore, MD 21201, 410-706-7480 (Fax: 410-706-4053). Hours: 8AM-4:30PM. Enrollment: 5800. Records go back to 1886. Alumni Records Office: 666 W Baltimore St, Baltimore, MD 21201. Degrees granted: Bachelors; Masters; Doctorate; Professional. Special programs- Dental Hygiene: Medical Tecnologist: Physical Therapy. Adverse incident record source- Dean of Students, 410-706-7460.

Attendance and degree information available by phone, fax, mail. Search requires name plus SSN, approximate years of attendance. There is no fee.

University of Maryland, University College (The), Records Office, University Blvd at Adelphi Rd, College Park, MD 20742, 301-985-7268 (Fax: 301-985-7364). Enrollment: 32000. Records go back to 1947. Alumni records are maintained here at the same phone number. Degrees granted: Associate; Bachelors; Masters. Adverse incident record source- Security.

Attendance and degree information available by phone. Search requires name plus SSN, exact years of attendance. There is no fee.

Villa Julie College, Registrar, 1525 Green Spring Valley Rd, Stevenson, MD 21153, 410-486-7000 X2207 (Fax: 410-486-3552). Hours: 8AM-4:30PM. Enrollment: 1800. Records go back to 1947. Alumni records are maintained here at the same phone number. Degrees granted: Bachelors; Masters.

Attendance and degree information available by phone, mail. Search requires name plus SSN, exact years of attendance. There is no fee.

Washington Bible College, Registrar, 6511 Princess Garden Pkwy, Lanham, MD 20706, 301-552-1400 (Fax: 301-552-2775). Hours: 8AM-4:30PM. Enrollment: 325. Records go back to 1938. Alumni records are maintained here at the same phone number. Degrees granted: Associate; Bachelors.

Attendance and degree information available by phone, fax, mail. Search requires name only. Also helpful: SSN, exact years of attendance. There is no fee.

Washington College, Registrar, 300 Washington Ave, Chestertown, MD 21620, 410-778-7299 (Fax: 410-778-7850). Hours: 8:30AM-4:30PM. Records go back to 1930. Alumni records are maintained here also. Call 410-778-7812. Degrees granted: Bachelors; Masters.

Attendance and degree information available by phone, fax, mail. Search requires name plus SSN, exact years of attendance. There is no fee.

Western Maryland College, Registrar, 2 College Hill, Westminster, MD 21157, 410-857-2215 (Fax: 410-857-2752). Hours: 8:30AM-4:30PM. Enrollment: 2400. Alumni records are maintained here also. Call 410-857-2296. Degrees granted: Bachelors; Masters. Adverse incident record source- Campus Safety, 410-857-2202.

Attendance and degree information available by phone, fax, mail. Search requires name only. Also helpful: SSN, date of birth, exact years of attendance. There is no fee.

Wor-Wic Community College, Registrar's Office Rm 109, 32000 Campus Dr, Salisbury, MD 21801, 410-334-2907 (Fax: 410-334-2954). Hours: 8:30PM-5PM Winter; 8AM-4:30PM Summer. Enrollment: 1900. Records go back to 1975. Degrees granted: Associate. Certification: Proficiency. Special programs- Continuing Education, 410-334-2815. Adverse incident record source- Dean of Students, 410-334-2893.

Attendance and degree information available by phone, fax, mail. Search requires name plus SSN, approximate years of attendance. Also helpful: date of birth, exact years of attendance. There is no fee.

Trade and Vocational Schools

Abbie Business Institute, 5310 Spectrum Dr, Frederick, MD 21701, 301-694-0211

Acupuncture School of Maryland, 4400 East-West Hwy #128, Bethesda, MD 20814, 301-907-8986

All-State Career School (Branch Campus), 201 S Arlington Ave, Baltimore, MD 21223, 410-566-7111

Army Ordinance Center and School, Bldg 3072 #217-C, Aberdeen Proving Ground, MD 21005, 410-278-2994

Arundel Institute of Technology, 1808 Edison Hwy, Baltimore, MD 21213, 410-327-6640

Broadcasting Institute of Maryland, 7200 Harford Rd, Baltimore, MD 21234, 410-254-2770

Bureau of Medicine and Surgery - US Navy, 2300 E St Bldg 2, Washington, MD 20372-5300, 202-762-3370

Diesel Institute of America, PO Box 69, Grantsville, MD 21536, 301-895-5139

Emergency Management Institute, 16825 S Seton Ave, Emmitsburg, MD 21727, 301-447-1240

Fleet Business School, 2530 Riva Rd, Annapolis, MD 21401, 410-266-8500

Johnston School of Practical Nursing, 201 E University Pkwy, Baltimore, MD 21218, 410-554-2327

Lincoln Technical Institute, 3200 Wilkens Ave, Baltimore, MD 21229, 410-646-5480

Lincoln Technical Institute, 7800 Central Ave, Landover, MD 20785, 301-336-7250

Maryland Drafting Institute, 2045 University Blvd E, Langley Park, MD 20783, 301-439-7776

Medix School (The), 1017 York Rd, Towson, MD 21204, 410-337-5155

National Cryptologic School, 9800 Savage Rd, Fort Meade, MD 20755, 410-859-6266

Naval Health Sciences Education and Training Command, 8901 Wisconsin Ave, Bethesda, MD 20889, 301-295-0203

Naval Health Sciences Education and Training Command (Dental School-Maxillofacial), Nat'l Naval Dental Ctr, Bethesda, MD 20889, 301-295-0064

Naval Health Sciences Education and Training Command (School of Health Science), Nat'l Naval Medical Ctr, Bethesda, MD 20889, 301-295-1204

New England Tractor Trailer Training School, 1410 Bush St, Baltimore, MD 21230, 410-783-0100

Rice Aviation, a Division of A&J Enterprises (Branch Campus), 701 Wilson Point Rd, Baltimore, MD 21220, 410-682-2226

TESST Electronics and Computer Institute, 5122 Baltimore Ave, Hyattsville, MD 20781, 301-864-5750

Ultrasound Diagnostic School (Branch Campus), 1320 Fenwick Ln, Silver Spring, MD 20910, 301-588-0786

Woodbridge Business Institute, 309 E Main St, Salisbury, MD 21801, 301-762-6700

State Licensing & Business Registration Quick Finder Index

Architecture, Engineering & Surveying
Architect, Partnerships, Corporations #10
(7144) .... ☎ 410-333-6322
Engineer #10 .... ☎ 410-333-6267
Landscape Architect #10 .... ☎ 410-333-6267
Surveyor #10 .... ☎ 410-333-6267

Business - Court & Legal Services
Attorney #1 .... ☎ 410-514-7044
Bondsman #8 .... ☎ 410-333-4074
Notary Public #23 (91865) .... ☎ 410-974-5520

Business - General Services
Fundraising Counsel #23 (130) .... ☎ 410-974-5534
Precious Metal & Gem Dealer/Secondhand #10
.... ☎ 410-333-6267
Professional Solicitor #23 (45) .... ☎ 410-974-5534
Public Accountant-CPA #10 .... ☎ 410-333-6267

Construction & Manufacturing
Contractor #9 .... ☎ 410-333-6309
Master Electrician #10 .... ☎ 410-333-6267
Plumber #10 .... ☎ 410-333-6267
Water Conditioner Installer #5 .... ☎ 410-631-3168

Education
School Administrator #4 410-333-2141
Teacher #4 410-333-2141

Environmental & Agriculture
Asbestos Abatement #5 .... ☎ 410-631-3200
Forester #10 .... ☎ 410-333-6267
Hazardous & Solid Waste #5 410-631-3343
Mining Foreman/Fire Boss #5 .... ☎ 410-631-3609
Pesticide Applicator #3 .... ☎ 410-841-5710
Pesticide Applicator/Consultant #15 ... ☎ 410-764-4725
Pesticide Applicator/Operator/Dealer #3 ...... ☎ 410-841-5710
Pesticide Consultant #3 .... ☎ 410-841-5710
Pesticide Dealer #3 .... ☎ 410-841-5710
Pesticide-Certified Consultant #3 ...... ☎ 410-841-5710
Pesticide-Private Applicator #3 .... ☎ 410-841-5710
Pump Installer #5 (65) .... ☎ 410-631-3168
Sewage Treatment #5 .... ☎ 410-631-3609
Veterinarian #2 (2200) .... ☎ 410-841-5862
Waste Water Treatment Superintendent #5
.... ☎ 410-631-3609
Well Driller #5 (520) .... ☎ 410-631-3168

Financial - Real Estate, Insurance & Banking
Collection Agency #9 (763) .... ☎ 410-333-6820
Insurance Agent #8 .... ☎ 410-333-4074
Insurance Broker/Advisor #8 .... ☎ 410-333-4074
Investment Adviser/Representative #24 .... ☒ 410-576-6360
Mortgage Broker #9 (2000) .... ☎ 410-333-6830
Real Estate Agent #9 410-333-6230
Real Estate Appraiser #9 (2800) .... ☒ 410-333-6590
Securities Broker/Dealer #24 .... ☒ 410-576-6360
Securities Sales Agent #24 .... ☒ 410-576-6360

Health & Beauty
Acupuncturist #15 (433) .... ☎ 410-764-4766
Audiologist #15 .... ☎ 410-764-4725
Barber #9 .... ☎ 410-333-6320
Chiropractor #15 .... ☎ 410-764-4727
Cosmetologist #9 .... ☎ 410-333-6801
Dentist #15 (5013) .... ☎ 410-764-4730
Dietitian #15 .... ☎ 410-764-4733
Electrologist #6 (214) .... ☒ 410-764-4702
Embalmer #15 .... ☎ 410-764-4725
Funeral Director #15 .... ☎ 410-764-4725
Funeral Establishment #15 .... ☎ 410-764-4792
Hearing Aid Dispenser #15 .... ☎ 410-764-4725
Medical Doctor #18 410-764-4761
Mortician #15 (738) .... ☎ 410-764-4792
Nurse #17 .... ☎ 410-764-4740
Nursing Home Administrator #15 ...... ☒ 410-764-4750
Occupational Therapist #15 .... ☎ 410-764-4727
Optometrist #15 .... ☎ 410-764-4725
Pesticide Business #3 .... ☎ 410-841-5710
Pharmacist #15 .... ☒ 410-764-4755
Physical Therapist #16 (2913) .... ☎ 410-764-4752
Physical Therapist Assistant #16 .... ☎ 410-764-4752
Podiatrist #16 (370) .... ☎ 410-764-4785
Radiation Therapy Technician #15 ..... ☎ 410-764-4725
Radiologic Technician #15 .... ☎ 410-764-4725
Respiratory Care Practitioner #15 ...... ☎ 410-764-4725
Sanitarian #5 .... ☎ 410-631-3167
Speech Pathologist #15 .... ☎ 410-764-4725

Investigations & Security
Corrections Officer #14 410-764-4070
Police Officer #14 410-764-4070
Private Investigator #22 .... ☎ 410-799-0191

Social Services
Counselor #16 .... ☎ 410-764-4732
Day Care Provider #19 410-767-8600
Foster Care Provider #20 .... ☎ 410-554-5797
Psychologist #16 .... ☎ 410-764-4787
Social Worker #16 (11181) .... ☎ 410-764-4788

Sports & Entertainment
Boxer #11 (800) .... ☎ 410-333-6315
Greyhound Racing #7 .... ☎ 410-333-6267
Harness Racing #7 .... ☎ 410-333-6267
Horse Racing #7 .... ☎ 410-333-6267
Lottery Retailer #21 410-764-5770
Referee #9 .... ☎ 410-333-6801
Sports Agent #9 .... ☎ 410-333-6210

Transportation
Airport #13 .... ☎ 410-859-7064
Airport License (Public and Private
Registration) #13 (36) .... ☎ 410-859-7064
Cab Driver #12 410-768-7254
Pilot #10 .... ☎ 410-333-6267

State Licensing & Business Registration Agency Information

(1) Board of Law Examiners, 100 Community Pl, People's Resource Cntr, Rm 1210, Crownsville, MD 21032-2026, 410-514-7044

(2) Board of Veterinary Medical Examiners, 50 Harry S Truman Pkwy, Annapolis, MD 21401, 410-841-5862, Fax: 410-841-5999

(3) Department of Agriculture, Pesticide Regulation Section, 50 Harry S Truman Pkwy, Annapolis, MD 21401, 410-841-5710, Fax: 410-841-2765

(4) Department of Education, Division of Certification & Accreditation, 200 W Baltimore St, Baltimore, MD 21201-2595, 410-333-2141

(5) Department of Environment, 2500 Broenig Hwy, Baltimore, MD 21224, 410-631-4477, Fax: 410-633-0456

(6) Department of Health & Mental Hygiene, Boards and Commissiong, 4201 Patterson Ave. Rm 304, Baltimore, MD 21215, Department of Licensing & Regulation, Division of Racing, 501 St Paul Place, Baltimore, MD 21202, 410-333-6267, Fax: 410-333-8308

(7) Department of Licensing & Regulation, Insurance Agent/Brokers Licensing & Investigation, 501 St Paul Place, Baltimore, MD 21202, 410-333-4074, Fax: 410-333-8258

(8) Department of Licensing & Regulation, Office of the Secretary, 501 St Paul Place, Baltimore, MD 21202, 410-333-6801

(9) Department of Licensing & Regulation, Office of the Secretary, 501 St Paul Place, Baltimore, MD 21202, 410-333-6323, Fax: 410-333-6314

(10) Department of Licensing & Regulation, State Athletic Commission, 501 St Paul Place 8th Floor, Baltimore, MD 21202, 410-333-6315, Fax: 410-333-6314

(11) Department of Transportation, Motor Vehicle Administration, 6601 Ritchie Hwy, Glen Burnie, MD 21062, 410-768-7254

(12) Department of Transportation, State Aviation Administration, PO Box 8766 BWI Airport, Baltimore, MD 21240, 410-859-7064, Fax: 410-8597287

(13) Dept of Public Safety & Correctional Services, Handgun Permit Review Board, 6776 Reisterstown Rd, Suite 310, Baltimore, MD 21215-2341, 410-764-4182, Fax: 410-764-4182

(14) Licensing Boards, 4201 Patterson Ave, Baltimore, MD 21215, 410-764-4792, Fax: 410-358-6571

(15) Licensing Boards, 4201 Patterson Ave, Baltimore, MD 21215, 410-764-4788, Fax: 410-358-2469

(16) Licensing Boards, 4201 Patterson Ave, Baltimore, MD 21215, 410-764-4740, Fax: 410-764-5989

(17) Licensing Boards, 4201 Patterson Ave, Baltimore, MD 21215, 410-764-4761, Fax: 410-764-2478

(18) Maryland Commission on Human Relations, Child Care Administration, 2701 N Charles St, 5th Floor, Baltimore, MD 21218, 410-767-8600

(19) Maryland Commission on Human Relations, Foster Care Review Board, 311 W Saratoga, Baltimore, MD 21201, 410-554-5797, Fax: 410-333-8699

(20) Maryland State Lottery Agency, 6776 Reisterstown Rd, Suite 204, Baltimore, MD 21215, 410-764-5770

(21) Maryland State Police, Licensing Division, 7751 Washington Blvd., Jessup, MD 20794, 410-799-0191, Fax: 410-799-5934

(22) Office of Secretary of State, 100 State Circle, Statehouse, Annapolis, MD 21401, 410-974-5520, Fax: 410-974-5527

(23) Securities Division, Attorney General's Office, 200 St Paul Pl, Baltimore, MD 21202, 410-576-6360, Fax: 410-576-6532

Massachusetts

Capitol: Boston (Suffolk County)	
State Population	6.1 Million
Number of Degree Granting Institutions:	133
Number of State Licensing & Business Registration Agencies:	168

Degree Granting Educational Institutions

American International College, Registrar, 1000 State St, Springfield, MA 01109, 413-737-6212 (Fax: 413-737-2803). Hours: 8:30AM-4:30PM. Enrollment: 1200. Records go back to 1885. Alumni records are maintained here also. Call 413-737-7000. Degrees granted: Associate; Bachelors; Masters; Doctorate.
Attendance and degree information available by phone, fax, mail. Search requires name plus SSN, exact years of attendance. There is no fee.

Amherst College, Registrar, Amherst, MA 01002, 413-542-2225 (Fax: 413-542-2327). Hours: 8:30AM-4:30PM. Enrollment: 1600. Records go back to 1800's. Alumni records are maintained here also. Call 413-542-5900. Degrees granted: Bachelors.
Attendance and degree information available by phone, fax, mail. Search requires name plus SSN. Also helpful: date of birth, exact years of attendance. There is no fee.

Andover Newton Theological School, Registrar, 210 Herrick Rd, Newton Centre, MA 02159, 617-964-1100 X212 (Fax: 617-965-9756). Hours: 8:30AM-4:30PM. Enrollment: 500. Records go back to 1919. Alumni records are maintained here also. Call 617-964-1100 X202. Degrees granted: Masters; Doctorate.
Attendance and degree information available by phone, fax, mail. Search requires name plus exact years of attendance. Also helpful: SSN, date of birth. There is no fee.

Anna Maria College, Registrar, Paxton, MA 01612-1198, 508-849-3400 (Fax: 508-849-3430). Hours: 8:30AM-4:30PM. Enrollment: 1073. Records go back to 1952. Alumni records are maintained here also. Call 508-849-3342. Degrees granted: Associate; Bachelors; Masters. Adverse incident record source- Dean of Students, 508-849-3386: Security, 508-849-3370
Attendance and degree information available by phone, mail. Search requires name plus SSN, approximate years of attendance. There is no fee.

Aquinas College at Milton, Registrar, 303 Adams St, Milton, MA 02186, 617-696-3100 (Fax: 617-696-8706). Enrollment: 255. Records go back to 1957. Alumni records are maintained here at the same phone number. Degrees granted: Associate; 1-year Certificates.
Attendance and degree information available by phone, mail. Search requires name plus SSN, exact years of attendance. There is no fee.

Aquinas College at Newton, Registrar, 15 Walnut Park, Newton, MA 02158, 617-969-4400 (Fax: 617-965-6393). Hours: 8AM-4PM. Enrollment: 210. Records go back to 1961. Alumni records are maintained here also. Call 617-969-4400 X25. Degrees granted: Associate.
Attendance and degree information available by phone, fax, mail. Search requires name plus SSN, exact years of attendance. There is no fee.

Art Institute of Boston, Registrar, 700 Beacon St, Boston, MA 02215, 617-262-1223 (Fax: 617-437-1226). Hours: 8AM-5PM. Enrollment: 350. Records go back to 1950. Alumni records are maintained here at the same phone number. Degrees granted: Bachelors.
Attendance and degree information available by phone, fax, mail. Search requires name plus SSN, date of birth, approximate years of attendance. Also helpful: exact years of attendance. There is no fee.

Arthur D. Little School of Management, Registrar, Acorn Park, Cambridge, MA 02140, 617-498-6200 (Fax: 617-498-7100). Hours: 8:30AM-5PM. Enrollment: 60. Records go back to 1965. Alumni records are maintained here at the same phone number. Degrees granted: Masters. Adverse incident record source- Registrar, 617-498-6200.
Attendance and degree information available by fax, mail. Search requires name plus approximate years of attendance. There is no fee.

Assumption College, Registrar, 500 Salisbury St, Worcester, MA 01609, 508-767-7355 (Fax: 508-799-5411). Hours: 8:30AM-4:30PM. Enrollment: 2150. Records go back to 1905. Alumni records are maintained here also. Call 508-767-7223. Degrees granted: Bachelors; Masters. Adverse incident record source- Dean of Students, 508-767-7325.
Attendance and degree information available by phone, fax, mail. Search requires name plus SSN. There is no fee.

Atlantic Union College, Registrar, PO Box 1000, South Lancaster, MA 01561, 508-368-2216 (Fax: 508-368-2015). Hours: 9AM-Noon,1-4PM M-Th; 9-11AM F. Enrollment: 886. Records go back to 1884. Alumni records are maintained here at the same phone number. Degrees granted: Associate; Bachelors; Masters.

Attendance and degree information available by phone, fax, mail. Search requires name plus SSN, date of birth, approximate years of attendance. Also helpful: exact years of attendance. There is no fee.

Babson College, Registrar, Babson Park, Wellesley, MA 02157, 617-239-4519 (Fax: 617-239-5618). Hours: 8:30AM-4:30PM. Enrollment: 3200. Records go back to 1921. Alumni records are maintained here also. Call 617-239-4562. Degrees granted: Bachelors. Adverse incident record source- Student Affairs, 617-239-4218.

Attendance and degree information available by phone, fax, mail. Search requires name plus SSN, date of birth, approximate years of attendance. There is no fee.

Bay Path College, Registrar, 588 Longmeadow St, Longmeadow, MA 01106, 413-567-0621 (Fax: 413-567-9324). Hours: 8:30AM-5PM. Enrollment: 600. Records go back to 1897. Alumni records are maintained here also. Call 413-567-0621 X421. Degrees granted: Associate; Bachelors.

Attendance and degree information available by phone, fax, mail. Search requires name plus SSN, exact years of attendance. There is no fee.

Bay State College, Registrar, 122 Commonwealth Ave, Boston, MA 02116, 617-236-8000 (Fax: 617-236-8023). Hours: 8AM-5PM. Enrollment: 655. Records go back to 1970's. Degrees granted: Associate.

Attendance and degree information available by phone, fax, mail. Search requires name plus SSN, exact years of attendance. Also helpful: date of birth. There is no fee.

Becker College, Registrar, 61 Sever St, Worcester, MA 01609, 508-791-9241 (Fax: 508-831-7505). Hours: 8:30AM-5PM. Enrollment: 1500. Records go back to 1930's. Alumni records are maintained here also. Call 508-791-9241. Degrees granted: Associate; Bachelors. Adverse incident record source- Dean of Students, 508-791-9241.

Attendance and degree information available by phone, fax, mail. Search requires name plus exact years of attendance. Also helpful: SSN, date of birth. There is no fee.

Becker College, (Branch), Registrar, 3 Paxton St, Leicester, MA 01524, 508-791-9241 X434 (Fax: 508-892-0330). Hours: 8:30AM-5PM. Enrollment: 400. Records go back to 1897. Degrees granted: Bachelors.

Attendance information available by phone, fax, mail. Search requires name plus SSN, exact years of attendance. There is no fee.

Degree information available by phone, fax, mail. Search requires name plus SSN, exact years of attendance. Also helpful: date of birth. There is no fee.

Bentley College, Registrar, 175 Forest St, Waltham, MA 02154-4705, 617-891-2146 (Fax: 617-891-3428). Hours: 8:30AM-6:30PM M-Th, 8:30AM-4:30PM. Enrollment: 4820. Records go back to 1917. Alumni records are maintained here also. Call 617-891-3444. Degrees granted: Associate; Bachelors. Adverse incident record source- Dean of Students, 617-891-2058.

Attendance and degree information available by phone, fax, mail. Search requires name plus SSN, exact years of attendance. There is no fee.

Berklee College of Music, Registrar, 1140 Boylston St, Boston, MA 02215, 617-266-1400 X355 (Fax: 617-247-8278). Hours: 9AM-5PM. Enrollment: 2495. Records go back to 1950. Degrees granted: Bachelors; 4 year Professional Diploma. Adverse incident record source- Dean of Students.

Attendance and degree information available by phone, fax, mail. Search requires name plus SSN, approximate years of attendance. Also helpful: date of birth, exact years of attendance. There is no fee.

Berkshire Christian College, Registrar, PO Box 826, Haverhill, MA 01831, 508-372-8122. Enrollment: 35. Records go back to 1897. Alumni records are maintained here at the same phone number. Certification: Religion. Special programs- Bible Theology. Adverse incident record source- Student Affairs.

Attendance and degree information available by phone, mail. Search requires name plus SSN, approximate years of attendance. There is no fee.

Berkshire Community College, Registrar, 1350 West St, Pittsfield, MA 01201, 413-499-4660 X236 (Fax: 413-496-9511). Hours: 8AM-8PM M-Th; 8AM-4PM F. Enrollment: 2300. Records go back to 1960. Alumni records are maintained here at the same phone number. Degrees granted: Associate.

Attendance information available by phone, fax, mail. Search requires name plus SSN. Also helpful: exact years of attendance. There is no fee.

Degree information available by phone, fax, mail. Search requires name plus SSN. Also helpful: exact years of attendance. There is no fee.

Boston Architectural Center, Registrar, 320 Newbury St, Boston, MA 02115, 617-536-3170 (Fax: 617-536-5829). Enrollment: 850. Records go back to 1950. Alumni records are maintained here at the same phone number. Degrees granted: Bachelors. Special programs- Liberal Arts: Architecture. Adverse incident record source- Student Services.

Attendance and degree information available by phone, fax, mail. Search requires name plus SSN, exact years of attendance. There is no fee.

Boston College, Registrar, Chestnut Hill, MA 02167-3934, 617-552-2300 (Fax: 617-552-4975). Hours: 8:45AM-4:45PM. Enrollment: 12855. Records go back to 1863. Alumni records are maintained here also. Call 617-552-3440. Degrees granted: Bachelors; Masters; Doctorate; Graduate Law School. Adverse incident record source- Dean, 617-552-3470.

Attendance information available by phone, fax, mail. Search requires name plus SSN, approximate years of attendance. There is no fee.

Degree information available by fax, mail. Search requires name plus SSN, approximate years of attendance. There is no fee.

Boston Conservatory, Registrar, 8 The Fenway, Boston, MA 02215, 617-536-6340 X146 (Fax: 617-536-3176). Hours: 9AM-5PM. Enrollment: 400. Records go back to 1920. Alumni records are maintained here also. Call 617-536-6340 X128. Degrees granted: Bachelors; Masters. Adverse incident record source- Student Services, 617-536-6340 X121.

Attendance and degree information available by phone, fax, mail. Search requires name plus SSN, exact years of attendance. There is no fee.

Boston University, Registrar, 147 Bay State Rd, Boston, MA 02215, 617-353-3616. Hours: 9AM-5PM. Enrollment: 12855. Records go back to 1800's. Alumni records are maintained here also. Call 617-353-2233. Degrees granted: Bachelors; Masters; Doctorate.

Attendance and degree information available by phone, mail. Search requires name plus SSN, date of birth. There is no fee.

Bradford College, Office of the Registrar, 320 S Main St, Bradford, MA 01835, 508-372-7161 X5262 (Fax: 508-521-0480). Hours: 8:30AM-4:30PM. Enrollment: 600. Records go back to 1920. Alumni records are maintained here also. Call 508-372-7161 X5212. Degrees granted: Bachelors. Special programs- English as Second Language. Adverse incident record source- Dean of Students, 508-372-7161 X222.

Attendance information available by phone, fax, mail. Search requires name plus approximate years of attendance. Also helpful: SSN, date of birth. There is no fee.

Degree information available by phone, fax, mail. Search requires name only. Also helpful: SSN, date of birth, approximate years of attendance. There is no fee.

Brandeis University, Registrar, Waltham, MA 02254-9110, 617-736-2010 (Fax: 617-736-3485). Hours: 9AM-5PM. Enrollment: 3897. Records go back to 1936. Alumni records are maintained here also. Call 617-736-4100. Degrees granted: Bachelors. Adverse incident record source- Office of Campus Life.

Attendance and degree information available by phone, fax, mail. Search requires name plus SSN. There is no fee.

Bridgewater State College, Registrar, Bridgewater, MA 02325, 508-697-1200. Hours: 8AM-5PM. Enrollment: 8000. Records go back to 1840. Alumni records are maintained here also. Call 508-697-1200. Degrees granted: Bachelors; Masters.

Attendance and degree information available by phone, mail. Search requires name plus SSN, exact years of attendance. There is no fee.

Bristol Community College, Registrar, 777 Elsbree St, Fall River, MA 02720-7395, 508-678-2811 X240 (Fax: 508-678-2811 X2055). Hours: 8AM-4:30PM. Enrollment: 3120. Records go back to 1965. Alumni records are maintained here also. Call 508-678-2811 X2169. Degrees granted: Associate.

Attendance and degree information available by phone, mail. Search requires name plus SSN, exact years of attendance. There is no fee.

Bunker Hill Community College, Registrar, 250 New Rutherford Ave, Boston, MA 02129, 617-228-2000 (Fax: 617-228-2082). Hours: 8AM-5PM. Enrollment: 6008. Records go back to 1973. Alumni records are maintained here also. Call 617-228-2000. Degrees granted: Associate.

Attendance and degree information available by phone, fax, mail. Search requires name plus SSN, date of birth, exact years of attendance. There is no fee.

Cambridge College, Registrar, 1000 Massachusetts Ave #128, Cambridge, MA 02138, 617-868-1000 X101 (Fax: 617-349-3545). Hours: 9AM-9PM M-Th, 9AM-4PM F. Enrollment: 1700. Records go back to 1971. Alumni records are maintained here also. Call 617-868-1000 X131. Degrees granted: Bachelors; Masters.

Attendance and degree information available by phone, mail. Search requires name plus SSN, exact years of attendance. There is no fee.

Cape Cod Community College, Registrar, Rte 132, West Barnstable, MA 02668, 508-362-2131 X313 (Fax: 508-362-3988). Hours: 8:30AM-4:30PM. Enrollment: 3700. Records go back to 1961. Alumni records are maintained here at the same phone number. Degrees granted: Associate. Adverse incident record source- Security, 508-362-2131.

Attendance and degree information available by phone, mail. Search requires name plus SSN, date of birth. There is no fee.

Clark University, Registrar, Worcester, MA 01610-1477, 508-793-7426 (Fax: 508-793-7500). Hours: 9AM-5PM. Enrollment: 2581. Records go back to 1900. Alumni records are maintained here also. Call 508-793-7166. Degrees granted: Bachelors; Masters; Doctorate. Special programs- Professional & Continuing Education, 508-793-7217.

Attendance and degree information available by phone, fax, mail. Search requires name only. Also helpful: SSN, date of birth, exact years of attendance. There is no fee.

College of Our Lady of the Elms, Registrar, 291 Springfield St, Chicopee, MA 01013-2839, 413-594-2761 X236 (Fax: 413-592-4871). Hours: 8:30AM-4:30PM. Enrollment: 1244. Records go back to 1928. Alumni records are maintained here also. Call 413-594-2761 X227. Degrees granted: Associate; Bachelors; Masters. Adverse incident record source- Peter Mascaro, 413-594-2761 X231.

Attendance information available by phone, fax, mail. Search requires name plus date of birth, exact years of attendance. Also helpful: SSN. There is no fee.

Degree information available by phone, fax, mail. Search requires name plus exact years of attendance. Also helpful: SSN. There is no fee.

College of the Holy Cross, Registrar, College Street, Worcester, MA 01610-2395, 508-793-2511 (Fax: 508-793-3790). Hours: 8:30AM-4:30PM. Enrollment: 2700. Records go back to 1907. Alumni records are maintained here also. Call 508-793-2418. Degrees granted: Bachelors. Adverse incident record source- Dean of Students, 508-793-2411.

Attendance and degree information available by phone, fax, mail. Search requires name plus SSN. Also helpful: exact years of attendance. There is no fee.

Conway School of Landscape Design, Registrar, Delabarre Ave, Conway, MA 01341, 413-369-4044. Hours: 8:30AM 4:30PM. Enrollment: 18. Records go back to 1972. Degrees granted: Masters.

Attendance and degree information available by phone, mail. Search requires name plus exact years of attendance. There is no fee.

Curry College, Registrar, Milton, MA 02186, 617-333-2348 (Fax: 617-333-6860). Hours: 8:30AM-4:30PM. Enrollment: 1160. Records go back to 1920. Alumni records are maintained here also. Call 617-333-2212. Degrees granted: Bachelors; Masters. Adverse incident record source- Student Life, 717-333-2254.

Attendance and degree information available by phone, fax, mail. Search requires name plus SSN. There is no fee.

Dean College, Registrar, Franklin, MA 02038, 508-528-9100 (Fax: 508-541-8726). Hours: 8:30AM-4:30PM. Enrollment: 1700. Records go back to 1865. Alumni records are maintained here at the same phone number. Degrees granted: Associate. Special programs- "Bridge" Program - Prep. for entrance to college. Adverse incident record source- Campus Life, 508-541-1551.

Attendance and degree information available by phone, fax, mail. Search requires name only. Also helpful: SSN, date of birth, exact years of attendance. There is no fee.

Eastern Nazarene College, Registrar, 23 E Elm Ave, Quincy, MA 02170-2999, 617-745-3476/745-3477. Hours: 8AM-5PM. Enrollment: 670. Records go back to 1919. Alumni records are maintained here at the same phone number. Degrees granted: Bachelors; Masters.

Attendance and degree information available by phone, mail. Search requires name plus date of birth, exact years of attendance. There is no fee.

Emerson College, Registrar, 100 Beacon St, Boston, MA 02116-1596, 617-578-8660 (Fax: 617-578-8619). Hours: 9AM-5PM. Enrollment: 3800. Records go back to 1965. Some records prior to 1965 stored on microfilm. Alumni records are maintained here also. Call 617-824-8535. Degrees granted: Bachelors; Masters.

Attendance and degree information available by phone, fax, mail. Search requires name plus approximate years of attendance. Also helpful: SSN, date of birth, exact years of attendance. There is no fee.

Emmanuel College, Registrar, 400 The Fenway, Boston, MA 02115, 617-735-9960 (Fax: 617-731-9877). Hours: 8:30AM-4:30PM. Enrollment: 1568. Records go back to 1921. Alumni records are maintained here also. Call 617-735-9771. Degrees granted: Bachelors; Masters. Adverse incident record source- Security, 617-735-9710.

Attendance and degree information available by phone, fax, mail. Search requires name only. Also helpful: SSN, approximate years of attendance. There is no fee.

Endicott College, Registrar, Beverly, MA 01915, 508-927-0585 X2064 (Fax: 508-927-0084). Hours: 9AM-5PM. Enrollment: 850. Records go back to 1939. Alumni records are maintained here at the same phone number. Degrees granted: Associate; Bachelors; Masters.

Attendance and degree information available by phone, fax, mail. Search requires name plus exact years of attendance. Also helpful: SSN. There is no fee.

Episcopal Divinity School, Registrar, 99 Brattle St, Cambridge, MA 02138, 617-868-3450 (Fax: 617-864-5385). Hours: 9AM-5PM. Enrollment: 127. Records go back to 1978. Alumni records are maintained here at the same phone number. Degrees granted: Masters; Doctorate.

Attendance and degree information available by phone, fax, mail. Search requires name plus approximate years of attendance. Also helpful: exact years of attendance. There is no fee.

Essex Agricultural and Technical Institute, Registrar, 562 Maple St, Hathorne, MA 01937, 508-774-0050 X224 (Fax: 508-774-6530). Hours: 8AM-4PM. Enrollment: 500. Records go back to 1960. Degrees granted: Associate.

Attendance and degree information available by phone, mail. Search requires name plus SSN, exact years of attendance. There is no fee.

Fisher College, Registrar, 118 Beacon St, Boston, MA 02116, 617-236-8826 (Fax: 617-236-8858). Hours: 8:30AM-4:30PM. Enrollment: 2415. Records go back to 1945. Alumni records are maintained here also. Call 617-262-3240. Degrees granted: Associate.

Attendance and degree information available by phone, fax, mail. Search requires name plus SSN, approximate years of attendance. There is no fee.

Fitchburg State College, Registrar, 160 Pearl St, Fitchburg, MA 01420, 508-345-2151 X3138 (Fax: 508-665-3683). Hours: 8AM-5PM. Enrollment: 3605. Records go back to 1960. Degrees granted: Bachelors; Masters.

Attendance and degree information available by phone, fax, mail. Search requires name plus approximate years of attendance. Also helpful: SSN, date of birth, exact years of attendance. There is no fee.

Forsyth School of Dental Hygienists, 140 Fenway, Boston, MA 02115, 617-262-5200 X211 (Fax: 617-262-4021). Enrollment: 120. Records go back to 1920. Alumni records are maintained here at the same phone number. Degrees granted: Associate; Bachelors. Adverse incident record source- Student Services.

Attendance and degree information available by phone, mail. Search requires name plus SSN, exact years of attendance. There is no fee.

Framingham State College, Registrar, 100 State St, Framingham, MA 01701-9101, 508-626-4545 (Fax: 508-626-4017). Hours: 8:30AM-4:30PM. Enrollment: 3624. Records go back to 1839. Degrees granted: Bachelors; Masters. Certification: Teachers Cert.

Attendance and degree information available by phone, mail. Search requires name plus SSN, exact years of attendance. Also helpful: date of birth. There is no fee.

Franklin Institute of Boston, Registrar, Boston, MA 02116, 617-423-4630 (Fax: 617-482-3706). Hours: 7:30AM-5PM. Records go back to 1908. Alumni records are maintained here at the same phone number. Degrees granted: Associate; Bachelors.

Attendance and degree information available by phone, fax, mail. Search requires name plus approximate years of attendance. Also helpful: SSN. There is no fee.

Franklin Institute of Boston, Registrar, 41 Berkley St, Boston, MA 02116, 617-423-4630 (Fax: 617-482-3706). Hours: 7:30AM-5PM. Enrollment: 300. Records go back to 1908. Alumni records are maintained here at the same phone number. Degrees granted: Associate; Bachelors. Special programs- Bachelors in Automative Technolgy, 617-423-4630. Adverse incident record source- Student Life, 617-423-4630.

Attendance and degree information available by phone, fax, mail. Search requires name only. Also helpful: SSN, date of birth, exact years of attendance. There is no fee.

Gordon College, Registrar, Wenham, MA 01984, 508-927-2300 X4208 (Fax: 508-524-3724). Hours: 8AM-4:30PM. Enrollment: 1200. Alumni records are maintained here at the same phone number. Degrees granted: Bachelors. Adverse incident record source- Public Safety.

Attendance and degree information available by phone, fax, mail. Search requires name only. Also helpful: date of birth, exact years of attendance. There is no fee.

Gordon-Conwell Theological Seminary, Registrar, 130 Essex St, South Hamilton, MA 01982, 508-468-5111 X380 (Fax: 508-468-6691). Hours: 9AM-4:30PM. Enrollment: 1015. Records go back to 1969. Degrees granted: Masters; Doctorate.

Attendance and degree information available by phone, fax, mail. Search requires name only. Also helpful: exact years of attendance. There is no fee.

Greenfield Community College, Registrar, One College Dr, Greenfield, MA 01301, 413-774-3131 (Fax: 413-773-5129). Hours: 8:30AM-5PM. Enrollment: 1810. Records go back to 1968. Alumni records are maintained here also. Call 413-774-3131 X523. Degrees granted: Associate.

Attendance and degree information available by phone, mail. Search requires name plus SSN, date of birth, exact years of attendance. Also helpful: approximate years of attendance. There is no fee.

Hampshire College, Central Records, Amherst, MA 01002, 413-582-5421 (Fax: 413-582-5584). Hours: 8:30AM-Noon, 1-4:30PM. Enrollment: 1100. Records go back to 1970. Alumni records are maintained here also. Call 413-582-5516. Degrees granted: Bachelors.

Attendance and degree information available by phone, fax, mail. Search requires name only. Also helpful: exact years of attendance. There is no fee.

Harvard Radcliffe, Registrar, 20 Garden St, Cambridge, MA 02138, 617-495-1544 (Fax: 617-495-0815). Hours: 9AM-5PM. Enrollment: 10000. Records go back to 1700's. Alumni records are maintained here also. Call 617-495-8641. Degrees granted: Bachelors; Masters; PhD. Adverse incident record source- Residential Dean.

Attendance and degree information available by phone, fax, mail. Search requires name plus approximate years of attendance. There is no fee.

Harvard University, (Faculty of Arts and Sciences), Office of the Registrar, 20 Garden St, Cambridge, MA 02138,

617-495-1543 (Fax: 617-495-0815). Hours: 9AM-5PM. Enrollment: 10000. Records go back to 1965. Earlier records are at Archives. Records for graduate schools other than arts and sciences are held separately. Call for information. Alumni Records Office: Alumni Association, Wadsworth House, Cambridge, MA 02138. Degrees granted: Bachelors; Masters; Doctorate.

Attendance and degree information available by phone, fax, mail. Search requires name only. Also helpful: date of birth, exact years of attendance. There is no fee.

Harvard University-Business School, Registrar,

Baker Library 5, Soldiers Field, Boston, MA 02163, 617-495-6205 (Fax: 617-496-3955). Enrollment: 1500. Records go back to 1920. Alumni records are maintained here at the same phone number. Degrees granted: Masters. Adverse incident record source- Security.

Attendance and degree information available by phone. Search requires name plus SSN, exact years of attendance. There is no fee.

Harvard University-Divinity School, Registrar,

45 Francis Ave, Cambridge, MA 02138, 617-495-5760 (Fax: 617-495-9489). Enrollment: 550. Records go back to 1900. Alumni records are maintained here also. Call 617-495-1778. Degrees granted: Masters; Doctorate.

Attendance and degree information available by phone, mail. Search requires name plus SSN, exact years of attendance. There is no fee.

Harvard University-Extension School, Regis-

trar, 51 Brattle St, Cambridge, MA 02138, 617-495-9522 (Fax: 617-495-2921). Enrollment: 5000. Records go back to 1909. Alumni records are maintained here at the same phone number. Adverse incident record source- Security.

Attendance and degree information available by phone, mail. Search requires name plus SSN, exact years of attendance. There is no fee.

Harvard University-JFK School of Government, Registrar, 79 JFK St, Cambridge, MA 02138, 617-495-

1150 (Fax: 617-496-3182). Enrollment: 800. Alumni records are maintained here at the same phone number. Degrees granted: Masters; Doctorate.

Attendance and degree information available by phone, fax, mail. Search requires name only. Also helpful: exact years of attendance. There is no fee.

Harvard University-Medical School, Registrar,

25 Shatteck St, Boston, MA 02115, 617-432-1515 (Fax: 617-432-0275). Enrollment: 900. Records go back to 1782. Alumni records are maintained here at the same phone number. Adverse incident record source- Student Services.

Attendance and degree information available by phone, mail. Search requires name plus SSN, exact years of attendance. There is no fee.

Harvard University-School of Dentistry, Reg-

istrar, 188 Longwood Ave, Boston, MA 02115, 617-432-1447 (Fax: 617-432-3881). Enrollment: 270. Alumni records are maintained here also. Call 617-432-1533. Degrees granted: Masters; Doctorate. Certification: Speciality. Special programs-Postdoctoral Education, 617-432-1376.

Attendance information available by mail. Search requires name plus approximate years of attendance. Also helpful: exact years of attendance. There is no fee.

Degree information available by phone, fax. Search requires name plus approximate years of attendance. Also helpful: exact years of attendance. There is no fee.

Harvard University-School of Design, Regis-

trar, 48 Quincy St, Cambridge, MA 02138, 617-496-1237 (Fax: 617-495-8449). Enrollment: 530. Records go back to 1946. Alumni records are maintained here at the same phone number.

Degrees granted: Masters; Doctorate. Special programs- Arts Design. Adverse incident record source- Student Services.

Attendance and degree information available by phone, mail. Search requires name plus SSN, date of birth, exact years of attendance. There is no fee.

Harvard University-School of Education,

Registrar, 13 Appian Way, Cambridge, MA 02138, 617-495-3418. Enrollment: 1200. Records go back to 1920. Alumni records are maintained here also. Call 617-495-4340. Degrees granted: Masters; Doctorate. Adverse incident record source- Student Services.

Attendance and degree information available by phone. Search requires name plus SSN, exact years of attendance. There is no fee.

Harvard University-School of Law, Registrar,

1525 Mass Ave, Cambridge, MA 02138, 617-495-4612 (Fax: 617-495-1110). Enrollment: 4000. Records go back to 1900. Alumni Records Office: Alumni Association, 1587 Mass. Ave, Baker House, Cambridge, MA 02138. Special programs- LLM, 617-495-2855: ITP, 617-495-4406.

Attendance and degree information available by phone, fax, mail. Search requires name only. Also helpful: SSN, date of birth, exact years of attendance. There is no fee.

Harvard University-School of Public Health,

Registrar, 677 Huntington Ave, Boston, MA 02115, 617-432-1032 (Fax: 617-432-2009). Enrollment: 800. Records go back to 1920. Alumni records are maintained here at the same phone number. Degrees granted: Masters; Doctorate. Special programs-Science: Health.

Attendance and degree information available by phone, mail. Search requires name plus SSN, exact years of attendance. There is no fee.

Harvard University-Summer School, Registrar,

51 Brattle St, Cambridge, MA 02138, 617-495-9522 (Fax: 617-495-2921). Enrollment: 5000. Records go back to 1909. Alumni records are maintained here at the same phone number. Degrees granted: Associate; Bachelors; Masters. Special programs- Liberal Arts. Adverse incident record source- Security.

Attendance and degree information available by phone, mail. Search requires name plus SSN, date of birth, exact years of attendance. There is no fee.

Hebrew College, Registrar, 43 Hawes St, Brookline, MA

02156, 617-278-4944 (Fax: 617-734-9769). Hours: 9AM-5PM. Enrollment: 38. Alumni records are maintained here at the same phone number. Degrees granted: Bachelors; Masters.

Attendance and degree information available by phone, fax, mail. Search requires name plus approximate years of attendance. Also helpful: SSN, date of birth. Fee is $3.00.

Hellenic College/Holy Cross Greek Orthodox School of Theology, Registrar, 50 Goddard Ave,

Brookline, MA 02146, 617-731-3500 (Fax: 617-232-7819). Hours: 9AM-5PM. Enrollment: 154. Records go back to 1937. Alumni records are maintained here at the same phone number. Degrees granted: Bachelors; Masters. Adverse incident record source- Student Life, 617-731-3500 X279.

Attendance and degree information available by phone, fax, mail. Search requires name plus SSN, date of birth, exact years of attendance. There is no fee.

Holyoke Community College, Registrar, 303

Homestead Ave, Holyoke, MA 01040, 413-552-2751 (Fax: 413-534-8975). Hours: 9AM-4:30PM. Enrollment: 3500. Records go back to 1946. Alumni records are maintained here also. Call 413-552-2253. Degrees granted: Associate.

Attendance information available by fax, mail. Search requires name plus SSN, approximate years of attendance, signed release.

Also helpful: date of birth, exact years of attendance. There is no fee.

Degree information available by phone, fax, mail. Search requires name plus SSN, approximate years of attendance. Also helpful: date of birth. There is no fee.

ITT Technical Institute, Registrar, 1671 Worcester Rd, Framingham, MA 01701-9465, 508-879-6266 (Fax: 508-879-9745). Hours: 8AM-5PM. Enrollment: 270. Records go back to 1991. Alumni Records Office: Alumni Association, ITT Technical Institute, 5975 Castle Creek Pkwy N Dr, Indianapolis, IN 46250. Degrees granted: Associate. Special programs- Electronics Technology: Computer-Aided Drafting Technology.

Attendance information available by phone, fax, mail. Search requires name plus SSN, date of birth. There is no fee.

Degree information available by phone, fax, mail. Search requires name plus SSN, date of birth. Also helpful: approximate years of attendance. There is no fee.

Katharine Gibbs School, Registrar, 126 Newbury St, Boston, MA 02116, 617-578-7114 (Fax: 617-262-6210). Hours: 8AM-5PM. Enrollment: 400. Records go back to 1918. Alumni records are maintained here also. Call 617-578-7125. Degrees granted: Associate.

Attendance information available by phone, fax, mail. Search requires name only. Also helpful: SSN, exact years of attendance. There is no fee.

Degree information available by fax, mail. Search requires name only. Also helpful: SSN, exact years of attendance. There is no fee.

Laboure College, Registrar, 2120 Dorchester Ave, Boston, MA 02124, 617-296-8300 X4025 (Fax: 617-296-7947). Hours: 8AM-4:30PM. Enrollment: 474. Records go back to 1895. Alumni records are maintained here also. Call 617-296-8300 X4030. Degrees granted: Associate.

Attendance and degree information available by phone, mail. Search requires name plus approximate years of attendance. Also helpful: SSN, exact years of attendance. There is no fee.

Lasell College, Registrar, Newton, MA 02166, 617-243-2133 (Fax: 617-243-2326). Hours: 8:30PM-4:30PM. Enrollment: 665. Records go back to 1851. Alumni records are maintained here also. Call 617-243-2141. Degrees granted: Associate; Bachelors. Adverse incident record source- Student Affairs, 617-243-2124: Academic Affairs, 617-243-2134

Attendance and degree information available by phone, fax, mail. Search requires name plus exact years of attendance. There is no fee.

Lesley College, Registrar, 29 Everett St, Cambridge, MA 02138-2790, 617-349-8740 (Fax: 617-349-8717). Hours: 9AM-7PM M-Th, 9AM-5PM F. Enrollment: 6600. Records go back to 1909. Alumni records are maintained here also. Call 617-349-8622. Degrees granted: Bachelors; Masters. Adverse incident record source- Student Affairs, 617-349-8530.

Attendance information available by mail. Search requires name plus SSN, signed release. Also helpful: date of birth, exact years of attendance. There is no fee.

Degree information available by phone, fax, mail. Search requires name plus SSN. Also helpful: date of birth, exact years of attendance. There is no fee.

MGH Institute of Health Professions, Registrar, 101 Merrimac St, Boston, MA 02114-4719, 617-726-3140 (Fax: 617-726-3136). Hours: 8:30AM-5PM. Enrollment: 544. Records go back to 1916. Alumni records are maintained here at the same phone number. Degrees granted: Masters. Certification: NP,PT.

Attendance and degree information available by phone, fax, mail. Search requires name only. Also helpful: SSN. There is no fee.

Marian Court College, Registrar, 35 Little's Point Rd, Swampscott, MA 01907, 617-595-6768 (Fax: 617-595-3560). Hours: 9AM-5PM. Enrollment: 203. Degrees granted: Associate.

Attendance and degree information available by phone, fax, mail. Search requires name plus SSN, exact years of attendance. There is no fee.

Massachusetts Bay Community College, Registrar, 50 Oakland St, Wellesley Hills, MA 02181-5399, 617-237-1100. Hours: 8AM-5PM. Enrollment: 3336. Records go back to 1961. Alumni records are maintained here at the same phone number. Degrees granted: Associate. Adverse incident record source- Student Services, 617-237-1100 X2750.

Attendance and degree information available by phone, mail. Search requires name plus SSN, approximate years of attendance. There is no fee.

Massachusetts College of Art, Registrar, 621 Huntington Ave, Boston, MA 02115, 617-232-1555 X243 (Fax: 617-566-4034). Hours: 9AM-5PM. Enrollment: 1430. Records go back to 1890's. Alumni records are maintained here also. Call 617-232-1555 X258. Degrees granted: Bachelors; Masters. Certification: Design Teaching.

Attendance and degree information available by fax, mail. Search requires name plus SSN, signed release. Also helpful: date of birth, exact years of attendance. There is no fee.

Massachusetts College of Pharmacy and Allied Health Services, Registrar, 179 Longwood Ave, Boston, MA 02115, 617-732-2855. Hours: 8:30AM-4:30PM. Enrollment: 1450. Records go back to 1915. Degrees granted: Associate; Bachelors; Masters; Doctorate. Special programs-Continuing Education, 617-732-2961.

Attendance and degree information available by phone, mail. Search requires name only. Also helpful: exact years of attendance. There is no fee.

Massachusetts Institute of Technology, Registrar's Office, E19-335, 77 Massachusetts Ave, Cambridge, MA 02139, 617-253-4784 (Fax: 617-253-7459). Hours: 9AM-5PM. Enrollment: 9960. Records go back to 1800's. Alumni records are maintained here at the same phone number. Degrees granted: Bachelors; Masters; Doctorate. Adverse incident record source-Committee in Discipline, 617-253-4052.

Attendance information available by phone, fax, mail. Search requires name only. Also helpful: SSN, exact years of attendance. There is no fee.

Degree information available by phone, fax, mail. Search requires name only. Also helpful: SSN, date of birth, exact years of attendance. There is no fee.

Massachusetts Maritime Academy, Registrar, Academy Dr, Buzzards Bay, MA 02532, 508-830-5036 (Fax: 508-830-5018). Hours: 8AM-4:30PM. Enrollment: 750. Records go back to 1896. Alumni Records Office: PO Box 1910, Boston, MA 02210. Degrees granted: Bachelors. Adverse incident record source- Commandant's Office, 508-830-5047

Attendance and degree information available by phone, fax, mail. Search requires name plus SSN. Also helpful: date of birth, approximate years of attendance. There is no fee.

Massachusetts School of Professional Psychology, Registrar, 221 Rivermore St, Boston, MA 02132, 617-327-6777 (Fax: 617-327-4447). Hours: 9AM-5PM. Enrollment: 180. Records go back to 1984. Degrees granted: Doctorate.

Attendance and degree information available by phone, fax, mail. Search requires name only. Also helpful: SSN, date of birth, exact years of attendance. There is no fee.

Massasoit Community College, Registrar, One Massasoit Blvd, Brockton, MA 02402, 508-588-9100 (Fax: 508-427-1255). Hours: 8AM-5PM. Enrollment: 3377. Records go back to 1966. Alumni records are maintained here also. Call 508-588-9100 X1005. Degrees granted: Associate.

Attendance and degree information available by phone, fax, mail. Search requires name plus SSN, approximate years of attendance. There is no fee.

Merrimack College, Registrar, 315 Turnpike St, North Andover, MA 01845, 508-837-5000 (Fax: 508-837-5222). Hours: 8:30AM-4:30PM. Enrollment: 2900. Records go back to 1947. Alumni records are maintained here also. Call 508-837-5000 X5440. Degrees granted: Associate; Bachelors. Adverse incident record source- Public Safety, 508-837-5294.

Attendance and degree information available by phone, mail. Search requires name plus approximate years of attendance. Also helpful: SSN. There is no fee.

Middlesex Community College, Registrar, Springs Rd, Bedford, MA 01730, 617-280-3614. Hours: 8:30AM-9:30PM M-Th, 8:30AM-5PM F, 8:30-11:30AM Sat. Enrollment: 7000. Records go back to 1970. Alumni records are maintained here also. Call 617-280-3523. Degrees granted: Associate.

Attendance and degree information available by phone, mail. Search requires name plus SSN, approximate years of attendance. There is no fee.

Middlesex Community College, (Lowell), Registrar, Kearney Square, Lowell, MA 01852, 508-656-3200 (Fax: 508-452-5559). Records are not housed here. They are located at Middlesex Community College, Registrar, Springs Rd, Bedford, MA 01730.

Montserrat College of Art, Registrar, 23 Exxex St, Beverly, MA 01915, 508-922-8222 (Fax: 508-922-4268). Hours: 9AM-4PM. Enrollment: 250. Records go back to 1971. Alumni records are maintained here also. Call 508-922-8222. Degrees granted: Bachelors.

Attendance and degree information available by fax, mail. Search requires name plus SSN, exact years of attendance, signed release. Also helpful: approximate years of attendance. There is no fee.

Mount Holyoke College, Registrar, South Hadley, MA 01075, 413-538-2025 (Fax: 413-538-3003). Hours: 8:30AM-5PM Winter; 8:30AM-4PM Summer. Enrollment: 1920. Records go back to 1898. Alumni records are maintained here also. Call 413-538-2303. Degrees granted: Bachelors; Masters.

Attendance and degree information available by phone, fax, mail. Search requires name only. Also helpful: SSN, date of birth, exact years of attendance. There is no fee.

Mount Ida College, Registrar, 777 Dedham St, Newton Centre, MA 02159, 617-928-4500 (Fax: 617-928-4760). Hours: 8AM-4:30PM. Enrollment: 1640. Records go back to 1899. Degrees granted: Associate; Bachelors.

Attendance and degree information available by phone, fax, mail. Search requires name plus SSN, approximate years of attendance. Also helpful: date of birth, exact years of attendance. There is no fee.

Mount Wachusett Community College, Registrar, 444 Green St, Gardner, MA 01440, 508-632-6600 (Fax: 508-632-6155). Hours: 8AM-5PM. Enrollment: 2800. Records go back to 1980. Alumni records are maintained here at the same phone number. Degrees granted: Associate.

Attendance information available by written request only. Search requires name plus SSN. There is no fee.

Degree information available by written request only. Search requires name plus SSN. Also helpful: approximate years of attendance. There is no fee.

New England Banking Institute, Registrar, One Lincoln Plaza, 89 South St, Boston, MA 02111, 617-951-2350 (Fax: 617-951-2533). Hours: 8:30AM-4:30PM. Enrollment: 439.

Records go back to 1970. Alumni records are maintained here at the same phone number. Degrees granted: Associate.

Attendance and degree information available by phone, fax, mail. Search requires name plus SSN, approximate years of attendance. There is no fee.

New England College of Optometry, Registrar, 424 Beacon St, Boston, MA 02115, 617-236-6272 (Fax: 617-424-9202). Hours: 9AM-4PM. Enrollment: 423. Records go back to 1900. Alumni records are maintained here also. Call 617-236-6285. Degrees granted: Bachelors; Doctorate. Special programs- Continuing Education, 617-286-6311.

Attendance information available by phone, mail. Search requires name plus SSN. Also helpful: date of birth, exact years of attendance. There is no fee.

Degree information available by phone, mail. Search requires name plus SSN, date of birth. Also helpful: exact years of attendance. There is no fee.

New England Conservatory of Music, Registrar, 290 Huntington Ave, Boston, MA 02115, 617-262-1120 (Fax: 617-272-0500). Hours: 9AM-5PM. Enrollment: 775. Records go back to 1900. Alumni records are maintained here at the same phone number. Degrees granted: Bachelors; Masters; Doctorate; Graduate Diploma, Artist Diploma.

Attendance and degree information available by fax, mail. Search requires name only. Also helpful: SSN, date of birth, exact years of attendance. There is no fee.

New England School of Law, Registrar, 154 Stuart St, Boston, MA 02116, 617-422-7215 (Fax: 617-422-7200). Hours: 9AM-5PM. Enrollment: 1100. Records go back to 1908. Alumni records are maintained here also. Call 617-422-7203. Degrees granted: Doctorate; J.D.

Attendance and degree information available by phone, fax, mail. Search requires name plus SSN. Also helpful: exact years of attendance. There is no fee.

Newbury College, Registrar, 129 Fisher Ave, Brookline, MA 02146, 617-730-7112 (Fax: 617-730-7095). Hours: 9AM-5PM. Enrollment: 2425. Records go back to 1962. Alumni records are maintained here also. Call 617-730-7210. Degrees granted: Associate; Bachelors.

Attendance and degree information available by phone, fax, mail. Search requires name plus SSN, approximate years of attendance. Also helpful: exact years of attendance. There is no fee.

Nichols College, Office of the Registrar, PO Box 5000, Dudley, MA 01571-5000, 508-943-1560. Hours: 8:30AM-4:30PM. Enrollment: 1700. Records go back to 1930's. Alumni records are maintained here at the same phone number. Degrees granted: Associate; Bachelors; Masters.

Attendance information available by phone, mail. Search requires name plus SSN, date of birth. There is no fee.

Degree information available by phone, mail. Search requires name only. There is no fee.

North Adams State College, Registrar, North Adams, MA 01247, 413-662-4611 (Fax: 413-662-5580). Hours: 8:30AM-4:45PM. Enrollment: 1500. Records go back to 1908. Alumni records are maintained here also. Call 413-662-5224. Degrees granted: Bachelors; Masters. Adverse incident record source- Registrar's Office .

Attendance and degree information available by phone, fax, mail. Search requires name plus SSN, approximate years of attendance. Also helpful: date of birth, exact years of attendance. There is no fee.

North Shore Community College, Registrar, One Ferncroft Rd, Danvers, MA 01923-4093, 508-762-4000 (Fax: 508-762-4021). Hours: 8AM-4PM. Enrollment: 3090. Records

go back to 1965. Alumni records are maintained here at the same phone number. Degrees granted: Associate.

Attendance and degree information available by phone, fax, mail. Search requires name plus SSN, approximate years of attendance. Also helpful: date of birth, exact years of attendance. There is no fee.

Northeastern University, Transcripts Office, 117 Hayden Hall, 360 Huntington Ave, Boston, MA 02115, 617-373-5411 (Fax: 617-373-5351). Hours: 8:30AM-4:30PM. Enrollment: 18459. Records go back to 1945. Alumni Records Office: Alumni Association, Northeastern University, 346 Richards Hall, Boston, MA 02115. Degrees granted: Associate; Bachelors; Masters; Doctorate.

Attendance and degree information available by phone, mail. Search requires name plus SSN, approximate years of attendance. Also helpful: date of birth, exact years of attendance. There is no fee.

Northern Essex Community College, Registrar, 100 Elliott Way, Haverhill, MA 01830, 508-374-3700 (Fax: 508-374-3729). Hours: 8AM-8PM M-Th; 8AM-4PM F. Enrollment: 3588. Records go back to 1965. Alumni records are maintained here also. Call 508-374-3862. Degrees granted: Associate. Adverse incident record source- Security, 508-374-3689.

Attendance and degree information available by phone, fax, mail. Search requires name plus SSN, date of birth. Also helpful: exact years of attendance. Fee is $1.00. Expedited service available for $1.00.

Pine Manor College, Registrar, 400 Heath St, Chestnut Hill, MA 02167, 617-731-7135 (Fax: 617-731-7199). Hours: 9AM-5PM. Enrollment: 400. Records go back to 1917. Alumni records are maintained here also. Call 617-731-7132. Degrees granted: Associate; Bachelors; Masters; MED.

Attendance and degree information available by phone, fax, mail. Search requires name plus SSN, exact years of attendance. There is no fee. Expedited service available for $10.00.

Pope John XXIII National Seminary, Registrar, 558 South Ave, Weston, MA 02193-2699, 617-899-5500 (Fax: 617-899-9057). Hours: 9AM-4:30PM. Enrollment: 63. Records go back to 1962. Alumni records are maintained here at the same phone number. Degrees granted: Masters.

Attendance information available by mail. Search requires name plus signed release. There is no fee.

Degree information available by phone, fax, mail. Search requires name only. There is no fee.

Quincy Junior College, Registrar, 34 Coddington St, Quincy, MA 02169, 617-984-1601 (Fax: 617-984-1789). Hours: 8AM-5PM. Enrollment: 5000. Records go back to 1958. Degrees granted: Associate. Adverse incident record source- Academic Dean, 617-984-1740.

Attendance information available by phone, fax. Search requires name plus SSN. There is no fee.

Degree information available by mail. Search requires name plus SSN. There is no fee.

Quinsigamond Community College, Registrar, 670 W Boylston St, Worcester, MA 01606, 508-853-2300 (Fax: 508-852-6943). Hours: 8AM-4:30PM. Enrollment: 2583. Records go back to 1965. Alumni records are maintained here also. Call 508-853-2300 X4281. Degrees granted: Associate.

Attendance and degree information available by phone, fax, mail. Search requires name plus SSN, approximate years of attendance. Also helpful: date of birth, exact years of attendance. There is no fee.

Regis College, Registrar, Weston, MA 02193, 617-768-7280 (Fax: 617-768-8339). Hours: 9AM-4:30PM Winter; 8AM-5PM Summer. Enrollment: 1200. Records go back to 1927.

Alumni records are maintained here also. Call 617-768-7243. Degrees granted: Bachelors; Masters.

Attendance and degree information available by phone, fax, mail. Search requires name plus approximate years of attendance. Also helpful: SSN, date of birth, exact years of attendance. There is no fee.

Roxbury Community College, Registrar, 1234 Columbus Ave, Roxbury Crossing, MA 02120-3400, 617-427-0060 (Fax: 617-541-5351). Hours: 8:30AM-5PM. Enrollment: 1898. Records go back to 1981. Degrees granted: Associate.

Attendance and degree information available by phone, fax, mail. Search requires name plus SSN, date of birth, exact years of attendance. There is no fee.

Salem State College, Registrar, 352 Lafayette St, Salem, MA 01970-4589, 508-741-6081 (Fax: 508-741-6336). Hours: 8:30AM-5PM. Enrollment: 10000. Records go back to 1915. Alumni records are maintained here also. Call 508-741-6605. Degrees granted: Bachelors; Masters. Adverse incident record source- Campus Police: Judicial Affairs

Attendance and degree information available by mail. Search requires name plus SSN, exact years of attendance, signed release. Also helpful: date of birth. There is no fee.

School of the Museum of Fine Arts, Boston, Registrar, 230 The Fenway, Boston, MA 02115-9975, 617-369-3621 (Fax: 617-424-6271). Hours: 9AM-5PM. Records go back to 1930. Alumni records are maintained here also. Call 617-369-3897. Degrees granted: Bachelors; Masters.

Attendance information available by phone, fax, mail. Search requires name plus SSN. Also helpful: date of birth. There is no fee.

Degree information available by phone, fax, mail. Search requires name plus SSN, approximate years of attendance. Also helpful: date of birth. There is no fee.

Simmons College, Registrar, 300 The Fenway, Boston, MA 02115, 617-521-2111 (Fax: 617-521-3144). Hours: 8:30AM-4:30PM M,T,Th,F; 8:30AM-6PM W. Enrollment: 4000. Records go back to 1905. Alumni records are maintained here also. Call 617-521-2321. Degrees granted: Bachelors; Masters; Doctorate.

Attendance information available by phone, fax, mail. Search requires name plus exact years of attendance. Also helpful: SSN. There is no fee.

Degree information available by phone, fax, mail. Search requires name plus exact years of attendance. Also helpful: SSN, date of birth. There is no fee.

Simon's Rock College of Bard, Registrar, Great Barrington, MA 01230-9702, 413-528-7201 (Fax: 413-528-7365). Hours: 9AM-5PM. Enrollment: 315. Records go back to 1966. Alumni records are maintained here at the same phone number. Degrees granted: Associate; Bachelors. Adverse incident record source- Dean, 413 528-7245.

Attendance and degree information available by phone, fax, mail. Search requires name only. Also helpful: date of birth, exact years of attendance. There is no fee.

Smith College, Registrar, Northampton, MA 01063, 413-585-2550 (Fax: 413-585-2557). Hours: 8AM-4:30PM. Enrollment: 2600. Records go back to 1800's. Alumni records are maintained here also. Call 413-585-2700. Degrees granted: Bachelors; Masters. Adverse incident record source- Dean, 413-585-4900.

Attendance and degree information available by phone, fax, mail. Search requires name plus SSN, date of birth, approximate years of attendance. There is no fee.

Springfield College, Registrar's Office, 263 Alden St, Springfield, MA 01109-3797, 413-748-3149 (Fax: 413-748-3764). Hours: 8:30AM-4:15PM. Enrollment: 3159. Records go

back to 1885. Alumni records are maintained here also. Call 413-748-3163. Degrees granted: Bachelors; Masters; Doctorate.

Attendance and degree information available by phone, fax, mail. Search requires name only. Also helpful: SSN, exact years of attendance. There is no fee.

Springfield Technical Community College,
Registrar, One Armory Square, Springfield, MA 01105, 413-781-7822 X3879 (Fax: 413-739-5066). Hours: 8AM-4PM. Enrollment: 3686. Alumni records are maintained here also. Call 413-781-7822 X3873. Degrees granted: Associate. Adverse incident record source- Dean of Students, 413-781-7822 X3454.

Attendance and degree information available by phone, fax, mail. Search requires name plus SSN. Also helpful: date of birth, exact years of attendance. There is no fee.

St. Hyacinth College and Seminary, Registrar,
Granby, MA 01033, 413-467-7191 X509 (Fax: 413-467-9609). Hours: 8:30AM-4:30PM. Enrollment: 23. Records go back to 1957. Degrees granted: Associate; Bachelors.

Attendance and degree information available by phone, fax, mail. Search requires name plus SSN, approximate years of attendance. There is no fee.

St. John's Seminary, Registrar, 127 Lake St, Brighton,
MA 02135, 617-254-2610 (Fax: 617-787-2336). Hours: 9-11:30AM, 1-3PM. Enrollment: 100. Records go back to 1900. Degrees granted: Masters.

Attendance and degree information available by mail. Search requires name plus exact years of attendance, signed release. Also helpful: SSN, date of birth. There is no fee.

Stonehill College, Registrar, North Easton, MA 02357,
508-565-1315 (Fax: 508-565-1434). Hours: 8AM-4:30PM. Enrollment: 2000. Records go back to 1952. Alumni records are maintained here also. Call 508-565-1343. Degrees granted: Bachelors. Adverse incident record source- Student Affairs, 508-565-1290.

Attendance information available by phone, fax, mail. Search requires name plus approximate years of attendance. Also helpful: date of birth, exact years of attendance. There is no fee.

Degree information available by phone, fax, mail. Search requires name only. Also helpful: date of birth, exact years of attendance. There is no fee.

Suffolk University, Registrar, 8 Ashburton Pl, Beacon
Hill, Boston, MA 02108, 617-573-8430 (Fax: 617-573-8703). Hours: 8AM-7PM M-Th, 8AM-4:45PM F. Enrollment: 9703. Records go back to 1985. Alumni records are maintained here also. Call 617-573-8443. Degrees granted: Associate; Bachelors; Masters; PhD.

Attendance and degree information available by phone, fax, mail. Search requires name plus SSN. Also helpful: date of birth, exact years of attendance. There is no fee.

Tufts University, Registrar, Medford, MA 02155, 617-
627-3267. Hours: 9AM-5PM. Enrollment: 7905. Records go back to 1856. Degrees granted: Bachelors; Masters; Doctorate.

Attendance and degree information available by phone, mail. Search requires name plus SSN, approximate years of attendance. Also helpful: date of birth. There is no fee.

University of Massachusetts Boston, Registrar,
100 Morrisey Blvd, Boston, MA 02125-3393, 617-287-6200 (Fax: 617-287-6242). Enrollment: 12000. Records go back to 1965. Alumni records are maintained here at the same phone number. Degrees granted: Bachelors; Masters; Doctorate.

Attendance and degree information available by phone, fax, mail. Search requires name only. Also helpful: SSN, date of birth, exact years of attendance. There is no fee.

University of Massachusetts Dartmouth,
Registrar, 285 Old Westport Rd, North Dartmouth, MA 02747,

508-999-8615 (Fax: 508-999-8901). Hours: 8AM-5PM. Enrollment: 5500. Records go back to 1950's. Alumni records are maintained here also. Call 508-999-8031. Degrees granted: Bachelors; Masters. Adverse incident record source- Campus Security, 508-999-8105.

Attendance information available by written request only. Search requires name plus SSN, exact years of attendance, signed release. Also helpful: date of birth. There is no fee.

Degree information available by written request only. Search requires name plus SSN, exact years of attendance, signed release. Also helpful: date of birth, approximate years of attendance. There is no fee.

University of Massachusetts Lowell, Registrar,
One University Ave, Lowell, MA 01854, 508-934-2550. Hours: 8:30AM-5PM. Records go back to 1890's. Alumni records are maintained here also. Call 508-454-6335. Degrees granted: Associate; Bachelors; Masters; Doctorate. Certification: C.E.

Attendance and degree information available by phone, mail. Search requires name plus SSN. There is no fee.

University of Massachusetts Medical Center at Worcester, Registrar, 55 Lake Ave N, Worcester,
MA 01655, 508-856-2267 (Fax: 508-856-1899). Hours: 9AM-5PM. Enrollment: 640. Records go back to 1974. Alumni records are maintained here also. Call 508-856-2129. Degrees granted: Doctorate; PhD.

Attendance and degree information available by phone, fax, mail. Search requires name plus SSN, approximate years of attendance. There is no fee.

University of Massachusetts Public Services School, Transcript Department, 100 Morrissey Blvd,
Boston, MA 02125, 617-287-6200 (Fax: 617-265-7173). Enrollment: 12000. Records go back to 1965. Alumni records are maintained here at the same phone number. Degrees granted: Bachelors; Masters; Doctorate. Special programs- Business. Adverse incident record source- Security.

Attendance and degree information available by phone, mail. Search requires name plus SSN. Also helpful: exact years of attendance. There is no fee.

University of Massachusetts at Amherst,
Graduate School, 530 Goodell Bldg, Amherst, MA 01003, 413-545-0024 (Fax: 413-577-0010). Hours: 8:30AM-5PM. Enrollment: 6000. Records go back to 1896. Alumni records are maintained here also. Call 413-545-2317. Degrees granted: Masters; Doctorate.

Attendance and degree information available by phone, fax, mail. Search requires name only. Also helpful: SSN, date of birth, exact years of attendance. There is no fee.

Wellesley College, Registrar, Wellesley, MA 02181,
617-283-2307 (Fax: 617-283-3680). Hours: 8:30AM-4:30PM. Enrollment: 2225. Records go back to 1920. Alumni records are maintained here also. Call 617-283-3331. Degrees granted: Bachelors. Adverse incident record source- Dean of Students.

Attendance and degree information available by phone, fax, mail. Search requires name plus approximate years of attendance. There is no fee.

Wentworth Institute of Technology, Office of
the Registrar, 550 Huntington Ave, Boston, MA 02115, 617-442-9010 X391 (Fax: 617-989-4591). Hours: 8:15AM-6PM M-Th; 8:15AM-4:45PM F; 9AM-1PM odd S. Enrollment: 2105. Records go back to 1920. Degrees granted: Associate; Bachelors.

Attendance and degree information available by phone, fax, mail. Search requires name plus SSN, approximate years of attendance. There is no fee.

Western New England College, Registrar, Spring-
field, MA 01119, 413-796-2080 (Fax: 413-796-2081). Hours:

8AM-7PM M-Th, 8:30AM-4:30PM F. Enrollment: 4700. Records go back to 1970. Alumni records are maintained here also. Call 413-782-1539. Degrees granted: Bachelors; Masters. Special programs- Weekend MBA, 413-782-1231. Adverse incident record source- Dean of Students, 413-782-1687.

Attendance and degree information available by phone, fax, mail. Search requires name plus SSN. There is no fee.

Westfield State College, Registrar, Western Ave, Westfield, MA 01086, 413-572-5240 (Fax: 413-562-3613). Hours: 8AM-5PM. Enrollment: 3710. Records go back to 1957. Alumni records are maintained here also. Call 413-568-3311 X5210. Degrees granted: Bachelors. Adverse incident record source- Student Affairs, 413-568-5403.

Attendance and degree information available by phone, fax, mail. Search requires name plus SSN, date of birth. There is no fee.

Weston School of Theology, Registrar, 3 Phillips Pl, Cambridge, MA 02138, 617-492-1960 (Fax: 617-492-5833). Hours: 8:30AM-4:30PM. Enrollment: 209. Records go back to 1950. Degrees granted: Masters.

Attendance and degree information available by phone, fax, mail. Search requires name plus SSN, approximate years of attendance. Also helpful: date of birth, exact years of attendance. There is no fee.

Wheaton College, Registrar, Norton, MA 02766, 508-285-8247 (Fax: 508-285-8276). Hours: 8:30AM-12:30PM, 1:30-4:30PM. Enrollment: 1360. Records go back to 1890's. Alumni records are maintained here at the same phone number. Degrees granted: Bachelors. Special programs- Center for Work and Learning, 508-286-3798. Adverse incident record source- Dean of Students.

Attendance and degree information available by phone, fax, mail. Search requires name plus SSN, approximate years of attendance. There is no fee.

Wheelock College, Registrar, 200 The Riverway, Boston, MA 02215-4176, 617-734-5200 X135 (Fax: 617-566-7369). Hours: 9AM-5PM. Enrollment: 1077. Records go back to 1900. Degrees granted: Associate; Bachelors; Masters; CAGS.

Attendance and degree information available by phone, fax, mail. Search requires name plus SSN, exact years of attendance. There is no fee.

Williams College, Registrar, Williamstown, MA 01267, 413-597-4286 (Fax: 413-597-4010). Hours: 8:30AM-4:30PM. Enrollment: 2000. Records go back to 1795. Alumni records are maintained here also. Call 413-597-4151. Degrees granted: Bachelors; Masters.

Attendance information available by fax, mail. Search requires name plus SSN, approximate years of attendance, signed release. There is no fee.

Degree information available by phone, fax, mail. Search requires name plus SSN, approximate years of attendance. There is no fee.

Worcester Polytechnic Institute, Registrar, 100 Institute Rd, Worcester, MA 01609-2280, 508-831-5211 (Fax: 508-831-5931). Hours: 9AM-4PM. Enrollment: 3345. Records go back to 1868. Alumni records are maintained here also. Call 508-831-5600. Degrees granted: Bachelors; Masters; PhD.

Attendance and degree information available by phone, fax, mail. Search requires name plus SSN. There is no fee.

Worcester State College, Registrar, 486 Chandler St, Worcester, MA 01602-2597, 508-793-8035 (Fax: 508-793-8196). Hours: 8:15AM-5PM. Enrollment: 3750. Records go back to 1874. Alumni records are maintained here at the same phone number. Degrees granted: Bachelors; Masters.

Attendance and degree information available by phone, fax, mail. Search requires name plus SSN, approximate years of attendance. There is no fee.

Trade and Vocational Schools

Bancroft School of Message Therapy, 50 Franklin St, Worcester, MA 01608, 508-757-7923

Bay State School of Appliances, 225 Turnpike St, Canton, MA 02021, 617-828-3434

Burdett School, 745 Boylston St, Boston, MA 02116, 617-859-1900

Burdett School (Branch Campus), 100 Front St, Worcester, MA 01608, 508-849-1900

Butera School of Art, 111 Beacon St, Boston, MA 02116, 617-536-4623

Cambridge School of Culinary Arts (The), 2020 Massachusetts Ave, Cambridge, MA 02140, 617-354-3836

Catherine E. Hinds Institute of Esthetics, 65 Riverside Pl, Woburn, MA 02155, 617-391-3733

Catherine E. Hinds Institute of Esthetics (Woburn Campus), 83 Olympia Ave, Woburn, MA 01801, 617-933-2501

Charles H. McCann Technical School, Hodges Crossroad, North Adams, MA 01247, 413-663-5383

Computer Learning Center, 5 Middlesex Ave, Somerville, MA 02145, 617-776-3500

Computer Learning Center (Branch Campus), 436 Broadway, Methuen, MA 01844, 508-794-0233

Computer Processing Institute, 615 Massachusetts Ave, Cambridge, MA 02139, 617-354-6900

East Coast Aero Technical School, 696 Virginia Rd, Concord, MA 01742, 508-371-9977

Forsyth School for Dental Hygienists, 140 The Fenway, Boston, MA 02115, 617-262-5200

Hallmark Institute of Photography, PO Box 308, Turners Falls, MA 01376, 413-863-2478

Hickox School, 200 Tremont St, Boston, MA 02116, 617-482-7655

Kinyon-Campbell Business School, 59 Linden St, New Bedford, MA 02740, 508-992-5448

Kinyon-Campbell Business School (Branch Campus), 1041 Pearl St, Brockton, MA 02401, 508-584-6869

Longy School of Music, Inc., One Follen St, Cambridge, MA 02138, 617-876-0956

Massachusetts School of Barbering & Men's Hairstyling, 152 Parkingway St, Quincy, MA 02169, 617-770-4444

Mildred Elley Business School (Branch Campus), 400 Columbus Ave, Pittsfield, MA 01201, 413-499-8618

National Education Center-Bryman Campus, 323 Boylston St, Brookline, MA 02146, 617-232-6035

New England Hair Academy, 492-500 Main St, Malden, MA 02148, 617-324-6799

New England Hair Academy (Haverhill Campus), 80 Merrimack St, Haverhill, MA 01830, 508-521-6200

New England School of Accounting, 155 Ararat St, Worcester, MA 01606, 508-853-8972

New England School of Acupuncture, 30 Common St, Watertown, MA 02172, 617-926-1788

New England School of Art and Design, 28 Newbury St, Boston, MA 02116-3276, 617-536-0383

New England School of Photography, 537 Commonwealt Ave, Boston, MA 02215, 617-437-1868

New England Tractor Trailer Training School of Massachusetts, 1093 N Montello St, Brockton, MA 02401, 508-587-1100

North Bennet Street School, 39 N Bennet St, Boston, MA 02113, 617-227-0155

Northeast Broadcasting School, 142 Berkeley St, Boston, MA 02116, 617-267-7910

Northeast Institute of Industrial Technology, 41 Phillips St, Boston, MA 02114, 617-523-2869

Pedigree Career Institute, Harbor Mall, Lynn, MA 01901, 617-592-3647

RETS Electronic Schools, 965 Commonwealth Ave, Boston, MA 02215, 617-783-1197

Salter School (The), 155 Ararat St, Worcester, MA 01606, 508-853-1074

Salter School (The) (Branch Campus), 458 Bridge St, Cambridge, MA 01103, 413-731-7353

Southeastern Technical Institute, 250 Foundry St, South Easton, MA 02375, 508-238-4374

St. John's School of Business, PO Box 1190, West Springfield, MA 01090, 413-781-0390

TAD Technical Institute, 45 Spruce St, Chelsea, MA 02150, 617-889-3600

Travel Education Center, 100 Cambridge Park Dr, Cambridge, MA 02140, 617-547-7750

Travel School of America, 1047 Commonwealth Ave, Boston, MA 02215, 617-787-1214

Ultrasound Diagnostic School (Branch Campus), 33 Boston Post Rd W #140, Marlborough, MA 01752, 508-485-1213

Wentworth Technical School, 1919 Spring Ave, Lexington, MA 02173, 617-674-1000

Worcester Technical Institute, 251 Belmont St, Worcester, MA 01605, 508-799-1945

State Licensing & Business Registration Quick Finder Index

Architecture, Engineering & Surveying

Architect #35 .... ☎ 617-727-3072
Engineer #7 (18000)..................................... ☎ 617-727-9956
Landscape Architect #7 617-727-3093

Business - Court & Legal Services

Attorney #2 (56503) .... ☎ 617-728-8800
Justice of the Peace #37.. ☎ 617-727-2795
Notary Public #37... ☎ 617-727-2795

Business - General Services

Auctioneer #36 (900)..................................... ☎ 617-727-3480
Car Dealer #41 .... ☎ 617-727-3141
Employment Agency #19 (52) .... ✉ 617-727-3696
Hawker/Peddler #36 (1200) .... ☎ 617-727-3480
Importer #9 .... ☎ 617-727-3040
Inspector of Tramways #25 617-727-3200
Modeling Agency #19 (52) .... ✉ 617-727-3696
Motion Picture Operator #22...................... ☎ 617-727-3200
Personal Agent #24.. 617-727-3692
Public Accountant-CPA #7 .... ☎ 617-727 1806
Solicitor #9... ☎ 617-727-3040
Transient Vendor #36 (300) .... ☎ 617-727-3480
Vending Machine #20 617-522-3700
Wholesale or Retail Seller of Cigarettes #27
(7500) .... ☎ 617-887-5090
Wholesaler #9 .... ☎ 617-727-3040

Construction & Manufacturing

Concrete Technician #3 617-727-3200
Concrete-Testing Laboratory #3........................ 617-727-3200
Construction/Maintenance/Repair of
Elevators #22.. 617-727-3200
Construction/Maintenance/Repair of
Escalators #22 617-727-3200
Electrician #7 617-727-9931
Elevator Operator #22................................... 617-727-3200
Hoisting Machinery (Forklift, Hydraulic, Crane)
Operator #23.. 617-727-3200
Inspector of Amusement Devices #22 617-727-3200
Inspector of Boilers/Pressure Vessels &
Amusement Devices #23.............................. 617-727-3200
Manufacturer #9.. ☎ 617-727-3040
Nuclear Power Plant Engineer & Operator #23
.... 617-727-3200
Painter #18 617-727-1932
Pipefitter #23.. 617-727-3200
Plumber & Gasfitter #7 (22000) .... ✉ 617-727-9952
Refrigeration & Oil Burner Technician #23........ 617-727-3200

Education

Administrator #12 .... ☎ 617-770-7467

Private Kindergarten #11 617-727-8898
School Age Child Care Program #11 617-727-8898
School Guidance Counselor #12 .... ☎ 617-770-7467
Teacher #12 .... ☎ 617-770-7467

Environmental & Agriculture
Asbestos Abatement #17 617-727-7047
Cattle Dealer & Transporter #15 .... ☎ 617-727-3018
Commercial Finfishing #29 (5000) .... ✉ 617-727-3193
Commercial Shellfishing #29 (3500) .... ✉ 617-727-3193
Equine Dealer #15 .... ☎ 617-727-3018
Exterminator #16 (7000) .... ☎ 617-727-3020
Farmer-Brewery #9 .... ☎ 617-727-3040
Farmer-Winery #9 .... ☎ 617-727-3040
Lobstering #29 (1200) .... ✉ 617-727-3193
Milk Plant #14 .... ✉ 617-727-3020
Nursery #13 .... ☎ 617-727-3020
Nursery Agent #13 .... ☎ 617-727-3020
Pasteurization Plant #14 (200) .... ✉ 617-727-3020
Pesticide Applicator or Dealer #14 .... ✉ 617-727-3020
Swine Dealer #15 .... ☎ 617-727-3018
Trapping #31 .... ☎ 617-727-3151
Veterinarian #7 617-727-3080

Financial - Real Estate, Insurance & Banking
Appraiser of Motor Vehicle Damage #40 ...... ✉ 617-727-7189
Auto Sales Finance Company #41 (106) .... ☎ 617-727-3141
Broker #9 .... ☎ 617-727-3040
Brokerage Firm #42 617-727-3548
Collection Agency #30 617-727-3141
Consumer Credit Grantor #30 617-727-3141
Cooperative Bank #30 617-727-3141
Credit Union #30 617-727-3141
Insurance Adviser/Adjuster #33 .... ☎ 617-727-7189
Insurance Agent #33 .... ☎ 617-727-7189
Insurance Broker #33 .... ☎ 617-727-7189
Insurance, Domestic & Foreign Company #34
.... ✉ 617-727-7189
Mortgage Broker & Lender #41 (348) .... ☎ 617-727-3141
Real Estate Appraiser #7 (3205) 617-727-3055
Real Estate Broker & Salesperson #7 (13000)
.... ☎ 617-727-2373
Sales Finance Company #41 (96) .... ☎ 617-727-3141
Securities Agent #42 617-727-3548
Securities Broker/Dealer #42 617-727-3548
Small Loan Company #41 (131) .... ☎ 617-727-3141
State-Chartered Savings Bank #30 617-727-3141
Stock Broker #42 617-727-3548
Trust Company #30 617-727-3141

Health & Beauty
Acupuncturist #5 (546) .... ☎ 617-727-3086
Allied Health Professions (Athletic
 Trainers, etc.) #6 (13000) .... ☎ 617-727-3071
Allied Mental Health & Human Services
 Professions #6 (5200) .... ☎ 617-727-3080
Ambulance Service #8 (289) .... ☎ 617-753-8300
Ambulance Service Attendant #8 .... ☎ 617-727-8338
Ambulatory Surgical Center #38 .... ✉ 617-727-5860
Barber Master/Apprentice #6 (6000) .... ☎ 617-727-7367
Birthing Center #38 .... ✉ 617-727-5860
Blood Bank #38 .... ✉ 617-727-5860
Chiropractor #6 (1589) .... ☎ 617-727-3093
Clinic #38 .... ✉ 617-727-5860
Comprehensive Out-Patient Rehabilitation
 Facility #38 .... ✉ 617-727-5860
Cosmetologist (Hairdresser, Manicurist,
 Aesthetician) #6 (60000) .... ✉ 617-727-3067
Dental Examiner #6 (6800) .... ✉ 617-727-9928
Dental Hygienist #4 (6000) .... ☎ 617-727-9928

Dentist #4 (9000) .... ☎ 617-727-9928
Dispensing Optician #7 (1953) .... ☎ 617-727-3093
Drug/Alcoholism Facility #1 .... ☎ 617-727-3040
Drug/Alcoholism Program #1 .... ☎ 617-727-1960
Electrologist #7 .... ☎ 617-727-9957
Embalmer & Funeral Director #7 .... ☎ 617-727-1718
Emergency Medical Technician #8 (17862)
.... ☎ 617-753-8300
End State Renal Dialysis #38 .... ✉ 617-727-5860
Health Officer (Certified) #7 (150) .... ☎ 617-727-3069
Hospice & Hospital #38 .... ✉ 617-727-5860
Laboratory #38 .... ✉ 617-727-5860
Lead Inspector #20 .... ☎ 617-753-8400
Mammography Radiologic Technologist #21
.... ☎ 617-727-6214
Nuclear Medicine Technologist (Radiologic
 Technologist-Nuclear Medicine) #21
 (616) .... ☎ 617-727-6214
Nurse (Licensed Practical & Registered Nurse,
 Midwife) #7 (120000) .... ☎ 617-727-9961
Nurses Aide in Long-Term Care Facilities #32
 (45000) .... ☎ 617-727-5860
Nursing Home & Rest Home #38 .... ✉ 617-727-5860
Nursing Home Administrator #7 (1500) .... ☎ 617-727-3069
Occupational Therapist #6 .... ☎ 617-727-3071
Optometrist #7 (2100) .... ☎ 617-727-1817
Pharmacist #7 (9000) .... ☎ 617-727-9953
Physical Therapist #38 .... ✉ 617-727-5860
Physician's Assistant #7 (700) .... ☎ 617-727-1183
Podiatrist #7 (900) .... ☎ 617-727-1817
Radiographer #21 .... ☎ 617-522-3700
Radiologic Technologist-Radiation
 Therapy #21 .... ☎ 617-727-6214
Radiologic Technologist/Radiographer #21
 (6326) .... ☎ 617-727-6214
Respiratory Care Therapist #7 .... ☎ 617-727-3090
Sanitarian #7 (800) .... ☎ 617-727-3072
Speech-Language Pathologist/Audiologist #7
 (3500) .... ☎ 617-727-1747

Investigations & Security
Fire Protection Sprinkler System Contractor &
 Fitter #23 617-727-3200
Firemen Engineer #23 617-727-3200
Guard or Hearing Dog Business #15 .... ☎ 617-727-3018
Private Detective #28 (570) .... ☎ 617-727-6128
Private Investigator #28 .... ☎ 617-727-3692
Security Guard Agency #28 (150) .... ☎ 617-727-6128

Social Services
Adoption Placement Agency #11 617-727-8898
Day Care Facility #11 617-727-8900
Family Day Care Home #11 617-727-8898
Foster Care Placement Agency #11 617-727-8898
Group Care Facility #11 617-727-8900
Nursery School #11 617-727-8898
Preschool Program #11 617-727-8898
Psychologist/Provider #7 (5000) .... ☎ 617-727-9925
Residential & Temporary Shelter Facility for
 Children #11 617-727-8898
Social Worker #7 (20000) .... ☎ 617-727-3073
State Child Care Center #11 617-727-8898
Temporary Shelter for Children #11 617-727-8900

Sports & Entertainment
Agent #9 .... ☎ 617-727-3040
Amusement Device Operator #23 617-727-3200
Boxer #43 617-727-3296
Boxing #43 617-727-3296
Chair Lift #25 617-727-3200
Horse/Greyhound #10 (10000) .... ☎ 617-727-2581
Jockey #10 (100) .... ☎ 617-568-3336

Pet Shop #15 .... ☎ 617-727-3018
Riding Instructor #15 .... ☎ 617-727-3018
Riding School #15 .... ☎ 617-727-3018
Simulcast & Inter-Track Wagering #10 .... ☎ 617-727-2581
Ski Tow #25 617-727-3200
Skimobile #25 617-727-3200
Stable (Horse & Buggy Operator) #15 .... ☎ 617-727-3018
Theatrical Booking Agent #24 617-727-3692
Ticket Reseller #24 617-727-3692
Track #10 (6) .... ☎ 617-727-2581
Trainer #10 (5000) .... ☎ 617-727-2581

Transportation

Airport #39 (50) .... ☎ 617-973-8881
Airport Manager #39 (50) .... ☎ 617-973-8881
Bus Driver #26 .... ☎ 617-727-3541
Heliport #39 (5) .... ☎ 617-973-8881
Motor Vehicle Repair Shop (Auto Body,
   Auto Glass, etc) #36 (2500) .... ☎ 617-727-3480
Railroad, Airlines & Steamship Transportation &
   Warehouse #9 .... ☎ 617-727-3040
Two & Multi-Car Aerial Passenger Cable
   Car #25 617-727-3200

State Licensing & Business Registration Agency Information

(1) Alcoholic Beverages Control Commission, Division of Substance Abuse Services, 100 Cambridge St, Rm 2204, Boston, MA 02202, 617-727-3040

(2) Board of Bar Examiners, Board of Overseers Reg Dept, 75 Federal St, Boston, MA 02110, 617-728-8800, Fax: 617-357-1872

(3) Board of Building Regulations & Standards, Executive Office of Public Safety, One Ashburton Place, 13th Floor, Boston, MA 02108, 617-727-3200

(4) Board of Registration in Dentistry, 100 Cambridge St, Rm 1514, Boston, MA 02202, 617-727-2197

(5) Board of Registration in Medicine, 10 West St, 3rd Floor, Boston, MA 02111, 617-727-3086

(6) Boards of Registration & Examination, Division of Registration, 100 Cambridge St, 15th Floor, Boston, MA 02202, 617-727-3071, Fax: 617-727-1627

(7) Boards of Registration & Examination, Division of Registration, 100 Cambridge St, 15th Floor, Boston, MA 02202, 617-727-9956

(8) Bureau of Health Care Systems - Public Health, Office of Emergency Medical Services, 470 Atlantic Avenue, 2nd Floor, Boston, MA 02210-2208, 617-753-8300, Fax: 617-753-8350

(9) Consumer Department, Alcoholic Beverages Control Commission, 100 Cambridge St, .22nd Floor, Boston, MA 02202, 617-727-3040, Fax: 617-727-1258

(10) Consumer Department, State Racing Commission, One Ashburton Place, 13th Floor, Boston, MA 02108, 617-727-2581, Fax: 617-227-6062

(11) Department for Children, 24 Farnsworth St., Boston, MA 02210, 617-727-8900, Fax: 617-727-2468

(12) Department of Education & Arts, Division of Educational Personnel, 350 Main, Malven, MA 02148, 617-388-3300 X665

(13) Department of Environment & Energy, 100 Cambridge St, 21st Floor, Boston, MA 02202, 617-727-3020

(14) Department of Food & Agriculture, 100 Cambridge St, 21st Flr, Rm 2103, Boston, MA 02202, 617-727-3018, Fax: 617-727-7235

(15) Department of Food & Agriculture, 100 Cambridge St, 21st Floor, Boston, MA 02202, 617-727-3018, Fax: 617-727-7235

(16) Department of Food & Agriculture, Pesticide Bureau, 100 Cambridge St, 21st Flr, Boston, MA 02202, 617-727-3020, Fax: 617-727-7235

(17) Department of Labor & Industries, Bureau of Technical Services/Licensing Division, 100 Cambridge St, 11th Floor, Boston, MA 02202, 617-727-1932

(18) Department of Labor & Industries, Bureau of Technical Services/Licensing Division, 100 Cambridge St, 11th Floor, Boston, MA 02202, 617-727-1932

(19) Department of Labor & Occupational Safety, 100 Cambridge St, 11th Flr, Rm 1107, Boston, MA 02202, 617-727-3452, Fax: 617-727-8022

(20) Department of Public Health, 470 Atlantic Ave, 2nd Flr, Boston, MA 02210-2224, 617-522-3700, Fax: 617-753-8436

(21) Department of Public Health, Radiation Control Program, 305 South St, Jamaica Plain, MA 02130, 617-727-6214, Fax: 617-727-2098

(22) Department of Public Safety, One Ashburton Place, 13th Floor Room 1301, Boston, MA 02108, 617-727-3200 ext. 623, Fax: 617-248-0813

(23) Department of Public Safety, One Ashburton Place, 13th Floor, Boston, MA 02108, 617-727-3200

(24) Department of Public Safety, One Ashburton Place, 13th Floor, Boston, MA 02108, 617-727-3692

(25) Department of Public Safety, One Ashburton Place, 13th Floor, Boston, MA 02108, 617-727-3200

(26) Department of Public Utilities, Transportation Division, 100 Cambridge St, Rm 1203, Boston, MA 02202, 617-305-3559, Fax: 617-723-7947

(27) Department of Revenue, Excises Unit, 100 Cambridge St, 3rd Floor, Boston, MA 02204, 617-887-5090, Fax: 617-887-5039

(28) Department of State Police, Special Licensing Unit, 20 Somerset Street, 9th Floor, Boston, MA 02108, 617-727-6128, Fax: 617-727-6021

(29) Dept of Fisheries, Wildlife & Environment, 100 Cambridge St, 19th Flr, Boston, MA 02202, 617-727-3193, Fax: 617-727-7988

(30) Division of Banks & Loan Agencies, 100 Cambridge St, 20th Flr, Boston, MA 02202, 617-727-3141, Fax: 617-727-0607

(31) Division of Fisheries & Wildlife, 100 Cambridge St, 19th Flr, Boston, MA 02202, 617-727-3151, Fax: 617-727-7288

(32) Division of Health Care Quality, Department of Public Health, 10 West St, Boston, MA 02111, 617-727-5860 X325, Fax: 617-338-0011

(33) Division of Insurance, 470 Atlantic Ave, Boston, MA 02110, 617-521-7446

(34) Division of Insurance, Consumer Department, 470 Atlantic Ave, Boston, MA 02110, 617-521-7446

(35) Division of Regulation of Architecture, 100 Cambridge St, #1406, Boston, MA 02108, 617-727-3072

(36) Division of Standards, One Ashburton Place, 11th Floor, Boston, MA 02108, 617-727-3480, Fax: 617-727-5705

(37) Governor's Council, State House, Room 184, Boston, MA 02133, 617-727-2795

(38) Health Care Quality, Department of Public Health, 10 West St, Boston, MA 02111, 617-727-5860 X304, Fax: 617-727-5141

(39) Massachusetts Aeronautics Commission, Executive Office of Transportation & Construction, 10 Park Plaza, Room 6620, Boston, MA 02116, 617-973-8881, Fax: 617-973-8889

(40) Motor Vehicle Damage Appraisers Licensing Board, Division of Insurance, 470 Atlantic Ave, Boston, MA 02110, 617-521-7446

(41) Office of the Bank Commissioner, 100 Cambridge St, Rm 2004, Boston, MA 02202, 617-727-3141 X337, Fax: 617-727-0607

(42) Office of the Secretary of State, Securities Division, One Ashburton Place, 17th Floor, Boston, MA 02108, 617-727-3548

(43) State Boxing Commission, One Ashburton Pl, Room 1310, Boston, MA 02108, 617-727-3296

Michigan

Capitol: Lansing (Eaton County)	
State Population	9.5 Million
Number of Degree Granting Institutions:	101
Number of State Licensing & Business Registration Agencies:	98

Degree Granting Educational Institutions

Academy of Court Reporting, (Branch), Registrar, 26111 Evergreen Rd Ste 101, Southfield, MI 48076, 810-353-4880 (Fax: 810-353-1670). Hours: 8:30AM-7PM. Records go back to 1991.

Attendance and degree information available by phone, fax, mail. Search requires name plus SSN, approximate years of attendance. There is no fee.

Adrian College, Registrar, 110 S Madison St, Adrian, MI 49221, 517-265-5161 (Fax: 517-264-3331). Hours: 8:30AM-5PM. Enrollment: 1100. Records go back to 1859. Alumni records are maintained here also. Call 517-265-5161. Degrees granted: Associate; Bachelors.

Attendance and degree information available by phone, fax, mail. Search requires name only. Also helpful: SSN, date of birth, exact years of attendance. There is no fee.

Albion College, Registrar, 611 E Porter St, Albion, MI 49224, 517-629-0477 (Fax: 517-629-0509). Hours: 8AM-5PM. Enrollment: 1500. Records go back to 1835. Alumni records are maintained here also. Call 517-629-0284. Degrees granted: Bachelors.

Attendance and degree information available by phone, fax, mail. Search requires name only. Also helpful: SSN, date of birth, exact years of attendance. There is no fee.

Alma College, Registrar, Alma, MI 48801, 517-463-7348 (Fax: 517-463-7993). Hours: 8AM-Noon,1-5PM. Enrollment: 1447. Records go back to 1886. Alumni records are maintained here at the same phone number. Degrees granted: Bachelors. Adverse incident record source- Dean of Students, 517-463-7333: Provost's Office, 517-463-7176

Attendance and degree information available by phone, fax, mail. Search requires name only. Also helpful: SSN, date of birth, exact years of attendance. There is no fee.

Alpena Community College, Registrar, 666 Johnson St, Alpena, MI 49707, 517-356-9021 (Fax: 517-356-0980). Hours: 8AM-4:30PM. Enrollment: 1800. Degrees granted: Associate.

Attendance and degree information available by phone, fax, mail. Search requires name plus SSN. Also helpful: date of birth, approximate years of attendance. There is no fee.

Andrews University, Registrar, Berrien Springs, MI 49104, 616-471-3399 (Fax: 616-471-6001). Hours: 8AM-Noon, 1-5PM. Enrollment: 3000. Records go back to 1874. Alumni records are maintained here also. Call 616-471-3591. Degrees granted: Associate; Bachelors; Masters; Doctorate.

Attendance and degree information available by phone, fax, mail. Search requires name only. Also helpful: SSN. There is no fee.

Aquinas College, Registrar, 1607 Robinson Rd SE, Grand Rapids, MI 49506, 616-459-8281 (Fax: 616-732-4435). Hours: 8:30AM-6PM. Enrollment: 2422. Records go back to 1931. Alumni records are maintained here at the same phone number. Degrees granted: Associate; Bachelors; Masters. Certification: Teaching - MI. Adverse incident record source- Campus Safety, 616-459-8281 X 3754.

Attendance and degree information available by phone, fax, mail. Search requires name only. Also helpful: SSN, date of birth, exact years of attendance. There is no fee.

Baker College of Flint, Registrar, G-1050 W Bristol Rd, Flint, MI 48507, 810-766-7600 (Fax: 810-766-4049). Hours: 8AM-6PM. Enrollment: 10185. Records go back to 1950. Degrees granted: Associate; Bachelors; Masters.

Attendance and degree information available by phone, fax, mail. Search requires name plus SSN. Also helpful: date of birth, exact years of attendance. There is no fee.

Baker College of Flint, (Baker College of Muskegon), Registrar, 123 E Apple Ave, Muskegon, MI 49442, 616-726-4904 (Fax: 616-728-1417). Hours: 7AM-9:40PM M-Th, 7AM-5PM F. Enrollment: 1650. Records go back to 1965. Alumni records are maintained here also. Call 616-726-4904. Degrees granted: Associate; Bachelors; Masters. Adverse incident record source- Security, 616-726-4904.

Attendance and degree information available by phone, fax, mail. Search requires name plus SSN. There is no fee.

Baker College of Mt. Clemens, Registrar, 34950 Little Mack, Clinton Township, MI 48035, 810-791-6610 (Fax: 810-791-0967). Enrollment: 965. Records go back to 1888. Degrees granted: Associate; Bachelors; Masters. Special programs- Business Arts: Sciences. Adverse incident record source- Security.

Attendance and degree information available by phone, mail. Search requires name plus SSN, exact years of attendance. There is no fee.

Baker College of Muskegon, Registrar's Office, 123 E Apple Ave, Muskegon, MI 49442, 616-726-4904 (Fax: 616-728-1417). Enrollment: 1600. Formerly Muskegon Business College Records go back to 1960. Degrees granted: Associate; Bachelors; Masters; Diplomas, Certificate. Adverse incident record source- 616-726-4904.

Attendance and degree information available by phone, fax, mail. Search requires name plus SSN. Also helpful: date of birth, exact years of attendance. There is no fee.

Baker College of Owosso, Registrar's Office, 1020 S Washington St, Owosso, MI 48867, 517-723-5251 (Fax: 517-723-3355). Hours: 8AM-6PM. Enrollment: 1800. Records go back to 1983. Degrees granted: Associate; Bachelors; Masters. Adverse incident record source- Security Department.

School will not confirm attendance information.

Degree information available by phone, fax, mail. Search requires name plus SSN. Also helpful: exact years of attendance. There is no fee.

Baker College of Pontiac, Registrar, 1500 University Dr, Auburn Hills, MI 48326, 810-340-0600 (Fax: 810-340-0608). Enrollment: 777. Records go back to 1990. Alumni records are maintained here at the same phone number. Degrees granted: Associate. Special programs- Allied Health Technicians: Business. Adverse incident record source- Student Services.

Attendance and degree information available by phone, mail. Search requires name plus SSN. There is no fee.

Baker College of Port Huron, Registrar, 3403 Lapeer Rd, Port Huron, MI 48060, 810-985-7000 (Fax: 810-985-7066). Enrollment: 400. Records go back to 1990. Degrees granted: Associate; Bachelors; Masters. Adverse incident record source- Student Services.

Attendance and degree information available by phone, mail. Search requires name plus SSN, exact years of attendance. There is no fee.

Bay de Noc Community College, Registrar, 2001 N Lincoln Rd, Escanaba, MI 49829, 906-786-5802 (Fax: 906-786-8515). Hours: 8AM-4:30PM. Enrollment: 2248. Records go back to 1962. Degrees granted: Associate. Adverse incident record source- Student Services, 906-786-5802.

Attendance and degree information available by phone, fax, mail. Search requires name plus SSN. Also helpful: date of birth, exact years of attendance. There is no fee.

Calvin College, Registrar, 3201 Burton St SE, Grand Rapids, MI 49546, 616-957-6155 (Fax: 616-957-8551). Hours: 8AM-5PM. Enrollment: 3840. Records go back to 1898. Alumni records are maintained here at the same phone number. Degrees granted: Bachelors. Special programs- Accounting, 616-9957-7191: Engineering, 616-957-6071: Nursing, 616-957-7076.

Attendance and degree information available by phone, fax, mail. Search requires name only. Also helpful: SSN, date of birth, exact years of attendance. There is no fee.

Calvin Theological Seminary, Registrar, 3233 Burton St SE, Grand Rapids, MI 49546, 616-957-6027 (Fax: 616-957-8621). Hours: 8AM-5PM. Enrollment: 250. Records go back to 1895. Alumni records are maintained here also. Call 616-

957-6141. Degrees granted: Masters; PhD. Adverse incident record source- Alumni Office, 616-957-6141.

Attendance and degree information available by phone, fax, mail. Search requires name plus approximate years of attendance. There is no fee.

Center for Creative Studies-College of Art and Design, Registrar, 201 E Kirby St, Detroit, MI 48202-4034, 313-872-3118 X226 (Fax: 313-872-8377). Hours: 8:30AM-4:30PM. Enrollment: 950. Records go back to 1906. Alumni records are maintained here also. Call 313-872-3118 X278. Degrees granted: Bachelors. Adverse incident record source- Dean of Studen Affairs, 313-872-3118 X289.

Attendance and degree information available by phone, fax, mail. Search requires name plus SSN, approximate years of attendance. There is no fee.

Center for Humanistic Studies, Registrar, 40 E Ferry Ave, Detroit, MI 48202, 313-875-7440 (Fax: 313-875-2610). Hours: 8:30AM-4PM. Enrollment: 70. Records go back to 1981. Degrees granted: Masters; Specialist. Adverse incident record source- WSU Police, 313-577-2222.

Attendance and degree information available by fax, mail. Search requires name plus signed release. Also helpful: SSN, date of birth, exact years of attendance. There is no fee.

Central Michigan University, Registrar, Mount Pleasant, MI 48859, 517-774-3261 (Fax: 517-774-3783). Hours: 8AM-5PM. Enrollment: 16500. Records go back to 1920. Alumni records are maintained here also. Call 517-774-3312. Degrees granted: Bachelors; Masters; Doctorate.

Attendance and degree information available by phone, fax, mail. Search requires name only. Also helpful: SSN, date of birth, exact years of attendance. There is no fee.

Charles Stewart Mott Community College, Registrar, 1401 E Court St, Flint, MI 48503, 810-762-0221 (Fax: 810-762-0257). Hours: 7:30AM-7PM M, 8AM-4:30PM T-F. Enrollment: 16000. Records go back to 1945. Record on microfiche from 1945. Alumni records are maintained here at the same phone number. Degrees granted: Associate. Adverse incident record source- Security, 810-762-0222.

Attendance and degree information available by phone, fax, mail. Search requires name plus SSN, approximate years of attendance. There is no fee.

Cleary College, Registrar, 2170 Washtenaw Ave, Ypsilanti, MI 48197, 313-483-4400 X3344 (Fax: 313-483-0090). Hours: 8AM-5PM. Enrollment: 680. Records go back to 1884. Alumni records are maintained here also. Call 313-483-4400 X3354. Degrees granted: Associate; Bachelors. Adverse incident record source- 313-483-4400 X3331.

Attendance and degree information available by fax, mail. Search requires name plus SSN, date of birth, approximate years of attendance, signed release. There is no fee.

Concordia College, Registrar, 4090 Geddes Rd, Ann Arbor, MI 48105, 313-995-7324 (Fax: 313-995-4610). Hours: 8AM-4:30PM. Enrollment: 600. Records go back to 1963. Alumni records are maintained here at the same phone number. Degrees granted: Associate; Bachelors. Certification: Teacher.

Attendance and degree information available by phone, fax, mail. Search requires name only. Also helpful: SSN, date of birth, exact years of attendance. There is no fee.

Cornerstone College and Grand Rapids Baptist Seminary, Registrar, 1001 E Beltline Ave NE, Grand Rapids, MI 49505, 616-222-1431 (Fax: 616-949-0875). Hours: 8AM-4PM. Enrollment: 1150. Records go back to 1941. Alumni records are maintained here also. Call 616-222--1439. Degrees granted: Associate; Bachelors; Masters; Doctorate.

Attendance and degree information available by phone, fax, mail. Search requires name only. Also helpful: SSN, date of birth, exact years of attendance. There is no fee.

Cranbrook Academy of Art, Registrar, 1221 Woodward Ave, Bloomfield Hills, MI 48303-0801, 810-645-3300 (Fax: 810-646-0046). Hours: 8:30AM-5PM. Enrollment: 140. Records go back to 1932. Degrees granted: Masters.

Attendance and degree information available by phone, fax, mail. Search requires name only. There is no fee.

Davenport College of Business, Registrar, 415 E Fulton St, Grand Rapids, MI 49503, 616-732-1210 (Fax: 616-732-1142). Hours: 8AM-6:30PM M-Th; 8AM-5PM F. Enrollment: 800. Records go back to 1920. Alumni records are maintained here also. Call 616-451-3511. Degrees granted: Associate; Bachelors. Adverse incident record source- Student Services, 616-451-3511.

Attendance and degree information available by phone, fax, mail. Search requires name plus date of birth. Also helpful: SSN, approximate years of attendance. There is no fee.

Davenport College of Business, (Branch), Registrar, 643 Waverly Rd, Holland, MI 49423, 616-395-4610 (Fax: 616-395-4698). Hours: 8AM-6:30PM M-Th; 8AM-5PM F. Enrollment: 2700. Records go back to 1945. Alumni Records Office: 415 E Fulton, Grand Rapids, MI 49503. Degrees granted: Associate; Bachelors.

Attendance and degree information available by phone, fax, mail. Search requires name plus SSN, exact years of attendance. There is no fee.

Davenport College of Business, (Branch), Registrar, 4123 N Main St, Kalamazoo, MI 49006, 616-382-2835 (Fax: 616-382-3541). Hours: 8AM-6PM. Records go back to 1981. Alumni records are maintained here at the same phone number. Degrees granted: Associate; Bachelors. Adverse incident record source- Human Resources, 616-382-2835.

Attendance and degree information available by phone, fax, mail. Search requires name only. Also helpful: SSN, date of birth, exact years of attendance. There is no fee.

Davenport College of Business, (Branch), Registrar, 220 E Kalamazoo St, Lansing, MI 48933, 517-484-2600 (Fax: 517-484-9719). Hours: 8AM-7PM. Records go back to 1966. Alumni records are maintained here at the same phone number. Degrees granted: Associate; Bachelors. Adverse incident record source- Security Department.

Attendance information available by phone, fax, mail. Search requires name plus SSN. Also helpful: date of birth. There is no fee.

Degree information available by fax, mail. Search requires name plus SSN. Also helpful: date of birth. There is no fee.

Delta College, Registrar, University Center, MI 48710, 517-686-9539 (Fax: 517-686-8736). Hours: 8AM-7PM M,Th; 8AM-4:30PM T,W,F. Enrollment: 9500. Records go back to 1961. Degrees granted: Associate.

Attendance and degree information available by phone, fax, mail. Search requires name only. Also helpful: SSN, exact years of attendance. There is no fee.

Detroit College of Business, Registrar, 4801 Oakman Blvd, Dearborn, MI 48126, 313-581-4400 (Fax: 313-581-6822). Hours: 8AM-8PM M-Th; 8AM-4PM F. Enrollment: 6000. Records go back to 1962. Alumni records are maintained here at the same phone number. Degrees granted: Associate; Bachelors.

Attendance and degree information available by phone, fax, mail. Search requires name plus SSN. Also helpful: date of birth. There is no fee.

Detroit College of Law, Registrar, 130 E Elizabeth St, Detroit, MI 48201, 313-226-0153 (Fax: 313-226-0196). Hours: 9AM-6PM M,T; 9AM-4:30PM W,T. Enrollment: 790. Files older than 3 years housed at Leonard Archives, 810-477-7007. Alumni records are maintained here also. Call 313-965-3264.

Attendance and degree information available by phone, fax. Search requires name plus approximate years of attendance. Also helpful: SSN. There is no fee.

Eastern Michigan University, Registrar, Ypsilanti, MI 48197, 313-487-1849 (Fax: 313-487-6808). Enrollment: 23000. Records go back to 1849. Alumni Records Office: Alumni Association, 115 Welch Hall, Ypsilanti, MI 48197. Degrees granted: Bachelors; Masters; Doctorate.

Attendance and degree information available by phone, fax, mail. Search requires name plus SSN. Also helpful: date of birth, approximate years of attendance. There is no fee.

Ferris State University, Registrar's Office, 420 Oak St, Big Rapids, MI 49307, 616-592-2790 (Fax: 616-592-2242). Hours: 8AM-5PM. Enrollment: 9767. Records go back to 1895. Alumni Records Office: Alumni Office, Ferris State University, 330 Oak St, 108 West Bldg, Big Rapids, MI 49307. Degrees granted: Associate; Bachelors; Masters; Doctorate. Adverse incident record source- Judicial Services, 616-592-3619.

Attendance and degree information available by phone, fax, mail. Search requires name only. Also helpful: SSN, date of birth, exact years of attendance. There is no fee.

GMI Engineering and Management Institute, Registrar, 1700 W Third Ave, Flint, MI 48504, 810-762-7862 (Fax: 810-762-9836). Hours: 8AM-5PM. Enrollment: 2600. Records go back to 1919. Alumni records are maintained here also. Call 810-762-9883. Degrees granted: Bachelors; Masters. Adverse incident record source- Campus Safety, 810-762-9501.

Attendance information available by phone, fax, mail. Search requires name plus SSN, date of birth. Also helpful: exact years of attendance. There is no fee.

Degree information available by phone, fax, mail. Search requires name plus SSN. Also helpful: date of birth, exact years of attendance. There is no fee.

Glen Oaks Community College, Registrar, 62249 Shimmel Rd, Centreville, MI 49032, 616-467-9945 (Fax: 616-467-4114). Hours: 8AM-4PM. Enrollment: 1100. Records go back to 1967. Degrees granted: Associate. Adverse incident record source- Dean of Administration, 616-467-9945 X237.

Attendance and degree information available by phone, fax, mail. Search requires name plus SSN. Also helpful: date of birth, exact years of attendance. There is no fee.

Gogebic Community College, Registrar, E-4946 Jackson Rd, Ironwood, MI 49938, 906-932-4231 X207 (Fax: 906-932-0868). Hours: 7:30AM-4:30PM. Enrollment: 875. Records go back to 1932. Degrees granted: Associate.

Attendance and degree information available by phone, fax, mail. Search requires name plus SSN. Also helpful: date of birth, exact years of attendance. There is no fee.

Grace Bible College, Registrar, 1011 Aldon St SW, PO Box 910, Grand Rapids, MI 49509-9990, 616-538-2330 (Fax: 616-538-0599). Hours: 8AM-4:30PM. Enrollment: 160. Records go back to 1939. Alumni records are maintained here at the same phone number. Degrees granted: Associate; Bachelors.

Attendance and degree information available by phone, fax, mail. Search requires name plus SSN. There is no fee.

Grand Rapids Community College, Registrar, 143 Bostwick St NE, Grand Rapids, MI 49503, 616-771-4120 (Fax: 616-771-4005). Hours: 7:30AM-5PM. Enrollment: 13000. Records go back to 1914. Alumni records are maintained here at the same phone number. Degrees granted: Associate. Adverse incident record source- Campus Safety, 616-771-4010.

Attendance and degree information available by fax, mail. Search requires name plus SSN, date of birth, approximate years of attendance, signed release. Also helpful: exact years of attendance. There is no fee.

Grand Valley State University, Registrar, One Campus Dr, Allendale, MI 49401, 616-895-3327 (Fax: 616-895-2000). Hours: 8AM-6PM M-Th; 8AM-5PM F. Enrollment: 14000. Records go back to 1963. Alumni records are maintained here also. Call 616-895-3590. Degrees granted: Bachelors; Masters.

Attendance and degree information available by phone, fax, mail. Search requires name only. Also helpful: SSN, date of birth, exact years of attendance. There is no fee.

Great Lakes Christian College, Registrar, 6211 W Willow Hwy, Lansing, MI 48917, 517-321-0242 (Fax: 517-321-5902). Hours: 8AM-5PM. Enrollment: 175. Records go back to 1949. Alumni records are maintained here at the same phone number. Degrees granted: Associate; Bachelors.

Attendance information available by fax, mail. Search requires name plus SSN, date of birth, signed release. Also helpful: exact years of attendance. There is no fee.

Degree information available by fax, mail. Search requires name plus SSN, signed release. Also helpful: date of birth, exact years of attendance. There is no fee.

Great Lakes Junior College, Registrar, 310 S Washington Ave, Saginaw, MI 48607, 517-755-3457 (Fax: 517-752-3453). Hours: 8AM-5PM. Enrollment: 1600. Records go back to 1957. Requests handled at last campus of attendance. Alumni records are maintained here at the same phone number. Degrees granted: Associate.

Attendance and degree information available by phone, fax, mail. Search requires name plus SSN. Also helpful: date of birth, approximate years of attendance. There is no fee.

Henry Ford Community College, Registrar, 5101 Evergreen Rd, Dearborn, MI 48128, 313-845-6403 (Fax: 313-845-6464). Hours: 8AM-7:30PM M-Th; 8AM-4:30PM F. Enrollment: 13500. Records go back to 1936. Alumni records are maintained here at the same phone number. Degrees granted: Associate. Adverse incident record source- 313-845-9770.

Attendance and degree information available by phone, fax, mail. Search requires name plus SSN, date of birth. Also helpful: exact years of attendance. There is no fee.

Highland Park Community College, Registrar, Glendale Ave at Third St, Highland Park, MI 48203, 313-252-0475 X240 (Fax: 313-252-0425). Hours: 8AM-4:30PM. Enrollment: 100. Records go back to 1920. Degrees granted: Associate. Adverse incident record source- Security, 313-252-0475 X220.

Attendance and degree information available by fax, mail. Search requires name plus SSN, date of birth, approximate years of attendance, signed release. Also helpful: exact years of attendance. There is no fee.

Hillsdale College, Registrar, 33 E College Ave, Hillsdale, MI 49242, 517-437-7341 (Fax: 517-437-0190). Hours: 8:30AM-5PM Fall; 8AM-4PM Summer. Enrollment: 1100. Records go back to 1877. Alumni records are maintained here also. Call 517-437-7341 X2461. Degrees granted: Bachelors.

Attendance and degree information available by phone, fax, mail. Search requires name plus approximate years of attendance. Also helpful: date of birth, exact years of attendance. There is no fee.

Hope College, Registrar, 141 E 12th St, PO Box 9000, Holland, MI 49422-9000, 616-395-7760 (Fax: 616-395-7680). Hours: 8AM-5PM. Enrollment: 2900. Records go back to 1866. Alumni records are maintained here also. Call 616-395-7860.

Degrees granted: Bachelors. Adverse incident record source- Director of Security, 616-395-7770.

Attendance and degree information available by phone, mail. Search requires name plus SSN, approximate years of attendance. Also helpful: date of birth, exact years of attendance. There is no fee.

ITT Technical Institute, (Branch of Fort Wayne, IN), Registrar, 1225 E Big Beaver Rd, Troy, MI 48083-1905, 810-524-1800 (Fax: 810-528-2218). Hours: 8AM-5PM. Enrollment: 450. Records go back to 1963. Alumni Records Office: ITT Technical Institute, 9511 Angola Ct, Indianapolis, IN 46268. Degrees granted: Associate. Special programs- Electronics. Adverse incident record source- Security.

Attendance and degree information available by phone, fax, mail. Search requires name plus SSN, exact years of attendance. There is no fee.

Jackson Community College, Registrar, 2111 Emmons Rd, Jackson, MI 49201, 517-787-0800 (Fax: 517-789-1631). Hours: 8AM-5PM. Enrollment: 7000. Records go back to 1928. Alumni records are maintained here also. Call 517-787-0800. Degrees granted: Associate.

Attendance and degree information available by phone, fax, mail. Search requires name plus SSN. There is no fee.

Kalamazoo College, Registrar, 1200 Academy St, Kalamazoo, MI 49007, 616-337-7204 (Fax: 616-337-7252). Hours: 8AM-5PM. Enrollment: 1200. Records go back to 1833. Alumni records are maintained here also. Call 616-337-7282. Degrees granted: Bachelors.

Attendance and degree information available by phone, fax, mail. Search requires name plus SSN. Also helpful: date of birth, exact years of attendance. There is no fee.

Kalamazoo Valley Community College, Registrar, PO Box 4070, Kalamazoo, MI 49003-4070, 616-372-5281. Hours: 8AM-4:30PM M,T,Th,F; 8AM-7PM W. Enrollment: 11000. Records go back to 1969. Degrees granted: Associate. Adverse incident record source- Department of Security.

Attendance and degree information available by phone, mail. Search requires name plus SSN. There is no fee.

Kellogg Community College, Registrar, 450 North Ave, Battle Creek, MI 49017-3397, 616-965-3931 X2612 (Fax: 616-965-8850). Hours: 9AM-7PM M-Th, 9AM-4:30PM F. Enrollment: 8000. Records go back to 1956. Degrees granted: Associate. Adverse incident record source- 616-965-3931 X2358.

Attendance and degree information available by phone, mail. Search requires name plus SSN, date of birth, approximate years of attendance. There is no fee.

Kendall College of Art and Design, Registrar, 111 Division Ave N, Grand Rapids, MI 49503, 616-451-2787 (Fax: 616-451-9867). Hours: 8AM-5PM. Enrollment: 500. Records go back to 1928. Alumni records are maintained here at the same phone number. Degrees granted: Bachelors.

Attendance and degree information available by written request only. Search requires name plus SSN, date of birth, exact years of attendance. There is no fee.

Kirtland Community College, Registrar, 10775 N St Helen Rd, Roscommon, MI 48653, 517-275-5121 X248 (Fax: 517-275-8210). Hours: 8AM-4:30PM. Enrollment: 1600. Records go back to 1968. Alumni records are maintained here also. Call 517-275-5121 X259. Degrees granted: Associate. Adverse incident record source- Director of Security.

Attendance and degree information available by fax, mail. Search requires name plus SSN, signed release. There is no fee.

Lake Michigan College, Registrar, 2755 E Napier St, Benton Harbor, MI 49022, 616-927-8614 (Fax: 616-927-6874).

Hours: 8AM-5PM. Enrollment: 3400. Records go back to 1946. Alumni records are maintained here at the same phone number. Degrees granted: Associate.

Attendance and degree information available by phone, fax, mail. Search requires name plus SSN. Also helpful: date of birth, exact years of attendance. There is no fee.

Lake Superior State University, Registrar, 1000 College Dr, Sault Ste. Marie, MI 49783, 906-635-2683 (Fax: 906-635-2111). Hours: 8AM-5PM. Enrollment: 3400. Records go back to 1946. Alumni records are maintained here also. Call 906-635-2831. Degrees granted: Associate; Bachelors; Masters. Adverse incident record source- Security, 906-635-2210: Student Services, 906-635-2684

Attendance and degree information available by phone, fax, mail. Search requires name plus SSN. Also helpful: date of birth, exact years of attendance. There is no fee.

Lansing Community College, 1110 Office of Registrar, PO Box 40010, Lansing, MI 48901-7210, 517-483-1266 (Fax: 517-483-9795). Hours: 8AM-5PM M-F; 8AM-8AM Th. Enrollment: 17000. Records go back to 1957. Alumni records are maintained here also. Call 517-483-1985. Degrees granted: Associate.

Attendance and degree information available by fax, mail. Search requires name plus signed release. Also helpful: SSN, date of birth, exact years of attendance. There is no fee.

Lawrence Technological University, Registrar, 21000 W Ten Mile Rd, Southfield, MI 48075, 810-204-3100 (Fax: 810-204-3727). Hours: 7:30AM-8PM M-Th; 7:30AM-5PM F. Enrollment: 4500. Records go back to 1932. Alumni records are maintained here at the same phone number. Degrees granted: Associate; Bachelors; Masters. Adverse incident record source- Registrar's Office, 810-204-3100 .

Attendance and degree information available by phone, fax, mail. Search requires name only. Also helpful: SSN, date of birth, exact years of attendance. There is no fee.

Lewis College of Business, Registrar, 17370 Meyers Rd, Detroit, MI 48235, 313-862-6300 X233 (Fax: 313-862-1027). Hours: 9AM-6PM Fall, 8AM-5:15PM Summer. Enrollment: 250. Records go back to 1939. Alumni records are maintained here also. Call 313-862-6300 X217. Degrees granted: Associate. Adverse incident record source- Business Office, 313-862-6300 X216.

Attendance and degree information available by phone, mail. Search requires name plus SSN, approximate years of attendance. There is no fee.

Macomb Community College, Registrar, 14500 E Twelve Mile Rd, Warren, MI 48093, 810-445-7225 (Fax: 810-445-7140). Hours: 8AM-7:15PM M,T; 8AM-4:30PM W,Th,F. Enrollment: 25185. Records go back to 1956. Degrees granted: Associate. Adverse incident record source- Campus Police, 810-445-7135.

Attendance and degree information available by phone, fax, mail. Search requires name plus SSN. Also helpful: date of birth, exact years of attendance. There is no fee.

Madonna University, Registrar, 36600 Schoolcraft Rd, Livonia, MI 48150, 313-432-5400 (Fax: 313-432-5405). Hours: 8AM-5PM. Enrollment: 3500. Records go back to 1947. Alumni records are maintained here also. Call 313-432-5601. Degrees granted: Associate; Bachelors; Masters.

Attendance information available by fax, mail. Search requires name plus signed release. Also helpful: SSN, exact years of attendance. There is no fee.

Degree information available by phone, fax, mail. Search requires name only. Also helpful: SSN, approximate years of attendance. There is no fee.

Marygrove College, Registrar, 8425 W McNichols Rd, Detroit, MI 48221, 313-862-8000 X400 (Fax: 313-864-6670). Hours: 9AM-5PM M; 9AM-6PM T,W; 9AM-5PM Th; 9AM-1PM F. Enrollment: 1800. Records go back to 1950. Alumni records are maintained here also. Call 313-862-8000 X568. Degrees granted: Associate; Bachelors; Masters. Adverse incident record source- Student Affairs, 313-862-2000 X273 or X277.

Attendance and degree information available by phone, mail. Search requires name plus SSN. There is no fee.

Michigan Christian College, Registrar, 800 W Avon Rd, Rochester Hills, MI 48307, 810-650-6035 (Fax: 810-650-6060). Hours: 8:30AM-5PM. Enrollment: 400. Records go back to 1959. Alumni records are maintained here also. Call 810-650-6013. Degrees granted: Associate; Bachelors.

Attendance and degree information available by phone, fax, mail. Search requires name only. Also helpful: SSN, date of birth, exact years of attendance. There is no fee.

Michigan State University, Registrar, 50 Administration Bldg, East Lansing, MI 48824, 517-355-3300 (Fax: 517-432-1649). Hours: 8AM-6PM M-Th; 8AM-5PM F. Enrollment: 40000. Records go back to 1855. Alumni records are maintained here also. Call 517-355-8314. Degrees granted: Bachelors; Masters; Doctorate. Certification: 2 year Agricultural Tech. Adverse incident record source- Student Affairs, 517-355-2264.

Attendance and degree information available by phone, fax, mail. Search requires name only. Also helpful: SSN, date of birth, exact years of attendance. There is no fee.

Michigan Technological University, Registrar, 1400 Townsend Dr, Houghton, MI 49931, 906-487-2319 (Fax: 906-487-3343). Hours: 8AM-5PM. Enrollment: 6390. Records go back to 1887. Alumni records are maintained here also. Call 906-487-2400. Degrees granted: Associate; Bachelors; Masters; Doctorate.

Attendance and degree information available by phone, fax, mail. Search requires name only. Also helpful: SSN, exact years of attendance. There is no fee.

Mid Michigan Community College, Registrar, 1375 S Clare Ave, Harrison, MI 48625, 517-386 6658 (Fax: 517-386-9088). Hours: 8AM-6:30PM M-Th; 8AM-4:30PM F. Enrollment: 3500. Records go back to 1968. Degrees granted: Associate. Adverse incident record source- Records Office, 517-386-6659.

Attendance and degree information available by phone, fax, mail. Search requires name only. Also helpful: SSN, date of birth, exact years of attendance. There is no fee.

Monroe County Community College, Registrar, 1555 S Raisinville Rd, Monroe, MI 48161, 313-242-7300 (Fax: 313-242-9711). Hours: 8AM-4:30PM. Enrollment: 3800. Records go back to 1964. Alumni records are maintained here also. Call 313-242-7300 X4111. Degrees granted: Associate.

Attendance and degree information available by phone, fax, mail. Search requires name plus SSN. Also helpful: date of birth, exact years of attendance. There is no fee.

Montcalm Community College, Registrar, 2800 College Dr SW, Sidney, MI 48885, 517-328-1230 (Fax: 517-328-2950). Hours: 8AM-4:30PM. Enrollment: 2200. Records go back to 1965. Degrees granted: Associate.

Attendance and degree information available by phone, fax, mail. Search requires name only. Also helpful: SSN, date of birth, exact years of attendance. There is no fee.

Muskegon Community College, Registrar, 221 S Quarterline Rd, Muskegon, MI 49442, 616-777-0364 (Fax: 616-777-0334). Hours: 8AM-4:30PM. Enrollment: 5000. Records go back to 1936. Alumni records are maintained here also. Call 616-

777-0341. Degrees granted: Associate. Adverse incident record source- Student Affairs.

Attendance information available by phone, fax, mail. Search requires name only. Also helpful: SSN, date of birth, exact years of attendance. There is no fee.

Degree information available by mail. Search requires name only. Also helpful: SSN, date of birth, exact years of attendance. There is no fee.

North Central Michigan College, Registrar, 1515
Howard St, Petoskey, MI 49770, 616-348-6605 (Fax: 616-348-6672). Hours: 8:30AM-5PM. Enrollment: 2000. Records go back to 1958. Alumni records are maintained here also. Call 616-348-6545. Degrees granted: Associate. Adverse incident record source- Business Office, 616-348-6602.

Attendance and degree information available by phone, fax, mail. Search requires name plus SSN, approximate years of attendance. There is no fee.

Northern Michigan University, Records Office, 301
Cohodas Bldg, 1401 Presque isle Ave, Marquette, MI 49855-5323, 906-227-2278 (Fax: 906-227-2231). Hours: 8AM-5PM. Enrollment: 7898. Records go back to 1899. Alumni records are maintained here at the same phone number. Degrees granted: Associate; Bachelors; Masters. Adverse incident record source- Dean of Students, 906-227-1700.

Attendance and degree information available by phone, mail. Search requires name plus SSN. Also helpful: date of birth, exact years of attendance. There is no fee.

Northwestern Michigan College, Records Office,
1701 E Front St, Traverse City, MI 49686-3061, 616-922-1047 (Fax: 616-922-1570). Hours: 8AM-5PM. Enrollment: 3900. Records go back to 1951. Alumni records are maintained here also. Call 616-922-1019. Degrees granted: Associate. Special programs- Maritime, 616-922-1202. Adverse incident record source- Educatiional Services, 616-922-1032.

Attendance and degree information available by phone, fax, mail. Search requires name only. Also helpful: SSN, exact years of attendance. There is no fee.

Northwood University, Registrar, 3225 Cook Rd,
Midland, MI 48640, 517-837-4216 (Fax: 517-832-9590). Hours: 8:30AM-5PM. Enrollment: 1200. Records go back to 1959. Alumni records are maintained here also. Call 517-837-4350. Degrees granted: Associate; Bachelors; Masters. Adverse incident record source- Dean of Students, 517-837-4398.

Attendance and degree information available by phone, fax, mail. Search requires name plus SSN. Also helpful: date of birth, exact years of attendance. There is no fee.

Oakland Community College, Registrar, 2480
Opdyke Rd, Bloomfield Hills, MI 48304-2266, 810-540-1548 (Fax: 810-540-1841). Hours: 8AM-8PM M-Th, 8AM-5PM F. Enrollment: 27130. Records go back to 1965. Alumni records are maintained here also. Call 810-540-1803. Degrees granted: Associate. Adverse incident record source- Records Office, 810-540-1548.

Attendance and degree information available by phone, fax, mail. Search requires name plus SSN. There is no fee.

Oakland Community College, (Highland Lakes),
Registrar, 7350 Cooley Lake Rd, Waterford, MI 48327-4187, 810-540-1500. Records are not housed here. They are located at Oakland Community College, Registrar, 2480 Opdyke Rd, Bloomfield Hills, MI 48304-2266.

Oakland Community College, (Orchard Ridge),
Registrar, 27055 Orchard Lake Rd, Farmington Hills, MI 48334, 810-540-1548 (Fax: 810-540-1841). Records are not housed here. They are located at Oakland Community College, Registrar, 2480 Opdyke Rd, Bloomfield Hills, MI 48304-2266.

Oakland University, Academic Records Office, 102
O'Dowd Hall, Rochester, MI 48309-4401, 810-370-3452 (Fax: 810-370-3461). Hours: 8AM-5PM M,T,Th,F; 8AM-6:30PM W. Enrollment: 13600. Records go back to 1959. Alumni Records Office: John Dodge House, Rochester, MI 48309-4401, 810-370-2158 (Fax: 810-370-4249). Degrees granted: Bachelors; Masters; Doctorate. Special programs- Continuing Education, 810-370-3120. Adverse incident record source- Dean of Students, 810-370-3352: OU Police, 810-370-3331

Attendance and degree information available by phone, fax, mail. Search requires name only. Also helpful: SSN, date of birth, exact years of attendance. There is no fee.

Olivet College, Registrar, Olivet, MI 49076, 616-749-7637 (Fax: 616-749-7178). Hours: 8:30AM-Noon, 1-5PM. Enrollment: 700. Records go back to 1844. Alumni records are maintained here also. Call 616-749-7644. Degrees granted: Bachelors. Adverse incident record source- Dean of Community Life, 616-749-7611.

Attendance information available by phone, fax, mail. Search requires name only. Also helpful: SSN, exact years of attendance. There is no fee.

Degree information available by phone, fax, mail. Search requires name only. Also helpful: SSN, date of birth, exact years of attendance. There is no fee.

Reformed Bible College, Registrar, 3333 E Beltline
Ave NE, Grand Rapids, MI 49505, 616-222-3000 (Fax: 616-222-3045). Hours: 8AM-5PM. Enrollment: 200. Records go back to 1940. Alumni records are maintained here at the same phone number. Degrees granted: Associate; Bacheolor of Religious Education, EXCEL Degree Completion.

Attendance and degree information available by phone, fax, mail. Search requires name only. There is no fee.

Sacred Heart Major Seminary, Registrar, 2701
Chicago Blvd, Detroit, MI 48206, 313-883-8500 (Fax: 313-868-6440). Hours: 8:30AM-4:30PM. Enrollment: 300. Records go back to 1926. Alumni records are maintained here at the same phone number. Degrees granted: Associate; Bachelors; Masters.

Attendance information available by phone, fax, mail. Search requires name plus SSN, date of birth. Also helpful: exact years of attendance. There is no fee.

Degree information available by phone, fax, mail. Search requires name plus SSN, date of birth. Also helpful: exact years of attendance. There is no fee.

Saginaw Valley State University, Registrar, 7400
Bay Rd, University Center, MI 48710, 517-790-4347 (Fax: 517-790-0180). Hours: 8AM-4:30PM. Enrollment: 7300. Records go back to 1964. Alumni records are maintained here also. Call 517-790-7075. Degrees granted: Bachelors; Masters.

Attendance and degree information available by mail. Search requires name only. Also helpful: SSN, date of birth, exact years of attendance. There is no fee.

Schoolcraft College, Registrar, 18600 Haggerty Rd,
Livonia, MI 48152, 313-462-4430 (Fax: 313-462-4506). Hours: 8AM-6PM M-Th;8AM-4:30PM F. Enrollment: 9465. Records go back to 1964. Alumni records are maintained here at the same phone number. Degrees granted: Associate. Adverse incident record source- VP for Student Services, 313-462-4400.

Attendance and degree information available by phone, fax, mail. Search requires name plus SSN. Also helpful: date of birth. There is no fee.

Siena Heights College, Registrar, 1247 E Siena
Heights Dr, Adrian, MI 49221, 517-264-7120 (Fax: 517-264-7704). Hours: 8AM-5PM. Enrollment: 1900. Records go back to 1919. Alumni records are maintained here also. Call 517-264-7140. Degrees granted: Associate; Bachelors; Masters. Adverse incident record source- Campus Security, 517-264-7194.

Attendance and degree information available by phone, fax, mail. Search requires name plus SSN, date of birth. Also helpful: exact years of attendance. There is no fee.

Southwestern Michigan College, Registrar, 58900 Cherry Grove Rd, Dowagiac, MI 49047-9793, 616-782-5113 (Fax: 616-782-8414). Hours: 8AM-8PM M-Th; 8AM-5PM F. Enrollment: 3500. Records go back to 1966. Alumni records are maintained here also. Call 616-782-5113. Degrees granted: Associate. Adverse incident record source- Student Services.

Attendance and degree information available by phone, fax, mail. Search requires name plus SSN. Also helpful: date of birth, exact years of attendance. There is no fee.

Spring Arbor College, Registrar, Spring Arbor, MI 49283, 517-750-6520 (Fax: 517-750-6534). Hours: 8AM-5PM. Enrollment: 2150. Records go back to 1938. Alumni records are maintained here also. Call 517-750-6398. Degrees granted: Associate; Bachelors; Masters.

Attendance and degree information available by phone, fax, mail. Search requires name plus SSN, date of birth, approximate years of attendance. Also helpful: exact years of attendance. There is no fee.

St. Clair County Community College, Registrar, 323 Erie St, PO Box 5015, Port Huron, MI 48061-5015, 810-984-3881. Hours: 8AM-4:30PM. Enrollment: 4500. Records go back to 1923. Alumni records are maintained here also. Call 810-984-3881. Degrees granted: Associate.

Attendance and degree information available by mail. Search requires name plus SSN, date of birth, approximate years of attendance, signed release. There is no fee.

St. Mary's College, Registrar, 3535 Indian Trail, Orchard Lake, MI 48324, 810-683-0522 (Fax: 810-683-0433). Hours: 9AM-5PM. Enrollment: 280. Records go back to 1920's. Alumni records are maintained here also. Call 810-683-0405. Degrees granted: Bachelors.

Attendance and degree information available by phone, fax, mail. Search requires name plus SSN. Also helpful: date of birth, approximate years of attendance. There is no fee.

Suomi College, Registrar, 601 Quincy St, Hancock, MI 49930, 906-487-7272 (Fax: 906-487-7509). Hours: 8AM-4:30PM. Enrollment: 400. Records go back to 1896. Alumni records are maintained here also. Call 906-487-7367. Degrees granted: Associate. Adverse incident record source- Dean of Students, 906-487-7370.

Attendance and degree information available by phone, fax, mail. Search requires name plus SSN, date of birth, approximate years of attendance. There is no fee.

Thomas M. Cooley Law School, Registrar, 507 Grand Ave, PO Box 13038, Lansing, MI 48901-3038, 517-371-5140 (Fax: 517-334-5716). Enrollment: 1536. Records go back to 1976. Alumni records are maintained here also. Call 517-371-5140 X584. Adverse incident record source- Dean, 517-371-5140.

Attendance and degree information available by phone, fax, mail. Search requires name only. Also helpful: exact years of attendance. Fee is $3.00.

University of Detroit Mercy, Registrar, 4001 W NcNichols Rd, PO Box 19900, Detroit, MI 48219, 313-993-3313 (Fax: 313-993-3317). Hours: 8:30AM-5PM. Enrollment: 7500. Records go back to 1877. Alumni records are maintained here also. Call 313-993-1250. Degrees granted: Associate; Bachelors; Masters; Doctorate.

Attendance and degree information available by phone, fax, mail. Search requires name plus SSN, approximate years of attendance. Also helpful: date of birth, exact years of attendance. There is no fee.

University of Michigan, Transcript Department, 555 LSA Building, Ann Arbor, MI 48109-1382, 313-763-9066 (Fax: 313-764-5556). Hours: 8AM-5PM. Enrollment: 36545. Records go back to 1817. Alumni Records Office: 200 Fletcher St, Ann Arbor, MI 48109-1007. Degrees granted: Bachelors; Masters; Doctorate. Special programs- Medical School, 313-764-0219: Dental School, 313-764-1512: Law, 313-764-6499.

Attendance and degree information available by phone, fax, mail. Search requires name only. Also helpful: SSN, date of birth, exact years of attendance. There is no fee.

University of Michigan-Dearborn, 240 SSC, Transcripts, 4901 Evergreen Rd, Dearborn, MI 48128-1591, 313-593-5210 (Fax: 313-593-5697). Hours: 8AM-6:30PM M&Th; 8AM-5PM TWF. Enrollment: 8500. Records go back to 1959. Alumni records are maintained here also. Call 313-593-5131. Degrees granted: Bachelors; Masters. Special programs- Graduate/Master degrees, Ann Arbor, 313-763-9066. Adverse incident record source- Campus Safety, 313-593-5333.

Attendance and degree information available by phone, fax, mail. Search requires name only. Also helpful: SSN, date of birth, exact years of attendance. There is no fee.

University of Michigan-Flint, Registrar, Flint, MI 48502, 810-762-3344 (Fax: 810-762-3346). Hours: 8AM-6:30PM M-Th; 8AM-5PM F. Enrollment: 6312. Records go back to 1956. Alumni records are maintained here at the same phone number. Degrees granted: Bachelors; Masters. Adverse incident record source- Student Services.

Attendance and degree information available by phone, fax, mail. Search requires name plus SSN. Also helpful: date of birth, exact years of attendance. There is no fee.

Walsh College of Accountancy and Business Administration, Registrar, 3838 Livernois Rd, PO Box 7006, Troy, MI 48007-7006, 810-689-8282 (Fax: 810-524-2520). Hours: 8:30AM-7PM. Enrollment: 3915. Records go back to 1922. Alumni records are maintained here at the same phone number. Degrees granted: Bachelors; Masters.

Attendance and degree information available by phone, fax, mail. Search requires name only. Also helpful: SSN, exact years of attendance. There is no fee.

Washtenaw Community College, Registrar, 4800 E Huron River Dr, PO Box D-1, Ann Arbor, MI 48106, 313-677-5159 (Fax: 313-677-5408). Hours: 8AM-7PM M-Th, 8AM-5PM F. Enrollment: 10000. Records go back to 1966. Alumni records are maintained here at the same phone number. Degrees granted: Associate. Adverse incident record source- Dean of Students, 313-973-3536.

Attendance and degree information available by phone, fax, mail. Search requires name plus SSN. There is no fee.

Wayne County Community College, Registrar, 801 W Fort St, Detroit, MI 48226-3010, 313-496-2862 (Fax: 313-961-2791). Hours: 9AM-4:30PM. Enrollment: 11000. Records go back to 1969. Alumni records are maintained here also. Call 313-496-2818. Degrees granted: Associate.

Attendance and degree information available by mail. Search requires name plus SSN, date of birth, signed release. Also helpful: exact years of attendance. There is no fee.

Wayne State University, Student Records, 2 W Helen Newberry Joy, SSC, Detroit, MI 48202, 313-577-3531 (Fax: 313-577-3769). Hours: 8:30AM-6PM M-Th; 8:30AM-5PM F. Degrees granted: Bachelors; Masters; Doctorate.

Attendance and degree information available by phone, fax, mail. Search requires name only. Also helpful: SSN, date of birth, exact years of attendance. There is no fee.

West Shore Community College, Student Records Office, 3000 N Stiles Rd, Scottville, MI 49454, 616-845-6211 (Fax: 616-845-0207). Hours: 8AM-4:30PM. Enrollment: 1500.

Alumni records are maintained here also. Call 616-845-6211 X3103. Degrees granted: Associate. Adverse incident record source- Business Office, 616-845-6211 X3123.

School will not confirm attendance information.

Degree information available by mail. Search requires name plus SSN. Also helpful: date of birth, exact years of attendance. There is no fee.

Western Michigan University, Registrar, Kalamazoo, MI 49008, 616-387-4300. Hours: 8AM-5PM. Enrollment: 26500. Records go back to 1904. Alumni records are maintained here also. Call 616-387-8777. Degrees granted: Bachelors; Masters; PhD. Adverse incident record source- Student Services.

Attendance information available by mail. Search requires name plus SSN, date of birth, signed release. There is no fee.

Degree information available by phone, mail. Search requires name plus SSN, date of birth. There is no fee.

Western Theological Seminary, Registrar, 101 E 13th St, Holland, MI 49423, 616-392-8555 (Fax: 616-392-7717). Hours: 8AM-5PM. Enrollment: 150. Records go back to 1900. Alumni records are maintained here at the same phone number. Degrees granted: Masters; Doctorate.

Attendance and degree information available by phone, fax, mail. Search requires name plus exact years of attendance. There is no fee.

William Tyndale College, Registrar, 35700 W Twelve Mile Rd, Farmington Hills, MI 48331, 810-553-7200 (Fax: 810-553-5963). Hours: 8AM-5PM. Enrollment: 625. Records go back to 1945. Degrees granted: Associate; Bachelors. Adverse incident record source- Student Services.

Attendance and degree information available by fax, mail. Search requires name plus SSN, exact years of attendance, signed release. Also helpful: date of birth. There is no fee.

Yeshiva Beth Yehuda-Yeshiva Gedolah of Greater Detroit, Registrar, 24600 Greenfield St, Oak Park, MI 48237, 810-968-3360 (Fax: 810-968-8613). Hours: 8:30AM-5:30PM. Enrollment: 45. Records go back to 1985. Degrees granted: Associate; Bachelors; Masters; Doctorate. Adverse incident record source- Student Affairs.

Attendance information available by phone, fax, mail. Search requires name plus SSN. There is no fee.

Degree information available by fax, mail. Search requires name plus SSN. There is no fee.

Trade and Vocational Schools

Academy of Health Careers, 27301 Dequindre Rd #200, Madison Heights, MI 48071, 810-547-8400

American Education Center, 26075 Woodward Ave, Huntington Woods, MI 48070, 810-399-5522

Ann Arbor School of Business, 3810 Packard Rd Ste 270, Ann Arbor, MI 48108, 313-973-9530

Black Forest Hall, PO Box 140, Harbor Springs, MI 49740, 616-526-7066

Carnegie Institute, 550 Stephenson Hwy #100, Troy, MI 48083, 810-589-1078

Center for Creative Studies-Institute of Music and Dance, 201 E Kirby St, Detroit, MI 48202, 313-872-3118

Detroit Business Institute, 1249 Washington Blvd #1200, Detroit, MI 48226, 313-962-6534

Detroit Business Institute-Downriver, 19100 Fort St, Riverview, MI 48192, 313-479-0660

Detroit Institute of Ophthalmology, 15415 E Jefferson Ave, Grosse Pointe Park, MI 48230, 313-824-4800

Dorsey Business School, 30821 Barrington Ave, Madison Heights, MI 48071, 810-585-9200

Dorsey Business School, 31542 Gratiot Ave, Roseville, MI 48066, 810-296-3225

Dorsey Business School, 15755 Northline Rd, Southgate, MI 48195, 313-285-5400

Dorsey Business School, 34841 Veteran's Plaza, Wayne, MI 48184, 313-595-1540

Educational Institute of the American Hotel and Motel Association, PO Box 1240, East Lansing, MI 48826, 517-353-5500

Flint Institute of Barbering, 3214 Flushing Rd, Flint, MI 48504, 313-232-4711

Grand Rapids Educational Center, 1750 Woodworth St NE, Grand Rapids, MI 49505, 616-364-8464

Grand Rapids Educational Center (Branch Campus), 5349 W Main St, Kalamazoo, MI 49009, 606-381-9616

Hawes Career Institute, 47884 D St, Belleville, MI 48111, 800-447-1310

ITT Technical Institute, 4020 Sparks Dr SE, Grand Rapids, MI 49546, 616-956-1060

Lansing Computer Institute, 501 N Marshall St #101, Lansing, MI 48912, 517-482-8896

Lawton School, 21800 Greenfield, Oak Park, MI 48237, 810-968-2421

Michigan Barber School, Inc., 8988-90 Grand River Ave, Detroit, MI 48204, 313-894-2300

Michigan Career Institute, 14520 Gratiot Ave, Detroit, MI 48205, 313-526-6600

Michigan School of Canine Cosmetology, 3022 S Ceder, Lansing, MI 48910, 517-393-6311

Motech Education Center, 35155 Industrial Rd, Livonia, MI 48150, 313-522-9510

National Education Center (Branch Campus), 4244 Oakman Blvd, Detroit, MI 48204, 313-581-4710

National Education Center-National Institute of Technology Campus, 18000 Newburgh Rd, Livonia, MI 48152, 313-464-7387

National Education Center-National Institute of Technology Campus, 2620 Remico St SW, Wyoming, MI 49509, 616-538-3170

Payne-Pulliam School of Trade and Commerce, 2345 Cass Ave, Detroit, MI 48201, 313-963-4710

Pontiac Business Institute, PO Box 459, Oxford, MI 48371, 810-628-4846

Ross Business Institute, 22293 Eureka Rd, Taylor, MI 48180, 313-374-2135

Ross Business Institute (Branch Campus), 37065 Gratiot, Clinton Township, MI 48036, 810-954-3083

Ross Business Institute (Branch Campus), 1285 N Telegraph Rd, Monroe, MI 48161, 313-243-5456

Ross Medical Education Center, 1036 Gilbert Rd, Flint, MI 48532, 810-230-1100

Ross Medical Education Center, 913 W Holmes Rd #260, Lansing, MI 48910, 517-887-0180

Ross Medical Education Center, 26417 Hoover Rd, Warren, MI 48089, 810-758-7200

Ross Medical Education Center (Branch Campus), 15670 E Eight Mile Rd, Detroit, MI 48205, 313-371-2131

Ross Medical Education Center (Branch Campus), 2035 28th St SE #O, Grand Rapids, MI 49508, 616-243-3070

Ross Medical Education Center (Branch Campus), 1188 N West Ave, Jackson, MI 49202, 517-782-7677

Ross Medical Education Center (Branch Campus), 950 W Norton Ave, Roosevelt Park, MI 48441, 616-739-1531

Ross Medical Education Center (Branch Campus), 4054 Bay Rd, Saginaw, MI 48603, 517-793-9800

Ross Medical Education Center (Branch Campus), 253 Summit Dr, Waterford, MI 48328, 810-683-1166

Ross Technical Institute, 5757 Whitmore Lake Rd #800, Brighton, MI 48116, 810-227-0160

Ross Technical Institute, 1553 Woodward Ave #650, Detroit, MI 48226, 313-965-7451

Ross Technical Institute (Branch Campus), 4703 Washtenaw Ave, Ann Arbor, MI 48108, 313-434-7320

Ross Technical Institute (Branch Campus), 20820 Greenfield Rd 1st Fl, Oak Park, MI 48237, 810-967-3100

SER Business and Technical Institute, 9301 Michigan Ave, Detroit, MI 48210, 313-846-2240

Saginaw Beauty Academy, PO Box 423, Saginaw, MI 48601, 517-752-9261

Sawyer School of Business, 26051 Hoover Rd, Warren, MI 48089, 810-758-2300

Sharp's Academy of Hairstyling, 115 Main St, Flushing, MI 48433, 810-659-3348

Sharp's Academy of Hairstyling (Branch Campus), 8166 Holly Rd, Grand Blanc, MI 48499, 810-695-6742

Specs Howard School of Broadcast Arts, Inc., 19900 W Eight Mile Rd #115, Southfield, MI 48075, 810-569-0101

Travel Education Institute, 24901 Northwestern Hwy Ste 110, Southfield, MI 48075, 810-352-4875

Travel Education Institute (Warren Campus), 30100 Van Dyke Ste 200, Warren, MI 48093, 810-751-5634

Travel Training Center, 5003-05 Schaefer Rd, Dearborn, MI 48126, 313-584-5000

State Licensing & Business Registration Quick Finder Index

Architecture, Engineering & Surveying
Architect #9 .... ☎ 517-335-1669
Engineer-Professional #10 .... ☎ 517-335-1669
Landscape Architect #10 .... ☎ 517-335-1669
Surveyor-Professional #10 .... ☎ 517-335-1669

Business - Court & Legal Services
Attorney #27 .... ☎ 517-346-4300
Notary Public #22 .... ☎ 517-373-2531

Business - General Services
Dealer #28 .... ☎ 517-373-9082
Employment Agency #10 (85) .... ☎ 517-373-1654
Public Accountant (CPA) #9 .... ☎ 517-373-0682

Construction & Manufacturing
Boiler Repairer #7 .... ☎ 517-322-1836
Boilermaker (Boiler Installer) #7 (1800) .... ☎ 517-322-1836
Electrician (4 types) #7 .... ☎ 517-322-1739
Elevator Service (5 types) #7 .... ✉ 517-322-1839
Mechanical Construction #7 .... ☎ 517-322-1798
Mobile Home Dealer #17 .... ☎ 517-373-9153
Mobile Home Installer/Repair #17 .... ☎ 517-373-9153
Plumber #7 .... ✉ 517-322-1804
Pump Installer #20 .... ☎ 517-335-8000

Education
Guidance Counselor #19 .... ☎ 517-373-6505
School Librarian #19 .... ☎ 517-373-6505
Teacher #19 .... ☎ 517-373-6505

Environmental & Agriculture
Asbestos Accreditation-Individual #12 .... ☎ 517-335-8246
Asbestos Licensing #12 (135) .... ☎ 517-335-8246
Food Licensing #2 .... ☎ 517-373-1060
Forester #10 .... ☎ 517-335-1669
Horologist #10 .... ☎ 517-373-0580
Pesticide Licensing (5 types) #2 .... ☎ 517-373-1086
Veterinarian #16 (3200) .... ☎ 517-373-3596
Well Contractor #20 .... ☎ 517-335-8000

Financial - Real Estate, Insurance & Banking
Assessor (Certification, Levels 1-4) #25
   (3000) .... ☎ 517-373-8320
Bank & Trust #14 (142) .... ☎ 517-373-7210
Collection Manager #9 (370) .... ☎ 517-373-1654
Credit Union #14 (325) .... ☎ 517-373-6930
Insurance Adjuster #5 .... ✉ 517-373-0234
Insurance Agent, Counselor, Solicitor,
   Administrator #5 .... ✉ 517-373-0234
Investment Advisor #13 (1026) .... ☎ 517-334-6209
Mobile Home Lessor #17 .... ☎ 517-373-9153
Real Estate #10 .... ☎ 517-373-0490
Real Estate Appraiser #10 (4098) .... ☎ 517-373-0580
Real Estate Broker/Salesperson #10 .... ☎ 517-335-4403
Securities Agent #13 (68350) .... ☎ 517-334-6209
Securities Broker-Dealer #13 .... ☎ 517-334-6209
Securities Broker/Dealer #13 (5000) .... ☎ 517-334-6215

Health & Beauty
Ambulance Attendant (Medical First
   Responders) #11 (13000) .... ☎ 517-335-8547
Barber #9 (7149) .... ☎ 517-373-0580
Cemetery #9 .... ☎ 517-373-3105
Chiropractor #15 .... ☎ 517-373-3596

Cosmetologist #9 (77498) .... ☎ 517-373-0580
Counselor #15 .... ☎ 517-373-7480
Dentist #15 (7700) .... ☎ 517-373-6650
EMT Instructor #11 (750) .... ☎ 517-335-8547
EMT, EMT Advanced, EMT Specialist #11
   (15000) .... ☎ 517-335-8547
Food Service Licensing #3 517-335-9181
Health Facilities/Laboratories #8 (8000) ...... ✉ 517-335-8505
Hearing Aid Dealer #10 (659) .... ☎ 517-335-4403
Massage #10 .... ☎ 517-373-0580
Medical Doctor #15 (30000) .... ☎ 517-335-0918
Mortuary Science #10 (2155) .... ☎ 517-373-0580
Nurse #15 .... ☎ 517-373-1600
Nursing Home Administrator #10 .... ☎ 517-335-4403
Occupational Therapist #15 (2781) .... ☎ 517-373-7480
Ocularist and Optometrist #10 (16) .... ☎ 517-373-0580
Osteopathic Physician #15 (5600) .... ☎ 517-373-6650
Pharmacist #15 .... ☎ 517-335-0918
Physical Therapist #15 .... ☎ 517-373-3596
Physician's Assistant #16 (1100) .... ☎ 517-373-6650
Podiatric Medicine & Surgery #16 .... ☎ 517-373-3596
Prepaid Funeral Contract Salesperson
   (Prepaid Funeral Contract Registration) #10
   (575) .... ☎ 517-373-0580
Sanitarian #16 .... ☎ 517-373-3596

Investigations & Security
Alarm System Services #23 (390) .... ☎ 517-322-1964
Corrections Officer #18 517-335-1426
Forensic Polygraph Examiner #10 (110) .... ☎ 517-335-4403
Parole/Probation Officer #18 517-335-1426
Private Detective #23 (1378) .... ☎ 517-322-1964
Private Security #23 (364) .... ☎ 517-322-1964

Social Services
Adoption Service #8 (300) .... ☎ 517-373-4549
Adult & Foster Care #8 (4500) .... ☎ 517-373-8580
Child Caring Institution #26 .... ☎ 517-373-8383
Child Day Care #8 (4600) .... ☎ 517-373-8300
Child Welfare Agency (Child Placing Agency) #26
   (250) .... ☎ 517-373-8383
Children's Camp/Adult Camp #26 .... ☎ 517-373-8383
Community Planner-Professional #9 .... ☎ 517-335-1669
Foster Care Program (Foster Family Home/Foster
   Family Group Home) #21 (7300) 517-335-6108
Marriage Counselor #10 .... ☎ 517-335-0918
Psychologist #16 (2200) .... ☎ 517-373-3596
Social Workers #10 .... ☎ 517-373-1653

Sports & Entertainment
Athletic Control #9 .... ☎ 517-373-3105
Carnival-Amusement #9 (1500) .... ☎ 517-373-7964
Charitable Gaming (Supplier) #1 (53) .... ☎ 517-335-5781
Liquor Distributor #6 517-322-1164
Lottery Retailer #1 (9000) .... ☎ 517-335-5619
Millionaire Party-Vegas Night #1 .... ☎ 517-335-5781
Racing #4 .... ☎ 313-462-2400
Raffle #1 .... ☎ 517-335-5781
Special Bingo #1 .... ☎ 517-335-5781
Weekly Bingo #1 .... ☎ 517-335-5781

Transportation
Aeronautics #24 .... ✉ 517-373-1834
Driver Training & Commercial #22 .... ☎ 517-373-0082

State Licensing & Business Registration Agency Information

(1) Bureau of State Lottery, PO Box 30023, 101 E Hillsdale, Lansing, MI 48909, 517-335-5781, Fax: 517-373-6863

(2) Department of Agriculture, PO Box 30017, Ottawa Bldg, 4th Flr, Lansing, MI 48909, 517-373-1060, Fax: 517-335-4540

(3) Department of Agriculture, Food Service Sanitation Section, PO Box 30017, 611 W Ottawa St, Lansing, MI 48909, 517-335-8000, Fax: 517-241-1185

(4) Department of Agriculture, Office of Racing Commissioner, 37650 Professional Center Dr, Livonia, MI 48154-1114, 313-462-2400, Fax: 313-462-2429

(5) Department of Commerce, Insurance Bureau, PO Box 30220, Ottawa Bldg, 2nd Floor, Lansing, MI 48909, 517-373-0234, Fax: 517-335-4978

(6) Department of Commerce, Liquor Control Commission, 7150 Harris Dr, Secondary Complex, PO Box 30005, Lansing, MI 48909, 517-322-1164

(7) Department of Consumer & Industry Services, Bureau of Construction Codes, PO Box 30254, 7150 Harris Dr, State Secondary Complex, Lansing, MI 48909, 517-373-1820, Fax: 517-322-1267

(8) Department of Consumer & Industry Services, Bureau of Health Systems, 3423 North MLK Jr. Blvd. PO Box 30195, Lansing, MI 48909, 517-335-8505, Fax: 517-335-8582

(9) Department of Consumer & Industry Services, Commercial Services/Licensing Division, Ottawa Bldg, 1st Floor PO Box 30018, Lansing, MI 48909, 517-373-7964, Fax: 517-373-7964

(10) Department of Consumer & Industry Services, Commercial Services/Licensing Division, Ottawa Bldg, 1st Floor PO Box 30018, Lansing, MI 48909, 517-373-0580, Fax: 517-373-2795

(11) Department of Consumer & Industry Services, Division of Emergency Medical Services, 3423 N Logan PO Box 30195, Lansing, MI 48909, 517-335-8547

(12) Department of Consumer & Industry Services, Division of Occupational Health, 3423 N ML King Jr. Blvd, PO BOX 30649, Lansing, MI 48909-8149, 517-335-8246, Fax: 517-335-9444

(13) Department of Consumer & Industry Services, Enforcement Division, PO Box 30222, Lansing, MI 48909, 517-334-6200, Fax: 517-334-6155

(14) Department of Consumer & Industry Services, Financial Institutions Bureau, 333 S Capital, Suite A PO Box 30224, Lansing, MI 48909, 517-373-6930, Fax: 517-373-9475

(15) Department of Consumer & Industry Services, Health Services Licensing Division, PO Box 30018, Ottawa Bldg, 4th Flr, Lansing, MI 48909, 517-373-3596, Fax: 517-373-2179

(16) Department of Consumer & Industry Services, Health Services Licensing Division, PO Box 30018, Ottawa Bldg, 4th Flr, Lansing, MI 48909, 517-335-0918, Fax: 517-373-2179

(17) Department of Consumer & Industry Services, Mobile Home and Land Resources Division, PO Box 30222, Lansing, MI 48909, 517-373-9153

(18) Department of Corrections, 206 E Michigan Ave, Lansing, MI 48909, 517-335-1426

(19) Department of Education, Office of Professional Preparation & Certification, PO Box 30008, Hannah Bldg, 4th Flr, Lansing, MI 48909, 517-373-3310, Fax: 517-373-0542

(20) Department of Health, Ground Water Quality Control Section, 3423 N Logan, Lansing, MI 48909, 517-335-8000

(21) Department of Social Services, 235 S Grand Ave, Grand Tower, PO Box 30037, Lansing, MI 48909, 517-373-2083

(22) Department of State, Office of the Great Seal, 717 W Allegan St, Lansing, MI 48918, 517-373-2531

(23) Department of State Police, Private Security & Investigator Unit, 7150 Harris Dr General Office Bldg., Lansing, MI 48913, 517-322-1964, Fax: 517-322-5551

(24) Department of Transportation, Bureau of Aeronautics, 2700 E Airport Service Dr, Lansing, MI 48906, 517-335-9283

(25) Department of Treasury, Treasury Building, Lansing, MI 48922, 517-373-3200

(26) Michigan Department of Consumer & Industry Svcs., Bureau of Regulatory Services, 7109 W. Saginaw, 2nd Floor PO Box 30650, Lansing, MI 48909-8150, 517-373-8383, Fax: 517-335-6121

(27) State Bar, 306 Townsend, Lansing, MI 48933, 517-346-4300, Fax: 517-482-6248

(28) State Department, 208 N Capitol Ave, Mutual Bldg, 2nd Floor, Lansing, MI 48918-1200, 517-373-9082, Fax: 517-373-0964

Minnesota

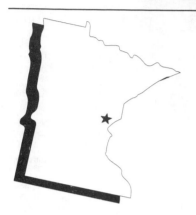

Capitol: St. Paul (Ramsey County)	
State Population	4.6 Million
Number of Degree Granting Institutions:	83
Number of State Licensing & Business Registration Agencies:	110

Degree Granting Educational Institutions

Alexandria Technical College, Registrar, 1601 Jefferson St, Alexandria, MN 56308, 320-762-4470 (Fax: 320-762-4430). Hours: 8AM-4:30PM. Enrollment: 1800. Records go back to 1965. Alumni records are maintained here also. Call 320-762-4439. Degrees granted: Associate.

Attendance and degree information available by phone, fax, mail. Search requires name plus approximate years of attendance. Also helpful: SSN. There is no fee.

Alfred Adler Institute of Minnesota, Registrar, 1001 Hwy 7 Ste 344, Hopkins, MN 55305, 612-988-4170 (Fax: 612-988-4171). Hours: 8:30AM-4:30pm. Enrollment: 190. Records go back to 1984. Alumni records are maintained here at the same phone number. Degrees granted: Masters. Adverse incident record source- Registrar, 612-988-4170.

Attendance and degree information available by mail. Search requires name plus approximate years of attendance. Fee is $5.00.

American Schools of Professional Psychology, (Minnesota School of Professional Psychology), Registrar, 3103 E 80th St Ste 290, Bloomington, MN 55420, 612-858-8800 (Fax: 612-858-3515). Hours: 8:30AM-5PM. Enrollment: 310. Records go back to 1987. Degrees granted: Masters; Doctorate.

Attendance and degree information available by phone, fax, mail. Search requires name plus SSN. Also helpful: exact years of attendance. There is no fee.

Anoka Technical College, Registrar, 1355 W Hwy 10, Anoka, MN 55303, 612-576-4700 (Fax: 612-422-0607). Hours: 8AM-8PM M-Th, 8AM-4PM F. Records go back to 1970.

Attendance and degree information available by phone, fax, mail. Search requires name plus SSN, approximate years of attendance. There is no fee.

Anoka-Ramsey Community College, Records Office, 11200 Mississippi Blvd, Coon Rapids, MN 55433, 612-422-3422 (Fax: 612-422-3636). Hours: 8AM-4:30PM T,W,F; 8AM-7PM M,Th. Enrollment: 4500. Records go back to 1931.

Degrees granted: Associate. Adverse incident record source-Bonnie Anderson, 612-422-3430.

Attendance and degree information available by phone, fax, mail. Search requires name plus SSN. Also helpful: date of birth, approximate years of attendance. There is no fee.

Augsburg College, Registrar, 2211 Riverside Ave, Minneapolis, MN 55454, 612-330-1036 (Fax: 612-330-1425). Hours: 8AM-4:30PM. Enrollment: 2549. Records go back to 1869. Records for past five years other than transcripts. Alumni Records Office: 2124 S 7th St, Minneapolis, MN 55454. Degrees granted: Bachelors; Masters. Special programs- Studies Abroad.

Attendance and degree information available by phone, fax, mail. Search requires name only. Also helpful: SSN, date of birth, approximate years of attendance. There is no fee.

Bemidji State University, Registrar, 1500 Birchmont Dr NE, Bemidji, MN 56601-2699, 218-755-2020 (Fax: 218-744-4048). Hours: 8AM-4PM. Enrollment: 4700. Records go back to 1919. Alumni records are maintained here also. Call 218-755-3989. Degrees granted: Associate; Bachelors; Masters. Adverse incident record source- Campus Security, 218-755-3888.

Attendance and degree information available by phone, fax, mail. Search requires name only. Also helpful: SSN, date of birth, exact years of attendance. There is no fee.

Bethany Lutheran College, Registrar, 734 Marsh St, Mankato, MN 56001, 507-386-5310 (Fax: 507-386-5376). Hours: 8AM-5PM. Enrollment: 400. Records go back to 1911. Alumni records are maintained here also. Call 507-386-5314. Degrees granted: Associate.

Attendance and degree information available by phone, fax, mail. Search requires name plus SSN. There is no fee.

Bethel College, Registrar, 3900 Bethel Dr, St Paul, MN 55112, 612-638-6250 (Fax: 612-638-6001). Hours: 8AM-4:30PM. Enrollment: 2400. Records go back to 1905. Alumni records are maintained here at the same phone number. Degrees granted: Associate; Bachelors; Masters. Adverse incident record source- Student Life, 612-638-6300.

Attendance and degree information available by phone, fax, mail. Search requires name plus SSN, exact years of attendance. Also helpful: date of birth. There is no fee.

Bethel Theological Seminary, Registrar, 3949 Bethel Dr, St Paul, MN 55112, 612-638-6181 (Fax: 612-638-6002). Hours: 8AM-4:30PM. Enrollment: 565. Records go back to 1930. Records prior to 1930 in archives. Alumni Records Office: Alumni Association, Bethel Theological Seminary, 3900 Bethel Dr, St Paul, MN 55112. Degrees granted: Masters; Doctorate.

Attendance and degree information available by phone, fax, mail. Search requires name only. Also helpful: SSN, date of birth, approximate years of attendance. There is no fee.

Brainerd Community College, Registrar, 501 W College Dr, Brainerd, MN 56401, 218-828-2508 (Fax: 218-828-2710). Hours: 8AM-4:30PM. Records go back to 1958. Alumni records are maintained here also. Call 218-828-2525. Degrees granted: Associate.

Attendance and degree information available by phone, fax, mail. Search requires name plus SSN, approximate years of attendance. There is no fee.

Carleton College, Registrar, One N College St, Northfield, MN 55057, 507-663-4289 (Fax: 507-663-5419). Hours: 8AM-5PM. Enrollment: 1800. Records go back to 1870. Pre-1953 are at school archives, 507-663-4270. Alumni records are maintained here also. Call 507-663-4205. Degrees granted: Bachelors.

Attendance and degree information available by phone, fax, mail. Search requires name only. Also helpful: SSN, date of birth, exact years of attendance. There is no fee.

Century College, Registrar, 3300 Century Ave, White Bear Lake, MN 55110, 612-779-3298 (Fax: 612-773-1708). Hours: 8AM-4PM Enrollment: 7000. Formerly Lakewood Community College Records go back to 1970. Alumni records are maintained here also. Call 612-779-3338. Degrees granted: Associate.

Attendance and degree information available by phone, mail. Search requires name plus SSN, date of birth. Also helpful: approximate years of attendance. There is no fee.

College of Associated Arts, Registrar, 344 Summit Ave, St Paul, MN 55102-2199, 612-224-3416 (Fax: 612-224-8854). Enrollment: 210. Records go back to 1954. Alumni records are maintained here at the same phone number. Degrees granted: Bachelors. Adverse incident record source- Business Manager.

Attendance and degree information available by phone, fax, mail. Search requires name plus SSN, date of birth. Also helpful: exact years of attendance. There is no fee.

College of St. Benedict, Registrar, 37 S College Ave, St Joseph, MN 56374, 612-363-3396 (Fax: 612-363-2714). Records are not housed here. They are located at St. John's University, Registrar, Collegeville, MN 56321.

College of St. Catherine, Registrar, 2004 Randolph Ave, St Paul, MN 55105, 612-690-6531. Hours: 9AM-3:30PM. Enrollment: 4035. Records go back to 1905. Alumni records are maintained here also. Call 612-690-6000. Degrees granted: Bachelors. Adverse incident record source- Dean of Students, 612-690-6000.

Attendance and degree information available by phone, mail. Search requires name plus SSN, approximate years of attendance. There is no fee.

College of St. Catherine-Minneapolis, (St. Mary's), Records & Accounts, 601 25th Ave S, Minneapolis, MN 55454, 612-690-7777 (Fax: 612-690-7849). Hours: 10AM-

6PM. Enrollment: 1200. Alumni records are maintained here also. Call 612-690-7759. Degrees granted: Associate; Masters.

Attendance information available by fax, mail. Search requires name only. Also helpful: SSN, approximate years of attendance. There is no fee.

Degree information available by phone, fax, mail. Search requires name only. Also helpful: SSN, approximate years of attendance. There is no fee.

College of St. Scholastica, Registrar, 1200 Kenwood Ave, Duluth, MN 55811, 218-723-6039 (Fax: 218-723-6290). Hours: 8AM-4:30PM. Enrollment: 2000. Records go back to 1945. Alumni records are maintained here also. Call 218-723-6033 X6658. Degrees granted: Bachelors; Masters. Adverse incident record source- Dean, 218-723-6033 X6038.

Attendance and degree information available by phone, fax, mail. Search requires name plus SSN. There is no fee.

Concordia College, Registrar, 901 S 8th St, Moorhead, MN 56562, 218-299-3250 (Fax: 218-229-3947). Hours: 8AM-5PM. Enrollment: 2958. Alumni records are maintained here also. Call 218-299-3743. Degrees granted: Bachelors. Adverse incident record source- Student Affairs, 218-299-3455.

Attendance and degree information available by phone, mail. Search requires name plus SSN. Also helpful: date of birth, exact years of attendance. There is no fee.

Concordia College, Registrar, 275 N Syndicate St, St Paul, MN 55104, 612-641-8223 (Fax: 612-659-0207). Hours: 8AM-4:30PM. Enrollment: 1200. Records go back to 1894. Alumni records are maintained here at the same phone number. Degrees granted: Associate; Bachelors; Masters. Adverse incident record source- Security, 612-641-8777.

Attendance and degree information available by phone, fax, mail. Search requires name plus SSN. Also helpful: date of birth, exact years of attendance. There is no fee.

Crown College, Registrar, 6425 County Rd 30, St Bonifacius, MN 55375, 612-446-4172 (Fax: 612-446-4149). Hours: 8AM-4:30PM. Enrollment: 620. Alumni records are maintained here at the same phone number. Degrees granted: Associate; Bachelors.

Attendance and degree information available by phone, fax, mail. Search requires name plus SSN, approximate years of attendance. There is no fee.

Dakota County Technical College, Registrar, 1300 145th St E, Rosemount, MN 55068, 612-423-8301 (Fax: 612-423-7028). Hours: 7AM-4PM. Enrollment: 2500. Records go back to 1972. Alumni records are maintained here at the same phone number. Degrees granted: Associate.

Attendance and degree information available by phone, fax, mail. Search requires name plus SSN. Also helpful: date of birth, exact years of attendance. There is no fee.

Fergus Falls Community College, Registrar, 1414 College Way, Fergus Falls, MN 56537, 218-739-7500 (Fax: 218-739-7472). Hours: 8AM-5PM. Records go back to 1960. Degrees granted: Associate.

Attendance and degree information available by phone, fax, mail. Search requires name plus SSN. Also helpful: date of birth, exact years of attendance. There is no fee.

Globe College of Business, Registrar, 175 Fifth St E Ste 201, Box 60, St Paul, MN 55101-2901, 612-224-4378 (Fax: 612-224-5684). Hours: 8AM-7:30PM M-Th; 8AM-4:30PM F. Degrees granted: Associate.

Attendance information available by phone, mail. Search requires name plus SSN, date of birth, exact years of attendance. There is no fee.

Degree information available by phone, mail. Search requires name plus SSN, date of birth. Also helpful: exact years of attendance. There is no fee.

Golden Valley Lutheran College, Registrar, 3718 Macalaster Dr NE, Minneapolis, MN 55421, 612-788-7616 (Fax: 612-789-1549). Records go back to 1919. This school closed 5/24/85. Degrees granted: Associate.

Attendance and degree information available by phone, fax, mail. Search requires name only. Also helpful: SSN, date of birth, exact years of attendance. There is no fee.

Gustavus Adolphus College, Registrar, 800 W College Ave, St Peter, MN 56082, 507-933-7495 (Fax: 507-933-6270). Hours: 8AM-4PM. Enrollment: 2362. Records go back to 1860. Alumni records are maintained here also. Call 507-933-7552. Degrees granted: Bachelors. Adverse incident record source- Dean of Students, 507-933-7526.

Attendance and degree information available by phone, fax, mail. Search requires name plus SSN, date of birth, approximate years of attendance. There is no fee.

Hamline University, Registrar, 1536 Hewitt Ave, St Paul, MN 55104, 612-641-2023 (Fax: 612-659-3043). Hours: 8AM-5PM. Enrollment: 2562. Records go back to 1864. Alumni records are maintained here also. Call 612-641-2015. Degrees granted: Bachelors; Masters. Adverse incident record source- Development Office, 612-641-2800.

Attendance and degree information available by phone, fax, mail. Search requires name plus SSN, approximate years of attendance. There is no fee.

Hibbing Community College, Records Office, 1515 E 25th St, Hibbing, MN 55746, 218-262-6700 (Fax: 218-262-6717). Hours: 8AM-4:30PM. Enrollment: 1000. Records go back to 1916. Alumni records are maintained here at the same phone number. Degrees granted: Associate. Special programs-A.D. Nursing, 218-262-6700: Computer Drafting, 218-262-6700. Adverse incident record source- Administration Office.

Attendance and degree information available by phone, fax, mail. Search requires name plus SSN, date of birth. There is no fee.

Inver Hills Community College, Registrar, 2500 E 80th St, Inver Grove Heights, MN 55076, 612-450-8405 (Fax: 612-450-8677). Hours: 7:30AM-4:30PM. Records go back to 1970. Degrees granted: Associate. Certification: Vocational.

Attendance and degree information available by phone, fax, mail. Search requires name only. Also helpful: SSN. There is no fee.

Itasca Community College, Registrar, 1851 E Hwy 169, Grand Rapids, MN 55744, 218-327-4468 (Fax: 218-327-4350). Hours: 8AM-4:30PM. Records go back to 1926. Degrees granted: Associate.

Attendance and degree information available by phone, fax, mail. Search requires name plus SSN. There is no fee.

Lake Superior College, Office of Student Records, 2101 Trinity Rd, Duluth, MN 55811-3399, 218-722-2801 (Fax: 218-722-2899). Hours: 8AM-4PM. Enrollment: 1290. Records go back to 1956. Known as Duluth Technical College before July 1995. Degrees granted: Associate.

Attendance and degree information available by phone, fax, mail. Search requires name plus SSN, approximate years of attendance. There is no fee.

Lowthian College, Registrar, 825 2nd Ave S, Minneapolis, MN 55402, 612-332-3361. Hours: 9AM-5PM. Enrollment: 120. Records go back to 1965. Alumni records are maintained here also. Call 612-332-3361. Degrees granted: Associate.

Attendance and degree information available by phone, mail. Search requires name plus approximate years of attendance. There is no fee.

Luther Seminary, Registrar, 2481 Como Ave, St Paul, MN 55108, 612-641-3473. Hours: 8:30-10AM, 10:40-Noon, 1-

3:30PM Closed for Chapel. Enrollment: 819. Records go back to 1869. Alumni records are maintained here also. Call 612-641-3451. Degrees granted: Masters. Adverse incident record source- Dean of Students, 612-641-3229.

Attendance and degree information available by phone, mail. Search requires name plus SSN, approximate years of attendance. There is no fee.

Macalester College, Registrar, 1600 Grand Ave, St Paul, MN 55105, 612-696-6200 (Fax: 612-696-6600). Hours: 8AM-4:30PM. Enrollment: 1768. Alumni records are maintained here also. Call 612-696-6295. Degrees granted: Bachelors. Adverse incident record source- Dean of Students, 612-696-6220.

Attendance and degree information available by phone, fax, mail. Search requires name only. Also helpful: SSN, date of birth, exact years of attendance. There is no fee.

Mankato State University, Registrar's Office, MSU 15, PO Box 8400, Mankato, MN 56002-8400, 507-389-6266 (Fax: 507-389-5917). Hours: 8AM-5PM. Enrollment: 12000. Records go back to 1876. Alumni records are maintained here also. Call 507-389-1515. Degrees granted: Associate; Bachelors; Masters.

Attendance and degree information available by phone, fax, mail. Search requires name plus SSN. Also helpful: date of birth, exact years of attendance. There is no fee.

Martin Luther College, Registrar, 1995 Luther Ct, New Ulm, MN 56073, 507-354-8221 (Fax: 507-354-8225). Hours: 8AM-4:30PM. Enrollment: 850. Records go back to 1884. Degrees granted: Bachelors.

Attendance and degree information available by phone, fax, mail. Search requires name only. Also helpful: SSN, date of birth, exact years of attendance. There is no fee.

Mayo Graduate School, Registrar, 200 First St SW, Rochester, MN 55905, 507-284-2220 (Fax: 507-284-0532). Hours: 8AM-5PM. Enrollment: 588. Records go back to 1940. Alumni records are maintained here also. Call 507-284-2317. Degrees granted: Masters; Doctorate.

Attendance and degree information available by fax, mail. Search requires name plus SSN, date of birth, approximate years of attendance. There is no fee.

Mesabi Community College, Registrar, 1001 Chestnut West, Virginia, MN 55792, 218-749-7762 (Fax: 218-749-0318). Hours: 8AM-4:30PM. Records go back to 1900. Alumni records are maintained here also. Call 800-657-3860. Degrees granted: Associate.

Attendance and degree information available by phone, fax, mail. Search requires name plus SSN, approximate years of attendance. There is no fee.

Metropolitan State University, Registrar, 700 E 7th St, St Paul, MN 55106-5000, 612-772-7772 (Fax: 612-772-7738). Hours: 8AM-5PM. Enrollment: 5510. Records go back to 1970. Alumni records are maintained here also. Call 612-772-7800. Degrees granted: Bachelors; Masters.

Attendance and degree information available by phone, fax, mail. Search requires name plus SSN, date of birth. There is no fee.

Minneapolis College of Art and Design, Registrar, 2501 Stevens Ave S, Minneapolis, MN 55404, 612-874-3727 (Fax: 612-874-3704). Hours: 8:30AM-5PM. Enrollment: 545. Records go back to 1912. Alumni records are maintained here also. Call 612-874-3792. Degrees granted: Bachelors; Masters.

Attendance and degree information available by phone, fax, mail. Search requires name plus SSN. There is no fee.

Minneapolis Community College, Records & Admissions, 1501 Hennepin Ave, Minneapolis, MN 55403, 612-

341-7006 (Fax: 612-341-7075). Hours: 8:30AM-4:30PM. Enrollment: 4498. Records go back to 1968. Degrees granted: Associate.

Attendance and degree information available by written request only. Search requires name plus SSN, approximate years of attendance, signed release. Also helpful: date of birth. There is no fee.

Minnesota Bible College, Registrar, 920 Mayowood Rd SW, Rochester, MN 55902, 507-288-4563 (Fax: 507-288-9046). Hours: 8AM-4:30PM. Enrollment: 110. Records go back to 1946. Alumni records are maintained here at the same phone number. Degrees granted: Associate; Bachelors.

Attendance and degree information available by phone, fax, mail. Search requires name plus SSN, approximate years of attendance. There is no fee.

Moorhead State University, Registrar, 1104 7th Ave S, Moorhead, MN 56563, 218-236-2565 (Fax: 218-236-2168). Hours: 8AM-4:30PM. Enrollment: 6355. Records go back to 1889. Alumni records are maintained here also. Call 218-236-3265. Degrees granted: Associate; Bachelors; Masters; Specialist. Adverse incident record source- Student Services, 218-236-2171.

Attendance information available by phone, fax, mail. Search requires name plus SSN, date of birth. Also helpful: exact years of attendance. There is no fee.

Degree information available by phone, fax, mail. Search requires name plus SSN. Also helpful: date of birth, exact years of attendance. There is no fee.

Normandale Community College, Registrar, 9700 France Ave S, Bloomington, MN 55431, 612-832-6314 (Fax: 612-832-6571). Hours: 8AM-9PM. Enrollment: 8171. Records go back to 1968. Degrees granted: Associate.

Attendance and degree information available by phone, fax, mail. Search requires name plus SSN. There is no fee.

North Central Bible College, Registrar, 910 Elliot Ave S, Minneapolis, MN 55404, 612-343-4409 (Fax: 612-343-4778). Hours: 8AM-4:30PM. Enrollment: 1100. Records go back to 1930. Alumni records are maintained here at the same phone number. Degrees granted: Associate; Bachelors. Special programs- Carlson Institute Correspondence Course Dept, 612-343-4430. Adverse incident record source- Security Office, 612-343-4444.

Attendance and degree information available by phone, fax, mail. Search requires name plus approximate years of attendance. Also helpful: SSN, exact years of attendance. There is no fee.

North Hennepin Community College, Registrar, 7411 85th Ave N, Brooklyn Park, MN 55445, 612-424-0719 (Fax: 612-424-0929). Hours: 8AM-7PM M-Th, 8AM-4:30PM F. Enrollment: 5500. Records go back to 1966. Degrees granted: Associate.

Attendance and degree information available by phone, fax, mail. Search requires name only. Also helpful: SSN, date of birth, approximate years of attendance. There is no fee.

Northland Community College, Registrar, Hwy 1 E, Thief River Falls, MN 56701, 218-681-0701 (Fax: 218-681-0724). Hours: 8AM-4:30PM. Enrollment: 1200. Records go back to 1965. Degrees granted: Associate.

Attendance and degree information available by phone, fax, mail. Search requires name plus SSN. There is no fee.

Northwest Technical College, Registrar, Hwy 200 N, PO Box 111, East Grand Forks, MN 56721, 218-773-3441 (Fax: 218-773-4502). Hours: 8AM-5PM. Enrollment: 1400. Records go back to 1972. Degrees granted: Associate.

Attendance information available by phone, fax, mail. Search requires name plus SSN. Also helpful: date of birth, exact years of attendance. There is no fee.

Degree information available by phone, fax, mail. Search requires name plus SSN, date of birth. Also helpful: exact years of attendance. There is no fee.

Northwest Technical College-Moorhead, Registrar, 1900 28th Ave S, Moorhead, MN 56560, 218-299-6593 (Fax: 218-236-0342). Hours: 9AM-4PM. Enrollment: 1250. Records go back to 1970. Degrees granted: Associate. Adverse incident record source- Dean of Students, 218-299-6503.

Attendance and degree information available by phone, fax, mail. Search requires name plus SSN. There is no fee.

Northwest Technical Institute, Registrar, 11995 Singletree Lane, Eden Prairie, MN 55344-5351, 612-944-0080 (Fax: 612-944-9274). Hours: 8AM-5PM. Enrollment: 160. Records go back to 1958. Alumni records are maintained here at the same phone number. Degrees granted: Associate. Special programs- Engineering Drafting & Design: Architectural Drafting & Desing.

Attendance and degree information available by phone, fax, mail. Search requires name plus SSN, approximate years of attendance. There is no fee.

Northwestern College, Registrar, 3003 N Snelling Ave, St Paul, MN 55113, 612-631-5248 (Fax: 612-631-5124). Hours: 8:15AM-4PM. Enrollment: 1269. Records go back to 1900. Degrees granted: Associate; Bachelors. Certification: Biblical Arts.

Attendance and degree information available by phone, fax, mail. Search requires name plus SSN, approximate years of attendance. There is no fee.

Northwestern College of Chiropractic, Registrar, 2501 W 84th St, Bloomington, MN 55431-1599, 612-888-4777 (Fax: 612-888-6713). Hours: 8AM-4:30PM. Enrollment: 650. Records go back to 1941. Alumni records are maintained here at the same phone number. Degrees granted: Bachelors; First Professional. Adverse incident record source- Registrar, 612-885-5440.

Attendance and degree information available by phone, fax, mail. Search requires name plus SSN, date of birth. Also helpful: exact years of attendance. There is no fee.

Oak Hills Bible College, Registrar, 1600 Oak Hills Rd SW, Bemidji, MN 56601, 218-751-8670w (Fax: 218-751-8825). Hours: 8AM-5PM. Enrollment: 135. Records go back to 1940's. Alumni records are maintained here at the same phone number. Degrees granted: Associate; Bachelors. Certification: 1 year Bible.

Attendance and degree information available by phone, fax, mail. Search requires name only. Also helpful: date of birth, exact years of attendance. There is no fee.

Pillsbury Baptist Bible College, Registrar, 315 S Grove, Owatonna, MN 55060, 507-451-2710 X276 (Fax: 507-451-6459). Enrollment: 200. Records go back to 1975. Alumni records are maintained here at the same phone number. Degrees granted: Associate; Bachelors; Practical Christian Workers Diploma. Adverse incident record source- Student Life, 507-451-2710 X202.

Attendance and degree information available by phone, fax, mail. Search requires name only. There is no fee.

Rainy River Community College, Registrar, 1501 Hwy 71, International Falls, MN 56649, 218-285-2207 (Fax: 218-285-2239). Hours: 8AM-4:30PM. Enrollment: 400. Records go back to 1967. Alumni records are maintained here also. Call 218-285-2213. Degrees granted: Associate. Adverse incident record source- Student Development.

Attendance and degree information available by phone, fax, mail. Search requires name only. Also helpful: SSN, date of birth. There is no fee.

Range Technical College, Registrar, 2900 E Beltline, Hibbing, MN 55746, 218-262-7212 (Fax: 218-262-7222). Hours: 7:30AM-4:30PM. Records go back to 1965. Degrees granted: Associate.

Attendance and degree information available by phone, fax, mail. Search requires name plus SSN. There is no fee.

Rasmussen Business College, Registrar, 3500 Federal Dr, Eagan, MN 55122, 612-687-9000 (Fax: 612-687-0507). Hours: 7AM-10PM. Records go back to 1975. Degrees granted: Associate.

Attendance and degree information available by phone, fax, mail. Search requires name plus SSN, approximate years of attendance. There is no fee.

Rasmussen Business College, Registrar, 501 Holly Ln, Mankato, MN 56001, 507-625-6556 (Fax: 507-625-6557). Hours: 8AM-9:30PM. Enrollment: 260. Records go back to 1983. Degrees granted: Associate.

Attendance information available by phone, fax, mail. Search requires name plus SSN. Also helpful: exact years of attendance. There is no fee.

Degree information available by phone, mail. Search requires name plus SSN. Also helpful: exact years of attendance. There is no fee.

Rasmussen Business College, Registrar, 12450 Wayzata Blvd Ste 315, Minnetonka, MN 55305-9845, 612-545-2000 (Fax: 612-545-7038). Hours: 8AM-9PM. Enrollment: 300. Records go back to 1966. Degrees granted: Associate. Special programs- Court Reporting.

Attendance and degree information available by fax. Search requires name plus SSN, approximate years of attendance, signed release. There is no fee.

Ridgewater College, Registrar, PO Box 1097, Willmar, MN 56201, 320-235-5114 (Fax: 320-231-7677). Hours: 8AM-4:30PM. Formerly Hutchinson Willman Regional Technical College Records go back to 1961. Alumni records are maintained here also. Call 320-231-2935. Degrees granted: Associate. Special programs- Student Services, 320-231-2915. Adverse incident record source- Student Affairs, 320-231-2915.

Attendance information available by fax, mail. Search requires name plus SSN, signed release. Also helpful: date of birth. There is no fee.

Degree information available by phone, fax, mail. Search requires name plus SSN. There is no fee.

Ridgewater College, Registrar, PO Box 1097, Willmar, MN 56201, 320-231-2923 (Fax: 320-231-6602). Hours: 8AM-4:30PM. Enrollment: 3000. Formerly Willmar Community College Records go back to 1962. Alumni records are maintained here also. Call 320-231-5115. Degrees granted: Associate. Adverse incident record source- 320-231-5176.

Attendance and degree information available by phone, fax, mail. Search requires name plus SSN. Also helpful: exact years of attendance. There is no fee.

Riverland Community College, Registrar, 1900 8th Ave NW, Austin, MN 55912, 507-433-0510 (Fax: 507-433-0370). Hours: 8AM-4:30PM. Enrollment: 2100. Formerly Austin Community College Records go back to 1940. Degrees granted: Associate. Adverse incident record source- Registrar's Office, 507-433-0510

Attendance and degree information available by phone, fax, mail. Search requires name only. Also helpful: SSN, date of birth, approximate years of attendance. There is no fee.

Rochester Community and Technical College, Admissions & Records, 851 30th Ave SE, Rochester, MN 55904-4999, 507-285-7265 (Fax: 507-285-7496). Hours: 8AM-4:30PM. Enrollment: 4500. Formerly Rochester Community College Records go back to 1915. Degrees granted: Associate. Adverse incident record source- Dir of Institutional Services, 507-285-7214.

Attendance information available by phone, fax, mail. Search requires name plus SSN. Also helpful: date of birth, exact years of attendance. There is no fee.

Degree information available by phone, fax, mail. Search requires name plus SSN. Also helpful: date of birth, exact years of attendance. There is no fee.

Southwest State University, Registrar, 1501 State St, Marshall, MN 56258, 507-537-6206 (Fax: 507-537-7154). Hours: 8:30AM-4:30PM. Enrollment: 2575. Records go back to 1967. Alumni records are maintained here at the same phone number. Degrees granted: Associate; Bachelors; Masters.

Attendance and degree information available by phone, fax, mail. Search requires name plus SSN. Also helpful: exact years of attendance. There is no fee.

Southwestern Technical College, Registrar, 1593 11th Ave, Granite Falls, MN 56241, 320-564-4511 (Fax: 320-564-2318). Hours: 8AM-4:30PM. Enrollment: 406. Records go back to 1965. Degrees granted: Associate.

Attendance and degree information available by fax, mail. Search requires name plus SSN, approximate years of attendance, signed release. Also helpful: exact years of attendance. There is no fee.

St Paul Seminary School of Divinity, St Thomas, Registrar, 2260 Summit Ave, Saint Paul, MN 55105, 612-962-5770 (Fax: 612-962-5790). Enrollment: 200. Formerly Saint Paul Seminary, School of Divinity Records go back to 1850. Alumni Records Office: Alumni Association, 2115 Summit Ave, Saint Paul, MN 55105. Degrees granted: Masters; Doctorate.

Attendance and degree information available by written request only. Search requires name plus SSN, exact years of attendance, signed release. Also helpful: date of birth. There is no fee.

St. Cloud State University, Registrar, 740 Fourth Ave S, St Cloud, MN 56301-4498, 612-255-2111. Hours: 8AM-4:30PM. Degrees granted: Associate; Bachelors; Masters.

Attendance information available by mail. Search requires name plus signed release. Also helpful: SSN. There is no fee.

Degree information available by phone, fax, mail. Search requires name only. Also helpful: SSN. There is no fee.

St. Cloud Technical College, Registrar, 1540 Northway Dr, St Cloud, MN 56303, 612-654-5075 (Fax: 612-654-5981). Hours: 7:30AM-5PM M-Th; 7:30AM-4PM F. Enrollment: 4000. Records go back to 1960. Alumni records are maintained here at the same phone number. Degrees granted: Associate.

Attendance and degree information available by phone, fax, mail. Search requires name only. Also helpful: SSN, exact years of attendance. There is no fee.

St. John's University, Registrar, Collegeville, MN 56321, 612-363-3395 (Fax: 612-363-2714). Hours: 8AM-4:30PM. Enrollment: 1800. Records go back to 1857. Alumni records are maintained here also. Call 612-363-2591. Degrees granted: Bachelors; Masters.

Attendance and degree information available by phone, fax, mail. Search requires name only. Also helpful: SSN, date of birth, exact years of attendance. There is no fee.

St. Mary's University of Minnesota, Registrar, 700 Terrace Heights, Winona, MN 55987-1399, 507-457-1428. Hours: 7:30AM-4PM Summer, 7:30AM-4:30PM Fall. Records

go back to 1912. Alumni records are maintained here also. Call 507-457-1499. Degrees granted: Bachelors; Masters. Adverse incident record source- Dean of Students, 507-457-1403.

Attendance and degree information available by phone, mail. Search requires name plus approximate years of attendance. Also helpful: SSN. There is no fee.

St. Olaf College, Registrar, 1520 St Olaf Ave, Northfield, MN 55057, 507-646-3014 (Fax: 507-646-3210). Hours: 8AM-5PM. Enrollment: 2900. Records go back to 1874. Alumni records are maintained here also. Call 507-646-3028. Degrees granted: Bachelors. Special programs- Continuing Education, 507-646-3066. Adverse incident record source- Dean of Students, 507-646-3023.

Attendance and degree information available by phone, mail. Search requires name plus date of birth. Also helpful: SSN, exact years of attendance. There is no fee.

St. Paul Technical College, Registrar, 235 Marshall Ave, St Paul, MN 55102, 612-221-1300 (Fax: 612-221-1416). Hours: 7:30AM-4PM. Enrollment: 7234. Records go back to 1919. Alumni records are maintained here at the same phone number. Degrees granted: Associate.

Attendance and degree information available by phone, fax, mail. Search requires name only. Also helpful: SSN, date of birth, exact years of attendance. There is no fee.

United Theological Seminary of the Twin Cities, Registrar, 3000 Fifth St NW, New Brighton, MN 55112, 612-633-4311 (Fax: 612-633-4315). Hours: 8AM-5PM. Enrollment: 256. Records go back to 1864. Degrees granted: Masters; Doctorate.

Attendance and degree information available by phone, fax, mail. Search requires name plus SSN. Also helpful: date of birth, exact years of attendance. There is no fee.

University of Minnesota-Crookston, Registrar, Hwys 2 and 75 N, Crookston, MN 56716, 218-281-8547 (Fax: 218-281-8050). Hours: 8AM-4:30PM. Enrollment: 1750. Records go back to 1966. Alumni records are maintained here at the same phone number. Degrees granted: Associate; Bachelors.

Attendance and degree information available by phone, fax, mail. Search requires name plus SSN. Also helpful: date of birth, exact years of attendance. There is no fee.

University of Minnesota-Duluth, Registrar's Office, Attn: Transcripts, 10 University Dr, Duluth, MN 55812, 218-726-8805 (Fax: 218-726-6389). Hours: 8AM-4:30PM. Enrollment: 7000. Records go back to 1950. Degrees granted: Bachelors; Masters. Adverse incident record source- Campus Police, 218-726-7000.

Attendance and degree information available by phone, fax, mail. Search requires name plus SSN, date of birth. Also helpful: exact years of attendance. There is no fee.

University of Minnesota-Morris, Registrar, 600 E Fourth St, Morris, MN 56267, 320-589-6030 (Fax: 320-589-6025). Hours: 8AM-4:30PM. Enrollment: 1800. Records go back to 1960. Alumni records are maintained here also. Call 320-589-6066. Degrees granted: Bachelors.

Attendance and degree information available by phone, fax, mail. Search requires name only. Also helpful: SSN, date of birth, exact years of attendance. There is no fee.

University of Minnesota-Twin Cities, Office of the Registrar, 150 Williamson Hall, 231 Pillsbury Dr SE, Min-

neapolis, MN 55455, 612-625-5333 (Fax: 612-625-4351). Hours: 9AM-5:30PM M; 8AM-4PM T-F. Enrollment: 48091. Records go back to 1880's. Alumni Records Office: 615 2nd Ave S, Minneapolis, MN 55402. Degrees granted: Associate; Bachelors; Masters; Doctorate. Adverse incident record source- University Police, 612-624-3550.

Attendance and degree information available by phone, mail. Search requires name plus SSN. Also helpful: date of birth, exact years of attendance. There is no fee.

University of St. Thomas, Registrar, 2115 Summit Ave, St Paul, MN 55105, 612-962-6707 (Fax: 612-962-6710). Hours: 8AM-4:30PM. Enrollment: 10160. Records go back to 1910. Alumni records are maintained here also. Call 612-962-6430. Degrees granted: Masters; Doctorate.

Attendance and degree information available by phone, fax, mail. Search requires name plus SSN. There is no fee.

Vermilion Community College, Registrar, 1900 E Camp St, Ely, MN 55731, 218-365-7223 (Fax: 218-365-7207). Hours: 8AM-4:30PM. Enrollment: 1000. Records go back to 1922. Degrees granted: Associate. Adverse incident record source- Student Services, 218-365-7249.

Attendance and degree information available by phone, fax, mail. Search requires name plus SSN. Also helpful: date of birth. There is no fee.

Walden University, Registrar, 155 S Fifth Ave, Minneapolis, MN 55401, 612-338-7224 (Fax: 612-338-5092). Hours: 8AM-5PM. Enrollment: 879. Records go back to 1970. Degrees granted: Doctorate.

Attendance and degree information available by phone, fax, mail. Search requires name plus approximate years of attendance. Also helpful: SSN. There is no fee.

William Mitchell College of Law, Registrar, 875 Summit Ave, St Paul, MN 55105, 612-290-6363 (Fax: 612-290-6414). Hours: 8:30AM-7:30PM M-Th; 8:30AM-6PM F. Enrollment: 1100. Records go back to 1900. Alumni records are maintained here also. Call 612-290-6371. Degrees granted: Masters; 1st Prof. (JD).

Attendance and degree information available by phone, fax, mail. Search requires name only. Also helpful: SSN, exact years of attendance. There is no fee.

Winona State University, Registrar, Winona, MN 55987, 507-457-5030 (Fax: 507-457-5578). Hours: 7:30AM-4:30PM. Enrollment: 7000. Records go back to 1880. Alumni records are maintained here also. Call 507-457-5027. Degrees granted: Bachelors; Masters. Adverse incident record source- Registrar's Office, 507-457-5090 .

Attendance and degree information available by phone, fax, mail. Search requires name only. Also helpful: SSN, date of birth, approximate years of attendance. There is no fee.

Worthington Community College, Registrar, 1450 Collegeway, Worthington, MN 56187, 507-372-3451 (Fax: 507-372-5801). Hours: 8AM-4:30PM. Enrollment: 900. Records go back to 1937. Alumni records are maintained here at the same phone number. Degrees granted: Associate.

Attendance and degree information available by phone, fax, mail. Search requires name plus SSN. Also helpful: date of birth, exact years of attendance. There is no fee.

Trade and Vocational Schools

Academy Education Center, 3050 Metro Dr #200, Minneapolis, MN 55425, 612-851-0066

Art Instruction Schools, 3309 Northeast St, Minneapolis, MN 55413, 612-339-6656

Avante School of Cosmetology, 1650 White Bear Ave, St. Paul, MN 55106, 612-772-1417

ConCorde Career Institute, 12 N 12th St, Minneapolis, MN 55403, 612-341-3850

Duluth Business University, 412 W Superior St, Duluth, MN 55802, 218-722-3361

Hennepin Technical College, 9000 Brooklyn Blvd, Brooklyn Park, MN 55455, 612-425-3800

Hurbert H Humphrey Job Corps Center, 1480 Snelling Ave, St Paul, MN 55108, 612-642-1133

Lakeland Medical-Dental Academy, 1402 W Lake St, Minneapolis, MN 55408, 612-827-5656

McConnell School (The), 831 Second Ave S, Minneapolis, MN 55402, 612-332-4238

Medical Institute of Minnesota, 5503 Green Valley Dr, Bloomington, MN 55437, 612-884-0064

Minneapolis Business College, 1711 W County Rd B, Roseville, MN 55113, 612-636-7406

Minneapolis Drafting School, 5700 W Broadway, Minneapolis, MN 55428, 612-535-8843

Minneapolis Technical College, 1415 Hennepin Ave S #446, Minneapolis, MN 55403, 612-370-9400

Minnesota Institute of Acupuncture and Herbal Studies, 5251 Chicago Ave S, Minneapolis, MN 55417-1731, 612-823-6235

Minnesota School of Barbering, 3615 E Lake St, Minneapolis, MN 55406, 612-722-1996

Minnesota School of Business, 1401 W 76th St #500, Richfield, MN 55423, 612-861-2000

Minnesota School of Business (Branch Campus), 6120 Earle Brown Dr, Brooklyn Center, MN 55430, 612-566-7777

Moler Barber School of Hairstyling, 1411 Nicollet Ave, Minneapolis, MN 55403, 612-871-3754

Music Tech, 304 N Washington Ave, Minneapolis, MN 55401, 612-338-0175

NEI College of Technology, 825 41st Ave NE, Columbia Heights, MN 55421, 612-781-4881

Rasmussen College St. Cloud, 245 N 37th Ave, St Cloud, MN 56303, 320-251-5600

School of Communication Arts, 2526 27th Ave S, Minneapolis, MN 55406, 612-721-5357

State Licensing & Business Registration Quick Finder Index

Architecture, Engineering & Surveying
Architect #35 .... ☎ 612-297-2208
Engineer #35 (9300) .... ☎ 612-296-2388
Surveyor #35 .... ☎ 612-296-7937

Business - Court & Legal Services
Attorney #38 (21000) .... ☎ 612-296-2254
Bondsman #22 .... ☎ 612-296-6319
Lobbyist #44 612-296-5148
Notary Public #22 .... ☎ 612-296-6319

Business - General Services
Auditor #19 .... ☎ 612-341-7537
Employment Agency Counselor #34 .... ☎ 612-296-4531
Employment Agency Manager #34 .... ☎ 612-296-4531
Public Accountant-CPA #37 (11863) .... ☎ 612-296-7937
Wholesaler, Manufacturer, Labels & Imports #32
 (483) .... ☎ 612-296-6939

Construction & Manufacturing
Boiler Inspector #34 (11) .... ☎ 612-296-4531
Electrician #6 .... ☎ 612-642-0800
Elevator Inspector #34 .... ☎ 612-296-4531
High Pressure Inspector #34 .... ☎ 612-296-4529
Manufactured Structures Section #36 (21) ..... ☎ 612-296-4628
Plumber #25 .... ☎ 612-627-5100
Residential Remodeler/Contractor #22 .... ☎ 612-296-6319

Education
Licensure Information #43 .... ☎ 612-296-0680
Teacher #17 (28000) .... ☎ 612-296-2415

Environmental & Agriculture
Asbestos Abatement Worker/Contractor #25
 .... ☎ 612-215-0900
Consumption & Display Information #32 ...... ☎ 612-296-6570
Livestock Weighing #20 .... ☎ 612-296-2292
Pesticide Applicator #21 612-297-2530
Public Water Supply Operator #25 .... ☎ 612-627-5100
Underground Storage Tank Contractor
 /Supervisor #41 .... ☎ 612-297-8679
Veterinarian #18 (2600) .... ☎ 612-642-0597
Waste Disposal Facility Inspector #41 .... ☎ 612-296-8868
Waste Water Disposal Facility Operator #41
 .... ☎ 612-296-8868
Water Conditioning Installer/Contractor #25
 .... ☎ 612-627-5100
Water Well Contractor #25 .... ☎ 612-627-5100

Financial - Real Estate, Insurance & Banking
Abstractor #24 .... ☎ 800-657-3978
Accredited Minnesota Assessor #1 .... ☎ 612-296-0209

Assessor (Certified Minnesota Assessor) #1
(600) .... ☎ 612-296-0209
Bank #23 (2) .... ✉ 612-297-3779
Certified Minnesota Assessor Specialist #1 ... ☎ 612-296-0209
Consumer Credit, Credit Union & Savings Association
(Consumer Credit, CU) #23 (250) .... ✉ 612-296-2297
Credit Union #23 .... ✉ 612-296-2297
Insurance Agent/Salesman #22 .... ☎ 612-296-6319
Real Estate Broker/Dealer #22 .... ☎ 612-296-6319
Securities/Investment Advisor #22 .... ☎ 612-296-6319
Senior Accredited Minnesota Assessor #1 ..... ☎ 612-296-0209

Health & Beauty

Audiologist #27 (195) .... ☎ 612-282-5625
Barber #2 (3000) .... ☎ 612-642-0489
Chiropractor #4 (1886) .... ☎ 612-642-0591
Cosmetologist #22 .... ☎ 612-296-6319
Cosmetology School/Shop #22 .... ☎ 612-296-6319
Dental Hygiene #5 .... ✉ 612-642-0579
Dentist #5 (3787) .... ✉ 612-642-0579
Embalmer #26 .... ☎ 612-623-5655
Emergency Medical Technician #27 612-627-6000
Esthetician #22 .... ☎ 612-296-6319
Funeral Director #26 (1600) .... ☎ 612-282-3829
Hearing Aid Dispenser #27 (253) .... ☎ 612-282-5625
LPA #37 .... ☎ 612-296-7937
Medical Doctor #9 612-642-0533
Nurse #10 .... ☎ 612-642-0572
Nursing Home Administrator #7 (900) .... ☎ 612-642-0595
Occupational Therapist #27 (800) .... ☎ 612-282-5625
Optometrist #11 (800) .... ☎ 612-642-0594
Pharmacist #13 (5200) .... ☎ 612-617-2201
Podiatrist (Licensed & Temporary Permit) #14
(150) .... ☎ 612-642-0401
Registered Dental Assistant #5 .... ✉ 612-642-0579
Respiratory Care Practitioner #27 .... ☎ 612-282-5620
Sanitarian #25 .... ☎ 612-627-5100
Speech-Language Pathologist #27 (585) .... ☎ 612-282-5625

Investigations & Security

Alarm & Communication System Contractor #6
.... ☎ 612-642-0800
Alarm & Communication System Installer #6
.... ☎ 612-642-0800
Part-time Peace Officer #12 .... ☎ 612-643-3060
Peace Officer #12 (13400) .... ☎ 612-643-3060
Private Detective/Investigator #42 (270) .... ☎ 612-215-1753

Social Services

Adoption & Guardianship #29 .... ☎ 612-296-6117
Applicant Background Study & Investigation #28
.... ☎ 612-296-6117
Child Care Facility #29 .... ☎ 612-296-6117
Children's Services #28 .... ☎ 612-296-3971
Developmental Disabilities Licensing #28 ..... ☎ 612-296-4727
Foster Care Program #29 .... ☎ 612-296-6117
Marriage & Family Therapist #8 (700) .... ☎ 612-643-3667
Mental Health, Chemical Dependency #28 .... ☎ 612-296-4727
Psychological Practitioner #15 .... ☎ 612-642-0587
Psychologist-Licensed #15 (3200) .... ☎ 612-642-0587
Social Worker #16 (9350) .... ☎ 612-643-2580

Sports & Entertainment

All-Terrain Vehicle Registration #30 612-296-2316
Amateur Boxing Coach #3 .... ✉ 612-296-2501
Amateur Boxing Referee #3 .... ✉ 612-296-2501
Amateur Boxing Show #3 .... ✉ 612-296-5310
Bingo Halls #33 (19) .... ☎ 612-639-4000
Boat & Canoe Registration #30 .... ☎ 612-296-2316
Boxing (Professional Boxers) #3 (87) .... ✉ 612-296-2501
County Fair #39 .... ☎ 612-496-7952
Equipment Manufacturing and Distribution #31
(36) .... ☎ 612-643-3006
Gaming Distributor #33 .... ☎ 612-639-4000
Gaming Manufacturer #33 .... ☎ 612-639-4000
Gaming Organizations #33 .... ☎ 612-639-4000
Kick Karate Professional #3 .... ✉ 612-296-2501
Lottery #40 612-635-8100
On-Sale Retail Municipal Liquor Store #32
.... ☎ 612-296-6939
Professional Cornermen #3 .... ✉ 612-296-2501
Professional Referee #3 .... ✉ 612-296-2501
Protective Agent #42 .... ☎ 612-215-1753
Race Track Operator #39 .... ☎ 612-496-7952
Racing (Racing Class "A"- Owners of Track) #39
(1) .... ☎ 612-496-7952
Racing-Occupational #39 .... ☎ 612-496-7952
Snowmobile Registration #30 612-296-2316
Wine, Strong Beer, Off-Sale Retail #32 .... ☎ 612-296-6430

Transportation

Boat Title #30 .... ☎ 612-297-1231
Off-Highway Motorcycle #30 .... ☎ 612-296-2316
Off-Road Vehicle #30 .... ☎ 612-296-2316
Watercraft #30 .... ☎ 612-296-2316

State Licensing & Business Registration Agency Information

(1) Board of Assessors, Mail Station 3340, St Paul, MN 55146-3340, 612-296-0209, Fax: 612-297-2166

(2) Board of Barber Examiners, 1885 University Ave, Suite 335, St Paul, MN 55104, 612-642-0489

(3) Board of Boxing, 133 E 7th St, St Paul, MN 55101, 612-296-2501, Fax: 612-297-5310

(4) Board of Chiropractic Examiners, 2829 University Ave SE, Minneapolis, MN 55414-3220, 612-617-2220, Fax: 612-617-2224

(5) Board of Dentistry, 2700 University Ave W, Suite 70, St Paul, MN 55114, 612-642-0579

(6) Board of Electricity, 1821 University Ave, Rm S-128, St Paul, MN 55104, 612-642-0800, Fax: 612-642-0441

(7) Board of Examiners for Nursing Home Administrators, 2700 University Ave W, Suite 104, St Paul, MN 55114-1082, 612-642-0595, Fax: 612-643-3414

(8) Board of Marriage & Family Therapy, 2700 University Ave, W, Suite 67, St Paul, MN 55114, 612-643-3667, Fax: 612-643-2164

(9) Board of Medical Practice, 2700 University Ave W, Suite 106, St Paul, MN 55114-1080, 612-642-0533

(10) Board of Nursing, 2824 University Ave SE, Suite 500, Minneapolis, MN 55414, 612-617-2270, Fax: 612-617-2190

(11) Board of Optometry, 2829 University Ave SE, Suite 550, Minneapolis, MN 55414, 612-617-2173, Fax: 612-617-2174

(12) Board of Peacc Officers Standards & Training, 1600 University Ave, Suite 200, St Paul, MN 55104, 612-643-3060, Fax: 612-643-3072

(13) Board of Pharmacy, 2829 University Ave SE, Suite 530, Minneapolis, MN 55414, 612-642-0541, Fax: 612-617-2212

(14) Board of Podiatric Medicine, 2700 University Ave W, Suite 40, St Paul, MN 55114, 612-642-0401

(15) Board of Psychology, 2829 University Avenue, SE, Minneapolis, MN 55414, 612-642-0587

(16) Board of Social Work, 2700 University Ave, W, Suite 225, St Paul, MN 55114, 612-643-2580, Fax: 612-643-3545

(17) Board of Teaching, Licensing Unit, 616 Capitol Square Bldg, 550 Cedar St, St Paul, MN 55101, 612-296-2046, Fax: 612-282-2403

(18) Board of Veterinary Medicine, 2829 University Ave SE, Minneapolis, MN 55414, 612-617-2170

(19) Department of Agriculture, Agriculture Certification Division, 90 W Plato Blvd, St Paul, MN 55107, 612-297-2980, Fax: 612-297-2504

(20) Department of Agriculture, Livestock Weighing & Licensing, 90 W Plato Blvd, St Paul, MN 55107, 612-296-2292, Fax: 612-297-2504

(21) Department of Agriculture, Pesticide Registration, 90 W Plato Blvd, St Paul, MN 55107, 612-297-2530

(22) Department of Commerce, 133 E 7th St, St Paul, MN 55101, 612-296-6319, Fax: 612-296-8591

(23) Department of Commerce, Division of Financial Examiners, 133 E 7th St, St Paul, MN 55101, 612-296-9410, Fax: 612-296-8591

(24) Department of Commerce, Licensing Unit for Abstractors, 133 E 7th St, St Paul, MN 55101, 800-657-3978

(25) Department of Health, Environmental Health Division, 121 E 7th Pl, PO Box 64975, St Paul, MN 55164-0975, 612-215-0900, Fax: 612-215-0975

(26) Department of Health, Mortuary Science, PO Box 64975, 121 E 7th Pl, Suite 400, St Paul, MN 55146-0975, 612-282-3829

(27) Department of Health Occupation Programs, Bureau of Health Resources, Managed Care System, 121 E 7th Pl, Suite 450, Metro Square Bldg, St Paul, MN 55101, 612-282-5629, Fax: 612-282-3839

(28) Department of Human Services, 444 Lafayette Rd, St Paul, MN 55155-3831, 612-296-6117, Fax: 612-297-1490

(29) Department of Human Services, 444 Lafayette Rd, St Paul, MN 55155-3831, 612-296-3971, Fax: 612-297-1490

(30) Department of Natural Resources, License Bureau, 500 Lafayette Rd, St Paul, MN 55155, 612-296-2316, Fax: 612-297-8851

(31) Department of Public Safety, Division of Gambling Enforcement, 1600 University Ave, Suite 306, St Paul, MN 55104, 612-643-3006, Fax: 612-649-5400

(32) Department of Public Safety, Liquor Control Division, 444 Cedar St, Suite 100L, St Paul, MN 55101, 612-296-6159, Fax: 612-297-5259

(33) Gambling Control Board, 1711 W County Rd B, Suite 300 S, Roseville, MN 55113, 612-639-4000

(34) Labor & Industry, Code & Inspection Services, 443 Lafayette Rd, St Paul, MN 55155-4304, 612-296-4531, Fax: 612-296-1140

(35) Licensing Boards, 85 E 7th Pl, Suite 160, St Paul, MN 55101, 612-296-2388, Fax: 612-297-5310

(36) Licensing Boards, 408 Metro Square Bldg, 121 7th Pl E, St Paul, MN 55101-2181, 612-296-7937

(37) Minnesota Board of Accountancy, 85 E 7th Pl, Suite 125, St Paul, MN 55101, 612-296-7937, Fax: 612-282-2644

(38) Minnesota Judical Center, Board of Law Examiners, 25 Constitution Ave, Suite 305, St Paul, MN 55155, 612-297-1800, Fax: 612-297-4149

(39) Minnesota Racing Commission, PO Box 630, Shakopee, MN 55379, 612-496-7952

(40) Minnesota State Lottery, 2645 Long Lake Rd, Roseville, MN 55113, 612-635-8100

(41) Pollution Control Agency, 520 Lafayette Rd N, St Paul, MN 55155, 612-296-7283, Fax: 612-297-8683

(42) Private Detective & Protective Agent Services Bd, 444 Cedar Street, Suite 100-P, St Paul, MN 55101, 612-215-1753, Fax: 612-297-5259

(43) State College & University Section, Licensing Unit, 550 Cedar St, St Paul, MN 55101, 612-296-0680, Fax: 612-296-4217

(44) State Ethical Practices Board, 658 Cedar St, Centennial Bldg, 1st Floor, St Paul, MN 55155, 612-296-5148, Fax: 612-296-1722

Mississippi

Capitol: Jackson (Hinds County)	
State Population	2.7 Million
Number of Degree Granting Institutions:	40
Number of State Licensing & Business Registration Agencies:	88

Degree Granting Educational Institutions

Alcorn State University, Registrar's Office, 1000 ASU Drive #420, Lorman, MS 39096-9402, 601-877-6170 (Fax: 601-877-6688). Hours: 8AM-5PM M-Th; 8AM-4PM F. Enrollment: 2712. Records go back to 1871. Degrees granted: Associate; Bachelors; Masters. Special programs- School of Nursing, Natchez Branch, 601-877-6550. Adverse incident record source-Security, 601-877-6390: Academic Affairs, 601-877-6142

Attendance and degree information available by phone, fax, mail. Search requires name plus SSN. Also helpful: date of birth, exact years of attendance. There is no fee.

Belhaven College, Registrar, 1500 Peachtree St, Jackson, MS 39202, 601-968-5922 (Fax: 601-968-9998). Hours: 8AM-5PM. Enrollment: 905. Records go back to 1900. Alumni records are maintained here also. Call 601-968-5930. Degrees granted: Bachelors. Adverse incident record source- Security, 601-968-5900.

Attendance information available by mail. Search requires name plus SSN, date of birth, signed release. Also helpful: exact years of attendance. There is no fee.

Degree information available by mail. Search requires name plus SSN, date of birth, signed release. Also helpful: exact years of attendance. There is no fee.

Blue Mountain College, Registrar's Office, PO Box 188, Blue Mountain, MS 38610, 601-685-4771 X2 (Fax: 601-685-4776). Hours: 8AM-5PM. Enrollment: 320. Records go back to 1910. Alumni records are maintained here at the same phone number. Alumni Records Office: PO Box 111, Blue Mountain, MS 38610. Degrees granted: Bachelors.

Attendance and degree information available by phone, mail. Search requires name only. Also helpful: SSN, date of birth, exact years of attendance. There is no fee.

Coahoma Community College, Registrar, 3240 Friars Point Rd, Clarksdale, MS 38614, 601-627-2571 (Fax: 601-627-2571). Hours: 8:30AM-4PM. Enrollment: 915. Records go back to 1949. Alumni records are maintained here at the same phone number. Degrees granted: Associate.

Attendance information available by phone, fax, mail. Search requires name plus SSN, date of birth, exact years of attendance. There is no fee.

Degree information available by phone, fax, mail. Search requires name plus SSN, exact years of attendance. Also helpful: date of birth. There is no fee.

Copiah-Lincoln Community College, Registrar, PO Box 457, Wesson, MS 39191, 601-643-8307 (Fax: 601-643-8212). Hours: 8AM-4:30PM. Enrollment: 2230. Records go back to 1928. Alumni records are maintained here at the same phone number. Degrees granted: Associate.

Attendance and degree information available by phone, fax, mail. Search requires name plus SSN, date of birth, exact years of attendance. There is no fee.

Delta State University, Registrar, Hwy 8 W, Cleveland, MS 38733, 601-846-4040 (Fax: 601-846-4016). Hours: 8AM-5PM. Enrollment: 3357. Records go back to 1924. Alumni records are maintained here also. Call 601-846-4705. Degrees granted: Bachelors; Masters; Doctorate. Adverse incident record source- Student Affairs, 601-846-4155.

Attendance and degree information available by phone, fax, mail. Search requires name plus SSN, date of birth, approximate years of attendance. There is no fee.

East Central Community College, Registrar, PO Box 129, Decatur, MS 39327, 601-635-2111 X206 (Fax: 601-635-2150). Hours: 8AM-4:30PM. Enrollment: 1698. Records go back to 1928. Alumni records are maintained here also. Call 601-635-2111 X202. Degrees granted: Associate; Bachelors. Adverse incident record source- Dean of Students, 601-635-2111 X204.

Attendance and degree information available by phone, fax, mail. Search requires name plus SSN. There is no fee.

East Mississippi Community College, Registrar, PO Box 158, Scooba, MS 39358, 601-476-8442 X219 (Fax: 601-476-5618). Hours: 8AM-4:30PM. Enrollment: 1050. Records go back to 1927. Alumni records are maintained here at the same phone number. Degrees granted: Associate.

Attendance information available by phone, fax, mail. Search requires name plus SSN, exact years of attendance. Also helpful: date of birth. There is no fee.

Degree information available by phone, fax, mail. Search requires name plus SSN, exact years of attendance. There is no fee.

Hinds Community College, Admissions & Records, Raymond, MS 39154, 601-857-3211 (Fax: 601-857-3539). Hours: 8AM-4:30PM. Enrollment: 13000. Records go back to 1940's. Alumni records are maintained here also. Call 601-857-3350. Degrees granted: Associate.

Attendance and degree information available by phone, fax, mail. Search requires name plus SSN, date of birth, exact years of attendance. There is no fee.

Holmes Community College, Registrar, PO Box 369, Goodman, MS 39079, 601-472-2312 X23 (Fax: 601-472-9852). Hours: 8AM-3PM. Enrollment: 1914. Records go back to 1925. Alumni records are maintained here also. Call 601-472-2312 X53. Degrees granted: Associate. Adverse incident record source- Dean of Students, 601-472-2312 X25.

Attendance and degree information available by phone, fax, mail. Search requires name plus SSN, approximate years of attendance. There is no fee.

Itawamba Community College, Registrar, 602 W Hill St, Fulton, MS 38843-1099, 601-862-3101 X234 (Fax: 601-862-9540). Hours: 8AM-4PM. Enrollment: 2702. Records go back to 1948. Alumni records are maintained here also. Call 601-862-3101 X225. Degrees granted: Associate. Adverse incident record source- Security, 601-862-3101 X201.

Attendance and degree information available by phone, fax, mail. Search requires name plus SSN. Also helpful: date of birth, exact years of attendance. There is no fee.

Jackson State University, Registrar, 1400 J R Lynch St, Jackson, MS 39217, 601-968-2300 (Fax: 601-968-2399). Hours: 8AM-5PM. Enrollment: 5772. Records go back to 1900's. Degrees granted: Bachelors; Masters; Doctorate.

Attendance information available by mail. Search requires name only. Also helpful: SSN, date of birth, exact years of attendance. There is no fee.

Degree information available by mail. Search requires name only. Also helpful: SSN, date of birth, exact years of attendance. There is no fee.

Jones County Junior College, Registrar, 900 S Court St, Ellisville, MS 39437, 601-477-4036 (Fax: 601-477-4212). Hours: 8AM-4:30PM. Enrollment: 3968. Records go back to 1911. Degrees granted: Associate.

Attendance and degree information available by phone, fax, mail. Search requires name plus SSN. Also helpful: date of birth, exact years of attendance. There is no fee.

Magnolia Bible College, Registrar, PO Box 1109, Kosciusko, MS 39090, 601-289-2896 (Fax: 601-289-1850). Hours: 8AM-4:30PM. Enrollment: 26. Records go back to 1976. Alumni records are maintained here also. Call 601-289-2896. Degrees granted: Bachelors. Adverse incident record source- Dean of Students.

Attendance information available by phone, fax, mail. Search requires name only. Also helpful: SSN, date of birth, exact years of attendance. Fee is $1.00.

Mary Holmes College, Registrar, PO Box 1257, Hwy 50 W, West Point, MS 39773, 601-494-6820 (Fax: 601-494-1881). Hours: 8AM-5PM. Enrollment: 375. Records go back to 1946. Alumni records are maintained here at the same phone number. Degrees granted: Associate.

Attendance information available by phone, fax, mail. Search requires name plus SSN, exact years of attendance. Also helpful: date of birth. There is no fee.

Degree information available by phone, fax, mail. Search requires name plus SSN, exact years of attendance. There is no fee.

Meridian Community College, Registrar, 910 Hwy 19 N, Meridian, MS 39307, 601-484-8636 (Fax: 601-484-8607). Hours: 8AM-4:30PM M-Th; 8AM-3:30PM F. Enrollment: 1950. Records go back to 1937. Degrees granted: Associate. Adverse incident record source- 601-484-8622.

Attendance and degree information available by phone, fax, mail. Search requires name plus SSN, date of birth, exact years of attendance. There is no fee.

Millsaps College, Office of Records, PO Box 150110, Jackson, MS 39210, 601-974-1120 (Fax: 601-974-1114). Hours: 8AM-4:30PM. Enrollment: 1240. Records go back to 1890. Alumni Records Office: PO Box 150552, Jackson, MS 39210. Degrees granted: Bachelors; Masters.

Attendance and degree information available by phone, fax, mail. Search requires name plus SSN. Also helpful: date of birth, exact years of attendance. There is no fee.

Mississippi College, Registrar, PO Box 4186, Clinton, MS 39058, 601-925-3210 (Fax: 601-925-3804). Hours: 8AM-4:30PM. Enrollment: 2857. Records go back to 1826. Degrees granted: Bachelors; Masters.

Attendance and degree information available by phone, fax, mail. Search requires name plus SSN, date of birth. Also helpful: approximate years of attendance. There is no fee.

Mississippi Delta Community College, Registrar, PO Box 668, Moorhead, MS 38761, 601-246-6306 (Fax: 601-246-6321). Hours: 8AM-4PM Summer, 8AM-4:30PM Fall. Enrollment: 3490. Records go back to 1940. Alumni records are maintained here also. Call 601-246-6457. Degrees granted: Associate. Certification: Vocational. Adverse incident record source- Dean of Students, 601-246-6444.

Attendance information available by phone, fax, mail. Search requires name plus SSN, date of birth, approximate years of attendance. There is no fee.

Degree information available by fax, mail. Search requires name plus SSN, date of birth, approximate years of attendance. There is no fee.

Mississippi Gulf Coast Community College, Registrar, PO Box 67, Perkinston, MS 39573, 601-928-5211 (Fax: 601-928-6345). Hours: 8AM-4:30PM. Enrollment: 953. Records go back to 1912. Alumni records are maintained here also. Call 601-928-6288. Degrees granted: Associate. Adverse incident record source- Student Services, 601-928-5211.

Attendance and degree information available by phone, fax, mail. Search requires name plus SSN, exact years of attendance. Also helpful: date of birth. There is no fee. Expedited service available for $5.00.

Mississippi State University, Registrar's Office, 112 Allen Hall, PO Box 5268, Mississippi State, MS 39762, 601-325-1843 (Fax: 601-325-1846). Hours: 8AM-5PM. Enrollment: 13651. Records go back to 1878. Degrees granted: Bachelors; Masters; Doctorate.

Attendance and degree information available by phone, fax. Search requires name plus SSN, date of birth. Also helpful: exact years of attendance. There is no fee.

Mississippi University for Women, Registrar, PO Box W-1605, Columbus, MS 39701, 601-329-7131 (Fax: 601-241-7481). Hours: 8AM-5PM. Enrollment: 3000. Records go back to 1884. Alumni Records Office: PO Box W-10, Columbus, MS 39701, 601-329-7295 (Fax: 601-329-7123). Degrees granted: Associate; Bachelors; Masters. Adverse incident record source- Security, 601-329-7436.

Attendance and degree information available by phone, fax, mail. Search requires name plus SSN, approximate years of attendance. Also helpful: date of birth, exact years of attendance. There is no fee.

Mississippi Valley State University, Registrar,
14000 Hwy 82 W, Itta Bena, MS 38941, 601-254-3325 (Fax: 601-254-7575). Hours: 8AM-5PM M,T,W,Th; 8AM-4PM F. Enrollment: 2100. Records go back to 1950. Alumni records are maintained here also. Call 601-254-3576. Degrees granted: Bachelors; Masters. Adverse incident record source- Student Services, 601-254-3636.

Attendance information available by phone, mail. Search requires name plus SSN. Also helpful: date of birth, exact years of attendance. There is no fee.

Degree information available by phone, mail. Search requires name only. Also helpful: SSN, date of birth, exact years of attendance. There is no fee.

Northeast Mississippi Community College,
Registrar, Cunningham Blvd, Booneville, MS 38829, 601-728-7751 (Fax: 601-728-1165). Hours: 8AM-4:30PM. Enrollment: 2735. Records go back to 1948. Alumni records are maintained here also. Call 601-720-7300. Degrees granted: Associate.

Attendance and degree information available by phone, fax, mail. Search requires name plus SSN, approximate years of attendance. There is no fee.

Northwest Mississippi Community College,
Registrar, 510 N Panola St, Senatobia, MS 38668, 601-562-3219 (Fax: 601-562-3221). Hours: 8AM-4:30PM. Enrollment: 3425. Records go back to 1900. Alumni records are maintained here also. Call 520-562-3222. Degrees granted: Associate.

Attendance and degree information available by phone, fax, mail. Search requires name plus SSN, exact years of attendance. Also helpful: date of birth. There is no fee.

Pearl River Community College, Registrar, 101
Hwy 11 N, Box 5559, Poplarville, MS 39470-2298, 601-795-6801 (Fax: 601-795-1129). Hours: 8AM-4PM. Enrollment: 2383. Records go back to 1909. Degrees granted: Associate.

Attendance and degree information available by phone, fax, mail. Search requires name plus SSN, date of birth. Also helpful: exact years of attendance. There is no fee.

Phillips Junior College, Registrar, 2680 Insurance
Center Dr, Jackson, MS 39216, 601-362-6341 (Fax: 601-366-9407). Hours: 8AM-4:30PM. Records go back to 1973. Degrees granted: Associate.

Attendance and degree information available by fax, mail. Search requires name plus SSN, exact years of attendance, signed release. There is no fee.

Reformed Theological Seminary, Registrar, 5422
Clinton Blvd, Jackson, MS 39209, 601-922-4988 X236 (Fax: 601-922-1153). Hours: 8AM-5PM. Enrollment: 507. Records go back to 1966. Degrees granted: Masters; Doctorate.

Attendance and degree information available by phone, fax, mail. Search requires name only. Also helpful: SSN, exact years of attendance. There is no fee.

Rust College, Registrar, 150 E Rust Ave, Holly Springs,
MS 38635, 601-252-8000 X4057 (Fax: 601-252-6107). Hours: 8AM-5PM. Enrollment: 1180. Records go back to 1957. Alumni records are maintained here also. Call 601-252-8000 X4015. Degrees granted: Associate; Bachelors.

Attendance and degree information available by phone, fax, mail. Search requires name plus SSN. There is no fee.

Southeastern Baptist College, Registrar, 4229
Hwy 15 N, Laurel, MS 39440, 601-426-6346 (Fax: 601-426-6347). Hours: 8AM-4:30PM. Enrollment: 100. Records go back to 1948. Alumni records are maintained here at the same phone number. Degrees granted: Associate; Bachelors.

Attendance and degree information available by phone, fax, mail. Search requires name only. Also helpful: SSN, date of birth, exact years of attendance. There is no fee.

Southwest Mississippi Community College,
Registrar, Summit, MS 39666, 601-276-2001 (Fax: 601-276-3888). Hours: 8AM-4:30PM. Enrollment: 1492. Records go back to 1932. Alumni records are maintained here at the same phone number. Degrees granted: Associate.

Attendance and degree information available by phone, fax, mail. Search requires name plus SSN. Also helpful: date of birth, exact years of attendance. There is no fee.

Tougaloo College, Registrar, 500 W County Line Rd,
Tougaloo, MS 39174, 601-977-7700 (Fax: 601-977-6185). Hours: 8AM-5PM. Enrollment: 980. Records go back to 1869. Alumni records are maintained here also. Call 601-977-7836. Degrees granted: Associate; Bachelors.

Attendance information available by phone, fax, mail. Search requires name only. Also helpful: SSN, date of birth, exact years of attendance. There is no fee.

Degree information available by phone, mail. Search requires name only. Also helpful: SSN, date of birth, exact years of attendance. There is no fee.

University of Mississippi, Registrar, University, MS
38677, 601-232-7226 (Fax: 601-232-5869). Hours: 8AM-5PM. Enrollment: 10500. Records go back to 1848. Alumni records are maintained here also. Call 601-232-7375. Degrees granted: Bachelors; Masters; Doctorate; PhD. Adverse incident record source- Dean of Students, 601-232-7247.

Attendance and degree information available by phone, fax, mail. Search requires name only. Also helpful: SSN, date of birth, approximate years of attendance. There is no fee.

University of Mississippi Medical Center,
Registrar, 2500 N State St, Jackson, MS 39216-4505, 601-984-1080 (Fax: 601-984-1079). Hours: 8AM-4:30PM. Enrollment: 1758. Records go back to 1955. Alumni records are maintained here at the same phone number. Degrees granted: Bachelors; Doctorate.

Attendance and degree information available by phone, mail. Search requires name plus SSN, date of birth. There is no fee.

University of Southern Mississippi, Registrar,
Box 5006, Hattiesburg, MS 39406-5001, 601-266-5006 (Fax: 601-266-5816). Hours: 8AM-5PM. Enrollment: 10465. Records go back to 1946. Alumni Records Office: Box 5013, Hattiesburg, MS 39406-5001. Degrees granted: Bachelors; Masters; Doctorate.

Attendance information available by phone, fax, mail. Search requires name plus SSN. Also helpful: exact years of attendance. There is no fee.

Degree information available by phone, fax, mail. Search requires name plus SSN, date of birth. Also helpful: exact years of attendance. There is no fee.

University of Southern Mississippi, (Gulf
Park), Registrar, 730 E Beach Blvd, Long Beach, MS 39560, 601-865-4503 (Fax: 601-865-4587). Hours: 8AM-4:30PM. Records go back to 1984. Alumni Records Office: PO Box 5013, Hattiesburg, MS 39406. Degrees granted: Bachelors; Masters. Certification: Education.

Attendance and degree information available by phone, mail. Search requires name plus SSN, date of birth. Also helpful: exact years of attendance. There is no fee.

Wesley Biblical Seminary, Registrar, 5980 Floral Dr,
Jackson, MS 39206, 601-957-1314 (Fax: 601-957-1314). Hours: 8AM-5PM. Enrollment: 100. Records go back to 1974. Alumni records are maintained here also. Call 601-957-1314. Degrees granted: Masters.

Attendance and degree information available by phone, fax, mail. Search requires name only. There is no fee.

Wesley College, Registrar, 111 Wesley Cir, PO Box 1070, Florence, MS 39073, 601-845-2265 (Fax: 601-845-2266). Enrollment: 110. Records go back to 1946. Degrees granted: Bachelors.

Attendance and degree information available by phone, fax, mail. Search requires name plus SSN. Also helpful: date of birth, exact years of attendance. There is no fee.

William Carey College, Registrar, 498 Tuscan Ave, Hattiesburg, MS 39401-5499, 601-582-6195 (Fax: 601-582-6196). Hours: 8AM-5PM. Enrollment: 2139. Records go back to 1911. Alumni records are maintained here also. Call 601-582-6107. Degrees granted: Bachelors; Masters.

Attendance information available by phone, fax, mail. Search requires name plus approximate years of attendance. Also help-ful: SSN, date of birth, exact years of attendance. There is no fee.

Degree information available by phone, fax, mail. Search requires name only. Also helpful: SSN, date of birth, exact years of attendance. There is no fee.

Wood College, Registrar, PO Box 289, Mathiston, MS 39752, 601-263-5352 (Fax: 601-263-4964). Hours: 8AM-4:30PM. Enrollment: 476. Formerly Wood Junior College Records go back to 1886. Alumni records are maintained here at the same phone number. Degrees granted: Associate. Adverse incident record source- Dean of Students, 601-263-8000.

Attendance and degree information available by phone, fax, mail. Search requires name plus SSN. There is no fee.

Trade and Vocational Schools

Amherst Career Center, 201 W Park Ave, Greenwood, MS 38930, 601-453-0480

Amherst Career Center (Branch Campus), 330 N Mart Plaza, Jackson, MS 37206, 601-336-0392

Antonelli College (Branch Campus), 1500 N 31st Ave, Hattiesburg, MS 39401, 601-583-4100

Batesville Job Corps Center, Hwy 51 S, Batesville, MS 38606, 601-563-4656

Delta Technical Institute, 323 Central Ave, Cleveland, MS 38732, 601-843-6063

Geiger's School of Cosmetology, 600 N 26th Ave, Hattiesburg, MS 39401, 601-583-2523

Gulfport Job Corps Center, 3300 20th St, Gulfport, MS 39501, 601-864-9691

Jackson Academy of Beauty, 2525 Robinson Rd, Jackson, MS 39209, 601-352-3003

Mississippi Job Corps Center, 400 Harmoney Rd, Crystal Springs, MS 39059, 601-892-3348

Moore Career College, 2460 Terry Rd, Jackson, MS 39204, 601-371-2900

Naval Constructions Training Center, 5510 CBC 8th St, Gulfport, MS 39501, 601-871-2531

Naval Technical Training Center, 740 Fletcher Rd #100, Meridian, MS 39309, 601-679-2161

North Mississippi EMS Authority, PO Box 377, Tupelo, MS 38802, 601-844-5870

Queen City College (Branch Campus), 800 Hwy 1 S, Greenville, MS 38701, 601-334-9120

Rice College (Branch Campus), 2525 Robinson Rd, Jackson, MS 39209, 601-355-8100

Southern Driver's Academy, 3906 I-55 S, Jackson, MS 39284, 601-371-1371

Southern Vocational Technical Institute, 905 Hardy St, Hattiesburg, MS 39404, 601-583-2523

State Licensing & Business Registration
Quick Finder Index

Architecture, Engineering & Surveying
Architect #3 (850)..☎ 601-359-6020
Engineer #10 (7043).....................................☎ 601-359-6160
Landscape Architect #3 (150).....................☎ 601-359-6020
Surveyor #10 (1074)....................................☎ 601-359-6160

Business - Court & Legal Services
Attorney (Certificate of Eligibility) #5..........☎ 601-354-6055
Lobbyist #30..☎ 601-359-1615
Notary Public #30 (20000)...........................☎ 601-359-1615
Shorthand Reporter #21................................. 601-374-5060

Business - General Services
Public Accountant-CPA #20 (4000) ....☎ 601-354-7320

Construction & Manufacturing
Boiler & Pressure Vessel Inspector #35 (200)
....☎ 601-960-7917
General Contractor #7 ....☎ 601-354-6161

Education
School Administrator #34 (3000)...................☎ 601-359-3483
Teacher #34 (2000)......................................☎ 601-359-3483

Environmental & Agriculture
Animal Technician #28 ....☎ 601-324-9380
Asbestos Contractor/Inspector #23 ....☎ 601-961-5100
Asbestos Management Planner/Project Designer #23
....☎ 601-961-5100
Asbestos Supervisor #23 ....☎ 601-961-5100
Asbestos Worker #23 ....☎ 601-961-5100
Commercial Fishing #25 ....☎ 601-362-9212
Veterinarian #28 (40)...................................☎ 601-324-9380
Veterinary Facility #28.................................☎ 601-324-9380
Veterinary Technician #28 ....☎ 601-324-9380

Financial - Real Estate, Insurance & Banking
Appraiser #29 (781)......................................☎ 601-987-4150
Banking #4.. 601-359-1031
General Real Estate Appraiser #29 ....☎ 601-987-4150
Insurance Sales Agent #26 ....☎ 601-359-3582
Insurance Solicitor/Advisor #26....................☎ 601-359-3582
Real Estate Broker #32 (4168) ....☎ 601-987-3969
Real Estate Salesperson #32 (5303) ....☎ 601-987-3969
Residential Real Estate Appraiser #29 ....☎ 601-987-4150
Savings Institution #24................................. 601-354-6135
Securities Agent #31 (34000)........................☎ 601-359-6363
Securities Broker/Dealer #31 (1140).............☎ 601-359-6363

Health & Beauty
Barber #6 (3500)...☎ 601-359-1015
Barber College #6...☎ 601-359-1015
Barber Instructor #6......................................☎ 601-359-1015
Barber Shop #6...☎ 601-359-1015
Chiropractor #33...☎ 601-773-4478
Cosmetologist #8 (11000) ....✉ 601-354-6623
Cosmetology Instructor #8 ....✉ 601-354-6623
Dental Hygienist #9 (800).............................☎ 601-944-9622
Dental Radiologist #9...................................☎ 601-944-9622
Dentist #9 (1422)..☎ 601-944-9622
Dietitian #35 ....☎ 601-987-4153

Emergency Medical Technician #35 ....☎ 601-987-3880
Emergency Medical Technician (Basic) #35
(2300) ....☎ 601-987-3880
Emergency Medical Technician-Intermediate #35
....☎ 601-987-3880
Emergency Medical Technician-Paramedic #35
....☎ 601-987-3880
Esthetician #8...✉ 601-354-6623
Eye Enucleator #35.......................................☎ 601-987-4153
Funeral Director #12 (750)............................☎ 601-354-6903
Funeral Service Practitioner #12 (550)..........☎ 601-354-6903
Health Facility #40.......................................✉ 601-987-3775
Hearing Aid Dealer (Specialist) #36 (95).......☎ 601-987-4153
Hearing Aid Specialist #35 ....☎ 601-987-4153
Manicurist #8...✉ 601-354-6623
Medical Doctor #13 ....☎ 601-354-6645
Nurse #14 (26500) ....☎ 601-359-6170
Nursing Home Administrator #15 601-359-6044
Occupational Therapist/Assistant #37 (485)
....☎ 601-987-4153
Occupational Therapist/Occupational Therapist
Assistant #35 ....☎ 601-987-4153
Optometrist #16 601-684-6241
Osteopathic Physician #13............................☎ 601-354-6645
Pharmacist #17...☎ 601-345-6750
Pharmacy Intern #17 ....☎ 601-345-6750
Physical Therapist/Assistant #37 (1178) ....☎ 601-987-4153
Physical Therapist/Physical Therapist
Assistant #35 ....☎ 601-987-4153
Physician's Assistant #13..............................☎ 601-354-6645
Podiatrist #13 ....☎ 601-354-6645
Practical Nurse #14 (11000) ....☎ 601-359-6170
Radiation Technician #35..............................☎ 601-987-4153
Respiratory Care Practitioner #13 ....☎ 601-354-6645
Salon #8 ....✉ 601-354-6623
Speech Pathologist/Audiologist #38...............☎ 601-987-4153
Speech-Language Pathologist/Audiologist #22
(656) ....☎ 601-987-4153
Speech/Language Pathologist, Audiologist #35
....☎ 601-987-4153

Investigations & Security
Polygraph Examiner #18 601-987-4202

Social Services
Child Care Facility #35 (1564)......................☎ 601-960-7613
Counselor, Licensed Professional #11 ....☎ 601-359-6630
Psychologist #19 ....☎ 601-353-8871
Social Worker #35 (3275) ....✉ 601-987-4153
Youth Camp #39 ....☎ 601-960-7740

Sports & Entertainment
Alcohol Beverage Employee #27 ....☎ 601-856-1330
Athletic Trainer #35.....................................☎ 601-987-4153
Gaming #27 (27)...☎ 601-351-2800
Liquor Control #2 (1200)...............................☎ 601-856-1310
Liquor Control, Alcoholic Beverate Retailers #1
(1500) ....☎ 601-856-1330
Tattoo Artist #35...☎ 601-987-4153

State Licensing & Business Registration Agency Information

(1) Alcohol Beverage Control Permits, PO Box 540, Madison, MS 39130-0540, 601-856-1330, Fax: 601-856-1390

(2) Alcoholic Beverage Control Board, PO Box 540, Madison, MS 39110-0540, 601-856-1310, Fax: 601-856-1390

(3) Board of Architecture, 239 N Lamar St, 502 Robert E Lee Bldg, Jackson, MS 39201, 601-359-6020, Fax: 601-359-6011

(4) Board of Banking Review, 550 High St, 304 Sillers Bldg, Jackson, MS 39205, 601-359-1031

(5) Board of Bar Admissions, 656 N. State Street, 1st Floor PO Box 1449, Court of Appeals Bldg., Jackson, MS 39215-1449, 601-354-6055, Fax: 601-354-6054

(6) Board of Barber Examiners, 510 George St, Room 234, Dickson Bldg, PO Box 603, Jackson, MS 39205, 601-359-1015, Fax: 601-359-1050

(7) Board of Contractors, 2001 Airport Rd, Suite 101, Jackson, MS 39208, 601-354-6161, Fax: 601-354-6915

(8) Board of Cosmetology, 1804 N State St, Jackson, MS 39202, 601-354-6623, Fax: 601-354-7076

(9) Board of Dental Examiners, 100 East Amite Street, Suite 100, Jackson, MS 39201-2801, 601-944-9622, Fax: 601-944-7622

(10) Board of Engineers & Land Surveyors, 501 Robert E Lee Bldg, 239 N Lamar St, Jackson, MS 39201, 601-359-6160, Fax: 601-359-6159

(11) Board of Examiners for Professional Counselors, 1101 Robert E. Lee Bldg., 239 N. Lamar St., Jackson, MS 39201, 601-359-6630, Fax: 601-359-6295

(12) Board of Funeral Service, 1307 E. Fortification St., Jackson, MS 39202, 601-354-6903, Fax: 601-354-6934

(13) Board of Medical Licensure, 3000 Old Canten Rd., Suite 111, Jackson, MS 39216, 601-354-6645, Fax: 601-987-4159

(14) Board of Nursing, 239 N. Lamar St., Suite 401, Jackson, MS 39201, 601-359-6170, Fax: 601-359-6185

(15) Board of Nursing Home Administrators, 1400 Lakeover Rd, #120, Jackson, MS 39213, 601-364-2310, Fax: 601-364-2306

(16) Board of Optometry, PO Box 688, McComb, MS 39648, 601-684-6241

(17) Board of Pharmacy, PO Box 24507, 2310 Hwy 80 W, Suite D, Jackson, MS 39225, 601-354-6071

(18) Board of Polygraph Examiners, PO Box 958, Jackson, MS 39205, 601-987-4202

(19) Board of Psychological Examiners, 812 N President St, Jackson, MS 39202, 601-353-8871, Fax: 601-352-4384

(20) Board of Public Accountancy, 653 North State St., Jackson, MS 39202, 601-354-7320, Fax: 601-354-7290

(21) CSR Contact Person, PO Box 1384, Biloxi, MS 39533, 601-374-5060

(22) Council of Advisors in Speech Pathology/Audiology, Department of Health, PO Box 1700, Jackson, MS 39215-1700, 601-987-4153, Fax: 601-987-3784

(23) Department of Environmental Quality, Pollution Control, PO Box 10385, Jackson, MS 39289, 601-961-5100, Fax: 601-354-6612

(24) Department of Savings Institutions, 633 N State St, Suite 201, Jackson, MS 39202, 601-354-6135

(25) Department of Wildlife, Fisheries & Parks, 2906 N State St, Jackson, MS 39216, 601-362-9212, Fax: 601-364-2009

(26) Insurance Department, Licensing Division, 1804 Sillers Bldg, 550 High St, Jackson, MS 39201, 601-359-3582, Fax: 601-359-2474

(27) Mississippi Gaming Commission, 202 E. Pearl St., Jackson, MS 39205, 601-351-2800, Fax: 601-351-2817

(28) Mississippi Board of Veterinary Medicine, 209 S Lafayette St, Starkville, MS 39759, 601-324-9380, Fax: 601-324-9380

(29) Mississippi Real Estate Appraiser, Licensing and Certification Board, 5176 Keele Street, PO Box 12685, Jackson, MS 39236-2685, 601-987-4150, Fax: 601-987-4173

(30) Office of Secretary of State, PO Box 136, Jackson, MS 39205-0136, 601-359-1615, Fax: 601-359-1607

(31) Office of Secretary of State, Securities Department, PO Box 136, Jackson, MS 39205, 601-359-6363, Fax: 601-359-2894

(32) Real Estate Commission, 1920 Dunbarton Dr, Jackson, MS 39216, 601-987-3969, Fax: 601-987-4984

(33) State Board of Chiropractic Examiners, PO Box 775, Louisville, MS 39339, 601-773-4478, Fax: 601-793-4433

(34) State Department of Education, Teacher Licensure/Certification, 802 Sillers Bldg, Jackson, MS 39201, 601-359-3483, Fax: 601-359-2778

(35) State Department of Health, 2423 N State St, PO Box 1700, Jackson, MS 39216, 601-987-4153, Fax: 601-987-3784

(36) State Department of Health, 2423 N State St, PO Box 1700, Jackson, MS 39216, 601-987-4153, Fax: 601-987-3784

(37) State Department of Health, 2423 N State St, PO Box 1700, Jackson, MS 39216, 601-960-4153, Fax: 601-987-3784

(38) State Department of Health, 500 B East Woodrow Wilson Blvd., Jackson, MS 39216, 601-960-7740, Fax: 601-987-3784

(39) State Department of Health, 2423 N State St, PO Box 1700, Jackson, MS 39216, 601-960-7740

(40) State Department of Health, Health Facilities Licensure & Certification, PO Box 1700, 4800 I-55 N, Jackson, MS 39215-1700, 601-354-7300, Fax: 601-354-7230

Missouri

Capitol: Jefferson City (Cole County)	
State Population	5.3 Million
Number of Degree Granting Institutions:	96
Number of State Licensing & Business Registration Agencies:	79

Degree Granting Educational Institutions

Aquinas Institute of Theology, Registrar, 3642 Lindell Blvd, St Louis, MO 63108-3396, 314-977-3883 (Fax: 314-977-7225). Hours: 8:30AM-5PM. Enrollment: 200. Degrees granted: Masters; Doctorate.

Attendance and degree information available by phone, fax, mail. Search requires name plus exact years of attendance. Also helpful: SSN, date of birth. There is no fee.

Assemblies of God Theological Seminary, Registrar, 1445 Boonville Ave, Springfield, MO 65802, 417-862-3344 X5608 (Fax: 417-862-3214). Hours: 8AM-4:30PM. Enrollment: 210. Records go back to 1973. Alumni records are maintained here also. Call 417-862-3344 X5640. Degrees granted: Masters.

Attendance and degree information available by phone, fax, mail. Search requires name plus SSN. There is no fee.

Avila College, Registrar, 11901 Wornall Rd, Kansas City, MO 64145, 816-942-8400 X2210 (Fax: 816-942-3362). Hours: 8AM-5PM. Enrollment: 1450. Records go back to 1916. Alumni records are maintained here also. Call 816-942-8400 X2236. Degrees granted: Bachelors; Masters. Adverse incident record source- Student Affairs, 816-942-8400 X2227.

Attendance and degree information available by phone, fax, mail. Search requires name plus SSN, approximate years of attendance. There is no fee.

Baptist Bible College, Registrar, 628 E Kearney St, Springfield, MO 65803, 417-268-6060 (Fax: 417-268-6694). Hours: 9AM-5PM. Enrollment: 400. Records go back to 1950. Alumni records are maintained here also. Call 417-268-6070. Degrees granted: Associate; Bachelors; Masters. Adverse incident record source- Dean.

Attendance information available by phone, fax, mail. Search requires name plus SSN. There is no fee.

Degree information available by phone, fax, mail. Search requires name plus SSN. There is no fee.

Calvary Bible College, Registrar, 15800 Calvary Rd, Kansas City, MO 64147-1341, 816-322-0110 (Fax: 816-331-4474). Hours: 8AM-4:30PM. Enrollment: 300. Records go back to 1931. Alumni records are maintained here at the same phone number. Degrees granted: Associate; Bachelors; Masters. Special programs- Christian Ministry. Adverse incident record source-Dean, 816-322-0110 X1327.

Attendance and degree information available by phone, fax, mail. Search requires name only. Also helpful: SSN, date of birth, exact years of attendance. There is no fee. Expedited service available for $15.00.

Central Bible College, Registrar, 3000 N Grant Ave, Springfield, MO 65803, 417-833-2551 (Fax: 417-833-5478). Enrollment: 900. Records go back to 1922. Alumni records are maintained here at the same phone number. Degrees granted: Associate; Bachelors.

Attendance and degree information available by phone, mail. Search requires name plus SSN, date of birth, exact years of attendance. There is no fee.

Central Christian College of the Bible, Registrar, 911 Urbandale Dr E, Moberly, MO 65270, 816-263-3900 (Fax: 816-263-3936). Hours: 8AM-Noon, 1-5PM. Enrollment: 140. Records go back to 1957. Degrees granted: Associate; Bachelors. Adverse incident record source- Registrar's Office .

Attendance information available by phone, fax, mail. Search requires name only. Also helpful: approximate years of attendance. There is no fee.

Degree information available by fax, mail. Search requires name only. Fee is $3.00.

Central Methodist College, Registrar, Fayette, MO 65248, 816-248-3391 X208 (Fax: 816-248-2622). Hours: 8AM-5PM. Enrollment: 899. Records go back to 1900. Alumni records are maintained here also. Call 816-248-3391 X230. Degrees granted: Bachelors.

Attendance and degree information available by phone, fax, mail. Search requires name plus SSN, approximate years of attendance. There is no fee.

Central Missouri State University, Registrar, Warrensburg, MO 64093, 816-543-4900 (Fax: 816-543-8400). Hours: 8AM-5PM. Enrollment: 10805. Records go back to 1871. Alumni records are maintained here also. Call 816-543-4025. Degrees granted: Associate; Bachelors; Masters; Education Specialist. Adverse incident record source- Student Affairs, 816-543-4111.

Attendance and degree information available by phone, mail. Search requires name only. Also helpful: SSN, date of birth, exact years of attendance. There is no fee.

Cleveland Chiropractic College, Registrar, 6401 Rockhill Rd, Kansas City, MO 64131, 816-333-8230 X232 (Fax: 816-361-0272). Hours: 8AM-5PM. Records go back to 1940. Alumni records are maintained here also. Call 816-333-8230. Degrees granted: Doctorate.

Attendance and degree information available by phone, fax, mail. Search requires name plus SSN. There is no fee.

College of the Ozarks, Registrar, Point Lookout, MO 65726, 417-334-6411 (Fax: 417-335-2618). Hours: 8AM-Noon, 1-5PM, 4PM in summer. Enrollment: 1500. Records go back to 1960. Alumni records are maintained here also. Call 417-334-6411. Degrees granted: Bachelors.

Attendance and degree information available by phone, fax, mail. Search requires name plus SSN, exact years of attendance. Also helpful: date of birth. There is no fee.

Columbia College, Registration, 1001 Rogers St, Columbia, MO 65216, 573-875-7507 (Fax: 573-875-7506). Hours: 8AM-5PM. Enrollment: 6335. Records go back to 1851. Alumni records are maintained here also. Call 573-875-7210. Degrees granted: Associate; Bachelors.

Attendance and degree information available by phone, fax, mail. Search requires name only. Also helpful: SSN, date of birth, exact years of attendance. There is no fee.

Conception Seminary College, Registrar, PO Box 502, Conception, MO 64433, 816-944-2218 (Fax: 816-944-2800). Hours: 8:30AM-3:30PM. Records go back to 1886. Alumni records are maintained here also. Call 816-944-2218. Degrees granted: Bachelors.

Attendance and degree information available by phone, fax, mail. Search requires name only. There is no fee.

Concordia Seminary, Registrar, 801 De Mun Ave, St Louis, MO 63105, 314-721-5934 (Fax: 314-721-5902). Hours: 8AM-Noon, 1-4:30PM. Enrollment: 500. Records go back to 1926. Alumni records are maintained here at the same phone number. Degrees granted: Masters; Doctorate.

Attendance and degree information available by phone, fax, mail. Search requires name only. Also helpful: exact years of attendance. There is no fee.

Cottey College, Registrar, 1000 W Austin St, Nevada, MO 64772, 417-667-8181 (Fax: 417-667-8103). Hours: 8AM-Noon, 1-5PM. Enrollment: 350. Records go back to 1884. Alumni records are maintained here at the same phone number. Degrees granted: Associate. Adverse incident record source-Business Office, 417-667-8181.

Attendance and degree information available by phone, fax, mail. Search requires name only. Also helpful: SSN, date of birth, exact years of attendance. There is no fee.

Covenant Theological Seminary, Registrar, 12330 Conway Rd, St Louis, MO 63141, 314-434-4044 (Fax: 314-434-4819). Hours: 8AM-4:30PM. Enrollment: 800. Records go back to 1956. Alumni records are maintained here at the same phone number. Degrees granted: Masters; Doctorate. Special programs- Extension Office, 314-434-4044.

Attendance and degree information available by phone, fax, mail. Search requires name only. Also helpful: SSN, date of birth, exact years of attendance. There is no fee.

Crowder College, Registrar, 6601 Laclede, Neosho, MO 64850, 417-451-3223 (Fax: 417-451-4280). Hours: 7:30AM-4:30PM. Records go back to 1966. Degrees granted: Associate.

Attendance and degree information available by phone, fax, mail. Search requires name plus SSN, date of birth. Also helpful: exact years of attendance. Fee is $1.00.

Culver-Stockton College, Registrar, Canton, MO 63435, 217-231-6339 (Fax: 217-231-6616). Hours: 8AM-Noon, 1-5PM. Enrollment: 1000. Records go back to 1853. Alumni records are maintained here at the same phone number. Degrees granted: Bachelors.

Attendance and degree information available by phone, fax, mail. Search requires name plus SSN, date of birth. Also helpful: exact years of attendance. There is no fee.

DeVry Institute of Technolgy, Kansas City, Registrar, 11224 Holmes Rd, Kansas City, MO 64131, 816-941-0430 (Fax: 816-941-0896). Hours: 8AM-5PM. Degrees granted: Associate; Bachelors.

Attendance and degree information available by phone, fax, mail. Search requires name plus SSN. Also helpful: date of birth, exact years of attendance. There is no fee.

DeVry Institutes, Registrar, 1224 Holmes Rd, Kansas City, MO 64131, 708-571-7700 (Fax: 708-941-0896). Hours: 8:30AM-7:30PM M-Th, 8:30AM-5PM F. Enrollment: 1965. Records go back to 1948. Alumni records are maintained here at the same phone number. Degrees granted: Associate; Bachelors.

Attendance and degree information available by phone, mail. Search requires name plus SSN, exact years of attendance. There is no fee.

Deaconess College of Nursing, Registrar, 6150 Oakland Ave, St Louis, MO 63139, 314-768-3044 X31 (Fax: 314-768-5673). Hours: 8:30AM-4:30PM. Enrollment: 425. Records go back to 1922. Alumni records are maintained here also. Call 314-768-3013. Degrees granted: Associate; Bachelors. Adverse incident record source- Student Services, 314-768-3862.

Attendance and degree information available by phone, fax, mail. Search requires name only. Also helpful: SSN, date of birth, exact years of attendance. There is no fee.

Drury College, Registrar, 900 N Benton Ave, Springfield, MO 65802, 417-873-7211 (Fax: 417-873-7529). Hours: 8AM-8:30PM M-Th; 8AM-5PM F. Enrollment: 1200. Records go back to 1874. Alumni records are maintained here also. Call 417-873-7217. Degrees granted: Associate; Bachelors; Masters.

Attendance and degree information available by fax, mail. Search requires name plus SSN, date of birth, approximate years of attendance, signed release. Also helpful: exact years of attendance. There is no fee.

East Central College, Registrar, PO Box 529, Union, MO 63084, 314-583-5193 (Fax: 314-583-1897). Hours: 7:30AM-8PM. Enrollment: 3000. Records go back to 1969. Alumni records are maintained here at the same phone number. Degrees granted: Associate.

Attendance and degree information available by phone, fax, mail. Search requires name only. Also helpful: SSN, date of birth. There is no fee.

Eden Theological Seminary, Registrar, 475 E Lockwood Ave, St Louis, MO 63119-3192, 314-961-3627 X339 (Fax: 314-961-5738). Enrollment: 200. Records go back to 1920's. Degrees granted: Masters; Doctorate.

Attendance and degree information available by phone, fax, mail. Search requires name plus SSN, exact years of attendance. There is no fee.

Evangel College, Registrar, 1111 N Glenstone Ave, Springfield, MO 65802, 417-865-2811 X7431 (Fax: 417-865-9599). Hours: 8AM-4:30PM. Enrollment: 1600. Records go back to 1955. Alumni records are maintained here also. Call 417-865-2811 X7333. Degrees granted: Associate; Bachelors. Adverse incident record source- Student Development, 417-865-2811 X7316.

Attendance and degree information available by phone, fax, mail. Search requires name plus SSN. There is no fee.

Fontbonne College, Registrar, 6800 Wydown Blvd, St Louis, MO 63105, 314-889-1421 (Fax: 314-889-1451). Hours: 8AM-4:30PM. Enrollment: 1801. Records go back to 1920. Alumni records are maintained here also. Call 314-889-1447. Degrees granted: Bachelors; Masters. Adverse incident record source- Business & Finance.

Attendance and degree information available by phone, fax, mail. Search requires name plus SSN. Also helpful: exact years of attendance. There is no fee.

Forest Institute of Professional Psychology, Registrar, 1322 S Campbell Ave, Springfield, MO 65807, 417-831-7902 (Fax: 417-831-6839). Hours: 8AM-5PM. Enrollment: 150. Records go back to 1979. Degrees granted: Masters; Doctorate.

Attendance and degree information available by fax, mail. Search requires name plus SSN, signed release. Also helpful: date of birth, approximate years of attendance. There is no fee.

Hannibal-LaGrange College, Registrar, 2800 Palmyra Rd, Hannibal, MO 63401, 573-221-3675 X207 (Fax: 573-221-6594). Hours: 8AM-5PM. Enrollment: 950. Records go back to 1921. Alumni records are maintained here also. Call 573-221-3675 X208. Degrees granted: Associate; Bachelors. Special programs- Admissions, 573-221-3675 X264: Business Office, 573-221-3675 X261: Financial Aid, 573-221-3675 X279. Adverse incident record source- Security, 573-221-3675 X231.

Attendance information available by phone, fax, mail. Search requires name plus SSN. Also helpful: exact years of attendance. There is no fee.

Degree information available by phone, mail. Search requires name only. Also helpful: SSN, date of birth, exact years of attendance. There is no fee.

Harris-Stowe State College, Registrar, 3026 Laclede Ave, St Louis, MO 63103, 314-340-3600 (Fax: 314-340-3322). Hours: 8AM-10PM M-Th, 8AM-4PM F,Sat. Enrollment: 1900. Records go back to 1919. Alumni records are maintained here also. Call 314-340-3375. Degrees granted: Bachelors.

Attendance and degree information available by phone, fax, mail. Search requires name plus SSN, date of birth, approximate years of attendance. Also helpful: exact years of attendance. There is no fee.

Hickey School, Registrar, 940 W Port Plaza, St Louis, MO 63146, 314-434-2212 (Fax: 314-434-1974). Hours: 7:30AM-5PM. Records go back to 1933. Degrees granted: Associate.

Attendance and degree information available by phone, fax, mail. Search requires name plus exact years of attendance. Also helpful: SSN. There is no fee.

ITT Technical Institute, Registrar, 13505 Lakefront Dr, Earth City, MO 63045-1416, 314-298-7800. Hours: 9AM-5PM. Records go back to 1936. Degrees granted: Associate; Bachelors.

Attendance and degree information available by phone, mail. Search requires name plus SSN. Also helpful: approximate years of attendance. There is no fee.

Jefferson College, Registrar, 1000 Viking Dr, Hillsboro, MO 63050-2441, 314-789-3951 (Fax: 314-789-5103). Hours: 8AM-4:30PM. Enrollment: 3900. Records go back to 1964. Alumni records are maintained here also. Call 314-942-3000 X104. Degrees granted: Associate. Adverse incident record source- Dean, 314-789-3951 X200.

Attendance information available by phone, fax, mail. Search requires name plus approximate years of attendance. Also helpful: SSN, exact years of attendance. There is no fee.

Degree information available by phone, fax, mail. Search requires name only. Also helpful: SSN, exact years of attendance. There is no fee.

Kansas City Art Institute, Registrar, 4415 Warwick Blvd, Kansas City, MO 64111-1874, 816-561-4852 X244 (Fax: 816-561-6404). Hours: 8:30AM-5PM. Enrollment: 559. Records go back to 1930. Alumni records are maintained here also. Call 816-561-4852. Degrees granted: Bachelors.

Attendance and degree information available by phone, fax, mail. Search requires name only. Also helpful: SSN, date of birth, exact years of attendance. There is no fee.

Keller Graduate School of Management, (Kansas City Downtown), Registrar, City Center Square, 1100 Main St, Kansas City, MO 64105-2112, 816-221-1300 (Fax: 816-474-0318). Records are not housed here. They are located at Keller Graduate School of Management, Registrar, 10 S Riverside Plaza, Chicago, IL 60606.

Keller Graduate School of Management, (Kansas City South), Registrar, 11224 Holmes Rd, Kansas City, MO 64131, 816-941-0367. Records are not housed here. They are located at Keller Graduate School of Management, Registrar, 10 S Riverside Plaza, Chicago, IL 60606.

Kemper Military School and College, Registrar, 701 Third St, Boonville, MO 65233, 816-882-5623 (Fax: 816-882-3332). Hours: 7:30AM-5PM. Enrollment: 490. Records go back to 1926. Alumni records are maintained here also. Call 816-882-5623 X3159. Degrees granted: Associate. Special programs- ESL: Aviation: Early Commission Program for Army. Adverse incident record source- Dean, 816-882-5623 X3116.

Attendance and degree information available by phone, fax, mail. Search requires name plus SSN, date of birth. Also helpful: exact years of attendance. There is no fee.

Kenrick-Glennon Seminary, Registrar, 5200 Glennon Dr, St Louis, MO 63119-4399, 314-644-0266 (Fax: 314-644-3079). Hours: 8AM-3:30PM. Enrollment: 60. Alumni records are maintained here at the same phone number. Degrees granted: Masters.

Attendance and degree information available by phone, fax, mail. Search requires name only. Also helpful: exact years of attendance. There is no fee.

Kirksville College of Osteopathic Medicine, Registrar, 800 W Jefferson Ave, Kirksville, MO 63501, 816-626-2356 (Fax: 816-626-2926). Hours: 8AM-5PM. Enrollment: 560. Records go back to 1892. Alumni records are maintained here also. Call 816-626-2307. Degrees granted: Doctorate. Special programs- Master of Science in Physical Therapy, 816-841-4077: Occupational Therapy, 816-841-4077: Physician Assistant, 816-841-4077: Sports Health Care, 816-841-4077.

Attendance and degree information available by phone, fax, mail. Search requires name only. Also helpful: SSN, exact years of attendance. There is no fee.

Lincoln University, Registrar, 820 Chestnut St, Jefferson City, MO 65102-0029, 573-681-5011 (Fax: 573-681-5013). Hours: 8AM-5PM. Enrollment: 3512. Records go back to 1912. Alumni records are maintained here also. Call 573-681-5570. Degrees granted: Associate; Bachelors; Masters. Adverse incident record source- Public Safety, PO Box 29, Jefferson City, MO 65102-0029.

Attendance and degree information available by phone, mail. Search requires name only. Also helpful: SSN, date of birth, exact years of attendance. There is no fee.

Lindenwood College, Registrar, 209 S Kingshighway Blvd, St Charles, MO 63301, 314-949-4954. Hours: 8AM-6PM M-Th, 8AM-5PM F. Records go back to 1827. Alumni records are maintained here also. Call 314-949-4906. Degrees granted: Bachelors; Masters. Adverse incident record source- Dean, 314-949-4984.

Attendance and degree information available by mail. Search requires name plus SSN, date of birth, approximate years of attendance, signed release. There is no fee.

Logan College of Chiropractic, Registrar, 1851
Schoettler Rd, PO Box 1065, Chesterfield, MO 63006-1065, 314-227-2100 (Fax: 314-207-2424). Hours: 7AM-4:30PM. Enrollment: 962. Records go back to 1939. Alumni records are maintained here at the same phone number. Degrees granted: Bachelors; Doctorate.

Attendance information available by phone, fax, mail. Search requires name plus exact years of attendance. Also helpful: SSN. There is no fee.

Degree information available by fax, mail. Search requires name plus exact years of attendance. Also helpful: SSN. There is no fee.

Longview Community College, Registrar, 500
Longview Rd, Lee's Summit, MO 64081, 816-672-2244 (Fax: 816-672-2040). Hours: 8AM-6PM. Enrollment: 6500. Records go back to 1969. Degrees granted: Associate.

Attendance and degree information available by phone, fax, mail. Search requires name plus SSN. Also helpful: date of birth, exact years of attendance. There is no fee.

Maple Woods Community College, Registrar,
2601 NE Barry Rd, Kansas City, MO 64156, 816-437-3100 (Fax: 816-437-3351). Hours: 8AM-7PM M-Th; 8AM-4:30PM F. Enrollment: 4600. Records go back to 1969. Alumni Records Office: Alumni Association, 3200 Broadway, Kansas City, MO 64110. Degrees granted: Associate.

Attendance and degree information available by phone, fax, mail. Search requires name only. Also helpful: SSN, date of birth. There is no fee.

Maryville University of St. Louis, Registrar, 13550
Conway Rd, St Louis, MO 63141, 314-529-9370 (Fax: 314-529-9925). Hours: 8AM-5PM. Records go back to 1926. Degrees granted: Bachelors; Masters.

Attendance and degree information available by fax, mail. Search requires name plus SSN. Also helpful: date of birth, exact years of attendance. There is no fee.

Midwestern Baptist Theological Seminary,
Registrar, 5001 N Oak St Trafficway, Kansas City, MO 64118, 816-453-4600 (Fax: 816-455-3528). Hours: 8AM-4:30PM. Enrollment: 550. Records go back to 1958. Alumni records are maintained here at the same phone number. Degrees granted: Masters; Doctorate.

Attendance and degree information available by phone, fax, mail. Search requires name only. Also helpful: SSN, date of birth, exact years of attendance. There is no fee.

Mineral Area College, Registrar, PO Box 1000, Hwy
67 and 32, Park Hills, MO 63601, 573-431-4593 (Fax: 573-431-2321). Hours: 8AM-4PM. Enrollment: 2400. Records go back to 1922. Alumni records are maintained here at the same phone number. Degrees granted: Associate.

Attendance and degree information available by phone, mail. Search requires name plus SSN. Also helpful: date of birth, exact years of attendance. There is no fee.

Missouri Baptist College, Records Office, One College Park Dr, St Louis, MO 63141, 314-434-1115 X2233 (Fax: 314-434-7596). Hours: 8AM-4:30PM. Enrollment: 2000. Records go back to 1968. Alumni records are maintained here also. Call 314-434-1115 X2302. Degrees granted: Associate; Bachelors. Special programs- Sports Medicine: Sports Management. Adverse incident record source- Dean, 314-434-1115 X2211.

Attendance and degree information available by phone, fax, mail. Search requires name plus SSN. Also helpful: exact years of attendance. There is no fee.

Missouri Southern State College, Registrar, 3950
Newman Rd, Joplin, MO 64801, 417-625-9340 (Fax: 417-625-3117). Hours: 8AM-5PM. Enrollment: 5500. Records go back to 1938. Alumni records are maintained here at the same phone number. Degrees granted: Associate; Bachelors. Adverse incident record source- Dean of Students.

Attendance and degree information available by phone, fax, mail. Search requires name plus SSN. Also helpful: date of birth, approximate years of attendance. There is no fee.

Missouri Valley College, Registrar, 500 E College Dr,
Marshall, MO 65340, 816-886-6924 (Fax: 816-886-9818). Hours: 8AM-5PM. Enrollment: 1300. Records go back to 1890. Alumni records are maintained here at the same phone number. Degrees granted: Associate; Bachelors.

Attendance and degree information available by phone, fax, mail. Search requires name only. Also helpful: SSN, date of birth, exact years of attendance. There is no fee.

Missouri Western State College, Registrar, 4525
Downs Dr, St Joseph, MO 64507, 816-271-4228. Hours: 8AM-4:30PM. Enrollment: 5100. Records go back to 1915. Alumni records are maintained here also. Call 816-271-4253. Degrees granted: Associate; Bachelors. Adverse incident record source- Dean of Students, 816-271-4432.

Attendance and degree information available by phone, mail. Search requires name plus SSN. Also helpful: date of birth. There is no fee.

Moberly Area Community College, Student
Services, College and Rollins Sts, Moberly, MO 65270, 816-263-4110 (Fax: 816-263-6448). Hours: 8AM-10PM M-Th; 8AM-8PM F. Records go back to 1927. Degrees granted: Associate. Certification: LPN.

Attendance and degree information available by phone, fax, mail. Search requires name only. Also helpful: SSN, date of birth, approximate years of attendance. There is no fee.

Nazarene Theological Seminary, Registrar, 1700
E Meyer Blvd, Kansas City, MO 64131, 816-333-6254 (Fax: 816-333-6271). Hours: 8AM-4:30PM. Enrollment: 277. Records go back to 1945. Alumni records are maintained here also. Call 816-333-6254. Degrees granted: Masters; Doctorate.

Attendance and degree information available by phone, fax, mail. Search requires name plus exact years of attendance. Also helpful: SSN, date of birth, approximate years of attendance. There is no fee.

North Central Missouri College, Registrar, 1301
Main St, Trenton, MO 64683, 816-359-3948. Hours: 8AM-4PM. Enrollment: 1100. Records go back to 1925. Degrees granted: Associate.

School will not confirm attendance information.

Degree information available by mail. Search requires name plus SSN. Also helpful: exact years of attendance. There is no fee.

Northwest Missouri State University, Registrar,
800 University Dr, Maryville, MO 64468-6001, 816-562-1151 (Fax: 816-562-1993). Hours: 8AM-5PM. Enrollment: 6000. Records go back to 1906. Degrees granted: Bachelors; Masters; Specialist in Education. Adverse incident record source- Dean of Students, 816-562-1154.

Attendance and degree information available by phone, fax, mail. Search requires name plus SSN. Also helpful: date of birth, exact years of attendance. There is no fee.

Ozark Christian College, Registrar's Office, 1111 N
Main St, Joplin, MO 64801, 417-624-2518 (Fax: 417-624-0090). Hours: 8AM-5PM. Enrollment: 527. Records go back to 1942. Alumni records are maintained here at the same phone number. Degrees granted: Associate; Bachelors. Adverse incident record source- Student Development, 417-624-2518.

Attendance and degree information available by phone, fax, mail. Search requires name only. Also helpful: SSN, date of birth, exact years of attendance. There is no fee.

Ozarks Technical Community College, Registrar, 1417 N Jefferson Ave, Springfield, MO 65802, 417-895-7195 (Fax: 417-895-7161). Hours: 8AM-4:30PM. Enrollment: 3500. Records go back to 1966. Alumni records are maintained here at the same phone number. Degrees granted: Associate.

Attendance and degree information available by mail. Search requires name plus SSN, approximate years of attendance, signed release. Also helpful: date of birth, exact years of attendance. There is no fee.

Park College, Registrar, 8700 River Park Dr, Parkville, MO 64152, 816-741-6270 (Fax: 816-587-5585). Hours: 8AM-4:30PM. Enrollment: 8494. Records go back to 1936. Alumni records are maintained here also. Call 816-714-2000 X211. Degrees granted: Bachelors; Masters. Special programs- School of Extended Learning,816-741-6242. Adverse incident record source- Human Resource, 816-741-6386.

Attendance and degree information available by phone, fax, mail. Search requires name plus SSN, approximate years of attendance. There is no fee.

Penn Valley Community College, Registrar, 3201 SW Trafficway, Kansas City, MO 64111, 816-759-4000 (Fax: 816-759-4478). Hours: 8AM-4:30PM Fall; 7AM-5:30PM M-Th Summer. Enrollment: 4100. Records go back to 1919. Degrees granted: Associate. Special programs- Allied Health Fields, 816-759-4234. Adverse incident record source- Security Office, 816-759-4123.

Attendance and degree information available by phone, fax, mail. Search requires name plus SSN. There is no fee.

Phillips Junior College, Registrar, 1010 W Sunshine St, Springfield, MO 65807, 417-864-7220 (Fax: 417-864-5697). Hours: 8AM-6PM. Enrollment: 400. Records go back to 1989. Degrees granted: Associate.

Attendance and degree information available by phone, fax, mail. Search requires name plus SSN, approximate years of attendance. Also helpful: date of birth, exact years of attendance. There is no fee.

Ranken Technical College, Registrar, 4431 Finney Ave, St Louis, MO 63113, 314-371-0236 X1180 (Fax: 314-371-0241). Hours: 7:30AM-6:30PM M,T,Th; 7:30AM-4PM W,F. Enrollment: 1500. Records go back to 1909. Alumni records are maintained here also. Call 314-371-0236 X1650. Degrees granted: Associate.

Attendance and degree information available by phone, fax, mail. Search requires name plus SSN, approximate years of attendance. There is no fee.

Rockhurst College, Registrar, 1100 Rockhurst Rd, Kansas City, MO 64110, 816-501-4057 (Fax: 816-501-4588). Hours: 8AM-6PM M-Th, 8AM-4:30PM F. Enrollment: 3000. Records go back to 1910. Alumni records are maintained here also. Call 816-501-4581. Degrees granted: Bachelors; Masters. Adverse incident record source- Rockhurst Security, 816-501-4000.

Attendance and degree information available by phone, fax, mail. Search requires name only. Also helpful: SSN, date of birth, approximate years of attendance. There is no fee.

Saint Louis Christian College, Registrar, 1360 Grandview Dr, Florissant, MO 63033, 314-837-6777 (Fax: 314-837-8291). Hours: 8AM-5PM. Enrollment: 175. Records go back to 1956. Alumni records are maintained here at the same phone number. Degrees granted: Associate; Bachelors. Adverse incident record source- Dean of Students.

Saint Louis Conservatory of Music, Registrar, 560 Trinity at Delmar, St. Louis, MO 63130, 314-863-3033 (Fax: 314-286-4421). Enrollment: 1200. Records go back to 1947. Alumni records are maintained here at the same phone number. Degrees granted. Adverse incident record source- Department of Student Services.

Attendance and degree information available by phone, fax, mail. Search requires name plus SSN, exact years of attendance. There is no fee.

Saint Mary's College of O'Fallon, Registrar, 4601 Mid Rivers Mall Dr, Saint Peters, MO 63376, 314-922-8000 (Fax: 314-922-8236). Enrollment: 5500. Records go back to 1987. Degrees granted: Associate. Special programs- Arts: Science. Adverse incident record source- Security.

Attendance and degree information available by phone, mail. Search requires name plus SSN, exact years of attendance. There is no fee.

Saint Mary's Seminary, Registrar, 1701 W St Joseph, Perryville, MO 63775, 573-547-6533 X261 (Fax: 573-547-2204). This school closed in May, 1985. Degrees granted.

Attendance and degree information available by phone, fax, mail. Search requires name plus approximate years of attendance. Also helpful: SSN, date of birth, exact years of attendance. Fee is $5.00.

Sanford-Brown Business College, Registrar, 12006 Manchester Rd, Des Peres, MO 63131, 314-822-7100 (Fax: 314-822-4017). Hours: 9AM-6PM. Enrollment: 1410. Records go back to 1987. Degrees granted: Associate.

Attendance and degree information available by fax, mail. Search requires name plus SSN, signed release. Also helpful: exact years of attendance. There is no fee.

Sanford-Brown Business College, (Branch), Registrar, 355 Brooks Dr, Hazelwood, MO 63042, 314-731-5200. Hours: 7AM-7PM M-Th, 7AM-4PM F. Records go back to 1985. Degrees granted: Associate.

Attendance and degree information available by phone, mail. Search requires name plus SSN, exact years of attendance. There is no fee.

Sanford-Brown Business College, (Branch), Registrar, 2702 Rockcreek Pkwy Ste 300, North Kansas City, MO 64117, 816-472-7400 (Fax: 816-472-0688). Degrees granted: Associate.

Attendance and degree information available by mail. Search requires name plus signed release. Also helpful: SSN, approximate years of attendance. There is no fee.

Sanford-Brown Business College, (Branch), Registrar, 3555 Franks Dr, St Charles, MO 63301, 314-949-2620 (Fax: 314-949-5081). Hours: 8AM-4PM. Enrollment: 1410. Degrees granted: Associate.

Attendance and degree information available by phone, fax, mail. Search requires name plus SSN, date of birth, exact years of attendance. There is no fee.

School of the Ozarks, Registrar, Point Lookout, MO 65726, 417-334-6411 X4223 (Fax: 417-335-2618). Enrollment: 1550. Records go back to 1960. Alumni records are maintained here at the same phone number. Degrees granted: Bachelors. Adverse incident record source- Security.

Attendance and degree information available by phone. Search requires name plus SSN, exact years of attendance. There is no fee.

Southeast Missouri State University, Registrar,
One University Plaza, Cape Girardeau, MO 63701, 573-651-2250 (Fax: 573-651-5155). Hours: 8AM-5PM. Enrollment: 8000. Records go back to 1921. Alumni records are maintained here also. Call 573-651-2259. Degrees granted: Associate; Bachelors; Masters.

Attendance and degree information available by phone, fax, mail. Search requires name plus SSN. Also helpful: date of birth, approximate years of attendance. There is no fee. Expedited service available for $2.00.

Southwest Baptist University, Registrar, 1601 S
Springfield St, Bolivar, MO 65613, 417-326-1605 (Fax: 417-326-1514). Hours: 8AM-5PM. Enrollment: 3000. Alumni records are maintained here also. Call 417-326-1837. Degrees granted: Associate; Bachelors; Masters.

Attendance and degree information available by phone, fax, mail. Search requires name only. Also helpful: SSN, date of birth, exact years of attendance. There is no fee.

Southwest Missouri State University, Registrar,
901 S National Ave, Springfield, MO 65804, 417-836-5519. Hours: 8AM-5PM. Enrollment: 15000. Records go back to 1908. 1908-1982 on microfilm; 1982 forward on computer. Alumni records are maintained here also. Call 417-836-5654. Degrees granted: Bachelors; Masters; Specialist. Adverse incident record source- Police.

Attendance and degree information available by phone, fax, mail. Search requires name plus SSN, date of birth. Also helpful: exact years of attendance. There is no fee.

St. Charles County Community College, Attn:
Records, 4601 Mid Rivers Mall Dr, St Peters, MO 63376, 314-922-8237 (Fax: 314-922-8236). Hours: 8AM-7PM M-Th; 8AM-4:30PM F. Enrollment: 4700. Records go back to 1989. Alumni records are maintained here also. Call 314-922-8473. Degrees granted: Associate. Special programs- Art: Applied Science: LPM: Clerical.

Attendance and degree information available by phone, fax, mail. Search requires name plus SSN. Also helpful: exact years of attendance. There is no fee.

St. Louis College of Pharmacy, Registrar, 4588
Parkview Pl, St Louis, MO 63110, 314-367-8700 X1067 (Fax: 314-367-2784). Hours: 8:30AM-5PM. Enrollment: 850. Records go back to 1926. Alumni records are maintained here also. Call 314-367-1046. Degrees granted: Bachelors; Masters; Pharm. D.

Attendance and degree information available by phone, fax, mail. Search requires name only. Also helpful: SSN, date of birth, exact years of attendance. There is no fee.

St. Louis Community College, Central Records,
5600 Oakland Ave Rm B-013, St Louis, MO 63110, 314-644-9670 (Fax: 314-644-9752). Enrollment: 25000. Records go back to 1962. Degrees granted: Associate.

Attendance and degree information available by phone, fax, mail. Search requires name only. Also helpful: SSN, date of birth. There is no fee.

St. Louis Community College at Florissant
Valley, Registrar, 3400 Pershall Rd, St Louis, MO 63135, 314-595-4244. Hours: 8AM-8PM M-Th, 8AM-4:30PM F. Records go back to 1962. Alumni records are maintained here also. Call 314-595-4556. Degrees granted: Associate. Adverse incident record source- President, 314-595-4208.

Attendance and degree information available by phone, mail. Search requires name plus SSN, date of birth. There is no fee.

St. Louis Community College at Meramec,
Registrar, 11333 Big Bend Blvd, Kirkwood, MO 63122, 314-984-7601 (Fax: 314-984-7117). Hours: 7:30AM-9PM M-Th, 7:30AM-5PM F. Enrollment: 13000. Records go back to 1973. Alumni records are maintained here also. Call 314-984-7641.

Degrees granted: Associate. Special programs- AAS: Horticulture: OTA: PTA: Interior Design: Court & Conference Reporting. Adverse incident record source- Student Development, 314-984-7661.

Attendance and degree information available by phone, fax, mail. Search requires name plus SSN, date of birth, approximate years of attendance. There is no fee.

St. Louis University, Registrar, 221 N Grand Blvd, St
Louis, MO 63103, 314-977-2269 (Fax: 314-977-3447). Hours: 8:30AM-5PM. Enrollment: 11243. Records go back to 1911. Alumni records are maintained here also. Call 314-977-2308. Degrees granted: Associate; Bachelors; Masters; Doctorate. Adverse incident record source- Public Safety, 314-977-3877.

Attendance and degree information available by phone, fax, mail. Search requires name plus SSN, date of birth, approximate years of attendance. Also helpful: exact years of attendance. There is no fee.

St. Paul School of Theology, Registrar, 5123 Tru-
man Rd, Kansas City, MO 64127, 816-483-9600 (Fax: 816-483-9605). Hours: 8AM-4:30PM. Enrollment: 298. Records go back to 1962. Alumni records are maintained here also. Call 816-483-9600. Degrees granted: Doctorate.

Attendance and degree information available by phone, fax, mail. Search requires name plus SSN, approximate years of attendance. There is no fee.

State Fair Community College, Registrar, 3201 W
16th St, Sedalia, MO 65301, 816-530-5800 X296 (Fax: 816-530-5820). Hours: 8AM-7PM M-Th, 8AM-4PM F. Enrollment: 2700. Records go back to 1968. Alumni records are maintained here also. Call 816-530-5800 X250. Degrees granted: Associate. Adverse incident record source- Dean of Students, 816-530-5800.

Attendance and degree information available by phone, fax, mail. Search requires name plus SSN. There is no fee.

Stephens College, Registrar, Columbia, MO 65215,
314-876-7277 (Fax: 314-876-7248). Hours: 8AM-Noon, 1-5PM. Enrollment: 889. Records go back to 1900. Alumni records are maintained here at the same phone number. Degrees granted: Associate; Bachelors.

Attendance and degree information available by phone, fax, mail. Search requires name only. Also helpful: SSN, date of birth, exact years of attendance. There is no fee.

TAD Technical Institute, Registrar, 7910 Troost Ave,
Kansas City, MO 64131, 816-361-5640 (Fax: 816-361-2140). Enrollment: 300. Formerly ITT Technical Institute Records go back to 1980's. Degrees granted. Adverse incident record source- Registrar, 816-361-5640.

Attendance and degree information available by fax, mail. Search requires name plus signed release. Also helpful: SSN, exact years of attendance. There is no fee.

Three Rivers Community College, Registrar,
2080 Three Rivers Blvd, Poplar Bluff, MO 63901, 573-840-9665 (Fax: 573-840-9604). Hours: 8AM-4PM. Enrollment: 2405. Records go back to 1967. Alumni records are maintained here also. Call 573-840-9695. Degrees granted: Associate.

Attendance information available by phone, fax, mail. Search requires name plus SSN. Also helpful: date of birth, exact years of attendance. There is no fee.

Degree information available by fax, mail. Search requires name plus SSN. Also helpful: date of birth, exact years of attendance. There is no fee.

Truman State University, Registrar, Kirksville, MO
63501, 816-785-4143 (Fax: 816-785-7396). Hours: 8AM-5PM. Enrollment: 6000. Formerly Northeast Missouri State University Records go back to 1867. Alumni records are maintained here at

the same phone number. Degrees granted: Bachelors; Masters. Adverse incident record source- Student Affairs, 816-785-4111.

Attendance and degree information available by phone, fax, mail. Search requires name plus SSN, exact years of attendance. Also helpful: date of birth. There is no fee.

University of Health Sciences, Registrar, 2105 Independence Blvd, Kansas City, MO 64124, 816-283-2332 (Fax: 816-283-2349). Hours: 8AM-4:30PM. Enrollment: 757. Records go back to 1916. Alumni records are maintained here also. Call 816-283-2360. Degrees granted: Bachelors; Masters. Special programs- Doctor of Osteopathy, 816-283-2332. Adverse incident record source- Student Services, 816-283-2332.

Attendance and degree information available by phone, fax, mail. Search requires name plus SSN, exact years of attendance. There is no fee.

University of Missouri-Columbia, Registrar, Columbia, MO 65211, 573-882-7881 (Fax: 573-884-4530). Enrollment: 23000. Records go back to 1800's. Alumni records are maintained here also. Call 573-882-6611. Degrees granted: Doctorate.

Attendance and degree information available by phone, fax, mail. Search requires name only. Also helpful: SSN, date of birth, approximate years of attendance. There is no fee.

University of Missouri-Kansas City, Records Office, 111 SSB, 4825 Troost, Kansas City, MO 64110, 816-235-1122 (Fax: 816-235-5513). Hours: 8AM-5PM. Records go back to 1933. Degrees granted: Bachelors; Masters; Doctorate. Adverse incident record source- Campus Police, 816-235-1515.

Attendance information available by fax, mail. Search requires name plus signed release. Also helpful: SSN, date of birth, exact years of attendance. There is no fee.

Degree information available by phone, fax, mail. Search requires name only. Also helpful: SSN, date of birth, exact years of attendance. There is no fee.

University of Missouri-Rolla, Registrar, 103 Parker Hall, Rolla, MO 65401, 314-341-4181 (Fax: 314-341-4362). Hours: 8AM-4PM. Records go back to 1930's. Alumni records are maintained here also. Call 314-341-4145. Degrees granted: Bachelors; Masters; Doctorate.

Attendance and degree information available by phone, fax, mail. Search requires name only. Also helpful: SSN, date of birth, exact years of attendance. There is no fee. Expedited service available for $3.00.

University of Missouri-St. Louis, Registrar, 8001 Natural Bridge Rd, St Louis, MO 63121, 314-516-5676 (Fax: 314-516-5310). Hours: 8AM-5PM. Enrollment: 12650. Records go back to 1963. Alumni records are maintained here at the same phone number. Degrees granted: Bachelors; Masters; Doctorate.

Attendance and degree information available by phone, fax, mail. Search requires name plus SSN, date of birth, approximate years of attendance. Also helpful: exact years of attendance. There is no fee.

Washington University, Registrar, One Brookings Dr, Box 1143, St Louis, MO 63130, 314-935-5919 (Fax: 314-935-4268). Hours: 8:30AM-5PM. Enrollment: 11482. Records go back to 1978. Records go back to 1853, on-line from 1978.

Alumni Records Office: Alumni Development, Box 1210, 1 Brookings, St Louis, MO 63130. Degrees granted: Associate; Bachelors; Masters; Doctorate. Adverse incident record source- Academic Dean, 314-935-5994.

Attendance and degree information available by fax, mail. Search requires name plus SSN, date of birth. Also helpful: exact years of attendance. Fee is $5.00.

Webster University, Registrar, 470 E Lockwood Ave, St Louis, MO 63119-3194, 314-968-7450 (Fax: 314-968-7112). Hours: 8:30AM-5:30PM M-Th, 8:30AM-4:30PM F. Enrollment: 3790. Records go back to 1915. Alumni records are maintained here also. Call 314-968-6955. Degrees granted: Bachelors; Masters; Doctorate. Special programs- Women's Studies: Media Studies: Paralegal Studies. Adverse incident record source- Public Safety, 314-968-4750.

Attendance and degree information available by fax, mail. Search requires name plus SSN, date of birth, signed release. Also helpful: exact years of attendance. There is no fee.

Wentworth Military Academy and Junior College, Registrar, 1880 Washington Ave, Lexington, MO 64067, 816-259-2221 X244 (Fax: 816-259-3780). Hours: 9AM-5PM. Enrollment: 827. Records go back to 1890. Alumni records are maintained here at the same phone number. Degrees granted: Associate. Special programs- Military Science. Adverse incident record source- Commandant, 816-259-2221 X400.

Attendance and degree information available by phone, fax, mail. Search requires name only. Also helpful: SSN, date of birth, exact years of attendance. There is no fee.

Westminster College, Registrar, 501 Westminster Ave, Fulton, MO 65251-1299, 573-592-1213 (Fax: 573-592-1217). Hours: 8AM-4:30PM. Enrollment: 572. Records go back to 1800's. Alumni records are maintained here also. Call 573-592-1319. Degrees granted: Bachelors.

Attendance and degree information available by phone, fax, mail. Search requires name plus approximate years of attendance. Also helpful: exact years of attendance. There is no fee.

William Jewell College, Registrar's Office, 500 College Hill, Liberty, MO 64068, 816-781-7700 (Fax: 816-781-3164). Hours: 8AM-5PM. Alumni records are maintained here at the same phone number. Degrees granted: Bachelors.

Attendance and degree information available by phone, fax, mail. Search requires name plus SSN, date of birth, approximate years of attendance. Also helpful: exact years of attendance. There is no fee.

William Woods University, Registrar, Fulton, MO 65251, 573-592-4248 (Fax: 573-592-1146). Hours: 8AM-4:30PM. Enrollment: 1100. Alumni records are maintained here also. Call 573-592-4219. Degrees granted: Associate; Bachelors; Masters. Special programs- Equestrian: Intreping: Paralegal. Adverse incident record source- Student Development, 573-592-4238.

Attendance and degree information available by phone, fax, mail. Search requires name plus date of birth, approximate years of attendance. Also helpful: SSN, exact years of attendance. There is no fee.

Trade and Vocational Schools

Aero Mechanics School, Riverside, MO 64150, 816-741-7700

Al-Med Academy, 10963 St Charles Rock Rd, St Louis, MO 63074, 314-739-4450

Bryan Career College, 520 W University St #B, Springfield, MO 65807, 417-862-5700

Bryan Career College (Grandview Campus), 12220 S Blue Ridge Blvd, Ste F, Grandview, MO , 816-763-1000

Bryan Institute, 12184 Natural Bridge Rd, Bridgeton, MO 63044, 314-291-0241

Cape Girardeau Area Vocational-Technical School, 301 N Clark St, Cape Girardeau, MO 63701, 573-334-3358

ConCorde Career Institute, 3239 Broadway, Kansas City, MO 64111, 816-531-5223

Diamond Council of America, 9140 Ward Pkwy, Kansas City, MO 64114, 816-444-3500

Dick Hill International Flight School, PO BOx 10603, Springfield, MO 65808, 417-485-3474

Eastern Jackson County College of Allied Health, 808 S 15th St, Blue Springs, MO 64015, 816-229-4720

Florissant Upholstery School, 1420 N Vandeventer St, St Louis, MO 63113, 314-534-1886

Hannibal Area Vocational-Technical School, 4500 McMasters Ave, Hannibal, MO 63401, 314-221-4430

IHM Health Studies Center, 2500 Abbott Pl, St Louis, MO 63143, 314-768-1234

Leonard Barber College, 4974 Natural Bridge Rd, St Louis, MO 63115, 314-382-3000

Metro Business College, 1732 N Kingshighway Blvd, Cape Girardeau, MO 63701, 573-334-9181

Metro Business College (Branch Campus), 1407 Southwest Blvd, Jefferson City, MO 65109, 573-635-6600

Metro Business College (Branch Campus), PO Box 839, Rolla, MO 65401, 573-364-8464

Midwest Institute for Medical Assistants, 10910 Manchester Rd, Kirkwood, MO 63122, 314-965-8363

Missouri School of Barbering and Hairstyling, 1125 N Hwy 67, Florissant, MO 63031, 314-839-0310

Missouri School of Barbering and Hairstyling, 3740 Noland Rd, Independence, MO 64055, 816-836-4118

Nichols Career Center, 609 Union St, Jefferson City, MO 65101, 314-659-3000

Patricia Stevens College, 1415 Olive St, St Louis, MO 63103, 314-421-0949

Rolla Area Vocational-Technical School, 1304 E Tenth St, Rolla, MO 65401, 314-364-3726

Southwest School of Broadcasting, 1031 E Battlefield Rd #212B, Springfield, MO 65807, 417-883-4060

St. Louis College of Health Careers, 4484 W Pine Blvd, St Louis, MO 63108, 314-652-0300

St. Louis Symphony Community Music School, 560 Trinity Ave, St Louis, MO 63130, 314-863-3033

St. Louis Tech, 9741 St Charles Rock Rd, St Louis, MO 63114, 314-427-3600

Ste. Genevieve Beauty College, 755 Market St, Ste. Genevieve, MO 63670, 314-883-5550

TAD Technical Institute, 7910 Troost Ave, Kansas City, MO 64131, 816-361-5140

Trans World Travel Academy, 11495 Natural Bridge Rd, St Louis, MO 63044, 314-895-6754

Vanderschmidt School (The), 4625 Lindell Blvd, St Louis, MO 63108, 314-361-6000

Vatterott Educational Centers, 3854 Washington Ave, St Louis, MO 63108, 314-534-2586

Wright Business School (Branch Campus), 5528 NE Antioch Rd, Kansas City, MO 64119, 816-452-4411

State Licensing & Business Registration Quick Finder Index

Architecture, Engineering & Surveying
Architect #2 .... ☎ 573-751-0047
Engineer #2 .... ☎ 573-751-0047
Landscape Architect #27 (364) .... ☎ 573-751-0039
Landscape Architect Corporation and
  Partnership #27 .... ☎ 573-751-0039
Surveyor #2 .... ☎ 573-751-0047

Business - Court & Legal Services
Attorney #39 (23000) .... ☎ 573-635-4128
Court Reporter #12 .... ☎ 573-751-4144
Lobbyist #33 .... ☎ 573-751-2783
Notary Public #33 .... ☎ 573-751-2783
Shorthand Reporter #13 .... ☎ 417-962-4520

Business - General Services
Public Accountant Partnerships #1 .... ☎ 573-751-0012
Public Accountant-CPA #1 (6894) .... ☎ 573-751-0012

Construction & Manufacturing
Heating & Air Conditioning Mechanic #24 573-751-0293

Education
School Counselor #25 .... ☎ 573-751-4234
School Librarian #25 .... ☎ 573-751-4234
School Principal #25 .... ☎ 573-751-4234
School Superintendent #25 .... ☎ 573-751-4234
Teacher #25 .... ☎ 573-751-4234

Environmental & Agriculture
Landfill Operator #37 .... ☎ 573-751-5401
Pesticide Applicator #20 (6436) .... ✉ 573-751-5504
Pesticide Dealer #20 (981) .... ✉ 573-751-5504
Pesticide Technician #20 (2108) .... ✉ 573-751-9198
Veterinarian #31 (2647) .... ☎ 573-751-0031
Veterinary Technician #31 (396) .... ☎ 573-751-0031
Waste Water Operator #37 .... ☎ 314-751-1600
Water Supply Opertor #37 .... ☎ 314-751-1600

Financial - Real Estate, Insurance & Banking
Insurance Agent/Broker #22 573-751-4126
Investment Advisor #34 .... ☎ 573-751-4310
Real Estate Appraiser #14 (1581) .... ☎ 573-751-0038
Real Estate Broker #35 .... ☎ 573-751-0099
Real Estate Sales Agent #35 .... ☎ 573-751-2628
Securities Agent #34 .... ☎ 573-751-4310
Securities Broker/Dealer #34 .... ☎ 573-751-4310

Health & Beauty
Barber #3 (3601) .... ☎ 573-751-0805
Barber Instructor #3 .... ☎ 573-751-0805
Barber Shop #3 .... ☎ 573-751-0805
Cemetery (Endowed Care Cemetary) #26
  (98) .... ☎ 573-751-0849

Chiropractor #4 (1855) .... ☎ 573-751-2104
Clinical Audiologist #17 .... ☎ 573-751-0098
Combined Speech/Clinical Audiologist #17
.... ☎ 573-751-0098
Cosmetologist #5 (42519) .... ☎ 573-751-1052
Cosmetology Instructor #5 .... ☎ 573-751-1052
Cosmetology School #5 .... ☎ 573-751-1052
Cosmetology Shop #5 .... ☎ 573-751-1052
Dental Hygienist #19 (2168) .... ☎ 573-751-0040
Dental Specialist #19 (639) .... ☎ 573-751-0040
Dentist #19 (3534) .... ☎ 573-751-0040
Embalmer #6 (1306) .... ☎ 573-751-0813
Emergency Medical Technician (Basic) #21
  (6871) .... ☎ 573-751-6356
Emergency Medical Technician-Paramedic #21
.... ☎ 573-751-6356
Funeral Director #6 (3066) .... ☎ 573-751-0813
Funeral Establishment #6 .... ☎ 573-751-0813
Funeral Preneed Provider #6 .... ☎ 573-751-0813
Funeral Preneed Seller #6 .... ☎ 573-751-0813
Hearing Aid Dealer/Fitter #18 .... ☎ 573-751-0240
Manicurist #5 .... ☎ 573-751-1052
Medical Doctor #11 (15951) .... ☎ 573-751-0098
Nurse #7 .... ☎ 573-751-0681
Nursing Home Administrator #32 (1701) ...... ☎ 573-751-3511
Occupational Therapist #40 (1576) .... ☎ 573-751-0877
Occupational Therapy Assistant #40 .... ☎ 573-751-0877
Optometrist #8 (981) .... ☎ 573-751-0814
Osteopathic Physician #11 (3237) .... ☎ 573-751-0098
Pharmacist/Pharmacy Intern #9 (7500) .... ☎ 573-751-0092
Physical Therapist #11 (3529) .... ☎ 573-751-0098
Physician's Assistant #11 (116) .... ☎ 573-751-0098
Podiatrist #10 (215) .... ☎ 573-751-0873
Practical Nurse #7 .... ☎ 573-751-0681
Respiratory Care Practitioner #41 573-751-0877
Speech Pathologist/Audiologist (Speech-
  Language Pathologist) #17 (1616) .... ☎ 573-751-0098

Social Services
Child Care Facility #29 (4200) .... ☎ 573-751-2450
Professional Counselor #16 (1500) .... ☎ 573-751-0018
Psychologist #36 .... ☎ 573-751-2628
Social Worker (Clinical) #15 (5000) .... ☎ 573-751-0885
Substance Abuse Counselor #38 .... ☎ 573-751-0018

Sports & Entertainment
Athletic Trainer (Registrants) #28 (260) .... ☎ 573-751-0098
Horse Racing #30 .... ☎ 573-751-3565
Liquor Control #23 .... ✉ 573-751-2333
Professional Nurse #7 .... ☎ 573-751-0681

State Licensing & Business Registration Agency Information

(1) Board of Accountancy, 3605 Missouri Blvd, PO Box 613, Jefferson City, MO 65102-0613, 573-751-0012, Fax: 573-751-0890

(2) Board of Architects, Engineers & Land Survey, 3605 Missouri Blvd, PO Box 184, Jefferson City, MO 65109-0184, 573-751-0047, Fax: 573-751-8046

(3) Board of Barbers, 3605 Missouri Blvd, PO Box 1335, Jefferson City, MO 65102-1335, 573-751-0805, Fax: 573-526-8782

(4) Board of Chiropractic Examiners, 3605 Missouri Blvd, PO Box 672, Jefferson City, MO 65102-0672, 573-751-2104, Fax: 573-751-0735

(5) Board of Comsetology, 3605 Missouri Blvd, PO Box 1062, Jefferson City, MO 65102-1062, 573-751-1052, Fax: 573-751-8167

(6) Board of Embalmers & Funeral Directors, 3605 Missouri Blvd, PO Box 423, Jefferson City, MO 65102-0423, 573-751-0813, Fax: 573-751-1155

(7) Board of Nursing, 3605 Missouri Blvd, PO Box 1337, Jefferson City, MO 65102, 573-751-0681, Fax: 573-751-0075

(8) Board of Optometry, 3605 Missouri Blvd, PO Box 672, Jefferson City, MO 65102-0423, 573-751-0814, Fax: 573-751-0735

(9) Board of Pharmacy, 3605 Missouri Blvd, PO Box 625, Jefferson City, MO 65102-0625, 573-751-0091, Fax: 573-526-3464

(10) Board of Podiatric Medicine, 3605 Missouri Blvd, PO Box 423, Jefferson City, MO 65102-0423, 573-751-0873, Fax: 573-751-1155

(11) Board of Registration for Healing Arts, 3605 Missouri Blvd, PO Box 4, Jefferson City, MO 65102-0004, 573-751-0098, Fax: 573-751-3166

(12) CCR Contact Person, PO Box 150, Jefferson City, MO 65102, 573-751-4144, Fax: 573-751-7514

(13) CSR Contact Person, PO Box 405, Cabool, MO 65689, 417-865-1214

(14) Commission of Real Estate Appraisers, 3605 Missouri Blvd, PO Box 1335, Jefferson City, MO 65102, 573-751-0038, Fax: 573-526-2831

(15) Committee for Licensed Clinical Social Workers, Division of Professional Registration, 3605 Missouri Blvd, Jefferson City, MO 65102, 573-751-0885

(16) Committee of Professional Counselors, 3605 Missouri Blvd, PO Box 1335, Jefferson City, MO 65102-1335, 573-751-0018, Fax: 573-751-4176

(17) Committee of Speech Pathology & Audiology, 3605 Missouri Boulevard, PO Box 4, Jefferson City, MO 65102, 573-751-0098, Fax: 573-751-3166

(18) Council for Hearing Aid Dealers & Fitters, 3605 Missouri Blvd, PO Box 1335, Jefferson City, MO 65102-1335, 573-751-0240, Fax: 573-526-3489

(19) Dental Board, 3605 Missouri Blvd, PO Box 1367, Jefferson City, MO 65102-1367, 573-751-0040

(20) Department of Agriculture, Divison of Plant Industries, Bureau of Pesticide, PO Box 630, Jefferson City, MO 65102, 573-751-2462, Fax: 573-751-0005

(21) Department of Health, Emergency Medical Services, 1738 E Elm St, PO Box 570, Jefferson City, MO 65102-0570, 573-751-6356, Fax: 573-526-4102

(22) Department of Insurance, Licensing Section, PO Box 690, Jefferson City, MO 65102-0690, 573-751-4126, Fax: 573-526-3416

(23) Department of Public Safety, Division of Liquor Control, Truman Bldg, Room 870, PO Box 837, Jefferson City, MO 65102-0837, 573-751-2333, Fax: 573-526-4540

(24) Division of Professional Registration, Department of Economic Development, PO Box 1335, Jefferson City, MO 65102, 573-751-0293, Fax: 573-751-4176

(25) Education, Elementary & Secondary Instruction, 205 Jefferson St, PO Box 480, Jefferson City, MO 65102-0480, 573-751-4234

(26) Endowed Care Cemeteries, 3605 Missouri Blvd, PO Box 1335, Jefferson City, MO 65102-1335, 573-751-0849, Fax: 573-751-4176

(27) Landscape Architectural Council, 3605 Missouri Blvd, PO Box 1335, Jefferson City, MO 65102-, 573-751-0039, Fax: 573-526-2831

(28) Missouri Board of Healing Arts, 3605 Missouri Blvd, PO Box 4, Jefferson City, MO 65102-4, 573-751-0098, Fax: 573-751-3166

(29) Missouri Department of Health, Bureau of Child Care Safety & Licensure, PO Box 570, Jefferson City, MO 65102, 573-751-2450, Fax: 573-751-6010

(30) Missouri Gaming Commission, 3417 Knipp Dr, Jefferson City, MO 65109, 573-526-4080, Fax: 573-526-4084

(31) Missouri Veterinary Medical Board, 3605 Missouri Blvd, PO Box 633, Jefferson City, MO 65102-0633, 573-751-0031, Fax: 573-526-3856

(32) Nursing Home Licensing, 615 Howerton Court, PO Box 1337, Jefferson City, MO 65102-1337, 573-751-3511, Fax: 573-751-8493

(33) Office of Secretary of State, PO Box 778, Jefferson City, MO 65102, 573-751-2783

(34) Secretary of State, Securities Division, 1600 W Main St, Jefferson City, MO 65101, 573-751-4310, Fax: 573-526-3124

(35) State Commission of Real Estate, 3605 Missouri Blvd, PO Box 1339, Jefferson City, MO 65102-1339, 573-751-2628, Fax: 573-751-2777

(36) State Committee of Psychology, PO Box 1335, 3605 Misouri Blvd, Jefferson City, MO 65102-0153, 573-751-0099, Fax: 573-527-3489

(37) State Department of Natural Resources, Div of Environmental Quality, Solid Waste Mgmt, 205 Jefferson St, Jefferson City, MO 65102, 573-751-5401, Fax: 573-526-3902

(38) Substance Abuse Counselors Certification Board, Divison of Professional Registration, 3605 Missouri Blvd, Jefferson City, MO 65102, 573-751-0018, Fax: 573-526-3489

(39) The Missouri Bar, PO Box 119, 326 Monroe St, Jefferson City, MO 65102-0119, 573-635-4128, Fax: 573-635-2811

(40) Therapist Boards, 3605 Missouri Blvd, PO Box 1335, Jefferson City, MO 65102-1335, 573-751-0877, Fax: 573-751-4176

(41) Therapist Boards, 3605 Missouri Blvd, PO Box 1335, Jefferson City, MO 65102-1335, 573-751-0877, Fax: 573-751-4176

Montana

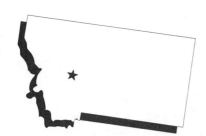

Capitol: Helena (Lewis and Clark County)	
State Population	**.8 Million**
Number of Degree Granting Institutions:	**22**
Number of State Licensing & Business Registration Agencies:	**94**

Degree Granting Educational Institutions

Blackfeet Community College, Registrar, Browning, MT 59417, 406-338-3197 (Fax: 406-338-7808). Hours: 8AM-4PM. Enrollment: 437. Degrees granted: Associate.

Attendance and degree information available by phone, fax, mail. Search requires name only. Also helpful: SSN, date of birth, exact years of attendance. There is no fee.

Carroll College, Registrar, N Benton Ave, Helena, MT 59625, 406-447-5435 (Fax: 406-447-4533). Hours: 9AM-4PM. Enrollment: 1412. Records go back to 1910. Alumni records are maintained here also. Call 406-447-5413. Degrees granted: Associate; Bachelors. Adverse incident record source- Student Affairs, 406-447-4531.

Attendance and degree information available by fax. Search requires name only. Also helpful: SSN, date of birth, exact years of attendance. There is no fee.

Dawson Community College, Registrar, Glendive, MT 59330, 406-365-3396 (Fax: 406-365-8132). Hours: 8AM-4:30PM. Enrollment: 700. Records go back to 1940. Alumni records are maintained here at the same phone number. Degrees granted: Associate.

Attendance information available by phone. Search requires name only. Also helpful: SSN, date of birth. There is no fee.

Degree information available by phone. Search requires name only. Also helpful: exact years of attendance. There is no fee.

Dull Knife Memorial College, Registrar, PO Box 98, Lame Deer, MT 59043, 406-477-6215 X305 (Fax: 406-477-6219). Enrollment: 300. Records go back to 1976. Degrees granted: Associate. Special programs- Business Office Management. Adverse incident record source- Academic Dean.

Attendance and degree information available by phone, mail. Search requires name plus SSN, exact years of attendance. There is no fee.

Flathead Valley Community College, Registrar, 777 Grandview Dr, Kalispell, MT 59901, 406-756-3822 (Fax: 406-756-3965). Hours: 8AM-5PM. Enrollment: 2000. Records go back to 1967. Alumni records are maintained here also. Call 406-756-3962. Degrees granted: Associate. Certification: Office Technology, Business Management, Accounting Technology, Law Management, Medical Assistant.

Attendance and degree information available by phone, fax, mail. Search requires name plus SSN. Also helpful: date of birth, exact years of attendance. There is no fee.

Fort Belknap College, Registrar, PO Box 159, Harlem, MT 59526-0159, 406-353-2607 X20 (Fax: 406-353-2898). Hours: 8AM-5PM. Enrollment: 385. Records go back to 1988. Degrees granted: Associate. Certification: Computer Applications. Special programs- Native American Languages, Cultural Courses. Adverse incident record source- Student Services.

Attendance and degree information available by phone, fax, mail. Search requires name plus SSN, exact years of attendance. There is no fee.

Fort Peck Community College, Registrar, PO Box 398, Poplar, MT 59255, 406-768-5551 (Fax: 406-768-5552). Hours: 8AM-4:30PM. Enrollment: 450. Records go back to 1980. Degrees granted: Associate.

Attendance and degree information available by phone, fax, mail. Search requires name only. Also helpful: SSN, date of birth. There is no fee.

Helena College of Technology of the University of Montana, Registrar, 115 N Roberts St, Helena, MT 59620, 406-444-6800 (Fax: 406-444-6892). Hours: 8AM-5PM. Records go back to 1939. Degrees granted: Associate.

Attendance and degree information available by phone, mail. Search requires name only. Also helpful: date of birth, exact years of attendance. There is no fee.

Little Big Horn College, Registrar, PO Box 370, Crow Agency, MT 59022, 406-638-7212 (Fax: 406-638-7213). Hours: 8AM-5PM. Enrollment: 250. Records go back to 1984. Degrees granted: Associate. Special programs- Pre Nursing & Pre Medical.

Attendance and degree information available by mail. Search requires name only. There is no fee.

Miles Community College, Registrar, Miles City, MT 59301, 406-232-3031 (Fax: 406-232-5705). Hours: 7:30AM-5PM. Enrollment: 550. Records go back to 1939. Alumni records are maintained here also. Call 406-732-3031 X16. Degrees granted: Associate. Special programs- Nursing Dept, 406-732-3031. Adverse incident record source- Dean of Student Services.

Attendance and degree information available by phone, fax, mail. Search requires name only. Also helpful: SSN, date of birth, exact years of attendance. There is no fee.

Montana State University College of Technology-Great Falls, Registrar, 2100 16th Ave S, Great Falls, MT 59405, 406-771-4300 (Fax: 406-453-6769). Hours: 8AM-5PM. Enrollment: 1100. Records go back to 1969. Degrees granted: Associate.

Attendance and degree information available by phone, mail. Search requires name plus SSN, date of birth, exact years of attendance. There is no fee.

Montana State University-Billings, Registrar, 1500 N 30th, Billings, MT 59101, 406-657-2880 (Fax: 406-657-2302). Hours: 8AM-5PM. Enrollment: 3700. Records go back to 1927. Alumni records are maintained here also. Call 406-657-2244. Degrees granted: Associate; Bachelors; Masters. Special programs- Vocational, 406-656-4445 X120. Adverse incident record source- Registrar's Office, 406-657-1600 .

Attendance and degree information available by phone, fax, mail. Search requires name plus SSN, date of birth. Also helpful: exact years of attendance. There is no fee.

Montana State University-Bozeman, Registrar, Bozeman, MT 59717, 406-994-0211 (Fax: 406-994-1972). Hours: 8AM-5PM. Enrollment: 11000. Records go back to 1893. Alumni Records Office: Alumni Association, 1501 S 11th, Bozeman, MT 59717. Degrees granted: Bachelors; Masters; Doctorate. Special programs- Architecture & Agriculture Programs. Adverse incident record source- Dean of Students.

Attendance and degree information available by phone, fax, mail. Search requires name plus SSN. Also helpful: date of birth, exact years of attendance. There is no fee.

Montana Tech of the University of Montana, Registrar, 1300 W Park St, Butte, MT 59701-8997, 406-496-4256 (Fax: 406-496-4710). Hours: 8AM-4:30PM. Enrollment: 1800. Records go back to 1900. Alumni records are maintained here also. Call 406-496-4278. Degrees granted: Associate; Bachelors; Masters. Special programs- Minerals, Energy & Invironmental Engineering, 406-496-4178.

Attendance information available by phone, fax, mail. Search requires name plus SSN, approximate years of attendance. Also helpful: exact years of attendance. There is no fee.

Degree information available by phone, fax, mail. Search requires name plus SSN, date of birth, approximate years of attendance. Also helpful: exact years of attendance. There is no fee.

Montana Tech of the University of Montana-College of Technology, Registrar, 25 Basin Creek Rd, Butte, MT 59701, 406-496-3732 (Fax: 406-496-3710). Hours: 7:30AM-5PM. Enrollment: 340. Records go back to 1969. Degrees granted: Associate. Adverse incident record source- Student Services, 406-496-3730.

Attendance and degree information available by phone, fax, mail. Search requires name only. Also helpful: SSN, date of birth, exact years of attendance. There is no fee.

Rocky Mountain College, Registrar, 1511 Poly Dr, Billings, MT 59102, 406-657-1030 (Fax: 406-259-9251). Hours: 10AM-Noon, 1-4:30PM. Enrollment: 800. Records go back to 1900. Alumni records are maintained here also. Call 406-657-1009. Degrees granted: Associate; Bachelors.

Attendance information available by phone, fax, mail. Search requires name plus SSN. There is no fee.

Degree information available by phone, fax, mail. Search requires name plus SSN. Also helpful: approximate years of attendance. There is no fee.

Salish Kootenai College, Registrar, PO Box 117, Pablo, MT 59855, 406-675-4800 (Fax: 406-675-4801). Enrollment: 100. Records go back to 1977. Alumni records are maintained here at the same phone number. Degrees granted: Associate; Bachelors. Special programs- Native American Studies: Nursing: Dental: Truck Driving. Adverse incident record source- Registrar.

Attendance and degree information available by phone, fax, mail. Search requires name plus SSN, date of birth. Also helpful: exact years of attendance. There is no fee.

Stone Child Community College, Registrar, RR 1 Box 1082, Box Elder, MT 59521-9796, 406-395-4313 (Fax: 406-395-4836). Hours: 8AM-4:30PM. Enrollment: 250. Records go back to 1990. Degrees granted: Associate. Adverse incident record source- Local Police, 406-395-4513.

Attendance information available by phone, fax, mail. Search requires name plus SSN. There is no fee.

Degree information available by phone, fax, mail. Search requires name plus SSN, date of birth. There is no fee.

University of Great Falls, Registrar, 1301 20th St S, Great Falls, MT 59405, 406-791-5200 (Fax: 406-791-5209). Hours: 8AM-4:30PM. Enrollment: 1400. Formerly College of Great Falls Records go back to 1932. Alumni records are maintained here also. Call 406-791-5291. Degrees granted: Associate; Bachelors; Masters.

Attendance and degree information available by phone, fax, mail. Search requires name plus approximate years of attendance. Also helpful: SSN, date of birth, exact years of attendance. There is no fee.

University of Montana, Registrar, Missoula, MT 59812, 406-243-2995 (Fax: 406-243-4087). Hours: 9AM-4PM. Enrollment: 11000. Records go back to 1893. Alumni records are maintained here also. Call 406-243-5211. Degrees granted: Associate; Bachelors; Masters; Doctorate. Certification: Elementary & Secondary Education. Adverse incident record source- Campus Police, 406-243-6131: Student Services

Attendance and degree information available by phone, fax, mail. Search requires name plus SSN, approximate years of attendance. Also helpful: date of birth, exact years of attendance. There is no fee.

University of Montana-Missoula/College of Technology, Registrar, 909 South Ave W, Missoula, MT 59801, 406-243-7887 (Fax: 406-243-7899). Enrollment: 650. Records go back to 1969. Alumni Records Office: Alumni Association, University of Montana-Missoula, Brantley Hall Rm 115, Missoula, MT 59812. Degrees granted: Associate; Certificates of Completion (programs under 2 years).

Attendance and degree information available by phone, fax, mail. Search requires name plus approximate years of attendance. Also helpful: SSN, date of birth, exact years of attendance. There is no fee.

Western Montana College of the University of Montana, Registrar's Office, 710 S Atlantic St, Dillon, MT 59725-3598, 406-683-7371 (Fax: 406-683-7493). Hours: 8AM-5PM. Enrollment: 1176. Records go back to 1897. Alumni records are maintained here at the same phone number. Degrees granted: Associate; Bachelors.

Attendance information available by written request only. Search requires name plus SSN, date of birth, signed release. Also helpful: exact years of attendance. There is no fee.

Degree information available by phone, fax, mail. Search requires name plus SSN. Also helpful: date of birth, exact years of attendance. There is no fee.

Trade and Vocational Schools

Big Sky College of Barber Styling, 750 Kensington Ave, Missoula, MT 59801, 406-721-5588

Billings Business College, 2520 Fifth Ave S, Billings, MT 59101, 406-256-1000

Billings School of Barbering and Hairstyling, 206 N 13th St, Billings, MT 59101, 406-259-9369

May Technical College, 1306 Central Ave, Billings, MT 59102, 406-259-7000

May Technical College (Branch Campus), 1807 Third St NW, Great Falls, MT 59404, 406-761-4000

Sage Technical Services, 1148 16th St W, Billings, MT 59102, 406-652-3030

State Licensing & Business Registration Quick Finder Index

Architecture, Engineering & Surveying
Architect #8 .... ☎ 406-444-3745
Engineer #9 .... ☎ 406-444-4285
Landscape Architect #8 (31) 406-444-5433
Surveyor #9... ☎ 406-444-4285

Business - Court & Legal Services
Attorney #2 (3400) .... ☎ 406-444-3858
Lobbyist #3 (800) .... ☎ 406-444-2942
Notary Public #19 (5) .... ☎ 406-444-5379
Shorthand Reporter #17 (7) .... ☎ 406-721-1143

Business - General Services
Employment Agency #9 .... ☎ 406-444-4370
Public Accountant #9 (1378).......................... ☎ 406-444-3739

Construction & Manufacturing
Construction Blaster #7 .... ☎ 406-494-4291
Contractor #20 .... ☎ 406-444-4395
Electrician #23 .... ☎ 406-444-4390
Plumber #1 .... ☎ 406-444-4390

Education
School Guidance Counselor #18 .... ☎ 406-444-3150
School Librarian #18 .... ☎ 406-444-3150
School Principal #18.. ☎ 406-444-3150
School Superintendent #18.............................. ☎ 406-444-3150
Teacher #18 .... ☎ 406-444-3150

Environmental & Agriculture
Asbestos Abatement Contractor/Supplier
  (Supervisor) #10.. ☎ 406-444-3671
Asbestos Abatement Project Designer #10 .... ☎ 406-444-3671
Asbestos Inspector/Worker (Asbestos Inspector
  /Asbestos Abatement Worker) #10............. ☎ 406-444-3671
Asbestos Management Planner #10 .... ☎ 406-444-3671
Fur/Hide Dealer #13 .... ☎ 406-444-4558
Milk & Cream Tester #16................................ ☎ 406-444-2043
Milk & Cream Weigher, Grader, Sampler #16
  .... ☎ 406-444-2043
Nurseryman #4 (750)....................................... ☎ 406-444-5400
Pesticide Applicator #4 (1500)........................ ☎ 406-444-5400
Pesticide Dealer #4 (500) .... ☎ 406-444-5400
Septic Tank Cleaner #10 .... ☎ 406-444-3671
Underground Storage Tank Inspector #10 ..... ☎ 406-444-3671
Underground Storage Tank Installer
  /Remover #10 .... ☎ 406-444-3671
Veterinarian #9 .... ☎ 406-444-5436
Water & Sewage Plant Operator #10 .... ☎ 406-444-3671
Weather Modifier #24 .... ☎ 406-444-6601

Financial - Real Estate, Insurance & Banking
Advisor Representative #21............................. ☎ 406-444-2040
Appraiser #8 (447)... ☎ 406-444-3561
Insurance Adjuster #21 .... ☎ 406-444-2040
Insurance Agent #21 .... ☎ 406-444-2040
Securities Broker/Salesperson #22 .... ☎ 406-444-2040
Solicitor/Advisor #21...................................... ☎ 406-444-2040
Timeshare Broker/Salesperson #9 .... ☎ 406-444-4294

Health & Beauty
Acupuncturist #9... ☎ 406-444-4285
Barber #8 (794)... ☎ 406-444-4288
Chiropractor #8 (214)...................................... 406-444-5433
Cosmetologist #8 (5086).................................. ☎ 406-444-4288
Dentistry #8.. ☎ 406-444-3745
Dietitian #9... ☎ 406-444-4285
Electrologist #9 .... ☎ 406-444-4285
Emergency Medical Technician #9 .... ☎ 406-444-4285
Hearing Aid Dispenser #8 (73)........................ 406-444-5433
Lay Midwife #9... ☎ 406-444-5436
Manicurist (Manager/Operator) #8 (451)........ ☎ 406-444-4288
Medical Doctor #9 .... ☎ 406-444-4284
Mortician #8 (149)... 406-444-5433
Nurse, RN/LPN #9 (14000)............................. ☎ 406-444-1696
Nutritionist #9... ☎ 406-444-4285
Occupational Therapist #9 (290) .... ☎ 406-444-3091
Optometrist #9 (250).. ☎ 406-444-1698
Osteopath Physician #9................................... ☎ 406-444-4285
Pharmacist #9 (1227) .... ☎ 406-444-1698
Physical Therapist #9 (883)............................. ☎ 406-444-3728
Podiatrist #9 .... ☎ 406-444-4285
Radiologic Technologists #9 (950) .... ☎ 406-444-3091
Respiratory Therapist #9 (400)........................ ☎ 406-444-3091
Sanitarian #9 (170).. ☎ 406-444-3091
Speech Pathologist/Audiologist #9 (320)........ ☎ 406-444-3091

Investigations & Security
Polygraph Examiner #9 .... ☎ 406-444-7763
Private Security Patrolman & Investigator #9
  (897) .... ☎ 406-444-3728

Social Services
Adoption Agency #12....................................... ☎ 406-444-6587
Chemical Dependency Counselor #14 (500)
  .... ☎ 406-444-2827
Child Care Agency #12.................................... ☎ 406-444-6587
Day Care Program #11 (2000)......................... ☎ 406-444-5919
Foster Care Program #12 (1000) .... ☎ 406-444-6587

Professional Counselor #9 .... ☎ 406-444-4285
Psychologists #9 .... ☎ 406-444-5436
Social Worker #9 .... ☎ 406-444-4285
Youth Group Home #12 .... ☎ 406-444-6587

Sports & Entertainment
Athletic Trainer #8 406-444-5433
Calcutta #15 .... ✉ 406-444-1971
Card Contractor #15 .... ✉ 406-444-1971
Card Dealer #15 .... ✉ 406-444-1971
Card Tournaments #15 .... ✉ 406-444-1791
Casino Night #15 .... ✉ 406-444-1971
Gambling Operator #15 (1752) .... ✉ 406-444-1971

Gaming Manufacturer/Distributor #15 .... ✉ 406-444-1971
Horse Racing #5 .... ☎ 406-444-4287
Jockey #5 .... ☎ 406-444-4287
Live Card Table #15 .... ✉ 406-444-1971
Lottery Retailer #6 (672) .... ☎ 406-444-5825
Outfitter #9 (300) .... ☎ 406-444-3738
Taxidermist #13 .... ☎ 406-444-4558
Video Gambling Machine #15 .... ✉ 406-444-1971

Transportation
Passenger Tramways #9 (73) .... ☎ 406-444-3561

State Licensing & Business Registration Agency Information

(1) Board of Plumbers, 1218 E 6th Ave, Helena, MT 59620, 406-444-4390

(2) Clerk of Superior Court, Bar Association, 215 N Sanders, Room 323, Justice Bldg, Helena, MT 59620, 406-444-3858, Fax: 406-444-5705

(3) Commissioner of Political Practices, Capitol Station, Helena, MT 59620, 406-444-2942, Fax: 406-444-1643

(4) Department of Agriculture, PO Box 200201, Helena, MT 59620, 406-444-2944, Fax: 406-444-5409

(5) Department of Commerce, Board of Horse Racing, 1520 E 6th Ave, Room 50, PO Box 200512, Helena, MT 59620-0512, 406-444-4287

(6) Department of Commerce, Montana Lottery, 2525 N Montana Ave, PO Box 200544, Helena, MT 59620-0544, 406-444-5825, Fax: 406-444-5830

(7) Department of Commerce, Occupational Professional Licensing, 111 Jackson Street, Helena, MT 59601, 406-444-4291

(8) Department of Commerce, Professional & Occupational Licensing Bureau, 111 N Jackson, PO Box 200513, Helena, MT 59620-0513, 406-444-7763, Fax: 406-444-1667

(9) Department of Commerce, Professional & Occupational Licensing Bureau, 111 N Jackson, PO Box 200513, Helena, MT 59620-0513, 406-444-5436, Fax: 406-444-1667

(10) Department of Environmental Quality, Permitting and Compliance Division, PO Box 200901, 1520 E. 6th Ave., Helena, MT 59620, 406-444-3671

(11) Department of Family Services, Early Childhood Unit Services, PO Box 8005, Helena, MT 59604-8005, 406-444-5919

(12) Department of Family Services, Research & Planning Bureau, 48 N Last Chance Gulch, PO Box 204001, Helena, MT 59620-4001, 406-444-6587, Fax: 406-444-5956

(13) Department of Fish, Wildlife & Parks, Licensing/Data Bureau, Fish, Wildlife & Parks Bldg, 1420 E 6th Ave, Helena, MT 59620-0701, 406-444-4558

(14) Department of Institutions, Chemical Dependancy Bureau, 1400 Broadway RM C-118, Helena, MT 59620, 406-444-2827, Fax: 406-444-4435

(15) Department of Justice, Gambling Control Division, 2687 Airport Rd, PO Box 201424, Helena, MT 59620-1424, 406-444-1971, Fax: 406-444-9157

(16) Department of Livestock, Capitol Station, Helena, MT 59620, 406-444-2043

(17) Jeffries Court Reporting, CSR Contact Person, 690 SW Higgins, Lewis & Clark Bldg, Missoula, MT 59801, 406-721-1143, Fax: 406-728-0888

(18) Office of Public Instruction, Certification Division, State Capitol, Room 106, PO Box 202501, Helena, MT 59620-2501, 406-444-3150, Fax: 406-444-2893

(19) Office of Secretary of State, 225 State Capitol, Helena, MT 59620, 406-444-5379, Fax: 406-444-3976

(20) Public Contractors Licensing, PO Box 200513, 111 N Jackson, Helena, MT 59620-0513, 406-444-4390

(21) State Auditor's Office, Insurance Licensing Division, Box 200301, Helena, MT 59620-0301, 406-444-2040

(22) State Auditor's Office, Securities Department, Box 200301, Helena, MT 59620-0301, 406-444-2040, Fax: 406-444-5558

(23) State Electrical Board, 111 N Jackson, Helena, MT 59620, 406-444-4390, Fax: 406-444-1667

(24) Water Resources Division, 58 North Last Chance Circle, Helena, MT 59620, 406-444-6601, Fax: 406-444-5918

Nebraska

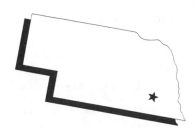

Capitol: Lincoln (Lancaster County)	
State Population	**1.6 Million**
Number of Degree Granting Institutions:	**39**
Number of State Licensing & Business Registration Agencies:	**89**

Degree Granting Educational Institutions

Bellevue University, Registrar, Galvin Rd at Harvell Dr, Bellevue, NE 68005, 402-293-3780 (Fax: 402-293-2020). Hours: 8AM-5PM. Enrollment: 2400. Records go back to 1966. Alumni records are maintained here also. Call 402-293-3707. Degrees granted: Bachelors; Masters. Adverse incident record source- Student Services, 402-293-2087.

Attendance and degree information available by phone, fax, mail. Search requires name only. Also helpful: SSN, date of birth, exact years of attendance. There is no fee.

Bishop Clarkson College, Registrar, 333 S 44th St, Omaha, NE 68131, 402-552-3033 (Fax: 402-552-6057). Enrollment: 500. Records go back to 1880. Alumni records are maintained here at the same phone number. Degrees granted: Associate; Bachelors; Masters. Special programs- Nursing: Administrative Health Services. Adverse incident record source- Security.

Attendance and degree information available by phone, mail. Search requires name plus SSN, approximate years of attendance. There is no fee.

Central Community College, Registrar, PO Box 4903, Grand Island, NE 68802-4903, 308-384-5220 (Fax: 308-389-6398). Enrollment: 1500. Records go back to 1976. Alumni Records Office: 2727 W 2nd #211, Hastings, NE 68101, 402-462-4000. Degrees granted: Associate. Adverse incident record source- Student Services, 308-389-6405.

Attendance and degree information available by mail. Search requires name plus SSN, approximate years of attendance. Also helpful: date of birth, exact years of attendance. There is no fee.

Central Technical Community College, Registrar, PO Box 1024, Hastings, NE 68902-1024, 402-463-9811 (Fax: 402-461-2454). Hours: 9AM-5PM. Enrollment: 1700. Records go back to 1966. Alumni Records Office: Alumni Association, Central Technical Community College, 2727 W 2nd, Hastings, NE 68901. Degrees granted: Associate. Adverse incident record source- Security Office, 402-461-4452.

Attendance and degree information available by phone, fax, mail. Search requires name plus approximate years of attendance. Also helpful: SSN, date of birth, exact years of attendance. There is no fee.

Chadron State College, Registrar, 1000 Main St, Chadron, NE 69337, 308-432-6221 (Fax: 308-432-6229). Hours: 8AM-5PM. Enrollment: 3200. Records go back to 1911. Alumni records are maintained here also. Call 308-432-6362. Degrees granted: Bachelors; Masters. Special programs- Health Opportunities Program, 888-298-2293. Adverse incident record source- Student Services, 308-432-6231.

Attendance and degree information available by phone, fax, mail. Search requires name plus SSN. Also helpful: date of birth, exact years of attendance. There is no fee.

Clarkson College, Registrar, 101 S 42nd St, Omaha, NE 68131, 402-552-3041 (Fax: 402-552-6057). Hours: 8AM-5PM. Enrollment: 600. Records go back to 1869. Alumni records are maintained here also. Call 402-552-3439. Degrees granted: Associate; Bachelors; Masters. Certification: Nurse Practitioner.

Attendance and degree information available by phone, fax, mail. Search requires name plus SSN, approximate years of attendance. Also helpful: date of birth, exact years of attendance. There is no fee.

College of St. Mary, Registrar, 1901 S 72nd St, Omaha, NE 68124, 402-399-2443 (Fax: 402-399-2341). Hours: 9AM-5PM. Enrollment: 1100. Records go back to 1923. Alumni records are maintained here also. Call 402-399-2456. Degrees granted: Associate; Bachelors. Adverse incident record source- Business Manager.

Attendance information available by phone, mail. Search requires name only. Also helpful: SSN, date of birth. There is no fee.

Degree information available by phone, mail. Search requires name only. There is no fee.

Concordia College, Registrar, 800 N Columbia Ave, Seward, NE 68434, 402-643-7230 (Fax: 402-643-4073). Hours: 8AM-5PM. Enrollment: 1150. Records go back to 1894. Alumni records are maintained here also. Call 402-643-7276. Degrees granted: Bachelors; Masters. Certification: Lutheran Teacher Diploma. Adverse incident record source- Student Services, 402-643-7231.

Attendance and degree information available by phone, fax, mail. Search requires name only. Also helpful: SSN, exact years of attendance. There is no fee.

Creighton University, Registrar, 2500 California Plaza, Omaha, NE 68178, 402-280-2701 (Fax: 402-280-2527). Hours: 8:30AM-4:30PM. Enrollment: 6300. Records go back to 1878. Alumni records are maintained here also. Call 402-280-2222. Degrees granted: Associate; Bachelors; Masters; Doctorate.

Attendance and degree information available by fax, mail. Search requires name only. Also helpful: SSN, date of birth, approximate years of attendance. There is no fee.

Dana College, Registrar, 2848 College Dr, Blair, NE 68008, 402-426-7209 (Fax: 402-426-7386). Hours: 8AM-5PM. Enrollment: 575. Records go back to 1930. Alumni records are maintained here also. Call 402-426-7235. Degrees granted: Bachelors.

Attendance and degree information available by phone, fax, mail. Search requires name plus approximate years of attendance. Also helpful: SSN, date of birth, exact years of attendance. There is no fee.

Doane College, Registrar, 1014 Boswell Ave, Crete, NE 68333, 402-826-8251 (Fax: 402-826-8600). Hours: 8AM-Noon, 12:30-4:30PM. Enrollment: 1700. Records go back to 1975. Alumni records are maintained here also. Call 402-826-8258. Degrees granted: Bachelors; Masters.

Attendance and degree information available by phone, fax, mail. Search requires name plus SSN. Also helpful: date of birth, exact years of attendance. There is no fee. Expedited service available for $5.00.

Grace University, Registrar, Ninth and William, Omaha, NE 68108, 402-449-2811 (Fax: 402-341-9587). Hours: 8AM-Noon, 1-5PM. Enrollment: 500. Records go back to 1943. Alumni records are maintained here also. Call 402-449-2815. Degrees granted: Associate; Bachelors; Masters.

Attendance information available by phone, fax, mail. Search requires name only. Also helpful: SSN, date of birth, exact years of attendance. There is no fee.

Degree information available by phone, mail. Search requires name only. Also helpful: SSN, date of birth, exact years of attendance. There is no fee.

Hastings College, Registrar, 800 N Turner Ave, PO Box 269, Hastings, NE 68902-0269, 402-461-7306 (Fax: 402-461-7490). Hours: 8AM-Noon, 1-5PM. Enrollment: 1165. Records go back to 1883. Alumni records are maintained here also. Call 402-461-7474. Degrees granted: Bachelors. Special programs- MAT Graduate Program, 402-461-7388. Adverse incident record source- Business Office, 402-461-7300.

Attendance information available by phone, fax, mail. Search requires name plus SSN. Also helpful: date of birth, exact years of attendance. There is no fee.

Degree information available by phone, fax, mail. Search requires name plus approximate years of attendance. Also helpful: SSN, date of birth, exact years of attendance. There is no fee.

ITT Technical Institute, (Branch of Earth City, MO), Registrar, 9814 M St, Omaha, NE 68127-2056, 402-331-2900 (Fax: 402-331-9495). Hours: 7:30AM-5PM. Enrollment: 150. Records go back to 1990. Degrees granted: Associate.

Attendance information available by phone. Search requires name plus approximate years of attendance. There is no fee.

Degree information available by fax, mail. Search requires name plus approximate years of attendance. There is no fee.

Lincoln School of Commerce, Registrar, PO Box 82826, 1821 K St, Lincoln, NE 68501-2826, 402-474-5315. Hours: 8AM-10PM. Records go back to 1885. Alumni records are maintained here at the same phone number. Degrees granted: Associate.

Attendance and degree information available by phone, fax, mail. Search requires name plus SSN, exact years of attendance. Also helpful: approximate years of attendance. There is no fee.

McCook Community College, Registrar, 1205 E Third St, McCook, NE 69001, 800-658-4348 (Fax: 308-345-3305). Hours: 8AM-5:30PM M-Th, 8AM-4PM F. Enrollment: 980. Records go back to 1926. Alumni records are maintained here at the same phone number. Degrees granted: Associate. Adverse incident record source- Student Services, 308-345-6303.

Attendance and degree information available by phone, mail. Search requires name plus SSN, date of birth, exact years of attendance. There is no fee.

Metropolitan Community College, Registrar, PO Box 3777, Omaha, NE 68103, 402-449-8400.

Attendance and degree information available by phone, fax, mail. Search requires name plus SSN. Also helpful: date of birth, exact years of attendance. There is no fee.

Mid-Plains Community College, Registrar's Office, 1101 Halligan Dr, North Platte, NE 69101, 308-532-8740 (Fax: 308-532-8494). Hours: 8AM-5PM. Enrollment: 2000. Records go back to 1965. Degrees granted: Associate.

Attendance and degree information available by phone, fax, mail. Search requires name plus SSN. Also helpful: date of birth, exact years of attendance. There is no fee.

Midland Lutheran College, Registrar, 900 Clarkson St, Fremont, NE 68025, 402-721-5480 X6220 (Fax: 402-721-0250). Hours: 8AM-4:30PM. Enrollment: 1030. Records go back to 1883. Alumni records are maintained here at the same phone number. Degrees granted: Associate; Bachelors. Adverse incident record source- Student Services.

Attendance information available by phone, fax, mail. Search requires name plus approximate years of attendance. Also helpful: SSN, date of birth, exact years of attendance. There is no fee.

Degree information available by phone, fax, mail. Search requires name only. Also helpful: SSN, date of birth, approximate years of attendance. There is no fee.

Nebraska Christian College, Registrar, 1800 Syracuse St, Norfolk, NE 68701, 402-371-5960 (Fax: 402-371-5967). Hours: 8AM-5PM. Enrollment: 150. Records go back to 1944. Alumni records are maintained here at the same phone number. Degrees granted: Bachelors. Adverse incident record source- Dean of Students, 402-371-5960.

Attendance and degree information available by phone, mail. Search requires name only. Also helpful: exact years of attendance. There is no fee.

Nebraska College of Business, Registrar, 3350 N 90th St, Omaha, NE 68134-4710, 402-553-8500 (Fax: 402-573-1341). Hours: 9AM-6PM. Enrollment: 300. Records go back to 1940's. Alumni records are maintained here at the same phone number. Degrees granted: Associate. Special programs- Medical Program, 402-553-8500. Adverse incident record source- Student Services, 402-553-8500.

Attendance and degree information available by phone, fax, mail. Search requires name plus SSN, date of birth, approximate years of attendance. Also helpful: exact years of attendance. There is no fee.

Nebraska College of Technical Agriculture, Registrar, Curtis, NE 69025, 308-367-4124 (Fax: 308-367-5203). Hours: 8AM-5PM. Enrollment: 325. Records go back to 1967. Alumni records are maintained here also. Call 308-367-4124. Degrees granted: Associate.

Attendance and degree information available by phone, mail. Search requires name plus SSN, exact years of attendance. There is no fee.

Nebraska Indian Community College, Registrar, PO Box 428, Macy, NE 68039, 402-878-2414 (Fax: 402-878-2522). Hours: 8AM-5PM. Enrollment: 100. Records go

back to 1980. Alumni records are maintained here at the same phone number. Degrees granted: Associate. Adverse incident record source- Registrar's Office, 402-878-2414 .

School will not confirm attendance or degree information.

Nebraska Methodist College of Nursing and Allied Health, Registrar, 8501 W Dodge Rd, Omaha, NE 68114, 402-390-4879. Enrollment: 453. Alumni records are maintained here also. Call 402-354-4952. Degrees granted: Associate; Bachelors.

Attendance information available by written request only. Search requires name plus signed release. Also helpful: SSN, exact years of attendance. There is no fee.

Degree information available by phone, fax, mail. Search requires name only. Also helpful: SSN, exact years of attendance. There is no fee.

Nebraska Wesleyan University, Registrar, 5000 St Paul Ave, Lincoln, NE 68504, 402-465-2242 (Fax: 402-465-2179). Hours: 8AM-5PM. Enrollment: 1600. Records go back to 1887. Alumni records are maintained here also. Call 402-465-2316. Degrees granted: Bachelors. Adverse incident record source- Student Affairs.

Attendance and degree information available by phone, fax, mail. Search requires name only. Also helpful: SSN, date of birth, exact years of attendance. There is no fee.

Northeast Community College, Dir, Enrollment Management, 801 E Benjamin Ave, PO Box 469, Norfolk, NE 68702-0469, 402-644-0415 (Fax: 402-644-0650). Hours: 8AM-5PM. Enrollment: 5000. Records go back to 1928. Alumni records are maintained here also. Call 402-644-0463. Degrees granted: Associate.

Attendance and degree information available by phone, fax, mail. Search requires name plus SSN. Also helpful: date of birth, exact years of attendance. There is no fee.

Peru State College, Registrar, Peru, NE 68421, 402-872-2239 (Fax: 402-872-2375). Hours: 8:30AM-4:30PM. Enrollment: 1900. Records go back to 1867. Alumni Records Office: PO Box 10, Peru, NE 68421. Degrees granted: Associate; Bachelors; Masters.

Attendance and degree information available by phone, mail. Search requires name plus SSN. Also helpful: date of birth, exact years of attendance. There is no fee.

Platte Valley Bible College, Registrar, Box 1227, Scottsbluff, NE 69363, 308-632-6933 (Fax: 308-632-8599). Enrollment: 85. Records go back to 1951. Alumni records are maintained here at the same phone number. Degrees granted: Associate; Bachelors. Special programs- Arts: Science. Adverse incident record source- Department of Student Affairs.

Attendance and degree information available by phone, mail. Search requires name plus SSN, exact years of attendance. There is no fee.

Southeast Community College, Registrar, 8800 O St, Lincoln, NE 68520, 402-437-2609 (Fax: 402-437-2404). Hours: 8AM-8PM M-Th; 8AM-5PM F. Enrollment: 4600. Records go back to 1970. Degrees granted: Associate. Special programs- Motorcycle/Small Engines Program: Health Trades: Fire Protection. Adverse incident record source- Corrections Division, 402-479-6144.

Attendance and degree information available by phone, fax, mail. Search requires name plus approximate years of attendance. Also helpful: SSN, date of birth, exact years of attendance. There is no fee.

Spencer School of Business, Registrar, PO Box 399, 410 W Second St, Grand Island, NE 68802, 308-382-8044 (Fax: 308-382-5072). Hours: 7:30AM-5PM. Enrollment: 125. Records go back to 1983. See alternate location before 1983.

Degrees granted: Associate. Adverse incident record source- Registrar, 308-382-8044.

Attendance and degree information available by phone, fax, mail. Search requires name plus SSN, exact years of attendance. There is no fee.

Union College, Records, 3800 S 48th St, Lincoln, NE 68506, 402-486-2509 (Fax: 402-486-2895). Hours: 8:30AM-Noon, 1-5PM. Enrollment: 600. Records go back to 1933. Alumni records are maintained here at the same phone number. Degrees granted: Associate; Bachelors.

Attendance and degree information available by phone, fax, mail. Search requires name only. Also helpful: SSN, date of birth, approximate years of attendance. There is no fee.

University of Nebraska Medical Center, Registrar, 600 S 42nd St, Omaha, NE 68198-4230, 402-559-7391 (Fax: 402-559-6796). Hours: 8AM-4:30PM. Enrollment: 2765. Records go back to 1902. Alumni records are maintained here also. Call 402-559-4354. Degrees granted: Bachelors; Masters; Doctorate.

Attendance and degree information available by phone, fax, mail. Search requires name only. Also helpful: SSN, date of birth, exact years of attendance. There is no fee.

University of Nebraska at Kearney, Registrar, Founders Hall, 905 W 25th St, Kearney, NE 68849, 308-865-8527 (Fax: 308-865-8484). Hours: 8AM-5PM. Enrollment: 8500. Records go back to 1903. Alumni Records Office: 2222 9th Ave, Kearney, NE 68849. Degrees granted: Bachelors; Masters. Adverse incident record source- Campus Security, 308-865-8517.

Attendance information available by phone, fax, mail. Search requires name plus SSN. Also helpful: date of birth, exact years of attendance. There is no fee.

Degree information available by phone, fax, mail. Search requires name only. Also helpful: SSN, date of birth, exact years of attendance. There is no fee.

University of Nebraska at Kearney, Registrar, 905 W 25th, Kearney, NE 68849, 308-865-8527. Enrollment: 8000. Formerly Kearney State College Records go back to 1904. Alumni records are maintained here also. Call 308-865-8474. Degrees granted: Bachelors; Masters; Specialist.

Attendance and degree information available by phone, mail. Search requires name plus SSN. Also helpful: date of birth, exact years of attendance. There is no fee.

University of Nebraska at Omaha, Registrar, 60th and Dodge Sts, Omaha, NE 68182, 402-554-2314 (Fax: 402-554-3472). Hours: 8AM-5PM. Enrollment: 16000. Records go back to 1906. Alumni records are maintained here also. Call 402-554-3367. Degrees granted: Associate; Bachelors; Masters; Doctorate.

Attendance and degree information available by phone, fax, mail. Search requires name only. Also helpful: SSN, date of birth, exact years of attendance. There is no fee.

University of Nebraska-Lincoln, Registration & Records, PO Box 880416, Lincoln, NE 68588-0416, 402-472-3684 (Fax: 402-472-8220). Hours: 8AM-5PM. Enrollment: 25000. Records go back to 1869. Alumni records are maintained here also. Call 402-472-2841. Degrees granted: Bachelors; Masters; Doctorate; Juris Doctor. Adverse incident record source- Student Judicial Affairs.

Attendance and degree information available by phone, mail. Search requires name plus SSN. Also helpful: exact years of attendance. There is no fee.

Wayne State College, Registrar, 1111 Main St, Wayne, NE 68787, 402-375-7241 (Fax: 402-375-7204). Hours: 8AM-5PM. Enrollment: 4000. Records go back to 1891. Alumni records are maintained here also. Call 402-375-7209. Degrees

granted: Bachelors; Masters; Ed Specialist. Adverse incident record source- Dean of Students, 402-375-7213.

Attendance and degree information available by phone, mail. Search requires name only. Also helpful: SSN, date of birth, exact years of attendance. There is no fee.

Western Nebraska Community College, Registrar, 1601 E 27th St, Scottsbluff, NE 69361, 308-635-6012 (Fax: 308-635-6100). Hours: 8AM-5PM. Enrollment: 3300. Records go back to 1926. Alumni records are maintained here also. Call 308-635-6080. Degrees granted: Associate. Adverse incident record source- Student Services, 308-635-3606.

Attendance and degree information available by phone, fax, mail. Search requires name plus SSN, date of birth. Also helpful: exact years of attendance. There is no fee.

York College, Registrar, 9th & Kiplinger Ave, York, NE 68467-2699, 402-363-5678 (Fax: 402-363-5623). Hours: 8AM-5PM. Enrollment: 525. Records go back to 1890. Alumni records are maintained here also. Call 402-363-5678. Degrees granted: Bachelors. Special programs- Human Resources Management, 402-363-5694. Adverse incident record source- Student Services, 402-363-5614.

Attendance and degree information available by phone, fax, mail. Search requires name plus SSN, approximate years of attendance. There is no fee.

Trade and Vocational Schools

College of Hair Design, 304 S 11th St, Lincoln, NE 68508, 402-474-4244

Dr. Welbes College of Message Therapy, 2602 J St, Omaha, NE 68107, 402-731-6768

Omaha College of Health Careers, 10845 Harney St, Omaha, NE 68154, 402-333-1400

Omaha Opportunities Industrialization Center, 2724 N 24th St, Omaha, NE 68110, 402-457-4222

Universal Technical Institute, 902 Capitol Ave, Omaha, NE 68102, 402-345-2422

State Licensing & Business Registration Quick Finder Index

Architecture, Engineering & Surveying
Architect #4 (1422)...................................☎ 402-471-2021
Engineer #4 (4806)...................................☎ 402-471-2021
Landscape Architect #33 (70).....................☎ 402-571-3500
Surveyor #5 (236)....................................☎ 402-471-2566

Business - Court & Legal Services
Attorney #35...☎ 402-475-7091
Lobbyist #13 (616)..................................☎ 402-471-2608
Notary Public #39 (30000).........................☎ 402-471-2558

Business - General Services
Auctioneer #11 (35).................................☎ 402-441-7437
Certified Public Accountant #9....................☎ 402-471-3595
Public Accountant-CPA #9 (5)......................☎ 402-471-3595
Vendor #29 (4000)...................................☎ 402-471-2571

Construction & Manufacturing
Air Conditioning/Heating Contractor #17 (80)
....☎ 402-441-7508
Boiler/Boilerhouse Inspector #26 (100).........☎ 402-471-4721
City Street Superintendent #3 (420).............☎ 402-479-4569
County Highway Superintendent #3 (600) ....☎ 402-479-4569
Electrician #41 (7000)..............................☎ 402-471-3550
Elevator Inspection Manager #31 (4000).......☎ 402-471-2239
General Contractor #24.............................☎ 402-471-5729
Industrial Safety Hygienist #19..................☎ 402-471-2115
Plumber Journeyman #12...........................☎ 402-466-5154

Education
Educational Media Specialist/Librarian #18
....☎ 402-471-2497
School Administrator/Supervisor #18...........☎ 402-471-2497

School Nurse #18....................................☎ 402-471-2497
Teacher #18...☎ 402-471-2497

Environmental & Agriculture
Animal Technician #7...............................☎ 402-471-2115
Exterminator #28....................................☎ 402-437-5080
Veterinarian #7......................................☎ 402-471-2115
Water Operator (Water Operator/Water Treatment
    Plant Operator) #27 (1385).....................☎ 402-471-2541
Water Treatment Plant Operator #27............☎ 402-471-2541
Well Driller/Pump Installer #27 (637)...........☎ 402-471-2541

Financial - Real Estate, Insurance & Banking
Abstractor #8...☎ 402-471-2383
Collection Agency #38 (130).......................☎ 402-471-2554
Debt Management Agency #38 (5).................☎ 402-471-2554
Insurance Agency #23...............................☎ 402-471-4913
Insurance Agent #23 (26278)......................☎ 402-471-4913
Insurance Broker #23................................☎ 402-471-4913
Insurance Consultant #23...........................☎ 402-471-4913
Investment Advisor #16 (277).....................☎ 402-471-2171
Investment Advisor Representative #16..........☎ 402-471-2171
Real Estate Appraiser #32 (965)...................☎ 402-471-9015
Real Estate Broker/Salesman #37 (7000)........☎ 402-471-2004
Securities Agent #16 (33012)......................☎ 402-471-2171
Securities Broker/Dealer #16 (1098)..............☎ 402-471-2171

Health & Beauty
Barber #2..☎ 402-471-2051
Chiropractor #6......................................☎ 402-471-2115
Cosmetologist #36 (8546)..........................☎ 402-471-2117
Dental Hygienist #19................................☎ 402-471-2115

Dentist #19 .... ☎ 402-471-2115
Dietitian (Medical Nutrition Therapist) #36
  (300) .... ☎ 402-471-2117
Educational Interpreter Performance-Hearing
  Empaired #14 .... ☎ 402-471-3593
Embalmer #19 .... ☎ 402-471-2115
Emergency Medical Technician #19 .... ☎ 402-471-2115
Funeral Director #19 .... ☎ 402-471-2115
Hearing Aid Dealer/Fitter #19 .... ☎ 402-471-2115
Hearing Assessment (EIPA) #14 .... ☎ 402-471-3593
Massage Therapist #19 .... ☎ 402-471-2115
Medical Doctor #21 .... ☎ 402-471-2115
Mental Health Practitioner #20 .... ☎ 402-471-2117
Nurse #21 .... ☎ 402-471-2115
Nursing Home Administrator #19 .... ☎ 402-471-2115
Occupational Therapist/Assistant #20 (335)
  .... ☎ 402-471-2117
Optometrist #21 .... ☎ 402-471-2115
Osteopathic Physician #21 .... ☎ 402-471-2115
Pharmacist #19 .... ☎ 402-471-2115
Physical Therapist #19 .... ☎ 402-471-2115
Physician's Assistant #21 .... ☎ 402-471-2115
Podiatrist #19 .... ☎ 402-471-2115
Quality Assurance Screening-Hearing
  Impaired #14 .... ☎ 402-471-3593
Radiologic Technologist #19 .... ☎ 402-471-2168
Respiratory Care Practitioner #19 .... ☎ 402-471-2115
Sanitarian #27 (73) .... ☎ 402-471-2299
Speech-Language Pathologist/Audiologist #19
  .... ☎ 402-471-2115

Investigations & Security
Fire Protection Sprinkler Contractor #10 .... ☎ 402-471-7791
Law Enforcement Officer #30 (160) .... ☎ 308-385-6030
Polygraph Examiner #38 (34) .... ☎ 402-471-2554
Private Detective #38 .... ☎ 402-471-2384

Social Services
Certified Professional Counselor #20 (747)
  .... ☎ 402-471-2117
Child Care Facility #25 .... ☎ 402-471-9138
Interpreter for the Hearing Impaired (National
  Registry of Interpreters) #14 (18) .... ☎ 402-471-3593
Marriage and Family Therapist #20 .... ☎ 402-471-2117
Psychologist #22 (348) .... ☎ 402-471-2117
Social Worker #20 .... ☎ 402-471-2117
Social Worker (Certified Master) #20 (623)
  .... ☎ 402-471-2117

Sports & Entertainment
Athletic Trainer #40 .... ☎ 402-471-2009
Boxer #40 (55) .... ☎ 402-471-2009
Boxing Promoter #40 (20) .... ☎ 402-471-2009
Carnival or State Fair #1 .... ☎ 402-474-5371
Racing #34 .... ☎ 402-471-4155

Transportation
Pilot #15 .... ☎ 402-471-2371

State Licensing & Business Registration Agency Information

(1) Board of Agriculture, State Fair Office, PO Box 81223, Lincoln, NE 68501-1223, 402-474-5371

(2) Board of Barber Examiners, PO Box 94723, 301 Centennial Mall S, 6th Floor, Lincoln, NE 68509-4723, 402-471-2051

(3) Board of County Highway & Street Superintendent, PO Box 94759, Lincoln, NE 68509-4759, 402-479-4569, Fax: 402-479-3975

(4) Board of Examiners for Engineers & Architects, PO Box 94751, 301 Centennial Mall, S, 6th Floor, Lincoln, NE 68509-4751, 402-471-2021, Fax: 402-471-0787

(5) Board of Examiners for Land Surveyors, 555 N Cotner Blvd, Lower Level, Lincoln, NE 68505, 402-471-2566, Fax: 402-471-3057

(6) Board of Examiners in Chiropractic, 301 Centennial Mall S, PO Box 95007, Lincoln, NE 68509, 402-471-2115, Fax: 402-471-3577

(7) Board of Examiners in Veterinary Medicine-Surgery, PO Box 95007, Lincoln, NE 68509, 402-471-2115, Fax: 402-471-3577

(8) Board of Examiners or Abstractors, PO Box 94944, 301 Centennial Mall S, 3rd Floor, Lincoln, NE 68509-4944, 402-471-2383

(9) Board of Public Accountancy, PO Box 94725, Lincoln, NE 68509, 402-471-3595, Fax: 402-471-4484

(10) Bureau of Fire Protection, 555 S 10th St, Lincoln, NE 68508, 402-471-7791, Fax: 402-471-7791

(11) City Clerk's Office, 555 S 10th St, Lincoln, NE 68508, 402-441-7437, Fax: 402-441-6513

(12) City Codes Administration, 555 S 10th St, Lincoln, NE 68508, 402-466-5154

(13) Clerk of the Legislature, PO Box 94604, State Capitol, Room 2014, Lincoln, NE 68509-4604, 402-471-2608, Fax: 402-471-2126

(14) Commission for the Hearing Impaired, 4600 Valley Rd, Lincoln, NE 68510, 402-471-3593, Fax: 402-471-3067

(15) Department of Aeronautics, PO Box 82088, Lincoln Municipal Airport, Lincoln, NE 68501, 402-471-2371, Fax: 402-471-2906

(16) Department of Banking & Finance, PO Box 95006, 1200 "N" St, Suite 311, The Atrium, Lincoln, NE 68509-5006, 402-471-2171

(17) Department of Building & Safety, 555 S 10th St, City County Bldg, Lincoln, NE 68508, 402-441-7508, Fax: 402-441-8214

(18) Department of Education, Teacher Accreditation/Certification Division, PO Box 94987, 301 Centennial Mall S, 6th Floor, Lincoln, NE 68509-4987, 402-471-2497, Fax: 402-471-0117

(19) Department of Health, PO Box 95007, 301 Centennial Mall S, 3rd Floor, Lincoln, NE 68509-5007, 402-471-2115, Fax: 402-471-3577

(20) Department of Health, Mental Health Consumer Services Section, PO Box 95007, 301 Centennial Mall S, 3rd Floor, Lincoln, NE 68509-5007, 402-471-2117, Fax: 402-471-3577

(21) Department of Health, Nursing & Specialized Medical Examining Boards, PO Box 95007, 301 Centennial Mall S, 3rd Floor, Lincoln, NE 68509-5007, 402-471-2115

(22) Department of Health, PSrofessional & Occupational Licensure Division, PO Box 95007, 301 Centennial Mall S, 3rd Floor, Lincoln, NE 68509-5007, 402-471-2117, Fax: 402-471-3577

(23) Department of Insurance, The Terminal Bldg, 941 "O" St, Suite 400, Lincoln, NE 68508, 402-471-2201, Fax: 402-471-6559

(24) Department of Revenue, PO Box 94818, Lincoln, NE 68509, 402-471-5729, Fax: 402-471-5608

(25) Department of Social Services, Licensing, PO Box 95026, 301 Centennial Mall, S, 5th Floor, Lincoln, NE 68509, 402-471-9138, Fax: 402-471-9435

(26) Division of Safety, Boiler Section, 301 Centennial Mall S, PO Box 95024, Lincoln, NE 68509, 402-471-4721, Fax: 402-471-5039

(27) Drinking Water & Environmental Sanitation Division, 301 Centennial Mall S, PO Bo x95007, Lincoln, NE 68509, 402-471-2541, Fax: 402-471-6436

(28) Environmental Protection Agency, 100 Centennial Mall N, Lincoln, NE 68508, 402-437-5080, Fax: Y

(29) Liquor Control Commission, PO Box 95046, 301 Centennial Mall, S, 5th Floor, Lincoln, NE 68509, 402-471-2571

(30) Nebraska Crime Commission, 3600 N. Academy Rd., Grand Island, NE 68801, 308-381-5700, Fax: 308-385-6032

(31) Nebraska Department of Labor, 301 Centennial Mall S, PO Box 95024, Lincoln, NE 68509, 402-471-2239, Fax: 402-471-5039

(32) Nebraska Real Estate Appraiser Board, PO Box 94963, 301 Centennial Mall S, 3rd Floor, Lincoln, NE 68509-4963, 402-471-9015, Fax: 402-471-9017

(33) Nebraska State Board of Landscape Architects, 4205 North 101st Street, Omaha, NE 68134, 402-571-3500, Fax: 402-571-3500

(34) Nebraska State Racing Commission, PO Box 95014, 301 Centennial Mall S, 4th Floor, Lincoln, NE 68509-5014, 402-471-4155, Fax: 402-471-2339

(35) Nebraska Supreme Court, 635 S. 14th, PO Box 81809, Lincoln, NE 68501, 402-475-7091, Fax: 402-475-7098

(36) Professional & Occupational Licensure Division, 301 Centennial Mall S, PO Box 95007, Lincoln, NE 68509-5007, 402-471-2117, Fax: 402-471-3577

(37) Real Estate Commission, PO Box 94667, Lincoln, NE 68509-4667, 402-471-2004

(38) Secretary of State, Licensing Division, PO Box 94608, State Capitol, Suite 2300, Lincoln, NE 68509-4608, 402-471-2554, Fax: 402-471-3237

(39) Secretary of State, Notary Division, PO Box 95104, Room 1303, Lincoln, NE 68509-5104, 402-471-2558, Fax: 402-471-4429

(40) State Athletic Commission, PO Box 94743, 301 Centennial Mall S, 3rd Floor, Lincoln, NE 68509-4743, 402-471-2009, Fax: 402-471-2009

(41) State Electrical Division, PO Box 95066, Lincoln, NE 68509-5066, 402-471-3550

Nevada

Capitol: Carson City (Carson City County)	
State Population	1.5 Million
Number of Degree Granting Institutions:	10
Number of State Licensing & Business Registration Agencies:	123

Degree Granting Educational Institutions

Community College of Southern Nevada, Registrar, 3200 E Cheyenne Ave, North Las Vegas, NV 89030, 702-651-4060 (Fax: 702-643-1474). Hours: 8AM-6PM. Enrollment: 22000. Records go back to 1971. Degrees granted: Associate.

Attendance information available by phone, mail. Search requires name plus SSN. There is no fee.

Degree information available by written request only. Search requires name plus SSN. There is no fee.

Deep Springs College, Registrar, HC 72, Box 45001, Dyer, NV 89010-9803, 619-872-2000 (Fax: 619-872-4466). Hours: 8AM-5PM. Enrollment: 26. Records go back to 1917. Alumni records are maintained here also. Call 619-873-6048. Degrees granted: Associate. Adverse incident record source-Registrar, 619-872-2000.

Attendance and degree information available by phone, fax, mail. Search requires name plus exact years of attendance. There is no fee.

Great Basin College, Registrar, 1500 College Pkwy, Elko, NV 89801, 702-753-2102 (Fax: 702-753-2311). Hours: 8AM-5PM. Enrollment: 3000. Formerly Northern Nevada Community College Records go back to 1969. Degrees granted: Associate.

Attendance information available by phone, fax, mail. Search requires name plus SSN. There is no fee.

School will not confirm degree information.

Morrison College-Reno, Records Dept, 140 Washington St, Reno, NV 89503, 702-323-4145 (Fax: 702-323-8495). Hours: 8:30AM-7:30PM M-Th; 8AM-5PM F. Enrollment: 225. Records go back to 1960. Alumni records are maintained here at the same phone number. Degrees granted: Associate; Bachelors. Adverse incident record source- Registrar, 702-323-4145.

Attendance and degree information available by phone, fax, mail. Search requires name plus approximate years of attendance. Also helpful: SSN, exact years of attendance. There is no fee.

Phillips Junior College of Las Vegas, Registrar, 3320 E Flamingo Rd Ste 30, Las Vegas, NV 89121-4306, 702-434-0486 (Fax: 702-434-8601). Hours: 7AM-4PM. Degrees granted: Associate.

Attendance and degree information available by fax, mail. Search requires name plus SSN, signed release. Also helpful: exact years of attendance. There is no fee.

Sierra Nevada College, Registrar, PO Box 4269, Incline Village, NV 89450-4269, 702-831-1314 (Fax: 702-831-1347). Hours: 8AM-5PM. Enrollment: 4300. Records go back to 1989. Degrees granted: Bachelors.

Attendance and degree information available by phone, fax, mail. Search requires name only. Also helpful: SSN, date of birth, exact years of attendance. There is no fee.

Truckee Meadows Community College, Registrar, 7000 Dandani Blvd, Reno, NV 89512, 702-673-7042 (Fax: 702-673-7028). Hours: 8AM-5PM M,Th,F; 8AM-7PM T,W. Enrollment: 9000. Records go back to 1972. Degrees granted: Associate. Adverse incident record source- 702-673-7000.

Attendance and degree information available by mail. Search requires name plus SSN, signed release. Also helpful: date of birth, approximate years of attendance. There is no fee.

University of Nevada, Las Vegas, Registrar, 4505 Maryland Pkwy, Las Vegas, NV 89154, 702-895-3771 (Fax: 702-895-4046). Hours: 8AM-5PM. Enrollment: 19769. Records go back to 1955. Alumni records are maintained here also. Call 702-895-3621. Degrees granted: Bachelors; Masters; Doctorate. Special programs- Continuing Education.

Attendance and degree information available by phone, mail. Search requires name plus SSN. Also helpful: date of birth. There is no fee.

University of Nevada, Reno, Admissions & Records, MS 120, Reno, NV 89557, 702-784-6865 (Fax: 702-784-4283). Hours: 8AM-4:30PM. Enrollment: 12350. Records go back to 1904. Alumni records are maintained here also. Call 702-784-6620. Degrees granted: Bachelors; Masters; Doctorate.

Attendance and degree information available by fax, mail. Search requires name plus SSN, date of birth, approximate years of attendance, signed release. Also helpful: exact years of attendance. There is no fee.

Western Nevada Community College, Registrar, 2201 W Nye Lane, Carson City, NV 89703, 702-887-3000 (Fax: 702-885-0642). Records go back to 1970's. Degrees granted: Associate.

Attendance and degree information available by phone, fax, mail. Search requires name plus SSN, date of birth, approximate years of attendance. Also helpful: exact years of attendance. There is no fee.

Trade and Vocational Schools

Academy of Medical Careers, 5243 W Charleston Blvd #11, Las Vegas, NV 89102, 818-896-2272

Interior Design Institute, 4225 S Eastern Ave #4, Las Vegas, NV 89119, 702-369-9944

International Dealers School, 503 E Fremont St, Las Vegas, NV 89101, 702-385-7665

National Academy for Casino Dealers, 557 S Sahara Ave #108, Las Vegas, NV 89104, 702-735-4884

Nevada Jewerly Manufacturing, 953 E Sahara Ste B 27, Las Vegas, NV 89104, 702-735-4191

PCI Dealers School, 920 S Valley View Blvd, Las Vegas, NV 89107, 702-877-4724

Professional Careers, 3305 Spring Mountain Rd #7, Las Vegas, NV 89193, 702-368-2338

Reno Tahoe Gaming Academy, One First St Ste 1405, Reno, NV 89501, 702-348-7700

Vegas Career School, 3333 S Maryland Pkwy, Las Vegas, NV 89102, 702-792-6299

State Licensing & Business Registration Quick Finder Index

Architecture, Engineering & Surveying
Architect #2 .... ☎ 702-486-7300
Engineer #42 (7880)...................................... ☎ 702-688-1231
Landscape Architect #10 (469) .... ☎ 702-829-8117
Surveyor #42 (1140)...................................... ☎ 702-688-1231

Business - Court & Legal Services
Attorney #46 .... ☎ 702-382-2200
Lobbyist #28 (658) .... ☎ 702-687-6800
Notary Public #40 (35000) .... ⊠ 702-687-5115
Shorthand Reporter #23................................ ☎ 702-384-1663

Business - General Services
Auditor #1.. ☎ 702-786-0231
Public Accountant #1 .... ☎ 702-786-0231
Registered Interior Designer #2 .... ☎ 702-486-7300
Residential Designer #2................................ ☎ 702-486-7300

Construction & Manufacturing
Bricklayer #48 .... ☎ 702-486-1100
Carpenter #48 .... ☎ 702-486-1100
Cement Mason #48 .... ☎ 702-486-1100
Contractor #48 .... ☎ 702-486-1100
Electrician #48.. ☎ 702-486-1100
Floor & Carpet Layer #48 .... ☎ 702-486-1100
Glazier #48... ☎ 702-486-1100
Heating & Air Conditioning Mechanic #48
.... ☎ 702-486-1100
Insulation Installer #48 .... ☎ 702-486-1100
Mobile Home Manufacturer #33 702-486-4135
Monitor Well Driller #51................................ ☎ 702-687-4380
Painter/Paper Hanger #48............................. ☎ 702-486-1100
Plasterer/Drywall Installer #48...................... ☎ 702-486-1100
Plumber #48... ☎ 702-486-1100
Roofer #48 .... ☎ 702-486-1100
Rotary Driller #25... 702-687-4380

Education
Program Administrator #49 .... ☎ 702-687-9200
School Administrator #49............................... ☎ 702-687-9200
School Counselor #49.................................... ☎ 702-687-9200
School Librarian #49 .... ☎ 702-687-9200
Teacher #49.. ☎ 702-687-9200

Environmental & Agriculture
Animal Caretaker #21 .... ☎ 702-322-9422
Animal Technician #21 (48).......................... ☎ 702-322-9422
Groundskeeper/Gardener #29 (500) .... ☎ 702-688-1180
Liquified Petroleum Gas (LPG) #44 (439).....⊠ 702-687-4890
Pest Control #29 (1100)................................ ☎ 702-688-1180
Veterinarian #21 (657).................................. ☎ 702-322-9422
Well Driller #51 (439) .... ☎ 702-687-4380

Financial - Real Estate, Insurance & Banking
Appraiser (MVD) #24.................................... ☎ 702-486-4009
Claims Adjuster #24 .... ☎ 702-486-4009
Collection Agency #30 .... ☎ 702-486-4120
Financial Advisor (Investment Advisor) #45
.... ☎ 702-486-2440
Insurance Agent #24 .... ☎ 702-486-4009
Investment Advisor #39................................... 702-486-6440
Real Estate Agent #41.................................. ☎ 702-486-4033
Real Estate Appraiser #41............................ ☎ 702-486-4033
Repossessor #38 (31).................................. ☎ 702-687-3535
Securities Broker/Dealer #39........................... 702-486-6440
Securities Registration #45 .... ☎ 702-486-2440
Securities Sales Representative #39 702-486-6440

Health & Beauty
Acupuncturist #15... 702-359-7025
Adult Day Care #22 .... ⊠ 702-687-4475
Adult Group Care #22................................... ⊠ 702-687-4475

Aesthetician #37 .... ☎ 702-486-6542
Ambulance Attendant #22 .... ✉ 702-687-4475
Ambulance Permit #22 .... ✉ 702-687-4475
Ambulatory Surgical Center #22.................... ✉ 702-687-4475
Apprentice Optician #5.................................. ☎ 702-345-1444
Barber #47 (639)... ☎ 702-731-1966
Blood Gas Technician #22 .... ✉ 702-687-4475
Blood Gas Technologist #22 .... ✉ 702-687-4475
Chiropractor #3.. ✉ 702-826-8574
Clinical Laboratory Technologist #22............ ✉ 702-687-4475
Cosmetologist #37 (20301) .... ☎ 702-486-6542
Dental Hygienist #4 .... ☎ 702-255-4211
Dentist #4.. ☎ 702-255-4211
Director (Medical Laboratory) #22 .... ✉ 702-687-4475
Electrologist #37 (117).................................. ☎ 702-486-6542
Embalmer #7 702-802-3005
Emergency Medical Technician #22.............. ✉ 702-687-4475
Euthanasia Technician #21 (48).................... ☎ 702-322-9422
First Responder EMT #22 .... ✉ 702-687-4475
Funeral Director #7....................................... 702-802-3005
Hair Stylist (Designer) #37 (15).................... ☎ 702-486-6542
Hearing Aid Specialist #8............................. ☎ 702-226-5716
Histologic Technician/Histotechnologist #22
.... ✉ 702-687-4475
Histotechnologist #22.................................... ✉ 702-687-4475
Histotogic Technician #22............................. ✉ 702-687-4475
Home Health Agency #22 .... ✉ 702-687-4475
Homeopathic Physician #9 .... ☎ 702-258-5487
Hospice #22 .... ✉ 702-687-4475
Hospital #22.. ✉ 702-687-4475
Independent Center for Emergency Care #22
.... ✉ 702-687-4475
Intermediate Care Facility/MR #22............... ✉ 702-687-4475
Laboratory Assistant/Blood Gas Assistant #22
.... ✉ 702-687-4475
Manicurist #37 .... ☎ 702-486-6542
Medical Doctor #11 702-688-2559
Medical Laboratory #22 .... ✉ 702-687-4475
Medical Technician #22 .... ✉ 702-687-4475
Nurse #12.. ☎ 702-786-2778
Nursing Facility #22 .... ✉ 702-687-4475

Nursing Pool Operator #22 .... ✉ 702-687-4475
Occupational Therapist/Assistant #13 (297)
.... ☎ 702-857-1700
Office Laboratory Assistant #22.................... ✉ 702-687-4475
Optician #5 (138)... ☎ 702-345-1444
Optometrist #14 .... ☎ 702-883-8367
Osteopathic Physician #16............................. ☎ 702-732-2147
Pathologist Assistant #22.............................. ✉ 702-687-4475
Pharmacist #17 (6500) .... ☎ 702-322-0691
Physical Therapist #18 (700)......................... ☎ 702-876-5535
Physician's Assistant #11.............................. 702-688-2559
Podiatrist #19 .... ✉ 702-733-7617
Public Sanitarian #43.................................... 702-328-2418
Registered Laboratory Certification #22 .... ✉ 702-687-4475
Rehabilitation Service #22............................. ✉ 702-687-4475
Respiratory Therapist #11............................. 702-688-2559
Speech Pathologist/Audiologist #31.............. ☎ 702-784-4887

Investigations & Security
Polygraph Examiner #38 (13)........................ ☎ 702-687-3535
Private Investigator #38 (223) .... ☎ 702-687-3535
Private Patrol #38.. ☎ 702-687-3535
Process Server #38.. ☎ 702-687-3535

Social Services
Alcohol and Drug Abuse Center #22 .... ✉ 702-687-4475
Marriage & Family Therapist #32 .... ☎ 702-486-7388
Psychologist #20 (240) .... ☎ 702-688-1268
Social Worker #6 .... ☎ 702-688-2555

Sports & Entertainment
Athletic Promoter #34.................................... ✉ 702-486-2575
Fishing Guide #27 (15).................................. ☎ 702-688-1539
Gaming License (By Company) #35 .... ☎ 702-687-6520
Racing #36 702-486-5888

Transportation
Bus Driver #26.. ☎ 702-687-5505
Taxicab Driver #50 (3266) .... ☎ 702-486-6532

State Licensing & Business Registration Agency Information

(1)   Board of Accountancy, 200 S Virginia St, #670, Reno, NV 89501, 702-786-0231, Fax: 702-786-0234

(2)   Board of Architecture, Interior & Residential Design, 2080 E Flamingo Rd, Suite 225, Las Vegas, NV 89119, 702-486-7300, Fax: 702-486-7304

(3)   Board of Chiropractic Examiners, 4600 Kietzke Lane, #M245, Reno, NV 89502, 702-329-2559

(4)   Board of Dental Examiners of Nevada, 2225 #E Renaissance Dr, Las Vegas, NV 89119, 702-486-7044

(5)   Board of Dispensing Opticians, PO Box 70503, Reno, NV 89570, 702-345-1444, Fax: 702-345-1444

(6)   Board of Examiners for Social Workers, 4600 Kietzke La, #A101, Reno, NV 89502, 702-688-2555, Fax: 702-688-2557

(7)   Board of Funeral Directors & Embalmers, 305 N. Carson St., Suite 201, Carson City, NV 89701, 702-882-3005, Fax: 702-882-5393

(8)   Board of Hearing Aid Specialists, 3172 N. Rainbow Blvd. #141, Las Vegas, NV 89108, 702-732-8721

(9)   Board of Homeopathic Medical Examiners, PO Box 41064, Reno, NV 89504, 702-258-5487, Fax: 702-258-5487

(10)   Board of Landscape Architecture, PO Box 40968, Reno, NV 89504, 702-829-8117, Fax: 702-829-8117

(11)   Board of Medical Examiners, 1105 Terminal Way, #301 (89502), PO Box 7238, Reno, NV 89510, 702-688-2559, Fax: 702-688-2321

(12)   Board of Nursing, 1755 E Plumb Way, Suite 1755, Reno, NV 89502, 702-786-2778

(13)   Board of Occupational Therapy, PO Box 70220, Reno, NV 89570-0220, 702-857-1700, Fax: 702-857-1700

(14)   Board of Optometry, PO Box 1687, Carson City, NV 89702, 702-883-8367

(15)   Board of Oriental Medicine, 434 10th St, Sparks, NV 89431, 702-642-3322

(16)   Board of Osteopathic Medicine, 2950 E Flamingo Rd, #E3, Las Vegas, NV 89121, 702-732-2147, Fax: 702-732-2079

(17)   Board of Pharmacy, 1201 Terminal Way, Suite 212, Reno, NV 89502, 702-322-0691, Fax: 702-322-0895

(18) Board of Physical Therapy Examiners, PO Box 81467, Las Vegas, NV 89180-1467, 702-876-5535, Fax: 702-876-2097

(19) Board of Podiatry, 2413 S Eastern Ave, #142, Las Vegas, NV 89104, 702-733-7617

(20) Board of Psychological Examiners, PO Box 2286, Reno, NV 89505-2286, 702-688-1268

(21) Board of Veterinary Medical Examiners, 1005 Terminal Way, Suite 246, Reno, NV 89502, 702-322-9422, Fax: 702-322-1926

(22) Bureau of Licensure & Certification, Medical Laboratory Services, 1550 College Parkway #158, Carson City, NV 89710, 702-687-4475, Fax: 702-687-6588

(23) Certified Court Reporters Board, PO Box 237, Las Vegas, NV 89125-0237, 702-384-1663

(24) Department of Business & Industry, Insurance Division, Bradley Building, 2501 E Sahara Ave, Rm 302, Las Vegas, NV 89104, 702-486-4595

(25) Department of Conservation & National Resources, 123 W Nye Ln, Capitol Complex, Carson City, NV 89710, 702-687-4380

(26) Department of Motor Vehicles & Public Safety, Records Section, 555 Wright Way, Carson City, NV 89711-0250, 702-687-5505

(27) Department of Wildlife, Fisheries Division, PO Box 10678 (1100 Valley Rd), Reno, NV 89520, 702-688-1530

(28) Director of Legislative Counsel Bureau, Capitol Complex, Legislative Bldg, Carson City, NV 89710, 702-687-6800, Fax: 702-687-5962

(29) Division of Agriculture, Pest Control Licensing Division, 350 Capitol Hill Ave., Reno, NV 89502, 702-688-1180, Fax: 702-688-1178

(30) Division of Financial Institutions, Collection Agency Advisory Board, 2501 E Sahara Ave, Suite 300, Las Vegas, NV 89104, 702-486-4120

(31) Examiners for Audiology & Speech Pathology, Department of Speech Pathology & Audiology, University of Nevada, School of Medicine, Reno, NV 89557-0046, 702-784-4887, Fax: 702-784-4095

(32) Examiners for Marriage & Family Therapists, PO Box 7258, Las Vegas, NV 89170, 702-486-7388

(33) Manufactured Housing Division, 2501 E Sahara Ave, Las Vegas, NV 89104, 702-486-4135, Fax: 702-486-4509

(34) Nevada Athletic Commission, 555 E. Washington Ave. Suite 1500, Las Vegas, NV 89109, 702-486-2575, Fax: 702-486-2577

(35) Nevada Gaming Control Board, 1150 E William St, Carson City, NV 89710, 702-687-6500, Fax: 702-687-5817

(36) Nevada Racing Commission, State Mail Room, Las Vegas, NV 89158, 702-486-5888

(37) Nevada State Board of Cosmetology, 1785 E Sahara Ave, Suite 255, Las Vegas, NV 89104, 702-486-6542, Fax: 702-369-8064

(38) Office of the Attorney General, Capitol Complex, Carson City, NV 89710, 702-687-3535, Fax: 702-687-5798

(39) Office of the Secretary of State, Securities Division, 555 E Washington Ave, Suite 5200, Las Vegas, NV 89502, 702-486-2440, Fax: 702-486-2454

(40) Office of the Secretary of State, Securities Division, Capital Complex, Carson City, NV 89710, 702-687-5115

(41) Real Estate Division, 2501 E Sahara Ave, Las Vegas, NV 89104, 702-486-4033

(42) Registered Professional Engineers & Land Surveyors, 1755 E Plumb Land, Suite 135, Reno, NV 89502, 702-688-1231, Fax: 702-688-2991

(43) Registration of Public Health Sanitarians, c/o Washoe County District Health Department, PO Box 11130, Reno, NV 89520, 702-328-2434, Fax: 702-328-6176

(44) Regulation of Liquefied Petroleum Gas, PO Box 338, Carson City, NV 89702, 702-687-4890, Fax: 702-687-3956

(45) Secretary of State Securities, 555 E. Washington, Ste 5200, Las Vegas,, NV 89101, 702-687-2440, Fax: 702-486-2452

(46) State Bar of Nevada, 201 Las Vegas Blvd South, Ste 200, Las Vegas, NV 89101, 702-382-2200, Fax: 702-385-2878

(47) State Barbers' Health & Sanitation Board, 606 E Sahara Ave, Las Vegas, NV 89104, 702-731-1966

(48) State Contractors' Board, 4220 Maryland Pkwy, Bldg. D Ste. 800, Las Vegas, NV 89119, 702-486-1100, Fax: 702-486-1190

(49) State Department of Education, 400 W King St, Carson City, NV 89710, 702-687-9200

(50) Taxicab Authority, 1785 E Sahara Ave, Suite 200, Las Vegas, NV 89104, 702-486-6532, Fax: 702-486-7350

(51) Well Drillers' Advisory Board, 123 W Nye Lane, Carson City, NV 89710, 702-687-4380, Fax: 702-687-6972

New Hampshire

Capitol: Concord (Merrimack County)	
State Population	1.1 Million
Number of Degree Granting Institutions:	30
Number of State Licensing & Business Registration Agencies:	104

Degree Granting Educational Institutions

Antioch University, **(Antioch New England Graduate School)**, Registrar, 40 Avon St, Keene, NH 03431, 603-357-3122 (Fax: 603-357-0718). Records are not housed here. They are located at College at Antioch University, Registrar, 795 Livermore St, Yellow Springs, OH 45387.

Castle College, Registrar, Searles Rd, Windham, NH 03087, 603-893-6111 (Fax: 603-898-0547). Hours: 8AM-5PM. Records go back to 1965. Alumni records are maintained here at the same phone number. Degrees granted: Associate.

Attendance and degree information available by phone, fax, mail. Search requires name plus SSN, approximate years of attendance. There is no fee.

Colby-Sawyer College, Registrar, 100 Main St, New London, NH 03257, 603-526-3673 (Fax: 603-526-2135). Hours: 8AM-5PM. Enrollment: 780. Records go back to 1940. Alumni records are maintained here also. Call 603-526-3727. Degrees granted: Associate; Bachelors. Adverse incident record source- Student Development, 603-526-3755.

Attendance information available by phone, fax, mail. Search requires name plus date of birth, exact years of attendance. Also helpful: SSN. There is no fee.

Degree information available by phone, fax, mail. Search requires name plus date of birth. Also helpful: SSN, exact years of attendance. There is no fee.

College for Lifelong Learning, Registrar, 125 N State St, Concord, NH 03301-6438, 603-228-3000 (Fax: 603-229-0964). Enrollment: 2400. Records go back to 1972. Alumni records are maintained here also. Call 603-228-3000 X329. Degrees granted: Associate; Bachelors.

Attendance and degree information available by phone, mail. Search requires name plus SSN. Also helpful: date of birth, approximate years of attendance. There is no fee.

Daniel Webster College, Registrar, Nashua, NH 03063, 603-577-6510 (Fax: 603-577-6001). Hours: 8:30AM-5PM. Enrollment: 1000. Records go back to 1965. Alumni records are maintained here also. Call 603-577-6620. Degrees granted: Associate; Bachelors. Adverse incident record source-Student Life, 603-577-6581: Security, 603-577-6529

Attendance information available by phone, fax, mail. Search requires name plus SSN. Also helpful: exact years of attendance. There is no fee.

Degree information available by phone, fax, mail. Search requires name plus SSN. Also helpful: exact years of attendance. There is no fee.

Dartmouth College, Registrar, Hanover, NH 03755, 603-646-2246 (Fax: 603-646-2247). Hours: 8AM-4PM. Enrollment: 4400. Records go back to 1769. Alumni records are maintained here also. Call 603-646-3643. Degrees granted: Bachelors; Masters; Doctorate. Adverse incident record source- Dean of Students, 603-646-2243.

Attendance and degree information available by phone, fax, mail. Search requires name plus SSN, exact years of attendance. Also helpful: date of birth. There is no fee.

Franklin Pierce College, Registrar, College Rd, Rindge, NH 03461, 603-899-4100 (Fax: 603-899-4308). Hours: 8AM-4:30PM. Enrollment: 2700. Records go back to 1962. Records on computer from 1980 on. Alumni records are maintained here also. Call 603-899-4100. Degrees granted: Associate; Bachelors; Masters.

Attendance and degree information available by phone, fax, mail. Search requires name plus SSN. Also helpful: date of birth, exact years of attendance. There is no fee.

Franklin Pierce Law Center, Registrar, 2 White St, Concord, NH 03301, 603-228-1541 X103 (Fax: 603-228-1074). Hours: 8AM-4:30PM. Enrollment: 400. Alumni records are maintained here also. Call 603-228-1541 X121. Degrees granted: Masters; Doctorate.

Attendance and degree information available by phone, fax, mail. Search requires name only. Also helpful: SSN, exact years of attendance. There is no fee.

Hesser College, Registrar, 3 Sundial Ave, Manchester, NH 03103, 603-668-6660 (Fax: 603-666-4722). Hours: 8AM-4:30PM. Enrollment: 2500. Records go back to 1915. Alumni records are maintained here at the same phone number. Degrees granted: Associate. Adverse incident record source- Dean of Student Affairs, 603-668-6660 X205.

Attendance and degree information available by phone, fax, mail. Search requires name plus SSN. Also helpful: date of birth, exact years of attendance. There is no fee.

Keene State College, Box 2607, Records Retrieval, 229 Main St, Keene, NH 03435-2607, 603-358-2321. Hours: 9AM-4:30PM. Enrollment: 4800. Records go back to 1909. Alumni records are maintained here also. Call 603-358-2369. Degrees granted: Associate; Bachelors; Masters. Adverse incident record source- Associate Dean of Student Affairs, 603-358-2842.

Attendance and degree information available by phone, mail. Search requires name plus SSN. Also helpful: date of birth, exact years of attendance. There is no fee.

Magdalen College, Registrar, 511 Kearsarge Mtn Rd, Warner, NH 03102, 603-456-2656. Enrollment: 70. Records go back to 1978. Degrees granted: Associate; Bachelors.

Attendance and degree information available by phone, mail. Search requires name plus exact years of attendance. Also helpful: SSN, date of birth. There is no fee.

McIntosh College, Registrar, 23 Cataract Ave, Dover, NH 03820, 603-742-1234 (Fax: 603-742-7292). Hours: 7:30AM-10:30PM. Records go back to 1920. Degrees granted: Associate.

Attendance and degree information available by phone, fax, mail. Search requires name plus SSN, date of birth. Also helpful: exact years of attendance. There is no fee.

New England College, Registrar, Henniker, NH 03242-0788, 603-428-2203 (Fax: 603-428-2266). Hours: 8:30AM-4:30PM. Enrollment: 1100. Records go back to 1947. Alumni records are maintained here also. Call 603-428-2300. Degrees granted: Bachelors; Masters.

Attendance and degree information available by phone, fax, mail. Search requires name only. Also helpful: SSN, approximate years of attendance. There is no fee.

New Hampshire College, Registrar, 2500 N River Rd, Manchester, NH 03106-1045, 603-668-2211 (Fax: 603-645-9665). Hours: 8AM-4:30PM. Enrollment: 6100. Alumni records are maintained here also. Call 603-645-9799. Degrees granted: Associate; Bachelors; Masters. Adverse incident record source- Student Affairs, 603-645-9608.

Attendance and degree information available by phone, fax, mail. Search requires name plus SSN. Also helpful: date of birth, exact years of attendance. There is no fee.

New Hampshire Community Technical College, Registrar, 505 Amerst St, PO Box 2052, Nashua, NH 03061-2052, 603-882-6923 (Fax: 603-882-8690). Hours: 8AM-4:30PM. Enrollment: 1060. Formerly New Hampshire Technical College at Nashua Records go back to 1969. Degrees granted: Associate.

Attendance and degree information available by phone, mail. Search requires name plus SSN, approximate years of attendance. Also helpful: exact years of attendance. There is no fee.

New Hampshire Community Technical College at Laconia, Registrar, Prescott Hill Rte 106, Laconia, NH 03246, 603-524-3207 (Fax: 603-524-8084). Hours: 8AM-4PM. Enrollment: 1000. Records go back to 1969. Alumni records are maintained here at the same phone number. Degrees granted: Associate. Adverse incident record source- Provost, 603-524-3207.

Attendance and degree information available by phone, fax, mail. Search requires name plus SSN, approximate years of attendance. Also helpful: exact years of attendance. There is no fee.

New Hampshire Community Technical College at Manchester, Registrar, 1066 Front St, Manchester, NH 03102, 603-668-6706 (Fax: 603-668-5354). Hours: 8AM-4PM. Enrollment: 1800. Records go back to 1945. Alumni records are maintained here at the same phone number.

Degrees granted: Associate. Adverse incident record source- Registrar, 603-668-6706.

Attendance information available by fax, mail. Search requires name plus SSN, signed release. Also helpful: exact years of attendance. There is no fee.

Degree information available by phone, fax, mail. Search requires name plus SSN. Also helpful: exact years of attendance. There is no fee.

New Hampshire Community Technical College at Stratham, Registrar, 277 Portsmouth Ave., Stratham, NH 03885, 603-772-1194 (Fax: 603-772-1198). Hours: 8AM-8PM M-Th, 8AM-4PM F. Enrollment: 1300. Records go back to 1945. Degrees granted: Associate. Adverse incident record source- Student Affairs, 603-772-1194.

Attendance and degree information available by phone, fax, mail. Search requires name plus SSN, approximate years of attendance. Also helpful: exact years of attendance. There is no fee.

New Hampshire Technical College, Registrar, One College Dr, Claremont, NH 03743-9707, 603-542-7744 (Fax: 603-543-1844). Hours: 8AM-4:30PM. Records go back to 1968. Degrees granted: Associate.

Attendance and degree information available by fax, mail. Search requires name only. Also helpful: SSN, date of birth, exact years of attendance. There is no fee.

New Hampshire Technical College at Berlin, Registrar, 2020 Riverside Dr, Berlin, NH 03570, 603-572-1113. Hours: 8AM-4:30PM. Enrollment: 590. Degrees granted: Associate.

Attendance and degree information available by phone, mail. Search requires name plus SSN, approximate years of attendance. Also helpful: exact years of attendance. There is no fee.

New Hampshire Technical Institute, Registrar, 11 Institute Dr, Concord, NH 03301-7412, 603-225-1800 (Fax: 603-225-1809). Hours: 8AM-4:30PM. Enrollment: 3000. Records go back to 1965. Alumni records are maintained here at the same phone number. Degrees granted: Associate. Special programs- Certificate Programs, 603-225-1877.

Attendance and degree information available by phone, mail. Search requires name plus SSN, approximate years of attendance. Also helpful: exact years of attendance. There is no fee.

Notre Dame College, Registrar, 2321 Elm St, Manchester, NH 03104-2299, 603-669-4298 (Fax: 603-644-8316). Hours: 8AM-5PM. Enrollment: 1350. Records go back to 1950. Alumni records are maintained here also. Call 603-669-4298. Degrees granted: Associate; Bachelors; Masters. Certification: Early Childhood Paralegal.

Attendance and degree information available by fax, mail. Search requires name plus signed release. Also helpful: SSN, date of birth, exact years of attendance. There is no fee.

Plymouth State College, Registrar, Plymouth, NH 03264, 603-535-2345 (Fax: 603-535-2724). Hours: 8AM-4:30PM. Enrollment: 4300. Records go back to 1870's. Alumni records are maintained here also. Call 603-535-2218. Degrees granted: Associate; Bachelors; Masters. Special programs- Meteorology. Adverse incident record source- Dean of Students, 603-535-2240.

Attendance and degree information available by phone, mail. Search requires name plus SSN. Also helpful: date of birth, exact years of attendance. There is no fee.

Plymouth State College, Registrar, Plymouth, NH 03264, 603-535-2345 (Fax: 603-535-2724). Enrollment: 4500. Formerly University of New Hampshire, Plymouth State Records go back to 1871. Alumni records are maintained here also. Call 603-535-2218. Degrees granted: Associate; Bachelors;

Masters. Adverse incident record source- Security, 603-535-2330.

Attendance and degree information available by phone, mail. Search requires name plus SSN. Also helpful: date of birth, exact years of attendance. There is no fee.

Rivier College, Registrar, 420 S Main St, Nashua, NH 03060-5086, 603-888-1311. Hours: 8AM-5PM. Enrollment: 2700. Records go back to 1937. Alumni records are maintained here also. Call 603-888-1311 X8522. Degrees granted: Associate; Bachelors; Masters.

Attendance and degree information available by phone, mail. Search requires name plus SSN, approximate years of attendance. Also helpful: exact years of attendance. There is no fee.

St. Anselm College, Registrar, Manchester, NH 03102-1310, 603-641-7000 (Fax: 603-641-7284 or 603-641-7116). Hours: 8:30AM-4:30PM. Enrollment: 2500. Records go back to 1800's. Alumni records are maintained here also. Call 603-641-7220. Degrees granted: Associate; Bachelors. Adverse incident record source- Dean of Students, 603-641-7600.

Attendance and degree information available by phone, fax, mail. Search requires name plus SSN, date of birth, approximate years of attendance. Also helpful: exact years of attendance. There is no fee.

University of New Hampshire, Registrar's Office, 11 Garrison Ave, Durham, NH 03824-3511, 603-862-1500 (Fax: 603-862-1817). Hours: 8AM-4:30PM. Records go back to 1866. Alumni Records Office: Alumni Association, Edgewood Rd, Durham, NH 03824. Degrees granted: Associate; Bachelors; Masters; Doctorate.

Attendance and degree information available by phone, fax, mail. Search requires name only. Also helpful: SSN, date of birth, exact years of attendance. There is no fee.

University of New Hampshire at Manchester, Registrar, 220 Hackett Hill Rd, Manchester, NH 03102, 603-668-0700 (Fax: 603-623-2745). Hours: 8AM-6:30PM M-Th, 8AM-4:30PM F. Enrollment: 2000. Records go back to 1988. All transcript information is kept in Durham. Records can be accessed as Transcript OFfice, 7 Garrison Ave, Durham, NH 03824 Alumni records are maintained here also. Call 603-862-2040. Degrees granted: Associate; Bachelors. Adverse incident record source- Counselling Office, 603-668-0700.

Attendance and degree information available by phone, mail. Search requires name plus SSN, approximate years of attendance. Also helpful: exact years of attendance. There is no fee.

University of New Hampshire, Keene State College, Registrar, 229 Main St, Keene, NH 03431, 603-535-2336 (Fax: 603-535-2528). Enrollment: 4000. Records go back to 1871. Alumni records are maintained here at the same phone number. Degrees granted: Associate; Bachelors; Masters. Special programs- Science: Education. Adverse incident record source- Security.

Attendance and degree information available by phone, mail. Search requires name plus SSN, exact years of attendance. There is no fee.

White Pines College, Registrar, Chester, NH 03036, 603-887-4401 (Fax: 603-887-1777). Hours: 8:30AM-4:30PM. Records go back to 1965. Degrees granted: Associate.

Attendance and degree information available by phone, fax, mail. Search requires name plus SSN, approximate years of attendance. Also helpful: date of birth, exact years of attendance. There is no fee.

Trade and Vocational Schools

Northeast Career Schools, 749 E Industrial Park Dr, Manchester, NH 03109, 603-622-2866

Travel Education Center (Branch Campus), 402 Amherst St, Nashua, NH 03063, 603-880-7200

State Licensing & Business Registration Quick Finder Index

Architecture, Engineering & Surveying
Architect #33 (1215) .... ☎ 603-271-2219
Engineer #33 (5633) .... ☎ 603-271-2219
Surveyor #33 (419) .... ☎ 603-271-2219

Business - Court & Legal Services
Attorney #47 (4000) .... ☎ 603-271-2646
Bondsman #4 (8) .... ☎ 603-271-1463
Lobbyist #34 .... ☎ 603-627-2071
Notary Public #46 (18000) .... ☎ 603-271-3242
Shorthand Reporter #5 603-669-7410

Business - General Services
Auctioneer #2 .... ☎ 603-271-3242
Itinerant Vendor #34 .... ☎ 603-627-2071
Public Accountant #32 (60) 603-271-3286
Public Accountant/CPA #40 (2500) .... ☎ 603-271-3286

Construction & Manufacturing
Boiler Inspector #30 (158) .... ☎ 603-271-2584
Electrician #31 (8000) .... ☎ 603-271-3748
Elevator Inspector #30 (250) .... ☎ 603-271-2656
Elevator Mechanic #30 .... ☎ 603-271-3171
Energy Facility Construction #8 603-271-3503
Energy Facility Siting #8 603-271-3503
Plumber #9 603-271-3267
Pump Installer #44 (424) .... ☎ 603-271-3406

Education
School Administrator #7 .... ☎ 603-271-3868
Teacher #7 .... ☎ 603-271-3868

Environmental & Agriculture
Forester #33 (243) .... ☎ 603-271-2219
Natural Scientist #33 (47) .... ☎ 603-271-2219

Pesticide Dealer #6 .... ☎ 603-271-3550
Pesticide Disposal #6 .... ☎ 603-271-3550
Pesticide Labeling #6 .... ☎ 603-271-3550
Pesticide Sale #6 .... ☎ 603-271-3550
Pesticide User #6 .... ☎ 603-271-3550
Veterinary Medicine #37 (853) .... ☎ 603-271-3706
Waste Water Treatment Plant Operator #44
.... ☎ 603-271-3406
Water Distribution System Operator #44 .... ☎ 603-271-3406
Water Well Contractor #44 (194) .... ☎ 603-271-3406

Financial - Real Estate, Insurance & Banking

Bank #1 .... ☎ 603-271-3561
Bank Holding Company #1 .... ☎ 603-271-3561
Business & Loan Association (Building & Loan Association/Cooperative Bank) #1 .... ☎ 603-271-3561
Credit Union #1 .... ☎ 603-271-3561
Debt Adjustor #1 .... ☎ 603-271-3561
First Mortgage Banker, Non-Depository #1
.... ☎ 603-271-3561
First Mortgage Broker #1 .... ☎ 603-271-3561
Insurance Adjuster #38 (3000) .... ☎ 603-271-2261
Insurance Advisor/Consultant #38 (225) .... ☎ 603-271-2261
Insurance Agent #38 (12500) .... ☎ 603-271-2261
Insurance Broker #38 (42000) .... ☎ 603-271-2261
Insurance Company #38 (1100) .... ☎ 603-271-2261
Investment Advisor #1 .... ☎ 603-271-3561
Loan Production Office #1 .... ☎ 603-271-3561
Morris Plan Bank #1 .... ☎ 603-271-3561
Mortgage Servicer #1 .... ☎ 603-271-3561
Out-of-State Trust Company #1 .... ☎ 603-271-3561
Real Estate Appraiser #35 .... ☎ 603-271-6186
Real Estate Broker #36 (5818) .... ☎ 603-271-2701
Real Estate Salesperson #36 (5790) .... ☎ 603-271-2701
Second Mortgage Home Loan Lender #1 ...... ☎ 603-271-3561
Securities Agent #1 .... ☎ 603-271-3561
Securities Dealer #1 .... ☎ 603-271-3561
Small Loan Company #1 .... ☎ 603-271-3561
Trust Company #1 .... ☎ 603-271-3561

Health & Beauty

Ambulance & Rescue Attendant #24 (7000)
.... ✉ 603-271-4568
Ambulance Service #24 .... ✉ 603-271-4568
Barber #3 (600) .... ☎ 603-271-3608
Chiropractor #15 (457) .... ☎ 603-271-4560
Cosmetologist #3 (8000) .... ☎ 603-271-3608
Dental Hygienist #16 (1057) .... ☎ 603-271-4561

Dentist #16 (1105) .... ☎ 603-271-4561
Electrologist #12 (200) .... ☎ 603-271-4604
Embalmer #18 .... ☎ 603-271-4651
Esthetician #3 (200) .... ☎ 603-271-3608
Funeral Director #18 .... ☎ 603-271-4651
Hearing Aid Dispenser/Fitter #27 .... ☎ 603-271-4816
Manicurist #3 (600) .... ☎ 603-271-3608
Massage Practitioner #13 (821) .... ✉ 603-271-4594
Midwife #26 .... ☎ 603-271-4537
Nurse #19 (30000) .... ☎ 603-271-2323
Nursing Home Administrator #17 .... ☎ 603-271-4728
Optician #14 (225) 603-271-4816
Optometrist #21 (5) .... ☎ 603-271-2428
Pharmacist #29 (1691) .... ☎ 603-271-2350
Podiatrist #20 (2) .... ☎ 603-271-1203
Residential Care Facility-Children #25 .... ☎ 603-271-4624
Respiratory Care Practitioner #22 (50) .... ☎ 603-271-1203
Speech-Language Pathologist #11 .... ☎ 603-271-1203

Investigations & Security

Private Investigator #41 .... ☎ 603-271-3575
Security Guard #43 .... ☎ 603-271-3575

Social Services

Alcohol/Drug Counselor #45 .... ☎ 603-271-6112
Child Care Facility #25 (1250) .... ☎ 603-271-4624
Child Placing Agency #10 .... ☎ 800-852-3345
Children & Youth Facility #23 .... ☎ 603-271-4453
Foster Family Home #10 .... ☎ 800-852-3345
Marital Mediator #42 .... ☎ 603-227-8043
Pastoral Counselor #28 (40) .... ☎ 603-271-6762
Psychologist #28 (550) .... ☎ 603-271-6762
Social Worker #28 (625) .... ☎ 603-271-6762

Sports & Entertainment

Bingo/Lottery #48 (360) .... ☎ 603-271-3391
Contestant #34 .... ☎ 603-627-2071
Liquor Licensing #39 (4374) .... ☎ 603-271-3521
Manager #34 .... ☎ 603-627-2071
Promoter #34 .... ☎ 603-627-2071
Referee #34 .... ☎ 603-627-2071
Second #34 .... ☎ 603-627-2071
Timekeeper #34 .... ☎ 603-627-2071

Transportation

Driver Education Instructor #7 (255) .... ☎ 603-271-3869
Motor Vehicle Retail Seller #1 .... ☎ 603-271-3561
Motor Vehicle Sales Finance Company #1 .... ☎ 603-271-3561

State Licensing & Business Registration Agency Information

(1) Banking Department, 169 Manchester St, Concord, NH 03301, 603-271-3561

(2) Board of Auctioneers, State House #24, Concord, NH 03301-4989, 603-271-3286

(3) Board of Barbering Cosmetology & Esthetics, 2 Industrial Park Drive, Concord, NH 03301, 603-271-3608, Fax: 603-271-6702

(4) Bureau of Securities Regulation, Department of State, State House, Room 204, Concord, NH 03301, 603-271-1463, Fax: 603-271-7933

(5) CSR Board, 235 A Black Brook Rd, Goffstown, NH 03045, 603-669-7410

(6) Department of Agriculture, 10 Ferry St, The Concord Center, Concord, NH 03301, 603-271-3550, Fax: 603-271-1109

(7) Department of Education, Division of Educational Improvement, 101 Pleasant St, State Office Park S, Concord, NH 03301, 603-271-3869, Fax: 603-271-1953

(8) Department of Environmental Services, 6 Hazen Dr, Concord, NH 03301, 603-271-3503

(9) Department of Environmental Services, Plumbers Licensing Board, PO Box 1386, Concord, NH 03302, 603-271-3267, Fax: 603-271-6656

(10) Department of Health & Human Services, 6 Hazen Dr, Concord, NH 03301, 800-852-3345, Fax: 603-271-4729

(11) Department of Health & Human Services, 6 Hazen Dr, Concord, NH 03301, 603-271-1203, Fax: 603-271-6702

(12) Department of Health & Human Services, Advisory Board of Electrologists, 6 Hazen Dr, Concord, NH 03301, 603-271-4604, Fax: 603-271-3745

(13) Department of Health & Human Services, Advisory Board of Massage Practitioners, 6 Hazen Dr, Concord, NH 03301, 603-271-4594, Fax: 603-271-4968

(14) Department of Health & Human Services, Advisory Council on Ophthalmic Despensing, 6 Hazen Dr, Concord, NH 03301, 603-271-4816, Fax: 603-271-3745

(15) Department of Health & Human Services, Board of Chiropractic Examiners, 6 Hazen Dr, Concord, NH 03301, 603-271-4560, Fax: 603-271-3745

(16) Department of Health & Human Services, Board of Dental Examiners, 2 Industrial Park Drive, Concord, NH 03301, 603-271-4561, Fax: 603-271-6702

(17) Department of Health & Human Services, Board of Examiners ofNursing Home Adminstrators, 2 Industrial Park Drive, Concord, NH 03301, 603-271-4728, Fax: 603-271-6702

(18) Department of Health & Human Services, Board of Funeral Directors & Embalmers, 6 Hazen Dr, Concord, NH 03301, 603-271-4651

(19) Department of Health & Human Services, Board of Nursing, 78 Regional Dr, Concord, NH 03301, 603-271-2323, Fax: 603-271-6605

(20) Department of Health & Human Services, Board of Podiatry, 6 Hazen Dr, Concord, NH 03301, 603-271-1203, Fax: 603-271-6702

(21) Department of Health & Human Services, Board of Registration in Optometry, 6 Hazen Dr, Concord, NH 03301, 603-271-2428, Fax: 603-271-6702

(22) Department of Health & Human Services, Board of Respiratory Care Examiners, 6 Hazen Dr, Concord, NH 03301, 603-271-1203, Fax: 603-271-6702

(23) Department of Health & Human Services, Bureau of Child Care Licensing, 6 Hazen Dr, Concord, NH 03301, 603-271-4443, Fax: 603-271-3745

(24) Department of Health & Human Services, Bureau of Emergency Medical Services, 6 Hazen Dr, Concord, NH 03301, 603-271-4568, Fax: 603-271-4567

(25) Department of Health & Human Services, Child Care Licensing, 6 Hazen Dr, Concord, NH 03301, 603-271-4624, Fax: 603-271-3745

(26) Department of Health & Human Services, Committee for the Practice of Lay-Midwifery, 6 Hazen Dr, Concord, NH 03301, 603-271-4537, Fax: 603-271-3827

(27) Department of Health & Human Services, Council on the Sale & Fitting of Hearing Aids, 6 Hazen Dr, Concord, NH 03301, 603-271-4816, Fax: 603-271-4141

(28) Department of Health & Human Services, Examiners of Psychology & Mental Health Practices, 105 Pleasant St., Concord, NH 03301, 603-271-6762

(29) Department of Health & Human Services, Pharmacy Board, 57 Regional Dr., Concord, NH 03301, 603-271-2350, Fax: 603-271-2856

(30) Department of Labor, 95 Pleasant St, State Office Park, S, Concord, NH 03301, 603-271-3171, Fax: 603-271-2668

(31) Department of Safety, Electricians' Board, 78 Regional Dr., Bldg. 1 PO Box 646, Concord, NH 03301, 603-271-3748

(32) Department of State, 57 Regional Dr, Concord, NH 03301, 603-271-3286

(33) Department of State, 57 Regional Dr, Concord, NH 03301, 603-271-2219

(34) Department of State, Boxing & Wrestling Commission, 1791 Bodwell Rd., Manchester, NH 03109, 603-627-2071

(35) Department of State, Real Estate Appraisal Board, 25 Capitol St, Rm 426, Concord, NH 03301-6312, 603-271-6186, Fax: 603-271-6513

(36) Department of State, Real Estate Commission, 95 Pleasant St, Spaulding Bldg, Concord, NH 03301, 603-271-2701, Fax: 603-271-1039

(37) Department of Veterinary Medicine, 25 Capital St., PO Box 2042, Concord, NH 03302-2042, 603-271-3706

(38) Insurance Department, Division of Licensing, 169 Manchester St, Concord, NH 03301, 603-271-2261, Fax: 603-271-1463

(39) Liquor Commission, Licensing & Enforcement, PO Box 503, Storrs St, Concord, NH 03302, 603-271-3521

(40) New Hampshire Board of Accountancy, 57 Regional Dr, Concord, NH 03301, 603-271-3286, Fax: 603-271-2856

(41) New Hampshire Department of Safety, 10 Hazen Dr, Concord, NH 03301, 603-271-3575, Fax: 603-271-1153

(42) New Hampshire Mediation Program, The Concord Center, 10 Ferry St #425, Concord, NH 03301, 603-224-8043, Fax: 603-224-8388

(43) New Hampshire State Police, License & Permits Division, 10 Hazen Dr, Jaems Hayes Safety Bldg, Concord, NH 03305, 603-271-3575, Fax: 605-271-1153

(44) New Hampshire Water Well Board, PO Box 2008, Concord, NH 03302-2008, 603-271-3406, Fax: 603-271-7894

(45) Office of Alcohol & Drug Abuse Prevention, 105 Pleasant St, Concord, NH 03301, 603-271-6112, Fax: 603-271-1116

(46) Office of Secretary of State, 107 N. Main St.,Statehouse Rm 204, Concord, NH 03301, 603-271-3242, Fax: 603-271-6316

(47) Supreme Court, 1 Noble Dr., Supreme Court, Concord, NH 03301, 603-271-2646, Fax: 603-271-6630

(48) Sweepstakes Commission, Bingo/Lucky 7 Division, 75 Fort Eddy Rd, Concord, NH 03301, 603-271-3391, Fax: 603-271-1160

New Jersey

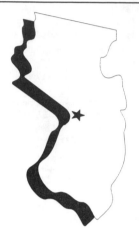

Capitol: Trenton (Mercer County)	
State Population	**7.9 Million**
Number of Degree Granting Institutions:	**87**
Number of State Licensing & Business Registration Agencies:	**103**

Degree Granting Educational Institutions

Assumption College for Sisters, Registrar, 350 Bernardsville Rd, Mallinckrodt Convent, Mendham, NJ 07945-0800, 201-543-6528 (Fax: 201-543-9459). Hours: 9AM-4PM. Enrollment: 321. Records go back to 1953. Degrees granted: Associate.

Attendance and degree information available by mail. Search requires name plus SSN, date of birth, exact years of attendance, signed release. There is no fee.

Atlantic Community College, Registrar, 5100 Black Horse Pike, Mays Landing, NJ 08330-2699, 609-343-5092 (Fax: 609-343-4914). Hours: 9AM-4:30PM. Enrollment: 5900. Records go back to 1969. Alumni records are maintained here at the same phone number. Degrees granted: Associate. Adverse incident record source- Dean of Students, 609-343-5083.

Attendance and degree information available by fax, mail. Search requires name plus signed release. Also helpful: SSN, date of birth, approximate years of attendance. There is no fee.

Bergen Community College, Registrar, 400 Paramus Rd, Paramus, NJ 07652, 201-447-7857 (Fax: 201-670-7973). Hours: 9AM-5PM. Records go back to 1968. Degrees granted: Associate.

Attendance and degree information available by mail. Search requires name plus SSN, signed release. Also helpful: date of birth, exact years of attendance. There is no fee.

Berkeley College of Business, (Waldwick Campus), Registrar, 100 W Prospect St, Waldwick, NJ 07463, 201-652-0388 (Fax: 201-670-7737). Hours: 7:30AM-4:30PM. Records go back to 1961. Alumni records are maintained here at the same phone number. Degrees granted: Associate. Adverse incident record source- 201-652-0388.

Attendance and degree information available by fax, mail. Search requires name plus SSN, approximate years of attendance. Also helpful: date of birth, exact years of attendance. There is no fee.

Berkeley College of Business, (West Paterson Campus), Office of the Registrar, 44 Rifle Camp Rd, West Paterson, NJ 07424, 201-278-5400 (Fax: 201-670-7737). Hours: 8:30AM-4:30PM. Records go back to 1945. Degrees granted: Associate.

School will not confirm attendance information.

Degree information available by fax, mail. Search requires name plus SSN, exact years of attendance, signed release. Also helpful: date of birth. There is no fee.

Berkeley College of Business, (Woodbridge Campus), Registrar, 430 Rahway Ave, Woodbridge, NJ 07095, 908-750-1800 (Fax: 908-750-0652). Hours: 7:30AM-4:30PM. Alumni records are maintained here at the same phone number. Degrees granted: Associate.

Attendance and degree information available by phone, fax, mail. Search requires name plus SSN, approximate years of attendance. Also helpful: exact years of attendance. There is no fee.

Beth Medrash Govoha, Registrar, 617 Sixth St, Lakewood, NJ 08701, 908-367-1060 (Fax: 908-367-7487). Hours: 9AM-1:40PM. Enrollment: 1900. Records go back to 1970. Alumni records are maintained here at the same phone number. Degrees granted: Bachelors; Masters; Advanced Talmudic, Rabbinic Ordination, Advanced Rabbinic.

Attendance and degree information available by fax. Search requires name plus signed release. Also helpful: SSN, date of birth, exact years of attendance. There is no fee.

Bloomfield College, Registrar, 467 Franklin St, Bloomfield, NJ 07003, 201-748-9000 (Fax: 201-743-3998). Hours: 7:30AM-5PM. Alumni records are maintained here at the same phone number. Degrees granted: Associate; Bachelors.

Attendance and degree information available by phone, fax, mail. Search requires name plus date of birth, exact years of attendance. There is no fee.

Brookdale Community College, Registrar, 47 Throckmorton St, Freehold, NJ 07728, 908-224-2268. Hours: 9AM-7PM M-Th; 9AM-5PM F; 9AM-1PM S. Records go back to 1970. Degrees granted: Associate.

Attendance and degree information available by mail. Search requires name plus SSN, signed release. There is no fee.

Brookdale Community College, Registrar, 765
Newman Springs Road, Lincroft, NJ 07738, 908-224-2710 (Fax: 908-224-2242). Hours: 9AM-7PM M-Th; 9AM-5PM F; 9AM-Noon S. Enrollment: 13000. Records go back to 1969. Alumni records are maintained here at the same phone number. Degrees granted: Associate.

Attendance and degree information available by mail. Search requires name plus SSN, exact years of attendance, signed release. There is no fee.

Brookdale Community College, Registrar, Newman Springs Rd, Lincroft, NJ 07738, 908-224-2000 (Fax: 908-224-2242). Hours: 8:30AM-7PM M-Th; 8:30AM-5PM F; 9AM-Noon S. Enrollment: 13000. Records go back to 1969. Alumni records are maintained here at the same phone number. Degrees granted: Associate. Adverse incident record source- Student Development, 908-224-2270.

Attendance and degree information available by fax, mail. Search requires name plus SSN, signed release. There is no fee.

Brookdale Community College, (Bayshore
Learning Center), Registrar, 311 Laurel Ave, West Keansburg, NJ 07734, 908-842-1900. Records are not housed here. They are located at Brookdale Community College, Registrar, Newman Springs Rd, Lincroft, NJ 07738.

Brookdale Community College, (Forth Monmouth Learning Center), Registrar, 918 Murphy Dr, Fort Monmouth, NJ 07703, 908-842-1900. Records are not housed here. They are located at Brookdale Community College, Registrar, Newman Springs Rd, Lincroft, NJ 07738.

Brookdale Community College, (Long Branch
Learning Center), Registrar, Third Ave and Broadway, Long Branch, NJ 07740, 908-842-1900. Records are not housed here. They are located at Brookdale Community College, Registrar, Newman Springs Rd, Lincroft, NJ 07738.

Burlington County College, Registrar, County Rte
530, Pemberton, NJ 08068-1599, 609-894-4900 (Fax: 609-894-9440). Alumni records are maintained here also. Call 609-894-9311 X7331. Degrees granted: Associate.

Attendance and degree information available by fax, mail. Search requires name plus SSN, approximate years of attendance, signed release. There is no fee.

Caldwell College, Registrar, 9 Ryerson Ave, Caldwell,
NJ 07006-6195, 201-228-4424 (Fax: 201-403-1784). Hours: 9AM-4:30PM. Enrollment: 1700. Records go back to 1939. Alumni records are maintained here at the same phone number. Degrees granted: Bachelors; Masters. Certification: EED, SNC.

Attendance and degree information available by fax, mail. Search requires name only. Also helpful: SSN, date of birth, exact years of attendance. There is no fee.

Camden County College, Registrar, PO Box 200,
Blackwood, NJ 08012, 609-227-7200 X4200 (Fax: 609-374-4917). Hours: 8:30AM-8:30PM. Records go back to 1968. Alumni records are maintained here at the same phone number. Degrees granted: Associate.

Attendance and degree information available by phone, fax, mail. Search requires name plus SSN. Also helpful: date of birth, approximate years of attendance. There is no fee.

Camden County College, (Branch Campus), Registrar, 200 N Broadway, Camden, NJ 08102-1102, 609-338-1817 (Fax: 609-756-0497). Records are not housed here. They are located at Camden County College, Registrar, PO Box 200, Blackwood, NJ 08012.

Centenary College, Registrar, 400 Jefferson St, Hackettstown, NJ 07840, 908-852-1400 (Fax: 908-852-3454). Hours: 8:30AM-6:45PM M-Th; 8:30AM-4:30PM F. Enrollment: 800. Alumni records are maintained here also. Call 908-852-1400. Degrees granted: Associate; Bachelors.

Attendance and degree information available by phone, fax, mail. Search requires name plus SSN, exact years of attendance. Also helpful: date of birth. There is no fee.

College of New Jersey (The), Registrar, Hollwood
Lakes, CN 4700, Trenton, NJ 08650, 609-771-1855 (Fax: 609-771-3484). Hours: 8:30AM-4:30PM. Enrollment: 7000. Formerly Trenton State College Records go back to 1900. Alumni records are maintained here also. Call 609-771-2393. Degrees granted: Bachelors; Masters.

Attendance and degree information available by phone, mail. Search requires name plus SSN, approximate years of attendance. There is no fee.

College of St. Elizabeth, Registrar, 2 Convent Rd,
Morristown, NJ 07960-7989, 201-605-7000 (Fax: 201-605-7499). Hours: 8AM-4:30PM. Alumni records are maintained here also. Call 201-292-6300. Degrees granted: Associate; Bachelors; Masters.

Attendance and degree information available by phone, fax, mail. Search requires name plus SSN, date of birth, exact years of attendance. There is no fee.

County College of Morris, Registrar, Rte 10 and
Center Grove Rd, Randolph, NJ 07869, 201-328-5198 (Fax: 201-328-5209). Hours: 8:30AM-4:30PM. Records go back to 1965. Alumni records are maintained here also. Call 201-328-5000. Degrees granted: Associate.

Attendance and degree information available by phone, fax, mail. Search requires name plus SSN. There is no fee.

Cumberland County College, Registrar, College
Dr, PO Box 517, Vineland, NJ 08360, 609-691-8600 (Fax: 609-691-9157). Hours: 8AM-5:30PM. Enrollment: 2700. Records go back to 1966. Alumni records are maintained here at the same phone number. Degrees granted: Associate. Special programs-Aquaculture: Aviation: Horticulture: Radiography: Quality Assurance. Adverse incident record source- Dean of Students, 609-691-8600 X211.

School will not confirm attendance information.

Degree information available by phone, fax, mail. Search requires name plus approximate years of attendance. Also helpful: SSN, exact years of attendance. There is no fee.

Drew University, Office of the Registrar, 36 Madison
Ave, Madison, NJ 07940, 201-408-3025 (Fax: 201-408-3044). Hours: 9AM-5PM. Enrollment: 2000. Records go back to 1917. Alumni Records Office: 120 Madison Ave, Madison, NJ 07940. Degrees granted: Bachelors; Masters; Doctorate. Certification: Medical Humanities. Adverse incident record source- Office of Student Life, 201-408-3390.

Attendance and degree information available by phone, fax, mail. Search requires name plus SSN. Also helpful: date of birth, exact years of attendance. There is no fee.

Essex County College, Registrar, 303 University Ave,
Newark, NJ 07102, 201-877-3111 (Fax: 201-623-6449). Hours: 8:30AM-7:30PM M-Th; 9AM-5PM F. Enrollment: 8500. Records go back to 1968. Alumni records are maintained here also. Call 201-877-3039. Degrees granted: Associate. Adverse incident record source- Security Office, 201-877-3131.

Attendance and degree information available by phone, fax, mail. Search requires name plus SSN. Also helpful: approximate years of attendance. There is no fee.

Essex County College, (West Essex Branch Campus), Registrar, 730 Bloomfield Ave, West Caldwell, NJ 07006, 201-403-2560 (Fax: 201-228-6181). Hours: 8AM-4:30PM.

Alumni records are maintained here also. Call 201-877-3039. Degrees granted: Associate. Adverse incident record source- 201-877-3131.

Attendance and degree information available by mail. Search requires name plus SSN, approximate years of attendance. There is no fee.

Fairleigh Dickinson University, Registrar, 1000 River Rd, Teaneck, NJ 07666, 201-692-2218. Hours: 9AM-5PM. Enrollment: 9500. Records go back to 1952. Alumni records are maintained here also. Call 201-692-7013. Degrees granted: Bachelors; Masters; Ph.D.

Attendance information available by mail. Search requires name plus SSN, approximate years of attendance, signed release. There is no fee.

Degree information available by phone, fax, mail. Search requires name plus SSN, approximate years of attendance. There is no fee.

Fairleigh Dickinson University, (Florham-Madison Campus), Offic of Enrollment Svcs, 285 Madison Ave, Madison, NJ 07940, 201-593-8600 (Fax: 201-593-8604). Hours: 9AM-5PM. Records go back to 1958. Alumni records are maintained here also. Call 201-443-7013. Degrees granted: Associate; Bachelors; Masters. Adverse incident record source-Madison & Teaneck Campuses.

Attendance and degree information available by phone, fax, mail. Search requires name plus SSN. Also helpful: date of birth, exact years of attendance. Fee is $5.00.

Fairleigh Dickinson University, (Rutherford Campus), Registrar, 223 Montrose Ave, Rutherford, NJ 07070, 201-460-5000. Records are not housed here. They are located at Fairleigh Dickinson University, (Teaneck-Hackensack Campus), Registrar, University Plaza 3, Hackensack, NJ 07840.

Fairleigh Dickinson University, (Teaneck-Hackensack Campus), Registrar, University Plaza 3, Hackensack, NJ 07840, 201-692-9170. Records are not housed here. They are located at Fairleigh Dickinson University, Registrar, 1000 River Rd, Teaneck, NJ 07666.

Felician College, Registrar, 262 S Main St, Lodi, NJ 07644, 201-778-1190 X6038 (Fax: 201-778-4111). Hours: 8:30AM-4:30PM MTF; 8:30AM-8PM WTh. Enrollment: 1150. Records go back to 1942. Alumni records are maintained here at the same phone number. Degrees granted: Associate; Bachelors; Masters.

Attendance and degree information available by phone, fax, mail. Search requires name plus SSN. Also helpful: approximate years of attendance. There is no fee.

Georgian Court College, Registrar's Office, Kingscote, Admin Bldg, 900 Lakewood Ave, Lakewood, NJ 08701-2697, 908-364-2200 X228 (Fax: 908-367-3920). Hours: 8:30AM-4:30PM. Enrollment: 2400. Records go back to 1908. Alumni records are maintained here also. Call 908-364-2200 X232. Degrees granted: Bachelors; Masters. Adverse incident record source- Student Services, 908-364-2200 X315.

Attendance and degree information available by phone, mail. Search requires name plus exact years of attendance. Also helpful: SSN, date of birth. There is no fee.

Gloucester County College, Registrar, 1400 Tanyard Rd, Sewell, NJ 08080, 609-468-5000 X282 (Fax: 609-848-8498). Hours: 8:30AM-5PM. Enrollment: 5000. Records go back to 1968. Alumni records are maintained here also. Call 609-468-5000 X273. Degrees granted: Associate.

Attendance and degree information available by phone, mail. Search requires name plus SSN, approximate years of attendance. Also helpful: date of birth, exact years of attendance. There is no fee.

Hudson County Community College, Registrar, 168 Sip Ave, Jersey City, NJ 07306, 201-714-2138 (Fax: 201-714-2136). Hours: 9AM-6PM M-Th; 9AM-5PM F. Enrollment: 3950. Records go back to 1974. Alumni records are maintained here also. Call 201-714-2228. Degrees granted: Associate.

Attendance and degree information available by mail. Search requires name plus SSN, approximate years of attendance, signed release. There is no fee.

Immaculate Conception Seminary, Registrar, 400 S Orange Ave, South Orange, NJ 07079, 201-761-9238. Hours: 9AM-5PM. Enrollment: 170. Records go back to 1945. Degrees granted: Masters.

Attendance and degree information available by mail. Search requires name plus SSN, signed release. There is no fee.

Jersey City State College, Registrar, 2039 Kennedy Blvd, Jersey City, NJ 07305, 201-200-3336 (Fax: 201-200-2044). Hours: 8:30AM-4:30PM. Enrollment: 10000. Records go back to 1993. Alumni records are maintained here also. Call 201-200-3196. Degrees granted: Bachelors; Masters.

Attendance and degree information available by phone, fax, mail. Search requires name plus SSN. Also helpful: date of birth. There is no fee.

Katharine Gibbs School, (Branch Campus), Registrar, 80 Kingsbridge Rd, Piscataway, NJ 08854, 908-885-1580 (Fax: 908-885-1235). Enrollment: 300. Records go back to 1984. Alumni records are maintained here at the same phone number. Degrees granted: Associate.

Attendance and degree information available by fax, mail. Search requires name plus SSN, exact years of attendance, signed release. There is no fee.

Katherine Gibbs School, Registrar, 33 Plymouth St, Montclair, NJ 07042, 201-744-2010 (Fax: 201-744-2298). Hours: 8AM-10PM. Enrollment: 400. Records go back to 1960. Alumni Records Office: 52 Vanderbilt Avenue, New York, NY 10017. Degrees granted: Associate. Special programs- Applied Sciences.

Attendance and degree information available by fax, mail. Search requires name plus SSN, approximate years of attendance, signed release. There is no fee.

Kean College of New Jersey, Registrar, 1000 Morris Ave, Union, NJ 07083, 908-527-2445 (Fax: 908-527-0423). Hours: 8:30AM-4:30PM. Enrollment: 12000. Records go back to 1960. Alumni records are maintained here also. Call 908-527-2526. Degrees granted: Bachelors; Masters. Adverse incident record source- Dean of Students, 908-527-2190.

Attendance and degree information available by phone, mail. Search requires name plus SSN. Also helpful: exact years of attendance. There is no fee.

Mercer County Community College, Registrar, 1200 Old Trenton Rd, Box B, Trenton, NJ 08690-0182, 609-586-4800 (Fax: 609-586-6944). Hours: 8AM-7PM M-Th; 8AM-5PM F. Enrollment: 8500. Alumni records are maintained here at the same phone number. Degrees granted: Associate.

Attendance and degree information available by fax, mail. Search requires name plus SSN, date of birth, signed release. Also helpful: exact years of attendance. There is no fee.

Mercer County Community College, (James Kerney Campus), Registrar, N Broad and Academy Sts, Trenton, NJ 08690, 609-586-4800 (Fax: 609-586-6944). Records are not housed here. They are located at Mercer County Community College, Registrar, 1200 Old Trenton Rd, Box B, Trenton, NJ 08690-0182.

Middlesex County College, Registrar's Office, 155 Mill Rd, PO Box 3050, Edison, NJ 08818-3050, 908-548-6000 (Fax: 908-494-8244). Enrollment: 10500. Records go back to

1966. Alumni records are maintained here also. Call 908-906-2564. Degrees granted: Associate. Special programs- Liberal Arts, 908-906-2528: Business Tech, 908-906-2502: Engineering & Science, 908-906-2501: Health Tech, 908-906-2533: Open College, 908-906-2533. Adverse incident record source- Student Services, 908-906-2514.

Attendance and degree information available by phone, mail. Search requires name only. Also helpful: SSN, date of birth, exact years of attendance. There is no fee.

Monmouth University, Registrar, Norwood and Cedar Aves, West Long Branch, NJ 07764-1898, 908-571-3477 (Fax: 908-571-7510). Hours: 9AM-5PM. Enrollment: 4500. Records go back to 1933. Alumni records are maintained here also. Call 908-571-3489. Degrees granted: Associate; Bachelors; Masters.

Attendance and degree information available by fax, mail. Search requires name plus SSN. Also helpful: date of birth, exact years of attendance. There is no fee.

Montclair State College, Registrar, Valley Rd and Normal Ave, Upper Montclair, NJ 07043-1624, 201-655-4376 (Fax: 201-655-7371). Hours: 8:30AM-4:30PM. Records go back to 1950. Alumni records are maintained here also. Call 201-655-4141. Degrees granted: Bachelors; Masters. Adverse incident record source- Dean of Students, 201-655-4118.

Attendance and degree information available by phone, fax, mail. Search requires name plus SSN, date of birth, approximate years of attendance. There is no fee.

New Brunswick Theological Seminary, Registrar, 17 Seminary Pl, New Brusnwick, NJ 08901-1196, 908-246-5593 (Fax: 908-249-5412). Hours: 8:30AM-4PM. Enrollment: 185. Records go back to 1920's. Alumni records are maintained here also. Call 908-246-5600. Degrees granted: Masters; M. Div. Special programs- Theology. Adverse incident record source- Office of President.

Attendance and degree information available by phone, fax, mail. Search requires name plus exact years of attendance. Also helpful: SSN, date of birth. There is no fee.

New Jersey Institute of Technology, Registrar, University Heights, Newark, NJ 07102-9938, 201-596-3236 (Fax: 201-802-1854). Hours: 8:30AM-4:30PM. Enrollment: 8000. Records go back to 1919. Alumni records are maintained here at the same phone number. Degrees granted: Bachelors; Masters; Doctorate. Adverse incident record source- Campus Police, 201-596-3111.

Attendance and degree information available by phone, fax, mail. Search requires name plus SSN, date of birth, approximate years of attendance. Also helpful: exact years of attendance. There is no fee.

Northeastern Bible Institute, Registrar, PO Box 676, Essex Fells, NJ 07021, 201-992-0730 (Fax: 201-992-1085). Formerly Northeastern Bible College Records go back to 1950. Closed as a degree-granting college 6/30/90, currently operating as a bible institute offering non-credit courses. Alumni Records Office: Alumni Association, PO Box 141, Essex Falls, NJ 07021.

Attendance and degree information available by phone, fax, mail. Search requires name only. Also helpful: SSN, date of birth, exact years of attendance. There is no fee.

Ocean County College, Admissions & Records, College Dr/PO Box 2001, Toms River, NJ 08754-2001, 908-255-0304. Hours: 8AM-9PM M-Th; 8AM-5PM F. Records go back to 1966. Alumni records are maintained here also. Call 908-255-0400. Degrees granted: Associate.

Attendance and degree information available by mail. Search requires name plus SSN, signed release. Also helpful: date of birth, exact years of attendance. There is no fee.

Passiac County Community College, Registrar, One College Blvd, Paterson, NJ 07505-1179, 201-684-6400 (Fax: 201-684-6778). Hours: 9AM-7PM M,Th; 9AM-5PM T,W,F. Enrollment: 3700. Records go back to 1971. Alumni records are maintained here also. Call 201-684-5656. Degrees granted: Associate. Adverse incident record source- Student Affairs.

Attendance and degree information available by phone, fax, mail. Search requires name plus SSN. Also helpful: approximate years of attendance. There is no fee.

Princeton Theological Seminary, Registrar, 64 Mercer St CN 821, Princeton, NJ 08542-0803, 609-497-7820 (Fax: 609-683-0741). Hours: 8:30AM-4:30PM. Records go back to 1920. Alumni records are maintained here at the same phone number. Degrees granted: Masters; Ph.D.

Attendance and degree information available by phone, fax, mail. Search requires name plus SSN, approximate years of attendance. There is no fee.

Princeton University, Office of the Registrar, Box 70, Princeton, NJ 08542, 609-258-6191 (Fax: 609-258-6328). Hours: 8:45AM-5PM. Enrollment: 6424. Records go back to 1909. Degrees granted: Bachelors; Masters; Doctorate.

Attendance and degree information available by phone, fax, mail. Search requires name only. Also helpful: SSN, approximate years of attendance. There is no fee.

Rabbinical College of America, Registrar, 226 Sussex Ave, Morristown, NJ 07960, 201-267-9404 (Fax: 201-267-5208). Hours: 9AM-5PM. Enrollment: 190. Records go back to 1965. Alumni records are maintained here at the same phone number. Degrees granted: Bachelors. Adverse incident record source- Registrar, 201-267-9404.

Attendance information available by phone, fax, mail. Search requires name plus approximate years of attendance. Also helpful: SSN, date of birth, exact years of attendance. There is no fee.

Degree information available by fax, mail. Search requires name plus approximate years of attendance. Also helpful: SSN, date of birth, exact years of attendance. There is no fee.

Ramapo College of New Jersey, Registrar, 505 Ramapo Valley Rd, Mahwah, NJ 07430-1680, 201-529-7700 (Fax: 201-529-7603). Hours: 8:30AM-4:30PM. Enrollment: 4600. Records go back to 1971. Alumni records are maintained here also. Call 201-529-7612. Degrees granted: Bachelors; Masters. Special programs- MALS (Graduate), 201 529 7423. Adverse incident record source- Dean of Students, 201-529-7700 X7457.

Attendance and degree information available by phone, fax, mail. Search requires name plus SSN, date of birth, exact years of attendance. There is no fee.

Raritan Valley Community College, Registrar's Office, PO Box 3300, Somerville, NJ 08876, 908-526-1200 X8869 (Fax: 908-231-8811). Hours: 8:30AM-4:30PM. Enrollment: 12000. Records go back to 1970. Alumni records are maintained here at the same phone number. Degrees granted: Associate. Adverse incident record source- Student Affairs, 908-526-1200.

Attendance and degree information available by phone, fax, mail. Search requires name plus SSN. Also helpful: approximate years of attendance. There is no fee.

Rider College, Registrar, 2083 Lawrenceville Rd, Lawrenceville, NJ 08648-3099, 609-896-5065 (Fax: 609-895-5447). Hours: 8:30AM-5PM. Records go back to 1925. Alumni records are maintained here also. Call 609-895-5340. Degrees granted: Bachelors; Masters. Adverse incident record source- Dean of Students, 609-895-5103.

Attendance and degree information available by phone, mail. Search requires name plus SSN, date of birth, approximate years of attendance. There is no fee.

Rider College, **(Westminster Choir College)**, Registrar, 101 Walnut Lane, Princeton, NJ 08540, 609-921-7100 X207 (Fax: 609-921-8829). Hours: 8:30AM-5PM. Enrollment: 375. Records go back to 1920. Alumni records are maintained here at the same phone number. Degrees granted: Bachelors; Masters.

Attendance and degree information available by phone, fax, mail. Search requires name only. There is no fee.

Rowan College, Transcript Registrar, Glassboro, NJ 08028, 609-756-4500 (Fax: 609-756-0497). Formerly Glassboro State College

Attendance and degree information available by phone, mail. Search requires name plus SSN, exact years of attendance. Also helpful: date of birth. There is no fee.

Rowan College of New Jersey, Registrar, 201 Mullica Hill Rd, Glassboro, NJ 08028-1701, 609-256-4350 (Fax: 609-256-4929). Hours: 8AM-4:30PM. Enrollment: 9000. Records go back to 1980. Alumni records are maintained here also. Call 609-256-4131. Degrees granted: Bachelors; Masters. Adverse incident record source- Dean of Students, 609-256-4040.

Attendance and degree information available by phone, fax, mail. Search requires name plus SSN. There is no fee.

Rowan College of New Jersey, **(Camden Campus)**, Registrar, One Broadway, Camden, NJ 08102, 609-756-5400. Records are not housed here. They are located at Rowan College of New Jersey, Registrar, 201 Mullica Hill Rd, Glassboro, NJ 08028-1701.

Rutgers, The State University of New Jersey Camden Campus, Registrar, 311 N Fifth St, Camden, NJ 08102, 609-225-6054 (Fax: 609-225-6453). Hours: 8:30AM-4:30PM. Enrollment: 5000. Records go back to 1934. Alumni Records Office: Capehart Bldg, Camden, NJ 08102, 609-225-6028. Degrees granted: Bachelors; Masters; School of Law J.D. Adverse incident record source- Student Affairs, Brunswick, NJ, 908-932-9090.

Attendance and degree information available by phone, fax, mail. Search requires name plus SSN. Also helpful: date of birth, exact years of attendance. There is no fee.

Rutgers, The State University of New Jersey New Brunswick Campus, Registrar, PO Box 1360, Piscateaway, NJ 08903, 908-445-2757 (Fax: 908-445-5948). Degrees granted: Bachelors; Masters; Doctorate.

Attendance information available by fax, mail. Search requires name plus SSN, signed release. Also helpful: exact years of attendance. There is no fee.

Degree information available by phone, fax, mail. Search requires name plus SSN, approximate years of attendance. Also helpful: exact years of attendance. There is no fee.

Rutgers, The State University of New Jersey Newark Campus, Registrar, 249 University Ave, Rm 309, Newark, NJ 07102, 201-648-5324 (Fax: 201-648-1357). Hours: 8:30AM-4:30PM. Enrollment: 10000. Records go back to 1940. Alumni records are maintained here also. Call 201-648-5242. Degrees granted: Bachelors; Masters.

Attendance and degree information available by phone, fax, mail. Search requires name plus SSN, approximate years of attendance. There is no fee.

Salem Community College, Registrar, 460 Hollywood Ave, Carneys Point, NJ 08069, 609-299-2100 (Fax: 609-299-9193). Hours: 8:30AM-7:30PM M-Th; 8:30AM-4:30PM F. Enrollment: 1150. Records go back to 1972. Alumni records are

maintained here at the same phone number. Degrees granted: Associate.

Attendance and degree information available by mail. Search requires name plus SSN, signed release. Also helpful: date of birth. There is no fee.

Seton Hall University, Registrar, 400 S Orange Ave, South Orange, NJ 07079, 201-761-9374 (Fax: 201-275-2040). Hours: 8:45AM-4:45PM. Alumni records are maintained here also. Call 201-761-9822. Degrees granted: Bachelors; Masters; Doctorate.

Attendance and degree information available by phone, mail. Search requires name plus SSN, approximate years of attendance. Also helpful: exact years of attendance. There is no fee.

Seton Hall University, **(School of Law)**, Registrar, One Newark Ctr, Newark, NJ 07102-5210, 201-642-8162 (Fax: 201-642-8734). Hours: 8:30AM-6PM. Enrollment: 1250. Records go back to 1930. Alumni records are maintained here also. Call 201-642-8711. Degrees granted: Doctorate. Adverse incident record source- Registrar, 201-642-8162.

Attendance and degree information available by phone, fax, mail. Search requires name plus SSN, approximate years of attendance. There is no fee.

St. Peter's College, Registrar, 2641 Kennedy Blvd, Jersey City, NJ 07306, 201-915-9035 (Fax: 201-915-9038). Hours: 9AM-8PM M-Th; 9AM-5PM F. Records go back to 1916. Alumni records are maintained here also. Call 201-915-9204. Degrees granted: Associate; Bachelors; Masters.

Attendance and degree information available by phone, fax, mail. Search requires name plus SSN. There is no fee.

St. Peter's College, **(Englewood Cliffs Campus)**, Registrar, Hudson Terrace, Englewood Cliffs, NJ 07632, 201-568-7730 (Fax: 201-568-6614). Records are not housed here. They are located at St. Peter's College,   Registrar, 2641 Kennedy Blvd, Jersey City, NJ 07306.

Stevens Institute of Technology, Registrar, Castle Point on the Hudson, Hoboken, NJ 07030, 201-216-5210 (Fax: 201-216-8030). Hours: 8AM-5PM. Records go back to 1870. Alumni records are maintained here also. Call 201-216-5163. Degrees granted: Bachelors; Masters; Doctorate.

Attendance and degree information available by phone, fax, mail. Search requires name plus SSN, approximate years of attendance. Also helpful: date of birth, exact years of attendance. There is no fee.

Stockton College of New Jersey, Registrar, Jimmy Leeds Rd, Pomona, NJ 80240, 609-652-1776 (Fax: 609-652-4958). Enrollment: 5000. Records go back to 1972. Alumni records are maintained here at the same phone number. Degrees granted: Bachelors. Special programs- Arts: Science. Adverse incident record source- Security.

Attendance and degree information available by mail. Search requires name plus SSN, date of birth, exact years of attendance, signed release. There is no fee.

Stockton State College, Registrar, Jimmy Leeds Rd, Pomona, NJ 08240, 609-652-4235 (Fax: 609-652-4598). Hours: 8:30AM-4:30PM. Records go back to 1975. Alumni records are maintained here also. Call 609-652-4468.

Attendance and degree information available by phone, fax, mail. Search requires name plus SSN, approximate years of attendance. Also helpful: date of birth, exact years of attendance. There is no fee.

Sussex County Community College, Registrar, College Hill, Newton, NJ 07860, 201-300-2215 (Fax: 201-579-5226). Hours: 8AM-8PM M-Th; 8AM-5PM F. Enrollment: 2300. Records go back to 1982. Degrees granted: Associate. Adverse incident record source- Dean of Students.

Attendance information available by phone, fax, mail. Search requires name only. There is no fee.

Degree information available by phone, fax, mail. Search requires name only. Also helpful: exact years of attendance. There is no fee.

Talmudical Academy of New Jersey, Registrar, Rte 524, Adelphia, NJ 07710, 908-431-1600 (Fax: 908-431-3951). Hours: 9AM-5PM. Records go back to 1971. Alumni records are maintained here at the same phone number. Degrees granted: Bachelors.

Attendance and degree information available by fax, mail. Search requires name plus SSN, date of birth, signed release. There is no fee.

Thomas A. Edison State College, Registrar, 101 W State St, Trenton, NJ 08608-1176, 609-784-1100 (Fax: 609-777-0477). Hours: 8AM-4:30PM. Enrollment: 8000. Records go back to 1972. Alumni records are maintained here also. Call 201-877-1458. Degrees granted: Associate; Bachelors.

Attendance and degree information available by phone, fax, mail. Search requires name plus SSN. There is no fee.

Union County College, Registrar, 1033 Springfield Ave, Cranford, NJ 07016, 908-709-7132 (Fax: 908-709-1392). Hours: 8:30AM-4:30PM. Enrollment: 9000. Records go back to 1933. Alumni records are maintained here also. Call 908-709-7113. Degrees granted: Associate. Adverse incident record source- Dean of Students, 908-709-7644.

Attendance information available by fax, mail. Search requires name plus SSN, approximate years of attendance, signed release. Also helpful: date of birth, exact years of attendance. There is no fee.

Degree information available by fax, mail. Search requires name plus SSN, approximate years of attendance. Also helpful: date of birth, exact years of attendance. There is no fee.

Union County College, (Elizabeth Campus), Registrar, 12 W Jersey St, Elizabeth, NJ 07206, 908-965-6050 (Fax: 908-709-1392). Records are not housed here. They are located at Union County College, Registrar, 1033 Springfield Ave, Cranford, NJ 07016.

Union County College, (Plainfield Campus), Registrar, 232 E Second St, Plainfield, NJ 07060, 908-889-8500. Records are not housed here. They are located at Union County College, Registrar, 1033 Springfield Ave, Cranford, NJ 07016.

University of Medicine Science of New Jersey, Registrar, 185 S Orange, Rm B640, Newark, NJ 07103-2714, 201-982-4640 (Fax: 201-982-6930). Hours: 8:30AM-4:30PM. Enrollment: 750. Records go back to 1960. Degrees granted: Doctorate.

Attendance and degree information available by phone, fax, mail. Search requires name only. There is no fee.

University of Medicine and Dentistry, ((New Jersey Dental School)), Registrar, 110 Bergen St, Newark, NJ 07103, 201-982-4728 (Fax: 201-982-3689). Hours: 8AM-4PM. Enrollment: 350. Records go back to 1956. Alumni records are maintained here also. Call 201-982-6883. Degrees granted: Doctorate.

Attendance and degree information available by phone, fax, mail. Search requires name only. Also helpful: SSN. There is no fee.

University of Medicine and Dentistry of New Jersey, (Graduate School of Biomedical Sciences), Registrar, 185 S Orange Ave, Newark, NJ 07103, 201-982-4300. Records are not housed here. They are located at University of Medicine Science of New Jersey, Registrar, 185 S Orange, Rm B640, Newark, NJ 07103-2714.

University of Medicine and Dentistry of New Jersey, (Medical School), Registrar, 185 S Orange Ave, Newark, NJ 07103, 201-982-2000. Records are not housed here. They are located at University of Medicine Science of New Jersey, Registrar, 185 S Orange, Rm B640, Newark, NJ 07103-2714.

University of Medicine and Dentistry of New Jersey, (Robert Wood Johnson Medical School), Registrar, 675 Hoes Lane, Piscataway, NJ 08854, 908-235-4565 (Fax: 908-235-5078). Hours: 8:30AM-5PM. Enrollment: 600. Records go back to 1974. Alumni records are maintained here also. Call 908-235-4898. Degrees granted: Masters; Doctorate.

Attendance and degree information available by phone, fax, mail. Search requires name only. Also helpful: SSN. There is no fee.

University of Medicine and Dentistry of New Jersey, (School of Health-Related Professions), Registrar, 65 Bergen St, Newark, NJ 07107, 201-456-5453. Records are not housed here. They are located at University of Medicine Science of New Jersey, Registrar, 185 S Orange, Rm B640, Newark, NJ 07103-2714.

University of Medicine and Dentistry of New Jersey, (School of Osteopathic Medicine), Registrar, Academic Ctr, One Medical Center Dr, Stratford, NJ 08084, 609-566-6995. Records are not housed here. They are located at University of Medicine Science of New Jersey, Registrar, 185 S Orange, Rm B640, Newark, NJ 07103-2714.

Upsala College, Registrar. 345 Prospect St, East Orange, NJ 07019, 201-266-7145. Degrees granted: Bachelors.

Attendance and degree information available by phone, mail. Search requires name plus SSN, approximate years of attendance. There is no fee.

Warren County Community College, Registrar, 475 Rte 57 W, Washington, NJ 07882, 908-689-1090 (Fax: 908-689-9262). Hours: 8:30AM-5PM. Records go back to 1981. Degrees granted: Associate.

Attendance and degree information available by mail. Search requires name plus SSN, signed release. Also helpful: exact years of attendance. There is no fee.

Westminster Choir College, Registrar, Hamilton Ave and Walnut Ln, Princeton, NJ 08540, 609-921-7100 X295 (Fax: 609-921-8829). Degrees granted.

Attendance and degree information available by phone, fax, mail. Search requires name plus SSN, approximate years of attendance. There is no fee.

William Paterson College of New Jersey, Office of the Registrar, College Hall 358 Hamburg Tpk, PO Box 913, Wayne, NJ 07470-0913, 201-595-3119. Hours: 8:30AM-4:30PM. Alumni Records Office: Alumni Office, 300 Pompton Rd, Wayne, NJ 07470. Degrees granted: Bachelors; Masters. Certification: Education.

Attendance and degree information available by phone, mail. Search requires name plus SSN, date of birth, exact years of attendance. There is no fee.

Trade and Vocational Schools

Academy of Professional Development, 98 Mayfield Ave, Edison, NJ 08837, 908-417-9100

Academy of Professional Development (Branch Campus), 934 Parkway Ave, Ewing, NJ 08618, 609-538-0400

American Business Academy, 66 Moore St, Hackensack, NJ 07601, 201-488-9400

Berdan Institute, 265 Rte 46 W, Totowa, NJ 07512, 201-256-3444

Boardwalk and Marina Casino Dealers School, 1923 Bacharan Blvd, Atlantic City, NJ 08401, 609-344-1986

Brick Computer Science Institute, 515 Hwy 70, Brick, NJ 08723, 908-477-0975

Business Training Institute, 4 Forest Ave, Paramus, NJ 07652, 201-845-9300

Cape May County Technical Institute, 188 Crest Haven Rd, Cape May Court House, NJ 08210, 609-465-3064

Chubb Institute (The), 8 Sylvan Wy, Parsippany, NJ 07054, 201-682-4900

Chubb Institute (The) (Branch Campus), 40 Journal Sq, Jersey City, NJ 07306, 201-656-0330

Cittone Institute, 1697 Oak Tree Rd, Edison, NJ 08820, 908-548-8798

Cittone Institute (Branch Campus), 523 Fellowship Rd #625, Mount Laurel, NJ 08054, 609-722-9333

Cittone Institute (Branch Campus), 100 Canal Pointe Blvd, Princeton, NJ 08540, 609-520-8798

Computer Learning Center, 160 E Rte 4, Paramus, NJ 07652, 201-845-6868

Divers Academy of the Eastern Seaboard, 2500 S Broadway, Camden, NJ 08104, 800-238-3483

Dover Business College, 15 E Blackwell St, Dover, NJ 07801, 201-366-6700

Dover Business College (Branch Campus), E 81 Rte 4 W, Paramus, NJ 07652, 201-712-0107

Drake College of Business, 125 Broad St, Elizabeth, NJ 07201, 908-352-5509

Drake College of Business (Branch Campus), 60 Evergreen Pl, East Orange, NJ 07018, 201-673-6009

Du Cret School of the Arts, 1030 Central Ave, Plainfield, NJ 07060, 908-757-7171

Empire Technical Schools of New Jersey, 576 Central Ave, East Orange, NJ 07018, 201-675-0565

Engine City Technical Institute, Rte 22 W Box 3116, Union, NJ 07083, 908-964-1450

General Technical Institute Welding Trade School, 1118 Baltimore Ave, Linden, NJ 07036, 908-486-9353

Harris School of Business, 654 Longwood Ave, Cherry Hill, NJ 08002, 609-662-5300

HoHoKus School, 50 S Frankling Tpke, Ramsey, NJ 07446, 201-327-8877

Joe Kubert School of Cartoon and Graphic Art, 37 Myrtle Ave, Dover, NJ 07801, 201-361-1327

Joe Kubert School of Cartoon and Graphic Art (Mahwah Campus), 70 McKee Dr, Mahwah, NJ 07430, 201-529-1414

Kane Business Institute, 206 Haddonfield Rd, Cherry Hill, NJ 08002, 609-488-1166

Lincoln Technical Institute, Haddonfield Rd, Pennsauken, NJ 08110, 609-665-3010

Lincoln Technical Institute, 2299 Vauxhall Rd, Union, NJ 07083, 908-964-7800

Lincoln Technical Institute (Mahwah Campus), 70 McKee Dr, Mahwah, NJ 07430, 201-529-1414

Metropolitan Technical Institute, 11 Daniel Rd, Fairfield, NJ 07004, 201-227-8191

National Education Center-RETS Campus, 103 Park Ave, Nutley, NJ 07110, 201-661-0600

Naval Air Technical Training Center (Branch Campus), Hanger 1, Lakehurst, NJ 08733, 908-323-7433

Omega Institute, 7050 Rte 30 E, Pennsauken, NJ 08109, 609-663-4299

Pennco Tech, PO Box 1427, Blackwood, NJ 08012, 609-232-0310

Plaza School (The), Bergen Mall, Paramus, NJ 07652, 201-843-0344

Star Technical Institute, 251 N Delsea Dr, Deptford, NJ 08096, 609-384-2888

Star Technical Institute, 2224 US Hwy, Edgewater Park, NJ 08010, 609-877-2727

Star Technical Institute, Somerdale Sq #2, Somerdale, NJ 08083, 609-435-7827

Star Technical Institute, 1386 S Delsea Dr, Vineland, NJ 08360, 609-696-0500

Star Technical Institute (Branch Campus), 1255 Rte 70 #12N, Lakewood, NJ 08701, 908-901-0001

Star Technical Institute (Branch Campus), 2105 Hwy 35, Ocean Township, NJ 07712, 908-493-1660

Stuart School of Business Administration, 2400 Belmar Blvd, Wall, NJ 07719, 908-681-7200

Technical Institute of Camden County, 343 Berlin-Cross Keys Rd, Sicklerville, NJ 08081, 609-767-7000

Teterboro School of Aeronautics, 80 Moonachie Ave, Teterboro, NJ 07608, 201-288-6300

Titan Helicopter Academy, Easterwood St Bldg 90, Millville, NJ 08332, 609-327-5203

Ultrasound Diagnostic School, 675 US Rte 1, 2nd Floor, Iselin, NJ 08830, 908-634-1131

State Licensing & Business Registration Quick Finder Index

Architecture, Engineering & Surveying
Architect #6 (8000)........................ ☎ 201-504-6385
Engineer #20 (18175)...................... ☎ 201-504-6460
Landscape Architect #6 (600) .... ☎ 201-504-6385
Surveyor #20 (1211)........................ ☎ 201-504-6460

Business - Court & Legal Services
Attorney #49 .... ✉ 609-984-7783
Court Reporter #24 .... ☎ 201-504-6490
Lobbyist #43 (570) .... ☎ 609-292-8700
Notary Public #39.......................... ☎ 609-530-6421
Shorthand Reporter #24 (1350)........ ☎ 201-504-6490

Business - General Services
Certified Public Accountant #5 .... ☎ 201-504-6380
Employment Agency #41 .... ☎ 201-504-6200
Public Accountant-CPA #5 (2000) ... ☎ 201-504-6380
Weigh Master #38 908-815-4845
Weights & Measures Mechanic #38 ... 908-815-4845

Construction & Manufacturing
Boiler Operator #36 (45000) .... ☎ 609-292-2921
Building Inspector #45 (1000) .... ☎ 609-530-8803
Construction Code Official #45 (2000)........ ☎ 609-530-8803
Crane Operator #36 (12000)............. ☎ 609-292-2921
Electrician #11 (16000) .... ☎ 201-504-6410
Home Repair Contractor/Salesperson #29 ..... ✉ 609-292-3420
Plumber #12 (7000)........................ 201-504-6420
Pump Installer #31 609-292-2885

Education
Director of Student Personnel Services #30
.... ✉ 609-292-0739
Educational Media Specialist/Librarian #30
.... ✉ 609-292-0739
School Administrator #30................. ✉ 609-292-0739
School Counselor #30...................... ✉ 609-292-0739
School Principal #30....................... ✉ 609-292-0739
School Supervisor #30..................... ✉ 609-292-0739
Teacher #30 .... ✉ 609-292-0739

Environmental & Agriculture
Asbestos Employee/Employer #35.......... ☎ 609-633-3760
Pesticide Applicator #32 (8000)........ ☎ 609-530-4070
Pesticide Dealer #32 (300) .... ☎ 609-530-4070
Pesticide Operator #32 (5000).......... ☎ 609-530-4070
Tree Expert #55 (230)..................... ☎ 609-292-2532
Veterinarian #26 .... ✉ 201-504-6500
Waste Water System Operator #31 609-292-2885
Well Driller #31............................. 609-292-2885

Financial - Real Estate, Insurance & Banking
Certified General Appraiser #23 .... ☎ 201-504-6480
Certified Residential Appraiser #23 ..... ☎ 201-504-6480
Check Casher/Seller #29 .... ✉ 609-292-5340
Check Cashier/Seller #28 609-292-5466
Consumer Lender #29 .... ✉ 609-292-5340
Insurance Agent (Insurance Producer) #34
    (83000) .... ✉ 609-292-4390
Investment Advisor #37 201-504-6200
Mortgage Banker/Broker #37.............. 201-504-6200
Public Insurance Adjuster #34 .... ✉ 609-292-4390
Real Estate Agent #48 .... ☎ 609-292-8280
Real Estate Appraiser/Apprentice #23 (246)
.... ☎ 201-504-6480

Real Estate Broker #48 (16000) .... ☎ 609-292-8280
Real Estate Instructor #48 (200) .... ☎ 609-292-8280
Real Estate Salesperson #48 (64000) .... ☎ 609-292-8280
Residential Appraiser #23................. ☎ 201-504-6480
Second Mortgage Lender #29........... ✉ 609-292-5340
Securities Agent #37....................... 201-504-6200
Securities Broker/Dealer #37............ 201-504-6200
Securities Issuer #37 201-504-6200

Health & Beauty
Acupuncturist #1 (62)..................... ☎ 609-826-7100
Bio-Analytical Lab Director #14 609-292-4843
Cemetery #46 (398) .... ☎ 201-504-6553
Chiropractor #8 .... ☎ 201-504-6395
Cosmetologist #9 (75000)................ ✉ 201-504-6400
Dental Assistant #10 .... ☎ 201-504-6405
Dental Hygienist #10 .... ☎ 201-504-6405
Dentist #10 .... ☎ 201-504-6405
Dentist/Dental Hygienist #10 (9838)........... ☎ 201-504-6405
Embalmer #15 .... ☎ 201-504-6425
Emergency Medical Technician #33 .... ✉ 609-633-3666
Funeral Director #15....................... ☎ 201-504-6425
Hearing Aid Dispenser/Fitter #44........ 609-292-4843
Implant Inspector #45 .... ☎ 609-530-8803
Midwife #14................................. 609-292-4843
Nurse #16 .... ✉ 201-504-6430
Nursing Home Administrator #50 .... ✉ 609-588-7771
Optician/Optician Technician #51 (2251)...... ☎ 201-504-6435
Optometrist #17 .... ☎ 201-504-6440
Orthopedist #14............................ 609-292-4843
Orthotics & Prosthetics #52.............. ☎ 201-504-6440
Pharmacist #18 (12000)................... ✉ 201-504-6450
Physical Therapist #19.................... ☎ 201-504-6455
Podiatrist #14 609-292-4843
Public Health Officer #31 (400) .... ☎ 609-588-3129
Radiation Therapy Technologist #31 .... ☎ 609-984-6070
Respiratory Care Practitioner #54 (30400)..... ☎ 201-504-6485
Sanitary Inspector #31 (1500) .... ☎ 609-588-3129
Speech-Language Pathologist/Audiologist #7
    (3500) .... ☎ 201-504-6390
X-Ray Technologist, Diagnostic #31 .... ☎ 609-984-6070

Investigations & Security
Fire Protection Inspector #45 (800)................ ☎ 609-530-8803
Private Detective #56 (1770).......................... ✉ 609-882-2000

Social Services
Alcohol Abuse Counselor #3 .... ☎ 908-919-7979
Drug Abuse Counselor #3 .... ☎ 908-919-7979
Marriage Counselor #13 (12000) .... ☎ 908-594-6415
Psychologist #22........................... 201-504-6470
Social Worker #25 .... ☎ 201-504-6495
Urban Planner #21 (4251) .... ☎ 201-504-6465

Sports & Entertainment
Athletic Trainer #4........................ ☎ 609-292-4843
Boxer #53.................................... ✉ 609-292-0317
Boxing Manager #53 .... ✉ 609-292-0317
Casino #27 (13)............................. ☎ 609-441-3865
Casino Employee #27 .... ☎ 609-441-3865
Liquor Control #40 .... ✉ 609-984-3231
Racing #47 .... ☎ 609-292-0613

Transportation
Auto Dealer #42 (5000)................... ✉ 609-292-4517
Mover/Warehouseman #2 (400) .... ☎ 201-504-6475

State Licensing & Business Registration Agency Information

(1) Acupuncture Examining Board, 140 E Front St, 2nd Floor, Trenton, NJ 08608, 609-826-7100

(2) Advisory Board of Public Movers & Warehousemen, 124 Halsey St (07102), PO Box 45018, Newark, NJ 07101, 201-504-6475, Fax: 201-648-3536

(3) Alcohol-Other Drugs of Abuse Counselor Cert Board, 1325 Campus Pkwy, #208, Wall, NJ 07753, 908-919-7979, Fax: 908-919-7118

(4) Athletic Training Advisory Commission, Board of Medical Examiners, 140 E Front St, Trenton, NJ 08625, 609-292-4843

(5) Board of Accountancy, 124 Halsey St, (07102), PO Box 45000, Newark, NJ 07101, 201-504-6380

(6) Board of Architects, PO Box 45001, (124 Halsey St 07102), Newark, NJ 07101, 201-504-6385, Fax: 201-648-3536

(7) Board of Audiology & Speech Language Pathology, 124 Halsey St (07102), PO Box 45002, Newark, NJ 07101, 201-504-6390, Fax: 201-648-3355

(8) Board of Chiropractic Examiners, 124 Halsey St (07102), PO Box 45004, Newark, NJ 07101, 201-504-6395, Fax: 201-648-3355

(9) Board of Cosmetology & Hairstyling, 124 Halsey St (07102), PO Box 45003, Newark, NJ 07101, 201-504-6400

(10) Board of Dentistry, 124 Halsey St (07102), PO Box 45005, Newark, NJ 07101, 201-504-6405, Fax: 201-648-3481

(11) Board of Examiners of Electrical Contractors, 124 Halsey St (07102), PO Box 45006, Newark, NJ 07101, 201-504-6410

(12) Board of Examiners of Master Plumbers, 124 Halsey St (07102), PO Box 45008, Newark, NJ 07101, 201-504-6420

(13) Board of Marriage & Family Therapy Examiners, 124 Halsey St (07102), PO Box 45007, Newark, NJ 07101, 201-504-6415, Fax: 201-648-3536

(14) Board of Medical Examiners, 140 E Front St, Trenton, NJ 08608, 609-292-4843

(15) Board of Mortuary Science, 124 Halsey St (07102), PO Box 45009, Newark, NJ 07101, 201-504-6425

(16) Board of Nursing, PO Box 45010, (124 Halsey St 07102), Newark, NJ 07101, 201-504-6430

(17) Board of Optometrists, PO Box 45012, (124 Halsey St 07102), Newark, NJ 07101, 201-504-6440, Fax: 201-645-3536

(18) Board of Pharmacy, 124 Halsey St (07102), PO Box 45013, Newark, NJ 07101, 201-504-6450

(19) Board of Physical Therapists, 124 Halsey St (07102), PO Box 45014, Newark, NJ 07101, 201-504-6455, Fax: 201-648-2536

(20) Board of Professional Engineers & Land Surveyors, PO Box 45015, (124 Halsey St 07102), Newark, NJ 07101, 201-504-6460, Fax: 201-648-3536

(21) Board of Professional Planners, 124 Halsey St (07102), PO Box 45016, Newark, NJ 07101, 201-504-6465

(22) Board of Psychological Examiners, 124 Halsey St (07102), PO Box 45017, Newark, NJ 07101, 201-504-6470

(23) Board of Real Estate Appraisers, 124 Halsey St, PO Box 45032, Newark, NJ 07101, 201-504-6480, Fax: 201-648-3536

(24) Board of Shorthand Reporting, 124 Halsey St (07102), PO Box 45019, Newark, NJ 07101, 201-504-6490, Fax: 201-648-3536

(25) Board of Social Work Examiners, PO Box 45033, Newark, NJ 07101, 201-504-6495, Fax: 201-648-3536

(26) Board of Veterinary Medical Examiners, 124 Halsey St (07102), PO Box 45020, Newark, NJ 07101, 201-504-6500, Fax: 201-648-3355

(27) Casino Control Commission, Arcade Bldg, Tennessee Ave & Boardwalk, Atlantic City, NJ 08401, 609-441-3799, Fax: 609-441-3752

(28) Department of Banking, Consumer Credit Bureau, 20 W State St, CN-040, Trenton, NJ 08625, 609-292-5466

(29) Department of Banking, Office of Consumer Finance, 20 W State St, CN-040, Trenton, NJ 08625, 609-292-5340, Fax: 609-292-5461

(30) Department of Education, State Board of Examiners, 225 E State St, Trenton, NJ 08625, 609-292-2045, Fax: 609-292-3768

(31) Department of Environmental Protection & Energy, Bureau of Revenu, 428 E State St, CN-402, Trenton, NJ 08625, 609-984-6070

(32) Department of Environmental Protection & Energy, Pesticide Control Program, CN-411, Trenton, NJ 08625-0411, 609-530-4070

(33) Department of Health, Division of Community Health Services, 50 E State St, CN-364, Trenton, NJ 08625, 609-588-3720

(34) Department of Insurance, License Processing, CN-327, Trenton, NJ 08625-0327, 609-292-4337

(35) Department of Labor, Office of Asbestos Control & Licensing, 28 Yard Ave, 3rd Floor, Trenton, NJ 08625-0054, 609-633-3760, Fax: 609-633-0664

(36) Department of Labor, Office of Boiler & Pressure Vessel Compliance, CN-392, Trenton, NJ 08625-0392, 609-292-2921

(37) Department of Law & Public Safety, 124 Halsey St, Newark, NJ 07102, 201-504-3645

(38) Department of Law & Public Safety, Office of Weights & Measures, 1261 Routes 1 & 9 South, Avanel, NJ 07001, 908-815-4845

(39) Department of State, Division of Community Recording, Notary Section, 820 Bear Tavern Rd, 2nd Floor, CN452, West Trenton, NJ 08625, 609-530-6421

(40) Division of Alcoholic Beverage Control, 140 E Front St, CN 087, Trenton, NJ 08625-0087, 609-984-2830

(41) Division of Consumer Affairs, Private Employment Agency Operator, PO Box 45028, 124 Halsey St, Newark, NJ 07101, 201-504-6200

(42) Division of Motor Vehicles, Dealer Licensing Section, 225 E State St, Trenton, NJ 08666, 609-292-4517

(43) Election Law Enforcement Commission, CN-185, Trenton, NJ 08625-0185, 609-292-8700, Fax: 609-633-9854

(44) Hearing Aid Dispensers Examining Committee, 140 E Front St, Trenton, NJ 08608, 609-292-4843

(45) NJ Department of Community Affairs, Bureau of Code Services, Attn: Licensing Unit, CN-816, Trenton, NJ 08625-0816, 609-530-8803, Fax: 609-530-8357

(46) New Jersey Cemetery Board, PO Box 45036, Newark, NJ 07101, 201-504-6553, Fax: 201-648-3536

(47) New Jersey Racing Commission, 140 E Front, CN-088, Trenton, NJ 08625, 609-292-0613, Fax: 609-599-1785

(48) New Jersey Real Estate Commission, 20 W State St, CN-328, Trenton, NJ 08625-0328, 609-292-8280, Fax: 609-292-0944

(49) New Jersey State Bar Association, Board of Bar Exams, CN 973, Trenton, NJ 08625, 609-984-7783

(50) Nursing Home Administrators Licensing Board, CN-367, Trenton, NJ 08625-0367, 609-588-7771, Fax: 609-588-7698

(51) Ophthalmic Dispensers & Ophthalmic Technicians, 124 Halsey St (07102), PO Box 45011, Newark, NJ 07101, 201-504-6435, Fax: 201-648-3355

(52) Orthotics & Prosthetics Board of Examiners, 124 Halsey St (07102), PO Box 45034, Newark, NJ 07101, 201-504-6440, Fax: 201-648-3536

(53) State Athletic Conrol Board, CN-180, Trenton, NJ 08625-0180, 609-292-0317, Fax: 609-292-3756

(54) State Board of Respiratory Care, PO Box 45031, 124 Halsey St, Newark, NJ 07101, 201-504-6485

(55) State Forestry Service, CN-404, Trenton, NJ 08625-0404, 609-292-2532, Fax: 609-984-0378

(56) State Police Department, Private Detective Division, River Rd, PO Box 7068, Trenton, NJ 08628, 609-882-2000, Fax: 609-637-9583

New Mexico

Capitol: Santa Fe (Santa Fe County)	
State Population	**1.7 Million**
Number of Degree Granting Institutions:	**36**
Number of State Licensing & Business Registration Agencies:	**96**

Degree Granting Educational Institutions

Albuquerque Technical-Vocational Institute, Records Office, 525 Buena Vista Dr SE, Albuquerque, NM 87108, 505-224-3202. Hours: 8AM-7PM M-Th; 8AM-5PM F. Enrollment: 15000. Records go back to 1965. Degrees granted: Associate. Adverse incident record source- Student Services, 505-224-3020.

Attendance and degree information available by phone, mail. Search requires name plus date of birth. Also helpful: exact years of attendance. There is no fee.

Clovis Community College, Registrar, 417 Schepps Blvd, Clovis, NM 88101, 505-769-4025 (Fax: 505-769-4190). Hours: 8AM-4:30PM. Enrollment: 4000. Records go back to 1970. Degrees granted: Associate. Adverse incident record source- Student Services, 505-769-4199.

Attendance and degree information available by phone, mail. Search requires name plus SSN. There is no fee.

College of Santa Fe, Registrar, 1600 St Michael's Dr, Santa Fe, NM 87501, 505-473-6317 (Fax: 505-473-6127). Hours: 8AM-5PM. Enrollment: 1450. Records go back to 1947. Alumni records are maintained here also. Call 505-473-6312. Degrees granted: Associate; Bachelors; Masters.

Attendance and degree information available by phone, fax, mail. Search requires name plus exact years of attendance. There is no fee.

College of the Southwest, Registrar, 6610 Lovington Hwy, Hobbs, NM 88240, 505-392-6561 (Fax: 505-392-6006). Hours: 8AM-5PM. Enrollment: 500. Records go back to 1956. Alumni records are maintained here at the same phone number. Degrees granted: Bachelors.

Attendance and degree information available by phone, fax, mail. Search requires name only. Also helpful: SSN, date of birth, exact years of attendance. There is no fee.

Dona Ana Branch Community College, Registrar, Box 30001, Las Cruces, NM 88003, 505-646-3411 (Fax: 505-646-6330). Hours: 8AM-5PM. Records go back to 1970. Alumni records are maintained here also. Call 505-646-3616. Degrees granted: Associate.

Attendance and degree information available by phone, fax, mail. Search requires name plus SSN, approximate years of attendance. There is no fee.

Eastern New Mexico University, Registrar, Portales, NM 88130, 505-562-2175 (Fax: 505-562-2566). Hours: 8AM-4PM. Records go back to 1950's. Degrees granted: Associate; Bachelors; Masters.

Attendance and degree information available by phone, fax, mail. Search requires name plus SSN, approximate years of attendance. Also helpful: date of birth. There is no fee.

Eastern New Mexico University-Roswell, Registrar, PO Box 6000, Roswell, NM 88202, 505-624-7145 (Fax: 505-624-7119). Hours: 8AM-5PM. Records go back to 1958. Degrees granted: Associate.

Attendance and degree information available by phone, fax, mail. Search requires name plus SSN, approximate years of attendance. Also helpful: date of birth, exact years of attendance. There is no fee.

ITT Technical Institute, (Branch of Tucson, AZ), Registrar, 5100 Masthead NE, Albuquerque, NM 87109-4366, 505-828-1114 (Fax: 505-828-1849). Hours: 8AM-5PM. Enrollment: 300. Records go back to 1907. Alumni records are maintained here at the same phone number. Degrees granted: Associate. Adverse incident record source- Education, 505-828-1114.

Attendance and degree information available by phone, fax, mail. Search requires name only. Also helpful: SSN, date of birth, exact years of attendance. There is no fee.

Institute of American Indian and Alaskan Native Culture and Arts, Registrar, St. Michael's Dr, Box 20007, Santa Fe, NM 87504, 505-988-6463 (Fax: 505-988-6446). Enrollment: 128. Records go back to 1962. Degrees granted: Associate.

Attendance and degree information available by phone, fax, mail. Search requires name plus date of birth, exact years of attendance. Also helpful: SSN. There is no fee.

International Institute of Chinese Medicine, Registrar, PO Box 4991, Santa Fe, NM 87502-4991, 505-473-

5233 (Fax: 505-471-5551). Hours: 9AM-5PM. Records go back to 1985. Degrees granted: Masters.

Attendance and degree information available by phone, fax, mail. Search requires name plus SSN, exact years of attendance. Also helpful: date of birth. Fee is $5.00.

Luna Vocational Technical Institute, Registrar, PO Drawer K, Las Vegas, NM 87701, 505-454-2548 (Fax: 505-454-2518). Hours: 8AM-4:30PM. Records go back to 1970. Degrees granted: Associate. Adverse incident record source-Student Services, 505-454-2554.

Attendance and degree information available by phone, fax, mail. Search requires name plus SSN, exact years of attendance. There is no fee.

Nazarene Bible College, (Nazarene Indian Bible College), Registrar, 2315 Markham Rd SW, Albuquerque, NM 87105, 505-877-0240 (Fax: 505-877-6214). Hours: 8AM-5PM Fall; 9AM-4:30PM Summer. Enrollment: 50. Records go back to 1955. Degrees granted: Associate; Bachelors. Adverse incident record source- Bookkeeper, 505-877-0240.

Attendance and degree information available by phone, fax, mail. Search requires name only. There is no fee.

New Mexico Highlands University, Registrar, National Ave, Las Vegas, NM 87701, 505-454-3424 (Fax: 505-454-3552). Hours: 8AM-5PM. Alumni records are maintained here at the same phone number. Degrees granted: Associate; Bachelors; Masters.

Attendance and degree information available by phone, fax, mail. Search requires name plus SSN. Also helpful: date of birth, exact years of attendance. There is no fee.

New Mexico Institute of Mining and Technology, Registrar, Socorro, NM 87801, 505-835-5133 (Fax: 505-835-6511). Hours: 8AM-5PM. Records go back to 1889. Alumni records are maintained here at the same phone number. Degrees granted: Associate; Bachelors; Masters; Doctorate. Adverse incident record source- Campus Police, 505-835-5434.

Attendance information available by phone, fax, mail. Search requires name plus SSN. There is no fee.

Degree information available by phone, fax, mail. Search requires name only. Also helpful: SSN, exact years of attendance. There is no fee.

New Mexico Junior College, Registrar, 5317 Lovington Hwy, Hobbs, NM 88240, 505-392-5113 (Fax: 505-392-2526). Hours: 8AM-5PM. Records go back to 1967. Alumni records are maintained here at the same phone number. Degrees granted: Associate.

Attendance and degree information available by phone, fax, mail. Search requires name plus SSN. Also helpful: date of birth. There is no fee.

New Mexico Military Institute, Registrar, 100 W College Blvd, Roswell, NM 88201, 505-624-8070 (Fax: 505-624-8058). Hours: 7:30AM-4:30PM. Enrollment: 850. Records go back to 1885. Degrees granted: Associate.

Attendance and degree information available by phone, fax, mail. Search requires name only. Also helpful: SSN, date of birth, exact years of attendance. There is no fee.

New Mexico State University, Registrar, Box 30001, Las Cruces, NM 88003, 505-646-3411 (Fax: 505-646-6330). Hours: 8AM-5PM. Alumni records are maintained here at the same phone number. Degrees granted: Associate; Bachelors; Masters; Doctorate.

Attendance and degree information available by phone, fax, mail. Search requires name plus SSN, approximate years of attendance. Also helpful: exact years of attendance. There is no fee.

New Mexico State University at Alamogordo, Registrar, PO Box 477, Alamogordo, NM 88311-0477, 505-439-3600 (Fax: 505-439-3760). Records are not housed here. They are located at Dona Ana Branch Community College, Registrar, Box 30001, Las Cruces, NM 88003.

New Mexico State University at Carlsbad, Registrar, 1500 University Dr, Carlsbad, NM 88220, 505-885-8831 (Fax: 505-885-4951). Hours: 8AM-5PM. Records go back to 1950. Degrees granted: Associate.

Attendance information available by phone, fax, mail. Search requires name plus SSN, exact years of attendance. Also helpful: date of birth, approximate years of attendance. There is no fee.

Degree information available by phone, fax, mail. Search requires name plus SSN, exact years of attendance. There is no fee.

New Mexico State University at Grants, Registrar, 1500 3rd St, Grants, NM 87020, 505-287-7981 (Fax: 505-287-2329). Records are not housed here. They are located at New Mexico State University, Registrar, Box 30001, Las Cruces, NM 88003.

Northern New Mexico Community College, Registrar, 1002 N Onate St, Espanola, NM 87532, 505-747-2112 (Fax: 505-747-2180). Hours: 8AM-5PM M,Th,F; 8AM-6PM T,Th. Enrollment: 2000. Records go back to 1970. Degrees granted: Associate. Adverse incident record source- Dean of Students, 504-747-2112.

Attendance and degree information available by fax, mail. Search requires name plus SSN, date of birth, approximate years of attendance, signed release. There is no fee.

Parks College, Registrar, 1023 Tijeras Ave NW, Albuquerque, NM 87102, 505-843-7500 (Fax: 505-242-1986). Hours: 8AM-9:30PM. Enrollment: 250. Records go back to 1978. Degrees granted: Associate. Adverse incident record source- Dean of Students, 505-843-7500.

Attendance and degree information available by phone, mail. Search requires name plus SSN, date of birth, exact years of attendance. There is no fee.

Pima Medical Institute, (Branch), Registrar, 2201 San Pedro Dr NE Bldg 3 Ste 100, Albuquerque, NM 87110, 505-881-1234.

Attendance and degree information available by phone, mail. Search requires name plus SSN. Also helpful: exact years of attendance.

San Juan College, Records Office, 4601 College Blvd, Farmington, NM 87402, 505-599-0320 (Fax: 505-599-0500). Hours: 8AM-5PM. Enrollment: 4700. Records go back to 1972. Degrees granted: Associate.

Attendance and degree information available by mail. Search requires name plus SSN, signed release. Also helpful: date of birth, exact years of attendance. There is no fee.

Sante Fe Community College, Registrar, PO Box 4187, Santa Fe, NM 87502-4187, 505-471-8200 (Fax: 505-438-1237). Hours: 8AM-5PM. Enrollment: 5500. Records go back to 1983. Degrees granted: Associate. Adverse incident record source- Dean of Student Services, 505-471-8200.

Attendance and degree information available by mail. Search requires name plus SSN, signed release. Also helpful: date of birth, exact years of attendance. There is no fee.

Southwest Acupuncture College, Registrar, 325 Paseo De Peralta #500, Santa Fe, NM 87501, 505-988-3538 (Fax: 505-988-5438). Hours: 9AM-5PM. Enrollment: 150. Records go back to 1981. Degrees granted: Masters. Adverse incident record source- 505-988-3538.

Attendance and degree information available by phone, fax, mail. Search requires name plus SSN, date of birth, exact years of attendance. Fee is $7.00. Expedited service available for $17.00.

Southwest Acupuncture College, (Branch Campus), Registrar, 4308 Carlisle Blvd NE Ste 205, Albuquerque, NM 87107, 505-888-8898. Records are not housed here. They are located at Southwest Acupuncture College, Registrar, 325 Paseo De Peralta #500, Santa Fe, NM 87501.

Southwestern Indian Polytechnic Institute, Registrar, 9169 Coors Rd NW, Box 10146, Albuquerque, NM 87184, 505-897-5346 (Fax: 505-897-5343). Hours: 8AM-4:30PM. Enrollment: 600. Records go back to 1971. Degrees granted: Associate.

Attendance information available by phone, fax, mail. Search requires name plus SSN. There is no fee.

Degree information available by phone. Search requires name plus SSN. There is no fee.

St. John's College, Registrar, Santa Fe, NM 87501-4599, 505-984-6075 (Fax: 505-984-6003). Hours: 9AM-5PM. Enrollment: 470. Records go back to 1964. Alumni records are maintained here also. Call 505-984-6103. Degrees granted: Bachelors; Masters. Adverse incident record source- Assistant Dean, 505-984-6086.

Attendance and degree information available by phone, fax, mail. Search requires name only. Also helpful: SSN, date of birth, exact years of attendance. There is no fee.

University of Albuquerque, Records Office-Rm 250, Student Service Center, Albuquerque, NM 87131, 505-277-2916 (Fax: 505-277-6809). Enrollment: 24000. Alumni Records Office: Hodgin Hall 1st Flr, Albuquerque, NM 87131. Degrees granted: Bachelors; Masters; Doctorate.

Attendance information available by phone, fax, mail. Search requires name only. Also helpful: SSN, date of birth, exact years of attendance. There is no fee.

Degree information available by phone, fax, mail. Search requires name only. Also helpful: SSN, date of birth, exact years of attendance. There is no fee.

University of New Mexico, Records Office, Student Services Ctr Rm 250, Albuquerque, NM 87131-2039, 505-277-2917 (Fax: 505-277-6809). Hours: 8AM-5PM. Enrollment: 25000. Records go back to 1889. Alumni records are maintained here also. Call 505-277-5808. Degrees granted: Associate;

Bachelors; Masters; Doctorate. Special programs- Law School: Medical School. Adverse incident record source- Dean of Students, 505-277-2917: Campus Police, 505-277-2917

Attendance and degree information available by phone, fax, mail. Search requires name plus SSN, exact years of attendance. Also helpful: date of birth. There is no fee.

University of New Mexico, (Gallup Branch), Registrar, 200 College Rd, Gallup, NM 87301, 505-843-7783 (Fax: 505-863-7610). Records are not housed here. They are located at University of New Mexico, Records Office, Student Services Ctr Rm 250, Albuquerque, NM 87131-2039.

University of New Mexico, (Los Alamos Branch), Registrar, 400 University Dr, Los Alamos, NM 87544, 505-662-5919. Records are not housed here. They are located at University of New Mexico, Records Office, Student Services Ctr Rm 250, Albuquerque, NM 87131-2039.

University of New Mexico, (Valencia Branch), Registrar, 280 La Entrada, Los Lunas, NM 87031, 505-925-8500 (Fax: 505-925-8501). Records are not housed here. They are located at University of New Mexico, Records Office, Student Services Ctr Rm 250, Albuquerque, NM 87131-2039.

University of Phoenix, (Albuquerque Main), Registrar, 7471 Pan American Fwy NE, Albuquerque, NM 87109, 505-821-4800 (Fax: 505-821-5551). Hours: 8AM-6PM. Enrollment: 1550. Records go back to 1986. Transcript records are housed at University of Phoenix, Registrar, PO Box 52069, Phoenix, AZ 85072. Degrees granted: Associate; Bachelors; Masters.

Attendance and degree information available by written request only. Search requires name plus SSN, approximate years of attendance. There is no fee.

Western New Mexico University, Registrar, PO Box 680, 1000 W College Ave, Silver City, NM 88062, 505-538-6118 (Fax: 505-538-6155). Hours: 8AM-4:30PM. Enrollment: 2500. Alumni records are maintained here also. Call 505-538-6336. Degrees granted: Associate; Bachelors; Masters.

Attendance and degree information available by phone, fax, mail. Search requires name plus SSN, approximate years of attendance. Also helpful: date of birth. There is no fee.

Trade and Vocational Schools

Albuquerque Barber College, 525 San Pedro Dr NE #104, Albuquerque, NM 87108, 505-266-4900

Albuquerque Job Corps Center, 1500 Indian School Rd NW, Albuquerque, NM 87104, 505-842-6500

Art Center (The), 2268 Wyoming Blvd NE, Albuquerque, NM 87112, 505-298-1828

AzTech College (Branch Campus), 2201 San Pedro Dr NE Bldg 3, Albuquerque, NM 87110, 505-884-8371

Computer Career Center (Branch Campus), 4121 Wyoming Blvd NE, Albuquerque, NM 87111, 505-271-8200

International Business College, 650 E Montana Ave #F, Las Cruces, NM 88001, 505-526-5579

Metropolitan College of Court Reporting, 2201 San Pedro St NE, Albuquerque, NM 87110, 505-888-3400

Western Business Institute, 3200 N White Sands Blvd, Alamogordo, NM 88310, 505-437-1854

State Licensing & Business Registration Quick Finder Index

Architecture, Engineering & Surveying
Architect #2 .... ☎ 505-827-6375
Engineer #48 505-827-7316
Landscape Architect #5 .... ☎ 505-827-7095
Surveyor #48 505-827-7316

Business - Court & Legal Services
Attorney #7 (600) .... ✉ 505-827-4860
Notary Public #54 .... ☎ 505-827-3600
Shorthand Reporter #4 505-827-4834

Business - General Services
Interior Decorator #14 .... ☎ 505-827-7163
Public Accountant-CPA #39 (2800) .... ☎ 505-841-9109

Construction & Manufacturing
Boiler Operator Journeyman #36 .... ☎ 505-841-8020
Contractor #13 .... ☎ 505-841-8020
Electrician #12 .... ☎ 505-841-8020
Manufactured Housing #34 505-827-7070
Mechanic #32 .... ☎ 505-827-7030

Education
School Administrator #11 .... ☎ 505-827-6587
School Counselor #11 .... ☎ 505-827-6587
Teacher #11 .... ☎ 505-827-6587

Environmental & Agriculture
Liquified Petroleum Gas (LPG) #31 .... ☎ 505-841-8394
Pesticide Applicator (3 types) #8 (1370) .... ☎ 505-646-2133
Pesticide Dealer #8 (103) .... ☎ 505-646-2133
Pesticide Management Consultant #8 (70) ..... ☎ 505-646-2133
Pesticide Operator #8 (647) .... ☎ 505-646-2133
Veterinarian #56 505-841-9112
Veterinary Artificial Insemination #56 505-841-9112
Veterinary Facilities #56 505-841-9112
Veterinary Technician #56 505-841-9112
Veterinary-Pregnancy Diagnosis #56 505-841-9112

Financial - Real Estate, Insurance & Banking
Bank #33 (40) .... ☎ 505-827-7100
Collection Agency #33 (124) .... ☎ 505-827-7100
Collection Agency Manager #51 (124) .... ☎ 505-827-7100
Consumer Credit #33 .... ☎ 505-827-7100
Credit Union #33 (25) .... ☎ 505-827-7100
General Real Estate Appraiser #27 .... ☎ 505-827-7554
Insurance Agent #10 (11000) .... ✉ 505-827-4349
Investment Advisor/Representative #52
(4000) .... ☎ 505-827-7140
Real Estate Agent/Sales #50 (5089) .... ☎ 505-841-9120
Real Estate Appraiser #27 (266) .... ☎ 505-827-7554
Real Estate Broker #50 .... ☎ 505-841-9120
Residential Real Estate Appraiser #27 .... ☎ 505-827-7554
Savings & Loan #33 (1) .... ☎ 505-827-7100
Securities Broker/Dealer #52 (1200) .... ☎ 505-827-7140
Securities Division Agents #35 (34000) .... ☎ 505-827-7140
Securities Sales Representative #52 (34000)
.... ☎ 505-827-7140

Health & Beauty
Acupuncturist #15 (365) .... ☎ 505-827-7554
Assistant Funeral Service Practitioner #30 .... ☎ 505-827-7013
Barber #3 (1000) .... ☎ 505-827-7550

Chiropractor #17 (600) .... ✉ 505-827-7171
Clinical Nurse Specialist #6 .... ☎ 505-841-8340
Cosmetologist #18 (9000) 505-827-7550
Dental Assistant #19 .... ☎ 505-827-7165
Dental Hygiene #19 .... ☎ 505-827-7165
Dentist #19 (900) .... ☎ 505-827-7165
Dietitian/Nutritionist #21 (230) .... ☎ 505-827-7169
Embalmer (Funeral Service Practitioner) #30
(162) .... ☎ 505-827-7013
Emergency Medical Technician #9 .... ☎ 505-827-4200
Funeral Director/Associate Funeral Service
Practitioner #30 (4) .... ☎ 505-827-7013
Funeral Service Intern #30 .... ☎ 505-827-7013
Hearing Aid Specialist #37 .... ☎ 505-827-7164
LPN #6 .... ☎ 505-841-8340
Massage Therapist #20 (1858) .... ☎ 505-827-7013
Massage Therapy Instructor #20 .... ☎ 505-827-7013
Massage Therapy School #20 .... ☎ 505-827-7013
Medical Doctor #40 (5382) .... ✉ 505-827-7317
Midwife #38 .... ☎ 505-827-2453
Midwife (CNM) #38 (250) .... ☎ 505-827-2453
Nuclear Medicine Technologist #43 (107) ..... ✉ 505-827-4300
Nurse (RN) #6 (14442) .... ☎ 505-841-8340
Nurse Practitioner #6 .... ☎ 505-841-8340
Nursing Home Administrator #41 (202) .... ☎ 505-827-7170
Occupational Therapist #22 (536) .... ✉ 505-827-7162
Occupational Therapy Assistant #22 .... ✉ 505-827-7162
Optometrist #45 .... ☎ 505-827-7170
Osteopathic Physician #23 (400) .... ✉ 505-827-7171
Perpetual Care Cemetery #33 (22) .... ☎ 505-827-7100
Pharmacist #46 (1298) .... ☎ 505-841-9102
Physical Therapist #24 (910) .... ✉ 505-827-7162
Physical Therapist Assistant #24 .... ✉ 505-827-7162
Podiatrist #25 (110) .... ☎ 505-827-7554
RN Anesthetist #6 .... ☎ 505-841-8340
Radiation Therapy Technologist #43 .... ✉ 505-827-4300
Radiologic Technologist #43 .... ✉ 505-827-2948
Respiratory Care Practitioner #53 (599) .... ☎ 505-827-7170
Speech-Language Pathologist/Audiologist
/Hearing Aid Dispenser #29 (850) .... ☎ 505-827-7554

Investigations & Security
Polygraph Examiner #47 (30) .... ☎ 505-827-7172
Private Investigator #26 .... ☎ 505-827-7172

Social Services
Provisional Social Worker #28 .... ☎ 505-827-7554
Psychologist #42 (500) .... ☎ 505-827-7163
Social Worker (LBSW) #28 (758) .... ☎ 505-827-7554
Social Worker-LI #28 .... ☎ 505-827-7554
Social Worker-LM #28 .... ☎ 505-827-7554

Sports & Entertainment
Athletic Commission #44 (1) .... ☎ 505-827-7172
Athletic Trainer #16 (90) .... ☎ 505-827-7554
Gambling #1 505-827-7088
Liquor Distributor #1 (78) .... ☎ 505-827-7066
Pyrotechnician (Retailers, Whslers, Distributors) #55
.... ✉ 505-827-3762
Racing #49 505-841-4644

State Licensing & Business Registration Agency Information

(1) Alcohol Gaming Division, 725 St. Michael's Dr, Santa Fe, NM 87503-7605, 505-827-7088

(2) Architect Examiners Board, PO Box 509, Santa Fe, NM 87504, 505-827-6375, Fax: 505-827-6373

(3) Barber & Cosmetology Licensing Board, 1599 St. Francis Dr., Santa Fe, NM 87504, 505-827-7550

(4) Board Governing Recording of Judicial Proceedings, PO Box 25883, Albuquerque, NM 87125, 505-797-6000, Fax: 505-843-8765

(5) Board of Landscape & Architects, PO Box 25101, Santa Fe, NM 87504, 505-827-7095

(6) Board of Nursing, 4206 Louisiana NE Suite A, Albuquerque, NM 87109, 505-842-8340

(7) Clerk of the Court, Supreme Court Bldg, Room 104, Santa Fe, NM 87503, 505-827-4860, Fax: 505-827-4837

(8) Department of Agriculture, Box 30005, Dept. 3AQ, Las Cruces, NM 88003, 505-646-2133, Fax: 505-646-5977

(9) Department of Health, Primary Care & EMS Bureau, 1190 St. Francis Dr, RM N1100, Santa Fe, NM 87502-6110, 505-827-4200, Fax: 505-827-4203

(10) Department of Insurance, Licensing Division, PO Drawer 1269, Santa Fe, NM 87504, 505-827-4349

(11) Education Department, Professional Licensure, 300 Don Gaspar, Education Bldg, Santa Fe, NM 87501-2786, 505-827-6587, Fax: 505-827-6696

(12) Electrical Bureau, 1650 University Blvd, NE Suite 201, Albuquerque, NM 87102-1731, 505-841-8020, Fax: 505-841-8019

(13) General Construction Bureau, 1650 University Blvd, NE, Albuquerque, NM 87102, 505-841-8020

(14) Interior Designers Licensing, 725 St. Michael's Dr, Santa Fe, NM 87504, 505-827-7163, Fax: 505-827-7017

(15) Licensing Boards, 1599 St. Francis Dr., Suite B, Santa Fe, NM 87505, 505-827-7000, Fax: 505-827-7560

(16) Licensing Boards, 725 St. Michael's Dr, Santa Fe, NM 87503, 505-827-7554

(17) Licensing Boards, 725 St. Michael's Dr, Santa Fe, NM 87503, 505-827-7171

(18) Licensing Boards, 725 St. Michael's Dr. PO Box 25101, Santa Fe, NM 87504, 505-827-7176

(19) Licensing Boards, PO Box 25101, Santa Fe, NM 87504, 505-827-7165, Fax: 505-827-7095

(20) Licensing Boards, 725 St. Michael's Dr, Santa Fe, NM 87503, 505-827-7013, Fax: 505-827-7095

(21) Licensing Boards, PO Box 25101, Santa Fe, NM 87504, 505-827-7169, Fax: 505-827-7095

(22) Licensing Boards, 725 St. Michael's Dr, Santa Fe, NM 87503, 505-827-7162, Fax: 505-827-7095

(23) Licensing Boards, 725 St. Michael's Dr, Santa Fe, NM 87503, 505-827-7171

(24) Licensing Boards, 725 St. Michael's Dr, Santa Fe, NM 87503, 505-827-7162, Fax: 505-827-7095

(25) Licensing Boards, 1599 St. Francis Dr., Ste B, Santa Fe, NM 87505, 505-827-7160, Fax: 505-827-7560

(26) Licensing Boards, 725 St. Michael's Dr, Santa Fe, NM 87503, 505-827-7172

(27) Licensing Boards, 1599 St. Francis Dr., Ste. B, Santa Fe, NM 87505, 505-827-7160, Fax: 505-827-7560

(28) Licensing Boards, 1599 St. Francis Dr., Santa Fe, NM 87504, 505-827-7554, Fax: 505-827-7560

(29) Licensing Boards, 725 St. Michael's Dr, Santa Fe, NM 87503, 505-827-7554, Fax: 505-827-7560

(30) Licensing Boards, 725 St. Michael's Dr, Santa Fe, NM 87503, 505-827-7013, Fax: 505-827-7095

(31) Licensing Boards, 725 St. Michael's Dr, Santa Fe, NM 87503, 505-827-8394, Fax: 505-841-8019

(32) Licensing Boards, 725 St. Michael's Dr, Santa Fe, NM 87503, 505-827-7030

(33) Licensing Boards, 725 St. Michael's Dr, Santa Fe, NM 87503, 505-827-7100, Fax: 505-827-7107

(34) Licensing Boards, 725 St. Michael's Dr, Santa Fe, NM 87504, 505-827-7070, Fax: 505-827-7074

(35) Licensing Boards, 725 St. Michael's Dr, Santa Fe, NM 87505, 505-827-7140, Fax: 505-984-0617

(36) Licensing Boards, Boiler Operator Journeyman, 1650 University NE, Suite 201, Albuquerque, NM 87102-1731, 505-841-8020, Fax: 505-841-8019

(37) Licensing Boards, Speech, Language Pathology & Audiology Board, 1599 St. Francis Dr., Santa Fe, NM 87504, 505-827-7554, Fax: 505-827-7560

(38) Mid Wifery Board, 1190 St. Frances Drive, S1260, Santa Fe, NM 87502, 505-827-2453, Fax: 505-827-1697

(39) New Meixico Board of Public Accountancy, 1650 University Blvd, NE, Suite 400-A, Albuquerque, NM 87102, 505-841-9108

(40) New Mexico Board of Medical Examiners, Lamy Bldg, 2nd Floor, 491 Old Santa Fe Trail, Santa Fe, NM 87501, 505-827-7317, Fax: 505-827-7317

(41) New Mexico Board of Optometry, PO Box 25101 725 St. Michaels Drive, Santa Fe, NM 87504, 505-827-7170, Fax: 505-827-7095

(42) New Mexico Board of Psychological Examiners, 725 St. Michael's Dr, Santa Fe, NM 87504, 505-827-7163, Fax: 505-827-7017

(43) New Mexico Environment Department, Radiologic Licensing & Registration Section, PO Box 26110, Santa Fe, NM 87505-6110, 505-827-4300, Fax: 505-821-4389

(44) New Mexico State Athletic Commission, PO Box 25101, Santa Fe, NM 87503, 505-827-7172, Fax: 505-827-7095

(45) Optometry Board of Regulation & Licensing, 725 St. Michael's Dr PO Box 25101, Santa Fe, NM 87504, 505-827-7170

(46) Pharmacy Board, 1650 University Blvd, NE, Suite 400-B, Albuquerque, NM 87102, 505-841-9102, Fax: 505-841-9113

(47) Polygraph Examiners Bureau, Department of Regulation & Licensing, PO Box 25101 (725 St. Michael's Dr 87503), Santa Fe, NM 87504, 505-827-7172

(48) Professional Engineer & Surveyors Board, 1010 Marquay Pl, Santa Fe, NM 87501, 505-827-7561, Fax: 505-827-7566

(49) Racing Commission, PO Box 8576, Highland Station, Albuquerque, NM 87198, 505-841-4644

(50)   Real Estate Commission, 1650 University Blvd, Suite 490, Albuquerque, NM 87102, 505-841-9120, Fax: 505-841-9126

(51)   Regulation & Licensing Department, Financial Institutions Division, PO Box 25101 (725 St. Michael's Dr 87503), Santa Fe, NM 87504, 505-827-7100, Fax: 505-827-7107

(52)   Regulation & Licensing Department, Securities Division, PO Box 25101, Santa Fe, NM 87504, 505-827-7140, Fax: 505-984-0617

(53)   Respiratory Care Advisory Board, Department of Regulation & Licensing, 725 St. Michael's Dr PO Box 25101, Santa Fe, NM 87504, 505-827-7170 x31 and x20, Fax: 505-827-7095

(54)   Secretary of State, Notary Public, State Capitol Bldg, Room 420, Santa Fe, NM 87503, 505-827-3600, Fax: 505-827-3611

(55)   State Corporation Commission, State Fire Marshal, PO Drawer :269, Santa Fe, NM 87504, 505-827-3762, Fax: 505-827-3778

(56)   Veterinary Examiners Board, 1650 University Blvd, NE, Suite 400-C, Albuquerque, NM 87102, 505-841-9112

New York

Capitol: Albany (Albany County)	
State Population	18.1 Million
Number of Degree Granting Institutions:	332
Number of State Licensing & Business Registration Agencies:	97

Degree Granting Educational Institutions

Adelphi University, Registrar, South Ave, Garden City, NY 11530, 516-877-3300 (Fax: 516-877-3326). Hours: 8:30AM-7PM M-Th; 8:30AM-4:30PM F.

Attendance and degree information available by phone, mail. Search requires name only. Also helpful: SSN, exact years of attendance. There is no fee.

Adirondack Community College, Registrar, Queensbury, NY 12804, 518-743-2280 (Fax: 518-745-1433). Hours: 8AM-5PM. Records go back to 1962. Alumni records are maintained here at the same phone number. Degrees granted: Associate.

Attendance and degree information available by phone, fax, mail. Search requires name plus SSN, date of birth, exact years of attendance. There is no fee.

Albany College of Pharmacy of Union University, Registrar, 106 New Scotland Ave, Albany, NY 12208, 518-445-7201 (Fax: 518-445-7202). Hours: 8:30AM-4:30PM. Enrollment: 700. Alumni records are maintained here also. Call 518-445-7251. Degrees granted: Bachelors; PharmD.

Attendance and degree information available by phone, fax, mail. Search requires name only. Also helpful: SSN, exact years of attendance. There is no fee.

Albany Law School, Registrar, 80 New Scotland Ave, Albany, NY 12208, 518-445-2330 (Fax: 518-445-2315). Hours: 8:30AM-4:30PM. Enrollment: 790. Records go back to 1930. Alumni records are maintained here at the same phone number. Degrees granted: Doctorate.

Attendance and degree information available by phone, fax, mail. Search requires name plus SSN, approximate years of attendance. There is no fee.

Albany Medical College of Union University, Registrar, 47 New Scotland Ave, Albany, NY 12208, 518-262-4970 X5523. Hours: 8AM-4PM. Enrollment: 169. Records go back to 1839. Alumni records are maintained here also. Call 518-262-5970 X5033. Degrees granted: Masters; Doctorate.

Attendance and degree information available by mail. Search requires name plus SSN, approximate years of attendance, signed release. There is no fee.

Alfred University, Registrar, Saxon Dr, Alfred, NY 14802, 607-871-2122 (Fax: 607-871-2347). Hours: 8:30AM-4:30PM. Enrollment: 2300. Records go back to 1925. Alumni records are maintained here also. Call 607-871-2144. Degrees granted: Masters; Doctorate; Ph.D. Adverse incident record source- Student Affairs, 607-871-2133.

Attendance information available by phone, fax, mail. Search requires name plus date of birth. Also helpful: exact years of attendance. There is no fee.

Degree information available by phone, fax, mail. Search requires name only. Also helpful: date of birth, exact years of attendance. There is no fee.

American Academy McAllister Institute of Funeral Service, Inc., Registrar, 450 W 56th St, New York, NY 10019, 212-757-1190. Hours: 9AM-3:30PM. Records go back to 1930. Degrees granted: Associate.

Attendance and degree information available by mail. Search requires name plus SSN, approximate years of attendance, signed release. There is no fee.

American Academy of Dramatic Arts, Registrar, 120 Madison Ave, New York, NY 10016, 212-686-0250 (Fax: 212-545-7934). Hours: 9AM-2PM, 3-5PM. Records go back to 1885. Degrees granted: Associate.

Attendance information available by fax, mail. Search requires name plus SSN, date of birth, exact years of attendance, signed release. There is no fee.

Degree information available by fax, mail. Search requires name plus exact years of attendance, signed release. There is no fee.

Associated Beth Rivkah Schools, Registrar, 310 Crown St, Brooklyn, NY 11225, 718-735-0414 (Fax: 718-735-0422). Enrollment: 100. Records go back to 1964. Alumni records are maintained here at the same phone number. Degrees granted: Judaic Teacher Training.

Attendance and degree information available by mail. Search requires name plus SSN, exact years of attendance, signed release. There is no fee.

Audrey Cohen College, Registrar, 345 Hudston St, New York, NY 10014-4598, 212-343-1234 X5008 (Fax: 212-

343-7399). Hours: 9AM-6PM M,W; 9AM-7PM T,Th; 9AM-5PM F. Enrollment: 1200. Records go back to 1964. Alumni records are maintained here also. Call 212-343-1234 X3202. Degrees granted: Bachelors; Masters.

Attendance and degree information available by fax, mail. Search requires name plus SSN, signed release. There is no fee.

Bank Street College of Education, Registrar, 610 W 112th St, New York, NY 10025, 212-875-4407 (Fax: 212-875-4753). Hours: 9AM-5PM. Enrollment: 900. Records go back to 1919. Alumni records are maintained here also. Call 212-875-4606. Degrees granted: Masters.

Attendance and degree information available by fax, mail. Search requires name plus SSN, date of birth, approximate years of attendance, signed release. There is no fee.

Bard College, Registrar, Annandale-On-Hudson, NY 12504, 914-758-7458 (Fax: 914-758-4294). Hours: 9AM-5PM. Enrollment: 1000. Records go back to 1940. Alumni records are maintained here also. Call 914-758-7407. Degrees granted: Bachelors; MA, MFA.

Attendance and degree information available by phone, fax, mail. Search requires name plus approximate years of attendance. Also helpful: SSN, exact years of attendance. There is no fee.

Barnard College, Registrar, 3009 Broadway, New York, NY 10027-6598, 212-854-2011 (Fax: 212-854-9470). Hours: 9:30AM-4:30PM. Enrollment: 2200. Records go back to 1892. Alumni records are maintained here also. Call 212-854-2005. Degrees granted: Bachelors.

Attendance and degree information available by phone, fax, mail. Search requires name plus SSN, date of birth, approximate years of attendance. There is no fee.

Berkeley College, Registrar, W Red Oak Lane, White Plains, NY 10604, 201-652-0388 X126 (Fax: 201-670-7737). Hours: 9AM-5PM. Enrollment: 550. Records go back to 1932. Alumni records are maintained here at the same phone number. Degrees granted: Associate.

Attendance and degree information available by phone, fax, mail. Search requires name plus SSN, approximate years of attendance. There is no fee.

Berkeley School of New York, Registrar, 3 E 43rd St, New York, NY 10017, 212-986-4343. Records are not housed here. They are located at Berkeley College of Business, (West Paterson Campus), Office of the Registrar, 44 Rifle Camp Rd, West Paterson, NJ 07424.

Bernard M. Baruch College, Registrar, 17 Lexington Ave, New York, NY 10010, 212-802-2182 (Fax: 212-802-2190). Hours: 9:15AM-7PM M-Th; 9:15AM-4:45PM F. Records go back to 1920. Alumni records are maintained here also. Call 212-387-1145. Degrees granted: Bachelors; Doctorate.

Attendance and degree information available by fax, mail. Search requires name plus SSN, date of birth, approximate years of attendance, signed release. There is no fee.

Beth HaTalmud Rabbinical College, Registrar, 2127 82nd St, Brooklyn, NY 11214, 718-259-2525. Hours: 9AM-2PM. Records go back to 1990.

Attendance and degree information available by phone, fax, mail. Search requires name plus SSN, approximate years of attendance. There is no fee.

Beth Hamedrash Shaarei Yosher, Registrar, 4102 16th Ave, Brooklyn, NY 11204, 718-854-2290. Hours: 8AM-5PM. Records go back to 1957. Adverse incident record source-Student Affairs.

Attendance and degree information available by phone, mail. Search requires name plus SSN, date of birth, exact years of attendance. There is no fee.

Beth Jacob Hebrew Teachers College, Registrar, 1213-23 Elm Ave, Brooklyn, NY 11230, 718-339-4747 (Fax: 718-998-5766). Degrees granted.

Attendance and degree information available by phone, fax, mail. Search requires name plus SSN, approximate years of attendance. There is no fee.

Beth Medrash Eeyun Hatalmud, Registrar, 14 Fred Eller Dr, Monsey, NY 10952, 914-356-0477 (Fax: 914-356-7867). Enrollment: 120.

Attendance and degree information available by fax, mail. Search requires name plus SSN, exact years of attendance, signed release. There is no fee.

Boricua College, Registrar, 3755 Broadway, New York, NY 10032, 212-694-1000 (Fax: 212-694-1015). Hours: 9:30AM-6PM. Records go back to 1976. Degrees granted: Associate; Bachelors.

Attendance information available by fax, mail. Search requires name plus SSN, signed release. Also helpful: date of birth, exact years of attendance. There is no fee.

Degree information available by mail. Search requires name plus SSN, approximate years of attendance, signed release. Also helpful: date of birth, exact years of attendance. There is no fee.

Borough of Manhattan Community College, Registrar, 199 Chambers St, New York, NY 10007, 212-346-8201 (Fax: 212-346-8110). Enrollment: 16500. Records go back to 1964. Alumni records are maintained here also. Call 212-346-8807. Degrees granted: Associate.

Attendance and degree information available by mail. Search requires name plus SSN, signed release. Also helpful: date of birth, exact years of attendance. There is no fee.

Bramson Ort Technical Institute, Registrar, 69-30 Austin St, Forest Hills, NY 11375, 718-261-5800 (Fax: 718-575-5120). Degrees granted.

Attendance and degree information available by phone, fax, mail. Search requires name plus SSN, date of birth, approximate years of attendance. There is no fee.

Briarcliffe College, Registrar, 250 Crossways Park Dr, Woodbury, NY 11797-2015, 516-364-2055 X435 (Fax: 516-364-7127). Hours: 9AM-5PM. Enrollment: 1243. Formerly Briarcliffe School, Inc. Records go back to 1966. Degrees granted: Associate.

Attendance and degree information available by phone, fax, mail. Search requires name plus SSN, approximate years of attendance. Also helpful: date of birth, exact years of attendance. There is no fee.

Briarcliffe School, Inc., (Branch Campus), Registrar, 10 Peninsula Blvd, Lynbrook, NY 11563, 516-596-1313. Records are not housed here. They are located at Briarcliffe College, Registrar, 250 Crossways Park Dr, Woodbury, NY 11797-2015.

Briarcliffe School, Inc., (Branch Campus), Registrar, 10 Lake St, Patchogue, NY 11772, 516-654-5300 (Fax: 516-654-5082). Records are not housed here. They are located at Briarcliffe College, Registrar, 250 Crossways Park Dr, Woodbury, NY 11797-2015.

Bronx Community College, Registrar, W 181st St and University Ave, Bronx, NY 10453, 718-289-5712 (Fax: 718-280-5100). Hours: 9AM-5PM. Records go back to 1960. Degrees granted: Associate. Adverse incident record source-Dean.

Attendance and degree information available by phone, mail. Search requires name plus SSN, date of birth. There is no fee.

Brooklyn College, Registrar, 2900 Bedford Ave, Brooklyn, NY 11210-2889, 718-951-5693. Hours: 10AM-4:30PM. Records go back to 1931. Alumni records are main-

tained here also. Call 718-951-5000 X5065. Degrees granted: Bachelors; Masters.

Attendance and degree information available by mail. Search requires name plus SSN, exact years of attendance, signed release. Also helpful: date of birth. There is no fee.

Brooklyn Law School, Registrar, 250 Joralemon St, Brooklyn, NY 11201, 718-780-7913 (Fax: 718-780-7548). Hours: 9AM-5PM M,W,Th,F; 8AM-6PM T. Records go back to 1901. Alumni records are maintained here also. Call 718-780-7966.

Attendance and degree information available by phone, fax, mail. Search requires name plus approximate years of attendance. Also helpful: SSN, date of birth. There is no fee.

Broome Community College, Registrar, Upper Front St, PO Box 1017, Binghamton, NY 13902, 607-778-5527 (Fax: 607-778-5310). Hours: 9AM-5PM. Enrollment: 5800. Records go back to 1947. Alumni records are maintained here at the same phone number. Degrees granted: Associate.

Attendance and degree information available by phone, fax, mail. Search requires name only. Also helpful: SSN, date of birth, exact years of attendance. There is no fee.

Bryant & Stratton Business Institute, Registrar, 1259 Central Ave, Albany, NY 12205, 518-437-1802 (Fax: 518-437-1048). Hours: 7:30AM-8PM. Enrollment: 500. Records go back to 1800's. Alumni records are maintained here also. Call 518-437-1802. Degrees granted: Associate. Adverse incident record source- 518-437-1802.

Attendance and degree information available by phone, fax, mail. Search requires name plus SSN. Also helpful: date of birth, exact years of attendance. There is no fee.

Bryant & Stratton Business Institute, Registrar, 1028 Main St, Buffalo, NY 14202, 716-884-9120 (Fax: 716-884-0091). Hours: 7:30AM-9PM. Records go back to 1932. Alumni records are maintained here at the same phone number. Degrees granted: Associate.

Attendance and degree information available by phone, fax, mail. Search requires name plus exact years of attendance. Also helpful: SSN. There is no fee.

Bryant & Stratton Business Institute, Registrar, 82 St Paul St, Rochester, NY 14604-1381, 716-884-8000 (Fax: 716-325-6805). Hours: 9:30AM-6PM. Enrollment: 265. Records go back to 1973. Alumni records are maintained here also. Call 518-437-1802. Degrees granted: Associate.

Attendance and degree information available by phone, fax, mail. Search requires name plus SSN. Also helpful: date of birth, exact years of attendance. There is no fee.

Bryant & Stratton Business Institute, Registrar, 953 James St, Syracuse, NY 13203-2502, 315-472-6603 (Fax: 315-474-4383). Hours: 8AM-7PM. Enrollment: 537. Records go back to 1950. Alumni records are maintained here at the same phone number. Degrees granted: Associate. Adverse incident record source- 315-472-6603.

Attendance and degree information available by phone, fax, mail. Search requires name plus SSN. Also helpful: date of birth, exact years of attendance. There is no fee.

Bryant & Stratton Business Institute, (Branch Campus), Registrar, 1214 Abbott Rd, Lackawanna, NY 14218-1989, 716-821-9331 (Fax: 716-821-9343). Hours: 8AM-6PM M-Th; 9AM-5PM F. Enrollment: 381. Records go back to 1988. Alumni records are maintained here also. Call 716-821-9331. Degrees granted: Associate. Adverse incident record source- 716-821-9331.

Attendance and degree information available by phone, fax, mail. Search requires name plus SSN. Also helpful: date of birth, exact years of attendance. There is no fee.

Bryant & Stratton Business Institute, (Branch Campus), Registrar, 200 Bryant and Stratton Way, Williamsville, NY 14221, 716-631-0260 X308 (Fax: 716-631-0273). Hours: 8AM-8:30PM. Records go back to 1988. Alumni records are maintained here at the same phone number. Degrees granted: Associate.

Attendance and degree information available by fax, mail. Search requires name plus SSN, approximate years of attendance, signed release. There is no fee.

Bryant & Stratton Business Institute, (Henrietta Campus), Registrar, 1225 Jefferson Rd, Rochester, NY 14623, 716-292-5627 (Fax: 716-292-6015). Hours: 7:30AM-8PM M-Th; 7:30AM-5PM F, 9AM-1PM S. Enrollment: 628. Records go back to 1985. Alumni records are maintained here at the same phone number. Degrees granted: Associate.

Attendance and degree information available by phone, fax, mail. Search requires name plus SSN. Also helpful: date of birth, exact years of attendance. There is no fee.

Bryant & Stratton Business Institute, (Penncan Campus), Registrar, 5775 S Bay Rd, Cicero, NY 13039, 315-452-1105 (Fax: 315-458-4536). Hours: 8AM-8PM. Enrollment: 369. Records go back to 1983. Alumni records are maintained here at the same phone number. Degrees granted: Associate. Adverse incident record source- 315-452-1105.

Attendance and degree information available by phone, fax, mail. Search requires name plus SSN. Also helpful: date of birth, exact years of attendance. There is no fee.

Canisius College, Registrar, 2001 Main St, Buffalo, NY 14208, 716-888-2990 (Fax: 716-888-2996). Hours: 8:30AM-7PM M-Th; 8:30AM-5PM F. Enrollment: 4900. Records go back to 1940. Alumni records are maintained here also. Call 716-888-2700. Degrees granted: Associate; Bachelors; Masters.

Attendance and degree information available by phone, mail. Search requires name plus SSN, approximate years of attendance. Also helpful: exact years of attendance. There is no fee.

Cayuga County Community College, Registrar, 197 Franklin St, Auburn, NY 13021, 315-255-1743 (Fax: 315-255-2117). Hours: 7:30AM-5PM. Enrollment: 2800. Records go back to 1954. Alumni records are maintained here also. Call 315-255-1743 X224. Degrees granted: Associate.

Attendance information available by phone, mail. Search requires name plus SSN, date of birth. There is no fee.

Degree information available by mail. Search requires name plus SSN, date of birth. There is no fee.

Cazenovia College, Registrar, Seminary St, Cazenovia, NY 13035, 315-655-9446 (Fax: 315-655-2190). Hours: 8:30AM-5PM. Enrollment: 1050. Records go back to 1900. Alumni records are maintained here at the same phone number. Degrees granted: Associate; Bachelors. Adverse incident record source- Student Affairs, 315-655-9446 X237.

Attendance and degree information available by phone, fax, mail. Search requires name plus SSN. Also helpful: exact years of attendance. There is no fee.

Central Yeshiva Tomchei Tmimlm-Lubavitch, Registrar, 841-853 Ocean Pkwy, Brooklyn, NY 11230, 718-859-2277. Hours: 9:30AM-5:30PM. Records go back to 1985. Alumni records are maintained here also. Call 718-859-2277. Degrees granted: Associate.

Attendance and degree information available by phone, mail. Search requires name plus SSN, date of birth. There is no fee.

Christ the King Seminary, Registrar, 711 Knox Rd, PO Box 607, East Aurora, NY 14052-0607, 716-652-8900 (Fax: 716-652-8903). Hours: 9AM-4PM. Enrollment: 110. Records go back to 1950. Some records prior to 1974 destroyed. Alumni records are maintained here at the same phone number. Degrees granted: Masters.

Attendance and degree information available by phone, fax, mail. Search requires name only. Also helpful: SSN, date of birth, exact years of attendance. There is no fee.

City College, Registrar, Convent Ave at 138th St, New York, NY 10031, 212-650-7850 (Fax: 212-650-6108). Hours: 9AM-5PM M,Th,F; 9AM-6:30PM T,W. Enrollment: 14000. Records go back to 1910. Alumni records are maintained here at the same phone number. Degrees granted: Bachelors; Masters. Special programs- BBA Degrees at Baruch College, 212-447-3000. Adverse incident record source- Dean of Students, 212-650-5426.

Attendance and degree information available by phone, fax, mail. Search requires name plus SSN, approximate years of attendance. Also helpful: date of birth, exact years of attendance. There is no fee.

City University of New York College, Registrar, 94-20 Guy R Brewer Blvd, Jamaica, NY 11451, 718-262-2145 (Fax: 718-262-2631). Alumni records are maintained here also. Call 718-262-2420. Degrees granted: Bachelors; Education Certifications.

Attendance and degree information available by fax, mail. Search requires name plus SSN, signed release. Also helpful: date of birth, exact years of attendance. There is no fee.

City University of New York John Jay College, Registrar, 445 W 59th St, New York, NY 10019, 212-237-8000 (Fax: 212-237-8777). Enrollment: 12000. Records go back to 1964. Alumni records are maintained here also. Call 212-237-8547. Degrees granted: Masters. Special programs- Liberal Arts. Adverse incident record source- Dean of Students.

Attendance and degree information available by phone, mail. Search requires name plus SSN, date of birth, exact years of attendance. There is no fee.

City University of New York-Manhattan College, Registrar, 199 Chambers St, Room S-310, New York, NY 10007, 212-346-8201 (Fax: 212-346-8110). Records go back to 1963. Alumni records are maintained here at the same phone number. Degrees granted: Associate. Special programs- Liberal Arts: Business. Adverse incident record source- Student Services.

Attendance and degree information available by written request only. Search requires name plus SSN, date of birth, exact years of attendance, signed release. There is no fee.

Clarkson University, Registrar's Office, Box 5575, Potsdam, NY 13699-5575, 315-268-6451 (Fax: 315-268-6452). Hours: 8AM-4:30PM. Enrollment: 2500. Records go back to 1900. Alumni Records Office: Box 5525, Potsdam, NY 13699-5575. Degrees granted: Bachelors; Masters; Doctorate. Adverse incident record source- Dean of Students, 315-268-6620.

Attendance and degree information available by phone, fax, mail. Search requires name only. Also helpful: SSN, date of birth, exact years of attendance. There is no fee.

Clinton Community College, Registrar, 136 Clifton Pt Dr, Plattsburgh, NY 12901, 518-562-4124 (Fax: 518-561-8621). Hours: 8AM-4PM. Enrollment: 1600. Records go back to 1976. Alumni records are maintained here also. Call 518-562-4195. Degrees granted: Associate. Adverse incident record source- Dean of Students, 518-562-4120.

Attendance and degree information available by phone, fax, mail. Search requires name plus SSN. Also helpful: exact years of attendance. There is no fee.

Cochran School of Nursing-St Johns, Registrar, 967 N Broadway, Yonkers, NY 10701, 914-964-4283 (Fax: 914-964-4971). Enrollment: 110. Records go back to 1894. Alumni records are maintained here at the same phone number.

Degrees granted: Associate. Special programs- Arts: Science. Adverse incident record source- Student Services.

Attendance and degree information available by phone, mail. Search requires name plus SSN, exact years of attendance. There is no fee.

Colgate Rochester Divinity School/Bexley Hall/Crozer Theo. Sem., Registrar, 1100 S Goodman St, Rochester, NY 14620, 716-271-1320 X243 (Fax: 716-271-2166). Hours: 8AM-5PM. Records go back to 1817. Alumni records are maintained here at the same phone number. Degrees granted: Masters; Doctorate.

Attendance and degree information available by phone, fax, mail. Search requires name only. Also helpful: exact years of attendance. There is no fee.

Colgate University, Registrar, 13 Oak Dr, Hamilton, NY 13346, 315-824-7406 (Fax: 315-824-7125). Hours: 8AM-4:30PM. Enrollment: 2800. Records go back to 1822. Alumni Records Office: Alumni Association, Colgate University, Merrill House, Hamilton, NY 13346. Degrees granted: Bachelors; Masters. Adverse incident record source- Dean of College, 315-824-7425.

Attendance and degree information available by phone, fax, mail. Search requires name only. Also helpful: SSN, date of birth, exact years of attendance. There is no fee.

College of Aeronautics, Registrar, La Guardia Airport, Flushing, NY 11371, 718-429-6600 X146 (Fax: 718-429-0256). Hours: 9AM-5PM. Records go back to 1932. Alumni records are maintained here also. Call 718-429-6600 X189. Degrees granted: Associate; Bachelors.

Attendance and degree information available by phone, fax, mail. Search requires name plus SSN, approximate years of attendance. There is no fee.

College of Insurance, Registrar, 101 Murray St, New York, NY 10007, 212-962-4111 (Fax: 212-732-5669). Hours: 9AM-5:30PM M-Th; 9AM-5PM F. Enrollment: 2500. Records go back to 1901. Alumni records are maintained here also. Call 212-962-4111 X229. Degrees granted: Associate; Bachelors; Masters.

Attendance and degree information available by fax, mail. Search requires name plus date of birth, approximate years of attendance, signed release. Also helpful: SSN, exact years of attendance. There is no fee.

College of Mount St. Vincent, Registrar, 6301 Riverdale Ave, Riverdale, NY 10471, 718-405-3267. Hours: 8:30AM-4:30PM. Enrollment: 1060. Records go back to 1913. Degrees granted: Associate; Bachelors; Masters.

School will not confirm attendance information.
School will not confirm degree information.

College of New Rochelle, Registrar, 29 Castle Pl, New Rochelle, NY 10805, 914-654-5214 (Fax: 914-654-5554). Hours: 9AM-6PM. Enrollment: 7000. Records go back to 1904. Alumni records are maintained here also. Call 914-654-5294. Degrees granted: Bachelors; Masters. Adverse incident record source- Security Dept.

Attendance and degree information available by phone, fax, mail. Search requires name plus SSN, date of birth, exact years of attendance. There is no fee.

College of New Rochelle, (Brooklyn Campus), Registrar, 1368 Fulton St, Brooklyn, NY 11216, 718-638-2500 (Fax: 718-230-4523). Records are not housed here. They are located at College of New Rochelle, Registrar, 29 Castle Pl, New Rochelle, NY 10805.

College of New Rochelle, (Co-op City Campus), Registrar, 950 Baychester Ave, Bronx, NY 10457, 718-320-0300 (Fax: 718-379-8633). Records are not housed here. They

are located at College of New Rochelle, Registrar, 29 Castle Pl, New Rochelle, NY 10805.

College of New Rochelle, (DC 37 Campus), Registrar, 125 Barclay St, New York, NY 10007, 212-815-1710 (Fax: 212-349-4089). Records are not housed here. They are located at College of New Rochelle, Registrar, 29 Castle Pl, New Rochelle, NY 10805.

College of New Rochelle, (New York Theological Seminary Campus), Registrar, 5 W 29th St, New York, NY 10001, 212-689-6208. Records are not housed here. They are located at College of New Rochelle, Registrar, 29 Castle Pl, New Rochelle, NY 10805.

College of New Rochelle, (Rosa Parks Campus), Registrar, 144 W 125th St, New York, NY 10024, 212-662-7500. Records are not housed here. They are located at College of New Rochelle, Registrar, 29 Castle Pl, New Rochelle, NY 10805.

College of New Rochelle, (South Bronx Campus), Registrar, 332 E 149th St, Bronx, NY 10451, 718-665-1310. Records are not housed here. They are located at College of New Rochelle, Registrar, 29 Castle Pl, New Rochelle, NY 10805.

College of St. Rose, Registrar, 432 Western Ave, Albany, NY 12203, 518-454-5213 (Fax: 518-454-2100). Hours: 9:30AM-2:30PM, 3:30-6PM M-Th; 9:30AM-4:30PM F. Enrollment: 4000. Records go back to 1920. Alumni records are maintained here also. Call 518-454-5105. Degrees granted: Bachelors; Masters. Adverse incident record source- Security, 518-454-5187.

Attendance and degree information available by phone, fax, mail. Search requires name plus SSN, approximate years of attendance. Also helpful: date of birth, exact years of attendance. There is no fee.

College of Staten Island, Registrar, 2800 Victory Blvd, Staten Island, NY 10314, 718-982-2121. Hours: 9AM-5PM. Enrollment: 12512. Records go back to 1955. Alumni records are maintained here also. Call 718-982-2290. Degrees granted: Associate; Bachelors; Masters. Adverse incident record source- Security, 718-982-2110.

Attendance and degree information available by mail. Search requires name plus SSN, approximate years of attendance, signed release. There is no fee.

College of Staten Island, (Sunnyside Campus), Registrar, 2800 Victory Blvd, Staten Island, NY 10314, 718-982-2120. Hours: 9AM-5PM. Records go back to 1956. Alumni records are maintained here also. Call 718-982-2250. Degrees granted: Associate; Bachelors; Masters.

Attendance and degree information available by mail. Search requires name plus SSN, signed release. Also helpful: date of birth, approximate years of attendance. There is no fee.

Columbia University, Registrar, 116th St and Broadway, New York, NY 10027, 212-854-1458. Hours: 9AM-5PM. Records go back to 1754. Alumni records are maintained here also. Call 212-870-2535. Degrees granted: Associate; Bachelors; Masters; Doctorate.

Attendance and degree information available by mail. Search requires name plus SSN, approximate years of attendance, signed release. There is no fee.

Columbia University Teachers College, Registrar, 525 W 120th St, New York, NY 10027, 212-678-4065 (Fax: 212-678-4048). Hours: 8AM-5PM. Records go back to 1898. Alumni records are maintained here at the same phone number. Degrees granted: Masters; Doctorate. Adverse incident record source- Dean of Students.

Attendance and degree information available by phone, fax, mail. Search requires name only. Also helpful: SSN, date of birth, exact years of attendance. There is no fee.

Columbia-Greene Community College, Registrar, 4400 Route 23, Hudson, NY 12534, 518-828-4181 (Fax: 518-828-2409). Hours: 8AM-5PM. Enrollment: 1660. Records go back to 1969. Degrees granted: Associate.

Attendance and degree information available by phone, fax, mail. Search requires name only. Also helpful: SSN, date of birth, exact years of attendance. There is no fee.

Concordia College, Registrar, 171 White Plains Rd, Bronxville, NY 10708-1998, 914-337-9300 X2103 (Fax: 914-395-4500). Hours: 9AM-5PM. Enrollment: 600. Records go back to 1881. Alumni records are maintained here also. Call 914-337-9300 X2167. Degrees granted: Associate; Bachelors. Adverse incident record source- Dean of Students, 914-337-9300 X2123.

Attendance and degree information available by phone, fax, mail. Search requires name only. Also helpful: SSN, date of birth, exact years of attendance. There is no fee.

Cooper Union for the Advancement of Science and Art, Registrar, 30 Cooper Square, New York, NY 10003, 212-353-4124 (Fax: 212-353-4343). Hours: 9AM-4:30PM. Enrollment: 1075. Records go back to 1859. Degrees granted: Bachelors; Masters. Adverse incident record source- Dean of Students, 212-353-4112.

Attendance and degree information available by phone, fax, mail. Search requires name plus approximate years of attendance. Also helpful: date of birth. There is no fee.

Cornell University, Registrar, 222 Day Hall, Ithaca, NY 14853, 607-255-4232 (Fax: 607-255-6262). Hours: 8AM-4:30PM; Open 9:30AM W. Enrollment: 18400. Records go back to 1885. Alumni Records Office: Alumni Association, 55 Brown Rd, Ithaca, NY 14853. Degrees granted: Bachelors; Masters; Doctorate. Special programs- M.D. at Cornell Univ. Medical College, 212-746-1056. Adverse incident record source- Public Safety, 607-255-1111.

Attendance and degree information available by phone, fax, mail. Search requires name plus SSN, exact years of attendance. There is no fee.

Cornell University Medical College, Registrar, 1300 York Ave Rm C-118, New York, NY 10021, 212-746-1056 (Fax: 212-746-5981). Enrollment: 400. Records go back to 1895. Alumni records are maintained here at the same phone number. Degrees granted: Doctorate; PhD. Adverse incident record source- Student Services.

Attendance and degree information available by phone, mail. Search requires name plus SSN, date of birth, exact years of attendance. There is no fee.

Cornell University School of Medical Sciences, Registrar, 445 E 69th St, Room 412, New York, NY 10021, 212-746-6565 (Fax: 212-746-8906). Enrollment: 230. Records go back to 1912. Alumni records are maintained here at the same phone number. Degrees granted: Doctorate. Special programs- Medical Science PhD. Adverse incident record source- Student Services.

Attendance and degree information available by phone, mail. Search requires name plus SSN, date of birth, exact years of attendance. There is no fee.

Cornell University Statutory Colleges, Registrar, 222 Day Hall, Ithaca, NY 14853, 607-255-4232 (Fax: 607-255-6262). Enrollment: 19000. Records go back to 1800. Alumni records are maintained here at the same phone number. Degrees granted: Bachelors; Masters; PhD. Special programs- Business: Liberal Arts. Adverse incident record source- Student Services.

Attendance and degree information available by phone, mail. Search requires name plus SSN, exact years of attendance. There is no fee.

Corning Community College, Registrar, 1 Academic Dr, Corning, NY 14830-3297, 607-962-9230 (Fax: 607-962-9456). Hours: 8AM-5PM M-Th; 8AM-4PM F. Enrollment: 5520. Records go back to 1956. Alumni records are maintained here also. Call 607-962-9320. Degrees granted: Associate. Adverse incident record source- Dean of Students, 607-962-9264.

Attendance and degree information available by phone, fax, mail. Search requires name plus SSN, approximate years of attendance. There is no fee.

Culinary Institute of America, Registrar, PO Box 53 N Rd, Hyde Park, NY 12538, 914-452-9600 X1347 (Fax: 914-451-1058). Enrollment: 2039. Alumni records are maintained here at the same phone number. Degrees granted: Associate; Bachelors.

Attendance and degree information available by phone, fax, mail. Search requires name only. Also helpful: SSN, exact years of attendance. There is no fee.

D'Youville College, Registrar, 320 Porter Ave, Buffalo, NY 14201, 716-881-7626 (Fax: 716-881-7790). Hours: 8:30AM-4:30PM. Enrollment: 1900. Records go back to 1908. Alumni Records Office: 631 Niagara St, Buffalo, NY 14201. Degrees granted: Bachelors; Masters.

Attendance and degree information available by phone, fax, mail. Search requires name plus SSN, approximate years of attendance. Also helpful: date of birth, exact years of attendance. There is no fee.

Daemen College, Registrar, 4380 Main St, Amherst, NY 14226-3592, 716-839-8214 (Fax: 716-839-8516). Hours: 8:30AM-4:30PM. Enrollment: 2150. Records go back to 1947. Alumni records are maintained here also. Call 716-839-8555. Degrees granted: Bachelors; Masters. Adverse incident record source- Student Affairs, 716-839-8332.

Attendance and degree information available by phone, fax, mail. Search requires name plus SSN. Also helpful: date of birth, exact years of attendance. There is no fee.

Darkei No'am Rabbinical College, Registrar, 2822 Ave J, Brooklyn, NY 11210, 718-338-6464 (Fax: 718-338-0622). Hours: 9AM-4PM. Enrollment: 50. Records go back to 1978. Degrees granted: Bachelors.

Attendance and degree information available by fax, mail. Search requires name plus SSN, signed release. There is no fee.

Derech Ayson Rabbinical Seminary, Registrar, 802 Hicksville Rd, Far Rockaway, NY 11691, 718-327-7600 (Fax: 718-327-1430). Enrollment: 150. Records go back to 1975.

Attendance and degree information available by phone, mail. Search requires name plus SSN, date of birth. There is no fee.

Dominican College of Blauvelt, Registrar, 470 Western Hwy, Orangeburg, NY 10962, 914-359-7800 (Fax: 914-359-2313). Hours: 8:30AM-5PM. Records go back to 1964. Alumni records are maintained here at the same phone number. Degrees granted: Associate; Bachelors; Masters.

Attendance and degree information available by phone, fax, mail. Search requires name plus SSN. Also helpful: exact years of attendance. There is no fee.

Dowling College, Registrar, Idle Hour Blvd, Oakdale, NY 11769-1999, 516-244-3250 (Fax: 516-589-6644). Hours: 8AM-8PM M-Th; 9AM-5PM F; 9AM-2PM S. Enrollment: 6000. Records go back to 1970. Alumni records are maintained here also. Call 516-244-3106. Degrees granted: Bachelors; Masters.

Attendance and degree information available by phone, fax, mail. Search requires name plus SSN. There is no fee.

Dutchess Community College, Registrar, 53 Pendell Rd, Poughkeepsie, NY 12601-1595, 914-471-4500 X1500 (Fax: 914-431-8983). Hours: 8AM-9PM. Records go back to 1957. Alumni records are maintained here also. Call 914-471-4500. Degrees granted: Associate.

Attendance and degree information available by fax, mail. Search requires name plus SSN, signed release. There is no fee.

Dutchess Community College, (Branch Campus), Registrar, Martha Lawrence Ext Sit, Spackenhill Rd, Poughkeepsie, NY 12603, 914-471-4500 X1500 (Fax: 914-471-4578). Hours: 8AM-9PM M-Th; 8AM-5PM F. Enrollment: 7025. Records go back to 1957. Degrees granted: Associate.

Attendance information available by fax, mail. Search requires name plus SSN, signed release. Also helpful: exact years of attendance. There is no fee.

Degree information available by fax, mail. Search requires name plus SSN, signed release. Also helpful: exact years of attendance. There is no fee.

Dutchess Community College, (South Campus), Registrar, Hollowbrook Plaza, Wappingers Falls, NY 12590, 914-298-0755. Records are not housed here. They are located at Dutchess Community College, Registrar, 53 Pendell Rd, Poughkeepsie, NY 12601-1595.

Elmira College, Registrar, 1 Park Place, Elmira, NY 14901, 607-735-1895 (Fax: 607-735-1758). Hours: 8:30AM-5PM. Enrollment: 2000. Records go back to 1855. Alumni records are maintained here also. Call 607-735-1855. Degrees granted: Associate; Bachelors; Masters. Adverse incident record source- Student Life, 607-735-1806.

Attendance and degree information available by phone, fax, mail. Search requires name only. There is no fee.

Erie Community College City Campus, Registrar, 121 Ellicott St, Buffalo, NY 14203, 716-851-1166 (Fax: 716-851-1129). Hours: 8AM-6PM M,T; 8AM-4PM W-F. Enrollment: 3200. Records go back to 1971. Alumni Records Office: 4041 Southwestern Blvd, Orchard Park, NY 14127-2155. Degrees granted: Associate. Special programs- Alcohol Counselling Technican. Adverse incident record source- Dean of Students, 716-851-1120.

Attendance and degree information available by phone, fax, mail. Search requires name plus SSN. Also helpful: date of birth, exact years of attendance. There is no fee.

Erie Community College North (Amherst) Campus, Registrar, 6205 Main St, Williamsville, NY 14221, 716-851-1467 (Fax: 716-851-1429). Hours: 8AM-4PM M,Th,F; 8AM-6PM T,W. Enrollment: 6000. Records go back to 1950. Alumni records are maintained here also. Call 716-851-1002. Degrees granted: Associate.

Attendance and degree information available by phone, fax, mail. Search requires name plus SSN, approximate years of attendance. There is no fee.

Erie Community College South Campus, Registrar, S-4041 Southwestern Blvd, Orchard Park, NY 14127-2199, 716-851-1668 (Fax: 716-851-1629). Hours: 8AM-4PM; 4-8PM W. Enrollment: 3500. Records go back to 1985. Alumni records are maintained here also. Call 716-851-1663. Degrees granted: Associate.

Attendance and degree information available by phone, fax, mail. Search requires name plus SSN. Also helpful: exact years of attendance. There is no fee.

Fashion Institute of Technology, Registrar, Seventh Ave at 27th St, New York, NY 10001-5992, 212-760-7676. Hours: 10AM-4PM. Records go back to 1945. Alumni records are maintained here also. Call 212-760-7158. Degrees granted: Associate; Bachelors; Masters. Adverse incident record source- Dean of Students, 212-760-7681.

Attendance and degree information available by mail. Search requires name plus SSN, exact years of attendance. Also helpful: date of birth. There is no fee.

Finger Lakes Community College, Registrar, 4355 Lake Shore Dr, Canandaigua, NY 14424, 716-394-3500 X290 (Fax: 716-394-5005). Hours: 8:30AM-5PM. Records go back to 1968. Alumni records are maintained here at the same phone number. Degrees granted: Associate.

Attendance and degree information available by phone, fax, mail. Search requires name plus SSN, approximate years of attendance. Also helpful: date of birth. There is no fee.

Five Towns College, Registrar, 305 N Service Rd, Dix Hills, NY 11746-6055, 516-424-7000 (Fax: 516-424-7006). Hours: 8AM-6PM M-Th, 8AM-4PM F. Enrollment: 600. Records go back to 1974. Alumni records are maintained here at the same phone number. Degrees granted: Associate; Bachelors.

Attendance and degree information available by phone, mail. Search requires name only. Also helpful: SSN, date of birth, exact years of attendance. There is no fee.

Fordham University, Registrar, E Fordham Rd, Bronx, NY 10458, 718-817-3901 (Fax: 718-367-9404). Hours: 9AM-4:45PM. Enrollment: 14000. Records go back to 1918. Alumni Records Office: 113 W 60th, New York, NY 10023. Degrees granted: Bachelors; Masters; Ph.D. Adverse incident record source- Dean of Students, 718-817-4731.

Attendance and degree information available by phone, fax, mail. Search requires name plus SSN, approximate years of attendance. There is no fee.

Friends World College Long Island University, Registrar, 239 Montauk Hwy, South Hampton, NY 11968, 516-283-4000 (Fax: 516-283-4081). Records go back to 1965. Alumni records are maintained here at the same phone number. Degrees granted: Bachelors.

Attendance and degree information available by phone, fax, mail. Search requires name plus SSN. Also helpful: exact years of attendance. There is no fee.

Fulton-Montgomery Community College, Registrar, Rte 67, Johnstown, NY 12095, 518-762-4651 X222 (Fax: 518-762-4334). Hours: 8AM-4PM. Enrollment: 1750. Records go back to 1964. Alumni records are maintained here at the same phone number. Degrees granted: Associate.

Attendance and degree information available by phone, fax, mail. Search requires name plus SSN. Also helpful: date of birth. Fee is $3.00.

General Theological Seminary, Registrar, 175 Ninth Ave, New York, NY 10011-4977, 212-243-5150 (Fax: 212-727-3907). Hours: 8:30AM-5PM. Enrollment: 120. Records go back to 1920. Alumni records are maintained here at the same phone number. Degrees granted: Masters; Ph.D.

Attendance information available by phone, fax, mail. Search requires name plus SSN. Also helpful: exact years of attendance. There is no fee.

Degree information available by phone, fax, mail. Search requires name plus SSN, approximate years of attendance. Also helpful: exact years of attendance. There is no fee.

Genesee Community College, Registrar, One College Rd, Batavia, NY 14020, 716-343-0055 X6218 (Fax: 716-343-6810). Hours: 8AM-6:30PM M-Th; 8AM-4:30PM F; 8:30-10:30AM S. Records go back to 1967. Alumni records are maintained here also. Call 716-343-0055-X6262. Degrees granted: Associate. Adverse incident record source- Dean of Students, 716-343-0055 X6219.

Attendance and degree information available by mail. Search requires name plus SSN, approximate years of attendance, signed release. Also helpful: date of birth, exact years of attendance. There is no fee.

Graduate School and University Center, Registrar, 33 W 42nd St, New York, NY 10036, 212-642-1600 (Fax: 212-642-2779). Hours: 9AM-5PM. Records go back to 1961. Alumni records are maintained here also. Call 212-642-2850. Degrees granted: Masters; Ph.D.

Attendance and degree information available by phone, fax, mail. Search requires name plus SSN, approximate years of attendance. There is no fee.

Hadar Hatorah Rabbinical Seminary, Registrar, 824 Eastern Pkwy, Brooklyn, NY 11213, 718-735-0250 (Fax: 718-735-4455). Enrollment: 300. Records go back to 1964. Alumni records are maintained here at the same phone number. Degrees granted: Bachelors. Adverse incident record source-Student Services.

Attendance and degree information available by mail. Search requires name plus SSN, exact years of attendance, signed release. There is no fee.

Hamilton College, Registrar, 198 College Hill Rd, Clinton, NY 13323, 315-859-4637 (Fax: 315-859-4632). Hours: 8:30AM-4:30PM. Enrollment: 1650. Records go back to 1810. Alumni records are maintained here also. Call 315-859-4412. Degrees granted: Bachelors. Adverse incident record source-Dean of Students, 315-859-4020.

Attendance and degree information available by phone, fax, mail. Search requires name only. Also helpful: exact years of attendance. There is no fee.

Hartwick College, Registrar, Oneonta, NY 13820, 607-431-4460 (Fax: 607-431-4006). Hours: 9AM-5PM. Enrollment: 1500. Records go back to 1928. Alumni records are maintained here also. Call 607-431-4010. Degrees granted: Bachelors.

Attendance and degree information available by phone, fax, mail. Search requires name only. Also helpful: SSN, date of birth, exact years of attendance. There is no fee.

Hebrew Union College-Jewish Institute of Religion, Registrar, One W Fourth St, New York, NY 10012, 212-674-5300 (Fax: 212-388-1720). Hours: 8:30AM-5:30PM. Enrollment: 150. Records go back to 1883. Degrees granted: Masters; Doctorate. Special programs- Hebrew Union College, Cincinnati, 513-221-1875. Adverse incident record source- Dean of Students.

Attendance and degree information available by phone, fax, mail. Search requires name plus exact years of attendance. There is no fee.

Helene Fuld School of Nursing, Registrar, 1879 Madison Ave, New York, NY 10035, 212-423-1000 X238 (Fax: 212-427-2453). Hours: 8AM-4PM. Records go back to 1946. Alumni records are maintained here also. Call 212-423-1000 X216. Degrees granted: Associate.

Attendance and degree information available by phone, fax, mail. Search requires name plus SSN, exact years of attendance. There is no fee.

Herbert H. Lehman College, Registrar, 250 Bedford Park Blvd W, Bronx, NY 10468, 718-960-8613. Hours: 9AM-5PM. Records go back to 1970. Alumni records are maintained here also. Call 718-960-8044. Degrees granted: Bachelors; Masters.

Attendance and degree information available by mail. Search requires name plus SSN, approximate years of attendance, signed release. There is no fee.

Herkimer County Community College, Registrar, Reservoir Rd, Herkimer, NY 13350, 315-866-0300 X280 (Fax: 315-866-7253). Hours: 8AM-4PM. Enrollment: 2300. Records go back to 1968. Alumni records are maintained here also. Call 315-866-0300 X259. Degrees granted: Associate. Adverse incident record source- Dean of Students, 315-866-0300 X276: Safety Office, 315-866-0300 X336

Attendance and degree information available by phone, fax, mail. Search requires name only. Also helpful: SSN, date of birth, approximate years of attendance. There is no fee.

Hilbert College, Registrar, 5200 S Park Ave, Hamburg, NY 14075-1597, 716-649-7900 (Fax: 716-649-0702). Hours: 8:30AM-5PM. Enrollment: 800. Records go back to 1957. Alumni records are maintained here at the same phone number. Degrees granted: Associate; Bachelors.

Attendance and degree information available by phone, fax, mail. Search requires name plus SSN. Also helpful: date of birth, approximate years of attendance. There is no fee.

Hobart & William Smith College, Registrar, Geneva, NY 14456, 315-781-3651 (Fax: 315-781-3920). Hours: 9AM-4PM. Enrollment: 1740. Records go back to 1908. Alumni records are maintained here also. Call 315-781-3700. Degrees granted: Bachelors.

Attendance and degree information available by phone, fax, mail. Search requires name plus SSN, approximate years of attendance. There is no fee.

Hofstra University, Office of Financial and Academic Records, Room 126, Hempstead, NY 11550, 516-463-6680 (Fax: 516-463-4936). Hours: 8AM-4:30PM. Enrollment: 12056. Records go back to 1936. Alumni records are maintained here at the same phone number. Degrees granted: Bachelors; Masters; Doctorate; Professional Diplomas. Adverse incident record source- Dean of Students, 516-463-6913.

Attendance and degree information available by fax, mail. Search requires name plus SSN, exact years of attendance. There is no fee.

Holy Trinity Orthodox Seminary, Registrar, PO Box 36, Jordanville, NY 13361, 315-858-0940 (Fax: 315-858-0945). Enrollment: 40. Records go back to 1948. Alumni records are maintained here at the same phone number. Degrees granted: Bachelors. Special programs- Theological Studies Conducted in Russian Language. Adverse incident record source- Department of Student Affairs.

Attendance and degree information available by phone, mail. Search requires name plus SSN, date of birth. Also helpful: approximate years of attendance. There is no fee.

Hostos Community College, Registrar, 475 Grand Concourse, Bronx, NY 10451, 718-518-6771 (Fax: 718-518-6548). Hours: 11AM-7PM. Records go back to 1970. Alumni records are maintained here also. Call 718-518-4306. Degrees granted: Associate.

Attendance and degree information available by phone, fax, mail. Search requires name plus SSN, exact years of attendance. There is no fee.

Houghton College, Registrar, Houghton, NY 14744, 716-567-9257 (Fax: 716-567-9572). Hours: 8AM-5PM. Records go back to 1883. Alumni records are maintained here also. Call 716-567-9353. Degrees granted: Bachelors. Adverse incident record source- Dean of Students.

Attendance and degree information available by phone, fax, mail. Search requires name plus SSN, approximate years of attendance. There is no fee.

Houghton College, (**Buffalo Suburban Campus**), Registrar, 910 Union Rd, West Seneca, NY 14224, 716-674-6363 (Fax: 716-674-6363 X764). Records are not housed here. They are located at Houghton College, Registrar, Houghton, NY 14744.

Hudson Valley Community College, Registrar, 80 Vandenburgh Ave, Troy, NY 12180, 518-270-1569 (Fax: 518-270-1576). Hours: 8AM-5PM. Enrollment: 10000. Records go back to 1988. Alumni records are maintained here also. Call

518-270-7556. Degrees granted: Associate. Adverse incident record source- Public Safety, 518-270-7210.

Attendance information available by phone, mail. Search requires name plus SSN. Also helpful: date of birth, exact years of attendance. There is no fee.

Degree information available by phone, mail. Search requires name plus SSN, date of birth. Also helpful: exact years of attendance. There is no fee.

Hunter College, Registrar, 695 Park Ave, New York, NY 10021, 212-772-4500. Hours: 10AM-6PM. Records go back to 1906. Alumni records are maintained here also. Call 212-772-4087. Degrees granted: Bachelors; Masters. Adverse incident record source- Dean of Students.

Attendance and degree information available by mail. Search requires name plus SSN, date of birth, approximate years of attendance, signed release. There is no fee.

Interboro Institute, Registrar, 450 W 56th St, New York, NY 10019, 212-399-0091 (Fax: 212-765-5772). Hours: 9AM-5PM. Enrollment: 900. Records go back to 1945. Degrees granted: Associate. Adverse incident record source- 212-399-0091.

Attendance and degree information available by fax, mail. Search requires name plus SSN, approximate years of attendance, signed release. There is no fee.

Iona College, Registrar, 715 North Ave, New Rochelle, NY 10801-1890, 914-633-2508 (Fax: 914-633-2182). Hours: 9AM-5PM. Enrollment: 5588. Records go back to 1941. Alumni Records Office: 115 Beechmont Dr, New Rochelle, NY 10801. Degrees granted: Associate; Bachelors; Masters.

Attendance and degree information available by phone, mail. Search requires name plus approximate years of attendance. Also helpful: SSN, date of birth, exact years of attendance. There is no fee.

Iona College, (**Manhattan Campus**), Registrar, 425 W 33rd St, New York, NY 10001, 212-630-0270 (Fax: 212-630-0275). Records are not housed here. They are located at Iona College, Registrar, 715 North Ave, New Rochelle, NY 10801-1890.

Iona College, (**Rockland Campus**), Registrar, One Dutch Hill Rd, Orangeburg, NY 10962, 914-359-2252 (Fax: 914-359-2261). Records are not housed here. They are located at Iona College, Registrar, 715 North Ave, New Rochelle, NY 10801-1890.

Iona College, (**Yonkers Campus**), Registrar, 1061 N Broadway, Yonkers, NY 10701, 914-378-8000. Records are not housed here. They are located at Iona College, Registrar, 715 North Ave, New Rochelle, NY 10801-1890.

Ithaca College, Office of the Registrar, Transcript Requests, 228 Job Hall, Ithaca, NY 14850-7014, 607-274-3127 (Fax: 607-274-1366). Hours: 8AM-5PM. Enrollment: 5700. Records go back to 1892. Degrees granted: Bachelors; Masters. Adverse incident record source- Campus Safety, 607-274-3333.

Attendance and degree information available by phone, fax, mail. Search requires name only. Also helpful: SSN, date of birth, exact years of attendance. There is no fee.

Jamestown Business College, Registrar, PO Box 429, Fairmount Ave, Jamestown, NY 14702-0429, 716-664-5100 (Fax: 716-664-3144). Hours: 8AM-5PM. Enrollment: 350. Records go back to 1920. Degrees granted: Associate. Adverse incident record source- Dean, 716-664-5100.

Attendance and degree information available by phone, fax, mail. Search requires name plus SSN. Also helpful: approximate years of attendance. There is no fee.

Jamestown Community College, Academic Transcripts, 525 Falconer St, Jamestown, NY 14701, 716-665-5220 X332 (Fax: 716-665-4115). Hours: 8:30AM-5PM. Enrollment: 3400. Records go back to 1950. Alumni records are maintained here at the same phone number. Degrees granted: Associate. Special programs- Financial Aid Transcripts: Financial Aids Office, 716-665-5220.

Attendance and degree information available by phone, fax, mail. Search requires name plus SSN, approximate years of attendance. Also helpful: date of birth. There is no fee.

Jamestown Community College, (**Cattaraugus County Campus**), Registrar, 525 Falconer Jamestown St, Olean, NY 14760, 716-665-5220 X332 (Fax: 716-665-4115). Hours: 8:30AM-4:30PM. Enrollment: 3800. Records go back to 1950. Alumni records are maintained here at the same phone number. Degrees granted: Associate.

Attendance and degree information available by phone, fax, mail. Search requires name plus SSN, date of birth. Also helpful: exact years of attendance. There is no fee.

Jefferson Community College, Registrar, Outer Coffeen St, Watertown, NY 13601, 315-786-2417 (Fax: 315-786-2459). Hours: 9AM-5PM. Enrollment: 3500. Records go back to 1961. Alumni records are maintained here also. Call 315-786-2327. Degrees granted: Associate. Adverse incident record source- Security, 315-786-2359.

Attendance and degree information available by phone, fax, mail. Search requires name plus SSN. Also helpful: date of birth, exact years of attendance. There is no fee.

Jewish Theological Seminary of America, Registrar, 3080 Broadway, New York, NY 10027, 212-678-8007 (Fax: 212-678-8947). Hours: 9AM-5PM. Records go back to 1885. Degrees granted: Bachelors; Masters; Doctorate; Rabbamic Ordination.

Attendance information available by phone, fax, mail. Search requires name plus SSN, date of birth, exact years of attendance. There is no fee.

Degree information available by fax, mail. Search requires name plus SSN, date of birth, exact years of attendance. There is no fee.

John Jay College of Criminal Justice, Registrar, 445 W 59th St Room 4113, New York, NY 10019, 212-237-8986 (Fax: 212-237-8777). Hours: 9AM-5PM. Enrollment: 10313. Records go back to 1965. Degrees granted: Associate; Bachelors; Masters.

Attendance and degree information available by phone, mail. Search requires name plus SSN, date of birth, exact years of attendance. There is no fee.

Julliard School, Registrar, 60 Lincoln Center Plaza, New York, NY 10023-6590, 212-799-5000 (Fax: 212-724-0263). Hours: 9AM-5PM. Records go back to 1905. Alumni records are maintained here also. Call 212-799--5000 X344. Degrees granted: Bachelors; Masters; Doctorate.

Attendance and degree information available by fax, mail. Search requires name only. There is no fee.

Katherine Gibbs School, Registrar, 535 Broad Hollow Rd, Melville, NY 11747, 516-293-2460 (Fax: 516-293-1276). Hours: 9AM-10PM. Enrollment: 350. Records go back to 1915. Alumni records are maintained here also. Call 516-293-1024. Degrees granted: Associate.

Attendance and degree information available by phone, fax, mail. Search requires name plus SSN. There is no fee.

Katherine Gibbs School, Registrar, 200 Park Ave, New York, NY 10166, 212-973-4954 (Fax: 212-338-9606). Hours: 8:30AM-8:30PM. Records go back to 1918. Alumni records are maintained here also. Call 212-745-9480. Degrees granted: Associate.

Attendance and degree information available by fax, mail. Search requires name plus SSN, exact years of attendance, signed release. There is no fee.

Kehilath Yakov Rabbinical Seminary, Registrar, 206 Wilson St, Brooklyn, NY 11211, 718-963-3940 (Fax: 718-387-8586). Hours: 9AM-5:30PM.

Attendance and degree information available by fax, mail. Search requires name plus SSN, approximate years of attendance, signed release. There is no fee.

Keuka College, Registrar, Keuka Park, NY 14478, 315-536-5204 (Fax: 315-536-5216). Hours: 8:30AM-4:30PM. Enrollment: 920. Records go back to 1900. Alumni records are maintained here also. Call 315-536-5238. Degrees granted: Bachelors.

Attendance and degree information available by phone, fax, mail. Search requires name only. Also helpful: SSN, exact years of attendance. There is no fee.

King's College, Registrar, Lodge Rd, Briarcliff Manor, NY 10510, 914-941-7200 (Fax: 914-941-9460). Hours: 8:30AM-5PM. Records go back to 1976. Alumni records are maintained here at the same phone number. Degrees granted: Associate; Bachelors. Certification: Teacher. Adverse incident record source- Dean of Students.

Attendance and degree information available by phone, fax, mail. Search requires name plus SSN, date of birth, exact years of attendance. There is no fee.

Kingsborough Community College, Registrar, 2001 Oriental Blvd, Manhattan Beach, Brooklyn, NY 11235, 718-368-5000 (Fax: 718-368-5692). Hours: 9AM-4:45PM. Enrollment: 14000. Records go back to 1963. Alumni records are maintained here at the same phone number. Degrees granted: Associate. Special programs- Marine Technology. Adverse incident record source- Dean of Students.

Attendance and degree information available by mail. Search requires name plus SSN, approximate years of attendance, signed release. There is no fee.

La Guardia Community College, Registrar, 31-10 Thomson Ave, Long Island City, NY 11101, 718-482-7232 (Fax: 718-482-5008). Hours: 9:30AM-5PM M,T; 2-8PM W; 9:30AM-8PM Th; Closed F. Enrollment: 11000. Records go back to 1971. Alumni records are maintained here also. Call 718-482-5054. Degrees granted: Associate.

Attendance and degree information available by written request only. Search requires name plus SSN, signed release. Also helpful: date of birth, exact years of attendance. There is no fee.

Laboratory Institute of Merchandising, Registrar, 12 E 53rd St, New York, NY 10022, 212-752-1530 (Fax: 212-832-6708). Hours: 9AM-4:30PM. Enrollment: 200. Records go back to 1939. Alumni records are maintained here at the same phone number. Degrees granted: Associate; Bachelors.

Attendance and degree information available by phone, fax, mail. Search requires name plus exact years of attendance. Also helpful: SSN, date of birth. There is no fee.

LeMoyne College, Registrar, Le Moyne Heights, Syracuse, NY 13214, 315-445-4100 (Fax: 315-445-4540). Records go back to 1946. Alumni records are maintained here also. Call 315-445-4545. Degrees granted: Bachelors; Masters. Adverse incident record source- Student Life.

Attendance and degree information available by phone, fax, mail. Search requires name plus date of birth. Also helpful: SSN, exact years of attendance. Fee is $3.00.

Long Island University, Registrar, 720 Northern Blvd, Brookville, NY 11548, 516-299-2756 (Fax: 516-299-2721). Hours: 9AM-5PM M,W,Th,F; 9AM-8PM T. Records go back to

1954. Degrees granted: Associate; Bachelors; Masters; Doctorate.

Attendance and degree information available by phone, fax, mail. Search requires name plus SSN. Also helpful: date of birth, exact years of attendance. There is no fee.

Long Island University, Registrar, 555 Broadway, Dobbs Ferry, NY 10522, 914-674-7445 (Fax: 914-674-7269). Hours: 9:30AM-7PM. Enrollment: 1000. Records go back to 1975. Alumni records are maintained here at the same phone number. Degrees granted: Masters.

Attendance and degree information available by fax, mail. Search requires name plus SSN, signed release. Also helpful: date of birth, exact years of attendance. There is no fee.

Long Island University, (Brentwood Campus), Registrar, Second Ave, Brentwood, NY 11717, 516-299-2756. Hours: 9AM-5PM M,W,Th,F; 9AM-8PM T. Records go back to 1954. Alumni records are maintained here also. Call 516-299-2525. Degrees granted: Bachelors; Masters.

Attendance and degree information available by phone, fax, mail. Search requires name plus SSN. Also helpful: date of birth, exact years of attendance. There is no fee.

Long Island University, (Brooklyn Campus), Registrar, University Plaza, Brooklyn, NY 11201, 718-488-1000. Enrollment: 9000. Records go back to 1926. Alumni records are maintained here at the same phone number. Degrees granted: Associate; Bachelors; Masters; Doctorate.

Attendance information available by mail. Search requires name plus SSN, exact years of attendance, signed release. Also helpful: date of birth. There is no fee.

Degree information available by mail. Search requires name plus SSN, date of birth, exact years of attendance, signed release. There is no fee.

Long Island University, (C.W. Post Campus), Registrar, Brookville, NY 11548, 516-299-2755 (Fax: 516-299-2721). Hours: 9AM-5PM M,W,Th,F; 9AM-8PM T. Enrollment: 8100. Records go back to 1954. Alumni records are maintained here also. Call 516-299-2263. Degrees granted: Associate; Bachelors; Masters; Doctorate.

Attendance and degree information available by phone, mail. Search requires name plus SSN. Also helpful: date of birth, exact years of attendance. There is no fee.

Long Island University, (Rockland Campus), Registrar, Rte 340, Orangeburg, NY 10962, 914-359-7200 (Fax: 914-359-7248). Hours: 9AM-8PM M-Th; 9AM-5PM F. Enrollment: 400. Records go back to 1990. Degrees granted: Masters. Certification: Adv. Business. Special programs- Graduate Records at C W Post, 516-299-2755. Adverse incident record source- Main Office, 914-359-7200.

Attendance and degree information available by phone, fax, mail. Search requires name plus SSN, date of birth. Also helpful: exact years of attendance. There is no fee.

Manhattan College, Registrar, Manhattan College Pkwy, Riverdale, NY 10471, 718-862-7312 (Fax: 718-862-7457). Hours: 9AM-4:30PM. Enrollment: 3200. Records go back to 1800. Alumni records are maintained here at the same phone number. Degrees granted: Bachelors; Masters. Adverse incident record source- Dean of Students, 718-862-7246.

Attendance and degree information available by phone, fax, mail. Search requires name plus exact years of attendance. Also helpful: SSN, date of birth. There is no fee.

Manhattan School of Music, Registrar, 120 Claremont Ave, New York, NY 10027, 212-749-2802 X469 (Fax: 212-749-5471). Hours: 9AM-5PM. Records go back to 1918. Alumni records are maintained here also. Call 212-749-2802 X502. Degrees granted: Bachelors; Masters; Doctorate. Adverse incident record source- Dean of Students.

Attendance and degree information available by mail. Search requires name plus SSN, date of birth, approximate years of attendance, signed release. There is no fee.

Manhattanville College, Registrar, 2900 Purchase St, Purchase, NY 10577, 914-694-2200 (Fax: 914-694-2386). Hours: 9AM-5PM. Records go back to 1914. Alumni records are maintained here also. Call 914-694-2200 X202. Degrees granted: Bachelors; Masters.

Attendance and degree information available by phone, mail. Search requires name plus SSN, approximate years of attendance. There is no fee.

Maria College of Albany, Registrar, Rm 100, 700 New Scotland Ave, Albany, NY 12208-1798, 518-438-3111 X24 (Fax: 518-438-7170). Hours: 8:30AM-4PM. Enrollment: 900. Records go back to 1963. Alumni records are maintained here also. Call 518-489-7436. Degrees granted: Associate. Adverse incident record source- 518-438-3111 X28.

Attendance and degree information available by phone, fax, mail. Search requires name only. Also helpful: SSN, date of birth, exact years of attendance. There is no fee.

Marist College, Registrar, 290 North Rd, Poughkeepsie, NY 12601, 914-575-2250 (Fax: 914-471-6212). Hours: 8AM-5PM. Enrollment: 4500. Records go back to 1945. Alumni records are maintained here at the same phone number. Degrees granted: Bachelors; Masters. Adverse incident record source- Dean of Students, 914-575-3000.

Attendance and degree information available by mail. Search requires name plus SSN, approximate years of attendance, signed release. There is no fee.

Maryknoll School of Theology, Archive Dept, Maryknoll, NY 10545, 914-941-7590 X2500 (Fax: 914-941-5753). This school closed in May, 1995. Degrees granted: Masters.

Attendance and degree information available by written request only. Search requires name plus SSN, date of birth, exact years of attendance, signed release. There is no fee.

Marymount College, Registrar, 100 Marymount Ave, Tarrytown, NY 10591-3796, 914-332-8211 (Fax: 914-631-8586). Hours: 9AM-5PM. Enrollment: 1000. Alumni records are maintained here also. Call 914-332-8353. Degrees granted: Bachelors.

Attendance and degree information available by phone, fax, mail. Search requires name plus SSN. Also helpful: date of birth, exact years of attendance. There is no fee.

Marymount Manhattan College, Registrar, 221 E 71st St, New York, NY 10021, 212-517-0400 (Fax: 212-517-0413). Hours: 8AM-4:30PM. Records go back to 1936. Alumni records are maintained here also. Call 212-517-0530. Degrees granted: Bachelors. Special programs- Continuing Education, 212-517-0564.

Attendance and degree information available by phone, fax, mail. Search requires name plus approximate years of attendance. Also helpful: SSN, date of birth, exact years of attendance. There is no fee.

Mater Dei College, Registrar, Rural Rte 2 Box 45, Ogdensburg, NY 13669-1034, 315-393-5930 (Fax: 315-393-5930 X440). Hours: 8AM-5PM. Enrollment: 350. Records go back to 1960. Alumni records are maintained here at the same phone number. Degrees granted: Associate. Adverse incident record source- Student Affairs.

Attendance and degree information available by mail. Search requires name plus SSN, date of birth, signed release. Also helpful: exact years of attendance. There is no fee.

Medaille College, Registrar, 18 Agassiz Circle, Buffalo, NY 14214, 716-884-3281 (Fax: 716-884-0291). Hours: 8AM-

8:15PM M,T; 8AM-6PM W,Th; 8AM-4PM F. Enrollment: 900. Records go back to 1937. Alumni records are maintained here also. Call 716-884-3281 X208. Degrees granted: Associate; Bachelors.

Attendance and degree information available by phone, fax, mail. Search requires name plus SSN, approximate years of attendance. There is no fee.

Medgar Evers College, Registrar's Office, 1150 Carroll St RC-101, Brooklyn, NY 11225, 718-270-6079 (Fax: 718-270-6496). Hours: 9AM-7PM M,Th; 9AM-2PM W; 9AM-5PM T; 10AM-5PM F. Records go back to 1975. Degrees granted: Associate; Bachelors.

Attendance and degree information available by fax, mail. Search requires name plus SSN, date of birth, exact years of attendance, signed release. There is no fee.

Mercy College, Registrar, 555 Broadway, Dobbs Ferry, NY 10522, 914-674-7265 (Fax: 914-693-9455). Hours: 9AM-7PM M-Th; 9AM-5PM F; 9AM-12:30PM S. Records go back to 1950's. Alumni records are maintained here also. Call 914-674-7314. Degrees granted: Associate; Bachelors; Masters.

Attendance and degree information available by phone, fax, mail. Search requires name plus exact years of attendance. Also helpful: SSN, date of birth. There is no fee.

Mercy College, (Bronx Campus), Registrar, 50 Antin Place, Bronx, NY 10462, 718-798-8952. Records are not housed here. They are located at Mercy College, Registrar, 555 Broadway, Dobbs Ferry, NY 10522.

Mercy College, (White Plains Campus), Registrar, Martine Ave and S Broadway, White Plains, NY 10601, 914-948-3666 (Fax: 914-948-6732). Records are not housed here. They are located at Mercy College, Registrar, 555 Broadway, Dobbs Ferry, NY 10522.

Mercy College, (Yorktown Campus), Registrar, 2651 Stang Blvd, Yorktown Heights, NY 10598, 914-245-6100. Records are not housed here. They are located at Mercy College, Registrar, 555 Broadway, Dobbs Ferry, NY 10522.

Mesivta Tifereth Jerusalem of America, Registrar, 141 E Broadway, New York, NY 10002, 212-964-2830 (Fax: 212-349-5213). Hours: 9AM-5PM. Enrollment: 87. Records go back to 1937. Alumni records are maintained here at the same phone number.

Attendance and degree information available by fax, mail. Search requires name plus SSN, approximate years of attendance, signed release. There is no fee.

Mesivta Torah Vodaath Rabbinical Seminary, Registrar, 425 E 9th St, Brooklyn, NY 11218, 718-941-8000 (Fax: 718-941-8032). Hours: 8AM-4PM.

Attendance and degree information available by mail. Search requires name plus SSN, date of birth, exact years of attendance. There is no fee.

Mirrer Yeshiva Central Institute, Registrar, 1791 S Ocean Pkwy, Brooklyn, NY 11223, 718-645-0536 (Fax: 718-645-9251). Hours: 8AM-4:30PM.

Attendance and degree information available by fax, mail. Search requires name plus SSN, exact years of attendance, signed release. There is no fee.

Mohawk Valley Community College, Registrar, 1101 Sherman Dr, Utica, NY 13501, 315-792-5336 (Fax: 315-792-5698). Hours: 8AM-7PM M-Th; 8AM-4:30PM F. Enrollment: 5300. Records go back to 1988. Alumni records are maintained here also. Call 315-792-5340. Degrees granted: Associate. Adverse incident record source- Dean of Students.

Attendance and degree information available by phone, fax, mail. Search requires name plus SSN, date of birth, exact years of attendance. There is no fee.

Mohawk Valley Community College, (Branch Campus), Registrar, Floyd Ave, Rome, NY 13440, 315-792-5494 (Fax: 315-792-5698). Hours: 8:M-7PM M-Th; 8AM-4:30PM F. Records go back to 1900's. Alumni records are maintained here also. Call 315-792-5340. Degrees granted: Associate. Adverse incident record source- Dean of Students.

Attendance and degree information available by phone, fax, mail. Search requires name plus SSN. Also helpful: date of birth, exact years of attendance. There is no fee.

Molloy College, Registrar, PO Box 5002, Rockville Centre, NY 11571-5002, 516-678-5000 X229 (Fax: 516-256-2232). Enrollment: 230. Records go back to 1955. Alumni records are maintained here also. Call 516-678-5000 X218. Degrees granted: Associate; Bachelors; Masters. Special programs- Nursing. Adverse incident record source- Dean's Office .

Attendance and degree information available by phone, mail. Search requires name plus SSN, exact years of attendance. Also helpful: date of birth, approximate years of attendance. There is no fee.

Monroe College, Registrar, 29 E Fordham Rd, Bronx, NY 10468, 718-933-6700 X317 (Fax: 718-220-3032). Hours: 8:30AM-7:30PM M-Th; 8:30AM-2PM F. Enrollment: 1926. Records go back to 1960. Alumni records are maintained here also. Call 718-933-6700 X310. Degrees granted: Associate.

Attendance and degree information available by phone, fax, mail. Search requires name plus SSN, approximate years of attendance. There is no fee.

Monroe College, (New Rochelle Campus), Registrar, 434 Main St, New Rochelle, NY 10801, 914-632-5400 (Fax: 914-632-5462). Hours: 8:30AM-7:30PM. Enrollment: 600. Records go back to 1983. Degrees granted: Associate.

Attendance information available by mail. Search requires name plus SSN, exact years of attendance, signed release. Also helpful: date of birth. There is no fee.

Degree information available by mail. Search requires name plus SSN, exact years of attendance, signed release. There is no fee.

Monroe Community College, Registrar, 1000 E Henrietta Rd, Rochester, NY 14623, 716-292-2300 (Fax: 716-292-3850). Hours: 8AM-4:30PM. Records go back to 1961. Alumni records are maintained here also. Call 716-292-2000. Degrees granted: Associate.

Attendance and degree information available by phone, fax, mail. Search requires name plus SSN. Also helpful: date of birth, exact years of attendance. There is no fee.

Mount Sinai School of Medicine, Registrar, One Gustave L Levy Pl, New York, NY 10029, 212-241-6691 (Fax: 212-369-6013). Enrollment: 485. Records go back to 1972. Alumni records are maintained here at the same phone number. Degrees granted: Bachelors; Masters; First Professional Degree.

Attendance and degree information available by phone, mail. Search requires name plus SSN, date of birth, exact years of attendance. There is no fee.

Mount St. Mary College, Registrar, 330 Powell Ave, Newburgh, NY 12550, 914-569-3258 (Fax: 914-562-6762). Hours: 8AM-5PM. Enrollment: 1900. Records go back to 1935. Alumni records are maintained here also. Call 914-569-3217. Degrees granted: Bachelors; Masters. Adverse incident record source- Dean of Students, 914-569-3114.

Attendance and degree information available by phone, fax, mail. Search requires name only. Also helpful: SSN, date of birth, exact years of attendance. There is no fee.

Nassau Community College, Registrar, One Education Dr, Garden City, NY 11530, 516-572-7205 (Fax: 516-572-7130). Hours: 8AM-7:30PM M-Th; 8AM-4:30PM F. Records go back to 1959. Alumni records are maintained here at the same phone number. Degrees granted: Associate. Adverse incident record source- Dean of Students.

Attendance and degree information available by fax, mail. Search requires name plus SSN, signed release. There is no fee.

Nazareth College of Rochester, Registrar, 4245 East Ave, Rochester, NY 14618-3790, 716-586-2525 X408 (Fax: 716-586-2452). Hours: 8:30AM-4:30PM M-Th,8AM-Noon Sat. Enrollment: 2800. Records go back to 1924. Alumni records are maintained here also. Call 716-389-2470. Degrees granted: Bachelors; Masters. Adverse incident record source- Student Affairs.

Attendance information available by phone, fax, mail. Search requires name plus approximate years of attendance. Also helpful: SSN, exact years of attendance. There is no fee.

Degree information available by phone, fax, mail. Search requires name plus approximate years of attendance. Also helpful: SSN, date of birth, exact years of attendance. There is no fee.

New School for Social Research, Registrar, 66 W 12th St, New York, NY 10011, 212-229-5600 (Fax: 212-229-5359). Hours: 7:30AM-4:30PM. Enrollment: 6500. Records go back to 1919. Alumni records are maintained here also. Call 212-229-5662. Degrees granted: Bachelors; Masters; Doctorate.

Attendance and degree information available by phone, fax, mail. Search requires name only. Also helpful: SSN, date of birth, exact years of attendance. There is no fee.

New School for Social Research, (Parsons School of Design), Registrar, 66 Fifth Ave, New York, NY 10011, 212-229-5762 (Fax: 212-229-5470). Hours: 9AM-6PM. Enrollment: 10000. Records go back to 1800's. Alumni records are maintained here also. Call 212-229-5662. Degrees granted: Associate; Bachelors; Masters; Doctorate; BPA, MSSC, MS, MPS, DSSC, MPA. Adverse incident record source- Registrar, 212-229-5762.

Attendance and degree information available by phone, fax, mail. Search requires name plus SSN, approximate years of attendance. Also helpful: date of birth, exact years of attendance. There is no fee.

New York Chiropractic College, Registrar, 2360 State Rte 89, Seneca Falls, NY 13148-0800, 315-568-3000. Enrollment: 950. Records go back to 1919. Alumni records are maintained here at the same phone number. Degrees granted: Doctorate.

Attendance and degree information available by fax, mail. Search requires name plus signed release. Also helpful: SSN, date of birth, exact years of attendance. There is no fee. Expedited service available for $11.00.

New York City Technical College, Registrar, 300 Jay St, Brooklyn, NY 11201, 718-260-5800 (Fax: 718-260-5198). Hours: 9:30AM-6:30PM M,W,Th; 9:30AM-4:30PM T; 9:30AM-3PM F. Enrollment: 1102. Records go back to 1940. Alumni records are maintained here also. Call 718-260-5402. Degrees granted: Associate; Bachelors. Adverse incident record source- Student Affairs.

Attendance information available by phone, fax, mail. Search requires name plus SSN, date of birth, approximate years of attendance. There is no fee.

Degree information available by fax, mail. Search requires name plus SSN, date of birth, approximate years of attendance. There is no fee.

New York College of Podiatric Medicine, Registrar, 1800 Park Avenue, New York, NY 10035, 212-410-8054 (Fax: 212-722-4918). Hours: 9AM-5PM. Enrollment: 485.

Records go back to 1911. Alumni records are maintained here at the same phone number. Degrees granted: Doctorate. Adverse incident record source- Dean.

Attendance and degree information available by fax, mail. Search requires name plus SSN, signed release. There is no fee.

New York Institute of Technology, Registrar, 268 Wheatley Rd, Old Westbury, NY 11568-1036, 516-686-7580. Hours: 9AM-5PM. Enrollment: 10000. Records go back to 1955. Alumni records are maintained here also. Call 516-626-7632. Degrees granted: Associate; Bachelors; Masters; D.O.

Attendance and degree information available by phone, fax, mail. Search requires name plus SSN. Also helpful: date of birth, exact years of attendance. There is no fee.

New York Institute of Technology, (Central Islip Campus), Registrar, 211 Carleton Ave, Central Islip, NY 11722, 516-686-7580 (Fax: 516-348-0912). Records are not housed here. They are located at New York Institute of Technology, Registrar, 268 Wheatley Rd, Old Westbury, NY 11568-1036.

New York Institute of Technology, (Manhattan Campus), Registrar, 1855 Broadway, New York, NY 10023, 212-261-1600 (Fax: 212-261-1646). Records are not housed here. They are located at New York Institute of Technology, Registrar, 268 Wheatley Rd, Old Westbury, NY 11568-1036.

New York Medical College, Registrar, Sunshine Cottage, Admin Bldg, Valhalla, NY 10595, 914-993-4495 (Fax: 914-993-4613). Hours: 9AM-5PM. Records go back to 1920. Alumni records are maintained here also. Call 914-993-4555. Degrees granted: Masters; Doctorate; Ph.D.

Attendance and degree information available by phone, mail. Search requires name plus SSN. There is no fee.

New York School of Interior Design, Registrar, 170 E 70th St, New York, NY 10021-5110, 212-472-1500 X17 (Fax: 212-472-3800). Hours: 9AM-5PM. Enrollment: 750. Alumni records are maintained here at the same phone number. Degrees granted: Associate; Bachelors. Adverse incident record source- Registrar, 212-472-1500 X17.

Attendance and degree information available by phone, fax, mail. Search requires name plus SSN, date of birth. Also helpful: exact years of attendance. There is no fee.

New York School of Law, Registrar, 57 Worth St, New York, NY 10013, 212-431-2100 (Fax: 212-343-2137). Hours: 9AM-7PM M-Th; 9AM-5PM F. Records go back to 1895. Alumni records are maintained here also. Call 212-431-2800. Degrees granted: Doctorate.

Attendance and degree information available by phone, fax, mail. Search requires name plus SSN. There is no fee.

New York Theological Seminary, Registrar, 5 W 29th St, New York, NY 10001-4599, 212-532-4012 (Fax: 212-684-0757). Hours: 9AM-5PM. Enrollment: 500. Records go back to 1906. Alumni records are maintained here at the same phone number. Degrees granted: Masters; Doctorate.

Attendance information available by fax. Search requires name plus SSN, signed release. Also helpful: date of birth, exact years of attendance. There is no fee.

Degree information available by fax. Search requires name plus SSN, date of birth, signed release. Also helpful: exact years of attendance. Fee is $5.00. Expedite service available for $5.00.

New York University, Registrar, PO Box 910, New York, NY 10276-0910, 212-998-4250 (Fax: 212-995-4587). Hours: 9AM-5PM. Records go back to 1913. Alumni records are maintained here also. Call 212-998-6965. Degrees granted: Bachelors; Masters; Doctorate; Ph.D. Adverse incident record source- Dean.

Attendance and degree information available by phone, fax, mail. Search requires name plus SSN. There is no fee.

Niagara County Community College, Registrar, 3111 Saunders Settlement Rd, Sanborn, NY 14132, 716-731-3271 (Fax: 716-731-4053). Hours: 8AM-5PM. Records go back to 1968. Alumni records are maintained here at the same phone number. Degrees granted: Associate. Adverse incident record source- Academic Affairs, 716-731-3271 X172.

Attendance and degree information available by phone, fax, mail. Search requires name only. Also helpful: SSN, date of birth, exact years of attendance. There is no fee.

Niagara University, Registrar, Niagara University, NY 14109, 716-286-8727 (Fax: 716-286-8733). Hours: 9AM-5PM. Records go back to 1856. Alumni Records Office: Barrows Hall, Devaux Campus, Niagara University, NY 14109. Degrees granted: Bachelors; Masters. Adverse incident record source- Student Affairs, 716-286-8566.

Attendance and degree information available by phone, fax, mail. Search requires name plus SSN, date of birth, approximate years of attendance. There is no fee.

North Country Community College, Registrar, 20 Winona Ave, PO Box 89, Saranac Lake, NY 12983, 518-891-2915 (Fax: 518-891-2915 X214). Enrollment: 1550. Records go back to 1967. Alumni records are maintained here also. Call 518-891-2915 X224. Degrees granted: Associate. Adverse incident record source- Student Affairs.

Attendance and degree information available by phone, fax, mail. Search requires name only. Also helpful: SSN. There is no fee.

North Country Community College, Registrar, PO Box 89, 20 Winona Ave, Saranac Lake, NY 12983, 518-891-2915 X245 (Fax: 518-891-2915 X214). Hours: 8:30AM-4:30PM. Records go back to 1967. Alumni records are maintained here also. Call 518-891-2915 X224. Degrees granted: Associate. Adverse incident record source- Dean of Admissions, 518-891-2915 X204.

Attendance and degree information available by phone, fax, mail. Search requires name plus SSN. There is no fee.

North Country Community College, (Branch Campus), Registrar, College Ave, Malone, NY 12953, 518-891-2915 (Fax: 518-891-2915 X214). Hours: 8:30PM-4:30PM. Records go back to 1967. Alumni records are maintained here also. Call 518-891-2915 X224. Degrees granted: Associate. Adverse incident record source- Dean of Admissions, 518-891-2915 X204.

Attendance information available by phone, fax, mail. Search requires name plus SSN. Also helpful: exact years of attendance. There is no fee.

Degree information available by phone, fax, mail. Search requires name only. Also helpful: SSN, date of birth, exact years of attendance. There is no fee.

Nyack College, Registrar, One South Blvd, Nyack, NY 10960-3698, 914-358-1710 X121 (Fax: 914-353-6429). Hours: 8:30AM-4:30PM M,T,Th,F; 8AM-Noon W. Enrollment: 900. Records go back to 1910. Alumni records are maintained here also. Call 914-358-1710 X361. Degrees granted: Associate; Bachelors. Special programs- Adult Degree Completion, 914-358-1710 X572. Adverse incident record source- Student Development, 914-358-1710.

Attendance and degree information available by phone, fax, mail. Search requires name only. Also helpful: SSN, exact years of attendance. There is no fee.

Ohr Hameir Theological Seminary, Registrar, Furnace Woods Rd, PO Box 2130, Peekskill, NY 10566, 914-736-1500 (Fax: 914-736-1055). Hours: 8AM-4:30PM. Enrollment: 100.

Attendance and degree information available by phone, mail. Search requires name plus SSN, exact years of attendance. There is no fee.

Ohr Somayach Institutions, Registrar, 244 Route 306, PO Box 334, Monsey, NY 10952, 914-425-1370 (Fax: 914-425-8865). Records go back to 1985. Alumni Records Office: 115 S Gate Dr, Spring Valley, NY 10977. Degrees granted: Associate; Bachelors.

Attendance and degree information available by phone, mail. Search requires name plus SSN, date of birth, exact years of attendance. There is no fee.

Olean Business Institute, Registrar, 301 N Union St, Olean, NY 14760, 716-372-7978 (Fax: 716-372-2120). Hours: 8AM-5PM. Enrollment: 200. Records go back to 1960. Degrees granted: Associate.

Attendance and degree information available by phone, fax, mail. Search requires name plus SSN, approximate years of attendance. There is no fee.

Onondaga Community College, Registration Office, Syracuse, NY 13215, 315-469-2357 (Fax: 315-469-6775). Hours: 8:30AM-4:30PM. Enrollment: 7100. Records go back to 1962. Alumni records are maintained here at the same phone number. Degrees granted: Associate. Adverse incident record source- Campus Security, 315-469-7741 X2478.

Attendance and degree information available by phone, fax, mail. Search requires name plus SSN. Also helpful: date of birth. There is no fee.

Orange County Community College, Registrar, 115 South St, Middletown, NY 10940, 914-343-1121 (Fax: 914-341-4999). Hours: 9AM-8PM M-Th;9AM-4:30PM F. Enrollment: 5500. Alumni records are maintained here also. Call 914-344-6222. Degrees granted: Associate. Adverse incident record source- Campus Security, 914-341-4932.

Attendance information available by phone, fax, mail. Search requires name plus SSN. Also helpful: date of birth, exact years of attendance. There is no fee.

Degree information available by phone, mail. Search requires name plus SSN. Also helpful: date of birth, exact years of attendance. There is no fee.

Pace University, Registrar, One Pace Plaza, New York, NY 10038, 212-356-1315 (Fax: 212-356-1643). Hours: 9AM-5PM. Records go back to 1905. Degrees granted: Associate; Bachelors; Masters; Doctorate.

Attendance and degree information available by phone, fax, mail. Search requires name plus SSN, exact years of attendance. Also helpful: date of birth. There is no fee.

Pace University, (Pleasantville/Briarcliff), Registrar, 861 Bedford Rd, Pleasantville, NY 10570, 914-773-3200 (Fax: 914-773-3862). Hours: 9AM-5PM. Enrollment: 4000. Records go back to 1960's. Alumni records are maintained here at the same phone number. Degrees granted: Associate; Bachelors; Masters. Certification: Teaching. Adverse incident record source- Dean of Students.

Attendance and degree information available by phone, fax, mail. Search requires name plus SSN. There is no fee.

Pace University, (White Plains), Registrar, 78 N Broadway, White Plains, NY 10603, 914-422-4213 (Fax: 914-422-4248). Records are not housed here. They are located at Pace University, (Pleasantville/Briarcliff), Registrar, 861 Bedford Rd, Pleasantville, NY 10570.

Pacific College of Oriental Medicine, (Branch), Registrar, 915 Broadway 3rd Fl, New York, NY 10010, 212-982-3456 (Fax: 212-982-6514). Hours: 8:30AM-5:30PM M-Th, 8:30AM-5PM F. Records go back to 1993. Degrees granted: Masters.

Attendance information available by fax, mail. Search requires name plus SSN, date of birth, signed release. Also helpful: exact years of attendance. There is no fee.

Degree information available by written request only. Search requires name plus SSN, date of birth, signed release. Also helpful: exact years of attendance. There is no fee.

Parsons School of Design, Registrar, 66 W 12th St, New York, NY 10011, 212-229-5720. Records go back to 1964. Degrees granted: Associate; Bachelors; Masters. Adverse incident record source- Dean of Students.

Attendance and degree information available by phone, fax, mail. Search requires name plus SSN, exact years of attendance. Also helpful: date of birth. There is no fee.

Paul Smith's College, Registrar, Paul Smiths, NY 12970, 518-327-6231 (Fax: 518-327-6161). Hours: 8AM-5PM. Enrollment: 750. Records go back to 1946. Alumni records are maintained here at the same phone number. Degrees granted: Associate. Certification: Baking. Special programs- Hotel Restaurant Management. Adverse incident record source- Student Affairs, 518-327-6222.

Attendance and degree information available by phone, fax, mail. Search requires name only. There is no fee.

Paul Smith's College of Arts and Sciences, Registrar, Paul Smiths, NY 12970, 518-327-6231. Records go back to 1931. Degrees granted: Associate. Adverse incident record source- Director of Academics.

Attendance and degree information available by phone, fax, mail. Search requires name plus SSN, exact years of attendance. Also helpful: date of birth. There is no fee.

Phillips Beth Israel School of Nursing, Registrar, 310 E 22nd St, New York, NY 10010, 212-614-6108 (Fax: 212-614-6109). Hours: 8AM-4:30PM. Enrollment: 140. Records go back to 1904. Alumni records are maintained here at the same phone number. Degrees granted: Associate. Adverse incident record source- Office of the Dean, 212-614-6107.

Attendance and degree information available by fax, mail. Search requires name plus SSN, exact years of attendance, signed release. Also helpful: date of birth. There is no fee.

Plaza Business Institute, Registrar, 74-09 37th Ave, Jackson Heights, NY 11372, 718-779-1430 (Fax: 718-779-7423). Hours: 8AM-8:30PM M,T,Th;8AM-5PM W,F. Records go back to 1970's. Alumni records are maintained here at the same phone number. Degrees granted: Associate.

Attendance and degree information available by mail. Search requires name plus SSN, approximate years of attendance, signed release. Fee is $10.00.

Polytechnic University, Office of the Registrar, 6 MetroTech Ctr, Brooklyn, NY 11201, 718-260-3486 (Fax: 718-260-3136). Hours: 9AM-6PM M,Th; 9AM-5PM T,W,F. Enrollment: 3253. Records go back to 1986. Alumni records are maintained here also. Call 718-260-3486 X3188. Degrees granted: Bachelors; Masters; Doctorate. Adverse incident record source- Dean of Students.

Attendance and degree information available by phone, fax, mail. Search requires name only. Also helpful: SSN, date of birth, exact years of attendance. There is no fee.

Polytechnic University, (Long Island Center), Office of the Registrar, Rte 100, Farmingdale, NY 11735, 516-755-4400. Records are not housed here. They are located at Polytechnic University, Office of the Registrar, 6 MetroTech Ctr, Brooklyn, NY 11201.

Polytechnic University, (Westchester Graduate Center), Registrar, 36 Saw Mill River Rd, Hawthorne, NY 10532, 718-260-3900 (Fax: 718-260-3136). Records are not housed here. They are located at Polytechnic University, Office of the Registrar, 6 MetroTech Ctr, Brooklyn, NY 11201.

Pratt Institute, Registrar, 200 Willoughby Ave, Brooklyn, NY 11205, 718-636-3534 (Fax: 718-636-3548). Hours: 9AM-5PM Winter; 9AM-4PM Summer. Enrollment: 3400. Records go back to 1887. Confirming from 1986 on is quick; before 1986 research must be done. Alumni records are maintained here also. Call 718-636-2531. Degrees granted: Associate; Bachelors; Masters.

Attendance and degree information available by phone, fax, mail. Search requires name only. Also helpful: SSN, date of birth, exact years of attendance. There is no fee.

Queens College, Transcript & Records Dept, Jefferson Hall Rm 100, 65-30 Kissena Blvd, Flushing, NY 11367, 718-997-4400 (Fax: 718-997-4439). Hours: 8AM-5PM. Enrollment: 17500. Records go back to 1946. Alumni records are maintained here also. Call 718-997-3930. Degrees granted: Bachelors; Masters. Adverse incident record source- Dean of Students, 718-997-5500: Incident reports: Security, 718-997-5412

Attendance and degree information available by phone, mail. Search requires name plus SSN, date of birth, exact years of attendance. There is no fee.

Queensborough Community College, Registrar, 222-05 56th Ave, Bayside, NY 11364-1497, 718-631-6212 (Fax: 718-281-5041). Hours: 9AM-5PM. Records go back to 1962. Alumni records are maintained here also. Call 718-631-6391. Degrees granted: Associate. Adverse incident record source- Dean, 718-631-6351.

Attendance and degree information available by fax, mail. Search requires name plus SSN, signed release. There is no fee.

Rabbinical Academy Mesivta Rabbi Chaim Berlin, Registrar, 1605 Coney Island Ave, Brooklyn, NY 11230, 718-377-0777 (Fax: 718-338-5578).

Attendance and degree information available by mail. Search requires name plus SSN, exact years of attendance. There is no fee.

Rabbinical College Beth Shraga, Registrar, 28 Saddle River Rd, Monsey, NY 10952, 914-356-1980 (Fax: 914-425-2604). Alumni records are maintained here at the same phone number. Degrees granted: Bachelors.

Attendance and degree information available by phone, mail. Search requires name plus SSN, date of birth, exact years of attendance. There is no fee.

Rabbinical College Bobover Yeshiva B'nei Zion, Registrar, 1577 48th St, Brooklyn, NY 11219, 718-438-2018 (Fax: 718-871-9031). Hours: 9AM-5PM. Enrollment: 387. Records go back to 1976. Alumni records are maintained here at the same phone number. Adverse incident record source- Discipline Department.

Attendance and degree information available by mail. Search requires name plus SSN, approximate years of attendance. There is no fee.

Rabbinical College Ch'san Sofer, Registrar, 1876 50th St, Brooklyn, NY 11204, 718-236-1171 (Fax: 718-236-1119).

Attendance and degree information available by mail. Search requires name plus SSN, exact years of attendance. There is no fee.

Rabbinical College of Long Island, Registrar, 201 Magnolia Blvd, Long Beach, NY 11561, 516-431-7304 (Fax: 516-431-8662). Hours: 9AM-5PM. Records go back to 1970's. Alumni records are maintained here at the same phone number.

Attendance and degree information available by phone, fax, mail. Search requires name plus SSN. There is no fee.

Rabbinical Seminary Adas Yereim, Registrar, 185 Wilson St, Brooklyn, NY 11211, 718-388-1751 (Fax: 718-388-3531). Hours: 9:30AM-5:30PM. Enrollment: 90. Records go back to 1990. Alumni records are maintained here at the same phone number.

Attendance and degree information available by phone, fax, mail. Search requires name plus SSN, approximate years of attendance. Also helpful: exact years of attendance. There is no fee.

Rabbinical Seminary M'kor Chaim, Registrar, 1571 55th St, Brooklyn, NY 11219, 718-851-0183 (Fax: 718-853-2967).

Attendance and degree information available by phone, mail. Search requires name plus SSN, date of birth. There is no fee.

Rabbinical Seminary of America, Registrar, 92-15 69th Ave, Forest Hills, NY 11375, 718-268-4700 (Fax: 718-268-4684).

Attendance and degree information available by mail. Search requires name only. There is no fee.

Regents College of the University of the State of New York, Registrar, 7 Columbia Cir, Albany, NY 12203-5159, 518-464-8500 (Fax: 518-464-8777). Hours: 9AM-5PM. Enrollment: 17270. Records go back to 1970's. Alumni records are maintained here at the same phone number. Degrees granted: Bachelors.

Attendance and degree information available by phone, fax, mail. Search requires name plus SSN. There is no fee.

Rensselaer Polytechnic Institute, Registrar, 110 Eighth St, Troy, NY 12180-3590, 518-276-6231 (Fax: 518-276-6180). Hours: 8:30AM-5PM Fall & Spring; 8AM-4:30PM Summer. Enrollment: 6400. Records go back to 1900's. Alumni records are maintained here also. Call 518-276-6205. Degrees granted: Bachelors; Masters; Doctorate. Special programs- Hartford Graduate Center, 275 Windsor St, Hartford, CT 06120. Adverse incident record source- Dean of Students.

Attendance and degree information available by phone, fax, mail. Search requires name plus SSN, exact years of attendance. Also helpful: date of birth. There is no fee. Expedited service available for $10.75.

Roberts Wesleyan College, Registrar, 2301 Westside Dr, Rochester, NY 14624-1997, 716-594-6220 (Fax: 716-594-6371). Hours: 8AM-5PM. Degrees granted: Associate; Bachelors; Masters. Special programs- MHR, OM, M.Ed, M.S.W., 716-594-6455.

Attendance and degree information available by phone, fax, mail. Search requires name plus SSN, exact years of attendance. Also helpful: date of birth. There is no fee.

Rochester Business Institute, Registrar, 1850 Ridge Rd E, Rochester, NY 14622, 716-266-0430 (Fax: 716-266-8243). Hours: 8AM-6PM M-Th, 8AM-5PM F. Records go back to 1920. Alumni records are maintained here at the same phone number. Degrees granted: Associate.

Attendance and degree information available by phone, fax, mail. Search requires name plus SSN. There is no fee.

Rochester Institute of Technology, Office of the Registrar, George Eastman Bldg, 27 Lomb Memorial Dr, Rochester, NY 14623-5603, 716-475-2885 (Fax: 716-475-7005). Hours: 8:30AM-6PM M-Th; 8:30AM-4:30PM F. Enrollment: 13000. Records go back to 1800's. Alumni Records Office: Alumni Association, 41 Lomb Memorial Dr, Rochester, NY 14623-5603. Degrees granted: Associate; Bachelors; Masters; Doctorate. Special programs- Industrial Design, 716-475-5944: Imaging Science, 716-475-5944. Adverse incident record source- Student Affairs.

Attendance and degree information available by phone, fax, mail. Search requires name only. Also helpful: SSN, date of birth, exact years of attendance. There is no fee.

Rockefeller University, Graduate Studies, 1230 York Ave, New York, NY 10021, 212-327-8000. Alumni records are maintained here at the same phone number. Degrees granted: Doctorate. Special programs- PhD Program in Science. Adverse incident record source- Director of Academics.

Attendance and degree information available by mail. Search requires name plus signed release. There is no fee.

Rockland Community College, Registrar, 145 College Rd, Suffern, NY 10901, 914-574-4328 (Fax: 914-574-4499). Hours: 8AM-8PM M-Th, 9AM-5PM. Enrollment: 7320. Records go back to 1959. Alumni Records Office: Rockland Community College, 145 College Rd, Rm 6206, Suffern, NY 10901. Degrees granted: Associate. Adverse incident record source- Dean, 914-574-4207.

Attendance and degree information available by fax, mail. Search requires name plus SSN, approximate years of attendance, signed release. There is no fee.

Rockland Community College, (Haverstraw Learning Center), Registrar, 36-39 Main St, Haverstraw, NY 10927, 914-942-0624. Records are not housed here. They are located at Rockland Community College, Registrar, 145 College Rd, Suffern, NY 10901.

Rockland Community College, (Nyack Learning Center), Registrar, 92-94 Main St, Nyack, NY 10960, 914-358-9392. Records are not housed here. They are located at Rockland Community College, Registrar, 145 College Rd, Suffern, NY 10901.

Rockland Community College, (Spring Valley Learning Center), Registrar, 185 N Main St, Spring Valley, NY 10977, 914-352-5535. Records are not housed here. They are located at Rockland Community College, Registrar, 145 College Rd, Suffern, NY 10901.

Russell Sage College Main Campus, Registrar, 45 Ferry St, Troy, NY 12180, 518-270-2205. Records go back to 1966. Alumni records are maintained here at the same phone number. Degrees granted: Associate; Bachelors; Masters.

Attendance and degree information available by mail. Search requires name plus SSN, exact years of attendance. There is no fee.

Sage Colleges, Registrar, 45 Ferry St, Troy, NY 12180, 518-270-2205 (Fax: 518-270-2460). Hours: 8:30AM-5PM. Enrollment: 1000. Records go back to 1917. Alumni records are maintained here also. Call 518-270-2242. Degrees granted: Associate; Bachelors; Masters. Special programs- Associate Level, 518-270-2000. Adverse incident record source- Russell Sage College, 518-270-2000.

Attendance and degree information available by phone, fax, mail. Search requires name plus SSN, approximate years of attendance. Also helpful: date of birth, exact years of attendance. There is no fee.

Sage Colleges, (Sage Junior College of Albany), Registrar, 140 New Scotland Ave, Albany, NY 12208, 518-445-1715 (Fax: 518-445-5414). Hours: 8:30AM-5PM; 8:30AM-4:30PM Summer. Enrollment: 800. Records go back to 1957. Alumni records are maintained here also. Call 518-445-1717. Degrees granted: Associate. Certification: Legal Studies, Computer Science.

Attendance and degree information available by phone, mail. Search requires name plus SSN. Also helpful: date of birth, exact years of attendance. There is no fee.

Sara Schenirer Teacher Seminary, Registrar, 4622 14th Ave, Brooklyn, NY 11219, 718-633-8557. Records go back to 1941. Alumni records are maintained here at the same phone number. Degrees granted. Adverse incident record source- Student Affairs.

Attendance information available by mail. Search requires name only. Also helpful: SSN. There is no fee.

Degree information available by fax, mail. Search requires name plus approximate years of attendance. Also helpful: SSN. There is no fee.

Sarah Lawrence College, Registrar, One Meadway, Bronxville, NY 10708, 914-395-2301. Hours: 9AM-5PM. Enrollment: 1306. Records go back to 1928. Alumni records are maintained here also. Call 914-395-2530. Degrees granted: Bachelors; Masters. Special programs- Center for Continuing Education, 914-395-2205. Adverse incident record source- Public Affairs, 914-395-2220.

Attendance and degree information available by phone, mail. Search requires name only. Also helpful: SSN. There is no fee.

Schenectady County Community College, Registrar, 78 Washington Ave, Schenectady, NY 12305, 518-381-1200 (Fax: 518-346-0379). Hours: 8:30AM-7:30PM M-Th, 8:30AM-4:30PM F. Records go back to 1970's. Alumni records are maintained here at the same phone number. Degrees granted: Associate.

Attendance and degree information available by fax, mail. Search requires name plus SSN, signed release. Also helpful: exact years of attendance. There is no fee.

School of Visual Arts, Registrar, 209 E 23rd St, New York, NY 10010, 212-592-2200 (Fax: 212-592-2069). Hours: 8AM-5:45PM. Enrollment: 5100. Records go back to 1940's. Alumni records are maintained here also. Call 212-592-2300. Degrees granted: Bachelors; Masters. Adverse incident record source- Student Services, 212-592-2140.

Attendance and degree information available by phone, fax, mail. Search requires name plus SSN. Also helpful: exact years of attendance. There is no fee.

Seminary of the Immaculate Conception, Registrar, 440 W Neck Rd, Huntington, NY 11743, 516-423-0483 (Fax: 516-423-2346). Hours: 8:30AM-4:30PM. Enrollment: 192. Records go back to 1936. Alumni records are maintained here at the same phone number. Degrees granted: Masters; Doctorate.

Attendance and degree information available by written request only. Search requires name plus SSN, date of birth, exact years of attendance, signed release. There is no fee.

Sh'or Yoshuv Rabbinical College, Registrar, 1526 Central Ave, Far Rockaway, NY 11691, 718-327-7444. Hours: 9AM-5PM. Enrollment: 110. Records go back to 1991. Degrees granted: Bachelors. Adverse incident record source- Dean.

Attendance and degree information available by phone, fax, mail. Search requires name only. Also helpful: SSN, date of birth, exact years of attendance. There is no fee.

Siena College, Registrar, 515 Loudon Rd, Loudonville, NY 12211-1462, 518-783-2310 (Fax: 518-786-5060). Hours: 8:30AM-4:30PM. Enrollment: 3232. Records go back to 1950's. Alumni records are maintained here also. Call 518-783-2430. Degrees granted: Bachelors. Adverse incident record source- Student Affairs, 518-783-2328.

Attendance and degree information available by phone, fax, mail. Search requires name plus SSN. There is no fee.

Simmons Institute of Funeral Service, Registrar, 1828 South Ave, Syracuse, NY 13207, 315-475-5142 (Fax: 315-475-3817). Hours: 8AM-3PM M-F, 8AM-Noon Sat. Enrollment: 70. Records go back to 1950's. Alumni records are maintained here at the same phone number. Degrees granted: Associate; NAOS. Special programs- Funeral Service. Adverse incident record source- Records & Registration, 315-475-5142.

Attendance information available by phone, fax, mail. Search requires name plus SSN. There is no fee.

Degree information available by phone, fax, mail. Search requires name plus SSN. Also helpful: exact years of attendance. There is no fee.

Skidmore College, Registrar, 815 N Broadway, Saratoga Springs, NY 12866-1632, 518-584-5000 X2210 (Fax: 518-584-7963). Hours: 8AM-4:30PM. Enrollment: 2100. Records go back to 1912. Alumni records are maintained here also. Call 518-584-5000 X2226. Degrees granted: Bachelors; Masters. Special programs- UWW, 518-584-5000 X2294: MALS, 518-584-5000 X2274. Adverse incident record source- Dean of Studies, 518-584-5000 X2203.

Attendance and degree information available by phone, mail. Search requires name plus exact years of attendance. Also helpful: SSN, date of birth. There is no fee.

Southampton College of Long Island University, Registrar Office, 239 Montauk Hwy, Southampton, NY 11968, 516-283-4000 X8325 (Fax: 516-283-4081). Hours: 8AM-5PM. Enrollment: 1400. Records go back to 1963. Alumni records are maintained here also. Call 516-283-4000 X8347. Degrees granted: Bachelors; Masters.

Attendance and degree information available by phone, fax, mail. Search requires name plus SSN. Also helpful: date of birth, exact years of attendance. There is no fee.

St Anthony On Hudson, Registrar, 517 Washington Ave, Rensselaer, NY 12144, 518-463-2261. Degrees granted. Adverse incident record source- Dean of Students.

Attendance and degree information available by phone, mail. Search requires name plus SSN, exact years of attendance. Also helpful: date of birth. There is no fee.

St. Bernard's Institute, Registrar, 1100 S Goodman St, Rochester, NY 14620, 716-271-3657 (Fax: 716-271-2045). Hours: 8:30AM-4:30PM. Enrollment: 150. Records go back to 1893. Alumni records are maintained here at the same phone number. Degrees granted: Bachelors; Masters.

Attendance and degree information available by phone, fax, mail. Search requires name plus SSN. Also helpful: exact years of attendance. There is no fee.

St. Bonaventure University, Registrar, Rte 417, St Bonaventure, NY 14778, 716-375-2020 (Fax: 716-375-2135). Hours: 8:30AM-4:30PM. Enrollment: 2489. Records go back to 1920's. Alumni records are maintained here also. Call 716-375-2375. Degrees granted: Masters.

Attendance and degree information available by phone, fax, mail. Search requires name only. Also helpful: SSN, date of birth, exact years of attendance. There is no fee.

St. Francis College, Registrar, 180 Remsen St, Brooklyn, NY 11201, 718-522-2300 X242 (Fax: 718-522-1274). Hours: 9AM-5PM. Enrollment: 2100. Records go back to 1930. Alumni records are maintained here also. Call 718-522-2300 X362. Degrees granted: Associate; Bachelors. Adverse incident record source- E. Boyd, 718-522-2300 X275.

Attendance and degree information available by fax, mail. Search requires name plus signed release. Also helpful: SSN, date of birth, exact years of attendance. There is no fee.

St. John Fisher College, Registrar, 3690 East Ave, Rochester, NY 14618, 716-385-8015 (Fax: 716-385-7303). Hours: 8:30AM-4:30PM. Enrollment: 1900. Records go back to 1951. Alumni records are maintained here also. Call 716-385-8001. Degrees granted: Bachelors; Masters. Certification: ACCT. Special programs- Academic Dean, 716-385-8116.

Adverse incident record source- Protective Services, 716-385-8025.

Attendance and degree information available by phone, fax, mail. Search requires name only. Also helpful: SSN, exact years of attendance. There is no fee.

St. John's University, Registrar, 8000 Utopia Pkwy, Jamaica, NY 11439, 718-990-1487 (Fax: 718-990-1677). Hours: 8:30AM-7:30PM M, 8:30AM-4:30PM T-Th, 8:30AM-3PM. Alumni records are maintained here also. Call 718-990-6232. Degrees granted: Associate; Bachelors; Masters; Doctorate. Adverse incident record source- Student Life, 718-990-6256.

Attendance and degree information available by phone, mail. Search requires name plus SSN. There is no fee.

St. John's University, (Branch), Registrar, 300 Howard Ave, Staten Island, NY 10301, 718-390-4545. Records are not housed here. They are located at St. John's University, Registrar, 8000 Utopia Pkwy, Jamaica, NY 11439.

St. Joseph's College, Registrar, 245 Clinton Ave, Brooklyn, NY 11205-3688, 718-636-6800 (Fax: 718-398-4936). Hours: 9AM-5PM. Enrollment: 1300. Records go back to 1921. Alumni records are maintained here at the same phone number. Degrees granted: Bachelors.

Attendance and degree information available by mail. Search requires name plus SSN. Also helpful: date of birth, exact years of attendance. There is no fee.

St. Joseph's College, (Suffolk), Registrar, 155 Roe Blvd, Patchogue, NY 11772, 516-447-3239 (Fax: 516-654-1782). Hours: 8:30AM-5PM. Records go back to 1920's. Alumni records are maintained here also. Call 516-447-3215. Degrees granted: Bachelors; Masters. Special programs- Graduate Files, 718-636-6800. Adverse incident record source- Dean of Students.

Attendance information available by phone, fax, mail. Search requires name plus SSN. Also helpful: exact years of attendance. There is no fee.

Degree information available by phone, fax, mail. Search requires name plus SSN, approximate years of attendance. Also helpful: exact years of attendance. There is no fee.

St. Joseph's Seminary, Registrar, 201 Seminary Ave, Yonkers, NY 10704, 914-968-6200 X8208 (Fax: 914-968-7912). Hours: 9AM-5PM. Records go back to 1896. Alumni records are maintained here at the same phone number. Degrees granted: Masters; M.Div.

Attendance and degree information available by phone, fax, mail. Search requires name plus SSN. There is no fee.

St. Lawrence University, Registrar, 23 Ramoda Dr, Canton, NY 13617, 315-379-5267 (Fax: 315-379-7424). Hours: 8AM-4:30PM. Enrollment: 1920. Records go back to 1856. Alumni records are maintained here also. Call 315-379-5513. Degrees granted: Bachelors; Masters. Adverse incident record source- Security Dept, 315-379-5555.

Attendance and degree information available by phone, fax, mail. Search requires name plus SSN. There is no fee.

St. Thomas Aquinas College, Records Office, 125 Rte 340, Sparkill, NY 10976, 914-398-4300. Hours: 8:30AM-5PM. Enrollment: 2500. Records go back to 1958. Alumni records are maintained here also. Call 914-398-4017. Degrees granted: Associate; Bachelors; Masters. Special programs- Continuing Education (HS), 914-398-4200. Adverse incident record source- Dean of Students, 914-398-4300: Security, 914-398-4080

Attendance and degree information available by phone, mail. Search requires name plus SSN. Also helpful: approximate years of attendance. There is no fee.

St. Vladimir's Orthodox Theological Seminary, Registrar, 575 Scarsdale Rd, Crestwood, NY 10707, 914-961-8313 (Fax: 914-961-4507). Hours: 9AM-3PM. Degrees granted: Masters; Doctorate.

Attendance and degree information available by phone, fax, mail. Search requires name plus approximate years of attendance. There is no fee.

State University College at Brockport, Registrar, 350 New Campus Dr, Brockport, NY 14420, 716-395-2211. Hours: 8AM-5PM. Enrollment: 9148. Records go back to 1940's. Alumni records are maintained here also. Call 716-395-5124. Degrees granted: Bachelors; Masters. Certification: ADV Study. Adverse incident record source- DEan of Students.

Attendance and degree information available by phone, mail. Search requires name plus SSN. There is no fee.

State University College at Cortland, Registrar, PO Box 2000, Cortland, NY 13045, 607-753-4701 (Fax: 607-753-5989). Hours: 8:30AM-4PM. Enrollment: 5700. Records go back to 1867. Alumni records are maintained here also. Call 607-753-2516. Degrees granted: Bachelors; Masters. Certification: CAS.

Attendance and degree information available by phone, fax, mail. Search requires name only. Also helpful: SSN, date of birth, exact years of attendance. There is no fee.

State University College at Fredonia, Registrar, Fredonia, NY 14063, 716-673-3323. Hours: 9AM-5PM. Enrollment: 4500. Records go back to 1900's. Alumni records are maintained here also. Call 716-673-3553. Degrees granted: Bachelors; Masters. Adverse incident record source- Student Affairs.

Attendance and degree information available by phone, mail. Search requires name plus SSN, exact years of attendance. There is no fee.

State University College at Geneseo, Records Office, Erwin 102, 1 College Circle, Geneseo, NY 14454, 716-245-5566 (Fax: 716-245-5005). Hours: 8AM-4:15PM. Enrollment: 5200. Records go back to 1800's. Alumni Records Office: Alumni Association, Schrader Bldg, Geneseo, NY 14454, 716-245-5566 X5506. Degrees granted: Bachelors; Masters. Adverse incident record source- Student Services.

Attendance and degree information available by phone, fax, mail. Search requires name only. Also helpful: SSN, exact years of attendance. There is no fee.

State University College at Old Westbury, Registrar, PO Box 210, Old Westbury, NY 11568, 516-876-3055 (Fax: 516-876-3209). Hours: 9AM-4:45PM. Enrollment: 4000. Records go back to 1976. Alumni records are maintained here also. Call 516-876-3140. Degrees granted: Bachelors. Adverse incident record source- Public Safety, 516-876-3333.

Attendance and degree information available by phone, mail. Search requires name plus SSN. There is no fee.

State University College at Oneonta, Registrar, Oneonta, NY 13820-4015, 607-436-2531 (Fax: 607-436-2164). Hours: 7:30AM-4:30PM. Enrollment: 5200. Records go back to 1889. Alumni records are maintained here also. Call 607-536-2526. Degrees granted: Bachelors; Masters. Adverse incident record source- Dean of Students, 607-436-2513.

Attendance and degree information available by phone, fax, mail. Search requires name plus SSN. Also helpful: exact years of attendance. There is no fee.

State University College at Oswego, Registrar, Oswego, NY 13126, 315-341-2234 (Fax: 315-341-3167). Hours: 8AM-5PM. Enrollment: 8500. Records go back to 1940. Alumni Records Office: Alumni Association, King Alumni Hall, Oswego, NY 13126, 315-341-2258. Degrees granted:

Bachelors; Masters. Adverse incident record source- Public Safety, 315-341-5555.

Attendance and degree information available by phone, fax, mail. Search requires name plus SSN, exact years of attendance. There is no fee.

State University College at Plattsburgh, Registrar, 101 Broad St, Plattsburgh, NY 12901, 518-564-2100 (Fax: 518-564-4900). Hours: 9AM-4PM. Enrollment: 6182. Records go back to 1890's. Alumni records are maintained here also. Call 518-564-2090. Degrees granted: Bachelors; Masters. Adverse incident record source- Student Affairs, 518-564-2280.

Attendance and degree information available by phone, fax, mail. Search requires name plus SSN. Also helpful: date of birth. There is no fee.

State University College at Potsdam, Registrar, Pierrepont Ave, Potsdam, NY 13676, 315-267-2154 (Fax: 315-267-2157). Hours: 8AM-4:30PM. Enrollment: 4294. Records go back to 1880's. Alumni records are maintained here also. Call 315-267-2120. Degrees granted: Bachelors; Masters. Adverse incident record source- Dean, 315-267-2117.

Attendance and degree information available by phone, mail. Search requires name plus SSN. There is no fee.

State University College at Purchase, Registrar, 735 Anderson Hill Rd, Purchase, NY 10577-1400, 914-251-6360 (Fax: 914-251-6373). Hours: 8:30AM-5PM. Enrollment: 2500. Records go back to 1970. Alumni records are maintained here also. Call 914-251-6054. Degrees granted: Bachelors; Masters. Special programs- Performing Arts (Theater and Film). Adverse incident record source- Statistics Div, 914-251-6018.

Attendance and degree information available by phone, fax, mail. Search requires name plus SSN. There is no fee.

State University of New York, (College of Environmental Science and Forestry), Registrar, Syracuse, NY 13210, 315-470-6655 (Fax: 315-470-6933). Hours: 8AM-4:30PM. Enrollment: 1566. Records go back to 1912. Alumni records are maintained here also. Call 315-470-6632. Degrees granted: Associate; Bachelors; Masters; Doctorate. Adverse incident record source- Student Affairs, 315-470-6658.

Attendance and degree information available by phone, fax, mail. Search requires name plus SSN. Also helpful: exact years of attendance. There is no fee.

State University of New York, (College of Optometry at New York City), Registrar, 100 E 24th St, Manhattan, NY 10010, 212-780-4900 (Fax: 212-780-5104). Hours: 8AM-5PM. Enrollment: 275. Records go back to 1972. Alumni records are maintained here at the same phone number. Degrees granted: Masters; Doctorate; O.D.

Attendance information available by mail. Search requires name plus SSN, approximate years of attendance, signed release. There is no fee.

Degree information available by mail. Search requires name plus SSN, signed release. There is no fee.

State University of New York College at Buffalo, Registrar, 1300 Elmwood Ave, Buffalo, NY 14222, 716-878-4811 (Fax: 716-878-3159). Hours: 8:15AM-5PM. Enrollment: 11528. Records go back to 1920's. Alumni records are maintained here also. Call 716-878-6001. Degrees granted: Bachelors; Masters. Adverse incident record source- Public Safety, 716-878-6333.

Attendance and degree information available by phone, fax, mail. Search requires name plus SSN, exact years of attendance. There is no fee.

State University of New York College at Farmingdale, Office of the Registrar, Greenley Hall, Melville Rd, Farmingdale, NY 11735-1021, 516-420-2776

(Fax: 516-420-2257). Hours: 8:30AM-8PM M-Th; 8:30AM-4:30PM F. Enrollment: 6718. Records go back to 1965. Alumni records are maintained here at the same phone number. Degrees granted: Associate; Bachelors. Adverse incident record source- Student Affairs.

Attendance and degree information available by phone, mail. Search requires name plus SSN. Also helpful: date of birth, approximate years of attendance. There is no fee.

State University of New York College of Ag and Tech at Cobleskill, Registrar, Cobleskill, NY 12043, 518-234-5521 (Fax: 518-234-5333). Hours: 8AM-4:15PM. Enrollment: 2400. Records go back to 1930's. Alumni records are maintained here also. Call 518-234-5628. Degrees granted: Associate; Bachelor of Technology. Adverse incident record source- Public Safety.

Attendance and degree information available by phone, fax, mail. Search requires name plus SSN, exact years of attendance. Also helpful: date of birth. There is no fee.

State University of New York College of Ag and Tech/Morrisville, Registrar, Morrisville, NY 13408, 315-684-6066 (Fax: 315-684-6421). Hours: 8AM-5PM. Enrollment: 3151. Records go back to 1920's. Alumni records are maintained here also. Call 315-684-6030. Degrees granted: Associate. Adverse incident record source- Dean, 315-684-6070.

Attendance and degree information available by phone, fax, mail. Search requires name plus SSN. Also helpful: exact years of attendance. There is no fee.

State University of New York College of Technology at Alfred, Registrar, Huntington Bldg, Alfred, NY 14802, 607-587-4796 (Fax: 607-587-3294). Hours: 8AM-4PM. Enrollment: 3493. Records go back to 1911. Alumni records are maintained here also. Call 607-587-4260. Degrees granted: Associate; Bachelors. Adverse incident record source- Student Affairs, 607-587-3247.

Attendance and degree information available by phone, fax, mail. Search requires name plus SSN. There is no fee.

State University of New York College of Technology at Canton, Registrar, Cornell Dr, Canton, NY 13617-1098, 315-386-7042 (Fax: 315-386-7930). Hours: 8AM-5PM Winter; 8AM-4PM Summer. Enrollment: 2000. Records go back to 1906. Alumni records are maintained here also. Call 315-386-7127. Degrees granted: Associate. Adverse incident record source- Dean of Students, 315-386-7120.

Attendance and degree information available by phone, mail. Search requires name plus SSN. Also helpful: date of birth, exact years of attendance. There is no fee.

State University of New York College of Technology at Delhi, Office of Records & Registration, 117 Bush Hall, Delhi, NY 13753, 607-746-4562 (Fax: 607-746-4208). Hours: 8AM-5PM. Enrollment: 2100. Records go back to 1968. Alumni records are maintained here also. Call 607-746-4603. Degrees granted: Associate. Adverse incident record source- Student Affairs, 607-746-4440.

Attendance and degree information available by mail. Search requires name plus SSN, signed release. Also helpful: exact years of attendance. There is no fee.

State University of New York Empire State College, Registrar, Two Union Ave, Saratoga Springs, NY 12866, 518-587-2100 X209 (Fax: 518-587-5404). Hours: 8:30AM-4:30PM. Degrees granted: Associate; Bachelors; Masters. Adverse incident record source- Dean of Students.

Attendance and degree information available by phone, fax, mail. Search requires name plus SSN. There is no fee.

State University of New York Empire State College, (Genessee Valley Regional Center), Registrar, 8

Prince St, Rochester, NY 14607, 716-244-3641. Records are not housed here. They are located at State University of New York Empire State College, Registrar, Two Union Ave, Saratoga Springs, NY 12866.

State University of New York Empire State College, (Hudson Valley Regional Center), Registrar, 200 N Central Ave, Hartsdale, NY 10530, 914-948-6206. Records are not housed here. They are located at State University of New York Empire State College, Registrar, Two Union Ave, Saratoga Springs, NY 12866.

State University of New York Empire State College, (Long Island Regional Center), Registrar, Trainor House, PO Box 130, Old Westbury, NY 11568, 516-997-4700. Records are not housed here. They are located at State University of New York Empire State College, Registrar, Two Union Ave, Saratoga Springs, NY 12866.

State University of New York Empire State College, (Metropolitan Regional Center), Registrar, 666 Broadway, New York, NY 10012, 212-598-0640. Records are not housed here. They are located at State University of New York Empire State College, Registrar, Two Union Ave, Saratoga Springs, NY 12866.

State University of New York Empire State College, (Niagara Frontier Regional Center), Registrar, 617 Main St Market Arcade, Buffalo, NY 14203-1498, 716-853-7700 (Fax: 716-853-7713). Records are not housed here. They are located at State University of New York Empire State College, Registrar, Two Union Ave, Saratoga Springs, NY 12866.

State University of New York Empire State College, (Northeast Center), Registrar, 845 Central Ave, Albany, NY 12206, 518-485-5964. Records are not housed here. They are located at State University of New York Empire State College, Registrar, Two Union Ave, Saratoga Springs, NY 12866.

State University of New York Health Science Center at Brooklyn, Registrar, 450 Clarkson Ave, Brooklyn, NY 11203, 718-270-1875 (Fax: 718-270-7592). Hours: 10AM-6PM. Enrollment: 1672. Alumni records are maintained here at the same phone number. Degrees granted: Bachelors; Masters; Doctorate. Adverse incident record source-Student Affairs.

Attendance information available by phone, fax, mail. Search requires name plus SSN. There is no fee.

Degree information available by phone, fax, mail. Search requires name plus SSN. Also helpful: approximate years of attendance. There is no fee.

State University of New York Health Science Center at Syracuse, Registrar, 155 Elizabeth Blackwell St, Syracuse, NY 13210, 315-464-4604 (Fax: 315-464-8867). Hours: 8:30AM-4:30PM. Enrollment: 1200. Records go back to 1902. Alumni records are maintained here also. Call 315-464-4361. Degrees granted: Associate; Bachelors; Masters; Doctorate. Special programs- College of Medicine Alumni, 315-464-4361: Health Related Professions Alumni, 315-464-4416.

Attendance and degree information available by phone, fax, mail. Search requires name plus SSN. Also helpful: date of birth, exact years of attendance. There is no fee.

State University of New York Institute of Technology / Utica/Rome, Registrar, PO Box 3050, Utica, NY 13504-3050, 315-792-7265 (Fax: 315-792-7804). Hours: 8AM-5PM. Enrollment: 2500. Records go back to 1966. Alumni records are maintained here also. Call 315-792-7110. Degrees granted: Bachelors; Masters.

Attendance and degree information available by phone, fax, mail. Search requires name plus SSN. Also helpful: date of birth, exact years of attendance. There is no fee.

State University of New York Maritime College, Registrar, Fort Schuyler, Throggs Neck, NY 10465, 718-409-7266 (Fax: 718-409-7392). Hours: 8:30AM-4:30PM. Enrollment: 810. Records go back to 1878. Alumni Records Office: Alumni Association, SUNY Maritime College, 6 Pennyfield Ave, Bronx, NY 10465. Degrees granted: Bachelors; Masters. Adverse incident record source- Public Safety, 718-409-7310: Regimental Office, 718-409-7451

Attendance and degree information available by phone, fax, mail. Search requires name plus exact years of attendance. There is no fee.

State University of New York Maritime College, (Stenotype Academy), Registrar, 15 Park Row #4FL, New York, NY 10038, 212-962-0002 (Fax: 212-608-8210). Hours: 8AM-7PM M-Th, 8AM-4PM F. Records go back to 1970's. Alumni records are maintained here at the same phone number. Degrees granted: Associate. Adverse incident record source- Dean of Students.

Attendance and degree information available by phone, fax, mail. Search requires name plus SSN. Also helpful: exact years of attendance. There is no fee.

State University of New York at Albany, Registrar, 1400 Washington Ave, Albany, NY 12222, 518-442-3070 (Fax: 518-442-2560). Hours: 9AM-5PM M-Th; 9AM-4PM F. Enrollment: 16616. Alumni records are maintained here at the same phone number. Degrees granted: Bachelors; Masters; Doctorate. Adverse incident record source- Dean of Students.

Attendance and degree information available by mail. Search requires name plus SSN, exact years of attendance, signed release. There is no fee.

State University of New York at Binghamton, Registrar, PO Box 6000, Binghamton, NY 13902-6000, 607-777-6087 (Fax: 607-777-6515). Hours: 9:30AM-4PM. Enrollment: 12089. Records go back to 1950's. Alumni records are maintained here also. Call 607-777-2431. Degrees granted: Bachelors; Masters; Doctorate. Adverse incident record source- Public Safety, 607-777-2275.

Attendance and degree information available by phone, fax, mail. Search requires name plus SSN. There is no fee.

State University of New York at New Paltz, Records & Registration, 75 S Manheim Blvd, New Paltz, NY 12561, 914-257-3100 (Fax: 914-257-3009). Hours: 8:30AM-4:30PM. Enrollment: 7852. Records go back to 1961. Alumni records are maintained here also. Call 914-257-3230. Degrees granted: Bachelors; Masters. Adverse incident record source- Dean of Students.

Attendance information available by fax, mail. Search requires name plus approximate years of attendance, signed release. Also helpful: SSN, date of birth, exact years of attendance. There is no fee.

Degree information available by phone, fax, mail. Search requires name plus approximate years of attendance. Also helpful: SSN, date of birth, exact years of attendance. There is no fee.

State University of New York at Stony Brook, Registrar Office, Stony Brook, NY 11794-1101, 516-632-6885 (Fax: 516-632-9685). Hours: 8:40AM-4PM. Records go back to 1961. Alumni records are maintained here also. Call 516-632-6330. Degrees granted: Bachelors; Masters; Doctorate. Adverse incident record source- Student Affairs, 516-632-6700.

Attendance and degree information available by phone, fax, mail. Search requires name plus SSN. Also helpful: date of birth. There is no fee.

Suffolk Community College, (Ammerman), Registrar, 533 College Rd, Selden, NY 11784, 516-451-4008 (Fax: 516-451-4015). Hours: 9AM-8PM M-Th, 9AM-5PM F. Enrollment: 19500. Records go back to 1985. Alumni records are maintained here also. Call 516-732-7979. Degrees granted: Associate.

Attendance information available by phone, fax, mail. Search requires name plus SSN. There is no fee.

Degree information available by fax, mail. Search requires name plus SSN. There is no fee.

Suffolk Community College, (Eastern), Registrar, Speonk-Riverhead Rd, Riverhead, NY 11901, 516-548-2500. Records are not housed here. They are located at Suffolk Community College, (Ammerman), Registrar, 533 College Rd, Selden, NY 11784.

Suffolk Community College, (Western), Registrar, Crooked Hill Rd, Brentwood, NY 11717, 516-434-6750. Records are not housed here. They are located at Suffolk Community College, (Ammerman), Registrar, 533 College Rd, Selden, NY 11784.

Sullivan County Community College, Registrar, PO Box 4002, Loch Sheldrake, NY 12759, 914-434-5750 (Fax: 914-434-4806). Enrollment: 2000. Records go back to 1964. Alumni records are maintained here at the same phone number. Degrees granted: Associate.

Attendance and degree information available by phone, fax, mail. Search requires name only. Also helpful: SSN, date of birth, approximate years of attendance. There is no fee.

Syracuse University, Registrar, Syracuse, NY 13244, 315-443-1870. Hours: 8AM-4:30PM. Enrollment: 18970. Alumni records are maintained here also. Call 315-443-3514. Degrees granted: Bachelors. Adverse incident record source- Student Affairs, 315-443-4263.

Attendance and degree information available by phone, mail. Search requires name plus exact years of attendance. Also helpful: SSN. There is no fee.

Talmudical Institute of Upstate New York, Registrar, 769 Park Ave, Rochester, NY 14607, 716-473-2810. Records go back to 1952. Adverse incident record source- Student Affairs.

Attendance and degree information available by phone, fax, mail. Search requires name plus SSN, exact years of attendance. Also helpful: date of birth. There is no fee.

Talmudical Seminary Oholei Torah, Registrar, 667 Eastern Pkwy, Brooklyn, NY 11213, 718-774-5050. Hours: 9:30AM-5PM. Enrollment: 232. Records go back to 1985. Alumni records are maintained here at the same phone number. Adverse incident record source- Student Affairs.

Attendance and degree information available by mail. Search requires name plus SSN, approximate years of attendance, signed release. There is no fee.

Taylor Business Institute, Registrar, 120 W 30th St, New York, NY 10001, 212-279-0510 (Fax: 212-947-9793). Hours: 9AM-5PM. Enrollment: 500. Records go back to 1970. Degrees granted: Associate. Adverse incident record source- Dean of Students.

Attendance and degree information available by mail. Search requires name plus SSN, date of birth, exact years of attendance, signed release. There is no fee.

Technical Career Institute, Registrar, 320 W 31st St, New York, NY 10001, 212-594-4000 X270 (Fax: 212-629-

3937). Hours: 8:45AM-6:45PM M, 8:45AM-4:45PM W-F. Enrollment: 3500. Records go back to 1940. Degrees granted: Associate.

Attendance and degree information available by fax, mail. Search requires name plus SSN, date of birth, approximate years of attendance, signed release. Also helpful: exact years of attendance. There is no fee.

Tompkins Cortland Community College, Registrar, PO Box 139, 170 North St, Dryden, NY 13053, 607-844-3211 X4301 (Fax: 607-844-9665). Hours: 8:30AM-4PM. Enrollment: 2925. Records go back to 1968. Alumni records are maintained here also. Call 607-844-8211 X4366. Degrees granted: Associate. Adverse incident record source- Dean of Students.

Attendance information available by mail. Search requires name plus SSN, signed release. Also helpful: date of birth, exact years of attendance. There is no fee.

Degree information available by phone, mail. Search requires name plus SSN. Also helpful: date of birth, exact years of attendance. There is no fee.

Torah Temimah Talmudical Seminary, Registrar, 555 Ocean Pkwy, Brooklyn, NY 11218, 718-438-5779. Enrollment: 248. Alumni records are maintained here at the same phone number. Degrees granted: Bachelors. Adverse incident record source- Dean of Students.

Attendance and degree information available by mail. Search requires name plus SSN, date of birth, exact years of attendance, signed release. There is no fee.

Touro College, Registrar, Empire State Bldg Ste 5122, 350 Fifth Ave, New York, NY 10118, 212-463-0400 X611 (Fax: 212-627-9542). Records are not housed here. They are located at Touro College, Registrar, 844 6th Ave, New York, NY 10001.

Touro College, Registrar, 844 6th Ave, New York, NY 10001, 212-463-0400 X634 (Fax: 212-627-9542). Hours: 8AM-5PM. Records go back to 1971. Alumni Records Office: Touro College, 350 Fifth Ave, Empire State Bldg Ste 5122, New York, NY 10118. Degrees granted: Bachelors.

Attendance and degree information available by phone, fax, mail. Search requires name plus SSN, date of birth, exact years of attendance. There is no fee.

Touro College, (Huntington Branch), Registrar, 300 Nassau Rd, Huntington, NY 11743, 516-421-2244 (Fax: 516-421-2675). Hours: 9AM-7PM M-Th, 9AM-3PM F. Enrollment: 896. Records go back to 1980. Alumni records are maintained here also. Call 516-421-2244 X315. Degrees granted: Masters; Doctorate. Adverse incident record source- Student Affairs, 516-421-2244.

Attendance information available by phone, mail. Search requires name plus SSN. There is no fee.

Degree information available by phone, mail. Search requires name plus SSN. There is no fee.

Trocaire College, Registrar, 110 Red Jacket Pkwy, Buffalo, NY 14220, 716-826-6110 (Fax: 716-826-4704). Hours: 8AM-7PM M-Th, 8AM-4PM F. Records go back to 1960. Alumni records are maintained here also. Call 716-826-1200 X306. Degrees granted: Associate. Adverse incident record source- Registrar, 716-826-1200 X224: Dean, 716-826-1200 X228

Attendance and degree information available by phone, fax, mail. Search requires name plus date of birth. Also helpful: SSN, exact years of attendance. There is no fee.

Ulster County Community College, Registrar, Stone Ridge, NY 12484, 914-687-5075. Hours: 8:30AM-7:30PM M-Th, 8:30AM-4:30PM F. Records go back to 1968. Alumni records are maintained here also. Call 914-687-5261.

Degrees granted: Associate. Adverse incident record source-Dean, 914-687-5078.

Attendance information available by phone, mail. Search requires name plus SSN. There is no fee.

Degree information available by phone, mail. Search requires name plus SSN. Also helpful: approximate years of attendance. There is no fee.

Union College, Registrar, Whitaker House, Schenectady, NY 12308, 518-388-6109 (Fax: 518-388-6173). Hours: 8:30AM-5PM. Enrollment: 2100. Records go back to 1938. Alumni records are maintained here also. Call 518-388-6109. Degrees granted: Bachelors; Masters; Doctorate. Special programs- Graduate, 518-388-6288. Adverse incident record source- Dean of Students, 518-388-6116.

Attendance information available by phone, fax, mail. Search requires name plus SSN, date of birth. Also helpful: exact years of attendance. There is no fee.

Degree information available by phone, fax, mail. Search requires name plus date of birth. Also helpful: SSN, exact years of attendance. There is no fee.

Union Theological Seminary, Registrar, 3041 Broadway, New York, NY 10027-5710, 212-280-1555 (Fax: 212-280-1416). Hours: 9AM-5PM. Enrollment: 310. Records go back to 1935. Alumni records are maintained here also. Call 212-280-1511. Degrees granted: Masters; Doctorate. Special programs- Library (Pre 1935), 212-280-1501. Adverse incident record source- Dean, 212-280-1550.

Attendance and degree information available by phone, fax, mail. Search requires name plus SSN, exact years of attendance. Also helpful: date of birth. There is no fee.

United States Merchant Marine Academy, Registrar, Steamboat Rd, Kings Point, NY 11024, 516-773-5000 (Fax: 516-773-5241). Enrollment: 900. Records go back to 1939. Alumni records are maintained here also. Call 516-773-5658. Degrees granted: Bachelors. Adverse incident record source- 516-773-5409.

Attendance and degree information available by phone, fax, mail. Search requires name plus SSN. Also helpful: date of birth, exact years of attendance.

United States Military Academy, Graduate Records Branch, Office of the Dean, West Point, NY 10996-5000, 914-938-3708 (Fax: 914-938-5438). Hours: 7:45AM-4:30PM. Enrollment: 4000. Records go back to 1920. Alumni records are maintained here also. Call 914-938-3700. Degrees granted: Bachelors.

Attendance and degree information available by phone, fax, mail. Search requires name only. Also helpful: SSN, date of birth, exact years of attendance. There is no fee.

United Talmudical Academy, Registrar, 82 Lee Ave, Brooklyn, NY 11211, 718-963-9260. Hours: 9AM-5PM. Records go back to 1985. Alumni records are maintained here at the same phone number.

Attendance and degree information available by mail. Search requires name plus SSN, signed release. There is no fee.

University of Rochester, Registrar, 129 Administration Bldg, Rochester, NY 14627-0038, 716-275-5131 (Fax: 716-275-2190). Hours: 8AM-5PM. Enrollment: 8500. Records go back to 1900's. Alumni records are maintained here also. Call 716-275-2121. Degrees granted: Bachelors; Masters; Doctorate. Special programs- Simon Business School: Eastman School of Music. Adverse incident record source- Residential Life, 716-275-3166.

Attendance and degree information available by phone, fax, mail. Search requires name plus SSN, exact years of attendance. There is no fee.

Utica College of Syracuse University, Registrar, 1600 Burrstone Rd, Utica, NY 13502-4892, 315-792-3195 (Fax: 315-792-3292). Hours: 8:30AM-5PM. Enrollment: 2000. Records go back to 1947. Alumni records are maintained here also. Call 315-792-3025. Degrees granted: Bachelors.

Attendance and degree information available by phone, mail. Search requires name only. Also helpful: SSN, date of birth, exact years of attendance. There is no fee.

Utica School of Commerce, Registrar, 201 Bleecker St, Utica, NY 13501, 315-733-2307 (Fax: 315-733-9281). Hours: 7:30AM-4:30PM. Records go back to 1896. Alumni records are maintained here at the same phone number. Degrees granted: Associate. Adverse incident record source- Dean of Students.

Attendance information available by fax, mail. Search requires name plus SSN, exact years of attendance, signed release. There is no fee.

Degree information available by fax, mail. Search requires name plus SSN, exact years of attendance, signed release. There is no fee.

Utica School of Commerce, (Branch), Registrar, PO Box 462, Canastota, NY 13032, 315-697-8200 (Fax: 315-697-2805). Records are not housed here. They are located at Utica School of Commerce, Registrar, 201 Bleecker St, Utica, NY 13501.

Utica School of Commerce, (Branch), Registrar, 17-19 Elm St, Oneonta, NY 13820, 607-432-7003 (Fax: 607-432-7004). Records are not housed here. They are located at Utica School of Commerce, Registrar, 201 Bleecker St, Utica, NY 13501.

Vassar College, Registrar, Raymond Ave, Box 11, Poughkeepsie, NY 12601, 914-437-5275 (Fax: 914-437-7050). Hours: 8AM-5PM. Enrollment: 2350. Records go back to 1865. Alumni records are maintained here also. Call 914-437-5445. Degrees granted: Bachelors; Masters. Adverse incident record source- Dean, 914-437-5255.

Attendance and degree information available by phone, fax, mail. Search requires name plus exact years of attendance. Also helpful: SSN. There is no fee.

Villa Maria College of Buffalo, Registrar, 240 Pine Ridge Rd, Buffalo, NY 14225-3999, 716-896-0700 X337 (Fax: 716-896-0705). Hours: 8AM-4PM. Records go back to 1964. Alumni records are maintained here also. Call 716-896-0700 X327. Degrees granted: Associate.

Attendance information available by fax, mail. Search requires name plus signed release. Also helpful: SSN, date of birth, exact years of attendance. Fee is $2.00. Expedited service available for $2.00.

Degree information available by phone, fax, mail. Search requires name only. Also helpful: SSN, date of birth, exact years of attendance. Fee is $2.00. Expedite service available for $2.00.

Wadhams Hall Seminary/College, Registrar, R D 4 Box 80, Ogdensburg, NY 13669, 315-393-4231 (Fax: 315-393-4249). Hours: 8AM-4PM. Enrollment: 30. Records go back to 1924. Alumni records are maintained here at the same phone number. Degrees granted: Bachelors. Certification: Christian Leadership, Pre-Theologate.

Attendance information available by phone. Search requires name plus SSN. Also helpful: date of birth, exact years of attendance. Fee is $4.00.

Degree information available by written request only. Search requires name plus SSN. Also helpful: date of birth, exact years of attendance. Fee is $4.00.

Wagner College, Registrar, Howard Ave and Campus Rd, Staten Island, NY 10301, 718-390-3208 (Fax: 718-390-

3344). Hours: 10AM-4PM. Enrollment: 1800. Alumni records are maintained here also. Call 718-390-3240. Degrees granted: Bachelors; Masters. Certification: Nursing. Adverse incident record source- Dean of Students, 718-390-3423.

Attendance and degree information available by fax, mail. Search requires name plus SSN. Also helpful: date of birth, exact years of attendance. There is no fee.

Webb Institute, Registrar, Crescent Beach Rd, Glen Cove, NY 11542, 516-671-2213 (Fax: 516-674-9838). Enrollment: 80. Alumni records are maintained here at the same phone number. Degrees granted: Bachelors.

Attendance and degree information available by phone, fax, mail. Search requires name plus exact years of attendance. Also helpful: SSN. There is no fee.

Wells College, Registrar, Aurora, NY 13026-0500, 315-364-3215 (Fax: 315-364-3229). Hours: 8:30AM-Noon, 1-4:30PM. Enrollment: 400. Records go back to 1900. Alumni records are maintained here also. Call 315-364-3200. Degrees granted: Bachelors. Adverse incident record source- Dean of Students, 315-364-3311.

Attendance and degree information available by phone, fax, mail. Search requires name plus SSN, date of birth. Also helpful: exact years of attendance. There is no fee.

Westchester Business Institute, Registrar, PO Box 710, 325 Central Ave, White Plains, NY 10600, 914-948-4442 (Fax: 914-948-8216). Hours: 8AM-11PM. Records go back to 1960. Alumni records are maintained here at the same phone number. Degrees granted: Associate. Adverse incident record source- Dean of Students.

Attendance and degree information available by fax, mail. Search requires name plus SSN, exact years of attendance, signed release. There is no fee.

Westchester Community College, Registrar, 75 Grasslands Rd, Valhalla, NY 10595, 914-785-6810. Hours: 9AM-8PM M-Th, 9AM-5PM F. Enrollment: 11211. Records go back to 1950. Alumni records are maintained here also. Call 914-785-6670. Degrees granted: Associate. Adverse incident record source- Student Affairs, 914-785-6731.

Attendance and degree information available by phone, mail. Search requires name plus SSN. There is no fee.

Wood Tobe Coburn School, Registrar, 8 E 40th St, New York, NY 10016, 212-686-9040 X36 (Fax: 212-686-9171). Hours: 8AM-5PM. Records go back to 1954. Alumni records are maintained here at the same phone number. Degrees granted: Associate. Adverse incident record source- Dean of Students.

Attendance and degree information available by phone, fax, mail. Search requires name plus SSN, date of birth, exact years of attendance. There is no fee.

Yeshiva Derech Chaim, Registrar, 1573 39th St, Brooklyn, NY 11218, 718-438-3070 (Fax: 718-435-9285). Enrollment: 165.

Attendance and degree information available by mail. Search requires name plus SSN. There is no fee.

Yeshiva Karlin Stolin Beth Aaron V'Israel Rabbinical Institute, Registrar, 1818 54th St, Brooklyn, NY 11204, 718-232-7800 (Fax: 718-331-4833). Enrollment: 50. Degrees granted: Bachelors; 1st Professional Degree.

Attendance and degree information available by mail. Search requires name plus SSN, signed release. There is no fee.

Yeshiva Mikdash Melech, Registrar, 1326 Ocean Pkwy, Brooklyn, NY 11230-5655, 718-339-1090 (Fax: 718-998-9321). Enrollment: 80.

Attendance and degree information available by phone, mail. Search requires name plus SSN, date of birth, exact years of attendance. There is no fee.

Yeshiva Shaar HaTorah Talmudic Research Institute, Registrar, 83-96 117th St, Kew Gardens, NY 11415, 718-846-1940 (Fax: 718-846-1942). Enrollment: 142. Alumni records are maintained here at the same phone number. Adverse incident record source- Dean of Students.

Attendance and degree information available by phone, mail. Search requires name plus exact years of attendance. There is no fee.

Yeshiva University, Registrar, 500 W 185th St, New York, NY 10033-3299, 212-960-5400. Hours: 9AM-5PM M,W; 1-5PM T,Th. Enrollment: 5279. Records go back to 1950. Alumni records are maintained here at the same phone number. Degrees granted: Associate; Bachelors; Masters; Doctorate. Adverse incident record source- Student Affairs.

Attendance and degree information available by phone, mail. Search requires name plus SSN. Also helpful: date of birth, exact years of attendance. There is no fee.

Yeshiva of Nitra-Rabbinical College Yeshiva Farm Settlement, Registrar, Pines Bridge Rd, Mount Kisco, NY 10549, 718-387-0422 (Fax: 718-387-9400). Hours: 9AM-5PM. Enrollment: 190. Alumni records are maintained here at the same phone number. Degrees granted: Bachelors; Rabbinic Degree. Adverse incident record source- Dean of Students.

Attendance and degree information available by fax, mail. Search requires name plus SSN, date of birth. There is no fee.

Yeshivas Novominsk, Registrar, 1569 47th St, Brooklyn, NY 11219, 718-438-2727 (Fax: 718-438-2472). Hours: 9AM-5PM. Enrollment: 113. Records go back to 1932. Adverse incident record source- Student Affairs.

Attendance information available by mail. Search requires name plus approximate years of attendance. Also helpful: SSN. There is no fee.

Degree information available by fax, mail. Search requires name plus approximate years of attendance. Also helpful: SSN. There is no fee.

Yeshivath Viznitz, Registrar, PO Box 446, Monsey, NY 10952, 914-356-1010 (Fax: 914-425-1730). Enrollment: 345.

Attendance and degree information available by mail. Search requires name plus SSN, date of birth, exact years of attendance, signed release. There is no fee.

Yesivath Zichron Moshe, Registrar, Laurel Park Rd, PO Box 580, South Fallsburg, NY 12779, 914-434-5240 (Fax: 914-434-1009). Enrollment: 120. Records go back to 1931. Alumni records are maintained here at the same phone number. Adverse incident record source- Student Affairs.

Attendance and degree information available by mail. Search requires name plus SSN, date of birth, exact years of attendance, signed release. There is no fee.

Trade and Vocational Schools

ASA Institute of Business and Computer Technology, 151 Lawrence St 2nd Fl, Brooklyn, NY 11201, 718-522-9073

Academy for Career Education, 55-05 Myrtle Ave, Ridgewood, NY 11385, 718-497-4900

Alvin Ailey American Dance Center (The), 211 W 61st St 3rd Fl, New York, NY 10023, 212-767-0940

American Ballet Center/Joffrey Balley School, 434 Ave of the Americas, New York, NY 10011, 212-254-8520

American Musical and Dramatic Academy (The), 2109 Broadway, New York, NY 10023, 212-787-5300

Apex Technical School, 635 Ave of the Americas, New York, NY 10011, 212-645-3300

Berk Trade and Business School, 312 W 36th St, New York, NY 10018, 212-629-3736

Blake Business School, PO Box 1052, New York, NY 10276, 212-254-1233

Blake Business School (Branch Campus), 145A 4th Ave, New York, NY 10003, 212-995-1711

Business Informatics Center, 134 S Central Ave, Valley Stream, NY 11580, 516-561-0050

Cashier Training Institute, 500 Eighth Ave, New York, NY 10018, 212-564-0500

Charles Stuart School of Diamond Setting, 1420 Kings Hwy, Brooklyn, NY 11229, 718-339-2640

Chauffeurs Training School, 12 Railroad Ave, Albany, NY 12205, 518-482-8601

Cheryl Fell's School of Business, 2541 Military Rd, Niagara Falls, NY 14304, 716-297-2750

Circle in the Square Theatre School, 1633 Broadway, New York, NY 10019, 212-307-3732

Commercial Driver Training, 600 Patton Ave, West Babylon, NY 11704, 516-249-1330

Computer Career Center, 474 Fulton Ave, Hempstead, NY 11550, 516-486-2526

Continental Dental Assistant School, 633 Jefferson Rd, Rochester, NY 14623, 716-272-8060

Cope Institute, 84 Williams St 4th Fl, New York, NY 10038, 718-809-5935

Dance Theatre of Harlem, Inc., 466 W 152nd St, New York, NY 10031, 212-690-2800

Drake Business School, 2122 White Plains, Bronx, NY 10452, 718-822-8080

Drake Business School, 36-09 Main St 6th Fl, Flushing, NY 11354, 718-353-3535

Drake Business School, 225 Broadway, New York, NY 10007, 212-349-7900

Drake Business School, 25 Victory Blvd, Staten Island, NY 10301, 718-447-1515

Elmira Business Institute, 180 Clemens Center Pkwy, Elmira, NY 14901, 607-733-7177

FEGS Trades and Business School, 17 Battery Pl #6N, New York, NY 10004, 212-440-8130

FEGS Trades and Business School (Branch Campus), 199 Jay St, Brooklyn, NY 11201, 718-448-0120

Folk Art Institute of the Museum of American Folk Art, 61 W 62nd St, New York, NY 10023, 212-977-7170

French Culinary Institute, 462 Broadway, New York, NY 10013, 212-219-8890

Gemological Institute of America (Branch Campus), 580 Fifth Ave, New York, NY 10036-4794, 212-944-5900

Global Business Institute, 1931 Mott Ave, Far Rockaway, NY 11691, 718-327-2220

Global Business Institute (Branch Campus), 209 W 125th St, New York, NY 10027, 212-663-1500

Globe Institute of Technology, 291 Broadway 4th Fl, New York, NY 10007, 212-349-4330

Globe Institute of Technology, 5 Beekman St Ste 501, New York, NY 10038, 212-349-9768

Hunter Business School, 3601 Hempstead Tpke, Levittown, NY 11756, 516-796-1000

Institute of Allied Medical Professions, 106 Central Park S #23D, New York, NY 10019, 212-757-0520

Institute of Audio Research, 64 University Pl, New York, NY 10003, 212-677-7580

Isabella G. Hart School of Practical Nursing, 1425 Portland Ave, Rochester, NY 14621, 716-338-4784

Island Drafting & Technical Institute, 128 Broadway, Amityville, NY 11701, 516-691-8733

Krissler Business Institute, 166 Mansion Sq Park, Poughkeepsie, NY 12601, 914-471-0330

Laban/Bartenieff Institute of Movement Studies, Inc., 11 E 4th St, New York, NY 10003, 212-477-4299

Lewis A. Wilson Technical Center, 17 Westminster Ave, Dix Hills, NY 11746, 516-667-6000

Long Island Business Institute, 6500 Jericho Tpke, Commack, NY 11725, 516-499-7100

Mandl School, 254 W 54th St, New York, NY 10019, 212-247-3434

Marion S. Whelan School of Practical Nursing, 196-198 North St, Geneva, NY 14456, 315-789-4222

Martha Graham School of Contemporary Dance, Inc., 316 E 63rd St, New York, NY 10021, 212-838-5886

Merce Cunningham Studio, 55 Bethune St, New York, NY 10014, 212-255-313-

Mildred Elley Business School, 2 Computer Dr S, Albany, NY 12205, 518-446-0595

Modern Welding School, 1740 Broadway, Schenectady, NY 12306, 518-374-1216

Munson-Williams-Proctor Institute, 310 Genesee St, Utica, NY 13502, 315-797-8260

National Shakespeare Conservatory, 591 Broadway, New York, NY 10012, 212-219-9874

National Tax Training School, PO Box 382, Monsey, NY 10952, 914-352-3634

National Tractor Trailer School, PO Box 208, Liverpool, NY 13088, 315-451-2430

National Tractor Trailer School (Branch Campus), 175 Katherine St, Buffalo, NY 14210, 716-849-6887

Neighborhood Playhouse School of Theatre, 340 E 54th St, New York, NY 10022, 212-688-3770

New School of Contemporary Radio, 50 Colvin Ave, Albany, NY 12206, 518-438-7682

New York Food & Hotel Management School, 154 W 14th St, New York, NY 10011, 212-675-6655

New York Institute of Business and Technology, 401 Park Ave S 2nd Fl, New York, NY 10016, 212-725-9400

New York Paralegal School, 299 Broadway Ste 200, New York, NY 10007, 212-349-8800

New York Restaurant School, 75 Varwick St, 16th Floor, New York, NY 10013, 212-226-5500

New York School for Medical/Dental Assistants, 116-16 Queens Blvd, Forest Hills, NY 11375, 718-793-2330

New York School of Dog Grooming, 248 E 34th St, New York, NY 10016, 212-685-3776

New York School of Dog Grooming (Branch Campus), 265-17 Union Tpke, New Hyde Park, NY 11040, 718-343-3130

Nikolais and Louis Dance Lab, 375 W Broadway 5th Fl, New York, NY 10012, 212-226-7000

Professional Business Institute, 125 Canal St, New York, NY 10002, 212-226-7300

Ridley-Lowell Business and Technical Institute, 116 Front St, Binghamton, NY 13905, 607-724-2941

Royal Barber & Beauty School, 108-112 Broadway, Schenectady, NY 12305, 518-346-2288

SCS Business and Technical Institute, 394 Bridge St, Brooklyn, NY 11201, 718-802-9500

SYRIT Computer School Systems, 1760 53rd St, Brooklyn, NY 11204, 718-853-1212

Sonia Moore Studio of the Theatre (The), 485 Park Ave #6A, New York, NY 10022, 212-755-5120

Sotheby's Educational Studies, 1334 York Ave, New York, NY 10021, 212-606-7822

Spanish-American Institute, 215 W 43rd St, New York, NY 10036, 212-840-7111

Spencer Business and Technical Institute, 200 State St, Schenectady, NY 12305, 518-374-7619

St. Francis School of Practical Nursing, 2221 W STate St, Olean, NY 14760, 716-375-7316

Stella Adler Conservatory of Acting, 419 Lafayette St 6thFl, New York, NY 10003, 212-260-0525

Stenotopia, the World of Court Reporting, 45 S Service Rd, Plainview, NY 11803, 516-777-1117

Suburban Technical School, 175 Fulton Ave, Hempstead, NY 11550, 416-481-6660

Suburban Technical School (Branch Campus), 2650 Sunrise Hwy, East Islip, NY 11730, 516-224-5001

Superior Career Institute, 116 W 14th St, New York, NY 10011, 212-675-2140

Swedish Institute (The), 226 W 26th St 5th FL, New York, NY 10001, 212-924-5900

Techno-Dent Training Center, 101 W 31st St 4th Fl, New York, NY 10001, 212-695-1818

Travel Institute, 15 Park Row #617, New York, NY 10038, 212-349-3331

Tri-State Institute of Traditional Chinese Acupuncture, 80 Avenue 4th Floor, New York, NY 10011, 212-242-2255

Ultrasound Diagnostic School, One Old Country Rd, Carle Place, NY 11514, 516-248-6060

Ultrasound Diagnostic School, 2269 Saw Mill River Rd, Elmsford, NY 10523, 914-347-6817

Ultrasound Diagnostic School, 121 W 27th St #504, New York, NY 10001, 212-645-9116

Universal Business and Media School, 220 E 106th St, New York, NY 10029, 212-360-1210

Westchester Conservatory of Music, 20 Soundview Ave, White Plains, NY 10606, 914-761-3715

State Licensing & Business Registration Quick Finder Index

Architecture, Engineering & Surveying
Architect #19 .... ☎ 518-474-3830
Engineer #19 .... ☎ 518-474-3830
Landscape Architect #19 .... ☎ 518-474-3830
Surveyor #19 .... ☎ 518-474-3830

Business - Court & Legal Services
Attorney #15 (172000) .... ☎ 212-417-5872
Bondsman #13 (54) .... ☎ 518-474-6630
Court Reporter #19 .... ☎ 518-474-3830
Lobbyist #18 (2075) .... ☎ 518-474-7126
Notary Public #11 .... ☎ 518-474-4429

Business - General Services
Charitable Organization #11 .... ☎ 518-474-4429
Interior Designer #19 .... ☎ 518-474-3830
Professional Fund Raiser #11 .... ☎ 518-474-4429
Public Accountant #19 .... ☎ 518-474-3830
Public Accountant-CPA #19 .... ☎ 518-474-3830

Construction & Manufacturing
Boiler & Pressure Vessel Inspector #8 (425)
.... ☎ 518-457-2722
Crane Operator #9 .... ☎ 718-797-7659
Mobil Laser Operator #9 .... ☎ 718-797-7659
Security & Fire Alarm Installer #11 .... ☎ 518-474-4429
Upholsters & Bedding Industry #11 .... ☎ 518-474-4429
Welder Field Cert. Structural SMAW #12 ... ☎ 518-457-7160
Welder, Shop Certification #12 .... ☎ 518-457-4525

Education
School Administrator/Supervisor #20 .... ✉ 518-474-3901
School Counselor #20 .... ✉ 518-474-3901
School Media Specialist #20 .... ✉ 518-474-3901
Teacher #20 .... ✉ 518-474-3901

Environmental & Agriculture
Asbestos Handler #9 .... ☎ 718-797-7659
Blaster #9 .... ☎ 718-797-7659
Pesticide Applicator #2 .... ✉ 518-457-7482
Pesticide Dealer #2 .... ✉ 518-457-7482
Pet Cemetery #11 .... ☎ 518-474-4429
Veterinarian #19 .... ☎ 518-474-3830
Waste Water Treatment Plant Operator #4 (4000)
.... ☎ 518-457-5968
Water Treatment Plant Operator #14 (410).. ☎ 518-458-6755

Financial - Real Estate, Insurance & Banking
Apartment Information Vendor #11 .... ☎ 518-474-4429
Apartment Manager/Vendor & Agent #11 ... ☎ 518-474-4429
Apartment Sharing Agent #11 .... ☎ 518-474-4429
Check Casher #1 (560) .... ☎ 212-618-6642
Insurance Agent/Consultant/Broker #13
(160504) .... ☎ 518-474-6630
Insurance Appraiser #13 (4299) .... ☎ 518-474-6630
Investment Advisor #10 212-416-8200
Lending Institution #1 (238) .... ☎ 212-618-6642
Mortgage Broker #1 (1790) .... ☎ 212-618-6642
Real Estate Salesperson/Broker/Appraiser #11
.... ☎ 518-474-4429
Securities Broker/Dealer #10 212-416-8200
Securities Salesperson #10 212-416-8200

Health & Beauty
Acupuncturist #19 .... ☎ 518-474-3830
Chiropractor #19 .... ☎ 518-474-3830
Cosmetologist/Barber #11 .... ☎ 518-474-4429
Cosmetology #11 .... ☎ 518-474-4429
Dental Anesthesologist #19 .... ☎ 518-474-3830
Dental Hygienist #19 .... ☎ 518-474-3830
Dentist #19 .... ☎ 518-474-3830
Dietitian #19 .... ☎ 518-474-3830
Emergency Medical Technician-Paramedic #7
(3504) .... ✉ 518-474-2219
Esthetics #11 .... ☎ 518-474-4429
Funeral Director #6 (5666) .... ☎ 518-453-1989
Health Club #11 .... ☎ 518-474-4429
Hearing Aid Dealer #11 .... ☎ 518-474-4429
Massage Therapist #19 .... ☎ 518-474-3830
Medical Doctor #19 .... ☎ 518-474-3830
Midwife #19 .... ☎ 518-474-3830
Nail Technology #11 .... ☎ 518-474-4429
Natural Hair Styling #11 .... ☎ 518-474-4429
Nurse #19 .... ☎ 518-474-3830
Nurse Practitioner #19 .... ☎ 518-474-3830
Nursing Home Administrator #5 (4100) .... ☎ 518-452-6822
Nutritionist #19 .... ☎ 518-474-3830
Occupational Therapist #19 .... ☎ 518-474-3830
Ophthalmic Dispenser #19 .... ☎ 518-474-3830
Optometrist #19 .... ☎ 518-474-3830
Osteopathic Physician #19 .... ☎ 518-474-3830
Parenteral Conscious Sedation #19 .... ☎ 518-474-3830
Pharmacist #19 .... ☎ 518-474-3830
Physical Therapist #19 .... ☎ 518-474-3830
Physical Therapy Assistant #19 .... ☎ 518-474-3830
Physician's Assistant #19 .... ☎ 518-474-3830
Podiatrist #19 .... ☎ 518-474-3830
Practical Nurse #19 .... ☎ 518-474-3830
Radiological Technologist #16 518-458-6476
Radiotherapy Technologist #16 518-458-6476
Respiratory Technician #19 .... ☎ 518-474-3830
Respiratory Therapist #19 .... ☎ 518-474-3830
Specialist Assistant #19 .... ☎ 518-474-3830
Speech Pathologist/Audiologist #19 .... ☎ 518-474-3830

Investigations & Security
Law Enforcement for Railroad/Steamboat #11
.... ☎ 518-474-4429
Private Investigator #11 .... ☎ 518-474-4429
Security Guard #11 .... ☎ 518-474-4429
Watch Dog/Patrol Agency #11 .... ☎ 518-474-4429
Watch Guard or Patrol Agency #11 .... ☎ 518-474-4429

Social Services
Psychologist #19 .... ☎ 518-474-3830
Social Worker #19 .... ☎ 518-474-3830

Sports & Entertainment
Athletic Trainer #19 .... ☎ 518-474-3830
Games of Chance Registration #11 .... ☎ 518-474-4429
Guide #3 (1725) .... ☎ 518-457-5740
Racing #17 212-417-4200
Wagering Employee #17 212-417-4200

Transportation
Hotel/Motel #11 .... ☎ 518-474-4429

State Licensing & Business Registration Agency Information

(1) Banking Department, Two Rector St, New York, NY 10006, 212-618-6642, Fax: 212-618-6923

(2) Department of Environmental Conservation, Bureau of Pesticide Radiation, 50 Wolf Rd, Room 498, Albany, NY 12233-7254, 518-457-7482

(3) Department of Environmental Conservation, Division of Forest Protection & Fire Mgmt., 50 Wolf Rd, Room 440C, Albany, NY 12233-2560, 518-457-5740, Fax: 518-485-8458

(4) Department of Environmental Conservation, Division of Water, Bureau of Watershed Compliance, 50 Wolf Rd, Room 320, Albany, NY 12233-3506, 518-457-5968, Fax: 518-485-7786

(5) Department of Health, Board of Examiners of Nursing Home Administrators, 1 Corporate Plaza, Suite 102, Albany, NY 12203-5499, 518-452-6822

(6) Department of Health, Bureau of Funeral Directing, Corning Tower, Albany, NY 12237-0763, 518-453-1989

(7) Department of Health, Emergency Medical Services, 1 Commerce Plaza, Room 126, Albany, NY 12260, 518-474-2219, Fax: 518-486-6216

(8) Department of Labor, Boiler Safety Bureau, State Campus, Bldg 12, Room 134, Albany, NY 12240, 518-457-2722, Fax: 518-485-1150

(9) Department of Labor, Division of Safety & Health, One Main St, Brooklyn, NY 11201, 718-797-7659, Fax: 718-797-7016

(10) Department of Law, Bureau of Investor Protection & Securities, 120 Broadway, 23rd Floor, New York, NY 10271, 212-416-8200

(11) Department of State, Division of Licensing Services, 84 Holland Ave, Albany, NY 12208, 518-474-4429, Fax: 518-473-6648

(12) Department of Transportation, Structures Division, Building 5, Mail Drop 0600, Albany, NY 12232, 518-457-7160, Fax: 518-457-6010

(13) Insurance Department, Empire State Plaza, Bldg 1, Albany, NY 12257, 518-474-6630

(14) New York State Department of Health, Bureau of Public Water Supply Protection, 2 University Pl, Room 410, Albany, NY 12203-3313, 518-458-6731

(15) New York State Office of Court Administration, PO Box 2806, Church Street Station, New York, NY 10008, 212-417-5872

(16) State Department of Health, Bureau of Environmental Radiation Protection, 2 University Pl, Room 325, Albany, NY 12203, 518-458-6482, Fax: 518-458-6434

(17) State Racing & Wagering Board, 120 Broadway, 13th Floor, New York, NY 10271, 212-417-4200, Fax: 212-417-4315

(18) Temporary State Commission on Lobbying, 2 Commerce Plaza, Suite 1701, Albany, NY 12223, 518-474-7126, Fax: 518-473-6492

(19) The State Education Department, Professional Licensing Services, Cultural Education Center, Madison Ave, Albany, NY 12230, 518-474-3830

(20) University of the State of New York, State Education Department, Licensing Unit, Cultural Education Center, Room 5A11, Madison Ave, Albany, NY 12230, 518-474-3901, Fax: 518-473-0271

North Carolina

Capitol: Raleigh (Grant County)	
State Population	7.2 Million
Number of Degree Granting Institutions:	118
Number of State Licensing & Business Registration Agencies:	48

Degree Granting Educational Institutions

Alamance Community College, Registrars Office, Student Services, PO Box 8000, Graham, NC 27253-8000, 910-578-2002 (Fax: 910-578-1987). Hours: 8AM-8PM M-Th; 8AM-5PM F. Enrollment: 3500. Records go back to 1959. Alumni records are maintained here at the same phone number. Degrees granted: Associate. Adverse incident record source-Security Chief, 910-578-2002 X4405.

Attendance and degree information available by phone, fax, mail. Search requires name only. Also helpful: SSN, date of birth, exact years of attendance. There is no fee.

Anson Community College, Registrar, PO Box 126, Polkton, NC 28135, 704-272-7635 (Fax: 704-272-8904). Hours: 8AM-5PM. Enrollment: 590. Records go back to 1950's. Alumni records are maintained here at the same phone number. Degrees granted: Associate.

Attendance and degree information available by phone, fax, mail. Search requires name plus SSN. There is no fee.

Appalachian State University, Registrar, Boone, NC 28608, 704-262-2000 (Fax: 704-262-3136). Hours: 8AM-5PM. Enrollment: 12000. Records go back to 1929. Alumni records are maintained here at the same phone number. Degrees granted: Bachelors; Masters; Doctorate; EDS. Adverse incident record source- Registrar's Office, 704-262-2050 .

Attendance and degree information available by phone, fax, mail. Search requires name plus SSN. Also helpful: date of birth, exact years of attendance. There is no fee.

Asheville-Buncombe Technical Community College, Registrar, 340 Victoria Rd, Asheville, NC 28801, 704-254-1921 X147 (Fax: 704-251-6718). Hours: 8:30AM-8PM M,W; 8:30AM-4:30PM T,Th,F. Enrollment: 2764. Records go back to 1959. Degrees granted: Associate. Special programs- Radiography.

Attendance and degree information available by phone, fax, mail. Search requires name plus SSN, date of birth. Also helpful: exact years of attendance. There is no fee.

Barber-Scotia College, Registrar, 145 Cabarrus Ave W, Concord, NC 28025, 704-786-5171 X221 (Fax: 704-793-

4950). Hours: 8:30AM-4:30PM. Alumni records are maintained here at the same phone number. Degrees granted: Bachelors.

Attendance and degree information available by mail. Search requires name plus exact years of attendance. There is no fee.

Barton College, Office of Registrar, College Station, Wilson, NC 27893, 919-399-6327 (Fax: 919-237-1620). Hours: 8:30AM-5PM. Enrollment: 1338. Records go back to 1902. Alumni records are maintained here also. Call 919-399-6360. Degrees granted: Bachelors. Adverse incident record source- Student Life Division, 919-399-6364.

Attendance and degree information available by phone, fax, mail. Search requires name plus SSN, approximate years of attendance. There is no fee.

Beaufort County Community College, Registrar, PO Box 1069, Washington, NC 27889, 919-946-6194 (Fax: 919-946-0271). Hours: 8:15AM-5PM M-Th; 8:15AM-4PM F. Enrollment: 1250. Records go back to 1970. Degrees granted: Associate. Adverse incident record source- Security Dept, 919-946-6194 X444.

Attendance information available by phone, fax, mail. Search requires name plus SSN, approximate years of attendance. Also helpful: exact years of attendance. There is no fee.

Degree information available by phone, fax, mail. Search requires name plus SSN, approximate years of attendance. Also helpful: date of birth, exact years of attendance. There is no fee.

Belmont Abbey College, Registrar, 100 Belmont-Mount Holly Rd, Belmont, NC 28012-2795, 704-825-6732 (Fax: 704-825-6727). Hours: 8:30AM-4:30PM. Enrollment: 900. Alumni records are maintained here also. Call 704-825-6889. Degrees granted: Bachelors; Masters.

Attendance information available by phone, mail. Search requires name only. Also helpful: SSN, date of birth, exact years of attendance. There is no fee.

Degree information available by phone, mail. Search requires name only. Also helpful: date of birth, exact years of attendance. There is no fee.

Bennett College, Records Office, 900 E Washington St, Greensboro, NC 27401-3239, 910-370-8620 (Fax: 910-272-7143). Hours: 8AM-5PM. Enrollment: 600. Records go back to

1928. Alumni records are maintained here also. Call 910-370-8620. Degrees granted: Bachelors.

Attendance information available by phone, fax, mail. Search requires name plus SSN. There is no fee.

Degree information available by phone, fax, mail. Search requires name plus SSN. Also helpful: approximate years of attendance. There is no fee.

Bladen Community College, Registrar, PO Box 266, Dublin, NC 28332-0266, 910-862-2164 (Fax: 910-862-7424). Hours: 8AM-4:30PM M-Th; 8AM-3PM F. Enrollment: 600. Records go back to 1967. Degrees granted: Associate.

Attendance and degree information available by phone, fax, mail. Search requires name plus SSN. Also helpful: exact years of attendance. There is no fee.

Blanton's College, Registrar, 126 College St, Asheville, NC 28801, 704-687-6883. Alumni records are maintained here at the same phone number. Degrees granted: Associate.

Attendance and degree information available by mail. Search requires name plus SSN, exact years of attendance. There is no fee.

Blue Ridge Community College, Registrar, College Dr, Flat Rock, NC 28731-9624, 704-692-3572 X217 (Fax: 704-692-2441). Hours: 8AM-8PM M-Th; 8AM-4:30PM F. Enrollment: 1606. Records go back to 1969. Degrees granted: Associate.

Attendance and degree information available by phone, fax, mail. Search requires name only. Also helpful: SSN, date of birth, exact years of attendance. There is no fee.

Brevard College, Registrar, 400 N Broad St, Brevard, NC 28712-3306, 704-883-8292 (Fax: 704-884-3790). Hours: 8AM-4:30PM. Enrollment: 650. Records go back to 1934. From 1986 records are on computer. Alumni records are maintained here at the same phone number. Degrees granted: Associate. Adverse incident record source- Campus Life, 704-884-8258.

Attendance and degree information available by phone. Search requires name plus SSN, approximate years of attendance. There is no fee.

Brookstone College of Business, Registrar, 7815 National Service Rd, Greensboro, NC 27409, 919-668-2627. Degrees granted: Associate.

Attendance and degree information available by phone, mail. Search requires name plus SSN, exact years of attendance. There is no fee.

Brunswick Community College, Registrar, PO Box 30, Supply, NC 28462-0030, 910-754-6900 X325 (Fax: 910-754-9609). Hours: 8AM-5PM. Enrollment: 900. Records go back to 1979. Alumni records are maintained here at the same phone number. Degrees granted: Associate.

Attendance and degree information available by phone, fax, mail. Search requires name plus SSN. Also helpful: date of birth, exact years of attendance. There is no fee.

Caldwell Community College and Technical Institute, Registrar, 2855 Hickory Blvd, Hudson, NC 28638, 704-726-2200 (Fax: 704-726-2216). Hours: 8AM-8PM M-Th, 8AM-5PM F. Enrollment: 3000. Records go back to 1960's. Degrees granted: Associate.

Attendance and degree information available by phone, fax, mail. Search requires name plus SSN. There is no fee.

Campbell University, Registrar's Office, PO Box 367, Buies Creek, NC 27506, 910-893-1200 (Fax: 910-893-1424). Hours: 8:30AM-5PM. Enrollment: 5800. Records go back to 1836. Alumni Records Office: Alumni Association, PO Box 158, Buies Creek, NC 27506. Degrees granted: Bachelors; Masters; Doctorate.

Attendance and degree information available by phone, fax, mail. Search requires name plus SSN. There is no fee.

Cape Fear Community College, Registrar, 411 N Front St, Wilmington, NC 28401-3993, 910-343-0481 (Fax: 910-763-2279). Hours: 8AM-6PM M-Th, 8AM-5PM F. Enrollment: 2730. Records go back to 1967. Degrees granted: Associate. Adverse incident record source- Records & Registration, 910-343-0481.

Attendance information available by phone, fax, mail. Search requires name plus SSN. Also helpful: exact years of attendance. There is no fee.

Degree information available by phone, fax, mail. Search requires name plus SSN. Also helpful: exact years of attendance. There is no fee.

Catawba College, Registrar, 2300 W Innes St, Salisbury, NC 28144, 704-637-4111 (Fax: 704-637-4777). Hours: 8:30AM-5PM. Enrollment: 1100. Alumni records are maintained here also. Call 704-637-4394. Degrees granted: Bachelors; Masters.

Attendance and degree information available by phone, fax, mail. Search requires name only. Also helpful: SSN, date of birth, exact years of attendance. There is no fee.

Catawba Valley Community College, Student Records, 2550 Hwy 70 SE, Hickory, NC 28602, 704-327-7009 (Fax: 704-327-7276 X224). Hours: 8AM-8PM M-Th; 8AM-5PM F. Enrollment: 3300. Records go back to 1960. Degrees granted: Associate. Adverse incident record source- Dean of Student Services, 704-327-7009 (Ext 219).

Attendance and degree information available by phone, fax, mail. Search requires name plus SSN. Also helpful: date of birth, exact years of attendance. There is no fee.

Cateret Community College, Student Services, 3505 Arendell St, Morehead City, NC 28557, 919-247-4142 (Fax: 919-247-2514). Hours: 8AM-8PM M-Th; 8AM-3:30PM F. Enrollment: 1400. Records go back to 1963. Degrees granted: Associate. Adverse incident record source- Director of Operations, 919-247-6000 X198.

Attendance and degree information available by phone, fax, mail. Search requires name plus SSN. Also helpful: date of birth, exact years of attendance. There is no fee.

Cecil's College, Registrar, 1567 Patton Ave, Asheville, NC 28806, 704-252-2486 (Fax: 704-252-8558). Hours: 9AM-6PM. Enrollment: 175. Records go back to 1930's. Degrees granted: Associate. Adverse incident record source- Records & Registration, 704-252-2486.

Attendance and degree information available by phone, fax, mail. Search requires name plus SSN. Also helpful: date of birth, exact years of attendance. There is no fee.

Central Carolina Community College, Registrar, 1105 Kelly Dr, Sanford, NC 27330, 919-775-5401 (Fax: 919-774-1500). Hours: 7:30AM-6PM M-Th; 7:30AM-3:30PM F. Enrollment: 3200. Records go back to 1962. Alumni records are maintained here at the same phone number. Degrees granted: Associate.

Attendance and degree information available by phone, mail. Search requires name plus SSN. Also helpful: exact years of attendance. There is no fee.

Central Piedmont Community College, Registrar, PO Box 35009, Charlotte, NC 28235, 704-342-2722. Hours: 8AM-5PM. Enrollment: 10916. Records go back to 1965. Alumni records are maintained here also. Call 704-342-6666. Degrees granted: Associate. Adverse incident record source- Dean, 704-342-6888.

Attendance and degree information available by phone, fax, mail. Search requires name plus SSN. There is no fee.

Chowan College, Registrar, PO Box 1848, Murfreesboro, NC 27855, 919-398-4101 (Fax: 919-398-1190). Hours: 8:30AM-5PM. Enrollment: 800. Records go back to 1846. Alumni records are maintained here at the same phone number.

Degrees granted: Associate; Bachelors. Adverse incident record source- 919-398-4101.

Attendance and degree information available by phone, fax, mail. Search requires name plus SSN. Also helpful: date of birth, exact years of attendance. There is no fee.

Cleveland Community College, Registrar, 137 S Post Rd, Shelby, NC 28152, 704-484-4099 (Fax: 704-484-4036). Hours: 8AM-8 PM M-Th, 8AM-4PM F. Enrollment: 1650. Records go back to 1965. Degrees granted: Associate.

Attendance and degree information available by fax, mail. Search requires name plus SSN, exact years of attendance. There is no fee.

Coastal Carolina Community College, Registrar, 444 Western Blvd, Jacksonville, NC 28546-6877, 910-938-6253 (Fax: 910-455-2767). Hours: 8AM-5PM. Enrollment: 3500. Records go back to 1967. Degrees granted: Associate.

Attendance and degree information available by phone, fax, mail. Search requires name plus SSN. Also helpful: date of birth, exact years of attendance. There is no fee.

College of the Albemarle, Registrar, PO Box 2327, Elizabeth City, NC 27906-2327, 919-335-0821 X252 (Fax: 919-335-2011). Hours: 8AM-4:30PM. Enrollment: 1900. Records go back to 1960. Degrees granted: Associate. Adverse incident record source- Records & Registration, 919-335-0821 X251.

Attendance and degree information available by phone, fax, mail. Search requires name plus SSN. Also helpful: date of birth, approximate years of attendance. There is no fee.

Craven Community College, Dean of Records, 800 College Ct, New Bern, NC 28562, 919-638-7223 (Fax: 919-638-4232). Hours: 8AM-10PM M-Th, 8AM-5PM F. Enrollment: 1545. Records go back to 1968. Alumni records are maintained here also. Call 919-638-4131. Degrees granted: Associate.

Attendance and degree information available by phone, fax, mail. Search requires name plus SSN. Also helpful: date of birth, exact years of attendance. There is no fee.

Davidson College, Registrar, PO Box 1719, Davidson, NC 28036, 704-892-2227 (Fax: 704-892-2005). Hours: 8:30AM-5PM. Enrollment: 1700. Records go back to 1837. Alumni records are maintained here also. Call 704-892-2111. Degrees granted: Bachelors. Adverse incident record source- Public Safety, 704-892-2178.

Attendance and degree information available by phone, mail. Search requires name plus SSN, date of birth. There is no fee.

Davidson County Community College, Student Records Office, PO Box 1287, Lexington, NC 27293-1287, 704-249-8186 (Fax: 704-249-0379). Hours: 8:30AM-5PM. Enrollment: 2500. Records go back to 1964. Degrees granted: Associate. Adverse incident record source- Student Development.

Attendance and degree information available by phone, fax, mail. Search requires name only. Also helpful: SSN, date of birth, exact years of attendance. There is no fee.

Duke University, Registrar, PO Box 90054, Durham, NC 27708-0001, 919-684-2813 (Fax: 919-684-4500). Hours: 8AM-5PM. Enrollment: 11000. Records go back to 1938. Degrees granted: Bachelors; Masters; Doctorate. Adverse incident record source- Same as above.

Attendance and degree information available by phone, mail. Search requires name only. Also helpful: SSN, date of birth, exact years of attendance. There is no fee.

Durham Technical Community College, Registrar, 1637 Lawson St, Durham, NC 27703, 919-686-3315 (Fax: 919-686-3669). Hours: 8AM-6PM M-Th; 8AM-5PM F.

Enrollment: 3183. Records go back to 1960's. Practical Nursing records available from 1940's. Degrees granted: Associate.

Attendance and degree information available by phone, fax, mail. Search requires name only. Also helpful: SSN, date of birth, exact years of attendance. There is no fee.

East Carolina University, Registrar, E. Fifth St, Greenville, NC 27858-4353, 919-328-6524 (Fax: 919-328-4232). Hours: 8AM-5PM. Enrollment: 16176. Records go back to 1907. Alumni records are maintained here also. Call 919-328-6072. Degrees granted: Bachelors; Masters; Doctorate; Med. School. Special programs- Medical School, 919-816-2201. Adverse incident record source- Dean, 919-328-6824.

Attendance and degree information available by phone, fax, mail. Search requires name plus SSN, approximate years of attendance. There is no fee.

East Coast Bible College, Registrar, 6900 Wilkinson Blvd, Charlotte, NC 28214, 704-394-2307 (Fax: 704-393-3689). Enrollment: 300. Records go back to 1976. Alumni records are maintained here at the same phone number. Degrees granted: Associate; Bachelors.

Attendance and degree information available by written request only. Search requires name plus signed release. Also helpful: SSN. There is no fee.

Edgecombe Community College, Registrar, 2009 W Wilson St, Tarboro, NC 27886, 919-823-5166 (Fax: 919-823-6817). College was formerly Edgecombe Technical College. Alumni records are maintained here at the same phone number. Degrees granted: Associate.

Attendance and degree information available by phone, fax, mail. Search requires name plus SSN, date of birth, approximate years of attendance. There is no fee.

Elizabeth City State University, Registrar, ECSU Box 953, Elizabeth City, NC 27909, 919-335-3300 (Fax: 919-335-3537). Hours: 8AM-5PM. Enrollment: 2000. Records go back to 1894. Alumni Records Office: Alumni Association, Campus Box 977, Elizabeth City, NC 27909. Degrees granted: Bachelors. Adverse incident record source- Student Affairs, 919-335-3276.

Attendance and degree information available by phone, fax, mail. Search requires name plus SSN, approximate years of attendance. There is no fee.

Elon College, Registrar, Campus Box 2106, Elon College, NC 27244, 910-584-2376 (Fax: 910-538-2735). Enrollment: 3500. Alumni Records Office: Alumni Relations, Elon College, Campus Box 2600, Elon College, NC 27244. Degrees granted: Bachelors; Masters.

Attendance and degree information available by phone, mail. Search requires name plus SSN. Also helpful: exact years of attendance. There is no fee.

Fayetteville State University, Registrar, 1200 Murchison Rd, Fayetteville, NC 28302, 910-486-1185 (Fax: 910-486-1599). Enrollment: 3719. Records go back to 1900. Alumni records are maintained here at the same phone number. Degrees granted: Associate; Bachelors; Masters; Doctorate.

Attendance and degree information available by phone, mail. Search requires name plus SSN. There is no fee.

Fayetteville Technical Community College, Registrar, PO Box 35236, 2201 Hull Rd, Fayetteville, NC 28303, 910-678-8416 (Fax: 910-484-6600).

Attendance and degree information available by phone, fax, mail. Search requires name plus SSN, approximate years of attendance. Also helpful: exact years of attendance. There is no fee.

Forsyth Technical Community College, Registrar, 2100 Silas Creek Pkwy, Winston-Salem, NC 27103, 910-723-0371 X7314 (Fax: 910-761-2098). Hours: 8AM-7PM M-Th; 8AM-3PM F. Enrollment: 4900. Records go back to 1960.

Alumni records are maintained here at the same phone number. Degrees granted: Associate; Arts & Science, Applied Science. Adverse incident record source- Student Development, 910-723-0371 X7236.

Attendance and degree information available by fax, mail. Search requires name plus SSN, approximate years of attendance, signed release. There is no fee.

Gardner-Webb University, Registrar, PO Box 997, Boiling Springs, NC 28017, 704-434-2361 X222. Enrollment: 1970. Degrees granted: Associate; Bachelors; Masters.

Attendance and degree information available by phone, mail. Search requires name plus SSN. There is no fee.

Gaston College, Registrar, 201 Hwy 321 S, Dallas, NC 28034, 704-922-6200 (Fax: 704-922-6233). Enrollment: 4000. Records go back to 1960. Degrees granted: Associate.

Attendance and degree information available by fax, mail. Search requires name plus signed release. Also helpful: SSN, exact years of attendance. There is no fee.

Greensboro College, Registrar, 815 W Market St, Greensboro, NC 27401, 910-373-7474 (Fax: 910-271-2237). Enrollment: 784. Alumni records are maintained here at the same phone number. Degrees granted: Bachelors.

Attendance and degree information available by phone, mail. Search requires name plus approximate years of attendance. There is no fee.

Guilford College, Registrar, 5800 W Friendly Ave, Greensboro, NC 27410-4171, 910-316-2000 (Fax: 910-316-2948). Hours: 8:30PM-5PM. Enrollment: 1558. Records go back to 1837. Alumni records are maintained here at the same phone number. Degrees granted: Bachelors.

Attendance and degree information available by phone, fax, mail. Search requires name only. Also helpful: SSN, date of birth, approximate years of attendance. There is no fee.

Guilford Technical Community College, Registrar, PO Box 309, Jamestown, NC 27282, 910-454-1126 X2235 (Fax: 910-454-2510). Hours: 8AM-7PM M-Th, 8AM-5PM F. Enrollment: 5900. Records go back to 1966. Alumni records are maintained here at the same phone number. Degrees granted: Associate. Adverse incident record source- Public Safety, 910-454-1126 X2398.

Attendance and degree information available by phone, fax, mail. Search requires name plus SSN. There is no fee.

Halifax Community College, Registrar, PO Drawer 809, Weldon, NC 27890, 919-536-7221 (Fax: 919-536-4144). Enrollment: 993. Alumni records are maintained here also. Call 919-536-7289. Degrees granted: Associate.

Attendance and degree information available by phone, mail. Search requires name plus SSN, date of birth, approximate years of attendance. There is no fee.

Haywood Community College, Registrar, Freedlander Dr, Clyde, NC 28721, 704-627-4507 (Fax: 704-627-4513). Hours: 8AM-7PM. Enrollment: 1300. Records go back to 1964. Degrees granted: Associate.

Attendance information available by mail. Search requires name plus date of birth. Also helpful: SSN, exact years of attendance. There is no fee.

Degree information available by phone, fax, mail. Search requires name plus date of birth. Also helpful: SSN, exact years of attendance. There is no fee.

High Point University, Registrar, University Station, Montlieu Ave, High Point, NC 27262-3598, 910-841-9131 (Fax: 910-841-4599). Hours: 8:30AM-5PM; 4:30 in Summer. Enrollment: 2500. Records go back to 1924. Alumni records are maintained here also. Call 910-841-9135. Degrees granted: Bachelors; Masters. Special programs- Home Furnishings Marketing, 910-841-9110. Adverse incident record source- Dean Evans, 910-841-9026.

Attendance and degree information available by phone, fax, mail. Search requires name only. Also helpful: exact years of attendance. There is no fee.

Isothermal Community College, Registrar, PO Box 804, Spindale, NC 28160, 704-286-3636 X240 (Fax: 704-286-8109). Hours: 8AM-8PM M-Th; 8AM-4:30PM F. Enrollment: 1800. Records go back to 1964. Alumni records are maintained here also. Call 704-286-3636 X261. Degrees granted: Associate. Adverse incident record source- Dean of Students, 704-286-3636 X238.

Attendance and degree information available by phone, fax, mail. Search requires name plus SSN, approximate years of attendance. Also helpful: date of birth, exact years of attendance. There is no fee.

James Sprunt Community College, Registrar, PO Box 398, Kenansville, NC 28349-0398, 910-296-2400 (Fax: 910-296-1222). Enrollment: 1000. Records go back to 1962. Degrees granted: Associate.

Attendance and degree information available by phone, fax, mail. Search requires name plus SSN, date of birth. Also helpful: exact years of attendance. There is no fee.

John Wesley College, Registrar, 2314 N Centennial St, High Point, NC 27265, 910-889-2262 (Fax: 910-889-2261). Hours: 8AM-5PM. Enrollment: 130. Alumni records are maintained here also. Call 910-889-2262. Degrees granted: Associate; Bachelors. Certification: Christian Workers.

Attendance and degree information available by phone, fax, mail. Search requires name plus SSN, date of birth. Also helpful: exact years of attendance. There is no fee.

Johnson C. Smith University, Registrar, 100 Beatties Ford Rd, Charlotte, NC 28216, 704-378-1013 (Fax: 704-330-1302). Hours: 8:15AM-5:15PM. Enrollment: 1400. Records go back to 1867. Alumni records are maintained here also. Call 704-378-1026. Degrees granted: Bachelors. Adverse incident record source- Mrs. Treva Norman, 704-378-1039.

Attendance information available by phone, fax, mail. Search requires name only. Also helpful: SSN, exact years of attendance. There is no fee.

Degree information available by phone, fax, mail. Search requires name only. Also helpful: exact years of attendance. There is no fee.

Johnston Community College, Registrar, PO Box 2350, Smithfield, NC 27577, 919-934-3051 (Fax: 919-934-2823). Hours: 8AM-9PM M-Th; 8AM-5PM F. Enrollment: 2700. Records go back to 1971. Degrees granted: Associate.

Attendance and degree information available by phone, fax, mail. Search requires name plus SSN. Also helpful: date of birth, approximate years of attendance. There is no fee.

Lees-McRae College, Registrar, PO Box 128, Banner Elk, NC 28604, 704-898-8738 (Fax: 704-898-8814). Hours: 8:30AM-4:30PM. Enrollment: 657. Records go back to 1932. Alumni records are maintained here at the same phone number. Degrees granted: Bachelors. Special programs- Performing Arts. Adverse incident record source- Student Development, 704-898-5241 X8211.

Attendance and degree information available by phone, fax, mail. Search requires name plus SSN, exact years of attendance. Also helpful: approximate years of attendance. There is no fee.

Lenoir Community College, Registrar, PO Box 188, Kinston, NC 28501, 919-527-6223 X306 (Fax: 919-527-1199). Hours: 8AM-5PM M-Th, 8AM-4PM F. Enrollment: 1545. Records go back to 1960's. Alumni records are maintained here at the same phone number. Degrees granted: Associate.

Attendance and degree information available by phone, fax, mail. Search requires name plus SSN. Also helpful: date of birth, exact years of attendance. There is no fee.

Lenoir-Rhyne College, Registrar, Seventh Ave and Eighth St NE, Hickory, NC 28603, 704-328-7278 (Fax: 704-328-7368). Hours: 8:30AM-5PM. Enrollment: 1500. Records go back to 1940's. Alumni records are maintained here at the same phone number. Degrees granted: Bachelors; Masters. Adverse incident record source- Dean, 704-328-7246.

Attendance and degree information available by phone, fax, mail. Search requires name plus SSN. There is no fee.

Louisburg College, Registrar Office, 501 N Main St, Louisburg, NC 27549, 919-496-2521 (Fax: 919-496-1788). Hours: 8:30AM-5PM. Enrollment: 568. Records go back to 1900's. Alumni records are maintained here at the same phone number. Degrees granted: Associate. Adverse incident record source- Student Affairs, 919-496-2521 X235.

Attendance and degree information available by phone, fax, mail. Search requires name plus SSN. There is no fee.

Mars Hill College, Registrar, Marshall St, Mars Hill, NC 28754, 704-689-1151 (Fax: 704-689-1437). Hours: 8AM-4:30PM. Enrollment: 1184. Alumni records are maintained here also. Call 704-689-1102. Degrees granted: Bachelors.

Attendance information available by phone, fax. Search requires name plus approximate years of attendance. Also helpful: SSN, exact years of attendance. There is no fee.

Degree information available by phone, fax. Search requires name only. There is no fee.

Martin Community College, Registrar, 1161 Kuhukee Park Rd, Williamston, NC 27892-9988, 919-792-1521 (Fax: 919-792-4425). Hours: 8AM-4:30PM. Enrollment: 800. Records go back to 1968. Degrees granted: Associate.

Attendance and degree information available by phone, fax, mail. Search requires name only. Also helpful: SSN, date of birth, approximate years of attendance. There is no fee.

Mayland Community College, Registrar, PO Box 547, Spruce Pine, NC 28777, 704-765-7351 (Fax: 704-765-0728). Hours: 8AM-5PM. Enrollment: 750. Records go back to 1972. Degrees granted: Associate. Adverse incident record source- MIS Department.

Attendance and degree information available by fax, mail. Search requires name plus SSN, signed release. Also helpful: date of birth, exact years of attendance. There is no fee.

McDowell Technical Community College, Registrar, Rte 1 Box 170, Marion, NC 28752, 704-652-6021 X401 (Fax: 704-652-1014). Hours: 9AM-8:30PM T,Th; 8AM-4PM M,W,F. Enrollment: 1000. Records go back to 1964. Degrees granted: Associate.

Attendance and degree information available by phone, fax, mail. Search requires name plus SSN. There is no fee.

Meredith College, Registrar, 3800 Hillsborough St, Raleigh, NC 27607-5298, 919-829-8593 (Fax: 919-829-2878). Hours: 8AM-5PM. Enrollment: 2011. Records go back to 1900's. Alumni records are maintained here also. Call 919-829-8391. Degrees granted: Bachelors; Masters. Special programs-Graduate Dept., 919-829-8353. Adverse incident record source-Dean of Students, 919-829-8521.

Attendance and degree information available by mail. Search requires name plus SSN. There is no fee.

Methodist College, Registrar, 5400 Ramsey St, Fayetteville, NC 28311-1420, 910-630-7036 (Fax: 910-630-2123). Hours: 8AM-5PM. Enrollment: 1600. Records go back to 1963. Alumni records are maintained here also. Call 910-630-7170. Degrees granted: Associate; Bachelors. Adverse incident record source- Security Office, 910-630-7149.

Attendance information available by phone, fax, mail. Search requires name plus SSN. There is no fee.

Degree information available by phone, fax, mail. Search requires name plus SSN, approximate years of attendance. There is no fee.

Mitchell Community College, Registrar, 500 W Broad St, Statesville, NC 28677, 704-878-3246 (Fax: 704-878-0872). Hours: 8AM-5PM. Enrollment: 1450. Records go back to 1930. Alumni records are maintained here also. Call 704-878-3356. Degrees granted: Associate.

Attendance and degree information available by phone, fax, mail. Search requires name plus SSN. Also helpful: date of birth, exact years of attendance. There is no fee.

Montgomery Community College, Registrar, PO Box 787, Troy, NC 27371, 910-576-6222 X225 (Fax: 910-576-2176). Hours: 8AM-5PM M-Th; 8AM-3PM F. Enrollment: 600. Records go back to 1967. Degrees granted: Associate.

Attendance and degree information available by written request only. Search requires name plus SSN, approximate years of attendance, signed release. Also helpful: date of birth, exact years of attendance. There is no fee.

Montreat-Anderson College, Registrar, PO Box 1267, Montreat, NC 28757, 704-669-8011 X3731 (Fax: 704-669-9554). Hours: 8AM-4:30PM. Enrollment: 1000. Records go back to 1916. Alumni records are maintained here also. Call 704-669-8011 X3703. Degrees granted: Associate. Adverse incident record source- Student Development, 704-669-8011 X3632.

Attendance and degree information available by phone, fax, mail. Search requires name plus SSN. Also helpful: date of birth, exact years of attendance. There is no fee.

Mount Olive College, Registrar, 634 Henderson St, Mount Olive, NC 28365, 919-658-7165 X3019 (Fax: 919-658-8934). Hours: 8AM-5PM. Enrollment: 1800. Records go back to 1951. Alumni records are maintained here also. Call 919-658-2502. Degrees granted: Associate; Bachelors. Special programs- Modular Programs, 800-653-0854. Adverse incident record source- Dean, 919-658-7167.

Attendance and degree information available by phone, fax, mail. Search requires name plus SSN. Also helpful: exact years of attendance. There is no fee.

Nash Community College, Registrar, PO Box 7488, Rocky Mount, NC 27804-0488, 919-443-4011 (Fax: 919-443-0828). Hours: 8AM-5PM M-Th; 8AM-4PM F. Enrollment: 1800. Records go back to 1968. Degrees granted: Associate.

Attendance and degree information available by phone, fax, mail. Search requires name plus SSN. Also helpful: date of birth, exact years of attendance. There is no fee.

North Carolina Agricultural and Technical State University, Office of the Registrar, Dowdy Bldg, 1601 E Market St, Greensboro, NC 27411, 910-334-7595 (Fax: 910-334-7466). Hours: 8AM-5PM M,Th,F; 8AM-7PM T,W. Enrollment: 7300. Records go back to 1930. Alumni records are maintained here also. Call 910-334-7583. Degrees granted: Bachelors; Masters; Doctorate. Adverse incident record source-University Police, 910-334-7675.

Attendance information available by phone, fax, mail. Search requires name plus SSN. Also helpful: exact years of attendance. There is no fee.

Degree information available by phone, fax, mail. Search requires name only. Also helpful: SSN, exact years of attendance. There is no fee.

North Carolina Central University, Registrar, 1801 Fayetteville St, Durham, NC 27707, 919-560-6262 (Fax: 919-560-5012). Hours: 8AM-5PM. Enrollment: 5000. Alumni records are maintained here also. Call 919-560-6363. Degrees granted: Bachelors; Masters. Adverse incident record source- Student Life, 919-560-6490.

School will not confirm attendance information.

Degree information available by phone, mail. Search requires name plus SSN. Also helpful: date of birth, exact years of attendance. There is no fee.

North Carolina School of the Arts, Registrar, 200 Waughtown St, PO Box 12189, Winston-Salem, NC 27117-2189, 910-770-3294. Hours: 8:30AM-5PM. Enrollment: 589. Records go back to 1965. Alumni records are maintained here also. Call 910-770-3332. Degrees granted: Bachelors; Masters.

Attendance and degree information available by phone, mail. Search requires name only. There is no fee.

North Carolina State University, Registrar, PO Box 7313, Raleigh, NC 27695-7313, 919-515-2572 (Fax: 919-515-2376). Hours: 8AM-5PM. Enrollment: 27500. Alumni Records Office: Alumni Association, PO Box 7503, Raleigh, NC 27695-7503. Degrees granted: Bachelors; Masters; Doctorate.

Attendance and degree information available by phone, fax, mail. Search requires name plus SSN. Also helpful: date of birth, exact years of attendance. There is no fee.

North Carolina Weselyan College, Registrar, 3400 N Wesleyan Blvd, Rocky Mount, NC 27804, 919-985-5124 (Fax: 919-977-3701). Hours: 8AM-5PM. Enrollment: 1800. Records go back to 1960. Alumni records are maintained here also. Call 919-985-5145. Degrees granted: Bachelors.

Attendance and degree information available by phone, fax, mail. Search requires name only. Also helpful: SSN, exact years of attendance. There is no fee.

Pamlico Community College, Registrar, PO Box 185, Hwy 306 S, Grantsboro, NC 28529, 919-249-1851 (Fax: 919-249-2377). Hours: 7:30AM-10PM. Enrollment: 205. Records go back to 1962. Alumni records are maintained here at the same phone number. Degrees granted: Associate.

Attendance and degree information available by mail. Search requires name plus SSN. Also helpful: date of birth, exact years of attendance. There is no fee.

Peace College, Registrar, 15 E Peace St, Raleigh, NC 27604, 919-508-2250 (Fax: 919-508-2326). Hours: 8:15AM-4:45PM. Enrollment: 450. Records go back to 1900. Alumni records are maintained here also. Call 919-508-2000. Degrees granted: Associate; Bachelors. Adverse incident record source-Business Office, 919-508-2000.

Attendance information available by phone, fax, mail. Search requires name plus SSN, date of birth, exact years of attendance. There is no fee.

Degree information available by phone, fax. Search requires name plus SSN, date of birth, exact years of attendance. There is no fee.

Pfeiffer University, Registrar, PO Box 960, Misenheimer, NC 28109-0960, 704-463-1360 X2056 (Fax: 704-463-1363). Hours: 8AM-Noon, 1-5PM. Enrollment: 1360. Records go back to 1955. Alumni records are maintained here at the same phone number. Degrees granted: Bachelors; Masters.

Attendance and degree information available by phone, fax, mail. Search requires name only. Also helpful: SSN, date of birth, exact years of attendance. There is no fee.

Piedmont Bible College, Registrar, 716 Franklin St, Winston-Salem, NC 27101, 910-725-8344 (Fax: 910-725-5522). Hours: 8AM-5PM. Enrollment: 300. Records go back to 1947. Alumni records are maintained here at the same phone number. Degrees granted: Associate; Bachelors; Masters. Adverse incident record source- Development Dept, 910-725-8344 X233.

Attendance and degree information available by phone, fax, mail. Search requires name only. Also helpful: approximate years of attendance. There is no fee.

Piedmont Community College, Registrar, PO Box 1197, Roxboro, NC 27573, 910-599-1181 (Fax: 910-597-3817). Hours: 8AM-5PM. Enrollment: 1200. Records go back to 1970. Alumni records are maintained here at the same phone number. Degrees granted: Associate.

Attendance and degree information available by phone, fax, mail. Search requires name only. Also helpful: SSN, exact years of attendance. There is no fee.

Pitt Community College, Registrar, PO Drawer 7007, Greenville, NC 27835-7007, 919-321-4232 (Fax: 919-321-4209). Hours: 8AM-5PM. Enrollment: 4700. Records go back to 1963. Alumni records are maintained here also. Call 919-321-4322. Degrees granted: Associate. Adverse incident record source- Campus Security, 919-321-4210.

Attendance and degree information available by fax, mail. Search requires name plus SSN. Also helpful: date of birth, exact years of attendance. There is no fee.

Queens College, Registrar, 1900 Selwyn Ave, Charlotte, NC 28274, 704-337-2211 (Fax: 704-337-2218). Hours: 8:30AM-6PM M-Th, 8:30AM-3PM F. Enrollment: 1600. Records go back to 1900. Alumni records are maintained here also. Call 704-337-2214. Degrees granted: Bachelors; MBA, MED, MAT. Adverse incident record source- Student Development, 704-327-2226.

Attendance and degree information available by phone, fax, mail. Search requires name plus SSN, date of birth. There is no fee.

Randolph Community College, Registrar, PO Box 1009, Asheboro, NC 27204-1009, 910-629-1471 (Fax: 910-629-4695). Hours: 8AM-5PM. Enrollment: 1400. Records go back to 1963. Degrees granted: Associate.

Attendance and degree information available by phone, fax, mail. Search requires name plus SSN. Also helpful: date of birth, exact years of attendance. There is no fee.

Richmond Community College, Registrar, PO Box 1189, Hamlet, NC 28345, 910-582-7113 (Fax: 910-582-7102). Hours: 8AM-5PM. Enrollment: 1600. Records go back to 1966. Alumni records are maintained here also. Call 910-582-7122. Degrees granted: Associate.

Attendance and degree information available by phone, fax, mail. Search requires name plus SSN, approximate years of attendance. Also helpful: date of birth, exact years of attendance. There is no fee.

Roanoke Bible College, Registrar, 714 First St, Elizabeth City, NC 27909, 919-338-5191 (Fax: 919-338-0801). Hours: 9AM-5PM. Enrollment: 160. Records go back to 1948. Alumni records are maintained here at the same phone number. Degrees granted: Associate; Bachelors.

Attendance and degree information available by phone, fax, mail. Search requires name plus SSN, date of birth. Also helpful: exact years of attendance. There is no fee.

Roanoke-Chowan Community College, Registrar, Rte 2 Box 46-A, Ahoskie, NC 27910, 919-332-5921 (Fax: 919-332-2210). Hours: 8:15AM-5PM. Enrollment: 500. Records go back to 1967. Alumni records are maintained here at the same phone number. Degrees granted: Associate; Curriculums. Adverse incident record source- Jack Henderson, 919-332-5921 X243.

Attendance and degree information available by phone, fax, mail. Search requires name plus SSN. Also helpful: date of birth, exact years of attendance. There is no fee.

Robeson Community College, Registrar, PO Box 1420, Lumberton, NC 28359, 910-738-7101 (Fax: 910-671-4143). Enrollment: 1450. Records go back to 1966. Degrees granted: Associate; Vocational Diploma.

Attendance and degree information available by mail. Search requires name plus SSN, signed release. Also helpful: date of birth, exact years of attendance. There is no fee.

Rockingham Community College, Registrar, PO Box 38, Wentworth, NC 27375-0038, 910-342-4261 X118 (Fax: 910-349-9986). Hours: 8AM-5PM. Enrollment: 2000. Records go back to 1966. Alumni records are maintained here at the same phone number. Degrees granted: Associate. Adverse incident record source- Dean of Student Services.

Attendance and degree information available by phone, fax, mail. Search requires name plus SSN, date of birth. There is no fee.

Rowan-Cabarrus Community College, Registrar, PO Box 1595, Salisbury, NC 28145, 704-637-0760 X270 (Fax: 704-633-6804). Enrollment: 3500. Records go back to 1963. Alumni records are maintained here also. Call 704-637-0760 X216. Degrees granted: Associate.

Attendance and degree information available by phone, fax, mail. Search requires name plus SSN. Also helpful: date of birth, approximate years of attendance. There is no fee.

Salem College, Registrar, Salem Station, PO Box 10548, Winston-Salem, NC 27180, 910-721-2618 (Fax: 910-917-5432). Hours: 8:30AM-5PM. Enrollment: 900. Records go back to 1925. Alumni records are maintained here also. Call 910-721-2608. Degrees granted: Bachelors; Masters.

Attendance and degree information available by phone, fax, mail. Search requires name only. Also helpful: SSN, date of birth, exact years of attendance. There is no fee.

Sampson Community College, Registrar, PO Drawer 318, Clinton, NC 28328, 910-592-8081. Enrollment: 995. Records go back to 1965. Degrees granted: Associate.

Attendance and degree information available by phone, fax, mail. Search requires name plus SSN. Also helpful: date of birth, exact years of attendance. There is no fee.

Sandhills Community College, Registrar, 2200 Airport Rd, Pinehurst, NC 28374, 910-695-3739 (Fax: 910-695-1823). Hours: 8AM-4:30PM. Enrollment: 2300. Records go back to 1963. Degrees granted: Associate.

Attendance information available by phone, mail. Search requires name plus SSN, approximate years of attendance. Also helpful: date of birth. There is no fee.

Degree information available by phone, mail. Search requires name plus SSN, approximate years of attendance. There is no fee.

Shaw University, Registrar, 118 E South St, Raleigh, NC 27601, 919-546-8415 (Fax: 919-546-8235). Hours: 8AM-5PM. Enrollment: 2432. Records go back to 1930. Alumni records are maintained here also. Call 919-546-8270. Degrees granted: Bachelors. Adverse incident record source- Dean of Students, 919-546-8270.

Attendance information available by phone, fax, mail. Search requires name plus SSN, approximate years of attendance. There is no fee.

Degree information available by fax, mail. Search requires name plus SSN, approximate years of attendance. There is no fee.

Southeastern Baptist Theological Seminary, Registrar, PO Box 1889, Wake Forest, NC 27588-1889, 919-556-3101 X215 (Fax: 919-556-0998). Hours: 8AM-4:30PM. Records go back to 1954. Degrees granted: Associate; Bachelors; Masters; Doctorate.

Attendance and degree information available by phone, fax, mail. Search requires name plus approximate years of attendance. Also helpful: SSN, exact years of attendance. There is no fee.

Southeastern Community College, Registrar, PO Box 151, Whiteville, NC 28472, 910-642-7141 (Fax: 910-642-5658). Hours: 8:30AM-5PM. Records go back to 1965. Degrees granted: Associate.

Attendance and degree information available by fax, mail. Search requires name plus SSN, date of birth, signed release. Also helpful: exact years of attendance. There is no fee.

Southwestern Community College, Registrar, 447 College Drive, Sylva, NC 28779, 704-586-4091 X219

(Fax: 704-586-3129). Hours: 8AM-5PM. Enrollment: 1140. Records go back to 1964. Alumni records are maintained here at the same phone number. Degrees granted: Associate. Special programs- Diploma-Electro-Neuro Diagnostics Technology. Adverse incident record source- Director of Counselling.

Attendance and degree information available by fax, mail. Search requires name plus SSN, date of birth, signed release. There is no fee.

St. Andrews Presbyterian College, Registrar, 1700 Dogwood Mile, Laurinburg, NC 28352, 910-277-5221 (Fax: 910-277-5020). Hours: 8:30AM-5PM. Enrollment: 750. Records go back to 1961. Alumni records are maintained here also. Call 910-277-5668. Degrees granted: Bachelors.

Attendance and degree information available by mail. Search requires name plus exact years of attendance, signed release. Also helpful: SSN, date of birth. There is no fee.

St. Augustine's College, Registrar, 1315 Oakwood Ave, Raleigh, NC 27610-2298, 919-516-4199 (Fax: 919-516-4415). Hours: 8AM-6PM. Enrollment: 1700. Records go back to 1920. Alumni records are maintained here also. Call 919-516-4023. Degrees granted: Bachelors. Adverse incident record source- Public Safety, 919-516-4220 or 919-516-4640.

Attendance and degree information available by phone, fax, mail. Search requires name plus SSN, exact years of attendance. Also helpful: date of birth. There is no fee.

St. Mary's College, Registrar, 900 Hillsborough St, Raleigh, NC 27603-1689, 919-839-4009 (Fax: 919-832-4831). Hours: 8:30AM-4:30PM. Enrollment: 215. Records go back to 1852. Alumni records are maintained here also. Call 919-839-4101. Degrees granted: Associate. Adverse incident record source- Dean, 919-839-4015.

Attendance and degree information available by phone, fax, mail. Search requires name plus SSN, date of birth, exact years of attendance. There is no fee.

Stanly Community College, Registrar, 141 College Dr, Albemarle, NC 28001, 704-982-0121 X237 (Fax: 704-982-0819). Hours: 8AM-5PM. Enrollment: 1800. Records go back to 1924. Degrees granted: Associate.

Attendance and degree information available by phone, fax, mail. Search requires name only. Also helpful: SSN, exact years of attendance. There is no fee.

Surry Community College, Dept of Student Services, PO Box 304, Dobson, NC 27017, 910-386-8121 (Fax: 910-386-8951). Hours: 8AM-8PM. Enrollment: 3200. Records go back to 1965. Alumni records are maintained here at the same phone number. Degrees granted: Associate. Adverse incident record source- Student Services, 910-386-8121 X238.

Attendance and degree information available by phone, fax, mail. Search requires name plus SSN, approximate years of attendance. Also helpful: exact years of attendance. There is no fee.

Tri-County Community College, Registrar, 2300 Hwy 64 E, Murphy, NC 28906, 704-837-6810 (Fax: 704-837-3266). Hours: 8AM-6:30PM. Enrollment: 900. Records go back to 1991. Degrees granted: Associate.

Attendance and degree information available by phone, fax, mail. Search requires name plus SSN. Also helpful: exact years of attendance. There is no fee.

University of North Carolina at Asheville, Registrar, One University Heights, Asheville, NC 28804, 704-251-6575 (Fax: 704-251-6841). Hours: 8AM-4:30PM. Enrollment: 3300. Records go back to 1930's. Alumni records are maintained here also. Call 704-251-6512. Degrees granted: Bachelors; Masters. Adverse incident record source- Student Affairs.

Attendance and degree information available by phone, fax, mail. Search requires name plus SSN. Also helpful: date of birth, exact years of attendance. There is no fee.

University of North Carolina at Chapel Hill,
Registrar, CB # 2100, 105 Hanes Hall, Chapel Hill, NC 27599-2100, 919-962-3954 (Fax: 919-962-3349). Hours: 8AM-4:30PM. Enrollment: 24468. Records go back to 1902. Alumni Records Office: Geo. Watts Hill Alumni Center, CB 9180, Chapel Hill, NC 27599-2100. Degrees granted: Bachelors; Masters; Doctorate. Adverse incident record source- Student Affairs, 919-962-4041.

Attendance and degree information available by phone, fax, mail. Search requires name plus SSN. Also helpful: date of birth. There is no fee.

University of North Carolina at Charlotte,
Registrar, 921 University City Blvd, Charlotte, NC 28223, 704-547-3658 (Fax: 704-547-3340). Hours: 8AM-5PM. Enrollment: 15708. Records go back to 1960. Alumni records are maintained here also. Call 704-547-2273. Degrees granted: Bachelors; Doctorate. Adverse incident record source- Dept. of Student Account, 704-547-2215: Dept. of Traffic, 704-547-4285

Attendance information available by phone, fax, mail. Search requires name plus SSN, date of birth, approximate years of attendance. There is no fee.

Degree information available by phone, fax, mail. Search requires name plus SSN, approximate years of attendance. There is no fee.

University of North Carolina at Greensboro,
Registrar, 1000 Spring Garden St, Greensboro, NC 27412, 910-334-5946 (Fax: 910-334-3649). Hours: 8AM-5PM. Enrollment: 12600. Records go back to 1891. Alumni records are maintained here also. Call 910-334-5696. Degrees granted: Doctorate. Adverse incident record source- Student Affairs.

Attendance and degree information available by phone, mail. Search requires name plus SSN. There is no fee.

University of North Carolina at Pembroke
(The), Registrar, One University Dr, PO Box 1510, Pembroke, NC 28372, 910-521-6303 (Fax: 910-521-6548). Hours: 8AM-5PM. Enrollment: 3000. Formerly Pembroke State University Records go back to 1900's. Alumni records are maintained here at the same phone number. Degrees granted: Masters. Adverse incident record source- Student Affairs.

Attendance and degree information available by phone, fax, mail. Search requires name plus SSN. Also helpful: exact years of attendance. There is no fee.

University of North Carolina at Wilmington,
Registrar, 601 S College Rd, Wilmington, NC 28403-3297, 910-962-3125 (Fax: 910-962-3887). Hours: 8AM-5PM. Enrollment: 7463. Records go back to 1947. Degrees granted: Bachelors; Masters.

Attendance information available by mail. Search requires name plus SSN, date of birth, approximate years of attendance, signed release. There is no fee.

Degree information available by fax, mail. Search requires name plus SSN, date of birth, approximate years of attendance, signed release. There is no fee.

Vance-Granville Community College, Registrar,
PO Box 917, Poplar Creek Rd, Henderson, NC 27536, 919-492-2061 (Fax: 919-430-0460). Enrollment: 2500. Records go back to 1970. Alumni records are maintained here at the same phone number. Degrees granted: Associate. Adverse incident record source- Dean of Students, 919-492-2061 X282.

Attendance and degree information available by phone, fax, mail. Search requires name plus SSN, date of birth. Also helpful: exact years of attendance. Fee is $1.00.

Wake Forest University, Registrar, PO Box 7207
Reynolds Station, Winston-Salem, NC 27109, 910-759-5206

(Fax: 910-759-6056). Hours: 8AM-5PM. Enrollment: 3860. Records go back to 1834. Alumni records are maintained here also. Call 910-759-5264. Degrees granted: Bachelors; Masters; Doctorate. Adverse incident record source- 91-759-5255.

Attendance and degree information available by phone, fax, mail. Search requires name plus SSN, exact years of attendance. Also helpful: date of birth. There is no fee.

Wake Technical Community College, Registrar,
9191 Fayetteville Rd, Raleigh, NC 27603-5696, 919-662-3253. Enrollment: 7000. Records go back to 1963. Degrees granted: Associate.

Attendance and degree information available by written request only. Search requires name plus SSN, date of birth. Also helpful: exact years of attendance. There is no fee.

Warren Wilson College, Registrar, PO Box 9000,
Asheville, NC 28815-9000, 704-298-3325 (Fax: 704-299-3326). Hours: 8AM-5PM. Enrollment: 620. Records go back to 1894. Alumni records are maintained here at the same phone number. Degrees granted: Bachelors; Masters.

Attendance and degree information available by phone, fax, mail. Search requires name plus SSN, date of birth. There is no fee.

Wayne Community College, Admissions & Records, Caller Box 8002, Goldsboro, NC 27533-8002, 919-735-5151 (Fax: 919-736-3204). Hours: 8AM-5PM. Enrollment: 2237. Degrees granted: Associate. Adverse incident record source- Security: Student Development

Attendance and degree information available by phone, fax, mail. Search requires name plus SSN. Also helpful: date of birth, exact years of attendance. There is no fee.

Western Carolina University, Registrar, Cullowhee,
NC 28723, 704-227-7232 (Fax: 704-227-7217). Hours: 8AM-5pm. Enrollment: 6500. Records go back to 1920. Alumni records are maintained here also. Call 704-227-7335. Degrees granted: Bachelors; Masters. Adverse incident record source- Public Safety, 704-227-7301.

Attendance and degree information available by phone, fax, mail. Search requires name only. Also helpful: SSN, date of birth, approximate years of attendance. There is no fee.

Western Piedmont Community College, Registrar, 1001 Burkemont Ave, Morganton, NC 28655-9978, 704-438-6041 (Fax: 704-438-6065). Hours: 8AM-5PM. Enrollment: 2500. Records go back to 1963. Degrees granted: Associate.

Attendance information available by phone, fax, mail. Search requires name plus SSN. Also helpful: date of birth, exact years of attendance. There is no fee.

Degree information available by phone, fax, mail. Search requires name only. Also helpful: SSN, date of birth, exact years of attendance. There is no fee.

Wilkes Community College, Registrar, PO Box 120,
Collegiate Dr, Wilkesboro, NC 28697-0120, 910-838-6140 (Fax: 910-838-6277). Hours: 8AM-5PM. Enrollment: 2162. Records go back to 1966. Alumni records are maintained here at the same phone number. Degrees granted: Associate.

Attendance and degree information available by phone, fax, mail. Search requires name plus SSN. Also helpful: date of birth, exact years of attendance. There is no fee.

Wilson Technical Community College, Registrar, 902 Herring Ave, PO Box 4305, Wilson, NC 27893, 919-291-1195 X277 (Fax: 919-243-7148). Hours: 8AM-5PM. Enrollment: 1300. Records go back to 1956. Alumni records are maintained here also. Call 919-291-1195 X276. Degrees granted: Associate. Adverse incident record source- Dean of Fiscal Affairs, 919-291-1195 X221.

Attendance and degree information available by phone, fax, mail. Search requires name only. Also helpful: SSN, exact years of attendance. There is no fee.

Wingate College, Registrar, Wingate, NC 28174-0157, 704-233-8126 (Fax: 704-233-8110). Hours: 8:30AM-5PM. Enrollment: 1400. Records go back to 1896. Alumni records are maintained here also. Call 704-233-8114. Degrees granted: Associate; Bachelors; Masters. Special programs- Winter National Program (Study Foreign Country/Visit): Wingate in London (1 Semester of study in London). Adverse incident record source- 704-233-8126.

Attendance and degree information available by phone, fax, mail. Search requires name plus SSN, date of birth, exact years of attendance. There is no fee.

Winston-Salem State University, Registrar, 601 Martin Luther King,Jr. Dr, Winston-Salem, NC 27110, 910-750-2000 (Fax: 910-750-3336). Degrees granted: Bachelors.

Attendance and degree information available by phone, fax, mail. Search requires name plus SSN, approximate years of attendance. Also helpful: exact years of attendance. There is no fee.

Trade and Vocational Schools

Academy of Artistic Hair Design, 314 Tenth St, North Wilkesboro, NC 28659, 910-838-4571

Alliance Tractor Trailer Training Center, PO Box 883, Arden, NC 28704, 704-684-4454

Alliance Tractor Trailer Training Centers II (Training Center V Campus), PO Box 579, Benson, NC 27504, 910-892-8370

American Business and Fashion Institute, 1515 Mockingbird Ln #600, Charlotte, NC 28209, 704-523-3738

American Education Institute of Cosmetology, 415 Seventh Ave SW, Hickory, NC 29601, 704-327-2887

Arnold's Beauty College, 3117 Shannon Rd, Durham, NC 27707, 919-493-9557

Black World College of Hair Design, PO Box 669403, Charlotte, NC 28266, 704-372-8172

Brookstone College of Business, 8307 Univers. Exec. Park Dr #240, Charlotte, NC 28262, 704-547-8600

Brookstone College of Business (Branch Campus), 7815 National Service Rd, Greensboro, NC 27409, 910-668-2627

Burke Academy of Cosmetic Art, 304 W Union St, Morganton, NC 28655, 704-437-1028

Burke Academy of Cosmetic Art (Branch Campus), 609 W 29th St, Newton, NC 28658, 704-465-7281

Carolina Beauty College, 801 English Rd, High Point, NC 27262, 910-886-4712

Carolina Beauty College (Branch Campus), 5430-0 N Tryon St, Charlotte, NC 28213, 704-597-5641

Carolina Beauty College (Branch Campus), 5106 N Roxboro Rd, Durham, NC 22704, 919-477-4014

Carolina Beauty College (Branch Campus), 2001 E Wendover Ave, Greensboro, NC 27405, 910-272-2966

Carolina Beauty College (Branch Campus), 1201 Stafford St #12, Monroe, NC 28110, 704-283-2514

Carolina Beauty College (Branch Campus), 19012 S Main St, Salisbury, NC 28144, 704-639-0382

Carolina Beauty College (Branch Campus), 7736-C Northpoint Blvd, Winston-Salem, NC 27127, 910-759-7969

Fayetteville Beauty College, 2018 Ft Bragg Rd, Fayetteville, NC 28303, 910-484-9370

Hairstyling Institute of Charlotte, 209-B S KIngs Dr, Charlotte, NC 28204, 704-334-5511

Kings College, 322 Lamar Ave, Charlotte, NC 28204, 704-372-0266

Lyndon B. Johnson Civilian Conservation Center, 466 Job Corps Dr, Franklin, NC 28734, 704-369-7338

Maria Parham Hospital, Inc., PO Drawer 59, Henderson, NC 27536, 919-438-4143

Mille-Motte Business College (Branch Campus), 606 S College Rd, Wilmington, NC 28403, 910-392-4660

Mr. David's School of Hair Design, 4348 Market St, Wilmington, NC 28403, 910-763-4418

Naval Health Sciences Education and Training Command (Field Medical Service School), Camp Lejeune, NC 28542, 910-451-0929

North Carolina Academy of Cosmetic Art, 131 Sixth Ave E, Hendersonville, NC 28792, 910-692-5211

Northern Hospital of Surry County School of Medical Technology, PO Box 1101, Mount Airy, NC 27030, 910-719-7124

Oconaluftee Job Corps Civilian Conservation Center, 200 Park Cir, Cherokee, NC 28719, 704-497-5411

Salisbury Business College, 1400 Jake Alexander Blvd W, Salisbury, NC 28147, 704-636-4071

Schnenck Civilian Conservation Center, 98 Schcnck Dr, Pisgah Forest, NC 28768, 704-877-3291

Skyland Academy, 170 Rosscraggon Rd, Skyland, NC 28776, 704-687-1643

Winston-Salem Barber School, 1531 Silas Creek Pkwy, Winston-Salem, NC 27127, 910-724-1459

State Licensing & Business Registration Quick Finder Index

Architecture, Engineering & Surveying.cc.
Architect #3 (4100) .... ☎ 919-733-9544
Engineer #48 (14000)................................... ☎ 919-781-9499
Geologist #46 .... ☎ 919-781-7240
Landscape Architect #44 .... ☎ 919-781-7759
Surveyor #48 (3000)..................................... ☎ 919-781-9499

Business - Court & Legal Services.cc.
Attorney #45... ☎ 919-828-4886
Lobbyist #40... ☎ 919-733-3406
Notary Public #40 (170000)......................... ☎ 919-733-3406
Shorthand Reporter #30 .... ☎ 919-733-7107

Business - General Services.cc.
Auctioneer #2 (3000) .... ☎ 919-981-5066
Public Accountant-CPA #37 .... ☎ 919-733-4222
Solicitor #22 (1541) .... ☎ 919-733-4510

Construction & Manufacturing.cc.
Boiler/Pressure Vessel Inspector #24 .... ☎ 919-662-4690
Electrical Contractor/Inspector #6 (13000).. ☎ 919-733-9042
Elevator Inspector #24 (13000)..................... ☎ 919-662-4744
General Contractor #33 (19000)................... ☎ 919-571-4183
Heating Contractor #32 .... ☎ 919-733-9350
Plumber #32 (11000)...................................... ☎ 919-733-9350

Education.cc.
School Librarian #29 (3000) .... ☎ 919-733-2570

Environmental & Agriculture.cc.
Pesticide Applicator #16 (10000)................. ☎ 919-733-3556
Pesticide Consultant #16 (100) .... ☎ 919-733-3556
Pesticide Dealer #16.................................... ☎ 919-733-3556
Private Applicator #16 .... ☎ 919-733-3556
Solid Waste Facility Operator #28 .... ☎ 919-733-4996
Veterinarian #50 (2683) .... ☎ 919-733-7689
Waste Water Treatment Plant Operator #28. ☎ 919-733-4996

Financial - Real Estate, Insurance & Banking.cc.
Bank #27 .... ☎ 919-733-6344
Banking Division #17 .... ☎ 919-733-3016
Insurance Agent #23..................................... ☎ 919-733-7487
Investment Advisor #27 .... ☎ 919-733-6344
Investment Representative #26 .... ☎ 919-733-3924
Real Estate Broker #39 (43056) .... ☎ 919-733-9580
Real Estate Dealer #39 .... ☎ 919-733-9580

Health & Beauty.cc.
Acupuncturist #47 .... ☎ 919-876-3885
Ambulance Attendant #21 .... ☎ 919-733-2285
Apprentice Barber #4 .... ☎ 919-715-5000
Barber #4 (12000) .... ☎ 919-715-5000
Barber Instructor #4..................................... ☎ 919-715-5000
Burial Division #18 (124) .... ☎ 919-733-3403
Cemetery #19 (178)....................................... ☎ 919-981-2536
Cemetery Salesperson #19 .... ☎ 919-981-2536
Chiropractor #41 919-828-0600

Crematory #7 .... ☎ 919-733-9380
DME (Rx Device) #11 .... ☎ 919-942-4454
Dental Hygienist #42 (4166)......................... ✉ 919-781-4901
Dentist #42 (3786) .... ✉ 919-781-4901
Electrologist #35 (239) .... ☎ 919-832-3429
Electrologist Instructor #35........................... ☎ 919-832-3429
Embalmer #7 .... ☎ 919-733-9380
Emergency Medical Service #22 .... ☎ 919-733-2285
Funeral Director #7 .... ☎ 919-733-9380
Funeral Home/Chapel #7 .... ☎ 919-733-9380
Funeral Service #7 .... ☎ 919-733-9380
Hearing Aid Dispenser/Fitter #43 .... ☎ 910-715-8750
Hospital #22.. ☎ 919-733-7461
Licensure #22.. ☎ 919-733-1610
Medical Doctor #47 .... ☎ 919-876-3885
Nurse #8.. ☎ 919-782-3211
Nursing Home #22... ☎ 919-733-7461
Nursing Home Administrator #5 (800) .... ✉ 919-571-4164
Occupational Therapist #9 (1350) .... ✉ 919-832-1380
Occupational Therapist Assistant #9............. ✉ 919-832-1380
Optometrist/Optician #10 (1000)................... ☎ 919-733-9321
Pharmacist #11 (7897).................................. ☎ 919-942-4454
Pharmacy #11 .... ☎ 919-942-4454
Physical Therapist #49 .... ☎ 919-489-7814
Physician's Assistant #47 .... ☎ 919-876-3885
Physician-Pharmacy #11............................... ☎ 919-942-4454
Podiatrist #12 (390) .... ☎ 919-468-8055
Provisional Occ. Therapist/Assistant #9 .... ✉ 919-832-1380
Sanitarian #14 .... ☎ 704-495-8593
Speech Pathologist/Audiologist #31 (2762) . ☎ 910-272-1828

Investigations & Security.cc.
Alarm Installer #1 919-779-1611
Alarm System Business License #1 919-779-1611
Armed Security Guard #38 .... ☎ 919-662-4387
Fire Sprinkler Contractor/Inspector #32 .... ☎ 919-733-9350
Polygraph Examiner #38............................... ☎ 919-662-4387
Private Investigator #38 .... ☎ 919-662-4387

Social Services.cc.
Counselor #13... ☎ 919-515-2244
Day Care Administrator #21 .... ☎ 919-733-2285
Day Care Teacher #21 .... ☎ 919-733-2285
Marital & Family Therapist (Marriage & Family Therapist) #34 (546) .... ☎ 910-724-1288
Psychological Associate #36......................... ☎ 704-262-2258
Psychologist #36 (1828) .... ☎ 704-262-2258
Social Worker #15 .... ☎ 910-625-1679

Sports & Entertainment.cc.
Alcoholic Beveral Control #20 .... ☎ 919-779-0700
Amusement Device #24................................. ☎ 919-662-4690
Bingo Registration #22 (323) 919-733-3029
Certification #22 .... ☎ 919-733-7461
Firearms Instructor #38................................. ☎ 919-662-4387
Taxidermist #25 .... ☎ 919-733-4984

State Licensing & Business Registration

(1) Alarm Systems Licensing Board, PO Box 29500, Raleigh, NC 27603, 919-779-1611

(2) Auctioneer Licensing Board, 1313 Navaho Dr, Suite 201, Raleigh, NC 27609, 919-981-5066, Fax: 919-981-5069

(3) Board of Architecture, 127 W Hargett St, Suite 304, Raleigh, NC 27601, 919-733-9544, Fax: 919-733-1272

(4) Board of Barber Examiners, 3000 G Industrial Dr, Raleigh, NC 27609, 919-715-5000

(5) Board of Examiners for Nursing Home Administrators, 3733 National Dr, Suite 228, Raleigh, NC 27612-3820, 919-571-4164, Fax: 919-571-4166

(6) Board of Examiners of Electrical Contractors, 1200 Front St, Suite 105, Raleigh, NC 27609-7554, 919-733-9042, Fax: 919-733-6105

(7) Board of Mortuary Science, 801 Hillsborough St, Ste 405 (27603), PO Box 27368, Raleigh, NC 27611, 919-733-9380, Fax: 919-733-8271

(8) Board of Nursing, PO Box 2129, Raleigh, NC 27602, 919-782-3211, Fax: 919-781-9461

(9) Board of Occupational Therapy, PO Box 2280, Raleigh, NC 27602, 919-832-1380, Fax: 919-833-1059

(10) Board of Opticians, 222 N Person St, Suite 102, PO Box 25336, Raleigh, NC 27611-5336, 919-733-9321

(11) Board of Pharmacy, PO Box 459, Carrboro, NC 27510, 919-942-4454, Fax: 919-967-5757

(12) Board of Podiatry Examiners, PO Box 1088, Raleigh, NC 27602, 919-829-8055, Fax: 919-468-8055

(13) Department of Public Instruction, 301 N Wilmington St, Education Bldg, Raleigh, NC 27601-2825, 919-733-4125

(13) Board of Registered Practicing Counselors, PO Box 21005, Raleigh, NC 27619-1005, 919-787-1980

(14) Board of Sanitarian Examiners, Route 8, Box 342, Taylorsville, NC 28681, 704-495-8593, Fax: 704-495-8593

(15) Certification Board for Social Workers, PO Box 1043, Asheboro, NC 27204, 910-625-1679, Fax: 910-625-1680

(16) Department of Agriculture, Pesticide Section, PO Box 27647, Raleigh, NC 27611, 919-733-3556, Fax: 919-733-9796

(17) Department of Commerce, 702 Oberlin Rd., Raleigh, NC 27605, 919-733-3016, Fax: 919-733-6918

(18) Department of Commerce, 430 N Salisbury St, Dobbs Bldg, Raleigh, NC 27603-5900, 919-733-3403, Fax: 919-733-0012

(19) Department of Commerce, 1100 Navaho Dr. GL-2, Raleigh, NC 27609, 919-981-2536, Fax: 919-981-2538

(20) Department of Commerce, Alcoholic Beverage Control Commission, 3322 Garner Rd, Raleigh, NC 27610-5631, 919-779-0700, Fax: 919-662-1946

(21) Department of Human Resources, 701 Borbour Dr, Raleigh, NC 27603, 919-733-2285, Fax: 919-733-7021

(22) Department of Human Resources, Division of Facility Services, 701 Barbour Dr., Raleigh, NC 27626-0530, 919-733-3029, Fax: 919-715-3073

(23) Department of Insurance, Regulatory Services, 430 N Salisbury St, Raleigh, NC 27603-5908, 919-733-7487, Fax: 919-715-3794

(24) Department of Labor, 4 W Edenton St, Labor Bldg, Raleigh, NC 27601-1092, 919-733-7394, Fax: 919-662-3588

(25) Department of Natural Resources & Community Dev, 512 N Salisbury St, Raleigh, NC 27611, 919-733-4984

(26) Department of State, Securities Divison, 300 N Salisbury St, Suite 404, Raleigh, NC 27603, 919-733-3924

(27) Department of State Treasurer, Investment & Banking Division, 325 N Salisbury St, Albemarle Bldg, Raleigh, NC 27603-1388, 919-733-0587, Fax: 919-733-6918

(28) Dept of Environment, Health & Natural Resources, 401 Oberlin, Suite 150, Raleigh, NC 27605, 919-733-4996, Fax: 919-715-3605

(29) Division of State Library, Department of Cultural Resources, 109 E Jones St, Raleigh, NC 27611, 919-733-2570, Fax: 919-733-8714

(30) Examiners for Court Reporting Standards & Testing, PO Box 2448, Raleigh, NC 27602, 919-733-7107, Fax: 919-715-5779

(31) Examiners for Speech Pathologists & Audiologists, PO Box 5545, Greensboro, NC 27435, 910-272-1828

(32) Examiners of Plumbing, Heating & Fire Sprinkler, Contractors, 801 Hillsborough St, Suite 403, Raleigh, NC 27603, 919-733-9350, Fax: 919-733-9357

(33) Licensing Board for General Contractors, 3739 National Dr, Suite 225, Raleigh, NC 27619, 919-571-4183, Fax: 919-571-4703

(34) Marital & Family Therapy Certification Board, 1001 S Marshall St, Suite 5, Winston-Salem, NC 27101-5893, 910-724-1288, Fax: 910-777-3603

(35) North Carolina Board of Electrolysis Examiners, PO Box 10834, Raleigh, NC 27605-0834, 919-832-3429

(36) North Carolina Psychology Board, 895 State Farm Road, Suite 102, Boone, NC 28607, 704-262-2258, Fax: 704-265-8611

(37) Noth Carolina State Board of CPA Examiners, 1101 Oberlin Rd, Suite 104, PO Box 12827, Raleigh, NC 27605-2827, 919-733-4222

(38) Private Protective Services Board, PO Box 29500, Raleigh, NC 27626, 919-662-4387, Fax: 919-662-4459

(39) Real Estate Commission, 1313 Navaho Dr, Raleigh, NC 27609-7460, 919-733-9580, Fax: 919-872-0038

(40) Secretary of State, Notary Public Division, 300 N Salisbury St, Legislative Office Bldg, Raleigh, NC 27603-5909, 919-733-3406

(41) State Board of Chiropractic Examiners, 720 W Hargett St, Raleigh, NC 27603.ll (42) State Board of Dental Examiners, PO Box 32270, Raleigh, NC 27622, 919-781-4901, Fax: 919-571-8457

(43) State Board of Hearing Aid Dispensers & Fitters, 136 Oakwood Dr, Winston-Salem, NC 27103, 919-715-8750, Fax: 919-715-8774

(44) State Board of Landscape Architecture, PO Box 41225, Raleigh, NC 27629, 919-981-0923, Fax: 919-872-1598

(45) State Board of Law Examiners, PO Box 2946, Raleigh, NC 27602, 919-828-4886, Fax: 919-828-2251

(46) State Board of Licensing Geologists, PO Box 41225, (3733 Benson Dr 27609), Raleigh, NC 27629, 919-850-9669, Fax: 919-872-1598

(47) State Board of Medical Examiners, PO Box 20007, Raleigh, NC 27619, 919-828-1212, Fax: 919-828-1295

(48) State Board of Registration for Prof Engineers, 3620 Six Forks Rd, Raleigh, NC 27609, 919-781-9499, Fax: 919-781-2035

(49) State Examining Committee of Physical Therapy, 18 W Colony Pl, #121, Durham, NC 27705, 919-490-6393, Fax: 919-490-5106

North Dakota

Capitol: Bismark (Burleigh County)	
State Population	.6 Million
Number of Degree Granting Institutions:	21
Number of State Licensing & Business Registration Agencies:	115

Degree Granting Educational Institutions

Bismarck State College, Registrar, 1500 Edwards Ave, Bismarck, ND 58501, 701-224-5429 (Fax: 701-224-5550). Hours: 8AM-5PM M-Th, 8AM-4PM F. Enrollment: 2350. Alumni records are maintained here also. Call 701-224-5431. Degrees granted: Associate.

Attendance and degree information available by phone, fax, mail. Search requires name plus SSN, date of birth, approximate years of attendance. There is no fee.

Dickinson State University, Registrar, 291 Campus Dr, Dickinson, ND 58601, 701-277-2331 (Fax: 701-227-2006). Hours: 7:45AM-4:30PM. Enrollment: 1600. Records go back to 1918. Alumni records are maintained here also. Call 701-227-2082. Degrees granted: Associate; Masters. Certification: Truck Driving.

Attendance and degree information available by phone, fax, mail. Search requires name only. Also helpful: SSN, date of birth, exact years of attendance. There is no fee. Expedited service available for $3.00.

Fort Berthold Community College, Registrar, PO Box 490, New Town, ND 58763, 701-627-3665 (Fax: 701-627-3609). Hours: 8AM-5PM. Enrollment: 210. Records go back to 1978. Degrees granted: Associate.

Attendance and degree information available by phone, fax, mail. Search requires name plus SSN, date of birth. There is no fee.

Jamestown College, Registrar, 600 College Ln, Jamestown, ND 58405, 701-252-3467 (Fax: 701-253-4318). Hours: 8AM-5PM. Enrollment: 1080. Records go back to 1920. Alumni records are maintained here also. Call 701-252-3467 X2557. Degrees granted: Bachelors.

Attendance and degree information available by phone, fax, mail. Search requires name only. Also helpful: SSN, date of birth, exact years of attendance. There is no fee.

Little Hoop Community College, Registrar, PO Box 269, Fort Totten, ND 58335, 701-766-4415 (Fax: 701-766-4077). Hours: 8AM-4:30PM. Enrollment: 150. Records go back to 1974. Degrees granted: Associate; Vocational.

Attendance and degree information available by fax, mail. Search requires name plus SSN, approximate years of attendance, signed release. There is no fee.

Mayville State University, Registrar, 330 Third St NE, Mayville, ND 58257, 701-786-4774 (Fax: 701-786-4748). Hours: 8AM-Noon, 12:30-4:30PM. Enrollment: 780. Records go back to 1889. Alumni records are maintained here also. Call 701-786-4854. Degrees granted: Associate; Bachelors. Adverse incident record source- Student Services, 701-786-4842.

Attendance and degree information available by phone, fax, mail. Search requires name plus SSN, date of birth. Also helpful: exact years of attendance. There is no fee.

Medcenter One College of Nursing, Registrar, 512 N Seventh St, Bismarck, ND 58501, 701-224-6271 (Fax: 701-224-6967). Hours: 8AM-4:30PM. Enrollment: 90. Records go back to 1909. Alumni records are maintained here also. Call 701-224-6283. Degrees granted: Bachelors.

Attendance and degree information available by phone, fax, mail. Search requires name plus date of birth, approximate years of attendance. Also helpful: SSN, exact years of attendance. There is no fee.

Minot State University, Registrar, Minot, ND 58707, 701-858-3340 (Fax: 701-839-6933). Hours: 7:30AM-4:30PM. Enrollment: 3761. Records go back to 1913. Alumni records are maintained here also. Call 701-858-3234. Degrees granted: Associate; Bachelors; Masters.

Attendance information available by phone, fax, mail. Search requires name only. Also helpful: SSN, date of birth, approximate years of attendance. There is no fee.

Degree information available by phone, fax, mail. Search requires name only. Also helpful: SSN, date of birth, exact years of attendance. There is no fee.

North Dakota State College of Science, Registrar, 800 N Sixth St, Wahpeton, ND 58076, 800-342-4325 X2203 (Fax: 701-671-2145). Hours: 7:45AM-4:45PM. Enrollment: 2500. Records go back to 1903. Alumni records are maintained here at the same phone number. Degrees granted: Associate. Adverse incident record source- Registrar's Office .

Attendance and degree information available by phone, fax, mail. Search requires name plus SSN, approximate years of attendance. Also helpful: date of birth. There is no fee.

North Dakota State University, Office of the Registrar, PO Box 5196, Fargo, ND 58105, 701-231-8295 (Fax: 701-231-8959). Hours: 8AM-5PM Sep-May; 7:30AM-4PM Jun-Aug. Enrollment: 9600. Records go back to 1896. Alumni Records Office: PO Box 5144, Fargo, ND 58105. Degrees granted: Bachelors; Masters; Doctorate. Adverse incident record source-Student Affairs.

Attendance and degree information available by phone, fax, mail. Search requires name only. Also helpful: SSN, date of birth, exact years of attendance. There is no fee.

North Dakota State University (Bottineau), Registrar, First St and Simrall Blvd, Bottineau, ND 58318, 701-228-5487 (Fax: 701-228-5499). Hours: 8AM-5PM. Enrollment: 370. Records go back to 1906. Alumni records are maintained here also. Call 701-228-5435. Degrees granted: Associate.

Attendance and degree information available by phone, fax, mail. Search requires name plus SSN, date of birth, approximate years of attendance. There is no fee.

Sitting Bull College, Registrar, HC1 Box 4, Fort Yates, ND 58538, 701-854-3861 (Fax: 701-854-3403). Hours: 8AM-4:30PM. Enrollment: 229. Formerly Standing Rock College Records go back to 1971. Alumni records are maintained here at the same phone number. Degrees granted: Associate.

Attendance and degree information available by phone, fax, mail. Search requires name plus SSN, date of birth, approximate years of attendance. There is no fee.

Tri-College University, Registrar, 306 Ceres Hall, North Dakota State University, Fargo, ND 58105, 701-231-8170 (Fax: 701-231-7205). Records are not housed here. They are located at North Dakota State College of Science, Registrar, 800 N Sixth St, Wahpeton, ND 58076.

Trinity Bible College, Academic Records Office, 50 S Sixth St, Ellendale, ND 58436, 701-349-3621 X2034 (Fax: 701-349-5443). Hours: 8AM-5PM. Enrollment: 354. Records go back to 1948. Alumni records are maintained here also. Call 701-349-5621 X2036. Degrees granted: Associate; Bachelors.

Attendance and degree information available by phone, fax, mail. Search requires name only. There is no fee.

Turtle Mountain Community College, Registrar, PO Box 340, Belcourt, ND 58316-0340, 701-477-5605 (Fax: 701-477-5028). Hours: 8AM-4:30PM. Enrollment: 440. Records go back to 1973. Degrees granted: Associate. Adverse incident record source- Student Support Services.

Attendance and degree information available by phone, fax, mail. Search requires name plus SSN. Also helpful: date of birth, exact years of attendance. There is no fee.

United Tribes Technical College, Registrar, 3315 University Dr, Bismarck, ND 58504, 701-255-3285 X216 (Fax: 701-255-7718). Hours: 8AM-5PM. Enrollment: 265. Records go back to 1969. Degrees granted: Associate.

Attendance and degree information available by phone, fax, mail. Search requires name plus SSN, date of birth, exact years of attendance. There is no fee.

University of Mary, Registrar's Office, 7500 University Dr, Bismarck, ND 58504-9652, 701-255-7500 X410 (Fax: 701-255-7687). Hours: 8AM-4:30PM. Enrollment: 1900. Records go back to 1959. Alumni records are maintained here at the same phone number. Degrees granted: Associate; Bachelors; Masters.

Attendance and degree information available by phone, fax, mail. Search requires name plus SSN. There is no fee.

University of North Dakota, Records & Registration, Box 8232, University Station, Grand Forks, ND 58202-8232, 701-777-2711 (Fax: 701-777-2696). Hours: 8AM-4:30PM. Enrollment: 10500. Records go back to 1883. Alumni records are maintained here also. Call 701-777-2611. Degrees granted: Associate; Bachelors; Masters; Doctorate. Adverse incident record source- Affirmative Action, 701-777-4171.

Attendance and degree information available by phone, fax, mail. Search requires name plus SSN, exact years of attendance. Also helpful: date of birth. There is no fee.

University of North Dakota (Lake Region), Registrar, N College Dr, Devils Lake, ND 58301, 701-662-1515 (Fax: 701-662-1570). Hours: 8AM-4:30PM. Enrollment: 700. Records go back to 1941. Alumni records are maintained here also. Call 701-662-1520. Degrees granted: Associate. Adverse incident record source- Student Services, 701-662-1513.

Attendance and degree information available by phone, fax, mail. Search requires name only. Also helpful: SSN, date of birth, exact years of attendance. There is no fee.

University of North Dakota (Williston), Registrar, PO Box 1326, Williston, ND 58801, 701-774-4212 (Fax: 701-774-4211). Hours: 8AM-5PM. Enrollment: 900. Records go back to 1961. Alumni records are maintained here at the same phone number. Degrees granted: Associate.

Attendance information available by written request only. Search requires name plus SSN, signed release. Also helpful: date of birth, exact years of attendance. There is no fee.

Degree information available by phone, fax, mail. Search requires name plus SSN. Also helpful: date of birth, exact years of attendance. There is no fee.

Valley City State University, Registrar, College St, Valley City, ND 58072, 701-845-7295 (Fax: 701-845-7245). Hours: 7:45AM-4:30PM. Enrollment: 1000. Records go back to 1892. Alumni records are maintained here also. Call 701-845-7411. Degrees granted: Bachelors.

Attendance and degree information available by phone, fax, mail. Search requires name only. Also helpful: SSN, date of birth, exact years of attendance. There is no fee.

Trade and Vocational Schools

Aaker's Business College, 201 N 3rd St, Grand Forks, ND 58203, 701-772-6646

Interstate Business College, 2720 32nd Ave SW, Fargo, ND 58103, 701-232-2477

Interstate Business College (Branch Campus), 520 E Main Ave, Bismarck, ND 58501, 701-255-0779

Meyer Vocational Technical School, PO Box 2126, Minot, ND 58702, 701-852-0427

Minot School for Allied Health, 110 Burdick Expy W, Minot, ND 58701, 701-857-5620

Moler Barber College of Hairstyling, 16 S Eighth St, Fargo, ND 58103, 701-232-6773

Travel Career Institute, 218 N 4th St, Bismarck, ND 58504, 701-258-9419

State Licensing & Business Registration Quick Finder Index

Architecture, Engineering & Surveying
Architect #45 (450)...☎ 701-852-4178
Engineer #38 (2000) ....☎ 701-258-0786
Engineer/Land Surveyor #38..........................☎ 701-258-0786
Land Surveyor #38 ....☎ 701-258-0786

Business - Court & Legal Services
Attorney #43 (1800) ....☎ 701-328-4201
Lobbyist #41 (500) ....☎ 701-328-3665
Notary Public #41 (10000) ....☎ 701-328-3666

Business - General Services
Auction Clerk #36 ....☎ 701-328-2400
Auctioneer #36 (300).......................................☎ 701-328-2400
Charitable Solicitation #41 (400) ....☎ 701-328-3665
Employment Agency #26 ....☎ 701-328-2660
Professional Fund Raiser #41 (100) ....☎ 701-328-3665
Public Accountant-CPA #44 (2300) ....☎ 701-775-7100
Transient Merchant #3 (51)............................☎ 701-328-2329
Weighman/Weighmaster #54 ....☎ 701-328-2400

Construction & Manufacturing
Contractor/General Contractor #41 (5000) ....☎ 701-328-3665
Electrician #28 (2647)....................................☎ 701-328-9522
General Contractor #41 ....☎ 701-328-3665
Heating & Air Conditioning Contractor #41
....☎ 701-328-3665
Heating & Air Conditioning Mechanic #41
....☎ 701-328-3665
Monitoring Well Contractor #52 (27) ....☎ 701-328-2754
Oil & Gas Wellhead Welder #42....................☎ 701-328-2910
Plumber #34 (1230)..☎ 701-328-9977
Sewer & Water Contractor/Installer #34
(490)...☎ 701-328-9977

Education
School Counselor #27.....................................☎ 701-328-2264
School Media Specialist #27 ....☎ 701-328-2264
School Principal #27..☎ 701-328-2264
School Superintendent #27..............................☎ 701-328-2264
Teacher #27 ....☎ 701-328-2264

Environmental & Agriculture
Abstractor #1 (200)..☎ 701-947-2446
Aerial Sprayer #32..☎ 701-328-9650
Asbestos Abatement Contractor #30..............☎ 701-328-5200
Asbestos Abatement Inspector #30 ....☎ 701-328-5200
Asbestos Abatement Project Planner #30 ......☎ 701-328-5200
Asbestos Abatement Supervisor #30..............☎ 701-328-5200

Asbestos Worker #30......................................☎ 701-328-5200
Landfill Operator #8 ....☎ 701-328-6140
Municipal Waste-Solid Waste Facility #8......☎ 701-328-6140
Pesticide Applicator #21.................................☎ 701-328-4756
Pesticide Dealer #21 ....☎ 701-328-4756
Soil Classifier #18..701-225-5113
Veterinarian #20 (400)....................................✉ 701-328-2655
Veterinary Technician #20...............................✉ 701-328-2655
Waste Water Incinerator Operator #24...........☎ 701-328-6628
Waste Water System Operator #24 (700).......☎ 701-328-6628
Water Conditioning Contractor/Installer #34
(40) ....☎ 701-328-9977
Water Distribution System Operator #24 (700)
....☎ 701-328-6628
Water Well Contract Driller #52 ....☎ 701-328-2754
Water Well Pump & Pitless Unit #52.............☎ 701-328-2754
Weather Modifier #2.......................................☎ 701-328-4940

Financial - Real Estate, Insurance & Banking
Abstract Company #1 ....☎ 701-947-2446
Check Seller #22 (13) ....☎ 701-328-9933
Debt Collector/Collection Agency #22 (100)
....☎ 701-328-9933
Insurance Agent #31 (11000) ....✉ 701-328-3548
Insurance Broker #31 (800).............................✉ 701-328-3548
Investment Advisor #42..................................☎ 701-328-2910
Oil & Gas Broker #42 ....☎ 701-328-2910
Real Estate Agent #37 (1200).........................☎ 701-328-9749
Real Estate Appraiser #37...............................☎ 701-222-1051
Real Estate Broker #37 (750) ....☎ 701-328-9749
Securities Agent #42.......................................☎ 701-328-2910
Securities Dealer #42......................................☎ 701-328-2910

Health & Beauty
Barber #6 (360)...☎ 701-523-3327
Beauty Shop Manager/Operator #9 (3740) ....✉ 701-224-9800
Chiropractor #7 (193) ....✉ 701-352-1690
Clinical Laboratory Scientist/Technician #8
....☎ 701-328-6140
Cosmetologist #9 (2225).................................✉ 701-224-9800
Cosmetologist Instructor #9 (55) ....✉ 701-224-9800
Dental Assistant #11 ....✉ 701-223-1474
Dental Hygienist #11 (420) ....✉ 701-223-1474
Dentist #11 (400) ....✉ 701-223-1474
Dietitian/Nutritionist (Registered Dietitian) #12
(260) ....☎ 701-777-3752
Electrologist #9 ....✉ 701-224-9800

Embalmer/Funeral Director #46 (289) .... ✉ 701-662-2511
Emergency Medical Technician #23 (2800)
.... ☎ 701-328-2388
Environmental Health Practitioner #8 .... ☎ 701-328-6140
Esthetician/Manicurist #9 (36) .... ✉ 701-224-9800
Funeral Director #46 .... ✉ 701-662-2511
Hearing Aid Dealer/Fitter #47 (4) .... ☎ 701-222-0201
Massage Therapist #48 701-235-9208
Medical Doctor #49 (2500) .... ☎ 701-328-6500
Nurse #33 .... ☎ 701-328-9777
Nursing Home Administrator #14 (175) .... ☎ 701-222-4867
Nutritionist #12 .... ☎ 701-777-3752
Occupational Therapist #50 .... ☎ 701-293-7971
Optometrist #51 .... ✉ 701-225-9333
Osteopathic Physician #49 .... ☎ 701-223-9485
Pharmacist #15 (250) .... ☎ 701-258-9535
Physical Therapist/Assistant #53 (800) .... ☎ 701-352-0125
Physician's Assistant #49 (150) .... ☎ 701-328-6500
Podiatrist #16 .... ☎ 701-252-1050
Respiratory Care Practitioner #39 (350) .... ☎ 701-255-4451
Sanitary Pumper #8 .... ☎ 701-328-6140
Speech-Language Pathologist/Audiologist #13
(650) .... ✉ 701-777-4421

Investigations & Security
Police Officer #3 .... ☎ 701-328-2210
Polygraph Operator #3 (16) .... ☎ 701-328-2329

Private Detective #35 (125) .... ☎ 701-222-3063

Social Services
Addiction Counselor #4 (240) .... ☎ 701-255-1439
Adoption Service #25 .... ☎ 701-328-4805
Day Care Service #25 .... ☎ 701-328-4809
Foster Care Program #25 .... ☎ 701-328-3587
Professional Counselor #10 .... ☎ 701-777-2729
Psychologist #17 (169) .... ✉ 701-663-2321
Social Worker #19 (2014) .... ☎ 701-222-0255

Sports & Entertainment
Alcoholic Beverage Control #3 (1401) .... ☎ 701-328-2329
Athletic Trainer #5 (80) .... ☎ 701-280-3460
Boxer/Kickboxer #40 (200) .... ☎ 701-328-3665
Boxing #40 .... ☎ 701-328-2219
Fishing Guide #29 (100) .... ✉ 701-328-6300
Racing #40 .... ☎ 701-328-2219
Taxidermist #29 (100) .... ✉ 701-328-6300

Transportation
Aircraft Registration #32 .... ☎ 701-328-9650
Aircraft Sales #32 .... ☎ 701-328-9650
Airport #32 .... ☎ 701-328-9650
Pilot Registration #32 .... ☎ 701-328-9650

State Licensing & Business Registration Agency Information

(1) Abstractors Board of Examiners, PO Box 551, New Rockford, ND 58356, 701-947-2446, Fax: 701-947-2443

(2) Atmospheric Resource Board, State Water Commission, 900 E Boulevard Ave, Bismarck, ND 58505, 701-328-2788, Fax: 701-328-4749

(3) Attorney General's Office, Alcoholic Beverage Licensing Division, 600 E Blvd Ave, State Capitol, 1st Floor, Bismarck, ND 58505, 701-328-2329, Fax: 701-328-3535

(4) Board of Addiction Counseling Examiners, 1120 College Dr, Suite 205, Bismarck, ND 58501, 701-255-1439, Fax: 701-255-1439

(5) Board of Athletic Trainers, Dakota Sports Medicine, 1702 S University Dr, Box 6001, Fargo, ND 58103, 701-280-3460, Fax: 701-298-6698

(6) Board of Barber Examiners, Box 885, Bowman, ND 58623, 701-523-3327, Fax: 701-574-3126

(7) Board of Chiropractic Examiners, PO Box 185, Grafton, ND 58237, 701-352-1690, Fax: 701-352-2258

(8) Board of Clinical laboratory Practices, Department of Health & Consolicated Laboratories, 2635 E Main (58501-0937), PO Box 937, Bismarck, ND 58502, 701-328-6140, Fax: 701-328-6145

(9) Board of Cosmetology, Box 2177, Bismarck, ND 58502, 701-224-9800, Fax: 701-222-8756

(10) Board of Counselor Examiners, PO Box 8255, Grand Forks, ND 58202, 701-777-2729

(11) Board of Dental Examiners, Box 7246, Bismarck, ND 58507, 701-223-1474, Fax: 701-224-0038

(12) Board of Dietetic Practice, PO Box 6142, Grand Forks, ND 58206, 701-777-3752, Fax: 701-777-3650

(13) Board of Examiners in Audiology/Speech Pathology, Box 7189, Grand Forks, ND 58202-7189, 701-777-4421, Fax: 701-777-4365

(14) Board of Examiners in Nursing Home Adminstrators, 120 W Thayer Ave, Bismarck, ND 58501, 701-222-4867, Fax: 701-223-0977

(15) Board of Pharmacy, PO Box 1354, Bismarck, ND 58502-1354, 701-328-9535, Fax: 701-328-9312

(16) Board of Podiatric Medicine, Dr Hofsommez, 1402 25th St. S, Fargo, ND 58103-3606, 701-232-5479, Fax: 701-237-9532

(17) Board of Psychologist Examiners, 1406 - 2nd St NW, Mandan, ND 58554, 701-663-2321, Fax: 701-663-2598

(18) Board of Registry for Professional Soil Classifier, 2493 - 4th Ave W, Dickinson, ND 58601.ll Board of Social Worker Examiners, PO Box 914, Bismarck, ND 58502, 701-222-0255, Fax: 701-224-9824

(19) Board of Veterinary Medical Examiners, 600 E Boulevard Ave, 6th Floor, Bismarck, ND 58505-, 701-328-2655, Fax: 701-328-4567

(20) Department of Agriculture, Pesticide Division, 600 E Boulevard Ave, 6th Floor, Bismarck, ND 58505-0020, 701-328-4756, Fax: 701-328-4567

(21) Department of Banking & Financial Institutions, 2900 North 19th Street, Suite 3, Bismarck, ND 58501-5305, 701-328-9933, Fax: 701-328-9955

(22) Department of Health, Division of Emergency Health Services, 600 E Boulevard Ave, State Capitol Bldg, Bismarck, ND 58545-0200, 701-328-2388, Fax: 701-328-4727

(23) Department of Health & Consolidated Laboratories, Environmental Health Section, 600 E Boulevard Ave, Bismarck, ND 58505-0200, 701-328-6628, Fax: 701-328-6206

(24) Department of Human Services, Children & Family Services, 600 E Boulevard Ave, 3rd Floor, Bismarck, ND 58505-0250, 701-328-4809, Fax: 701-328-2359

(25) Department of Labor, 600 E Boulevard Ave, Bismarck, ND 58505, 701-328-2660, Fax: 701-328-2031

(26) Department of Public Instruction, Certification Division, 600 E Boulevard Ave, 9th Floor, Bismarck, ND 58505-0440, 701-328-2264, Fax: 701-328-4770

(27) Electrical Board, PO Box 857, Bismarck, ND 58502, 701-328-9522, Fax: 701-328-9524

(28) Game & Fish Department, 100 N Bismarck Expwy, Bismarck, ND 58501-5095, 701-328-6300, Fax: 701-328-6352

(29) Health & Consolidated Laboratories, Registration Divsion, 1200 Missouri Ave., Bismarck, ND 58506, 701-328-5200, Fax: 701-328-5188

(30) Insurance Department, 600 E Boulevard Ave, 5th Floor, Bismarck, ND 58505-0320, 701-328-2440, Fax: 701-328-4880

(31) North Dakota Aeronautics Commission, Municipal Airport, PO Box 5020, Bismarck, ND 58502, 701-328-9650, Fax: 701-328-9656

(32) Nursing Board, 919 S 7th St, Suite 504, Bismarck, ND 58504, 701-328-9777, Fax: 701-328-9785

(33) Plumbing Board, 204 W Thayer Ave, Bismarck, ND 58501, 701-328-9977, Fax: 701-328-9979

(34) Private Investigators Licensing, PO Box 7026, Bismarck, ND 58507, 701-222-3063, Fax: 701-222-3063

(35) Public Service Commission, State Capitol, 12th Floor, Bismarck, ND 58505-0480, 701-328-2400, Fax: 701-328-2410

(36) Real Estate Commission, 314 E Thayer (58501), PO Box 727, Bismarck, ND 58502-0727, 701-328-9749, Fax: 701-328-9750

(37) Registration for Prof. Engineers & Land Surveyors, Box 1375, Bismarck, ND 58502-1357, 701-258-0786, Fax: 701-258-0786

(38) Respiratory Care Examining Board, 1912 N Bell, Bismarck, ND 58501, 701-255-4451, Fax: 701-255-9149

(39) Secretary of State, Licensing Division, 600 E Boulevard Ave, 1st Floor, Bismarck, ND 58505-0040, 701-328-3665, Fax: 701-328-2992

(40) Secretary of State, Licensing Division, Capitol Bldg, 600 E Boulevard Ave, 1st Floor, Bismarck, ND 58505-0500, 701-328-3666, Fax: 701-328-2992

(41) Securities Commissioner, 600 E Boulevard Ave, 5th Floor, Bismarck, ND 58505-0510, 701-328-2910, Fax: 701-255-3113

(42) State Bar Board, 600 E Boulevard Ave, 1st Floor-Judicial Wing, Bismarck, ND 58505-0530, 701-328-4201, Fax: 701-328-4480

(43) State Board of Accountancy, 2701 S Columbia Rd, Grand Forks, ND 58201, 701-775-7100

(44) State Board of Architects, 2705 - 4TH Ave, NW, Minot, ND 58703, 701-852-4178, Fax: 701-852-4179

(45) State Board of Funeral Directors, PO Box 632, Devil's Lake, ND 58201, 701-662-2511

(46) State Board of Hearing Aid Dealers & Fitters, 1929 N Washington St, Bismarck, ND 58501, 701-222-0201, Fax: 701-258-9652

(47) State Board of Massage, 22 Fremont Dr SW, Fargo, ND 58103, 701-235-9208

(48) State Board of Medical Examiners, 418 E Broadway Ave, Suite 12, Bismarck, ND 58501, 701-328-6500, Fax: 701-328-6505

(49) State Board of Occupational Therapy Pratice, 1837 S 15th St, Fargo, ND 58103, 701-293-7971, Fax: 701-293-7971

(50) State Board of Optometry, 45 Eight St, Dickinson, ND 58601, 701-225-0460, Fax: 701-225-9333

(51) State Board of Water Well Contractors, 900 E Boulevard Ave, Bismarck, ND 58505, 701-328-2754, Fax: 701-328-3696

(52) State Examining Committee of Physical Therapists, PO Box 69, Grafton, ND 58237, 701-352-0125, Fax: 701-352-3093

(53) Testing and Safety Division, Public Service Commission, State Capitol, 12th Fl, Bismarck, ND 58505, 701-328-2400, Fax: 701-328-2410

Ohio

Capitol: Columbus (Franklin County)	
State Population	11.1 Million
Number of Degree Granting Institutions:	171
Number of State Licensing & Business Registration Agencies:	93

Degree Granting Educational Institutions

Academy of Court Reporting, Registrar, 614 Superior Ave NW, Cleveland, OH 44113, 216-861-3222. Hours: 8AM-5PM. Records go back to 1978. Degrees granted: Associate.

Attendance and degree information available by mail. Search requires name plus SSN, date of birth, approximate years of attendance, signed release. There is no fee.

Academy of Court Reporting, (Branch), Registrar, 2930 W Market St, Akron, OH 44313, 216-861-3222 (Fax: 216-861-4517). Hours: 8AM-5PM. Records go back to 1970. Degrees granted: Associate.

Attendance and degree information available by mail. Search requires name plus SSN, date of birth, approximate years of attendance, signed release. There is no fee.

Academy of Court Reporting, (Branch), Registrar, 630 E Broad St, Columbus, OH 43215, 614-221-7770 (Fax: 614-221-8429). Hours: 8AM-5PM. Records go back to 1975. Degrees granted: Associate.

Attendance and degree information available by mail. Search requires name plus SSN, date of birth, exact years of attendance, signed release. There is no fee.

Air Force Institute of Technology, Registrar, 2950 P St, Wright-Patterson AFB, OH 45433, 513-255-2816 (Fax: 513-255-2791). Hours: 7:30AM-5PM. Enrollment: 625. Records go back to 1951. Alumni records are maintained here also. Call 513-255-9623. Degrees granted: Masters; Doctorate.

Attendance and degree information available by phone, fax, mail. Search requires name plus SSN, date of birth, approximate years of attendance. There is no fee.

Antonelli Institute of Art and Photography, Registrar, 124 E Seventh St, Cincinnati, OH 45202-2592, 513-241-4338 (Fax: 513-241-9396). Hours: 8AM-5PM M-Th, 8AM-4PM. Records go back to 1988. Degrees granted: Associate.

Attendance and degree information available by phone, fax, mail. Search requires name plus SSN, exact years of attendance. There is no fee.

Art Academy of Cincinnati, Registrar, 1125 St. Gregory St, Cincinnati, OH 45202, 513-562-8749 (Fax: 513-562-8778). Hours: 8:30AM-5PM M,W,Th. Enrollment: 187. Alumni records are maintained here also. Call 513-562-8746. Degrees granted: Associate; Bachelors; Masters.

Attendance information available by phone, fax, mail. Search requires name plus approximate years of attendance. Also helpful: SSN, exact years of attendance. There is no fee.

Degree information available by phone, fax, mail. Search requires name only. Also helpful: SSN, exact years of attendance. There is no fee.

Ashland University, Registrar, 401 College Ave, Ashland, OH 44805, 419-289-5028 (Fax: 419-289-5333). Hours: 7:30AM-5PM. Enrollment: 3155. Records go back to 1921. Alumni records are maintained here also. Call 419-289-5040. Degrees granted: Associate; Bachelors; Masters. Special programs- Seminary, 419-289-5907.

Attendance and degree information available by phone, fax, mail. Search requires name only. Also helpful: SSN, date of birth, exact years of attendance. There is no fee.

Athenaeum of Ohio, Registrar, 6616 Beechmont Ave, Cincinnati, OH 45230-2091, 513-231-2223 (Fax: 513-231-3254). Hours: 8:30AM-5PM. Enrollment: 258. Alumni records are maintained here at the same phone number. Degrees granted: Masters.

Attendance and degree information available by phone, fax, mail. Search requires name only. Also helpful: SSN, approximate years of attendance. There is no fee.

Baldwin-Wallace College, Registrar, 275 Eastland Rd, Berea, OH 44017, 216-826-2126 (Fax: 216-826-6522). Hours: 8:30AM-4:30PM. Enrollment: 4716. Records go back to 1956. Alumni records are maintained here at the same phone number. Degrees granted: Bachelors; Masters.

Attendance and degree information available by phone, fax, mail. Search requires name plus SSN. Also helpful: exact years of attendance. There is no fee.

Belmont Technical College, Registrar, 120 Fox-Shannon Pl, St. Clairsville, OH 43950, 614-695-9500 (Fax: 614-

695-2247). Hours: 8AM-4:30PM. Enrollment: 1790. Records go back to 1971. Degrees granted: Associate.

Attendance and degree information available by phone, fax, mail. Search requires name plus SSN. Also helpful: exact years of attendance. There is no fee.

Bluffton College, Registrar, 280 W College Ave, Bluffton, OH 45817-1196, 419-358-3322 (Fax: 419-358-3323). Hours: 8AM-Noon, 1-5PM. Enrollment: 1000. Records go back to 1900. Alumni records are maintained here also. Call 419-358-3245. Degrees granted: Bachelors. Adverse incident record source- Student Affairs, 419-358-3248.

Attendance and degree information available by phone, fax, mail. Search requires name plus SSN, approximate years of attendance. Also helpful: exact years of attendance. There is no fee.

Bohecker's Business College, Registrar, 326 E Main St, Ravenna, OH 44266, 330-297-7319. Hours: 8AM-7PM M-Th, 8AM-3PM F. Enrollment: 150. Records go back to 1922. Degrees granted: Associate.

Attendance and degree information available by mail. Search requires name plus SSN, exact years of attendance, signed release. There is no fee.

Bowling Green State University, Office of Registration & Records, 110 Administration Bldg, Bowling Green, OH 43403, 419-372-7973 (Fax: 419-372-7977). Hours: 8AM-5PM. Enrollment: 16450. Records go back to 1914. Alumni records are maintained here at the same phone number. Degrees granted: Associate; Bachelors; Masters; Doctorate. Adverse incident record source- Student Life, 419-372-2843.

Attendance information available by phone, mail. Search requires name plus SSN. There is no fee.

Degree information available by phone, fax, mail. Search requires name plus SSN. There is no fee.

Bowling Green State University, (Firelands College), Registrar, 901 Rye Beach Rd, Huron, OH 44839, 419-433-5560 (Fax: 419-433-9696). Records are not housed here. They are located at Bowling Green State University, Office of Registration & Records, 110 Administration Bldg, Bowling Green, OH 43403.

Bradford School, Registrar, 6170 Busch Blvd, Columbus, OH 43229, 614-846-9410 (Fax: 614-846-9656). Hours: 8AM-5PM. Enrollment: 200. Records go back to 1940's. School was previously called Office Training School and Columbus Business University. Degrees granted: Associate.

Attendance and degree information available by phone, fax, mail. Search requires name plus SSN, exact years of attendance. There is no fee.

Bryant & Stratton Business Institute, Registrar, 12955 Snow Rd, Parma, OH 44130-1013, 216-265-3151 (Fax: 216-265-0325). Hours: 8AM-5PM. Records go back to 1852. Degrees granted: Associate.

Attendance and degree information available by mail. Search requires name plus SSN, exact years of attendance. There is no fee.

Bryant & Stratton Business Institute, (Branch), Registrar, Sears Bldg 3rd Fl, 691 Richmond Rd, Richmond Heights, OH 44143, 216-461-3151. Records are not housed here. They are located at Bryant & Stratton Business Institute, Registrar, 12955 Snow Rd, Parma, OH 44130-1013.

Capital University, Registrar, 2199 E Main St, Columbus, OH 43209, 614-236-6150 (Fax: 614-236-6820). Hours: 8AM-4:30PM. Enrollment: 2708. Records go back to 1850. Alumni records are maintained here also. Call 614-236-6701. Degrees granted: Bachelors; Masters; JD. Adverse incident record source- Student Services, 614-236-6611.

Attendance and degree information available by phone, fax, mail. Search requires name plus SSN, date of birth, exact years of attendance. There is no fee.

Case Western Reserve University, Registrar's Office, 10900 Euclid Ave, 223 Pardee Hall, Cleveland, OH 44106-7042, 216-368-4337 (Fax: 216-368-8711). Hours: 9AM-4PM. Enrollment: 9000. Records go back to 1896. For M.D. Degrees prior to 5/92,216-368-6621. Alumni Records Office: Alumni Association, 10900 Euclid Ave, Baker Bldg 316, Cleveland, OH 44106-7035. Degrees granted: Bachelors; Masters; Doctorate.

Attendance and degree information available by fax, mail. Search requires name plus SSN, exact years of attendance. Also helpful: date of birth. There is no fee.

Cedarville College, Registrar, N Main St, Box 601, Cedarville, OH 45314-0601, 513-766-7710 (Fax: 513-766-7663). Hours: 8AM-5PM. Enrollment: 2297. Records go back to 1800's. Alumni records are maintained here also. Call 513-766-7858. Degrees granted: Associate; Bachelors. Adverse incident record source- Student Services, 513-766-7812.

Attendance information available by phone, fax, mail. Search requires name only. Also helpful: SSN, exact years of attendance. There is no fee.

Degree information available by phone, fax, mail. Search requires name only. Also helpful: SSN, exact years of attendance. There is no fee.

Center for Pastoral Leadership Cleveland Diocese, Records Office, 28700 Euclid Ave, Wickliffe, OH 44092, 216-943-7600 (Fax: 216-943-7577). Enrollment: 90. Formerly Borromeo College of Ohio Records go back to 1957. Degrees granted: Masters. Special programs- Arts: Theological Studies. Adverse incident record source- Records Office.

Attendance and degree information available by mail. Search requires name plus SSN, exact years of attendance, signed release. There is no fee.

Central Ohio Technical College, Registrar, 1179 University Dr, Newark, OH 43055-1767, 614-366-9208 X208 (Fax: 614-366-5047). Hours: 8AM-5PM. Enrollment: 1712. Records go back to 1971. Alumni records are maintained here at the same phone number. Degrees granted: Associate.

Attendance information available by phone. Search requires name plus SSN. Also helpful: date of birth, exact years of attendance. There is no fee.

Degree information available by phone, fax, mail. Search requires name plus SSN. Also helpful: date of birth, exact years of attendance. There is no fee.

Central State University, Registrar, 1400 Brush Row Rd, Wilberforce, OH 45384, 513-376-6231 (Fax: 513-376-6530). Hours: 9AM-4PM. Enrollment: 2700. Records go back to 1947. Degrees granted: Associate; Bachelors; Masters. Adverse incident record source- Campus Police.

Attendance and degree information available by mail. Search requires name plus SSN, date of birth, exact years of attendance, signed release. There is no fee.

Chatfield College, Registrar, 20918 State Rte 251, St Martin, OH 45118, 513-875-3344 (Fax: 513-875-3912). Hours: 8AM-5PM. Enrollment: 300. Records go back to 1968. Degrees granted: Associate. Adverse incident record source- President.

Attendance and degree information available by phone, fax, mail. Search requires name plus SSN, approximate years of attendance. Also helpful: date of birth, exact years of attendance. There is no fee.

Cincinnati Bible College and Seminary, Registrar, 2700 Glenway Ave, Cincinnati, OH 45204, 513-244-8170 (Fax: 513-244-8140). Hours: 8:30AM-4:30PM. Enrollment: 900. Records go back to 1924. Alumni records are maintained here also. Call 513-244-8113. Degrees granted: Associate; Bachelors; Masters.

Attendance and degree information available by phone, fax, mail. Search requires name plus SSN. Also helpful: date of birth, exact years of attendance. There is no fee.

Cincinnati College of Mortuary Science, Registrar, Cohen Ctr, 3860 Pacific Ave, Cincinnati, OH 45207-1033, 513-745-3631 (Fax: 513-745-1909). Hours: 8AM-4PM. Records go back to 1989. Degrees granted: Associate; Bachelors.

Attendance information available by written request only. Search requires name plus signed release. Also helpful: SSN, exact years of attendance. There is no fee.

Degree information available by phone, fax, mail. Search requires name only. Also helpful: SSN, exact years of attendance. There is no fee.

Cincinnati State Technical & Community College, Registrar, 3520 Central Pkwy, Cincinnati, OH 45223, 513-569-1500 (Fax: 513-569-1495). Hours: 8AM-7PM M-Th, 8AM-5PM F. Enrollment: 5500. Records go back to 1968. Alumni records are maintained here at the same phone number. Degrees granted: Associate.

Attendance and degree information available by phone, fax, mail. Search requires name plus SSN. Also helpful: approximate years of attendance. There is no fee.

Circleville Bible College, Registrar, 1476 Lancaster Pike, PO Box 458, Circleville, OH 43113, 614-477-7740 (Fax: 614-477-7755). Hours: 8:30AM-4:30PM. Enrollment: 180. Records go back to 1948. Alumni records are maintained here also. Call 614-477-7760. Degrees granted: Associate; Bachelors.

Attendance information available by phone, fax, mail. Search requires name plus SSN, date of birth. Also helpful: exact years of attendance. There is no fee.

Degree information available by phone, mail. Search requires name plus SSN, date of birth. Also helpful: exact years of attendance. There is no fee.

Clark State Community College, Registrar, 570 E Leffels Lane, PO Box 570, Springfield, OH 45505, 513-328-6014. Hours: 8AM-5PM. Enrollment: 2200. Records go back to 1962. Degrees granted: Associate.

Attendance and degree information available by phone, fax, mail. Search requires name plus SSN. Also helpful: approximate years of attendance. There is no fee.

Cleveland College of Jewish Studies, Registrar, 26500 Shaker Blvd, Beachwood, OH 44122, 216-464-4050 (Fax: 216-464-5827). Hours: 8:30AM-4PM. Enrollment: 1000. Alumni records are maintained here at the same phone number. Degrees granted: Bachelors; Masters.

Attendance and degree information available by phone, fax, mail. Search requires name plus SSN. There is no fee.

Cleveland Institute of Art, Registrar, 11411 East Blvd, Cleveland, OH 44106, 216-421-7321 (Fax: 216-421-7333). Hours: 8:30AM-5PM. Records go back to 1882. Alumni records are maintained here also. Call 216-421-7412. Degrees granted: Bachelors. Adverse incident record source- Dean, 216-421-7428: Operations, 216-421-7314

Attendance and degree information available by phone, fax, mail. Search requires name plus SSN, date of birth, approximate years of attendance. There is no fee.

Cleveland Institute of Electronics, Inc., Registrar, 1776 E 17th St, Cleveland, OH 44114, 216-781-9400 (Fax: 216-781-0331). Hours: 8:30AM-4:45PM. Enrollment: 5600. Records go back to 1934. Degrees granted: Associate.

Attendance and degree information available by phone, fax, mail. Search requires name only. Also helpful: SSN, exact years of attendance. There is no fee.

Cleveland Institute of Music, Registrar, 11021 East Blvd, Cleveland, OH 44106, 216-795-3203 (Fax: 216-791-1530). Hours: 9AM-5PM. Records go back to 1920. Alumni records are maintained here at the same phone number. Degrees granted: Bachelors; Masters; Doctorate.

Attendance information available by fax, mail. Search requires name plus approximate years of attendance. Also helpful: SSN, date of birth, exact years of attendance. There is no fee.

Degree information available by phone, fax, mail. Search requires name plus approximate years of attendance. Also helpful: SSN, date of birth, exact years of attendance. There is no fee.

Cleveland State University, Registrar, Euclid Ave at 24th St, Cleveland, OH 44115, 216-687-3700 (Fax: 216-687-5501). Hours: 8AM-6PM M-Th; 8AM-5PM F. Degrees granted: Bachelors; Masters; Doctorate.

Attendance and degree information available by phone, fax, mail. Search requires name plus SSN, date of birth, approximate years of attendance. There is no fee.

College at Antioch University, Registrar, 795 Livermore St, Yellow Springs, OH 45387, 513-767-6401 (Fax: 513-767-7452). Hours: 8:30AM-4PM. Enrollment: 625. Formerly Antioch University Records go back to 1860. Alumni records are maintained here also. Call 513-767-6381. Degrees granted: Bachelors; Masters; Doctorate. Special programs- Antioch Education Abroad, 513-767-6366.

Attendance and degree information available by phone, mail. Search requires name plus SSN, exact years of attendance. There is no fee.

College of Mount St. Joseph, Registrar's Office, 5701 Delhi Rd, Cincinnati, OH 45233, 513-244-4621 (Fax: 513-244-4222). Hours: 8:30AM-4:30PM. Records go back to 1920. Alumni records are maintained here also. Call 513-244-4425. Degrees granted: Associate; Bachelors; Masters.

Attendance information available by phone, fax, mail. Search requires name plus SSN, approximate years of attendance. Also helpful: date of birth, exact years of attendance. There is no fee.

Degree information available by phone, fax, mail. Search requires name plus SSN. Also helpful: date of birth, exact years of attendance. There is no fee.

College of Wooster, Registrar, Wooster, OH 44691, 330-263-2366 (Fax: 330-263-2260). Hours: 8AM-Noon, 1-4:30PM. Enrollment: 1600. Records go back to 1866. Alumni records are maintained here also. Call 330-263-2324. Degrees granted: Bachelors. Adverse incident record source- Dean of Students, 330-263-2545.

Attendance and degree information available by phone, fax, mail. Search requires name plus SSN, approximate years of attendance. There is no fee.

Columbus College of Art and Design, Registrar, 107 N Ninth St, Columbus, OH 43215, 614-224-9101 (Fax: 614-222-4040). Hours: 8:30AM-5PM. Enrollment: 1760. Records go back to 1960. Alumni records are maintained here at the same phone number. Degrees granted: Bachelors. Adverse incident record source- Student Affairs, 614-224-9101.

Attendance information available by mail. Search requires name plus SSN, approximate years of attendance. There is no fee.

Degree information available by mail. Search requires name only. There is no fee.

Columbus Para-Professional Institute, Registrar, 1077 Lexington Ave, Columbus, OH 43201, 614-891-5030. Hours: 8:30AM-6PM. Records go back to 1975.

Attendance and degree information available by fax, mail. Search requires name plus SSN, date of birth, exact years of attendance, signed release. There is no fee.

Columbus State Community College, Registrar, 550 E Spring St, PO Box 1609, Columbus, OH 43216-1609, 614-227-2643 (Fax: 614-227-5117). Hours: 8AM-7:30PM M-Th; 8AM-4:30PM F. Records go back to 1963. Degrees granted: Associate.

Attendance and degree information available by mail. Search requires name only. Also helpful: SSN, exact years of attendance. There is no fee.

Cuyahoga Community College, (Eastern), Registrar, 4250 Richmond Rd, Highland Hills, OH 44122, 216-987-2021 (Fax: 216-987-2214). Hours: 8:30AM-8PM M-Th; 8:30AM-5PM F; 11AM-1PM S. Records go back to 1963. Degrees granted: Associate.

Attendance and degree information available by phone, mail. Search requires name plus SSN, date of birth. There is no fee.

Cuyahoga Community College, (Metropolitan), Registrar, 2900 Community College Ave, Cleveland, OH 44115, 216-987-4030 (Fax: 216-696-2567). Hours: 8:30AM-8PM. Records go back to 1969. Alumni Records Office: Cuyahoga Community College, 700 Carnegie Ave, Cleveland, OH 44115. Degrees granted: Associate. Adverse incident record source- Health Services, 216-987-4650.

Attendance and degree information available by phone, fax, mail. Search requires name plus SSN, approximate years of attendance. There is no fee.

Cuyahoga Community College, (Western), Admissions & Records, 11000 W Pleasant Valley Rd, Parma, OH 44130, 216-987-5150 (Fax: 216-987-5071). Hours: 8AM-8:30PM M-Th; 8AM-5PM F. Alumni Records Office: 700 Carniggi Ave, Cleveland, OH 44115. Degrees granted: Associate.

Attendance and degree information available by phone, fax, mail. Search requires name plus SSN, date of birth. Also helpful: exact years of attendance. There is no fee.

David N. Myers College, Office of Registrar, 112 Prospect Ave SE, Cleveland, OH 44115, 216-696-9000 X823 (Fax: 216-696-6430). Hours: 8:30AM-5PM. Enrollment: 1362. Formerly Dyke College Records go back to 1848. Alumni records are maintained here also. Call 216-696-9000 X861. Degrees granted: Associate; Bachelors.

Attendance and degree information available by phone, fax, mail. Search requires name plus SSN, approximate years of attendance. Also helpful: date of birth, exact years of attendance. There is no fee.

Davis College, Registrar, 4747 Monroe St, Toledo, OH 43623, 419-473-2700 (Fax: 419-473-2472). Hours: 9AM-6PM. Enrollment: 462. Records go back to 1945. Degrees granted: Associate.

Attendance and degree information available by phone, fax, mail. Search requires name plus SSN, approximate years of attendance. There is no fee.

DeVry Institute of Technology, Columbus, Registrar, 1350 Alum Creek Dr, Columbus, OH 43209, 614-253-7291 (Fax: 614-252-4108). Alumni records are maintained here at the same phone number. Degrees granted: Bachelors.

Attendance and degree information available by phone, mail. Search requires name plus SSN. There is no fee.

Defiance College, Registrar, 701 N Clinton St, Defiance, OH 43512, 419-783-2357 (Fax: 419-784-0426). Hours: 8AM-4:30PM. Enrollment: 884. Records go back to 1906. Alumni records are maintained here also. Call 419-783-3306. Degrees granted: Associate; Bachelors; Masters.

Attendance and degree information available by phone, fax, mail. Search requires name plus approximate years of attendance. Also helpful: SSN, date of birth, exact years of attendance. There is no fee.

Denison University, Registrar, PO Box B, Granville, OH 43023, 614-587-6530 (Fax: 614-587-6417). Hours: 8:30AM-4:30PM. Enrollment: 1736. Records go back to 1940. Alumni records are maintained here also. Call 614-587-6576. Degrees granted: Bachelors. Special programs- Prior to 1940; Archives, 614-587-6399. Adverse incident record source- Student Affairs (active only), 614-587-6567.

Attendance and degree information available by phone, fax, mail. Search requires name only. Also helpful: SSN, date of birth, exact years of attendance. There is no fee.

ETI Technical College, Registrar, 4300 Euclid Ave, Cleveland, OH 44103-9932, 216-431-4300. Hours: 8AM-9PM. Records go back to 1940's. Degrees granted: Associate; Bachelors.

Attendance information available by phone, fax, mail. Search requires name plus SSN, approximate years of attendance. Also helpful: exact years of attendance. There is no fee.

Degree information available by phone, fax, mail. Search requires name plus SSN. Also helpful: exact years of attendance. There is no fee.

ETI Technical College, Registrar, 1320 W Maple St NW, North Canton, OH 44720, 216-494-1214 (Fax: 216-494-8112). Hours: 9AM-5PM. Enrollment: 160. Records go back to 1983. Degrees granted: Associate. Adverse incident record source- President, 216-494-1214.

Attendance and degree information available by phone, fax, mail. Search requires name only. Also helpful: SSN. There is no fee.

ETI Technical College, (Niles), Registrar, 2076-86 Youngstown-Warren Rd, Niles, OH 44446-4398, 216-652-9916 X16 (Fax: 216-652-4399). Hours: 9AM-6PM. Enrollment: 240. Records go back to 1989. Degrees granted: Associate.

Attendance and degree information available by phone, fax, mail. Search requires name plus SSN, approximate years of attendance. There is no fee.

Edison State Community College, Registrar, 1973 Edison Dr, Piqua, OH 45356, 513-778-8600 (Fax: 513-778-1920). Hours: 8AM-5PM. Enrollment: 2755. Records go back to 1973. Degrees granted: Associate.

Attendance and degree information available by phone, fax, mail. Search requires name only. Also helpful: SSN, date of birth. There is no fee.

Franciscan University of Steubenville, Registrar, University Blvd, Steubenville, OH 43952, 614-283-6207 (Fax: 614-283-6472). Hours: 8:30AM-4:30PM. Enrollment: 2000. Records go back to 1946. Alumni records are maintained here also. Call 614-283-3771 X6414. Degrees granted: Associate; Bachelors; Masters. Special programs- MBA 4+1, 614-283-6270: Pre-Theology, 614-283-6226. Adverse incident record source- Dean, 614-283-6441.

Attendance and degree information available by phone, fax, mail. Search requires name plus SSN, approximate years of attendance. Also helpful: date of birth, exact years of attendance. There is no fee.

Franklin University, Registrar, 201 S Grant Ave, Columbus, OH 43215-5399, 614-341-6242 (Fax: 614-224-0434). Hours: 8AM-6PM M-Th; 8AM-5PM F. Enrollment: 5000. Records go back to 1950. Alumni records are maintained here also. Call 614-341-6409. Degrees granted: Associate; Bachelors; Masters.

Attendance and degree information available by phone, fax, mail. Search requires name plus SSN, approximate years of attendance. Also helpful: date of birth, exact years of attendance. There is no fee. Expedited service available for $10.00.

God's Bible College, Registrar, 1810 Young St, Cincinnati, OH 45210, 513-721-7944 X298 (Fax: 513-721-3971).

Hours: 8AM-5PM. Enrollment: 170. Records go back to 1900. Alumni records are maintained here also. Call 513-721-7944 X251. Degrees granted: Bachelors.

Attendance information available by written request only. Search requires name plus approximate years of attendance, signed release. There is no fee.

Degree information available by phone, fax, mail. Search requires name plus approximate years of attendance. There is no fee.

Hebrew Union College-Jewish Institute of Religion, Registrar, 3101 Clifton Ave, Cincinnati, OH 45220, 513-221-1875 (Fax: 513-221-0321). Enrollment: 130. Records go back to 1906. Alumni records are maintained here at the same phone number. Degrees granted: Masters; Doctorate; M.Phil.

Attendance information available by phone, fax, mail. Search requires name plus SSN, approximate years of attendance. Also helpful: exact years of attendance. There is no fee.

Degree information available by phone, fax, mail. Search requires name plus SSN, approximate years of attendance. Also helpful: exact years of attendance. There is no fee.

Heidelberg College, Registrar, 310 E Market St, Tiffin, OH 44883, 419-448-2090 (Fax: 419-448-2124). Hours: 8AM-5PM. Enrollment: 1300. Records go back to 1900. Alumni records are maintained here also. Call 419-448-2383. Degrees granted: Bachelors; Masters; Master of Arts in Counseling, Master of Arts in Education, Master of Business Administration. Adverse incident record source- Student Services, 419-448-2058.

Attendance and degree information available by phone, fax, mail. Search requires name plus exact years of attendance. There is no fee.

Hiram College, Registrar, Hiram, OH 44234, 330-569-5210 (Fax: 330-569-5211). Hours: 8:30AM-5PM. Enrollment: 1000. Alumni records are maintained here also. Call 330-569-5283. Degrees granted: Bachelors. Adverse incident record source- Dean of Students, 330-569-5233.

Attendance and degree information available by phone, fax, mail. Search requires name plus SSN. There is no fee.

Hocking Technical College, Registrar, 3301 Hocking Pkwy, Nelsonville, OH 45764, 614-753-3591 (Fax: 614-753-2586). Hours: 8AM-5:30PM M-Th, 8AM-4:30PM F. Enrollment: 5995. Records go back to 1968. Alumni records are maintained here at the same phone number. Degrees granted: Associate; LPN.

Attendance and degree information available by phone, fax, mail. Search requires name plus SSN, approximate years of attendance. There is no fee.

ITT Technical Institute, Registrar, 3325 Stop Eight Rd, Dayton, OH 45414-9915, 513-454-2267 (Fax: 513-454-2278). Hours: 8AM-5PM. Records go back to 1948. Degrees granted: Associate.

Attendance and degree information available by phone, mail. Search requires name plus approximate years of attendance. Also helpful: exact years of attendance. There is no fee.

ITT Technical Institute, Registrar, 1030 N Meridian Rd, Youngstown, OH 44509-4017, 330-747-5555 (Fax: 330-747-7718). Hours: 8AM-10PM. Records go back to 1968. Degrees granted: Associate.

Attendance and degree information available by fax, mail. Search requires name plus approximate years of attendance, signed release. There is no fee.

International College of Broadcasting, Registrar, 6 S Smithville Rd, Dayton, OH 45431-1833, 513-258-8251 (Fax: 513-258-8714). Hours: 8AM-8PM. Records go back to 1933. Degrees granted: Associate.

Attendance information available by phone, fax, mail. Search requires name only. Also helpful: SSN, date of birth, exact years of attendance. There is no fee.

Degree information available by phone, fax. Search requires name only. Also helpful: SSN, date of birth, exact years of attendance. There is no fee.

Jefferson Community College, Registrar, 4000 Sunset Blvd, Steubenville, OH 43952, 614-264-5591 (Fax: 614-264-1338). Hours: 8AM-7:30PM. Enrollment: 1550. Formerly Jefferson Technical College Records go back to 1969. Alumni records are maintained here at the same phone number. Degrees granted: Associate.

Attendance and degree information available by phone, fax, mail. Search requires name plus SSN. There is no fee.

John Carroll University, Registrar, 20700 N Park Blvd, University Heights, OH 44118, 216-397-4291 (Fax: 216-397-3049). Hours: 8:30AM-5PM. Enrollment: 3482. Records go back to 1886. Alumni records are maintained here also. Call 216-397-4322. Degrees granted: Bachelors; Masters. Adverse incident record source- Dean, 216-397-4401.

Attendance and degree information available by phone, fax, mail. Search requires name plus SSN, date of birth, approximate years of attendance. There is no fee.

Kent State University, Registrar, PO Box 5190, Kent, OH 44242, 330-672-3131 (Fax: 330-672-4836). Hours: 8AM-5PM. Enrollment: 26796. Records go back to 1921. Alumni records are maintained here also. Call 216-672-5368. Degrees granted: Associate; Bachelors; Masters; Doctorate. Adverse incident record source- Student Conduct, 216-672-4054.

Attendance information available by phone, fax, mail. Search requires name plus SSN, exact years of attendance. Also helpful: date of birth, approximate years of attendance. There is no fee.

Degree information available by phone, fax, mail. Search requires name plus SSN. Also helpful: date of birth, approximate years of attendance. There is no fee.

Kent State University, (Ashtabula), Registrar, Ms. Bates, 3325 W 13th St, Ashtabula, OH 44004, 216-964-4216 (Fax: 216-964-4269). Hours: 8AM-5PM. Records go back to 1921. Degrees granted: Associate; Bachelors.

Attendance and degree information available by fax, mail. Search requires name plus SSN, date of birth, approximate years of attendance, signed release. Also helpful: exact years of attendance. There is no fee.

Kent State University, (East Liverpool), Registrar, 400 E Fourth St, East Liverpool, OH 43920, 330-385-3805 (Fax: 330-385-3857). Hours: 8AM-8PM M-Th, 8AM-5PM F. Records go back to 1963. Alumni records are maintained here at the same phone number. Degrees granted: Associate.

Attendance and degree information available by phone, fax, mail. Search requires name plus SSN, approximate years of attendance. There is no fee.

Kent State University, (Geuaga), Registrar, 14111 Claridon-Troy Rd, Burton Township, OH 44021, 216-834-4187 (Fax: 216-834-8846). Hours: 8AM-8PM M-Th, 8AM-5PM F, 8AM-2PM Sat. Enrollment: 26800. Records go back to 1960. Degrees granted: Associate.

Attendance and degree information available by fax, mail. Search requires name plus SSN, approximate years of attendance, signed release. There is no fee.

Kent State University, (Salem), Registrar, 2491 State Rte 45 S, Salem, OH 44460, 330-332-0361 (Fax: 330-332-9256). Hours: 9AM-8PM M, 9AM-6PM T-Th, 9AM-4:30PM F. Records go back to 1965. Degrees granted: Associate; Bachelors.

Attendance and degree information available by phone, fax, mail. Search requires name plus SSN, approximate years of attendance. There is no fee.

Kent State University, (Stark), Registrar, 6000 Frank Ave NW, Canton, OH 44720, 330-499-9600 (Fax: 330-494-6121). Hours: 8AM-7:30PM M-Th, 8AM-5PM F. Enrollment: 25. Records go back to 1950. Alumni records are maintained here at the same phone number. Degrees granted: Associate; Bachelors. Adverse incident record source- Business, 330-499-9600 X231.

Attendance and degree information available by phone, fax, mail. Search requires name plus SSN, approximate years of attendance. There is no fee.

Kent State University, (Trumbull), Registrar, 4314 Mahoning Ave NW, Warren, OH 44483, 330-847-0571 (Fax: 330-847-6172). Hours: 8AM-6PM M-Th, 8AM-5PM F, 9AM-1PM Sat. Records go back to 1960. Degrees granted: Associate.

Attendance information available by fax, mail. Search requires name plus SSN, exact years of attendance. There is no fee.

Degree information available by phone, fax, mail. Search requires name plus SSN, exact years of attendance. There is no fee.

Kent State University, (Tuscarawas), Registrar, 330 University Dr NE, New Philadelphia, OH 44663-9447, 330-339-3391 (Fax: 330-339-3321). Hours: 8AM-8PM M-Th; 8AM-5PM F and when not in session. Enrollment: 1200. Records go back to 1962. Alumni Records Office: Alumni Association, Williamson Alumni Center, Kent, OH 44242. Degrees granted: Associate. Adverse incident record source- Same as above.

Attendance and degree information available by phone, fax, mail. Search requires name plus SSN. Also helpful: date of birth, exact years of attendance. There is no fee.

Kenyon College, Registrar, Gambier, OH 43022-9623, 614-427-5121 (Fax: 614-427-5615). Hours: 8:30AM-4:30PM. Enrollment: 1500. Records go back to 1930. Alumni records are maintained here also. Call 614-427-5121. Degrees granted: Bachelors. Adverse incident record source- Dean of Students, 614-427-5136.

Attendance and degree information available by phone, fax, mail. Search requires name only. Also helpful: SSN, date of birth, exact years of attendance. There is no fee.

Kettering College of Medical Arts, Registrar, 3737 Southern Blvd, Kettering, OH 45429, 513-296-7289 (Fax: 513-296-4238). Hours: 9AM-4PM M,Th; 10AM-6PM T; 9AM-Noon F. Enrollment: 625. Records go back to 1967. Alumni Records Office: Alumni Association, 3535 Southern Blvd, Kettering, OH 45429. Degrees granted: Associate.

Attendance and degree information available by phone, fax, mail. Search requires name plus SSN, exact years of attendance. There is no fee.

Lake Erie College, Registrar, 391 W Washington St, Painesville, OH 44077, 216-639-7825 (Fax: 216-352-3533). Hours: 8AM-5PM M-F; 8AM-7PM T. Enrollment: 669. Records go back to 1856. Alumni records are maintained here also. Call 216-639-7831. Degrees granted: Bachelors; Masters. Adverse incident record source- 216-639-7823.

Attendance information available by phone, fax, mail. Search requires name plus exact years of attendance. Also helpful: SSN. There is no fee.

Degree information available by phone, fax, mail. Search requires name only. Also helpful: SSN, exact years of attendance. There is no fee.

Lakeland Community College, Registrar, 7700 Clocktower Dr, Mentor, OH 44060, 216-953-7100 (Fax: 216-975-4330). Hours: 8AM-8:30PM M-Th, 7:30AM-5PM F, 8:30AM-12:30PM Sat. Enrollment: 8200. Records go back to

1967. Degrees granted: Associate. Adverse incident record source- Security Office, 216-953-7246.

Attendance and degree information available by phone, fax, mail. Search requires name plus SSN. There is no fee.

Lima Technical College, Registrar, 4240 Campus Dr, Lima, OH 45804, 419-221-1112 X319 (Fax: 419-995-8098). Hours: 8AM-5PM. Enrollment: 2583. Records go back to 1974. Alumni records are maintained here at the same phone number. Degrees granted: Associate. Adverse incident record source- Security, 419-221-1112 X499.

Attendance information available by fax, mail. Search requires name plus SSN. There is no fee.

Degree information available by phone, fax, mail. Search requires name plus SSN. There is no fee.

Lorain County Community College, Admissions & Records, 1005 N Abbe Rd, Elyria, OH 44035, 800-995-5222 (Fax: 216-365-6519). Hours: 8:30AM-7:30PM M-Th; 8:30AM-4:30PM F. Enrollment: 7000. Records go back to 1965. Alumni records are maintained here at the same phone number. Degrees granted: Associate. Adverse incident record source- Student Life, 800-995-5222 X7646: Campus Services, 800-995-5222 X7530

Attendance and degree information available by phone, fax, mail. Search requires name plus SSN, date of birth. Also helpful: exact years of attendance. There is no fee.

Lourdes College, Registrar, 6832 Convent Blvd, Sylvania, OH 43560, 419-885-4917 X207 (Fax: 419-882-3987). Hours: 8:30AM-6PM M-Th, 8:30AM-4:30PM, 9AM-1PM Sat. Enrollment: 1600. Records go back to 1958. Alumni records are maintained here at the same phone number. Degrees granted: Bachelors. Adverse incident record source- Student Services, 419-885-4917 X200.

Attendance information available by fax, mail. Search requires name plus SSN, date of birth, approximate years of attendance, signed release. There is no fee.

Degree information available by phone, fax, mail. Search requires name plus SSN, date of birth, approximate years of attendance. There is no fee.

MTI Business College, Registrar, 1140 Euclid Ave, Cleveland, OH 44115, 216-621-8228 (Fax: 216-621-6488). Hours: 7:30AM-5:30PM. Enrollment: 125. Records go back to 1961. Alumni records are maintained here at the same phone number. Degrees granted: Associate.

Attendance and degree information available by phone, fax, mail. Search requires name plus approximate years of attendance. Also helpful: SSN, date of birth, exact years of attendance. There is no fee.

Malone College, Registrar, 515 25th St NW, Canton, OH 44709, 330-471-8129 (Fax: 330-454-6977). Hours: 8AM-5PM. Enrollment: 2016. Records go back to 1892. Alumni records are maintained here also. Call 330-471-8237. Degrees granted: Bachelors; Masters.

Attendance and degree information available by phone, fax, mail. Search requires name plus SSN, date of birth. There is no fee.

Marietta College, Registrar, Marietta, OH 45750, 614-376-4728 (Fax: 614-376-4896). Hours: 8:30AM-5PM. Enrollment: 1100. Records go back to 1835. Alumni records are maintained here at the same phone number. Degrees granted: Associate; Bachelors; Masters. Adverse incident record source- Dean of Students, 614-376-4736.

Attendance and degree information available by phone, fax, mail. Search requires name plus SSN. Also helpful: date of birth, exact years of attendance. There is no fee.

Marion Technical College, Student Records, 1467 Mt Vernon Ave, Marion, OH 43302-5694, 614-389-4636 (Fax: 614-

389-6136). Hours: 8AM-6PM. Enrollment: 1800. Records go back to 1971. Degrees granted: Associate. Adverse incident record source- President's Office, 614-389-4636 .

Attendance information available by fax, mail. Search requires name plus SSN, signed release. Also helpful: date of birth, exact years of attendance. There is no fee.

Degree information available by phone, fax, mail. Search requires name plus SSN. Also helpful: date of birth, exact years of attendance. There is no fee.

McGregor School of Antioch University (The), Registrar, 800 Livermore St, Yellow Springs, OH 45387-1609, 513-767-6321 (Fax: 513-767-6461). Hours: 8:30AM-5PM M-F, 7AM-3PM Sat. Enrollment: 920. Antioch University (School for Adult and Experiential Learning) Records go back to 1987. Degrees granted: Bachelors; Masters.

Attendance and degree information available by phone, fax, mail. Search requires name plus SSN, approximate years of attendance. Also helpful: date of birth, exact years of attendance. There is no fee.

Medical College of Ohio at Toledo, Registrar, Caller Svc No. 10008, Toledo, OH 43699, 419-381-4172 (Fax: 419-381-1008). Hours: 8:30AM-5PM. Enrollment: 1029. Records go back to 1955. Alumni records are maintained here at the same phone number. Degrees granted: Masters; Doctorate. Adverse incident record source- Written Management, 419-381-4172.

Attendance and degree information available by phone, fax, mail. Search requires name plus SSN, date of birth, approximate years of attendance. Also helpful: exact years of attendance. There is no fee.

Methodist Theological School in Ohio, Registrar, PO Box 1204, 3081 Columbus Pike, Delaware, OH 43015-0931, 614-362-3344 (Fax: 614-362-3135). Hours: 8:30AM-4:30PM. Enrollment: 245. Records go back to 1960. Alumni records are maintained here also. Call 614-363-1146. Degrees granted: Masters. Adverse incident record source- Dean, 614-363-1146.

Attendance and degree information available by fax, mail. Search requires name plus SSN, exact years of attendance, signed release. There is no fee.

Miami University, Office of the Registrar, Oxford, OH 45056, 513-529-1809 (Fax: 513-529-7255). Hours: 8AM-5PM. Enrollment: 17900. Records go back to 1826. Degrees granted: Associate; Bachelors; Masters; Doctorate. Adverse incident record source- Student Affairs, 513-529-1417.

Attendance and degree information available by phone, fax, mail. Search requires name only. Also helpful: SSN, date of birth, exact years of attendance. There is no fee.

Miami University, (Hamilton), Registrar, 1601 Peck Blvd, Hamilton, OH 45011, 513-863-8833 (Fax: 513-863-1655). Records are not housed here. They are located at Miami University, Office of the Registrar, Oxford, OH 45056.

Miami University, (Middletown), Records & Registration, 4200 E University Blvd, Middletown, OH 45042, 513-727-3217 (Fax: 513-727-3220). Hours: 9AM-5PM. Enrollment: 2444. Records go back to 1976. Alumni records are maintained here also. Call 513-529-5957. Degrees granted: Associate.

Attendance and degree information available by mail. Search requires name plus SSN. Also helpful: date of birth, exact years of attendance. There is no fee.

Miami-Jacobs College, Registrar, PO Box 1433, 400 E Second St, Dayton, OH 45402, 513-461-5174 (Fax: 513-461-3384). Hours: 8AM-4:30PM. Enrollment: 300. Records go back to 1960. Degrees granted: Associate. Adverse incident record source- Finance, 513-461-5174 X156.

Attendance information available by fax, mail. Search requires name plus SSN. There is no fee.

Degree information available by fax, mail. Search requires name only. There is no fee.

Mount Union College, Registrar, 1972 Clark Ave, Alliance, OH 44601, 330-823-6018 (Fax: 330-823-5097). Hours: 8AM-5PM. Enrollment: 1532. Records go back to 1800's. Degrees granted: Bachelors.

Attendance and degree information available by phone, fax, mail. Search requires name plus SSN, date of birth. Also helpful: exact years of attendance. There is no fee.

Mount Vernon Nazarene College, Registrar, 800 Martinsburg Rd, Mount Vernon, OH 43050, 614-397-1244 X4530 (Fax: 614-397-2769). Hours: 8AM-4:30PM. Enrollment: 1450. Records go back to 1968. Alumni records are maintained here at the same phone number. Degrees granted: Associate; Bachelors; Masters.

Attendance information available by written request only. Search requires name plus signed release. There is no fee.

Degree information available by fax. Search requires name plus signed release. There is no fee.

Muskingum Area Technical College, Registrar, 1555 Newark Rd, Zanesville, OH 43701, 614-454-2501 (Fax: 614-454-0035). Hours: 8AM-5PM. Enrollment: 2135. Records go back to 1971. Degrees granted: Associate.

Attendance information available by fax, mail. Search requires name plus signed release. Also helpful: SSN, date of birth, exact years of attendance. There is no fee.

Degree information available by phone, fax, mail. Search requires name only. Also helpful: SSN, date of birth, exact years of attendance. There is no fee.

Muskingum College, Registrar, New Concord, OH 43762, 614-826-8164 (Fax: 614-826-8404). Hours: 8AM-Noon, 1-5PM. Enrollment: 1100. Records go back to 1904. Alumni records are maintained here at the same phone number. Degrees granted: Bachelors; Masters.

Attendance and degree information available by phone, mail. Search requires name plus approximate years of attendance. Also helpful: SSN, date of birth, exact years of attendance. There is no fee.

North Central Technical College, Registrar, PO Box 698, 2411 Kenwood Circle, Mansfield, OH 44901-0698, 419-755-4837 (Fax: 419-755-4729). Hours: 8:30AM-7:45PM M-Th; 8:30AM-4:30PM F. Enrollment: 2857. Records go back to 1966. Degrees granted: Associate.

Attendance and degree information available by fax, mail. Search requires name plus SSN. Also helpful: date of birth, exact years of attendance. There is no fee.

Northeastern Ohio Universities College of Medicine, Registrar, 4209 State Rte 44, PO Box 95, Rootstown, OH 44272-0095, 330-325-2511 (Fax: 330-325-2159). Hours: 7:30AM-5PM. Enrollment: 425. Records go back to 1977. Alumni records are maintained here at the same phone number.

Attendance and degree information available by phone, fax, mail. Search requires name only. Also helpful: SSN, date of birth, exact years of attendance. There is no fee.

Northwest State Community College, Registrar, 22-600 State Rte 34, Archbold, OH 43502, 419-267-5511 (Fax: 419-267-2688). Hours: 8AM-4PM. Enrollment: 2000. Formerly Northwest Technical College Records go back to 1965. Degrees granted: Associate.

Attendance information available by phone, fax, mail. Search requires name plus SSN. There is no fee.

Degree information available by mail. Search requires name plus SSN. There is no fee.

Northwestern College, Registrar, 1441 N Cable Rd, Lima, OH 45805, 419-998-3141 (Fax: 419-229-6926). Hours: 7:30AM-4:30PM. Enrollment: 1700. Records go back to 1925. Degrees granted: Associate.

Attendance and degree information available by phone, fax, mail. Search requires name only. Also helpful: SSN, exact years of attendance. There is no fee.

Notre Dame College, Registrar, 4545 College Rd, South Euclid, OH 44121, 216-381-1680 X243 (Fax: 216-381-3802). Hours: 8:30AM-4:30PM. Enrollment: 640. Records go back to 1922. Alumni records are maintained here at the same phone number. Degrees granted: Associate; Bachelors; Masters. Certification: Bus. Admin., Gerontology. Adverse incident record source- Geri Cahill, 216-381-1680 X204.

Attendance and degree information available by phone, mail. Search requires name only. Also helpful: SSN, exact years of attendance. There is no fee.

Oberlin College, Registrar, Oberlin, OH 44074, 216-775-8450 (Fax: 216-775-8800). Hours: 8AM-4:30PM. Enrollment: 2745. Records go back to 1985. Alumni records are maintained here also. Call 216-775-8692. Degrees granted: Bachelors; Masters; Performance Diploma. Special programs- Student Health Office, 216-775-1651. Adverse incident record source-Student Support, 216-775-8464.

Attendance and degree information available by mail. Search requires name plus SSN, date of birth, exact years of attendance, signed release. There is no fee.

Ohio College of Podiatric Medicine, Student Records, 10515 Carnegie Ave, Cleveland, OH 44106, 216-231-3300 X348 (Fax: 216-231-1005). Hours: 9AM-4PM. Enrollment: 500. Records go back to 1917. Alumni records are maintained here also. Call 216-231-3300 X269. Degrees granted: Doctorate.

Attendance and degree information available by phone, fax, mail. Search requires name plus approximate years of attendance. Also helpful: SSN, exact years of attendance. There is no fee.

Ohio Dominican College, Registrar's Office, 1216 Sunbury Rd, Columbus, OH 43219, 614-251-4650 (Fax: 614-252-0776). Hours: 8AM-4:30PM. Enrollment: 1732. Records go back to 1911. Alumni records are maintained here also. Call 614-251-4617. Degrees granted: Associate; Bachelors.

School will not confirm attendance information.

Degree information available by phone, fax, mail. Search requires name only. Also helpful: SSN, date of birth, exact years of attendance. There is no fee.

Ohio Northern University, Registrar, 525 S Main St, Ada, OH 45810, 419-772-2024. Hours: 8AM-5PM. Enrollment: 2900. Records go back to 1871. Alumni records are maintained here also. Call 419-772-2038. Degrees granted: Bachelors; PharmD, JD.

Attendance and degree information available by phone, mail. Search requires name plus SSN. Also helpful: date of birth, exact years of attendance. There is no fee.

Ohio State University, Registrar, 205 Bricker Hall, 190 N Oval Drive, Columbus, OH 43210, 614-292-8500 (Fax: 614-292-2363). Hours: 9:30AM-5PM M,T,Th,F; 9:30AM-6PM W. Enrollment: 41818. Records go back to 1873. Alumni Records Office: Alumni House, 567 Fawcett Center, 2400 Olintangy Rd, Columbus, OH 43201. Degrees granted: Bachelors; Masters; Doctorate; Medical.

Attendance and degree information available by phone, fax, mail. Search requires name plus SSN, date of birth, exact years of attendance. There is no fee.

Ohio State University, (Agricultural Technical Institute), Registrar, 1328 Dover Rd, Wooster, OH 44691, 330-264-

3911 (Fax: 330-262-7634). Records are not housed here. They are located at Ohio State University, Registrar, 205 Bricker Hall, 190 N Oval Drive, Columbus, OH 43210.

Ohio State University, (Lima), Registrar, 4240 Campus Dr, Lima, OH 45804, 419-221-1641. Records are not housed here. They are located at Ohio State University, Registrar, 205 Bricker Hall, 190 N Oval Drive, Columbus, OH 43210.

Ohio State University, (Mansfield), Registrar, 1680 University Dr, Mansfield, OH 44906, 419-755-4011. Records are not housed here. They are located at Ohio State University, Registrar, 205 Bricker Hall, 190 N Oval Drive, Columbus, OH 43210.

Ohio State University, (Marion), Registrar, 1465 Mount Vernon Ave, Marion, OH 43302, 614-389-2361 (Fax: 614-292-5817). Records are not housed here. They are located at Ohio State University, Registrar, 205 Bricker Hall, 190 N Oval Drive, Columbus, OH 43210.

Ohio State University, (Newark), Registrar, University Dr, Newark, OH 43055, 614-366-3321. Records are not housed here. They are located at Ohio State University, Registrar, 205 Bricker Hall, 190 N Oval Drive, Columbus, OH 43210.

Ohio University, Registrar, Chubb Hall, Athens, OH 45701-2979, 614-593-4180 (Fax: 614-593-4184). Hours: 8AM-5PM. Enrollment: 24309. Records go back to 1893. Alumni records are maintained here also. Call 614-593-4300. Degrees granted: Associate; Bachelors; Masters; PhD. Adverse incident record source- Legal Affairs, 614-593-2626.

Attendance and degree information available by phone, fax, mail. Search requires name plus SSN, date of birth, approximate years of attendance. There is no fee.

Ohio University, (Chillicothe), Student Records, Chillicothe, OH 45601, 614-774-7240 (Fax: 614-774-7214). Records are not housed here. They are located at Ohio University, Registrar, Chubb Hall, Athens, OH 45701-2979.

Ohio University, (Eastern), Registrar, St Clairsville, OH 43950, 614-695-1720 (Fax: 614-695-7079). Records are not housed here. They are located at Ohio University, Registrar, Chubb Hall, Athens, OH 45701-2979.

Ohio University, (Lancaster), Registrar, 1570 Granville Pike, Lancaster, OH 43130, 614-654-6711. Records are not housed here. They are located at Ohio University, Registrar, Chubb Hall, Athens, OH 45701-2979.

Ohio University, (Southern), Registrar, 1804 Liberty Ave, Ironton, OH 45638, 614-533-4600 (Fax: 614-533-4632). Hours: 9AM-6PM. Degrees granted: Associate; Bachelors; Masters; Doctorate.

Attendance and degree information available by phone, fax, mail. Search requires name plus SSN, date of birth, exact years of attendance. There is no fee.

Ohio University, (Zanesville), Registrar, Zanesville, OH 43701, 614-453-0762 (Fax: 614-453-6161). Records are not housed here. They are located at Ohio University, Registrar, Chubb Hall, Athens, OH 45701-2979.

Ohio Valley Business College, Registrar, PO Box 7000, 500 Maryland Ave, East Liverpool, OH 43920, 330-385-1070 (Fax: 330-385-4606). Hours: 8AM-4PM. Records go back to 1921. Degrees granted: Associate. Special programs- Administration, 216-385-1070.

Attendance and degree information available by mail. Search requires name plus SSN. There is no fee.

Ohio Wesleyan University, Registrar, 61 S Sanusky St, Delaware, OH 43015, 614-368-3201 (Fax: 614-368-3210).

Hours: 8:30AM-Noon, 1-5PM. Enrollment: 1800. Records go back to 1946. Alumni records are maintained here also. Call 614-368-3318. Degrees granted: Bachelors. Adverse incident record source- Dean of Students, 614-368-3136.

Attendance and degree information available by phone, fax, mail. Search requires name only. Also helpful: SSN, date of birth, approximate years of attendance. There is no fee.

Otterbein College, Registrar, Westerville, OH 43081, 614-823-1350 (Fax: 614-823-1009). Hours: 8:30AM-5PM. Enrollment: 2488. Records go back to 1847. Alumni records are maintained here also. Call 614-823-1400. Degrees granted: Bachelors; Masters.

Attendance and degree information available by phone, fax, mail. Search requires name plus SSN, date of birth. There is no fee.

Owens Community College, Registrar, PO Box 10000, 30335 Oregon Rd, Toledo, OH 43699, 419-661-7323 (Fax: 419-661-7607). Hours: 8AM-7:30PM M,Th; 8AM-5PM T,W; 8AM-4:30PM F. Enrollment: 11000. Records go back to 1965. Alumni records are maintained here also. Call 419-661-7114. Degrees granted: Associate.

Attendance and degree information available by phone, fax, mail. Search requires name plus SSN, approximate years of attendance. Also helpful: date of birth, exact years of attendance. There is no fee.

Owens Community College, (Branch), Registrar, 300 Davis St, Findlay, OH 45840, 419-423-6827 (Fax: 419-423-0246). Hours: 8AM-5PM. Records go back to 1989. Degrees granted: Associate. Special programs- Toledo Campus, 419-661-7220.

Attendance information available by phone, fax, mail. Search requires name plus SSN, approximate years of attendance. There is no fee.

Degree information available by fax, mail. Search requires name plus SSN, approximate years of attendance. There is no fee.

Pontifical College Josephinum, Registrar, 7625 N High St, Columbus, OH 43235, 614-885-5585 (Fax: 614-885-2307). Hours: 8AM-5:30PM. Enrollment: 53. Alumni records are maintained here at the same phone number. Degrees granted: Bachelors; Masters.

Attendance and degree information available by phone, fax, mail. Search requires name plus SSN, date of birth, exact years of attendance. There is no fee.

RETS Technical Center, Registrar, 116 Westpark Rd, Centerville, OH 45459, 513-433-3410 (Fax: 513-435-6516). Enrollment: 380. Records go back to 1953. Degrees granted: Associate. Adverse incident record source- Department of Student Services.

Attendance and degree information available by phone, mail. Search requires name plus SSN, approximate years of attendance. Also helpful: exact years of attendance. There is no fee.

Rabbinical College of Telshe, Registrar, 28400 Euclid Ave, Wickliffe, OH 44092, 216-943-5300 (Fax: 216-943-5303). Hours: 8AM-5PM. Enrollment: 150. Degrees granted: Masters; Doctorate.

Attendance and degree information available by mail. Search requires name plus SSN, date of birth, exact years of attendance. There is no fee.

Shawnee State University, Registrar, 940 Second St, Portsmouth, OH 45662, 614-355-2262 (Fax: 614-355-2593). Hours: 7AM-6PM M-Th, 7AM-5PM F. Enrollment: 3185. Records go back to 1970. Alumni records are maintained here also. Call 614-355-2257. Degrees granted: Associate; Bachelors.

Attendance and degree information available by phone, fax, mail. Search requires name plus SSN. There is no fee.

Sinclair Community College, Registrar, 444 W Third St, Dayton, OH 45402, 513-226-2736 (Fax: 513-449-5370). Hours: 8AM-7PM M-Th; 8AM-5PM F. Enrollment: 19800. Alumni records are maintained here also. Call 513-226-3030. Degrees granted: Associate. Adverse incident record source- Student Activities, 513-226-2509.

Attendance and degree information available by phone, mail. Search requires name plus SSN. Also helpful: exact years of attendance. There is no fee.

Southeastern Business College, Registrar, 1855 Western Ave, Chillicothe, OH 45601, 614-774-6300 (Fax: 614-774-6317). Hours: 8:30AM-10PM. Enrollment: 130. Records go back to 1985. Degrees granted: Associate. Adverse incident record source- Education, 614-774-6300.

Attendance and degree information available by phone, fax, mail. Search requires name plus SSN, exact years of attendance. There is no fee.

Southeastern Business College, Registrar, 1176 Jackson Pike Ste 312, Gallipolis, OH 45631, 614-446-4367. Records are not housed here. They are located at Southeastern Business College, Registrar, 1855 Western Ave, Chillicothe, OH 45601.

Southeastern Business College, Registrar, 1907 N Ridge Rd, Lorain, OH 44055, 216-277-0021 (Fax: 216-277-7989). Hours: 8:30AM-5PM. Records go back to 1971. Degrees granted: Associate.

Attendance and degree information available by phone, fax, mail. Search requires name plus SSN. Also helpful: exact years of attendance. There is no fee.

Southeastern Business College, (Branch), Registrar, 420 E Main St, Jackson, OH 45640, 614-286-1554 (Fax: 614-286-4476). Records are not housed here. They are located at Southeastern Business College, Registrar, 1855 Western Ave, Chillicothe, OH 45601.

Southeastern Business College, (Branch), Registrar, 1522 Sheridan Dr, Lancaster, OH 43130, 614-687-6126. Records are not housed here. They are located at Southeastern Business College, Registrar, 1855 Western Ave, Chillicothe, OH 45601.

Southeastern Business College, (Branch), Registrar, 3879 Rhodes Ave, New Boston, OH 45662, 614-456-4124 (Fax: 614-456-5163). Hours: 8:30AM-5PM. Enrollment: 200. Records go back to 1981. Also have some (not all) records from Portsmouth Interstate Business College from 1940's. Degrees granted: Associate.

Attendance and degree information available by phone, fax, mail. Search requires name plus approximate years of attendance. Also helpful: SSN, date of birth, exact years of attendance. There is no fee.

Southeastern Business College, (Branch), Registrar, 4020 Milan Rd, Sandusky, OH 44870, 419-627-8345. Records are not housed here. They are located at Southeastern Business College, Registrar, 1855 Western Ave, Chillicothe, OH 45601.

Southern Ohio College, Registrar, 1011 Glendale Milford Rd, Cincinnati, OH 45237, 513-242-3791 (Fax: 513-242-4774). Hours: 9AM-5:30PM. Enrollment: 1035. Degrees granted: Associate.

Attendance and degree information available by phone, fax, mail. Search requires name plus SSN, exact years of attendance. There is no fee.

Southern Ohio College, (Branch), Registrar, 2791 Mogadore Rd, Akron, OH 44312, 216-733-8766 X51 (Fax: 216-733-5853). Hours: 8AM-5PM T,Th,F; 8AM-6:30PM M,W.

Enrollment: 200. Records go back to 1975. Formerly Buckeye College Degrees granted: Associate.

Attendance and degree information available by phone, fax, mail. Search requires name plus SSN, date of birth. There is no fee.

Southern State Community College, Registrar,
200 Hobart Dr, Hillsboro, OH 45133, 513-393-3431 (Fax: 513-393-9831). Hours: 8AM-5PM. Enrollment: 1500. Records go back to 1976. Alumni records are maintained here at the same phone number. Degrees granted: Associate.

Attendance and degree information available by phone, fax, mail. Search requires name only. Also helpful: SSN. There is no fee.

Southwestern College of Business, Registrar,
9910 Princeton-Glendale Rd, Cincinnati, OH 45246, 513-874-0432 (Fax: 513-874-0123). Hours: 9AM-7PM. Enrollment: 160. Records go back to 1977. Degrees granted: Associate. Adverse incident record source- Director, 513-874-0432.

Attendance information available by phone, fax, mail. Search requires name plus SSN, exact years of attendance. There is no fee.

Degree information available by fax, mail. Search requires name plus SSN, exact years of attendance. There is no fee.

Southwestern College of Business, Registrar,
225 W First St, Dayton, OH 45402, 513-224-0061 X14. Hours: 9AM-7PM M-Th, 9AM-1PM F. Records go back to 1976. Degrees granted: Associate. Special programs- Corporate Office, 513-874-0432.

Attendance information available by phone, mail. Search requires name plus SSN, approximate years of attendance. Also helpful: exact years of attendance. There is no fee.

Degree information available by phone, mail. Search requires name plus SSN, approximate years of attendance. Also helpful: date of birth, exact years of attendance. There is no fee.

Southwestern College of Business, (Branch),
Registrar, 632 Vine St, Suite 200, Cincinnati, OH 45202, 513-874-0432. Hours: 8AM-7PM. Records go back to 1977. Degrees granted: Associate.

Attendance and degree information available by mail. Search requires name plus date of birth, signed release. Also helpful: SSN, exact years of attendance. Fee is $2.00. Expedited service available for $4.00.

Southwestern College of Business, (Branch),
Registrar, 631 S Briel Blvd, Middletown, OH 45044, 513-423-3346 (Fax: 513-874-0123). Hours: 8:30AM-6:30PM M-Th, 9AM-1PM F. Records go back to 1979. Degrees granted: Associate.

Attendance and degree information available by phone, fax, mail. Search requires name plus SSN, approximate years of attendance. There is no fee.

St. Mary Seminary, Registrar, 28700 Euclid Ave, Wickliffe, OH 44092-2585, 216-943-7667 (Fax: 216-943-7577). Hours: 8AM-4PM. Enrollment: 73. Records go back to 1976. Degrees granted: Masters.

Attendance information available by mail. Search requires name plus signed release. Also helpful: SSN, date of birth, exact years of attendance. There is no fee.

Degree information available by phone, fax, mail. Search requires name only. Also helpful: SSN, date of birth, exact years of attendance. There is no fee.

Stark State College of Technology, Registrar,
6200 Frank Ave NW, Canton, OH 44720, 330-966-5460 X211 (Fax: 330-966-6594). Hours: 8AM-8PM. Enrollment: 4300. Formerly Stark Technical College Records go back to 1966. Alumni records are maintained here also. Call 330-966-5460 X211. Degrees granted: Associate.

Attendance and degree information available by fax, mail. Search requires name plus SSN, signed release. There is no fee.

Stautzenberger College (Central), Registrar,
5355 Southwyck Blvd, Toledo, OH 43614, 419-866-0261 (Fax: 419-867-9821). Hours: 8AM-10PM M-Th, 9AM-5PM F, 9AM-5PM Sat. Enrollment: 225. Degrees granted: Associate. Special programs- Medical Assisting: Dental Assisting: Veterinary Assisting: Novell Network.

Attendance and degree information available by phone, fax, mail. Search requires name plus SSN, approximate years of attendance. There is no fee.

Stautzenberger College (Findlay), Registrar,
1637 Tiffin Ave, Findlay, OH 45840, 419-423-2211 (Fax: 419-423-0725). Hours: 8AM-5PM. Enrollment: 150. Records go back to 1988. Degrees granted: Associate.

Attendance information available by mail. Search requires name plus SSN, date of birth, approximate years of attendance, signed release. Also helpful: exact years of attendance. There is no fee.

Degree information available by phone, fax, mail. Search requires name plus SSN, date of birth. Also helpful: exact years of attendance. There is no fee.

Terra State Community College, Registrar, 2830
Napoleon Rd, Fremont, OH 43420, 419-334-8400 X333 (Fax: 419-334-9035). Hours: 8AM-5:30PM M-Th, 8AM-4:30PM F. Enrollment: 2500. Records go back to 1970. Alumni records are maintained here also. Call 419-334-8400 X345. Degrees granted: Associate.

Attendance and degree information available by phone, fax, mail. Search requires name plus SSN, approximate years of attendance. There is no fee.

Tiffin University, Registrar, 155 Miami St, Tiffin, OH
44883, 419-447-6442 X216 (Fax: 419-443-5006). Hours: 8AM-5PM. Enrollment: 1023. Records go back to 1924. Degrees granted: Associate; Bachelors; Masters. Adverse incident record source- Dean, 419-447-6442.

Attendance and degree information available by phone, fax, mail. Search requires name plus SSN, date of birth, approximate years of attendance. There is no fee.

Trinity Lutheran Seminary, Registrar, 2199 E Main
St, Columbus, OH 43209-2334, 614-235-4136 (Fax: 614-238-0263). Hours: 8AM-4:30PM. Enrollment: 261. Degrees granted: Masters.

Attendance and degree information available by phone, fax, mail. Search requires name plus approximate years of attendance. Also helpful: exact years of attendance. There is no fee.

Trumbull Business College, Registrar, 3200 Ridge
Rd, Warren, OH 44484, 330-369-3200 (Fax: 330-369-6792). Hours: 7:30AM-5PM. Enrollment: 200. Records go back to 1972. Degrees granted: Associate. Adverse incident record source- 330-369-3200 X11.

Attendance and degree information available by fax, mail. Search requires name plus SSN, approximate years of attendance, signed release. There is no fee.

Union Institute, Registrar, 440 E McMillan St, Cincinnati,
OH 45206-1947, 513-861-6400 (Fax: 513-861-0779). Hours: 9AM-5PM. Enrollment: 1800. Records go back to 1969. Alumni records are maintained here at the same phone number. Degrees granted: Bachelors; PhD. Adverse incident record source- Dean, 513-861-6400.

Attendance and degree information available by phone, fax, mail. Search requires name plus SSN. There is no fee.

United Theological Seminary, Registrar, 1810
Harvard Blvd, Dayton, OH 45406, 513-278-5817 (Fax: 513-278-

1218). Hours: 8:30AM-4:30pm. Enrollment: 560. Records go back to 1874. Degrees granted: Masters; Doctorate.

Attendance and degree information available by phone, fax, mail. Search requires name plus exact years of attendance. Also helpful: SSN. There is no fee.

University of Akron, Registrar, Akron, OH 44325, 330-972-7844 (Fax: 330-972-7097). Hours: 8AM-5PM. Enrollment: 24000. Records go back to 1800's. Alumni Records Office: 138 Fir Hill, Akron, OH 44325. Degrees granted: Associate; Bachelors; Masters; Doctorate. Adverse incident record source- Student Discipline, 330-972-7021.

Attendance and degree information available by phone, fax, mail. Search requires name plus SSN, date of birth, exact years of attendance. There is no fee.

University of Cincinnati, Registrar, 2624 Clifton Ave, Cincinnati, OH 45221-0060, 513-556-9900. Hours: 8AM-5PM. Enrollment: 36000. Records go back to 1900. Alumni records are maintained here also. Call 513-556-4641 or 4344. Degrees granted: Associate; Bachelors; Masters; Doctorate; PhD.

Attendance and degree information available by phone, mail. Search requires name plus SSN, approximate years of attendance. There is no fee.

University of Cincinnati-Clermont College, Registrar, 4200 Clermont College Dr, Batavia, OH 45103, 513-732-5200 (Fax: 513-732-5303). Hours: 9AM-6PM M-Th, 9AM-5PM F. Records go back to 1920. Alumni Records Office: Alumni Association, University of Cincinnati, Alumni Center, PO Box 210024, Cincinnati, OH 45221-0024. Degrees granted: Associate. Adverse incident record source- Business office, 513-732-5200.

Attendance and degree information available by phone, fax, mail. Search requires name plus SSN. There is no fee.

University of Cincinnati-Raymond Walters College, Registrar, 9555 Plainfield Rd, Cincinnati, OH 45236, 513-745-5600 (Fax: 513-745-5768). Hours: 8AM-7PM M-Th, 8AM-5PM F. Enrollment: 3850. Alumni Records Office: Alumni Association, University of Cincinnati, PO Box 210024, Cincinnati, OH 45221-0024. Degrees granted: Associate. Special programs- University of Cincinnati, 513-556-9900.

Attendance and degree information available by phone, fax, mail. Search requires name plus SSN, date of birth, exact years of attendance. There is no fee.

University of Dayton, Registrar, 300 College Park Ave, Dayton, OH 45469, 513-229-4141. Hours: 8:30AM-4:30PM. Enrollment: 6435. Records go back to 1989. Alumni Records Office: Alumni Impaired Relations, Alumni House, Dayton, OH 45469-2710. Degrees granted: Bachelors; Masters; Doctorate. Adverse incident record source- Student Development, 513-229-3311.

Attendance and degree information available by phone, mail. Search requires name plus SSN, approximate years of attendance. There is no fee.

University of Findlay, Registrar, 1000 N Main St, Findlay, OH 45840, 419-424-4556 (Fax: 419-424-4822). Hours: 8:30AM-5PM. Enrollment: 3300. Records go back to 1983. Alumni records are maintained here also. Call 419-424-4516. Degrees granted: Associate; Bachelors; Masters. Adverse incident record source- Dean, 419-424-4553.

Attendance and degree information available by phone, fax, mail. Search requires name plus SSN, approximate years of attendance. There is no fee.

University of Rio Grande, Registrar, E College Ave, Rio Grande, OH 45674, 614-245-7368 (Fax: 614-245-7445). Hours: 8AM-5PM M,T,W,F; 8AM-6PM Th. Enrollment: 2032. Records go back to 1920. Alumni records are maintained here also. Call 614-245-7527. Degrees granted: Associate; Bachelors;

Masters. Adverse incident record source- Student Development, 614-245-7234.

Attendance and degree information available by phone, fax, mail. Search requires name plus SSN, approximate years of attendance. There is no fee.

University of Toledo, Registrar, 2801 W Bancroft St, Toledo, OH 43606, 419-530-2701 (Fax: 419-530-7251). Hours: 9AM-5PM M,Th,F; 9AM-7PM T,W. Enrollment: 21353. Records go back to 1800's. Alumni records are maintained here also. Call 419-527-2601. Degrees granted: Associate; Bachelors; Masters; Doctorate; PhD. Adverse incident record source- Dean, 419-530-2256.

Attendance and degree information available by phone, fax, mail. Search requires name plus SSN, date of birth, exact years of attendance. There is no fee.

Urbana University, Registrar, One College Wy, Urbana, OH 43078, 513-484-1353 (Fax: 513-484-1322). Hours: 8AM-4:30PM. Enrollment: 1073. Records go back to 1950. Alumni records are maintained here also. Call 513-484-1323. Degrees granted: Associate; Bachelors. Adverse incident record source- Dean of Students, 513-484-1378.

Attendance and degree information available by phone, mail. Search requires name plus SSN, date of birth, approximate years of attendance. Also helpful: exact years of attendance. There is no fee.

Ursuline College, Registrar, 2550 Lander Rd, Pepper Pike, OH 44124, 216-646-8131 (Fax: 216-646-8129). Hours: 8:30AM-5PM. Records go back to 1950. Alumni records are maintained here also. Call 216-646-8375. Degrees granted: Bachelors; Masters.

Attendance and degree information available by phone, fax, mail. Search requires name plus SSN. Also helpful: date of birth, exact years of attendance. There is no fee.

Virginia Marti College of Fashion and Art, Registrar, 11724 Detroit Ave, Lakewood, OH 44107, 216-221-8584 (Fax: 216-221-2311). Enrollment: 150. Records go back to 1966. Degrees granted: Associate. Adverse incident record source- Student Services.

Attendance and degree information available by phone, mail. Search requires name plus SSN. Also helpful: approximate years of attendance. There is no fee.

Walsh University, Registrar, 2020 Easton St NW, Canton, OH 44720, 330-490-7194 (Fax: 330-490-7185). Hours: 8AM-4PM. Enrollment: 1241. Records go back to 1960. Alumni records are maintained here also. Call 330-490-7111. Degrees granted: Associate; Bachelors; Masters. Certification: Teacher Prep.

Attendance and degree information available by phone, fax, mail. Search requires name plus SSN, date of birth. Also helpful: approximate years of attendance. There is no fee.

Washington State Community College, Records Office, 710 Colegate Dr, Marietta, OH 45750, 614-374-8716 (Fax: 614-373-7496). Hours: 7:30AM-4:30PM. Enrollment: 2100. Records go back to 1972. Degrees granted: Associate.

Attendance and degree information available by phone, fax, mail. Search requires name plus SSN. There is no fee.

West Side Institute of Technology, Registrar, 9801 Walford Ave, Cleveland, OH 44102, 216-651-1656 X22 (Fax: 216-651-4077). Enrollment: 300. Records go back to 1957. Alumni records are maintained here at the same phone number. Degrees granted: Associate. Adverse incident record source- Student Services.

Attendance and degree information available by phone, mail. Search requires name plus SSN, exact years of attendance. There is no fee.

Wilberforce University, Registrar, Wilberforce, OH 45384, 513-376-2911 (Fax: 513-376-2627). Hours: 8AM-4:30PM. Enrollment: 958. Alumni records are maintained here also. Call 513-376-2911 X707. Degrees granted: Bachelors. Adverse incident record source- Campus Police, 513-376-2911 X701.

Attendance and degree information available by phone, fax, mail. Search requires name only. Also helpful: SSN, date of birth, exact years of attendance. There is no fee.

Wilmington College, Dir Academic Records, Pyle Center Box 1286, Wilmington, OH 45177, 513-382-6661 X213 (Fax: 513-382-7077). Hours: 8AM-5PM. Enrollment: 1000. Records go back to 1900. Alumni Records Office: Alumni Association, Pyle Center Box 1307, Wilmington, OH 45177. Degrees granted: Bachelors. Adverse incident record source- Student Services, 513-382-6661 X339.

Attendance and degree information available by phone, fax, mail. Search requires name plus SSN, date of birth, exact years of attendance. There is no fee.

Winebrenner Theological Seminry, Registrar, 701 E Melrose Ave, PO Box 478, Findlay, OH 45839, 419-422-4824 (Fax: 419-422-3999). Hours: 8AM-5PM. Enrollment: 110. Records go back to 1842. Alumni records are maintained here at the same phone number. Degrees granted: Masters. Special programs- Master of Divinity: MA in Christian Ed: MA (Theological Studies).

Attendance and degree information available by phone, fax, mail. Search requires name only. Also helpful: approximate years of attendance. There is no fee.

Wittenberg University, Registrar, PO Box 720, Springfield, OH 45501, 513-327-6132 (Fax: 513-327-6340). Hours: 8AM-5PM. Enrollment: 2180. Records go back to 1900. Alumni Records Office: Alumni Association, PO Box 720, Springfield, OH 45501. Degrees granted: Bachelors. Adverse incident record source- Dean, 513-327-7800.

Attendance information available by phone, fax, mail. Search requires name plus SSN, date of birth, exact years of attendance. There is no fee.

Degree information available by phone, fax, mail. Search requires name only. There is no fee.

Wright State University, Registrar, 3640 Colonel Glenn Hwy, Dayton, OH 45435, 513-873-5588 (Fax: 513-873-5795). Hours: 8:30AM-7PM M-Th, 8:30AM-5PM F. Enrollment: 15900. Records go back to 1964. Alumni records are maintained here also. Call 513-873-2251. Degrees granted: Associate; Bachelors; Masters; Doctorate; Medicine, Psy D. Special programs- School Medicine, 513-873-3013. Adverse incident record source- Public Safety, 513-873-2056.

Attendance and degree information available by phone, fax, mail. Search requires name plus SSN, approximate years of attendance. There is no fee.

Wright State University, **(Lake)**, Registrar, 7600 State Rte 703, Celina, OH 45822, 419-586-0324 (Fax: 419-586-0358). Records are not housed here. They are located at Wright State University, Registrar, 3640 Colonel Glenn Hwy, Dayton, OH 45435.

Xavier University, Registrar, 3800 Victory Pkwy, Cincinnati, OH 45207, 513-745-3941 (Fax: 513-745-2969). Hours: 8AM-7PM M-Th; 8AM-5PM F. Enrollment: 6200. Records go back to 1920's. Alumni records are maintained here also. Call 513-745-3337. Degrees granted: Associate; Bachelors; Masters. Adverse incident record source- Safety and Security, 513-745-1000.

Attendance and degree information available by phone, fax, mail. Search requires name only. Also helpful: SSN, date of birth, exact years of attendance. There is no fee.

Youngstown State University, Records Office, 410 Wick Ave, Youngstown, OH 44555, 330-742-3182 (Fax: 330-742-1408). Hours: 8AM-5PM. Enrollment: 13000. Records go back to 1908. Alumni records are maintained here also. Call 330-742-3497. Degrees granted: Associate; Bachelors; Masters; Doctorate.

Attendance and degree information available by phone, fax, mail. Search requires name plus SSN, date of birth. Also helpful: approximate years of attendance. There is no fee.

Trade and Vocational Schools

Academy of Hair Design, 1440 Whipple Ave, Canton, OH 44708, 216-477-6695

Akron Barber College, 3200 S Arlington Rd #2, Akron, OH 44312, 216-644-9114

Akron Machining Institute, Inc., 2959 Barber Rd, Barberton Rd, OH 44203, 216-745-1111

Akron Machining Institute, Inc. (Cleveland Machining Institute), 2500 Brookpark Rd, Cleveland, OH 44134, 216-741-1100

Akron School of Practical Nursing, 619 Sumner St, Akron, OH 44311, 216-376-4129

Akron-Medical-Dental Institute, 733 W Market St, Akron, OH 44303, 216-762-9788

Allstate Hairstyling and Barber College, 2546 Lorain Ave, Cleveland, OH 44113, 216-241-6684

American School of Nail Techniques & Cosmetology, 924 E Tallmadge Ave, Akron, OH 44310, 216-633-9427

American School of Technology, 4599-4605 Morse Center Dr, Columbus, OH 43229, 614-436-4820

Central School of Practical Nursing, 3300 Chester Ave, Cleveland, OH 44114, 216-391-8434

Choffin Career Center, 200 E Wood St, Youngstown, OH 44503, 216-744-8700

Cleveland Institute of Dental-Medical Assistants, Inc., 1836 Euclid Ave #401, Cleveland, OH 44115, 216-241-2930

Cleveland Institute of Dental-Medical Assistants, Inc. (Branch Campus), 5564 Mayfield Rd, Lyndhurst, OH 44124, 216-473-6273

Cleveland Institute of Dental-Medical Assistants, Inc. (Branch Campus), 5733 Hopkins Rd, Mentor, OH 44060, 216-946-9530

Columbus Para-Professional Institute, 1077 Lexington Ave, Columbus, OH 43201, 614-299-0200

Connecticut School of Broadcasting, 4790 Red Bank Expy #102, Cincinnati, OH 45227, 216-271-6060

Connecticut School of Broadcasting, 6701 Rockside Rd #204, Independence, OH 44131, 216-447-9117

Fairfield Career Center, 4000 Columbus-Lancaster Rd, Carroll, OH 43112, 614-837-9443

Hamrick Truck Driving School, 1156 Medina Rd, Medina, OH 44256, 216-239-2229

Hannah E. Mullins School of Practical Nursing, 2094 E State St, Salem, OH 44460, 216-332-8940

Hobart Institute of Welding Technology, Trade Sq E, Troy, OH 45373, 513-332-5214

Hospitality Training Center, 220 N Main St, Hudson, OH 44236, 216-653-9151

Institute of Medical and Dental Technology, 375 Glensprings Dr #201, Cincinnati, OH 45246, 513-851-8500

Institute of Medical and Dental Technology (Branch Campus), 4452 Eastgate Blvd #209, Cincinnati, OH 45244, 513-753-5030

International College of Broadcasting, 6 S Smithville Rd, Dayton, OH 45431, 513-258-8251

Knox County Career Center, 306 Martinsburg Rd, Mount Vernon, OH 43050, 614-397-5820

Marymount School of Practical Nursing, 12300 McCracken Rd, Garfield Heights, OH 44125, 216-587-8160

Medina County Career Center, 1101 W Liberty St, Medina, OH 44256, 216-953-7118

NHRAW Home Study Institute, PO Box 16790, Columbus, OH 43216, 614-488-1835

National Education Center-National Institute of Technology Campus, 1225 Orlen Ave, Cuyahoga Falls, OH 44221, 216-923-9959

Ohio Auto-Diesel Technical Institute, 1421 E 49th St, Cleveland, OH 44103, 216-881-1700

Ohio College of Massotherapy, 1018 Kenmore Blvd, Akron, OH 44314, 216-745-6170

Ohio State College of Barber Styling, 329 Superior St, Toledo, OH 43604, 419-241-5618

Ohio State College of Barber Styling (Branch Campus), 4614 E Broad St, Columbus, OH 43223, 614-868-1015

Professional Skills Institute, 20 Arco Dr, Toledo, OH 43607, 419-531-9610

Raedel College and Industrial Welding School, 137 Sixth St NE, Canton, OH 44702, 216-454-9006

School of Advertising Art, 2900 Acosta St, Kettering, OH 45420, 513-294-0592

TDDS, 1688 N Princetown Rd, Diamond, OH 44412, 216-538-2216

Technology Education Center, 288 S Hamilton Rd, Columbus, OH 43213, 614-759-7700

Total Technical Institute, 6500 Pearl Rd, Parma Heights, OH 44130, 216-843-2323

Ultrasound Diagnostic School (Branch Campus), 4700 Rockside Rd, Independence, OH 44131, 216-573-5833

State Licensing & Business Registration Quick Finder Index

Architecture, Engineering & Surveying
Architect #14 (6150)............................... ☎ 614-466-2316
Engineer #29 (30401).................................. ☎ 614-466-3650
Landscape Architect #14 (500) .... ☎ 614-466-2316
Surveyor #29 (1835).................................. ☎ 614-466-3650

Business - Court & Legal Services
Attorney #2 (44659) .... ☎ 614-644-1553
Executive Agency Lobbyist #39 614-728-5100
Legislative Agent #39.................................... 614-728-5100
Lobbyist (Executive Agency Lobbyist) #39
(1595) 614-728-5100
Notary Public #38 (200000) .... ☎ 614-466-2566

Business - General Services
Auctioneer #34 (3000)................................... ☎ 614-466-4130
Pawn/Mortgage Broker #33 (1000)................ ☎ 614-466-2221
Public Accountant/CPA #1 (41442)................ ☎ 614-752-8248

Construction & Manufacturing
Automatic Sprinkler System Inspector #41.... ☎ 614-644-2253

Boiler Inspector #41... ☎ 614-644-2236
Electrical Safety Inspector #41 .... ☎ 614-644-2253
Elevator Inspector #41 .... ☎ 614-644-2244
Factory & Building Inspector #41 .... ☎ 614-644-2622
Furniture Manufacturer #41........................... ☎ 614-644-2253
Plans Examiner #41 .... ☎ 614-644-2253

Education
School Administrator #43............................... ☎ 614-466-3593
School Counselor #43..................................... ☎ 614-466-3593
School Principal #43....................................... ☎ 614-466-3593
Teacher #43.. ☎ 614-466-3593

Environmental & Agriculture
Milk Hauler/Tester #8 (660)............................. 614-466-5550
Milk Processor #6 .... ☎ 614-466-5550
Milk Producer #6 .... ☎ 614-466-5550
Mine Fire Boss #41 .... ☎ 614-644-2253
Mine Foreman #41 .... ☎ 614-644-2253
Mine Inspector #41 .... ☎ 614-644-2253
Pesticide Applicator #5 (30000) .... ☎ 614-728-6200

Pesticide Dealer #5 (2900) .... ☎ 614-728-6200
Pesticide Operator #5............................... ☎ 614-728-6200
Solid Waste Facility Operator #13 614-644-3020
Surface Blaster #41................................ ☎ 614-644-2253
Veterinarian #32 .... ☎ 614-644-5281

Financial - Real Estate, Insurance & Banking

Banking #33.................................... ☎ 614-466-2932
Credit Union #33 (500) .... ☎ 614-466-2384
Insurance Agent #10 (75000)............................ 614-644-2665
Insurance Solicitor #10 (3000)......................... 614-644-2665
Non Resident Insurance Broker #10 614-644-2665
Public Adjuster #10 (50) 614-644-2665
Real Estate Appraiser #35 (2776) .... ☎ 216-787-3100
Real Estate Broker #35 (7670).................... ☎ 614-466-4100
Real Estate Sales Agent #35 (36261)............. ☎ 614-466-4100
Savings & Loan Association #36 .... ☎ 614-466-3723
Securities Dealer #37 (2008)...................... ☎ 614-466-3466
Securities Salesperson #37 (82370) .... ☎ 614-466-3466

Health & Beauty

Barber #15 (100017)............................... ☎ 614-466-5003
Chiropractor #16 (1775).............................. ☎ 614-644-7032
Cosmetologist/Managing Cosmetologist #3
  (94973) 614-644-6099
Cosmetology/Manicuring/Esthetician Instructor #3
  614-644-6099
Dental Assistant Radiologist #17 614-466-2580
Dental Hygienist #17................................. 614-466-2580
Dentist #17 (6137)................................... 614-466-2580
Dietitian #18 (3021) .... ☎ 614-466-3291
Embalmer #19 (1600)............................... ☎ 614-466-4252
Emergency Medical Technician #12 (36000)
  .... ☎ 614-466-9447
Esthetician/Managing Esthetician #3 614-644-6099
Funeral Director #19 (1600)....................... ☎ 614-466-4252
Hearing Aid Dealer/Fitter #7 (800) .... ✉ 614-466-5215
Manicurist/Managing Manicurist #3 614-644-6099
Masseur/Masseuse #21 .... ✉ 614-466-3934

Medical Doctor #21 .... ✉ 614-466-3934
Nurse #22 .... ✉ 614-466-3947
Nursing Home Administrator #6 (2000)......... ☎ 614-466-5114
Occupational Therapist/Assistant #23 (2585)
  .... ☎ 614-466-3774
Optical Dispenser #24 (3800) .... ☎ 614-466-9707
Optometrist #25 (254)............................... 614-466-5115
Optometrist-Diagnostic #25.......................... 614-466-5115
Optometrist-Therapeutic #25 614-466-5115
Pharmacist #26 (12000)............................ ☎ 614-466-4143
Physical Therapist/Assistant #23 (8000)........ ☎ 614-466-3774
Podiatrist #21 .... ✉ 614-644-6191
Respiratory Therapist #30 (6000).................. ☎ 614-753-9218
Speech Pathologist/Audiologist #31.............. ☎ 614-466-3145

Investigations & Security

Private Investigator #34 (750) .... ☎ 614-466-4130
Security Guard #34 .... ☎ 614-466-4130

Social Services

Adoption #9 (312)................................ ☎ 614-466-9274
Child Day Care #9 (4000)............................ 614-466-3822
Children's Services #9 (9000)..................... ☎ 614-466-3438
Counselor #4 (8000) .... ☎ 614-466-0912
Psychologist #27 (5150) 614-466-8808
School Psychologist #27............................. 614-466-8808
Social Worker #4 (27000) .... ☎ 614-466-0912

Sports & Entertainment

Athletic Trainer #23 (1072)....................... ☎ 614-466-3774
Boxer #40 (100) 330-742-5120
Boxing Manager/Trainer/Second #40 330-742-5120
Boxing Official #40 330-742-5120
Boxing Promoter/Matchmaker #40 330-742-5120
Fishing Guide #11................................ ☎ 614-265-7040
Liquor Control #20 614-466-3132
Lottery Retailer #42............................. ✉ 216-787-3200
Racing #28 (20000) .... ☎ 614-466-2757

State Licensing & Business Registration Agency Information

(1) Accountancy Board of Ohio, 77 S High St, 18th Floor, Columbus, OH 43266-0301, 614-752-8248, Fax: 614-466-6828

(2) Board of Bar Examiners, Office of Attorney Registration, 30 E Broad St, Columbus, OH 43266-0419, 614-644-1553, Fax: 614-728-0930

(3) Board of Cosmetology, 8 E Long St, Suite 1000, Columbus, OH 43215, 614-644-6099

(4) Counselor and Social Worker Board, 77 S High St, 16th Floor, Columbus, OH 43266, 614-466-0912, Fax: 614-728-7790

(5) Department of Agriculture, 8995 E Main St, Reynoldsburg, OH 43068, 614-728-6200, Fax: 614-728-4235

(6) Department of Health, 246 N High St, PO Box 118, Columbus, OH 43266-0118, 614-466-5114, Fax: 614-466-0271

(7) Department of Health, 246 N High St, PO Box 118, Columbus, OH 43266-0588, 614-466-5215

(8) Department of Health, 246 N High St, PO Box 118, Columbus, OH 43266-0588, 614-466-5550

(9) Department of Human Services, Office of Child Care & Family Services, 65 E State St, 5th Floor, Columbus, OH 43215, 614-466-9274, Fax: 614-466-0164

(10) Department of Insurance, 2100 Stella Court, Columbus, OH 43266-0566, 614-644-2665

(11) Department of Natural Resources, Division of Wildlife, 1840 Belcher Dr, Columbus, OH 43224, 614-265-7040, Fax: 614-262-1143

(12) Department of Public Safety, 240 Parsons ave, PO Box 7167, Columbus, OH 43205-0167, 614-466-9447, Fax: 614-466-0433

(13) Hazardous Waste Facility Board, 1800 WaterMark Dr, PO Box 1049, Columbus, OH 43216-1049, 614-644-3020, Fax: 614-644-3439

(14) Licensing Boards, 77 S High St, 16th Floor, Columbus, OH 43266, 614-466-2316, Fax: 614-644-9048

(15) Licensing Boards, 77 S High St, 16th Floor, Columbus, OH 43266-0304, 614-466-5003

(16) Licensing Boards, 77 S High St, 16th Floor, Columbus, OH 43266, 614-644-7032, Fax: 614-752-2539

(17) Licensing Boards, 77 S High St, 18th Floor, Columbus, OH 43266-0550, 614-466-2580

(18) Licensing Boards, 77 S High St, 18th Floor, Columbus, OH 43266-0337, 614-466-3291, Fax: 614-728-0723

(19) Licensing Boards, 77 S High St, 16th Floor, Columbus, OH 43266, 614-466-4252, Fax: 614-728-6825

(20) Licensing Boards, 77 S High St, 18th Floor, Columbus, OH 43266-0565, 614-466-3132

(21) Licensing Boards, 77 S High St, 17th Floor, Columbus, OH 43215, 614-644-6191

(22) Licensing Boards, 77 S High St, 17th Floor, Columbus, OH 43215, 614-466-3947

(23) Licensing Boards, 77 S High St, 16th Floor, Columbus, OH 43266-0317, 614-466-3774, Fax: 614-644-8112

(24) Licensing Boards, 77 S High St, 16th Floor, Columbus, OH 43266-0328, 614-466-9707, Fax: 614-644-8112

(25) Licensing Boards, 77 S High St, 16th Floor, Columbus, OH 43266-0318, 614-466-5115

(26) Licensing Boards, 77 S High St, 17th Floor, Columbus, OH 43266-0320, 614-466-4143, Fax: 614-752-4836

(27) Licensing Boards, 77 S High St, 18th Floor, Columbus, OH 43266-0321, 614-466-8808

(28) Licensing Boards, 77 S High St, 18th Floor, Columbus, OH 43266-0416, 614-466-2757, Fax: 614-466-1000

(29) Licensing Boards, 77 S High St, 16th Floor, Columbus, OH 43266, 614-466-3650, Fax: 614-728-3059

(30) Licensing Boards, 77 S High St, 18th Floor, Columbus, OH 43266, 614-753-9218, Fax: 614-644-8112

(31) Licensing Boards, 77 S High St, 16th Floor, Columbus, OH 43266-0324, 614-466-3145

(32) Licensing Boards, 77 S High St, 16th Floor, Columbus, OH 43266-0116, 614-644-5281, Fax: 614-644-8112

(33) Licensing Boards, Division of Financial Institutions, 77 S High St, 22nd Floor, Columbus, OH 43266-0121, 614-466-2221, Fax: 614-466-1631

(34) Licensing Boards, Division of Licensing, 77 S High St, 20th Floor, Columbus, OH 43266-0544, 614-466-4130

(35) Licensing Boards, Division of Real Estate, 77 S High St, 20th Floor, Columbus, OH 43266, 614-466-4100, Fax: 614-644-0584

(36) Licensing Boards, Division of Savings & Loan Associations, 77 S High St, 21st Floor, Columbus, OH 43266-0121, 614-466-3723, Fax: 614-466-2631

(37) Licensing Boards, Division of Securities, 77 S High St, 22nd Floor, Columbus, OH 43266-0549, 614-466-7381, Fax: 614-466-3316

(38) Office of Governor, 77 S High St, Level B-1, Columbus, OH 43215, 614-466-2566

(39) Office of Legislative Inspector General, 50 W Broad St, Ste 1308, Columbus, OH 43215-3365, 614-728-5100

(40) Ohio Boxing Commission, 2545 Belmont Ave, Union Square Plaza, Youngstown, OH 44505, 216-742-5120

(41) Ohio Department of Commerce, Division of Industrial Compliance, 6606 Tussing Rd., PO Box 4009, Renoldsburg, OH 43068-9009, 614-644-2622, Fax: 614-644-2428

(42) Ohio Lottery Commission, 615 W Superior Ave, NW Frank J. Lausche Bldg, Cleveland, OH 44113, 216-787-3200, Fax: 216-787-3718

(43) State Department of Education, Division of Teacher Education & Certification, 65 S Front St, Room 1012, Columbus, OH 43266-0308, 614-466-3593, Fax: 614-466-1999

Oklahoma

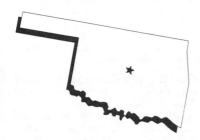

Capitol: Oklahoma City (Oklahoma County)	
State Population	3.3 Million
Number of Degree Granting Institutions:	44
Number of State Licensing & Business Registration Agencies:	124

Degree Granting Educational Institutions

Bacone College, Registrar, 2299 Old Bacone Rd, Muskogee, OK 74403-1597, 918-683-4581 X275-277 (Fax: 918-687-5913). Hours: 8AM-4:30PM. Enrollment: 500. Records go back to 1880. Alumni records are maintained here at the same phone number. Degrees granted: Associate. Adverse incident record source- Dean, 918-683-4581.

Attendance and degree information available by phone, fax, mail. Search requires name plus SSN, approximate years of attendance. Also helpful: date of birth. There is no fee.

Bartlesville Wesleyan College, Registrar, 2201 Silver Lake Rd, Bartlesville, OK 74006, 918-333-6151 (Fax: 918-335-6229). Hours: 8AM-Noon, 1-5PM. Enrollment: 550. Records go back to 1909. Alumni records are maintained here at the same phone number. Degrees granted: Associate; Bachelors. Adverse incident record source- Student Development, 918-333-6151.

Attendance information available by phone, fax, mail. Search requires name only. Also helpful: SSN, date of birth, exact years of attendance. There is no fee.

Degree information available by fax, mail. Search requires name only. Also helpful: SSN, date of birth, exact years of attendance. There is no fee.

Cameron University, Registrar, 2800 Gore Blvd, Lawton, OK 73505, 405-581-2238 (Fax: 405-581-5514). Hours: 8AM-5Pm. Enrollment: 5600. Records go back to 1920. Alumni records are maintained here also. Call 405-581-2988. Degrees granted: Associate; Bachelors; Masters. Special programs-Teacher Certification, 405-581-2339. Adverse incident record source- Dean, 405-581-2209.

Attendance and degree information available by mail. Search requires name plus SSN, exact years of attendance. There is no fee.

Carl Albert State College, Registrar, 1507 S McKenna, Poteau, OK 74953-5208, 918-647-1300 (Fax: 918-647-1201). Hours: 8AM-4:30PM. Enrollment: 2000. Records go back to 1934. Alumni records are maintained here also. Call 918-647-1213. Degrees granted: Associate. Special programs- Nursing-RN, 918-647-1350: Physical Therapist Assistant, 918-647-1357. Adverse incident record source- Student Affairs, 918-647-1370.

Attendance and degree information available by phone, fax, mail. Search requires name plus SSN, date of birth, exact years of attendance. There is no fee.

Connors State College, Registrar, Rte 1 Box 1000, Warner, OK 74469, 918-463-6241 (Fax: 918-463-6272). Hours: 8AM-4:30PM. Enrollment: 2200. Records go back to 1927. Alumni Records Office: Alumni Association, 2501 N 41st St E, Muskogee, OK 74403. Degrees granted: Associate. Adverse incident record source- Ed Hardeman, 918-463-6217.

Attendance and degree information available by phone, fax, mail. Search requires name only. Also helpful: SSN, date of birth, exact years of attendance. There is no fee.

East Central University, Registrar, Ada, OK 74820, 405-332-8000 (Fax: 405-436-5495). Hours: 8AM-5PM. Enrollment: 4500. Records go back to 1907. Alumni records are maintained here also. Call 405-332-8000 X611. Degrees granted: Bachelors; Masters. Adverse incident record source- Student Services, 405-332-8000 X208.

Attendance information available by phone, fax, mail. Search requires name plus SSN, approximate years of attendance. Also helpful: date of birth, exact years of attendance. There is no fee.

Degree information available by phone, fax, mail. Search requires name plus SSN. Also helpful: date of birth, exact years of attendance. There is no fee.

Eastern Oklahoma State College, Registrar, 1301 W Main St, Wilburton, OK 74578, 918-465-2361 X346 (Fax: 918-465-2431). Hours: 7:30AM-4:30PM. Enrollment: 2400. Records go back to 1911. Alumni records are maintained here also. Call 918-465-2361 X215. Degrees granted: Associate.

Attendance and degree information available by fax, mail. Search requires name plus signed release. Also helpful: SSN, exact years of attendance. There is no fee.

Hilldale Free Will Baptist College, Registrar, PO Box 7208, Moore, OK 73153, 405-794-6661 (Fax: 405-794-6663). Enrollment: 150. Records go back to 1959. Alumni records are maintained here at the same phone number. Degrees granted: Associate; Bachelors; Bible Certificate. Adverse incident record source- Dean of Students, 405-794-6661 X224.

Attendance and degree information available by phone, fax, mail. Search requires name only. Also helpful: SSN, date of birth, exact years of attendance. There is no fee.

Langston University, Registrar, PO Box 907, Langston, OK 73050-0907, 405-466-3225 (Fax: 405-466-3381). Hours: 8AM-5PM. Enrollment: 4070. Records go back to 1910. Alumni records are maintained here also. Call 405-466-3201 X2999. Degrees granted: Associate; Bachelors; Masters. Adverse incident record source- Student Affairs, 405-466-3444.

Attendance and degree information available by phone, fax, mail. Search requires name plus SSN. Also helpful: date of birth, exact years of attendance. There is no fee.

Mid-America Bible College, Registrar, 3500 SW 119th St, Oklahoma City, OK 73170-9797, 405-691-3800 (Fax: 405-692-3165). Hours: 8:30AM-4PM. Enrollment: 450. Records go back to 1956. Alumni records are maintained here at the same phone number. Degrees granted: Associate; Bachelors.

Attendance and degree information available by phone, fax, mail. Search requires name only. Also helpful: SSN, exact years of attendance. There is no fee.

Murray State College, Registrar, 1100 S Murray, Tishomingo, OK 73460, 405-371-2371 X108 (Fax: 405-371-9844). Hours: 8AM-4:30PM. Enrollment: 1700. Alumni records are maintained here at the same phone number. Degrees granted: Associate.

Attendance information available by phone, fax, mail. Search requires name plus SSN, date of birth, exact years of attendance. There is no fee.

Degree information available by fax, mail. Search requires name plus SSN, date of birth, exact years of attendance. There is no fee.

Northeastern Oklahoma A&M College, Registrar, 200 I St NE, Miami, OK 74354, 918-542-8441 (Fax: 918-542-9759). Hours: 8AM-4:30PM. Enrollment: 2381. Records go back to 1940's. Alumni records are maintained here also. Call 918-542-8441 X385. Degrees granted: Associate.

Attendance and degree information available by phone, mail. Search requires name plus SSN, date of birth. Also helpful: exact years of attendance. There is no fee.

Northeastern State University, Registrar, Tahlequah, OK 74464, 918-456-5511 X2200 (Fax: 918-456-2342). Hours: 8AM-Noon, 1-5PM. Enrollment: 9300. Records go back to 1900. Alumni records are maintained here also. Call 918-456-5511 X4200. Degrees granted: Bachelors; Masters. Special programs- Doctor of Optometry, 918-456-5511 X4000.

Attendance and degree information available by mail. Search requires name plus SSN, date of birth. Also helpful: exact years of attendance. There is no fee.

Northern Oklahoma College, Registrar, PO Box 310, 1220 E Grand Ave, Tonkawa, OK 74653-0310, 405-628-6200 (Fax: 405-628-5260). Hours: 8AM-5PM. Enrollment: 2232. Degrees granted: Associate.

Attendance and degree information available by mail. Search requires name plus SSN, date of birth. There is no fee.

Northwestern Oklahoma State University, Registrar, 709 Oklahoma Blvd, Alva, OK 73717, 405-327-8553 (Fax: 405-327-1881). Hours: 8AM-5PM. Enrollment: 2000. Records go back to 1897. Alumni records are maintained here also. Call 405-327-8593. Degrees granted: Bachelors; Masters. Adverse incident record source- Dean of Students, 405-327-8414: Alva Police, 405-327-2121

Attendance and degree information available by phone, fax, mail. Search requires name only. Also helpful: SSN, date of birth, exact years of attendance. There is no fee.

Oklahoma Baptist University, Registrar, OBU Box 61173, Shawnee, OK 74801, 405-878-2023 (Fax: 405-878-2046). Hours: 8AM-5PM. Enrollment: 2400. Records go back to 1910. Alumni Records Office: OBU Box 61275, Shawnee, OK 74801, 405-878-2706. Degrees granted: Associate; Bachelors;

Masters. Adverse incident record source- Dean of Students, 405-878-4206.

Attendance and degree information available by phone, fax, mail. Search requires name plus SSN, date of birth. Also helpful: exact years of attendance. There is no fee.

Oklahoma Christian University of Science and Arts, Registrar, PO Box 11000, Oklahoma City, OK 73136, 405-425-5200 (Fax: 405-425-5208). Hours: 8AM-5PM. Enrollment: 1445. Records go back to 1951. Alumni records are maintained here also. Call 405-425-5120. Degrees granted: Bachelors; Masters. Adverse incident record source- Student Development, 405-425-5220.

Attendance and degree information available by phone, fax, mail. Search requires name only. Also helpful: SSN, date of birth, exact years of attendance. There is no fee.

Oklahoma City Community College, Registrar, 7777 S May Ave, Oklahoma City, OK 73159, 405-682-7512 (Fax: 405-682-7521). Hours: 8AM-8PM M; 8AM-6PM T,W; 11:30AM-6PM Th; 8AM-5PM F. Enrollment: 600. Records go back to 1990. Alumni records are maintained here also. Call 405-682-7523. Degrees granted: Associate. Adverse incident record source- Dean, 405-682-7590.

Attendance and degree information available by phone, fax, mail. Search requires name plus SSN, approximate years of attendance. There is no fee.

Oklahoma City University, Registrar, 2501 N Blackwelder Ave, Oklahoma City, OK 73106, 405-521-5296 (Fax: 405-521-5264). Hours: 8AM-6PM M, 8AM-5PM T-F. Enrollment: 2237. Records go back to 1904. Alumni records are maintained here at the same phone number. Degrees granted: Bachelors; Masters.

Attendance information available by mail. Search requires name plus SSN, exact years of attendance, signed release. Also helpful: date of birth. There is no fee.

Degree information available by phone, fax, mail. Search requires name plus SSN, exact years of attendance. Also helpful: date of birth. There is no fee.

Oklahoma Panhandle State University, Registrar, Box 430, Goodwell, OK 73939, 405-349-2611 X223 (Fax: 405-349-2302). Hours: 8AM-4:30PM. Enrollment: 1150. Records go back to 1921. Alumni records are maintained here also. Call 405-349-2611. Degrees granted: Associate; Bachelors.

Attendance information available by phone, fax, mail. Search requires name plus SSN. Also helpful: date of birth, approximate years of attendance. There is no fee.

Degree information available by phone, fax, mail. Search requires name only. Also helpful: SSN, date of birth, approximate years of attendance. There is no fee.

Oklahoma State University, Registrar's Office, 103 Whitehurst, Stillwater, OK 74078, 405-744-6888 (Fax: 405-744-8426). Hours: 8AM-5PM. Enrollment: 18000. Records go back to 1900. Alumni Records Office: 212 Student Union, Stillwater, OK 74078, 405-744-5368. Degrees granted: Bachelors; Masters; Doctorate. Adverse incident record source- Student Conduct Officer: University Counseling

Attendance and degree information available by phone, fax, mail. Search requires name plus SSN, approximate years of attendance. Also helpful: date of birth, exact years of attendance. There is no fee.

Oklahoma State University (Oklahoma City), Registrar, 900 N Portland Ave, Oklahoma City, OK 73107, 405-945-3291 (Fax: 405-945-3277). Hours: 8AM-6PM. Enrollment: 4159. Records go back to 1961. Alumni records are maintained here also. Call 405-945-8618. Degrees granted: Associate.

Attendance and degree information available by phone, fax, mail. Search requires name plus SSN, date of birth, approximate years of attendance. There is no fee.

Oklahoma State University (Okmulgee), Registrar, 1801 E Fourth St, Okmulgee, OK 74447, 918-756-6211 (Fax: 918-756-4157). Hours: 7:30AM-4:30PM. Enrollment: 2188. Alumni records are maintained here also. Call 918-756-6211. Degrees granted: Associate. Adverse incident record source- Student Services, 918-756-6211 X364.

Attendance information available by phone, fax. Search requires name plus SSN, date of birth, approximate years of attendance. There is no fee.

Degree information available by phone, fax, mail. Search requires name plus SSN, date of birth, approximate years of attendance. There is no fee.

Oklahoma State University College of Osteopathic Medicine, Registrar, 1111 W 17th St, Tulsa, OK 74107, 800-677-1972 (Fax: 918-561-8243). Hours: 8AM-5PM. Enrollment: 271. Records go back to 1977. Alumni records are maintained here also. Call 918-582-1972.

Attendance and degree information available by phone, fax, mail. Search requires name plus SSN, exact years of attendance. Also helpful: date of birth. There is no fee.

Oral Roberts University, Registrar, 7777 S Lewis Ave, Tulsa, OK 74171, 918-495-6549. Hours: 8AM-4:30PM. Records go back to 1960. Alumni records are maintained here also. Call 918-495-6627. Degrees granted: Bachelors; Masters; Doctorate.

Attendance and degree information available by phone, mail. Search requires name plus SSN. There is no fee.

Phillips Graduate Seminary, Registrar, 102 University Dr, PO Box 2335 University Station, Enid, OK 73702, 405-548-2239 (Fax: 405-237-7686). Records are not housed here. They are located at Phillips University, Registrar, 100 S University Ave, Enid, OK 73701.

Phillips University, Registrar, 100 S University Ave, Enid, OK 73701, 405-548-2272 (Fax: 405-237-1607). Hours: 8:30AM-4PM. Enrollment: 1606. Records go back to 1906. Alumni records are maintained here also. Call 405-548-2293. Degrees granted: Bachelors; Masters.

Attendance and degree information available by phone, mail. Search requires name plus SSN, approximate years of attendance. There is no fee.

Redlands Community College, Registrar, 1300 S Country Club Rd, El Reno, OK 73036-0370, 405-262-2552 (Fax: 405-422-1200). Hours: 8AM-5PM. Enrollment: 2100. Records go back to 1938. Alumni records are maintained here at the same phone number. Degrees granted: Associate.

Attendance and degree information available by phone, fax, mail. Search requires name only. Also helpful: SSN, date of birth, exact years of attendance. There is no fee.

Rogers State College, Registrar, Will Rogers and College Hill, Claremore, OK 74017, 918-343-7540 (Fax: 918-343-7595). Hours: 8AM-5PM. Enrollment: 3000. Records go back to 1908. Alumni records are maintained here also. Call 918-343-7769. Degrees granted: Associate. Adverse incident record source- Student Services, 918-343-7579.

Attendance and degree information available by phone, fax, mail. Search requires name plus SSN. Also helpful: date of birth, exact years of attendance. There is no fee.

Rose State College, Registrar, 6420 SE 15th St, Midwest City, OK 73110, 405-733-7308 (Fax: 405-733-7440). Hours: 8AM-8PM M-Th, 8AM-6PMF. Records go back to 1971. Alumni records are maintained here also. Call 405-736-0313. Degrees granted: Associate.

Attendance and degree information available by phone, mail. Search requires name plus SSN. There is no fee.

Seminole State College, Registrar, PO Box 351, Seminole, OK 74868-0351, 405-382-9950 X248 (Fax: 405-382-3122). Hours: 8AM-5PM. Enrollment: 1600. Formerly Seminole Junior College Records go back to 1970. Alumni records are maintained here also. Call 405-382-9218. Degrees granted: Associate. Adverse incident record source- Campus Police, 405-382-9500.

Attendance information available by phone, fax, mail. Search requires name plus SSN, approximate years of attendance. Also helpful: date of birth, exact years of attendance. There is no fee.

Degree information available by phone, fax, mail. Search requires name plus SSN, approximate years of attendance. Also helpful: exact years of attendance. There is no fee.

Southeastern Oklahoma State University, Registrar, PO Box 4139, Durant, OK 74701-0609, 405-924-0121 (Fax: 405-920-7472). Hours: 8AM-5PM. Enrollment: 4000. Records go back to 1909. Alumni records are maintained here at the same phone number. Degrees granted: Bachelors; Masters. Adverse incident record source- Student Affairs.

Attendance and degree information available by phone, fax, mail. Search requires name only. Also helpful: SSN, date of birth, exact years of attendance. There is no fee.

Southern Nazarene University, Registrar's Office, 6729 NW 39th Expwy, Bethany, OK 73008, 405-491-6386 (Fax: 405-491-6381). Hours: 8AM-5PM. Enrollment: 1834. Records go back to 1900's. Alumni records are maintained here also. Call 405-491-6312. Degrees granted: Bachelors; Masters. Adverse incident record source- Student Development, 405-491-6336.

Attendance and degree information available by phone, fax, mail. Search requires name plus SSN. Also helpful: date of birth. There is no fee.

Southwestern College of Christian Ministries, Registrar, PO Box 340, Bethany, OK 73008, 405-789-7661 X3423 (Fax: 405-789-7661 X3432). Hours: 8:30AM-4:30PM. Records go back to 1946. Alumni records are maintained here at the same phone number. Degrees granted: Associate; Bachelors; Masters.

Attendance and degree information available by phone, fax, mail. Search requires name plus SSN. Also helpful: date of birth, exact years of attendance. There is no fee.

Southwestern Oklahoma State University, Registrar, 100 Campus Dr, Weatherford, OK 73096, 405-772-6611 (Fax: 405-774-3795). Hours: 8AM-5PM. Enrollment: 5000. Records go back to 1918. Alumni records are maintained here also. Call 405-774-3267. Degrees granted: Associate; Bachelors; Masters. Special programs- Associate, 405-928-5533. Adverse incident record source- Public Safety, 405-774-3785.

Attendance information available by phone, fax, mail. Search requires name plus SSN. There is no fee.

Degree information available by phone, fax, mail. Search requires name plus SSN, approximate years of attendance. There is no fee.

Southwestern Oklahoma State University, (Sayre), Registrar, 409 E Mississippi, Sayre, OK 73662, 405-928-5533 (Fax: 405-928-5533). Hours: 8AM-5PM. Enrollment: 531. Records go back to 1938. Degrees granted: Associate. Adverse incident record source- Registrar, 405-928-5533.

Attendance and degree information available by phone, fax, mail. Search requires name plus SSN. There is no fee.

St. Gregory's College, Registrar, 1900 W MacArthur, Shawnee, OK 74801, 405-878-5433 (Fax: 405-878-5198). Hours: 8AM-4:30PM. Enrollment: 425. Records go back to 1920. Alumni records are maintained here also. Call 405-878-

5172. Degrees granted: Associate. Adverse incident record source- Dean, 405-878-5400.

Attendance information available by phone, fax, mail. Search requires name plus SSN. Also helpful: date of birth. There is no fee.

Degree information available by fax, mail. Search requires name plus SSN. Also helpful: date of birth. There is no fee.

Tulsa Community College, (Metro), Registrar's Office, 909 S Boston, Tulsa, OK 74119, 918-595-7226 (Fax: 918-595-7347). Hours: 8AM-7PM M-Th, 8AM-5PM F. Enrollment: 21500. Formerly Tulsa Junior College (Metro) Records go back to 1970. Degrees granted: Associate. Adverse incident record source- Security, 918-631-7263.

Attendance and degree information available by mail. Search requires name plus SSN, signed release. There is no fee.

University of Central Oklahoma, Registrar, 100 N University Dr, Bos 158, Edmond, OK 73060, 405-341-2980 X2331 (Fax: 405-341-4964). Hours: 8AM-7:30PM M; 8AM-5PM T-F. Enrollment: 15000. Records go back to 1891. All records are maintained here at the same phone number. Degrees granted: Bachelors; Masters. Adverse incident record source- Student Services.

Attendance and degree information available by phone, fax. Search requires name plus SSN, approximate years of attendance. Also helpful: date of birth, exact years of attendance. There is no fee.

University of Oklahoma, Registrar's Office, 1000 Asp Ave, Norman, OK 73019, 405-325-2012 (Fax: 405-325-7047). Hours: 8AM-5PM. Enrollment: 16455. Records go back to 1940. Alumni Records Office: Alumni Association, University of Oklahoma, 900 Asp Ave, Norman, OK 73019. Degrees granted: Bachelors. Adverse incident record source- Registrar, 405-325-2012.

Attendance and degree information available by phone, fax, mail. Search requires name plus SSN, exact years of attendance. There is no fee.

University of Oklahoma Health Sciences Center, Registrar, PO Box 26901, Oklahoma City, OK 73126-0901, 405-271-1537 (Fax: 405-271-2480). Hours: 8AM-5PM. Enrollment: 3000. Records go back to 1900's. Alumni records are maintained here at the same phone number. Degrees granted: Bachelors; Masters; Doctorate. Adverse incident record source- Campus Police, 405-271-4300.

Attendance and degree information available by phone, fax, mail. Search requires name only. Also helpful: SSN, date of birth, exact years of attendance. There is no fee.

University of Science and Arts of Oklahoma, Registrar, PO Box 82345, Chickasha, OK 73018, 405-224-3140 X204 (Fax: 405-521-6244). Hours: 8AM-5PM. Enrollment: 1600. Records go back to 1911. Alumni records are maintained here also. Call 405-224-3140 X290. Degrees granted: Bachelors.

Attendance and degree information available by phone, mail. Search requires name plus SSN. Fee is $1.00.

University of Tulsa, Registrar, 600 S College Ave, Tulsa, OK 74104, 918-631-2253 (Fax: 918-631-2622). Hours: 8AM-6PM M-Th; 8AM-5PM F. Enrollment: 3168. Alumni records are maintained here also. Call 918-631-2555. Degrees granted: Bachelors; Masters; Doctorate; J.D.

Attendance information available by phone, fax, mail. Search requires name plus SSN, approximate years of attendance. Also helpful: date of birth, exact years of attendance. There is no fee.

Degree information available by fax, mail. Search requires name plus SSN, approximate years of attendance. Also helpful: date of birth, exact years of attendance. There is no fee.

Western Oklahoma State College, Admissions and Registrar, 2801 N Main St, Altus, OK 73521, 405-477-2000 (Fax: 405-521-6154). Hours: 7:30AM-4:30PM. Enrollment: 1703. Records go back to 1926. Alumni records are maintained here at the same phone number. Degrees granted: Associate. Adverse incident record source- Student Affairs.

Attendance and degree information available by phone, fax, mail. Search requires name plus SSN. There is no fee.

Trade and Vocational Schools

Advance Barber College, 5301 S Penn, Oklahoma City, OK 73118, 405-685-0172

Bryan Institute, 2843 E 51st St, Tulsa, OK 74105, 918-749-6891

Career Point Business School (Branch Campus), 3138 S Garnett Rd, Tulsa, OK 74146, 918-622-4100

Central Oklahoma Area Vocational-Technical Center, 3 CVT Cir, Drumright, OK 74030, 918-352-2551

Climate Control Institute, 708 S Sheridan Rd, Tulsa, OK 74112, 918-836-6656

Francis Tuttle Vocational-Technical Center, 12777 N Rockwell Ave, Oklahoma City, OK 73142, 405-722-7799

Great Plains Area Vocational-Technical Center, 4500 W Lee Blvd, Lawton, OK 73505, 405-355-6371

Hollywood Cosmetology Center, PO Box 890488, Oklahoma City, OK 73189, 405-364-3375

Indian Meridian Vocational-Technical Center, 1312 S Sangre Rd, Stillwater, OK 74074, 405-377-3333

Meridian Technology Center, 1312 S Sangre St, Stillwater, OK 74074, 405-377-3333

Metropolitan College of Court Reporting, 2525 Northwest Expy #215, Oklahoma City, OK 73112, 405-840-2181

Metropolitan College of Legal Studies, 2865 E Skelly Dr, Tulsa, OK 74105, 918-745-9946

Mid-Del College, 3420 S Sunny Ln, Del City, OK 73115, 405-677-8311

Miss Shirley's Beauty College, 309 SW 59th St #305, Oklahoma City, OK 73109, 405-631-0055

O.T. Autry Area Vocational-Technical Center, 1201 W Willow St, Enid, OK 73703, 405-242-2750

Oklahoma Farrier's College, Rte 2 Box 88, Sperry, OK 74073, 918-288-7221

Oklahoma State Horseshoeing School, Rte 1 Box 28B, Ardmore, OK 73401, 405-223-0064

Platt College, 4821 S 72nd E Ave, Tulsa, OK 74145, 918-663-9000

Platt College (Branch Campus), 3737 N Portland Ave, Oklahoma City, OK 73112, 405-942-8683

State Barber & Hair Design College, Inc., 2514 S Agnew Ave, Oklahoma City, OK 73108, 405-631-8621

Tulsa Technology Center, 3420 S Memorial Dr, Tulsa, OK 74145, 918-627-7200

Tulsa Welding School, 3038 Southwest Blvd, Tulsa, OK 74107, 918-587-6789

United States Coast Guard Institute, 5900 SW 64th Rm 235, Oklahoma City, OK 73169, 405-680-4262

Wright Business School, 2219 SW 74th St #122, Oklahoma City, OK 73159, 405-681-2300

State Licensing & Business Registration Quick Finder Index

Architecture, Engineering & Surveying
Architect #25 (1880)..................................... ☎ 405-751-6512
Engineer #15... ☎ 405-521-2874
Landscape Architect #25 (125) .... ☎ 405-751-6512
Surveyor #15.. ☎ 405-521-2874

Business - Court & Legal Services
Attorney #28 (12585) 405-524-2365
Attorney, Active #28 405-524-2365
Attorney, Active-Associate #28 405-524-2365
Attorney, Legal Intern #28 405-524-2365
Attorney, Senior #28...................................... 405-524-2365
Bondsman #32 (363) .... ☎ 405-521-6610
Lobbyist #26 .... ☎ 405-521-3911
Notary Public #26... ☎ 405-521-3911
Shorthand Reporter #11.................................. ☎ 405-521-2450

Business - General Services
Employment Agency #24 .... ☎ 405-528-1500
Pawnbroker #23 (519).................................... 405-521-3653
Precious Metal & Gem Dealer #23 (31).............. 405-521-3653
Public Accountant #16 (220).......................... ☎ 405-521-2397
Public Accountant-CPA #16 (10840) .... ☎ 405-521-2397
Rent to Own Dealer #23 405-521-3653

Construction & Manufacturing
Building Inspector #39 (378) .... ☎ 405-271-5217
Electrical Contractor/Journeyman #39 405-271-5217
Electrical Inspector #39.................................. 405-271-5217
Mechanical Contractor/Journeyman #38........ ☎ 405-271-5217
Mechanical Inspector #38............................. ☎ 405-271-5217
Plumbing Contractor/Journeyman #38........... ☎ 405-271-5217
Plumbing Inspector #38................................ ☎ 405-271-5217
Weld Testing Laboratory #24...................... ☎ 405-528-1500
Welder #24.. ☎ 405-528-1500

Education
School Accreditation #42 .... ✉ 405-521-3301
School Transportation #42 .... ✉ 405-521-3301
Teacher #42 .... ✉ 405-521-3301

Environmental & Agriculture
Agricultural Marketing #22............................ ✉ 405-521-3864
Agricultural Promoting #22............................ ✉ 405-521-3864
Animal Industry #22.................................... ✉ 405-521-3864
Animal Technician #19 .... ☎ 405-843-0843
Asbestos Abatement Contractor/Worker #24
.... ☎ 405-528-1500
Forester-Registered #17 (118)...................... ☎ 405-521-3864

Ground Water & Observation Water Well Driller #40 .... ☎ 405-521-3859
Liquified Petroleum Dealers #33 (280).......... ☎ 405-521-2458
Liquified Petroleum Managers #33 (398) ...... ☎ 405-521-2458
Liquified Petroleum Manufacturer/Others #33 (1512) .... ☎ 405-521-2458
Liquified Petroleum System Installer (and Bobtail Drivers) #33 (1391)...................... ☎ 405-521-2458
Mining Operation for Land Reclamation #34 (400) .... ☎ 405-521-3859
Pump Installer #40...................................... ☎ 405-521-3859
Veterinarian #19... ☎ 405-843-0843
Waste Water Operator #40 .... ☎ 405-521-3859
Water Operator #40..................................... ☎ 405-521-3859
Well Driller/Monitor #40............................. ☎ 405-521-3859

Financial - Real Estate, Insurance & Banking
Consumer Finance Company #23 (1127)............ 405-521-3653
Credit Services Organization #23.................... 405-521-3653
Credit Union #37 .... ☎ 405-521-2783
Insurance Adjuster #32................................. ☎ 405-521-6610
Insurance Agent/Representative #32 .... ☎ 405-521-6610
Insurance Consultant #32 .... ☎ 405-521-6610
Investment Adviser #36 (516) 405-521-2451
Investment Adviser Representative #36 405-521-2451
Money Order Agent #37................................ ☎ 405-521-2783
Real Estate Appraiser #35............................. ☎ 405-521-6610
Real Estate Broker #35 (8643) .... ☎ 405-521-6610
Real Estate Salesperson #35 (9157) .... ☎ 405-521-3387
Savings & Loan Association #37 .... ☎ 405-521-2783
Securities Agent (41534)................................ 405-521-2451
Securities Broker/Dealer #36 (1283) 405-521-2451
State Chartered Bank #37 .... ☎ 405-521-2783
Trust Company #37...................................... ☎ 405-521-2783

Health & Beauty
Audiologist #6 (235)..................................... ☎ 405-840-2774
Barber #39... 405-271-5217
Beauty School #4 (1600) .... ☎ 405-521-2441
Beauty Shop #4 (2500)................................. ☎ 405-521-2441
Chiropractor #3 (680) .... ☎ 405-528-5505
Cosmetology Instructor #4 (1192).................. ☎ 405-521-2441
Cosmetology Student & Apprentice #4 (8).... ☎ 405-521-2441
Dental Assistant #29 (1690) .... ☎ 405-848-1364
Dental Hygienist #29 (1220) .... ☎ 405-848-1364
Dentist #29 (1832) .... ☎ 405-848-1364
Dietitian #10.. 405-848-6841

Dietitian (and Provisional Licensed Dietitian) #10
(779) 405-848-6841
Electrologist #10 (28) 405-848-6841
Embalmer #5 (500) .... ☎ 405-525-0158
Emergency Medical Technician #39 .... ☎ 405-271-5217
Facial Operator #4 (1920) .... ☎ 405-521-2441
Funeral Director #5 (500) .... ☎ 405-525-0158
Health Spa #23 (68) 405-521-3653
Hearing Aid Dealer/Fitter #39 .... ☎ 405-271-5217
Manicurist #4 (1949) .... ☎ 405-521-2441
Medical Doctor #10 (7502) 405-848-6841
Nurse #30 (24128) .... ✉ 405-525-2076
Nurse Anesthetist #30 (378) .... ✉ 405-525-2076
Nurse Midwife #30 (21) .... ✉ 405-525-2076
Nursing Home Administrator #2 405-848-8338
Occupational Therapist/Assistant #10 (726) 405-848-6841
Optometrist #7 (635) .... ☎ 405-733-7836
Osteopathic Physician #12 (1400) .... ☎ 405-528-8625
Pharmacist #13 405-521-3815
Pharmacy #13 405-521-3815
Physical Therapist/Assistant #10 (1744) 405-848-6841
Physician Assistant #10 405-848-6841
Physician's Assistant #10 (318) 405-848-6841
Podiatrist #14 (85) .... ☎ 405-848-6841
Practical Nurse #30 (13251) .... ✉ 405-525-2076
Respiratory Care Practitioner #10 405-848-6841
Sanitarian/Environmental Specialist #43 (621)
.... ☎ 405-271-5217
Speech Pathologist #6 (2207) .... ☎ 405-840-2774

Investigations & Security
Alcohol & Drug Influence Tester #18 (4000) 405-271-2270
Burglar Alarm Salesman #39 405-271-5217
Burglar Alarm Service/Installer #39 405-271-5217
Fire Alarm Salesman #39 .... ☎ 405-271-5217
Fire Alarm Service/Installer #39 .... ☎ 405-271-5217
Polygraph Examiner/Intern #41 (74) .... ☎ 405-425-2778
Private Investigator #21 405-425-2750
Private Investigator Agency #21 405-425-2750
Security Guard #21 405-425-2750
Security Guard Agency #21 405-425-2755

Social Services
Children & Youth Private Agency #20 405-521-3561
Children & Youth Public Agency #20 405-521-3561
Counselor LPC/LM&T #44 405-271-6030
Counselor (LPC) #44 (1200) 405-271-6030
Psychologist #8 (460) .... ✉ 405-271-6118
Social Worker #9 405-946-7230

Sports & Entertainment
Athletic Trainer & Apprentice #10 405-848-6841
Athletic Trainer/Apprentice Athletic Trainer #10
(153) 405-848-6841
Horse Racing #31 (10000) .... ✉ 405-943-6472
Liquor Industry #1 .... ☎ 405-521-3484

Transportation
Airport Development Project #27 405-521-2377

State Licensing & Business Registration Agency Information

(1) Alcoholic Beverage Laws Enforcement Commission, 4545 N Lincoln Dr, #270, Oklahoma City, OK 73105, 405-521-3484

(2) Board for Nursing Home Administrators, 3033 N Walnut, #100E, Oklahoma City, OK 73105, 405-521-0991, Fax: 405-528-3483

(3) Board of Chiropractic Examiners, 310 NE 28th St, Suite 205, Oklahoma City, OK 73105, 405-528-5505, Fax: 405-528-5447

(4) Board of Cosmetology, 2200 Classen Blvd, Suite 1530, Oklahoma City, OK 73106, 405-521-2441, Fax: 405-528-8310

(5) Board of Embalmers & Funeral Directors, 4545 N Lincoln Blvd, Suite 175, Oklahoma City, OK 73105, 405-525-0158, Fax: 405-557-1844

(6) Board of Examiners for Speech Pathology/Audiology, 1140 NW 63rd, Suite 305, PO Box 53592, Oklahoma City, OK 73152, 405-840-2774, Fax: 405-840-2774

(7) Board of Examiners in Optometry, 310 S. Highland Avenue, Oklahoma City, OK 73110, 405-733-7836, Fax: 405-741-3060

(8) Board of Examiners of Psychologists, PO Box 53551, 1000 NE 10th, Room 504, Oklahoma City, OK 73152, 405-271-6118, Fax: 405-271-6137

(9) Board of Licensed Social Workers, 4145 NW 61st Terrace, Oklahoma City, OK 73112, 405-946-7230

(10) Board of Medical Licensure & Supervision, 5104 N Francis, Suite C, PO Box 18256, Oklahoma City, OK 73154-0256, 405-848-6841

(11) Board of Official Shorthand Reporters, 1915 N Stiles, Room 305, Oklahoma City, OK 73105, 405-521-2450, Fax: 405-521-3815

(12) Board of Osteopathic Examiners, 4848 N Lincoln, Suite 100, Oklahoma City, OK 73105, 405-528-8625, Fax: 405-528-8625

(13) Board of Pharmacy, 4545 N Lincoln Blvd, Suite 112 North Terrace, Oklahoma City, OK 73105-3488, 405-521-3815

(14) Board of Podiatry, 5104 N Francis, Suite C, Box 18256, Oklahoma City, OK 73154-0256, 405-848-6841, Fax: 405-848-8240

(15) Board of Prof. Engineers & Land Surveyors, Oklahoma Engineering Center, 201 NE 27th St Rm 120, Oklahoma City, OK 73105, 405-521-2874, Fax: 405-523-3135

(16) Board of Public Accountancy, 4545 N Lincoln Blvd, Suite 165, Oklahoma City, OK 73105, 405-521-2397, Fax: 405-521-3118

(17) Board of Registration for Foresters, c/o Agriculture Building, 2800 N Lincoln Blvd, Oklahoma City, OK 73105-4298, 405-521-3864 ext 296, Fax: 405-522-4583

(18) Board of Tests for Alcohol & Drug Influence, State Department of Public Safety, 3600 Martin Luther King Ave, PO Box 11415, Oklahoma City, OK 73136, 405-271-2270, Fax: 405-271-3798

(19) Board of Veterinary Medical Examiners, 5104 N Francis, Suite F, Oklahoma City, OK 73118, 405-843-0843, Fax: 405-840-4501

(20) Commission on Children & Youth, 4545 N Lincoln Blvd, Suite 114, Oklahoma City, OK 73105, 405-521-3561, Fax: 405-524-0417

(21) Council on Law Enforcement Education & Training, PO Box 11476, Cimarron Station, Oklahoma City, OK 73136-0476, 405-425-2750

(22) Department of Agriculture, 2800 N Lincoln Blvd, Oklahoma City, OK 73105, 405-521-3864, Fax: 405-521-4912

(23) Department of Consumer Credit, Commission of Consumer Credit, 4545 N Lincoln Blvd, Suite 104, Oklahoma City, OK 73105, 405-521-3653

(24) Department of Labor, 4001 N Lincoln Blvd, Oklahoma City, OK 73105, 405-528-1500, Fax: 405-528-5751

(25) Licensed Architects & Landscape Architects, 11212 N. May, Suite 110, Oklahoma City, OK 73120, 405-751-6512, Fax: 405-755-6391

(26) Office of Secretary of State, 101 State Capitol Bldg, Oklahoma City, OK 73105, 405-521-3911

(27) Oklahoma Aeronautics Commission, Department of Transportation, 200 NE 21st, B-7 1st Floor, Oklahoma City, OK 73105, 405-521-2377, Fax: 405-521-2379

(28) Oklahoma Bar Association, 1901 Lincoln Blvd, PO Box 53036, Oklahoma City, OK 73152, 405-524-2365

(29) Oklahoma Board of Dentistry, 6501 N. Boradway, #220, Oklahoma City, OK 73116, 405-848-1364, Fax: 405-848-3279

(30) Oklahoma Board of Nursing, 2915 N Classen Blvd, Suite 524, Oklahoma City, OK 73106, 405-525-2076, Fax: 405-521-6089

(31) Oklahoma Horse Racing Commission, 2614 Villa Prom, Shephard Mall, Oklahoma City, OK 73107, 405-943-6472, Fax: 405-943-6474

(32) Oklahoma Insurance Commission, 3814 N. Santa Fe Ave., Oklahoma City, OK 73152, 405-521-6610, Fax: 405-521-6652

(33) Oklahoma Liquified Petroleum Gas Administration, Jim Thorpe Bldg, Room B-45, 2101 N Lincoln Blvd, Oklahoma City, OK 73105, 405-521-2458, Fax: 405-521-6037

(34) Oklahoma Mining Commission/Dept. of Mines, 4040 N Lincoln, Suite 107, Oklahoma City, OK 73105, 405-521-3859, Fax: 405-427-9646

(35) Oklahoma Real Estate Commission, 4040 Lincoln Blvd, Oklahoma City, OK 73105-5283, 405-521-3387, Fax: 405-424-1534

(36) Oklahoma Securities Commission, 621 N Robinson, Suite 400, Oklahoma City, OK 73102, 405-521-2451

(37) Oklahoma State Banking Department, 4545 N Lincoln Blvd, #164, Oklahoma City, OK 73105, 405-521-2783, Fax: 405-525-9701

(38) Oklahoma State Department of Health, Occupational Licensing Division, 1000 NE Tenth, Oklahoma City, OK 73117-1299, 405-271-5217, Fax: 405-571-5254

(39) Oklahoma State Health Department, 1000 NE Tenth, Oklahoma City, OK 73152, 405-271-5217, Fax: 405-271-5254

(40) Oklahoma Water Resources Board, 3800 Classen Blvd., Oklahoma City, OK 73118, 405-530-8800, Fax: 405-530-8900

(41) Polygraph Examiners Board, PO Box 11476, Cimarron Station, Oklahoma City, OK 73136-0476, 405-425-2778, Fax: 405-425-2773

(42) State Department of Education, Oliver Hodge Bldg, 2500 N Lincoln Blvd, Oklahoma City, OK 73105-4599, 405-521-3301

(43) State Department of Health, OLS-0203, 1000 NE Tenth, PO Box 53551, Oklahoma City, OK 73117, 405-271-5217, Fax: 405-271-5254

(44) State Department of Health, Professional Counselor Licensing, 1000 NE Tenth, Oklahoma City, OK 73152, 405-271-6030

Oregon

Capitol: Salem (Marion County)	
State Population	3.1 Million
Number of Degree Granting Institutions:	47
Number of State Licensing & Business Registration Agencies:	153

Degree Granting Educational Institutions

Bassist College, Registrar, 2000 SW Fifth Ave, Portland, OR 97201, 503-228-6528 (Fax: 503-228-4227). Hours: 7:30AM-5PM. Enrollment: 125. Records go back to 1981. Alumni records are maintained here at the same phone number. Degrees granted: Associate; Bachelors. Adverse incident record source- Registrar, 800-547-0937.

Attendance and degree information available by phone, fax, mail. Search requires name plus date of birth, exact years of attendance. Also helpful: SSN. There is no fee.

Blue Mountain Community College, Registrar, PO Box 100, Pendleton, OR 97801, 503-276-1260 (Fax: 503-276-6118). Hours: 8AM-5PM. Records go back to 1916. Degrees granted: Associate.

Attendance and degree information available by phone, fax, mail. Search requires name plus SSN, approximate years of attendance. There is no fee.

Central Oregon Community College, Registrar, 2600 NW College Way, Bend, OR 97701, 503-383-7250 (Fax: 503-383-7506). Hours: 8AM-5PM. Enrollment: 3200. Records go back to 1949. Alumni records are maintained here at the same phone number. Degrees granted: Associate.

Attendance and degree information available by phone, fax, mail. Search requires name plus SSN. Also helpful: date of birth, exact years of attendance. There is no fee.

Chemeketa Community College, Registrar, PO Box 14007, Salem, OR 97309, 503-399-5001 (Fax: 503-399-3918). Hours: 8AM-4:30PM. Enrollment: 18400. Records go back to 1955's. Transcripts available from 1970 on. Alumni records are maintained here at the same phone number. Degrees granted: Associate. Adverse incident record source- Security Office, 503-399-5023.

Attendance and degree information available by phone, fax, mail. Search requires name plus SSN. Also helpful: date of birth. There is no fee.

Clackamas Community College, Registrar, 19600 S Molalla Ave, Oregon City, OR 97045, 503-657-6958 (Fax: 503-650-6654). Hours: 8AM-5PM. Enrollment: 27000. Records go back to 1966. Degrees granted: Associate. Special programs-

Nursing, 503-657-6958 X2214: Accelerated Degree, 503-657-6958 X2214. Adverse incident record source- Instructional Services, 503-657-6958 X2406.

Attendance information available by fax, mail. Search requires name plus SSN. Also helpful: date of birth, exact years of attendance. There is no fee.

Degree information available by phone, fax, mail. Search requires name plus SSN. Also helpful: date of birth, exact years of attendance. There is no fee.

Clatsop Community College, Registrar, 1653 Jerome Ave, Astoria, OR 97103, 503-325-0910 (Fax: 503-325-5738). Hours: 8AM-5PM. Enrollment: 2500. Records go back to 1958. Degrees granted: Associate.

Attendance and degree information available by phone, fax, mail. Search requires name plus SSN. There is no fee.

Concordia University, Registrar, 2811 NE Holman St, Portland, OR 97211, 503-280-8510 (Fax: 503-280-8531). Hours: 8AM-6PM M-Th, 8AM-4:30PM F. Enrollment: 986. Formerly Concordia College Records go back to 1905. Alumni records are maintained here also. Call 503-280-8505. Degrees granted: Associate; Bachelors; Masters of Education. Special programs-Environmental Remediation: Hazardous Material Management. Adverse incident record source- Security, 503-280-8517.

Attendance and degree information available by phone, fax, mail. Search requires name plus SSN, approximate years of attendance. There is no fee.

Eastern Oregon State College, Registrar, La Grande, OR 97850, 541-962-3519 (Fax: 541-962-3799). Hours: 8AM-5PM. Enrollment: 1850. Records go back to 1929. Alumni records are maintained here also. Call 541-962-3844. Degrees granted: Associate; Bachelors; MTE. Adverse incident record source- Security, 541-962-3350.

Attendance and degree information available by phone, fax, mail. Search requires name plus SSN, approximate years of attendance. There is no fee.

Eugene Bible College, Registrar, 2155 Bailey Hill Rd, Eugene, OR 97405, 503-485-1780 (Fax: 503-485-5801). Hours: 8AM-5PM. Enrollment: 250. Records go back to 1989. Alumni records are maintained here at the same phone number. Degrees granted: Bachelors. Certification: Bible.

Attendance and degree information available by phone, fax, mail. Search requires name plus approximate years of attendance. Also helpful: SSN, exact years of attendance. There is no fee.

George Fox College, Registrar, Newberg, OR 97132, 503-538-8383 (Fax: 503-538-3867). Hours: 8AM-5PM. Enrollment: 1420. Alumni records are maintained here also. Call 503-538-8383. Degrees granted: Bachelors; Masters; Doctorate.

Attendance and degree information available by phone, fax, mail. Search requires name plus SSN, date of birth, approximate years of attendance. Also helpful: exact years of attendance. There is no fee.

ITT Technical Institute, Registrar, 6035 NE 78th Ct, Portland, OR 97218-2854, 503-255-6500 (Fax: 503-255-6135). Records go back to 1979. Alumni records are maintained here at the same phone number. Degrees granted: Bachelors.

Attendance and degree information available by phone, fax, mail. Search requires name plus SSN, date of birth, approximate years of attendance. There is no fee.

Lane Community College, Registrar, 4000 E 30th Ave, Eugene, OR 97405, 541-726-2213 (Fax: 541-744-3995). Hours: 8AM-4:45PM M,T,W,F; 9AM-4:45PM Th. Enrollment: 9917. Records go back to 1964. Degrees granted: Associate. Adverse incident record source- Student Services, 541-741-3075: Security, 541-747-4501 X2558

Attendance and degree information available by phone, fax, mail. Search requires name plus SSN. Also helpful: date of birth. There is no fee.

Lewis and Clark College, College of Arts & Sciences, 0615 SW Palatine Hill Rd, Portland, OR 97219, 503-768-7334 (Fax: 503-768-7333). Hours: 8AM-4:30PM. Enrollment: 1700. Alumni records are maintained here also. Call 503-768-7950. Degrees granted: Bachelors; Masters. Adverse incident record source- Dean of Students, 503-768-7115.

Attendance and degree information available by phone, fax, mail. Search requires name only. Also helpful: SSN, exact years of attendance. There is no fee.

Linfield College, Office of the Registrar, Unit D - 900 S Baker, McMinnville, OR 97128, 503-434-2200 (Fax: 503-434-2215). Hours: 8AM-5PM. Enrollment: 2200. Records go back to 1847. Alumni records are maintained here also. Call 503-434-2200. Degrees granted: Bachelors; Masters.

Attendance information available by phone, fax, mail. Search requires name plus SSN. Also helpful: exact years of attendance. There is no fee.

Degree information available by phone, fax, mail. Search requires name plus SSN. Also helpful: exact years of attendance. There is no fee.

Linn-Benton Community College, Registrar, 6500 SW Pacific Blvd, Albany, OR 97321, 541-917-4812 (Fax: 541-917-4811). Hours: 8:30AM-4:30PM. Enrollment: 25000. Records go back to 1967. Degrees granted: Associate. Adverse incident record source- Dean, 503-917-4999.

Attendance and degree information available by phone, fax, mail. Search requires name plus SSN. There is no fee.

Marylhurst College, Registrar, PO Box 261, Marylhurst, OR 97036, 503-699-6267 X3316 (Fax: 503-636-9526). Hours: 8AM-5PM. Enrollment: 1660. Records go back to 1893. Alumni records are maintained here at the same phone number. Degrees granted: Bachelors; Masters. Special programs- Masters Art Therapy, 503-699-6244: Early Scholars Program. Adverse incident record source- Student Services, 503-699-6268.

Attendance information available by phone, fax, mail. Search requires name only. Also helpful: SSN, exact years of attendance. There is no fee.

Degree information available by phone, fax, mail. Search requires name only. Also helpful: SSN, approximate years of attendance. There is no fee.

Mount Angel Seminary, Records & Registration, St. Benedict, OR 97373, 503-845-3951 (Fax: 503-845-3126). Hours: 8AM-5PM. Enrollment: 150. Records go back to 1900's. Alumni records are maintained here at the same phone number. Degrees granted: Bachelors; Masters.

Attendance and degree information available by phone, fax, mail. Search requires name plus SSN, approximate years of attendance. Also helpful: date of birth, exact years of attendance. There is no fee.

Mount Hood Community College, Admissions Office, 26000 SE Stark St, Gresham, OR 97030, 503-667-6422 (Fax: 503-667-7388). Hours: 8AM-7:30PM M-Th, 8AM-4:30PM F. Enrollment: 12000. Records go back to 1965. Alumni records are maintained here at the same phone number. Degrees granted: Associate. Adverse incident record source- 503-667-7316.

Attendance information available by phone, fax, mail. Search requires name plus SSN, approximate years of attendance. Also helpful: date of birth, exact years of attendance. There is no fee.

Degree information available by phone, fax, mail. Search requires name plus SSN. Also helpful: date of birth, exact years of attendance. There is no fee.

Multnomah Bible College, Registrar, 8435 NE Glisan St, Portland, OR 97220, 503-255-0332 X372 (Fax: 503-254-1268). Hours: 8AM-5PM. Enrollment: 725. Records go back to 1936. Alumni records are maintained here at the same phone number. Degrees granted: Bachelors; Masters.

Attendance and degree information available by phone, fax, mail. Search requires name plus SSN. There is no fee.

Northwest Christian College, Registrar, 828 E 11th Ave, Eugene, OR 97401, 503-343-1641 X15 (Fax: 503-343-9159). Hours: 8AM-5PM. Enrollment: 400. Records go back to 1895. Alumni records are maintained here also. Call 503-343-1641. Degrees granted: Associate; Bachelors; Masters. Adverse incident record source- Registrar, 503-343-1641.

Attendance and degree information available by phone, fax, mail. Search requires name plus SSN. There is no fee.

Oregon College of Oriental Medicine, Registrar, 10525 Cherry Blossom Dr, Portland, OR 97216, 503-253-3443 (Fax: 503-253-2701). Hours: 9AM-5PM. Enrollment: 150. Records go back to 1983. Alumni records are maintained here at the same phone number. Degrees granted: Masters.

Attendance and degree information available by phone, mail. Search requires name plus SSN, exact years of attendance. There is no fee.

Oregon Graduate Institute of Science and Technology, Registrar, PO Box 91000, Portland, OR 97291-1000, 503-690-1121 (Fax: 503-690-1285). Hours: 8AM-5PM. Enrollment: 350. Records go back to 1965. Alumni records are maintained here also. Call 503-690-1144. Degrees granted: Masters; Doctorate. Adverse incident record source- Facilities, 503-690-1508.

Attendance and degree information available by phone, mail. Search requires name plus SSN. There is no fee.

Oregon Health Sciences University, Registrar's Office L109A, 3181 SW SamJacksonPark Rd, Portland, OR 97201, 503-494-7800 (Fax: 503-494-4629). Hours: 7:30AM-4PM. Degrees granted: Bachelors; Masters; Ph.D.,DMD,MD. Special programs- School of Dentistry, 503-494-8825.

Attendance and degree information available by phone, fax, mail. Search requires name only. Also helpful: exact years of attendance. There is no fee.

Oregon Institute of Technology, Registrar, Klamath Falls, OR 97601-8801, 541-885-1300 (Fax: 541-885-1274). Hours: 8AM-5PM. Enrollment: 2400. Records go back to 1947. Alumni records are maintained here also. Call 503-885-1130. Degrees granted: Associate; Bachelors; Masters. Adverse incident record source- Security, 503-885-1111.

Attendance and degree information available by phone, fax, mail. Search requires name plus date of birth. Also helpful: SSN, approximate years of attendance. There is no fee.

Oregon Polytechnic Institute, Registrar, 900 SE Sandy Blvd, Portland, OR 97214, 503-234-9333 (Fax: 503-233-0195). Hours: 8AM-5PM. Records go back to 1947. Degrees granted: Associate.

Attendance and degree information available by phone, fax, mail. Search requires name plus approximate years of attendance. Also helpful: SSN, exact years of attendance. There is no fee.

Oregon State University, Registrar, Corvallis, OR 97331, 541-737-4331 (Fax: 541-737-2482). Hours: 8AM-5PM. Enrollment: 14000. Records go back to 1868. Alumni records are maintained here also. Call 541-737-2351. Degrees granted: Bachelors; Masters; Doctorate.

Attendance and degree information available by phone, fax, mail. Search requires name only. Also helpful: SSN. Fee is $3.00.

Pacific Northwest College of Art, Registrar, 1219 SW Park Ave, Portland, OR 97205, 503-226-4391 (Fax: 503-226-4842). Hours: 9AM-5PM. Enrollment: 269. Records go back to 1911. Alumni records are maintained here at the same phone number. Degrees granted: Bachelors. Adverse incident record source- Student Services.

Attendance and degree information available by phone, fax, mail. Search requires name plus SSN, approximate years of attendance. There is no fee.

Pacific University, Registrar, 2043 College Way, Forest Grove, OR 97116, 503-359-2234 (Fax: 503-359-2242). Hours: 8AM-5PM. Records go back to 1900's. Alumni records are maintained here also. Call 503-359-6151 X2206. Degrees granted: Bachelors; Masters; Doctorate. Adverse incident record source- Records & Registration, 503-359-2234.

Attendance and degree information available by phone, fax, mail. Search requires name plus SSN, approximate years of attendance. Also helpful: date of birth. There is no fee.

Portland Community College, Student Records, PO Box 19000, Portland, OR 97280, 503-614-7100 (Fax: 503-645-0894). Hours: 8AM-5PM. Enrollment: 38000. Records go back to 1961. Degrees granted: Associate; High School Completion.

Attendance and degree information available by fax, mail. Search requires name plus SSN, signed release. Also helpful: date of birth, exact years of attendance. There is no fee.

Portland State University, Registrar, PO Box 751, Portland, OR 97207-0751, 503-725-3435 (Fax: 503-725-5525). Hours: 8AM-6:30PM. Enrollment: 17200. Records go back to 1907. Alumni Records Office: Alumni Association, PO Box 751, Portland, OR 97207. Degrees granted: Bachelors; Masters; Doctorate.

Attendance information available by fax, mail. Search requires name only. Also helpful: SSN, date of birth, exact years of attendance. There is no fee.

Degree information available by phone, fax, mail. Search requires name only. Also helpful: SSN, date of birth, exact years of attendance. There is no fee.

Reed College, Registrar, 3203 SE Woodstock Blvd, Portland, OR 97202, 503-771-1112 X7793 (Fax: 503-777-7795). Hours: 10AM-5PM. Records go back to 1930. Second phone number is 503-777-7293. Alumni records are maintained here also. Call 503-771-7589. Degrees granted: Bachelors; Masters.

Attendance and degree information available by phone, fax, mail. Search requires name plus SSN, approximate years of attendance. There is no fee.

Rogue Community College, Student Records, 3345 Redwood Hwy, Grants Pass, OR 97527, 503-471-3500 (Fax: 503-471-3588). Hours: 9AM-4PM. Records go back to 1971. Degrees granted: Associate. Adverse incident record source- In student file.

Attendance information available by phone, fax, mail. Search requires name plus SSN, exact years of attendance. There is no fee.

Degree information available by phone, fax, mail. Search requires name plus SSN. Also helpful: approximate years of attendance. There is no fee.

Southern Oregon State College, Registrar, 1250 Siskiyou Blvd, Ashland, OR 97520, 541-552-6600 (Fax: 541-552-6329). Hours: 8AM-5PM. Enrollment: 4500. Records go back to 1920. Alumni records are maintained here also. Call 541-552-6361. Degrees granted: Associate; Bachelors; Masters. Certification: Education, Accounting, Anthropolgy. Adverse incident record source- Student Affairs, 541-552-6221.

Attendance and degree information available by phone, fax, mail. Search requires name plus SSN. Also helpful: date of birth, exact years of attendance. There is no fee.

Southwestern Oregon Community College, Registrar, 1988 Newmark, Coos Bay, OR 97420, 541-888-7339 (Fax: 541-888-7247). Hours: 8AM-5PM. Enrollment: 4700. Records go back to 1962. Alumni records are maintained here also. Call 541-888-7210. Degrees granted: Associate. Adverse incident record source- Dean, 541-888-7416.

Attendance information available by phone, mail. Search requires name plus SSN, date of birth. There is no fee.

Degree information available by mail. Search requires name plus SSN, date of birth. There is no fee.

Treasure Valley Community College, Registrar, 650 College Blvd, Ontario, OR 97914, 541-889-6493 X234 (Fax: 541-881-2721). Hours: 8AM-5PM M-Th summer hours. Enrollment: 3094. Records go back to 1962. Degrees granted: Associate. Adverse incident record source- Dean, 503-889-6493.

Attendance and degree information available by fax, mail. Search requires name plus SSN, date of birth, approximate years of attendance, signed release. There is no fee.

Umpqua Community College, Registrar, Roseburg, OR 97470, 503-440-4604 (Fax: 503-440-4612). Hours: 8AM-4PM. Enrollment: 6885. Records go back to 1964. Degrees granted: Associate.

Attendance and degree information available by mail. Search requires name only. There is no fee.

University of Oregon, Office of Registrar, Eugene, OR 97403-5257, 541-346-3243 (Fax: 541-346-5815). Hours: 8AM-5PM. Enrollment: 17500. Records go back to 1875. Alumni records are maintained here also. Call 541-346-3178. Degrees granted: Bachelors; Masters; Doctorate; JD, Certificates. Special programs- Law, 541-346-3852. Adverse incident record source- Dean of Student Life,v541-346-2822.

Attendance information available by phone, fax, mail. Search requires name only. Also helpful: SSN, exact years of attendance. There is no fee.

Degree information available by phone, fax, mail. Search requires name only. Also helpful: SSN, exact years of attendance. There is no fee.

University of Portland, Registrar, 5000 N Willamette Blvd, Portland, OR 97203, 503-283-7321 (Fax: 503-283-7508). Hours: 8:30AM-4:30PM. Enrollment: 2535. Records go back to 1901. Alumni records are maintained here also. Call 520-283-7328. Degrees granted: Bachelors; Masters. Adverse incident record source- Student Services, 503-283-7207.

Attendance and degree information available by phone, fax, mail. Search requires name only. Also helpful: SSN, date of birth, exact years of attendance. There is no fee.

Warner Pacific College, Registrar, 2219 SE 68th Ave, Portland, OR 97215, 503-775-4366 X611 (Fax: 503-788-7425). Hours: 8AM-5PM. Enrollment: 700. Records go back to 1937. Alumni records are maintained here also. Call 503-788-7492. Degrees granted: Associate; Bachelors; Masters. Adverse incident record source- 503-788-7427.

Attendance and degree information available by phone, fax, mail. Search requires name plus SSN, approximate years of attendance. Also helpful: exact years of attendance. There is no fee.

Western Baptist College, Registrar, 5000 Deer Park Dr SE, Salem, OR 97301-9891, 503-375-7014 (Fax: 503-585-4316). Hours: 8AM-5PM. Records go back to 1935. Alumni records are maintained here at the same phone number. Degrees granted: Associate; Bachelors.

Attendance and degree information available by phone, fax, mail. Search requires name plus date of birth. Also helpful: SSN, exact years of attendance. There is no fee.

Western Business College, Registrar, 505 S W 6th Ave, Portland, OR 97204, 503-222-3225 (Fax: 503-228-6926). Enrollment: 500. Records go back to 1955. Degrees granted: Associate. Adverse incident record source- Student Services.

Attendance and degree information available by phone, mail. Search requires name plus SSN, exact years of attendance. There is no fee.

Western Conservative Baptist Seminary, Registrar, 5511 SE Hawthorne Blvd, Portland, OR 97215, 503-233-8561 (Fax: 503-239-4216). Hours: 8:30AM-4PM. Records go back to 1926. Degrees granted: Masters; Doctorate.

Attendance and degree information available by phone, fax, mail. Search requires name plus SSN, approximate years of attendance. There is no fee.

Western Culinary Institute, Registrar, 1316 S W 13th Ave, Portland, OR 97201, 503-223-2245 (Fax: 503-223-0126). Enrollment: 430. Records go back to 1984. Alumni records are maintained here at the same phone number. Adverse incident record source- Student Services.

Attendance and degree information available by phone, mail. Search requires name plus SSN, exact years of attendance. There is no fee.

Western Evangelical Seminary, Registrar, 12753 SW 68th Ave, Tigard, OR 97223, 503-538-8383 (Fax: 503-598-4338). Hours: 8:30AM-4:30PM. Enrollment: 300. Records go back to 1949. Alumni records are maintained here at the same phone number. Degrees granted: Masters.

Attendance and degree information available by phone, fax, mail. Search requires name plus SSN. Also helpful: date of birth, exact years of attendance. There is no fee.

Western Oregon State College, Registrar's Office, Monmouth, OR 97361, 503-838-8415 (Fax: 503-838-8923). Hours: 8AM-5PM. Enrollment: 3848. Records go back to 1890. Alumni records are maintained here also. Call 503-838-8153. Degrees granted: Associate; Bachelors; Masters. Adverse incident record source- Dean of Students, 503-838-8221.

Attendance and degree information available by phone, fax, mail. Search requires name only. Also helpful: SSN, date of birth, exact years of attendance. There is no fee.

Western States Chiropractic College, Registrar, 2900 NE 132nd Ave, Portland, OR 97230, 503-251-5706 (Fax: 503-251-5723). Hours: 8AM-4:30PM. Enrollment: 460. Records go back to 1904. Alumni records are maintained here also. Call 503-251-5713. Degrees granted: Bachelors; Doctor of Chiropractic.

Attendance and degree information available by phone, fax, mail. Search requires name only. Also helpful: date of birth, exact years of attendance. There is no fee.

Willamette University, Registrar, 900 State St, Salem, OR 97301, 503-370-6206 (Fax: 503-375-5395). Hours: 8AM-Noon, 1-5PM. Enrollment: 2525. Records go back to 1900's. Alumni records are maintained here also. Call 503-370-6340. Degrees granted: Bachelors; Masters; Doctorate.

Attendance and degree information available by phone, fax, mail. Search requires name plus SSN. There is no fee.

Trade and Vocational Schools

Airman Proficiency Center, 3565 NE Cornell Rd, Hillsboro, OR 97124, 503-648-2831

Apollo College of Medical-Dental Careers, 2600 SE 98th St, Portland, OR 97266, 503-761-6100

Broadcast Professionals Complete School of Radio Broadcasting, 11507-D SW Pacific Hwy, Portland, OR 97223, 503-244-5113

College of Legal Arts, 527 SW Hall St #308, Portland, OR 97201, 503-223-5100

CollegeAmerica, 921 SW Washington St #200, Portland, OR 97205, 503-242-9000

Commercial Training Services, 2416 N Marine Dr, Portland, OR 97217, 503-285-7542

ConCorde Career Institute, 1827 NE 44th Ave, Portland, OR 97213, 503-281-4181

Diesel Truck Driver Training School, 90801 Hwy 99 N, Eugene, OR 97402, 800-888-7075

Moler Barber College, 517 SW Fourth St, Portland, OR 97204, 503-223-9818

Oregon School of Arts and Crafts, 824t SW Barnes Rd, Portland, OR 97225, 503-297-5544

Paramedic Training Institute, PO Box 1878, Beaverton, OR 97075, 503-297-5592

Pioneer Pacific College, 25195 SW Parkway Ave, Wilsonville, OR 97070, 503-682-3903

Tara Lara Academy of K-9 Hair Design, 16307 SE McLoughlin Blvd, Portland, OR 97267, 503-653-7134

West Coast Training, 11919 N Jensen Ave #292, Portland, OR 97217, 503-289-8661

West Coast Training (Branch Campus), 2525 SE Stubb St, Milwaukie, OR 97222, 503-659-5181

Western Business College, 425 SW Washington St, Portland, OR 97204, 503-222-3225

Western Culinary Institute, 1316 SW 13th Ave, Portland, OR 97201, 503-223-2245

Western Truck School, 8145 SE 82nd Ave, Portland, OR 97266, 503-788-0203

State Licensing & Business Registration Quick Finder Index

Architecture, Engineering & Surveying
Architect #6 (2300) .... ☎ 503-378-4270
Engineer #11 503-378-4180
Engineering Geologist #12 503-378-4180
Geologist #12 503-378-4180
Landscape Architect #53 (250) .... ☎ 503-378-4270
Surveyor #11 503-378-4180

Business - Court & Legal Services
Attorney #46 (10831) .... ✉ 503-620-0222
Lobbyist #43 (850) .... ☎ 503-378-5105
Notary Public #40 (40000) .... ☎ 503-986-2200

Business - General Services
Bakery #23 (644) .... ✉ 503-986-4720
Employment Agency (Private) #20 (115) 503-731-4074
Employment Agency-Private #20 503-731-4074
Municipal Auditor #5 .... ☎ 503-378-4181
Pawnbroker #27 503-378-4387
Public Accountant #5 (118) .... ☎ 503-378-4181
Public Accountant-CPA #5 (6500) .... ☎ 503-378-4181
Retail Food Establishment #23 (3523) .... ✉ 503-986-4720
Tax Consultant/Preparer #17 (4000) .... ☎ 503-378-4034

Construction & Manufacturing
Building Official #19 (1000) .... ☎ 503-373-1249
Construction Contractor & Subcontractor #21
   (37000) .... ☎ 503-378-4621
Electrical Installation #19 (18000) .... ☎ 503-373-1249
Inspector #19 (4300) .... ☎ 503-373-1249
Inspector, Structural/Mechanical #19 .... ☎ 503-373-1249
Landscape Contractor #28 (4500) .... ☎ 503-378-4621
Limited Pump Installation Contractor #21 (200)
   .... ☎ 503-378-4621
Limited Sign Contractor #21 (200) .... ☎ 503-378-4621
Manufactured Housing Construction #19 ...... ☎ 503-373-1249
Plans Examiner #19 .... ☎ 503-373-1249
Plumber #19 (4000) .... ☎ 503-373-1249

Education
School Administrator #56 (769) .... ☎ 503-378-6813
School Counselor #56 (313) .... ☎ 503-378-6813
School Superintendent #56 (50) .... ☎ 503-378-6813
School Supervisor #56 (13) .... ☎ 503-378-6813
Teacher #56 (11634) .... ☎ 503-378-6813

Environmental & Agriculture
Animal-Euthanasia Technician #38 (100) ...... ✉ 503-731-4051
Animal-Health Technician #38 (475) .... ✉ 503-731-4051
Brand Recording #22 (13000) .... ☎ 503-986-4681
Dairy #23 (480) .... ✉ 503-986-4720
Farm Labor Contractor #21 .... ☎ 503-378-4621
Farm/Forest Labor Contractors #20 503-731-4074
Food Exporter #24 .... ✉ 503-986-4720
Food Processing Facility #23 (1199) .... ✉ 503-986-4720
Food Storage Facility #23 (471) .... ✉ 503-986-4720

Forest Labor Contractor #21 .... ☎ 503-378-4621
Nursery/Christmas Tree Industry #25 (7000)
   .... ☎ 503-986-4644
Veterinarian #38 (1350) .... ✉ 503-731-4051
Water Rights Examiner #52 503-378-4180

Financial - Real Estate, Insurance & Banking
Bank #26 503-378-4140
Broker-Dealer #26 503-378-4140
Check & Money Order Seller #26 503-378-4140
Collection Agency #26 503-378-4140
Consumer Finance Company #26 503-378-4140
Credit Services Organization #26 503-378-4140
Credit Union #26 503-378-4140
Debt Collection Agency #27 503-378-4387
Debt Consolidating Agency #27 503-378-4387
Escrow Agent & Agency #49 (266) .... ☎ 503-378-4170
Investment Advisor #26 503-378-4140
Mortgage Banker/Broker #26 503-378-4140
Mortgage Broker #26 503-378-4140
Pawn Broker #26 503-378-4140
Property Manager #49 (421) .... ☎ 503-378-4170
Real Estate Appraiser #4 .... ☎ 503-373-1505
Real Estate Branch Office #49 (291) .... ☎ 503-378-4170
Real Estate Broker #49 (6447) .... ☎ 503-378-4170
Real Estate Salesperson #49 (12937) .... ☎ 503-378-4170
Savings & Loan Association #26 503-378-4140
Security Salesperson #26 503-378-4387
Special Qualifications Corporation #27 503-378-4387
Trust Company #26 503-378-4140
Water Right Examiner #11 503-378-4180

Health & Beauty
Acupuncturist #32 503-229-5770
Apprentice Embalmer #55 503-731-4040
Apprentice Funeral Service Practitioner #55 503-731-4040
Barber #7 (25000) .... ☎ 503-378-8667
Cemetery #55 (386) 503-731-4040
Chiropractic Assistant #8 (492) .... ☎ 503-378-5816
Chiropractor #8 (1336) .... ☎ 503-378-5816
Crematorium #55 (45) 503-731-4040
Dental Hygienist #9 (2674) .... ☎ 503-229-5520
Dental Specialist #9 (159) .... ☎ 503-229-5520
Dentist #9 (3143) .... ☎ 503-229-5520
Denturist #10 (132) 503-378-8667
Diagnostic Radiologic Technologist #42 .... ☎ 503-731-4088
Diagnostic/Therapeutic Technologist #42 ...... ☎ 503-731-4088
Dietitian #30 (325) .... ☎ 503-731-4085
Drug Manufacturer #15 .... ☎ 503-731-4032
Drug Wholesaler #15 .... ☎ 503-731-4032
Electrologist #1 (176) .... ☎ 503-378-8667
Electrology Facility #1 .... ☎ 503-378-8667
Electrology Instructor #1 (7) .... ☎ 503-378-8667
Electrology School #1 .... ☎ 503-378-8667

Embalmer #55 (489)..................................... 503-731-4040
Facial Technologist #7 .... ☎ 503-378-8667
Funeral Establishment #55 (167) 503-731-4040
Funeral Preneed Salespersons #55 503-731-4040
Funeral Service Practitioner #55 (594) 503-731-4040
Hair Salon #7 (3600) .... ☎ 503-378-8667
Hairdresser #7.................................... ☎ 503-378-8667
Hearing Aid Dispenser #2 .... ☎ 503-378-8667
Immediate Disposition Company #55 (24) 503-731-4040
Limited FSP Apprentice #55 503-731-4040
Limited Funeral Service Practitioner #55 (2)...... 503-731-4040
Limited Permit Radiologic Technologist #42
.... ☎ 503-731-4088
Manicurist #7 .... ☎ 503-378-8667
Massage Technician #41 (2874)..................... ☎ 503-731-4064
Medical Doctor/Surgeon #31 503-229-5770
Medical Examiner #54................................. 503-280-6061
Naturopathic Physician #39........................... 503-731-4045
Nurse #13.. 503-731-4745
Nurse Practitioner #13............................... 503-731-4745
Nursing Assistant #13................................ 503-731-4745
Nursing Home Administrator #36 (500) .... ☎ 503-731-4046
Occupational Therapist #37 (835) .... ☎ 503-731-4048
Occupational Therapy Assistant #37............... ☎ 503-731-4048
Optometrist #14 (1375) .... ☎ 503-373-7721
Osteopathic Physician #31 503-229-5770
Over-the-Counter Drug Outlet #15 .... ☎ 503-731-4032
Pathologist #10 (107) 503-378-8667
Pharmacist #15 (3500)............................... ☎ 503-731-4032
Pharmacy #15 (900)................................. ☎ 503-731-4032
Physical Therapist #48 (2240)..................... ☎ 503-731-4047
Physical Therapist/Assistant #48 (735).......... ☎ 503-731-4047
Physician's Assistant #33............................. 503-229-5770
Podiatrist #34.. 502-229-5770
Practical Nurse #13.................................. 503-731-4745
Respiratory Care Practitioner #35 503-229-5770

Sanitarian #50 (179)............................... ☎ 503-378-8667
Sanitarian Trainee #50 (30) .... ☎ 503-378-8667
Therapy Radiologic Technologist #42 (35).... ☎ 503-731-4088

Investigations & Security
Polygraph Examiner #18 503-378-2100

Social Services
Clinical Social Worker #51 .... ☎ 503-378-5735
Counselor #29 (1101) .... ☎ 503-378-5499
Marriage & Family Therapist #29 (347) .... ☎ 503-378-5499
Psychologist #16 (943) .... ☎ 503-378-4154
Psychologist Associate #16 .... ☎ 503-378-4154

Sports & Entertainment
Amusement Ride Inspector #19..................... ☎ 503-373-1249
Boxer #47.. 503-682-0582
Brewery #44.. ☎ 503-872-5124
Dog Racing #45 .... ☎ 503-731-4052
Horse Racing #45.................................. ☎ 503-731-4052
Liquor Control #44 .... ☎ 503-653-3056
Liquor Salesman/Agent #44 .... ☎ 503-872-5123
Liquor-Wide Shipper #44 .... ☎ 503-872-5124
Winery #44... ☎ 503-872-5124
Wrestler #47... 503-682-0582

Transportation
Aircraft Landing Area #3 (20) .... ☎ 503-378-4880
Aircraft Registration #3............................ ☎ 503-378-4880
Airport #3.. ☎ 503-378-4880
Airport- Public Licensed/Private Registered Use #3
.... ☎ 503-378-4880
Heliport #3 (90).................................... ☎ 503-378-4880
Pilot #3 (8052) .... ☎ 503-378-4880
Travel Agent #26 503-378-4140

State Licensing & Business Registration Agency Information

(1) Advisory Council for Electrologists, Permanent Color Technicians & Tattoo Artists, 750 Front St, NE, Suite 200, Salem, OR 97310, 503-378-8667

(2) Advisory Council on Hearing Aids, 750 Front St, NE, Suite 200, Salem, OR 97310, 503-378-8667

(3) Aeronautics Section, 3040 25th St, SE, Salem, OR 97310, 503-378-4880, Fax: 503-373-1688

(4) Appraiser Certification & Licensure Board, 350 Winter St. NE Room 21, Salem, OR 97310, 503-373-1505, Fax: 503-378-6576

(5) Board of Accountancy, 3218 Pringle Rd. SE #110, Salem, OR 97302, 503-378-4181, Fax: 503-378-3575

(6) Board of Architect Examiners, 750 Front St, NE, Suite 260, Salem, OR 97310, 503-378-4270, Fax: 503-378-6091

(7) Board of Barbers & Hairdressers, Health Division Licensing Programs, 750 Front St, NE, Suite 200, Salem, OR 97310, 503-378-8667, Fax: 503-585-9114

(8) Board of Chiropractic Examiners, 3218 Pringle Rd. SE, Sutie 50, Salem, OR 97302-6311, 503-378-5816, Fax: 503-378-3575

(9) Board of Dentistry, 1515 SW 5th Ave, Suite 602, Portland, OR 97201, 503-229-5520, Fax: 503-229-6606

(10) Board of Denture Technology, 750 Front St, NE, Suite 200, Salem, OR 97310, 503-378-8667

(11) Board of Engineering Examiners, 750 Front St, NE, #240, Salem, OR 97310, 503-378-4180

(12) Board of Geologist Examiners, 750 Front St, NE, #240, Salem, OR 97310, 503-378-4180

(13) Board of Nursing, 800 NE Oregon St, #25, Suite 465, Portland, OR 97232, 503-731-4745

(14) Board of Optometry, 3218 Pringle Rd SE Suite 100, Salem, OR 97310, 503-373-7721, Fax: 503-378-3616

(15) Board of Pharmacy, 800 NE Oregon St, #9, State Office Bldg, #425, Portland, OR 97232, 503-731-4032

(16) Board of Psychologist Examiners, 895 Summer St, NE, Salem, OR 97310, 503-378-4154, Fax: 503-378-3575

(17) Board of Tax Service Examiners, , Salem, OR 97310, 503-378-4034, Fax: 503-378-3575

(18) Board on Public Safety Standards & Training, Polygraphic Examiner Licensing, 550 N Monmouth Ave, Monmouth, OR 97361, 503-378-2100, Fax: 503-838-8907

(19) Building Codes Agency, Certification & Training Advisory Board, 1535 Edgewater St, NW, Salem, OR 97310, 503-373-1249, Fax: 503-378-2322

(20) Bureau of Labor & Industries, Private Employment Agencies Advisory Board, 800 NE Oregon St, #32, Portland, OR 97232, 503-731-4074

(21)   Construction Contractors Boards, 700 Summer St, NE, Suite 300, PO Box 14140, Salem, OR 97309-5052, 503-378-4621 x 4900, Fax: 503-373-2003

(22)   Department of Agriculture, 635 Capitol St, NE, Salem, OR 97310-0110, 503-986-4681, Fax: 503-986-4734

(23)   Department of Agriculture, Bakery and Related Licensing, 635 Capitol St, NE, Salem, OR 97310-0110, 503-986-4720, Fax: 503-986-4729

(24)   Department of Agriculture, Food Exporter Licensing, 635 Capitol St, NE, Salem, OR 97310-0110, 503-986-4720, Fax: 503-986-4729

(25)   Department of Agriculture, Nursery & Related Licensing, 635 Capitol St, NE, Salem, OR 97310-0110, 503-986-4644, Fax: 503-986-4786

(26)   Department of Insurance & Finance, Division of Finance & Corporate Securities, Labor & Industries Bldg, 350 Winter St., NE, Salem, OR 97310, 503-378-4387

(27)   Department of Insurance & Finance, Division of Finance & Corporate Securities, Labor & Industries Bldg, Salem, OR 97310, 503-378-4387

(28)   Landscape Contractors Board, 700 Summer St, NE, Suite 300, PO Box 14140, Salem, OR 97309-5052, 503-378-4621 x4900, Fax: 503-373-2003

(29)   Licensed Professional Counselors & Therapists, 3218 Pringle Rd. SE #160, Salem, OR 97302-6312, 503-378-5499

(30)   Medical Boards, 800 NE Oregon, #21, Suite 407, Portland, OR 97232, 503-731-4085, Fax: 503-731-4207

(31)   Medical Boards, 1500 SW 1st Ave, Crown Plaza Bldg. Suite 620, Portland, OR 97201, 503-229-5770, Fax: 503-229-6543

(32)   Medical Boards, 620 Crown Plaza, 1500 SW 1st Ave, Portland, OR 97201, 503-229-5770

(33)   Medical Boards, 620 Crown Plaza, 1500 SW 1st Ave, Portland, OR 97201, 503-229-5770

(34)   Medical Boards, 620 Crown Plaza, 1500 SW 1st Ave, Portland, OR 97201, 502-229-5770

(35)   Medical Boards, 1500 SW 1st Ave, Crown Plaza Bldg., Suite 620, Portland, OR 97201, 503-229-5770, Fax: 503-229-6543

(36)   Medical Boards, 800 NE Oregon, #21, Suite 407, Portland, OR 97232, 503-731-4046, Fax: 503-731-4207

(37)   Medical Boards, 800 NE Oregon, #21, Suite 407, Portland, OR 97232, 503-731-4048, Fax: 503-731-4207

(38)   Medical Boards, 800 NE Oregon, #21, Suite 407, Portland, OR 97232, 503-731-4051, Fax: 503-731-4207

(39)   Naturopathic Board of Examiners, 407-B State Office Bldg, 800 NE Oregon St, #21, Portland, OR 97232, 503-731-4045

(40)   Office of Secretary of State, 255 Capitol St. NE, Suite 151, Salem, OR 97310, 503-986-2200, Fax: 503-373-1166

(41)   Oregon Board of Massage Technicians, 800 NE Oregon, #21, Suite 407, Portland, OR 97232, 503-731-4064, Fax: 503-731-4207

(42)   Oregon Board of Radiologic Technology, Health Related Licensing Board, 800 NE Oregon, Suite 407, Portland, OR 97232, 503-731-4088, Fax: 503-531-4207

(43)   Oregon Government Standards & Pracrices Comm., 700 Pringle Pkwy SE, 1st Fl, Salem, OR 97310-1360, 503-378-5105, Fax: 503-373-1456

(44)   Oregon Liquor Control Commission, Regulatory Licensing & Compliance Division, PO Box 22297, Portland, OR 97222, 503-872-5140, Fax: 503-872-5018

(45)   Oregon Racing Commission, 800 NE Oregon, #11, Suite 310, Portland, OR 97232, 503-731-4052, Fax: 503-731-4053

(46)   Oregon State Bar Association, PO Box 1689, Lake Oswego, OR 97035-0899, 503-620-0222, Fax: 503-684-1366

(47)   Oregon State Boxing & Wrestling Commission, 9450 SW Commerce Circle, Wilsonville, OR 97070, 503-682-0582

(48)   Physical Therapy Licensing Board, 800 NE Oregon, #21, Suite 407, Portland, OR 97232, 503-731-4047

(49)   Real Estate Agency, Commerce Bldg, 158 12th St, NE, Salem, OR 97310, 503-378-4170

(50)   Sanitarians Registration Board, 700 Summer St. NE, Suite 100, Salem, OR 97310, 503-378-8667, Fax: 503-585-9114

(51)   State Board of Clinical Social Workers, 3218 Pringle Rd., SE, Suite 140, Salem, OR 97302-6310, 503-378-5735, Fax: 503-378-3575

(52)   State Board of Examiners for Engineering & Land, Surveying, 750 Front St NE, #240, Salem, OR 97310, 503-378-4180

(53)   State Landscape Architect Board, 750 Front St, NE, Suite 260, Salem, OR 97310, 503-378-4270, Fax: 503-378-6091

(54)   State Medical Examiner Advisory Board, 301 NE Knott St, Portland, OR 97212, 503-280-6061

(55)   State Mortuary & Cemetery Board, Portland State Bldg, Suite 430, 800 NE Oregon, #21, Portland, OR 97232, 503-731-4040

(56)   Teacher Standards & Practices Commission, 580 State St, #203, Salem, OR 97310, 503-378-6813, Fax: 503-378-4448

Pennsylvania

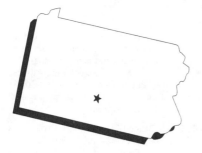

Capitol: Harrisburg (Dauphin County)	
State Population	**12.1 Million**
Number of Degree Granting Institutions:	**244**
Number of State Licensing & Business Registration Agencies:	**99**

Degree Granting Educational Institutions

Academy of the New Church College, Registration, PO Box 717, Bryn Athyn, PA 19009, 215-947-4200. Hours: 8AM-4:30PM. Enrollment: 160. Degrees granted: Associate; Bachelors.

Attendance and degree information available by phone, mail. Search requires name plus SSN, date of birth. There is no fee.

Albright College, Registrar, PO Box 15234, Reading, PA 19612-5234, 610-921-2381 (Fax: 610-921-7530). Hours: 8AM-5PM. Enrollment: 1050. Records go back to 1930. Alumni records are maintained here also. Call 610-921-2381. Degrees granted: Bachelors. Adverse incident record source- Dean of Students, 610-921-2381.

Attendance and degree information available by phone, fax, mail. Search requires name only. Also helpful: SSN, exact years of attendance. There is no fee.

Allegheny College, Registrar, 520 N Main St, Meadville, PA 16335, 814-332-2357 (Fax: 814-337-0988). Hours: 8AM-5PM. Enrollment: 800. Records go back to 1821. Alumni Records Office: Alumni Association, 400 N Main St, Meadville, PA 16335. Degrees granted: Bachelors. Special programs- Studies Abroad. Adverse incident record source- Dean of Students, 814-332-4356.

Attendance and degree information available by phone, fax, mail. Search requires name plus exact years of attendance. Also helpful: SSN, date of birth. There is no fee.

Allentown College of St. Francis de Sales, Registrar, 2755 Station Ave, Center Valley, PA 18034, 610-282-1100 X1223 (Fax: 610-282-2206). Hours: 8:30AM-4:45PM. Enrollment: 2220. Records go back to 1965. Alumni records are maintained here also. Call 610-282-1100 X1245. Degrees granted: Bachelors; Masters. Adverse incident record source- Student Affairs, 610-282-1100 X1261.

Attendance and degree information available by phone, fax, mail. Search requires name only. Also helpful: SSN, exact years of attendance. There is no fee.

Altoona School of Commerce, Registrar, 508 58th St, Altoona, PA 16602, 814-944-6134 (Fax: 814-944-4684). Hours: 8AM-5PM. Enrollment: 108. Records go back to 1960.

Alumni records are maintained here also. Call 814-944-6134. Degrees granted: Associate.

Attendance and degree information available by phone, fax, mail. Search requires name plus SSN. There is no fee.

Alvernia College, Registrar, 400 St Bernadine St, Reading, PA 19607, 610-796-8201 (Fax: 610-777-6632). Hours: 8AM-4:30PM. Enrollment: 1250. Records go back to 1962. Alumni records are maintained here also. Call 610-796-8212. Degrees granted: Associate; Bachelors. Adverse incident record source- Student Services, 610-796-8289.

Attendance and degree information available by phone, fax, mail. Search requires name plus approximate years of attendance. Also helpful: SSN. There is no fee.

American College, Registrar, 270 Bryn Mawr Ave, Bryn Mawr, PA 19010, 610-526-1462 (Fax: 610-526-1486). Hours: 8:30AM-5PM M-Th, 8:30AM-4PM F. Enrollment: 35000. Records go back to 1927. Degrees granted: Masters. Adverse incident record source- Registrar, 610-526-1462.

Attendance and degree information available by phone, fax, mail. Search requires name plus SSN. Also helpful: date of birth. There is no fee.

American Institute of Design, Registrar, 1616 Orthodox St, Philadelphia, PA 19124-3706, 215-288-8200 X23 (Fax: 215-288-0466). Hours: 8AM-5PM. Records go back to 1967. Degrees granted: Associate.

Attendance and degree information available by phone, fax, mail. Search requires name plus SSN, date of birth, exact years of attendance. There is no fee.

Antonelli Institute, Registrar, 2910 Jolly Rd, Plymouth Meeting, PA 19462-0570, 610-275-3040 (Fax: 610-836-2794). Hours: 8:30AM-5PM. Records go back to 1938. Degrees granted: Associate.

Attendance and degree information available by fax, mail. Search requires name plus SSN, exact years of attendance, signed release. There is no fee.

Art Institute of Philadelphia, Records Office, 1622 Chestnut St, Philadelphia, PA 19103-5198, 215-567-7080 (Fax: 215-246-3339). Hours: 8AM-5PM. Records go back to 1976.

Alumni records are maintained here at the same phone number. Degrees granted: Associate.

Attendance and degree information available by phone, fax, mail. Search requires name plus exact years of attendance. Also helpful: SSN. There is no fee.

Art Institute of Pittsburgh, Registrar, 526 Penn Ave, Pittsburgh, PA 15222-3269, 412-263-6600 (Fax: 412-263-3715). Hours: 7:30AM-7PM M, 7:30AM-5PM T-F. Enrollment: 2100. Records go back to 1966. Alumni records are maintained here also. Call 412-263-6600 X271. Degrees granted: Associate.

Attendance information available by phone, fax, mail. Search requires name plus SSN. Also helpful: exact years of attendance. There is no fee.

Degree information available by phone, fax, mail. Search requires name only. Also helpful: SSN, exact years of attendance. There is no fee.

Baptist Bible College and Seminary, Registrar, PO Box 800, 538 Venard Rd, Clarks Summit, PA 18411, 717-586-2400 X217 (Fax: 717-586-1753). Hours: 8AM-5PM. Records go back to 1932. Alumni records are maintained here at the same phone number. Degrees granted: Associate; Bachelors; Masters; Doctorate.

Attendance and degree information available by phone, fax, mail. Search requires name only. Also helpful: SSN, date of birth, approximate years of attendance. There is no fee.

Beaver College, Registrar, 450 S Easton Rd, Glenside, PA 19038-3295, 215-572-2100 (Fax: 215-572-2126). Hours: 8:30AM-8PM M-Th, 8:30AM-5PM F. Enrollment: 2600. Records go back to 1949. Alumni records are maintained here also. Call 215-572-2160. Degrees granted: Associate; Bachelors; Masters; Post Bac. Adverse incident record source- Security Dept., 215-572-2800.

Attendance and degree information available by phone, fax, mail. Search requires name plus SSN, exact years of attendance. There is no fee.

Berean Institute, Registrar, 1901 W Girard Ave, Philadelphia, PA 19130-1599, 215-763-4833 (Fax: 215-236-6011). Hours: 9AM-5PM. Enrollment: 500. Records go back to 1940. Alumni records are maintained here at the same phone number. Degrees granted: Associate. Adverse incident record source- Student Affairs, 215-763-4833.

Attendance and degree information available by phone, fax, mail. Search requires name plus SSN. There is no fee.

Biblical Theological Seminary, Registrar, 200 N Main St, Hatfield, PA 19440, 215-368-5000 (Fax: 215-368-7002). Hours: 8:30AM-4:30PM. Enrollment: 300. Records go back to 1972. Alumni records are maintained here at the same phone number. Degrees granted: Masters; Doctorate.

Attendance and degree information available by phone, mail. Search requires name plus SSN, exact years of attendance. There is no fee.

Bloomsburg University of Pennsylvania, Registrar, 400 E Second St, Bloomsburg, PA 17815, 717-389-4263 (Fax: 717-389). Hours: 8AM-4:30PM. Enrollment: 7000. Records go back to 1888. Alumni records are maintained here also. Call 717-389-4058. Degrees granted: Associate; Bachelors; Masters. Adverse incident record source- Student Standards, 717-389-4734: Campus Police, 717-389-4168

Attendance and degree information available by phone, fax, mail. Search requires name plus SSN. Also helpful: date of birth, exact years of attendance. There is no fee.

Bradford School, Registrar, 707 Grant St, Gulf Tower, Pittsburgh, PA 15219, 412-391-6710. Hours: 7AM-4PM. Records go back to 1957. Degrees granted: Associate.

Attendance and degree information available by phone, fax, mail. Search requires name plus SSN, approximate years of attendance. Also helpful: date of birth, exact years of attendance. There is no fee.

Bradley Academy for the Visual Arts, Registrar, 625 E Philadelphia St, York, PA 17403-1625, 717-848-1447 (Fax: 717-845-6016). Hours: 7:30AM-5:30PM. Enrollment: 300. Records go back to 1988. Alumni records are maintained here also. Call 717-848-1447. Degrees granted: Associate.

Attendance and degree information available by phone, fax, mail. Search requires name plus SSN. There is no fee.

Bryn Mawr College, Registrar's Office, 101 N Merion Ave, Bryn Mawr, PA 19010, 610-526-5141 (Fax: 610-526-5133). Hours: 9AM-5PM. Enrollment: 1850. Records go back to 1885. Alumni records are maintained here also. Call 610-526-5227. Degrees granted: Bachelors; Masters; Doctorate. Adverse incident record source- Security(Public Safety), 610-526-7302.

Attendance and degree information available by phone, fax, mail. Search requires name plus SSN. There is no fee.

Bucknell University, Office of the Registrar, 102 Marts Hall, Lewisburg, PA 17837-2086, 717-524-1201 (Fax: 717-524-3922). Hours: 8:30AM-4:30PM. Enrollment: 3600. Records go back to 1846. Alumni records are maintained here also. Call 717-524-3223. Degrees granted: Bachelors; Masters. Adverse incident record source- Registrar, 717-524-1201.

Attendance information available by phone, mail. Search requires name only. Also helpful: SSN, exact years of attendance. There is no fee.

Degree information available by phone, mail. Search requires name only. Also helpful: SSN, exact years of attendance. There is no fee.

Bucks County Community College, Registrar, Swamp Rd, Newtown, PA 18940, 215-968-8101. Hours: 7:45AM-4:30PM M-Th, 7:45AM-4PM F. Records go back to 1965. Alumni records are maintained here also. Call 215-968-8461. Degrees granted: Associate.

Attendance and degree information available by phone, fax, mail. Search requires name plus SSN. Also helpful: exact years of attendance. There is no fee.

Butler County Community College, Registrar, College Dr, Oak Hills, PO Box 1203, Butler, PA 16003-1203, 412-287-8711 X331 (Fax: 412-285-6047). Hours: 8AM-6:30PM M-Th; 8AM-4PM F. Enrollment: 3000. Records go back to 1965. Degrees granted: Associate. Adverse incident record source- Dean of Students, 412-287-8711.

Attendance information available by phone, fax, mail. Search requires name plus SSN. Also helpful: date of birth, exact years of attendance. There is no fee.

Degree information available by phone, fax, mail. Search requires name plus SSN. Also helpful: date of birth, exact years of attendance. There is no fee.

Cabrini College, Registrar's Office, 610 King of Prussia Rd, Radnor, PA 19087-3699, 610-902-8545 (Fax: 610-902-8309). Hours: 8AM-7PM M,T,W,Th; 8AM-5PM F. Enrollment: 2000. Records go back to 1957. Alumni records are maintained here at the same phone number. Degrees granted: Masters. Adverse incident record source- Dean of Students, 610-902-8406.

Attendance and degree information available by phone, fax, mail. Search requires name plus SSN. Also helpful: date of birth, exact years of attendance. There is no fee.

California Institute of Pennsylvania, Academic Records, 250 University, California, PA 15419-1934, 412-938-4434 (Fax: 412-938-4340). Hours: 8AM-4PM. Records go back to 1950. Alumni records are maintained here at the same phone number. Degrees granted: Associate; Bachelors; Masters; Registered Nurse Program. Adverse incident record source- Student Development, 412-938-4439: Public Safety, 412-938-4299

Attendance information available by phone, fax, mail. Search requires name plus SSN. Also helpful: exact years of attendance. There is no fee.

Degree information available by phone, mail. Search requires name plus SSN. Also helpful: exact years of attendance. There is no fee.

California University of Pennsylvania, Academic Records, 250 University Ave, California, PA 15419, 412-938-4434 (Fax: 412-938-4340). Enrollment: 6200. Records go back to 1852. Alumni records are maintained here at the same phone number. Degrees granted: Associate; Bachelors; Masters. Special programs- Arts: Science. Adverse incident record source- Security.

Attendance and degree information available by phone, mail. Search requires name plus SSN. Also helpful: date of birth, exact years of attendance. There is no fee.

Cambria-Rowe Business College, Registrar, 221 Central Ave, Johnstown, PA 15902, 814-536-5168 (Fax: 814-536-5160). Hours: 8AM-5PM. Records go back to 1897. Degrees granted: Associate. Adverse incident record source- Executive Director or President, 814-536-5168.

Attendance and degree information available by phone, fax, mail. Search requires name plus SSN. There is no fee.

Cambria-Rowe Business College, (Indiana), Registrar, 422 S 13th St, Indiana, PA 15701, 412-463-0222 (Fax: 412-463-7246). Hours: 8AM-5PM. Enrollment: 140. Records go back to 1993. Degrees granted: Associate.

Attendance and degree information available by phone, fax, mail. Search requires name plus SSN, date of birth. Also helpful: exact years of attendance. There is no fee.

Carlow College, Registrar's Office, 3333 Fifth Ave, Pittsburgh, PA 15213-3165, 412-578-6084. Hours: 8AM-5PM. Records go back to 1929. Alumni records are maintained here also. Call 412-578-6087. Degrees granted: Bachelors; Masters.

Attendance and degree information available by phone, mail. Search requires name plus SSN, date of birth. There is no fee.

Carnegie Mellon University, Registrar, 5000 Forbes Ave, Warner Hall 201, Pittsburgh, PA 15213, 412-268-2000 X2004 (Fax: 412-268-6651). Hours: 8:30AM-5PM. Records go back to 1920. Alumni records are maintained here also. Call 412-268-2063. Degrees granted: Bachelors; Masters; Doctorate. Adverse incident record source- Student Affairs, 412-268-2076.

Attendance and degree information available by phone, fax, mail. Search requires name plus SSN, exact years of attendance. Also helpful: date of birth. There is no fee.

Cedar Crest College, Registrar, 100 College Dr, Allentown, PA 18104, 610-740-3765 (Fax: 610-740-3766). Hours: 8:30AM-4:30PM. Enrollment: 1700. Records go back to 1900's. Alumni records are maintained here also. Call 610-606-4609. Degrees granted: Bachelors.

Attendance and degree information available by phone, fax, mail. Search requires name plus SSN, exact years of attendance. Also helpful: date of birth. There is no fee.

Center for Degree Studies, Registrar, Oak and Pawnee Streets, Scranton, PA 18515, 717-342-7701 (Fax: 717-961-4871). Records go back to 1980. Degrees granted: Associate. Adverse incident record source- Student Services.

Attendance and degree information available by phone, mail. Search requires name plus SSN, date of birth. There is no fee.

Central Pennsylvania Business School, Registrar, College Hill Rd, Summerdale, PA 17093-0309, 717-728-2205 (Fax: 717-732-5254). Hours: 8AM-5PM. Enrollment: 574. Records go back to 1960. Alumni records are maintained here at the same phone number. Degrees granted: Associate.

Attendance and degree information available by phone, fax, mail. Search requires name only. Also helpful: SSN, exact years of attendance. There is no fee.

Chatham College, Registrar's Office, Woodland Rd, Pittsburgh, PA 15232, 412-365-1121 (Fax: 412-365-1505). Hours: 9AM-5PM. Records go back to 1920. Alumni records are maintained here also. Call 412-365-1255. Degrees granted: Bachelors; Masters.

Attendance and degree information available by phone, fax, mail. Search requires name plus SSN. Also helpful: exact years of attendance. There is no fee.

Chestnut Hill College, Registrar's Office, 9601 Germantown Ave, Philadelphia, PA 19118-2695, 215-248-7005 (Fax: 215-248-7155). Hours: 8:30AM-4:30PM. Enrollment: 1100. Records go back to 1953. Alumni records are maintained here also. Call 215-248-7144. Degrees granted: Associate; Bachelors; Masters. Adverse incident record source- Student Life.

Attendance and degree information available by phone, fax, mail. Search requires name plus SSN, approximate years of attendance. There is no fee.

Cheyney University of Pennsylvania, Registrar's Office, Cheyney and Creek Rds, Cheyney, PA 19319, 610-399-2225 (Fax: 610-399-2415). Hours: 8AM-5PM. Enrollment: 1357. Records go back to 1837. Alumni records are maintained here also. Call 610-399-2000. Degrees granted: Bachelors; Masters.

Attendance and degree information available by phone, fax, mail. Search requires name plus SSN, exact years of attendance. There is no fee.

Chubb Institute-Keystone School, Registrar, 965 Baltimore Pike, Springfield, PA 19064, 610-543-1747 (Fax: 610-543-7479). Hours: 9AM-5PM. Enrollment: 500. Records go back to 1950. Alumni records are maintained here also. Call 610-543-1747. Degrees granted: Associate. Adverse incident record source- Education Office, 610-543-1747.

Attendance and degree information available by phone, fax, mail. Search requires name plus SSN, exact years of attendance. There is no fee.

Churchman Business School, Registrar, 355 Spring Garden St, Easton, PA 18042, 610-258-5345 (Fax: 610-250-9547). Hours: 7:30AM-4PM. Enrollment: 180. Records go back to 1911. Alumni records are maintained here at the same phone number. Degrees granted: Associate. Adverse incident record source- Administrator, 610-258-5345.

Attendance and degree information available by phone, fax, mail. Search requires name plus SSN. There is no fee.

Clarion University of Pennsylvania, Registrar's Office, 122 Carrier Hall, Clarion, PA 16214, 814-226-2229 (Fax: 814-226-2039). Hours: 8:30AM-4:30PM. Records go back to 1870. Alumni Records Office: Alumni Association, Clarion University of Pennsylvania, Alumni House, Clarion, PA 16214. Degrees granted: Associate; Bachelors; Masters. Adverse incident record source- Registrar, 814-226-2229.

Attendance and degree information available by phone, fax, mail. Search requires name only. Also helpful: SSN, exact years of attendance. There is no fee.

Clarion University of Pennsylvania, (Venango), Registrar, W First St, Oil City, PA 16301, 814-676-6591. Records are not housed here. They are located at Clarion University of Pennsylvania, Registrar's Office, 122 Carrier Hall, Clarion, PA 16214.

College Misericordia, Registrar, 301 Lake St, Dallas, PA 18612-1098, 717-674-6756 (Fax: 717-675-2441). Hours: 8:30AM-4:30PM. Enrollment: 1800. Records go back to 1920's.

Alumni records are maintained here also. Call 717-674-6248. Degrees granted: Associate; Bachelors; Masters.

Attendance information available by written request only. Search requires name plus signed release. Also helpful: SSN, exact years of attendance. There is no fee.

Degree information available by phone, fax, mail. Search requires name plus approximate years of attendance. Also helpful: SSN, date of birth, exact years of attendance. There is no fee.

Community College of Allegheny County,
(Allegheny), Registrar, 808 Ridge Ave, Byers Hall 211, Pittsburgh, PA 15212, 412-237-2525. Hours: 8AM-5PM. Records go back to 1966. Alumni Records Office: Alumni Association, 800 Alumni Affairs, Pittsburgh, PA 15212. Degrees granted: Associate.

Attendance and degree information available by phone, fax, mail. Search requires name plus SSN. There is no fee.

Community College of Allegheny County,
(Boyce), Registrar, 595 Beatty Rd, Monroeville, PA 15146, 412-325-6674 (Fax: 412-325-6797). Hours: 8:30AM-4:30PM. Records go back to 1966. Alumni records are maintained here also. Call 412-371-8651. Degrees granted: Associate.

Attendance and degree information available by phone, fax, mail. Search requires name plus SSN. There is no fee.

Community College of Allegheny County,
(North), Registrar, 8701 Perry Hwy, Pittsburgh, PA 15237, 412-369-3700 (Fax: 412-369-3635). Hours: 8:30AM-4:30PM. Records go back to 1966. Alumni records are maintained here also. Call 412-366-7000. Degrees granted: Associate.

Attendance and degree information available by phone, fax, mail. Search requires name plus SSN. Also helpful: exact years of attendance. There is no fee.

Community College of Allegheny County,
(South), Registrar, 1750 Clairton Rd Rte 885, West Mifflin, PA 15122, 412-469-6202 (Fax: 412-469-6371). Hours: 8:30AM-4:30PM. Records go back to 1960. Alumni records are maintained here also. Call 412-469-6243. Degrees granted: Associate.

Attendance and degree information available by mail. Search requires name plus SSN, signed release. There is no fee.

Community College of Beaver County, Registrar, One Campus Dr, Monaca, PA 15061-2588, 412-775-8561 (Fax: 412-775-4055). Hours: 8AM-4:30PM. Enrollment: 2500. Records go back to 1969. Alumni records are maintained here also. Call 412-775-8561. Degrees granted: Associate. Adverse incident record source- Campus Police, 412-775-8561.

Attendance and degree information available by mail. Search requires name plus SSN, signed release. There is no fee.

Community College of Philadelphia, Registrar, 1700 Spring Garden St, Philadelphia, PA 19130-3991, 215-751-8261 (Fax: 215-751-8001). Hours: 9AM-4:45PM M-W, 9AM-3:45PM R. Enrollment: 18305. Records go back to 1964. Degrees granted: Associate.

Attendance and degree information available by phone, fax, mail. Search requires name plus SSN. Also helpful: exact years of attendance. There is no fee.

Computer Tech, Registrar, 107 Sixth St, Pittsburgh, PA 15222, 412-391-4197 (Fax: 412-391-4224). Hours: 8AM-5PM. Enrollment: 600. Records go back to 1967. Degrees granted: Associate. Adverse incident record source- 412-391-4197.

Attendance and degree information available by phone, fax, mail. Search requires name plus SSN. Also helpful: date of birth, exact years of attendance. Fee is $5.00.

Consolidated School of Business, Registrar, 2124 Ambassador Circle, Lancaster, PA 17601, 717-394-6211 (Fax: 717-394-6213). Hours: 8AM-5PM. Records go back to 1986. Degrees granted: Associate.

Attendance information available by fax, mail. Search requires name plus SSN, exact years of attendance, signed release. There is no fee.

Degree information available by phone, fax, mail. Search requires name plus SSN, exact years of attendance. There is no fee.

Consolidated School of Business, Registrar, 1605 Clugston Rd, York, PA 17404, 717-764-9550 (Fax: 717-764-9469). Hours: 9AM-5:30PM. Enrollment: 175. Records go back to 1976. Alumni records are maintained here at the same phone number. Degrees granted: Associate. Adverse incident record source- Registrar's Office .

Attendance and degree information available by fax, mail. Search requires name plus SSN, approximate years of attendance, signed release. Also helpful: exact years of attendance. There is no fee.

Curtis Institute of Music, Registrar, 1726 Locust St, Philadelphia, PA 19103, 215-893-5252 (Fax: 215-893-9065). Hours: 9AM-5PM. Records go back to 1926. Alumni records are maintained here at the same phone number. Degrees granted: Bachelors; Masters. Adverse incident record source- Business Office, 215-893-5252.

Attendance information available by phone, fax, mail. Search requires name plus SSN. There is no fee.

Degree information available by phone, fax, mail. Search requires name plus SSN. There is no fee.

Dean Institute of Technology, Registrar, 1501 W Liberty Ave, Pittsburgh, PA 15226, 412-531-4433 (Fax: 412-531-4435). Hours: 7:45AM-4PM M-Th, 7:45AM-3PM F. Enrollment: 230. Records go back to 1974. Degrees granted: Associate. Special programs- Construction Engineering. Adverse incident record source- Registrar, 412-531-4433.

Attendance and degree information available by phone, fax, mail. Search requires name plus SSN. There is no fee.

Delaware County Community College, Registrar, 901 S Media Line Rd, Media, PA 19063, 610-359-5336 (Fax: 610-359-5343). Hours: 9AM-9PM. Records go back to 1967. Alumni records are maintained here also. Call 610-359-7399. Degrees granted: Associate.

Attendance and degree information available by phone, fax, mail. Search requires name only. Also helpful: SSN. There is no fee.

Delaware Valley College of Science and Agriculture, Registrar's Officd, 700 E Butler Ave, Doylestown, PA 18901, 215-345-1500 X2378 (Fax: 215-230-2962). Hours: 8:30AM-4:30PM. Enrollment: 2200. Records go back to 1896. Alumni records are maintained here also. Call 215-345-1500 X2424. Degrees granted: Associate; Bachelors. Adverse incident record source- Dean, 215-345-1500 X2215: Registrar, 215-345-1500 X2378

Attendance and degree information available by phone, mail. Search requires name plus SSN. There is no fee.

Dickinson College, Registrar, Carlisle, PA 17013, 717-245-1315 (Fax: 717-245-1534). Hours: 8AM-Noon, 1-4:30 PM. Enrollment: 1850. Records go back to 1783. Alumni Records Office: Alumni Association, 249 W Loother St, Carlisle, PA 17013. Degrees granted: Bachelors.

Attendance and degree information available by phone, fax, mail. Search requires name only. Also helpful: SSN, date of birth, exact years of attendance. There is no fee.

Dickinson School of Law, Registrar, 150 S College St, Carlisle, PA 17013, 717-240-5210 (Fax: 717-243-4366). Hours: 8AM-5PM. Records go back to 1925. Alumni records are maintained here also. Call 717-240-5250. Degrees granted: Doctorate.

Attendance and degree information available by phone, mail. Search requires name plus SSN, exact years of attendance. There is no fee.

Douglas School of Business, Registrar, 130 Seventh St, Monessen, PA 15062, 412-684-7644 (Fax: 412-684-7463). Hours: 8AM-5PM. Records go back to 1904. Degrees granted: Associate.

Attendance and degree information available by phone, fax, mail. Search requires name plus exact years of attendance. Also helpful: SSN, date of birth. There is no fee.

Drexel University, Registrar, 32nd and Chestnut Sts, Philadelphia, PA 19104, 215-895-2300. Hours: 9AM-5PM. Records go back to 1891. Degrees granted: Bachelors; Masters; Doctorate.

Attendance and degree information available by phone, fax, mail. Search requires name only. Also helpful: SSN, date of birth, exact years of attendance. There is no fee.

DuBois Business College, Registrar, One Beaver Dr, Du Bois, PA 15801, 814-371-6920 (Fax: 814-371-3974). Hours: 8:30AM-5PM. Records go back to 1960. Alumni records are maintained here also. Call 814-371-6920. Degrees granted: Associate. Adverse incident record source- Registrar, 814-371-6920.

Attendance and degree information available by phone, fax, mail. Search requires name plus SSN, approximate years of attendance. There is no fee.

Duff's Business Institute, Registrar, 110 Ninth St, Pittsburgh, PA 15222, 412-261-4530 (Fax: 412-261-4546). Hours: 8AM-4PM. Enrollment: 450. Records go back to 1925. Degrees granted: Associate.

Attendance information available by phone, fax, mail. Search requires name plus SSN. Also helpful: exact years of attendance. There is no fee.

Degree information available by phone, fax, mail. Search requires name plus SSN, approximate years of attendance. Also helpful: exact years of attendance. There is no fee.

Duquesne University, Registrar, 600 Forbes Ave, Pittsburgh, PA 15282, 412-396-6212 (Fax: 412-396-5622). Hours: 8:30AM-4:30PM. Records go back to 1846. Alumni records are maintained here also. Call 412-396-6209. Degrees granted: Bachelors; Masters; Doctorate. Adverse incident record source- Registrar, 412-396-6212.

Attendance information available by phone, mail. Search requires name plus SSN, date of birth, exact years of attendance. There is no fee.

Degree information available by phone, fax, mail. Search requires name plus SSN, date of birth, exact years of attendance. There is no fee.

East Stroudsburg University of Pennsylvania, Registrar, 200 Prospect St, East Stroudsburg, PA 18301, 717-422-3148 (Fax: 717-422-3842). Hours: 8AM-4:30PM. Enrollment: 5500. Records go back to 1890's. Alumni records are maintained here also. Call 909-424-3533. Degrees granted: Associate; Bachelors; Masters. Special programs- Graduate School, 717-422-3536. Adverse incident record source- Registrar, 717-422-3148.

Attendance and degree information available by phone, fax, mail. Search requires name plus SSN, approximate years of attendance. There is no fee.

Eastern Baptist Theological Seminary, Registrar, 6 Lancaster Ave, Wynnewood, PA 19096-3494, 610-645-9329 (Fax: 610-649-3834). Hours: 8:30AM-6:30PM. Records go back to 1925. Alumni records are maintained here also. Call 610-896-5000. Degrees granted: Masters. Certification: Christian Ministry.

Attendance information available by phone, fax, mail. Search requires name plus approximate years of attendance. Also helpful: SSN, exact years of attendance. There is no fee.

Degree information available by phone, fax, mail. Search requires name only. Also helpful: exact years of attendance. There is no fee.

Eastern College, Registrar, 10 Fairview Dr, St Davids, PA 19087-3696, 610-341-5854 (Fax: 610-341-1707). Hours: 8AM-8PM. Enrollment: 2300. Records go back to 1952. Alumni records are maintained here also. Call 610-341-5936. Degrees granted: Associate; Bachelors; Masters. Adverse incident record source- Dean of Students, 610-341-5822.

Attendance and degree information available by phone, fax, mail. Search requires name only. Also helpful: SSN, approximate years of attendance. There is no fee.

Edinboro University of Pennsylvania, Records & Registration, Edinboro, PA 16444, 814-732-2726 (Fax: 814-732-2680). Hours: 8AM-4:30PM. Enrollment: 7500. Records go back to 1900. Alumni records are maintained here also. Call 814-732-2715. Degrees granted: Associate; Bachelors; Masters. Adverse incident record source- Academic Affairs, 814-732-2825.

Attendance and degree information available by phone, fax, mail. Search requires name plus SSN. There is no fee.

Electronic Institutes, Registrar, 19 Jamesway Plaza, Middletown, PA 17057-4851, 717-944-2731 (Fax: 717-944-2734). Hours: 8AM-3PM. Enrollment: 180. Records go back to 1959. Degrees granted: Associate.

Attendance and degree information available by phone, fax, mail. Search requires name plus SSN. Also helpful: exact years of attendance. There is no fee.

Electronic Institutes, Registrar, 4634 Browns Hill Rd, Pittsburgh, PA 15217-2919, 412-521-8686 (Fax: 412-521-9277). Hours: 8AM-3:30PM. Records go back to 1966. Degrees granted: Associate.

Attendance and degree information available by phone, fax, mail. Search requires name plus SSN, date of birth. Also helpful: exact years of attendance. There is no fee.

Elizabethtown College, Registrar, One Alpha Dr, Elizabethtown, PA 17022-2298, 717-361-1409 (Fax: 717-361-1485). Hours: 8:30AM-5PM. Enrollment: 1500. Records go back to 1899. Alumni records are maintained here also. Call 717-361-1403. Degrees granted: Bachelors.

Attendance and degree information available by phone, fax, mail. Search requires name plus SSN, approximate years of attendance. Also helpful: exact years of attendance. There is no fee.

Erie Business Center, Registrar, 246 W Ninth St, Erie, PA 16501, 814-456-7504 (Fax: 814-456-4882). Hours: 8AM-5PM. Records go back to 1955. Alumni records are maintained here also. Call 814-456-7504. Degrees granted: Associate. Adverse incident record source- Registrar, 814-456-7504.

Attendance and degree information available by phone, fax, mail. Search requires name plus SSN, approximate years of attendance. There is no fee.

Erie Business Center, (Erie Business Center South), Registrar, 700 Moravia St, New Castle, PA 16101, 412-658-3595 (Fax: 412-658-3083). Hours: 9AM-5PM. Enrollment: 85. Records go back to 1970. Degrees granted: Associate.

Attendance and degree information available by phone, fax, mail. Search requires name plus SSN, exact years of attendance. There is no fee.

Evangelical School of Theology, Registrar, 121 S College St, Myerstown, PA 17067, 717-866-5775 (Fax: 717-866-4667). Hours: 8AM-4PM. Enrollment: 125. Records go

back to 1953. Alumni records are maintained here also. Call 717-866-5775. Degrees granted: Bachelors; Masters.

Attendance and degree information available by phone, mail. Search requires name plus SSN. There is no fee.

Franklin & Marshall College, Registrar, PO Box 3003, Lancaster, PA 17604-3003, 717-291-4168 (Fax: 717-399-4413). Hours: 8:30AM-4:30PM. Records go back to 1853. Alumni records are maintained here also. Call 717-291-3955. Degrees granted: Bachelors.

Attendance and degree information available by phone, fax, mail. Search requires name only. Also helpful: SSN, date of birth, exact years of attendance. There is no fee.

Gannon University, Registrar's Officd, University Square, Erie, PA 16541, 814-871-7243 (Fax: 814-871-7338). Hours: 8AM-4:30PM. Records go back to 1930. Alumni records are maintained here also. Call 814-871-7473. Degrees granted: Associate; Bachelors; Masters. Adverse incident record source- Student Living, 814-871-7660.

Attendance and degree information available by phone, fax, mail. Search requires name plus SSN, date of birth. There is no fee.

Geneva College, Registrar, 3200 College Ave, Beaver Falls, PA 15010, 412-847-6600 (Fax: 412-847-6696). Hours: 8AM-4:30PM. Enrollment: 1600. Records go back to 1900. Alumni records are maintained here also. Call 412-847-6525. Degrees granted: Associate; Bachelors; Masters.

Attendance and degree information available by phone, fax, mail. Search requires name only. Also helpful: SSN, date of birth, exact years of attendance. There is no fee.

Gettysburg College, Registrar, 300 N Washington St, Gettysburg, PA 17325-1486, 717-337-6240 (Fax: 717-337-6906). Hours: 8AM-5PM. Records go back to 1832. Alumni records are maintained here also. Call 717-337-6518. Degrees granted: Bachelors. Adverse incident record source- Academic Advising Files, 717-337-6579.

Attendance and degree information available by phone, fax, mail. Search requires name plus exact years of attendance. There is no fee.

Gratz College, Registrar, Old York Rd and Melrose Ave, Melrose Park, PA 19126, 215-635-7300 (Fax: 215-635-7320). Hours: 9AM-5PM M-Th, 9AM-3PM F. Enrollment: 125. Records go back to 1940. Alumni records are maintained here at the same phone number. Degrees granted: Bachelors; Masters. Adverse incident record source- Vice President, 215-635-7300.

Attendance and degree information available by phone, fax, mail. Search requires name plus exact years of attendance. There is no fee.

Grove City College, Registrar, 100 Campus Dr, Grove City, PA 16127-2104, 412-458-2172 (Fax: 412-458-3368). Hours: 8AM-Noon, 1-5PM. Records go back to 1896. Alumni records are maintained here also. Call 412-458-2300. Degrees granted: Bachelors; Masters.

Attendance and degree information available by phone, fax, mail. Search requires name plus SSN, exact years of attendance. Also helpful: date of birth. There is no fee.

Gwynedd-Mercy College, Registrar, Gwynedd Valley, PA 19437, 215-646-7300 (Fax: 215-641-5573). Hours: 8AM-4PM. Enrollment: 1900. Records go back to 1949. Alumni records are maintained here also. Call 215-646-7300 X178. Degrees granted: Associate; Bachelors; Masters.

Attendance and degree information available by phone, fax, mail. Search requires name plus approximate years of attendance. Also helpful: SSN, date of birth, exact years of attendance. There is no fee.

Harcum College, Registrar, 750 Montogomery Ave, Bryn Mawr, PA 19010-3476, 610-526-6007. Hours: 9AM-5PM. Records go back to 1921. Alumni records are maintained here also. Call 610-526-6006. Degrees granted: Associate.

Attendance and degree information available by phone, fax, mail. Search requires name plus SSN. There is no fee.

Harrisburg Area Community College, Registrar, One HACC Dr, Harrisburg, PA 17110-2999, 717-780-2370 (Fax: 717-231-7674). Hours: 8AM-8PM M-Th; 8AM-5PM F; 9AM-1PM S. Enrollment: 11000. Records go back to 1964. Alumni records are maintained here also. Call 717-780-2583. Degrees granted: Associate.

Attendance and degree information available by phone, fax, mail. Search requires name only. Also helpful: SSN, date of birth, exact years of attendance. There is no fee.

Harrisburg Area Community College, (Lancaster), Registrar, 1008 New Holland Ave, Lancaster, PA 17604, 717-293-5000 (Fax: 717-293-8967). Hours: 9AM-7:30PM M,T; 9AM-5PM W,Th; 9AM-4:30PM F. Records go back to 1989. Alumni records are maintained here also. Call 717-780-2400. Degrees granted: Associate. Adverse incident record source- Dean, 717-295-2975.

Attendance information available by mail. Search requires name plus SSN, exact years of attendance. There is no fee.

Degree information available by mail. Search requires name plus SSN, exact years of attendance. There is no fee.

Harrisburg Area Community College, (Lebanon), Registrar, 735 Cumberland St, Lebanon, PA 17042, 717-270-4222 (Fax: 717-270-6385). Hours: 7:30AM-8PM M-Th, 7:30AM-5PM F, 8AM-1PM Sat. Records go back to 1980. Alumni records are maintained here also. Call 717-780-2400. Degrees granted: Associate.

Attendance information available by mail. Search requires name plus SSN. Also helpful: exact years of attendance. There is no fee.

Degree information available by phone, fax, mail. Search requires name plus SSN. Also helpful: exact years of attendance. There is no fee.

Haverford College, Registrar, 370 Lancaster Ave, Haverford, PA 19041-1392, 610-896-1022 (Fax: 610-896-1224). Hours: 9AM-5PM Academic year; 8:30AM-4:30PM Summer. Records go back to 1883. Transcripts available to early 1900s. Alumni records are maintained here also. Call 610-896-1001. Degrees granted: Bachelors.

Attendance and degree information available by phone, fax, mail. Search requires name only. Also helpful: SSN, date of birth, exact years of attendance. There is no fee.

Holy Family College, Registrar's Office, Grant and Frankford Aves, Philadelphia, PA 19114-2094, 215-637-4851 (Fax: 215-281-9067). Hours: 8AM-7:30PM M-Th, 8AM-4:30PM F, 8:30AM-12:30PM Sat. Enrollment: 2800. Records go back to 1950. Alumni records are maintained here also. Call 215-637-7700. Degrees granted: Associate; Bachelors; Masters. Adverse incident record source- Dean, 215-637-3971.

Attendance information available by phone, mail. Search requires name plus SSN. Also helpful: exact years of attendance. There is no fee.

Degree information available by phone, mail. Search requires name plus SSN. Also helpful: exact years of attendance. There is no fee.

Hussian School of Art, Registrar, 1118 Market St, Philadelphia, PA 19107-3679, 215-981-0900 (Fax: 215-864-9115). Hours: 9AM-3PM. Enrollment: 140. Records go back to 1946. Alumni records are maintained here at the same phone number. Degrees granted: Associate.

Attendance and degree information available by fax, mail. Search requires name plus signed release. Also helpful: SSN, date of birth, exact years of attendance. There is no fee.

ICM School of Business, Registrar, 10 Wood St, Pittsburgh, PA 15222, 412-261-2647 (Fax: 412-261-6491). Hours: 8AM-4:30PM. Enrollment: 500. Records go back to 1960. Degrees granted: Associate. Adverse incident record source- Registrar, 412-261-2647.

Attendance and degree information available by phone, fax, mail. Search requires name plus SSN, exact years of attendance. There is no fee.

ITT Technical Institute, (Branch of Youngstown, OH), Registrar, 8 Parkway Ctr, Pittsburgh, PA 15220, 412-937-9150. Hours: 8AM-6PM. Records go back to 1992. Degrees granted: Associate.

Attendance and degree information available by mail. Search requires name plus SSN, date of birth, exact years of attendance, signed release. There is no fee.

Immaculata College, Registrar, Immaculata, PA 19345, 610-647-4400 X3009 (Fax: 610-251-1668). Hours: 8:30AM-4:30PM. Enrollment: 2000. Records go back to 1925. Alumni records are maintained here also. Call 610-647-4400 X3135. Degrees granted: Associate; Bachelors; Masters; Doctorate.

Attendance and degree information available by phone, fax, mail. Search requires name plus SSN, approximate years of attendance. Also helpful: date of birth, exact years of attendance. There is no fee.

Indiana University of Pennsylvania, Registrar's Office, 68 Sutton Hall, Indiana, PA 15705, 412-357-2217 (Fax: 412-357-4858). Hours: 8AM-4:30PM. Records go back to 1940. Alumni records are maintained here also. Call 412-357-7942. Degrees granted: Bachelors; Masters; Doctorate.

Attendance and degree information available by phone, fax, mail. Search requires name plus SSN, approximate years of attendance. There is no fee.

Indiana University of Pennsylvania, (Armstrong County), Registrar, Kittanning, PA 16201, 412-543-1078. Records are not housed here. They are located at Indiana University of Pennsylvania, Registrar's Office, 68 Sutton Hall, Indiana, PA 15705.

Indiana University of Pennsylvania, (Punxsutawney), Registrar, Punxsutawney, PA 15767, 814-938-6711. Records are not housed here. They are located at Indiana University of Pennsylvania, Registrar's Office, 68 Sutton Hall, Indiana, PA 15705.

Jefferson Medical College, Registrar, 1015 Walnut St G22, Philadelphia, PA 19107, 215-955-6748 (Fax: 215-923-6974). Enrollment: 915. Formerly Thomas Jefferson University Records go back to 1900's. Alumni records are maintained here at the same phone number. Degrees granted: Masters; Doctorate. Special programs- Graduate, 215-955-8982: Allied Health Sciences, 215-955-8893.

Attendance and degree information available by phone, mail. Search requires name plus exact years of attendance. Also helpful: SSN, date of birth. There is no fee.

Johnson Technical Institute, Registrar, 3427 N Main Ave, Scranton, PA 18508-1495, 717-342-6404. Hours: 8AM-5PM. Records go back to 1920. Alumni records are maintained here also. Call 717-342-6404 X51. Degrees granted: Associate. Adverse incident record source- President, 717-342-6404 X12.

Attendance and degree information available by phone, fax, mail. Search requires name plus SSN, exact years of attendance. There is no fee.

Johnson Technical Institute, (Branch), Registrar, 200 Shady Lane, Philipsburg, PA 16866, 814-342-5680. Records are not housed here. They are located at Johnson Technical Institute, Registrar, 3427 N Main Ave, Scranton, PA 18508-1495.

Juniata College, Registrar, 1700 Moore St, Huntingdon, PA 16652, 814-643-4310 X270 (Fax: 814-641-3199). Hours: 8:30AM-5PM. Records go back to 1932. Alumni records are maintained here also. Call 814-643-4310. Degrees granted: Bachelors.

Attendance and degree information available by phone, fax, mail. Search requires name plus SSN, exact years of attendance. There is no fee.

Keystone Junior College, Registrar, PO Box 50, La Plume, PA 18440-0200, 717-945-5141 X2301 (Fax: 717-945-6961). Hours: 9AM-5PM. Records go back to 1868. Alumni records are maintained here also. Call 717-945-5141. Degrees granted: Associate.

Attendance and degree information available by phone, mail. Search requires name plus SSN, exact years of attendance. Also helpful: date of birth. There is no fee.

King's College, Registrar, 133 N River St, Wilkes-Barre, PA 18711, 717-826-5870 (Fax: 717-825-9049). Hours: 8:30AM-4:30PM. Enrollment: 2300. Records go back to 1946. Alumni records are maintained here also. Call 717-826-5900. Degrees granted: Bachelors; Masters. Adverse incident record source-Registrar, 717-826-5870.

Attendance and degree information available by phone, mail. Search requires name plus SSN, date of birth, exact years of attendance. There is no fee.

Kutztown University of Pennslyvania, Registrar's Office, Kutztown, PA 19530, 610-683-4485. Hours: 8AM-4PM. Records go back to 1867. Alumni records are maintained here also. Call 610-683-4110. Degrees granted: Bachelors; Masters. Adverse incident record source- Public Safety, 610-683-4002.

Attendance and degree information available by phone, fax, mail. Search requires name plus SSN, exact years of attendance. There is no fee.

La Roche College, Registrar, 9000 Babcock Blvd, Pittsburgh, PA 15237, 412-367-9248 (Fax: 412-367-9368). Hours: 8:30AM-6:30PM M, 8:30AM-4:30PM T-Th. Enrollment: 1630. Records go back to 1963. Alumni records are maintained here also. Call 412-367-9300 X140. Degrees granted: Bachelors; Masters. Special programs- Accelerated B.S., 412-367-9360 X359. Adverse incident record source- Dean, 412-367-9300 X147.

Attendance and degree information available by phone, mail. Search requires name plus SSN, approximate years of attendance. There is no fee.

La Salle University, Registrar, 1900 W Olney Ave, Philadelphia, PA 19141, 215-951-1020. Hours: 8:30AM-4:30PM. Enrollment: 5228. Records go back to 1863. Degrees granted: Associate; Bachelors; Masters.

Attendance and degree information available by phone, mail. Search requires name plus SSN, date of birth, approximate years of attendance. Also helpful: exact years of attendance. There is no fee.

Lackawanna Senior College, Registrar's Office, 901 Prospect Ave, Scranton, PA 18505, 717-961-7840 (Fax: 717-961-7858). Hours: 9AM-6PM M,Th; 9AM-5PM T,W; 9AM-4:30PM F. Records go back to 1900's. Alumni records are maintained here also. Call 717-961-7829. Degrees granted: Associate.

Attendance and degree information available by fax, mail. Search requires name plus SSN, signed release. Also helpful: date of birth, exact years of attendance. There is no fee.

Lafayette College, Registrar, High St, Easton, PA 18042, 610-250-5090 (Fax: 610-250-1975). Hours: 8:45AM-5PM Fall-Spring hours; 8:15AM-4:30PM Summer hours. Enrollment: 2000. Records go back to 1800. Alumni records are maintained here also. Call 610-250-5040. Degrees granted: Bachelors. Adverse incident record source- Dean, 610-250-5080.

Attendance and degree information available by phone, fax, mail. Search requires name plus SSN, approximate years of attendance. Also helpful: exact years of attendance. There is no fee.

Lake Erie College of Osteopathic Medicine, Registrar, 1858 W Grandview Blvd, Erie, PA 16509, 814-866-8115 (Fax: 814-864-8699). Hours: 8AM-4:30PM. Enrollment: 325. Records go back to 1993. Degrees granted: Doctorate.

Attendance and degree information available by phone, fax, mail. Search requires name plus SSN. There is no fee.

Lancaster Bible College, Registrar, 901 Eden Rd, Lancaster, PA 17601, 717-569-7071 (Fax: 717-560-8211). Hours: 8AM-4PM. Enrollment: 650. Records go back to 1930. Alumni records are maintained here at the same phone number. Degrees granted: Associate; Bachelors; Masters.

Attendance and degree information available by phone, mail. Search requires name plus SSN, exact years of attendance. Also helpful: date of birth. Fee is $5.00.

Lancaster Theological Seminary, Registrar, 555 W James St, Lancaster, PA 17603-2897, 717-290-8718 (Fax: 717-393-4254). Hours: 8AM-5PM. Records go back to 1900's. Alumni records are maintained here also. Call 717-290-8729. Degrees granted: Masters; Doctorate.

Attendance and degree information available by fax, mail. Search requires name plus SSN, exact years of attendance, signed release. There is no fee.

Lansdale School of Business, Registrar, 201 Church Rd, North Wales, PA 19454, 215-699-5700 (Fax: 215-699-8770). Hours: 8AM-10PM. Records go back to 1950. Degrees granted: Associate. Adverse incident record source- President, 215-699-5700.

Attendance and degree information available by phone, fax, mail. Search requires name plus SSN, exact years of attendance. There is no fee.

Laurel Business Institute, Registrar, 11-15 Penn St, Uniontown, PA 15401, 412-439-4900. Hours: 8AM-5PM. Degrees granted: Associate.

Attendance and degree information available by written request only. Search requires name plus SSN, date of birth, approximate years of attendance, signed release. There is no fee.

Lebanon Valley College, Registrar, 101 N College Ave, Annville, PA 17003-0501, 717-867-6215 (Fax: 717-867-6018). Hours: 8AM-4:30PM. Enrollment: 1875. Records go back to 1883. Alumni records are maintained here also. Call 717-867-6320. Degrees granted: Associate; Bachelors; Masters. Adverse incident record source- Security Office, 717-867-6111.

Attendance and degree information available by phone, fax, mail. Search requires name plus SSN. Also helpful: date of birth, exact years of attendance. There is no fee.

Lehigh Carbon Community College, Registrar, 4525 Education Park Dr, Schnecksville, PA 18078-2598, 610-799-1174 (Fax: 610-799-1173). Hours: 8AM-9PM. Records go back to 1968. Alumni records are maintained here also. Call 610-799-2121. Degrees granted: Associate. Adverse incident record source- Security, 610-799-1169.

Attendance and degree information available by phone, mail. Search requires name only. Also helpful: SSN, date of birth, exact years of attendance. There is no fee.

Lehigh University, Registrar, 27 Memorial Dr W, Bethlehem, PA 18015, 610-758-3200 (Fax: 610-758-3198). Hours: 8:15AM-4:45PM. Enrollment: 6300. Records go back to 1860. Alumni records are maintained here also. Call 610-758-3200. Degrees granted: Bachelors; Masters; PhD. Adverse incident record source- Dean, 610-758-4159.

Attendance and degree information available by phone, fax, mail. Search requires name plus SSN, exact years of attendance. Also helpful: date of birth. There is no fee.

Lincoln University, Registrar, Lincoln University, PA 19352-0999, 610-932-3283 (Fax: 610-932-7659). Hours: 8AM-5PM. Enrollment: 1500. Records go back to 1930. Alumni records are maintained here at the same phone number. Degrees granted: Bachelors; Masters.

Attendance and degree information available by phone, fax, mail. Search requires name plus SSN. Also helpful: exact years of attendance. There is no fee.

Lock Haven University, Student Records, Sullivan Hall 207, Lock Haven, PA 17745, 717-893-2006 (Fax: 717-893-2432). Hours: 8AM-4PM. Enrollment: 3300. Records go back to 1935. Alumni records are maintained here also. Call 717-893-2021. Degrees granted: Associate; Bachelors; Masters. Certification: Teacher Education.

Attendance and degree information available by phone, fax, mail. Search requires name plus SSN. Also helpful: date of birth, exact years of attendance. There is no fee.

Lutheran Theological Seminary at Gettysburg, Registrar, 61 NW Confederate Ave, Gettysburg, PA 17325-1795, 717-334-6286 X201 (Fax: 717-334-3469). Hours: 8:30AM-4:30PM. Records go back to 1900. Alumni records are maintained here also. Call 717-334-3469 X210. Degrees granted: Masters; STM. Adverse incident record source- Dean, 717-334-3469 X202.

Attendance and degree information available by fax, mail. Search requires name plus approximate years of attendance. There is no fee.

Lutheran Theological Seminary at Philadelphia, Registrar, 7301 Germantown Ave, Philadelphia, PA 19119, 215-248-4616 (Fax: 215-248-4577). Hours: 9AM-4:30PM; Summer hours 8:30AM-4PM. Records go back to 1864. Alumni records are maintained here also. Call 215-248-4616. Degrees granted: Masters; Doctorate; Doctor of Ministry, Academic Master.

Attendance and degree information available by phone, fax, mail. Search requires name plus SSN, approximate years of attendance. There is no fee.

Luzerne County Community College, Registrar, 1333 S Prospect St, Nanticoke, PA 18634, 717-829-7340 (Fax: 717-735-6130). Hours: 8AM-5PM. Records go back to 1968. Alumni records are maintained here also. Call 717-829-7387. Degrees granted: Associate. Adverse incident record source- Dean, 717-829-7344.

Attendance information available by phone, fax, mail. Search requires name plus SSN, exact years of attendance. There is no fee.

Degree information available by phone, mail. Search requires name plus SSN, exact years of attendance. There is no fee.

Lycoming College, Registrar's Office, 700 College Pl, Williamsport, PA 17701, 717-321-4045 (Fax: 717-321-4337). Hours: 8AM-4:30PM. Enrollment: 1400. Records go back to 1812. Alumni records are maintained here also. Call 717-321-4035. Degrees granted: Bachelors. Adverse incident record source- Student Affairs, 717-321-4039.

Attendance and degree information available by phone, fax, mail. Search requires name plus SSN, exact years of attendance. There is no fee.

Manor Junior College, Registrar, 700 Fox Chase Rd, Jenkintown, PA 19046, 215-885-2360 X51. Hours: 9AM-5PM. Enrollment: 659. Records go back to 1948. Degrees granted: Associate.

Attendance and degree information available by phone, mail. Search requires name plus SSN, date of birth, exact years of attendance. Also helpful: approximate years of attendance. There is no fee.

Mansfield University of Pennsylvania, Registrar's Office, 112 S Hall, Mansfield, PA 16933, 717-662-4202 (Fax: 717-662-4122). Hours: 8AM-4:15PM. Enrollment: 2800. Records go back to 1950. Alumni records are maintained here also. Call 717-662-4292. Degrees granted: Bachelors; Masters.

Attendance and degree information available by phone, fax, mail. Search requires name plus SSN. There is no fee.

Marywood College, Registrar, 2300 Adams Ave, Scranton, PA 18509, 717-348-6280 X482 (Fax: 717-961-4758). Hours: 8:30AM-6PM M-Th, 8:30AM-4:30PM F. Records go back to 1915. Alumni records are maintained here also. Call 717-348-6206. Degrees granted: Bachelors; Masters.

Attendance and degree information available by fax, mail. Search requires name plus SSN. There is no fee.

McCann School of Business, Registrar, Main and Pine Sts, Mahanoy City, PA 17948, 717-773-1820 (Fax: 717-773-0483). Hours: 8AM-5PM. Records go back to 1897. Alumni records are maintained here at the same phone number. Degrees granted: Associate; Paralegal.

Attendance and degree information available by phone, fax, mail. Search requires name plus SSN, date of birth, exact years of attendance. There is no fee.

McCann School of Business, (Branch), Registrar, 2004 Wyoming Ave, Wyoming, PA 18644, 717-773-1820 (Fax: 717-773--0483). Hours: 8:30AM-4:30PM. Records go back to 1932. Alumni records are maintained here at the same phone number. Degrees granted: Associate.

Attendance and degree information available by fax, mail. Search requires name plus SSN, date of birth, exact years of attendance. There is no fee.

McCarrie Schools of Health Sciences and Technology Inc., Registrar, 512-520 S Broad St, Philadelphia, PA 19146-1613, 215-545-7772. Hours: 8AM-4PM. Records go back to 1917. Degrees granted: Associate.

Attendance information available by mail. Search requires name plus SSN, exact years of attendance, signed release. There is no fee.

Degree information available by fax, mail. Search requires name plus SSN, exact years of attendance, signed release. There is no fee.

Median School of Allied Health Careers, Registrar, 125 Seventh St, Pittsburgh, PA 15222-3400, 412-391-7021 (Fax: 412-232-4348). Hours: 8AM-4:30PM. Enrollment: 320. Records go back to 1970. Degrees granted: Associate.

Attendance and degree information available by phone, fax, mail. Search requires name plus exact years of attendance. Also helpful: SSN. There is no fee.

Medical College of Pennsylvania and Hahnemann University, Registrar's Office, 2900 Queen Lane, Philadelphia, PA 19129, 215-991-8206 (Fax: 215-843-5780). Hours: 8:30AM-4:30PM. Enrollment: 800. Records go back to 1940. Alumni records are maintained here at the same phone number. Degrees granted: Doctorate.

Attendance and degree information available by phone, mail. Search requires name plus SSN. There is no fee.

Mercyhurst College, Registrar, 501 E 38th St, Erie, PA 16546, 814-824-2250 (Fax: 814-824-2438). Hours: 8AM-4:30PM. Records go back to 1926. Alumni records are maintained here also. Call 814-824-2538. Degrees granted: Bachelors; Masters.

Attendance and degree information available by phone, mail. Search requires name plus SSN. There is no fee.

Messiah College, Registrar, Grantham, PA 17027, 717-691-6074 (Fax: 717-796-5373). Hours: 8AM-Noon, 1-5PM. Enrollment: 2400. Alumni records are maintained here also. Call 717-691-6019. Degrees granted: Bachelors.

Attendance and degree information available by phone, fax. Search requires name plus SSN, date of birth, approximate years of attendance. There is no fee.

Messiah College, (Philadelphia), Registrar, 2026 N Broad St, Philadelphia, PA 19121, 717-691-6074 (Fax: 717-691-6025). Records are not housed here. They are located at Messiah College, Registrar, Grantham, PA 17027.

Millersville University of Pennsylvania, Registrar, PO Box 1002, Millersville, PA 17551-1002, 717-872-3035 (Fax: 717-872-3016). Hours: 8AM-5PM. Alumni records are maintained here also. Call 717-872-3352. Degrees granted: Associate; Bachelors; Masters.

Attendance and degree information available by phone, fax, mail. Search requires name only. Also helpful: SSN, date of birth, exact years of attendance. There is no fee.

Montgomery County Community College, Office of Admissions, PO Box 400, Blue Bell, PA 19422-0796, 215-641-6551 (Fax: 215-641-6681). Hours: 8:30AM-7PM M-Th; 8:30AM-5PM F. Enrollment: 8500. Records go back to 1966. Alumni records are maintained here also. Call 215-641-6359. Degrees granted: Associate. Adverse incident record source- Student Activities.

Attendance and degree information available by fax, mail. Search requires name plus signed release. Also helpful: SSN, date of birth, exact years of attendance. There is no fee.

Moore College of Art and Design, Registrar, The Parkway at 20th St, Philadelphia, PA 19103, 215-568-4515 (Fax: 215-568-8017). Hours: 9AM-5PM. Records go back to 1844. Alumni records are maintained here at the same phone number. Degrees granted: Bachelors.

Attendance and degree information available by phone, fax, mail. Search requires name plus SSN, exact years of attendance. There is no fee.

Moravian College, Registrar, 1200 Main St, Bethlehem, PA 18018, 610-861-1350 (Fax: 610-861-3919). Hours: 8AM-4:30PM. Enrollment: 1800. Records go back to 1742. Alumni records are maintained here also. Call 610-861-1366. Degrees granted: Bachelors; Masters. Adverse incident record source- Campus Security, 610-861-1421: Dean, 610-861-1503

Attendance and degree information available by phone, mail. Search requires name plus SSN. Also helpful: date of birth, exact years of attendance. There is no fee.

Mount Aloysius College, Registration & Records, 7373 Admiral Peary Hwy, Cresson, PA 16630, 814-886-6343 (Fax: 814-886-2978). Hours: 8:30AM-4:30PM. Enrollment: 1160. Records go back to 1939. Alumni records are maintained here also. Call 814-886-6408. Degrees granted: Associate; Bachelors; Diplomas. Adverse incident record source- Dean, 814-886-6472.

Attendance and degree information available by phone, fax, mail. Search requires name plus SSN. There is no fee.

Muhlenberg College, Registrar, 2400 Chew St, Allentown, PA 18104, 610-821-3190 (Fax: 610-821-3234). Hours: 8AM-5PM. Records go back to 1900's. Alumni records are maintained here also. Call 610-821-3305. Degrees granted: Bachelors. Adverse incident record source- Dean, 610-821-3182.

Attendance and degree information available by phone, fax, mail. Search requires name plus SSN, exact years of attendance. There is no fee.

National Education Center Thompson Campus, Registrar, 5650 Derry St, Harrisburg, PA 17111-4112, 717-564-8710 (Fax: 717-564-3779). Hours: 8:30AM-4:30PM. Enrollment: 400. Records go back to 1918. Degrees granted: Associate.

Attendance and degree information available by mail. Search requires name plus exact years of attendance. There is no fee.

Neumann College, Registrar, Concord Rd, Aston, PA 19014, 610-558-5522 (Fax: 610-459-1370). Hours: 9AM-5PM. Enrollment: 1300. Records go back to 1965. Alumni records are maintained here also. Call 610-558-5524. Degrees granted: Associate; Bachelors; Masters. Adverse incident record source- Registrar, 610-558-5522.

Attendance and degree information available by phone, mail. Search requires name plus SSN, exact years of attendance. There is no fee.

Newport Business Institute, Registrar, 945 Greensburg Rd, Lower Burrell, PA 15068, 412-339-7542 (Fax: 412-339-2950). Hours: 8AM-5PM. Formerly New Kensington Commercial School Records go back to 1946. Alumni records are maintained here at the same phone number. Degrees granted: Associate.

Attendance information available by mail. Search requires name plus SSN, approximate years of attendance, signed release. Also helpful: exact years of attendance. There is no fee.

Degree information available by phone, fax, mail. Search requires name plus SSN. Also helpful: exact years of attendance. There is no fee.

Northampton County Area Community College, Registrar, 3835 Green Pond Rd, Bethlehem, PA 18017, 610-861-5494 (Fax: 610-861-5551). Hours: 8AM-7PM M-Th, 8AM-4PM F; Summer closed on Friday. Enrollment: 6000. Records go back to 1967. Alumni records are maintained here also. Call 610-861-5453. Degrees granted: Associate. Adverse incident record source- Campus Safety, 610-861-5324.

Attendance and degree information available by phone, fax, mail. Search requires name plus SSN. There is no fee.

Northeast Institute of Education, Registrar, 314 Adams Ave, Scranton, PA 18501-0470, 717-346-6666. Hours: 8AM-5PM. Records go back to 1936. Alumni records are maintained here at the same phone number. Degrees granted: Bachelors; Masters.

Attendance and degree information available by phone, mail. Search requires name plus SSN, exact years of attendance. There is no fee.

Northeast Institute of Education, (Branch), Registrar, Fountain Ct Rte 611 Box 574, Bartonsville, PA 18321, 717-629-5555. Records are not housed here. They are located at Northeast Institute of Education, Registrar, 314 Adams Ave, Scranton, PA 18501-0470.

Pace Institute, Registrar, 606 Court St, Reading, PA 19601, 610-375-1212 (Fax: 610-375-1924). Hours: 10AM-5PM two days, 7AM-3PM three days. This varies. Records go back to 1977. Degrees granted: Associate.

Attendance and degree information available by phone, fax, mail. Search requires name plus SSN, approximate years of attendance. There is no fee.

Penn Technical Institute, Registrar, 110 Ninth St, Pittsburgh, PA 15222-3618, 412-355-0455. Hours: 8AM-5PM T,Th,F; 5-9PM M,W. Records go back to 1949. Degrees granted: Associate. Adverse incident record source- Director, 412-355-0455.

Attendance information available by phone, mail. Search requires name plus SSN, approximate years of attendance. There is no fee.

Degree information available by phone, fax, mail. Search requires name plus SSN, approximate years of attendance. There is no fee.

Pennco Tech, Registrar, 3815 Otter St, Bristol, PA 19007-3696, 215-824-3200 X42 (Fax: 215-785-1945). Hours: 8AM-4:30PM. Records go back to 1970. Degrees granted: Associate.

Attendance and degree information available by fax, mail. Search requires name plus SSN, approximate years of attendance, signed release. There is no fee.

Pennsylvania Academy of the Fine Arts, Registrar, 1301 N Cherry St, Philadelphia, PA 19102, 215-972-7600 X3501 (Fax: 215-569-0153). Hours: 9AM-5PM. Records go back to 1806. Alumni records are maintained here at the same phone number. Degrees granted: Masters. Adverse incident record source- School Office, 215-972-7623 X3215.

Attendance and degree information available by phone, fax, mail. Search requires name plus SSN, date of birth, approximate years of attendance. There is no fee.

Pennsylvania Business Institute, Registrar, 81 Robinson St, Pottstown, PA 19464, 610-326-6150 (Fax: 610-326-4142). Hours: 8AM-5PM. Records go back to 1986. Degrees granted: Associate.

Attendance and degree information available by fax, mail. Search requires name plus signed release. Also helpful: SSN, exact years of attendance. There is no fee.

Pennsylvania Business Institute, (Branch), Registrar, One Angelini Ave, Nesquehoning, PA 18240, 800-220-7241 (Fax: 717-326-4142). Records are not housed here. They are located at Pennsylvania Business Institute, Registrar, 81 Robinson St, Pottstown, PA 19464.

Pennsylvania College of Optometry, Registrar, 1200 W Godfrey Ave, Philadelphia, PA 19141, 215-276-6260. Hours: 8:30AM-4:30PM. Enrollment: 650. Records go back to 1919. Alumni records are maintained here also. Call 215-276-6230. Degrees granted: Bachelors; Masters; Doctorate.

Attendance information available by mail. Search requires name only. Also helpful: SSN, date of birth, approximate years of attendance. There is no fee.

Degree information available by mail. Search requires name plus date of birth. Also helpful: SSN, approximate years of attendance. There is no fee.

Pennsylvania College of Podiatric Medicine, Registrar, 8th and Race Sts, Philadelphia, PA 19107, 215-625-5444 (Fax: 215-627-2815). Hours: 8:30AM-5PM. Enrollment: 430. Records go back to 1967. Alumni records are maintained here also. Call 215-625-5411. Degrees granted: Doctorate. Adverse incident record source- Registrar, 215-625-5444: Educational Affairs, 215-625-5251

Attendance and degree information available by phone, fax, mail. Search requires name plus SSN, approximate years of attendance. There is no fee.

Pennsylvania College of Technology, Registrar, 1 College Ave, Williamsport, PA 17701, 717-327-4772 (Fax: 717-321-5536). Hours: 8AM-4:30PM Summer hours 7:30AM-5:30PM M-W, 7:30AM-5PM Th. Records go back to 1963. Alumni records are maintained here at the same phone number. Degrees granted: Associate; Bachelors. Adverse incident record source- Security, 717-321-5527.

Attendance and degree information available by phone, fax, mail. Search requires name plus SSN, approximate years of attendance. There is no fee.

Pennsylvania College of Technology, Registrar, One College Ave, Williamsport, PA 17701, 717-326-3761 (Fax: 717-321-5536). Records go back to 1965. Alumni records are maintained here at the same phone number. Degrees granted: Bachelors. Adverse incident record source- Campus Police.

Attendance and degree information available by phone, fax, mail. Search requires name only. Also helpful: SSN, date of birth, exact years of attendance. There is no fee.

Pennsylvania Institute of Technology, Registrar, 800 Manchester Ave, Media, PA 19063, 610-892-1525 (Fax: 610-892-1510). Hours: 8AM-8PM. Enrollment: 500. Records go back to 1950. Alumni records are maintained here also. Call 610-892-1554. Degrees granted: Associate. Adverse incident record source- Academic Dean.

Attendance and degree information available by phone. Search requires name only. Also helpful: SSN. There is no fee.

Pennsylvania State University, Registrar, 112 Shields Bldg, University Park, PA 16802, 814-865-6357 (Fax: 814-865-6359). Hours: 8AM-5PM. Records go back to 1800's. Alumni Records Office: Alumni Association, The Pennsylvania State University, 101 Old Main, University Park, PA 16802. Degrees granted: Associate; Bachelors; Masters; Doctorate. Adverse incident record source- Conduct Standards & Judicial Affairs, 814-863-0342.

Attendance and degree information available by phone, fax, mail. Search requires name plus SSN, exact years of attendance. There is no fee.

Pennsylvania State University, Registrar's Office, 112 Shields Bldg, University Park, PA 16802-1271, 814-863-8500 (Fax: 814-865-6359). Enrollment: 70000. Formerly Pennsylvania State University (McKeesport Campus) Records go back to 1865. Transcript records are located at the main campus, 112 Shields Bldg, University Park, PA 16802. Alumni Records Office: 105 Old Main, University Park, PA 16802-1271. Degrees granted: Associate; Bachelors; Masters; Doctorate.

Attendance and degree information available by phone, fax, mail. Search requires name plus SSN, approximate years of attendance. There is no fee.

Pennsylvania State University, (Allentown), Registrar, 8380 Mohr Lane, Fogelsville, PA 18051, 610-285-5000 (Fax: 610-285-5220). Enrollment: 600. Records go back to 1980. Transcript records are located at the main campus, 112 Shields Bldg, University Park, PA 16802. Alumni Records Office: Alumni Association, 105 Old Main, University Park, PA 16802. Degrees granted: Associate.

Attendance and degree information available by phone, fax, mail. Search requires name plus SSN, approximate years of attendance. There is no fee.

Pennsylvania State University, (Altoona), Registrar, Ivyside Park, Altoona, PA 16001-3760, 814-949-5000 (Fax: 814-949-5702). Records go back to 1984. Transcript records are located at the main campus, 112 Shields Bldg, University Park, PA 16802. Alumni records are maintained here also. Call 814-949-5105. Degrees granted: Associate; Bachelors; Masters; Doctorate.

Attendance and degree information available by phone, fax, mail. Search requires name plus SSN, date of birth. There is no fee.

Pennsylvania State University, (Beaver), Registrar, Brodhead Rd, Monaca, PA 15061, 412-773-3500 (Fax: 412-773-3557). Enrollment: 900. Transcript records are located at the main campus, 112 Shields Bldg, University Park, PA 16802.

Alumni records are maintained here also. Call 412-773-3815. Degrees granted: Associate.

Attendance and degree information available by phone, fax, mail. Search requires name plus SSN, approximate years of attendance. Also helpful: date of birth, exact years of attendance.

Pennsylvania State University, (Berks), Registrar, Tulpehocken Rd, Reading, PA 19610, 610-320-4800 (Fax: 610-865-6359). Records go back to 1988. Transcript records are located at the main campus, 112 Shields Bldg, University Park, PA 16802. Alumni records are maintained here also. Call 610-320-4890. Degrees granted: Bachelors.

Attendance and degree information available by phone, fax, mail. Search requires name plus SSN, approximate years of attendance. There is no fee.

Pennsylvania State University, (Delaware Campus), Registrar, 25 Yearsley Mill Rd, Media, PA 19063, 610-892-1350. Transcript records are located at the main campus, 112 Shields Bldg, University Park, PA 16802. Degrees granted: Associate; Bachelors; Masters; Doctorate.

Attendance and degree information available by phone, fax, mail. Search requires name plus SSN, approximate years of attendance.

Pennsylvania State University, (DuBois), Registrar, College Pl, Du Bois, PA 15801, 814-375-4700. Transcript records are located at the main campus, 112 Shields Bldg, University Park, PA 16802. Degrees granted: Associate; Bachelors; Masters; Doctorate.

Attendance and degree information available by phone, fax, mail. Search requires name plus SSN, approximate years of attendance.

Pennsylvania State University, (Erie-Behrend College), Registrar, Station Rd, Erie, PA 16563, 814-898-6000 (Fax: 814-898-6382). Enrollment: 3200. Transcript records are located at the main campus, 112 Shields Bldg, University Park, PA 16802. Alumni records are maintained here also. Call 814-898-6159. Degrees granted: Associate; Bachelors; Masters. Adverse incident record source- Student Affairs, 814-898-6111.

Attendance and degree information available by phone, fax, mail. Search requires name plus SSN, approximate years of attendance. There is no fee.

Pennsylvania State University, (Fayette), Registrar, PO Box 519, Rte 119 N, Uniontown, PA 15401, 412-430-4100 (Fax: 412-430-4184). Records go back to 1982. Transcript records are located at the main campus, 112 Shields Bldg, University Park, PA 16802. Alumni records are maintained here at the same phone number. Degrees granted: Associate; Bachelors; Masters; Doctorate.

Attendance and degree information available by phone, fax, mail. Search requires name plus SSN. There is no fee.

Pennsylvania State University, (Great Valley Graduate Center), Registrar, 30 E Swedesford Rd, Malvern, PA 19355, 610-648-3242. Transcript records are located at the main campus, 112 Shields Bldg, University Park, PA 16802. Degrees granted: Associate; Bachelors; Masters; Doctorate.

Attendance and degree information available by phone, fax, mail. Search requires name plus SSN, approximate years of attendance.

Pennsylvania State University, (Harrisburg-Capital College), Registrar, Rte 230, Middletown, PA 17057, 717-948-6020 (Fax: 717-948-6325). Hours: 8AM-6PM M,Th; 8AM-5PM T,W,F. Enrollment: 3500. Records go back to 1969. Transcript records are located at the main campus, 112 Shields Bldg, University Park, PA 16802. Alumni records are maintained here at the same phone number. Degrees granted: Associate; Bachelors; Masters; Doctorate.

Attendance and degree information available by phone, fax, mail. Search requires name plus SSN, approximate years of attendance. There is no fee.

Pennsylvania State University, (Hazleton), Registrar, Highacres, Hazleton, PA 18201, 717-450-3000. Records go back to 1986. Transcript records are located at the main campus, 112 Shields Bldg, University Park, PA 16802. Alumni records are maintained here at the same phone number. Degrees granted: Associate; Bachelors; Masters; Doctorate.

Attendance and degree information available by phone, fax, mail. Search requires name plus SSN, approximate years of attendance. There is no fee.

Pennsylvania State University, (Hershey Medical Center), Registrar, 500 University Dr, Hershey, PA 17033, 717-531-8521. Transcript records are located at the main campus, 112 Shields Bldg, University Park, PA 16802. Degrees granted: Associate; Bachelors; Masters; Doctorate.

Attendance and degree information available by phone, mail. Search requires name plus SSN, approximate years of attendance. There is no fee.

Pennsylvania State University, (Mont Alto Campus), Registrar, Campus Dr, Mont Alto, PA 17237, 717-749-6000. Transcript records are located at the main campus, 112 Shields Bldg, University Park, PA 16802. Degrees granted: Associate; Bachelors; Masters; Doctorate.

Attendance and degree information available by phone, fax, mail. Search requires name plus SSN, date of birth, approximate years of attendance. There is no fee.

Pennsylvania State University, (New Kensington Campus), Registrar, 3550 Seventh Street Rd, New Kensington, PA 15068, 412-339-5466 (Fax: 412-339-5434). Hours: 8AM-5PM. Records go back to 1800's. Transcript records are located at the main campus, 112 Shields Bldg, University Park, PA 16802. Alumni records are maintained here at the same phone number. Degrees granted: Bachelors; Masters; Doctorate.

Attendance and degree information available by phone, fax, mail. Search requires name plus SSN, approximate years of attendance. There is no fee.

Pennsylvania State University, (Ogontz Campus), Registrar, 1600 Woodland Rd, Abington, PA 19001, 215-881-7332 (Fax: 215-881-7317). Hours: 8AM-5PM. Records go back to 1983. Transcript records are located at the main campus, 112 Shields Bldg, University Park, PA 16802. Alumni Records Office: The Pennsylvania State University, 105 Old Main, University Park, PA 16802. Degrees granted: Associate; Bachelors. Adverse incident record source- Abington Twp Police, 215-885-4450.

Attendance and degree information available by phone, fax, mail. Search requires name plus SSN, approximate years of attendance. There is no fee.

Pennsylvania State University, (Schuylkill Campus), Registrar, 200 University Dr, Schuylkill Haven, PA 17972, 717-385-6000 (Fax: 717-385-3672). Enrollment: 1100. Records go back to 1983. Transcript records are located at the main campus, 112 Shields Bldg, University Park, PA 16802. Alumni records are maintained here at the same phone number. Degrees granted: Associate. Adverse incident record source- Student Affairs.

Attendance and degree information available by phone, fax, mail. Search requires name plus SSN, approximate years of attendance. There is no fee.

Pennsylvania State University, (Shenango Campus), Registrar, 147 Shenango Ave, Sharon, PA 16146, 412-983-5860. Transcript records are located at the main campus, 112 Shields Bldg, University Park, PA 16802. Degrees granted: Associate; Bachelors; Masters; Doctorate.

Attendance and degree information available by phone, fax, mail. Search requires name plus SSN, approximate years of attendance. There is no fee.

Pennsylvania State University, (Wilkes-Barre Campus), Registrar, PO Box PSU, Lehman, PA 18627, 717-675-2171. Transcript records are located at the main campus, 112 Shields Bldg, University Park, PA 16802. Alumni records are maintained here at the same phone number. Degrees granted: Associate; Bachelors; Masters; Doctorate.

Attendance and degree information available by phone, fax, mail. Search requires name plus SSN, approximate years of attendance. There is no fee.

Pennsylvania State University, (Worthington-Scranton Campus), Registrar, 120 Ridge View Dr, Dunmore, PA 18512, 717-963-4757. Transcript records are located at the main campus, 112 Shields Bldg, University Park, PA 16802. Alumni records are maintained here at the same phone number. Degrees granted: Associate; Bachelors; Masters; Doctorate.

Attendance and degree information available by phone, fax, mail. Search requires name plus SSN, approximate years of attendance. There is no fee.

Pennsylvania State University, (York Campus), Registrar, 1031 Edgecomb Ave, York, PA 17403, 717-771-4057 (Fax: 717-771-4062). Hours: 8AM-5PM. Enrollment: 2100. Records go back to 1984. Transcript records are located at the main campus, 112 Shields Bldg, University Park, PA 16802. Alumni records are maintained here also. Call 717-771-4127. Degrees granted: Associate.

Attendance and degree information available by phone, fax, mail. Search requires name plus SSN, approximate years of attendance. There is no fee.

Philadelphia College of Bible, Records Office, 200 Manor Ave, Langhorne, PA 19047-2990, 215-752-5800 (Fax: 215-702-4341). Hours: 8AM-7:30PM. Records go back to 1913. Alumni records are maintained here at the same phone number. Degrees granted: Associate; Bachelors; Masters. Adverse incident record source- Student Development.

Attendance information available by phone, fax, mail. Search requires name only. Also helpful: SSN, date of birth, exact years of attendance. There is no fee.

Degree information available by fax, mail. Search requires name only. Also helpful: SSN, date of birth, exact years of attendance. There is no fee.

Philadelphia College of Osteopathic Medicine, Registrar, 4170 City Ave, Philadelphia, PA 19131, 215-871-6700 (Fax: 215-871-6719). Enrollment: 975. Alumni records are maintained here also. Call 215-871-6120.

Attendance and degree information available by phone, fax, mail. Search requires name plus SSN, exact years of attendance. There is no fee.

Philadelphia College of Pharmacy and Science, Registrar, 600 S 43rd St, Philadelphia, PA 19104-4495, 215-596-8813 (Fax: 215-895-1177). Records go back to 1821. Alumni records are maintained here also. Call 215-596-8856. Degrees granted: Bachelors; Masters; Doctorate.

Attendance and degree information available by phone, mail. Search requires name plus SSN, approximate years of attendance. There is no fee.

Philadelphia College of Textiles and Science, Registrar, 4201 Henry Ave, Philadelphia, PA 19144, 215-951-2700 (Fax: 215-951-2615). Hours: 8AM-4:30PM. Records go back to 1884. Alumni records are maintained here also. Call 215-951-2710. Degrees granted: Bachelors; Masters.

Attendance information available by phone, fax, mail. Search requires name plus SSN, exact years of attendance. There is no fee.

Degree information available by mail. Search requires name plus SSN, exact years of attendance. There is no fee.

Pierce Junior College, Registrar, 1420 Pine St, Philadelphia, PA 19102, 215-545-6400 (Fax: 215-546-5996). Hours: 8:30AM-5PM. Enrollment: 1400. Records go back to 1940's. Alumni records are maintained here also. Call 215-545-6400. Degrees granted: Associate. Certification: Proficiency.

Attendance and degree information available by phone, fax, mail. Search requires name plus SSN, approximate years of attendance. Also helpful: date of birth. There is no fee.

Pittsburgh Institute of Aeronautics, Registrar, PO Box 10897, Pittsburgh, PA 15236-0897, 412-462-9011 (Fax: 412-466-0513). Hours: 8AM-4:30PM. Records go back to 1930's. Degrees granted: Associate.

Attendance and degree information available by phone, fax, mail. Search requires name plus SSN, exact years of attendance. There is no fee.

Pittsburgh Institute of Mortuary Science, Registrar, 5808 Baum blvd, Pittsburgh, PA 15206, 412-362-8500 (Fax: 412-362-1684). Hours: 8AM-4PM. Records go back to 1939. Alumni records are maintained here at the same phone number. Degrees granted: Associate; Bachelors.

Attendance information available by phone, mail. Search requires name plus SSN, date of birth, exact years of attendance. There is no fee.

Degree information available by phone, fax, mail. Search requires name plus SSN, date of birth, exact years of attendance. There is no fee.

Pittsburgh Technical Institute, Registrar, 635 Smithfield St, Pittsburgh, PA 15222-2560, 412-741-1011 (Fax: 412-471-9014). Hours: 7AM-6PM. Records go back to 1970's. Degrees granted: Associate.

Attendance and degree information available by phone, fax, mail. Search requires name plus SSN, approximate years of attendance. Also helpful: date of birth, exact years of attendance. There is no fee.

Pittsburgh Theological Seminary, Registrar, 616 N Highland Ave, Pittsburgh, PA 15206, 412-362-5610 (Fax: 412-363-3260). Hours: 8:30AM-4:30PM. Enrollment: 309. Records go back to 1910. Alumni records are maintained here at the same phone number. Degrees granted: Masters; Doctorate. Adverse incident record source- Business Office, 412-362-5610.

Attendance and degree information available by phone, fax, mail. Search requires name plus approximate years of attendance. There is no fee.

Point Park College, Registrar, 201 Wood St, Pittsburgh, PA 15222, 412-392-3861 (Fax: 412-391-1980). Hours: 8:30AM-4:30PM. Records go back to 1960. Alumni records are maintained here also. Call 412-392-3816. Degrees granted: Associate; Bachelors; Masters. Adverse incident record source- Security, 412-392-3960.

Attendance and degree information available by phone, fax, mail. Search requires name plus SSN, approximate years of attendance. Also helpful: date of birth. There is no fee.

Reading Area Community College, Registrar, PO Box 1706, 10 S 2nd St, Reading, PA 19603-1706, 610-372-4721 X224 (Fax: 610-375-8255). Hours: 8AM-5PM. Records go back to 1971. Alumni records are maintained here at the same phone number. Degrees granted: Associate.

Attendance and degree information available by phone, mail. Search requires name plus SSN. There is no fee.

Reconstructionist Rabbinical College, Registrar, Greenwood Ave and Church Rd, Wyncote, PA 19095, 215-576-0800 (Fax: 215-576-6143). Hours: 9AM-5PM. Enrollment:

75. Records go back to 1970. Degrees granted: Masters; Doctorate; Rabbi.

Attendance and degree information available by phone, fax, mail. Search requires name only. Also helpful: exact years of attendance. There is no fee.

Robert Morris College, Director Student Records, Narrows Run Rd, Coraopolis, PA 15108, 412-262-8274. Hours: 8AM-9PM. Enrollment: 5221. Records go back to 1940's. Alumni records are maintained here also. Call 412-262-8481. Degrees granted: Associate; Bachelors; Masters. Adverse incident record source- Campus Police, 412-262-8352.

Attendance and degree information available by phone, fax, mail. Search requires name plus SSN. Also helpful: exact years of attendance. There is no fee.

Robert Morris College, (Pittsburgh College), Registrar, Coraopolis, PA 15108, 412-227-8256. Hours: 8AM-5PM. Enrollment: 5000. Records go back to 1962. Alumni records are maintained here at the same phone number. Degrees granted: Associate; Bachelors; Masters.

Attendance and degree information available by phone, mail. Search requires name plus SSN, date of birth, exact years of attendance. There is no fee.

Rosemont College, Registrar, 1400 Montgomery Ave, Rosemont, PA 19010-1699, 610-527-0200 X2306 (Fax: 610-526-2984). Hours: 8AM-5PM. Records go back to 1922. Alumni records are maintained here at the same phone number. Degrees granted: Bachelors; Masters.

Attendance and degree information available by phone, fax, mail. Search requires name plus SSN. There is no fee.

Saintt Francis College, Office of the Registrar, PO Box 600, Loretto, PA 15940, 814-472-3009. Hours: 9AM-Noon, 12:30-4:30PM. Enrollment: 1700. Records go back to 1895. Alumni records are maintained here also. Call 814-472-3015. Degrees granted: Associate; Bachelors; Masters.

Attendance and degree information available by phone, fax, mail. Search requires name plus SSN. Also helpful: date of birth, approximate years of attendance. There is no fee.

Sawyer School, Registrar, 717 Liberty Ave, Pittsburgh, PA 15222, 412-261-5700 (Fax: 412-261-5039). Hours: 8AM-5PM. Enrollment: 400. Records go back to 1970. Alumni records are maintained here at the same phone number. Degrees granted: Associate. Special programs- Health Information Technology, 412-261-5700 X248. Adverse incident record source- Student Services, 412-261-5700 X235.

Attendance and degree information available by fax, mail. Search requires name plus SSN, approximate years of attendance, signed release. Also helpful: exact years of attendance. There is no fee.

Schuylkill Business Institute, Registrar, 2400 W End Ave, Pottsville, PA 17901, 717-622-4835. Hours: 8AM-5PM. Records go back to 1977. Alumni records are maintained here at the same phone number. Degrees granted: Associate.

Attendance and degree information available by phone, mail. Search requires name plus SSN, exact years of attendance. There is no fee.

Seton Hill College, Registrar, Greensburg, PA 15601, 412-838-4218 (Fax: 412-830-4611). Hours: 8AM-6PM M-Th; 8AM-4PM F. Enrollment: 950. Records go back to 1920. Alumni records are maintained here also. Call 412-838-4226. Degrees granted: Bachelors; Masters.

Attendance and degree information available by phone, fax, mail. Search requires name only. Also helpful: SSN, date of birth, exact years of attendance. Fee is $2.00.

Shenango Valley School of Business, Registrar, 335 Boyd Dr, Sharon, PA 16146, 412-983-0700 (Fax: 412-

983-8355). Hours: 8:30AM-4:30PM. Records go back to 1985. Degrees granted: Associate.

Attendance and degree information available by written request only. Search requires name plus SSN, exact years of attendance, signed release. Fee is $5.

Shenango Valley School of Business, (Branch Campus), Registrar, RD 1 Schoolhouse Rd, Pulaski, PA 16143, 412-654-1976 (Fax: 412-964-8128). Hours: 8AM-4PM. Records go back to 1977. Alumni records are maintained here at the same phone number. Degrees granted: Associate.

Attendance and degree information available by phone, mail. Search requires name plus SSN, exact years of attendance. There is no fee.

Shenango Valley School of Business, (Branch Campus), Registrar, 124 W Spring St, Titusville, PA 16354, 814-827-9567. Hours: 8AM-4PM. Records go back to 1955. Alumni records are maintained here at the same phone number. Degrees granted: Associate.

Attendance and degree information available by phone, mail. Search requires name plus SSN, exact years of attendance. There is no fee.

Shippensburg University of Pennsylvania, Registrar, Shippensburg, PA 17257, 717-532-1381 (Fax: 717-532-1388). Hours: 8AM-4:30PM. Records go back to 1930's. Alumni records are maintained here also. Call 717-532-1381 X1218. Degrees granted: Bachelors; Masters.

Attendance and degree information available by phone, mail. Search requires name plus SSN, exact years of attendance. There is no fee.

Slippery Rock University of Pennsylvania, Academic Records, Slippery Rock, PA 16057, 412-738-2010 (Fax: 412-738-2936). Hours: 8AM-4:30PM. Enrollment: 7500. Records go back to 1890's. Alumni records are maintained here also. Call 412-738-2018. Degrees granted: Bachelors; Masters. Special programs- Doctorate in Physical Therapy.

Attendance and degree information available by phone, fax, mail. Search requires name plus SSN. Also helpful: date of birth, exact years of attendance. There is no fee.

South Hills Business School, Registrar, 480 Waupelani Dr, State College, PA 16801-4516, 814-234-7755. Hours: 8AM-5PM. Enrollment: 350. Records go back to 1966. Degrees granted: Associate.

Attendance and degree information available by mail. Search requires name plus SSN, exact years of attendance, signed release. There is no fee.

St. Charles Borromeo Seminary, Registrar, 1000 E Wynnewood Rd, Wynnewood, PA 19096-3099, 610-667-3394 (Ext 572). Hours: 8:30AM-4:30PM. Enrollment: 450. Alumni records are maintained here at the same phone number. Degrees granted: Bachelors; Masters.

Attendance and degree information available by phone, mail. Search requires name plus SSN, date of birth, exact years of attendance. There is no fee.

St. Joseph's University, Registrar, 5600 City Line Ave, Philadelphia, PA 19131, 610-660-1010 (Fax: 610-660-1019). Enrollment: 7000. Records go back to 1851. Alumni records are maintained here at the same phone number. Degrees granted: Bachelors; Masters.

Attendance and degree information available by phone, fax, mail. Search requires name plus SSN, exact years of attendance. Also helpful: date of birth. There is no fee.

St. Vincent College and Seminary, Registrar, Frazier Purchase Rd, Latrobe, PA 15650, 412-537-4559 (Fax: 412-537-4554). Hours: 9AM-4PM. Records go back to 1871.

Degrees granted: Bachelors; Masters. Adverse incident record source- Dean of Students, 412-537-4564.

Attendance and degree information available by phone, fax, mail. Search requires name only. Also helpful: SSN, date of birth, exact years of attendance. There is no fee.

Susquehanna University, Office of the Registrar, Selinsgrove, PA 17870, 717-372-4109 (Fax: 717-372-2722). Hours: 8:15AM-Noon, 1-4:30PM. Enrollment: 1550. Records go back to 1950. Alumni records are maintained here also. Call 717-372-4115. Degrees granted: Bachelors. Adverse incident record source- Student Life, 717-372-4135.

Attendance and degree information available by phone, fax, mail. Search requires name only. Also helpful: SSN, exact years of attendance. There is no fee.

Swarthmore College, Registrar, 500 College Ave, Swarthmore, PA 19081, 610-328-8000. Alumni records are maintained here at the same phone number. Degrees granted: Bachelors; Masters.

Attendance and degree information available by phone, mail. Search requires name plus approximate years of attendance. Also helpful: exact years of attendance. There is no fee.

Talmudical Yeshiva of Philadelphia, Registrar, 6063 Drexel Rd, Philadelphia, PA 19131, 215-477-1000 (Fax: 215-477-5065). Hours: 8AM-5PM. Enrollment: 115. Records go back to 1975. Alumni records are maintained here at the same phone number.

Attendance and degree information available by phone, mail. Search requires name plus SSN. There is no fee.

Temple University, Registrar, Broad and Montgomery Sts, Philadelphia, PA 19122, 215-204-7517. Enrollment: 30040. Degrees granted: Bachelors; Masters; Doctorate.

Attendance and degree information available by phone, mail. Search requires name plus SSN, exact years of attendance. There is no fee.

Thaddeus Stevens State School of Technology, Registrar, 750 E King St, Lancaster, PA 17602, 717-299-7796. Hours: 8AM-4PM. Records go back to 1913. Alumni records are maintained here at the same phone number. Degrees granted: Associate. Adverse incident record source- Dean of Students.

Attendance information available by phone, fax, mail. Search requires name plus approximate years of attendance. Also helpful: SSN, exact years of attendance. There is no fee.

Degree information available by phone, fax, mail. Search requires name plus approximate years of attendance. Also helpful: exact years of attendance. There is no fee.

Thiel College, Registrar, 75 College Ave, Greenville, PA 16125, 412-589-2110 (Fax: 412-589-2850). Hours: 8AM-4:30PM. Enrollment: 1000. Records go back to 1866. Alumni records are maintained here also. Call 412-589-2140. Degrees granted: Associate; Bachelors. Special programs- Respiratory Care Certificate Program, 412-589-2186. Adverse incident record source- Security, 412-589-2222.

Attendance and degree information available by phone, fax, mail. Search requires name only. There is no fee.

Thompson Institute, (Branch), Registrar, University City Science Ctr, 3440 Market St, Philadelphia, PA 19104, 215-387-1530 (Fax: 215-387-0106). Enrollment: 500. Formerly National Education Center Thompson Campus Records go back to 1987. Degrees granted: Associate. Special programs- Medical Assisting; Medical Office Management.

Attendance and degree information available by mail. Search requires name plus SSN, exact years of attendance. There is no fee.

Titusville Campus, Registrar, 504 E Main St, Titusville, PA 16354, 814-827-4482 (Fax: 814-827-4448). Hours: 8:30AM-5PM. Records go back to 1969. Degrees granted: Associate. Adverse incident record source- Student Affairs, 814-827-4460.

Attendance information available by phone, fax, mail. Search requires name only. Also helpful: SSN, approximate years of attendance. There is no fee.

Degree information available by phone, fax, mail. Search requires name only. Also helpful: SSN. There is no fee.

Tri-State Business Institute, Registrar, 5757 W 26th St, Erie, PA 16506, 814-88-7673. Hours: 8AM-5PM. Records go back to 1984. Degrees granted: Associate.

Attendance and degree information available by phone, mail. Search requires name plus SSN, exact years of attendance. There is no fee.

Triangle Tech, Registrar, PO Box 551, Du Bois, PA 15801-0551, 814-371-2090 (Fax: 814-371-9227). Hours: 8AM-5PM. Records go back to 1944. Alumni records are maintained here at the same phone number. Degrees granted: Associate.

Attendance and degree information available by phone, fax, mail. Search requires name plus SSN, date of birth, exact years of attendance. There is no fee.

Triangle Tech, Registrar, 2000 Liberty St, Erie, PA 16502-9987, 814-453-6016. Hours: 8AM-5PM. Records go back to 1944. Alumni Records Office: 1940 Perrysville Ave, Pittsburgh, PA 15214-3897. Degrees granted: Associate.

Attendance and degree information available by mail. Search requires name plus SSN, exact years of attendance, signed release. There is no fee.

Triangle Tech, Registrar, 222 E Pittsburgh St, Greensburg, PA 15601-9944, 412-832-1050 (Fax: 412-834-0325). Hours: 7:30AM-4PM. Records go back to 1978. Degrees granted: Associate.

Attendance and degree information available by phone, fax, mail. Search requires name only. Also helpful: SSN, exact years of attendance. There is no fee.

Triangle Tech, (**Business Careers Institute**), Registrar, 22 E Pittsburgh St, Greenburg, PA 15601, 412-832-1050 (Fax: 412-834-0325). Hours: 8AM-8PM. Records go back to 1944. Alumni Records Office: 1940 Perrysville Ave, Pittsburgh, PA 15214-3897. Degrees granted: Associate.

Attendance and degree information available by phone, fax, mail. Search requires name plus SSN, exact years of attendance. There is no fee.

Triangle Tech, (**Main**), Registrar, 1940 Perrysville Ave, Pittsburgh, PA 15214-3897, 412-359-1000 X197 (Fax: 412-359-1012). Hours: 8AM-5PM. Enrollment: 387. Records go back to 1947. Alumni records are maintained here at the same phone number. Degrees granted: Associate. Adverse incident record source- Corp of Education, 412-359-1000 X7196.

Attendance information available by phone, fax, mail. Search requires name plus SSN, date of birth, exact years of attendance. There is no fee.

Degree information available by phone, fax, mail. Search requires name plus SSN, date of birth, exact years of attendance. There is no fee.

Triangle Tech, (**Monroeville School of Business**), Registrar, 105 Mall Blvd Expo Mart 3rd Fl, Monroeville, PA 15146-2229, 412-856-8040. Hours: 8AM-6PM M-Th, 8AM-4PM F. Records go back to 1989. Alumni records are maintained here at the same phone number. Degrees granted: Associate.

Attendance and degree information available by phone, mail. Search requires name plus exact years of attendance. There is no fee.

Trinity Episcopal School for Ministry, Registrar, 311 Eleventh St, Ambridge, PA 15003, 412-266-3838 (Fax: 412-266-4617). Hours: 8:30AM-5PM. Enrollment: 150. Records go back to 1976. Alumni records are maintained here at the same phone number. Degrees granted: Masters; Basic Christian Studies, Anglican Studies.

Attendance and degree information available by phone, fax, mail. Search requires name only. Also helpful: SSN, date of birth, exact years of attendance. There is no fee.

Univerisity of Pittsburgh Titusville Campus, Registrar, PO Box 287, Titusville, PA 16354, 814-827-4400 (Fax: 814-827-4448). Enrollment: 300. Records go back to 1969. Degrees granted: Associate.

Attendance and degree information available by phone, fax, mail. Search requires name only. Also helpful: SSN, approximate years of attendance. There is no fee.

University of Pennsylvania, Registrar, 3451 Walnut St, Franklin Bldg Room 221, Philadelphia, PA 19104, 215-898-1561. Hours: 8AM-5PM. Enrollment: 22700. Records go back to 1740. Alumni records are maintained here also. Call 215-898-7811. Degrees granted: Bachelors; Masters; Doctorate.

Attendance and degree information available by phone, mail. Search requires name plus SSN, exact years of attendance. There is no fee.

University of Pennsylvania-Center for Judaic Studies, Registrar, 420 Walnut St, Philadelphia, PA 19106, 215-238-1290. Formerly Annenberg Research Institute Records go back to 1911.

Attendance information available by phone, mail. Search requires name plus exact years of attendance. There is no fee.

Degree information available by written request only. Search requires name plus exact years of attendance. There is no fee.

University of Pittsburgh, Registrar, G 3 Thackerey Hall, Pittsburgh, PA 15260, 412-624-7660. Hours: 8AM-4:30PM. Enrollment: 26328. Records go back to 1787. Alumni records are maintained here also. Call 412-624-8222. Degrees granted: Bachelors; Masters; Doctorate.

Attendance and degree information available by phone, mail. Search requires name plus SSN, exact years of attendance. There is no fee.

University of Pittsburgh, (**Bradford Campus**), Registrar, 300 Campus Dr, Bradford, PA 16701, 814-362-7600. Hours: 8AM-5PM. Enrollment: 1200. Records go back to 1963. Alumni records are maintained here also. Call 814-362-7655. Degrees granted: Bachelors.

Attendance and degree information available by phone, mail. Search requires name plus SSN. There is no fee.

University of Pittsburgh, (**Greensburg Campus**), Registrar, 1150 Mount Pleasant Rd, Greensburg, PA 15601, 412-836-9900 (Fax: 412-836-7176). Hours: 8:30AM-7PM M-Th; 8:30AM-5PM F. Enrollment: 1100. Records go back to 1963. Alumni records are maintained here also. Call 412-836-9905. Degrees granted: Bachelors. Adverse incident record source- Security Dept, 412-836-9865.

Attendance and degree information available by fax, mail. Search requires name plus SSN, date of birth, signed release. Also helpful: exact years of attendance. Fee is $3.00. Expedited service available for $8.00.

University of Pittsburgh, (**Johnstown Campus**), Registrar, 6PJ, 132 Biddle Hall, Johnstown, PA 15956, 814-269-7060 (Fax: 814-269-7068). Hours: 8AM-4PM. Records go back to 1927. Alumni records are maintained here at the same phone number. Degrees granted: Associate; Bachelors.

Attendance and degree information available by phone, fax, mail. Search requires name plus SSN, exact years of attendance.

Also helpful: date of birth. Fee is $3.00. Expedited service available for $10.00.

University of Scranton, Registrar, 800 Linden St, Scranton, PA 18510-4501, 717-941-7720 (Fax: 717-941-4148). Hours: 8:30AM-4:30PM. Enrollment: 5000. Records go back to 1930. Alumni records are maintained here also. Call 717-941-7660. Degrees granted: Associate; Bachelors; Masters.

Attendance and degree information available by phone, fax, mail. Search requires name only. Also helpful: SSN, date of birth, exact years of attendance. There is no fee.

University of the Arts, Registrar, 320 S Broad St, Philadelphia, PA 19102, 215-875-4848. Hours: 9AM-5PM. Enrollment: 1300. Year records start varies depending on school. Alumni records are maintained here also. Call 215-875-4826. Degrees granted: Associate; Bachelors; Masters. Special programs- New Studies Center (now PIE), 215-875-3350. Adverse incident record source- Student Services, 215-875-2256.

Attendance and degree information available by phone, mail. Search requires name plus SSN, date of birth, exact years of attendance. There is no fee.

Ursinus College, Registrar, Box 1000, Main Street, Collegeville, PA 19426-1000, 610-409-3000 X2225 (Fax: 610-489-0627). Hours: 8:39AM-5PM. Enrollment: 1250. Records go back to 1869. Alumni records are maintained here also. Call 610-409-3585. Degrees granted: Bachelors.

Attendance and degree information available by phone, mail. Search requires name only. Also helpful: SSN. There is no fee.

Valley Forge Christian College, Registrar, 1401 Charlestown Rd, VFCC Box 51, Phoenixville, PA 19460, 610-935-0450 (Fax: 610-935-9353). Hours: 8AM-4:30PM. Enrollment: 500. Records go back to 1938. Alumni records are maintained here at the same phone number. Degrees granted: Associate; Bachelors.

Attendance and degree information available by phone. Search requires name only. Also helpful: SSN, exact years of attendance. There is no fee.

Valley Forge Military College, Registrar, 1001 Eagle Rd, Wayne, PA 19087-3695, 610-989-1455 (Fax: 610-989-1550). Hours: 8:30AM-4:30PM. Enrollment: 225. Alumni records are maintained here at the same phone number. Degrees granted: Associate.

Attendance and degree information available by phone, fax, mail. Search requires name plus SSN. Also helpful: exact years of attendance. There is no fee.

Villanova University, Registrar, 800 Lancaster Ave, Villanova, PA 19085, 610-519-4032 (Fax: 610-519-4033). Hours: 9AM-5PM. Records go back to 1855. Degrees granted: Associate; Bachelors; Masters; Doctorate.

Attendance and degree information available by phone, fax, mail. Search requires name plus SSN, approximate years of attendance. Also helpful: date of birth, exact years of attendance. There is no fee.

Washington and Jefferson College, Registrar, 45 S Lincoln St, Washington, PA 15301, 412-223-6017. Hours: 9AM-Noon, 1-5PM. Enrollment: 1100. Records go back to 1901. Alumni records are maintained here also. Call 412-223-6079. Degrees granted: Associate; Bachelors.

Attendance information available by phone, mail. Search requires name plus exact years of attendance. Also helpful: SSN. There is no fee.

Degree information available by mail. Search requires name plus exact years of attendance. Also helpful: SSN. There is no fee.

Waynesburg College, Registrar, 51 W College St, Waynesburg, PA 15370, 412-852-3252. Hours: 8AM-4:30PM.

Records go back to 1849. Alumni records are maintained here also. Call 412-852-3300. Degrees granted: Bachelors; Masters.

Attendance and degree information available by phone, mail. Search requires name plus date of birth, exact years of attendance. There is no fee.

West Chester University of Pennsylvania, Registrar, EO Bull Center Room 154, West Chester, PA 19383, 610-436-3541 (Fax: 610-436-2370). Hours: 8AM-5PM. Records go back to 1971. Alumni records are maintained here also. Call 610-436-2813. Degrees granted: Bachelors; Masters.

Attendance and degree information available by phone, fax, mail. Search requires name plus SSN, date of birth, exact years of attendance. There is no fee.

West Virginia Career College, (Branch Campus), Registrar, 200 College Dr, Lemont Furnace, PA 15456, 412-437-4600. Records are not housed here. They are located at West Virginia Career College, Registrar, 148 Willey St, Morgantown, WV 26505.

Westminster College, Registrar's Office, South Market St, New Wilmington, PA 16172, 412-946-7136 (Fax: 412-946-7171). Hours: 8AM-4:30PM. Enrollment: 1500. Records go back to 1800's. Alumni records are maintained here also. Call 412-946-7008. Degrees granted: Bachelors; Masters. Adverse incident record source- Student Affairs, 412-946-7110.

Attendance and degree information available by phone, mail. Search requires name only. Also helpful: SSN, date of birth, exact years of attendance. There is no fee.

Westminster Theological Seminary, Registrar, Church Rd and Willow Grove Ave, Glenside, PA 19038, 215-572-3809 (Fax: 215-887-5404). Hours: 8:30AM-4:30PM. Enrollment: 560. Records go back to 1930's. Alumni records are maintained here at the same phone number. Degrees granted: Masters; Doctorate. Adverse incident record source- VP Student Affairs, 215-887-5511.

Attendance and degree information available by phone, fax, mail. Search requires name plus SSN. Also helpful: date of birth, exact years of attendance. There is no fee.

Westmoreland County Community College, Registrar, Armbrust Rd, Youngwood, PA 15697-1895, 412-925-4069 (Fax: 412-925-4292). Hours: 8AM-5PM. Enrollment: 6000. Records go back to 1970. Degrees granted: Associate.

Attendance and degree information available by phone, fax, mail. Search requires name plus SSN. There is no fee.

Widener University, Registrar, One University Pl, Chester, PA 19013-5792, 610-499-4140 (Fax: 610-499-4576). Hours: 8AM-4:30PM. Records go back to 1876. Alumni records are maintained here also. Call 610-499-1154. Degrees granted: Bachelors; Masters; Doctorate.

Attendance and degree information available by phone, fax, mail. Search requires name plus SSN. There is no fee.

Widener University at Harrisburg, (School of Law), Registrar, 3800 Vartan Way, Harrisburg, PA 17106, 717-541-3904 (Fax: 717-541-1923). Hours: 8:30AM-6:50PM M,T; 8:30AM-5PM W-F. Enrollment: 500. Records go back to 1989. Alumni Records Office: Alumni Office, Widener University, One University Place, Chester, PA 19013.

Attendance and degree information available by mail. Search requires name plus approximate years of attendance, signed release. Also helpful: SSN, exact years of attendance. There is no fee.

Wilkes University, Registrar, 267 S Franklin St, Wilkes-Barre, PA 18766, 717-831-4856 (Fax: 717-823-9470). Hours: 8:30AM-4:30PM. Records go back to 1933. Alumni Records Office: Evans Alumni House, Wilkes University, 110 S River St, Wilkes-Barre, PA 18766. Degrees granted: Bachelors; Masters;

PharmD. Adverse incident record source- Student Affairs, 717-831-4100.

Attendance and degree information available by phone, fax, mail. Search requires name plus SSN, date of birth. Also helpful: exact years of attendance. There is no fee.

Williamson Free School of Mechanical Trades, Registrar, 106 S Middletown Road Rt 352, Media, PA 19063, 610-566-1776 (Fax: 610-566-6502). Enrollment: 254. Records go back to 1911. Alumni records are maintained here at the same phone number. Degrees granted: Associate; Diplomas in Brickmasonry, Carpentry, Painting/Wallcovering.

Attendance and degree information available by phone, fax, mail. Search requires name plus exact years of attendance. There is no fee.

Williamsport School of Commerce, Registrar, 941 W Third St, Williamsport, PA 17701, 717-326-2869. Hours: 8AM-4PM. Records go back to 1955. Degrees granted: Associate.

Attendance and degree information available by phone, mail. Search requires name plus SSN. There is no fee.

Wilson College, Registrar, 1015 Philadelphia Ave, Chambersburg, PA 17201-1285, 717-264-4141 X355 (Fax: 717-264-1578). Hours: 8AM-4:30PM. Records go back to 1869. Alumni records are maintained here also. Call 717-264-3182. Degrees granted: Bachelors.

Attendance and degree information available by phone, fax, mail. Search requires name plus SSN, exact years of attendance. There is no fee.

Yeshiva Beth Moshe, Registrar, 930 Hickory St, Scranton, PA 18505, 717-346-1747. Hours: 8AM-5PM. Records go back to 1965.

Attendance and degree information available by mail. Search requires name plus SSN, date of birth, exact years of attendance, signed release. There is no fee.

York College of Pennsylvania, Records Office, Country Club Rd, York, PA 17405-7199, 717-846-7788 (Fax: 717-849-1607). Hours: 8AM-5PM M-Th, 8-11:30AM F. Records go back to 1788. Alumni records are maintained here also. Call 717-846-7788 X1500. Degrees granted: Associate; Bachelors; Masters.

Attendance and degree information available by phone, fax, mail. Search requires name plus SSN. Also helpful: date of birth, exact years of attendance. There is no fee.

Yorktowne Business Institute, Registrar, W Seventh Ave, York, PA 17404, 717-846-5000 (Fax: 717-848-4584). Hours: 8AM-5PM. Enrollment: 220. Records go back to 1977. Degrees granted: Associate.

Attendance and degree information available by phone, fax, mail. Search requires name only. Also helpful: SSN, date of birth, exact years of attendance. There is no fee.

Trade and Vocational Schools

Academy of Medical Arts and Business, 279 Boas St, Harrisburg, PA 17102, 717-233-2172

All-State Career School, 501 Seminole St, Lester, PA 19029, 610-521-1818

Allegheny Business Institute, 239 Fourth Ave #617, Pittsburgh, PA 15222, 412-456-7100

Allied Medical Careers, 104 Woodward Hill Rd, Edwardsville, PA 18704, 717-288-8400

Allied Medical Careers (Branch Campus), 2901 Pittston Ave, Scranton, PA 18505, 717-342-8000

Antonelli Medical and Professional Institute, 1700 Industrial Hwy, Pottstown, PA 19464, 610-323-7270

Automotive Training Center, 114 Pickering Wy, Exton, PA 19341, 610-363-6716

Bamberg Job Corps Center, 200 S Carlisle St, Bamberg, PA 29003, 803-552-3670

Barber Styling Institute, 3433 Simpson Ferry Rd, Camp Hill, PA 17011, 717-763-4787

Berks Technical Institute, 832 N Park Rd, Wyomissing, PA 19610, 610-372-1722

Beta Training Services, 225 S Chester Rd Ste 5, Swarthmore, PA 19081, 614-543-5000

Bidwell Training Center, 1815 Metropolitan St, Pittsburgh, PA 15233, 412-323-4000

Career Institute (The), 1825 John F. Kennedy Blvd, Philadelphia, PA 19103, 215-561-7600

Career Training Academy, 703 Fifth Ave, New Kensington, PA 15068, 412-337-1000

Career Training Academy (Branch Campus), 244 Center Rd, Monroeville, PA 15146, 412-372-3900

Computer Learning Center, 3600 Market St, Philadelphia, PA 19104, 215-222-6450

Computer Learning Network, 1110 Fernwood Ave, Camp Hill, PA 17011, 717-761-1481

Computer Learning Network (Branch Campus), 2900 Fairway Dr, Altoona, PA 16602, 814-944-5643

Delaware County Institute of Training, 615 Ave of the States, Chester, PA 19013, 610-874-1888

Delaware Valley Academy of Medical and Dental Assistants, 3330 Grant Ave, Philadelphia, PA 19114, 215-676-1200

Franklin Academy, 324 N Centre St, Pottsville, PA 17901, 717-622-8370

Garfield Business Institute, 709 Third Ave, New Brighton, PA 15066, 412-728-4050

Gateway Technical Institute, 100 Seventh St, Pittsburgh, PA 15222, 412-281-4111

Gleim Technical Institute, 200 S Spring Garden St, Carlisle, PA 17013, 800-922-8399

Greater Johnstown Area Vocational-Technical School, 445 Schoolhouse Rd, Johnstown, PA 15904, 814-266-6073

J.H. Thompson Academies, 2908 State St, Erie, PA 16508, 814-456-6217

JNA Marketing, 1212 S Broad St, Philadelphia, PA 19146, 215-468-8838

James Martin Adult Health Occupations, 2600 Red Lion Rd, Philadelphia, PA 19114, 215-961-2131

Joseph Donahue International School of Hairstyling, 2485 Grant Ave, Philadelphia, PA 19114, 215-969-1313

Learning and Evaluation Center, PO Box 616, Bloomsburg, PA 17815, 717-784-5220

Lifetime Career Schools, 101 Harrison St, Archbald, PA 18403, 717-876-6340

Lincoln Technical Institute, 9191 Torresdale Ave, Philadelphia, PA 19136, 215-335-0800

National Education Center Allentown Campus, 1501 Lehigh St, Allentown, PA 18103, 610-791-5100

Naval Damage Control Training Center, Naval Base, Philadelphia, PA 19112, 215-897-5677

New England Tractor Trailer Training School, 3715 E Thompson St, Philadelphia, PA 19137, 215-288-7800

North Hills School of Health Occupations, 1500 Northway Mall, Pittsburgh, PA 15237, 412-367-8003

Oakbridge Academy of Arts, 401 Ninth St, New Kensington, PA 15068, 412-335-5336

Orleans Technical Institute, 1330 Rhawn St, Philadelphia, PA 19111, 215-728-4700

Orleans Technical Institute (Court Reporting Institute), 1845 Walnut St 7th Floor, Philadelphia, PA 19103, 215-854-1823

Orleans Technical Institute (The Court Reporting Institute), 1845 Walnut St Ste 700, Philadelphia, PA 19103-4707, 215-854-1823

PJA School (The), 7900 W Chester Pike, Upper Darby, PA 19082, 610-789-6700

Penn Commercial College, 82 S Main St, Washington, PA 15301, 412-222-5330

Pennsylvania Gunsmith School, 812 Ohio River Blvd, Pittsburgh, PA 15202, 412-766-1812

Pennsylvania Institute of Culinary Arts, 717 LIberty Ave, Pittsburgh, PA 15222, 412-566-2433

Pennsylvania Institute of Taxidermy, Rural Rte 3 Box 188, Ebensburg, PA 15931, 814-472-4510

Pennsylvania School of Art and Design, 204 N Prince St, Lancaster, PA 17603, 717-396-7833

Philadelphia Wireless Technical Institute, 1533 Pine St, Philadelphia, PA 19102, 215-546-0745

Quaker City Institute of Aviation, 2565 Grays Ferry Ave, Philadelphia, PA 19146, 215-545-7518

Ralph Amodei INternational Institute of Hair Design & Technology, 4451 Frankford Ave, Philadelphia, PA 19124, 215-289-4433

Rosedale Technical Institute, 4634 Browns Hill Rd, Pittsburgh, PA 15217, 412-521-6200

Settlement Music School, 416 Queen St, Philadelphia, PA 19147, 215-336-0400

Shirley Rock School of the Pennsylvania Ballet (The), 1101 S Broad St, Philadelphia, PA 19147, 215-551-7000

Star Technical Institute, 9149 Roosevelt Blvd, Philadelphia, PA 19114, 610-969-5877

Star Technical Institute, 1570 Garrett Rd, Upper Darby, PA 19082, 610-626-2700

Star Technical Institute, 34 S Main St Ste 22, Wilkes Barre, PA 18701, 717-829-6960

Star Technical Institute (Branch Campus), 2102 Union Blvd, Allentown, PA 18103, 610-434-9963

Star Technical Institute (Branch Campus), 212 Wyoming Ave, Kingston, PA 18704, 717-287-9777

Star Technical Institute (Branch Campus), 1600 Nay Aug Ave, Scranton, PA 18509, 717-963-0144

Swanson's Driving Schools, Inc., 9915 Frankstown Rd, Pittsburgh, PA 15235, 412-241-6963

Tri-City Barber School, 128 E Main St, Norristown, PA 19401, 610-279-4432

Tri-City Barber School, 5901 N Broad St, Philadelphia, PA 19141, 215-927-3232

Ultrasound Diagnostic School (Branch Campus), 5830 Ellsworth Ave #102, Pittsburgh, PA 15232, 412-362-9404

Ultrasound Diagnostic School (Trevose Campus), 3 Neshaminy Interplex, Ste 117, Trevose, PA 19053, 215-244-4906

Welder Training and Testing Institute, 100 Pennslyvania Ave, Selinsgrove, PA 17870, 800-326-9306

Western School of Health and Business Careers, 327 5th Ave 2nd Flr, Pittsburgh, PA 15222, 412-281-2600

Western School of Health and Business Careers (Branch Campus), 421 7th Ave, Pittsburgh, PA 15219, 412-373-6400

Wilma Boyd Career Schools, 1412 Beer School Rd, Pittsburgh, PA 15219, 412-299-2200

York Technical Institute, 3351 Whiteford Rd, York, PA 17402, 717-757-1100

State Licensing & Business Registration Quick Finder Index

Architecture, Engineering & Surveying

Architect #22 (6982)	☎ 717-783-3397
Engineer #22 (34228)	☎ 717-783-7049
Landscape Architect #22 (711)	☎ 717-783-3397

Business - Court & Legal Services

Attorney #1 (52153)	☎ 717-731-7073
Court Reporter #2	717-255-2839
Lobbyist #19	☎ 717-787-5920
Notary Public #23 (82000)	☎ 717-787-5280

Business - General Services

Auctioneer #22 (2203)	☎ 717-783-3397
Public Accountant Corporation #22	☎ 717-783-1404
Public Accountant-CPA #22 (35077)	✉ 717-783-1404
Public Accountant-PA #22	✉ 717-783-1404
Public Accounting Partnership #22	☎ 717-783-1404

Education

Education Specialist #6	☎ 717-787-2967
Private School Staff #7 (375)	☎ 717-783-8228
School Administrator #6	☎ 717-787-2967
School Intermediate Unit Executive Director #6	☎ 717-787-2967
School Superintendent #6	☎ 717-787-2967
School Supervisor #6	☎ 717-787-2967
Teacher #6	☎ 717-787-2967

Environmental & Agriculture

Pest Management Consultant #3	✉ 717-787-4392
Pesticide Applicator #3 (32000)	✉ 717-787-4843
Pesticide Technician #3 (2000)	✉ 717-787-4843
Veterinarian #22 (7850)	☎ 717-783-1389
Veterinarian Technician #22	☎ 717-783-1389

Financial - Real Estate, Insurance & Banking

Bank #5	☎ 717-783-4721
Consumer Discount Company #5	☎ 717-787-3717
Debt Collector-Repossessor #5	☎ 717-787-3717
First Mortgage Banker #5	☎ 717-787-3717
Installment Loan Seller #5	☎ 717-787-3717
Insurance Agent #13 (180000)	☎ 717-783-2181
Insurance Supervisor/Broker #12 (20)	☎ 717-783-3840
Investment Adviser #18	☎ 717-787-5675
Licensing Division #12 (1600)	☎ 717-787-1879
Money Transmitter #5	☎ 717-787-3717
Mortgage Broker #22	☎ 717-787-8503
Pawnbroker #5	☎ 717-787-3717
Real Estate Agent #22 (1217)	☎ 717-783-4866
Real Estate Appraiser #22	☎ 717-783-4866
Real Estate Auctioneer #22	☎ 717-787-8503
Real Estate Broker #22	☎ 717-783-3658
Real Estate Salesperson #22	☎ 717-783-3658
Residential Appraiser #22	☎ 717-783-4866
Sales Finance Company #5	☎ 717-787-3717
Secondary Mortgage Lender #5	☎ 717-787-3717
Secondary Mortgage Loan Broker #5	☎ 717-787-3717
Secondary Mortgage Loan Broker Agent #5	☎ 717-787-3717
Securities Agent #18	☎ 717-787-5675
Securities Broker/Dealer #18	☎ 717-787-5675

Health & Beauty

Acupuncturist #22	☎ 717-787-8503
Ambulance Service #10	☎ 717-787-8740
Amphetamine Program #22	717-787-2568
Barber #22 (2729)	☎ 717-783-3402
Chiropractor #22	☎ 717-783-7156
Cosmetologist/Cosmetician #22 (85773)	☎ 717-783-7130
Dental Assistant-Expanded Function #22	☎ 717-783-7162
Dental Hygiene #22	☎ 717-783-7162
Dental Hygienist #22 (7120)	☎ 717-787-8503
Dentist #20 (11502)	☎ 717-783-7162
Emergency Medical Technician #10	☎ 717-787-8740
Emergency Medical Technician-Paramedic #10	☎ 717-787-8740
First Responder-EMT #10	☎ 717-787-8740
Funeral Director #22 (3846)	☎ 717-783-3397
Health Professional #10	☎ 717-787-8740
Hearing Aid Dealer #9 (573)	☎ 717-787-8015
Hearing Aid Fitter #9	☎ 717-787-8015
Hearing Aid Fitter-Apprentice #9	☎ 717-787-8015
Medical Doctor #22	717-787-2381
Medical Laboratories #8	☎ 717-462-8500
Midwife #22	☎ 717-787-8503
Nuclear Medicine Technologist #22	☎ 717-787-8503
Nurse #22	☎ 717-787-8503
Nursing Home Administrator #22 (1703)	☎ 717-783-7155
Nursing Home Licenses #11 (48)	☎ 610-594-8041
Occupational Therapist #22 (6599)	☎ 717-783-1389
Optometrist #22	☎ 717-783-7134
Osteopathic Physician #22	☎ 717-783-4858
Osteopathic Physician Assistant #22	☎ 717-783-4858
Pharmacist #22 (14785)	☎ 717-783-7157
Physical Therapist #22	☎ 717-783-7134
Physician's Assistant #22	☎ 717-787-8503
Podiatrist #22	☎ 717-783-4858
Prehospital RN #10	☎ 717-787-8740
Radiation Therapy Technician #22	☎ 717-787-8503
Radiologic Technologist #22	☎ 717-787-8503
Respiratory Care Practitioner #22	☎ 717-783-4858
Speech Pathologist/Audiologist (Speech, Language, Hearing) #22 (6407)	☎ 717-783-7156
Temporary Hearing Aid Apprentice #9	☎ 717-787-8015

Investigations & Security

Private Investigator #17 (32)	☎ 717-255-2692

Social Services

Child Day Care #14 (7880)	☎ 717-787-8691
Social Worker #22 (10005)	☎ 717-783-1389

Sports & Entertainment

Athletic Trainer #22	☎ 717-787-8503
Boat Registration #15 (330440)	☎ 717-657-4551
Harness Racing #4 (3500)	☎ 717-787-5196
Horse Racing #4 (6000)	☎ 717-787-1942
Liquor Distributor #16	☎ 717-783-8250
Retail Liquor #16	☎ 717-787-5428
Wholesale Liquor #16	☎ 717-787-5428

Transportation

Vehicle Dealer #21	☎ 717-783-1697
Vehicle Salesperson #21 (33682)	☎ 717-783-1697

State Licensing & Business Registration Agency Information

(1) Administrationn Office of PA Courts, Lawyer Assessment, PO Box 46, Camphill, PA 17001-0046, 717-238-7073, Fax: 717-231-7080

(2) CCR Court Reporter, 2846 N 2nd St, Harrisburg, PA 17110, 717-255-2839

(3) Department of Agriculture, Bureau of Plant Industry, 2301 N Cameron St, Harrisburg, PA 17110-9408, 717-787-4843, Fax: 717-783-3275

(4) Department of Agriculture, State Racing Commission, Agriculture Office Bldg, 2301 N Cameron St, Harrisburg, PA 17110-9408, 717-787-5196, Fax: 717-787-2271

(5) Department of Banking, Bureau of Licensing & Consumer Compliance, 333 Market St, 16th Floor, Harrisburg, PA 17101-2290, 717-783-3717, Fax: 717-787-8773

(6) Department of Education, Bureau of Teacher Certification & Preparation, 333 Market St,, Harrisburg, PA 17126-0333, 717-787-2967, Fax: 717-783-6736

(7) Department of Education, State Board of Private Licensed Schools, 333 Market St, 12th Floor, Harrisburg, PA 17126-0333, 717-783-8228, Fax: 717-783-0583

(8) Department of Health, PO Box 500, Exton, PA 19341-0500, 717-783-1927, Fax: 610-436-3346

(9) Department of Health, Bureau of Quality Assurance, Hearing Aid Program, Health & Welfare Bldg, Room 930, Harrisburg, PA 17120, 717-787-8015, Fax: 717-787-1491

(10) Department of Health, Division of Emergency Medical Services, PO Box 90, Harrisburg, PA 17120, 717-787-8740, Fax: 717-772-0910

(11) Department of Health, Division of Nursing Care, PO Box 500, Exton, PA 19341-0500, 610-594-8041, Fax: 610-436-3346

(12) Department of Insurance, Bureau of Licensing, 1345 Strawberry Sq, Harrisburg, PA 17120, 717-787-3840, Fax: 717-787-8557

(13) Department of Insurance, Bureau of Licensing, 1300 Strawberry Square, Harrisburg, PA 17120, 717-783-2181, Fax: 717-787-8553

(14) Department of Public Welfare, Bureau of Child Day Care Services, PO Box 2675, Harrisburg, PA 17105-2675, 717-787-8691, Fax: 717-787-1529

(15) Fish & Boat Commission, Division of Boat Registration, 3517 Walnut St, PO Box 68900, Harrisburg, PA 17106, 717-657-4551, Fax: 717-657-4449

(16) Pennsylvania Liquor Control Board, Licensing Administrative Div., PO Box 8940, Harrisburg, PA 17105-8940, 717-787-5428, Fax: 717-772-2165

(17) Pennsylvania Private Detective Licensing, Clerk of Courts, Dauphin County Courthouse, Front & Market Sts, Harrisburg, PA 17108, 717-255-2692

(18) Pennsylvania Securities Commission, Division of Licensing & Compliance, 1010 N 7th St, Eastgate-2nd Floor, Harrisburg, PA 17102-1410, 717-787-5675, Fax: 717-783-5122

(19) Secretary of Senate, Chief Clerk of the House, State Capitol, Room 460, Main Capitol Bldg, Harrisburg, PA 17120, 717-787-5920

(20) State Board of Dentistry, PO Box 2649, Harrisburg, PA 17105-2649, 717-783-7162, Fax: 717-787-7769

(21) State Board of Vehicle Manufacturers, Dealers &, Bureau of Professional & Occupational Affairs, 124 Pine St, Transportation & Safety Bldg, 6th Fl, Harrisburg, PA 17101, 717-783-1697, Fax: 717-787-0250

(22) State Department, PO Box 2649, Harrisburg, PA 17005, 717-787-8503, Fax: 717-787-7769

(23) State Department, Bureau of Commissions, Elections & Legislation, North Office Bldg, Room 304, Harrisburg, PA 17120, 717-787-5280

Rhode Island

Capitol: Providence (Providence County)	
State Population	.9 Million
Number of Degree Granting Institutions:	14
Number of State Licensing & Business Registration Agencies:	107

Degree Granting Educational Institutions

Brown University, Registrar, Box K, Providence, RI 02912, 401-863-1851. Hours: 8AM-4PM. Enrollment: 7000. Records go back to 1764. Alumni records are maintained here also. Call 401-863-3307. Degrees granted: Bachelors; Masters; Doctorate.

Attendance and degree information available by phone, mail. Search requires name plus exact years of attendance. There is no fee.

Bryant College, Academic Records Office, 1150 Douglas Pike, Smithfield, RI 02917-1284, 401-232-6080 (Fax: 401-232-6065). Hours: 8AM-4:30PM. Alumni records are maintained here also. Call 401-232-6040. Degrees granted: Associate; Bachelors; Masters.

Attendance and degree information available by phone, fax, mail. Search requires name plus date of birth, exact years of attendance. Also helpful: SSN. There is no fee.

Community College of Rhode Island, Registrar, 400 East Ave, Warwick, RI 02886-1805, 401-825-2125 (Fax: 401-825-2394). Hours: 8AM-7PM M-Th; 8AM-4PM F (when in session); 8AM-4PM (otherwise). Enrollment: 15000. Records go back to 1964. Alumni records are maintained here also. Call 401-825-2181. Degrees granted: Associate.

Attendance and degree information available by phone, fax, mail. Search requires name plus SSN. There is no fee.

Johnson & Wales University, Registrar, 8 Abbott Park Pl, Providence, RI 02903, 401-598-1000 (Fax: 401-598-2837). Hours: 8:30AM-4:30PM. Enrollment: 8000. Records go back to 1952. Inactive records: "Dept of Inactive Records," same address. Alumni records are maintained here at the same phone number. Degrees granted: Associate; Bachelors; Masters. Adverse incident record source- Student Affairs, 401-598-1109.

Attendance and degree information available by fax, mail. Search requires name plus signed release. Also helpful: SSN, date of birth, exact years of attendance. There is no fee.

Katharine Gibbs School, Registrar, 178 Butler Ave, Providence, RI 02906, 401-861-1420 (Fax: 401-421-6230). Hours: 9AM-5PM. Enrollment: 300. Records go back to 1911. Degrees granted. Special programs- Executive Assistant Program: Legal Executive Program: Medical Executive Program.

Attendance and degree information available by fax, mail. Search requires name plus SSN, exact years of attendance. Also helpful: date of birth. There is no fee.

Naval War College, Registrar, 686 Cushing Rd, Newport, RI 02841-5010, 401-841-6597 (Fax: 401-841-3084). Hours: 7:30AM-4PM. Enrollment: 500. Records go back to 1884. Alumni records are maintained here at the same phone number. Degrees granted: Masters. Special programs- CCE, 401-841-2134.

Attendance and degree information available by phone, fax, mail. Search requires name plus SSN, exact years of attendance. Also helpful: date of birth. There is no fee.

New England Institute of Technology, Registrar, 2500 Post Rd, Warwick, RI 02886-2251, 401-739-5000 (Fax: 401-738-5122). Hours: 8:30AM-5:30PM. Enrollment: 2000. Records go back to 1985. Degrees granted: Associate; Bachelors.

Attendance and degree information available by phone, fax, mail. Search requires name plus approximate years of attendance. Also helpful: SSN, date of birth, exact years of attendance. There is no fee.

Providence College, Registrar, Providence, RI 02918, 401-865-2366. Hours: 8AM-5PM. Enrollment: 5557. Records go back to 1919. Alumni records are maintained here also. Call 401-865-2414. Degrees granted: Associate; Bachelors; Masters; Doctorate. Adverse incident record source- 401-865-2366.

Attendance and degree information available by phone, mail. Search requires name plus SSN, exact years of attendance. There is no fee.

Rhode Island College, Registrar, Providence, RI 02908, 401-456-8212 (Fax: 401-456-8379). Hours: 8AM-4:30PM. Enrollment: 9000. Records go back to 1854. Alumni records are maintained here also. Call 401-456-8000. Degrees granted: Bachelors; Masters; Doctorate; CAGS.

Attendance and degree information available by written request only. Search requires name plus SSN, signed release. Also helpful: exact years of attendance. There is no fee.

Rhode Island School of Design, Registrar, 2 College St, Providence, RI 02903, 401-454-6151. Hours: 8:30AM-4:30PM. Enrollment: 1987. Records go back to 1930's. Alumni records are maintained here also. Call 401-454-6620. Degrees granted: Bachelors; Masters.

Attendance and degree information available by phone, fax, mail. Search requires name only. Also helpful: SSN, date of birth, exact years of attendance. There is no fee.

Roger Williams College Providence Branch,

Registrar, 612 Academy Ave, Providence, RI 02908, 401-274-2200 (Fax: 401-254-3480). Enrollment: 3400. Records go back to 1919. Degrees granted: Associate; Bachelors. Special programs- Arts: Science. Adverse incident record source- Security.

Attendance and degree information available by phone, mail. Search requires name plus SSN, exact years of attendance. There is no fee.

Roger Williams University, Registrar, One Old Ferry

Rd, Bristol, RI 02809-2921, 401-254-3033 (Fax: 401-254-3480). Hours: 8AM-5PM. Records go back to 1948. Degrees granted: Associate; Bachelors.

Attendance and degree information available by phone, fax, mail. Search requires name plus approximate years of attendance. Also helpful: SSN, date of birth, exact years of attendance. There is no fee.

Salve Regina University, Registrar, 100 Ochre Point

Ave, Newport, RI 02840-4192, 401-847-6650. Hours: 8AM-5PM. Enrollment: 2200. Records go back to 1947. Alumni records are maintained here also. Call 401-847-6650. Degrees granted: Associate; Bachelors; Masters; Doctorate. Adverse incident record source- Dean of Students, 401-847-6650.

Attendance and degree information available by phone, mail. Search requires name plus approximate years of attendance. Also helpful: SSN, date of birth, exact years of attendance. There is no fee.

University of Rhode Island, Registrar, Administra-

tion Bldg, Kingston, RI 02881-0806, 401-792-2835 (Fax: 401-874-2910). Hours: 8:30AM-4:30PM. Enrollment: 10400. Records go back to 1892. Alumni records are maintained here also. Call 401-792-2242. Degrees granted: Bachelors; Masters; Doctorate.

Attendance and degree information available by phone, mail. Search requires name plus SSN, date of birth, exact years of attendance. There is no fee.

Trade and Vocational Schools

Nasson Institute, 286 Main St, Pawtucket, RI 02860, 401-728-1570

Nasson Institute (Branch Campus), 361 Resorvoir Ave, Providence, RI 02907, 401-941-0557

Nasson Institute (Branch Campus), 191 Social St, Woonsocket, RI 02895, 401-769-2066

New England Technical College, 2500 Post Rd, Warwick, RI 02886, 401-739-5000

New England Tractor Trailer Training School of Rhode Island, 10 Dunnell Ln, Pawtucket, RI 02860, 401-725-1220

Ocean State Business Institute, 140 Point Judith Rd, Narragansett, RI 02882, 401-789-0287

Sawyer School, 101 Main St, Pawtucket, RI 02860, 401-272-8400

Sawyer School (Branch Campus), 1222 Warwick Ave, Warwick, RI 02888, 401-463-3555

School of Medical and Legal Secretarial Sciences, 60 S Angell St, Providence, RI 02906, 401-331-1711

State Licensing & Business Registration Quick Finder Index

Architecture, Engineering & Surveying
Architect #2 401-272-1730
Engineer #6 (2400) .... ☎ 401-277-2565
Surveyor #4 (231) .... ☎ 401-277-2038

Business - Court & Legal Services
Attorney #22 .... ☎ 401-277-3272
Bondsman #19 401-277-3212
Lobbyist #16 (739) 401-277-2249
Notary Public #16 (25000) 401-277-2249
Shorthand Reporter #19 401-277-3212

Business - General Services
Auctioneer #11 .... ☎ 401-277-3857
Public Accountant-CPA #1 (1800) .... ☎ 401-277-3185

Construction & Manufacturing
Building Contractor #5 (7440) .... ☎ 401-277-1268
Electric Sign Installer #5 .... ☎ 401-277-1268
Electrical Contractor #5 .... ☎ 401-277-1268
Electrician #13 .... ☎ 401-457-1860
Hoisting Engineer #13 .... ☎ 401-457-1860
Journeyman Plumber #15 .... ✉ 401-277-2827
Master Plumber #15 .... ✉ 401-277-2827
Pipefitter #13 .... ☎ 401-457-1860
Refrigeration Technician #13 .... ☎ 401-457-1860

Education
School Guidance Counselor #17 .... ☎ 401-277-4600
School Principal #17 .... ☎ 401-277-4600
School Superintendent #17 .... ☎ 401-277-4600
School Supervisor #17 .... ☎ 401-277-2675
Teacher #17 .... ☎ 401-277-4600

Environmental & Agriculture
Arborist #10 (400) .... ☎ 401-647-3367
Asbestos Abatement Contractor/Supervisor /Worker #5 .... ☎ 401-277-1268
Blaster #20 (159) .... ☎ 401-277-2335
Lead Hazard Abatement Contractor/Supervisor /Worker #5 .... ☎ 401-277-1268
Sewage Disposal System Installer #9 (1000) .... ☎ 401-277-6820
Veterinarian #15 .... ✉ 401-277-2827

Waste Water Treatment Facility Operator #9 (300) .... ☎ 401-277-6820

Financial - Real Estate, Insurance & Banking
Bank #6 .... ✉ 401-277-2405
Insurance Adjuster #6 .... ✉ 401-277-2405
Insurance Appraiser #6 .... ✉ 401-277-2405
Insurance Broker #6 .... ✉ 401-277-2405
Insurance Producer #6 .... ✉ 401-277-2223
Insurance Solicitor #6 .... ✉ 401-277-2405
Investment Advisor #6 .... ✉ 401-277-2405
Money & Mortgage Broker #6 .... ✉ 401-277-2405
Real Estate Appraiser #6 (447) .... ☎ 401-277-2416
Securities Broker/Dealer #6 (1240) .... ☎ 401-277-3048
Securities Broker/Dealer Sales Representative #6 .... ✉ 401-277-3048
Securities Sales Representative #6 .... ✉ 401-277-2405

Health & Beauty
Acupuncturist #14 .... ✉ 401-277-2827
Audiologist #14 .... ✉ 401-277-2827
Barber #14 .... ✉ 401-277-2827
Barber Instructor #14 .... ✉ 401-277-2827
Barber Shop #14 .... ✉ 401-277-2827
Beauty Shop #14 .... ✉ 401-277-2827
Chiropractor #14 .... ✉ 401-277-2827
Clinical Histologic Technician #8 (60) .... ☎ 401-277-2827
Clinical Laboratory Scientist #8 .... ☎ 401-277-2877
Clinical Laboratory Scientist-Cytogenetics #8 .... ☎ 401-277-2827
Clinical Laboratory Scientist/Election Miccroscopy #8 (4) .... ☎ 401-277-2827
Clinical Laboratory Technician #8 (179) .... ☎ 401-277-2827
Dental Hygienist #14 .... ✉ 401-277-2827
Dentist #14 .... ✉ 401-277-2827
Dentist (Limited) #15 .... ✉ 401-277-2827
Dietitian #15 .... ✉ 401-277-2827
Electrologist #15 .... ✉ 401-277-2827
Embalmer #15 .... ✉ 401-277-2827
Emergency Medical Technician #14 .... ✉ 401-277-2827
Esthetician #15 .... ✉ 401-277-2827
Funeral Director #15 .... ✉ 401-277-2827
Hairdresser #15 .... ✉ 401-277-2827

Hairdresser Instructor #15 ....✉ 401-277-2827
Hearing Aid Dispenser #14 ....✉ 401-277-2827
Manicuring Shop #15 ....✉ 401-277-2827
Manicurist #15 ....✉ 401-277-2827
Massage Therapist #15 ....✉ 401-277-2827
Midwife #15 ....✉ 401-277-2827
Nurse #15..✉ 401-277-2827
Nurse Practitioner #15 ....✉ 401-277-2827
Nursing Assistant #15..........................✉ 401-277-2827
Nursing Home Administrator #15.........✉ 401-277-2827
Occupational Therapist #15..................✉ 401-277-2827
Optician #15 ....✉ 401-277-2827
Optometrist #15 ....✉ 401-277-2827
Osteopathic Physician #14 ....✉ 401-277-2827
Pharmacist #3 (2499)..........................✉ 401-277-2837
Pharmacy Technician #3 ....✉ 401-277-2837
Physical Therapist #15 ....✉ 401-277-2827
Physical Therapy Assistant #15 ....✉ 401-277-2827
Physician's Assistant #15.....................✉ 401-277-2827
Podiatrist #15 ....✉ 401-277-2827
Practical Nurse #15.............................✉ 401-277-2827
Prosthetist #15 ....✉ 401-277-2827
Respiratory Care Practitioner #15 ....✉ 401-277-2827
Sanitarian #15 ....✉ 401-277-2827
Speech Pathologist #15.......................✉ 401-277-2827

Investigations & Security

Burglar & Holdup Alarm Agent #11 (500) ....☎ 401-277-3857
Fire Alarm Installer #20.................................☎ 401-457-1860
Fire Extinguisher Installer/Service #20 (161)
....☎ 401-277-2335

Social Services

Chemical Dependency Professional #7 401-233-2215
Marriage Therapist #15......................................✉ 401-277-2827
Mental Health Counselor #15...........................✉ 401-277-2827
Psychologist #15 ....✉ 401-277-2827
Social Worker #18 (1324) ....☎ 401-464-2421

Sports & Entertainment

Athletic Trainer #14...✉ 401-277-2827
Fireworks Shooter #20 (59) ....☎ 401-277-2335
Lifeguard #12 (800) ....☎ 401-277-2632
Liquor Control #6 (1037)..................................☎ 401-277-2562
Pyrotechnic Operator #20 (6) ....☎ 401-277-2335
Racing #6 401-277-6541
Vendor Employee #6 ....✉ 401-277-2405

Transportation

Ship Pilot #21 (15)...☎ 401-277-3429
Travel Agent #6 ....✉ 401-277-3154

State Licensing & Business Registration Agency Information

(1)   Board of Accountancy, Department of Business Regulation, 233 Richmond St, Providence, RI 02903-4236, 401-277-3185, Fax: 401-277-6654

(2)   Board of Examinations & Registration of Architects, 50 Holden St, Providence, RI 02908, 401-942-9364, Fax: 401-273-7156

(3)   Board of Pharmacy, 3 Capitol Hill, Room 304, Providence, RI 02908, 401-277-2837, Fax: 401-277-2499

(4)   Board of Registration for Professional Surveyors, 10 Orms St, Suite 324, Charles Orms Bldg, Providence, RI 02904-2228, 401-277-2038

(5)   Building Contractor Registration Board, Residential Contractors Division, One Capitol Hill, Providence, RI 02908, 401-277-1270, Fax: 401-277-2599

(6)   Business Regulation Department, 233 Richmond St, Providence, RI 02903, 401-277-6541

(7)   Certification of Chemical Dependency Professionals, 345 Waterman Ave, Smithfield, RI 02917, 401-233-2215, Fax: 401-233-0690

(8)   Clinical Laboratory Advisory Board, Division of Professional Regulation, 3 Capitol Hill, Room 104, Providence, RI 02908, 401-277-2827, Fax: 401-277-1272

(9)   Division of Air & Hazardous Materials, ISDS Section, Dept of Environmental Management, 235 Promenade St, Providence, RI 02908, 401-277-6820, Fax: 401-277-6177

(10)   Division of Forest Environment, Department of Environmental Management, 1037 Hartford Pike, North Scituate, RI 02857, 401-647-3367, Fax: 401-647-3590

(11)   Division of Licensing & Consumer Protection, Department of Business Regulations, 233 Richmond St, Providence, RI 02903, 401-277-3857

(12)   Division of Parks & Recreation, Department of Environmental Management, 2321 Hartford Ave, Johnston, RI 02919, 401-277-2632, Fax: 401-934-0610

(13)   Division of Professional Regulation, 610 Manton Ave, Providence, RI 02909, 401-457-1860

(14)   Health Department, Professional Regulation Division, 3 Capitol Hill, Providence, RI 02908-5097, 401-277-2827, Fax: 401-277-1272

(15)   Health Department, Professional Regulation Division, 3 Capitol Hill, Providence, RI 02908-5097, 401-277-2827

(16)   Office of Secretary of State, Notary Division, 217 State House, Providence, RI 02903, 401-277-2249

(17)   Office of Teacher Certification, State Department of Education, 22 Hayes St, Providence, RI 02908, 401-277-2675, Fax: 401-277-2048

(18)   Rhode Island Department of Health, 3 Capitol Hill, Rm 104, Providence, RI 02908-5097, 401-277-2827

(19)   Rhode Island Superior Court, 250 Benefit St, Providence, RI 02903, 401-277-3212, Fax: 401-272-4645

(20)   State Fire Marshall's Office, Division of Fire Safety, 272 W Exchange St, North Providence, RI 02903, 401-277-2335, Fax: 401-273-1222

(21)   State Pilotage Commission, Division of Coastal Resources, 83 Park Street, Providence, RI 02903, 401-277-3429, Fax: 401-454-0765

(22)   Supreme Court, 250 Benefit St., Providence, RI 02903, 401-277-3272, Fax: 401-277-3599

South Carolina

Capitol: Columbia (Richland County)	
State Population	3.7 Million
Number of Degree Granting Institutions:	60
Number of State Licensing & Business Registration Agencies:	90

Degree Granting Educational Institutions

Aiken Technical College, Registrar, PO Box 696, Aiken, SC 29802-0696, 803-593-9231 (Fax: 803-593-6641). Hours: 7:30AM-7PM. Enrollment: 2200. Records go back to 1972. Alumni records are maintained here also. Call 803-593-9231 X1263. Degrees granted: Associate. Adverse incident record source- VP of Students.

Attendance and degree information available by phone, fax, mail. Search requires name plus SSN, approximate years of attendance. Also helpful: date of birth, exact years of attendance. There is no fee.

Allen University, Registrar, 1530 Harden St, Columbia, SC 29204, 803-254-4165 (Fax: 803-376-5709). Hours: 9AM-5PM. Records go back to 1906. Degrees granted: Associate; Bachelors. Adverse incident record source- Student Affairs, 803-376-5714.

Attendance and degree information available by fax, mail. Search requires name plus SSN, signed release. Also helpful: date of birth, exact years of attendance. There is no fee.

Anderson College, Registrar, 316 Blvd, Anderson, SC 29621, 864-231-2120 (Fax: 864-231-2004). Hours: 8:30AM-4:30PM. Enrollment: 800. Records go back to 1945. Alumni records are maintained here also. Call 864-231-2064. Degrees granted: Associate; Bachelors.

Attendance information available by phone, fax, mail. Search requires name plus SSN, exact years of attendance. Also helpful: date of birth. There is no fee.

Degree information available by phone, fax, mail. Search requires name plus SSN. Also helpful: date of birth, exact years of attendance. There is no fee.

Benedict College, Registrar, 1600 Harden St, Columbia, SC 29204, 803-253-5143 (Fax: 803-253-5167). Records go back to 1870. Alumni records are maintained here at the same phone number. Degrees granted: Bachelors.

Attendance and degree information available by phone, fax, mail. Search requires name plus SSN, date of birth, exact years of attendance. There is no fee.

Bob Jones University, Registrar, Greenville, SC 29614, 803-242-5100 X2010 (Fax: 1-800-2-FAXBJU). Enrollment: 4400. Records go back to 1927. Alumni records are maintained here at the same phone number. Degrees granted: Associ-

ate; Bachelors; Masters; Doctorate. Special programs- Liberal Arts. Adverse incident record source- Security.

Attendance and degree information available by phone, mail. Search requires name plus SSN, date of birth, exact years of attendance. There is no fee.

Central Carolina Technical College, Registrar, 506 N Guignard Dr, Sumter, SC 29150-2499, 803-778-1961 X430 (Fax: 803-773-4859). Enrollment: 2200. Records go back to 1963. Alumni records are maintained here at the same phone number. Degrees granted: Associate. Adverse incident record source- Student Affairs, 803-778-6600: Security, 803-778-3304

Attendance information available by phone, mail. Search requires name plus SSN, exact years of attendance. Also helpful: date of birth. There is no fee.

Degree information available by phone, mail. Search requires name plus SSN, exact years of attendance. There is no fee.

Charleston Southern University, Registrar, PO Box 118087, Charleston, SC 29423, 803-863-8060 (Fax: 803-863-8023). Enrollment: 2600. Records go back to 1969. Alumni records are maintained here at the same phone number. Degrees granted: Bachelors; Masters. Special programs- Air Force ROTC, 803-863-7149. Adverse incident record source- Security & Housing, 803-863-7104.

Attendance and degree information available by phone, fax, mail. Search requires name plus SSN. Also helpful: date of birth, exact years of attendance. There is no fee.

Chesterfield-Marlboro Technical College, Registrar, 1201 Chesterfield Hwy #9 W, PO Drawer 1007, Cheraw, SC 29520-1007, 803-921-6900 (Fax: 803-537-6148). Hours: 8AM-7PM M-Th; 8AM-1:30PM F. Enrollment: 1025. Records go back to 1969. Degrees granted: Associate.

Attendance and degree information available by phone, fax, mail. Search requires name plus SSN. Also helpful: date of birth, exact years of attendance. There is no fee.

Citadel Military College of South Carolina, Registrar, Citadel Station 171 Moultrie St, Charleston, SC 29409, 803-953-6969 (Fax: 803-953-7630). Hours: 8AM-5PM. Enrollment: 4300. Records go back to 1842. Alumni records are maintained here also. Call 803-953-5000. Degrees granted: Bachelors; Masters. Adverse incident record source- Commandant's Office, 803-953-5003 .

Attendance and degree information available by phone, fax, mail. Search requires name plus SSN. Also helpful: date of birth, exact years of attendance. There is no fee.

Claflin College, Registrar, 700 College Ave NE, Orangeburg, SC 29115, 803-534-2710 (Fax: 803-531-2860). Degrees granted: Bachelors. Adverse incident record source- Campus Security.

Attendance and degree information available by phone, fax, mail. Search requires name plus SSN, exact years of attendance. There is no fee.

Clemson University, Transcripts, 104 Sikes Hall, Clemson, SC 29634, 803-656-2174 (Fax: 803-656-0622). Hours: 8AM-4:30PM. Alumni Records Office: Box 345603, Clemson, SC 29634. Degrees granted: Bachelors; Masters; Doctorate.

Attendance and degree information available by phone, fax, mail. Search requires name only. Also helpful: SSN, exact years of attendance. There is no fee.

Coastal Carolina University, Registrar, PO Box 261954, Conway, SC 29528-6054, 803-349-2025 (Fax: 803-349-2909). Hours: 8AM-5PM. Enrollment: 4500. Records go back to 1993. Records prior to July 1, 1993 are housed at University of South Carolina. Alumni records are maintained here also. Call 803-349-2006. Degrees granted: Bachelors; Masters. Certification: Gerontology. Adverse incident record source- Campus Police, 803-349-2177.

Attendance and degree information available by phone, fax, mail. Search requires name plus SSN, date of birth. Also helpful: exact years of attendance. There is no fee.

Coker College, Registrar, 300 E College Ave, Hartsville, SC 29550, 803-383-8022 (Fax: 803-383-8095). Enrollment: 800. Degrees granted: Bachelors.

Attendance and degree information available by mail. Search requires name plus SSN, exact years of attendance. There is no fee.

College of Charleston, Registrar's Office, 66 George St, Charleston, SC 29424, 803-953-5668 (Fax: 803-953-6560). Hours: 8:30AM-5PM. Enrollment: 10000. Alumni records are maintained here also. Call 803-953-5630. Degrees granted: Bachelors; Masters.

Attendance and degree information available by phone, fax, mail. Search requires name plus SSN, approximate years of attendance. Also helpful: date of birth, exact years of attendance. There is no fee.

Columbia College, Registrar, 1301 Columbia College Dr, Columbia, SC 29203, 803-786-3672 (Fax: 803-786-3771). Hours: 8:30AM-5PM. Degrees granted: Bachelors; Masters.

Attendance and degree information available by phone, fax, mail. Search requires name plus SSN, approximate years of attendance. Also helpful: date of birth, exact years of attendance. There is no fee.

Columbia International University, Registrar, PO Box 3122, Columbia, SC 29203-3122, 803-754-4100 (Fax: 803-786-4209). Hours: 8AM-5PM. Records go back to 1927. Alumni records are maintained here also. Call 803-754-4100 X3004. Degrees granted: Associate; Bachelors; Masters; Doctorate.

Attendance and degree information available by phone, mail. Search requires name only. Also helpful: SSN, date of birth, exact years of attendance. There is no fee.

Columbia Junior College of Business, Registrar, PO Box 1196, 3810 Main St, Columbia, SC 29202, 803-799-9082 (Fax: 803-799-9005). Hours: 8AM-5:30PM. Records go back to 1935. Degrees granted: Associate.

Attendance and degree information available by phone, fax, mail. Search requires name plus SSN, approximate years of

attendance. Also helpful: date of birth, exact years of attendance. There is no fee.

Converse College, Registrar, 580 E Main St, Spartanburg, SC 29302-0006, 864-596-9094. Hours: 8:30AM-5PM. Enrollment: 1200. Records go back to 1800's. Alumni records are maintained here at the same phone number. Degrees granted: Bachelors; Masters; EDS.

Attendance and degree information available by fax, mail. Search requires name plus SSN, date of birth. Also helpful: exact years of attendance. There is no fee.

Denmark Technical College, Registrar, PO Box 327, Denmark, SC 29042, 803-793-3301 (Fax: 803-793-5942). Hours: 8:30AM-5PM. Degrees granted: Associate. Adverse incident record source- Dean of Students, 803-793-3301 X230: Public Safety, 803-793-3301 X273

Attendance and degree information available by mail. Search requires name plus SSN, date of birth, exact years of attendance, signed release. There is no fee.

Erskine College Seminary, Registrar, 2 Washington St, Due West, SC 29639, 864-379-8872. Hours: 8AM-5PM. Enrollment: 750. Records go back to 1890's. Alumni records are maintained here also. Call 803-379-8881. Degrees granted: Bachelors; Masters; Doctorate. Certification: Theology.

Attendance and degree information available by phone, fax, mail. Search requires name only. There is no fee.

Florence-Darlington Technical College, Registrar, PO Box 100548, Florence, SC 29501-0548, 803-661-8090 (Fax: 803-661-8041). Hours: 8:30AM-8PM M-Th, 8:30AM-5PM F. Enrollment: 3000. Records go back to 1963. Alumni records are maintained here also. Call 803-661-8000. Degrees granted: Associate. Special programs- Continuing Education, 803-661-8126. Adverse incident record source- Security Guard House, 803-661-8210: Student Disciplinary Reports, 803-661-8150

Attendance and degree information available by phone, fax, mail. Search requires name plus SSN. Also helpful: date of birth, exact years of attendance. There is no fee.

Forrest Junior College, Registrar, 601 E River St, Anderson, SC 29624, 864-225-7653 (Fax: 864-261-7471). Hours: 8AM-9PM. Enrollment: 110. Records go back to 1960. Degrees granted: Associate.

Attendance information available by phone, fax, mail. Search requires name plus SSN, exact years of attendance. Also helpful: approximate years of attendance. There is no fee.

Degree information available by phone, fax, mail. Search requires name plus SSN, exact years of attendance. There is no fee.

Francis Marion College, Registrar, PO Box 100547, Florence, SC 29501-0547, 803-661-1175 (Fax: 803-661-1219). Enrollment: 4000. Records go back to 1970. Alumni records are maintained here also. Call 803-661-1228. Degrees granted: Bachelors; Masters.

Attendance and degree information available by mail. Search requires name plus SSN. There is no fee.

Furman University, Registrar, 3300 Poinsett Hwy, Greenville, SC 29613, 864-294-2031 (Fax: 864-294-3551). Enrollment: 2500. Records go back to 1826. Alumni records are maintained here also. Call 864-294-3464. Degrees granted: Bachelors; Masters.

Attendance and degree information available by fax, mail. Search requires name plus SSN, exact years of attendance. There is no fee.

Greenville Technical College, Registrar, PO Box 5616, Greenville, SC 29606, 864-250-8117 (Fax: 864-250-8535). Hours: 8AM-7PM M-Th; 8AM-1PM F. Enrollment: 8000. Records go back to 1963. Alumni Records Office: Alumni

Association, Greenville Technical College, PO Box 5616, Greenville, SC 29606-5161. Degrees granted: Associate. Adverse incident record source- Student Services, 803-250-8100.

Attendance and degree information available by phone, fax, mail. Search requires name plus SSN. Also helpful: date of birth, exact years of attendance. There is no fee.

Horry-Georgetown Technical College, Registrar, PO Box 1966, Conway, SC 29526, 803-347-3186 (Fax: 803-347-2962). Hours: 8AM-8:30PM M-Th; 8AM-4:30PM F. Enrollment: 3200. Records go back to 1966. Alumni records are maintained here at the same phone number. Degrees granted: Associate. Adverse incident record source- Dean of Students, 803-349-5247.

Attendance and degree information available by phone, fax, mail. Search requires name plus SSN, date of birth. Also helpful: exact years of attendance. There is no fee.

ITT Technical Institute, Education Department, One Marcus Dr Ste 402, Greenville, SC 29615, 803-288-0777 (Fax: 803-297-0930). Hours: 8AM-5PM. Enrollment: 285. Records go back to 1992. Alumni records are maintained here at the same phone number. Degrees granted: Associate.

Attendance and degree information available by mail. Search requires name plus signed release. Also helpful: approximate years of attendance. There is no fee.

Johnson & Wales University, (Branch Campus), Registrar, 701 E Bay St, BTC Box 1409, Charleston, SC 29403, 803-727-3063 (Fax: 803-727-3094). Hours: 8:30AM-4:30PM. Enrollment: 1100. Records go back to 1984. Alumni Records Office: 8 Abbott Park Pl, Providence, RI 02903. Degrees granted: Associate; Bachelors. Special programs- Culinary Arts: Pastry Arts: Hotel Management. Adverse incident record source- Student Life, 803-727-3026.

Attendance and degree information available by phone, fax, mail. Search requires name plus SSN. Also helpful: exact years of attendance. There is no fee.

Lander University, Registrar, 320 Stanley Ave, Greenwood, SC 29649-2099, 864-229-8398 (Fax: 864-388-8890). Hours: 8AM-5PM. Records go back to 1872. Alumni records are maintained here also. Call 803-229-8351. Degrees granted: Bachelors; Masters.

Attendance and degree information available by phone, fax, mail. Search requires name plus SSN, exact years of attendance. There is no fee.

Limestone College, Registrar, 1115 College Dr, Gaffney, SC 29340, 864-489-7151 (Fax: 864-487-8706). Hours: 8:30AM-5PM. Records go back to 1895. Alumni records are maintained here also. Call 864-489-7151 X604. Degrees granted: Associate; Bachelors.

Attendance and degree information available by phone, fax, mail. Search requires name only. Also helpful: SSN, date of birth, exact years of attendance. There is no fee.

Lutheran Theological Southern Seminary, Registrar, 4201 N Main St, Columbia, SC 29203, 803-786-5150 X210 (Fax: 803-786-6499). Hours: 8:30AM-4:30PM. Records go back to 1880's. Alumni records are maintained here at the same phone number. Degrees granted: Bachelors; Masters.

Attendance and degree information available by phone, fax, mail. Search requires name plus SSN, exact years of attendance. There is no fee.

Medical University of South Carolina, Registrar, 171 Ashley Ave, Charleston, SC 29425, 803-792-3281 (Fax: 803-792-3764). Hours: 8AM-5PM. Enrollment: 2276. Records go back to 1946. Alumni records are maintained here also. Call 803-792-7979. Degrees granted: Bachelors; Masters; Doctorate.

Attendance information available by phone, fax, mail. Search requires name plus SSN. Also helpful: date of birth, exact years of attendance. There is no fee.

Degree information available by fax, mail. Search requires name plus SSN. Also helpful: date of birth, exact years of attendance. There is no fee.

Midlands Technical College, Registrar, PO Box 2408, Columbia, SC 29202, 803-738-7703 (Fax: 803-738-7880). Hours: 8AM-6:30PM M-Th; 8AM-4:30PM F. Enrollment: 9300. Records go back to 1905. Alumni records are maintained here also. Call 803-732-5333. Degrees granted: Associate. Adverse incident record source- SDS, 803-738-7699.

Attendance and degree information available by phone, fax, mail. Search requires name plus SSN. Also helpful: date of birth, approximate years of attendance. There is no fee.

Morris College, Registrar, 100 W College St, Sumter, SC 29150-3599, 803-775-9371 X225 (Fax: 803-773-3687). Enrollment: 900. Records go back to 1912. Alumni records are maintained here also. Call 803-775-9371 X226. Degrees granted: Bachelors. Adverse incident record source- Student Affairs, 803-775-9371 X217.

Attendance and degree information available by fax, mail. Search requires name plus SSN, exact years of attendance, signed release. There is no fee.

Newberry College, Registrar, 2100 College St, Newberry, SC 29108, 803-321-5124 (Fax: 803-321-5627). Hours: 8AM-4:30PM. Enrollment: 650. Alumni records are maintained here also. Call 803-321-5143. Degrees granted: Bachelors.

Attendance and degree information available by phone, fax, mail. Search requires name only. Also helpful: exact years of attendance. There is no fee.

North Greenville College, Records Office, PO Box 1892, Tigerville, SC 29688, 864-977-7009 (Fax: 864-977-7021). Hours: 8:30AM-5PM M-Th; 8:30AM-Noon F. Degrees granted: Associate; Bachelors.

Attendance information available by phone. Search requires name plus SSN. Also helpful: date of birth, exact years of attendance. There is no fee.

School will not confirm degree information.

Orangeburg-Calhoun Technical College, Registrar, 3250 St Matthews Rd, Orangeburg, SC 29115, 803-536-0311 (Fax: 803-535-1388). Hours: 8:30AM-5PM. Enrollment: 1780. Records go back to 1968. Degrees granted: Associate. Adverse incident record source- Campus Security, 803-535-1336.

Attendance information available by phone, fax, mail. Search requires name plus SSN, approximate years of attendance. Also helpful: date of birth. There is no fee.

Degree information available by fax, mail. Search requires name plus SSN, approximate years of attendance. Also helpful: date of birth. There is no fee.

Piedmont Technical College, Student Records, Emerald Rd, Greenwood, SC 29648, 864-941-8364 (Fax: 864-941-8566). Hours: 8AM-8:30PM M-Th; 8AM-5PM F. Enrollment: 3300. Records go back to 1966. Alumni records are maintained here also. Call 864-941-8304. Degrees granted: Associate. Adverse incident record source- Student Development, 803-941-8358.

Attendance and degree information available by phone, fax, mail. Search requires name plus SSN. Also helpful: exact years of attendance. There is no fee.

Presbyterian College, Registrar, S Broad St, PO Box 975, Clinton, SC 29325, 864-833-8224 (Fax: 864-833-8481). Hours: 9AM-5PM. Alumni records are maintained here also. Call 864-833-8211. Degrees granted: Bachelors. Adverse incident record source- Dean of Students, 864-833-8275.

Attendance and degree information available by phone, fax, mail. Search requires name only. Also helpful: SSN, date of birth, exact years of attendance. There is no fee.

Sherman College of Straight Chiropractic, Registrar, 2020 Springfield Rd, PO Box 1452, Spartanburg, SC 29304, 864-578-8770 (Fax: 864-599-7145). Hours: 8AM-4:30PM. Enrollment: 288. Records go back to 1976. Alumni records are maintained here at the same phone number. Degrees granted: Doctorate. Adverse incident record source- Dean of Student Services.

Attendance and degree information available by phone, fax, mail. Search requires name only. Also helpful: SSN, date of birth, exact years of attendance. There is no fee.

South Carolina State University, Registrar, 300 College Ave NE, PO Box 1627, Orangeburg, SC 29117, 803-536-7185 (Fax: 803-536-8990). Hours: 8AM-5PM. Records go back to 1896. Alumni records are maintained here also. Call 803-536-8946. Degrees granted: Bachelors; Masters; Doctorate.

Attendance and degree information available by phone, mail. Search requires name plus SSN, date of birth, exact years of attendance. There is no fee.

Southern Wesleyan University, Registrar, PO Box 1020, Central, SC 29630-1020, 864-639-2453 X325 (Fax: 864-639-1956). Hours: 8AM-4:30PM. Enrollment: 1271. Formerly Central Wesleyan College Records go back to 1906. Alumni records are maintained here also. Call 864-639-2453 X368. Degrees granted: Bachelors; Masters. Adverse incident record source- Student Life, 864-639-2453 X340.

Attendance and degree information available by phone, fax, mail. Search requires name plus SSN. There is no fee.

Spartanburg Methodist College, Registrar, 1200 Textile Rd, Spartanburg, SC 29301-0009, 864-587-4232 (Fax: 864-587-4355). Hours: 8AM-5PM. Records go back to 1911. Alumni records are maintained here also. Call 864-587-4220. Degrees granted: Associate. Adverse incident record source- STudent Affairs, 864-584-4264.

Attendance and degree information available by phone, fax, mail. Search requires name plus exact years of attendance. Also helpful: SSN. There is no fee.

Spartanburg Technical College, Registrar, PO Drawer 4386, Spartanburg, SC 29305-4386, 864-591-3680 (Fax: 864-591-3689). Hours: 8AM-6:30PM M,T; 8AM-5PM W,Th; 8AM-1:30PM F. Enrollment: 2476. Records go back to 1962. Degrees granted: Associate.

Attendance and degree information available by phone, fax, mail. Search requires name plus SSN. Also helpful: exact years of attendance. There is no fee.

Technical College of the Lowcountry, Registrar, 921 S Ribaut Rd, PO Box 1288, Beaufort, SC 29902, 803-525-8210 (Fax: 803-525-8285). Hours: 8:30AM-5PM. Enrollment: 1356. Records go back to 1988. Alumni records are maintained here at the same phone number. Degrees granted: Associate. Adverse incident record source- Student Development, 803-525-8228.

Attendance information available by phone, fax, mail. Search requires name plus SSN. Also helpful: date of birth, exact years of attendance. There is no fee.

Degree information available by phone. Search requires name only. Also helpful: SSN. There is no fee.

Tri-County Technical College, Student Records, PO Box 587, Pendleton, SC 29670, 864-646-8361 X2198 (Fax: 864-646-8256). Hours: 8AM-9PM. Records go back to 1961. Alumni records are maintained here at the same phone number. Degrees granted: Associate.

Attendance information available by phone, fax, mail. Search requires name plus SSN. Also helpful: exact years of attendance. There is no fee.

Degree information available by phone, fax, mail. Search requires name plus SSN. Also helpful: date of birth, exact years of attendance. There is no fee.

Trident Technical College, Admissions & Records, AM-M, PO Box 118067, Charleston, SC 29423-8067, 864-572-6129 (Fax: 864-569-6483). Hours: 8AM-6:30PM M-Th; 8AM-1PM F. Records go back to 1970's. TTC from 1970's; Berkeley, Charlston, Dorchester Tech to 1950's; Palmer College from 1970's. Degrees granted: Associate. Adverse incident record source- Public Safety, 864-572-6024.

Attendance information available by phone, fax, mail. Search requires name plus SSN, date of birth. Also helpful: exact years of attendance. There is no fee.

Degree information available by phone, fax, mail. Search requires name plus SSN, date of birth, approximate years of attendance. Also helpful: exact years of attendance. There is no fee.

University of South Carolina-Aiken, Registrar, 171 University Pkwy, Aiken, SC 29801, 803-648-6851 (Fax: 803-641-3494). Hours: 8AM-5PM. Transcript records are housed at University of South Carolina, Registrar, Columbia, SC, 29208. Alumni records are maintained here also. Call 803-641-3480. Degrees granted: Associate; Bachelors. Adverse incident record source- Public Safety, 803-648-6851.

Attendance and degree information available by phone, fax, mail. Search requires name plus SSN. There is no fee.

University of South Carolina-Beaufort, Registrar, 801 Carteret St, Beaufort, SC 29902, 803-521-4100 (Fax: 803-521-4198). Hours: 8:30AM-5PM. Enrollment: 1350. Transcript records are housed at University of South Carolina, Registrar, Columbia, SC, 29208. Alumni records are maintained here at the same phone number. Degrees granted: Associate. Adverse incident record source- Student Services.

Attendance and degree information available by phone, fax, mail. Search requires name plus SSN. Also helpful: approximate years of attendance. There is no fee.

University of South Carolina-Columbia, Registrar, Columbia, SC 29208, 803-777-5555 (Fax: 803-777-6349). Enrollment: 38000. Records go back to 1801. Alumni records are maintained here also. Call 803-777-4111. Degrees granted: Associate; Bachelors; Doctorate; MD, JD.

Attendance and degree information available by phone, fax, mail. Search requires name plus SSN. Also helpful: date of birth, exact years of attendance. There is no fee.

University of South Carolina-Lancaster, Registrar, PO Box 889, Lancaster, SC 29721, 803-285-7471 (Fax: 803-289-7116). Hours: 8:30AM-5PM. Enrollment: 1200. Transcript records are housed at University of South Carolina, Registrar, Columbia, SC, 29208. Alumni records are maintained here at the same phone number. Degrees granted: Associate; Nursing, Criminal Justice, Business (2yr Associate Degrees).

Attendance information available by phone, fax, mail. Search requires name plus SSN. Also helpful: date of birth, exact years of attendance. There is no fee.

Degree information available by written request only. Search requires name plus SSN. Also helpful: date of birth, exact years of attendance. There is no fee.

University of South Carolina-Salkehatchie, Registrar, PO Box 617, Allendale, SC 29810, 803-584-3446. Records are not housed here. They are located at University of South Carolina-Columbia, Registrar, Columbia, SC 29208.

University of South Carolina-Spartanburg, Registrar, 800 University Wy, Spartanburg, SC 29303, 864-503-5220 (Fax: 864-503-5727). Enrollment: 3300. Records go back

to 1967. Transcript records are housed at University of South Carolina, Registrar, Columbia, SC, 29208. Alumni records are maintained here also. Call 864-503-5235. Degrees granted: Associate; Bachelors; Masters. Adverse incident record source-Student Affairs, 864-503-5194.

Attendance information available by phone, fax, mail. Search requires name plus SSN. There is no fee.

Degree information available by written request only. Search requires name plus SSN. There is no fee.

University of South Carolina-Sumter, Registrar, 200 Miller Rd, Sumter, SC 29150, 803-777-3871 (Fax: 803-777-6349). Hours: 8:30AM-5PM. Enrollment: 1200. Transcript records are housed at University of South Carolina, Registrar, Columbia, SC, 29208. Alumni records are maintained here also. Call 803-775-6341. Degrees granted: Associate.

Attendance and degree information available by phone, fax, mail. Search requires name plus SSN. Also helpful: exact years of attendance. There is no fee.

University of South Carolina-Union, Registrar, PO Drawer 729, Union, SC 29379, 864-429-8728 (Fax: 864-427-3682). Enrollment: 400. Records go back to 1965. Transcript records are housed at University of South Carolina, Registrar, Columbia, SC, 29208. Alumni records are maintained here at the same phone number. Degrees granted: Associate.

Attendance information available by phone, fax, mail. Search requires name plus SSN. There is no fee.

Degree information available by written request only. Search requires name plus SSN. Fee is $5.00.

Voorhees College, Registrar, 1141 Voorhees Rd, PO Box 678, Denmark, SC 29042, 803-793-3351 X7309 (Fax: 803-793-4584). Hours: 8AM-5PM. Enrollment: 715. Records go back to 1897. Alumni records are maintained here also. Call 803-793-3351. Degrees granted: Bachelors.

Attendance and degree information available by phone, mail. Search requires name plus SSN, exact years of attendance. There is no fee.

Williamsburg Technical College, Registrar, 601 Martin Luther King Jr. Ave, Kingstree, SC 29556-4197, 803-354-2021 X165 (Fax: 803-354-7269). Hours: Noon-8PM M,W,Th,F. Enrollment: 622. Records go back to 1969. Alumni records are maintained here at the same phone number. Degrees granted: Associate.

Attendance and degree information available by phone, fax, mail. Search requires name plus SSN. Also helpful: date of birth, exact years of attendance. There is no fee.

Winthrop University, Records & Registration, 101 Tillman Hall, Rock Hill, SC 29733, 803-323-2194 (Fax: 803-323-4600). Hours: 8:30AM-5PM. Enrollment: 5000. Records go back to 1886. Alumni Records Office: 304 Tillman Hall, Rock Hill, SC 29733, 803-323-2145. Degrees granted: Bachelors; Masters. Adverse incident record source- Public Safety, 803-323-3333.

Attendance information available by phone, fax, mail. Search requires name plus SSN, approximate years of attendance. Also helpful: exact years of attendance. There is no fee.

Degree information available by phone, fax, mail. Search requires name plus SSN. Also helpful: date of birth, exact years of attendance. There is no fee.

Wofford College, Registrar, 429 N Church St, Spartanburg, SC 29303-3663, 864-597-4030 (Fax: 864-597-4019). Hours: 8:30AM-5PM. Enrollment: 1100. Records go back to 1854. Alumni records are maintained here at the same phone number. Degrees granted: Bachelors. Adverse incident record source- Public Safety, 864-597-4350: Student Affairs, 864-592-4040

Attendance and degree information available by phone, fax, mail. Search requires name only. There is no fee.

York Technical College, Student Records, 452 S Anderson Rd, Rock Hill, SC 29730, 803-327-8002 (Fax: 803-327-8059). Hours: 8AM-7PM M-Th; 8AM-5PM F. Enrollment: 500. Records go back to 1964. Degrees granted: Associate. Adverse incident record source- Security Office, 803-327-8013.

Attendance and degree information available by phone, fax, mail. Search requires name plus SSN. Also helpful: exact years of attendance. There is no fee.

Trade and Vocational Schools

Alpha Beauty School, 10 Liberty Ln, Greenville, SC 29607, 864-370-0693

Alpha Beauty School (Branch Campus), 2619 S Main St, Anderson, SC 29624, 864-224-8338

Alpha Beauty School (Branch Campus), 85 Tunnell Rd, Asheville, SC 28805, 704-253-2875

Betty Stevens Cosmetology Institute, 301 Rainbow Dr, Florence, SC 29501, 803-669-4452

Camden Lugoff - Elgin Cosmetology College, PO Box 1419, Lugoff, SC 29078, 803-408-0050

Charleston Cosmetology Institute, 8484 Dorchester Rd, Charleston, SC 29420, 803-552-3670

Charzzanne Beauty College, 1549 Hwy 72 E, Greenwood, SC 29649, 803-223-7321

Dudley Beauty College, 505 Seventh Ave N, Myrtle Beach, SC 29577, 803-665-4602

Dudley Beauty College (Branch Campus), 1125 15-401 By-Pass #A, Bennettsville, SC 29512, 803-479-4076

Dudley Beauty College (Branch Campus), 1810-B Second Loop Rd, Florence, SC 29501, 803-665-4602

Dudley Beauty College (Branch Campus), 1235 S Pleasantburg Dr #A, Greenville, SC 29605, 803-299-0000

Dudley Beauty College (Branch Campus), Martintown Plaza, North Augusta, SC 29841, 803-278-1238

Dudley Beauty College (Branch Campus), 1930 N Cherry Rd, Rock Hill, SC 29730, 803-328-1838

Dudley Beauty College (Branch Campus), 256 S Pike Rd, Sumter, SC 29150, 803-773-8481

Farah's Beauty School, 520 Bush River Rd, Columbia, SC 29210, 803-772-0101

North American Institute of Aviation, PO Box 680, Conway, SC 29526, 803-397-9111

Professional Hair Design Academy, 1540 Wade Hampton Blvd, Greenville, SC 29607, 803-232-2676

Royal Academy of Hair Design, 200 W Main St, Clinton, SC 29325, 864-833-6976

South Carolina Criminal Justice Academy, 5400 Broad River Rd, Columbia, SC 29210, 803-737-7779

Sumter Beauty College, 921 Carolina Ave, Sumter, SC 29150, 803-773-7311

State Licensing & Business Registration Quick Finder Index

Architecture, Engineering & Surveying

Architect #3 .... ☎ 803-734-9752
Architecture Business Corporations #3......... ☎ 803-734-9752
Architecture Partnership or LLP #3 .... ☎ 803-734-9752
Architecture Professional Corp/Assoc. or Lic #3
.... ☎ 803-734-9752
Engineer #7.................................... ☎ 803-737-9260
Geologist #20.................................. ☎ 803-734-4231
Landscape Architect #7 .... ☎ 803-734-9169
Surveyor #7 (17660)............................ ☎ 803-737-9260

Business - Court & Legal Services

Attorney #48 (9000) .... ☎ 803-799-6653
Lobbyist #36 (700) .... ☎ 803-253-4193
Notary Public #36.............................. ☎ 803-734-2119

Business - General Services

Auctioneer #50 .... ☎ 803-734-4233
Public Accountant-CPA #2 (4000) .... ☎ 803-734-4228
Weighmaster #25 (3000) .... ☎ 803-734-2210

Construction & Manufacturing

Contractor #24 .... ☎ 803-734-4274
Electrician #42 (1940) .... ☎ 803-799-9574
Elevator Service #39 (6000).................... ☎ 803-734-9711
Mobile Home Manufacturer #41 (600) .... ☎ 803-734-4170
Plumbing #42................................... ☎ 803-799-9574
Residential Home Builder #45 (9000)........... ☎ 803-734-4255
Sheet Metal & Pipefitting #42.................. ☎ 803-799-9574

Education

School Guidance Counselor #26 .... ☎ 803-734-8466
School Media Communications Specialist #26
.... ☎ 803-734-8466
School Principal/Supervisor #26................ ☎ 803-734-8466
School Superintendent #26...................... ☎ 803-734-8466
Teacher #26 .... ☎ 803-734-8466

Environmental & Agriculture

Agricultural Dealer & Handler #25 (200)...... ☎ 803-734-2210
Forester #37 (900) .... ☎ 803-734-4224
Municipal Solid Waste Landfill Operator #30
(300) .... ✉ 803-896-4207
Percolation Test Technician #35 (29) 803-734-9113
Pesticide Applicator #33 (4000).................... ☎ 803-646-2155
Pesticide Dealer #33 (330) .... ☎ 803-646-2155
Soil Classifier #40 (26)........................ ☎ 803-734-9100
Veterinarian #23 .... ☎ 803-734-4170
Waste Water Treatment Plant Operator #35 803-734-9113
Well Driller #35............................... 803-734-9113

Financial - Real Estate, Insurance & Banking

Financial Institution #10 (54)................... ☎ 803-734-2001
Insurance Agent #31............................. ✉ 803-737-6095
Investment Advisor #47 (640)................... ☎ 803-734-1095

Real Estate Appraiser #43..................... ☎ 803-734-4170
Real Estate Broker #44 (30000) .... ☎ 803-737-0700
Securities Agent #47 (50310) .... ☎ 803-734-1095
Securities Broker/Dealer #47 (1387).............. ☎ 803-734-1095

Health & Beauty

Apprentice Optician #14....................... ☎ 803-734-4162
Barber #46 (50)............................... ☎ 803-737-9114
Barber Apprentice #46......................... ☎ 803-734-4224
Chiropractor #4 (1)............................ ☎ 803-734-4246
Cosmetologist #5 .... ☎ 803-734-9660
Dental Hygienist #6 803-734-8904
Dental Specialist #6 803-734-8904
Dental Techician #6 803-734-8904
Dentist #6.................................... 803-734-8904
EMS (Ambulance Co) #27 .... ☎ 803-737-7204
Embalmer #11 .... ☎ 803-734-4238
Emergency Medical Technician #27 (5500)
.... ☎ 803-737-7204
Funeral Director #11 .... ☎ 803-734-4238
Hearing Aid Dispenser/Fitter #29 (72).......... ☎ 803-737-7202
Heating & Air/Gas Fitting #42 .... ☎ 803-799-9574
Manicurist #46 .... ☎ 803-734-4224
Master Hair Care Specialist #46................ ☎ 803-734-4224
Medical Doctor #38 .... ☎ 803-737-9300
Nurse #12..................................... ☎ 803-731-1648
Nursing Home Administrator #32 (294)........✉ 803-737-9253
Occupational Therapist #13 (760) .... ☎ 803-734-4175
Optician #14 (668)............................. ☎ 803-734-4162
Optometrist #9 .... ☎ 803-734-4162
Osteopathic Physician #38...................... ☎ 803-737-9300
Pharmacist/Pharmacy Stores #15 (5000)....... ☎ 803-734-1010
Physical Therapist #16......................... ☎ 803-734-4170
Physician Assistant #38........................ ☎ 803-737-9300
Podiatrist #17................................. ☎ 803-734-4170
Psychologist #18.............................. ☎ 803-734-4170
Registered Barber #46 .... ☎ 803-734-4224
Respiratory Care Practitioner #38 .... ☎ 803-737-9300
Sanitarian #28 803-935-7958
Speech Pathologist/Audiologist #22............. ☎ 803-734-4170

Investigations & Security

Burglar Alarm Contractor #24.................. ☎ 803-734-4274
Fire Protection Contractor #24 .... ☎ 803-734-4274
Polygraph Examiner #51 .... ☎ 803-737-9000
Private Detective #51.......................... ☎ 803-737-9000

Social Services

Community Residential Care #32................✉ 803-737-9253
Marriage & Family Therapist #8 (300) .... ☎ 803-734-4244
Professional Counselor #8 (1000) .... ☎ 803-734-4244
Social Worker #21 (4000) .... ☎ 803-734-4241

Sports & Entertainment

Alcoholic Beverage Control #34 .... ☎ 803-734-0470
Amusement Rides #39 (900) .... ☎ 803-734-9711
Athletic Trainer #49........................... ☎ 803-734-9015

Pyrotechnic Technician #19 .... ☎ 803-734-4170
Swimming Pool/Spa Operator #35 803-737-9113

Transportation
Pilot #1 803-822-5400

State Licensing & Business Registration Agency Information

(1) Aeronautics Commission, Flight Operations, PO Box 280068, Columbia, SC 29228-0068, 803-822-5400, Fax: 803-822-4312

(2) Board of Accountancy, 3600 Forest Dr, Suite 101, PO Box 11329 (28211), Columbia, SC 29204, 803-734-4228, Fax: 803-734-9571

(3) Board of Architectural Examiners, 3710 Landmark Dr, Suite 206, Columbia, SC 29204, 803-734-9752, Fax: 803-734-9731

(4) Board of Chiropractic Examiners, PO Box 11329, Columbia, SC 29210-1329, 803-731-4246, Fax: 803-734-4824

(5) Board of Cosmetology, 3600 Forest Dr., Suite 101, Columbia, SC 29204, 803-734-9660, Fax: 803-734-4284

(6) Board of Dentistry, PO Box 11329, Columbia, SC 29211-1329, 803-734-4215, Fax: 803-734-4216

(7) Board of Engineers & Land Surveyors, 3700 Forest Dr., Suite 404, Columbia, SC 29204, 803-737-9260, Fax: 803-737-9270

(8) Board of Examiners, Prof. Counselors & Marital & Family Therapists, PO Box 11329 3600 Forest Dr., Suite 101, Columbia, SC 29211, 803-734-4244, Fax: 803-734-4284

(9) Board of Examiners in Optometry, PO Box 11329, Columbia, SC 29211, 803-734-4162

(10) Board of Financial Institutions, Examining Division, 1015 Sumter St., Columbia, SC 29201, 803-734-2001, Fax: 803-734-2013

(11) Board of Funeral Service, 3600 Forest Dr, Suite 101, PO Box 11329, Columbia, SC 29211-1329, 803-734-4238, Fax: 803-734-4284

(12) Board of Nursing, 220 Executive Center Dr, Suite 220, Columbia, SC 29210, 803-731-1648, Fax: 803-731-1647

(13) Board of Occupational Therapy, PO Box 11329 3600 Forest Dr., Columbia, SC 29211, 803-734-4175, Fax: 803-734-4218

(14) Board of Opticianry Examiners, PO Box 11329, Columbia, SC 29211, 803-734-4162, Fax: 803-734-4218

(15) Board of Pharmacy, PO Box 11927 1026 Sumter St., Suite 208, Columbia, SC 29211, 803-734-1010, Fax: 803-734-1552

(16) Board of Physical Therapy Examiners, 3600 Forest Dr., Suite 203 PO Box 11329, Columbia, SC 29204, 803-734-4170, Fax: 803-734-4218

(17) Board of Podiatry Examiners, 1410 Westway Dr, PO Box 11329, Columbia, SC 29211, 803-734-4170

(18) Board of Psychology Examiners, PO Box 11329, Columbia, SC 29211, 803-734-4170

(19) Board of Pyrotechnic Safety, PO Box 11329, Columbia, SC 29211, 803-734-4170

(20) Board of Registration for Geologists, PO Box 11329 3600 Forest Dr., Columbia, SC 29204, 803-734-4231, Fax: 803-734-4284

(21) Board of Social Work Examiners, PO Box 11329, Columbia, SC 29211, 803-734-4241, Fax: 803-634-4251

(22) Board of Speech-Language Pathology & Audiology, PO Box 11329, Columbia, SC 29211, 803-734-4170

(23) Board of Veterinary Medical Examiners, PO Box 11329, Columbia, SC 29211, 803-734-4170

(24) Contractor's Licensing Board, PO Box 11329, Columbia, SC 29211, 803-734-4274, Fax: 803-734-4269

(25) Department of Agriculture, Adminstration Division, 1101 William St., Columbia, SC 29201, 803-734-2210, Fax: 803-737-9703

(26) Department of Education, 1429 Senate St, 1015 Rutledge Bldg, Columbia, SC 29201, 803-734-8466, Fax: 803-734-2873

(27) Department of Health & Environmental Control, Division of Emergency Medical Services, 2600 Bull St, Columbia, SC 29201, 803-737-7204, Fax: 803-737-7212

(28) Department of Health & Environmental Control, Division of Environmental Health/Food, 2600 Bull St, Columbia, SC 29201, 803-935-7958, Fax: 803-935-7825

(29) Department of Health & Environmental Control, Division of Health Licensing, 2600 Bull St, Columbia, SC 29201, 803-737-7202, Fax: 803-737-7212

(30) Department of Health & Environmental Control, Division of Solid Waste Management, 2600 Bull St, Columbia, SC 29201, 803-896-4000, Fax: 803-896-4001

(31) Department of Insurance, Licensing & Taxation, 1612 Marion St., Columbia, SC 29201, 803-737-6095, Fax: 803-737-6232

(32) Department of LLR, Board of Long Term Health Care Administrators, 3700 Forest Drive, Suite 105, Columbia, SC 29204, 803-737-9253, Fax: 803-737-9251

(33) Department of Pesticide Regulation, Clemson University, Agricultural Center, 511 Westinghouse Rd., P, Penlleton, SC 29670, 864-646-2155, Fax: 864-646-2179

(34) Department of Revenue & Taxation, Alcoholic Beverage Licensing Division, PO Box 125 301 Gervais St., Columbia, SC 29214, 803-734-0470, Fax: 803-734-1401

(35) Environmental Certification Board, , Columbia, SC 29205, 803-734-9140, Fax: 803-737-9255

(36) Ethics Commission, PO Box 11926 500 Thurman Mall, Suite 250, Columbia, SC 29201, 803-253-4193, Fax: 803-253-7539

(37) LLR Board of Registration for Foresters, PO Box 11329, Columbia, SC 29211, 803-734-4224, Fax: 803-734-4284

(38) LLR SC State Board of Medical Examiners, PO Box 11289, Columbia, SC 29211-1289, 803-737-9300

(39) Labor Department, Licensing, 3600 Forest Dr., Columbia, SC 29204, 803-734-9711, Fax: 803-737-9119

(40) Land Resources Conservation Commission, Soil Classifiers Registration, 2221 Devine St, Suite 222, Columbia, SC 29205-2474, 803-734-9100, Fax: 803-734-9200

(41) Manufactured Housing Board, 3600 Forest Dr., Suite 100, Columbia, SC 29204, 803-734-4255, Fax: 803-734-4267

(42) Municipal Association of South Carolina, 1529 Washington St (29201), PO Box 12109, Columbia, SC 29211, 803-799-9574 ext. 1209, Fax: 803-799-9520

(43) Real Estate Appraisal Board, PO Box 11329, Columbia, SC 29211, 803-734-4170

(44) Real Estate Commission, 1201 Main St, Suite 1500, Columbia, SC 29201, 803-737-0700, Fax: 803-737-0848

(45) Residential Home Builders Commission, 3600 Forest Dr., Suite 100, Columbia, SC 29204, 803-734-4255, Fax: 803-734-4267

(46) SC Dept. Labor, Licensing & Regulation, PO Box 11329, Columbia, SC 29211-1329, 803-734-4224, Fax: 803-734-4284

(47)   Secretary of State, Securities Division, PO Box 11549, Columbia, SC 29211-1549, 803-734-1095

(48)   South Carolina State Supreme Court, PO Box 608 950 Taylor Street, Columbia, SC 29201, 803-799-6653, Fax: 803-799-4118

(49)   State Athletic Commission, 3600 Forest Dr. Suite 101, PO Box 11329, Columbia, SC 29211, 803-734-9015, Fax: 803-734-4284

(50)   State Auctioneer's Commission, 3600 Forest Dr, Suite 101, PO Box 11329, Columbia, SC 29211, 803-734-4233, Fax: 803-734-4284

(51)   State Law Enforcement Division, Regulatory Services, 4400 Broad River Rd, Columbia, SC 29210, 803-737-9000, Fax: 803-896-7041

South Dakota

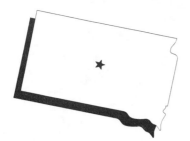

Capitol: Pierre (Hughs County)	
State Population	.7 Million
Number of Degree Granting Institutions:	24
Number of State Licensing & Business Registration Agencies:	77

Degree Granting Educational Institutions

Augustana College, Registrar, 29th St and Summit Ave, Sioux Falls, SD 57197, 605-336-4121 (Fax: 605-336-4450). Hours: 8AM-5PM. Enrollment: 1700. Records go back to 1889. Alumni records are maintained here also. Call 605-336-5230. Degrees granted: Associate; Bachelors; Masters. Adverse incident record source- Student Services, 605-336-4124.

Attendance and degree information available by phone, fax, mail. Search requires name plus SSN, approximate years of attendance. Also helpful: date of birth, exact years of attendance. There is no fee.

Black Hills State University, Admissions & Records, 1200 University Ave, USB 9502, Spearfish, SD 57799-9502, 605-642-6011 (Fax: 605-642-6214). Hours: 7AM-4PM. Enrollment: 2700. Records go back to 1885. Alumni records are maintained here also. Call 605-642-6228. Degrees granted: Associate; Bachelors; Masters. Adverse incident record source- Student Life, 605-642-6464.

Attendance and degree information available by fax, mail. Search requires name plus SSN, signed release. Also helpful: date of birth, exact years of attendance. There is no fee.

Dakota State University, Registrar, 820 N Washington St, Madison, SD 57042, 605-256-5145 (Fax: 605-256-5020). Hours: 8AM-5PM. Records go back to 1881. Alumni records are maintained here also. Call 605-256-5122. Degrees granted: Associate; Bachelors.

Attendance and degree information available by phone, fax, mail. Search requires name only. Also helpful: SSN, date of birth, exact years of attendance. There is no fee.

Dakota Wesleyan University, Registrar, 1200 W University, Campus Box 903, Mitchell, SD 57301, 605-995-2642 (Fax: 605-995-2643). Hours: 8AM-Noon, 1-5PM. Enrollment: 600. Records go back to 1896. Also have records from Methodist School of Nursing. Alumni records are maintained here at the same phone number. Alumni Records Office: PO Box 908, Mitchell, SD 57301. Degrees granted: Associate; Bachelors; Masters. Adverse incident record source- Campus Life.

Attendance and degree information available by phone, fax, mail. Search requires name only. Also helpful: SSN, date of birth, exact years of attendance. There is no fee.

Huron University, Registrar, 333 Ninth St SW, Huron, SD 57350, 605-352-8721 (Fax: 605-352-7421). Hours: 8AM-5PM. Enrollment: 1200. Records go back to 1883. Alumni records are maintained here at the same phone number. Degrees granted: Associate; Bachelors; Masters.

Attendance and degree information available by phone, fax, mail. Search requires name only. Also helpful: SSN, date of birth, exact years of attendance. There is no fee.

Kilian Community College, Registrar, 224 S Phillips Ave, Sioux Falls, SD 57102, 605-336-1711 (Fax: 605-336-2606). Hours: 8AM-5PM. Enrollment: 180. Records go back to 1977. Alumni records are maintained here at the same phone number. Degrees granted: Associate.

Attendance and degree information available by phone, fax, mail. Search requires name only. Also helpful: SSN, date of birth, approximate years of attendance. Fee is $2.00.

Lake Area Vocational-Technical Institute, Registrar, 230 11th St NE, Watertown, SD 57201, 605-882-5284 (Fax: 605-882-6299). Hours: 8AM-5PM. Enrollment: 1200. Records go back to 1965. Alumni records are maintained here at the same phone number. Degrees granted: Associate.

Attendance and degree information available by phone, fax, mail. Search requires name only. Also helpful: SSN, exact years of attendance. There is no fee.

Mitchell Technical Institute, Registrar, 821 N Capital St, Mitchell, SD 57301, 605-995-3024 (Fax: 605-996-3299). Hours: 8AM-5PM. Enrollment: 700. Records go back to 1968. Degrees granted: Associate.

Attendance and degree information available by phone, mail. Search requires name plus SSN, exact years of attendance. There is no fee.

Mount Marty College, Registrar, 1105 W Eighth St, Yankton, SD 57078, 605-668-1515 (Fax: 605-668-1607). Hours: 8AM-5PM. Enrollment: 1000. Records go back to 1936. Alumni records are maintained here also. Call 605-668-1526. Degrees granted: Associate; Bachelors; Masters. Certification: Secretarial, Computer Management.

Attendance and degree information available by phone, fax, mail. Search requires name plus SSN, date of birth. Also helpful: exact years of attendance. There is no fee.

National College, Registrar's Office, PO Box 1780, Rapid City, SD 57709, 605-394-4907 (Fax: 605-394-4869). Hours: 8AM-5PM. Enrollment: 2000. Records go back to 1950's. Degrees granted: Associate; Bachelors.

Attendance and degree information available by phone, fax, mail. Search requires name only. Also helpful: SSN, date of birth, exact years of attendance. There is no fee.

Nettleton Junior College, Registrar, 100 S Spring Ave, Sioux Falls, SD 57104, 605-336-1837 (Fax: 605-336-7626). Hours: 8AM-9:30PM. Enrollment: 150. Records go back to 1919. Alumni records are maintained here at the same phone number. Degrees granted: Associate. Adverse incident record source- Director's Office .

Attendance and degree information available by phone, fax, mail. Search requires name plus approximate years of attendance. Also helpful: SSN, date of birth, exact years of attendance. There is no fee.

North American Baptist Seminary, Registrar, 1525 S Grange Ave, Sioux Falls, SD 57105-1599, 605-336-6588 (Fax: 605-335-9090). Hours: 8AM-4:30PM. Degrees granted: Masters; Doctorate.

Attendance and degree information available by phone, fax, mail. Search requires name only. Also helpful: exact years of attendance. There is no fee.

Northern State University, Registrar, 1200 S Jay St, Aberdeen, SD 57401, 605-626-2012 (Fax: 605-626-2587). Hours: 8AM-5PM; 7:30AM-4:30PM Summer. Enrollment: 2700. Records go back to 1902. Alumni records are maintained here at the same phone number. Degrees granted: Associate; Bachelors; Masters. Adverse incident record source- Student Affairs, 605-626-2530.

Attendance and degree information available by phone, fax, mail. Search requires name only. Also helpful: SSN, date of birth, exact years of attendance. There is no fee.

Oglala Lakota College, Registrar, PO Box 490, Kyle, SD 57752, 605-455-2321 X236 (Fax: 605-455-2787). Hours: 8:30AM-5PM. Enrollment: 1000. Records go back to 1978. Degrees granted: Associate; Bachelors; Masters. Special programs- Lakota Studies, 605-455-2321 X236. Adverse incident record source- Registrar's Office .

Attendance information available by phone, fax, mail. Search requires name plus SSN. Also helpful: exact years of attendance. There is no fee.

Degree information available by phone, mail. Search requires name plus SSN. Also helpful: exact years of attendance. There is no fee.

Presentation College, Registrar, 1500 N Main St, Aberdeen, SD 57401, 605-229-8426 X424 (Fax: 605-229-8489). Hours: 8AM-4:30PM. Enrollment: 380. Records go back to 1950. Alumni records are maintained here also. Call 605-229-8442. Degrees granted: Associate; Bachelors. Adverse incident record source- Registrar's Office .

Attendance and degree information available by phone, fax, mail. Search requires name only. Also helpful: SSN, exact years of attendance. There is no fee.

Sinte Gleska University, Registrar, PO Box 490, Rosebud, SD 57570, 605-747-2263 (Fax: 605-747-2098). Hours: 9AM-5PM. Enrollment: 780. Records go back to 1972. Degrees granted: Associate; Bachelors; Masters.

Attendance information available by phone, fax, mail. Search requires name plus SSN, date of birth. Also helpful: exact years of attendance. There is no fee.

Degree information available by phone, fax, mail. Search requires name plus SSN. Also helpful: date of birth, exact years of attendance. There is no fee.

Sioux Falls College, Registrar, 1501 S Prairie, Sioux Falls, SD 57105, 605-331-5000 (Fax: 605-361-6615). Enrollment: 1000. Records go back to 1883. Alumni records are maintained here at the same phone number. Degrees granted: Bachelors. Adverse incident record source- Security.

Attendance and degree information available by phone, mail. Search requires name plus SSN, exact years of attendance. There is no fee.

Sisseton-Wahpeton Community College, Registrar, PO Box 689 Old Agency, Agency Village, SD 57262, 605-698-3966 (Fax: 605-698-3132). Hours: 8AM-5PM. Enrollment: 200. Records go back to 1979. Alumni records are maintained here at the same phone number. Degrees granted: Associate. Adverse incident record source- Student Services, 605-698-8966 X14.

Attendance and degree information available by phone, mail. Search requires name plus SSN, exact years of attendance. There is no fee.

South Dakota School of Mines and Technology, Registrar, 501 E St. Joseph St, Rapid City, SD 57701, 605-394-2414 (Fax: 605-394-6131). Hours: 7:30AM-4:30PM. Enrollment: 2500. Records go back to 1800's. Alumni records are maintained here also. Call 605-394-2347. Degrees granted: Bachelors; Masters; Doctorate. Adverse incident record source- Dean of Students.

Attendance and degree information available by phone, fax, mail. Search requires name only. Also helpful: SSN, date of birth. There is no fee.

South Dakota State University, Registrar, Box 2201 University Station, Brookings, SD 57007, 605-688-4121 (Fax: 605-688-6384). Hours: 8AM-5PM. Enrollment: 9323. Records go back to 1881. Alumni Records Office: Alumni Association, PO Box 515, Brookings, SD 57007. Degrees granted: Associate; Bachelors; Masters; Doctorate. Adverse incident record source- Registrar's Office .

Attendance and degree information available by phone, fax, mail. Search requires name only. Also helpful: SSN, date of birth, approximate years of attendance. There is no fee.

Southeast Technical Institute, Registrar, 2301 Career Pl, Sioux Falls, SD 57107, 605-367-7624 (Fax: 605-367-8305). Enrollment: 2600. Records go back to 1968. Degrees granted: Associate. Adverse incident record source- Administration, 605-367-7624 X225.

School will not confirm attendance information.

Degree information available by phone, fax, mail. Search requires name only. Also helpful: SSN, date of birth. There is no fee.

University of Sioux Falls, Registrar, 1101 W 22nd St, Sioux Falls, SD 57105, 605-331-6650 (Fax: 605-331-6615). Hours: 8AM-5PM. Enrollment: 950. Records go back to 1883. Alumni records are maintained here also. Call 605-331-6608. Degrees granted: Associate; Bachelors; Masters. Adverse incident record source- Student Affairs, 605-331-6620.

Attendance and degree information available by phone, fax, mail. Search requires name only. Also helpful: SSN, exact years of attendance. There is no fee.

University of South Dakota, Registrar, 414 E Clark St, Vermillion, SD 57069-2390, 605-677-5301 (Fax: 605-677-6753). Hours: 8AM-5PM. Enrollment: 7500. Records go back to 1882. Alumni records are maintained here also. Call 605-677-6715. Degrees granted: Bachelors; Masters; Doctorate. Adverse incident record source- Dean of College.

Attendance and degree information available by phone, mail. Search requires name plus SSN, date of birth, exact years of attendance. There is no fee.

Western Dakota Technical Institute, Registrar, 800 Mickelson Dr, Rapid City, SD 57701-4178, 605-394-4034 (Fax: 605-394-1789). Hours: 7:30AM-4PM. Enrollment: 850. Records go back to 1968. Degrees granted: Associate.

Attendance information available by phone, fax, mail. Search requires name only. Also helpful: SSN, date of birth, exact years of attendance. There is no fee.

Degree information available by phone, fax, mail. Search requires name plus approximate years of attendance. Also helpful: SSN, date of birth, exact years of attendance. There is no fee.

Trade and Vocational Schools

Stenotype Institute of South Dakota, 705 West Ave N, Sioux Falls, SD 57104, 605-336-1442

State Licensing & Business Registration Quick Finder Index

Architecture, Engineering & Surveying
Architect #21 (560)	☎ 605-394-2510
Engineer #21 (2475)	☎ 605-394-2510
Engineer-Petroleum Environmental #21	☎ 605-394-2510
Landscape Architect #21 (15)	☎ 605-394-2510
Surveyor #21 (350)	☎ 605-394-2510

Business - Court & Legal Services
Attorney #32	☎ 605-224-7554
Lobbyist #27 (500)	☎ 605-773-5666
Notary Public #27 (1090)	☎ 605-773-5666

Business - General Services
Public Accountant-CPA #2 (600)	☎ 605-367-5770

Construction & Manufacturing
Electrical Inspector #33 (65)	☎ 605-773-3573
Electrician #33 (3500)	☎ 605-773-3573
Plumber #34 (1000)	☎ 605-773-3429
Sewage & Water Installation Contractor/Installer #34 (200)	☎ 605-773-3429

Education
School Counselor #20	☎ 605-773-3553
School Principal #20	☎ 605-773-3553
School Superintendant #20	☎ 605-773-3553
Teacher #20	☎ 605-773-3553

Environmental & Agriculture
Pesticide Applicator #17 (2884)	☎ 605-773-4432
Pesticide Dealer #17 (290)	☎ 605-773-4432
Veterinarian #13	☎ 605-773-3321
Veterinary Corporation #13	☎ 605-773-3321
Veterinary Technician #13	☎ 605-773-3321
Waste Distribution System Operator #10	☎ 605-773-4208
Waste Water Collection System Operator #10	☎ 605-773-4208
Waste Water Treatment Plant Operator #10	☎ 605-773-4208
Water Treatment Plant Operator #10	☎ 605-773-4208

Financial - Real Estate, Insurance & Banking
Abstractor #1 (150)	☎ 605-869-2269
Insurance Agent #15	☎ 605-773-3371
Money Order Business #14 (15)	☎ 605-773-3421
Mortgage Broker #28	☎ 605-773-3600
Notary Lender #14 (87)	☎ 605-773-3421
Property Manager #32	☎ 605-224-7554
Real Estate Appraiser #32	☎ 605-224-7554
Real Estate Auctioneer #32	☎ 605-224-7554
Real Estate Broker #32	☎ 605-224-7554
Real Estate Sales Agent #32	☎ 605-224-7554
Securities Agent #31	☎ 605-733-4013
Small Installment Loan & Consumer Finance #14	☎ 605-773-3421
Water Conditioning Plumbing Installer #34 (100)	☎ 605-773-3429

Health & Beauty
Barber #26 (400)	☎ 605-224-6281
Barber Shop #26	☎ 605-224-6281
Chiropractor #3 (322)	☎ 605-997-3733
Clinical Nurse Specialist #9	☎ 605-367-5940
Cosmetologist #16 (8000)	☎ 605-773-6193
Dental Hygienist #5	✉ 605-224-1282
Dentist #5 (300)	605-224-1282
Emergency Medical Technician #18 (3300)	☎ 605-773-4031
Funeral Director-Embalmer #29	☎ 605-642-1600
Funeral Establishment #29	☎ 605-642-1600
Funeral Service #25	☎ 605-642-1600
Hearing Aid Dispenser #30	☎ 605-642-1600
Medical Assistant #8	☎ 605-334-8343
Medical Doctor #8	☎ 605-334-8343
Nurse Anesthetist, Certified Registered Nurse Anesthetist #9	☎ 605-367-5940
Nurse Midwife #9	☎ 605-367-5940
Nurse Practitioner #9	☎ 605-367-5940
Nurse, RN, Licensed Practical Nurse #9 (33000)	☎ 605-367-5940
Nursing Home Administrator #6 (200)	☎ 605-339-2071
Occupational Therapist/Assistant #8	☎ 605-334-8343
Optometrist #7 (150)	☎ 605-347-2136
Osteopathic Physician #8	☎ 605-334-8343
Pharmacist #11 (1550)	✉ 605-224-2338
Physical Therapist #8	☎ 605-334-8343
Physician's Assistant/Medical Assistant #8	☎ 605-334-8343
Podiatrist #12	☎ 605-336-7753
Respiratory Care Practitioners #8	☎ 605-334-8343
Salon #16	☎ 605-773-6193

Investigations & Security
Polygraph Examiner #23	☎ 605-773-3584

Social Services
Counselor #4 (500)	☎ 605-331-2927
Psychologist #24	☎ 605-642-1600
Social Worker #25	☎ 605-642-1600

Sports & Entertainment

Alcoholic Beverage Distribution #19.................. 605-773-3311
Athletic Trainer #8.. ☎ 605-334-8343
Cigarette Wholesaler #19 605-773-3311
Gaming #22 .... ☎ 605-773-6050

Racing #22 (400) .... ☎ 605-773-6050

Transportation

Motor Vehicle Retail Installment Sales #14... ☎ 605-773-3421

State Licensing & Business Registration Agency Information

(1)   Abstractors Board of Examiners, PO Box 187, Kennebec, SD 57544-0187, 605-734-4275, Fax: 605-869-2269

(2)   Board of Accountancy, 301 E 14th St, Suite 200, Sioux Falls, SD 57104-5022, 605-367-5770

(3)   Board of Chiropractic Examiners, 109 E 2nd Ave, Flandreau, SD 57028-1222, 605-997-3733, Fax: 605-997-3733

(4)   Board of Counselor Examiners, PO Box 1822, Sioux Falls, SD 57101-1822, 605-331-2927

(5)   Board of Dentistry, 106 W Capitol, PO Box 1037, Pierre, SD 57501, 605-224-1282

(6)   Board of Examiners for Nursing Home Administrators, 804 N Western Ave, Sioux Falls, SD 57104-2098, 605-339-2071, Fax: 605-339-1354

(7)   Board of Examiners in Optometry, PO Box 370, Sturgis, SD 57785, 605-347-2136, Fax: 605-347-5823

(8)   Board of Medical & Osteopathic Examiners, 1323 S Minnesota Ave, Sioux Falls, SD 57105-0685, 605-334-8343, Fax: 605-336-0270

(9)   Board of Nursing, 3307 S Lincoln Ave, Sioux Falls, SD 57105-5224, 605-367-5940, Fax: 605-367-5945

(10)   Board of Operator Certification, 523 E Capitol Ave, Foss Bldg, Pierre, SD 57501, 605-773-4208, Fax: 605-773-5286

(11)   Board of Pharmacy, PO Box 518, Pierre, SD 57501-0518, 605-224-2338, Fax: 605-224-1280

(12)   Board of Podiatry Examiners, 808 S Minnesota Ave, Sioux Falls, SD 57104-4829, 605-336-7753

(13)   Board of Veterinary Medical Examiners, 411 Fort St, Pierre, SD 57501-4503, 605-773-3321, Fax: 605-773-5459

(14)   Commerce & Regulations Department, 500 E. Capitol Ave.s Bldg, Pierre, SD 57501, 605-773-3421, Fax: 605-773-5367

(15)   Commerce & Regulations Department, Division of Insurance, 910 E Sioux, Pierre, SD 57501, 605-733-3371

(16)   Cosmetology Commission, 111 E Capitol, Pierre, SD 57501-3105, 605-773-6193, Fax: 605-224-5072

(17)   Department of Agriculture, Office of Agronomy Services, 523 E Capitol, Foss Bldg, Pierre, SD 57501, 605-773-4432, Fax: 605-773-3481

(18)   Department of Health, Emergency Medical Services Program, 445 E. Capitol Ave., Pierre, SD 57501-3185, 605-773-4031

(19)   Department of Revenue, Special Tax Division (Alcoholic Beverage Dept), 700 Governors Dr, Pierre, SD 57501, 605-773-3311

(20)   Education & Cultural Affairs Department, Teacher Education & Certification, 700 Governors Dr, Pierre, SD 57501-2291, 605-773-3553, Fax: 605-773-6139

(21)   Engineering, Architectural & Land Surveying Exams, 2040 W Main St, Suite 304, Rapid City, SD 57702-2447, 605-394-2510, Fax: 605-395-2509

(22)   Gaming Commission, 500 E Capitol Ave, State Capitol, Pierre, SD 57501-5070, 605-773-6050

(23)   Law Enforcement Standards & Training Commission, Division of Criminal Justice Training Center, , Pierre, SD 57501, 605-773-3584

(24)   Licensing Boards, PO Box 654, Spearfish, SD 57783-0654, 605-642-1600

(25)   Licensing Boards, PO Box 654, Spearfish, SD 57783-0654, 605-642-1600

(26)   Licensing Boards, PO Box 1115, Pierre, SD 57501-1115, 605-224-6281

(27)   Office of Secretary of State, 500 E Capitol Ave, Ste 204, State Capitol Bldg, Pierre, SD 57501, 605-773-5666, Fax: 605-773-6580

(28)   Real Estate Commission, PO Box 490, Pierre, SD 57501-0490, 605-773-3600, Fax: 605-777-4356

(29)   South Dakota Board of Funeral Services, PO Box 654, 132 East Illinois, Spearish, SD 57783, 605-642-1600

(30)   South Dakota Board of Licensing, PO Box 654, Spearfish, SD 57783-0654, 605-642-1600

(31)   South Dakota Securities, 118 West Capitol Ave., Pierre, SD 57501-2017, 605-773-4823, Fax: 605-773-5953

(32)   South Dakota State Bar, 222 E Capitol, Pierre, SD 57501, 605-224-7554, Fax: 605-224-0282

(33)   State Electrical Commission, 302 S Pawnee, Pierre, SD 57501-3136, 605-773-3573, Fax: 605-773-6213

(34)   State Plumbing Commission, PO Box 807, Pierre, SD 57501-0807, 605-773-3429, Fax: 605-773-5405

Tennessee

Capitol: Nashville (Davidson County)	
State Population	5.3 Million
Number of Degree Granting Institutions:	77
Number of State Licensing & Business Registration Agencies:	79

Degree Granting Educational Institutions

Aguinas College, Registrar, 4210 Harding Rd, Nashville, TN 37205, 615-297-7545 (Fax: 615-297-7557). Hours: 8AM-3:40PM. Enrollment: 400. Records go back to 1961. Degrees granted: Associate; Bachelors.

Attendance information available by phone, fax, mail. Search requires name plus SSN. Also helpful: date of birth. There is no fee.

Degree information available by phone, fax, mail. Search requires name plus SSN. Also helpful: date of birth, exact years of attendance. There is no fee.

American Baptist College, Registrar, 1800 Baptist World Ctr, Nashville, TN 37207, 423-224-7877. Hours: 8AM-4:30PM. Records go back to 1924. Alumni records are maintained here also. Call 615-228-7877. Degrees granted: Bachelors.

Attendance and degree information available by phone, mail. Search requires name plus exact years of attendance. There is no fee.

American Technical Institute, Registrar, PO Box 8, Brunswick, TN 38014, 901-382-5857 (Fax: 901-385-7627). Hours: 9AM-5PM. Enrollment: 150. Records go back to 1985. Degrees granted: Associate; Bachelors.

Attendance and degree information available by written request only. Search requires name plus SSN, signed release. Also helpful: date of birth, exact years of attendance. There is no fee.

Austin Peay State University, Registrar, 601 College St, Clarksville, TN 37044-4448, 615-648-7121 (Fax: 615-648-6264). Hours: 8AM-4:30PM. Enrollment: 7500. Records go back to 1927. Alumni records are maintained here also. Call 615-648-7979. Degrees granted: Associate; Bachelors; Masters. Adverse incident record source- Admissions, 615-648-7661: Public Safety, 615-648-7786

Attendance and degree information available by phone, fax, mail. Search requires name plus SSN. Also helpful: date of birth, exact years of attendance. There is no fee.

Belmont University, Registrar, 1900 Belmont Blvd, Nashville, TN 37212-3757, 615-460-6619 (Fax: 615-460-5415). Hours: 8AM-4:30PM. Enrollment: 3000. Records go back to 1955. Alumni records are maintained here also. Call 615-460-5723. Degrees granted: Associate; Bachelors; Masters.

Attendance and degree information available by phone, fax, mail. Search requires name plus SSN, exact years of attendance. Also helpful: date of birth. There is no fee.

Bethel College, Registrar, 325 Cherry Ave, McKenzie, TN 38201, 901-352-1000 (Fax: 901-352-1008). Hours: 8AM-4:30PM. Enrollment: 550. Records go back to 1842. Alumni records are maintained here also. Call 901-352-1000. Degrees granted: Bachelors; Masters. Adverse incident record source- Dean of Students, 901-352-1000.

Attendance and degree information available by phone, fax, mail. Search requires name only. Also helpful: SSN, date of birth. There is no fee.

Bryan College, Registrar, Box 7000, Dayton, TN 37321-7000, 423-775-7237 (Fax: 423-775-7330). Hours: 8AM-5PM. Enrollment: 450. Records go back to 1930's. Alumni records are maintained here also. Call 423-775-7312. Degrees granted: Associate; Bachelors. Adverse incident record source- Student Development, 423-775-7209.

Attendance and degree information available by phone, fax, mail. Search requires name plus exact years of attendance. Also helpful: SSN, approximate years of attendance. There is no fee.

Carson-Newman College, Registrar, Box 71985, Jefferson City, TN 37760, 423-471-3240 (Fax: 423-471-3502). Hours: 8:30AM-5PM. Enrollment: 2100. Records go back to 1930's. Alumni Records Office: Box 71988, Jefferson City, TN 37760, 423-471-3222. Degrees granted: Associate; Bachelors; Masters.

Attendance and degree information available by phone, fax, mail. Search requires name only. Also helpful: SSN, date of birth, exact years of attendance. There is no fee.

Chattanooga State Technical Community College, Registrar, 4501 Amnicola Hwy, Chattanooga, TN 37406, 423-697-4404 (Fax: 423-697-4709). Hours: 7:30AM-5:30PM M-Th; 7:30AM-4:30PM F. Enrollment: 8676. Records go back to 1965. Alumni records are maintained here at the same phone number. Degrees granted: Associate.

Attendance and degree information available by phone, fax, mail. Search requires name plus SSN. Also helpful: date of birth, exact years of attendance. There is no fee.

Christian Brothers University, Registrar, 650 East Pkwy S, Memphis, TN 38104, 901-321-3239 (Fax: 901-321-

). Hours: 8AM-4:30PM. Enrollment: 1800. Records go back to 1950's. Alumni records are maintained here at the same phone number. Degrees granted: Bachelors; Masters.

Attendance and degree information available by phone, fax, mail. Search requires name plus approximate years of attendance. Also helpful: SSN, date of birth, exact years of attendance. There is no fee.

Church of God School of Theology, Registrar,
PO Box 3330, 900 Walker St NE, Cleveland, TN 37311, 423-478-1131 X7725 (Fax: 423-478-7711). Hours: 8AM-5PM. Enrollment: 275. Records go back to 1975. Alumni records are maintained here also. Call 423-478-1132 X7707. Degrees granted: Masters. Adverse incident record source- Student Services, 615-478-1131 X7933.

Attendance and degree information available by phone, fax, mail. Search requires name only. Also helpful: SSN, exact years of attendance. There is no fee.

Cleveland State Community College, Registrar,
PO Box 3570, Cleveland, TN 37320-3570, 423-472-7141 X268 (Fax: 423-478-6255). Hours: 8AM-6PM M-Th, 8AM-4:30PM F. Enrollment: 3600. Records go back to 1967. Alumni records are maintained here at the same phone number. Degrees granted: Associate.

Attendance and degree information available by phone, mail. Search requires name plus SSN. Also helpful: exact years of attendance. There is no fee.

Columbia State Community College, Registrar,
PO Box 1315, Hwy 412 W, Columbia, TN 38402-1315, 615-540-2545 (Fax: 615-540-2535). Hours: 7:45PM-4:15PM. Enrollment: 3600. Records go back to 1966. Alumni records are maintained here also. Call 615-540-2514. Degrees granted: Associate. Adverse incident record source- Student Services, 615-540-2545.

Attendance and degree information available by phone, mail. Search requires name plus SSN. There is no fee.

Crichton College, Registrar, PO Box 757830, Memphis,
TN 38157-7830, 901-367-9800 (Fax: 901-367-3866). Hours: 8AM-5PM. Records go back to 1945. Degrees granted: Bachelors. Special programs- Continuing Education. Adverse incident record source- Student Services, 901-367-9800.

Attendance and degree information available by phone, fax, mail. Search requires name plus SSN, exact years of attendance. There is no fee.

Cumberland University, Registrar, S Greenwood St,
Lebanon, TN 37087-3554, 615-444-2562 (Fax: 615-444-2569). Hours: 8AM-4:30PM. Enrollment: 1000. Records go back to 1900. Alumni records are maintained here also. Call 615-444-2562 X238. Degrees granted: Associate; Bachelors; Masters. Adverse incident record source- Student Services, 615-444-2562 X224.

Attendance and degree information available by phone, fax, mail. Search requires name plus SSN, exact years of attendance. There is no fee.

David Lipscomb University, Registrar, 3901 Granny
White Pike, Nashville, TN 37204-3951, 615-269-1788 (Fax: 615-269-1808). Hours: 7:45AM-4:30PM. Degrees granted: Bachelors; Masters. Adverse incident record source- Dean of Students.

Attendance and degree information available by phone, fax, mail. Search requires name only. Also helpful: SSN, date of birth, exact years of attendance. There is no fee.

Draughons Junior College, Registrar, Plus Park at
Pavilion Blvd, Nashville, TN 37217, 615-361-7555 (Fax: 615-367-2736). Hours: 8AM-6PM M-Th; 8AM-2PM F. Enrollment: 300. Records go back to 1940's. Degrees granted: Associate.

Attendance and degree information available by phone, fax, mail. Search requires name plus SSN. Also helpful: date of birth, exact years of attendance. There is no fee.

Draughons Junior College, (Branch Campus),
Registrar, 1860 Wilma Rudolph Blvd, Clarksville, TN 37040, 615-552-7600 (Fax: 615-552-3624). Hours: 7:30AM-4:30PM. Records go back to 1954. Degrees granted: Associate.

Attendance and degree information available by phone, fax, mail. Search requires name plus SSN, exact years of attendance. There is no fee.

Dyersburg State Community College, Admissions & Records, 1510 Lake Rd, Dyersburg, TN 38024, 901-286-3330 (Fax: 901-286-3333). Hours: 8AM-4:30PM. Enrollment: 2000. Records go back to 1969. Alumni records are maintained here also. Call 901-286-3247. Degrees granted: Associate.

Attendance and degree information available by phone, fax, mail. Search requires name only. Also helpful: SSN, date of birth, exact years of attendance. There is no fee.

East Tennessee State University, Registrar, PO
Box 70561, Johnson City, TN 37614-0561, 423-439-4230 (Fax: 423-439-6604). Hours: 8AM-4:30PM. Enrollment: 11500. Records go back to 1911. Alumni Records Office: ETSU Elumni Assocation, Box 70709, Johnson City, TN 37614. Degrees granted: Associate; Bachelors; Masters; Doctorate. Certification: Respiratory Therapy, Surgican Technician, Dental Assistant. Adverse incident record source- Student Affairs.

Attendance and degree information available by phone, fax, mail. Search requires name plus SSN. Also helpful: date of birth, exact years of attendance. There is no fee.

Emmanuel School of Religion, Registrar, One
Walker Dr, Johnson City, TN 37601, 423-461-1520 (Fax: 423-926-6198). Hours: 8AM-5PM Winter; 8AM-4PM Summer. Records go back to 1965. Degrees granted: Masters; Doctorate. Adverse incident record source- President's Office, 615-461-1510 .

Attendance and degree information available by phone, fax, mail. Search requires name plus date of birth. Also helpful: SSN, exact years of attendance. There is no fee.

Fisk University, Registrar, 1000 17th Ave N, Nashville,
TN 37208-3051, 423-239-8586. Hours: 9AM-5PM. Degrees granted: Bachelors; Masters.

Attendance and degree information available by written request only. Search requires name plus SSN, exact years of attendance, signed release. Also helpful: date of birth. There is no fee.

Free Will Baptist Bible College, Registrar, PO Box
50117, Nashville, TN 37205, 615-383-1340 (Fax: 615-269-6028). Hours: 8AM-4:30PM. Records go back to 1942. Alumni Records Office: 3606 West End Ave, Nashville, TN 37205. Degrees granted: Associate. Certification: Teacher Ed. Special programs- Sports Medicine. Adverse incident record source- Dean of Students.

Attendance and degree information available by phone, fax, mail. Search requires name plus SSN, date of birth, exact years of attendance. There is no fee.

Freed-Hardeman University, Registrar, 158 E Main
St, Henderson, TN 38340-2399, 901-989-6648 (Fax: 901-989-6650). Hours: 8AM-5PM. Enrollment: 1500. Records go back to 1900's. Alumni records are maintained here also. Call 901-989-6022. Degrees granted: Bachelors; Masters.

Attendance and degree information available by phone, fax, mail. Search requires name only. Also helpful: SSN, date of birth, exact years of attendance. There is no fee.

Fugazzi College, (Branch), Registrar, 5042 Lindbar Dr,
Nashville, TN 37211, 615-333-3344 (Fax: 615-333-3429).

Hours: 8AM-5PM. Enrollment: 160. Records go back to 1989. Degrees granted: Associate.

Attendance and degree information available by phone, fax, mail. Search requires name plus SSN, approximate years of attendance. There is no fee.

Harding University Graduate School of Religion, Registrar, 1000 Cherry Rd, Memphis, TN 38117, 901-761-1353 (Fax: 901-761-1358). Hours: 8AM-5PM. Enrollment: 200. Records go back to 1958. Alumni records are maintained here at the same phone number. Degrees granted: Masters; Doctorate.

Attendance and degree information available by phone, fax, mail. Search requires name only. Also helpful: SSN, date of birth, exact years of attendance. There is no fee.

Hiwassee College, Registrar, HC Box 646, 225 Hiwassee College Dr, Madisonville, TN 37354, 423-442-2001 X215 (Fax: 423-442-3520). Hours: 8AM-5PM. Records go back to 1849. Alumni records are maintained here also. Call 423-442-2091. Degrees granted: Associate.

Attendance and degree information available by phone, mail. Search requires name plus SSN. There is no fee.

ITT Technical Institute, Registrar, 10208 Technology Dr, Knoxville, TN 37932, 423-671-2800 (Fax: 423-671-2811). Hours: 8AM-5PM. Records go back to 1988. Alumni Records Office: ITT Technical Institute, 9511 Angola Ct, Indianapolis, IN 46268. Degrees granted: Associate.

Attendance and degree information available by mail. Search requires name plus SSN, date of birth, exact years of attendance. There is no fee.

ITT Technical Institute, Registrar, 441 Donelson Pike, Nashville, TN 37214-8029, 615-889-8700 (Fax: 615-872-7209). Hours: 8AM-5PM. Enrollment: 350. Records go back to 1985. Alumni records are maintained here also. Call 317-594-4274. Degrees granted: Associate; Bachelors.

Attendance information available by mail. Search requires name plus SSN, date of birth, exact years of attendance, signed release. There is no fee.

Degree information available by phone, mail. Search requires name plus SSN, date of birth, exact years of attendance. There is no fee.

Jackson State Community College, Records Office, 2046 North Pkwy, Jackson, TN 38301-3797, 901-425-2654 (Fax: 901-425-2647). Hours: 8AM-4:30PM. Enrollment: 3500. Records go back to 1967. Degrees granted: Associate.

Attendance and degree information available by phone, fax, mail. Search requires name plus SSN. Also helpful: approximate years of attendance. There is no fee.

John A. Gupton College, Registrar, 1616 Church St, Nashville, TN 37203, 615-327-3927 (Fax: 615-321-4518). Hours: 8:30AM-4:30PM. Records go back to 1946. Degrees granted: Associate.

Attendance and degree information available by phone, fax, mail. Search requires name plus SSN, approximate years of attendance. There is no fee.

Johnson Bible College, Registrar, 7900 Johnson Dr, Knoxville, TN 37998, 423-579-2302 (Fax: 423-579-2337). Hours: 8AM-5PM. Enrollment: 450. Records go back to 1893. Alumni records are maintained here also. Call 423-579-2353. Degrees granted: Associate; Bachelors; Masters.

Attendance and degree information available by phone, mail. Search requires name only. There is no fee.

King College, Registrar, 1350 King College Rd, Bristol, TN 37620, 423-652-4739 (Fax: 423-968-4456). Hours: 8AM-5PM. Enrollment: 600. Records go back to 1800's. Alumni records are maintained here also. Call 423-652-4717. Degrees granted: Bachelors.

Attendance and degree information available by phone, fax, mail. Search requires name only. There is no fee.

Knoxville Business College, Registrar, 720 N Fifth Ave, Knoxville, TN 37917, 423-524-3043 X45 (Fax: 423-637-1027). Hours: 8AM-9:30PM. Records go back to 1882. Degrees granted: Associate.

Attendance and degree information available by phone, mail. Search requires name plus SSN, date of birth, exact years of attendance. There is no fee.

Lambuth University, Registrar, 705 Lambuth Blvd, Jackson, TN 38301, 901-425-3207 (Fax: 901-423-1990). Hours: 8:30AM-Noon, 1-4:30PM. Enrollment: 1200. Records go back to 1920's. Alumni records are maintained here also. Call 901-425-3354. Degrees granted: Bachelors. Adverse incident record source- Student Life, 901-425-3211.

Attendance and degree information available by phone, fax, mail. Search requires name only. Also helpful: SSN, date of birth, exact years of attendance. There is no fee.

Lane College, Registrar, 545 Lane Ave, Jackson, TN 38301-4598, 901-426-7600 (Fax: 901-427-3987). Hours: 8AM-5PM. Enrollment: 626. Records go back to 1882. Alumni records are maintained here also. Call 901-426-7523. Degrees granted: Bachelors. Adverse incident record source- Student Affairs, 901-426-7600.

Attendance and degree information available by phone, mail. Search requires name plus SSN, exact years of attendance. There is no fee.

LeMoyne-Owen College, Registrar, 807 Walker Ave, Memphis, TN 38126, 901-942-7321 (Fax: 901-942-7810). Hours: 8AM-6PM. Enrollment: 1500. Records go back to 1915. Alumni records are maintained here at the same phone number. Degrees granted: Bachelors; Masters. Adverse incident record source- Student Affairs.

Attendance and degree information available by phone, fax, mail. Search requires name plus SSN, approximate years of attendance. Also helpful: date of birth, exact years of attendance. There is no fee.

Lee College, Registrar, PO Box 3450, Cleveland, TN 37320-3450, 423-478-7319 (Fax: 423-478-7075). Hours: 9AM-Noon; 1-5PM. Enrollment: 2500. Records go back to 1947. Alumni records are maintained here at the same phone number. Degrees granted: Bachelors; Masters.

Attendance and degree information available by fax, mail. Search requires name plus SSN, signed release. Also helpful: date of birth, exact years of attendance. Fee is $5.00.

Lincoln Memorial University, Registrar, Cumberland Gap Pkwy, Harrogate, TN 37752-0901, 423-869-6212 (Fax: 423-869-6387). Hours: 8AM-4PM. Enrollment: 2000. Records go back to 1915. Alumni records are maintained here at the same phone number. Degrees granted: Associate; Bachelors; Masters; Ed.S.

Attendance and degree information available by phone, fax, mail. Search requires name plus SSN. Also helpful: date of birth, exact years of attendance. There is no fee.

Martin Methodist College, Registrar, 433 W Madison St, Pulaski, TN 38478, 915-363-9809 (Fax: 915-363-9818). Hours: 8AM-4:30PM. Enrollment: 500. Records go back to 1870. Alumni records are maintained here also. Call 423-363-7456. Degrees granted: Bachelors.

Attendance and degree information available by phone, mail. Search requires name plus SSN, exact years of attendance. There is no fee.

Maryville College, Registrar, 502 E Lamar Alexander Pkwy, Maryville, TN 37804, 423-981-8212 (Fax: 423-981-8010). Hours: 8AM-5PM. Enrollment: 900. Records go back to 1819. Alumni records are maintained here also. Call 423-981-8199. Degrees granted: Bachelors. Adverse incident record source- Student Development, 423-981-8213.

Attendance and degree information available by phone, fax, mail. Search requires name plus SSN, exact years of attendance. There is no fee.

Meharry Medical College, Admissions & Records, 1005 D.B. Todd Blvd, Nashville, TN 37208, 615-327-6223 (Fax: 615-327-6228). Hours: 8:30AM-5PM. Enrollment: 867. Records go back to 1897. Alumni records are maintained here also. Call 615-327-6266. Adverse incident record source- Academic Affairs, School of Medicine,615-327-6413: Academic Affairs, School of Dentistry,615-327-6182

Attendance and degree information available by phone, fax, mail. Search requires name plus SSN. There is no fee.

Memphis College of Art, Registrar, 1930 Poplar Ave, Overton Park, Memphis, TN 38104, 901-726-4085 X29 (Fax: 901-726-9371). Hours: 8AM-5PM. Enrollment: 250. Records go back to 1936. Alumni records are maintained here at the same phone number. Degrees granted: Bachelors; Masters. Adverse incident record source- Student Life, 901-726-4085.

Attendance and degree information available by fax, mail. Search requires name plus SSN, exact years of attendance, signed release. There is no fee.

Memphis Theological Seminary, Registrar, 168 East Pkwy S, Memphis, TN 38104, 901-458-8232 (Fax: 901-452-4051). Enrollment: 230. Degrees granted: Masters; Doctorate.

Attendance and degree information available by phone, fax, mail. Search requires name plus approximate years of attendance. Also helpful: SSN, date of birth, exact years of attendance. There is no fee.

Mid-America Baptist Theological Seminary, Registrar's Office, 1255 Poplar Ave, Memphis, TN 38104, 901-726-9171 (Fax: 901-726-6791). Hours: 8AM-4:30PM. Records go back to 1971. Alumni records are maintained here at the same phone number. Degrees granted: Associate; Masters; Doctorate.

Attendance and degree information available by phone, fax, mail. Search requires name plus SSN, approximate years of attendance. Also helpful: date of birth, exact years of attendance. There is no fee.

Middle Tennessee State University, Registrar, Murfreesboro, TN 37132, 615-898-2600 (Fax: 615-898-5538). Hours: 8AM-4:30PM. Records go back to 1926. Alumni records are maintained here also. Call 615-898-2922. Degrees granted: Bachelors; Masters; Doctorate.

Attendance and degree information available by phone, mail. Search requires name plus SSN, date of birth. There is no fee.

Milligan College, Registrar, PO Box 52, Milligan College, TN 37682, 423-461-8788 (Fax: 423-461-8716). Hours: 8AM-Noon, 1-5PM. Enrollment: 866. Records go back to 1913. Alumni records are maintained here also. Call 423-461-8718. Degrees granted: Associate; Bachelors; Masters. Adverse incident record source- Student Development, 615-461-8760.

Attendance and degree information available by phone, fax, mail. Search requires name only. Also helpful: SSN, date of birth, exact years of attendance. There is no fee.

Motlow State Community College, Admissions & Records, PO Box 88100, Tullahoma, TN 37388-8100, 615-393-1500 (Fax: 615-393-1681). Hours: 8AM-4:30PM. Enrollment: 3200. Records go back to 1969. Alumni records are maintained here also. Call 615-393-1690. Degrees granted: Associate.

Attendance and degree information available by phone, fax, mail. Search requires name plus SSN. Also helpful: date of birth, exact years of attendance. There is no fee.

Nashville State Technical Institute, Registrar, 120 White Bridge Rd, Nashville, TN 37209-4515, 615-353-3210 (Fax: 615-353-3202). Hours: 8AM-4:30PM. Records go back to 1970. Alumni records are maintained here at the same phone number. Degrees granted: Associate.

Attendance and degree information available by phone, fax, mail. Search requires name plus SSN. There is no fee.

Northeast State Technical Community College, Registrar, PO Box 246, 2425 Hwy 75, Blountville, TN 37617-0246, 423-323-3191 (Fax: 423-323-3083). Degrees granted: Associate.

Attendance and degree information available by phone, fax, mail. Search requires name plus SSN. Also helpful: date of birth, exact years of attendance. There is no fee.

O'More College of Design, Registrar, 423 S Margin St, PO Box 908, Franklin, TN 37065, 615-794-4254 (Fax: 615-790-1662). Hours: 8AM-4:30PM. Records go back to 1970. Alumni records are maintained here at the same phone number. Degrees granted: Bachelors.

Attendance and degree information available by phone, mail. Search requires name plus SSN, exact years of attendance. There is no fee.

Pellissippi State Technical Community College, Registrar, 10915 Hardin Valley Rd, PO Box 22990, Knoxville, TN 37933-0990, 423-694-6632 (Fax: 423-694-6435). Enrollment: 8000. Records go back to 1994. Alumni records are maintained here at the same phone number. Degrees granted: Associate.

Attendance and degree information available by phone, fax, mail. Search requires name only. Also helpful: SSN. There is no fee.

Rhodes College, Registrar, 2000 North Pkwy, Memphis, TN 38112, 901-726-3885 (Fax: 901-726-3576). Hours: 8:30AM-3:30PM. Enrollment: 1430. Records go back to 1848. Alumni records are maintained here also. Call 901-726-3845. Degrees granted: Bachelors; Masters.

Attendance and degree information available by phone, fax, mail. Search requires name only. Also helpful: SSN, date of birth, exact years of attendance. There is no fee.

Roane State Community College, Registrar, Rte 8 Box 69, Patton Lane, Harriman, TN 37748, 423-882-4523 (Fax: 423-882-4562). Hours: 8:30AM-5PM. Records go back to 1971. Alumni records are maintained here at the same phone number. Degrees granted: Associate.

Attendance and degree information available by phone, fax, mail. Search requires name plus SSN. There is no fee.

Scarritt Foundation, Registrar, 1008 19 Ave S, Nashville, TN 37212, 615-340-7500. Records go back to 1900. College closed in 1988; transcripts available. Alumni records are maintained here at the same phone number. Degrees granted: Bachelors; Masters; Diploma.

Attendance information available by phone, fax, mail. Search requires name plus approximate years of attendance. Also helpful: SSN, date of birth. There is no fee.

School will not confirm degree information.

Shelby State Community College, Registrar, PO Box 40568, Memphis, TN 38174-0568, 901-544-5668 (Fax: 901-544-5520). Hours: 8AM-7PM. Enrollment: 6361. Records go back to 1992. Alumni Records Office: Alumni Association, 1256 Union Ave, Memphis, TN 38104. Degrees granted: Associate. Adverse incident record source- 901-544-5555.

Attendance and degree information available by phone, fax, mail. Search requires name plus SSN. Also helpful: date of birth, exact years of attendance. There is no fee.

Southern College of Optometry, Registrar, 1245 Madison Ave, Memphis, TN 38104, 901-722-3228 (Fax: 901-722-3279). Hours: 8:30AM-4:30PM. Enrollment: 480. Records go back to 1932. Alumni records are maintained here also. Call 901-722-3217. Degrees granted: Doctorate.

Attendance and degree information available by phone, fax, mail. Search requires name plus SSN, exact years of attendance. Also helpful: date of birth. There is no fee.

Southern College of Seventh-Day Adventists, Registrar, PO Box 370, Collegedale, TN 37315-0370, 423-238-2111 (Fax: 423-238-3003). Hours: 8AM-Noon, 1-5PM. Enrollment: 1590. Records go back to 1892. Alumni records are maintained here at the same phone number. Degrees granted: Associate; Bachelors. Certification: Auto Body & Auto Mechanics, M.S. Ed.

Attendance and degree information available by phone, fax, mail. Search requires name plus SSN. Also helpful: date of birth, exact years of attendance. There is no fee.

State Technical Institute at Memphis, Records Office, 5983 Macon Cove, Memphis, TN 38134-7693, 901-383-4190 (Fax: 901-383-4473). Hours: 8AM-7PM M-Th; 8AM-4:30PM F. Enrollment: 10000. Records go back to 1976. Alumni records are maintained here at the same phone number. Degrees granted: Associate. Adverse incident record source- Student Services, 901-383-4179.

Attendance and degree information available by fax, mail. Search requires name plus SSN. Also helpful: date of birth, exact years of attendance. There is no fee.

Tennessee Institute of Electronics, Registrar, 3203 Tazewell Pike, Knoxville, TN 37918, 423-688-9422 (Fax: 423-688-2419). Enrollment: 200. Records go back to 1947. Degrees granted: Associate. Adverse incident record source- Student Services.

Attendance and degree information available by phone, mail. Search requires name plus SSN, exact years of attendance. There is no fee.

Tennessee State University, Registrar's Office, 3500 John Merritt Blvd, Nashville, TN 37209-1561, 615-963-5131 (Fax: 615-963-5108). Hours: 8AM-4:30pm. Records go back to 1912. Alumni records are maintained here also. Call 615-963-5880. Degrees granted: Associate; Bachelors; Masters; Doctorate.

Attendance and degree information available by phone, mail. Search requires name plus SSN, approximate years of attendance. Also helpful: date of birth, exact years of attendance. There is no fee.

Tennessee Technological University, Registrar, Office of Records, Box 5097, Cookeville, TN 38505, 615-372-3317 (Fax: 615-372-6111). Hours: 8AM-4:30PM. Enrollment: 8000. Records go back to 1915. Alumni Records Office: Box 5157, Cookeville, TN 38505, 615-372-3205 (Fax: 615-372-6365). Degrees granted: Associate; Bachelors; Masters; Doctorate. Adverse incident record source- Student Activities, 615-372-3237.

Attendance and degree information available by phone, fax, mail. Search requires name only. Also helpful: SSN, date of birth, exact years of attendance. There is no fee.

Tennessee Temple University, Registrar, 1815 Union Ave, Chattanooga, TN 37404, 423-493-4100 (Fax: 423-493-4497). Enrollment: 600. Records go back to 1946. Alumni records are maintained here also. Call 423-493-4464. Degrees granted: Associate; Bachelors; Masters. Adverse incident record source- Campus Security, 423-493-4370.

Attendance information available by phone, fax, mail. Search requires name plus approximate years of attendance. Also helpful: SSN, exact years of attendance. There is no fee.

Degree information available by phone, fax, mail. Search requires name plus approximate years of attendance. Also helpful: SSN, date of birth, exact years of attendance. There is no fee.

Tennessee Wesleyan College, Registrar, PO Box 40, Athens, TN 37371, 423-745-7504 X5282 (Fax: 423-744-9968). Hours: 8:30AM-4:30PM. Enrollment: 633. Records go back to 1857. Alumni records are maintained here also. Call 423-745-7504 X5202. Degrees granted: Bachelors. Adverse incident record source- Dean of Students, 423-745-7504 X5203.

Attendance and degree information available by phone, fax, mail. Search requires name plus SSN. Also helpful: date of birth, approximate years of attendance. There is no fee.

Trevecca Nazarene College, Registrar, 333 Murfreesboro Rd, Nashville, TN 37210, 615-248-1267 (Fax: 615-248-7799). Hours: 8AM-4:30PM. Enrollment: 1537. Alumni records are maintained here also. Call 615-248-1350. Degrees granted: Associate; Bachelors; Masters. Adverse incident record source- Student Services, 615-248-1245.

School will not confirm attendance information.

Degree information available by phone, fax, mail. Search requires name only. Also helpful: SSN, exact years of attendance. There is no fee.

Tusculum College, Registrar, PO Box 5050, Greeneville, TN 37743, 423-636-7300 (Fax: 423-638-5181). Hours: 8AM-5PM. Enrollment: 1500. Records go back to 1900. Alumni records are maintained here at the same phone number. Degrees granted: Bachelors; Masters. Adverse incident record source- Campus Life, 615-636-7300 X315.

Attendance and degree information available by phone, fax, mail. Search requires name plus SSN. Also helpful: date of birth, exact years of attendance. There is no fee.

Union University, Academic Center, 2447 Hwy 45 By-Pass N, Jackson, TN 38305, 901-661-5040 (Fax: 901-661-5187). Hours: 8AM-5PM. Enrollment: 2200. Records go back to 1925. Alumni records are maintained here also. Call 901-661-5208. Degrees granted: Associate; Bachelors; Masters. Adverse incident record source- Student Services, 901-661-5040.

Attendance and degree information available by phone, fax, mail. Search requires name only. Also helpful: SSN, date of birth, exact years of attendance. There is no fee.

University of Memphis, Office of the Registrar, Campus Box 526620, Memphis, TN 38152-6620, 901-678-3927 (Fax: 901-678-3249). Hours: 7:30AM-6PM M-Th; 7:30AM-4:30PM F; 8:30AM-Noon S. Enrollment: 20000. Records go back to 1912. Evening and Saturday phone number is 901-678-2671. Alumni records are maintained here also. Call 901-678-2586. Degrees granted: Bachelors; Masters; Doctorate. Certification: Paralegal. Adverse incident record source- Judicial Affairs, 901-678-2298.

Attendance and degree information available by phone, fax, mail. Search requires name only. Also helpful: SSN, date of birth, exact years of attendance. There is no fee.

University of Memphis, Office of the Registrar, Admin Bldg 143, Memphis, TN 38152, 901-678-2671 (Fax: 901-678-3249). Enrollment: 19000. Records go back to 1912. Alumni Records Office: Alumni Association, Alumni Center, Memphis, TN 38152. Degrees granted: Bachelors; Masters; Doctorate; J.D. Adverse incident record source- Public Safety, 901-678-3848.

Attendance and degree information available by phone, fax, mail. Search requires name plus SSN. Also helpful: date of birth, exact years of attendance. There is no fee.

University of Tennessee at Chattanooga, Registrar, 615 McCallie Ave, Chattanooga, TN 37403-2598,

423-755-4416 (Fax: 423-785-2172). Hours: 8AM-5PM. Enrollment: 8300. Alumni records are maintained here at the same phone number. Degrees granted: Bachelors; Masters.

Attendance and degree information available by phone, fax, mail. Search requires name plus SSN, exact years of attendance. Also helpful: date of birth. There is no fee.

University of Tennessee at Martin, Registrar, University St, Martin, TN 38238, 901-587-7049 (Fax: 901-587-7048). Hours: 8AM-5PM. Enrollment: 5800. Records go back to 1927. Alumni records are maintained here also. Call 901-587-7610. Degrees granted: Bachelors; Masters.

Attendance and degree information available by phone, fax, mail. Search requires name only. Also helpful: SSN, date of birth, approximate years of attendance. There is no fee.

University of Tennessee, Knoxville, Registrar, 209 Student Services Bldg, Knoxville, TN 37796-0200, 423-974-2101 (Fax: 423-974-6341). Hours: 8AM-5PM. Records go back to 1880. Alumni records are maintained here at the same phone number. Degrees granted: Bachelors; Masters; Doctorate. Adverse incident record source- Student Services, 615-974-3171.

Attendance and degree information available by phone, fax, mail. Search requires name plus SSN, date of birth, approximate years of attendance. Also helpful: exact years of attendance. There is no fee.

University of Tennessee, Memphis, Registrar's Office, 119 Randolph Hall, Memphis, TN 38163, 901-448-5563 (Fax: 901-448-7772). Hours: 8AM-5PM. Enrollment: 2080. Records go back to 1912. Alumni records are maintained here at the same phone number. Degrees granted: Bachelors; Masters; Doctorate.

Attendance and degree information available by phone, fax, mail. Search requires name plus SSN, exact years of attendance. There is no fee.

University of the South, Registrar, 735 University Ave, Sewanee, TN 37375-1000, 615-598-1314 (Fax: 615-598-

1145). Hours: 8AM-4:30PM. Records go back to 1858. Alumni records are maintained here also. Call 615-598-1402. Degrees granted: Bachelors; Masters; Doctorate. Adverse incident record source- Dean of Students, 615-598-1000.

Attendance and degree information available by mail. Search requires name plus SSN, date of birth, exact years of attendance, signed release. There is no fee.

Vanderbilt University, Registrar, 242 Alexander Hall, Nashville, TN 37240, 615-322-7701 (Fax: 615-343-7709). Hours: 8AM-5PM. Records go back to 1875. Alumni records are maintained here also. Call 615-322-4219. Degrees granted: Bachelors; Masters; Doctorate.

Attendance and degree information available by phone, fax, mail. Search requires name plus SSN. There is no fee.

Volunteer State Community College, Registrar, 1480 Nashville Pike, Gallatin, TN 37066, 615-452-8600 X3461 (Fax: 615-230-3645). Records go back to 1971. Alumni records are maintained here at the same phone number. Degrees granted: Associate. Adverse incident record source- Student Services, 615-452-8600 X3441.

Attendance and degree information available by phone, fax, mail. Search requires name plus SSN, date of birth. Also helpful: exact years of attendance. There is no fee.

Walters State Community College, Registrar, 500 S Davy Crockett Pkwy, Morristown, TN 37813-6899, 423-585-0828 (Fax: 423-585-2631). Hours: 8AM-4:30PM. Enrollment: 5800. Records go back to 1970. Alumni records are maintained here at the same phone number. Degrees granted: Associate. Adverse incident record source- Student Affairs, 423-585-2680.

Attendance and degree information available by phone, fax, mail. Search requires name plus SSN. Also helpful: approximate years of attendance. There is no fee.

Trade and Vocational Schools

American Academy of Nutrition, 1429 Cherokee Blvd, Knoxville, TN 37919, 423-524-8079

Arnold's Beauty School, 1179 S Second St, Milan, TN 38358, 901-686-7351

Artiste School of Cosmetology, 129 Springbrook Dr, Johnson City, TN 37601, 423-282-2279

Bobbie's School of Beauty Arts, 108 Decatur Pike, Athens, TN 37371, 423-745-8929

Chattanooga Barber College, 405 Market St, Chattanooga, TN 37402, 423-266-7013

Climate Control Institute (Travel Careers Division Campus), 150 Collins St, Memphis, TN 38111, 901-761-5730

ConCorde Career Institute, 5100 Poplar Ave #132, Memphis, TN 38137, 901-761-9494

Cumberland School of Technology, 1065 E Tenth St, Cookeville, TN 38501, 615-526-3660

Fort Sanders School of Nursing, 1915 White Ave, Knoxville, TN 37916, 423-541-1290

Jett College of Cosmetology & Barbering, 3740 N Watkins St, Memphis, TN 38127, 901-357-0388

Jett College of Cosmetology & Barbering, 524 S Cooper St, Memphis, TN 38104, 901-358-5121

Jett College of Cosmetology & Barbering, 1286 Southbrook Mall, Memphis, TN 38116, 901-332-7330

Knoxville Institute of Hair Design, 1221 N Central St, Knoxville, TN 37917, 423-971-1529

Knoxville Job Corps Center, 621 Dale Ave, Knoxville, TN 37921, 423-544-5600

Medical Career College, 537 Main St, Nashville, TN 37206, 615-255-7531

Mid-State Barber Styling College, Inc., 510 Jefferson St, Nashville, TN 37208, 615-242-9300

Mille-Motte Business College, 1820 Business Park Dr, Clarksville, TN 37040, 615-553-0071

Mister Wayne's School of Unisex Hair Design, 170 S Willow Ave, Cookeville, TN 38501, 615-526-1478

Nashville Career School, 51 Century Blvd Ste 350, Nashville, TN 37214-3609, 615-885-9770

National School of Hair Design, 3641 Brainerd Rd, Chattanooga, TN 37411-3604, 615-624-6451

Naval Air Technical Training Center, Naval Air Station, Memphis, Millington, TN 38054, 901-873-5106

North Central Institute, 2469 Fort Campbell Blvd, Clarksville, TN 37042, 615-552-6200

O'More College of Design, 423 S Margin St, PO Box 908, Franklin, TN 37065-0908, 615-794-4254

Pro-Way Hair School (Branch Campus), 3099 S Perkins Rd, Memphis, TN 38118, 901-363-3553

Queen City College, 1594 Fort Campbell Blvd, Clarksville, TN 37042, 615-645-2361

Rice College, 2485 Union Ave, Memphis, TN 38112, 901-324-7423

Rice College (Branch Campus), 1515 Magnolia Ave, Knoxville, TN 37917, 423-637-9899

Seminary Extension Independent Study Institute, 901 Commerce St #500, Nashville, TN 37203, 615-242-2453

Southeastern Paralegal Institute, 2416 21st Ave S #300, Nashville, TN 37212, 615-269-9900

Tennessee Technology Center at Athens, 1634 Vo-Tech Dr, Athens, TN 37371, 423-744-2814

Tennessee Technology Center at Covington, 1600 Hwy 51 S, Covington, TN 38019, 901-476-8634

Tennessee Technology Center at Crossville, 715 N Miller Ave, Crossville, TN 38555, 615-484-7502

Tennessee Technology Center at Dickson, 740 Hwy 46, Dickson, TN 37055, 615-446-4710

Tennessee Technology Center at Elizabethton, 1500 Arney St, Elizabethton, TN 37641, 423-542-4174

Tennessee Technology Center at Harriman, Hwy 27 N, Harriman, TN 37748, 423-882-6703

Tennessee Technology Center at Hartsville, 716 McMurry blvd, Hartsville, TN 37074, 615-374-2147

Tennessee Technology Center at Hohenwald, 813 W Main St, Hohenwald, TN 38462, 615-796-5351

Tennessee Technology Center at Jacksboro, Rte 1 Elkins Rd, Jacksboro, TN 37757, 423-562-8648

Tennessee Technology Center at Jackson, 2468 Westover Rd, Jackson, TN 38305, 901-424-0691

Tennessee Technology Center at Knoxville, 1100 Liberty St, Knoxville, TN 37919, 423-546-5567

Tennessee Technology Center at Livingston, Airport Rd, Livingston, TN 38570, 615-823-5525

Tennessee Technology Center at McKenzie, 905 Highland Dr, McKenzie, TN 38201, 901-352-5364

Tennessee Technology Center at McMinnville, 1507 Vo-Tech Dr, McMinnville, TN 37110, 615-473-5587

Tennessee Technology Center at Memphis, 550 Alabama, Memphis, TN 38105, 901-543-6100

Tennessee Technology Center at Memphis, 2752 Winchester Rd, Memphis, TN 38116, 901-345-1995

Tennessee Technology Center at Morristown, 821 W Louise Ave, Morristown, TN 37813, 423-586-5771

Tennessee Technology Center at Morristown, 316 E Main St, Rogersville, TN 37857, 423-272-2100

Tennessee Technology Center at Murfreesboro, 1303 Old Fort Pkwy, Murfreesboro, TN 37129, 615-898-8010

Tennessee Technology Center at Nashville, 100 White Bridge Rd, Nashville, TN 37209, 615-741-1241

Tennessee Technology Center at Nashville, 7204 Cockrill Bend Rd, Nashville, TN 37209, 615-350-6224

Tennessee Technology Center at Newbern, 340 Washington St, Newbern, TN 38059, 901-627-2511

Tennessee Technology Center at Oneida, 120 Eli Ln, Oneida, TN 37841, 423-569-8338

Tennessee Technology Center at Paris, 312 S Wilson St, Paris, TN 38242, 901-642-7552

Tennessee Technology Center at Pulaski, 1233 E College St, Pulaski, TN 38478, 423-363-1588

Tennessee Technology Center at Ripley, S Industrial Park, Ripley, TN 38063, 901-635-3368

Tennessee Technology Center at Savannah, Hwy 64 W, Crump, TN 38327, 901-632-3393

Tennessee Technology Center at Shelbyville, 1405 Madison St, Shelbyville, TN 37160, 615-685-5013

Tennessee Technology Center at Whiteville, 330 Hwy 100, Whiteville, TN 38075, 901-254-8521

University of Beauty, 1701-G S Lee Plaza, Cleveland, TN 37311, 423-472-1702

University of Beauty (Branch Campus), 5798-A Brainerd Rd, Chattanooga, TN 37411, 423-899-0246

West Tennessee Business College, 1186 Hwy 45 By-Pass, Jackson, TN 38301, 901-668-7240

William R. Moore School of Technology, 1200 Poplar Ave, Memphis, TN 38104, 901-726-1977

State Licensing & Business Registration Quick Finder Index

Architecture, Engineering & Surveying
Architect #3 .... ☎ 615-741-9771
Engineer #3 .... ☎ 615-741-9771
Geologist #4 .... ☎ 615-741-2241
Landscape Architect #3 .... ☎ 615-741-9771
Surveyor #4 .... ☎ 615-741-2241

Business - Court & Legal Services
Attorney #12 615-741-3234
Court Reporter/Stenographer #2 ....
Lobbyist #10 (482) .... ✉ 615-741-7959
Notary Public #9 (69000) .... ✉ 615-741-3699
Shorthand Reporter #2 ....

Business - General Services
Auctioneer #3 .... ☎ 615-741-9771
Personnel Consultant #4 .... ☎ 615-741-2241
Public Accountant #3 .... ☎ 615-741-9771
Public Weigher #11 .... ☎ 615-360-0120
Weighmaster #11 .... ☎ 615-360-0120

Construction & Manufacturing
Alarm Contractor #3 .... ☎ 615-741-9771
Boiler Operator #8 (1074) .... ✉ 901-385-5054
Contractor #3 .... ☎ 615-741-9771

Education
School Administrative Supervisor #5 615-532-4885
School Counselor #5 615-532-4885
School Librarian #5 615-532-4885
Teacher #5 615-532-4885

Environmental & Agriculture
Animal Dealer #11 (285) .... ☎ 615-360-0120
Environmentalist #7 .... ✉ 615-367-6213
Milk Tester/Sampler #11 .... ☎ 615-360-0120
Pest Control Operator #11 .... ☎ 615-360-0120
Service Technician #11 .... ☎ 615-360-0120
Veterinarian #7 .... ✉ 615-367-6213

Financial - Real Estate, Insurance & Banking
Collection Agent #3 .... ☎ 615-741-9771
Insurance Agent/Company #4 .... ☎ 615-741-2241
Investment Advisor #3 .... ☎ 615-741-9771
Real Estate Appraiser #4 .... ☎ 615-741-2241
Real Estate Broker #4 .... ☎ 615-741-2241
Real Estate Sales Agent #3 .... ☎ 615-741-9771
Securities Agent #3 .... ☎ 615-741-9771
Securities Broker/Dealer #3 .... ☎ 615-741-9771
Time Share Agent #3 .... ☎ 615-741-9771

Health & Beauty
Barber #3 .... ☎ 615-741-9771

Burial Service #3 .... ☎ 615-741-9771
Chiropractor #6 .... ☎ 615-741-1954
Clinical Laboratory Technician #6 .... ☎ 615-741-1954
Cosmetology #3 .... ☎ 615-741-9771
Dentist #6 .... ☎ 615-741-1954
Dietitian/Nutritionist #6 .... ☎ 615-741-1954
Disciplinary Tracking #7 .... ✉ 615-367-6213
Dispensing Optician #7 .... ✉ 615-367-6213
Electrologist #3 .... ☎ 615-741-9771
Electrology #7 .... ✉ 615-367-6213
Embalmer #4 .... ☎ 615-741-2241
Emergency Medical Service #7 .... ✉ 615-367-6213
Health Care Facility #7 .... ✉ 615-367-6213
Health Related Boards Administration #7 ...... ✉ 615-367-6213
Hearing Aid Dispenser #7 .... ✉ 615-367-6213
Medical Doctor #6 .... ☎ 615-741-1954
Medical Laboratory Personnel #6 .... ☎ 615-741-1954
Nurse Registered Nurse/Licensed Practical Nurse #7
  (65000) .... ✉ 615-367-6232
Nursing Home Administrator #7 .... ✉ 615-367-6213
Occupational Therapist #7 .... ✉ 615-367-6213
Optometrist #7 .... ✉ 615-367-6213
Osteopathic Physician #6 .... ☎ 615-741-1954
Pharmacy #4 .... ☎ 615-741-2241
Physical Therapist #7 .... ✉ 615-367-6213
Physician's Assistant #6 .... ☎ 615-741-1954
Podiatrist #6 .... ☎ 615-741-1954
Radiation Therapy Technician #6 .... ☎ 615-741-1954
Radiologic Technologist #6 .... ☎ 615-741-1954
Respiratory Care Practitioner #6 .... ☎ 615-741-1954
Speech Pathologist/Audiologist #7 .... ✉ 615-367-6213

Investigations & Security
Fire Protection Sprinkler System Contractor
  /Responisble Employee #3 .... ☎ 615-741-9771
Investigation #7 .... ✉ 615-367-6213
Polygraph Examiner #4 .... ☎ 615-741-2241
Private Investigator #4 .... ☎ 615-741-2241
Private Security Guard #4 .... ☎ 615-741-2241

Social Services
Professional Counselor & Marriage/Family
  Therapist #7 .... ✉ 615-367-6213
Psychologist #7 .... ✉ 615-367-6213
Social Worker #7 .... ✉ 615-367-6213

Sports & Entertainment
Athletic Trainer #6 .... ☎ 615-741-1954
Boxing & Racing #3 .... ☎ 615-741-9771
Liquor Control #1 .... ☎ 615-741-1602

State Licensing & Business Registration Agency Information

(1) Alcoholic Beverage Commission, 226 Capitol Blvd Bldg, Suite 300, Nashville, TN 37243-0755, 615-741-1602, Fax: 615-741-0847

(2) CSR Board, PO Box 447, Chattanooga, TN 37401.ll Commerce & Insurance Department, Regulatory Boards Division, 500 James Robertson Pky, 2nd Floor, Nashville, TN 37243, 615-741-9771, Fax: 615-532-2965

(3) Commerce & Insurance Department, Regulatory Boards Division, 500 James Robertson Pky, 2nd Floor, Nashville, TN 37243, 615-741-2241

(4) Department of Education, Office of Teaching Licensing, 710 James Robertson Pky, 5th Fl, Gateway Plaza, Nashville, TN 37243-0377, 615-532-4885

(5) Department of Health, Health Related Boards, 283 Plus Park Blvd, Nashville, TN 37247-1010, 615-367-6231

(6) Department of Health, Health Related Boards, 283 Plus Park Blvd, Nashville, TN 37247-1010, 615-367-6232

(7) Mechanical Licensing Board, 6465 Mullins Station Rd, Memphis, TN 38134, 901-385-5054, Fax: 901-385-5198

(8) Office of Secretary of State, James K Polk Bldg, Ste 1800, Nashville, TN 37243-0306, 615-741-3699, Fax: 615-741-7310

(9) Registry of Election Finance, 404 James Robertson Pky, Ste 1614, Nashville, TN 37243, 615-741-7959

(10) Tennessee Department of Agriculture, Animal Industries, PO Box 40627, Melrose Station, Nashville, TN 37204, 615-360-0120, Fax: 615-781-5309

(11) Tennessee State Board of Law Examiners, Nashville City Center, 511 Union St, Suite 1420, Nashville, TN 37243-0740, 615-741-3234

Texas

Capitol: Austin (Travis County)	
State Population	18.7 Million
Number of Degree Granting Institutions:	190
Number of State Licensing & Business Registration Agencies:	117

Degree Granting Educational Institutions

Abilene Christian University, Registrar, ACU Station Box 7940, Abilene, TX 79699, 915-674-2235 (Fax: 915-674-2238). Hours: 8AM-Noon, 1-5PM. Enrollment: 4200. Records go back to 1906. Alumni Records Office: ACU Box 8381, Abilene, TX 79699, 915-674-2622. Degrees granted: Bachelors; Masters; Doctorate. Adverse incident record source- Student Services, 914-674-2630.

Attendance and degree information available by phone, fax, mail. Search requires name plus SSN, date of birth. Also helpful: exact years of attendance. There is no fee.

Abilene Intercollegiate School of Nursing, Registrar, 2149 Hickory, Abilene, TX 79601, 915-672-2441 (Fax: 915-672-5026). Hours: 8AM-5PM. Enrollment: 150. Records go back to 1975. Alumni records are maintained here also. Call 915-672-2441. Degrees granted: Bachelors; Masters. Adverse incident record source- Admissions Office, 915-672-5026.

Attendance and degree information available by phone, fax, mail. Search requires name plus SSN, date of birth, exact years of attendance. There is no fee.

Alvin Community College, Director, A&R, 3110 Mustang Rd, Alvin, TX 77511-4898, 713-388-4616 (Fax: 713-388-4929). Hours: 8AM-5PM. Enrollment: 3800. Records go back to 1949. Alumni records are maintained here also. Call 713-388-4615. Degrees granted: Associate.

Attendance and degree information available by phone, fax, mail. Search requires name plus SSN, date of birth. There is no fee.

Amarillo College, Registrar, PO Box 447, Amarillo, TX 79178, 806-371-5030 (Fax: 806-371-5066). Hours: 8AM-4:30PM. Enrollment: 6000. Records go back to 1929. Alumni records are maintained here also. Call 806-371-5000. Degrees granted: Associate. Adverse incident record source- Student Services, 806-371-5300.

Attendance and degree information available by phone, fax, mail. Search requires name plus SSN, date of birth, exact years of attendance. There is no fee.

Amber University, Registrar, 1700 Eastgate Dr, Garland, TX 75041, 214-279-6511 (Fax: 214-279-9773). Hours: 8AM-4:30PM. Enrollment: 1300. Records go back to 1982. Alumni records are maintained here at the same phone number. Degrees granted: Bachelors; Masters.

Attendance and degree information available by mail. Search requires name plus SSN, exact years of attendance, signed release. There is no fee.

Angelina College, Registrar, PO Box 1768, Lufkin, TX 75902, 409-639-1301 (Fax: 409-639-4299). Hours: 8AM-9PM M-Th. Enrollment: 4000. Records go back to 1968. Alumni records are maintained here at the same phone number. Degrees granted: Associate.

Attendance and degree information available by phone, fax, mail. Search requires name plus SSN. Also helpful: date of birth, approximate years of attendance. There is no fee.

Angelo State University, Registrar, 2601 West Ave N, San Angelo, TX 76909, 915-942-2043 (Fax: 915-942-2078). Hours: 8AM-5PM. Enrollment: 6200. Records go back to 1928. Alumni records are maintained here also. Call 915-942-2122. Degrees granted: Associate; Bachelors; Masters. Certification: Teaching.

Attendance and degree information available by phone, mail. Search requires name plus SSN, exact years of attendance. Also helpful: date of birth. There is no fee.

Arlington Baptist College, Registrar, 3001 W Division St, Arlington, TX 76012-3425, 817-461-8741 (Fax: 817-274-1138). Hours: 8AM-4PM. Enrollment: 200. Records go back to 1939. Alumni records are maintained here at the same phone number. Degrees granted: Bachelors. Certification: Bible.

Attendance and degree information available by phone, fax, mail. Search requires name plus exact years of attendance. Also helpful: SSN, date of birth. Fee is $3.00. Expedited service available for $3.00.

Art Institute of Houston, Registrar, 1900 Yorktown, Houston, TX 77056, 713-623-2040 X750 (Fax: 713-966-2700). Enrollment: 900. Records go back to 1978. Alumni records are maintained here at the same phone number. Degrees granted: Associate. Adverse incident record source- Student Affairs.

Attendance and degree information available by phone, mail. Search requires name plus SSN, exact years of attendance. There is no fee.

Austin College, Registrar, 900 N Grand Ave, Sherman, TX 75090-4440, 903-813-2371 (Fax: 903-813-2378). Hours: 8AM-5PM. Enrollment: 1100. Records go back to 1919. Alumni records are maintained here at the same phone number. Degrees granted: Bachelors; Masters. Adverse incident record source- Vice President of Student Life, 903-813-2226.

Attendance and degree information available by phone, fax, mail. Search requires name plus SSN. Also helpful: date of birth, exact years of attendance. There is no fee.

Austin Community College, Registrar, 5930 Middle Fiskville Rd, Austin, TX 78752-4390, 512-223-7000 (Fax: 512-483-7791). Hours: 8AM-4:30PM. Enrollment: 14949. Degrees granted: Associate.

Attendance and degree information available by phone, fax, mail. Search requires name plus SSN, date of birth, exact years of attendance. There is no fee.

Austin Presbyterian Theological Seminary, Registrar, 100 E 27th St, Austin, TX 78705-5797, 512-472-6736 (Fax: 512-479-0738). Hours: 8:30AM-5PM. Enrollment: 330. Records go back to 1902. Alumni records are maintained here at the same phone number. Degrees granted: Masters; Doctorate. Adverse incident record source- Business Office, 512-472-6736.

Attendance and degree information available by phone, fax, mail. Search requires name only. Also helpful: SSN, date of birth. There is no fee.

Baptist Missionary Association Theological Seminary, Registrar, 1530 E Pine St, Jacksonville, TX 75766, 903-586-2501 (Fax: 903-586-0378). Hours: 9AM-4PM. Enrollment: 60. Records go back to 1965. Degrees granted: Associate; Bachelors; Masters.

Attendance information available by phone, fax, mail. Search requires name plus SSN. Also helpful: exact years of attendance. There is no fee.

Degree information available by phone, fax, mail. Search requires name plus approximate years of attendance. Also helpful: SSN, exact years of attendance. There is no fee.

Baylor College of Dentistry, Registrar, PO Box 660, Dallas, TX 75246-0677, 214-828-8230 (Fax: 214-828-8346). Hours: 8AM-4:30PM. Records go back to 1905. Alumni records are maintained here at the same phone number. Degrees granted: Doctorate. Adverse incident record source- Associate Dean of Student Services, 214-828-8230.

Attendance and degree information available by mail. Search requires name plus SSN, exact years of attendance, signed release. There is no fee.

Baylor College of Medicine, Registrar, One Baylor Plaza, Houston, TX 77030, 713-798-4600 (Fax: 713-798-7951). Hours: 8AM-5PM. Enrollment: 1145. Records go back to 1900. Alumni records are maintained here also. Call 713-798-4054. Degrees granted: Masters; Doctorate. Adverse incident record source- Dean of Student Affairs, 713-798-4600.

Attendance and degree information available by phone, fax, mail. Search requires name plus SSN. Also helpful: date of birth. There is no fee.

Baylor University, Registrar, PO Box 97068, Waco, TX 76798, 817-755-1181 (Fax: 817-755-2233). Hours: 8AM-5PM. Enrollment: 12800. Records go back to 1900. Alumni records are maintained here also. Call 817-755-1121. Degrees granted: Bachelors; Masters; Doctorate.

Attendance and degree information available by phone, fax, mail. Search requires name only. Also helpful: SSN, date of birth, exact years of attendance. There is no fee.

Bee County College, Registrar, 3800 Charco Rd, Beeville, TX 78102, 512-358-3130 X2245 (Fax: 512-358-3130 X2254). Hours: 8AM-4:30PM. Enrollment: 5500. Records go

back to 1967. Degrees granted: Associate. Adverse incident record source- Studet Services, 512-358-3130 X2720.

Attendance and degree information available by mail. Search requires name plus SSN, exact years of attendance. There is no fee.

Blinn College, Admissions & Records, 902 College Ave, Brenham, TX 77833, 409-830-4140 (Fax: 409-830-4110). Hours: 8AM-5PM. Enrollment: 9300. Alumni records are maintained here also. Call 409-830-4180. Degrees granted: Associate. Adverse incident record source- 409-830-4190.

Attendance information available by phone, fax, mail. Search requires name plus SSN. Also helpful: approximate years of attendance. There is no fee.

Degree information available by phone, fax, mail. Search requires name plus SSN. Also helpful: exact years of attendance. There is no fee.

Brazosport College, Registrar, 500 College Dr, Lake Jackson, TX 77566, 409-265-6131 X221. Hours: 8AM-5PM. Enrollment: 1860. Records go back to 1947. Alumni records are maintained here at the same phone number. Degrees granted: Associate.

Attendance and degree information available by phone, mail. Search requires name plus SSN, exact years of attendance. There is no fee.

Brookhaven College, Registrar, 3939 Valley View Lane, Farmers Branch, TX 75244-4997, 214-860-4700 (Fax: 214-860-4897). Hours: 8AM-4:30PM. Enrollment: 7000. Records go back to 1977. Alumni records are maintained here at the same phone number. Degrees granted: Associate. Adverse incident record source- Student Affairs, 214-860-4801.

Attendance and degree information available by phone, fax, mail. Search requires name plus SSN, exact years of attendance. There is no fee.

Cedar Valley College, Registrar, 3030 N Dallas Ave, Lancaster, TX 75134, 214-372-8200 (Fax: 214-372-8207). Hours: 8AM-4:30PM. Records go back to 1966. Degrees granted: Associate.

Attendance and degree information available by phone, mail. Search requires name plus SSN. There is no fee.

Central Texas College, Registrar, PO Box 1800, Killeen, TX 76540-9990, 817-526-1308 (Fax: 817-526-1481). Hours: 8AM-5PM. Records go back to 1968. Alumni records are maintained here also. Call 817-526-1306. Degrees granted: Associate. Special programs- Hanau, German, 011-49-6181-95060: Camp Market, Korea, 011-82-32-523-5110.

Attendance and degree information available by phone, fax, mail. Search requires name only. Also helpful: SSN, date of birth, exact years of attendance. There is no fee.

Cisco Junior College, Registrar, Rte 3 Box 3, Cisco, TX 76437, 817-442-2567 (Fax: 817-442-2546). Hours: 8AM-4PM. Enrollment: 2550. Records go back to 1920's. Degrees granted: Associate. Adverse incident record source- Student Affairs, 817-442-2567.

Attendance and degree information available by phone, fax, mail. Search requires name plus SSN, date of birth, exact years of attendance. There is no fee.

Clarendon College, Registrar, PO Box 968, Clarendon, TX 79226, 806-874-3571 (Fax: 806-874-3201). Hours: 8AM-4:30PM. Enrollment: 850. Records go back to 1925. Alumni records are maintained here at the same phone number. Degrees granted: Associate. Special programs- Ranch Operations: Electronics. Adverse incident record source- Dean of Students, 806-874-3571.

Attendance and degree information available by phone, fax, mail. Search requires name plus SSN, date of birth. Also helpful: exact years of attendance. There is no fee.

College of the Mainland, Admissions Office, 1200 Amburn Rd, Texas City, TX 77591, 409-938-1211 X263 (Fax: 409-938-1306). Hours: 8AM-5PM. Records go back to 1968. Alumni records are maintained here at the same phone number. Degrees granted: Associate.

Attendance and degree information available by phone, fax, mail. Search requires name plus SSN. Also helpful: date of birth, approximate years of attendance. There is no fee.

Collin County Community College, Registrar, 2200 W University Dr, PO Box 8001, McKinney, TX 75070, 214-548-6744 (Fax: 214-548-6702). Hours: 8AM-5PM M,T,Th,F; 8AM-8PM W. Records go back to 1985. Alumni records are maintained here at the same phone number. Degrees granted: Associate. Adverse incident record source- Dean of Students, 214-881-5790.

Attendance and degree information available by phone, fax, mail. Search requires name plus SSN. Also helpful: date of birth. There is no fee.

Commonwealth Institute of Funeral Service, Registrar, 415 Barren Springs Dr, Houston, TX 77090, 713-873-0262 (Fax: 713-873-5232). Hours: 8AM-4PM. Enrollment: 150. Records go back to 1945. Degrees granted: Associate. Adverse incident record source- Registrar, 713-873-0262: Dean of Student Affairs

Attendance information available by phone, mail. Search requires name only. Also helpful: SSN, exact years of attendance. There is no fee.

Degree information available by phone, mail. Search requires name only. Also helpful: exact years of attendance. There is no fee.

Community College of the Air Force, (Branch), 882 TRSS/TSOR, 939 Missile Rd #1003, Sheppard AFB, TX 76311-2260, 817-676-6640 (Fax: 817-676-4025). Hours: 7AM-4PM. Enrollment: 9000. Records go back to 1966. Degrees granted: Associate. Certification: Certificate of Training.

Attendance information available by mail. Search requires name plus SSN, exact years of attendance, signed release. There is no fee.

School will not confirm degree information.

Concordia Lutheran College, Registrar, 3400 I H 35 N, Austin, TX 78705, 512-452-7661 (Fax: 512-459-8517). Hours: 8AM-5PM M,T,Th,F; 8AM-6PM W. Enrollment: 700. Records go back to 1926. Alumni records are maintained here at the same phone number. Degrees granted: Associate; Bachelors. Adverse incident record source- Dean of Students, 512-452-7661.

Attendance and degree information available by phone, fax, mail. Search requires name only. Also helpful: SSN, date of birth, exact years of attendance. There is no fee.

Criswell College, Enrollment Services, 4010 Gaston Ave, Dallas, TX 75246, 214-821-5433 (Fax: 214-818-1310). Hours: 8AM-4:30PM. Enrollment: 450. Records go back to 1970. Alumni records are maintained here at the same phone number. Degrees granted: Associate; Bachelors; Masters. Adverse incident record source- Enrollment Services, 214-821-5433.

Attendance information available by fax, mail. Search requires name plus SSN, signed release. Also helpful: date of birth, exact years of attendance. There is no fee.

Degree information available by fax, mail. Search requires name plus SSN, signed release. Also helpful: date of birth, exact years of attendance. There is no fee.

Dallas Baptist University, Registrar, 3000 Mountain Creek Pkwy, Dallas, TX 75211-9299, 214-333-5334 (Fax: 214-

333-5142). Hours: 8AM-6PM M-T; 8AM-5PM W-F;9AM-1PM 2nd Sat of each month. Records go back to 1965. Alumni records are maintained here also. Call 214-333-5166. Degrees granted: Associate; Bachelors; Masters; Police Adacemy. Adverse incident record source- Student Affairs, 214-333-5101.

Attendance and degree information available by phone, fax, mail. Search requires name plus SSN. Also helpful: exact years of attendance. There is no fee.

Dallas Christian College, Registrar, 2700 Christian Pkwy, Dallas, TX 75234, 214-241-3371 (Fax: 214-241-8021). Hours: 8AM-5PM. Enrollment: 200. Records go back to 1950. Alumni records are maintained here at the same phone number. Degrees granted: Associate; Bachelors.

Attendance information available by phone, fax, mail. Search requires name only. Also helpful: SSN, date of birth, exact years of attendance. There is no fee.

Degree information available by phone, fax, mail. Search requires name plus approximate years of attendance. Also helpful: SSN, date of birth, exact years of attendance. There is no fee.

Dallas Theological Seminary, Registrar, 3909 Swiss Ave, Dallas, TX 75204, 214-841-3608 (Fax: 214-841-3664). Hours: 8AM-4:30PM. Enrollment: 1564. Records go back to 1924. Alumni records are maintained here also. Call 214-841-3606. Degrees granted: Masters; Doctorate. Adverse incident record source- Public Relations, 214-841-3556.

Attendance information available by phone, fax, mail. Search requires name only. Also helpful: SSN, exact years of attendance. There is no fee. Expedited service available for $15.00.

Degree information available by phone, fax, mail. Search requires name only. Also helpful: SSN, exact years of attendance. There is no fee. Expedite service available for $15.00.

DeVry Institute of Technology, Dallas, Registrar, 4801 Regent Blvd, Irving, TX 75063-2440, 214-929-6777 (Fax: 214-929-6778). Hours: 8AM-7PM M,T; 8AM-5PM W-F. Enrollment: 2300. Records go back to 1969. Alumni Records Office: Alumni Association, DeVry Institute of Technology, One Tower Lane,, Oakbrook Terrace, IL 60181-4624. Degrees granted: Associate; Bachelors. Adverse incident record source- Student Services, 214-929-6777.

Attendance and degree information available by phone, mail. Search requires name plus SSN. Also helpful: date of birth, exact years of attendance. There is no fee.

Del Mar College, Registrar, 101 Baldwin Blvd, Corpus Christi, TX 78404-3897, 512-886-1248 (Fax: 512-886-1595). Hours: 7:30AM-7:30PM M-Th; 7:30AM-Noon F. Records go back to 1935. Degrees granted: Associate.

Attendance and degree information available by phone, fax, mail. Search requires name plus SSN. Also helpful: date of birth, exact years of attendance. There is no fee.

East Texas Baptist University, Registrar, 1209 N Grove Ave, Marshall, TX 75670-1498, 903-935-7963 (Fax: 903-938-1705). Hours: 8AM-4:30PM. Enrollment: 1300. Records go back to 1917. Alumni records are maintained here at the same phone number. Degrees granted: Associate; Bachelors; Masters. Adverse incident record source- Student Affairs, 903-935-7963 X274.

Attendance and degree information available by phone, fax, mail. Search requires name only. Also helpful: SSN, date of birth, exact years of attendance. There is no fee.

East Texas State University, Registrar, ETSU Station, Commerce, TX 75429-3011, 903-886-5448 (Fax: 903-886-5888). Hours: 8AM-5PM. Records go back to 1915. Degrees granted: Bachelors; Masters; Doctorate.

Attendance and degree information available by phone, fax, mail. Search requires name only. Also helpful: SSN, date of birth, exact years of attendance. There is no fee.

East Texas State University at Texarkana,
Admissions, ETSU-T, 2600 N Robison Rd, Texarkana, TX 75505, 903-838-6514 (Fax: 903-832-8890). Hours: 8AM-5PM. Enrollment: 1184. Records go back to 1971. Alumni records are maintained here at the same phone number. Degrees granted: Bachelors; Masters.
Attendance and degree information available by phone, fax, mail. Search requires name only. Also helpful: SSN. There is no fee.

Eastfield College, Registrar, 3737 Motley Dr, Mesquite,
TX 75150-2099, 214-860-7100. Hours: 8AM-5PM. Enrollment: 8458. Records go back to 1970. Degrees granted: Associate.
Attendance and degree information available by mail. Search requires name plus SSN. There is no fee.

El Centro College, Registrar, Main and Lamar Sts, Dallas, TX 75202-3604, 903-765-2311 (Fax: 903-746-2335). Hours: 8AM-7PM. Enrollment: 4800. Records go back to 1966. Degrees granted: Associate. Adverse incident record source- Student Services, 214-746-2017.
Attendance and degree information available by phone, fax, mail. Search requires name plus SSN. Also helpful: date of birth, approximate years of attendance. There is no fee.

El Paso Community College, Registrar, PO Box
20500, El Paso, TX 79998, 915-594-2300 (Fax: 915-594-2161). Hours: 8AM-5PM M-F; 8AM-Noon S. Enrollment: 20000. Records go back to 1970. Degrees granted: Associate. Adverse incident record source- Security, 915-594-2200.
Attendance and degree information available by phone, fax, mail. Search requires name plus SSN. Also helpful: date of birth, exact years of attendance. There is no fee.

Episcopal Theological Seminary of the Southwest, Registrar, PO Box 2247, Austin, TX 78768-2247, 512-472-4133 (Fax: 512-472-3098). Hours: 8:15AM-2PM. Enrollment: 65. Records go back to 1955. Alumni records are maintained here at the same phone number. Degrees granted: Masters.
Attendance and degree information available by phone, fax, mail. Search requires name only. Also helpful: SSN, exact years of attendance. There is no fee.

Fashion And Art Institute of Dallas, Registrar, 2
N Park E, 8080 Park Ln, Dallas, TX 75231, 214-692-8080 (Fax: 214-750-9460). Enrollment: 1200. Records go back to 1986. Alumni records are maintained here at the same phone number. Degrees granted: Associate. Special programs- Arts: Science. Adverse incident record source- Student Services.
Attendance and degree information available by phone, mail. Search requires name plus SSN, exact years of attendance. There is no fee.

Frank Phillips College, Registrar, PO Box 5118, Borger, TX 79008-5118, 806-274-5311 (Fax: 806-274-6835). Hours: 8AM-5PM. Records go back to 1948. Degrees granted: Associate. Adverse incident record source- Dean of Student Life, 806-274-5311.
Attendance and degree information available by written request only. Search requires name plus SSN, signed release. Also helpful: date of birth, exact years of attendance. There is no fee.

Galveston College, Registrar, 4015 Ave Q, Galveston,
TX 77550, 409-763-6551 (Fax: 409-762-9367). Hours: 8:30AM-7PM. Alumni records are maintained here at the same phone number. Degrees granted: Associate. Adverse incident record source- Security, 409-763-7552 X364: Dean of Student Services, 409-763-6551 X206
Attendance and degree information available by fax, mail. Search requires name plus SSN, signed release. There is no fee.

Grayson County College, Registrar, 6161 Grayson
Dr, Denison, TX 75020, 903-463-8650 (Fax: 903-463-5284). Hours: 8AM-4PM. Enrollment: 3200. Records go back to 1965. Degrees granted: Associate. Adverse incident record source- Student Services, 903-463-8644.
Attendance and degree information available by phone, fax, mail. Search requires name plus SSN. There is no fee.

Hardin-Simmons University, Registrar, Sandefer
Memorial Bldg, Box 16190, Abilene, TX 79698, 915-670-1200 (Fax: 915-670-1261). Hours: 9AM-5PM. Enrollment: 2400. Records go back to 1891. Alumni Records Office: Box 15300, Abilene, TX 79698, 915-670-1377 (Fax: 915-670-1574). Degrees granted: Associate; Bachelors; Masters. Adverse incident record source- Campus Police, 915-670-1461.
Attendance and degree information available by phone, fax, mail. Search requires name only. Also helpful: SSN, exact years of attendance. There is no fee.

Hill College, Registrar, PO Box 619, Hillsboro, TX 76645,
817-582-2555 (Fax: 817-582-7591). Hours: 8AM-4PM. Enrollment: 2600. Records go back to 1923. Alumni records are maintained here at the same phone number. Degrees granted: Associate. Adverse incident record source- Dean, 817-582-2555.
Attendance information available by phone, fax, mail. Search requires name plus SSN. Also helpful: exact years of attendance. There is no fee.
Degree information available by phone, fax, mail. Search requires name plus SSN. Also helpful: exact years of attendance. There is no fee.

Houston Baptist University, Registrar, 7502 Fondren Rd, Houston, TX 77074-3298, 713-774-7661. Alumni records are maintained here at the same phone number. Degrees granted: Bachelors; Masters.
Attendance and degree information available by mail. Search requires name plus SSN, signed release. Also helpful: date of birth, exact years of attendance. There is no fee.

Houston Community College, Registrar, PO Box
7819, Houston, TX 77270-7849, 713-868-0763 (Fax: 713-869-5743). Hours: 8AM-4:30PM. Enrollment: 23330. Records go back to 1971. Degrees granted: Associate.
Attendance and degree information available by mail. Search requires name plus SSN, signed release. Also helpful: exact years of attendance. There is no fee.

Houston Community College, (Central College),
Registrar, 1300 Holman Ave, PO Box 7849, Houston, TX 77004, 713-523-2825. Hours: 8AM-5PM. Enrollment: 23330. Alumni records are maintained here at the same phone number. Degrees granted: Associate.
Attendance and degree information available by mail. Search requires name plus SSN, exact years of attendance, signed release. There is no fee.

Houston Community College, (College Without
Walls), Registrar, 4310 Dunlavy St, Houston, TX 77270, 713-868-0795. Records are not housed here. They are located at Houston Community College, (Central College), Registrar, 1300 Holman Ave, PO Box 7849, Houston, TX 77004.

Houston Community College, (Northeast College), Registrar, 4638 Airline Dr, PO Box 7849, Houston, TX 77270-7849, 713-694-5384. Records are not housed here. They are located at Houston Community College, (Central College), Registrar, 1300 Holman Ave, PO Box 7849, Houston, TX 77004.

Houston Community College, (Southeast College), Registrar, 6815 Rustic St, Houston, TX 77012, 713-641-2725. Records are not housed here. They are located at Houston

Community College, (Central College), Registrar, 1300 Holman Ave, PO Box 7849, Houston, TX 77004.

Houston Community College, (Southwest College), Registrar, 5407 Gulfton St, Houston, TX 77081, 713-661-4589. Records are not housed here. They are located at Houston Community College, (Central College), Registrar, 1300 Holman Ave, PO Box 7849, Houston, TX 77004.

Houston Community College System, Registrar, PO Box 7849, Houston, TX 77270, 713-718-2000 (Fax: 713-869-5743). Hours: 8AM-4:30PM. Enrollment: 23330. Records go back to 1971. Degrees granted: Associate.

Attendance and degree information available by fax, mail. Search requires name plus SSN, date of birth, signed release. Also helpful: exact years of attendance. There is no fee. Expedited service available for $15.00.

Houston Graduate School of Theology, Registrar, 1311 Holman St., Suite 200, Houston, TX 77004, 713-942-9505 (Fax: 713-942-9506). Hours: 8AM-5PM. Enrollment: 100. Records go back to 1986. Alumni records are maintained here at the same phone number. Degrees granted: Masters; Doctorate.

Attendance and degree information available by phone, fax, mail. Search requires name plus SSN. Also helpful: exact years of attendance. There is no fee.

Howard College, Admissions Office, 1001 Birdwell Lane, Big Spring, TX 79720, 915-264-5000 (Fax: 915-264-5082). Hours: 8AM-6PM M-Th; 8AM-3PM F. Enrollment: 2500. Records go back to 1945. Alumni records are maintained here also. Call 915-264-5000. Degrees granted: Associate. Adverse incident record source- Student Services, 915-26-5028.

Attendance and degree information available by mail. Search requires name plus signed release. Also helpful: SSN, date of birth, exact years of attendance. There is no fee.

Howard Payne University, Registrar, 1000 Fisk Ave, Brownwood, TX 76801, 915-649-8011 (Fax: 915-649-8901). Hours: 8AM-5PM. Enrollment: 1480. Records go back to 1889. Alumni records are maintained here at the same phone number. Degrees granted: Bachelors.

Attendance and degree information available by phone, fax, mail. Search requires name plus SSN, date of birth. Also helpful: exact years of attendance. There is no fee.

Huston-Tillotson College, Registrar, 900 Chicon St, Austin, TX 78702, 512-505-3082 (Fax: 512-505-3190). Hours: 8:30AM-5:30PM. Enrollment: 620. Alumni records are maintained here at the same phone number. Degrees granted: Bachelors.

Attendance information available by phone, fax, mail. Search requires name only. Also helpful: SSN, date of birth, exact years of attendance. There is no fee.

Degree information available by phone, fax, mail. Search requires name only. Also helpful: exact years of attendance. There is no fee.

ICI University, Registrar, 6300 N Belt Line Rd, Irving, TX 75063, 214-751-1111 (Fax: 214-714-8185). Hours: 8AM-4:30PM. Records go back to 1973. Degrees granted: Associate; Bachelors; Masters.

Attendance information available by written request only. Search requires name plus date of birth, signed release. Also helpful: exact years of attendance. There is no fee.

Degree information available by written request only. Search requires name plus date of birth. Also helpful: exact years of attendance. There is no fee.

ITT Technical Institute, Registrar, 2201 Arlington Downs Rd, Arlington, TX 76011-6319, 817-640-7100 (Fax: 817-649-8078). Hours: 8AM-5PM. Enrollment: 400. Records go

back to 1963. Alumni Records Office: 9511 Angola Ct, Indianapolis, IN 46268. Degrees granted: Associate. Special programs-Electrical Engineering: Computer Drafting. Adverse incident record source- Security, 817-640-7100.

Attendance and degree information available by mail. Search requires name plus SSN, date of birth, exact years of attendance, signed release. There is no fee.

ITT Technical Institute, Registrar, 1640 Eastgate Dr, Garland, TX 75041-5585, 214-279-0500 (Fax: 214-613-4523). Hours: 8AM-5PM. Enrollment: 350. Records go back to 1990. Alumni records are maintained here at the same phone number. Degrees granted: Associate.

Attendance and degree information available by phone, fax, mail. Search requires name plus SSN, approximate years of attendance. Also helpful: date of birth. There is no fee.

ITT Technical Institute, Registrar, 2950 S. Gessner, Houston, TX 77063, 713-952-2294 (Fax: 713-952-2393). Hours: 8AM-10PM. Enrollment: 500. Records go back to 1986. Alumni Records Office: 9511 Angola Ct, Indianapolis, IN 46268. Degrees granted: Associate. Special programs- Computer Design: Chemical Technology.

Attendance and degree information available by mail. Search requires name plus SSN, date of birth, exact years of attendance. There is no fee.

ITT Technical Institute, Registrar, 4242 Piedras Dr E Ste 100, San Antonio, TX 78228-1414, 210-737-1881. Hours: 8AM-5PM. Records go back to 1970's. Alumni Records Office: 9511 Angola Ct, Indianapolis, IN 46268. Degrees granted: Associate.

Attendance and degree information available by phone, mail. Search requires name plus SSN. There is no fee.

ITT Technical Institute, (Branch of Indianapolis, IN), Registrar, 6330 Hwy 290E #150, Austin, TX 78723-9975, 512-467-6800 (Fax: 512-467-6677). Hours: 8AM-6PM. Enrollment: 500. Records go back to 1981. Alumni Records Office: 6330 Hwy 290E, S150, Austin, TX 78723-9975. Degrees granted: Associate. Adverse incident record source- Education Supervisor, 512-467-6800.

Attendance and degree information available by phone, fax, mail. Search requires name plus SSN, date of birth. Also helpful: exact years of attendance. There is no fee.

ITT Technical Institute, (Branch of Indianapolis, IN), Registrar, 15621 Blue Ash Dr Ste 160, Houston, TX 77090-5818, 713-873-0512 (Fax: 713 873 0518). Hours: 8AM-4:30PM. Enrollment: 400. Records go back to 1970. Alumni Records Office: ITT Technical Institute, 9511 Angola Ct, Indianapolis, IN 46268. Degrees granted: Associate. Special programs- Engineering Technology.

Attendance and degree information available by phone, fax, mail. Search requires name plus SSN, exact years of attendance. There is no fee.

Institute for Christian Studies, Registrar, 1909 University Ave at 20th St, Austin, TX 78705, 512-476-2772 (Fax: 512-476-3919). Hours: 8AM-5PM. Enrollment: 75. Records go back to 1977. Alumni records are maintained here at the same phone number. Degrees granted: Bachelors; Masters; SACS accredits bachelor degree programs at ICS, an off-campus graduate degree program through Abilene Christian University.

Attendance and degree information available by phone, fax, mail. Search requires name plus SSN. Also helpful: date of birth, exact years of attendance. There is no fee.

Jacksonville College, Registrar, 105 B.J. Albritton Dr, Jacksonville, TX 75766-4759, 903-589-2801 (Fax: 903-586-0743). Hours: 8AM-5PM. Enrollment: 350. Records go back to 1899. Alumni records are maintained here also. Call 903-586-2518. Degrees granted: Associate.

Attendance and degree information available by phone, fax, mail. Search requires name only. Also helpful: SSN, approximate years of attendance. There is no fee.

Jarvis Christian College, Registrar, PO Drawer G, Hawkins, TX 75765-9989, 903-769-5700 (Fax: 903-769-4842). Hours: 8AM-5PM. Enrollment: 500. Records go back to 1912. Alumni records are maintained here also. Call 903-769-5711. Degrees granted: Bachelors.

Attendance and degree information available by phone, fax, mail. Search requires name plus SSN. Also helpful: exact years of attendance. There is no fee.

KD Studio, Registrar, 2600 Stemmons Fwy #117, Dallas, TX 75207, 214-638-0484 (Fax: 214-630-5140). Hours: 8AM-6PM. Enrollment: 140. Records go back to 1979. Degrees granted: Associate. Adverse incident record source- Registrar, 214-638-0484.

Attendance and degree information available by mail. Search requires name plus SSN. There is no fee.

Kilgore College, Registrar, 1100 Broadway, Kilgore, TX 75662-3299, 903-984-8531 (Fax: 903-983-8607). Hours: 8AM-4:30PM. Enrollment: 4300. Records go back to 1935. Alumni records are maintained here also. Call 903-983-8187. Degrees granted: Associate. Adverse incident record source- Student Services, 903-983-8189.

Attendance and degree information available by phone, fax, mail. Search requires name plus SSN, date of birth, exact years of attendance. There is no fee.

Kingwood College, Registrar, 20000 Kingwood Dr, Kingwood, TX 77339, 713-359-1600 (Fax: 713-359-0477). Hours: 8AM-9:30 PM M-Th;8AM-4:s30PM F. Enrollment: 3400. Records go back to 1974. Alumni records are maintained here at the same phone number. Degrees granted: Associate. Adverse incident record source- Student Services.

Attendance and degree information available by phone, fax, mail. Search requires name plus SSN. Also helpful: approximate years of attendance. There is no fee.

Lamar University at Beaumont, Registrar, 4400 Martin Luther King, Jr. Pkwy Blvd, Beaumont, TX 77710, 409-880-8365 (Fax: 409-880-8463). Enrollment: 8414. Records go back to 1923. Alumni records are maintained here at the same phone number. Degrees granted: Bachelors; Masters; Doctorate. Adverse incident record source- Student Affairs, 409-880-8458.

Attendance and degree information available by phone, mail. Search requires name plus SSN, date of birth. There is no fee.

Lamar University at Orange, Registrar, 410 W Front St, Orange, TX 77630, 409-883-7750. Hours: 8AM-5PM. Enrollment: 1500. Records go back to 1984. Degrees granted: Associate. Adverse incident record source- Dean of Student Services, 409-882-3341.

Attendance and degree information available by phone, mail. Search requires name plus SSN. There is no fee.

Lamar University at Port Arthur, Registrar, PO Box 310, Port Arthur, TX 77641-0310, 409-983-4921 (Fax: 409-984-6000). Hours: 8AM-5PM M,T,Th,F:8AM-6PM W. Enrollment: 2500. Records go back to 1975. Degrees granted: Associate. Adverse incident record source- Dean of Student Services, 409-984-6156.

Attendance and degree information available by phone, fax, mail. Search requires name plus SSN, approximate years of attendance. Also helpful: date of birth, exact years of attendance. There is no fee.

Laredo Community College, Registrar, W End Washington St, Laredo, TX 78040-4395, 210-721-5109 (Fax: 210-721-5493). Hours: 8AM-5PM. Enrollment: 7000. Records

go back to 1947. Degrees granted: Associate. Adverse incident record source- Dean of Student Services, 210-721-5417.

Attendance and degree information available by phone, fax, mail. Search requires name plus SSN, date of birth. There is no fee.

LeTourneau University, Registrar, PO Box 7001, Longview, TX 75607, 903-233-3450 (Fax: 903-233-3411). Hours: 8AM-5PM. Records go back to 1946. Alumni records are maintained here also. Call 903-233-3670. Degrees granted: Associate; Bachelors; Masters.

Attendance and degree information available by phone, fax, mail. Search requires name only. Also helpful: SSN, date of birth, exact years of attendance. There is no fee.

Lee College, Admissions & Records, PO Box 818, Baytown, TX 77522, 713-425-6393 (Fax: 713-425-6831). Hours: 7:30AM-7:30PM M,T; 7:30AM-5PM W,Th; 7:30AM-12:30PM F. Enrollment: 5700. Records go back to 1934. Alumni records are maintained here at the same phone number. Degrees granted: Associate. Special programs- Administrative Services, 713-425-6348. Adverse incident record source- Administrative Services, 713-425-6348.

Attendance and degree information available by phone, mail. Search requires name only. Also helpful: SSN, date of birth, exact years of attendance. There is no fee.

Lon Morris College, Registrar, 800 College Ave, Jacksonville, TX 75766, 903-589-4005 (Fax: 903-586-8562). Hours: 8:30AM-5PM. Enrollment: 350. Records go back to 1900. Alumni records are maintained here at the same phone number. Degrees granted: Associate. Adverse incident record source- Dean of Student Services, 903-589-4005.

Attendance and degree information available by mail. Search requires name plus SSN, exact years of attendance. There is no fee.

Lubbock Christian University, Registrar, 5601 19th St, Lubbock, TX 79407-2099, 806-796-8800 X225 (Fax: 806-796-8917). Enrollment: 1200. Records go back to 1957. Alumni records are maintained here also. Call 806-796-8800 X378. Degrees granted: Bachelors; Masters.

Attendance and degree information available by phone, fax, mail. Search requires name plus SSN, exact years of attendance. Also helpful: date of birth. There is no fee.

McLennan Community College, Registrar, 1400 College Dr, Waco, TX 76708, 817-299-8660 (Fax: 817-299-8653). Hours: 8AM-8PM M-Th; 8AM-5PM F. Enrollment: 6000. Records go back to 1966. Degrees granted: Associate. Adverse incident record source- Campus Police, 817-299-8911.

Attendance and degree information available by fax, mail. Search requires name plus SSN, approximate years of attendance, signed release. Also helpful: date of birth. There is no fee.

McMurry University, Registrar, PO Box 338, McMurry Station, Abilene, TX 79697, 915-691-6400 (Fax: 915-691-6599). Hours: 8AM-5PM. Enrollment: 1500. Records go back to 1923. Alumni Records Office: PO Box 938, Abilene, TX 79697, 915-691-6387. Degrees granted: Associate; Bachelors.

Attendance and degree information available by phone, mail. Search requires name plus SSN. Also helpful: exact years of attendance. There is no fee.

Midland College, Registrar, 3600 N Garfield St, Midland, TX 79705, 915-685-4508 (Fax: 915-685-4714). Hours: 8AM-4:30PM. Degrees granted: Associate.

Attendance and degree information available by phone, fax, mail. Search requires name plus SSN, approximate years of attendance. There is no fee.

Midwestern State University, Registrar & Admissions, 3410 Taft Blvd, Wichita Falls, TX 76308-2099, 817-689-

4321 (Fax: 817-689-4042). Hours: 8AM-5PM. Enrollment: 5833. Records go back to 1922. Alumni records are maintained here also. Call 817-689-4121. Degrees granted: Associate; Bachelors; Masters. Certification: Teacher Cert. Adverse incident record source- Dean of Students, 817-689-4291.

Attendance and degree information available by phone, mail. Search requires name plus SSN. Also helpful: date of birth, exact years of attendance. There is no fee.

Miss Wade's Fashion Merchandising College, Registrar, PO Box 586343, Dallas Apparel Mart Ste M5120, Dallas, TX 75258, 214-637-3520 (Fax: 214-637-0827). Hours: 8AM-4:30PM. Enrollment: 280. Degrees granted: Associate.

Attendance and degree information available by phone, fax, mail. Search requires name plus SSN, exact years of attendance. There is no fee.

Mountain View College, Registrar, 4849 W Illinois Ave, Dallas, TX 75211-6599, 214-860-8600 (Fax: 214-333-8570). Hours: 8AM-8PM M-Th; 8AM-5PM F. Enrollment: 6100. Records go back to 1965. Degrees granted: Associate.

Attendance and degree information available by fax, mail. Search requires name plus SSN. There is no fee.

Navarro College, Registrar, 3200 W Seventh Ave, Corsicana, TX 75110, 903-874-6501 (Fax: 903-874-4636). Hours: 8AM-7PM M-Th;8AM-5PM F. Enrollment: 320. Records go back to 1946. Alumni records are maintained here at the same phone number. Degrees granted: Associate. Adverse incident record source- Dean of Students, 903-874-6501.

Attendance and degree information available by phone, fax, mail. Search requires name plus SSN. There is no fee.

North Central Texas College, Registrar, 1525 W California St, Gainesville, TX 76240, 817-668-4222 (Fax: 817-668-6049). Hours: 8AM-8PM in session. Enrollment: 4000. Records go back to 1924. Alumni records are maintained here also. Call 817-668-4213. Degrees granted: Associate. Adverse incident record source- Gainesville Police, 817-668-7777.

Attendance and degree information available by phone, fax, mail. Search requires name only. Also helpful: SSN, exact years of attendance. There is no fee.

North Harris College, Registrar, 2700 W. Thorne, Houston, TX 77073, 713-443-5420. Degrees granted: Associate.

Attendance and degree information available by phone, mail. Search requires name plus SSN, exact years of attendance. There is no fee.

North Harris Montgomery Community College, Registrar, 250 N Sam Houston Pkwy E, Houston, TX 77060, 713-591-3573 (Fax: 713-591-9301). Hours: 8AM-5PM. Records go back to 1975. Degrees granted: Associate.

Attendance and degree information available by phone, fax, mail. Search requires name plus SSN, approximate years of attendance. There is no fee.

North Lake College, Registrar, 5001 N MacArthur Blvd, Irving, TX 75038-3899, 214-273-3310. Hours: 8AM-8PM M-Th; 8AM-4:30PM F. Enrollment: 3252. Records go back to 1977. Degrees granted: Associate.

Attendance and degree information available by mail. Search requires name plus SSN. There is no fee.

Northeast Texas Community College, Registrar, PO Drawer 1307, Mount Pleasant, TX 75456-1307, 903-572-1911 (Fax: 903-572-6712). Hours: 8AM-6PM M-Th; 8AM-Noon F. Enrollment: 1935. Records go back to 1985. Alumni records are maintained here at the same phone number. Degrees granted: Associate.

Attendance and degree information available by phone, fax, mail. Search requires name only. There is no fee.

Northwood University, (Branch), Registrar, 1114 W FM 1382, PO Box 58, Cedar Hill, TX 75104, 214-291-1541 (Fax: 214-291-3824). Hours: 8AM-5PM. Enrollment: 1050. Records go back to 1946. Alumni records are maintained here at the same phone number. Degrees granted: Associate; Bachelors. Adverse incident record source- Student Services.

Attendance and degree information available by phone, mail. Search requires name plus SSN. There is no fee.

Oblate School of Theology, Registrar, 285 Oblate Dr, San Antonio, TX 78216-6693, 210-341-1366 X212 (Fax: 210-341-4519). Hours: 8AM-Noon, 1-3PM. Enrollment: 130. Records go back to 1930's. Degrees granted: Masters; Doctorate.

Attendance and degree information available by mail. Search requires name plus SSN, date of birth, signed release. Also helpful: exact years of attendance. Fee is $3.00.

Odessa College, Registrar, 201 W University Blvd, Odessa, TX 79764, 915-335-6404 (Fax: 915-335-6303). Hours: 8AM-6PM. Enrollment: 5000. Records go back to 1946. Degrees granted: Associate.

Attendance and degree information available by fax, mail. Search requires name plus SSN, date of birth, exact years of attendance, signed release. There is no fee.

Our Lady of the Lake University, Registrar, 411 SW 24th St, San Antonio, TX 78207-4689, 210-434-6711 X316 (Fax: 210-436-2314). Enrollment: 3300. Records go back to 1920's. Alumni records are maintained here also. Call 210-434-6711 X469. Degrees granted: Bachelors; Masters; Doctorate. Adverse incident record source- Campus Police, 210-434-6711 X360.

Attendance and degree information available by phone, fax, mail. Search requires name only. Also helpful: SSN, date of birth, exact years of attendance. There is no fee.

Palo Alto College, Registrar, 1400 W Villaret Blvd, San Antonio, TX 78224-2499, 210-921-5000 (Fax: 210-921-5310). Hours: 8AM-5PM. Degrees granted: Associate.

Attendance and degree information available by phone, fax, mail. Search requires name plus SSN, approximate years of attendance. There is no fee.

Pan American University, Admissions Office, 1201 W University Dr, Edinburg, TX 78539, 210-381-2206 (Fax: 210-381-2212). Enrollment: 13366. Records go back to 1952. Alumni records are maintained here also. Call 210-381-2326. Degrees granted: Associate; Bachelors; Masters; Doctorate. Special programs- Liberal Arts & Science. Adverse incident record source- Department of Security.

Attendance and degree information available by phone, mail. Search requires name plus SSN, exact years of attendance. There is no fee.

Panola College, Registrar, 1109 W Panola St, Carthage, TX 75633, 903-693-2038 (Fax: 903-693-5588). Hours: 8AM-4:30PM. Enrollment: 1725. Records go back to 1947. Alumni records are maintained here also. Call 903-693-2044. Degrees granted: Associate. Special programs- Forest Technology, 903-693-2034: Associate Degree Nursing, 903-693-2034. Adverse incident record source- 903-693-2038.

Attendance and degree information available by phone, fax, mail. Search requires name plus SSN. Also helpful: date of birth, exact years of attendance. There is no fee.

Paris Junior College, Records Office, 2400 Clarksville St, Paris, TX 75460, 903-784-9212 (Fax: 903-784-9309). Hours: 8AM-5PM. Enrollment: 2400. Records go back to 1924. Alumni records are maintained here also. Call 903-785-9574. Degrees granted: Associate. Adverse incident record source- Student Life, 903-784-9402.

Attendance and degree information available by phone, fax, mail. Search requires name plus SSN. Also helpful: date of birth, exact years of attendance. There is no fee.

Parker College of Chiropractic, Registrar, 2500 Walnut Hill Lane, Dallas, TX 75229-5668, 214-438-6932 (Fax: 214-352-8425). Hours: 8AM-5PM. Enrollment: 193. Records go back to 1982. Degrees granted: Bachelors; Masters; Doctorate; First Professional Degree. Adverse incident record source- Registrar.

Attendance and degree information available by phone, fax, mail. Search requires name plus SSN. Also helpful: date of birth. There is no fee.

Paul Quinn College, Registrar, 3837 Simpson Stuart Rd, PO Box 411238, Dallas, TX 75241, 214-302-3540 (Fax: 214-302-3613). Hours: 8AM-6PM. Enrollment: 800. Records go back to 1880. Alumni records are maintained here also. Call 214-302-3580. Degrees granted: Bachelors. Adverse incident record source- Student Affairs, 214-302-3631.

Attendance and degree information available by phone, fax, mail. Search requires name only. Also helpful: SSN, date of birth. There is no fee.

Prairie View A&M University, Registrar, PO Box 2610, Prairie View, TX 77446, 409-857-2690 (Fax: 409-857-2699). Hours: 8AM-5PM. Enrollment: 5099. Records go back to 1930's. Alumni records are maintained here also. Call 409-857-4516. Degrees granted: Bachelors; Masters. Adverse incident record source- Student Affairs, 409-587-2693.

Attendance and degree information available by phone, fax, mail. Search requires name plus SSN. Also helpful: date of birth, exact years of attendance. There is no fee.

Ranger College, Registrar, College Cir, Ranger, TX 76470-3298, 817-647-3234 (Fax: 817-647-1656). Enrollment: 875. Records go back to 1926. Degrees granted: Associate.

Attendance and degree information available by phone, fax, mail. Search requires name only. Also helpful: SSN, date of birth, exact years of attendance. There is no fee.

Rice University, Office of the Registrar, 6100 Main St, Houston, TX 77005-1892, 713-527-4999 (Fax: 713-285-5323). Hours: 8:30PM-5PM. Records go back to 1916. Alumni records are maintained here at the same phone number. Degrees granted: Bachelors; Masters; Doctorate. Adverse incident record source- Dean of Students.

Attendance and degree information available by phone, fax, mail. Search requires name plus SSN, approximate years of attendance. Also helpful: date of birth, exact years of attendance. There is no fee.

Richland College, Registrar, 12800 Abrams Rd, Dallas, TX 75243-2199, 214-238-6051 (Fax: 214-238-6149). Hours: 8:30AM-7PM M-Th; 8:30AM-5PM F. Records go back to 1972. Degrees granted: Associate. Adverse incident record source- 214-238-6911.

Attendance and degree information available by mail. Search requires name plus SSN, signed release. There is no fee.

Sam Houston State University, Registrar, PO Box 2029, Huntsville, TX 77341, 409-294-1035 (Fax: 409-294-1097). Hours: 8AM-5PM. Enrollment: 12400. Records go back to 1800's. Alumni records are maintained here also. Call 409-294-1841. Degrees granted: Bachelors; Masters; Doctorate. Certification: Teacher.

Attendance and degree information available by phone, fax, mail. Search requires name plus SSN. Also helpful: date of birth, approximate years of attendance. There is no fee.

San Antonio College, Registrar, 1300 San Pedro Ave, San Antonio, TX 78212-4299, 210-733-2000. Hours: 8AM-4:30PM. Records go back to 1960's. Degrees granted: Associate.

Attendance and degree information available by phone, mail. Search requires name plus SSN. Also helpful: date of birth, approximate years of attendance. There is no fee.

San Jacinto College, Registrar, 8060 Spencer Hwy, Pasadena, TX 77505, 713-476-1844 (Fax: 713-476-1892). Hours: 8AM-4:30PM. Enrollment: 10000. Records go back to 1961. Degrees granted: Associate.

Attendance and degree information available by phone, mail. Search requires name plus SSN. Also helpful: date of birth, exact years of attendance. There is no fee.

San Jacinto College North Campus, Registrar, 5800 Uvalde Rd, Houston, TX 77049, 713-459-7102 (Fax: 713-459-7132). Enrollment: 50. Records go back to 1974. Degrees granted: Associate. Special programs- Arts: Science. Adverse incident record source- Security.

Attendance and degree information available by phone. Search requires name plus SSN, exact years of attendance. There is no fee.

Schreiner College, Registrar, 2100 Memorial Blvd, Kerrville, TX 78028, 210-896-5411 X224 (Fax: 210-896-3232). Hours: 8AM-5PM. Enrollment: 650. Records go back to 1923. Alumni records are maintained here also. Call 210-896-5411 X200. Degrees granted: Associate; Bachelors. Certification: Voc. Nursing.

Attendance and degree information available by phone, fax, mail. Search requires name plus SSN. Also helpful: date of birth, exact years of attendance. There is no fee.

South Plains College, Registrar, 1401 College Ave, Levelland, TX 79336, 806-894-9611 X2370 (Fax: 806-897-3167). Hours: 8AM-4PM. Enrollment: 5800. Alumni records are maintained here also. Call 806-894-9611 X2217. Degrees granted: Associate.

Attendance and degree information available by phone, fax, mail. Search requires name plus SSN. Also helpful: exact years of attendance. There is no fee.

South Texas College of Law, Registrar, 1303 San Jacinto St, Houston, TX 77002-7000, 713-659-8040. Hours: 9AM-5PM. Enrollment: 1250. Records go back to 1920's. Alumni records are maintained here at the same phone number. Degrees granted: Doctorate; First Professional Degree. Adverse incident record source- Registrar's Office, 713-659-8040 .

Attendance and degree information available by mail. Search requires name plus SSN, exact years of attendance, signed release. There is no fee.

Southern Methodist University, Registrar, PO Box 750276, Dallas, TX 75275-0276, 214-768-2045 (Fax: 214-768-2507). Hours: 8:30AM-5PM. Enrollment: 9172. Records go back to 1913. Alumni Records Office: Alumni Relations, PO Box 750173, Dallas, TX 75275. Degrees granted: Bachelors; Masters; Doctorate. Adverse incident record source- Student Life, 214-768-4564: DPS, 214-768-2490

Attendance and degree information available by phone, fax, mail. Search requires name plus SSN, approximate years of attendance. Also helpful: date of birth, exact years of attendance. There is no fee.

Southwest Texas Junior College, Registrar, 2401 Garner Field Rd, Uvalde, TX 78801-6297, 210-591-7276 (Fax: 210-591-7396). Hours: 8AM-6PM M-Th; 8AM-5PM F. Enrollment: 3250. Records go back to 1945. Degrees granted: Associate. Adverse incident record source- Registrar.

Attendance and degree information available by phone, fax, mail. Search requires name plus SSN. Also helpful: date of birth, exact years of attendance. There is no fee.

Southwest Texas State University, Registrar, 601 University Dr, San Marcos, TX 78666-4606, 512-245-2728

(Fax: 512-245-8126). Hours: 8AM-5PM. Enrollment: 20000. Records go back to 1900's. Alumni records are maintained here also. Call 512-245-2371. Degrees granted: Associate; Bachelors; Masters; Doctorate. Adverse incident record source- Police Admin, 512-245-2890: Student Justice, 512-245-2126

Attendance and degree information available by phone, fax, mail. Search requires name plus SSN. Also helpful: date of birth, exact years of attendance. There is no fee.

Southwestern Adventist College, Registrar, PO Box 567, Keene, TX 76059, 817-645-3921 X221 (Fax: 817-556-4744). Hours: 8AM-4:30PM. Enrollment: 1000. Records go back to 1893. Alumni records are maintained here at the same phone number. Degrees granted: Bachelors; Masters. Adverse incident record source- Registrar.

Attendance and degree information available by phone, fax, mail. Search requires name only. Also helpful: SSN, date of birth. There is no fee.

Southwestern Assemblies of God University, Registrar, 1200 Sycamore St, Waxahachie, TX 75165, 214-937-4010 X142 (Fax: 214-923-0488). Hours: 8AM-5PM. Enrollment: 1150. Records go back to 1930's. Alumni records are maintained here at the same phone number. Degrees granted: Associate; Bachelors. Adverse incident record source- Business Office, 214-937-4010 X104.

Attendance and degree information available by phone, fax, mail. Search requires name only. Also helpful: SSN, date of birth, exact years of attendance. There is no fee.

Southwestern Baptist Theological Seminary, Registrar, PO Box 22000, Fort Worth, TX 76122, 817-923-1921 X2000 (Fax: 817-923-1921 X2119). Hours: 8AM-Noon, 1-5PM. Enrollment: 3500. Records go back to 1908. Alumni records are maintained here also. Call 817-923-1921 X2380. Degrees granted: Masters; Doctorate.

Attendance and degree information available by phone, fax, mail. Search requires name only. Also helpful: SSN, date of birth, exact years of attendance. There is no fee.

Southwestern Christian College, Registrar, PO Box 10, Terrell, TX 75160, 214-524-3341 X128 (Fax: 214-563-7133). Hours: 8AM-5PM. Enrollment: 205. Records go back to 1950. Alumni records are maintained here at the same phone number. Degrees granted: Associate; Bachelors.

Attendance and degree information available by phone, fax, mail. Search requires name plus SSN, date of birth, exact years of attendance. There is no fee.

Southwestern University, Registrar, University Ave at Maple St, Georgetown, TX 78626, 512-863-1952 (Fax: 512-863-5788). Hours: 8AM-Noon, 1-5PM. Enrollment: 1200. Records go back to 1880's. Alumni records are maintained here at the same phone number. Degrees granted: Bachelors.

Attendance and degree information available by phone, fax, mail. Search requires name only. Also helpful: SSN, date of birth, exact years of attendance. There is no fee.

St. Edward's University, Registrar, 3001 S Congress Ave, Austin, TX 78704, 512-448-8750 (Fax: 512-448-8492). Enrollment: 2410. Records go back to 1885. Alumni records are maintained here also. Call 512-448-8512. Degrees granted: Bachelors; Masters.

Attendance and degree information available by phone, fax, mail. Search requires name plus exact years of attendance. There is no fee.

St. Mary's University, Registrar, One Camino Santa Maria, San Antonio, TX 78228-8576, 210-436-3701 (Fax: 210-431-2217). Hours: 8AM-5PM Winter; 8AM-4PM Summer. Enrollment: 4000. Records go back to 1930. Alumni records are maintained here also. Call 210-436-3325. Degrees granted: Bachelors; Masters; Doctorate; JD. Special programs- Continu-

ing Studies, 210-436-3321. Adverse incident record source- Dean of Students, 210-436-3714.

Attendance and degree information available by phone, fax, mail. Search requires name only. Also helpful: SSN, exact years of attendance. There is no fee.

St. Philip's College, Registrar, 1801 Martin Luther King, San Antonio, TX 78203, 210-531-3219 (Fax: 210-531-3235). Hours: 7:30AM-7PM M-Th; 7:30AM-5PM F. Enrollment: 7250. Records go back to 1940's. Alumni records are maintained here at the same phone number. Degrees granted: Associate. Adverse incident record source- Student Affairs, 210-531-3200.

Attendance and degree information available by phone, fax, mail. Search requires name plus SSN, date of birth. There is no fee.

Stephen F. Austin State University, Office of the Registrar, SFA PO Box 13050, Nacogdoches, TX 75962, 409-468-2501 (Fax: 409-468-2261). Hours: 8AM-5PM. Enrollment: 11800. Records go back to 1923. Alumni Records Office: SFA PO Box 6096, Nacogdoches, TX 75962, 409-468-3407. Degrees granted: Bachelors; Masters; Doctorate. Certification: In Forestry. Adverse incident record source- Student Development, 409-468-2703.

Attendance information available by phone, mail. Search requires name plus SSN. Also helpful: date of birth, approximate years of attendance. There is no fee.

Degree information available by phone, mail. Search requires name plus SSN. Also helpful: date of birth. There is no fee.

Sul Ross State University, Admissions & Records, Box C-2, Alpine, TX 79832, 915-837-8050 (Fax: 915-837-8431). Hours: 8AM-5PM. Enrollment: 3100. Records go back to 1924. Alumni Records Office: Box C-187, Alpine, TX 79832, 915-837-8059. Degrees granted: Associate; Bachelors; Masters. Adverse incident record source- Public Safety, 915-837-8100.

Attendance and degree information available by phone, fax, mail. Search requires name only. Also helpful: SSN, date of birth, exact years of attendance. There is no fee.

Sul Ross State University, (Rio Grande College), Registrar, Rt 3 Box 1200, Eagle Pass, TX 78852, 210-773-8974 (Fax: 210-773-8996). Hours: 8AM-5PM. Enrollment: 800. Alumni records are maintained here at the same phone number. Degrees granted: Bachelors; Masters. Adverse incident record source- Dean,210-278-3339.

Attendance and degree information available by phone, mail. Search requires name plus SSN. There is no fee.

Tarleton State University, Registrar, 1297 W Washington St, Tarleton Station, Stephenville, TX 76402, 817-968-9121 (Fax: 817-968-9389). Hours: 8AM-5PM. Enrollment: 6600. Alumni Records Office: Alumni Association, Box T-0060, Stephenville, TX 76402. Degrees granted: Associate; Bachelors; Masters.

Attendance and degree information available by phone, fax, mail. Search requires name plus SSN. Also helpful: date of birth, exact years of attendance. There is no fee.

Tarrant County Junior College, Dir. Admissions & Records, 1500 Houston St, Fort Worth, TX 76102-6599, 817-882-5291 (Fax: 817-882-5278). Hours: 8AM-5PM. Records go back to 1967. Degrees granted: Associate.

Attendance and degree information available by phone, fax, mail. Search requires name plus SSN. Also helpful: date of birth. There is no fee.

Tarrant County Junior College, (Northeast Campus), Registrar, 828 Harwood Rd, Hurst, TX 76054, 817-788-6965 (Fax: 817-788-6988). Hours: 8AM-7PM M-Th; 8AM-5PM F (Aug-May); 7:30AM-7PM M-Th (Jun-Jul). Enrollment: 11500. Records go back to 1967. Degrees granted: Associate.

Attendance and degree information available by phone, fax, mail. Search requires name plus SSN. Also helpful: date of birth, exact years of attendance. There is no fee.

Tarrant County Junior College, (Northwest Campus), Registrar, 4801 Marine Creek Pkwy, Fort Worth, TX 76179, 817-232-2900 (Fax: 817-232-7732). Hours: 8AM-5PM. Enrollment: 26000. Records go back to 1976. Degrees granted: Associate. Special programs- Criminal Justice: Fire Tech: Aviation Maintenance. Adverse incident record source- Campus Police, 812-232-7760: Dean's Office, 812-232-7701

Attendance and degree information available by phone, fax, mail. Search requires name plus SSN. Also helpful: date of birth. There is no fee.

Tarrant County Junior College, (South Campus), Registrar, 5301 Campus Dr, Fort Worth, TX 76119, 817-531-4590. Hours: 8AM-5PM. Records go back to 1967. Alumni records are maintained here at the same phone number. Degrees granted: Associate. Adverse incident record source- Dean of Students, 817-531-4504.

Attendance and degree information available by phone, mail. Search requires name plus SSN. There is no fee.

Temple Junior College, Registrar, 2600 S First St, Temple, TX 76504-7435, 817-773-0888 (Fax: 817-773-5265). Hours: 8AM-4:30PM. Enrollment: 2544. Degrees granted: Associate.

Attendance and degree information available by phone, mail. Search requires name plus SSN, exact years of attendance. There is no fee.

Texarkana College, Registrar, 2500 N Robinson Rd, Texarkana, TX 75599, 903-838-4541 (Fax: 903-832-5040). Hours: 8AM-5PM. Enrollment: 4500. Records go back to 1927. Degrees granted: Associate.

Attendance and degree information available by fax, mail. Search requires name plus SSN, exact years of attendance. There is no fee.

Texas A&M International University, Registrar, 5201 University Blvd, Laredo, TX 78041-1999, 210-326-2001 (Fax: 210-326-2199). Hours: 8AM-5PM. Enrollment: 2500. Records go back to 1970. Alumni records are maintained here at the same phone number. Degrees granted: Bachelors; Masters.

Attendance and degree information available by phone, fax, mail. Search requires name plus SSN, date of birth, exact years of attendance. There is no fee.

Texas A&M University, Registrar, College Station, TX 77843, 409-845-1003 (Fax: 409-845-0727). Hours: 8AM-5PM. Enrollment: 42000. Records go back to 1876. Alumni records are maintained here also. Call 409-845-7514. Degrees granted: Bachelors; Masters; Doctorate.

Attendance and degree information available by phone, fax, mail. Search requires name plus SSN, date of birth, exact years of attendance. There is no fee.

Texas A&M University at Galveston, Registrar, PO Box 1675, Galveston, TX 77553, 409-740-4414 (Fax: 409-740-4731). Hours: 8AM-5PM. Enrollment: 1250. Records go back to 1983. Official transcripts requested and produced from main campus at College Station. Degrees granted: Bachelors. Special programs- Corps of Cadets, 409-740-4588.

Attendance and degree information available by phone, fax, mail. Search requires name only. Also helpful: SSN, exact years of attendance. There is no fee.

Texas A&M University-Corpus Christi, Registrar, 6300 Ocean Dr, Corpus Christi, TX 78412, 512-991-6810 (Fax: 512-994-5887). Hours: 8AM-7PM M-Th; 8AM-3PM F. Enrollment: 5800. Records go back to 1947. Alumni records are maintained here also. Call 512-994-2420. Degrees granted:

Bachelors; Masters; Doctorate. Adverse incident record source-Student Affairs, 512-994-2612.

Attendance and degree information available by phone, fax, mail. Search requires name plus SSN. There is no fee.

Texas A&M University-Kingsville, Registrar, Campus Box 105, Kingsville, TX 78363, 512-593-2811 (Fax: 512-593-2195). Hours: 8AM-5PM. Enrollment: 6000. Records go back to 1925. Alumni records are maintained here at the same phone number. Degrees granted: Bachelors; Masters; Doctorate.

Attendance and degree information available by phone, fax, mail. Search requires name plus SSN, approximate years of attendance. Also helpful: date of birth. There is no fee.

Texas Arts and Industry University, Registrar, Campus Box 105, Waco, TX 78363, 512-593-2811 (Fax: 512-593-2195). Enrollment: 6000. Records go back to 1925. Alumni records are maintained here at the same phone number. Degrees granted: Bachelors; Masters. Special programs- Liberal Arts & Science: Business Engineering. Adverse incident record source-Security.

Attendance and degree information available by phone, mail. Search requires name plus SSN, exact years of attendance. Also helpful: approximate years of attendance. Fee is $.

Texas Chiropractic College, Registrar, 5912 Spencer Hwy, Pasadena, TX 77505, 713-487-1170 (Fax: 713-487-2009). Hours: 8AM-5PM. Enrollment: 525. Records go back to 1930. Alumni records are maintained here at the same phone number. Degrees granted: Bachelors; Doctorate.

Attendance and degree information available by fax, mail. Search requires name plus SSN. Also helpful: date of birth, exact years of attendance. There is no fee.

Texas Christian University, Registrar, PO Box 297004, Fort Worth, TX 76129, 817-921-7828 (Fax: 817-921-7333). Hours: 8AM-5PM. Enrollment: 6900. Records go back to 1890. Alumni Records Office: Alumni Association, 2901 Princeton St, Fort Worth, TX 76129. Degrees granted: Doctorate. Adverse incident record source- Student Life, 817-921-7820.

Attendance and degree information available by phone, fax, mail. Search requires name plus approximate years of attendance. Also helpful: SSN, date of birth, exact years of attendance. There is no fee.

Texas College, Registrar, 2404 N Grand Ave, Tyler, TX 75712, 903-593-8311 X215 (Fax: 903-593-0588). Hours: 8AM-5PM. Enrollment: 324. Records go back to 1900's. Alumni records are maintained here at the same phone number. Degrees granted: Bachelors. Adverse incident record source- Student Affairs, 903-593-8311 X212.

Attendance and degree information available by written request only. Search requires name plus SSN, date of birth, signed release. Also helpful: exact years of attendance. There is no fee.

Texas Lutheran College, Registrar, 1000 W Court St, Seguin, TX 78155, 210-372-8040 (Fax: 210-372-8096). Hours: 8AM-5PM. Enrollment: 1240. Records go back to 1925. Alumni records are maintained here also. Call 210-372-8025. Degrees granted: Associate; Bachelors.

Attendance and degree information available by phone, fax, mail. Search requires name plus SSN, date of birth. Also helpful: exact years of attendance. There is no fee.

Texas Southern University, Registrar, 3100 Cleburne St, Houston, TX 77004, 713-313-7080 (Fax: 713-313-1878). Hours: 8AM-5PM. Alumni records are maintained here at the same phone number. Degrees granted: Bachelors; Masters; Doctorate. Adverse incident record source- TSU Police, 713-527-1000.

Attendance information available by phone, fax, mail. Search requires name plus SSN, approximate years of attendance. There is no fee.

Degree information available by phone, fax, mail. Search requires name only. Also helpful: SSN, date of birth, approximate years of attendance. There is no fee.

Texas State Technical College-Amarillo,
Registrar, PO Box 11197, Amarillo, TX 79111, 806-335-2316 X268. Hours: 8AM-5PM. Degrees granted: Associate.

Attendance and degree information available by mail. Search requires name plus SSN, exact years of attendance. There is no fee.

Texas State Technical College-Harlingen,
Registrar, 2424 Boxwood, Harlingen, TX 78550-3697, 210-425-0669 (Fax: 210-425-0698). Hours: 8AM-7PM. Enrollment: 3056. Records go back to 1974. Alumni records are maintained here at the same phone number. Degrees granted: Associate. Adverse incident record source- Dean of Students, 210-425-0613: Security Dept, 210-425-0683

Attendance information available by phone, fax, mail. Search requires name plus SSN. Also helpful: exact years of attendance. There is no fee.

Degree information available by phone, mail. Search requires name plus SSN, approximate years of attendance. Also helpful: exact years of attendance. There is no fee.

Texas State Technical College-Sweetwater,
Registrar, 300 College Dr, Sweetwater, TX 79556, 915-235-7377 (Fax: 915-235-7416). Hours: 9AM-5PM. Enrollment: 900. Records go back to 1970. Alumni records are maintained here at the same phone number. Degrees granted: Associate. Adverse incident record source- Campus Security, 915-235-7400.

Attendance and degree information available by phone, fax, mail. Search requires name only. Also helpful: SSN, exact years of attendance. There is no fee.

Texas State Technical College-Waco,
Registrar, 3801 Campus Dr, Waco, TX 76705, 817-867-2366 (Fax: 817-867-2250). Hours: 8AM-5PM. Enrollment: 3300. Records go back to 1965. Alumni records are maintained here at the same phone number. Degrees granted: Associate. Adverse incident record source- Counseling, 817-867-3609.

Attendance information available by mail. Search requires name plus SSN, signed release. Also helpful: date of birth, exact years of attendance. There is no fee.

Degree information available by phone, fax, mail. Search requires name plus SSN. Also helpful: date of birth, exact years of attendance. There is no fee.

Texas Tech University,
Registrar, PO Box 45015, Lubbock, TX 79409-5015, 806-742-3652 (Fax: 806-742-0355). Hours: 8AM-5PM. Enrollment: 24000. Records go back to 1925. Alumni Records Office: Alumni Association, Texas Tech University, PO Box 45001, Lubbock, TX 79409-5001. Degrees granted: Bachelors; Masters; Doctorate.

Attendance and degree information available by phone, mail. Search requires name only. Also helpful: SSN, date of birth, approximate years of attendance. There is no fee.

Texas Tech University Health Sciences Center,
Registrar, 3601 Fourth St, Lubbock, TX 79430, 806-743-2300 (Fax: 806-743-3027). Hours: 8AM-5PM. Records go back to 1972. Alumni records are maintained here at the same phone number. Degrees granted: Bachelors; Masters; Doctorate. Certification: EMT.

Attendance and degree information available by phone, fax, mail. Search requires name only. Also helpful: SSN, date of birth, exact years of attendance. There is no fee.

Texas Wesleyan University,
Registrar, 1201 Wesleyan St, Fort Worth, TX 76105-1536, 817-531-4414 (Fax: 817-531-4464). Hours: 8AM-5PM. Enrollment: 2800. Records go back to 1890's. Alumni records are maintained here also. Call 817-531-4414. Degrees granted: Bachelors; Masters; Doctorate.

Special programs- TX Wesleyan School of Law, 214-579-1071. Adverse incident record source- Dean of Students, 817-531-4857.

Attendance and degree information available by phone, fax, mail. Search requires name plus SSN. Also helpful: exact years of attendance. There is no fee.

Texas Women's University,
Registrar, PO Box 425559, Denton, TX 76204, 817-898-3036 (Fax: 817-898-3072). Hours: 8AM-5PM. Enrollment: 10000. Records go back to 1901. Alumni Records Office: PO Box 425795, Denton, TX 76204, 817-898-2586. Degrees granted: Bachelors; Masters; Doctorate. Adverse incident record source- Public Safety, 817-898-2911.

Attendance and degree information available by phone, fax, mail. Search requires name only. Also helpful: SSN, exact years of attendance. There is no fee.

Tomball College,
Registrar, 30555 Tomball Pkwy, Tomball, TX 77375-4036, 713-351-3310 (Fax: 713-351-3384). Hours: 8AM-9:30PM M-Th; 8AM-4:30PM F. Enrollment: 3500. Records go back to 1988. Degrees granted: Associate. Adverse incident record source- Student Services.

Attendance and degree information available by phone, fax, mail. Search requires name plus SSN. There is no fee.

Trinity University,
Registrar, 715 Stadium Dr, San Antonio, TX 78212-7200, 210-736-7201 (Fax: 210-736-7202). Hours: 8AM-5PM. Records go back to 1895. Alumni records are maintained here also. Call 210-736-8404. Degrees granted: Bachelors; Masters.

Attendance and degree information available by phone, fax, mail. Search requires name plus approximate years of attendance. Also helpful: SSN, date of birth, exact years of attendance. There is no fee.

Trinity Valley Community College,
Registrar, 500 S Prairieville, Athens, TX 75751, 903-677-8822 (Fax: 903-675-6316). Enrollment: 3143. Records go back to 1946. Degrees granted: Associate.

Attendance and degree information available by phone, fax, mail. Search requires name only. Also helpful: SSN, date of birth, exact years of attendance. There is no fee.

Tyler Junior College,
Registrar, PO Box 9020, Tyler, TX 75711, 903-510-2397 (Fax: 903-510-2634). Hours: 8AM-8PM M-Th; 8AM-5PM F. Enrollment: 7800. Records go back to 1926. Alumni records are maintained here also. Call 903-510-2497. Degrees granted: Associate. Adverse incident record source- Campus Safety, 903-510-2258.

Attendance and degree information available by fax, mail. Search requires name plus SSN. Also helpful: date of birth, exact years of attendance. There is no fee.

University of Central Texas,
Records Office, PO Box 1416, Killeen, TX 76540, 817-526-8262 X253 (Fax: 817-526-8403). Hours: 8AM-7PM. Records go back to 1973. Alumni records are maintained here at the same phone number. Degrees granted: Bachelors; Masters. Adverse incident record source- Student Services, 817-526-8262.

Attendance and degree information available by phone, fax, mail. Search requires name only. Also helpful: SSN, date of birth, exact years of attendance. There is no fee.

University of Dallas,
Registrar, 1845 E Northgate Dr, Irving, TX 75061-4799, 214-721-5221 (Fax: 214-721-5132). Hours: 8AM-4:30PM. Enrollment: 2700. Records go back to 1956. Alumni records are maintained here also. Call 214-721-5066. Degrees granted: Bachelors; Masters; Doctorate.

Attendance and degree information available by phone, mail. Search requires name plus SSN. Also helpful: date of birth, exact years of attendance. There is no fee.

University of Houston, Transcript Office, 4800 Calhoun Blvd, Houston, TX 77204-2161, 713-743-1010 (Fax: 713-743-9050). Hours: 8AM-7PM M,T; 8AM-5PM W-F. Records go back to 1927. Alumni records are maintained here also. Call 713-743-9550. Degrees granted: Bachelors; Masters; Doctorate. Adverse incident record source- Dean of Students, 713-743-5470.

Attendance and degree information available by phone, fax, mail. Search requires name plus SSN, date of birth. Also helpful: exact years of attendance. There is no fee.

University of Houston-Clear Lake, Office of Enrollment Services, 2700 Bay Area Blvd, Box 13, Houston, TX 77058-1098, 713-283-2534 (Fax: 713-283-2530). Hours: 10AM-7PM M-Th; 8AM-5PM F. Enrollment: 7000. Records go back to 1974. Alumni Records Office: 2700 Bay Area Blvd Box 318, Houston, TX 77059-1098, 713-283-2023. Degrees granted: Bachelors; Masters.

Attendance and degree information available by phone, fax, mail. Search requires name only. Also helpful: SSN, date of birth, exact years of attendance. There is no fee.

University of Houston-Downtown, Registrar, One Main St, Houston, TX 77002, 713-221-8999 (Fax: 713-221-8157). Hours: 8AM-6PM M-Th; 8AM-5PM F. Enrollment: 8000. Records go back to 1956. Alumni records are maintained here at the same phone number. Degrees granted: Bachelors. Special programs- Urban Education: Criminal Justice. Adverse incident record source- Student Affairs, 713-221-8100.

Attendance and degree information available by phone, fax, mail. Search requires name plus SSN. Also helpful: date of birth, exact years of attendance. There is no fee.

University of Houston-Victoria, Registrar, 2506 E Red River, Victoria, TX 77901-4450, 512-788-6222 (Fax: 512-572-9377). Hours: 8AM-5PM. Enrollment: 1500. Records go back to 1973. Alumni records are maintained here at the same phone number. Degrees granted: Bachelors; Masters.

Attendance and degree information available by phone, fax, mail. Search requires name plus SSN. Also helpful: date of birth, exact years of attendance. There is no fee.

University of Mary Hardin-Baylor, Registrar, Box 8425, Belton, TX 76513, 817-939-4510 (Fax: 817-933-5052). Hours: 8AM-5PM. Enrollment: 2200. Records go back to 1845. Alumni Records Office: Box 8427, Belton, TX 76513, 817-939-4599 (Fax: 817-939-4535). Degrees granted: Bachelors; Masters. Adverse incident record source- Student Development, 817-939-4590.

Attendance and degree information available by phone, fax, mail. Search requires name only. Also helpful: SSN, date of birth, exact years of attendance. There is no fee.

University of North Texas, Registrar's Office, PO Box 13766, Denton, TX 76203, 817-565-2111 (Fax: 817-565-4463). Hours: 8AM-5PM. Enrollment: 26000. Alumni Records Office: Alumni Association, PO Box 13557, Denton, TX 76203-6557. Degrees granted: Bachelors; Masters; Doctorate.

Attendance and degree information available by phone, mail. Search requires name only. Also helpful: date of birth, exact years of attendance. There is no fee.

University of North Texas Health Science Center at Fort Worth, Registrar, 3500 Camp Bowie Blvd, Fort Worth, TX 76107-2970, 817-735-2201 (Fax: 817-735-2568). Hours: 8AM-5PM. Enrollment: 550. Records go back to 1974. Alumni records are maintained here also. Call 817-735-2559. Degrees granted: Bachelors; Masters; Doctorate.

Attendance information available by phone, fax, mail. Search requires name plus SSN, approximate years of attendance. Also helpful: exact years of attendance. There is no fee.

Degree information available by phone, fax, mail. Search requires name plus SSN, approximate years of attendance. Also helpful: date of birth, exact years of attendance. There is no fee.

University of St. Thomas, Registrar, 3800 Montrose Blvd, Houston, TX 77006-4696, 713-522-7911 (Fax: 713-525-2125). Hours: 8:30AM-5:30PM M-Th; 8:30AM-5PM F. Records go back to 1946. Alumni records are maintained here also. Call 713-525-3115. Degrees granted: Bachelors; Masters; Doctorate. Adverse incident record source- Student Services, 713-525-3575.

Attendance and degree information available by phone, fax, mail. Search requires name plus SSN. Also helpful: exact years of attendance. There is no fee.

University of Texas Health Science Center at San Antonio, Registrar, 7703 Floyd Curl Dr, San Antonio, TX 78284-7702, 210-567-2621 (Fax: 210-567-2685). Hours: 8AM-4:30PM. Enrollment: 426. Alumni records are maintained here at the same phone number. Degrees granted: Bachelors; Masters; Doctorate.

Attendance and degree information available by phone, fax, mail. Search requires name plus SSN, exact years of attendance. There is no fee.

University of Texas Medical Branch at Galveston, Registrar, 301 University Blvd, Galveston, TX 77555-1305, 409-772-1215 (Fax: 409-772-5056). Hours: 8AM-5PM. Enrollment: 2300. Records go back to 1891. Alumni records are maintained here also. Call 409-772-1215. Degrees granted: Bachelors; Masters; Doctorate.

Attendance and degree information available by phone, fax, mail. Search requires name plus date of birth. Also helpful: SSN, exact years of attendance. There is no fee.

University of Texas Southwestern Medical Center at Dallas, Registrar, 5323 Harry Hines Blvd, Dallas, TX 75235, 214-648-3606 (Fax: 214-648-3289). Hours: 8AM-4:30PM. Enrollment: 1700. Records go back to 1944. Alumni records are maintained here at the same phone number. Degrees granted: Doctorate.

Attendance and degree information available by phone, fax, mail. Search requires name plus SSN. There is no fee.

University of Texas at Arlington, Registrar, PO Box 19088, Arlington, TX 76019, 817-272-3372 (Fax: 817-272-3223). Hours: 8AM-7PM M-Th; 8AM-5PM F. Enrollment: 22000. Records go back to 1917. Alumni records are maintained here also. Call 817-272-2594. Degrees granted: Bachelors; Masters; Doctorate. Adverse incident record source- Discipline Coordinator, 817-272-2354: Student Affairs, 817-272-3361

Attendance and degree information available by phone, fax, mail. Search requires name plus SSN. There is no fee.

University of Texas at Austin, Registrar, Main Bldg Room 1, Austin, TX 78712, 512-475-7575. Hours: 8AM-4:30PM. Enrollment: 48000. Records go back to 1883. Alumni records are maintained here also. Call 512-471-3812. Degrees granted: Bachelors; Masters; Doctorate. Adverse incident record source- Dean of Students, 512-471-1201.

Attendance and degree information available by phone, mail. Search requires name plus SSN. Also helpful: exact years of attendance. There is no fee.

University of Texas at Brownsville, Registrar, 80 Fort Brown, Brownsville, TX 78520, 210-544-8254 (Fax: 210-544-8832). Hours: 7:30AM-7PM M-Th; 7:30AM-1:30PM F. Enrollment: 8000. Records go back to 1991. Alumni records are maintained here at the same phone number. Degrees granted: Bachelors; Masters. Adverse incident record source- V.P. Student Affairs, 210-544-8213.

Attendance and degree information available by fax, mail. Search requires name plus date of birth, signed release. Also helpful: SSN, exact years of attendance. There is no fee.

University of Texas at Dallas, Records & Registration, PO Box 830688 MCII, Richardson, TX 75083-0688, 214-883-2111 (Fax: 214-883-6335). Hours: 8AM-7PM M-Th; 8AM-5PM F. Enrollment: 5918. Records go back to 1969. Alumni records are maintained here at the same phone number. Degrees granted: Bachelors; Masters; Doctorate. Certification: Teacher Education. Adverse incident record source- Student Life, 214-883-2098.

Attendance and degree information available by phone, fax, mail. Search requires name only. Also helpful: SSN, date of birth, approximate years of attendance. There is no fee.

University of Texas at El Paso, Registrar, 500 W University Ave, El Paso, TX 79968, 915-747-5550 (Fax: 915-747-5012). Hours: 8AM-5PM M-F. Records go back to 1915. Degrees granted: Bachelors; Masters; Doctorate. Adverse incident record source- Dean of Students, 915-747-5648: Registrar, 915-747-5550

Attendance and degree information available by phone, fax, mail. Search requires name plus SSN, date of birth. Also helpful: exact years of attendance. There is no fee.

University of Texas at San Antonio, Registrar, 6900 N Loop 1604 W, San Antonio, TX 78249-0616, 210-691-4530. Hours: 8AM-5:00PM. Alumni records are maintained here at the same phone number. Degrees granted: Bachelors; Masters; Doctorate.

Attendance and degree information available by phone, mail. Search requires name plus SSN, exact years of attendance. There is no fee.

University of Texas at Tyler, Registrar, 3900 University Blvd, Tyler, TX 75799, 903-566-7000 (Fax: 903-566-7173). Hours: 8AM-5PM. Enrollment: 4477. Records go back to 1971. Alumni records are maintained here also. Call 903-566-7411. Degrees granted: Bachelors; Masters.

Attendance and degree information available by phone, fax, mail. Search requires name plus SSN. Also helpful: date of birth. There is no fee.

University of Texas of the Permian Basin, Registrar, 4901 E University Blvd, Odessa, TX 79762, 915-552-2635 (Fax: 915-552-2621). Hours: 8AM-6PM M-Th; 8AM-5PM F. Enrollment: 2400. Records go back to 1972. Alumni Records Office: Alumni Association, Development Office, Odessa, TX 79762. Degrees granted: Bachelors; Masters. Adverse incident record source- Student Services, 915-552-2600.

Attendance and degree information available by phone, fax, mail. Search requires name plus SSN. There is no fee.

University of Texas-Houston Health Science Center, Registrar, PO Box 20036, 7000 Fannin Ste 2250, Houston, TX 77225, 713-792-7444 (Fax: 713-794-5701). Hours: 8AM-5PM. Enrollment: 3097. Records go back to 1948. Alumni records are maintained here at the same phone number. Degrees granted: Bachelors; Masters; Doctorate. Adverse incident record source- Student Affairs, 713-792-7444.

Attendance and degree information available by phone, fax, mail. Search requires name plus SSN, exact years of attendance. There is no fee.

University of Texas-Pan American, Registrar, 1201 W University Dr, Edinburg, TX 78539-2999, 210-381-2011. Hours: 8AM-5PM. Enrollment: 14000. Alumni records are maintained here also. Call 210-381-3667. Degrees granted: Associate; Bachelors; Masters; Doctorate. Adverse incident record source- Dean of Student Affairs, 210-381-2262.

Attendance and degree information available by phone, mail. Search requires name plus SSN. Also helpful: date of birth, exact years of attendance. There is no fee.

University of the Incarnate Word, Registrar, 4301 Broadway, San Antonio, TX 78209, 210-829-6006 (Fax: 210-829-3922). Hours: 8AM-5PM. Formerly Incarnate Word College Records go back to 1910. Alumni records are maintained here also. Call 210-829-6014. Degrees granted: Bachelors; Masters.

Attendance and degree information available by phone, fax, mail. Search requires name only. Also helpful: SSN, date of birth, exact years of attendance. There is no fee.

Vernon Regional Junior College, Registrar, 4400 College Dr, Vernon, TX 76384, 817-552-6291 X204. Hours: 8AM-5PM. Enrollment: 1800. Records go back to 1972. Degrees granted: Associate. Adverse incident record source- Registrar, 817-552-6291.

Attendance and degree information available by phone, mail. Search requires name plus SSN. Also helpful: date of birth, exact years of attendance. There is no fee.

Victoria College, Registrar, 2200 E Red River St, Victoria, TX 77901-4494, 512-572-6411 (Fax: 512-572-3850). Enrollment: 3700. Alumni records are maintained here also. Call 512-573-3291 X440. Degrees granted: Associate.

Attendance and degree information available by phone, fax, mail. Search requires name plus SSN. Also helpful: date of birth, exact years of attendance. There is no fee.

Wayland Baptist University, Office of the Registrar, WBU #735, Plainview, TX 79072, 806-296-4706 (Fax: 806-296-4580). Hours: 8:30AM-5PM. Enrollment: 3500. Alumni records are maintained here also. Call 806-296-4844. Degrees granted: Associate; Bachelors; Masters. Certification: Secretarial. Adverse incident record source- Student Development, 806-296-4724.

Attendance and degree information available by phone, fax, mail. Search requires name plus SSN, date of birth. Also helpful: exact years of attendance. There is no fee.

Weatherford College, Registrar, 308 E Park Ave, Weatherford, TX 76086, 817-594-5471 (Fax: 817-594-9435). Hours: 8AM-5PM M-Th; 8AM-4PM F. Records go back to 1920's. Alumni records are maintained here at the same phone number. Degrees granted: Associate.

Attendance and degree information available by phone, fax, mail. Search requires name plus SSN. Also helpful: date of birth, exact years of attendance. There is no fee.

West Texas A&M University, Registrar, 2501 Fourth Ave, PO Box 877 W.T. Station, Canyon, TX 79016, 806-656-2022 (Fax: 806-656-2936). Hours: 8AM-5PM. Records go back to 1911. Alumni records are maintained here at the same phone number. Degrees granted: Bachelors; Masters. Certification: Education/Teacher. Adverse incident record source- University Police, 806-656-2300.

Attendance and degree information available by phone, fax, mail. Search requires name plus SSN. Also helpful: date of birth, approximate years of attendance. There is no fee.

Western Texas College, Registrar, 6200 S College Ave, Snyder, TX 79549, 915-573-8511 (Fax: 915-573-9321). Hours: 8AM-Noon, 1-5PM. Enrollment: 1100. Records go back to 1970. Alumni records are maintained here at the same phone number. Degrees granted: Associate.

Attendance and degree information available by phone, fax, mail. Search requires name plus SSN. Also helpful: date of birth, exact years of attendance. There is no fee.

Wharton County Junior College, Registrar, 911 Boling Hwy, Wharton, TX 77488, 409-532-6382. Hours: 8AM-5PM. Enrollment: 3700. Records go back to 1946. Alumni rec-

ords are maintained here also. Call 409-532-6322. Degrees granted: Associate. Adverse incident record source- Dean of Student Affairs, 409-532-6385.

Attendance and degree information available by phone, fax, mail. Search requires name plus SSN. Also helpful: exact years of attendance. There is no fee.

Wiley College, Registrar, 711 Wiley Ave, Marshall, TX 75670, 903-927-3221 (Fax: 903-938-8100). Hours: 8AM-5PM.

Enrollment: 600. Records go back to 1900's. Alumni records are maintained here also. Call 903-927-3225. Degrees granted: Bachelors. Adverse incident record source- Student Affairs, 903-927-3233.

Attendance and degree information available by mail. Search requires name plus SSN, date of birth, exact years of attendance. There is no fee.

Trade and Vocational Schools

A-Professional, 9225 Katy Frwy No 114, Houston, TX 77024, 713-468-4600

AIMS Academy, 1106 N Hwy 360 #305, Grand Prairie, TX 75050, 214-988-3202

AIMS Academy (Branch Campus), 6510 Abrams Rd, Dallas, TX 75232, 214-988-3202

ATI - American Trades Institutes, 6627 Maple Ave, Dallas, TX 75235, 214-352-2222

ATI Career Training Center, 2351 W Northwest Hwy, Dallas, TX 75229, 214-688-0467

ATI Career Training Center, 235 NE Loop 820 #110, Hurst, TX 76053, 817-284-1141

Academy of Oriental Medicine, 4105 S First St, Austin, TX 78745, 512-444-6744

Action Career Training, Rte 3 Box 41, Merkel, TX 79536, 915-676-3136

Advanced Career Training, 8800 N Central Expy #120, Dallas, TX 75231, 214-692-5400

Allied Health Careers, 5424 Hwy 29 W #105, Austin, TX 78735, 512-892-5210

American Commercial College, 402 Butternut St, Abilene, TX 79602, 915-672-8495

American Commercial College, 2007 34th St, Lubbock, TX 79411, 806-747-4339

American Commercial College, 2115 E Eighth St, Odessa, TX 79761, 915-332-0768

American Commercial College, 3177 Executive Dr, San Angelo, TX 76904, 915-942-6797

American Institute of Commerce, 9330 LJB Fwy #350, Dallas, TX 75243, 214-690-1978

American Weld Testing School, 921 Broadway, Pasedena, TX 77506, 713-475-2300

Arlington Court Reporting College, 901 Ave K, Grande Prairie, TX 75050, 214-647-1607

Army Academy of Health Sciences, 2250 Stanley Rd Bldg 2840, San Antonio, TX 78234, 210-221-8542

Bellaire Beauty College, 5014 Bellaire Blvd, Bellaire, TX 77401, 713-666-2318

Bradford School of Business, 4669 Southwest Fwy #300, Houston, TX 77027, 713-629-8940

Brown College of Court Reporting & Medical Transcription (Branch Campus), 501 Spur St #B-3, Longview, TX 75601, 903-757-4338

Bryan Institute (Branch Campus), 1719 W Pioneer Pkwy, Arlington, TX 76013, 817-265-5588

Business Skills Training Center, 616 Fort Worth Dr #B, Denton, TX 76201, 817-382-7922

Capitol City Careers, 4630 Westgate Blvd, Austin, TX 78745, 512-892-4270

Capitol City Trade & Technical School, 205 E Riverside Dr, Austin, TX 78704, 512-444-3257

Career Academy, 32 Oaklawn Village, Texarkana, TX 75501, 903-832-1021

Career Centers of Texas - El Paso, 8375 Burnham Rd, El Paso, TX 79907, 915-595-1935

Career Development Center, 413 S Chestnut St, Lufkin, TX 75901, 409-635-1740

Career Point Business School, 485 Spencer Ln, San Antonio, TX 78201, 210-732-3000

Careers Unlimited, 335 S Bonner St, Tyler, TX 75702, 903-593-4424

Careers Unlimited Beauty School, 1225 Lone Star St, Henderson, TX 75652, 903-657-0048

Center for Advanced Legal Studies, 3015 Richmond Ave, Houston, TX 77098, 713-529-2778

Central Texas Commercial College, PO Box 1324, Brownwood, TX 76801, 915-646-0521

Central Texas Commercial College (Branch Campus), 9400 N Central Expy #200, Dallas, TX 75231, 214-368-3680

Chenier, 6300 Richmond Ave #300, Houston, TX 77057, 713-886-3102

Chenier, 2819 Loop 306, San Angelo, TX 76904, 915-944-4404

Computer Career Center, 6101 Montana, El Paso, TX 79925, 915-779-8031

Court Reporting Institute of Dallas, 8585 N Stemmons Fwy #200, Dallas, TX 75247, 214-350-9722

Dalfort Aircraft Tech, 7701 Lemmon Ave, Dallas, TX 75209, 214-358-7820

Dallas Institute of Funeral Services, 3909 S Buckner Blvd, Dallas, TX 75227, 214-388-5466

David L. Carrasco Job Corps Center, 11155 Gateway W, El Paso, TX 79935, 915-594-0022

Delta Career Institute, 1310 Pennsylvania Ave, Beaumont, TX 77701, 409-833-6161

Euro Hair School, 2301-A Morgan Ave, Corpus Christi, TX 78405, 512-887-8494

European Health & Sciences Institute, 1201 Airway A-2, El Paso, TX 79925, 915-772-4243

Gary Job Corps Center, Hwy 21, San Marcos, TX 78667, 512-396-6652

Gulf Coast Trades Center, FM 1375 W, New Waverly, TX 77358, 409-344-6677

Health Institute of Louisville (The) (Branch Campus), 6800 Park Ten Blvd #160 S, San Antonio, TX 78213, 210-580-3660

Houston Allied Health Careers, Inc., 2800 San Jacinto St, Houston, TX 77004, 713-650-6155

Houston Ballet Academy, PO Box 130487, Houston, TX 77219, 713-523-6300

Houston Training School, 704 Shotwell St, Houston, TX 77020, 713-675-4300

Houston Training School (Branch Campus), 1260 Blalock, Houston, TX 77055, 713-464-1659

Houston Training School (Branch Campus), 6969 Gulf Fwy #200, Houston, TX 77087, 713-649-5050

Interactive College of Technology, 8585 N Stemmons Fwy #M50, Dallas, TX 75247, 214-637-3377

Interactive College of Technology (Branch Campus), 10200 Richmond Ave, Houston, TX 77042, 713-782-5161

International Aviation and Travel Academy, 48465 Collins Blvd, Arlington, TX 76018, 817-784-7000

International Aviation and Travel Academy, 17340 Chanute Rd, Houston, TX 77032, 800-627-4379

International Aviation and Travel Academy (Branch Campus), 5757 Alpha Rd #101, Dallas, TX 75240, 214-387-0553

International Business College, 4121 Montana Ave, El Paso, TX 79903, 915-566-8644

International Business College, 4630 50th St, Lubbock, TX 79414, 806-797-1933

International Business College (Branch Campus), 1030 N Zaragosa Rd, El Paso, TX 79907, 915-859-3986

International Business College (Business School - Denton), 3801 I-35N #138, Denton, TX 76205, 817-380-0024

International Business College (Business School - Sherman), 4107 N Texoma Pkwy, Sherman, TX 75090, 806-893-6604

Iverson Institute of Court Reporting, 1200 Copeland Rd #305, Arlington, TX 76011, 817-274-6465

Le Hair Design College, 217 Pleasant Grove Shopping Ctr, Dallas, TX 75217, 214-398-5905

Le Hair Design College, 505 Golden Triangle Shopping C, Dallas, TX 75224, 214-375-0592

Le Hair Design College, 1125 E Seminary Dr, Fort Worth, TX 76115, 817-926-7555

Le Hair Design College, 2410 W Walnut St, Garland, TX 75042, 214-272-8283

Le Hair Design College, 5201 E Belknap, Haltom City, TX 76117, 817-831-7261

LeChef College of Hospitality Careers, 6020 Dillard Cir, Austin, TX 78752, 512-323-2511

Lincoln Technical Institute, 2501 E Arkansas Ln, Grand Prairie, TX 75051, 214-660-5701

M & M Word Processing Institute, 5050 Westheimer Rd #300, Houston, TX 77056, 713-961-0500

M. Weeks Welding Laboratory Testing & School, 4405 Hwy 347, Nederland, TX 77627, 409-727-7640

Mid Cities Barber College, 411 Marshall Plaza, Grand Prairie, TX 75050, 214-642-1892

National Education Center (Fort Worth Campus), 300 E Loop 820, Fort Worth, TX 76112, 817-451-0017

National Education Center-National Institute of Technology Campus, 3622 Fredericksburg Rd, San Antonio, TX 78201, 210-733-6000

Nell Institute (The), 2101 IH 35S 3rd Fl, Austin, TX 78741, 512-447-9415

Occupational Safety Training Institute, 8415 W Bellfort St #300, Houston, TX 77031, 713-270-6882

Ocean Corporation (The), 10840 Rockley Rd, Houston, TX 77099, 713-530-0202

Office Careers Centre (The), 7001 Grapevine Hwy #202, Fort Worth, TX 76180, 817-284-8107

PCI Health Training Center, 8101 John Carpenter Fwy, Dallas, TX 75247, 214-630-0568

Polytechnic Institute, 4625 North Fwy #109, Houston, TX 77022, 713-694-6027

Professional Court Reporting School, 1401 N Central Expy, Richardson, TX 75080, 214-231-9502

R/S Institute, 7122 Lawndale Ave, Houston, TX 77023, 713-923-6968

RHDC Hair Design College, 3209 N Main St, Fort Worth, TX 76106, 817-624-0871

Rice Aviation, a Division of A&J Enterprises, 8880 Telephone Rd, Houston, TX 77061, 713-644-6616

Rice Aviation, a Division of A&J Enterprises (Branch Campus), 7811 N Shepherd Dr #100, Houston, TX 77088, 713-591-2908

S.W. School of Business & Technical Careers, 272 Commerical St, Eagle Pass, TX 78852, 210-733-1373

S.W. School of Business & Technical Careers, 505 E Travis, San Antonio, TX 78205, 210-225-7287

S.W. School of Business & Technical Careers, 602 W Southcross Blvd, San Antonio, TX 78221, 210-921-0951

S.W. School of Business & Technical Careers (Branch Campus), 122 W North St, Uvalde, TX 78801, 210-278-4103

San Antonio College of Medical & Dental Assistants, 4205 San Pedro Ave, San Antonio, TX 78212, 210-733-0777

San Antonio College of Medical & Dental Assistants (Branch Campus), 3900 N 23rd St, Mcallen, TX 78501, 210-360-1499

San Antonio College of Medical & Dental Assistants (Branch Campus), 5280 Medical Dr #100, San Antonio, TX 78229, 210-692-3829

San Antonio Trade School, 120 Playmoor St, San Antonio, TX 78210, 210-533-9126

San Antonio Trade School (Branch Campus), 117 W Martin, Del Rio, TX 78840, 210-774-5646

San Antonio Training Division, 9350 S Presa, San Antonio, TX 78223, 210-633-1000

San Antonio Training Division (Branch Campus), Kelly AFB Bldg 210, San Antonio, TX 78241, 210-633-2893

San Antonio Training Division (Branch Campus), Hemisfair Park Bldg 277, San Antonio, TX 78291, 210-633-1000

School of Automotive Machinists, 1911 Antoine Dr, Houston, TX 77055, 713-683-3817

School of Health Care Sciences, 917 Missile Rd, Sheppard Afb, TX 76311, 817-676-4033

Sebring Career Schools, 2212 Ave I, Huntsville, TX 77340, 409-291-6299

Sebring Career Schools (Branch Campus), 6715 Bissonnet St, Houston, TX 77074, 713-772-6209

Sebring Career Schools (Branch Campus), 6672 Hwy 6S, Houston, TX 77413, 713-561-6352

Seguin Beauty School, 102 E Court St, Seguin, TX 78155, 210-372-0935

Seguin Beauty School (Branch Campus), 214 W San Antonio St, New Braunfels, TX 78130, 210-620-1301

South Texas Vo-Tech Institute, 2255 N Coria St, Brownsville, TX 78520, 210-546-0353

South Texas Vo-Tech Institute, 2901 N 23rd St, Mcallen, TX 78501, 210-631-1107

South Texas Vo-Tech Institute, 2419 E Haggar Ave, Weslaco, TX 78596, 210-969-1564

Southeastern Paralegal Institute, 5440 Harvest Hill Rd #200, Dallas, TX 75230, 214-385-1446

Southern Careers Institute, 2301 S Congress Ave #27, Austin, TX 78704, 512-326-1415

Southern Careers Institute (Branch Campus), 5333 Everhart Rd #C, Corpus Christi, TX 78415, 210-857-5700

Southern Careers Institute (Branch Campus), 3233 N 38th St, Mcallen, TX 78501, 210-687-1415

Southern Careers Institute (Branch Campus), 1414 N Jackson Rd, Pharr, TX 78577, 210-687-1415

Southern Careers Institute (San Antonio Campus), 1405 N Main #100, San Antonio, TX 78212, 210-271-0096

Taylor's Institute of Cosmetology, 842C W 7th Ave, Corsicana, TX 75110, 903-874-7312

Temple Academy of Cosmetology, 5 S First St, Temple, TX 76501, 817-778-2221

Temple Academy of Cosmetology (Branch Campus), 1408 W Marshall Ave, Longview, TX 76504, 903-753-4717

Texas Barber College, 531 W Jefferson Blvd, Dallas, TX 75208, 214-943-7255

Texas Barber College (Branch Campus), 2406 Gus Thomason Rd, Dallas, TX 75228, 214-324-2851

Texas Barber College (Branch Campus), 525 W Arapaho Rd, Richardson, TX 75080, 214-644-4106

Texas Institute of Traditional Chinese Medicine, 4005 Manchaca Rd Ste 200, Austin, TX 78704, 512-444-8082

Texas School of Business, 711 Airtex Blvd, Houston, TX 77073, 713-876-2888

Texas School of Business - Southwest, 10250 Bissonnet St, Houston, TX 77036, 713-771-1177

Texas Vocational School, 3107 N Sugar, Pharr, TX 78577, 210-533-0150

Texas Vocational School, 1913 S Flores St, San Antonio, TX 78204, 210-225-3253

Texas Vocational Schools, 1921 E Red River, Victoria, TX 77902, 512-575-4768

Texas Vocational Schools (Branch Campus), 201 E Rio Grande, Victoria, TX 77902, 512-575-4768

Ultrasound Diagnostic School (Branch Campus), 6575 W Loop S #200, Bellaire, TX 77401, 713-664-9632

Ultrasound Diagnostic School (Branch Campus), 580 Decker Ct #211, Irving, TX 75062, 214-791-1120

Vanguard Institute of Technology, 221 N Eighth St, Edinburg, TX 78539, 210-380-3264

Vanguard Institute of Technology (Branch Campus), 603 Ed Carey Dr, Harlingen, TX 78550, 210-428-4999

Business - Court & Legal Services
Attorney #28 (60863) .... ☎ 512-463-1463
Court Reporter #11 .... ☎ 512-463-1630
Lobbyist #35 (1800) .... ☎ 512-463-5800
Notary Public #20 (327000) .... ☎ 512-463-5705
Shorthand Reporter #11 (3336) .... ☎ 512-463-1630

Business - General Services
Auctioneer #16 .... ☎ 512-463-5522
Pawnbroker #9 .... ☎ 512-479-1280
Public Accountant-CPA #30 (57600) .... ☎ 512-505-5500

Construction & Manufacturing
Air Conditioning & Refrigeration Contractor #16
.... ☎ 512-463-5522
Boiler Inspector #16 .... ☎ 512-463-5522
Industrialized Housing #16 .... ☎ 512-463-5522
Manufactured Housing #16 .... ☎ 512-463-5522
Plumber #5 (17500) .... ☎ 512-458-2145
Plumber Journeyman #5 .... ☎ 512-458-2145
Plumbing Inspector #5 .... ☎ 512-458-2145

Education
County Librarian #31 (700) .... ☎ 512-463-5466
Teacher #29 (2) .... ☎ 512-469-3000

Environmental & Agriculture
Air Monitoring Technician #14 (535) .... ☎ 512-834-6600
Asbestos Abatement Contractor #14 (187) .... ☎ 512-834-6600
Asbestos Consultant/Inspector #14 (800) ...... ☎ 512-834-6600
Asbestos Management Planner #14 (202) ...... ☎ 512-834-6600
Asbestos Worker #14 .... ☎ 512-834-6600
Fish Farmer #13 .... ☎ 512-463-7624
Pesticide Applicator #12 (30000) .... ☎ 512-463-4624
Structural Pest Control Technician #12 .... ☎ 512-451-7200
Veterinarian #18 (5600) .... ✉ 512-305-7555

Financial - Real Estate, Insurance & Banking
Appraiser #33 (4300) 512-465-3950
Bank #3 (457) .... ☎ 512-475-1300
Currency Exchange #3 .... ☎ 512-475-1300
Insurance Adjustor #34 (26958) .... ☎ 512-322-3503
Insurance Agency #34 .... ☎ 512-322-3503
Insurance Agent #34 (187070) .... ☎ 512-322-3503
Insurance Broker #34 .... ☎ 512-463-6169
Insurance Company #34 (2119) .... ☎ 512-322-3507
Investment Advisor #27 .... ☎ 512-305-8300
Property Tax Consultant #16 .... ☎ 512-463-5522
Real Estate Broker #37 (44359) .... ☎ 512-459-6544
Real Estate Inspector #37 (1379) .... ☎ 512-459-6544
Real Estate Salesperson #37 (71529) .... ☎ 512-459-6544
Sale of Checks #3 .... ☎ 512-475-1300
Savings & Loan Association #25 .... ✉ 512-475-1350
Savings Bank #25 .... ✉ 512-475-1350
Securities Broker #27 .... ☎ 512-305-8300
Securities Dealer #27 .... ☎ 512-305-8300
Securities Salesperson #27 .... ☎ 512-305-8322
Trust Companies #3 (98) .... ☎ 512-475-1300

Health & Beauty
Advanced Practice Nurse #19 .... ☎ 512-305-7400
Audiologist #19 (757) .... ☎ 512-834-6627
Audiology Assistant #19 .... ☎ 512-834-6627
Audiology Filters/Dispensers #19 .... ☎ 512-834-6627
Barber #4 (18000) .... ☎ 512-305-8475
Barber School #4 .... ☎ 512-305-8475
Barber Shop #4 (10000) .... ☎ 512-305-8475
Beauty Shop #10 .... ✉ 512-454-4674

Chiropractor #19 (3000) .... ☎ 512-305-8500
Cosmetologist #10 .... ✉ 512-454-4674
Dentist/Dental Hygienist #19 (14400) .... ☎ 512-463-6400
Dietitian #19 .... ☎ 512-834-6601
Embalmer #17 (100) .... ☎ 512-479-7222
Emergency Medical Technician #19 (25688)
.... ☎ 512-834-6700
Funeral Director #17 (100) .... ☎ 512-479-7222
Funeral Director/Embalmer #17 .... ☎ 512-479-7222
Funeral Facility #17 (1200) .... ☎ 512-479-7222
Health Facility #18 .... ✉ 512-834-6687
Hearing Aid Dispenser/Fitter #19 .... ☎ 512-834-6784
Home Health Aide #19 512-458-7240
Laboratory Certification #19 .... ☎ 512-463-6400
Manicurist #10 .... ✉ 512-454-4674
Massage Therapist #19 (9300) .... ☎ 512-834-6616
Medical Doctor #19 512-305-7010
Medication Aide #15 (7000) .... ☎ 512-834-6618
Midwife, Direct Entry #19 (250) .... ☎ 512-458-7700
Nurse, Registered Nurse #19 (65000) .... ☎ 512-305-7400
Nursing Home Administrator #19 (2835) ...... ☎ 512-834-6787
Occupational Therapist #16 .... ☎ 512-463-5522
Occupational Therapist/Assistant #18 .... ✉ 512-305-6900
Optometrist #36 (2772) .... ☎ 512-305-8500
Osteopathic Physician #19 .... ☎ 512-834-6687
Pharmacist #19 .... ☎ 512-305-8000
Physical Therapist\Assistant #18 (13000) ...... ✉ 512-305-6900
Physician's Assistant #19 .... ☎ 512-834-6687
Podiatrist #18 (740) .... ☎ 512-305-7000
Prepaid Funeral Permit Holders #3 .... ☎ 512-475-1300
Radiologic Technologist #19 (13000) .... ☎ 512-834-6617
Respiratory Care Practitioner #19 .... ☎ 512-834-6687
Sanitarian #19 (500) 512-834-6635
Speech Pathologist #19 (5458) .... ☎ 512-834-6627
Vocational Nurse #18 512-305-7400

Investigations & Security
Fire Alarm System Contractor #38 (3298) ..... ☎ 512-918-7224
Fire Extinguisher Contractor #38 (2136) .... ☎ 512-918-7220
Fire Protection Sprinkler System Contractor #38
(448) .... ☎ 512-918-7222
Firefighter #38 (17735) .... ☎ 512-918-7200
Polygraph Examiner #21 512-465-2058
Private Investigator #22 512-463-5545
Private Security Agency #22 512-463-5545

Social Services
Child Care Worker #23 .... ☎ 512-438-3269
Day Care Center #23 (8000) .... ☎ 512-438-3269
Interpreter for the Deaf #8 (1228) .... ☎ 512-451-8494
Marriage & Family Therapist #19 (5000) ...... ☎ 512-834-6657
Professional Counselor #19 (8500) .... ☎ 512-834-6658
Psychologist #18 (4723) .... ☎ 512-305-7700
Psychologist Associate #19 .... ☎ 512-305-7700
Specialist in School Psychology #19 .... ☎ 512-305-7700

Sports & Entertainment
Alcoholic Beverage Distributor #1 512-206-3360
Alcoholic Beverage Manufacturer #1 512-206-3360
Alcoholic Beverage Vendor #1 512-206-3360
Athletic Agent #26 .... ☎ 512-475-1769
Athletic Trainer #19 (1150) .... ☎ 512-834-6615
Boxing #16 .... ☎ 512-463-5522
Dog Racing #24 512-833-6697
Fireworks Display #38 .... ☎ 512-918-7100
Fishing Guide #32 (1475) .... ☎ 512-389-4820
Horse Racing #24 512-833-6697

Sports & Entertainment

Alcoholic Beverage Distributor #1	512-206-3360
Alcoholic Beverage Manufacturer #1	512-206-3360
Alcoholic Beverage Vendor #1	512-206-3360
Athletic Agent #26	☎ 512-475-1769
Athletic Trainer #19 (1150)	☎ 512-834-6615
Boxing #16	☎ 512-463-5522
Dog Racing #24	512-833-6697
Fireworks Display #38	☎ 512-918-7100
Fishing Guide #32 (1475)	☎ 512-389-4820
Horse Racing #24	512-833-6697

State Licensing & Business Registration Agency Information

(1)   Alcoholic Beverage Commission, 5806 Mesa Dr, PO Box 13127, Austin, TX 78711, 512-206-3360, Fax: 512-206-3399

(2)   Architectural Examiner's Board, 333 Guadalupe, Suite 2-350, Austin, TX 78701-3942, 512-458-9000, Fax: 512-305-8900

(3)   Banking Department, 2601 N Lamar Blvd, Austin, TX 78705-4294, 512-475-1300, Fax: 512-475-1313

(4)   Board of Barber Examiners, 333 Guadalupe, Suite 2-110, Austin, TX 78701, 512-305-8475, Fax: 512-305-6800

(5)   Board of Plumbing Examiners, PO Box 4200 (78765), 929 E 41st, Austin, TX 78765, 512-458-2145, Fax: 512-450-0637

(6)   Board of Professional Land Surveying, 7701 N Lamar, Suite 400, Austin, TX 78752, 512-452-9427

(7)   Board of Registration for Professional Engineers, PO Box 18329 (78760), 1917 IH35, S, Austin, TX 78741, 512-440-7723, Fax: 512-442-1414

(8)   Commission for the Deaf & Hard of Hearing, Board of Evaluation of Interpreters, PO Box 12904, Austin, TX 78711, 512-451-8494 V/TTY, Fax: 512-451-9316

(9)   Consumer Credit Commission, 2601 N Lamar, Austin, TX 78705, 512-479-1280, Fax: 512--479-1293

(10)   Cosmetology Commission, PO Box 26700 (78755-0700), 5717 Balcones Dr, Austin, TX 78731, 512-454-4674, Fax: 512-454-0339

(11)   Court Reporter Certification Board, PO Box 13131, Austin, TX 78711, 512-463-1630, Fax: 512-463-1117

(12)   Department of Agriculture, Certificate & Training, PO Box 12847, 1700 Congress Ave., Austin, TX 78711, 512-463-4624, Fax: 512-475-1618

(13)   Department of Agriculture, Fish Farmer Progra, 17th & Congress, Austin, TX 78701, 512-463-7624, Fax: 512-463-7582

(14)   Department of Health, Toxic Substances Control Division, 1100 W 49th St, Austin, TX 78756, 512-834-6600, Fax: 512-834-6644

(15)   Department of Human Services, PO Box 14930 (Mail Code 4979), Austin, TX 79714-9030, 512-834-6618, Fax: 512-834-6764

(16)   Department of Licensing & Regulation, PO Box 12157, Austin, TX 78711, 512-463-5522, Fax: 512-475-2854

(17)   Funeral Service Commission, 510 S. Congress Ave., Suite 206, Austin, TX 78704, 512-479-7222, Fax: 512-479-5064

(18)   Health Department, 1100 W 49th St, Austin, TX 78756, 512-305-7700, Fax: 512-305-7701

(19)   Health Department, Health Facility & Related Licensing, 1100 W 49th St, Austin, TX 78756, 512-586-7111, Fax: 512-834-6277

(20)   Office of Secretary of State, PO Box 12079, 1019 Brazos, Austin, TX 78701, 512-463-5705

(21)   Polygraph Examiner Board, PO Box 4087, Austin, TX 78773, 512-465-2058

(22)   Private Investigators/Security Agencies Board, PO Box 13509, Capitol Station, Austin, TX 78711, 512-463-5545

(23)   Protective and Regulatory Services, 701 W 51st St, #E-550, Austin, TX 78754, 512-438-3269, Fax: 512-438-3848

(24)   Racing Commission, 8505 Cross Park Drive, Suite 110, Austin, TX 78754, 512-794-8461

(25)   Savings & Loan Department, Corporate Activities, 2601 N Lamar Blvd, Suite 201, Austin, TX 78705, 512-475-1350, Fax: 512-475-1360

(26)   Secretary of State, Athletic Agent Registration, PO Box 12887, Austin, TX 78711-2887, 512-475-1769, Fax: 512-463-7552

(27)   Securities Board, 221 W 6th St, Suite 700, Austin, TX 78701, 512-305-8322, Fax: 512-305-8340

(28)   State Bar of Texas, 1414 Colorado, Suite 300, PO Box 12487, Austin, TX 78711, 512-463-1400

(29)   State Board for Educator Certification, 1001 Trivits, Austin, TX 78701, 512-469-3000, Fax: 512-469-3016

(30)   State Board of Public Accountancy, 333 Guadalupe St, Tower III, Suite 900, Austin, TX 78701, 512-505-5500, Fax: 512-505-5575

(31)   State Library & Archives Commission, Library Development Division, PO Box 12927, 1201 Brazos, Austin, TX 78711, 512-463-5466, Fax: 512-463-8800

(32)   State Parks & Wildlife Department, 4200 Smith School Rd, Austin, TX 78744, 512-389-4820, Fax: 512-389-4349

(33)   Texas Appraisers Licensing & Certification Board, Appraiser Licensing, 1101 Camino La Costa, Austin, TX 78752, 512-465-3950, Fax: 512-465-3953

(34)   Texas Department of Insurance, 333 Guadalupe PO Box 149104, Austin, TX 78714-9104, 512-463-6169, Fax: 512-322-3553

(35)   Texas Ethics Commission, PO Box 12070, Austin, TX 78711-2070, 512-463-5800, Fax: 512-463-5777

(36)   Texas Optometry Board, 333 Guadalupe St, Suite 2-420, Austin, TX 78701-3942, 512-835-1938, Fax: 512-305-8501

(37)   Texas Real Estate Commission, PO Box 12188, Austin, TX 78711, 512-459-6544, Fax: 512-465-3916

(38)   Texas State Fire Marshall, 12675 Research Blvd, Austin, TX 78759, 512-918-7100, Fax: 512-918-7106

Utah

Capitol: Salt lake City (Salt Lake County)	
State Population	1.9 Million
Number of Degree Granting Institutions:	17
Number of State Licensing & Business Registration Agencies:	98

Degree Granting Educational Institutions

Brigham Young University, Records Dept B150 ASB, Provo, UT 84602, 801-378-2631 (Fax: 801-378-6583). Enrollment: 30000. Records go back to 1875. Alumni Records Office: Alumni Services, 146 Alum, Provo, UT 84602. Degrees granted: Bachelors; Masters; Doctorate.

Attendance and degree information available by phone, fax, mail. Search requires name plus SSN, date of birth, approximate years of attendance. There is no fee.

College of Eastern Utah, Registrar, 451 E 400 N, Price, UT 84501, 801-637-2120 X5205 (Fax: 801-637-4102). Hours: 8AM-5PM. Enrollment: 3000. Records go back to 1938. Alumni records are maintained here also. Call 801-637-2120 X5246. Degrees granted: Associate.

Attendance and degree information available by phone, fax, mail. Search requires name plus SSN, date of birth, exact years of attendance. There is no fee.

Dixie College, Registrar, 225 S 700 E, St George, UT 84770, 801-673-4811 X348 (Fax: 801-656-4005). Hours: 9AM-4:30PM. Enrollment: 5000. Records go back to 1911. Alumni records are maintained here also. Call 801-652-7538. Degrees granted: Associate. Special programs- Aeronautics: Nursing. Adverse incident record source- Counseling, 801-652-7690.

Attendance and degree information available by phone, fax, mail. Search requires name plus SSN. Also helpful: exact years of attendance. There is no fee.

ITT Technical Institute, Registrar, 920 W LeVoy Dr, Murray, UT 84123-2500, 801-263-3313 (Fax: 801-263-3497). Hours: 8AM-8PM. Enrollment: 530. Records go back to 1970's. Alumni Records Office: 9511 Angola Ct, Indianapolis, IN 46286. Degrees granted: Associate; Bachelors. Special programs- Electronics Industrial Design.

Attendance and degree information available by phone, fax, mail. Search requires name plus SSN. Also helpful: date of birth, exact years of attendance. There is no fee.

LDS Business College, Registrar, 411 E S Temple St, Salt Lake City, UT 84111, 801-524-8140 (Fax: 801-524-1900). Hours: 8AM-5PM. Records go back to 1930. Prior records in archives. Alumni records are maintained here at the same phone number. Degrees granted: Associate.

Attendance and degree information available by phone, fax, mail. Search requires name plus exact years of attendance. Also helpful: SSN, date of birth. There is no fee.

Phillips Junior College, Registrar, 3098 Highland Dr, Salt Lake City, UT 84106, 801-485-0221 (Fax: 801-485-0057). Hours: 8:30AM-8PM. Records go back to 1982. Degrees granted: Associate.

Attendance information available by phone, fax, mail. Search requires name plus SSN, date of birth. Also helpful: exact years of attendance. There is no fee.

Degree information available by phone, fax, mail. Search requires name plus SSN, date of birth, approximate years of attendance. Also helpful: exact years of attendance. There is no fee.

Salt Lake Community College, Registrar's Office, PO Box 30808, Salt Lake City, UT 84130, 801-957-4298 (Fax: 801-957-4958). Hours: 8AM-8PM M-Th; 8AM-4:30PM F. Enrollment: 20000. Records go back to 1948. Alumni records are maintained here also. Call 801-957-4555. Degrees granted: Associate. Adverse incident record source- Security Office, 801-957-4270.

Attendance and degree information available by phone, fax, mail. Search requires name plus SSN. Also helpful: date of birth, exact years of attendance. There is no fee.

Snow College, Registrar, Ephraim, UT 84627, 801-283-4021 (Fax: 801-283-6874). Hours: 9AM-4PM. Records go back to 1888. Alumni records are maintained here at the same phone number. Degrees granted: Associate.

Attendance and degree information available by phone, fax, mail. Search requires name only. Also helpful: SSN, date of birth, exact years of attendance. There is no fee.

Southern Utah University, Registrar, 351 W Center, Cedar City, UT 84720, 801-586-7715 (Fax: 801-865-8223). Hours: 8AM-5PM. Enrollment: 5500. Records go back to 1896. Alumni records are maintained here at the same phone number. Degrees granted: Bachelors; Masters.

Attendance and degree information available by phone, mail. Search requires name plus SSN, date of birth, exact years of attendance. There is no fee.

Stevens College of Business, Registrar, 2168 Washington Blvd, Ogden, UT 84401-1467, 801-394-7791. Hours: 8AM-5PM. Enrollment: 250. Records go back to 1950. Degrees granted: Associate. Adverse incident record source- Program Director.

Attendance information available by phone, fax, mail. Search requires name plus SSN, date of birth. There is no fee.

Degree information available by phone, fax, mail. Search requires name plus SSN. There is no fee.

Stevens-Henager College of Business, (Branch Campus), Registrar, 25 E 1700 S, Provo, UT 84606-6157, 801-375-5455 (Fax: 801-375-9836). Records are not housed here. They are located at Stevens College of Business, Registrar, 2168 Washington Blvd, Ogden, UT 84401-1467.

University of Phoenix, (Salt Lake City Main), Registrar, 5251 Green St, Salt Lake City, UT 84123, 801-263-1444 (Fax: 801-269-9766). Enrollment: 2000. Transcript records are housed at University of Phoenix, Registrar, PO Box 52069, Phoenix, AZ 85072. Alumni records are maintained here at the same phone number. Degrees granted: Bachelors; Masters.

Attendance and degree information available by written request only. Search requires name plus SSN, approximate years of attendance.

University of Utah, Registrar, Student Services Bldg Room 250, Salt Lake City, UT 84112, 801-581-8965 (Fax: 801-585-7860). Hours: 7:30AM-5:30PM. Enrollment: 27000. Records go back to 1850. Alumni records are maintained here also. Call 801-581-6995. Degrees granted: Bachelors; Masters; Doctorate. Adverse incident record source- Campus Police, 801-581-7944: Dean of Students, 801-581-7066

Attendance and degree information available by phone, fax, mail. Search requires name plus SSN, date of birth. Also helpful: exact years of attendance. There is no fee.

Utah State University, Registrar, Logan, UT 84322-1400, 801-797-3988 (Fax: 801-797-3880). Alumni records are maintained here also. Call 801-797-2055. Degrees granted: Bachelors; Masters; Doctorate.

Attendance and degree information available by phone, fax, mail. Search requires name plus SSN, date of birth, exact years of attendance. There is no fee.

Utah Valley State College, Registrar, 800 W 1200 S, Orem, UT 84058, 801-222-8468 (Fax: 801-225-4677). Hours: 8AM-5PM. Enrollment: 14000. Records go back to 1963. Alumni records are maintained here also. Call 801-222-8205. Degrees granted: Bachelors. Special programs- Professional Driving, 801-222-7568. Adverse incident record source- Campus Police, 801-222-8187.

Attendance and degree information available by phone, fax, mail. Search requires name plus SSN, exact years of attendance. There is no fee.

Weber State University, Registrar, 3750 Harrison Blvd, Ogden, UT 84408, 801-626-6751 (Fax: 801-626-6679). Hours: 8AM-7:30PM. Records go back to 1913. Alumni records are maintained here also. Call 801-626-6564. Degrees granted: Associate; Bachelors; Masters.

Attendance and degree information available by mail. Search requires name only. Also helpful: SSN, date of birth, exact years of attendance. There is no fee.

Westminster College of Salt Lake City, Registrar, 1840 S 1300 E, Salt Lake City, UT 84105, 801-488-4100 (Fax: 801-495-1989). Hours: 8AM-5PM M,W,F; 8AM-6PM T,Th. Enrollment: 1773. Records go back to 1985. Alumni records are maintained here at the same phone number. Degrees granted: Bachelors; Masters. Certification: Teaching. Adverse incident record source- 801-488-1665.

Attendance and degree information available by phone, fax, mail. Search requires name only. Also helpful: SSN, date of birth, exact years of attendance. There is no fee.

Trade and Vocational Schools

American Institute of Medical-Dental Technology, 1675 N Freedom Blvd #4, Provo, UT 84604, 801-377-2900

American Institute of Medical-Dental Technology, 640 E 700 S, St George, UT 84770, 801-652-0900

Bryman School (The), 1144 W 3300 S, Salt Lake City, UT 84119, 801-975-7000

Intermountain College of Court Reporting, 5980 S 300 E, Murray, UT 84107, 801-268-9271

Myotherapy Institute of Utah, 3350 S 2300 E, Salt Lake City, UT 84109, 801-484-7624

Provo College, 1450 W 820 N, Provo, UT 84601, 801-375-1861

State Licensing & Business Registration Quick Finder Index

Architecture, Engineering & Surveying
Architect #4 .... ☎ 801-530-6628
Engineer #4... ☎ 801-530-6628
Geologist #7.. 801-537-3300
Landscape Architect #4 .... ☎ 801-530-6628
Surveyor #4.. ☎ 801-530-6628

Business - Court & Legal Services
Attorney #9... ☎ 801-531-9077
Notary Public #5 (30000) .... ☎ 801-530-6078
Shorthand Reporter #4............................. ☎ 801-530-6628

Business - General Services
Public Accountant-CPA #4 .... ☎ 801-530-6628
Public Accountant-Certificate Holder #4....... ☎ 801-530-6628
Weights & Measures #3 .... ☎ 801-538-7121

Construction & Manufacturing
Apprentice Electrician #4......................... ☎ 801-530-6628
Apprentice Plumber #4............................. ☎ 801-530-6628
Contractor #4 .... ☎ 801-530-6628
Journeyman Electrician & Plumber #4........... ☎ 801-530-6628
Manufactured Housing Dealer & Salesperson #4
.... ☎ 801-530-6628
Master Electrician #4............................... ☎ 801-530-6628
Residential Apprentice Plumber #4 .... ☎ 801-530-6628
Residential Electrican Trainee #4.............. ☎ 801-530-6628
Residential Journeyman Plumber #4 .... ☎ 801-530-6628
Residential Master Electrician #4.............. ☎ 801-530-6628

Education
School Administrator #6............................ ☎ 801-538-7751
School Librarian #6 .... ☎ 801-538-7751
Teacher #6 (24000)................................... ☎ 801-538-7751

Environmental & Agriculture
Bee Keeper #3.. ☎ 801-538-7121
Brand & Meat Inspection #3 .... ☎ 801-538-7121
Egg & Poultry #3...................................... ☎ 801-538-7121
Feed #3.. ☎ 801-538-7121
Food & Dairy #3....................................... ☎ 801-538-7121
Grain & Seed #3 .... ☎ 801-538-7121
Pesticide Dealer/Applicator #3................. ☎ 801-538-7121
Veterinarian #4 .... ☎ 801-530-6628
Veterinary Pharmaceutical Outlet #4 .... ☎ 801-530-6628

Financial - Real Estate, Insurance & Banking
Bank #10 (26).. ☎ 801-538-8835
Credit Union #10 (103) .... ☎ 801-538-8840
Escrow Agent #10 .... ☎ 801-538-8836
Insurance Agent #8 (15000) .... ✉ 801-538-3855
Insurance Establishment #8 (2500) .... ✉ 801-538-3802
Real Estate Agent #2 (10982) .... ☎ 801-530-6747
Real Estate Appraiser #2 .... ☎ 801-530-6747
Real Estate Broker #2 (3137) .... ☎ 801-530-6747
Real Estate Establishment #4 .... ☎ 801-530-6628
Savings & Loan #10 (2) .... ☎ 801-538-8842
Securities Broker/Dealer #4 .... ☎ 801-530-6628
Third Party Payment Issuer #10 .... ☎ 801-538-8836

Health & Beauty
Acupuncturist #4...................................... ☎ 801-530-6628

Agency Performing Euthanasia #4 .... ☎ 801-530-6628
Audiologist #4.. ☎ 801-530-6628
Branch Pharmacy #4 .... ☎ 801-530-6628
Chiropractor #4 .... ☎ 801-530-6628
Cosmetologist/Barber #4 .... ☎ 801-530-6628
Cosmetologist/Barber School #4 .... ☎ 801-530-6628
Dental Hygienist #4 .... ☎ 801-530-6628
Dentist #4.. ☎ 801-530-6628
Dietitian #4... ☎ 801-530-6628
Electrologist #4 .... ☎ 801-530-6628
Endowment Care-Cemetery #4................... ☎ 801-530-6628
Funeral Service Apprentice & Director #4..... ☎ 801-530-6628
Funeral Service Establishment #4 .... ☎ 801-530-6628
Health Facility Administrator #4 .... ☎ 801-530-6628
Hearing Aid Specialist #4......................... ☎ 801-530-6628
Hospital & Institutional Pharmacy #4 .... ☎ 801-530-6628
Massage Apprentice & Technician #4........... ☎ 801-530-6628
Medical Doctor/Surgeon #4...................... ☎ 801-530-6628
Naturopathic Physician #4........................ ☎ 801-530-6628
Nuclear Pharmacy #4 .... ☎ 801-530-6628
Nurse #4.. ☎ 801-530-6628
Nurse Midwife #4 .... ☎ 801-530-6628
Occupational Therapist/Assistant #4 .... ☎ 801-530-6628
Optometrist #4 .... ☎ 801-530-6628
Osteopathic Physician #4.......................... ☎ 801-530-6628
Out-of-State Mail Service Pharmacy #4........ ☎ 801-530-6628
Pharmaceutical Teaching Organization #4..... ☎ 801-530-6628
Pharmaceutical Wholesaler/Distributor #4..... ☎ 801-530-6628
Pharmacist #4 .... ☎ 801-530-6628
Pharmacist Intern #4 .... ☎ 801-530-6628
Physical Therapist #4............................... ☎ 801-530-6628
Physician's Assistant #4........................... ☎ 801-530-6628
Podiatrist #4 .... ☎ 801-530-6628
Practical Nurse #4 .... ☎ 801-530-6628
Radiology Practical Technician #4............. ☎ 801-530-6628
Radiology Technologist #4........................ ☎ 801-530-6628
Respiratory Care Practitioner #4 .... ☎ 801-530-6628
Retail Pharmacy #4 .... ☎ 801-530-6628
Sanitarian #4 .... ☎ 801-530-6628
Speech Pathologist/Audiologist #4................ ☎ 801-530-6628

Investigations & Security
Pharmaceutical Dog Trainer, Manufacturer &
   Researcher #4 .... ☎ 801-530-6628
Private Probation Provider #4........................ ☎ 801-530-6628

Social Services
Clinical Social Worker #4......................... ☎ 801-530-6628
Marriage & Family Therapist #4 .... ☎ 801-530-6628
Psychologist #4.. ☎ 801-530-6628
Recreational Therapist #4......................... ☎ 801-530-6628
Social Service Aide #4............................. ☎ 801-530-6628
Social Service Worker #4 .... ☎ 801-530-6628
Social Worker #4 .... ☎ 801-530-6628

Sports & Entertainment
Boxer/Judge/Manager/Promoter/Referee #4
.... ☎ 801-530-6628
Liquor Licensing #1 (1400)...................... ☎ 801-973-7770
Recreational Vehicle Dealer #4 .... ☎ 801-530-6628

State Licensing & Business Registration Agency Information

(1) Alcoholic Beverage Control Department, PO Box 30408, Salt Lake City, UT 84130-0408, 801-973-6800, Fax: 801-977-6888

(2) Commerce Department, Division of Real Estate, 160 E 300 S, 4th Floor, Salt Lake City, UT 84145-0806, 801-530-6747

(3) Department of Agriculture, Brand Section, 350 N Redwood Rd, Salt Lake City, UT 84116, 801-538-7100, Fax: 801-538-7126

(4) Department of Commerce, Division of Occupational & Professional Licensing, Heber M Wells Bldg, 160 E 300 S, PO Box 146741, Salt Lake City, UT 84114-6741, 801-530-6628, Fax: 801-530-6511

(5) Division of Corporation/Commercial Code, 160 E 300 S, PO Box 14G705, Salt Lake City, UT 84145-0801, 801-530-6078, Fax: 801-530-6430

(6) Education Office, Instructional Services, 250 E 500 S, Salt Lake City, UT 84111, 801-538-7751

(7) Geological Survey Department, 1500 W. North Tempe, Suite 3110, Salt Lake City, UT 84109-6100, 801-537-3300, Fax: 801-537-3400

(8) Insurance Department, 3110 State Office Bldg, Salt Lake City, UT 84114, 801-538-3645, Fax: 801-538-3829

(9) Utah State Bar Association, 645 S 20 E, Salt Lake City, UT 84111, 801-531-9077

(10) Utah State Deparptment of Financial Institutions, 324 S State, Suite 201, PO Box 89, Salt Lake City, UT 84110-0089, 801-538-8836, Fax: 801-538-8894

Vermont

Capitol: Montpelier (Washington County)	
State Population	.5 Million
Number of Degree Granting Institutions:	24
Number of State Licensing & Business Registration Agencies:	75

Degree Granting Educational Institutions

Bennington College, Registrar, Bennington, VT 05201, 802-442-5401 X242 (Fax: 802-442-6164). Hours: 9AM-5PM. Enrollment: 380. Records go back to 1932. Alumni records are maintained here at the same phone number. Degrees granted: Bachelors; Masters.

Attendance and degree information available by fax, mail. Search requires name plus date of birth, signed release. Also helpful: exact years of attendance. There is no fee.

Burlington College, Registrar, 95 North Ave, Burlington, VT 05401-8477, 802-862-9616 (Fax: 802-658-0071). Hours: 9AM-5PM. Enrollment: 170. Records go back to 1972. Degrees granted: Associate; Bachelors. Special programs- Independent Degree Program (IDP), 802-862-9616: Cinema Studies & Film Production Program, 802-862-9616.

Attendance information available by phone, fax, mail. Search requires name only. Also helpful: SSN. There is no fee.

Degree information available by phone, fax, mail. Search requires name only. Also helpful: SSN, date of birth. There is no fee.

Castleton State College, Registrar, Castleton, VT 05735, 802-468-5611 X209 (Fax: 802-468-5237). Hours: 8AM-4:30PM. Enrollment: 2000. Records go back to 1787. Alumni records are maintained here at the same phone number. Degrees granted: Bachelors; Masters; CAGS; Associate.

Attendance and degree information available by phone, fax, mail. Search requires name plus SSN, exact years of attendance. There is no fee.

Champlain College, Registrar's Office, 163 S Willard St, PO Box 670, Burlington, VT 05402-0670, 802-860-2715 (Fax: 802-860-2761). Hours: 8:30AM-5PM. Enrollment: 1300. Records go back to 1965. Alumni records are maintained here also. Call 802-860-2747. Degrees granted: Associate; Bachelors. Certification: Secretarial and Concentrated Study. Adverse incident record source- Security Office, 802-658-0800.

Attendance and degree information available by phone, fax, mail. Search requires name plus approximate years of attendance. Also helpful: SSN, exact years of attendance. There is no fee.

College of St. Joseph, Registrar, Rutland, VT 05701, 802-773-5900 X241 (Fax: 802-773-5900 X258). Hours: 8:30AM-7:30PM. Enrollment: 500. Records go back to 1964. Alumni records are maintained here at the same phone number. Degrees granted: Associate; Bachelors; Masters. Adverse incident record source- Student Services.

Attendance and degree information available by phone, mail. Search requires name plus approximate years of attendance. Also helpful: SSN, date of birth, exact years of attendance. There is no fee.

Community College of Vermont, Registrar, Waterbury, VT 05676, 802-241-3535 (Fax: 802-241-3526). Hours: 8:30AM-4:30PM. Enrollment: 4800. Records go back to 1975. Degrees granted: Associate. Adverse incident record source- Academic Dean, 802-241-3535.

Attendance information available by phone, mail. Search requires name plus SSN, date of birth. There is no fee.

Degree information available by mail. Search requires name plus SSN, date of birth. There is no fee.

Goddard College, Registrar, Plainfield, VT 05667, 802-454-8311 X13 (Fax: 802-454-1029). Hours: 8AM-4:30PM. Records go back to 1938. Alumni records are maintained here at the same phone number. Degrees granted: Bachelors; Masters. Adverse incident record source- Student Affairs, 802-454-8311.

Attendance and degree information available by phone, fax, mail. Search requires name plus SSN, exact years of attendance. There is no fee.

Green Mountain College, Registrar, 16 College St, Poultney, VT 05764, 802-287-8215 (Fax: 802-287-8099). Hours: 8AM-4:30PM. Enrollment: 600. Records go back to 1834. Alumni records are maintained here at the same phone number. Degrees granted: Bachelors.

Attendance and degree information available by phone, mail. Search requires name plus exact years of attendance. There is no fee.

Johnson State College, Registrar, Johnson, VT 05656, 802-635-2356 X229 (Fax: 802-635-1248). Hours: 8AM-5PM. Enrollment: 1400. Records go back to 1828. Alumni records are maintained here at the same phone number. Degrees granted: Bachelors; Masters. Adverse incident record source-Academic Dean, 802-635-2356.

Attendance and degree information available by phone, fax, mail. Search requires name plus SSN, exact years of attendance. There is no fee.

Landmark College, Registrar, Putney, VT 05346, 802-387-4767. Hours: 8AM-4:30PM. Degrees granted: Associate.

Attendance and degree information available by phone, mail. Search requires name plus SSN. Also helpful: approximate years of attendance. There is no fee.

Lyndon State College, Registrar, Vail Hill, Lyndonville, VT 05851, 802-626-9371 X194 (Fax: 802-626-9770). Hours: 9AM-4PM. Enrollment: 1200. Records go back to 1911. Alumni records are maintained here at the same phone number. Degrees granted: Bachelors; Masters. Adverse incident record source- Student Affairs.

Attendance and degree information available by phone, mail. Search requires name plus SSN, exact years of attendance. There is no fee.

Marlboro College, Registrar, Marlboro, VT 05344, 802-257-4333 X233 (Fax: 802-257-4154). Hours: 8AM-4:30PM. Enrollment: 275. Records go back to 1946. Alumni records are maintained here at the same phone number. Degrees granted: Bachelors.

Attendance and degree information available by phone, fax, mail. Search requires name only. There is no fee.

Middlebury College, Registrar, Old Chapel Bldg, Middlebury, VT 05753, 802-388-3711 X5389 (Fax: 802-388-9646). Hours: 8AM-5PM. Records go back to 1800. Alumni records are maintained here at the same phone number. Degrees granted: Bachelors; Masters; Doctorate.

Attendance and degree information available by phone, fax, mail. Search requires name plus SSN, approximate years of attendance. There is no fee.

Norwich University, Registrar, Northfield, VT 05663, 802-485-2035 (Fax: 802-485-2042). Hours: 8AM-4:30PM. Alumni records are maintained here at the same phone number. Degrees granted: Associate; Bachelors; Masters. Special programs- Graduate Programs & Adult Degree BA, 802-828-8725.

Attendance information available by phone, fax, mail. Search requires name plus SSN, approximate years of attendance. Also helpful: exact years of attendance. There is no fee. Expedited service available for $2.50.

Degree information available by phone, fax, mail. Search requires name plus SSN, date of birth, approximate years of attendance. Also helpful: exact years of attendance. There is no fee. Expedite service available for $2.50.

School for International Training, Registrar, PO Box 676, Brattleboro, VT 05301, 802-257-7751 (Fax: 802-258-3500). Hours: 8:30AM-4:30PM. Enrollment: 1600. Records go back to 1964. Alumni records are maintained here at the same phone number. Degrees granted: Bachelors; Masters.

Attendance and degree information available by phone, fax, mail. Search requires name only. Also helpful: SSN, date of birth, exact years of attendance. There is no fee.

Southern Vermont College, Registrar, Monument View Rd, Bennington, VT 05201, 802-442-5427 X228 (Fax: 802-442-5529). Hours: 8AM-4:30PM. Enrollment: 600. Records go back to 1926. Alumni records are maintained here at the same phone number. Degrees granted: Bachelors.

Attendance and degree information available by phone, mail. Search requires name plus SSN, exact years of attendance. There is no fee.

St. Michael's College, Registrar, Winooski Park, Colchester, VT 05439, 802-654-2571 (Fax: 802-655-3680). Hours: 8AM-4PM. Enrollment: 2300. Records go back to 1901. Alumni records are maintained here also. Call 802-654-2527. Degrees granted: Bachelors; Masters. Special programs- School of International Studies, 802-654-2300. Adverse incident record source-Student Life, 802-654-2566.

Attendance and degree information available by phone, fax, mail. Search requires name plus date of birth, approximate years of attendance. Also helpful: SSN, exact years of attendance. There is no fee.

Sterling College, Registrar, Craftsbury Common, VT 05827, 802-586-7711 (Fax: 802-586-2596). Hours: 9AM-5PM. Enrollment: 80. Records go back to 1958. Degrees granted: Associate. Special programs- Resource Management (Experimental). Adverse incident record source- Dean of Students.

Attendance and degree information available by phone, fax, mail. Search requires name only. Also helpful: SSN, date of birth, exact years of attendance. There is no fee.

Trinity College of Vermont, Registrar, 208 Colchester Ave, Burlington, VT 05401, 802-658-0337 X247 (Fax: 802-658-5446). Hours: 8AM-4:30PM. Records go back to 1925. Alumni records are maintained here at the same phone number. Degrees granted: Bachelors; Masters.

Attendance and degree information available by phone, fax, mail. Search requires name plus SSN, date of birth, exact years of attendance. There is no fee.

University of Vermont, Academic Transcript, Burlington, VT 05405-0160, 802-656-2045 (Fax: 802-656-8230). Hours: 8AM-5PM. Records go back to 1791. Alumni records are maintained here also. Call 802-656-2010. Degrees granted: Bachelors; Masters; Doctorate.

Attendance and degree information available by phone, fax, mail. Search requires name plus SSN, exact years of attendance. There is no fee.

Vermont College of Norwich University, Registrar, College St, Montpelier, VT 05602, 802-828-8727 (Fax: 802-828-8585). Hours: 8AM-4:30PM. Enrollment: 1000. Records go back to 1934. Alumni records are maintained here also. Call 802-485-2100. Degrees granted: Bachelors; Masters.

Attendance and degree information available by phone, mail. Search requires name plus SSN, date of birth. There is no fee.

Vermont Law School, Asst Registrar, PO Box 96, South Royalton, VT 05068, 802-763-8303 (Fax: 802-763-7071). Hours: 8:30AM-5PM. Enrollment: 500. Records go back to 1973. Alumni records are maintained here at the same phone number. Degrees granted: Masters; JD.

Attendance and degree information available by phone, fax, mail. Search requires name only. Also helpful: SSN, exact years of attendance. There is no fee.

Vermont Technical College, Registrar, Randolph Center, VT 05061, 802-728-1302 (Fax: 802-728-1390). Hours: 8AM-4:30PM; 8AM-4PM Summers. Enrollment: 750. Records go back to 1900. Alumni records are maintained here also. Call 802-728-1261. Degrees granted: Associate; Bachelors.

Attendance and degree information available by phone, fax, mail. Search requires name only. Also helpful: SSN, date of birth, exact years of attendance. There is no fee.

Woodbury College, Registrar, 660 Elm St, Montpelier, VT 05602, 802-229-0516 (Fax: 802-229-2141). Hours: 8AM-

5PM. Alumni records are maintained here at the same phone number. Degrees granted: Associate.

Attendance and degree information available by phone, fax, mail. Search requires name plus SSN, approximate years of attendance. There is no fee.

Trade and Vocational Schools

Fanny Allen Memorial School of Practical Nursing, 125 College Pkwy, Colchester, VT 05446, 802-655-2540

Thompson School of Practical Nursing, 30 Maple St, Brattleboro, VT 05301, 802-254-5570

State Licensing & Business Registration Quick Finder Index

Architecture, Engineering & Surveying
Architect #14 .... ☎ 802-828-2363
Engineer #14 .... ☎ 802-828-2363
Surveyor #14 .... ☎ 802-828-2363

Business - Court & Legal Services
Attorney #2 .... ☎ 802-828-3281
Lobbyist #13 .... ☎ 802-828-2464
Notary Public #12 (15500) .... ☎ 802-828-2308

Business - General Services
Auctioneer #14 .... ☎ 802-828-2363
Peddler #14 .... ☎ 802-828-2363
Photographer, Itinerant #14 .... ☎ 802-828-2363
Public Accountant-CPA #14 .... ☎ 802-828-2363
Vendor-Itinerant #14 .... ☎ 802-828-2363

Construction & Manufacturing
Blaster #1 802-241-3822
Boiler & Pressure Vessel Inspector #8 .... ☎ 802-828-2107
Dealer/Repairer Weighing & Measuring Devices #4
.... ☎ 802-244-4510
Electrician #8 .... ☎ 802-828-2107
Plumber #8 .... ☎ 802-828-2107
Precision Tank Tester #1 802-241-3822

Education
School Guidance Counselor #6 .... ☎ 802-828-2445
School Librarian/Media Specialist #6 .... ☎ 802-828-2445
School Principal #6 .... ☎ 802-828-2445
School Superintendent #6 .... ☎ 802-828-2445
Teacher #6 .... ☎ 802-828-2445
Vocational Education Teacher #6 .... ☎ 802-828-2445

Environmental & Agriculture
Laboratory #4 .... ☎ 802-244-4510
Livestock Laboratory #4 .... ☎ 802-244-4510
Meat Inspection Laboratory #4 .... ☎ 802-244-4510
Milk & Cream Tester #4 .... ☎ 802-244-4510
Pesticide Applicator #4 .... ☎ 802-244-4510
Veterinarian #14 .... ☎ 802-828-2363
Waste Water Management #1 802-241-3822
Well Driller #1 802-241-3822

Financial - Real Estate, Insurance & Banking
Insurance Adjuster #5 (3350) .... ✉ 802-828-3303
Insurance Agent/Consultant #5 (48000) .... ✉ 802-828-3303
Insurance Appraiser #5 (200) .... ✉ 802-828-3303
Insurance Broker #5 (2000) .... ✉ 802-828-3303
Public Adjuster #5 (75) .... ✉ 802-828-3303
Real Estate Appraiser #11 .... ☎ 802-828-3228
Real Estate Broker/Agent #11 .... ☎ 802-828-3228
Securities Broker/Dealer #5 .... ☎ 802-828-3420
Securities Sales Representative #5 .... ☎ 802-828-3420

Health & Beauty
Acupuncturist #14 .... ☎ 802-828-2363
Barber #14 .... ☎ 802-828-2363
Chiropractor #14 .... ☎ 802-828-2363
Cosmetologist #14 .... ☎ 802-828-2363
Dentist #14 .... ☎ 802-828-2363
Emergency Care Attendant #7 .... ☎ 802-863-7310
Emergency Medical Tech-Intermediate, Defib,
   Paramedic #7 (2500) .... ☎ 802-863-7310
Funeral Service Director #14 .... ☎ 802-828-2363
Hearing Aid Dispenser #14 .... ☎ 802-828-2363
Medical Doctor/Surgeon #14 (3500) .... ☎ 802-828-2673
Nurse/Nurse Practitioner/LNA #14 (15000)
.... ☎ 802-828-2396
Nursing Home Administrator #14 .... ☎ 802-828-2363
Optician #14 .... ☎ 802-828-2363
Optometrist #14 .... ☎ 802-828-2363
Osteopathic Physician #14 .... ☎ 802-828-2363
Pharmacist #14 .... ☎ 802-828-2363
Physical Therapist #14 .... ☎ 802-828-2363
Podiatrist #14 .... ☎ 802-828-2363
Radiologic Technologist #14 .... ☎ 802-828-2363

Investigations & Security
Armed Courier #14 .... ☎ 802-828-2363
Fire Detection System Installer/Dealer #8 ...... ☎ 802-828-2107
Guard Dog Handler #14 .... ☎ 802-828-2363
Lightning Rod Installer/Dealer #8 .... ☎ 802-828-2107
Polygraph Examiner #3 (20) .... ☎ 802-244-8781
Private Investigator #14 .... ☎ 802-828-2363
Security Guard #14 .... ☎ 802-828-2363

Social Services
Clinical Mental Health Counselors #14 .... ☎ 802-828-2363
Clinical Social Worker #14 .... ☎ 802-828-2363
Psychologist #14 .... ☎ 802-828-2363

Sports & Entertainment

Boxing #14 .... ☎ 802-828-2363
Liquor Distributor #9 .... ✉ 802-828-2345
Lottery Retailer #15 (850) .... ☎ 802-479-5686
Race Driver/Track Personnel #14 .... ☎ 802-828-2363
Racing #16 (500) .... ☎ 802-786-5050

Transportation

Commercial Driving Instructor/School #10 (40)
.... ☎ 802-828-2000

State Licensing & Business Registration Agency Information

(1) Agency of Natural Resources, Department of Environmental Conservation, 103 S Main St, The Sewing Bldg, Waterbury, VT 05671-0401, 802-241-3822

(2) Board of Bar Examiners, 104 State St,, Montpelier, VT 05609-0702, 802-828-3281, Fax: 802-828-3457

(3) Commission of Public Safety, State Police Headquarters, 103 S Main St, Waterbury State Complex, Waterbury, VT 05676, 802-244-8781, Fax: 802-244-1106

(4) Department of Agriculture, Plant Industry, Laboratories & Consumer Assurance, 103 S Main St, Waterbury, VT 05671, 802-244-4510, Fax: 802-82802361

(5) Department of Banking, Insurance & Securities, 89 Main St (City Ctr), Drawer 20, Montpelier, VT 05620-3101, 802-828-3420, Fax: 802-828-2896

(6) Department of Education, Teacher Licensing & Certification, 120 State St, Montpelier, VT 05620-2501, 802-828-2445, Fax: 802-828-3140

(7) Department of Health, Emergency Medical Services, PO Box 70, 108 Cherry St., Burlington, VT 05402, 802-863-7310, Fax: 802-863-7577

(8) Department of Labor & Industry, Fire Prevention Division, National Life Bldg, Drawer 20, Montpelier, VT 05620-3401, 802-828-2107

(9) Department of Liquor Control, Green Mountain Dr, Drawer 20, Montpelier, VT 05620-4501, 802-828-2339, Fax: 802-828-2803

(10) Department of Motor Vehicles, 120 State St, Montpelier, VT 05603, 802-828-2114, Fax: 802-828-2092

(11) Real Estate Commission, 26 Terrace St, Drawer 9, Montpelier, VT 05609-1106, 802-828-3228, Fax: 802-828-2484

(12) Secretary of State, 109 State St, Montpelier, VT 05609-1103, 802-828-2308, Fax: 802-828-2496

(13) Secretary of State, Attn: Elections, 109 State St, Montpelier, VT 05609-1101, 802-828-2464, Fax: 802-828-5171

(14) Secretary of State, Board of, Professional Regulation & Licensing Department, 109 State St, Montpelier, VT 05609-1101, 802-828-2673, Fax: 802-828-5450

(15) Vermont Lottery Commission, Route 14, PO Box 420, South Barre, VT 05670, 802-828-5686, Fax: 802-479-4294

(16) Vermont Racing Commission, 128 Merchant Row, Rutland, VT 05701, 802-786-5059, Fax: 802-786-5051

Virginia

Capitol: Richmond (Richmond City County)	
State Population	6.6 Million
Number of Degree Granting Institutions:	95
Number of State Licensing & Business Registration Agencies:	75

Degree Granting Educational Institutions

Averett College, Registrar, 420 W Main St, Danville, VA 24541, 804-791-5600 (Fax: 804-799-0658). Hours: 8AM-5PM. Enrollment: 2500. Records go back to 1859. Alumni records are maintained here also. Call 804-791-5600. Degrees granted: Bachelors; Masters.

Attendance and degree information available by phone, mail. Search requires name plus SSN, exact years of attendance. Also helpful: date of birth. There is no fee.

Blue Ridge Community College, Registrar, PO Box 80, Weyers Cave, VA 24486, 540-234-9261 (Fax: 540-234-9231). Hours: 8:15AM-5PM. Enrollment: 2500. Records go back to 1967. Alumni records are maintained here at the same phone number. Degrees granted: Associate. Adverse incident record source- Department of Security.

Attendance and degree information available by phone, fax, mail. Search requires name plus SSN. Also helpful: date of birth, exact years of attendance. There is no fee.

Bluefield College, Registrar, 3000 College Dr, Bluefield, VA 24605, 540-326-3682 (Fax: 540-326-4288). Hours: 8:30AM-Noon, 1-5PM. Enrollment: 850. Records go back to 1922. Alumni records are maintained here at the same phone number. Degrees granted: Associate; Bachelors. Adverse incident record source- Student Development.

Attendance and degree information available by phone, mail. Search requires name plus SSN, exact years of attendance. Also helpful: date of birth. There is no fee.

Bridgewater College, Registrar, Bridgewater, VA 22812, 540-828-2501 (Fax: 540-828-5479). Hours: 8AM-5PM. Records go back to 1920. Degrees granted: Bachelors.

Attendance and degree information available by phone, fax, mail. Search requires name only. Also helpful: SSN, date of birth, exact years of attendance. There is no fee.

Central Virginia Community College, Registrar, 3506 Wards Rd, Lynchburg, VA 24502-2498, 804-386-4576 (Fax: 804-386-4681). Hours: 8:30AM-4:30PM. Enrollment: 3700. Records go back to 1967. Alumni records are maintained here also. Call 804-386-4535. Degrees granted: Associate. Adverse incident record source- Department of Security.

Attendance and degree information available by phone, fax, mail. Search requires name plus SSN. Also helpful: date of birth, exact years of attendance. There is no fee.

Christendom College, Registrar, 134 Christendon Dr, Front Royal, VA 22630, 540-636-2900 (Fax: 540-636-1655). Hours: 8:30AM-4:30PM. Enrollment: 200. Records go back to 1977. Alumni records are maintained here at the same phone number. Degrees granted: Associate; Bachelors. Adverse incident record source- Student Services.

Attendance and degree information available by phone, fax, mail. Search requires name only. Also helpful: SSN, date of birth, exact years of attendance. There is no fee.

Christopher Newport College, Registrar, 50 Shoe Lane, Newport News, VA 23606-2998, 804-594-7155 (Fax: 804-594-7711). Hours: 8AM-5PM. Enrollment: 4800. Records go back to 1971. Alumni records are maintained here also. Call 804-594-7712. Degrees granted: Bachelors.

Attendance and degree information available by phone, fax, mail. Search requires name plus SSN. There is no fee.

Clinch Valley College of the University of Virginia, Registrar, #1 College Ave, Wise, VA 24293, 540-328-0116 (Fax: 540-328-0115). Hours: 8AM-4:30PM. Enrollment: 1500. Records go back to 1954. Alumni records are maintained here at the same phone number. Degrees granted: Bachelors. Adverse incident record source- Dean of Students, 540-328-0214.

Attendance and degree information available by phone, fax, mail. Search requires name plus SSN. Also helpful: date of birth, exact years of attendance. There is no fee.

College of William and Mary, Registrar, PO Box 8795, Williamsburg, VA 23187-8795, 804-221-2815 (Fax: 804-221-2799). Hours: 8AM-4:30PM. Enrollment: 6600. Records go back to 1693. Alumni records are maintained here also. Call 804-221-1842. Degrees granted: Bachelors; Masters; Doctorate. Adverse incident record source- Department of Security.

Attendance and degree information available by phone, mail. Search requires name plus SSN, date of birth, exact years of attendance. There is no fee.

Commonwealth College, Registrar, 301 Centre Pointe Drive, Virginia Beach, VA 23462, 804-499-7900 (Fax: 804-499

9977). Hours: 8AM-5PM. Enrollment: 261. Records go back to 1960's. Degrees granted: Associate.

Attendance and degree information available by phone, fax, mail. Search requires name plus SSN. Also helpful: exact years of attendance. There is no fee.

Commonwealth College, (Branch Campus), Registrar, 1120 W Mercury Blvd, Hampton, VA 23666-3309, 804-838-2122 (Fax: 804-838-4708). Hours: 8AM-5PM. Enrollment: 300. Records go back to 1981. Alumni records are maintained here at the same phone number. Degrees granted: Associate. Adverse incident record source- Student Affairs.

Attendance and degree information available by fax, mail. Search requires name plus SSN, signed release. There is no fee.

Commonwealth College, (Branch Campus), Registrar, 300 Boush St, Norfolk, VA 23510-1216, 757-499-7900 (Fax: 757-499-9977). Enrollment: 400. Records go back to 1981. Alumni records are maintained here at the same phone number. Degrees granted: Associate. Adverse incident record source- Student Services.

Attendance and degree information available by phone, fax, mail. Search requires name plus SSN, exact years of attendance. Also helpful: date of birth. There is no fee.

Commonwealth College, (Branch Campus), Registrar, 5579 Portsmouth Blvd, Portsmouth, VA 23701, 804-484-2121 (Fax: 804-686-5173). Hours: 8AM-5PM. Enrollment: 18000. Records go back to 1968. Degrees granted: Associate.

Attendance and degree information available by fax, mail. Search requires name plus SSN, signed release. There is no fee.

Commonwealth College, (Branch Campus), Registrar, 8141 Hull St Rd, Richmond, VA 23235-6411, 804-745-2444 (Fax: 804-745-6884). Hours: 8AM-5PM. Enrollment: 320. Records go back to 1960's. Alumni records are maintained here at the same phone number. Degrees granted: Associate. Adverse incident record source- Student Affairs.

Attendance and degree information available by fax, mail. Search requires name plus SSN, signed release. There is no fee.

Community Hospital of Roanoke Valley College of Health Sciences, Registrar, PO Box 13186, Roanoke, VA 24016, 540-985-8206. Hours: 8AM-5PM. Enrollment: 375. Records go back to 1982. Alumni records are maintained here also. Call 540-985-9031. Degrees granted: Associate.

Attendance and degree information available by phone, mail. Search requires name plus SSN, exact years of attendance. There is no fee.

Dabney S. Lancaster Community College, Registrar, PO Box 1000, Clifton Forge, VA 24422-1000, 540-862-4246 (Fax: 540-862-2398). Hours: 8AM-5PM. Enrollment: 1800. Records go back to 1967. Alumni records are maintained here at the same phone number. Degrees granted: Associate. Adverse incident record source- Department of Security.

Attendance and degree information available by phone. Search requires name only. There is no fee.

Danville Community College, Registrar, 1008 S Main St, Danville, VA 24541, 804-797-3553 (Fax: 804-797-8541). Hours: 8AM-5PM. Enrollment: 4000. Records go back to 1968. Alumni records are maintained here at the same phone number. Degrees granted: Associate. Adverse incident record source- Department of Security.

Attendance and degree information available by phone, mail. Search requires name plus SSN, exact years of attendance. There is no fee.

Eastern Mennonite University, Registrar, 1200 Park Rd, Harrisonburg, VA 22801-2462, 540-432-4110 (Fax: 540-432-4444). Hours: 8AM-5PM. Enrollment: 1200. Records go back to 1917. Alumni records are maintained here also. Call 540-432-4206. Degrees granted: Associate; Bachelors; Masters; First Professional Degree. Special programs- Adult Degree Completion Program, 540-432-4983.

Attendance and degree information available by phone, mail. Search requires name plus date of birth. Also helpful: SSN, exact years of attendance. There is no fee.

Eastern Shore Community College, Registrar, 29300 Lankford Hwy, Melfa, VA 23410, 757-787-5900 X15 (Fax: 757-787-5919). Hours: 8AM-5PM. Enrollment: 700. Records go back to 1971. Alumni records are maintained here at the same phone number. Degrees granted: Associate. Adverse incident record source- Records, 757-787-5915.

Attendance and degree information available by phone, fax, mail. Search requires name plus SSN, exact years of attendance. There is no fee.

Eastern Virginia Medical School, Office of the Registrar, 721 Fairfax Ave #117, PO Box 1980, Norfolk, VA 23501-1980, 804-446-5813 (Fax: 804-446-5817). Hours: 8AM-4:30PM. Enrollment: 602. Records go back to 1972. Alumni records are maintained here also. Call 804-446-5805. Degrees granted: Masters; Doctorate.

Attendance and degree information available by phone, mail. Search requires name plus SSN. Also helpful: date of birth. There is no fee.

Emory and Henry College, Registrar, PO Box 947, Emory, VA 24327, 540-944-6128 (Fax: 540-944-4438). Hours: 8AM-4PM. Enrollment: 885. Records go back to 1902. Alumni records are maintained here at the same phone number. Degrees granted: Bachelors.

Attendance and degree information available by phone, fax, mail. Search requires name plus SSN, exact years of attendance. There is no fee.

Ferrum College, Registrar, Ferrum, VA 24088, 540-365-4275 (Fax: 540-365-4278). Hours: 8AM-5PM. Enrollment: 1100. Records go back to 1913. Alumni records are maintained here also. Call 540-365-4216. Degrees granted: Bachelors. Adverse incident record source- Department of Security.

Attendance and degree information available by phone, mail. Search requires name plus SSN, exact years of attendance. There is no fee.

George Mason University, Registrar, 4400 University Dr, Fairfax, VA 22030-4444, 703-993-2448. Hours: 8AM-5PM. Enrollment: 15000. Records go back to 1972. Alumni records are maintained here also. Call 703-993-8696. Degrees granted: Bachelors; Masters; Doctorate.

Attendance and degree information available by phone, mail. Search requires name plus SSN, exact years of attendance. There is no fee.

Germanna Community College, Registrar, PO Box 339, Locust Grove, VA 22508, 540-727-3000 (Fax: 540-423-1009). Hours: 8AM-5PM. Enrollment: 2700. Records go back to 1970. Alumni records are maintained here at the same phone number. Degrees granted: Associate. Adverse incident record source- Department of Security.

Attendance and degree information available by phone, fax, mail. Search requires name plus SSN. There is no fee.

Hampden-Sydney College, Registrar's Office, Hampden-Sydney, VA 23943, 804-223-6274. Hours: 8:30AM-5PM. Enrollment: 970. Degrees granted: Bachelors. Adverse incident record source- Dean of Students, 804-223-6164.

Attendance information available by phone, mail. Search requires name plus date of birth, approximate years of attendance. Also helpful: SSN. There is no fee.

Degree information available by phone, mail. Search requires name only. Also helpful: exact years of attendance. There is no fee.

Hampton University, Registrar, East Queen St, Hampton, VA 23668, 757-727-5324 (Fax: 757-727-5095). Hours: 8AM-5PM. Enrollment: 6000. Records go back to 1868. Alumni records are maintained here also. Call 804-727-5485. Degrees granted: Bachelors; Masters; Doctorate. Adverse incident record source- University Police, 757-727-5259.

Attendance and degree information available by mail. Search requires name plus SSN, exact years of attendance. There is no fee.

Hollins College, Registrar, PO Box 9708, Roanoke, VA 24020, 540-362-6311 (Fax: 540-362-6642). Hours: 8:30AM-4:30PM. Enrollment: 871. Records go back to 1800's. Alumni Records Office: Alumni Affairs, PO Box 9626, Roanoke, VA 24020. Degrees granted: Bachelors; Masters.

Attendance information available by phone, fax, mail. Search requires name plus SSN. Also helpful: exact years of attendance. There is no fee.

Degree information available by phone, fax, mail. Search requires name plus SSN. Also helpful: date of birth, exact years of attendance. There is no fee.

ITT Technical Institute, (Branch of Evansville, IN), Registrar, 863 Glenrock Rd, Norfolk, VA 23502, 757-466-1260 (Fax: 757-466-7630). Hours: 8AM-5PM. Enrollment: 21467. Records go back to 1988. Alumni Records Office: ITT Technical Institute, 9511 Angola Ct, Indianapolis, IN 46268. Degrees granted: Associate; Bachelors. Adverse incident record source- Student Services.

Attendance and degree information available by phone, mail. Search requires name plus SSN, date of birth, exact years of attendance. There is no fee.

Institute of Textile Technology, Registrar, PO Box 391, Charlottesville, VA 22902, 804-296-5511 (Fax: 804-296-2957). Hours: 8AM-4:30PM. Enrollment: 27. Records go back to 1971. Alumni records are maintained here at the same phone number. Degrees granted: Masters. Adverse incident record source- Dean of Academics, 804-296-5511 fX277.

Attendance and degree information available by phone, mail. Search requires name plus SSN, approximate years of attendance. There is no fee.

J. Sargeant Reynolds Community College, Registrar, PO Box 85622, Richmond, VA 23285-5622, 804-371-3029 (Fax: 804-371-3631). Hours: 8:15AM-5PM. Enrollment: 9000. Records go back to 1972. Degrees granted: Associate. Adverse incident record source- Student Affairs.

Attendance and degree information available by phone, fax, mail. Search requires name plus SSN. Also helpful: date of birth. There is no fee.

James Madison University, Registrar, Harrisonburg, VA 22807, 540-568-6281 (Fax: 540-568-7954). Hours: 8AM-4:30PM. Enrollment: 13000. Records go back to 1908. Alumni records are maintained here also. Call 540-568-3628. Degrees granted: Bachelors; Masters. Adverse incident record source- Dept of Security, 540-568-6281 X3300.

Attendance and degree information available by phone, mail. Search requires name plus SSN. There is no fee.

John Tyler Community College, Admissions & Records, 13101 Jefferson Davis Hwy, Chester, VA 23831-5399, 804-796-4151 (Fax: 804-796-4163). Hours: 7:40AM-7PM M-Th; 7:45AM-5PM F. Enrollment: 4000. Records go back to 1967. Alumni records are maintained here at the same phone number. Degrees granted: Associate. Adverse incident record source- Department of Security.

Attendance and degree information available by phone, mail. Search requires name plus SSN. Also helpful: date of birth, approximate years of attendance. There is no fee.

Johnson & Wales University, (Branch Campus), Registrar, 2428 Almeda Ave Stes 316-318, Norfolk, VA 23513, 757-853-3508 (Fax: 757-857-4869). Hours: 8:30AM-4:30PM. Enrollment: 550. Records go back to 1987. Alumni Records Office: 8 Abbott Park Pl, Providence, RI 02903. Degrees granted: Associate. Special programs- Culinary Arts. Adverse incident record source- Security, 757-855-3883.

Attendance and degree information available by phone, mail. Search requires name plus SSN, exact years of attendance. There is no fee.

Judge Advocate General's School, Registrar, 600 Massie Rd, Charlottesville, VA 22903-1781, 804-972-6310. Hours: 8AM-4:30PM. Enrollment: 84. Records go back to 1950. Alumni records are maintained here at the same phone number. Degrees granted: Masters.

Attendance and degree information available by phone, mail. Search requires name plus SSN. There is no fee.

Liberty University, Registrar, PO Box 20000, Lynchburg, VA 24506-8001, 804-582-2397 (Fax: 804-582-2187). Hours: 8:30AM-4PM. Enrollment: 8000. Records go back to 1971. Alumni records are maintained here also. Call 804-582-2834. Degrees granted: Associate; Bachelors; Masters; Doctorate. Adverse incident record source- Department of Security, 804-582-2397 X7641.

Attendance and degree information available by phone, fax, mail. Search requires name plus SSN. Also helpful: date of birth, exact years of attendance. There is no fee.

Longwood College, Registrar, 201 High St, Farmville, VA 23909, 804-395-2095 (Fax: 804-395-2252). Hours: 8:15AM-5PM. Enrollment: 3200. Records go back to 1884. Alumni records are maintained here also. Call 804-395-2044. Degrees granted: Bachelors; Masters. Adverse incident record source- Campus Police, 804-395-2612.

Attendance information available by phone, fax, mail. Search requires name plus SSN, exact years of attendance. Also helpful: date of birth. There is no fee.

Degree information available by phone, mail. Search requires name plus SSN, date of birth, exact years of attendance. There is no fee.

Lord Fairfax Community College, Registrar, PO Box 47, Middletown, VA 22645, 540-869-1120 X126 (Fax: 540-869-7881). Hours: 8AM-5PM. Enrollment: 3000. Records go back to 1970. Alumni records are maintained here at the same phone number. Degrees granted: Associate. Adverse incident record source- Student Affairs.

Attendance and degree information available by mail. Search requires name plus SSN, signed release. There is no fee.

Lynchburg College, Registrar, 1501 Lakeside Dr, Lynchburg, VA 24501-3199, 804-522-8100 X218 (Fax: 804-522-0658). Hours: 8AM-5PM. Enrollment: 1600. Records go back to 1903. Alumni records are maintained here at the same phone number. Degrees granted: Bachelors; Masters. Adverse incident record source- Student Affairs.

Attendance and degree information available by phone, mail. Search requires name plus SSN. There is no fee.

Mary Baldwin College, Registrar, Frederick and New St, Staunton, VA 24401, 540-887-7071 (Fax: 540-886-5561). Hours: 8AM-5PM. Enrollment: 2140. Records go back to 1842. Alumni records are maintained here also. Call 540-887-7007. Degrees granted: Bachelors; Masters. Adverse incident record source- Department of Security, 540-887-7000.

Attendance and degree information available by phone, mail. Search requires name plus SSN. There is no fee.

Mary Washington College, Registrar, 1301 College Ave, Fredericksburg, VA 22401-5358, 540-654-1063. Hours: 8AM-5PM. Enrollment: 4000. Records go back to 1911. Alumni records are maintained here also. Call 540-899-4648. Degrees granted: Bachelors; Masters. Certification: Education. Adverse incident record source- Student Affairs.

Attendance and degree information available by phone, mail. Search requires name plus SSN. Also helpful: date of birth, exact years of attendance. There is no fee.

Marymount University, Registrar, 2807 N Glebe Rd, Arlington, VA 22207, 703-284-1520 (Fax: 703-516-4505). Hours: 8AM-6PM F-Th; 8AM-5PM F. Enrollment: 4000. Records go back to 1950. Alumni records are maintained here also. Call 703-284-1541. Degrees granted: Associate; Bachelors; Masters. Adverse incident record source- Student Affairs.

Attendance and degree information available by phone, fax, mail. Search requires name plus SSN. Also helpful: date of birth, exact years of attendance. There is no fee.

Mountain Empire Community College, Registrar, PO Drawer 700, Big Stone Gap, VA 24219, 540-523-2400 X209 (Fax: 540-523-2400 X323). Hours: 8AM-4:30PM. Enrollment: 3000. Records go back to 1972. Alumni records are maintained here at the same phone number. Degrees granted: Associate. Adverse incident record source- Student Services.

Attendance and degree information available by phone, fax, mail. Search requires name plus SSN. There is no fee.

National Business College, Registrar, PO Box 6400, Roanoke, VA 24017, 800-666-6221 (Fax: 504-389-5239). Records are not housed here. They are located at National Business College, (Corporate Office), Registrar, Transcripts, 1813 E Main St, Salem, VA 24153.

National Business College, (Branch Campus), Registrar, 100 Logan St, Bluefield, VA 24605, 540-326-3621. Records are not housed here. They are located at National Business College, (Corporate Office), Registrar, Transcripts, 1813 E Main St, Salem, VA 24153.

National Business College, (Branch Campus), Registrar, 300A Piedmont Ave, Bristol, VA 24201, 540-669-5333. Records are not housed here. They are located at National Business College, (Corporate Office), Registrar, Transcripts, 1813 E Main St, Salem, VA 24153.

National Business College, (Branch Campus), Registrar, 1819 Emmet St, Charlottesville, VA 22903, 804-295-0136. Records are not housed here. They are located at National Business College, (Corporate Office), Registrar, Transcripts, 1813 E Main St, Salem, VA 24153.

National Business College, (Branch Campus), Registrar, 734 Main St, Danville, VA 24541, 804-793-6822. Records are not housed here. They are located at National Business College, (Corporate Office), Registrar, Transcripts, 1813 E Main St, Salem, VA 24153.

National Business College, (Branch Campus), Registrar, 51-B Burgess Rd, Harrisonburg, VA 22801, 540-432-0943. Records are not housed here. They are located at National Business College, (Corporate Office), Registrar, Transcripts, 1813 E Main St, Salem, VA 24153.

National Business College, (Branch Campus), Registrar, 104 Candlewood Ct, Lynchburg, VA 24502, 804-239-3500. Records are not housed here. They are located at National Business College, (Corporate Office), Registrar, Transcripts, 1813 E Main St, Salem, VA 24153.

National Business College, (Corporate Office), Registrar, Transcripts, 1813 E Main St, Salem, VA 24153, 800-666-6221 (Fax: 540-986-1344). Enrollment: 400. Records go

back to 1886. Alumni records are maintained here at the same phone number. Degrees granted: Associate. Adverse incident record source- Student Affairs.

Attendance and degree information available by phone, fax, mail. Search requires name plus SSN. Also helpful: exact years of attendance. There is no fee.

New River Community College, Registrar, PO Drawer 1127, Dublin, VA 24084, 540-674-3603 (Fax: 540-674-3644). Hours: 8AM-5PM. Enrollment: 3435. Records go back to 1969. Alumni records are maintained here also. Call 540-674-3600. Degrees granted: Associate. Adverse incident record source- Department of Security.

Attendance and degree information available by phone, mail. Search requires name plus SSN. There is no fee.

Norfolk State University, Registrar, 2401 Corprew Ave, Norfolk, VA 23504, 804-683-8229 (Fax: 804-683-8907). Hours: 8AM-4:30PM. Enrollment: 8000. Records go back to 1935. Alumni records are maintained here also. Call 804-683-8135. Degrees granted: Bachelors; Masters; Doctorate. Adverse incident record source- Student Affairs, 804-683-8141.

Attendance and degree information available by phone, fax, mail. Search requires name plus SSN. Also helpful: exact years of attendance. There is no fee.

Northern Virginia Community College, (Alexandria Campus), Registrar, 3001 N Beauregard St, Alexandria, VA 22311, 703-845-6200. Hours: 8AM-5:30PM. Records go back to 1970's. Degrees granted: Associate.

Attendance and degree information available by phone, mail. Search requires name plus SSN. There is no fee.

Northern Virginia Community College, (Annandale Campus), Registrar, 8333 Little River Tpke, Annandale, VA 22003, 703-323-3328 (Fax: 703-323-3367). Hours: 9AM-6PM M-Th, 9AM-4PM F. Enrollment: 15000. Records go back to 1965. Alumni records are maintained here also. Call 703-323-3747. Degrees granted: Associate. Adverse incident record source- Department of Security.

Attendance and degree information available by phone, mail. Search requires name plus SSN. There is no fee.

Northern Virginia Community College, (Loudon Campus), Registrar, 1000 Harry Flood Byrd Hwy, Sterling, VA 22170, 703-450-2500 (Fax: 703-451-2536). Hours: 8AM-5:30PM. Enrollment: 4200. Records go back to 1974. Alumni records are maintained here also. Call 703-323-2364. Degrees granted: Associate. Adverse incident record source- Student Affairs.

Attendance and degree information available by phone, mail. Search requires name plus SSN. There is no fee.

Northern Virginia Community College, (Manassas Campus), Registrar, 6901 Sudley Rd, Manassas, VA 22110, 703-257-6600 (Fax: 703-257-9296). Hours: 8AM-5:30PM. Enrollment: 3800. Records go back to 1970's. Alumni records are maintained here at the same phone number. Degrees granted: Associate. Adverse incident record source- Student Affairs.

Attendance and degree information available by phone, mail. Search requires name plus SSN. There is no fee.

Northern Virginia Community College, (Woodbridge Campus), Registrar, 15200 Neabsco Mills Rd, Woodbridge, VA 22191, 703-878-5700 (Fax: 703-670-8433). Hours: 8AM-5PM. Enrollment: 5500. Records go back to 1970's. Alumni records are maintained here at the same phone number. Degrees granted: Associate. Adverse incident record source- Student Affairs.

Attendance and degree information available by phone, mail. Search requires name only. Also helpful: SSN. There is no fee.

Old Dominion University, Registrar, 5215 Hampton Blvd, Norfolk, VA 23529, 804-683-4425 (Fax: 804-683-5357). Hours: 8AM-5PM. Enrollment: 17000. Records go back to 1930. Alumni records are maintained here also. Call 804-683-3097. Degrees granted: Bachelors; Masters; Doctorate.

Attendance and degree information available by phone, mail. Search requires name plus SSN, date of birth, exact years of attendance. There is no fee.

Patrick Henry Community College, Registrar, PO Drawer 5311, Martinsville, VA 24115, 540-638-8777 (Fax: 540-656-0320). Enrollment: 2000. Records go back to 1971. Degrees granted: Associate.

Attendance and degree information available by phone, fax, mail. Search requires name only. Also helpful: SSN, date of birth, exact years of attendance. There is no fee.

Paul D. Camp Community College, Registrar, 100 N College Dr, PO Box 737, Franklin, VA 23851-0737, 804-569-6722 (Fax: 804-569-6795). Hours: 8AM-4:30PM. Enrollment: 1500. Records go back to 1970. Degrees granted: Associate.

Attendance information available by written request only. Search requires name plus SSN, approximate years of attendance, signed release. Also helpful: exact years of attendance. There is no fee.

Degree information available by written request only. Search requires name plus SSN, signed release. Also helpful: exact years of attendance. There is no fee.

Piedmont Virginia Community College, Registrar, Rte 6 Box 1, Charlottesville, VA 22902, 804-977-3900. Enrollment: 4900. Degrees granted: Associate.

Attendance and degree information available by phone, mail. Search requires name plus SSN. Also helpful: date of birth. There is no fee.

Presbyterian School of Christian Education, Registrar, 1205 Palmyra Ave, Richmond, VA 23227, 804-254-8054. Hours: 9AM-5PM. Records go back to 1915. Alumni records are maintained here at the same phone number. Degrees granted: Masters; Doctorate; Ed. S.

Attendance information available by phone, fax. Search requires name only. Also helpful: exact years of attendance. There is no fee. Expedite fee is based on cost of service.

Degree information available by phone, fax, mail. Search requires name only. Also helpful: exact years of attendance. There is no fee. Expedite fee is based on cost of service.

Protestant Episcopal Theological Seminary in Virginia, Registrar, 3737 Seminary Rd, Alexandria, VA 22304, 703-370-6600 (Fax: 703-370-6234). Hours: 8:45AM-4:45PM. Enrollment: 150. Records go back to 1985. Alumni records are maintained here also. Call 703-370-6600 X1712. Degrees granted: Masters; Doctorate. Adverse incident record source- Student Affairs.

Attendance and degree information available by phone, fax, mail. Search requires name plus SSN. Also helpful: date of birth, exact years of attendance. There is no fee.

Radford University, Registrar, PO Box 6904, Radford, VA 24142, 540-831-5271 (Fax: 540-831-5138). Hours: 8AM-5PM. Enrollment: 8500. Records go back to 1910. Alumni records are maintained here also. Call 540-831-5248. Degrees granted: Bachelors; Masters. Adverse incident record source-Department of Security.

Attendance and degree information available by phone, mail. Search requires name plus SSN. There is no fee.

Randolph-Macon College, Registrar, PO Box 5005, Ashland, VA 23005-5505, 804-752-7227 (Fax: 804-752-7231). Hours: 8:30AM-4:30PM. Enrollment: 1080. Records go back to

1875. Alumni records are maintained here also. Call 804-752-7222. Degrees granted: Bachelors.

Attendance and degree information available by phone, fax, mail. Search requires name plus SSN, approximate years of attendance. Also helpful: exact years of attendance. There is no fee.

Randolph-Macon Woman's College, Registrar, 2500 Rivermont Ave, Lynchburg, VA 24503-1526, 804-947-8143 (Fax: 804-947-8999). Hours: 8:30AM-4:30PM. Enrollment: 730. Records go back to 1891. Alumni records are maintained here also. Call 804-947-8102. Degrees granted: Bachelors.

Attendance and degree information available by phone, mail. Search requires name plus approximate years of attendance. Also helpful: SSN, date of birth, exact years of attendance. There is no fee.

Rappahannock Community College, Registrar, PO Box 287, Glenns, VA 23149, 804-758-6700 (Fax: 804-758-3852). Hours: 8AM-5PM. Enrollment: 2000. Records go back to 1970. Alumni records are maintained here at the same phone number. Degrees granted: Associate. Adverse incident record source- Department of Security.

Attendance and degree information available by phone, fax, mail. Search requires name plus SSN, exact years of attendance. There is no fee.

Regent University, Registrar, 1000 Centerville Tpke, Virginia Beach, VA 23464, 804-579-4094 (Fax: 804-575-5317). Hours: 8AM-5PM. Enrollment: 450. Records go back to 1977. Alumni records are maintained here also. Call 804-579-4461. Degrees granted: Bachelors; Masters; Doctorate. Adverse incident record source- Student Services.

Attendance and degree information available by phone, fax, mail. Search requires name plus SSN. There is no fee.

Richard Bland College, Registrar, 11301 Johnson Rd, Petersburg, VA 23805, 804-862-6206 (Fax: 804-862-6189). Hours: 8AM-5PM. Enrollment: 1200. Records go back to 1961. Alumni records are maintained here also. Call 804-862-6215. Degrees granted: Associate.

Attendance and degree information available by phone, fax, mail. Search requires name plus SSN, exact years of attendance. Also helpful: date of birth. There is no fee.

Roanoke College, Registrar, 221 College Lane, Salem, VA 24153-3794, 540-375-2210 (Fax: 540-375-2213). Hours: 8AM-4:30PM. Enrollment: 1700. Records go back to 1982. Alumni records are maintained here at the same phone number. Degrees granted: Bachelors. Adverse incident record source-Campus Safety, 540-375-2310.

Attendance and degree information available by phone, fax, mail. Search requires name plus SSN, date of birth, approximate years of attendance. Also helpful: exact years of attendance. There is no fee.

Shenandoah University, Registrar, 1460 University Dr, Winchester, VA 22601, 540-665-5585 (Fax: 540-665-5446). Hours: 9AM-5PM. Enrollment: 1800. Records go back to 1930. Alumni records are maintained here also. Call 540-665-4511. Degrees granted: Associate; Bachelors; Masters; Doctorate.

Attendance and degree information available by phone, fax, mail. Search requires name only. Also helpful: SSN, date of birth, exact years of attendance. There is no fee.

Southern Virginia College, Registrar, One College Hill Dr, Buena Vista, VA 24416, 540-261-8400 (Fax: 540-261-8451). Hours: 8AM-4PM. Enrollment: 180. Records go back to 1950's. Alumni records are maintained here at the same phone number. Degrees granted: Associate. Adverse incident record source- Dean of Academics.

Attendance and degree information available by phone, mail. Search requires name plus SSN, exact years of attendance. Also helpful: approximate years of attendance. There is no fee.

Southside Virginia Community College, Admissions & Records, 109 Campus Dr, Alberta, VA 23821, 804-949-1014 (Fax: 804-949-7863). Hours: 8AM-4:30PM. Enrollment: 3000. Records go back to 1970. Degrees granted: Associate. Adverse incident record source- Department of Security.

Attendance and degree information available by phone, fax, mail. Search requires name plus SSN. Also helpful: date of birth, exact years of attendance. There is no fee.

Southwest Virginia Community College, Registrar, PO Box SVCC, Richlands, VA 24641, 540-964-2555 X294 (Fax: 540-964-9307). Hours: 8AM-4:30PM. Enrollment: 4235. Records go back to 1968. Alumni records are maintained here at the same phone number. Degrees granted: Associate. Adverse incident record source- Department of Security.

Attendance and degree information available by phone, mail. Search requires name plus SSN. There is no fee.

St. Paul's College, Registrar, 406 Winsor Ave, Lawrenceville, VA 23868, 804-848-4356 (Fax: 804-848-0303). Hours: 8AM-5PM. Enrollment: 700. Records go back to 1888. Alumni records are maintained here at the same phone number. Degrees granted: Bachelors. Adverse incident record source- Student Services.

Attendance and degree information available by phone, mail. Search requires name plus SSN. There is no fee.

Strayer College, Registrar, 3045 Columbia Pike, Arlington, VA 22204, 703-679-2657 (Fax: 703-679-2640). Hours: 9AM-6PM. Enrollment: 7419. Records go back to 1920's. Alumni records are maintained here also. Call 703-769-2676. Degrees granted: Associate; Bachelors; Masters. Adverse incident record source- Registrar's Office   .

Attendance and degree information available by phone, fax, mail. Search requires name plus SSN. Also helpful: date of birth, exact years of attendance. There is no fee.

Sweet Briar College, Registrar, Sweet Briar, VA 24595, 804-381-6179 (Fax: 804-381-6484). Hours: 8AM-5PM. Enrollment: 585. Records go back to 1901. Alumni records are maintained here also. Call 804-381-6131. Degrees granted: Bachelors. Adverse incident record source- Student Affairs.

Attendance and degree information available by phone, mail. Search requires name plus SSN, exact years of attendance. There is no fee.

Thomas Nelson Community College, Records Office, PO Box 9407, Hampton, VA 23670, 804-825-2843 (Fax: 804-825-2763). Hours: 8AM-7PM M-Th; 8AM-5PM F; 8AM-12:30PM Summer. Enrollment: 7500. Records go back to 1968. Degrees granted: Associate.

Attendance and degree information available by phone, fax, mail. Search requires name plus SSN, approximate years of attendance. Also helpful: exact years of attendance. There is no fee.

Tidewater Community College, Registrar, 7000 College Dr, Portsmouth, VA 23703, 804-484-2121 (Fax: 804-686-5173). Hours: 9AM-6PM. Enrollment: 3500. Records go back to 1968. Alumni records are maintained here at the same phone number. Degrees granted: Associate. Adverse incident record source- Department of Security.

Attendance and degree information available by mail. Search requires name plus SSN, signed release. There is no fee.

Union Theological Seminary in Virginia, Registrar, 3401 Brook Rd, Richmond, VA 23227, 804-355-0671 X233 (Fax: 804-355-3919). Hours: 8AM-4:30PM. Enrollment: 250. Records go back to 1898. Alumni records are maintained

here at the same phone number. Degrees granted: Masters; Doctorate. Adverse incident record source- Student Services.

Attendance and degree information available by phone, mail. Search requires name plus SSN. There is no fee.

Univerity of Virginia Clinch Valley College, Registrar, Wise, VA 24293, 540-328-0116 (Fax: 540-328-0115). Enrollment: 1300. Records go back to 1954. Alumni records are maintained here at the same phone number. Degrees granted: Bachelors. Special programs- Arts: Science. Adverse incident record source- Student Services.

Attendance and degree information available by phone. Search requires name plus SSN, exact years of attendance. There is no fee.

University of Richmond, Registrar, Richmond, VA 23173, 804-289-8639 (Fax: 804-287-6578). Hours: 8AM-5PM. Enrollment: 2700. Records go back to 1830. Alumni records are maintained here also. Call 804-289-8473. Degrees granted: Bachelors; Masters; Doctorate. Adverse incident record source- Department of Security.

Attendance and degree information available by phone, mail. Search requires name plus SSN, exact years of attendance. There is no fee.

University of Virginia, Registrar, PO Box 9009, Charlottesville, VA 22906, 804-924-4122 (Fax: 804-924-4156). Hours: 8AM-5PM. Enrollment: 18000. Records go back to 1819. Alumni records are maintained here also. Call 804-971-9721. Degrees granted: Bachelors; Masters; Doctorate.

Attendance and degree information available by phone, mail. Search requires name plus SSN, exact years of attendance. There is no fee.

Virginia College, Registrar, 2163 Apperson Dr, Salem, VA 24153-7235, 540-776-0755 (Fax: 540-776-0764). Hours: 9AM-6PM M-Th, 8AM-5PM F. Enrollment: 80. Records go back to 1925. Degrees granted: Associate. Adverse incident record source- Student Services.

Attendance and degree information available by phone, mail. Search requires name plus SSN, exact years of attendance. There is no fee.

Virginia Commonwealth University, Registrar, 910 W Franklin St, PO Box 2520, Richmond, VA 23284, 804-367-1349. Degrees granted: Bachelors; Masters; Doctorate.

Attendance and degree information available by phone, mail. Search requires name plus SSN, exact years of attendance. There is no fee.

Virginia Highlands Community College, Admissions Office, PO Box 828, Abingdon, VA 24210, 540-628-6094 (Fax: 540-628-7576). Hours: 8AM-5PM. Enrollment: 1800. Records go back to 1969. Alumni records are maintained here at the same phone number. Degrees granted: AAS, AA&S. Adverse incident record source- Department of Security, 540-628-6094 X248.

Attendance and degree information available by phone, fax, mail. Search requires name plus SSN. Also helpful: date of birth, exact years of attendance. There is no fee.

Virginia Intermont College, Registrar, 1013 Moore St, Bristol, VA 24201, 540-669-6101 (Fax: 540-669-5763). Hours: 8:30AM-Noon, 1-4:30PM. Enrollment: 500. Records go back to 1800's. Alumni records are maintained here at the same phone number. Degrees granted: Associate; Bachelors. Adverse incident record source- Department of Security, 540-669-6101 X329.

Attendance and degree information available by phone, fax, mail. Search requires name only. Also helpful: SSN, date of birth, exact years of attendance. There is no fee.

Virginia Military Institute, Registrar, Lexington, VA 24450, 540-464-7213 (Fax: 540-464-7726). Enrollment: 1200. Alumni records are maintained here also. Call 540-464-7221. Degrees granted: Bachelors. Adverse incident record source-Registrar's Office, 540-464-7213 .

Attendance and degree information available by phone, fax, mail. Search requires name plus SSN, exact years of attendance. There is no fee.

Virginia Polytechnic Institute and State University, Office of the Registrar, Enrollment Services, 248 Burruss Hall, Blacksburg, VA 24061-0134, 540-231-5611 (Fax: 540-231-5527). Hours: 8AM-5PM. Enrollment: 25000. Records go back to 1896. Alumni records are maintained here at the same phone number. Degrees granted: Bachelors; Masters; Doctorate. Adverse incident record source- Department of Security.

Attendance information available by phone. Search requires name plus SSN, approximate years of attendance. Also helpful: exact years of attendance. There is no fee.

Degree information available by phone, fax, mail. Search requires name plus SSN, date of birth. Also helpful: exact years of attendance. There is no fee.

Virginia State University, Registrar, PO Box 9217, One Hayden Dr, Petersburg, VA 23806, 804-524-5275 (Fax: 804-524-6758). Hours: 8AM-5:30PM. Enrollment: 4000. Records go back to 1882. Alumni records are maintained here also. Call 804-524-5906. Degrees granted: Bachelors; Masters. Adverse incident record source- Police Dept, 804-524-5411.

Attendance and degree information available by phone, fax, mail. Search requires name plus SSN, exact years of attendance. There is no fee.

Virginia Union University, Registrar, 1500 N Lombardy St, Richmond, VA 23220-1711, 804-257-5845 (Fax: 804-257-5797). Hours: 8:30AM-4:30PM. Enrollment: 1400. Records go back to 1800's. Alumni records are maintained here also. Call 804-329-7403. Degrees granted: Bachelors; Masters; Doctorate. Adverse incident record source- Student Affairs, 804-257-5875.

Attendance and degree information available by phone, mail. Search requires name plus SSN, approximate years of attendance. Also helpful: date of birth, exact years of attendance. There is no fee.

Virginia Wesleyan College, Office of the Registrar, 1584 Wesleyan Dr, Norfolk, VA 23502-5599, 757-455-3200 (Fax: 757-461-0370). Hours: 8:30AM-4:30PM. Enrollment: 1500. Records go back to 1966. Alumni records are maintained here also. Call 757-455-3298. Degrees granted: Bachelors. Adverse incident record source- Dean of Students, 804-455-3273: Campus Security, 804-455-3349

Attendance and degree information available by phone, fax, mail. Search requires name plus SSN. Also helpful: date of birth, exact years of attendance. There is no fee.

Virginia Western Community College, Registrar, 3095 Colonial Ave SW, PO Box 14065, Roanoke, VA 24038, 540-857-7236 (Fax: 540-857-7544). Hours: 7:30AM-5PM. Enrollment: 1850. Records go back to 1966. Alumni records are maintained here at the same phone number. Degrees granted: Associate; Career Studies. Adverse incident record source- Department of Security.

Attendance and degree information available by phone, fax, mail. Search requires name plus SSN. There is no fee.

Washington and Lee University, Registrar's Office, Reid Hall, Lexington, VA 24450-0303, 540-463-8455 (Fax: 540-463-8045). Hours: 8:30AM-4:30PM. Enrollment: 2000. Records go back to 1845. Alumni records are maintained here also. Call 540-463-8464. Degrees granted: Bachelors; BA,BS,JD. Former degrees: MA,MS (to 1948).

Attendance and degree information available by phone, fax, mail. Search requires name only. Also helpful: SSN, date of birth, exact years of attendance. There is no fee.

Wytheville Community College, Registrar, 1000 E Main St, Wytheville, VA 24382, 540-223-4700 (Fax: 540-228-6506). Hours: 8AM-5PM. Enrollment: 1800. Records go back to 1968. Alumni records are maintained here at the same phone number. Degrees granted: Associate. Adverse incident record source- Department of Security.

Attendance information available by phone. Search requires name plus SSN. Also helpful: exact years of attendance. There is no fee.

Degree information available by phone, fax, mail. Search requires name plus SSN. Also helpful: date of birth, exact years of attendance. There is no fee.

Trade and Vocational Schools

AEGIS Training Center, Dahlgren, VA 22448, 540-653-8531

ATI - Hollywood, 3024 Trinkle Ave, Roanoke, VA 24012, 540-362-9338

ATI - Hollywood (Branch Campus), 1108 Brandon Ave SW, Roanoke, VA 24015, 540-343-0153

ATI - Hollywood (Branch Campus), 109 E Main St, Salem, VA 24153, 540-389-1500

ATI Career Institute, 7777 Leesburg Pike #100 S, Falls Church, VA 22043, 703-821-8570

ATI Career Institute (Branch Campus), Marine Corps Ed. Cmnd., Quantico, VA 22134, 703-640-0738

Alliance Tractor Trailer Training Centers II, PO Box 804, Wytheville, VA 24382, 540-228-6101

Anthony's Barber Styling College, 1307 Jefferson Ave, Newport News, VA 23607, 804-244-2311

Applied Career Training, Inc., 1100 N Wilson Blvd, Rosslyn, VA 22209, 703-527-6660

Apprentice School-Newport News Shipbuilding, 4101 Washington Ave, Newport News, VA 23607, 804-380-2682

Army Institute for Professional Development (The), US Army Training Support Ctr, Fort Eustis, VA 23604, 804-878-4774

Army Quartermaster Center and School, Fort Lee, VA 23801, 804-734-3683

Army Transportation and Aviation Logistics School, Bldg 2731, Fort Eustis, VA 23604, 804-878-4802

Braxton School (The), 4917 Augusta Ave, Richmond, VA 23230, 804-353-4458

Career Training Center, 4000 W Broad St, Richmond, VA 23230, 804-342-1190

Career Training Center (Branch Campus), 2600 Memorial Ave #201, Lynchburg, VA 24501, 804-845-7949

Career Training Center (Branch Campus), 3223 Brandon Ave SW, Roanoke, VA 24018, 540-981-0925

Catholic Home Study Institute (The), 781 Catoctin Ridge, Paeonian Springs, VA 22129, 540-883-3737

Central School of Practical Nursing, 1330 N Military Hwy, Norfolk, VA 23502, 804-441-5625

Computer Dynamics Institute, 5361 Virginia Beach Blvd, Virginia Beach, VA 23462, 804-499-4900

Computer Learning Center, 6295 Edsall Rd #210, Alexandria, VA 22312, 703-823-0300

Defense Mapping School, 5825 21st St #106, Fort Belvoir, VA 22060, 703-805-2557

Dominion Business School, 933 Reservoir St, Harrisonburg, VA 22801, 540-433-6977

Dominion Business School, 4142-1 Melrose Ave NW #1, Roanoke, VA 24017, 540-362-7738

Dominion Business School, 825 Richmond Rd, Staunton, VA 24401, 540-886-3596

Flatwoods Civilian Conservation Center, Rte 1 Box 211, Coeburn, VA 24230, 540-395-3384

Maryland Drafting Institute (Branch Campus), 8001 Forbes Pl, North Springfield, VA 22151, 703-321-9777

Medical Careers Institute, 605 Thimble Shoals Blvd #209, Newport News, VA 23606, 804-873-2423

Microcomputer Technology Center, 14904 Jefferson Davis Hwy, Ste 411, Woodbridge, VA 22190, 703-491-0393

Morgantown Skills Training Center, 1644 Mileground, Morgantown, VA 26505, 304-296-3548

National Education Center - Kee Business College, 803 Dilligence Dr, Newport News, VA 23606, 804-873-1111

Naval Guided Missiles School, 2025 Tartar Ave, Virginia Beach, VA 23461, 804-433-6628

Naval Health Sciences Education and Training Command (Opthalmis Support and Training), Yorktown, VA 23691, 804-887-7611

Naval Health Sciences Education and Training Command (School of Health Science), Portsmouth, VA 23708, 804-398-5032

Naval Surface Warfare Training Center, 5395 First St, Dahlgren, VA 22448-5190, 540-653-1023

Navy and Marine Corps Intelligence Training Center, 2088 Regulus Ave #420, Virginia Beach, VA 23461, 804-433-8001

Norfolk Skills Center, 922 W 21st St, Norfolk, VA 23517, 804-441-2665

Omege Travel School, 3102 Omega Office Park, Fairfax, VA 22031, 703-359-8830

Phillips Business College, PO Box 169, Lynchburg, VA 24505, 804-847-7701

Portsmouth General Health Career Center, 1000 Leckie St, Portsmouth, VA 23704, 804-398-4646

Potomac Academy of Hair Design, 9101 Center St, Manassas, VA 22110, 703-361-7775

Reporting Academy of Virginia, Pembroke One Ste 600, Virginia Beach, VA 23462, 804-499-5447

Reporting Academy of Virginia (Branch Campus), 1001 Boulders Pkwy #305, Richmond, VA 23225, 804-323-1020

Reporting Academy of Virginia (Branch Campus), 5501 Backlick Rd #250, Springfield, VA 22151, 703-658-0588

Rice Aviation, a Division of A&J Enterprises (Branch Campus), 5202 W Military Hwy Hanger 7, Chesapeake, VA 23321, 804-465-2813

Richard M. Milburne High School, 14416 Jefferson Davis Hwy #12, Woodbridge, VA 22191, 703-494-0147

Southside Training Skills Center, Hwy 460 E, Crewe, VA 23930, 804-645-7471

TESST Electronics and Computer Institute, 1400 Duke St, Alexandria, VA 22314, 703-548-4800

Tidewater Tech, 2697 Dean Dr #100, Virginia Beach, VA 23452, 804-340-2121

Tidewater Tech (Branch Campus), 932 B Ventures Wy #310, Chesapeake, VA 23320, 804-548-2828

Tidewater Tech (Branch Campus), 616 Denbigh Blvd, Newport News, VA 23402, 804-874-2121

Tidewater Tech (Branch Campus), 1760 E Little Creek Rd, Norfolk, VA 23518, 804-588-2121

Virginia Hair Academy, 3312 Williamson Rd NW, Roanoke, VA 24012, 540-563-2015

Virginia School of Cosmetology, 1516 Willow Lawn Dr, Richmond, VA 23226, 804-288-7923

Washington Business School of Northern Virginia, 1980 Gallows Rd, Vienna, VA 22182, 703-556-8888

Washington County Adult Skill Center, 848 Thompson Dr, Abingdon, VA 24210, 540-676-1948

Woodrow Wilson Rehabilitation Center, Fishersville, VA 22939, 540-332-7265

State Licensing & Business Registration Quick Finder Index

Architecture, Engineering & Surveying
Architect #10 (5009)...................................... ☎ 804-367-8500
Engineer #10 (17480)..................................... ☎ 804-367-8500
Geologist #10 (802)....................................... ☎ 804-367-8500
Landscape Architect #10 (392)...................... ☎ 804-367-8500
Surveyor #10... ☎ 804-367-8500

Business - Court & Legal Services
Attorney/Associates #14 (20766).................. ☎ 804-775-0500
Lobbyist #11 (1450)...................................... ☎ 804-781-2441
Notary Public #9... ☎ 804-786-2441
Shorthand Reporter #3................................... 703-768-8122

Business - General Services
Accountant #10 (12544)................................. ☎ 804-367-8500
Auctioneer #10 (1637)................................... ☎ 804-367-8500
Employment Agency #10................................ ☎ 804-367-8500
Interior Designer #10 (407)........................... ☎ 804-367-8500

Construction & Manufacturing
Contractor #10 (27940)................................. ☎ 804-367-8500
Heating & Air Conditioning Mechanic #10... ☎ 804-367-8500

Education
School Guidance Counselor #8...................... ☎ 804-225-2022
School Library Media Specialist #8............... ☎ 804-225-2022
School Principal #8.. ☎ 804-225-2022
School Superintendant #8............................... ☎ 804-225-2022
Teacher #8.. ☎ 804-225-2022

Environmental & Agriculture
Asbestos Related Occupation #10 (5356)...... ☎ 804-367-8500
Pesticide Applicator #4 (24000).................... ☎ 804-786-3798
Pesticide Dealer #4 (2000)............................ ☎ 804-786-3798
Soil Scientist #10 (81).................................. ☎ 804-367-8500
Veterinarian #6 (3000).................................. ☎ 804-662-9915
Veterinary Facility #6.................................... ☎ 804-662-9915
Veterinary Technician #6............................... ☎ 804-662-9915
Waste Management Facility Operator #10 (456)
.... ☎ 804-367-8500
Waste Water Works Operator #10 (2599)...... ☎ 804-367-8500

Financial - Real Estate, Insurance & Banking
Insurance Agent #2....................................... ☎ 804-371-9631
Investment Advisor #12................................. ☎ 804-371-9686
Investment Advisor Reprsentative #12........... ☎ 804-371-9686
Real Estate Agent & Appraiser #10 (2483)... ☎ 804-367-8500
Securities Broker/Dealer #12........................ ☎ 804-371-9686
Securities Broker/Dealer Agent #12.............. ☎ 804-371-9686

Health & Beauty
Acupuncturist #7... ☎ 804-662-9925

Barber #10 (3369)... ☎ 804-367-8500
Certified Nurse Aides #6............................... ☎ 804-662-9909
Chiropractor #6... ☎ 804-662-9073
Clinical Nurse Specialist #6........................... ☎ 804-662-9909
Cosmetologist #10 (35942)............................ ☎ 804-367-8500
Dentist #6 (5170).. ☎ 804-662-9906
Embalmer #6... ☎ 804-662-9073
Emergency Medical Technician #15 (25277)
.... ☎ 804-371-3500
Funeral Director #6....................................... ☎ 804-662-9073
Hearing Aid Dealer & Fitter #10 (436)......... ☎ 804-367-8500
Licensed Nurse Practitioner #6...................... ☎ 804-662-9909
Licensed Practical Nurse #6........................... ☎ 804-662-9909
Medical Doctor #7... ☎ 804-662-9925
Medical Equipment Supplier #6..................... ☎ 804-662-9921
Nurse #6 (72820).. 804-662-9909
Nursing Home Administrator #6..................... ☎ 804-662-9073
Occupational Therapist #7............................. ☎ 804-662-9925
Optician #10 (1518)...................................... ☎ 804-367-8500
Optometrist #6.. ☎ 804-662-9910
Osteopathic Physician #7............................... ☎ 804-662-9925
Pharmacist #6 (4980).................................... ☎ 804-662-9921
Pharmacy #6... ☎ 804-662-9921
Physical Therapist #7.................................... ☎ 804-662-9925
Physician #6... ☎ 804-662-9921
Podiatrist #7... ☎ 804-662-9925
Rehabilitation Provider #6............................. ☎ 804-662-7328
Respiratory Care Practitioner #7................... ☎ 804-662-9925
Speech Pathologist/Audiologist #6 (1897)..... ☎ 804-662-7390

Investigations & Security
Polygraph Examiner #10 (203)...................... ☎ 804-367-8500
Private Investigator #5.................................. ☎ 804-786-4000

Social Services
Professional Counselor #6 (1896)................. ✉ 804-662-9912
Psychologist, Cliinical, Applied, School #6
(1900).. ☎ 804-662-9913
Social Worker, Clinical Social Worker #6 (2100)
.... ☎ 804-662-9914
Substance Abuse Counselor #6...................... ☎ 804-662-7328

Sports & Entertainment
Alcoholic Beverage Distributor #1 (13000)... ☎ 804-367-0605
Boxer #10... ☎ 804-367-8500
Racing #13 (3000)... ☎ 804-371-7363
Wrestler #10... ☎ 804-367-8500

Transportation
Harbor Pilot #10 (40).................................... ☎ 804-367-8500

State Licensing & Business Registration Agency Information

(1) Alcoholic Beverage Control Board, 2901 Hermitage Rd, Richmond, VA 23220, 804-367-0605, Fax: 804-367-2554

(2) Bureau of Insurance, Licensing Department, PO Box 1157, Richmond, VA 23209, 804-371-9631, Fax: 804-371-9349

(3) CSR Contact Person, 2404 Belle Haven Meadows, Alexandria, VA 22306, 703-768-8122, Fax: 703-768-8921

(4) Department of Agriculture & Consumer Services, Office of Pesticide Services, PO Box 1163, Room 403, Richmond, VA 23218, 804-786-3798, Fax: 804-371-8598

(5) Department of Criminal Justice, Licensing Division, 805 E Broad St, 9th Floor, Richmond, VA 23219, 804-786-4000, Fax: 804-786-6344

(6) Department of Health Professions, 6606 W Broad St, 4th Floor, Richmond, VA 23230-1717, 804-662-9908, Fax: 804-662-9943

(7) Department of Health Professions, Board of Medicine, 6606 W Broad St, 4th Floor, Richmond, VA 23230-1717, 804-662-9925

(8) Office of Professional Licensure, Department of Education, PO Box 2120, Richmond, VA 23218-2120, 804-225-2022

(9) Office of Secretary of Commonwealth, Notary Public Division, PO Box 1795, Richmond, VA 23214-1795, 804-786-2441, Fax: 804-371-0017

(10) Professional & Occupational Regulatory Boards Dept, 3600 W Broad St, Richmond, VA 23230, 804-367-8500, Fax: 804-367-2475

(11) Secretary of the Commonwealth, PO Box 2454, Richmond, VA 23201-2454, 804-781-2441, Fax: 804-371-0017

(12) State Corporation Commission, Securities Division, PO Box 1197, Richmond, VA 23218, 804-786-7751, Fax: 804-371-9911

(13) Virginia Racing Commission, PO Box 1123, Richmond, VA 23208, 804-371-7363, Fax: 804-371-6127

(14) Virginia State Bar Association, 707 E Main St, Suite 1500, Richmond, VA 23219-2803, 804-775-0500, Fax: 804-775-0501

(15) Virginia State Department of Health, 1538 E. Parham Rd., Richmond, VA 23228, 804-371-3500, Fax: 804-371-3543

Washington

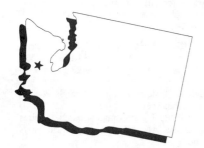

Capitol: Olympia (Thurston County)	
State Population	5.4 Million
Number of Degree Granting Institutions:	xx
Number of State Licensing & Business Registration Agencies:	xx

Degree Granting Educational Institutions

Antioch University, (Antioch Seattle), Registrar, 2607 Second Ave, Seattle, WA 98121, 206-441-5352 X771 (Fax: 206-441-3307). Hours: 9AM-5PM. Enrollment: 800. Records go back to 1985. Pre-1985 records are housed at Antioch University, 795 Livermore St., Yellow Springs, OH 45387, 513-767-6401. Alumni records are maintained here also. Call 206-441-5352 X5105. Degrees granted: Bachelors; Masters. Certification: Ed. Adverse incident record source- Registrar's Office .

Attendance information available by phone, fax, mail. Search requires name plus SSN. Also helpful: approximate years of attendance. There is no fee.

Degree information available by phone, fax, mail. Search requires name only. Also helpful: SSN, approximate years of attendance. There is no fee.

Art Institute of Seattle, Registrar, 2323 Elliott Ave, Seattle, WA 98121-1633, 206-448-0900 X884. Hours: 8AM-4PM. Enrollment: 2000. Records go back to 1982. Records to 1982 for AIS, to 1955 for Burnley School of Professional Art. Alumni records are maintained here at the same phone number. Degrees granted: Associate.

Attendance and degree information available by phone, mail. Search requires name plus SSN. Also helpful: exact years of attendance. There is no fee.

Bastyr University, Registrar, 144 NE 54th St, Seattle, WA 98105, 206-523-9585 X29. Hours: 8AM-4:30PM. Enrollment: 860. Records go back to 1978. Alumni records are maintained here at the same phone number. Degrees granted: Bachelors; Masters; First Professional Degree.

Attendance information available by phone, mail. Search requires name only. Also helpful: exact years of attendance. There is no fee.

Degree information available by phone, mail. Search requires name only. Also helpful: date of birth, exact years of attendance. There is no fee.

Bellevue Community College, Enrollment Services, 3000 Landerholm Cir SE, Mainstop B125, Bellevue, WA 98007-6484, 206-641-2761 (Fax: 206-641-2230). Hours: 8AM-5PM. Enrollment: 17000. Records go back to 1966. Alumni records are maintained here also. Call 206-641-2386. Degrees granted: Associate. Adverse incident record source- Dean of Students, 206-641-2326.

Attendance and degree information available by phone, fax, mail. Search requires name plus SSN, date of birth, exact years of attendance. There is no fee.

Big Bend Community College, Registrar, 7662 Chanute St, Moses Lake, WA 98837-3299, 509-762-6226 (Fax: 509-762-6243). Hours: 8AM-4:30PM. Enrollment: 3000. Records go back to 1962. Degrees granted: Associate. Special programs- Commercial Pilot, 509-762-6256.

Attendance and degree information available by phone, fax, mail. Search requires name plus SSN. Also helpful: date of birth, exact years of attendance. There is no fee.

Central Washington University, Registrar, Mitchell Hall, 400 E 8th Ave, Ellensburg, WA 98926-7463, 509-963-3001 (Fax: 509-963-3022). Hours: 8AM-5PM. Enrollment: 8500. Records go back to 1890. Alumni records are maintained here also. Call 509-963-2752. Degrees granted: Bachelors; Masters.

Attendance and degree information available by phone, fax, mail. Search requires name plus date of birth. Also helpful: SSN, exact years of attendance. There is no fee.

Centralia College, Registrar, 600 W Locust St, Centralia, WA 98531, 360-736-9391 X221. Hours: 8AM-4:30PM. Enrollment: 3300. Records go back to 1925. Alumni records are maintained here at the same phone number. Degrees granted: Associate. Special programs- Nursing Program: Air/Engineering Program. Adverse incident record source- Registrar's Office

Attendance information available by phone, mail. Search requires name only. Also helpful: SSN, date of birth, exact years of attendance. There is no fee.

Degree information available by phone, mail. Search requires name only. Also helpful: SSN, date of birth, exact years of attendance. There is no fee.

City University, Registrar, 335 116th Ave SE, Bellevue, WA 98004, 800-426-5596 (Fax: 206-450-4665). Hours: 8AM-4:30PM. Enrollment: 13000. Records go back to 1731. Alumni Records Office: Alumni Association, 919 SW Grady Wy 2nd Flr, Renton, WA 98055. Degrees granted: Associate; Bachelors; Masters.

Attendance and degree information available by phone, fax, mail. Search requires name plus SSN, exact years of attendance. Also helpful: date of birth. There is no fee.

Clark College, Registrar, 1800 E McLoughlin Blvd, Vancouver, WA 98663, 360-992-2136 (Fax: 360-992-2876). Hours: 8AM-4:30PM. Enrollment: 11000. Records go back to 1935. Alumni records are maintained here at the same phone number. Degrees granted: Associate.

Attendance and degree information available by phone, fax, mail. Search requires name plus SSN. Also helpful: exact years of attendance. There is no fee.

Columbia Basin College, Registrar, 2600 N 20th Ave, Pasco, WA 99302, 509-547-0511 (Fax: 509-546-0401). Hours: 7:30AM-4:30PM. Enrollment: 5000. Records go back to 1955. Degrees granted: Associate.

Attendance and degree information available by phone, fax, mail. Search requires name plus SSN. Also helpful: date of birth, exact years of attendance. There is no fee.

Cornish College of the Arts, Registrar, 710 E Roy St, Seattle, WA 98102, 206-323-1400 (Fax: 206-720-1011). Hours: 9AM-4PM. Enrollment: 642. Records go back to 1914. Alumni records are maintained here at the same phone number. Degrees granted: Bachelors. Certification: Acting.

School will not confirm attendance information.

Degree information available by phone, fax, mail. Search requires name only. There is no fee.

Eastern Washington University, Registrar, 526 5th St MS 150, Cheney, WA 99004, 509-359-6202 (Fax: 509-359-6153). Hours: 8AM-5PM. Records go back to 1912. Alumni records are maintained here also. Call 509-359-6303. Degrees granted: Bachelors; Masters. Certification: Educ. Adverse incident record source- Campus Police, 509-359-6300.

School will not confirm attendance information.

Degree information available by phone. Search requires name only. Also helpful: SSN, date of birth, exact years of attendance. There is no fee.

Edmonds Community College, Registrar, 20000 68th Ave W, Lynnwood, WA 98036, 206-640-1456 (Fax: 206-771-3366). Hours: 8AM-5PM. Enrollment: 18800. Records go back to 1967. Degrees granted: Associate. Adverse incident record source- Dean of Students, 206-640-1668.

Attendance and degree information available by mail. Search requires name plus SSN, date of birth, exact years of attendance. There is no fee.

Everett Community College, Registrar, 801 Wetmore Ave, Everett, WA 98201-1327, 206-388-9206 (Fax: 206-388-9129). Hours: 9AM-5PM. Records go back to 1954. Alumni records are maintained here at the same phone number. Degrees granted: Associate.

Attendance and degree information available by phone, fax, mail. Search requires name plus SSN. Also helpful: approximate years of attendance. There is no fee.

Evergreen State College, Registration & Records, Library 1100, Olympia, WA 98505, 360-866-6000 X6180 (Fax: 360-866-6680). Hours: 9AM-4PM. Enrollment: 3600. Records go back to 1970. Personal files are kept for 7 years after student leaves. Alumni records are maintained here also. Call 360-866-6000 X6551. Degrees granted: Bachelors; Masters. Adverse incident record source- Student Affairs.

Attendance and degree information available by phone, fax, mail. Search requires name plus SSN, date of birth. Also helpful: exact years of attendance. There is no fee.

Gonzaga University, University Registrar, Spokane, WA 99258, 509-328-4220 X3192 (Fax: 509-324-2818). Hours: 8AM-5PM. Enrollment: 5100. Records go back to 1887. Alumni records are maintained here at the same phone number. Degrees granted: Bachelors; Masters; Doctorate. Adverse incident record source- Student Life, 509-328-4220 X4100.

Attendance and degree information available by phone, fax, mail. Search requires name plus SSN, date of birth, exact years of attendance. There is no fee.

Grays Harbor College, Records Office, 1620 Edward P. Smith Dr, Aberdeen, WA 98520, 360-538-4060 (Fax: 360-538-4299). Hours: 8AM-4:30PM M,W,Th,F; 8AM-7PM T. Enrollment: 2700. Records go back to 1930. Degrees granted: Associate. Special programs- Natural Fisheries Tech.

Attendance and degree information available by phone, fax, mail. Search requires name plus SSN. Also helpful: date of birth, exact years of attendance. There is no fee.

Green River Community College, Registrar, 12401 SE 320th St, Auburn, WA 98002, 206-833-9111 X2511 (Fax: 206-288-3454). Hours: 8AM-5PM. Records go back to 1965. Degrees granted: Associate.

Attendance information available by fax, mail. Search requires name plus SSN, signed release. There is no fee.

Degree information available by fax, mail. Search requires name plus SSN, signed release. Also helpful: approximate years of attendance. There is no fee.

Henry Cogswell College, Registrar, 2802 Wetmore Ave, Everett, WA 98201, 206-258-3351 (Fax: 206-822-1006). Hours: 9AM-6PM. Enrollment: 200. Formerly Cogswell College North Records go back to 1979. Alumni records are maintained here at the same phone number. Degrees granted: Bachelors. Adverse incident record source- Registrar, 206-258-3351.

Attendance information available by fax, mail. Search requires name plus signed release. Also helpful: SSN, exact years of attendance. There is no fee.

Degree information available by phone, fax, mail. Search requires name only. Also helpful: SSN, exact years of attendance. There is no fee.

Heritage College, Registrar, 3240 Fort Rd, Toppenish, WA 98948, 509-865-2244 X1605 (Fax: 509-865-4469). Hours: 8AM-4:30PM. Enrollment: 1100. Records go back to 1982. Alumni records are maintained here at the same phone number. Degrees granted: Bachelors; Masters.

Attendance and degree information available by phone, fax, mail. Search requires name plus SSN, date of birth. There is no fee.

Highline Community College, Registrar, PO Box 98000, Des Moines, WA 98198-9800, 206-878-3710 X3244 (Fax: 206-870-3782). Hours: 8AM-4:30PM. Enrollment: 10000. Records go back to 1961. Alumni records are maintained here at the same phone number. Degrees granted: Associate. Adverse incident record source- Dean's Office

Attendance information available by mail. Search requires name plus SSN, signed release. Also helpful: date of birth, exact years of attendance. There is no fee.

Degree information available by phone, mail. Search requires name plus SSN. Also helpful: date of birth, exact years of attendance. There is no fee.

ITT Technical Institute, Registrar, 12720 Gateway Dr Ste 100, Seattle, WA 98168-3333, 206-244-3300 (Fax: 206-246-7635). Hours: 8AM-8PM. Enrollment: 400. Records go back to 1969. Alumni Records Office: Alumni Association, PO Box 50472, Indianapolis, IN 46250. Degrees granted: Associate; Bachelors.

Attendance and degree information available by phone, fax, mail. Search requires name plus exact years of attendance. Also helpful: SSN, date of birth. There is no fee.

ITT Technical Institute, Education Dept, N 1050 Argonne Rd, Spokane, WA 99212-2610, 509-926-2900 (Fax: 509-926-2908). Hours: 8AM-5PM. Enrollment: 250. Records go back to 1985. Alumni Records Office: 9511 Angola Ct, Indianapolis, IN 46268. Degrees granted: Associate. Special programs-

Electronics Enginnering: Computer Training. Adverse incident record source- Registrar's Office .

Attendance and degree information available by phone, mail. Search requires name plus SSN, date of birth, exact years of attendance. There is no fee.

Lake Washington Technical College, Registrar,
11605 132nd Ave NE, Kirkland, WA 98034, 206-828-5619 (Fax: 206-828-5648). Hours: 9AM-7PM. Enrollment: 8500. Records go back to 1949. Degrees granted: Associate.

Attendance and degree information available by mail. Search requires name plus SSN, exact years of attendance. There is no fee.

Lower Columbia College, Admissions Office, PO
Box 3010, 1600 Maple St, Longview, WA 98632-0310, 360-577-2303 (Fax: 360-578-5470). Hours: 9AM-5PM. Enrollment: 4000. Records go back to 1934. Alumni records are maintained here at the same phone number. Degrees granted: Associate. Adverse incident record source- Registrar's Office .

Attendance and degree information available by phone, fax, mail. Search requires name only. Also helpful: SSN, date of birth, exact years of attendance. There is no fee.

Lutheran Bible Institute of Seattle, Registrar,
4221 228th Ave SE, Issaquah, WA 98029, 206-392-0400 (Fax: 206-392-0404). Hours: 8AM-5PM. Enrollment: 180. Records go back to 1945. Alumni records are maintained here at the same phone number. Degrees granted: Associate; Bachelors.

Attendance and degree information available by phone, fax, mail. Search requires name only. Also helpful: exact years of attendance. There is no fee.

North Seattle Community College, Registrar,
9600 College Way N, Seattle, WA 98103, 206-527-3669 (Fax: 206-527-3635). Hours: 8AM-4:30PM. Enrollment: 8500. Records go back to 1970. Alumni records are maintained here also. Call 206-527-3604. Degrees granted: Associate. Adverse incident record source- Student Development, 206-527-3606.

Attendance and degree information available by phone, fax, mail. Search requires name plus SSN. Also helpful: exact years of attendance. There is no fee.

Northwest College of the Assemblies of God, Registrar, PO Box 579, Kirkland, WA 98083, 206-822-
8266 X5230 (Fax: 206-827-0148). Hours: 8AM-4:30PM. Enrollment: 850. Records go back to 1934. Alumni records are maintained here also. Call 206-889-5206. Degrees granted: Bachelors.

Attendance and degree information available by phone, fax, mail. Search requires name plus SSN, exact years of attendance. There is no fee.

Northwest Indian College, Registrar, 2522 Kwina
Rd, Bellingham, WA 98226, 360-676-2772 (Fax: 360-738-0136). Hours: 8AM-5PM. Enrollment: 600. Records go back to 1983. Alumni records are maintained here at the same phone number. Degrees granted: Associate. Adverse incident source- Student Records Office.

Attendance and degree information available by phone, fax, mail. Search requires name plus SSN, exact years of attendance. There is no fee.

Northwest Institute of Acupuncture and Oriental Medicine, Registrar, 1307 N 45th St, Seattle,
WA 98103, 206-633-2419 (Fax: 206-633-5578). Hours: 9AM-6PM M-Th. Enrollment: 150. Records go back to 1981. Degrees granted: Masters. Special programs- Acupuncture Masters. Adverse incident record source- Academic Dean.

Attendance and degree information available by phone, fax, mail. Search requires name only. Also helpful: date of birth, approximate years of attendance. There is no fee.

Olympic College, Registrar, 1600 Chester Ave, Bremer-
ton, WA 98337, 360-478-4542 (Fax: 360-792-2135). Hours: 8AM-6PM. Enrollment: 8000. Records go back to 1946. Degrees granted: Associate.

Attendance information available by fax, mail. Search requires name plus SSN, date of birth, signed release. There is no fee.

Degree information available by phone, fax, mail. Search requires name plus SSN, date of birth. There is no fee.

Pacific Lutheran University, Registrar's Office,
Tacoma, WA 98447, 206-535-7136 (Fax: 206-535-8320). Hours: 8AM-6PM M-Th; 8AM-5PM F. Degrees granted: Masters; Doctorate. Certification: Teaching. Adverse incident record source- Student Life, 206-535-7191.

Attendance and degree information available by phone, fax, mail. Search requires name plus SSN. Also helpful: exact years of attendance. There is no fee.

Peninsula College, Registrar, 1502 E Lauridsen Blvd,
Port Angeles, WA 98362, 360-452-9277 (Fax: 360-457-8100). Hours: 8AM-5PM. Degrees granted: Associate.

Attendance and degree information available by phone, fax, mail. Search requires name plus SSN. Also helpful: exact years of attendance. There is no fee.

Pierce College, Transcripts/Records, 9401 Farwest Dr
SW, Tacoma, WA 98498, 206-964-6500 (Fax: 206-964-6427). Enrollment: 13000. Records go back to 1967. Degrees granted: Associate. Adverse incident record source- Dean of Students.

Attendance and degree information available by phone, fax, mail. Search requires name plus SSN. Also helpful: date of birth, exact years of attendance. There is no fee.

Pima Medical Institute, Registrar, 1627 Eastlake Ave
E, Seattle, WA 98102, 206-322-6100 (Fax: 206-324-1985). Hours: 7:30AM-6PM. Enrollment: 250. Records go back to 1990. Degrees granted: Associate.

Attendance and degree information available by phone, fax, mail. Search requires name plus SSN, exact years of attendance. There is no fee.

Puget Sound Christian College, Registrar, 410
Fourth Ave N, Edmonds, WA 98020, 206-775-8686 (Fax: 206-775-8688). Hours: 7:30AM-4:30PM. Enrollment: 180. Records go back to 1950. Alumni records are maintained here at the same phone number. Degrees granted: Associate; Bachelors. Adverse incident record source- Business Office.

Attendance and degree information available by phone, fax, mail. Search requires name only. Also helpful: SSN. There is no fee.

Renton Technical College, Registrar, 3000 Fourth St
NE, Renton, WA 98056, 206-235-2352 (Fax: 206-235-2372). Enrollment: 14000. Records go back to 1942. Degrees granted: Associate; Associates & Applied Science.

Attendance and degree information available by fax, mail. Search requires name plus SSN, date of birth, approximate years of attendance, signed release. Also helpful: exact years of attendance. Fee is $3.00.

Seattle Central Community College, Registrar,
1701 Broadway, Seattle, WA 98122, 206-587-6918 (Fax: 206-344-4390). Hours: 8AM-5PM. Enrollment: 10000. Records go back to 1966. Degrees granted: Associate. Adverse incident record source- Dean of Students.

Attendance and degree information available by fax, mail. Search requires name plus SSN, date of birth, exact years of attendance. There is no fee.

Seattle Community College, South Campus,
Registrar, 6000 16th Ave S W, Seattle, WA 98106, 206-764-5300 (Fax: 206-764-7947). Enrollment: 6000. Records go back to 1972. Alumni records are maintained here at the same phone

number. Degrees granted: Associate. Adverse incident record source- Security.

Attendance and degree information available by phone, mail. Search requires name plus SSN, exact years of attendance. There is no fee.

Seattle Pacific University, Registrations & Records, 3307 Third Ave W, Seattle, WA 98119, 206-281-2034 (Fax: 206-281-2669). Hours: 8:30AM-4:30PM M,T,W,F; 9:30AM-4:30PM Th. Enrollment: 3400. Records go back to 1891. Alumni records are maintained here also. Call 206-281-2586. Degrees granted: Bachelors; Masters; Doctorate. Adverse incident record source- Dean of Students.

Attendance and degree information available by phone, fax, mail. Search requires name plus SSN. Also helpful: date of birth, exact years of attendance. There is no fee.

Seattle University, Registrar, 12th Ave and E Columbia St, Seattle, WA 98122, 206-296-5850 (Fax: 206-296-2443). Hours: 8AM-6PM. Records go back to 1897. Alumni records are maintained here also. Call 206-296-6127. Degrees granted: Bachelors; Masters; Doctorate.

Attendance and degree information available by phone, mail. Search requires name plus SSN, date of birth, exact years of attendance. There is no fee.

Shoreline Community College, Records Office, 16101 Greenwood Ave N, Seattle, WA 98133, 206-546-5623 (Fax: 206-546-5835). Hours: 8AM-4:30PM. Enrollment: 7500. Records go back to 1964. Call 206-546-4614 for transcripts. Degrees granted: Associate.

Attendance and degree information available by phone, fax, mail. Search requires name only. Also helpful: SSN, date of birth, exact years of attendance. There is no fee.

Skagit Valley College, Registrar, 2405 E College Way, Mount Vernon, WA 98273, 360-428-1261 (Fax: 360-416-7890). Hours: 8AM-5PM. Enrollment: 6496. Records go back to 1926. Degrees granted: Associate. Special programs- Nursing: Firefighter Training: Paralegal. Adverse incident record source- Student Programs, 360-416-7633.

Attendance and degree information available by phone, fax, mail. Search requires name plus SSN. There is no fee.

South Puget Sound Community College, Registrar, 2011 Mottman Rd SW, Olympia, WA 98512, 360-754-7711 X243 (Fax: 360-586-6054). Hours: 8AM-5PM. Enrollment: 5000. Records go back to 1965. Alumni records are maintained here at the same phone number. Degrees granted: Associate.

Attendance and degree information available by phone, fax, mail. Search requires name plus SSN. Also helpful: date of birth, exact years of attendance. There is no fee.

South Seattle Community College, Records, 6000 16th Ave SW, Seattle, WA 98106, 206-764-5399 (Fax: 206-764-7947). Hours: 7:30AM-5PM. Records go back to 1975. Degrees granted: Associate.

Attendance and degree information available by phone, fax, mail. Search requires name plus SSN. Also helpful: date of birth, approximate years of attendance. There is no fee.

Spokane Community College, Registrar, 1810 N Greene St MS2150, Spokane, WA 99207-5399, 509-533-7011 (Fax: 509-533-8839). Hours: 7:30AM-4:30PM. Records go back to 1970. Degrees granted: Associate; AAS.

Attendance and degree information available by phone, fax, mail. Search requires name plus SSN. Also helpful: exact years of attendance. There is no fee.

Spokane Falls Community College, Registrar, W 3410 Fort George Wright Dr, Spokane, WA 99224-5288, 509-533-3518 (Fax: 509-533-3237). Hours: 8AM-4:30PM. Enroll-

ment: 6000. Records go back to 1971. Degrees granted: Associate.

Attendance information available by phone, fax, mail. Search requires name plus SSN. There is no fee.

Degree information available by phone, fax, mail. Search requires name plus SSN. There is no fee.

St. Martin's College, Registrar, Lacey, WA 98503, 360-438-4356 (Fax: 360-438-4514). Hours: 8AM-7PM. Enrollment: 1100. Records go back to 1920. Alumni records are maintained here also. Call 360-438-4366. Degrees granted: Associate; Bachelors; Masters. Adverse incident record source- Safety & Security, 360-438-4555.

Attendance and degree information available by phone, fax, mail. Search requires name plus SSN. Also helpful: date of birth, exact years of attendance. There is no fee.

Tacoma Community College, Registrar, 6501 S 19th St, Tacoma, WA 98466, 206-566-5036 (Fax: 206-566-6011). Hours: 8AM-4:30PM. Enrollment: 800. Records go back to 1965. Alumni records are maintained here at the same phone number. Degrees granted: Associate.

Attendance and degree information available by phone, fax, mail. Search requires name plus SSN. Also helpful: date of birth, exact years of attendance. There is no fee.

University of Puget Sound, Office of the Registrar, Records Unit, 1500 N Warner, Tacoma, WA 98416, 206-756-3160 (Fax: 206-756-3500). Hours: 8:30AM-4:30PM. Records go back to 1888. Alumni records are maintained here also. Call 206-756-3245. Degrees granted: Bachelors; Masters. Adverse incident record source- Dean of Students, 206-756-3360: Security Services, 206-756-3311

Attendance and degree information available by phone, fax, mail. Search requires name plus SSN. Also helpful: date of birth, exact years of attendance. There is no fee.

University of Washington, Registrar, 1400 NE Campus Park Way, Seattle, WA 98195, 206-543-8580 (Fax: 206-685-3660). Hours: 8AM-4:30PM. Enrollment: 34000. Records go back to 1869. Alumni records are maintained here also. Call 206-543-0540. Degrees granted: Bachelors; Masters; Doctorate.

Attendance and degree information available by phone, fax, mail. Search requires name plus SSN, date of birth, exact years of attendance. There is no fee.

Walla Walla College, Registrar, 204 S College Ave, College Place, WA 99324, 509-527-2811 (Fax: 509-527-2574). Hours: 8:30AM-Noon, 1-4:30PM M-Th; 8:30AM-Noon F. Enrollment: 1700. Records go back to 1905. Alumni records are maintained here also. Call 509-527-2093. Degrees granted: Associate; Bachelors; Masters.

Attendance and degree information available by phone, fax, mail. Search requires name only. Also helpful: SSN, date of birth, exact years of attendance. There is no fee.

Walla Walla Community College, Registrar, 500 Tausick Way, Walla Walla, WA 99362, 509-527-4283 (Fax: 509-527-3661). Hours: 8AM-5PM. Enrollment: 3000. Records go back to 1967. Degrees granted: Associate. Adverse incident record source- Registrar's Office, 509-527-4283　.

Attendance and degree information available by phone, fax, mail. Search requires name plus SSN. Also helpful: date of birth. There is no fee.

Washington State Community College District 17, Transcript Department, Spokane, WA 99207, 509-533-7012 (Fax: 509-533-8839). Enrollment: 4000. Records go back to 1964. Alumni records are maintained here at the same phone number. Degrees granted: Associate. Adverse incident record source- Security.

Attendance and degree information available by phone, mail. Search requires name plus SSN. Also helpful: approximate years of attendance. There is no fee.

Washington State University, Registrar, PO Box 641035, Pullman, WA 99164-1035, 509-335-5330 (Fax: 509-335-7823). Hours: 8AM-5PM. Enrollment: 17000. Records go back to 1890. Alumni Records Office: Alumni Association, PO Box 646150, U;llman, WA 99164-6150. Degrees granted: Bachelors; Masters; Doctorate; Vet Med. Adverse incident record source- Campus Police, 509-335-4555.

Attendance and degree information available by phone, fax, mail. Search requires name only. Also helpful: SSN, date of birth, exact years of attendance. There is no fee.

Wenatchee Valley College, Registrar, 1300 Fifth St, Wenatchee, WA 98801, 509-662-1651 X2136 (Fax: 509-664-2576). Enrollment: 4000. Records go back to 1939. Alumni records are maintained here at the same phone number. Degrees granted: Associate. Special programs- Tree Fruit Production. Adverse incident record source- Student Support Services, 509-662-1651 X2173.

Attendance and degree information available by phone, fax, mail. Search requires name only. Also helpful: SSN, exact years of attendance. There is no fee.

Western Business College(Branch), Registrar, 6625 East Mill Plain Blvd, Vancouver, WA 98661, 306-694-3225 (Fax: 306-737-7719). Enrollment: 85. Records go back to 1956. Degrees granted: Associate. Adverse incident record source- Student Services.

Attendance and degree information available by phone, mail. Search requires name plus SSN, date of birth, exact years of attendance. There is no fee.

Western Washington University, Registrar, 516 High St, Bellingham, WA 98225, 360-650-3430 (Fax: 360-650-7327). Hours: 8AM-5PM. Enrollment: 10708. Records go back to 1899. Alumni records are maintained here at the same phone number. Degrees granted: Bachelors; Masters. Special programs-Hixley College of Environmental Studies: Center for Small Business. Adverse incident record source- Student Affairs, 360-650-3839.

Attendance and degree information available by phone, mail. Search requires name only. Also helpful: SSN, exact years of attendance. There is no fee.

Whatcom Community College, Registrar, 237 W Kellogg Rd, Bellingham, WA 98226, 360-676-2170 (Fax: 360-676-2171). Hours: 8AM-5PM. Enrollment: 4500. Records go back to 1970. Degrees granted: Associate.

Attendance and degree information available by phone, fax, mail. Search requires name only. Also helpful: SSN, approximate years of attendance. There is no fee.

Whitman College, Registrar, Walla Walla, WA 99362, 509-527-5179 (Fax: 509-527-4967). Hours: 8:30AM-Noon, 1-4:30PM. Enrollment: 1300. Records go back to 1859. Alumni records are maintained here also. Call 509-527-5167. Degrees granted: Bachelors. Adverse incident record source- Security, 509-527-5777.

Attendance and degree information available by phone, fax, mail. Search requires name only. Also helpful: SSN, date of birth, exact years of attendance. There is no fee.

Whitworth College, Academic Records, W 300 Hawthorne, Spokane, WA 99251, 509-466-3201 (Fax: 509-466-3773). Hours: 9AM-4PM. Enrollment: 1568. Records go back to 1896. Alumni records are maintained here also. Call 509-466-3799. Degrees granted: Bachelors; Masters. Certification: Educ. Adverse incident record source- Student Life Office.

Attendance and degree information available by phone, fax, mail. Search requires name only. Also helpful: date of birth, exact years of attendance. There is no fee.

Yakima Valley Community College, Registrar, PO Box 1647, Yakima, WA 98907, 509-574-4700 (Fax: 509-574-6860). Hours: 7:30AM-5PM. Enrollment: 5995. Records go back to 1928. Alumni records are maintained here also. Call 509-575-2442. Degrees granted: Associate. Adverse incident record source- Security, 509-574-4610.

Attendance and degree information available by phone, fax, mail. Search requires name only. Also helpful: SSN. There is no fee.

Trade and Vocational Schools

Bates Technical College, 1101 S Yakima Ave, Tacoma, WA 98405, 206-596-1500

Bellingham Technical College, 3028 Lindbergh Ave, Bellingham, WA 98225, 360-738-0221

Career Floral Design Institute, 14350 NE 21st St Ste 1, Bellevue, WA 98005, 206-746-8340

Clover Park Technical College, 4500 Steilacoom Blvd SW, Tacoma, WA 98499, 206-589-5800

Commercial Training Services, 24325 Pacific Hwy S, Des Moines, WA 98198, 206-824-3970

Court Reporting Institute, 929 N 130th St #2, Seattle, WA 98133, 206-363-8300

Crown Academy, 8739 S Hosmer St, Tacoma, WA 98444, 206-531-3123

Divers Institute of Technology, PO Box 70667, Seattle, WA 98107, 206-783-5542

Emil Fries Piano & Training Center, 2510 E Evergreen Blvd, Vancouver, WA 98661, 360-693-1511

Eton Technical Institute, 3649 Frontage Rd, Port Orchard, WA 98306, 360-479-3866

Eton Technical Institute (Branch Campus), 209 E Casino Rd, Everett, WA 98208, 206-353-4888

Eton Technical Institute (Branch Campus), 31919 Sixth Ave S, Federal Way, WA 98063, 206-941-5800

Fox Travel Institute, 520 Pike St #2800, Seattle, WA 98101, 206-224-7800

International Air Academy, 2901 E Mill Plain Blvd, Vancouver, WA 98661, 360-695-2500

Northwest School of Wooden Boatbuilding, 251 Otto St, Port Townsend, WA 98368, 360-385-4948

Pacific Northwest Ballet School, 4649 Sunnyside Ave N, Seattle, WA 98103, 206-547-5910

Perry Technical Institute, 2011 W Washington Ave, Yakima, WA 98903, 509-453-0374

Pima Medical Institute, 1627 Eastlake Ave E, Seattle, WA 98102, 206-322-6100

Trident Training Facility, Silverdale, WA 98315, 360-396-4068

Vocational Training Institute, 6400M NE Hwy 99, Vancouver, WA 98665, 360-695-5186

Western Business College (Branch Campus), 6625 E Mill Plain Blvd, Vancouver, WA 98661, 360-694-3225

State Licensing & Business Registration Quick Finder Index

Architecture, Engineering & Surveying
Architect, Landscape, Corporations #22 (200) ... 360-753-1153
Engineer #22 360-753-6966
Surveyor #13 .... ☎ 360-753-6928

Business - Court & Legal Services
Attorney #21 .... ☎ 206-727-8200
Notary Public #15 (70000) .... ☎ 360-753-3836

Business - General Services
Public Accountant-CPA #1 (4045) .... ☎ 360-753-2585
Weights & Measures #3 .... ☎ 360-902-1856

Construction & Manufacturing
Boiler Inspector #11 (165)..................... ☎ 360-902-5270
Dealer & Manufacturer #13 (2424).............. ☎ 360-902-3703
Electrical Administrator #10 (6000).............✉ 360-902-5269
Electrical Contractor #10 (4000)................✉ 360-902-5269
Electrician #10 (19000) .... ☎ 360-902-5800
General Contractor #10 (50000).................. ☎ 360-902-5226

Education
School Administrator #19.......................... ☎ 360-753-6773
School Counselor #19............................. ☎ 360-753-6773
School Principal #19.............................. ☎ 360-753-6773
School Superintendent #18.......................✉ 360-753-6773
Teacher #19 .... ☎ 360-753-6773

Environmental & Agriculture
Animal Technician #8 (1034)..................... ☎ 360-586-6355
Commercial Fishing #6 (6500)...................✉ 360-902-2253
Egg Inspector #22 360-902-1830
Fruit/Vegetable Inspector #22 360-902-1832
Grain Inspector #22 360-902-1827
Livestock Brand Recording #3.................... ☎ 360-902-1855
Meat Inspector #13 .... ☎ 360-902-1878
Pesticide Operators & Applicators #4 (22415)
.... ☎ 360-902-2020
Veterinarian #8 .... ☎ 360-586-5846

Financial - Real Estate, Insurance & Banking
Bank #5... ✉ 360-902-8704
Credit Union #5 .... ✉ 360-902-8701
Insurance Agent #24............................. ☎ 360-407-0341
Insurance Broker #24 .... ☎ 360-407-0341
Real Estate Appraiser #13 360-753-1062
Real Estate Salesperson #13...................... 360-753-2250
Real Estate/Escrow #13.......................... 360-753-2262
Securities Broker/Dealer #5 ....✉ 360-902-8760
Securities Dealer #5............................. ✉ 360-902-8760

Health & Beauty
Acupuncturist #8 (300)........................... ☎ 360-586-7759

Audiologist #9................................... ☎ 360-753-1817
Barber #16......................................✉ 360-586-6387
Cemetery & Funeral Board #22 (350)............... 360-586-4905
Chiropractor #8 (3293) .... ☎ 360-753-0776
Cosmetologist #16 ....✉ 360-586-6387
Dental Hygienist #8 (6700)....................... ☎ 360-586-1867
Dentist #8 (8600) .... ☎ 360-586-6898
Dietitian #8 (926)............................... ☎ 360-586-6351
Emergency Medical Technician #8 (18000) ..☎ 360-705-6700
Health Care Assistant #8 (14000)................. ☎ 360-753-1230
Hearing Instrument Fitter/Dispenser #9 (400)
.... ☎ 360-753-1817
Home Health Care Agency #7 (156) .... ☎ 360-705-6611
Hospital #7 (93) .... ☎ 360-705-6611
Hypnotherapist #9............................... 360-586-8584
Manicurist #16 ....✉ 360-586-6387
Massage Therapist #9 (10247)..................... ☎ 360-586-6351
Medical Doctor #9 (16895) .... ☎ 360-753-2287
Midwife #9...................................... ☎ 360-664-4216
Naturopathic Physician #9 (293) .... ☎ 360-664-3230
Nuclear Medicine Technologist #8................. ☎ 360-586-5846
Nurse #9.. 360-586-1923
Nursing Assistant #9............................. 360-586-1923
Nursing Home #7................................. ☎ 360-705-6652
Nursing Home Administrator #9 .... ☎ 360-753-3729
Occupational Therapist #9 (2000) .... ☎ 360-664-8662
Ocularist #9 (9) .... ☎ 360-753-3576
Optician #9 (877) .... ☎ 360-753-3576
Optometrist #9 .... ☎ 360-753-4614
Osteopahtic Physician #9 (587) .... ☎ 360-586-8438
Pharmacist #8 (5779) .... ☎ 360-753-6834
Physical Therapist #9 (4000) .... ☎ 360-753-0876
Physician Assistant #9 .... ☎ 360-753-2287
Podiatrist #9 (229) .... ☎ 360-586-8438
Practical Nurse #9 360-753-2807
Radiologic Technologist #9 (3387) .... ☎ 360-586-6100
Respiratory Therapist #9 (2300).................. ☎ 360-586-8437
Speech Language Pathology #9..................... ☎ 360-753-1817
X-Ray Technician #9 (2611) .... ☎ 360-586-6100

Social Services
Counselor #8.................................... ☎ 360-664-9098
Mental Health Counselor #8...................... ☎ 360-664-9098
Psychologist #9................................. ☎ 360-753-2147
Sexual Offender Treatment Provider #9 (150)
.... ☎ 360-753-2147

Sports & Entertainment
Gaming #23 (11000) .... ☎ 360-438-7654
Horse Racing #20................................ ☎ 360-459-6462
Liquor Control #17 (11000) .... ☎ 360-664-0012
Professional Athlete #14......................... 360-753-3713
Recreational Vehicle Dealer #12 .... ☎ 360-902-3703

Recreational Vehicle Manufacturer #12 .... ☎ 360-902-3703
Sport Fishing #6 (400000).................................. 360-902-2253

Miscellaneous Vehicle Dealer #12 .... ☎ 360-902-3703
Mobile Home Travel Trailer Dealer #12 .... ☎ 360-902-3703

Transportation
Commercial Marine Pilot #2 (59).................. ☎ 206-515-3904

State Licensing & Business Registration Agency Information

(1) Board of Accountancy, PO Box 9131, Olympia, WA 98507-9131, 360-753-2585

(2) Board of Pilotage Commissioners, 801 Alaskan Way, Pier 52, Mail Stop TB-32, Seattle, WA 98104-1487, 206-515-3904, Fax: 206-515-3969

(3) Department of Agriculture, 1111 Washington St, PO Box 42560, Olympia, WA 98504-2560, 360-902-1855, Fax: 360-902-2086

(4) Department of Agriculture, Pesticide Management Division, PO Box 42589, Olympia, WA 98504-2589, 360-902-2010, Fax: 360-902-2093

(5) Department of Financial Institutions, Division of Bank, PO Box 41200, Olympia, WA 98504-1200, 360-902-8700

(6) Department of Fish & Wildlife, 600 Capitol Way, N., Olympia, WA 98501-1091, 360-902-2253, Fax: 360-902-2171

(7) Department of Health, Facility & Services Licensing, PO Box 47852, Olympia, WA 98504-7852, 360-705-6611, Fax: 360-705-6654

(8) Department of Health, Professional Licensing Services, PO Box 47860, Olympia, WA 98504-7860, 360-586-5846

(9) Department of Health, Professional Licensing Services, PO Box 47860, Olympia, WA 98504-7860, 360-753-3576, Fax: 360-586-0745

(10) Department of Labor & Industries, Building & Construction Safety Inspection Service, PO Box 44000, Olympia, WA 98504-4000, 360-902-5800, Fax: 360-902-5292

(11) Department of Labor & Industries, Building & Construction Safety Inspection Service, PO Box 44410, Olympia, WA 98504-4410, 360-902-5270, Fax: 360-902-5292

(12) Department of Licensing, General Adm. Bldg, 210 11th St SW, PO Box 48001, Olympia, WA 98504-8001, 360-753-6928

(13) Department of Licensing, 1125 Washington St. SE PO Box 9039, Olympia, WA 98507-9039, 360-902-3600, Fax: 360-586-6703

(14) Department of Licensing, Professional Athletic Section, PO Box 9027, Olympia, WA 98507, 360-753-3713

(15) Department of Licensing, Professional Licensing, Notary Section, PO Box 9027, Olympia, WA 98507-9027, 360-586-4575

(16) Department of Professional Licensing, 405 Black Lake Blvd, Olympia, WA 98504, Liquor Control Board, License Regulation Services, 1025 E Union Ave, PO Box 43075, Olympia, WA 98504-3075, 360-753-6640, Fax: 360-753-2710

(17) Superintendent of Public Instruction, State Board of Education Administration, Old Capitol Bldg, PO Box 47200, Olympia, WA 98504-7200, 360-753-6773, Fax: 360-580-0145

(18) Teacher Certification, PO Box 47200, Olympia, WA 98504-7200, 360-753-6773, Fax: 360-586-0145

(19) Washington Horse Racing Commission, 7912 Martin Way, Suite D, Olympia, WA 98506, 360-459-6462, Fax: 360-459-6461

(20) Washington State Bar Association, 500 Westin Bldg, 2001 6th Ave, Seattle, WA 98121-2599, 206-727-8200, Fax: 206-727-8300

(21) Washington State Business Licensing Service, PO Box 9034, Olympia, WA 98507-9034, 360-586-8368

(22) Washington State Gambling Commission, PO Box 42400, Olympia, WA 98504-2400, 360-438-7654 x315, x372, Fax: 360-438-7503

(23) Washington State Insurance Licensing, Bldg. 5, 4224 6 Ave. SE, Olympia, WA 98503, 360-753-7300

West Virginia

Capitol: Charleston (Kanawha County)	
State Population	1.8 Million
Number of Degree Granting Institutions:	36
Number of State Licensing & Business Registration Agencies:	73

Degree Granting Educational Institutions

Alderson-Broaddus College, Registrar, Philippi, WV 26416, 304-457-6278 (Fax: 304-457-6239). Hours: 8AM-4:30PM. Enrollment: 850. Records go back to 1895. Alumni records are maintained here also. Call 304-457-6202. Degrees granted: Associate; Bachelors; Masters. Adverse incident record source- Student Life.

Attendance and degree information available by phone, fax, mail. Search requires name only. Also helpful: SSN, exact years of attendance. There is no fee.

Appalachian Bible College, Registrar, PO Box ABC, Bradley, WV 25818, 304-877-6428 (Fax: 304-877-5082). Hours: 8AM-Noon, 1-5PM. Enrollment: 250. Records go back to 1950. Alumni records are maintained at the same phone number. Degrees granted: Associate; Bachelors. Adverse incident record source- Dean of Students.

Attendance and degree information available by phone, fax, mail. Search requires name only. Also helpful: SSN, exact years of attendance. There is no fee.

Bethany College, Registrar, Bethany, WV 26032, 304-829-7831 (Fax: 304-829-7108). Hours: 8AM-4:30PM. Enrollment: 750. Records go back to 1900. Alumni records are maintained here also. Call 304-829-7411. Degrees granted: Bachelors. Adverse incident record source- Dean of Students, 304-829-7631.

Attendance and degree information available by phone, fax, mail. Search requires name only. Also helpful: date of birth, exact years of attendance. There is no fee.

Bluefield State College, Registrar, 219 Rock St, Bluefield, WV 24701, 304-327-4060 (Fax: 304-325=7747). Hours: 8AM-4PM. Enrollment: 2500. Records go back to 1930's. Degrees granted: Associate; Bachelors. Adverse incident record source- Student Services, 304-327-4068.

Attendance and degree information available by phone, fax, mail. Search requires name only. Also helpful: SSN, approximate years of attendance. There is no fee.

College of West Virginia, Registrar, 609 S Kanawha St, Beckley, WV 25802, 304-253-7351 X35 (Fax: 304-253-5072). Enrollment: 2000. Records go back to 1933. Alumni records are maintained here at the same phone number. Degrees granted: Associate; Bachelors. Adverse incident record source- Dean of Student Services, 304-253-7351 X358.

Attendance and degree information available by phone, mail. Search requires name plus SSN, date of birth. Also helpful: exact years of attendance. There is no fee.

College of West Virginia (The), Registrar, 609 S Kanawha St, Beckley, WV 25802, 304-253-7351 (Fax: 304-253-5072). Enrollment: 2000. Formerly Beckley College Alumni records are maintained here at the same phone number. Degrees granted: Associate; Bachelors; Certificate. Special programs-Nursing: Physician Assistant: Diagnostic Medical Sonography: Physical Therapy Assistant: Criminal Justice: Computer Information Systems.

Attendance and degree information available by phone, fax, mail. Search requires name only. Also helpful: SSN, date of birth, exact years of attendance. There is no fee.

Computer Tech, **(Branch)**, Registrar, Country Club Rd Ext, Fairmont, WV 26554, 304-363-5100 (Fax: 304-366-9948). Hours: 8:30AM-6PM. Records go back to 1988. Degrees granted: Associate. Adverse incident record source- Registrar, 304-363-5100.

Attendance and degree information available by phone, fax, mail. Search requires name plus SSN. There is no fee.

Concord College, Registrar, PO Box 1000, Athens, WV 24712, 304-384-5237. Degrees granted: Bachelors.

Attendance and degree information available by phone, mail. Search requires name plus SSN, exact years of attendance. There is no fee.

Davis & Elkins College, Registrar, 100 Campus Dr, Elkins, WV 26241, 304-636-1900 (Fax: 304-636-8624). Hours: 8:30AM-5PM. Records go back to 1904. Degrees granted: Associate; Bachelors. Special programs- Practical Nursing, 304-636-3300.

Attendance information available by phone, fax, mail. Search requires name only. Also helpful: SSN. There is no fee.

Degree information available by phone, fax, mail. Search requires name only. Also helpful: SSN, date of birth. There is no fee.

Fairmont State College, Registrar, Locust Ave, Fairmont, WV 26554, 304-367-4141 (Fax: 304-367-4789). Hours: 8AM-4PM. Enrollment: 6300. Records go back to 1900. Alumni records are maintained here also. Call 304-363-0387. Degrees granted: Bachelors.

Attendance and degree information available by mail. Search requires name plus SSN, signed release. Also helpful: date of birth, exact years of attendance. There is no fee. Expedited service available for $9.00.

Glenville State College, Registrar, 200 High St, Glenville, WV 26351, 304-462-4117 (Fax: 304-462-8619). Hours: 8AM-4PM. Enrollment: 2400. Records go back to 1880. Alumni records are maintained here also. Call 304-462-7361 X122. Degrees granted: Associate; Bachelors. Adverse incident record source- Campus Security, 304-462-7361 X132.

Attendance and degree information available by phone, fax, mail. Search requires name plus SSN. Also helpful: date of birth, exact years of attendance. There is no fee.

Huntington Junior College, Registrar, 900 Fifth Ave, Huntington, WV 25701, 304-697-7550 (Fax: 304-697-7554). Degrees granted: Associate.

Attendance and degree information available by phone, mail. Search requires name plus SSN, exact years of attendance. There is no fee.

Marshall University, Registrar, Huntington, WV 25701, 304-696-6410 (Fax: 304-696-2252). Hours: 8AM-4:30PM. Alumni records are maintained here at the same phone number. Degrees granted: Bachelors; Masters; First Professional Degree.

Attendance and degree information available by fax, mail. Search requires name plus SSN, exact years of attendance. There is no fee.

Mountain State College, Registrar, Spring at 16th St, Parkersburg, WV 26101, 304-485-5487. Hours: 8AM-5PM. Records go back to 1888. Degrees granted: Associate.

Attendance and degree information available by phone, mail. Search requires name plus SSN, date of birth, exact years of attendance. There is no fee.

National Education Center-Institute of Technoloy, Registrar, 5514 Big Tyler Rd, Cross Lanes, WV 25313, 304-776-6290 X18 (Fax: 304-776-6262). Enrollment: 308. Records go back to 1979. Degrees granted: Associate. Adverse incident record source- Education Dept, 304-776-6290.

Attendance information available by written request only. Search requires name plus SSN, exact years of attendance, signed release. There is no fee.

Degree information available by phone, fax, mail. Search requires name plus SSN, exact years of attendance. There is no fee.

Ohio Valley College, Registrar, 4501 College Pkwy, Parkersburg, WV 26101, 304-485-7384 (Fax: 304-485-3106). Hours: 8AM-5PM. Enrollment: 280. Records go back to 1960. Alumni records are maintained here also. Call 304-485-7384. Degrees granted: Associate; Bachelors. Special programs- NCJC records at King of Prussia, 610-337-7328. Adverse incident record source- Student Services, 304-485-7384: Parkersburg Police, 304-424-8444

Attendance and degree information available by phone, fax, mail. Search requires name only. Also helpful: SSN, date of birth, exact years of attendance. There is no fee.

Potomac State College of West Virginia University, Registrar, Fort Ave, Keyser, WV 26726, 304-788-6800 (Fax: 304-788-6940). Hours: 8AM-4:30PM. Records go back to 1901. Alumni records are maintained here at the same phone number. Degrees granted: Associate.

Attendance and degree information available by phone, mail. Search requires name plus SSN, exact years of attendance. There is no fee.

Salem-Teikyo University, Registrar, 223 W Main St, Salem, WV 26426, 304-782-5297 (Fax: 304-782-5297). Enrollment: 800. Records go back to 1888. Alumni records are maintained here also. Call 304-782-5351. Degrees granted: Bachelors; Masters.

Attendance information available by phone, fax, mail. Search requires name only. Also helpful: SSN, date of birth, exact years of attendance. There is no fee.

Degree information available by phone, fax, mail. Search requires name only. Also helpful: SSN, date of birth, exact years of attendance. There is no fee.

Shepherd College, Registrar, Shepherdstown, WV 25443, 304-876-5463 (Fax: 304-876-5136). Hours: 8AM-4:30PM. Records go back to 1871. Alumni records are maintained here also. Call 304-876-5157. Degrees granted: Associate; Bachelors.

Attendance and degree information available by phone, fax, mail. Search requires name plus SSN. Also helpful: date of birth, exact years of attendance. There is no fee.

Southern West Virginia Community & Technical College, Registrar, PO Box 2900, Mt Gay, WV 25637, 304-792-7098 (Fax: 304-792-7056). Hours: 8AM-4:30PM. Enrollment: 3100. Records go back to 1971. Degrees granted: Associate.

Attendance and degree information available by phone, fax, mail. Search requires name plus SSN, exact years of attendance. There is no fee.

University of Charleston, Registrar, 2300 MacCorkle Ave, Charleston, WV 25304, 304-357-4740 (Fax: 304-357-4715). Records go back to 1900's. Alumni records are maintained here at the same phone number. Degrees granted: Associate; Bachelors; Masters. Adverse incident record source- Security, 304-357-4857.

Attendance information available by phone, fax, mail. Search requires name only. Also helpful: SSN, date of birth, exact years of attendance. There is no fee.

Degree information available by phone, fax, mail. Search requires name only. Also helpful: SSN, exact years of attendance. There is no fee.

Webster College, Registrar, 412 Fairmont Ave, Fairmont, WV 26554, 304-363-8824. Hours: 8AM-4PM. Records go back to 1926. Degrees granted: Associate.

Attendance and degree information available by phone, mail. Search requires name plus SSN, exact years of attendance. There is no fee.

West Liberty State College, Registrar, West Liberty, WV 26074, 304-336-8007 (Fax: 304-336-8285). Hours: 8AM-4PM. Records go back to 1925. Alumni records are maintained here also. Call 304-336-8124. Degrees granted: Associate; Bachelors. Adverse incident record source- Dean of Students, 304-336-8016.

Attendance and degree information available by phone, fax, mail. Search requires name only. Also helpful: SSN, exact years of attendance. There is no fee.

West Virginia Business College, Registrar, 116 Pennsylvania Ave, Nutter Fort, WV 26301, 304-624-7695. Hours: 8AM-5PM. Records go back to 1880. Degrees granted: Associate.

Attendance and degree information available by phone, mail. Search requires name plus SSN, exact years of attendance. There is no fee.

West Virginia Business College, (Branch Campus), Registrar, 1052 Main St, Wheeling, WV 26003, 304-232-0631. Hours: 8AM-5PM. Records go back to 1920. Degrees granted. Associate.

Attendance and degree information available by phone, mail. Search requires name plus SSN, exact years of attendance. There is no fee.

West Virginia Career College, Registrar, 1000 Virginia St E, Charleston, WV 25301, 304-345-2820. Hours: 8AM-4PM. Degrees granted: Associate.

Attendance and degree information available by phone, mail. Search requires name plus exact years of attendance. Also helpful: SSN, date of birth. There is no fee.

West Virginia Career College, Registrar, 148 Willey St, Morgantown, WV 26505, 304-296-8882. Hours: 8AM-4PM. Enrollment: 250. Degrees granted: Associate.

Attendance and degree information available by phone, mail. Search requires name plus SSN, date of birth, exact years of attendance. There is no fee.

West Virginia Graduate College, Registrar, 100 Angus E Peyton Dr, South Charleston, WV 25303-1600, 304-746-2500. Hours: 8AM-5PM. Enrollment: 2895. Records go back to 1958. They existed as a branch of another campus from 1958 to 1972, then became independent in 1972. Alumni records are maintained here at the same phone number. Degrees granted: Bachelors; Masters.

Attendance and degree information available by phone, mail. Search requires name plus SSN. There is no fee.

West Virginia Institute of Technology, Registrar, Montgomery, WV 25136, 304-442-3151 (Fax: 304-442-3097). Hours: 8AM-4:30PM. Enrollment: 2300. Records go back to 1895. Alumni records are maintained here also. Call 304-422-1005. Degrees granted: Associate; Bachelors; Masters. Adverse incident record source- Dean of Students, 304-442-3158.

Attendance and degree information available by phone, fax, mail. Search requires name plus SSN. Also helpful: exact years of attendance. There is no fee.

West Virginia Northern Community College, Registrar, 1704 Market St, Wheeling, WV 26003, 304-233-5900 X4211 (Fax: 304-233-0965). Hours: 8:30AM-5PM. Enrollment: 2700. Records go back to 1972. Alumni records are maintained here also. Call 304-233-5900 X4265. Degrees granted: Associate. Adverse incident record source- Institutional Research, 304-233-5900 X4261.

Attendance and degree information available by mail. Search requires name plus SSN, signed release. Also helpful: date of birth, exact years of attendance. There is no fee.

West Virginia School of Osteopathic Medicine, Registrar, 400 N Lee St, Lewisburg, WV 24901, 304-647-6230 (Fax: 304-645-4859). Hours: 8AM-4:30PM. Records go back to 1974. Alumni records are maintained here also. Call 304-647-6382. Degrees granted: Bachelors; Masters; First Professional Degree.

Attendance and degree information available by phone, mail. Search requires name plus SSN, date of birth, exact years of attendance. There is no fee.

West Virginia State College, Registrar, Institute, WV 25112, 304-766-3144 (Fax: 304-766-4104). Hours: 8AM-4:30PM. Records go back to 1958. Alumni records are maintained here at the same phone number. Degrees granted: Bachelors.

Attendance and degree information available by phone, fax, mail. Search requires name plus SSN, date of birth, exact years of attendance. There is no fee.

West Virginia University, Admissions & Records, PO Box 6009, Morgantown, WV 26506-6009, 304-293-2124 (Fax: 304-293-3080). Hours: 8:15AM-4:45PM. Alumni Records Office: PO Box 4269, Morgantown, WV 26506-6009, 304-293-4731 (Fax: 304-293-4733). Degrees granted: Bachelors; Masters; Doctorate. Adverse incident record source- Student Life, 304-293-5611.

Attendance and degree information available by phone, fax, mail. Search requires name plus SSN. Also helpful: date of birth, exact years of attendance. Fee is $5.00. Expedited service available for $8.00.

West Virginia University at Parkersburg, Registrar, Rte 5 Box 167-A, Parkersburg, WV 26101, 304-424-8220 (Fax: 304-424-8332). Hours: 8AM-4:30PM. Enrollment: 3612. Records go back to 1961. Alumni records are maintained here at the same phone number. Degrees granted: Bachelors. Adverse incident record source- Dean of Students, 304-424-8209.

Attendance and degree information available by phone, fax, mail. Search requires name plus SSN. Also helpful: date of birth, exact years of attendance. There is no fee.

West Virginia Wesleyan College, Registrar, College Ave, Buckhannon, WV 26201, 304-473-8470 (Fax: 304-473-8531). Hours: 8AM-4PM. Enrollment: 1650. Records go back to 1890. Alumni records are maintained here also. Call 304-473-8509. Degrees granted: Bachelors; Masters. Special programs- Outreach Education, 304-473-8430. Adverse incident record source- Dean of Students, 304-473-8440.

Attendance and degree information available by phone, fax, mail. Search requires name only. Also helpful: SSN, date of birth, exact years of attendance. There is no fee.

Wheeling Jesuit College, Registrar, 316 Washington Ave, Wheeling, WV 26003, 304-243-2238 (Fax: 304-243-2500). Hours: 8:30AM-5PM. Records go back to 1955. Alumni records are maintained here also. Call 304-243-2205. Degrees granted: Bachelors; Masters.

Attendance and degree information available by phone, fax, mail. Search requires name only. Also helpful: SSN, date of birth, exact years of attendance. There is no fee.

Trade and Vocational Schools

B.M. Spurr School of Practical Nursing, 800 Wheeling Ave, Glen Dale, WV 26038, 304-845-3211

Boone County Career Center, Box 50B, Danville, WV 25053, 304-369-4585

Carver Career and Technical Education Center, 4799 Midland Dr, Charleston, WV 25306, 304-348-1965

Clarksburg Skills Training Center, 120 Linden Ave, Clarksburg, WV 26301, 304-623-6036

Monongalia Country Technical Education Center, 1000 Mississippi St, Morgantown, WV 26505, 304-291-9240

Wheeling College of Hair Design, 1122 Main St, Wheeling, WV 26003, 304-232-1957

Wood County Vocational School, 1511 Blizzard Dr, Parkersburg, WV 26101, 304-420-9501

State Licensing & Business Registration Quick Finder Index

Architecture, Engineering & Surveying
Architect #2 (950)... ☎ 304-528-5825
Engineer #33 304-558-3554
Landscape Architect #13 304-293-2141
Surveyor #7.. ☎ 304-574-2980

Business - Court & Legal Services
Attorney #14 .... ☎ 304-558-7815
Lobbyist #39 (500) .... ✉ 304-558-0664
Notary Public #36 (35000) .... ✉ 304-558-6000
Shorthand Reporter #37................................... 304-558-3456

Business - General Services
Public Accountant-CPA; Non-resident CPA #1
(1700) .... ✉ 304-558-3557

Construction & Manufacturing
Electrician #40 304-558-2191
General Contractor #24 304-558-7890

Education
School Counselor #26...................................... ☎ 800-982-2378
School Principal #26.. ☎ 800-982-2378
School Social Services/Attendance
Investigator #26 .... ☎ 800-982-2378
School Superintendent #26............................... ☎ 800-982-2378
Supervisor of Instruction #26 .... ☎ 800-982-2378
Teacher #26 .... ☎ 800-982-2378
Vocational Administrator #26 .... ☎ 800-982-2378

Environmental & Agriculture
Animal Technician #23 (50)............................. ☎ 304-558-2016
Forester #20 304-924-6266
Mine Electrician #27 304-348-3500
Mine Surveyor/Foreman #27............................ 304-348-3500
Miner #27.. 304-348-3500
Pesticide Applicator #25.................................. 304-558-2209
Shot Firer #27 304-348-3500
Veterinarian #23 (500) .... ☎ 304-558-2016

Financial - Real Estate, Insurance & Banking
Insurance Agent #31 304-558-3354
Insurance Broker #31 304-558-3354
Insurance Solicitor #31.................................... 304-558-3354
Investment Advisor; Representatives #38 (2400)
.... ☎ 304-558-2257
Real Estate Appraiser #34 .... ☎ 304-558-3919
Real Estate Broker/Salesperson #35.................. 304-558-3555

Securities Agent #38 (31732) .... ☎ 304-558-2257
Securities Broker/Dealer #38 (1085) .... ☎ 304-558-2257

Health & Beauty
Barber #3... 304-558-2924
Chiropractor #4 .... ✉ 304-527-6335
Cosmetologist #3 304-558-2924
Dental Hygienist #6 (1000) .... ☎ 304-252-8266
Dentist #6 (1400) .... ☎ 304-252-8266
Educational Audiologist #26 .... ☎ 304-558-7010
Embalmer #5 .... ✉ 304-558-0302
Emergency Medical Technician-Basic; Paramedic #28
(5500) .... ☎ 304-558-3956
Funeral Director; Funeral Homes #5 (700) ....✉ 304-558-0302
Hearing Aid Specialist #12 304-558-7886
Manicurist #3 304-558-2924
Medical Doctor #15 304-558-2921
Nurse #8 304-558-3596
Nurse Anesthetist #8....................................... 304-558-3596
Nurse Midwife #8 304-558-3596
Nursing Home Administrator #32 304-558-1414
Occupational Therapist/Assistant #16 (409)
.... ✉ 304-329-0480
Optometrist #15 304-558-3596
Osteopathic Physician/Assistants #17 (700)
.... ☎ 304-723-4638
Pharmacist #18.. 304-558-0558
Physical Therapist/Assistant #19 (800) ....✉ 304-745-4161
Physician's Assistant #15................................. 304-558-3596
Podiatrist #15 304-558-3596
Practical Nurse #8 304-558-3572
Radiologic Technologist #9 (2210) .... ☎ 304-256-6985
Sanitarian-Registered; In Training #21 (200)
.... ☎ 304-558-2981
School Nurse #26 .... ☎ 304-558-7010
Speech/Language Pathologist #26.................... ☎ 304-558-7010

Investigations & Security
Polygraph Examiner #29 .... ✉ 304-558-7890
Private Detective #36 (631) .... ✉ 304-558-6000

Social Services
Professional Counselor #10 (1250) ....✉ 304-746-2512
Psychologist #11 304-366-5170
Social Worker #22 .... ☎ 304-558-8816

Sports & Entertainment
Athletic Trainer #26.. ☎ 800-982-2378
Boating & Canoe Expedition Provider #30....☎ 304-558-2783

Commercial Shooting Reserve #30 .... ☎ 304-558-2783
Commercial Whitewater Boating #30 .... ☎ 304-558-2783
Fishing Guide #30 (40) .... ☎ 304-558-2783

Whitewater Rafting Outfitter #30 .... ☎ 304-558-2783

State Licensing & Business Registration Agency Information

(1) Board of Accountancy, L&S Bldg, Suite 201, 812 Quarrier St, Charleston, WV 25301-2695, 304-558-3557

(2) Board of Architects, 910 4th Ave, Suite 412, Huntington, WV 25701-1434, 304-528-5825, Fax: 304-528-5826

(3) Board of Barbers & Cosmetologists, 1716 Pennsylvania Ave, Suite 7, Charleston, WV 25302, 304-558-2924

(4) Board of Chiropractic Examiners, PO Box 153, St Albans, WV 25177, 304-722-1424

(5) Board of Embalmers & Funeral Directors, 179 Summers St, Suite 305, Charleston, WV 25301-2131, 304-558-0302

(6) Board of Examiners for Dentists/Dental Hygienists, PO Drawer 1459, Beckley, WV 25802-1459, 304-252-8266, Fax: 304-252-2779

(7) Board of Examiners for Land Surveyors, PO Box 925, Fayetteville, WV 25840-0925, 304-574-2980

(8) Board of Examiners for Nurses, 101 Dee Dr, Charleston, WV 25311-1620, 304-558-3572

(9) Board of Examiners for Radiologic Technology, 3049 Robert C. Byrd Dr, Room 303, Beckley, WV 25801, 304-256-6985, Fax: 304-256-6985

(10) Board of Examiners in Counseling, 100 Angus E. Peyton Drive, South Charleston, WV 25303-1600, 304-345-3852, Fax: 305-746-1942

(11) Board of Examiners of Psychologists, PO Box 910, Barrackville, WV 26559-0910, 304-366-5170

(12) Board of Hearing-Aid Dealers, 701 Jefferson Rd, South Charleston, WV 25309-1638, 304-558-7886

(13) Board of Landscape Architects, Agricultural Sciences Bldg, WVU, PO Box 6108, Morgantown, WV 26506-6108, 304-293-2141

(14) Board of Law Examiners, Bldg 1, Room E400, 1900 Kanawha Blvd, E, Charleston, WV 25305-0837, 304-558-7815, Fax: 304-558-1212

(15) Board of Medicine, 101 Dee Dr, Charleston, WV 25311-1620, 304-558-2921

(16) Board of Occupational Therapy, 119 South Price St., Kingwood, WV 26537, 304-329-0480

(17) Board of Osteopathy, 334 Penco Rd, Weirton, WV 26062-3813, 304-723-4638, Fax: 304-723-2877

(18) Board of Pharmacy, 236 Capitol St, Charleston, WV 25301-2206, 304-558-0558

(19) Board of Physical Therapy, Rt 1 Box 306, Lost Creek, WV 26385-9717, 304-745-4161

(20) Board of Registration for Foresters, 8 Kepner St, Buckhannon, WV 26201-2153, 304-924-6266

(21) Board of Registration for Sanitarians, Environmental Health Services, Public Health Div., 815 Quarrier St, Charleston, WV 25301, 304-558-2981, Fax: 304-558-1071

(22) Board of Social Work Examiners, PO Box 5459, Charleston, WV 25361, 304-558-8816, Fax: 304-558-4189

(23) Board of Veterinary Medicine, 1900 Kanawha Blvd, E, Charleston, WV 25305-0119, 304-558-2016, Fax: 304-558-0891

(24) Contractor Licensing Board, State Capitol Complex, Bldg 3, Room 319, Charleston, WV 25305, 304-558-7890

(25) Department of Agriculture, Pesticide Division, Guthrie Center, State Capitol Complex, Charleston, WV 25305, 304-558-2209

(26) Department of Education, Office of Educational Personal Development, 1900 Washington St E, Charleston, WV 25305, 800-982-2378, Fax: 304-558-2584

(27) Department of Energy, State Capitol Building, Charleston, WV 25305, 304-348-3500

(28) Department of Health, Office of Emergency Medical Services, 1411 Virginia St E, Charleston, WV 25301, 304-558-3956, Fax: 304-558-1437

(29) Department of Labor, 1800 Washington St E, Charleston, WV 25305, 304-558-7890, Fax: 304-558-3797

(30) Division of Natural Resources, Law Enforcement Section, 1900 Kanawha Blvd, East Bldg 3, Room 837, Charleston, WV 25305, 304-558-2783, Fax: 304-558-1170

(31) Insurance Commissioner, 2100 Washington St E, Charleston, WV 25305, 304-558-3354

(32) Nursing Home Administrators Licensing Board, 236 Capitol St, Charleston, WV 25301, 304-558-1414

(33) Professional Board of Registration for Engineers, 608 Union Bldg, 723 Kanawha Blvd, E, Charleston, WV 25301-2104, 304-558-3554

(34) Real Estate Appraiser Licensing & Certification Bd, 210 Kanawah Blvd E, #101, Charleston, WV 25311, 304-558-3919

(35) Real Estate Commission, 1033 Quarrier St, Suite 400, Charleston, WV 25301-2315, 304-558-3555

(36) Secretary of State, Bldg 1, Suite 157-K, 1900 Kanawha Blvd, Charleston, WV 25305-0770, 304-558-6000, Fax: 304-558-0900

(37) Secretary of State, State Capitol, Charleston, WV 25305, 304-558-3456

(38) State Auditor's Office, Security Division, State Capitol, Room W-118, Charleston, WV 25305, 304-558-2257, Fax: 304-558-4211

(39) West Virginia Ethics Commission, 1207 Quarrier St, 4th Floor, Charleston, WV 25301, 304-558-0664, Fax: 304-558-2169

(40) West Virginia State Fire Marshall, 2100 Washington St E, Charleston, WV 25305, 304-558-2191

Wisconsin

Capitol: Madison (Dane County)	
State Population	5.1 Million
Number of Degree Granting Institutions:	85
Number of State Licensing & Business Registration Agencies:	79

Degree Granting Educational Institutions

Alverno College, Registrar, PO Box 343922, 3401 S 39th St, Milwaukee, WI 53234-3922, 414-382-6370 (Fax: 414-382-6354). Hours: 8AM-5PM. Enrollment: 2151. Records go back to 1950's. Alumni records are maintained here also. Call 414-382-6090. Degrees granted: Associate; Bachelors.

Attendance and degree information available by phone, fax, mail. Search requires name only. Also helpful: SSN, approximate years of attendance. There is no fee.

Bellin College of Nursing, Registrar, PO Box 1700, 929 Cass St, Green Bay, WI 54305, 414-433-3560. Hours: 8AM-4:30PM. Records go back to 1970's. Degrees granted: Associate.

Attendance and degree information available by phone, mail. Search requires name plus SSN. There is no fee.

Beloit College, Registrar, 700 College St, Beloit, WI 53511, 608-363-2640 (Fax: 608-363-2718). Enrollment: 1200. Alumni records are maintained here also. Call 608-363-2218. Degrees granted: Bachelors; Masters.

Attendance and degree information available by phone, fax, mail. Search requires name plus date of birth, exact years of attendance. Also helpful: SSN. There is no fee.

Blackhawk Technical College, Records, PO Box 5009, Janesville, WI 53547-5009, 608-757-7668 (Fax: 608-757-9407). Hours: 8AM-4:30PM. Enrollment: 2530. Records go back to 1968. Degrees granted: Associate. Adverse incident record source- Rock County Sheriff, 608-757-8000.

School will not confirm attendance information.

Degree information available by phone, fax, mail. Search requires name plus SSN, approximate years of attendance. Also helpful: date of birth, exact years of attendance. There is no fee.

Cardinal Stritch College, Registrar, 6801 N Yates Rd, Milwaukee, WI 53217, 414-352-5400. Hours: 8AM-5PM. Enrollment: 5176. Records go back to 1937. Alumni records are maintained here at the same phone number. Degrees granted: Bachelors; Masters.

Attendance and degree information available by mail. Search requires name plus SSN, date of birth, exact years of attendance. There is no fee.

Carroll College, Registrar, 100 N East Ave, Waukesha, WI 53186, 414-524-7208 (Fax: 414-524-7139). Hours: 8AM-4:30PM. Enrollment: 2240. Records go back to 1926. Records are available further back if necessary. Degrees granted: Bachelors; Masters.

Attendance and degree information available by phone, fax, mail. Search requires name plus SSN. Also helpful: date of birth, approximate years of attendance. There is no fee.

Carthage College, Registrar, 2001 Alford Dr, Kenosha, WI 53140, 414-551-6100 (Fax: 414-551-6208). Hours: 8AM-4:30PM. Enrollment: 2200. Alumni records are maintained here also. Call 414-551-5700. Degrees granted: Bachelors; Masters; Paralegal. Adverse incident record source- 414-551-8500.

Attendance and degree information available by phone, fax, mail. Search requires name plus approximate years of attendance. Also helpful: SSN, date of birth, exact years of attendance. There is no fee.

Chippewa Valley Technical College, Registrar, 620 W Clairemont Ave, Eau Claire, WI 54701, 715-833-6269 (Fax: 715-833-6470). Hours: 7:30AM-8:30PM. Records go back to 1940's. Alumni records are maintained here at the same phone number. Degrees granted: Associate.

Attendance information available by mail. Search requires name plus SSN, signed release. Also helpful: exact years of attendance. There is no fee.

Degree information available by phone, fax, mail. Search requires name only. Also helpful: SSN, exact years of attendance. There is no fee.

Columbia College of Nursing, Registrar, 2121 E Newport Ave, Milwaukee, WI 53211, 414-961-3530 (Fax: 414-961-4121). Hours: 8AM-4PM. Enrollment: 400. Alumni records are maintained here also. Call 414-961-4012. Degrees granted: Associate. Adverse incident record source- 414-961-3530.

Attendance and degree information available by mail. Search requires name plus SSN. There is no fee.

Concordia University Wisconsin, Registrar, 12800 N Lake Shore Dr, Mequon, WI 53097, 414-243-4345

(Fax: 414-243-4351). Hours: 8AM-4:30PM. Enrollment: 3700. Records go back to 1800's. Alumni records are maintained here at the same phone number. Degrees granted: Associate; Bachelors; Masters.

Attendance and degree information available by phone, fax, mail. Search requires name only. Also helpful: SSN, date of birth, exact years of attendance. There is no fee.

District One Technical Institute, Registrar, 620 W Clairemont Ave, Eau Claire, WI 54701, 715-833-6269 (Fax: 715-833-6470). Enrollment: 600. Records go back to 1911. Alumni records are maintained here at the same phone number. Degrees granted: Associate. Adverse incident record source-Student Services.

Attendance and degree information available by phone, fax, mail. Search requires name plus SSN, date of birth, exact years of attendance. There is no fee.

Edgewood College, Registrar's Office, 855 Woodrow St, Madison, WI 53711, 608-257-4861 (Fax: 608-257-1455). Hours: 8AM-4:30PM. Enrollment: 2000. Alumni records are maintained here at the same phone number. Degrees granted: Associate; Bachelors; Masters.

Attendance and degree information available by phone, fax, mail. Search requires name only. Also helpful: SSN, date of birth, exact years of attendance. There is no fee.

Fox Valley Technical Institute, Registrar, 1825 N Bluemound Dr, PO Box 2277, Appleton, WI 54913-2277, 414-735-5712 (Fax: 414-735-4713). Hours: 8AM-8PM. Enrollment: 4500. Records go back to 1930's. Degrees granted: Associate.

Attendance and degree information available by phone, fax, mail. Search requires name plus SSN. Also helpful: date of birth, approximate years of attendance. There is no fee.

Gateway Technical College, Registrar, 3520 30th Ave, Kenosha, WI 53144-1690, 414-656-8972 (Fax: 414-656-7209). Enrollment: 10000. Alumni records are maintained here also. Call 414-656-7233. Degrees granted: Associate; Vocational Diplomas. Adverse incident record source- Student Services, 414-656-6984.

Attendance and degree information available by phone, fax, mail. Search requires name plus SSN, date of birth, exact years of attendance. There is no fee.

Herzing College of Technology, Registrar, 1227 N Sherman Ave, Madison, WI 53704, 608-249-6611 (Fax: 608-249-8593). Enrollment: 425. Formerly Wisconsin of Electronics Records go back to 1948. Alumni records are maintained here at the same phone number. Degrees granted: Associate; Bachelors.

Attendance information available by written request only. Search requires name plus SSN, date of birth, signed release. Also helpful: exact years of attendance. There is no fee.

Degree information available by phone, fax. Search requires name plus SSN, date of birth. Also helpful: exact years of attendance. There is no fee.

ITT Technical Institute, Registrar, 6300 W Layton Ave, Greenfield, WI 53220-4612, 414-282-9494 (Fax: 414-282-9698). Hours: 8AM-4PM. Records go back to 1970's. Alumni Records Office: 9511 Angola Ct, Indianapolis, IN 46268. Degrees granted: Associate; Bachelor's Degree-Electronics.

Attendance and degree information available by phone, mail. Search requires name plus SSN, exact years of attendance. There is no fee.

Keller Graduate School of Management, (Milwaukee Center), Registrar, 100 E Wisconsin Ave #2550, Milwaukee, WI 53202, 414-278-7677 (Fax: 414-278-0137). Records are not housed here. They are located at Keller Graduate School of Management, Registrar, 10 S Riverside Plaza, Chicago, IL 60606.

Keller Graduate School of Management, (Waukesha Center), Registrar, 20935 Swenson Dr, Waukesha, WI 53186, 414-798-9889 (Fax: 414-798-9912). Records are not housed here. They are located at Keller Graduate School of Management, Registrar, 10 S Riverside Plaza, Chicago, IL 60606.

LacCourte Oreilles Ojibwa Community College, Registrar, Rte 2 Box 2357, Hayward, WI 54843, 715-634-4790 (Fax: 715-634-5049). Hours: 8AM-4:30PM. Enrollment: 400. Records go back to 1981. Degrees granted: Associate.

Attendance and degree information available by mail. Search requires name plus SSN, date of birth, exact years of attendance, signed release. There is no fee. Expedited service available for $15.00.

Lakeland College, Registrar, PO Box 359, Sheboygan, WI 53082-0359, 414-565-1216 (Fax: 414-565-1206). Hours: 8AM-4:30PM. Records go back to 1920. Alumni records are maintained here at the same phone number. Degrees granted: Bachelors; Masters. Adverse incident record source- Student Affairs, 414-565-1248.

Attendance information available by phone, fax, mail. Search requires name only. Also helpful: SSN, date of birth, exact years of attendance. There is no fee.

Degree information available by phone, fax, mail. Search requires name only. Also helpful: SSN, date of birth, exact years of attendance. There is no fee.

Lakeshore Technical College, Registrar/Records, 1290 North Ave, Cleveland, WI 53015, 414-458-4183 X115 (Fax: 414-693-3561). Hours: 7:30AM-3:45PM. Enrollment: 2000. Records go back to 1940. Alumni records are maintained here at the same phone number. Degrees granted: Associate.

Attendance and degree information available by fax, mail. Search requires name plus SSN, date of birth, exact years of attendance, signed release. There is no fee.

Lawrence University, Registrar, PO Box 599, Appleton, WI 54912, 414-832-6578 (Fax: 414-832-6606). Hours: 8AM-Noon, 1-5PM. Enrollment: 1200. Records go back to 1920. Alumni records are maintained here also. Call 414-832-6521. Degrees granted: Bachelors. Adverse incident record source- Dean of Students, 414-832-6530.

Attendance and degree information available by phone, fax, mail. Search requires name plus approximate years of attendance. Also helpful: SSN, date of birth, exact years of attendance. There is no fee.

Madison Area Technical College, Registrar, 3350 Anderson St, Madison, WI 53704, 608-246-6210 (Fax: 608-246-6880). Degrees granted: Associate.

Attendance and degree information available by phone, mail. Search requires name plus SSN, exact years of attendance. There is no fee.

Madison Junior College of Business, Registrar, 31 S Henry St, Madison, WI 53703, 608-251-6522 (Fax: 608-251-6590). Hours: 7AM-4PM. Records go back to 1905. Degrees granted: Associate. Adverse incident record source- Student Services, 608-251-6522.

Attendance and degree information available by phone, fax, mail. Search requires name only. Also helpful: date of birth, exact years of attendance. There is no fee.

Marantha Baptist Bible College, Registrar, 745 W Main St, Watertown, WI 53094, 414-261-9300 X363 (Fax: 414-261-9109). Hours: 8AM-5PM. Records go back to 1968. Alumni records are maintained here at the same phone number. Degrees granted: Associate; Bachelors; Masters. Certification: P.C.T. Adverse incident record source- Dean's Office, 414-261-9300 X323 .

Attendance and degree information available by phone, fax, mail. Search requires name only. Also helpful: exact years of attendance. There is no fee.

Marian College of Fond du Lac, Registrar, 45 S National Ave, Fond Du Lac, WI 54935, 414-923-7618 (Fax: 414-923-7154). Hours: 8AM-6PM M-Th; 8AM-4:30PM F. Enrollment: 2500. Records go back to 1938. Alumni records are maintained here also. Call 414-923-8133. Degrees granted: Bachelors; Masters.

Attendance and degree information available by phone, fax, mail. Search requires name plus SSN, date of birth, approximate years of attendance. Also helpful: exact years of attendance. There is no fee.

Marquette University, Registrar, MH 310, PO Box 1881, Milwaukee, WI 53201-1881, 414-288-7034 (Fax: 414-288-1773). Hours: 8AM-4:30PM. Enrollment: 10781. Records go back to 1881. Alumni Records Office: 1212 W Wisconsin Ave, Milwaukee, WI 53201-1881, 414-288-7441 (Fax: 414-288-3956). Degrees granted: Bachelors; Masters; Doctorate.

Attendance and degree information available by phone, mail. Search requires name plus SSN, date of birth, exact years of attendance. There is no fee.

Medical College of Wisconsin, Registrar, 8701 Watertown Plank Rd, Milwaukee, WI 53226, 414-456-8296. Hours: 8AM-5PM. Enrollment: 800. Alumni records are maintained here at the same phone number. Degrees granted: Bachelors; Masters; Doctorate.

Attendance and degree information available by phone, mail. Search requires name plus exact years of attendance. There is no fee.

Mid-State Technical College, Registrar, 500 32nd St N, Wisconsin Rapids, WI 54494, 715-422-5502 (Fax: 715-422-5345). Hours: 7:30AM-4:30PM. Records go back to 1967. Alumni records are maintained here also. Call 715-422-5528. Degrees granted: Associate.

Attendance and degree information available by phone, fax, mail. Search requires name plus SSN. There is no fee.

Milwaukee Area Technical College, Registrar, 700 W State St, Milwaukee, WI 53233, 414-297-6470 (Fax: 414-297-6371). Hours: 7AM-4PM. Records go back to 1920. Alumni records are maintained here also. Call 414-297-6624. Degrees granted: Associate. Adverse incident record source- 414-297-6470.

Attendance and degree information available by phone, fax, mail. Search requires name plus SSN. Also helpful: date of birth, exact years of attendance. Fee is $3.00. Expedited service available for $5.00.

Milwaukee Institute of Art and Design, Registrar, 273 E Erie St, Milwaukee, WI 53202, 414-276-7889 X680 (Fax: 414-291-8077). Hours: 8AM-4:30PM. Enrollment: 500. Records go back to 1974. Alumni records are maintained here also. Call 414-276-7889. Degrees granted: Bachelors.

Attendance and degree information available by phone, fax, mail. Search requires name plus SSN, date of birth, approximate years of attendance. Also helpful: exact years of attendance. There is no fee.

Milwaukee School of Engineering, Registrar, 1025 N Broadway, Milwaukee, WI 53202-3109, 414-277-7220 (Fax: 414-277-6914). Enrollment: 2900. Alumni records are maintained here at the same phone number. Degrees granted: Associate; Bachelors; Masters.

Attendance and degree information available by phone, fax, mail. Search requires name only. Also helpful: SSN, exact years of attendance. There is no fee.

Moraine Park Technical College, Registrar, PO Box 1940, 235 N National Ave, Fond Du Lac, WI 54936-1940, 414-924-3308 (Fax: 414-924-3421). Degrees granted: Associate. Certification: Diplomas.

Attendance and degree information available by phone, mail. Search requires name plus SSN, date of birth. Also helpful: exact years of attendance. There is no fee.

Mount Mary College, Registrar, 2900 N Menomonee River Pkwy, Milwaukee, WI 53222, 414-258-4810 X281 (Fax: 414-256-1224). Hours: 8AM-4:30PM. Records go back to 1915. Alumni records are maintained here also. Call 414-258-4810. Degrees granted: Bachelors; Masters.

Attendance and degree information available by phone, fax, mail. Search requires name plus SSN. Also helpful: date of birth, exact years of attendance. There is no fee.

Mount Senario College, Registrar, 1500 W College Ave, Ladysmith, WI 54848, 715-532-5511 X120 (Fax: 715-532-7690). Hours: 8AM-4:30PM. Enrollment: 760. Records go back to 1964. Alumni records are maintained here also. Call 715-532-5511 X107. Degrees granted: Associate; Bachelors. Special programs- Outreach Department, 715-532-5511 X189.

Attendance and degree information available by phone, fax, mail. Search requires name plus SSN. Also helpful: exact years of attendance. There is no fee.

Nashotah House, Registrar, 2777 Mission Rd, Nashotah, WI 53058-9793, 414-646-3371 (Fax: 414-646-2215). Hours: 8:30AM-4:30PM. Enrollment: 40. Records go back to 1921. Degrees granted: Masters; Anglican Studies.

Attendance information available by phone. Search requires name only. Also helpful: exact years of attendance. There is no fee.

Degree information available by phone, mail. Search requires name only. Also helpful: exact years of attendance. There is no fee.

Nicolet Area Technical College, Registrar, Box 518, Rhinelander, WI 54501, 715-365-4422 (Fax: 715-365-4411). Hours: 8AM-4PM. Enrollment: 1700. Records go back to 1968. Degrees granted: Associate. Adverse incident record source- Student Services, 715-365-4456.

Attendance and degree information available by phone, fax, mail. Search requires name plus SSN, date of birth. There is no fee.

North Central Technical College, Registrar, 1000 Campus Dr, Wausau, WI 54401, 715-675-3331 (Fax: 715-675-9776). Hours: 8AM-6PM M-Th, 8AM-4:30PM F. Records go back to 1912. Alumni records are maintained here at the same phone number. Degrees granted: Associate.

Attendance and degree information available by phone, fax, mail. Search requires name plus SSN, approximate years of attendance. There is no fee.

Northeast Wisconsin Technical College, Registrar, PO Box 19042, 2740 W Mason St, Green Bay, WI 54307, 414-498-5579 (Fax: 414-498-6242). Hours: 8AM-5PM. Records go back to 1913. Alumni records are maintained here also. Call 414-498-5426. Degrees granted: Associate.

Attendance and degree information available by phone, mail. Search requires name plus SSN. There is no fee.

Northland College, Registrar, 1411 Ellis Ave, Ashland, WI 54806, 715-682-1227 (Fax: 715-682-1308). Hours: 8AM-Noon, 1-4PM. Enrollment: 850. Records go back to 1892. Alumni records are maintained here also. Call 715-682-1497. Degrees granted: Bachelors.

Attendance and degree information available by phone, mail. Search requires name plus SSN, date of birth. Also helpful: approximate years of attendance. There is no fee.

Ripon College, Registrar, PO Box 248, 300 Seward St, Ripon, WI 54971, 414-748-8119 (Fax: 414-748-9262). Hours: 8AM-5PM. Enrollment: 750. Records go back to 1851. Alumni records are maintained here also. Call 414-748-8126. Degrees granted: Bachelors. Adverse incident record source- Dean of Students, 414-748-8111.

Attendance and degree information available by phone, mail. Search requires name plus exact years of attendance. There is no fee.

Sacred Heart School of Theology, Registrar, PO Box 429, 7335 S Hwy 100, Hales Corners, WI 53130-0429, 414-425-8300 X7228. Hours: 8AM-5PM. Records go back to 1968. Alumni records are maintained here at the same phone number. Degrees granted: Bachelors; Masters; First Professional Degree.

Attendance and degree information available by mail. Search requires name only. There is no fee.

Saint Francis Seminary, Registrar, 3257 S Lake Dr, St Francis, WI 53235, 414-747-6450 (Fax: 414-747-6442). Hours: 8AM-5PM. Records go back to 1845. Alumni records are maintained here at the same phone number. Degrees granted: Bachelors; Masters. Special programs- Liturgy & Music.

Attendance and degree information available by phone, mail. Search requires name only. Also helpful: SSN, date of birth, exact years of attendance. There is no fee.

Silver Lake College, Registrar, 2406 S Alverno Rd, Manitowoc, WI 54220, 414-684-6691 (Fax: 414-684-7082). Hours: 8AM-4:30PM. Enrollment: 1200. Records go back to 1930's. Alumni records are maintained here at the same phone number. Degrees granted: Associate; Bachelors; Masters. Special programs- Business:·Education. Adverse incident record source- Student Services, 414-684-6691.

Attendance and degree information available by phone, fax, mail. Search requires name only. Also helpful: SSN, date of birth, approximate years of attendance. There is no fee.

Southwest Wisconsin Technical College, Registrar, 1800 Bronson Blvd, Fennimore, WI 53809, 608-822-3262 (Fax: 608-822-6019). Hours: 7:30AM-4PM. Records go back to 1969. Degrees granted: Associate. Adverse incident record source- 608-822-3262.

Attendance and degree information available by phone, fax, mail. Search requires name only. Also helpful: SSN, date of birth, exact years of attendance. There is no fee.

St. Norbert College, Registrar, 100 Grant St, De Pere, WI 54115-2099, 414-403-3216 (Fax: 414-403-4033). Hours: 8AM-Noon, 1-4:30PM. Enrollment: 200. Records go back to 1902. Alumni records are maintained here also. Call 414-337-3022. Degrees granted: Bachelors; Masters.

Attendance and degree information available by phone, mail. Search requires name plus SSN. Also helpful: date of birth, exact years of attendance. There is no fee.

Stratton College, Registrar, 1300 N Jackson St, Milwaukee, WI 53202-2608, 414-276-5200 X6 (Fax: 414-276-3930). Hours: 8AM-5PM. Records go back to 1863. Alumni records are maintained here at the same phone number. Degrees granted: Associate.

Attendance and degree information available by phone, mail. Search requires name plus SSN, exact years of attendance. There is no fee.

University of Wisconsin, Registrar, Room 130 Patterson Bldg., 750 University Ave., Madison, WI 53706, 608-262-3811 (Fax: 608-262-6002). Hours: 8AM-5PM. Enrollment: 39000. Records go back to 1848. Alumni records are maintained here at the same phone number. Degrees granted: Bachelors; Masters; Doctorate. Adverse incident record source- Deans Office.

Attendance and degree information available by phone, fax, mail. Search requires name only. Also helpful: SSN, date of birth, exact years of attendance. There is no fee.

University of Wisconsin-Baraboo-Sauk County, Registrar, 1006 Connie Rd, Baraboo, WI 53913, 608-356-8351 (Fax: 608-356-4074). Hours: 8AM-5PM. Enrollment: 400. Records go back to 1968. Degrees granted: Associate. Adverse incident record source- 608-356-8351.

Attendance and degree information available by phone, fax, mail. Search requires name only. Also helpful: SSN, exact years of attendance. There is no fee.

University of Wisconsin-Barron County, Registrar, 1800 College Dr, Rice Lake, WI 54868, 715-234-8176. Hours: 8AM-5PM. Enrollment: 500. Records go back to 1968. Alumni records are maintained here at the same phone number. Degrees granted: Associate. Adverse incident record source- 715-234-8176.

Attendance and degree information available by phone, mail. Search requires name plus SSN, date of birth, exact years of attendance. There is no fee.

University of Wisconsin-Eau Claire, Registrar, S 130, Eau Claire, WI 54702, 715-836-5912 (Fax: 715-836-2380). Hours: 7:45AM-4:30PM. Enrollment: 10000. Records go back to 1916. Alumni Records Office: Alumni Association, UWEC, S2116, Eau Claire, WI 54702. Degrees granted: Associate; Bachelors; Masters. Certification: Ed.

Attendance and degree information available by phone, fax, mail. Search requires name plus SSN. Also helpful: date of birth, exact years of attendance. There is no fee.

University of Wisconsin-Fond du Lac, Registrar, Campus Dr, Fond Du Lac, WI 54935, 414-929-3606 (Fax: 414-929-3626). Records are not housed here. They are located at University of Wisconsin, Registrar, Room 130 Patterson Bldg., 750 University Ave., Madison, WI 53706.

University of Wisconsin-Fox Valley, Registrar, PO Box 8002, Menasha, WI 54952-8002, 414-832-2600. Hours: 8AM-5PM. Enrollment: 1250. Alumni records are maintained here at the same phone number. Degrees granted: Associate.

Attendance and degree information available by phone, mail. Search requires name plus SSN. There is no fee.

University of Wisconsin-Green Bay, Registrar, 2420 Nicolet Dr, Green Bay, WI 54311, 414-465-2055 (Fax: 414-465-2765). Hours: 9AM-4:30PM. Enrollment: 5400. Records go back to 1969. Alumni records are maintained here also. Call 414-465-2586. Degrees granted: Associate; Bachelors; Masters. Adverse incident record source- Dean of Students, 414-465-2152.

Attendance and degree information available by fax, mail. Search requires name plus SSN. Also helpful: exact years of attendance. There is no fee.

University of Wisconsin-La Crosse, Registrar, 1725 State St, La Crosse, WI 54601, 608-785-8576 (Fax: 608-785-6695). Hours: 8AM-4:30PM. Enrollment: 8700. Records go back to 1906. Alumni records are maintained here also. Call 608-785-8489. Degrees granted: Associate; Bachelors; Masters. Adverse incident record source- Student Life, 608-785-8062.

Attendance and degree information available by phone, fax, mail. Search requires name only. Also helpful: SSN, date of birth, exact years of attendance. There is no fee.

University of Wisconsin-Madison, Registrar, 750 University Ave, AW Peterson Ofc Bldg Room 60, Madison, WI 53706, 608-262-3722 (Fax: 608-262-0123). Hours: 7:45AM-4:30PM. Enrollment: 40000. Records go back to 1848. Alumni records are maintained here also. Call 608-262-2551. Degrees granted: Bachelors; Masters; Doctorate.

Attendance and degree information available by phone, mail. Search requires name plus SSN, date of birth, exact years of attendance. There is no fee.

University of Wisconsin-Manitowoc County,
Registrar, 705 Viebahn St, Manitowoc, WI 54220-6699, 414-683-4700 (Fax: 414-683-4776). Hours: 8AM-5PM. Enrollment: 500. Alumni records are maintained here also. Call 414-683-4713. Degrees granted: Associate. Adverse incident record source- 414-683-4700.

Attendance and degree information available by phone, fax, mail. Search requires name plus SSN, date of birth. There is no fee.

University of Wisconsin-Marathon County,
Registrar, 518 S Seventh Ave, Wausau, WI 54401-5396, 715-845-9602 (Fax: 715-261-6333). Hours: 8AM-5PM. Alumni records are maintained here also. Call 715-261-6296. Degrees granted: Associate.

Attendance and degree information available by phone, mail. Search requires name plus SSN. There is no fee.

University of Wisconsin-Marinette County,
Registrar, 750 W Bay Shore St, Marinette, WI 54143, 715-735-4300 (Fax: 715-735-4307). Hours: 8AM-5PM. Enrollment: 350. Records go back to 1968. Alumni records are maintained here at the same phone number. Degrees granted: Associate.

Attendance and degree information available by phone, mail. Search requires name plus SSN. There is no fee.

University of Wisconsin-Marshfield-Wood County,
Registrar, PO Box 150, Marshfield, WI 54449, 715-389-6530 (Fax: 715-389-6517). Hours: 7:45AM-4:30PM. Enrollment: 550. Records go back to 1964. Degrees granted: Associate. Adverse incident record source- Student Services, 715-389-6530.

Attendance and degree information available by phone, fax, mail. Search requires name plus SSN. There is no fee.

University of Wisconsin-Milwaukee,
Registrar, PO Box 729, Milwaukee, WI 53201, 414-229-5774 (Fax: 414-229-6940). Hours: 8AM-4:30PM. Enrollment: 22000. Records go back to 1956. Alumni records are maintained here at the same phone number. Degrees granted: Bachelors; Masters; Doctorate. Adverse incident record source- Student Life, 414-229-4830.

Attendance and degree information available by phone, fax, mail. Search requires name plus SSN, exact years of attendance. Also helpful: date of birth. There is no fee.

University of Wisconsin-Oshkosh,
Records Office, 800 Algoma Blvd, Oshkosh, WI 54901, 414-424-0325 (Fax: 414-424-1098). Hours: 8:30AM-3:30PM. Enrollment: 11000. Records go back to 1850's. Alumni records are maintained here also. Call 414-424-3414. Degrees granted: Associate; Bachelors; Masters. Adverse incident record source- Dean of Students, 414-424-3100.

Attendance and degree information available by phone, mail. Search requires name plus SSN, approximate years of attendance. Also helpful: date of birth. There is no fee.

University of Wisconsin-Parkside,
Registrar, Box 2000, Kenosha, WI 53141-2000, 414-595-2284. Hours: 8AM-5PM. Enrollment: 4851. Records go back to 1968. Alumni records are maintained here also. Call 414-595-2414. Degrees granted: Bachelors; Masters.

Attendance and degree information available by phone, mail. Search requires name plus SSN, date of birth, exact years of attendance. There is no fee.

University of Wisconsin-Platteville,
Registrar, One University Plaza, Platteville, WI 53818-3099, 608-342-1321 (Fax: 608-342-1389). Hours: 7:45AM-4:45PM. Enrollment: 5000. Records go back to 1800's. Alumni records are

maintained here also. Call 608-342-1181. Degrees granted: Associate; Bachelors; Masters. Special programs- Masters Program Graduate Office, 608-342-1321. Adverse incident record source- Student Affairs, 608-342-1854.

Attendance information available by phone, mail. Search requires name plus SSN. Also helpful: date of birth, exact years of attendance. There is no fee.

Degree information available by phone, mail. Search requires name plus SSN, date of birth. Also helpful: exact years of attendance. There is no fee.

University of Wisconsin-Richland,
Registrar, Hwy 14 W, Richland Center, WI 53581, 608-647-6186 (Fax: 608-647-6225). Hours: 8AM-5PM. Enrollment: 375. Records go back to 1967. Alumni records are maintained here at the same phone number. Degrees granted: Associate.

Attendance and degree information available by phone, mail. Search requires name plus SSN. There is no fee.

University of Wisconsin-River Falls,
Registrar, River Falls, WI 54022, 715-425-3342 (Fax: 715-425-3352). Hours: 8AM-4:30PM. Enrollment: 5600. Records go back to 1874. Alumni records are maintained here also. Call 715-425-3505. Degrees granted: Bachelors; Masters. Adverse incident record source- Dean of Students, 715-425-3711.

Attendance and degree information available by phone, mail. Search requires name plus SSN, date of birth. There is no fee.

University of Wisconsin-Rock County,
Registrar, 2909 Kellogg Ave, Janesville, WI 53546, 608-758-6522 (Fax: 608-758-6564). Hours: 8AM-5PM. Enrollment: 800. Records go back to 1968. Alumni records are maintained here also. Call 608-758-6522. Degrees granted: Associate.

Attendance and degree information available by phone, mail. Search requires name plus SSN. There is no fee.

University of Wisconsin-Sheboygan County,
Registrar, One University Dr, Sheboygan, WI 53081, 414-459-6633 (Fax: 414-459-6602). Hours: 8AM-5PM. Enrollment: 550. Records go back to 1950. Degrees granted: Associate.

Attendance and degree information available by phone, fax, mail. Search requires name plus SSN. Also helpful: date of birth, exact years of attendance. There is no fee.

University of Wisconsin-Stevens Point,
Registrar, Stevens Point, WI 54481, 715-346-4301 (Fax: 715-346-2558). Hours: 7:45AM-4:30PM. Enrollment: 8400. Records go back to 1894. Alumni records are maintained here also. Call 715-346-3811. Degrees granted: Associate; Bachelors; Masters. Adverse incident record source- Student Rights & Responsibilities, 715-346-4566.

Attendance and degree information available by phone, fax, mail. Search requires name only. Also helpful: SSN, date of birth, exact years of attendance. There is no fee.

University of Wisconsin-Stout,
Registrar, Menomonie, WI 54751-0790, 715-232-2121 (Fax: 715-232-2436). Hours: 8AM-4:30PM. Enrollment: 7200. Records go back to 1893. Alumni records are maintained here also. Call 715-232-1151. Degrees granted: Bachelors; Masters. Special programs- Provosts Office, 715-232-2421.

Attendance and degree information available by phone, fax, mail. Search requires name plus SSN. Also helpful: date of birth, exact years of attendance. There is no fee.

University of Wisconsin-Superior,
Registrar, 1800 Grand Ave, Superior, WI 54880, 715-394-8228 (Fax: 715-394-8040). Hours: 8AM-5PM. Enrollment: 2000. Records go back to 1922. Alumni records are maintained here also. Call 715-394-8101. Degrees granted: Bachelors; Masters.

Attendance and degree information available by phone, mail. Search requires name plus SSN, exact years of attendance. There is no fee.

University of Wisconsin-Washington County, Registrar, 400 University Dr, West Bend, WI 53095, 414-335-5200 (Fax: 414-335-5220). Enrollment: 634. Records go back to 1968. Degrees granted: Associate.

Attendance and degree information available by phone, mail. Search requires name plus SSN. There is no fee.

University of Wisconsin-Waukesha County, Registrar, 1500 University Dr, Waukesha, WI 53188, 414-521-5200 (Fax: 414-521-5491). Hours: 8AM-5PM. Enrollment: 1600. Records go back to 1966. Alumni records are maintained here also. Call 414-521-5435. Degrees granted: Associate. Adverse incident record source- 414-521-5200.

Attendance and degree information available by phone, mail. Search requires name plus SSN, date of birth, exact years of attendance. There is no fee.

University of Wisconsin-Whitewater, Registrar, 800 W Main St, Whitewater, WI 53190, 414-472-1580 (Fax: 414-472-1515). Hours: 7:45AM-4:30PM. Enrollment: 10500. Records go back to 1885. Alumni records are maintained here also. Call 414-472-1105. Degrees granted: Associate; Bachelors; Masters. Adverse incident record source- Student Affairs, 414-472-1051.

Attendance and degree information available by phone, fax, mail. Search requires name only. Also helpful: SSN, date of birth, exact years of attendance. There is no fee.

Viterbo College, Registrar, 815 S Ninth St, La Crosse, WI 54601, 608-796-3180 (Fax: 608-796-3050). Hours: 8AM-4:30PM. Enrollment: 1600. Alumni records are maintained here also. Call 608-791-0471. Degrees granted: Bachelors; Masters. Adverse incident record source- 608-796-3180.

Attendance information available by mail. Search requires name only. Also helpful: SSN, date of birth. There is no fee.

Degree information available by phone, mail. Search requires name only. Also helpful: SSN, date of birth. There is no fee.

Waukesha County Technical College, Registrar, 800 Main St, Pewaukee, WI 53072, 414-691-5266 (Fax: 414-691-5123). Hours: 8AM-7:30PM. Enrollment: 35004. Records go back to 1960. Alumni records are maintained here also. Call 414-691-5295. Degrees granted: Associate. Special programs- Associate Degree: Technical Diploma, 414-691-5280. Adverse incident record source- Risk Management, 414-691-5283: Office of the President, 414-691-5346

Attendance information available by fax, mail. Search requires name plus SSN, signed release. Also helpful: exact years of attendance. There is no fee.

Degree information available by phone, fax, mail. Search requires name plus SSN. Also helpful: exact years of attendance. There is no fee.

Western Wisconsin Technical College, Registrar, 304 N Sixth St, La Crosse, WI 54601, 608-785-9149 (Fax: 608-789-9094). Hours: 8AM-8PM. Enrollment: 7000. Records go back to 1917. Alumni records are maintained here also. Call 608-785-9892. Degrees granted: Associate; Applied Sciences and Technical Diplomas. Special programs- Instructional Services, 608-785-9102. Adverse incident record source- 608-785-9444.

Attendance information available by phone, fax, mail. Search requires name only. Also helpful: SSN, date of birth, exact years of attendance. Fee is $3.00. Expedited service available for $10.00.

Degree information available by phone, fax, mail. Search requires name only. Also helpful: SSN, date of birth, exact years of attendance. Fee is $3.00. Expedite service available for $10.00.

Wisconsin Conservatory of Music, Registrar, 1584 N Prospect Ave, Milwaukee, WI 53202, 414-276-5760 (Fax: 414-276-6076). Enrollment: 1400. Records go back to 1899. Alumni records are maintained here at the same phone number. Degrees granted: Bachelors. Special programs- Fine Arts. Adverse incident record source- Student Affairs.

Attendance and degree information available by phone, mail. Search requires name plus SSN, date of birth, exact years of attendance. There is no fee.

Wisconsin Indianhead Tech College in Superior, Educational Services, 600 N 21st St, Superior, WI 54880, 715-394-6677 (Fax: 715-394-3771). Enrollment: 500. Records go back to 1915. Alumni records are maintained here at the same phone number. Degrees granted: Associate. Adverse incident record source- Student Services.

Attendance and degree information available by phone, mail. Search requires name plus SSN, date of birth, approximate years of attendance. There is no fee.

Wisconsin Indianhead Tech Institute in Ashland, Admissions and Records Office, 2100 Beaser Ave, Ashland, WI 54806, 715-682-4591 (Fax: 715-682-8040). Enrollment: 350. Records go back to 1921. Alumni records are maintained here at the same phone number. Degrees granted: Associate. Adverse incident record source- Student Services.

Attendance and degree information available by phone, mail. Search requires name plus SSN, exact years of attendance. There is no fee.

Wisconsin Indianhead Tech Institute in New Richmond, Registrar, 1019 S Knowles, New Richmond, WI 54017, 715-246-6561 (Fax: 715-246-2777). Enrollment: 300. Records go back to 1969. Alumni records are maintained here at the same phone number. Degrees granted: Associate. Adverse incident record source- Security Department.

Attendance and degree information available by phone, mail. Search requires name plus SSN, exact years of attendance. There is no fee.

Wisconsin Indianhead Tech Institute in Rice Lake, Student Services, 1900 College Dr, Rice Lake, WI 54868, 715-234-7082 (Fax: 715-234-5172). Enrollment: 625. Alumni records are maintained here at the same phone number. Degrees granted: Associate.

Attendance information available by phone, fax, mail. Search requires name plus SSN, exact years of attendance.

Degree information available by phone, fax, mail. Search requires name plus SSN, exact years of attendance.

Wisconsin Indianhead Technical College, Registrar, 505 Oine Ridge Drive, Shell Lake, WI 54871, 715-468-2815 (Fax: 715-468-2819). Hours: 8AM-4:30PM. Enrollment: 7000. Records go back to 1972. Alumni records are maintained here at the same phone number. Degrees granted: Associate. Special programs- Cable Television System Service: Marine Repair Technician: Aarchitectural Commercial Design: Automated Packaging Systems Technician: Wood Techniques. Adverse incident record source- Human Resources Department, 715-468-2815.

Attendance and degree information available by phone, fax, mail. Search requires name plus SSN, exact years of attendance. There is no fee.

Wisconsin Lutheran College, Registrar, 8800 W Bluemond Rd, Milwaukee, WI 53226, 414-443-8817 (Fax: 414-443-8514). Hours: 7:30AM-3:30PM. Enrollment: 425. Records go back to 1973. Alumni records are maintained here at the same phone number. Degrees granted: Bachelors. Adverse incident record source- Academic Dean, 414-443-8816.

Attendance and degree information available by phone, fax, mail. Search requires name only. Also helpful: SSN, date of birth, exact years of attendance. There is no fee.

Wisconsin School of Professional Psychology, Registrar, 9120 W Hampton Ave Ste 212, Milwaukee, WI 53225, 414-464-9777 (Fax: 414-358-5590). Hours: 9AM-5PM. Enrollment: 90. Records go back to 1980. Alumni records are maintained here at the same phone number. Degrees granted: Doctorate. Adverse incident record source- Dean, 414-464-9777.

Attendance and degree information available by written request only. Search requires name plus SSN, date of birth, signed release. There is no fee.

Trade and Vocational Schools

Acme Institute of Technology, 102 Revere Dr, Manitowoc, WI 54220, 414-682-6144

Acme Institute of Technology, 819 S 60th St, West Allis, WI 53214, 414-257-1011

Capri College (Madison Campus), 6414 Odana Rd, Madison, WI 53719, 608-274-5390

Diesel Truck Driver Training School, Hwy 151, Rte 2, Sun Prairie, WI 53590, 608-837-7800

MBTI Business Training Institute, 606 W Wisconsin Ave, Milwaukee, WI 53203, 414-272-2192

MBTI Business Training Institute (Branch Campus), 237 South St, Waukesha, WI 53186, 414-257-3221

Midwest Center for the Study of Oriental Medicine, 6226 Bankers Rd #5, Racine, WI 53403, 414-554-2010

Trans American School of Broadcasting, 600 Williamson St, Madison, WI 53703, 608-257-4600

Wisconsin Conservatory of Music, Inc., 1584 N Prospect Ave, Milwaukee, WI 53202, 414-276-5760

Wisconsin School of Professional Pet Grooming, 34197 Wisconsin Ave, Okauchee, WI 53069, 414-569-9492

State Licensing & Business Registration Quick Finder Index

Architecture, Engineering & Surveying
Architect #1 (4400).................................☎ 608-266-0609
Engineer #1 (18800)..............................☎ 608-266-0609
Geologist #1..☎ 608-266-0609
Landscape Architect #1 ....☎ 608-266-0609
Surveyor #1 (1400)................................☎ 608-266-0609

Business - Court & Legal Services
Attorney #17 ....☎ 608-257-3838
Lobbyist #12 (600) ....☎ 608-266-8123
Notary Public #15 (17000) ....☎ 608-266-5594

Business - General Services
Auction Company #2..............................☎ 608-267-1816
Auctioneer #2 ....☎ 608-267-1816
Charitable Organization #2 (4544)..........☎ 608-267-7132
Designer #1 (800) ....☎ 608-266-0609
Peddler #5 (25) 608-267-7132
Professional Fund Raiser #2 (90) ....☎ 608-267-7132
Public Accountant #1 (9500)..................☎ 608-266-0609

Education
School Counselor #16.............................☎ 608-266-1027
School Librarian/Media Specialist #16 ....☎ 608-266-1027
School Principal #16...............................☎ 608-266-1027
School Superintendent #16......................☎ 608-266-1027
Teacher #16 ....☎ 608-266-1027

Environmental & Agriculture
Animal Technician #4 (577)................................608-266-1626
Pesticide Applicator, Private, Commercial
Certification #10 (35500)..........................☎ 602-224-4548

Pesticide Dealer #10 (500).............................☎ 602-224-4548
Pesticide-Commercial Application Business #10
....☎ 608-224-4548
Veterinarian #4 (1873).................................608-266-1626
Veterinary Clinic #10.................................☎ 608-224-4548

Financial - Real Estate, Insurance & Banking
Debt Collector #6 (2474)..............................☎ 608-261-9555
Insurance Intermediary #14 (60000) ....☎ 608-266-8699
Investment Advisor #11 (765)........................☎ 608-266-3693
Loan Solicitor/Originator #5.............................608-266-1621
Mortgage Banker #5 608-266-1621
Private Detective Agency #2 (605).................☎ 608-266-0829
Real Estate Appraiser #1 (700)......................☎ 608-266-0609
Real Estate Broker #5 (16994) 608-267-1816
Real Estate Salesperson #2 ....☎ 608-267-1816
Securities Agent #11 (58028) ....☎ 608-266-3693
Securities Broker/Dealer #11 (1442).............☎ 608-266-3693
Time Share Salesperson #5 (239) 608-267-1816

Health & Beauty
Acupuncturist #3 (62)......................................608-267-7222
Barber #1 (19500)...☎ 608-266-0609
Cemetery #2 (70) ....☎ 608-267-7132
Cemetery Salesperseon #2 ....☎ 608-267-7132
Chiropractor #3 (1288)....................................608-267-7222
Cosmetologist #1 ....☎ 608-266-0609
Dental Hygienist #4 ....☎ 602-266-0483
Dentist #4 (3432)...608-266-5441
Dietitian #4..☎ 608-266-0483
Emergency Medical Technician #7 ....☎ 608-266-1568

Funeral Director #1 .... ☎ 608-266-0609
Funeral Preneed Seller #2 .... ☎ 608-267-7132
Hearing Instrument Specialist #4 .... ☎ 608-266-0483
Medical Doctor/Surgeon #4 .... ✉ 602-266-0483
Nurse #3 (340) 608-266-8957
Nurse Midwife #3 (62) 608-266-8957
Nursing Home Administrator #1 (1100) .... ☎ 608-266-0609
Occupational Therapist #4 .... ☎ 608-266-0483
Optometrist #3 (722) 608-267-7222
Osteopathic Physician #4 (1161) .... ☎ 608-266-2812
Pharmacist #4 .... ☎ 608-266-0483
Physical Therapist #4 (2583) 608-267-9377
Physician's Assistant #4 (542) .... ☎ 608-266-2812
Podiatrist #4 (217) .... ☎ 608-266-2812
Respiratory Care Practitioner #4 .... ☎ 608-266-0483
Speech Pathologist/Audiologist #4 .... ☎ 608-266-0483

Investigations & Security
Private Detective #2 (1201) .... ☎ 608-266-0829

Social Services
Marriage & Family Therapist #3 (449) .... ✉ 608-267-7212
Professional Counselor #3 (2130) .... ✉ 608-267-7212
Psychologist #3 (1115) 608-266-0070
Rehabilitation Counselor #3 .... ✉ 608-267-7212
Social Worker #3 (5400) .... ✉ 608-267-7212

Sports & Entertainment
Beer Wholesale #9 .... ☎ 608-266-8772
Boxing, Clerks #2 (40) .... ☎ 608-266-5521
Charitable Gaming #13 .... ☎ 608-264-6607
Dog Racing #13 (3) .... ☎ 608-264-6607
Fishing Guide #8 (1025) .... ☎ 608-266-2105
Liquor (Wholesale) #9 (66) .... ☎ 608-267-1350
Public Wine Distributor #9 .... ☎ 608-266-8772
Racing #13 .... ☎ 608-266-7777
Racing Vendor #13 .... ☎ 608-264-6607

State Licensing & Business Registration Agency Information

(1) Bureau of Business & Design Professions, PO Box 8935, 1400 E. Washington, Madison, WI 53708, 608-266-0609, Fax: 608-267-3816

(2) Bureau of District Licensing & Real Estate, PO Box 8935, Madison, WI 53708, 608-267-7132, Fax: 608-267-3816

(3) Bureau of Health Services Professions, 1400 E Washington Ave, PO Box 8935, Madison, WI 53708, 608-267-7212

(4) Bureau of Health Services Professions, 1400 E Washington Ave, PO Box 8935, Madison, WI 53708, 608-266-0483, Fax: 608-267-0644

(5) Department of Financial Institutions, PO Box 7876, Madison, WI 53707-7876, 608-266-1621

(6) Department of Financial Institutions, Division of Banking, PO Box 7876, Madison, WI 53707-7876, 608-261-9555

(7) Department of Health & Social Services, Division of Health, Emergency Medical Services Sec, 1414 E Washington, Rm 227, Madison, WI 53703, 608-266-1568, Fax: 608-261-6392

(8) Department of Natural Resources, Licensing Section, 101 S Webster, PO Box 7921, Madison, WI 53707, 608-266-2105, Fax: 608-264-6130

(9) Department of Revenue, Liquor (Wholesale) Licensing Division, PO Box 8902   4638 University Ave., Madison, WI 53708, 608-267-1350, Fax: 608-261-6226

(10) Dept of Agriculture, Trade & Consumer Protection, Applicator Certification & Licensing, 2811 Agriculture Dr, PO Box 8911, Madison, WI 53708-8911, 602-224-4548, Fax: 608-224-4656

(11) Division of Securities, Compliance Section, 101 E Wilson St, 4th Floor PO Box 768, Madison, WI 53701, 608-266-3693, Fax: 608-256-1259

(12) Ethics Board, 44 E Misslin St, Ste 601, Madison, WI 53703-2800, 608-266-8123, Fax: 608-264-9309

(13) Gaming Board, PO Box 8979, 1802 Beluino Hwy., Madison, WI 53708, 608-264-6607

(14) Insurance Commission, Agent Licensing Section, PO Box 7872, Madison, WI 53707-7872, 608-266-3585

(15) Office of Secretary of State, PO Box 7848, Madison, WI 53707-7848, 608-266-5594

(16) Teacher Education, Licensing & Placement, Box 7841, Madison, WI 53707-7841, 608-266-1027, Fax: 608-264-9558

(17) Wisconsin State Bar Association, PO Box 7158, Madison, WI 53707, 608-257-3838, Fax: 608-257-5502

Wyoming

Capitol: Cheyenne (xxx County)	
State Population	**.4 Million**
Number of Degree Granting Institutions:	**8**
Number of State Licensing & Business Registration Agencies:	**70**

Degree Granting Educational Institutions

Casper College, Registrar, 125 College Dr, Casper, WY 82601, 307-268-2211 (Fax: 307-268-2611). Hours: 8AM-5PM. Enrollment: 3800. Records go back to 1945. Alumni records are maintained here also. Call 307-268-2218. Degrees granted: Associate. Adverse incident record source- Dean of Students, 307-268-2210.

Attendance and degree information available by phone, fax, mail. Search requires name only. Also helpful: SSN, date of birth, exact years of attendance. There is no fee.

Central Wyoming College, Registrar, 2660 Peck Ave, Riverton, WY 82501, 307-856-9291 (Fax: 307-856-2264). Hours: 8AM-5PM. Records go back to 1966. Alumni records are maintained here at the same phone number. Degrees granted: Associate.

Attendance and degree information available by phone, fax, mail. Search requires name plus SSN, date of birth, exact years of attendance. There is no fee.

Eastern Wyoming College, Registrar, 3200 W C St, Torrington, WY 82240, 307-532-8257 (Fax: 307-532-8222). Hours: 8AM-4:30PM. Enrollment: 1800. Records go back to 1948. Alumni records are maintained here also. Call 307-532-8304. Degrees granted: Associate.

Attendance and degree information available by phone, fax, mail. Search requires name plus SSN, date of birth. Also helpful: exact years of attendance. There is no fee.

Laramie County Community College, Registrar, 1400 E College Dr, Cheyenne, WY 82007, 307-778-5222 (Fax: 307-778-1350). Hours: 8AM-5PM. Enrollment: 4000. Records go back to 1968. Alumni records are maintained here also. Call 307-778-1213. Degrees granted: Associate.

Attendance and degree information available by mail. Search requires name plus SSN, exact years of attendance, signed release. There is no fee.

Northern Wyoming Community College District, (Gillette Campus), Registrar, 720 W 8th St, Gillette, WY 82716, 307-686-0254 X403 (Fax: 307-687-7141). Hours: 8AM-5PM. Degrees granted: Associate.

Attendance and degree information available by phone, fax, mail. Search requires name plus SSN, date of birth. Also helpful: exact years of attendance. There is no fee.

Northwest College, Registrar, 231 W Sixth St, Powell, WY 82435, 307-754-3149 (Fax: 307-754-6700). Hours: 8AM-5PM. Records go back to 1946. Degrees granted: Associate.

Attendance and degree information available by phone, fax, mail. Search requires name plus SSN, date of birth, exact years of attendance. There is no fee.

University of Wyoming, Registrar, PO Box 3964, University Station, Laramie, WY 82071, 307-766-5272. Hours: 8AM-5PM. Records go back to 1886. Alumni Records Office: PO Box 3137, Laramie, WY 82071, 307-766-4166. Degrees granted: Bachelors; Masters; Doctorate.

Attendance and degree information available by phone, mail. Search requires name plus SSN, date of birth, exact years of attendance. There is no fee.

Western Wyoming College, Registrar, PO Box 428, Rock Springs, WY 82901, 307-382-1641 (Fax: 307-382-1636). Hours: 8AM-5PM. Enrollment: 2000. Records go back to 1959. Alumni records are maintained here also. Call 307-382-1600. Degrees granted: Associate. Adverse incident record source- Security, 307-382-1690.

Attendance and degree information available by phone, fax, mail. Search requires name only. Also helpful: SSN, date of birth, exact years of attendance. There is no fee.

Trade and Vocational Schools

Cheyenne Aero Tech, 1204 Airport Pkwy, Cheyenne, WY 82001, 307-632-1090

Sage Technical Services, 190 Pronghorn St, Casper, WY 82604, 307-234-0242

Wyoming Technical Institute, 4373 N Third St, Laramie, WY 82070, 307-742-3776

State Licensing & Business Registration Quick Finder Index

Architecture, Engineering & Surveying
Architect #2 (950) .... ☎ 304-528-5825
Engineer #33 304-558-3554
Landscape Architect #13 304-293-2141
Surveyor #7 .... ☎ 304-574-2980

Business - Court & Legal Services
Attorney #14 .... ☎ 304-558-7815
Lobbyist #39 (500) .... ✉ 304-558-0664
Notary Public #36 (35000) .... ✉ 304-558-6000
Shorthand Reporter #37 304-558-3456

Business - General Services
Public Accountant-CPA; Non-resident CPA #1
(1700) .... ✉ 304-558-3557

Construction & Manufacturing
Electrician #40 304-558-2191
General Contractor #24 304-558-7890

Education
School Counselor #26 .... ☎ 800-982-2378
School Principal #26 .... ☎ 800-982-2378
School Social Services/Attendance
Investigator #26 .... ☎ 800-982-2378
School Superintendent #26 .... ☎ 800-982-2378
Supervisor of Instruction #26 .... ☎ 800-982-2378
Teacher #26 .... ☎ 800-982-2378
Vocational Administrator #26 .... ☎ 800-982-2378

Environmental & Agriculture
Animal Technician #23 (50) .... ☎ 304-558-2016
Forester #20 304-924-6266
Mine Electrician #27 304-348-3500
Mine Surveyor/Foreman #27 304-348-3500
Miner #27 304-348-3500
Pesticide Applicator #25 304-558-2209
Shot Firer #27 304-348-3500
Veterinarian #23 (500) .... ☎ 304-558-2016

Financial - Real Estate, Insurance & Banking
Insurance Agent #31 304-558-3354
Insurance Broker #31 304-558-3354
Insurance Solicitor #31 304-558-3354
Investment Advisor; Representatives #38 (2400)
.... ☎ 304-558-2257
Real Estate Appraiser #34 .... ☎ 304-558-3919
Real Estate Broker/Salesperson #35 304-558-3555
Securities Agent #38 (31732) .... ☎ 304-558-2257
Securities Broker/Dealer #38 (1085) .... ☎ 304-558-2257

Health & Beauty
Barber #3 304-558-2924
Chiropractor #4 .... ✉ 304-527-6335
Cosmetologist #3 304-558-2924
Dental Hygienist #6 (1000) .... ☎ 304-252-8266
Dentist #6 (1400) .... ☎ 304-252-8266
Educational Audiologist #26 .... ☎ 304-558-7010
Embalmer #5 .... ✉ 304-558-0302
Emergency Medical Technician-Basic; Paramedic #28
(5500) .... ☎ 304-558-3956
Funeral Director; Funeral Homes #5 (700) .... ✉ 304-558-0302
Hearing Aid Specialist #12 304-558-7886
Manicurist #3 304-558-2924
Medical Doctor #15 304-558-2921
Nurse #8 304-558-3596
Nurse Anesthetist #8 304-558-3596
Nurse Midwife #8 304-558-3596
Nursing Home Administrator #32 304-558-1414
Occupational Therapist/Assistant #16 (409)
.... ✉ 304-329-0480
Optometrist #15 304-558-3596
Osteopathic Physician/Assistants #17 (700)
.... ☎ 304-723-4638
Pharmacist #18 304-558-0558
Physical Therapist/Assistant #19 (800) .... ✉ 304-745-4161
Physician's Assistant #15 304-558-3596
Podiatrist #15 304-558-3596
Practical Nurse #8 304-558-3572
Radiologic Technologist #9 (2210) .... ☎ 304-256-6985
Sanitarian-Registered; In Training #21 (200)
.... ☎ 304-558-2981
School Nurse #26 .... ☎ 304-558-7010
Speech/Language Pathologist #26 .... ☎ 304-558-7010

Investigations & Security
Polygraph Examiner #29 .... ✉ 304-558-7890
Private Detective #36 (631) .... ✉ 304-558-6000

Social Services
Professional Counselor #10 (1250) .... ✉ 304-746-2512
Psychologist #11 304-366-5170
Social Worker #22 .... ☎ 304-558-8816

Sports & Entertainment
Athletic Trainer #26 .... ☎ 800-982-2378
Boating & Canoe Expedition Provider #30 .... ☎ 304-558-2783
Commercial Shooting Reserve #30 .... ☎ 304-558-2783
Commercial Whitewater Boating #30 .... ☎ 304-558-2783
Fishing Guide #30 (40) .... ☎ 304-558-2783
Whitewater Rafting Outfitter #30 .... ☎ 304-558-2783

State Licensing & Business Registration Agency Information

(1) Board of Barber Examiners, 441 Sunlight Drive., Powell, WY 82435, 307-754-5237

(2) Board of Cosmetology, 6101 Yellowstone Rd., Suite 452, Cheyenne, WY 82002, 307-777-3534, Fax: 307-777-6005

(3) Board of Dental Examiners, PO Box 272, Kemmerer, WY 83101, 307-877-9649, Fax: 307-877-9649

(4) Board of Embalming, 2020 Carey Ave., Suite 201, Cheyenne, WY 82002, 307-377-7788, Fax: 307-777-3508

(5) Board of Hearing Aid Specialists, 2020 Carey Ave., Suite 201, Cheyenne, WY 82002, 307-777-7788, Fax: 307-777-3508

(6) Board of Insurance Agents Examiners, Insurance Department, Herschler Bldg, 3rd Floor, E, Cheyenne, WY 82002, 307-777-7319, Fax: 307-777-5895

(7) Board of Law Examiners, Wyoming State Bar, PO Box 109 500 Randall Ave., Cheyenne, WY 82003, 307-632-9061, Fax: 307-630-3737

(8) Board of Outfitters & Professional Guides, 1750 Westland Rd, Cheyenne, WY 82002, 307-777-5323, Fax: 307-777-6715

(9) Board of Pharmacy, 1720 S Poplar St, Suite 5, Casper, WY 82601, 307-234-0294, Fax: 307-234-7226

(10) Board of Registration for Professional Geologists, Box 3008, University Station, Laramie, WY 82071, 307-766-2490, Fax: 307-766-2713

(11) Board of Veterinary Medicine, 2020 Carey Ave., Suite 201, Cheyenne, WY 82002, 307-777-6529, Fax: 307-777-3508

(12) Child Care Certification Board, Division of Juvenile Services, 2300 Capitol Ave., 325 Hathaway Bldg., Cheyenne, WY 82002, 307-777-6595, Fax: 307-777-3659

(13) Deparptment of Audit, 122 W 25th St., Herschber Bldg, 3rd Floor, Cheyenne, WY 82002, 307-777-6605, Fax: 307-777-3555

(14) Department of Agriculture, Licensing & Registrations Section, 2219 Carey Ave, Cheyenne, WY 82002, 307-777-7321, Fax: 307-777-6593

(15) Department of Audit, Collection Agency Board, Herschler Bldg, 3rd Floor, E, Cheyenne, WY 82002, 307-777-7797, Fax: 307-777-3555

(16) Department of Education, 2300 Capitol Ave Hathaway Bldg, Cheyenne, WY 82002, 307-777-6265

(17) Department of Revenue, Herschler Bldg, 2nd Floor, W, Cheyenne, WY 82002, 307-777-6989

(18) Electrical Board, Herschler Bldg, 1st Floor, W, Cheyenne, WY 82002, 307-777-7288, Fax: 307-777-7119

(19) Engineers & Professional Land Surveyors, 122 West 25th St., Cheyenne, WY 82002, 307-777-6155, Fax: 307-777-3403

(20) Examiners for Speech Pathology & Audiology, 2020 Carey Ave., Suite 201, Cheyenne, WY 82002, 307-777-7788, Fax: 307-777-3508

(21) Legislative Service Office, 213 State Capitol, Cheyenne, WY 82002, 307-777-7881, Fax: 307-777-5466

(22) Licensing Boards, 2020 Carey Ave., Suite 100, Cheyenne, WY 82002, 307-777-7551, Fax: 307-777-3796

(23) Licensing Boards, 2020 Carey Ave., Suite 201, Cheyenne, WY 82002, 307-777-7788, Fax: 307-777-3508

(24) Licensing Boards, 2020 Carey, Suite 201, Cheyenne, WY 82002, 307-777-6529, Fax: 307-777-3508

(25) Licensing Boards, 211 W. 19th St. Colony Bldg, 2nd Floor, Cheyenne, WY 82002, 307-778-7053, Fax: 307-778-2069

(26) Licensing Boards, 2020 Carly Ave., Suite 110, Cheyenne, WY 82002, 307-777-7601, Fax: 307-777-3519

(27) Licensing Boards, 2020 Carey Ave., Suite 201, Cheyenne, WY 82002, 307-777-7788, Fax: 307-777-3508

(28) Licensing Boards, Barrett Bldg, Cheyenne, WY 82002, 307-777-6313

(29) Licensing Boards, 2020 Carey Ave. Suite 201, Cheyenne, WY 82002, 307-777-3507, Fax: 307-777-3508

(30) Licensing Boards, 2020 Carey Ave., Suite 201, Cheyenne, WY 82002, 307-777-6529, Fax: 307-777-6529

(31) Licensing Boards, 2020 Carey Ave. Suite 201, Cheyenne, WY 82002, 307-777-3507, Fax: 307-777-3508

(32) Licensing Boards, 2020 Carey Ave. Suite 201, Cheyenne, WY 82002, 307-777-6529, Fax: 307-777-3508

(33) Licensing Boards, Barrett Bldg, Cheyenne, WY 82002, 307-777-6529

(34) Licensing Boards, 2020 Carey Ave., Suite 201, Cheyenne, WY 82002, 307-777-7142, Fax: 307-777-3706

(35) Licensing Boards, Social Workers Addiction Dependency, 2020 Carey Ave., Suite 201, Cheyenne, WY 82002, 307-777-7788, Fax: 307-777-3508

(36) Mining Board of Wyoming, PO Box 1094 79 Winston Ave., Rock Springs, WY 82901, 307-362-5222, Fax: 307-362-3177

(37) Office of Secretary of State, The Capitol 200 W. 24th St., Cheyenne, WY 82002-0020, 307-777-5342, Fax: 307-777-5339

Appendix I—Sample Release Form

This release form serves as an all encompassing document for doing many types of background checks or verification. You can change the wording (line 2-3) to include specific types of verifications you wish to pursue. Also, if the signature of the applicant is required to be notarized, you can add such a line at the bottom.

Under the provisions of the Fair Credit Reporting Act U.S.C., Sec. 1681, et seq. notice is hereby given that a consumer report or investigative consumer report may be made which may include information pertaining to your employment history, educational background, credit worthiness, character, general reputation, driving record, criminal record, personal characteristics, and mode of living, which will be used for employment purposes. An investigation into your worker's compensation or industrial accident claims background may also be conducted under the guidelines of the Americans with Disabilities Act.

You are further advised under said act that any person who procures or causes to be prepared an investigative consumer report on any consumer shall, upon written request by the consumer within a reasonable period of time after the receipt by him of the disclosure required by subsection 1681 (d), shall make a complete and accurate disclosure of the nature and scope of the investigation requested. This disclosure shall be made in writing, mailed or otherwise delivered, to the consumer five days after the date on which the request for such disclosure was received from the consumer or such report was first requested, whichever is the latter.

You are further advised that if you are denied employment, either wholly or partly, because of information contained in a consumer report as that term is defined in the Fair Credit Reporting Act, that a disclosure will be made to you of the name and address of the consumer reporting agency making such report.

I, the undersigned, have read the above and foregoing notice and understanding same, I hereby authorize _____(your name)_____ to investigate and verify facts stated by me on the attached application.

Signed this_____day of _____, 199_____

Applicant Name (sign): _____ SSN: _____

Address:_____

This order form has been reproduced with the permission of LABORCHEX Companies of Jackson, MS (601) 362-0366.

Appendix II—Telephone Area Code Changes 1996-97

Telephone companies have been assigning new area codes at a frantic pace recently. Every attempt has been made to reflect in this publication the present effective area code for each government agency. Following is a list of recent and planned changes as of publication date.

Suburban Chicago • Effective August 3, 1996, Code 630 was created from Code 780. The region for 630 is western suburban Chicago including Du Page and Kane counties, the northern part of Kendall county and the western part of Cook county. The overlap period ends Nov. 30, 1996.

Cayman Islands • Effective September 1, 1996 Code 345 was created from Code 809. The islands will now have their own code. The overlap period ends August 31, 1997.

Dallas Suburbs • Effective September 14, 1996, Code 972 was created from Code 214. Dallas proper remains 214, the rest of 214 changes. The cities effected include Carrollton, Garland, Irving, Richardson, and Plano. The overlap period ends March 15, 1997.

Southwestern Ohio • Effective September 28, 1996, Code 937 was created from Code 513. 13 counties are effected. Cities effected include the Springfield, Dayton, and Troy areas. The Cincinnati area remains the same. The overlap period ends June 14, 1997.

Bahamas • Effective October 1, 1996, Code 242 was created from Code 809. The Bahamas now have their own code. The overlap period ends March 31, 1997.

Chicago • Effective October 12, 1996, Code 773 was created from Code 312. The boundary area is North of North Ave, South of 35th Street, West of West Ave, and East of Lakefront. The overlap period ends January 11, 1997.

British Columbia • Effective October 19, 1996, the island and the northern interior section stretching to Alberta changed to Code 250 from Code 604. The overlap period ends April 6, 1997.

Houston • Effective November 2, 1996, Code 281 was created from Code 713. Within the beltway, Houston remains 713; the suburbs outside of the beltway change. The overlap period ends May 3, 1997.

Southern California • Effective January 25, 1997, Code 562 will be created from the eastern side of Code 310. The cities effected include most of Long beach, Paramount, Downey, Lakewood, Norwalk, La Habra and Alamitos. The overlap period ends July 26, 1997.

Southern California • Effective March 22, 1997, Code 760 will be created from Code 619. This effects the northern part of San Diego County and parts of Riverside, San Bernardino, and Inyo counties. The overlap period ends September 27, 1997.

Appendix III—Privacy - What is, What isn't, and Why?

It seems appropriate to include in this book a discussion of records, privacy and regulations. Of course, not all information about a company or individual is public. The boundaries between public and private information are not well understood, and are these boundaries undergoing intense scrutiny lately. Here is an introduction to the subject for the viewpoint of a professional public record searcher.

How Do Records Get into the Public Domain

Here are three definitions you should understand—

Public Record	Public Records are records of **incidents** or **actions** filed or recorded with a government agency for the purpose of notifying others– the "public." The **deed** to your house **recorded** at the county recorder's office is a **public record**—it is a legal requirement that you record it with the county recorder. Anyone requiring details about your property may review or copy the documents.
Public Information	Your **telephone listing** in the phone book is **public information**; that is, you freely furnished the information to ease the flow of commercial and private communications.
Personal Information	Any information about a person or business that the person or business **might consider** private and confidential in nature such as your social security number is personal information. Such information will remain private to a limited extent unless it is disclosed to some outside entity that could make it public. **Personal information may be found in either public records or in public information.**

There are two ways that personal information can enter the public domain—statutory and voluntary. In a **voluntary** transaction, you **share** personal information of your own free will. In a **statutory** transaction, you **disclose** personal information because the law requires you to.

Personal information may be **shared** or **disclosed** to government agencies or to private enterprises. Here are a few examples—

Statutory
- Your weight, height, eye color and date of birth on a driver's license application
- Your Social Security Number, income and children's names and ages on your tax return
- Your address on a deed

Voluntary
- Your telephone number to be listed in the telephone directory
- Your Social Security Number on an application to obtain a credit card
- Your estimated annual income on a magazine subscription form

Disclosure of information by government agencies is controlled by either **statute** or **usage** (traditional practice). Disclosure of information by private companies is either **unregulated** (uncontrolled) or **regulated** by statute. Examples are—

Statute (gov't)
- The Freedom of Information Act and The Privacy Act dictate the rules for dissemination of information by federal agencies.
- The Drivers Privacy Protection Act of 1994 directs the state to impose restrictions on access to drivers records.
- Most states have statutes limiting access to certain types of court records, such as juvenile and adoption cases.

Usage (gov't)
- Most court records, civil and criminal, are open to public inspection by historical tradition.

Regulated (business)
- The Fair Credit Reporting Act limits access to individuals' credit histories to specific permissible purposes.

Unregulated (business)
- Some businesses sell their customer lists for solicitation by other businesses.
- Many businesses collect customer demographics, which they consider highly confidential.

Depending on these statutes, regulations, usage, and company policies, personal information may be **fully open** to access by the public, **restricted** in some way, or kept **closed** (entirely confidential).

Government Records — Open vs. Restricted vs. Closed

Records held by government agencies fall into these three categories. The only truly public information is that which is entirely **open** without restriction to anyone who wants to find it (if they can).

Typically, **restrictions** are placed by law and by tradition on some kinds of information where there is some public purpose that is served by keeping the information out of some hands.

Further, there are two typical types of restrictions: **prior approval** and **use**. Access to many records, both public and business, require the **prior approval** of the subject. For example, many colleges will not release a transcript without the notarized permission of the student. **Use** restrictions require whoever wants to obtain the information to jump through some legal or regulatory hoop, subject to penalties for breaking the rules. For example, many states restrict the use of voter registration data only to political solicitations. Frequently this kind of restrictive legislation includes exemptions from the rules, which information brokers and public record searchers should be aware of.

Even **closed** records are not entirely inaccessible. They can be defined as records accessible only **by or through** government officials authorized by law. For example, the FBI's national criminal information database, NCIC, is legally accessible only **by** law enforcement officials for specific investigative uses, and a juvenile court case record can only be released to someone **through** an order of the court.

Private Enterprise Records—Unregulated vs. Regulated

This is the vocabulary for the accessibility by the public of information held by private organizations, businesses, associations, etc. **Unregulated** information held by an organization about its customers, members or others may be kept confidential or disclosed at will. The organization makes up (and can change) its own rules about this information. **Regulated** information consists of information held by a private organization access to which is controlled by law or government regulation, such as the Fair Credit Reporting Act.

Frequently, information in the hands of private organizations is, in fact, the same information as that in the hands of a government agency such as your date of birth. With the availability of on–line information systems containing literally billions of pieces of information about people and businesses, the users of these systems often do not even think about whether the source of the information is government or a private organization.

The Right of Access

Access to public records are essential to the success of every user of this book. The availability of such information is dependent on unfettered access by every link in the information chain (i.e. government agency sources, vendors, search firms, etc.). Even the private companies who collect information are performing industry functions by taking public government data, adding value to it, and reselling it to others.

The courts have held that the "laws, regulations, and policies governing public access to government information should apply equally to all information regardless of the media in which it exists." This means that, if the information exists on an electronic media, the public may have access to it and not be required to access a large, unwieldy paper copy of the same material.

The legal framework surrounding the right to access rests on three major tenets:

- The public has a broad right of access to government information.

- The government may not discriminate in the dissemination of public information.

- Copyright-like restrictions on the use of public information are antithetical to the goal of widely disseminated government information.

Many members of the information community believe that since public use of government information is a right, any person who acquires public information is free to use it, sell it or otherwise disseminate it without penalty, fee or royalty. They believe there is no requirement that an individual show a "need" for the information requested as a precursor to receiving access, unless such access is precluded by Privacy Act restrictions, and that the government is bound to facilitate the public's access to governmental information. On the other side are those who feel that their right to privacy is being jeopardized when some kinds of government–held information is open to the public.

A Few Thoughts on Privacy

One of the problems with people's expectation of privacy is that they do not understand when they are giving up personal information to the public domain. They fail to notice, for example, the little word "optional" on the voter registration application over the Social Security Number and telephone boxes. Consider these points—

- Once an item of personal information is in the hands of a government agency or private business, it may or may not be subject to disclosure regulations.

- Once personal information has been shared with an unregulated private enterprise, the information should no longer be considered private.

Once it is released by the individual, information has begun the process of entering the public domain, whether or not it is later disclosed or remains confidential to the private enterprise that collected the information. If disclosed, the information will end up in a computer database accessible by anyone with a need to use it or, indeed, anyone with a password allowing access. And, in a world of computers, once an item of personal information becomes public, there is no reliable way to regain to its personal, private status.

Federal Acts Impacting Privacy

Acts which impact the content of public records

Privacy Act—
*5 USCA Section
552A (1974)*

The Privacy Act was enacted because:

- The collection and use of personal information by the US Government infringes on personal privacy;

- The increased use of computers and sophisticated technology enhances the possibility of harm to individual privacy;

- The misuse of information can threaten employment, insurance, and credit opportunities;

- The right to privacy is a fundamental personal right of all citizens, even though it is not stated expressly in the US Constitution.

The Act protects the individual who decides what records kept by the Government are important to him/her and permits him/her to insist that those records be used only for their intended purpose. The Privacy Act pertains only to personal records in the custody of the Executive Branch of the US Government, and the requested record must pertain to the requester or the requester must be the legal guardian of the individual of record. Each agency is required to publish a descriptive list of the record systems from which information can be retrieved using a personal identifier. The Federal Register has material concerning how information is stored and maintained, and how it can be retrieved. The Privacy Act is a companion act to the Freedom of Information Act (FOIA) and an individual can preclude release under the FOIA by citing the Privacy Act.

**The Right to
Financial
Privacy Act
(RFPA)—**
*12 USCA Section
3401 et seq (1978)*

The RFPA protects the right of customers in financial institutions to keep financial records private and free from unjustified governmental investigation. While this act appears to have no direct impact of information requests from private individuals, we feel it is important for readers to be aware of the existence of this Act.

Freedom of Information Act (FOIA)—
5 USCA Section 552 (l966) et seq (1976) et seq (1986)

Fundamentally, FOIA provides for public disclosure of information held by administrative agencies of the US Government. Thus, it allows access to all records in custody of the Executive Branch (meaning, armed forces, CIA, cabinet departments, etc., but not the federal court system or congress) unless specifically exempted. Such disclosure may be withheld when disclosure would cause harm to a governmental function; eg, invasion of privacy, trade secret disclosure, etc. Specifically, the most commonly recognized exceptions are: personal information which clearly invades personal privacy; commercial trade information belonging to a private entity which the government has because of a contract or for regulatory purposes; and information withheld for security reasons; e.g., government investigative files. FOIA is considered a general access statute and is the broadest of all such statutes. The requestor need not have any personal interest in the information requested nor need there be a reason for the request. Most Federal agencies have issued implementing instructions which covers what constitutes "readily available" information and how to get it, how to get "other" information, and the "right of review" process in cases when access is denied. The Federal Register and the Code of Federal Regulation (CFR) have material concerning how information is stored in Federal administrative agencies, how it is maintained, and how it can be retrieved.

If you are going to request information concerning FOIA, here are some suggestions—

- Do your homework—it may be helpful to first find and talk to the FOIA Officer of the agency. perhaps this information is readily available through another agency or department. They may even honor your request immediately if they know you are invoking the FOIA.

- Be sure to address the letter to the FOIA Officer of the agency in question.

- Be as specific as possible in your letter. Your request could be denied if it is too vague or unclear.

- Specify if you want both electronic and paper records.

- Send your request to both the field agency involved and to the agency headquarters.

- Ask if there are any fees involved.

The FOIA Officer must acknowledge your request within 10 days. Don't give the officer cause to deny it.

Driver's Privacy Protection Act (DPPA) Title XXXI—
Protection of Privacy of Information in State Motor Vehicle Records (1994)

The Driver's Privacy Protection Act, also known as the Driver's Privacy Protection Act of 1994 (DPPA), was an amendment to the Violent Crime Control Act of 1994 and was signed by President Clinton late in the summer of 1994. The intent of the DPPA is to protect the personal privacy of persons licensed to drive, by prohibiting certain disclosures of information maintained by the states. States were given three years (September 1997) to comply. This is the first time the federal government has regulated state level decisions regarding access to state held public records sold in significant quantity.

The bill prohibits disclosure of personal information from the driver history, vehicle registration, title files held by state DMVs, except for 14 specific "permissible uses." Personal information is defined as—

"...information that identifies an individual, including an individual's photograph, social security number, driver identification number, name, address (but not the 5-digit zip code), telephone number, and medical or disability information, but does not include information on vehicular accidents, driving violations, and driver's status."

The permissible uses do, in general, permit ongoing, legitimate businesses and individuals to obtain full record data, but with added compliance procedures. In reality, the states may continue to sell information to entities for purposes other than the 14 permissible uses, provided the individual, whose record is involved, has the ability to "waive or opt out." This means individuals can request that the state not release their address information to requesters not covered under the permissible uses. An example of such a requester is a firm collecting data for mail list purposes or a firm who purchases the data to be merged into a proprietary databases. Thus, if the individual chooses not to prohibit the release of their personal information, it can be sold by the state as mentioned above.

The DPPA will preempt state law where it provides greater privacy protection than the existing state law. Otherwise, state law disclosure restrictions remain in effect if they are equal to or more restrictive than the federal law. Because state legislatures are now forced to look at their access and restriction laws, states may pass legislation that is more restrictive than the federal version.

Recent Interest in Information Regulation by the Feds

Recent media attention to the availability of Social Security Numbers on private on–line databases has resulted in major privacy concerns expressed by the US Congress and by several federal agencies. Recently, congressional legislative proposals have led to creation of a task force to perform a study of the manner which private organizations—other than those subject to the *Fair Credit Reporting Act (FCRA)*—are making "sensitive consumer information" available to the public. *Consumer information* can be defined as SSNs, names, addresses, maiden names, and phone numbers, among other personal identifiers. If the study finds such information is being made available inappropriately, the Federal Reserve System is then instructed to determine the potential for fraud and/or risk of loss to insured depository institutions and whether changes in Federal law are necessary to address these risks. The study will be conducted by the Federal Trade Commission (FTC), the Federal Reserve System (Fed), and certain other federal banking agencies.

Social Security Numbers— Public or Private?

This attention by the federal government stems, in part, from LEXIS's P-TRAK program. This on–line service allowed a client to enter a name and receive the corresponding SS#. The program created such an outcry that the company suspended search capability of the program within two weeks of its introduction. The ensuing media attention and flood of mis-information on the Internet caught the eye of both Congress and a number of federal regulators.

The legislated study is actually a compromise between: (1) an FTC position of requiring that the SS# be removed from credit bureau "header" data (which is very open) and placed in the body of the credit information (governed by the FTC and severely restricted); and (2) a proposal to adopt a sense of congress resolution stating the congressional interest in and intent to further investigate these issues.

Private Sector Concerns

The significance of the study is enormous to the public records industry. A thoughtful assessment comes from an article written by Alden Schacher of the Information Industry Association (IIA) for the association's October Issue of *Policy Matters!*

- ■ "By adopting this legislation, Congress, for the first time, has required a Federal entity to study the information dissemination activities of companies not already regulated by the FCRA.

■ In addition, should the report ultimately suggest government regulation of private sector use of information, it would mean a new era in U.S. policy regarding information regulation.

■ In addition, the study's recommendations could set the course for the other privacy initiatives which are being driven by the Clinton Administration."

It appears that our country, while trying to address legitimate consumer concerns, is heading closer to federal regulation of private sector use of public information. The potential for decreasing the ability of businesses and consumers to access such information has major implications. The Driver's Privacy Protection Act is an example of regulation of the release of **government information to the private sector**. The study described above concerns the regulation of the release of **private sector information to the private sector**.

Those of us in the information community know that a SS# is no longer sacred. It is widely available from a variety of sources as a verification tool. Any efforts by a federal government study panel to turn an SS# into a secretive, restricted piece of information is too late!

What's Down the Road?

We foresee action occurring on several fronts:

■ A multitude of new privacy legislation will be introduced in the ensuing year at the state and federal levels. The intent will be to block or regulate both private source and public source data such as addresses and phone numbers. There will be complicated plans presented to determine who can or cannot have full or limited access and for what purposes.

■ Besides data such as addresses and phone numbers, talk could center on additional items now considered public record (real estate recordings, court records, etc.)

■ There will be talk of a new personal authentication tool, such as a retina scan, fingerprint or national ID.

How to Become Involved

For those of you who have a strong interest or economic concerns, voicing your concerns to your congressmen is a start. We recommend becoming involved with major trade associations. The Information Industry Association (202-986-0280) in Washington, DC is a major player (and we thank them for permission to quote their text in this article). Also, watch for task forces and working groups organized at the state level. We will continue to keep BRB customers informed in future issues of our newsletter *on-the-record*.

Notes

Send Me A COPY!

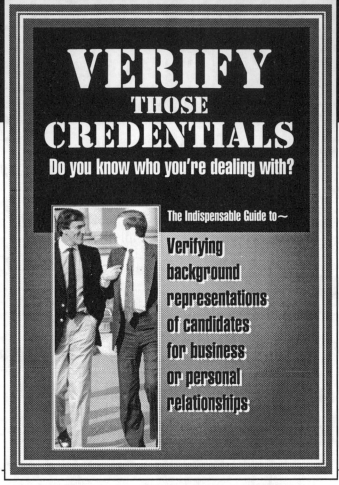

VERIFY THOSE CREDENTIALS
Do you know who you're dealing with?

The Indispensable Guide to~

Verifying background representations of candidates for business or personal relationships